ONE-HIT HIT WONDERS

Revised and Expanded

WAYNE JANCIK

To my son,

Matthew,

and my cousin,

Roy Thedford,

for their love and support

Wayne Jancik is by day a clinical social worker with the Chicago Public School system. He is possessed of possibly the largest privately owned recorded music collection in the known world – hundreds of thousands of 33s, 45s, 78s, 8-tracks, cassettes, CDs and the rest. Despite the responsibility and profundity of such an auditory gathering, Jancik is certifiably "normal" and quite the active advocate of mental health. He is the co-author of Cult Rockers and Noise; was the editor of DISCoveries magazine and has been a columnist with The Chicago Sun Times, RPM and the Music Express. His verbiage has appeared in the Chicago Daily News, Record Review, Illinois Entertainer and Goldmine Magazine.

Jancik can be heard monthly on "Life After Dark," the Steve King & Johnnie Putnam all-night program heard on WGN Radio 720 (AM). For those outside of Canada and the 38 US state coverage, the program can be heard via RealAudio at http://www.wgnradio.com. Wayne can be contacted at onehitbook@sbcglobal.net.

ISBN: 1-4196-8764-6
ISBN-13: 978-1419687648

ACKNOWLEDGMENTS

This survey was made possible by the many participants who gave me their time, their stories, their insights, their written materials, and their photographs. I am, of course, indebted to everyone I talked to, but the following individuals were especially helpful: Carl Perkins, Frank Pizani (of the Highlights), George Lanuis (of the Crescendos), Johnny Otis, Frankie Ford, Phil Phillips, Bo Diddley, Dr. Walter Nadel (of the Islanders), Jimmy Wisner (a.k.a. Kokomo), Sylvester Potts (of the Contours), Johnny Thunder, Johnny Cymball (a.k.a. Derek), P. F. Sloan, Roy Hensley (of the Castaways), Bob Kuban, John McElrath (of the Swingin' Medallions), Chip Taylor, Jim Post (of Friend & Lover), Rene Ornelas (of René & René), Denny Craswell (of the Castaways and Crow), Tommy James, Pepe Cardona (of Alive 'N Kickin'), Sammi Smith, Mike Brewer & Tom Shipley, Rupert Holmes, Dr. John, Mike Love (of the Beach Boys/Celebration), Dan McCafferty (of Nazareth), Phil Lynott (of Thin Lizzy), T.C. Furlong (of Jump'N The Saddle), Gene Allison, Eric Sorrentino (of Bullet), Scepter/Wand owner Florence Greenberg, Dr. Bruce Milner (of Every Mother's Son), John Fred, Terry Cashman & Tommy West, Deon Jackson, Beau Charles (of the Knickerbockers), Eric Darlin (of the Tarriers), Del-Fi Records' Bob Keene, Bonnie Guitar, B.B. Cunningham (of the Hombres), Jim Peterik (of the Ides of March), Dick St. John (of Dick & DeeDee), James Dunn (of the Dreamlovers), Pirkle Lee Moses (of the El Dorados), Jimmy Elledge, David Essex, John Zacherly, Ed Townsend, John Byrne (of Count Five), Dodie Stevens, Norman Greenbaum, Fire/Fury Records' Bobby Robinson, Tony Bellus, Jewel Akins, Rod Prince (of Bubble Puppy), Rick Lewis (of the Silhouettes), Mike Zero and Vinny Corella (of Randy & the Rainbows), Danny O'Keefe, Gene Hughes (of the Casinos), Tony Burrows, Sil Austin, Joey Levine (of Reunion), Rick Majors (of Majors), Margo Sylvia (of the Tuneweavers), Joe Valino, Pete Wingfield, Virgil Johnson (of the Velvets), Paul Balon (of Rockin' Rebels), Buck Wilkin and Buzz Cason (of Ronnie & the Daytonas), Nick Morinelli (of Shades of Blue), Joe Sicurella (of the Tassels), Bobby Marchan, Larry Verne, William Powers (of the Paradons), Troy Shondell, Lesley West, Sid Holmes (of the Cavaliers), Phyllis Carr and William Ferguson (of the Quintones), Gayle McCormick (of Smith), Unique's Joe Stampley, Little Johnny Taylor, Alvin Lee (of Ten Years After), Hal Miller (of the Rays), Nick Todd, Travis Pritchett (of Travis & Bob), Otto Nush (of the Riveras), Trade Martin, Tobin Matthews (a.k.a. Willie Hensen), Rick Nesta (of Music Explosion), Jimmy C. Newman, and Sonny Geraci (of Climax).

This project was made much easier by the band of rock-and-roll researchers who at every request were generous with their help. Special thanks to my good, good friend, *Goldmine* magazine's R&B editor, Bob Pruter, who went well beyond the call of duty in tracking down countless articles and bits of historic scraps. Bob has been there from the idea's inception, through nearly-daily phone calls, armchair strategy sessions, and my dark days of doubt. Thanks, Bob.

Special thanks to WGN's Steve King and Johnnie Putman and their producers, Bob Kessler and Paula Cooper, for their continuing interest, support, and camaraderie. Skip Rose, a collector who hoards every known—and unknown—rock-and-roll photograph, provided names, places, and otherwise unavailable pictures. I also want to thank: Paul Surratt at Research Video, for his enthusiasm and ready supply of one-hit video performances; Jeff Hubbard, for his many leads; and Pete Grendysa, for his article clippings and feedback on the manuscript. Thanks also to *DISCoveries'* founder, Brian Bukantis; his assistant, Aaron Roeth; and the editor and creator of those invaluable collectors' guides, Jerry Osborne; *Goldmine's* former rock editor, Jeff Tamakin; and Joel Whitburn, for his irreplaceable series of books on *Billboard* chartings.

I must not forget my dear friends who have listened to hours of my yapping about this project: Sam Mandel; Richard Schutz; Roy Thedford; Bill Kincade; Ronnie Rice; Warren Simon; "Chuckie" Bankel; Dave Fremon; "Radio & TV Dave" Milberg; Bob Sladek; Len Bukowski; Howard DeWitt; Ron Gordon; Michael "Doc Rock" Kelly; psycho-peers Vicki Wesley, Adaria Powell, and James Branch; and my bosom buddy, Commander Pickle. Also helpful with word-spreading, Harvey Moshman and Will Clinger, "Wild Chicago" Public TV producer and host, respectively. Paul Mawhinney helped with the discographies. I also want to acknowledge the collectors and behind-the-scenes movers: Phil Schwartz, editor of *Recorder* magazine; Jack Baker (of the Busters) and Aaron Mintz at radio station WHAI; Gerry Granahan; Bobby Poe (of the Chartbusters); Fred Masotti; Jerry Schollenberger; Paul Grenyo; Gene Bernardo; Fred Bronson; Jay Warner; Marty Pekar; and William Menor.

Thanks also to the project's original editor, former Billboard Books Senior Editor Tad Lathrop, whose great genius and visionary insight saved this project from oblivion; and the first edition's copy editor, former Billboard Books Associate Editor Fred Weiler, for his gentle proddings and skills in cleaning up my dangling modifiers, split infinitives, and often-uncontrolled uses of what all have come to call "Wayne-isms." Many thanks to the second edition's editors, Billboard Books Senior Editor, Bob Nirkind, and Billboard Books Editor, Liz Harvey, for their patience and continued belief in the book.

Finally, a loving thanks to my wife, Charlene, and my son, Matt, who have endured my absentmindedness, my late evenings at the Macintosh, and the house-cluttering resultants of my admitted vinyl-addictive tendencies. Thanks, honey.

CONTENTS

FOREWORD

Karma—believe in it? This book was written by a man fulfilling his karma. Wayne Jancik was destined to write this book from that preteen summer when he was confined to bed while running the gamut of childhood illnesses. The only thing that made the chickenpox itch a little less or the measles a little less annoying was the sound of each new 45 Wayne's dad brought home as a present for his ailing son. Something about the then-new rock-and-roll records Wayne heard not only helped him to feel better but seemed to be opening up a whole new world that he just had to explore.

As time and illness passed, Wayne accumulated more and more 45s and was soon thoroughly caught up in the excitement of Elvis, the Beatles, and the many individuals who followed them to achieve rock-legend status. But it wasn't just the legends; it was the music that was important. And as Wayne soon discovered, unlike Elvis and company, many of those who made some of the most memorable music that found its way into the upper reaches of the charts were able to accomplish that feat only once.

As an adult, Wayne might have left his childhood toys behind but not his records. He continued to accumulate more and more and more records (approaching 200,000 at last count!). But he has matured into a man who is capable of making extraordinary sacrifices for his wife, Charlene—(make that "Saint Charlene"). Why, just recently, he allowed one complete room of their house to be totally without records, and he gets the shakes only a little when he walks through it—quickly.

For the past several years, starting shortly after the publication of the first edition of *One Hit Wonders*, Wayne has been a monthly guest on our radio show. We've come to understand that this is a man who doesn't just write about and enjoy the artists and the music; he is PASSIONATE about them. He wonders about the stories—the hows, the whys, the accidents, the jokes, the loves, the frustrations—whatever it was that resulted in that one hit. Somewhere in the deep recesses of Wayne's mind there is probably a jukebox that needs this information in order to be able to play the final chorus of each song.

This book is the result of Wayne's fascination with the music and the people who made it. These are the stories of those who had a single moment in the spotlight. In a way, this book is also a diary of Wayne's passion and the artists who supplied the soundtrack to it. If you are a child of any of the rock-and-roll generations, then this soundtrack is yours, too. So, sit back, relax, pop a quarter into the jukebox of your mind, and let the pages, the records, and the memories start turning.

STEVE KING AND JOHNNIE PUTMAN
Co-hosts of Chicago's #1 All-Night
Radio Show on WGN-AM Radio 720
October, 1997

INTRODUCTION

A "one-hit wonder" is an act that has won a position on Billboard's national, pop, Top 40 just once. All of our rich heritage of one-off winners are here between the covers; all, that is, except for those I omitted by establishing two criteria: 1)*The Billboard Book of One-Hit Wonders* restricts its interest to the "rock-and-roll era" (here defined as beginning on January 1, 1955), and 2) a "grace" or "lag period" of five years was utilized to give the recent one-off hit-makers an interval in which to attempt come up with that second scoring (the cutoff point was set at December 31, 1992).

I omitted from consideration as a one-hit wonder all one-time pairings, usually duets, such as Barbra Streisand and Donna Summers. In such cases, when the individuals weren't intended to be perceived as an enduring "act," I disregarded their lone hits. I also omitted acts that had a one-time hit under a "cosmetic" name change, such as Harvey & the Moonglows. Under this modified moniker, the group earned only one Top 40 placement; however, recording earlier as simply the Moonglows, the group had two hit records.

I included all "studio acts," pseudo-groups usually put together by songwriters or producers to meet some felt musical need, such as the Pipkins, Edison Lighthouse, and the Cowboy Church Sunday School. I also cover "double" one-hit wonders, that is, artists who under the veil of different guises have two (or more) different publicly perceived careers. For example, the names Johnny Cymball and Derek refer to the same individual. And the Jayhawks and the Marathons are composed of basically the same individuals but radio programmers and the public alike regarded them as two distinct acts, hence their presentation here as two "different" one-hit wonders.

Billboard began publishing on November 1, 1894. But it wasn't until July 20, 1940, that this "international newsweekly of music and home entertainment" began its "Music Popularity Chart" ("I'll Never Smile Again" by Tommy Dorsey was the very first number one disk), a weekly reporting on the best-selling records in America. To complicate matters, *Billboard* published more than one pop chart each week. After awhile there were several charts: "Best Sellers in Stores," "Most Played in Jukeboxes," "Most Played by Jockeys," and the "Honor Roll of Hits." Although a "Top 100" was published as early as November 12, 1955, pop historians begin with August 4, 1958; the true test of a record's popularity was indicated by the "Best Sellers in Stores" list because it was based on the actual retail sales. The records included and the positions secured by these recordings up through August 4, 1958, were tabulated by Joel Whitburn, the author of *Top Pop Singles: 1955-1993*. All such positions reflect Whitburn's system of integrating these competing charts.

On August 4, 1958, *Billboard* debuted its "Hot 100" chart. Since that date, the magazine's Hot 100 has been acclaimed as the definitive source for the weekly ratings of the nation's most popular records. All chart positions noted in this work after August 4, 1958, are identical to those of *Billboard*'s Hot 100 listings.

WAYNE JANCIK

The 50s

JULIE LONDON

JOAN WEBER
LET ME GO LOVER
(Jenny Lou Carson, Al Hill)
Columbia 40366
No. 1 *January 1, 1955*

"Joan Weber had a five-and-dime voice," Mitch Miller told *Circular*'s Harvey Geller. "She sounded like every girl you ever heard singin' behind the counter in a five-and-dime store."

Joan Weber was born in 1936, raised in Paulsboro, New Jersey, and married to a young bandleader. She was pregnant in 1954 when she hit the streets of New York to audition. She stumbled upon Eddie Joy, the right man with the right ideas—a manager who brought her around to music publishers in the famed Brill Building.

"She was a wide-eyed, virginal, vulnerable, 105-pound waif," CHARLES RANDOLPH GREAN, Weber's discoverer, recalled. One day, Ginny Gibson, one of Grean's most-used demo singers, was unavailable; Weber was available. "Joan did a credible job on this song 'Marionette,' but it was no Grammy winner." Grean took the tape around to various labels and found Mitch Miller of Columbia Records most interested—not in "Marionette," but in that five-and-dime voice.

The producers of the long-running CBS program "Studio One" were planning a drama about shady activities in the record industry and needed a torchy song to provide some musical counterpoint. They approached Miller, who in turn approached Hill & Range Songs. Arnold Shaw, then general manager of the music publishing house, offered Miller a tune that had bombed a year earlier for Georgie Shaw, "Let Me Go, Devil." When Miller turned it down, Shaw had a team of house writers under the pseudonym "Al Hill" rewrite the country ode, eliminating references to lust for that demon rum. "I wanted to cut ["Lover"] with a voice nobody knew, so the audience wouldn't be distracted from the story line," Miller recalled. Before Joan's baby was due, the 18-year-old was in front of a microphone and Jimmy Carroll's Orchestra.

The big day arrived for the excited songstress and mother-to-be. On November 15, 1954, Joan's song appeared and reappeared six times in the "Studio One" presentation. The response was immediate: within two weeks, her first recording had sold half a million copies. Reportedly, this was the first time a song shot overnight into the nation's hit parade solely by means of a lone television plug. Despite successive cover versions of this lover's dirge by the well-established Teresa Brewer, Patti Page, and Sunny Gale, Joan's version out-distanced all the others, rocketed to the top, and held down *Billboard*'s sacred number-one position for four weeks.

On the same Monday that "Let Me Go Lover" hit number one, Joan's first-born arrived prematurely. The following Sunday she sang on "The Ed Sullivan Show." Within a month, she was co-starring with Jack Carter at the Copacabana, reportedly for $10,000 a week. "It May Sound Silly" and "Gone" were issued; neither single charted, despite the promotion as well as the extensive diction and vocal classes that she took.

Eighteen months after her dizzying ride to the top, Joan's record contract was terminated and her marriage ended. She performed in nameless bars in Philadelphia, worked as a clerk in a public library in New Jersey, and, according to rumors at the time, she was confined to a state mental hospital. "Let Me Go Lover" appeared on several anthology LPs, and in 1969, Columbia mailed Weber a sizable royalty check. It was returned; the envelope stamped "address unknown." Weber died on May 13, 1981.

PENGUINS
EARTH ANGEL (WILL YOU BE MINE)
(Curtis Williams)
DooTone 348
No. 8 *February 5, 1955*

True, Toronto's Crew-Cuts did create a Caucasian cover version (#3, 1955) and stole much of the initial action on the Penguins' "Earth Angel." But by now, all is nearly forgiven, and sales of the original rendering may well have exceeded the 10 million mark. Recorded in eight or nine takes, amid the bicycle pumps and scrapwood in someone's backyard garage, "Earth Angel" has become one of the most cherished of all rock and roll records. The tune is also reportedly the very first R & B record to ever crack the nation's Top 10 pop chart.

Lead singer Cleveland "Cleve" Duncan (b. July 23, 1935) and tenor Dexter Tisby formed the Penguins with bass Curtis Williams and baritone Bruce Tate in 1954. After many rehearsals, the quartet approached Dootsie Williams, owner of DooTone/Dooto Records, to record a song that Curtis had written, "Earth Angel."

"It's comical," Duncan told Bim Bam Boom's Steve Flam and Sal Mondrone. "We couldn't pick out a name. One of the fellows just happened to be smoking a pack of Kools and we got to kidding each other about the picture of 'Willie the Penguin' on it, and that's how we came by the name." Before "Earth Angel," DooTone issued a pair of Penguin tracks, "Ain't No News Today" b/w "When I Am Gone." "It was really a demonstration record for someone else," Duncan explained. "Dootsie had the rights on it and when we did it, it was a demo."

"After 'Earth Angel' was released—I imagine that we had gotten somewhere within the Top 10, and the

the cool, cool PENGUINS

group became in need of a small advance on royalties—Dootsie denied the group. Dootsie would not advance us any money whatsoever ... not even $50."

Discouraged and angered, the Penguins sought out the help of Buck Ram, manager of their friends, the Platters. Buck signed on as their representative and negotiated a recording contract with Mercury for the Penguins; as part of the agreement, the then-unsuccessful Platters were tossed into the deal. In the interim, Dootsie issued two follow-ups ("Ookey Ook" and "Baby Let's Make Some Love") which both flopped. Bruce Tate left the group after being involved in an auto accident in which he struck a pedestrian; his replacement was Teddy Harper.

Mercury/Wing eventually issued eight disks by the group, but not one of these 45s nudged the nation's notice. Atlantic shipped one single by the Penguins (a cover of KEN COPELAND's "Pledge of Love") that proved fairly successful on the R & B charts. Thereafter, the classic bird group returned to Dootsie's DooTone/ Dooto. After one single, Curtis Williams left, to be replaced by Randolph Jones. Dootsie issued two more 45s and an EP. The group broke up in 1963. Months later, FRANK ZAPPA managed to coax Cleve back into the studios and produced Zappa's "Memories of El Monte" and later "Heavenly Angel," both credited to the Penguins, for original sound.

Cleve did a one-off single with the Radiants; Harper, Jones, and Tisby later toured with Cornell Gunter's Coasters. According to Duncan, all of the original members of the Penguins "have given up entertaining all together."

DEJOHN SISTERS
(MY BABY DON'T LOVE ME) NO MORE
(Julie DeJohn, Dux DeJohn, Leo J. DeJohn)
Epic 9085
No. 6 *February 12, 1955*

Dux and Julie DeGiovanni worked behind the counter at Sears, Roebuck & Co. in Chester, Pennsylvania. The girls had dreams of things you don't see every day, and dreams of things you just can't buy at Sears, Roebuck. From their mid-teens onward, they would get together in their spare time and sing. Mom and Dad had a dry-cleaning shop; they hoped the girls would come to their senses and join the family business.

In the mid '50s, the Four Aces were the hometown heroes, but when Decca Record scouts heard the Aces and took the boys off to stardom, the Ukrainian Club—which the foursome had been using as their base of operations—needed a new attraction. Dux (b. Jan. 21, 1933) and Julie (b. Mar. 18, 1931) approached the club, and much to their surprise, they were offered a slot there. Their name went up in lights, and Chester had a new group to cheer about. Representatives from Epic Records came sniffing about in search of another Four Aces-type grouping, and decided to give the gals from Sears a chance.

"(My Baby Don't Love Me) No More" made the Chester girls big stuff for a while. The song—with hiccups and all—went Top 10 nationally. But nothing the Pennsylvania kids ever tried for Okeh, Sunbeam, Columbia, Capitol, or United Artists Records even again went Top 40. Hopefully, "No More" brought the girls some of those dreams money can't buy. And hopefully, Dux and Julie got to taste some of that good money, because after "No More," there was no more.

JOHNNY ACE
PLEDGING MY LOVE
(Ferdinard Washington, Don Robey)
Duke 136
No. 17 *March 19, 1955*

Johnny Ace killed himself with a gun while playing Russian Roulette one month before the release of what would become his lone pop hit. He has been called rock and roll's first fatality, by some; others whisper of Johnny being the victim of some sinister plot. But all have called his passing an extreme tragedy.

Here was a singer who could mix blues and ballads with a profound sadness and in a manner unheard of, before and since. James Mattis, his manager, struggling to define Ace's unique talent, told *Whiskey, Women And . . .* : "He had that funny voice surrounded by soft pur-

JOHNNY ACE

ple-sounds. Ah, [like] Nat Cole. It wasn't a style . . . it was something natural."

Johnny had spent two short but solid years atop *Billboard's* R & B listings, with "My Song" (R&B: #1, 1952), "Cross My Heart" (R&B: #3, 1953), "The Clock" (R&B: #1, 1953), "Saving My Love For You" (R&B: #2, 1954), "Please Forgive Me" (R&B: #6, 1954), and "Never Let Me Go" (R&B: #9, 1954). Everything he recorded charted, and his following, though largely black, was becoming massive. White radio was discovering the Platters and Fats Domino, and no doubt would soon find Ace to be equally accessible.

But all that changed on Christmas Eve of 1954 at Houston's Civic Auditorium. It was just before midnight, and Ace had just finished his performance. An audience of 2,000-plus was still jumping and jiving when Johnny went backstage to celebrate with his band. B. B. King, Willie Mae "Big Mama" Thornton, and possibly a dozen others were in his dressing room when Johnny pulled out his recently purchased gun, put it to his right temple . . . and pulled the trigger, once.

St. Clair Ace (a.k.a. Buddy Ace), John's younger brother and fellow Duke Recording artist, believes that his sib was murdered. "I don't want to mention names," he told *The Chicago Sun Times'* Dave Hoekstra, "because the guy might not be dead, but one of [the musicians] who played in his band told me the murder wasn't like they said it was. Taxes had Don Robey [then-owner of Duke Records] tied up. I was told he was putting a lot of trips [for Ace] down for places that he never played."

Johnny's sister, Norma Williams, now a secretary at a Memphis school, disputes this appraisal. "We thought about foul play until we talked to [Johnny's girlfriend]," Williams told Hoekstra. "She told us she was seated in Johnny's lap when he got the gun and she put her temple against his head. The bullet went in one side of his temple, but didn't come through.

"She told us they had been doing this on the road show. During intermission, they would go back in the dressing room and each person took turns with the gun. She didn't say how many people had pulled the trigger, but they certainly had been engaged in the game before it got to Johnny."

Johnny Ace was born John Marshall Alexander in Memphis on June 9, 1929. After completing some years at Booker T. Washington High, he enlisted in the Navy. During his absence, Johnny's mom had purchased a piano and after his discharge in 1947, he took a serious interest in the sounds that box could make. By 1949, he was playing well enough to win a slot with Adolph Duncan's band (a unit that evolved into the Beale Streeters, with sometime members that included Bobby "Blue" Bland, Earl Forrest, Roscoe Gordon, and B. B. King) and later, a job with B. B. King's group.

When B. B. hit paydirt and the road in 1951 with his "3 O'Clock Blues," Johnny auditioned for a position as a studio pianist at Memphis's radio WDIA. One of the executives at the station, David James Mattis, noticed the kid and his smooth style, and asked him to work as an accompanist on some sessions he had planned. Mattis had formed Duke Records largely to show off the talents of another WDIA staple, Roscoe Gordon, and his chauffeur, Bobby "Blue" Bland.

During one session, Bland had difficulties getting his performance together, so Mattis asked John if he would like to try a take on the tune. The song was "My Song," the first record—and first R & B hit—for Johnny Ace, as he was now known (after the Four Aces). Two years of R & B chartings followed before his tragic end. Duke issued the phenomenally successful "Pledging My Love" and other disks after Ace's death, but only one further offering, "Anymore" (R&B: #7, 1955), fared well.

COWBOY CHURCH SUNDAY SCHOOL
OPEN UP YOUR HEART
(AND LET THE SUNSHINE IN)
(Stuart Hamblen)
Decca 29367
No. 8 *April 2, 1955*

"Stuart Hamblen had this record label called Voss," said music researcher and writer Robert L. Synder in an exclusive interview. "He recorded this group; actually they were never what you would call a show business act. In fact, there really was no group to it. 'Open Up Your Heart' was a solo record by this little girl named Carole Sue. She didn't get billing on the label, but she did on the sheet music. They were all probably some kids who attended the same church that Stu did, and he had this song and probably thought this girl had a good voice . . ." Decca leased the master and the Cowboy Church Sunday School had their mini-moment. A few other disks were printed, but nothing sold very well and peace returned to the valley.

Stuart Hamblen's (b. Carl Hamblin, Oct. 20, 1908, Kellerville, TX) daddy was a traveling minister. The constant roaming encouraged the lad to want to be a cowboy. He learned to rope and ride; appearing at rodeos while tending to college studies to become a teacher. Instead Stu became a singing cowboy star who began recording in the late '20s for RCA. In 1928, he moved to Hollywood, where for the next two decades he made spot appearances in b-movies, usually as the villain, and performed on the radio—as Country Joe, and as a member of radio's first Western singing group, Zeke Manner's Beverly Hill Billies. Later, he hosted such programs as "Covered Wagon Jubilee" and "King Cowboy and His Woolly West Review." Sponsors were often called upon to spring the boy from the jailblock, where Stu was held for brawling or shooting out street lights.

Stu turned gospel singer in 1949, after evangelist Billy Graham at a prayer meeting held in L.A. inspired him at a tent meeting to give up his evil ways. He even ran for president on the Prohibition ticket in 1952; missing out on the gig by approximately 27 million votes.

Country fans probably remember Stu best for a tasty tune he wrote and recorded but didn't want released, "(I Won't Go Huntin' With You Jake) But I'll Go Chasin' Women" (C&W: #3, 1950). Having just become a born-again Christian, Hamblen asked Columbia Records not to issue the disk. Disregarding his heartfelt wishes, the company pressed thousands of copies. Its success was followed by Stu's renditions of three of his finest compositions: "(Remember Me) I'm The One Who Loves You" (C&W: #2, 1950), "It's No Secret (What God Can Do)" (C&W: #8, 1951), and "This Ole House" (C&W: #2, 1954).

"It's No Secret," one of the best-known gospels of the 20th century, Stu claims he wrote after a chance conversation with his old drinking buddy, John Wayne. The story goes that John found Stu's born-again stance hard to swallow and in an off-manner replied, "Well, it's no secret what God can do." Hamblen claims the line struck him like a brick.

Although he claimed he had retired decades back, he began a popular Sunday morning network radio show over KLAC in 1971. "The Cowboy Church Of The Air" remained on air for more than a decade. Stu Hamblen died at age 81 on March 8, 1989, during surgery for a brain tumor.

LENNY DEE
PLANTATION BOOGIE
(Lenny Dee)
Decca 29360
No. 19 *May 4, 1955*

"He makes it laugh and weep, pulse and pound, soothe and sway—in short he makes his organ do everything but sit up and beg . . ." wrote a Decca Record publicist of Lenny Dee, their keyboard wiz.

For years, Dee would amaze audiences with his organ playing, commanding his mightly, modified vintage 1933 "White Hammond" to flap like a bass fiddle, beat like a tom-tom, and strum like a banjo. Hi-Fi buffs were enthralled with his Dee-series of album sound experimentations, *Dee-lirious*, *Dee-Most*, *Dee-Licious*, *Hi-Dee-Fi* . . .

He was born in the '20s in Illinois, was raised in Florida, and took to making music early. When he was seven, Len started to study the piano and accordion. For fun, he'd pluck a banjo for his friends. After three years of service on an aircraft carrier, Dee took advantage of the G. I. Bill to enroll at the Music Conservatory of Chicago.

With his studies behind him, Lenny landed a series of bookings at hotels and nightclubs. After hearing Lenny at the Plantation Club in Nashville, Red Foley encouraged Decca Records to sign him to a recording contract. Dee remained a viable recording act, and stayed with the label for 20 years. Oddly enough, "Plantation Boogie," Dee's only charting record, would also be his very first recording. And *Dee-rightful!*, the album from which the "Boogie" was extracted, would become Lenny's largest-selling LP. No way to be considered a rock'n'roller, Dee worked the growing "Middle of the road" circuit, appearing with the Jimmy Dorsey and Ray Anthony bands; guesting on the "Ed Sullivan Show," and with Jack Parr, Joey Bishop, and Johnny Carson.

When last spotted, Lenny—"the Leprechaun of the organ"—and his talented dog Miss Muffet were still entertaining the masses at Dee's supper club, Dolphin Den, in St. Petersburg, Florida.

CATERINA VALENTE
THE BREEZE AND I
(Al Stillman, Ernesto Lecuona, Tutti Carmarata)
Decca 29467
No. 8 *May 14, 1955*

Caterina (b. Jan. 14, 1931, Paris) was born into a world of entertainment. Her Italian mama Maria, billed as "The Female Grock," was a famous clown; Daddy, a Spaniard, was an accordion virtuoso who went by the name of Di Zazzo. As her show biz family toured about, Caterina learned to play guitar and to speak and sing fluently in English, French, German, Italian, Japanese, and Swedish.

In 1952, Caterina married a German juggler named Eric Van Aro and became a circus singer. The following year, she auditioned and won the front spot in Kurt Edelhagen's band. Her second disk, "The Breeze And I," a Cuban song (written by Ernesto Lecuona, known also for writing "Malaguena") sung in German, became her prime pop moment in the United States. No further recordings charted. She toured the U.S. and performed on "The Colgate Comedy Hour," but turned down the offer to appear in any American films. In 1964, she co-starred with comedians Carol Burnett and Bob Newhart in the syndicated variety series "The Entertainers" (1964-1965).

In the '60s, she scored numerous European hits with such tunes as "Itsy Bitsy Teenie Weenie," "Quando, Quando, Quando," and "Pepe." In the mid '70s, Caterina married British jazz man Roy Budd, her music director and producer of her album *Caterina 86* (1988), a project that featured the Count Basie Orchestra.

While her visibility has diminished in this country, Caterina Valente is well known in Europe as a singer, dancer, and actress.

SUNNYSIDERS
HEY, MR. BANJO
(Freddy Morgan, Norman Milkin)
Kapp 113
No. 12 *June 18, 1955*

"I don't think he copied anybody," said Sunnysider frontman Freddy Morgan's widow to author Jordan R. Young. "I think he was a natural born idiot."

Freddy (b. Phillip Fred Morganstein, Nov. 7, 1910, New York City) was a banjo man and a member of Spike Jones & The City Slickers from 1947 to 1958. Morgan also fancied himself a songwriter, and penned tunes like "I Love You Fair Dinkum" and "Er War Ein Schoner Monsieur."

Freddy, who was raised in Cleveland, began picking banjo with Leo Livingston—as Morgan and Stone—in 1924. Three years later, they were under contract to play New York's Paramount Theatre for 51 consecutive weeks; followed by an elongated stay at the Palace Theater and much European travel. During WWII, Fred co-started, with Bebe Daniels and Ben Lyons, the European Theatre Artists Group—the forerunner of the American U.S.O. After tour time in Tokyo, Fred joined Spike Jones's City Slickers in 1947. Young, author of *Spike Jones: Off the Record*, reports, he was to become known for his "Chinese Mule Train" (#16, 1950) and "Poet and Peasant" routines, his appearance in the flick *Fireman, Save My Child* (1932) and his stabilizing presence in Spike's radio and TV series.

In 1955, as an outlet for his compositional brainstorms, he formed the Sunnysiders with Norman Milkin, MARGIE RAYBURN, and Jad Paul; the latter later to be Fred's replacement in the City Slickers. "Hey, Mr. Banjo" was reportedly the group's first recording—Fred had previously recorded with fellow-Slicker Mousie Garner as the Alley Singers—and was their only tangle with Top 40 success.

For the next two years, Morgan picked his brain in search of that follow-up. Assisting him was his occasional collaborator, Norman Milkin, then the spouse to lone female Sunnysider Margie Rayburn. Once the Sunnysiders' days were behind them, Margie would have her lone solo success with "I'm Available," a sensuous Patti Page-like platter, and in 1962, Milkin would reappear on the charts as the writer and producer of JACK ROSS' "Cinderella."

The Sunnysiders continued to work that banjo motif with "Banjo Pickers Ball" and "The Lonesome Banjo (In the Pawn Shop Window)," but nothing further charted. Morgan did, however, write "Japanese Farewell Song (Sayonara)"—not the Irving Berlin number popularized by Eddie Fisher and used in the like-titled Marlon Brando flick (1957). Fred returned to European trekking in the early '60s. Liberty issued a few in a projected series of "Bunch of Banjo" albums. When unoccupied, Fred was a voice on ABC-TV's "Beany and Cecil Show."

Jad who appeared on the syndicated TV show "Polka Party," had recorded as the Banjomaniacs and would go on to recording as a soloist for Liberty and could be heard on soundtracks, such as *Doctor Zhivago* (1965) and *Paint Your Wagon* (1970).

Morgan died of a heart attack on stage on December 21, 1970. Rayburn last recorded in 1963. Paul is still actively picking.

EDDIE BARCLAY
THE BANDIT (O'CANGACEIRO)
(Alfredo Ricardo de Nascimento)
Tico 249
No. 18 *July 16, 1955*

Surprise, surprise! Not 10 months after Percy Faith (#25, 1954), the Johnston Brothers (#26, 1954), and Tex Ritter (#30, 1954) raided the charts with their versions of this tune from a Mexican flick called *O'Cangaceiro* (1954), a young Parisian named Eddie Barclay was back like a bandit to snatch yet some more gold dust.

Eddie (b. Jan. 26, 1921, Paris) was schooled at the Ecole Massillon in Paris. He was a conductor, composer, and record producer, and he eventually became the president of the French record label Compagnie Phonographique Française.

PRISCILLA WRIGHT
THE MAN IN THE RAINCOAT
(Warwick Webster)
Unique 303
No. 16 *August 6, 1955*

Not many people have heard this ode to a shadowy being in shiny, squeaky, pitch-black plastic. While the title suggests a song about a flasher, the Wright reading is period-appropriate and quite innocuous.

At the time of her mini-moment, Cilla was only 14 and had a face full of braces. Her father was Don Wright, the leader of a choir in London, Ontario. Priscilla fooled around with her dad's tape machine, leaving some rough vocal tracks. On a chance listen, Don Knight heard Priscilla's moody and broody singing—here was a young voice with the sting of a worldly Eartha Kitt. Wright excitedly raced about for weeks in search of the right vehicle for his daughter, sifting through more than 120 numbers before choosing "The Man in the Raincoat." Sparton Records released the disk in Canada; the Unique label picked up the platter's distribution, and "The Man in the Raincoat" successfully crossed the border.

Marion Marlowe, known for her "Whither Thou Goest" (#27, 1954), also worked up a version of this musical mystery. Marion was a "friend" on the popular boob-tube bonanza "Arthur Godfrey and His Friends." Her "Raincoat" waxing (#14, 1955) competed with Cilla's, and likewise placed in the nation's Top 40.

Vinyl voyeurs note that Cilla was last captured, cloaked, and disseminated by 20th Century Fox Records in 1959.

CLIFFIE STONE
THE POPCORN SONG
(Bob Roubian)
Capitol 3131
No. 14 *August 20, 1955*

The son of banjo-plunkin' comedian, movie maker, and kennel owner Herman the Hermit, Clifford Gilpin Snyder was born in Stockton, California, on March 1, 1917. Truly, one of country music's most versatile, though largely invisible, kingpins, Mr. Stone—nicknamed "Cliffie Stonehead," by his pop—worked until the late '70s as a singer, composer, manager, bandleader, bass player, recording artist, comedian, disk jockey, TV host, consultant for Capitol Records, and founder of the independents Lariat (where he made the debut recordings on Merle Travis and Stan Freberg) and still-pumping Grante label.

To the pop-music audience, "The Popcorn Song" (with a lead vocal by the songs creator, Bob Roubian) was a fluke hit, an old-timey cornball throwback, a one-off hillbilly novelty. Country folk knew Cliffie for his "Silver Stars, Purple Sage, Eyes of Blue" (C&W: #4, 1947), "Peepin' Through the Keyhole" (C&W: #4, 1948) and "When My Blue Moon Turns Gold" (C&W: #11, 1948). Some of them probably knew of him as the co-author of such notables as "Divorce Me C. O. D.," "Steel Guitar Rag," and "So Round, So Firm, So Fully Packed." As a youth, Cliffie performed as a comedian and as a member of Ken Murray's Hollywood Blackouts, and once appeared in a sketch with fellow Blackout member and future singer-songwriter legend Gene Austin. He played bass in big bands with Anson Weeks and Freddie Slack, and worked for years on L.A. country radio stations as a disk jockey, emcee, and performer.

In the late '40s, Cliffie aligned himself with the newly formed Capitol Records as their C & W consultant and producer, where he helped the careers of Tennessee Ernie Ford, Hank Thompson, Merle Travis, Tex Williams, and Jimmy Wakely. His '50s TV program "Hometown Jamboree" (originally titled, "The Dinner Bell Round-Up") was a proving ground for artists like Billy Strange, Molly Bee, and JEANNE BLACK. A half-dozen albums and a good pile of singles were released over the years with Cliffie Stone's name on them, but "The Popcorn Song" was his lone crossover onto the Hot 100.

"Hometown Jamboree" ended in the early '60s, leaving Cliffie time to manage his publishing concerns, Snyder Music and American Music/Eastern Music. Capitol purchased both companies in the '70s, when his attentions turned to running ATV Music, founding Grante Records and later managing Gene Autry Music. In 1989, Cliffie Stone and his charge who he managed through many years—Tennessee Ernie Ford—were inducted into the Country Music Hall of Fame. His son Curtis Stone is the bassist with Highway 101.

CHUCK MILLER
THE HOUSE OF BLUE LIGHTS
(Don Raye, Frank Slack)
Mercury 70627
No. 9 *August 27, 1955*

Chuck was a scat-singing hep cat who played that eight-to-the-bar boogie woogie piano. He was born, bred, and based in California. Chuck played the lounge scene, and when the lights were low and the hour was late, he'd "blow piano." He'd take standards like "I Can't Give You Anything but Love" and alter them, syncopate them, drag them out. The result wasn't really jazz, but then it wasn't squeaky-clean pop, either. When rock and roll took hold, Miller sounded like he belonged with spit-curl Haley, duck-walkin' Berry, and all those pompadoured boys. His remake of Frank Slack's 1946 hit "The House of Blue Lights" found receptive ears, but "Hawk-Eye," a follow-up with the feel of a scotch-and-soda, seemed a bit antiquated.

After "Lights" went off the charts, Miller targeted his sounds to younger minds and bodies. "Bang Tang Ding Dong," "Bright Red Convertible," and "Cool It, Baby" approached rock and roll. His country cover of "The Auctioneer" charted at number 59 in 1956, and "Plaything," his cover of NICK TODD's hit, closed out Miller's recording career.

Prior to Chuck's momentary popularity with beatniks and teens, he had cut some collectible sides for Capitol Records. "Hopahula Boogie" is one to find, as is "Rogue River Valley."

LILLIAN BRIGGS
I WANT YOU TO BE MY BABY
(Jon Hendricks)
Epic 9115
No. 18 *October 1, 1955*

From the age of 12 on, Philly Lillie spent all her spare time messin' with the instruments: the accordion, piano, violin, and, in high school, the trombone. Lill became so good on the trombone that she represented her school at a district festival. In her senior year, she joined the Swingettes, an all-girl boogie-woogie band. After graduation, she worked the window at a movie theater and continued making rounds with the Swingettes. When the group broke up, Lill formed her own orchestra, playing the Philadelphia night spots and appearing weekly on radio WAEB. By day, she drove a truck.

In April of 1954, Briggs, joining Joy Cayler and her All-Girl Orchestra, started singing. Alan Freed discovered her during her New York City singing debut at the Arcadia, "The Million Dollar Ballroom." Legend has it that Freed—attracted to Lill's vocal talents as well as her skin-tight silver- and gold-lamé dresses—helped Briggs get an audition with the folks at Epic Records. The boys there liked her, too, and waxed her in absolutely no time flat.

"I Want You to Be My Baby" was Lillian's first offering, and, unfortunately, her only hit recording. If not for Georgia Gibbs's competing rendition, "I Want You" might have wriggled its way into the Top 10. The seasonal "Rock 'n' Rol-y Poly Santa Claus" failed to break any chart ground. Next up and quickly down was Lillian's cover of "Eddie My Love." Competing with the original version by THE TEEN QUEEN and covers by the Chordettes and the Fontane Sisters, Briggs' tasty take flopped. ABC-Paramount, Coral, and Sunbeam all tried their best to mold her into a choice chart item, but nothing worked.

For some years thereafter, Lillian Briggs continued working Alan Freed's many New York rock and roll shows. Perhaps, determined as she was, she is still out there somewhere, rockin' her stuff in an all-girl boogie-woogie bar band.

EL DORADOS
AT MY FRONT DOOR (CRAZY LITTLE MAMA)
(J. Moore, E. Abner)
Vee-Jay 147
No. 17 *November 12, 1955*

"It was different then . . ." said Pirkle Lee Jones, lead singer for the El Dorados in an exclusive interview. "We'd walk down the street singing, sing in the vacant lot, in the park; and people then enjoyed it. They'd pass by 'n throw money. There weren't TV 'n air conditioning. Nobody shot at ya, 'n they'd say, 'Sing that one again.' There was more respect then, one for 'nother. It was different. . . ."

The El Dorados were born and raised on Chicago's South Side. When Louis Bradley (tenor), Robert Glasper (bass), Jewel Jones (second tenor, baritone), James Maddox (baritone, bass), and Pirkle Lee Moses (lead vocals) came together in 1952, all were attending Englewood High. Johnny Moore, the school custodian,

The El Dorados

became their manager. They sang in the streets and the pool halls as the Five Stars.

"It started for me long, long ago, when I was in grammar school," said Pirkle Lee. "We got our sound by rehearsing a lot; experimenting. Jewel Jones was a piano player, and we would practice making sounds against the chords he'd play and with blend [our voices]."

By the time Vivian Carter of Vee-Jay Records heard them at a talent contest, the group was six in number— Glasper had left to join the Air Force, and Arthur Basset (tenor) and Richard Nickens (baritone, bass) had joined up—and was now named after their favorite set of wheels, the 1954 Cadillac El Dorado.

"We'd do songs by the Dominos and the Orioles. Things like 'The Bells of St. Mary's,' 'White Christmas' . . . Miss Vivian was impressed with us; not just our singing but our showmanship. She signed us and it all happened.

"We'd go to Al Smith's basement before we'd record; to get it just right. Vee-Jay was just a storefront, across the street and a half a block from Chess Records. All the guys backing us were jazz musicians. They'd pick it up real quick. We had Lefty Bates [guitar], Red Holloway [sax] . . . they each do their own thing, too; but we laid out the structure [of the tunes]."

What little mainstream success did visit this now legendary group came with the release of their fourth 45, "At My Front Door." Once they had charted, the El Dorados became a hot property. "We did the 'Ed Sullivan Show'—told ourselves it was just another show or we wouldn't a been able to do the show. Did Alan Freed shows. He was the one who labeled it 'rock 'n' roll'; cause we were doing rhythm 'n' blues. If he hadn't called it that we wouldn't a got as big."

The double-sided follow-up, "I'll Be Forever Loving You" b/w "I Began to Realize," should have done well on the nation's pop listings, but didn't. No other El Dorados 45 even made the Top 100, and by early 1957, all of the group's original members save Pirkle Lee Moses were gone.

Over the years, the El Dorados reappeared in a number of different incarnations. Carter set up a new El Dorados with Pirkle Lee (lead vocals), Doug Brown (second tenor), Johnny Carter (bass), Teddy Long (second tenor, baritone), and John McCall (first tenor). Brown, Carter, Long, and McCall had already recorded together—with Dee Clark singing lead—as the Kool Gents and the Delegates. "Lights Are Low" and "Boom Diddle Boom" bombed, so this edition of the El Dorados broke up. In 1958, Bradley, Jones, Maddox, and Marvin Smith recorded one single as the Four El Dorados and one as the Tempos. Johnny Carter assembled yet another El Dorados (Spencer Goulsby, Jr., Eugene Huff, Lee Toussaint, and Willie Williams) for the release of a few 45s on Paula in 1971.

Meanwhile, Pirkle Lee reformed his group with Melvin Morrow and George Prayer, both former members of the Moroccos; their lone single for Torrid died an unkind death. The El Dorados story has yet to see its conclusion. In 1978, Pirkle Lee and yet another edition of the El Dorados—Tony Charles, Billy Henderson, George Prayer, and Norman Palm, a one-time member of the PASTELS—had a hard-to-find 45 issued on the Delano label. Richard Nickens of the original line-up has since rejoined the group.

Pirkle Lee and a new line-up of seasoned peers continue to perform; particularly on the East Coast and in Europe. A new package of blues, rock' and roll and gospel numbers was recorded for George Paulus' St. George Records and issued in 1995.

"Forty years later, here we are, with a new record," said Pirkle Lee. "I took it 'round to radio stations. They laughed at me. Program directors there were babies when we came out. they don't know us from Adam . . . ya hear. But All for One, Take 6, Boys II Men are copying our music. We're original, but we can't get treated fair. . . . Now, there's rules for gettin' heard; 'n bein' old 'n not so pretty means ya don't get heard."

BONNIE LOU
DADDY-O
(Louis Innis, Charlie Gore, Buford Abner)
King 4835
No. 14 *December 3, 1955*

Bonnie was born Mary Kath on October 27, 1924, in Towanda, Illinois. For more than 20 years, she was a favorite of country fans in the Midwest. Her big break came by chance when *Billboard*'s Bill Sachs and WLW-Cincinnati talent scout Bill McCluskey—en route to the 1944 International Showman's Convention in Chicago—overheard a salesman on the radio singing the praises of this little guitar-picking yodeler. McCluskey sought out Sally (then a regular on Kansas City's KMBC), gave her a listen, and hired her for his station's "Midwestern Hayride."

A decade later came Bonnie Lou's lone pop hit, "Daddy-O," a take-off on a hip phrase then in teen currency. The lyrics were, to youthful 1955 ears, thought to be "like the most, Dad." The arrangement was rock and roll Cincinnati-country style, meaning it included clarinet and accordion. The vocal featured Bonnie squealing in her best Teresa Brewer manner.

For years before and thereafter, Bonnie Lou had local chartings and some country hits. is still delighting fans with concert and nightclub appearances.

JULIE LONDON
CRY ME A RIVER
(Arthur Hamilton)
Liberty 55006
No. 9 *December 17, 1955*

"'Cry Me a River' was an instant smash hit, and I could taste the smell of success," said Si Waronker, founder of Liberty Records, to author "Doc Rock" Kelley. "When the disc jockeys got their copies of that album [*Julie Is My Name*, her debut], they almost invariably talked about the cover. I must say it certainly was provocative. There was a certain dirty appeal about it. It was cleavage like you never saw . . . I'll never forget Al Jarvis, a popular disc jockey at the time, saying on the radio, 'Today, I have a surprise. I'm not going to play Julie's record—I'm going to play her album cover.'"

Julie's (b. Sept. 26, 1926, Santa Rosa, CA) parents were vaudeville song-and-dance entertainers, Jack and Josephine Peck. Between gigs, the couple ran a photographic studio and shopped their tot around. At age three, Julie Peck made her radio debut singing "Falling in Love Again." School never agreed with Julie's sensibilities; by the age of 15, she was on her way up-and down-as an elevator operator in L.A. While working in a department store on Hollywood Boulevard, Alan Ladd's wife spotted the budding beauty and suggested that Julie attend a screen test for a bit part in something then called *The Girl and the Gorilla*.

For the remainder of the decade, London appeared in a number of minor flicks like *Jungle Girl* (1944), *Nabonga* (1945), *A Night in Paradise* (1946), *The Red House* (1947), *Tap Roots* (1948), *Task Force* (1949), *Return of the Frontiersman* (1950), and *The Fat Man* (1951). All the while, she kept her $19-a-week job at the department store. In 1947, she married radio announcer Jack Webb. When Jack came up with "Dragnet," a boob-tube success, in 1950, Julie retired to raise two daughters, Lisa and Stacy. The marriage ended in divorce in 1953.

The following year, Julie met songwriter ("Daddy," "Route 66," "The Meaning of the Blues") and jazz musician Bobby Troup. "I met Julie when she came to see me at the Club Golden Celebrity Room," said Troup, to *Liberty Records* author "Doc Rock." "I was stricken. I thought she was wonderful. I thought, God, I'd like to marry her. I didn't know who she was, but I thanked her for coming to see me. She said, 'I didn't come to see you, I came to see your guitarist.'" Later that night she sang "Little Girl Blue." "I just couldn't believe it! That anyone that pretty could sing, because beautiful women usually don't have that much talent."

At the least, Bobby encouraged her singing endeavors and made arrangements with Waronker's newly formed Liberty label that would culminate in the haunting "Cry Me a River"—which Julie crawled through in the rock flick *The Girl Can't Help It* (1956)—as well as scads of titillatingly covered, breathy LPs:*Julie Is Her Name* (1955), *Lonely Girl* (1956), *Calendar Girl* (1956), *About the Blues* (1957), *The End of the World* (1963), and *The Wonderful World of Julie London* (1963).

"Julie was a fixture at Liberty Records. She really was Miss Liberty, because before Julie was on it, Liberty Records was nothin'," said Troup, to "Doc Rock."

Before her retirement, London recorded and decorated 30-plus albums for Liberty, the only label that would ever legally bear her name. Julie, according to "Doc Rock" Kelley, "did not get royalties for her record sales. She was on a flat fee for six years. She made about $50,000 a year, plus any money she made herself in clubs or films."

During the '50s and early '60s, Julie made numerous appearances for such TV fillers as the "Zane Grey Theatre" and "Adventures in Paradise," fleshing out the role of a dangerous blackjack queen in "Laramie." For five years in the '70s, London was a regular, Nurse Dixie McCall on ABC-TV's "Emergency," a notable Saturday-night favorite. Interestingly enough, the series was produced by Jack Webb, her ex-husband, and co-starred Bobby Troup, her then-current mate, as Dr. Joe Early.

In answer to the circulating Triva Pursuit question: Only two musicians are heard accompanying Julie— Barney Kessel (guitar) and Ray Leatherwood (bass). Each was paid the minimum session fee of $10 an hour, for the three hours need to create "Cry Me a River," "S'Wonderful," and two other tunes. As for, who was Arthur Hamilton, the songwriter of "Cry Me a River"—the answer: an old school chum of London's who later wrote GLORIA LYNN's one-moment, "He Needs Me," and Peggy Lee's "Sing a Rainbow," introduced in Jack Webb's *Pete Kelley's Blues* (1955).

BARRY GORDON
NUTTIN' FOR CHRISTMAS
(Sid Tepper, Roy C. Bennett)
MGM 12092
No. 6 *December 31, 1955*

Barry Gordon was born in Brookline, Massachusetts, on December 21, 1948. At the age of three, he made his TV debut on Ted Mack's "Original Amateur Hour." In the '50s, he appeared on "The Jackie Gleason Show" and on Benny Goodman and Francis Langford's musical variety program "Star Time." When the need arose at MGM Records to find a kid to sing the new Tepper & Bennett Christmas tune, seven-year-old Barry was chosen. "Nuttin' for Christmas" was rapidly covered by JOE WARD, RICKY ZAHND, Stan Freberg, Homer & Jethro, and the Fontane Sisters, to name a few. Barry's platter would outchart them all, eventually selling more than 2 million copies.

Barry's follow-up—"Rock Around Mother Goose" (#52, 1956)—would be his swan song from the music listings. Gordon continued recording throughout his adolescence and young adult years. In 1968, Barry even donned a Dylan look and sang folk-rock songs for the Dunhill label.

"Nuttin' for Christmas" opened a lot of doors for Barry. During the '50s and '60s, he appeared on "The Jack Benny Show," "The Danny Thomas Show," and "Alfred Hitchcock Presents." He appeared as the "newspaper brat" in the famed Jayne Mansfield—JULIE LONDON rock and roll flick *The Girl Can't Help It* (1956), won a Tony nomination for his role in the show *A Thousand Clowns* (1963) with Sandy Dennis and Jason Robards, also appearing in the movie. Gordon played an ad agency salesman on "The Don Rickles Show" (1972), a soap-opera writer on "The New Dick Van Dyke Show" (1973-1974), and a social worker on "Fish" (1977-1978). When last spotted, Gordon was Archie's accountant on "Archie Bunker's Place" (1981-1983).

JOE WARD
NUTTIN' FOR CHRISTMAS
(Sid Tepper, Roy C. Bennett)
King 4854
No. 20 *December 31, 1955*

"Nuttin' for Christmas" was absolutely the hottest Christmas tune of the year. Who can ever forget those endearing lines: "I'm gettin' nuttin' for Christmas/ Mommy and Daddy are mad." Every label in the land was out to find a kid to sing those words. Columbia had RICKY ZAHND. MGM had BARRY GORDON. Next to jump on the bandwagon was the Cincinnati-based King company. Syd Nathan had found a lad of a few years named Joe Ward. Joe's not singing anymore, or so it seems. His artsy rendering sold some copies and earned a place on *Billboard*'s Top 40—but when the Christmas tree came down, Joe was out of a job and back in school.

KIT CARSON
BAND OF GOLD
(Bob Musel, Jack Taylor)
Capitol 3283
No. 11 *January 7, 1956*

The real Kit Carson—the American frontiersman and Union general—died in 1868. This Kit, a fair-haired female, was born and raised under the name Liza

Morrow. In the '40s, she and Alan Dale were vocalists with George Paxton's big band. George's many platters for Guild, Major, and MGM never caught on. Discouraged, Paxton shut the show down late in the decade. He went on to arrange for Vaughn Monroe and Charlie Spivak, then formed the Coed label in 1958. Thanks to George's musical and business abilities, the Crests, the Duprees, and Adam Wade became hot recording artists. Alan Dale had a few big-selling duet disks in the early '50s, and in 1955 clicked twice with "Sweet and Gentle" (#10) and "Cherry Pink And Apple Blossom White" (#11), the latter from the Jane Russell-Jayne Mansfield film frolic *Underwater!* (1955).

Kit's recording career, however, proved to be less successful. Except for her providing the vocals to Benny Goodman's "Symphony" (#2, 1946), Carson's waxings went largely without notice. Capitol Records offered her a catchy number by Bob Musel and Jack Taylor—

"Band of Gold"—and although it did well, a cover version by Don Cherry out-distanced her effort. Musel and Taylor returned the following year with another *Billboard*-bound tune called "Earthbound." Kit didn't cover it, but Sammy Davis, Jr., did, and charted with it. By year's end, Carson was off the label and out of sight.

BOBBY SCOTT
CHAIN GANG
(Sol Quasha, Herb Yakus)
ABC-Paramount 9658
No. 13 *February 18, 1956*

Bobby Scott was born on January 29, 1937, in Mount Pleasant, New York. He attended Dorothea Anderson Follette's School of Music; studied classical composition with Edward Moritz, a student of Claudia Debussy. In his teens, he played piano in dance bands, worked the Big Apple's jazz circuit, accompanied Tony Scott, LOUIS PRIMA, and toured with the Gene Krupa Orchestra; recording sides for Verve with the latter. In 1955, Bobby met with the cigar-chompin' big cats at ABC-Paramount, who politely gave him a listen and signed him to a contract. "Chain Gang" was an early release, and it clicked.

Further recordings did not sell as well, and Scott turned to arranging for Harry Belafonte, Bobby Darin, and Sarah Vaughan. He also took to songwriting, and hit paydirt when his incidental music for Shelagh Delaney's play, *A Taste of Honey,* won a Grammy Award for "Best Instrumental Theme" in 1962. Three years later, Herb Alpert revived Scott's tune, and "A Taste of Honey" won three more Grammy Awards: "Record of the Year," "Best Instrumental Performance-Non-jazz," and "Best Instrumental Arrangement."

Bobby Scott's solo career continued through the '60s on MGM, Mercury, and Columbia. Scott has since worked as a music director for Dick Haymes and as a producer of sessions for Aretha Franklin, Marvin Gaye and Johnny Mathis. As a songwriter, he penned hits like "A Natural Woman" for Aretha Franklin, "He Ain't Heavy, He's My Brother" for the Hollies, and "Where Are You Going?" for Jerry Butler. Scott also recorded with Chet Baker, Larry Elgart, and Quincy Jones, and has been credited with the discovery of both Bobby "Sunny" Hebb and Perry Miller (a.k.a. Jesse Colin Young) of THE YOUNGBLOODS. Bobby died of lung cancer on November 5, 1990.

BONNIE SISTERS
CRY BABY
(Unknown)
Rainbow 328
No. 18 *March 3, 1956*

In the winter of 1955, three sisters checked out of Bellevue Hospital. The sisters—Sylvia, Jean, and Pat—were nurses at the facility who sang together on the side. Mickey "Guitar" Baker (later of MICKEY & SYLVIA) heard them and offered them a contract with Rainbow Records. The girls left their jobs. As the Bonnie Sisters, they issued a pop moaner, "Cry Baby," that remained in the Top 40 for only three weeks. "Track That Cat" was the follow-up single. And weeks later, quite probably, Sylvia, Jean, and Pat were back at Bellevue.

In 1990 off-beat director John Waters named a flaky flick after the Bellevue belles hit. *Cry Baby* featured JOEY HEATHERTON, porno-popster Traci Lords, talk show hostess Ricki Lake, and star-to-be Johnny Depp.

FOUR VOICES
LOVELY ONE
(Fred Weismantel)
Columbia 40643
No. 20 *March 17, 1956*

From somewhere in the U.S.A. came four voices. They were what was called, in their time, "sweet singers." The mid-'50s were hot on that tight four-part harmony. The Four Aces, Four Coins, Four Esquires, Four Preps, Four Lads . . . whenever one turned on the TV, there'd be men in clusters of four, short hair greased into place, and mouths open.

Allan Chase (tenor), Frank Fosta (bass baritone), Sal Mayo (tenor), and Bill McBride (baritone) did their stuff for the "Arthur Godfrey's Talent Scouts!" TV show and won top honors. Mitch Miller, A & R man over at Columbia Records, happened to hear their cheerful sounds, and in 1955 signed the guys to his label to make hits. But other than "Lovely One" and a nibble on "Dancing With My Shadow" (#50, 1958), the prefab foursome sidestepped stardom.

After five years of zips—including among them the original version of "Sealed With a Kiss"—Chase decided to move on and do some solo recordings, which fared poorly. Meanwhile, the three other voices cooled on ice. The wise thing was done in 1962 when the original guys got together again for Mr. Peacock Records and rerecorded their lone moment in the sun. It sounded good, but by this time, it was too late. The Four Voices dispersed, each Voice returning to his respective hometown.

BLUE STARS
LULLABYE OF BIRDLAND
(George Shearing)
Mercury 70742
No. 16 *March 24, 1956*

Blossom Dearie—yes, that's her real name—was the brains, if not the brawn, behind the short-lived Blue Stars. She was born on April 28, 1926, in East Durham, New York. Daddy was a bartender in the Catskill Mountains; Mommy a piano-toucher began Blossom's musical instruction at age two. By age 10, Dearie was dreaming of a life as a classical pianist. All would change when she heard Benny Goodman's vocalist, Martha Tilton. In the '40s, she sang with the Penn State—Fred Waring group, Woody Herman's Blue Flames, and Alvino Rey's Blue Reys. In 1952, after some wearying gigs as a cocktail piano player and after an encouraging meeting with Nicole Barclay, an owner of Barclay Records, Dearie fled to Paris, where her solo singing career flourished.

Two years later, Dearie began thinking of forming an octet of French, jazzy vocalists. She dreamed up some musical arrangements, and with an eye to her earlier bands, she labeled the chirpy eightsome the Blue Stars—members included Bob Dorough and Christiane Legrand, Michel Legrand's sister. Their unusual scat rendition of George Shearing's "Lullabye of Birdland"—sung in French and arranged by Michel Legrand—caught the responsive ear of French and American audiences alike. The follow-up, "Speak Low (Tout Bas)," plus other experimental excursions, fell flat saleswise. The language barrier and what Dearie called the "mercurial French temperament," lead to friction within the group. While in Paris, she meet jazz impresario Norman Granz, who signed her to a solo contract with Verve. About this time, Blossom fell in love with Bobby Jaspar, a Belgian flutist/tenor saxophonist. Months later, the lovebirds married in Liege and took flight to New York, shelving the Blue Stars concept. Members later reformed the act as the Double Six of Paris, and still later as the Swingle Singers.

After a half-dozen LPs for Verve, Blossom—feeling that her sophisticated music was being underappreciated by the existing labels—formed her own record company, Daffodil. In 1985, she became the first recipient of the Mabel Mercer Foundation Award, an annual accolade given to an outstanding cabaret or super club performer.

Bobby Jaspar—who went on to work with Miles Davis and J. J. Johnson—died in 1963, following heart surgery. Dearie never remarried.

In the years since, when the whim strikes her, Dearie unpacks her baggage, hits the night spots, and sings in her soothing one-of-a-kind style. "There have always

been hard times financially," said Dearie recently, "but perhaps things will get off the ground now. I'd sort of like to become the rage for a while."

TEDDI KING
MR. WONDERFUL
(Jerry Block, Larry Holoflener, George Weiss)
RCA 6392
No. 18 *March 24, 1956*

For a jazz-influenced songstress, Teddi King did well commercially when she charted with "Mr. Wonderful," from the Broadway musical of the same name, followed by "Married I Can Always Be" (#75, 1956) and "Say It Isn't So" (#98, 1957). "I worked the big rooms and was on network TV and the public became aware of my name," King told Whitney Balliett in *American Singers*. "But it wasn't me. I was doing pop pap, and I was in musical despair. I didn't have my lovely jazz music and the freedom it gives." Teddi quickly walked away from the glare of the limelight. For much of the '60s, she worked the Playboy Club in New York City. In 1970, she was diagnosed as suffering from systemic lupus. Singing engagements diminished in number, and King died of the debilitating disease on November 18, 1977.

Teddi was born Theodora King in Boston on September 18, 1929. After graduating from high school, she joined the Tributary Theatre and eventually won RKO's Dinah Shore sing-alike contest. She briefly studied classical singing, as well as classical and jazz piano; she worked with bands led by Jack Edwards and George Graham. Her recording debut came in 1951 with the taping of a set by Nat Pierce's band. Before going solo, Teddi toured for two years and recorded with George Shearing. It was her solo appearances at Chicago's Mr. Kelly's and Philadelphia's Rendezvous that brought her to the attention of RCA and her subsequent "pop pap" recordings.

Months before Teddi's death, the Audiophile label issued two albums of what King referred to as "my lovely jazz music." Both *Lovers and Losers* and *Someone to Light Up Your Life* are still in print.

TEEN QUEENS
EDDIE MY LOVE
(Aaron Collins, Maxwell Davis, Sam Ling)
RPM 453
No. 14 *March 31, 1956*

Aaron Collins and Maxwell Davis were sure they had a hit on their hands. Collins was a member of THE CADETS/Jacks (Modern/RPM/Flair Records' house group) and Davis was the label's arranger. Along with

Willie Davis, Will "Dub" Jones, Lloyd McCraw, and Austin "Ted" Taylor, Collins and Davis—as the Jacks—had an R & B hit in 1955 with a cover of the Feather's "Why Don't You Write Me?" (#3). In just a few months, the very same group, recording as The Cadets, would chart with their cover of THE JAYHAWKS'"Stranded in the Jungle" (#15). Now, however, Collins and Davis had an original, a catchy rock-a-ballad called "Eddie My Love," that they brought to Modern/RPM/Flair's Sam Bihari. Auditioning the tune were Aaron's sisters, Betty and Rose. Sam heard the number and rushed the girls into the Modern Studios in Culver City.

Despite the competition from "whitened" cover versions by both the Chordettes and the Fontane Sisters, Betty and Rose went Top 40 with "Eddie My Love." Their follow-ups were arguably as high quality as "Eddie"; their jump tunes, like "Rock Everybody," were especially pleasing. Nothing, however, charted, and not even a move to a major like RCA Victor helped gain the girls the further notice. The duo broke up in 1961.

TEEN QUEENS

CARL PERKINS
BLUE-SUEDE SHOES
(Carl Perkins)
Sun 234
No. 2 *May 19, 1956*

Carl Perkins (b. Apr. 9, 1932) was born the son of a dirt-poor sharecropper in Tiptonville, Tennessee. His father, Buck, was crippled, and suffered from ill health after the removal of a lung. Times were tough; by age 11, Carl was helping his family pick cotton 14 hours a day. When the crops were good and Carl's parents could afford it, they would buy batteries for the radio, and Carl would listen closely.

"I started playing guitar when I was about six or seven," Carl recalled in an exclusive interview. "I always loved the sound of the guitar, and finally got me this old one from a black man named Uncle John, who lived on the same plantation that my family did. I used to go over and listen to him play a simple blues-type thing. I loved the way he pushed the strings. I'd practice up on Bill Monroe and Ernest Tubb's 'Walking the Floor Over You,' and I'd add Uncle John's blues licks. That's where my style came from."

In 1953, Carl formed his first band, the Perkins Brothers, with siblings Jay (rhythm guitar) and Clayton (bass fiddle), plus "Fluke" Holland on drums. Forced to leave school to support his family, Carl worked in a bakery, on a dairy farm, and in a battery factory—but all the while, the brothers kept practicing.

The group sent some homemade demo tapes around to various labels, including Sam Phillips' Sun Records. In December 1954, Phillips granted the guys a 10-minute listen, and immediately thereafter, a recording contract. "Movie Magg" b/w "Turn Around" (issued on Sun's Flip subsidiary) and its follow-up, "Gone, Gone, Gone" b/w "Let the Jukeboxes Keep on Playing," both sold only locally. Carl's next single, however, proved to be a winner.

"It was the easiest song I ever wrote. Elvis and Johnny [Cash] and myself were playing Perkins, Arkansas, when John said to me, 'Carl, you oughta write a song called "Blue Suede Shoes" . . . [Cash] said, 'In the Army, guys would line up for chow in their combat boots and somebody'd always say, "Man, don't step on my suedes."' I thought about it, and about three weeks later, I was watching this couple jitterbug. I noticed that this cat had on suedes, and at one point, he says to her, 'Don't step on my suedes.' I knew what I was gonna say right then . . . I couldn't find any paper, so I took three potatoes out of a brown paper sack, and wrote 'Blue Suede Shoes' on that sack, exactly as it is today."

"Blue Suede Shoes," released on New Year's Day of 1956, sold over a million copies, and by March of that year, it was number one on the pop, R & B, and coun-

CARL PERKINS

anybody . . . I did lay there thinking, 'what if?'—but Elvis had the looks on me. He was hittin' em with his sideburns, flashy clothes, and no ring on his finger; I was married, with three kids. There was no way of keepin' Elvis from being the man."

With most of his money gone to pay the hospital bills, Carl's career momentum stalled. Depressed at the loss of his brother—who had also been in the car accident and died of complications months later—Carl started drinking heavily. He appeared in one of the earliest rock and roll flicks *Jamboree* (1957), also writing and recording songs like "Boppin' the Blues" (#70, 1956), "Your True Love" (#67, 1957), "Pink Pedal Pushers" (#91, 1958), and "Pointed Toe Shoes" (#93, 1959). "Matchbox," "Honey Don't," and "Everybody's Trying to Be My Baby," three of his compositions, were recorded by The Beatles in one late-night session that Perkins attended in 1963; the tracks appeared on *The Beatles for Sale* (1964) (U.S. version: *Beatles '65*). Perkins also toured with Johnny Cash's traveling show from 1964 through 1976.

Perkins who is still active performing and recording today—with sons Greg (bass) and Stan (drums)—co-authored his biography, *Go Cat Go* in 1997. When time allows, Carl can be spotted at his restaurant, the Suede, in Jackson, Tennessee, or the Exchange Club Carl Perkins Center for the Prevention of Child Abuse, founded in 1980.

Acclaimed as one of rock and roll's surviving legends, Carl was admitted into the Rock and Roll Hall of Fame in 1987. He has been called one of the originators of rockabilly. But Carl steadfastly refuses to take primary credit for this accomplishment.

"[Sam] Phillips, Elvis, and I didn't create rockabilly; it was just the white man's response to the black man's spiritualness. It was born in the South. People working those cotton fields as I did as a youngster would hear black people singing . . . There's a lot of cats that was doin' our things, and maybe better, that were never heard of—they're the ones that created rockabilly, the ones who never even got on record. We're just the lucky ones."

try charts. The same month, Elvis Presley recorded a hit version of the song. Carl was set to appear on "The Perry Como Show" as the first rockabilly artist on national TV But en route to the show, fate stepped in and dealt Perkins a cruel blow—he had a serious car accident that killed his manager, knocked him unconscious for three days, and laid him up with four broken ribs and a fractured right shoulder.

"They were gonna give me a gold record. Sam Phillips was already in New York . . . He was gonna surprise me and announce to the world on 'The Perry Como Show' that my record was number one on all three charts—something that rarely ever happened then.

"As a result of the wreck, I didn't get to make the show. I watched Elvis from my hospital bed do 'Blue Suede Shoes.' I've been asked many times how I felt about that. I always admired Elvis; I liked what he did. I knew he had the same feel for the music that I did; we loved the same type of things. And nobody was topping

GEORGE CATES
MOONGLOW AND THEME FROM *PICNIC*
(Will Hudson, Eddie De Lange, Irving Mills, STEVE ALLEN, George W. Duning)
Coral 61618
No. 4 *June 2, 1956*

Both titles were taken from the Academy Award-winning film *Picnic* (1956). Based on a play by William Inge and directed by Joshua Logan, *Picnic* utilized a basketful of movie stars (such as William Holden, Kim

Novak, Cliff Robertson, and Rosalind Russell) to tell the heart-warming story of a good-for-zip guy who appears in town one day to steal his best friend's damsel. MORRIS STOLOFF, musical director for the film, beat George to the top of the charts with his rendition of this medley. Both versions sold a million copies before the picnic was over.

George Cates (b. Oct. 19, 1911, New York City) began his musical education at the age of four, with violin lessons, followed by extensive study on the clarinet, flute, and saxophone. He attended New York University, initially with the notion of becoming a lawyer. Growing bored with legal study, George dropped out of school to work with various pick-up bands.

After arranging and conducting a musical for Olsen & Johnson, George served for three years in the dual role of arranger and sax man for Henry Busse's orchestra. Besides working as a composer, freelance conductor, and producer, Cates labored for years—beginning in 1950—as a music director for Coral and later Dot Records. He did arrangements for the Andrews Sisters, Teresa Brewer, Bing Crosby, and Russ Morgan; he also served for 25 years as music director for Lawrence Welk's long-running TV show.

Months before his lone Top 40 landing, Cates appeared on two other chart numbers: the mildly popular Champ Butler disk "Someone on My Mind" (#77, 1955) and STEVE ALLEN's "Autumn Leaves" (#35, 1955). George Cates continued recording throughout the '70s, but only his immediate follow-up, "Where There's Life" (#75, 1956), made the Top 100.

DON ROBERTSON
THE HAPPY WHISTLER
(Don Robertson)
Capitol 3391
No. 6 *June 2, 1956*

Donald Irwin Robertson (b. Dec. 5, 1922, Peking, China) has become known and respected in the industry as one of the best postwar C & W tunesmiths, and has been credited with creating the "country piano" or "Nashville piano" style that was largely popularized by Floyd Cramer. Yet Don never managed to have his own C & W hit, and were it not for "The Happy Whistler," the public-at-large might never have taken notice of the man.

Don's father was a distinguished physician who once headed the Department of Medicine at Peking Union Medical College. When Dr. Robertson was offered a position at the University of Chicago, the family moved there; Don was four years old, and began taking piano and composition lessons. The Robertson family summered in Birchwood Beach, Michigan,

where Carl Sandburg, a family friend, lived. Carl's *American Songbag*, an anthology of almost 300 folk songs assembled during the poet's years of wandering the nation's farmlands, was published in 1927, and with Sandburg's aid, Don learned many of these tunes.

Don played in school bands, and by the age of 14 was playing piano in local dance bands. After dropping out of a pre-med program and studying at the Chicago Musical College, Robertson worked as a musical arranger for radio WGN. In 1955, he moved to L. A., where he landed a position as a rehearsal and demo keyboardist for Capitol Records.

"The Happy Whistler," Robertson's first solo side, was a full-fledged fluke hit. The whistled instrumental, while not quite countrified and hardly mainstream pop, was a memorably melodic march just gorged with gaiety. The closest Don ever got to the Hot 100 again came with the release of "Born to Be With You" (1960) and "The Tennessee Waltz" (1961). The former, a one-off duet with BONNIE GUITAR, was recorded under the name of the Echoes [not to be confused with THE ECHOES responsible for "Baby Blue"].

As a C & W songwriter, Robertson has been phenomenally prosperous. Elvis recorded a dozen of his tunes, including "Anything That Is a Part of You" (#31, 1962), "I'm Yours" (#11, 1965), "I Really Don't Want to Know" (#21, 1971), "They Remind Me Too Much of You" (#53, 1963), and "There's Always Me" (#56, 1967). His songs have also been recorded by Eddie Arnold, the Chordettes, LORNE GREENE, Sonny James, HANK LOCKLIN, and Les Paul & Mary Ford.

When the Country Music Hall of Fame was opened in 1967, Don Robertson's name was in its Walkway of the Stars.

MORRIS STOLOFF
MOONGLOW AND THEME FROM *PICNIC*
(Will Hudson, Eddie De Lange, Irving Mills, STEVE ALLEN, George W. Duning)
Decca 29888
No. 2 *June 2, 1956*

Born on August 1, 1898, and raised in Philadelphia, Morris studied violin with Leopold Auer and Theodore Speiring. After a position as concertmaster of the Paramount Studio Orchestra, Stoloff in 1936 began his reign as composer-conductor and general music director for Columbia Pictures. His film scores for *Cover Girl* (1944), *The Jolson Story* (1946), and *Song Without End* (1960) won Academy Awards. Stoloff's rendition of this medley of tunes from the film *Picnic* was the more successful of the two versions that charted, the other being by GEORGE CATES. In addition to composing the pop songs "A Song to Remember," "Dream

Awhile With Me," and "Love Comes but Once in Awhile," Morris also created the film scores to *The Eddie Duchin Story* (1956), *Gidget* (1959), *They Came to Condura* (1959), and *The Last Angry Man* (1974).

Morris Stoloff died on April 16, 1980, at the age of 82.

CATHY CARR
IVORY TOWER
(Jack Fulton, Lois Steele)
Fraternity 734
No. 2 *June 16, 1956*

Cathy Carr was born Angela Helen Catherine Cordovano in the Bronx, New York, on June 28, 1938. From the age of six, she took extensive dance and singing lessons, and appeared on the locally popular "Horn & Hardart Children's Hour." After graduating from Christopher Columbus High School, she joined a U.S.O. troupe as a singer and dancer. On her return, Cathy fronted the orchestras of Johnny Dee, Sammy Kaye, and Larry Fotine.

While touring with Fotine, she leveled with him: She wanted to be a single act, a songstress, a star. Recognizing Cathy's talent, Fotine offered to become her manager. Coral Records signed the bubbly blond to

CATHY CARR

their roster in 1953. Nothing Carr recorded moved the nation—or the vinyl off the record-store shelves—until Cathy cut a cover of Otis Williams & The Charms' R & B hit "Ivory Tower." Cathy's sweetened and polished cover cut into the chart success of the Charms' version, but not by much; Williams and his group were already known to the ever-growing rock and roll audience for their big-time hits "Hearts of Stone" and "Ling Ting Tong."

For years, Cathy Carr continued recording pretty pop things in a Teresa Brewer/Patti Page vein, usually with a mini-touch of rock and roll piano or a youthful vocal-group backing. In 1959, her teen tune "First Anniversary" (#42) almost wormed its way into Top 40 land. An album issued by Dot Records in 1966 was the last noted Carr waxing.

Cathy Carr died in November 1988.

ROVER BOYS
GRADUATION DAY
(Joe Sherman)
ABC-Paramount 9700
No. 16 *June 23, 1956*

In 1950, Doug Wells (second tenor) moved from his birthplace in Southampton, England, to Toronto. With the voice of a cherub and an interest in money, Dougie quickly fashioned the idea of forming a pop group along the lines of his heroes, the Four Aces. He had already spotted Larry Amato (first tenor) at the United Music Center and Al Osten (bass) wiggling his vocal cords on a local TV program. Larry and Al thought Doug's idea was swell.

After some practice sessions, the Rovers three wandered to Long Island and a night spot called the Top Hat. Prior to the gig, the chaps enlisted a Brooklyn boy, Billy Albert (lead), to flesh out their sound. At the Top Hat, they sang *a cappella*. The people drank and danced to it. And one night in September 1954, a local disk jockey named Bill Silbert heard their vocalizing and rushed them to the studios of Coral Records to record their first single (and first flop), "Show Me."

At the Stage Coach Inn in Hackensack, New Jersey, the Rover Boys carried on and created such a din of delight that Sid Feller, an ABC-Paramount rep, signed them to the label. "Come to Me" moved but a few to buy a copy; "My Queen" stiffed in the stall. But "Graduation Day" made an appreciable mark on the charts, despite competition from a cover of the ballad by the more well-known Four Freshmen. The follow-up, "Little Did I

Know," did little, although "From a School Ring to a Wedding Ring" later in 1956 made a brief chart appearance at number 79. RCA and United Artists each gave a mini-whirl on the Rovers, but nothing further ever cracked *Billboard's* Top 100.

The Beach Boys did a remake of the perennial; as did the charting Bobby "Boris" Pickett (#88, 1963) and THE ARBORS (#59, 1967).

JAYHAWKS
STRANDED IN THE JUNGLE
(James Johnson, Ernest Smith)
Flash 109
No. 18 *July 28, 1956*

Carver Bunkum (bass), Carl Fisher (tenor), Dave Govan (baritone), and Jimmy Johnson (lead) met each other while serving time in their local L.A. high school, and soon became the jumpin', jivin' Jayhawks. With tunes in each of their heads and the urge for bread, the guys drifted over one afternoon to the Flash Record Store on Vernon Avenue. The store's owner liked their vocal vibrations, in particular something called "Counting My Teardrops," and took the Jayhawks into a nearby garage/studio, where a half-dozen sides were recorded.

"Stranded in the Jungle," the group's second disk on the Flash label, was a big seller and burned its way into rock and roll history as one of the decade's finest R & B novelty numbers. Unfortunately for the fellows, a quickly constructed but similar-sounding cover version by another local group, THE CADETS, surpassed the Jayhawks' original in record sales. Follow-ups like "Love Train" and the honkin' "Johnny's House Party" failed to catch much of a listen.

By 1960, Bunkum had left the group to be replaced by Don Bradley (bass) and Richard Owens (tenor), and the unit's name had changed. Feeling that they wanted to do more ballad material and that the "Jayhawks!" name was typecasting them as a novelty act, the fellows decided to call themselves the Vibrations. They then hit the Top 40 with two rock and roll notables, "The Watusi" (#25, 1961) and "My Girl Sloopy" (#26, 1964), the original rendition of the McCoys classic "Hang on Sloopy." In 1961, with an urge to go gimmicky again and an itch for some spending change, the same basic line-up did a one-off recording of "Peanut Butter" as THE MARATHONS.

CADETS
STRANDED IN THE JUNGLE
(James Johnson, Ernest Smith)
Modern 994
No. 15 *August 4, 1956*

They started in L.A. in 1954, intending to be a spiritual group. For a moment, they called themselves the Santa Monica Soul Seekers. Their main man and manager from Arkansas, baritone Lloyd McCraw, had a gospel-belting history dating back to the mid-'40s; he had sung with the Royal Four and the Dixie Humming-birds. Soon after their formation, McCraw, lead vocal-

The Cadets

ist Aaron Collins, second tenor Willie Davis, bass Will "Dub" Jones, and first tenor Austin "Ted" Taylor shifted to secular singing. As the Jacks, they approached the Bihari brothers at Modern/RPM/Flair.

Joe Bihari was impressed with their abilities, and in April of 1955, he walked the group into Modern's studios in Culver City, California. Joe had heard and picked NAPPY BROWN'S "Don't Be Angry" for the group to record. In an effort to capture some action on the tune, Bihari had McCraw and his music movers cover the tune as "The Cadets." "Angry" did not chart for the unit, but a cover of the Feathers' "Why Don't You Write Me?" (#82), released just weeks later under the Jacks name, did.

For the next year and a half, the public—and, more importantly, the nation's radio programmers—had no idea that the very same group was issuing disks under two different names. Cadets records were pressed on the Modern label; according to music researchers Donn Fileti and Marv Goldberg, these usually featured either Aaron Collins or "Dub" Jones on lead vocals. Smoothies and jumpers by The Jacks were issued on RPM, and usually featured Willie Davis.

The Cadets/Jacks then became Bihari's house band and started cutting ballads, jump tunes, or calypsos. They accompanied other Modern acts such as Donna Hightower, Young Jessie, and possibly even Paul Anka. As "Kings of the Covers," they rerecorded happening disks by Elvis ("Heartbreak Hotel"), Peppermint Harris ("I Got Loaded"), JOHNNIE & JOE ("I'll Be Spinning"), the Marigolds ("Rollin' Stone'), the Willows ("Church Bells May Ring"), and, for their most publicly known pinching, THE JAYHAWKS ("Stranded in the Jungle").

After "Stranded," not one of the group's fine records ever managed to regain a spot on the nation's pop or R & B listings. The Jacks name was shelved in mid-'56 when McCraw and Taylor left the group. Thomas "Pete" Fox and sometime member Prentice Moreland were brought in as their respective replacements. Shortly after, *Jumpin' With the Jacks*, one of the very first albums by an R & B group, was released. With this line-up, the Cadets continued on for another half-dozen singles and a highly sought-after album, *Rock and Rollin' With the Cadets*.

By 1958, the Modern Record Company complex was in financial difficulties. McCraw, Jones, and Collins formed their short-lived NUC label and issued one single as the Rocketeers. Minus Collins, the dwindling group (with George Hollis and Tommy Miller of the FLARES) recorded as the Cadets for the Sherwood ("Lookin' for a Job") and Jan-Lar ("Car Crash") labels. In 1962, they cut two singles as the Thor-Ables for McCraw's own Titantic label.

Ted Taylor went on to solo success; before his death in an auto accident on November 22, 1987, a number of

his hard-soul singles—"Stay Away From My Baby" (#14, 1965), "It's Too Late" (#30, 1969), and "Something Strange Is Goin' on in My House" (#26, 1970)—placed quite well on the R & B charts. "Dub" Jones joined the Coasters in 1958, remaining with the classic comedians until 1968. In 1961, Buck Ram, the Platters' producer and manager, asked Collins and Davis to write some tunes, and he eventually invited them to join his Flairs/Flares group. One interesting footnote: Aaron Collins's sisters, Betty and Rose, gained their own spot on the charts as THE TEEN QUEENS with the original take on "Eddie My Love."

SANFORD CLARK
THE FOOL
(Naomi Ford)
Dot 15481
No. 7 *September 22, 1956*

Sanford Clark (b. 1935, Tulsa, OK) certainly was a mystery man, then as now. Seldom was he seen, and almost never were his recordings given mass airings. He had a distinctive style that was engaging enough to rival that of BO DIDDLEY, Jerry Lee Lewis, and Elvis. Sounding as despondent as Johnny Cash in his blackest prime, Clark on record was encased in a sparse, echoey accompaniment of Sun-sounding rockabilly. "The Fool," his debut single, made the pop, R & B, and country charts all at once. His follow-ups were of equal or better quality. So what happened?

Even to click but once, all the necessary elements had to be present. Lee Hazlewood, a promising young DJ from Mannford, Oklahoma, had recently moved with Naomi Ford, his songwriting wife, to Phoenix and radio KTYL. Hazlewood, who had already tried marketing some rock and roll tracks while stationed in Tucson, Arizona, soon became friends with the leader of the Arizona Hayriders, guitarist Al Casey. It was Casey who had first heard Clark, and Casey introduced Clark to both Hazlewood and Naomi's mournful song.

The Hazlewoods, Casey, and Clark pooled their resources and bought some time at Floyd Ramsey's Audio Recording Studios in Phoenix (later known as the house that created all those twangy-guitar hits for Duane Eddy, a sometime accompanist on some of Clark's waxings). Present on the session were drummer Connie Conway, bassist Jimmy Wilcox, and guitarists Al Casey and wife Corky. Using the eerie guitar lick, Al has admitted lifting in part from Howlin' Wolf's "Smokestack Lightnin'." MCI Records was formed by these interested parties to issue "The Fool." The response was immediate and positive, and soon Dot Records had acquired the rights to distribute the record nationally.

Despite quitting his job delivering Canada Dry soda, Clark apparently did too little in the way of promoting his nation-shakin' hit. Some touring with Gene Vincent, Jerry Lee Lewis and CARL PERKINS followed. "Carl was a nice guy . . . drunk all the time. We all stayed drunk at the time," explained Clark to liner note writer Rick Kienzie.

Things looked bright as Sanford successfully passed a screen test for a Gordon MacRae flick with Universal International. "It was like those Presley movies," Clark said. "I had the wardrobe, the script, and everything, and then they decided they weren't gonna do it. They were gonna give me a $1,000 a week . . ."

"A Cheat" (#74, 1956) charted, but nothing further would ever again garner mainline pop, R & B, or country attention. By 1960, Sanford had joined the U.S. Air Force, again. On his return, he reportedly became a croupier, continuing to sing on the side. His subsequent performances were issued by the Dot, Jamie, 3-Trey, Project, Warner Bros., Ramco, and LHI labels. Only the latter company, owned by Hazlewood, released an LP, *Return of the Fool.*

"I never made any money to speak of," said Sanford. "I did a lot of record hops and then when I got my royalties, I owed all these damn airplane fares and clothes I hadda buy and hotels . . . and what not."

Asked if he knew then that he'd be considered one of rockabilly's finest acts, Clark said, "Shit, no. We was just havin' a good time. We partied all the time. No thought to it, we just knew how to do it and had a lotta fun doin' it."

HELMUT ZACHARIAS AND HIS MAGIC VIOLINS
WHEN THE WHITE LILACS BLOOM AGAIN
(Fritz Rotter, Franz Doelle)
Decca 30039
No. 12 *September 22, 1956*

Helmut Zacharias (b. Jan. 27, 1920, Germany) was handed his first violin at the age of three. The family was most encouraging; his father was a professional violinist. At 17, Helmut's virtuosity won him the Fritz Kreisler Award. Before his teen years were played out the lad was fronting his own orchestra. By his mid '20s, Helmut was hooked on jazz and soon acclaimed "Germany's top jazz violinist—Europe's hottest fiddler." This, too, would pass, as Helmut moved through his developmental stages and discovered "mood music." By the mid-'50s, Zacharias and His Magic Violins were quite popular throughout Europe. A representative from Decca Records brought some of Zach's zingers over to the U.S., and the label's Milt Gabler approved their stateside release. "China Boogie" shook no one,

but Zach's "Lilacs" number, a tune written in 1928, played on the emotions of many post-teens. Leroy Holmes, Billy Vaughn, Lawrence Welk, and Florian Zabach all rushed their string men into the studios to record their own renditions. Helmut's hummer, however, was the hit.

Well into the '60s, additional singles, EPs, and LPs by Helmut Zacharias were sporadically issued by Philips, RCA, and Capitol.

JANE POWELL
TRUE LOVE
(Cole Porter)
Verve 2018
No. 15 *October 27, 1956*

Jane Powell was born Suzanne Bruce in Portland, Oregon, on April 1, 1929. She performed on the radio from early childhood, and at the tender age of 15 made her film debut in *Song of the Open Road* (1944) with W. C. Fields, Edgar Bergen, and Charlie McCarthy. As a very innocent and sugary blue-eyed blond, Jane became an adolescent star in several light romances and movie musicals during the late '40s and early '50s. With a stiff whiff of purity, Jane moved through productions with teasing titles like *Rich, Young and Pretty* (1951), *The Girl Most Likely* (1957), and *The Female Animal* (1958). Her career reached a pinnacle with her lead role opposite Howard Keel in *Seven Brides for Seven Brothers* (1954).

In the musical *Royal Wedding* (1951), Jane Powell sang a ditty with Fred Astaire, "How Could You Believe Me When I Said I Loved You When You Know I've Been a Liar All My Life?" The duet, a pre-rock-and-roll-era hit (#30, 1951), eventually sold a million copies. Over the years, other twosomes and solo settings were tried, but only a filler of a flip side would fill the bill and give Jane her lone hit as a solo artist. Bing Crosby had lustfully sung "True Love" to Grace Kelly in what he later considered his favorite scene in his favorite movie, *High Society* (1954). While Jane's cover version of this Crosby tune, originally intended as the "B" side for a single, did not outsell the crown crooner's original, Powell surprised many when her recording charted only paces behind Bing's. But storm clouds were gathering, rock and roll was on the horizon, and Jane, with her distinctively mellow and mature style, was never to place another record on *Billboard*'s Top 100.

Jane Powell occasionally appears at nightclubs, in summer stock, and in TV specials; she has vacationed on "The Love Boat" and "Fantasy Island." She married her fifth husband, former child star Dickie Moore in 1988. None of her recordings are currently in print.

EDDIE COOLEY & THE DIMPLES
PRISCILLA
(Eddie Cooley)
Royal Roost 621
No. 20 *November 24, 1956*

Eddie was a New York City songwriter. He is known for only one song, "Fever"—a tune that he co-wrote with Otis Blackwell and that was popularized by Little Willie John, Peggy Lee, and the McCoys. Cooley also concocted "Priscilla," and legend has it that he liked the song so much that he and three unnamed ladies (the Dimples) recorded the tune for Royal Roost Records. Judging from the sound of "Priscilla," it seems like Cooley might have been a true rarity: a black man with rockabilly roots.

In the late '80s, Blackwell laid claim to writing "Priscilla." "Priscilla is a comic book character," Blackwell told the authors of *The Songwriter Speaks.* "I read a lot of comic books 'cause at the time I wanted to be a cartoonist; 'til my eyes went really bad on me. Comic book titles would give me an idea. I used to read them not for the story, but for the ideas about love. Then I'd add a little country bit to it. They gave me a sense of direction . . . [That 'Priscilla'] she was a bad little broad, too!"

Despite its chart status, "Priscilla" remains one of the least played of all hits from the '50s. And Cooley, whose name is difficult to locate in the annals of pop history, continues to live in obscurity.

Eddie Cooley made three more singles—"A Spark Met a Flame," "Hey You," and "Leona"—before his ride into the shadows.

HIGHLIGHTS
CITY OF ANGELS
(Nick Joven, Bev Dusham)
Bally 1016
No. 19 *November 24, 1956*

"The Highlights. God, I haven't seen any of those guys in years, years," said Frank Pizani (b. Jan. 24, 1935, Chicago), the group's lead voice, in an exclusive interview. "Nobody has even asked me of them in ages, ages.

While attending DePaul University as an education major, Frank worked as an usher for Chicago's answer to Philadelphia's "American Bandstand." "I ushered for Jim Lounsbury's 'Bandstand.' This show was starting to get out of hand. Now and then, they'd have like a riot, so what I did was sing to them while they were waiting in line outside the studio to get let in. One day, some of the kids asked Jim to put me on the show. I remember I sang 'Sh-Boom', *a cappella.* Now, the show's producer Holly Christensen and another fellow Jim Cross heard

me and lined it up for me to make a record; 'Cry Baby,' it was called. For Klick records, yeah. I recorded it with the George Rank Orchestra. On the other side was this instrumental, 'Tic Toc Melody.' You won't find that record. I don't even have a copy. It got some play on the show and did okay, locally."

Meanwhile at DePaul, Pizani met Frank Calzaretta (lead vocals) "He had a group with his brother Tony (tenor) and a couple of other guys [Bill Melshimer (baritone) and Jerry Oleski (bass)] that he called the Highlights. They'd do hops and high school dances. I knew a Frank McNulty [music coordinator for the "Oprah Winfrey Show"] and had done some demos for him. He had this song he wanted me to do called 'Jingle-Lo'; with all kinds of complex parts. I told him, 'I know this group and together I think we can do a good number on it.' So we went downstairs in the hallway of WGN Studios. There was this great echolike chamber sound and with the help of Joe Scotti on piano we did a take on the song right there in this hallway on Michigan Avenue. Scotti had cerebral palsy. He was a genius, but he'd hit the wrong notes; he couldn't help it. McNulty said, 'This is great' and took the tape around. He brought it to Bally Records, and they liked it and wanted to sign us up, immediately. Immediately! It was all happening fast.

"Now, from my way of looking at it, this was the beginning of the end for the Highlights. Frank [Calzaretta] wanted to sign as a group, without me, Frank Pizani. There was some friction as to who was going to sing lead and all that, but we did sign up. Unfortunately, looking back, we had a really big hit record with 'City of Angels', the very first thing we cut. The group was still not happy. They wanted to be their own group, not some back-up for me. So the fellows' parents got a lawyer, and they took the name away. They then approached the label and me and said that if I wanted to record with them I'd have to work for them. I wasn't happy with this and left. . . . Ah, what are ya gonna do? Even if we had had our problems most of the guys were still underage and in high school so we wouldn't have been able to travel or work the nightclubs. Hey, it wasn't meant to be"

Bally had "To Be With You," with Frank singing lead, in the can and issued it posthumously. It charted (#84, 1957). Pizani was signed on as a solo act and charted with "Angry" (#70, 1957). "Indiana Style," the first and only Pizani-less Highlights record, was released during the summer of 1957. It bombed and the group broke up. Pizani, meanwhile, went into the service. "When I returned, Bally Records was gone. The other guys, well, they finished their schooling and college and got 9-to-5 jobs. Jerry, he's an insurance salesman. Billy is a high school coach. Tony works at Ditka's [a night spot owned by former Chicago Bears coach Mike Ditka] as their entertainment director. His brother, Tony is off doing business type stuff somewhere."

Before his momentary retirement, Pizani had a few singles issued ("Wanna Dance" for Afton and Warwick and "You're Breakin' My Heart" for Carlton) and then returned to college to complete the requirements for his teaching certificate. For years in the '60s and '70s, he taught in Chicago's grammar schools. Most recently, Frank has appeared in a number of local TV commercials, worked as a comedian, and for some years was the Vice President of Carl Bonedfede's Chi-Town Records. The label and Pizani's own Happyday label released a few Pizani obscurities ["Fighting Jane (Byrne)", "I Love You Papa". . .]. In the '80s, he signed up with Ron Smith's Look-a-Likes, as a Tony Bennett imitator. In that capacity he briefly appeared in the Rick Springfield flick *Hard to Hold* (1984) crooning, "Yeah, you guessed it, 'I Left My Heart in San Francisco.' They didn't even include me on the soundtrack album. That Springfield, he was an ass."

Pizani also heads Custom Phone Announcements, a firm that creates personalized celebrity impersonation messages. Their motto: "We Touch Tone Your Funny Bone." (For further information, interested parties can reach Frank via P.O. Box 46207, Chicago, IL 60646.)

SONNY KNIGHT
CONFIDENTIAL
(Dorinda Morgan)
Dot 15507
No. 17 *November 24, 1956*

Joey C. Smith (b. 1934, Maywood, IL) was going to be an author, or a jazzman. Joey would practice some on Ma's piano and listen to Dizzy Gillespie on the jukebox. One story has him saved from an untimely death by Dinah Washington. He and a buddy had snuck into one of her band's practice sessions. Some older punks spotted the 12-year-old and flipped Joey over a balcony railing, when Dinah intervened and stopped his possible termination.

By the early '50s, Joey and his family were living in L.A. There he attended Belmont High and L.A. City College, wrote a novel that would be rejected, and played local theaters and talent shows with a drummer. "There was this one particular girl who used to come in and listen to me," Knight told *Goldmine*'s Randall C. Hill. "She suggested I get into recording, that I was as good as the folks who were getting airplay. So I looked in the L.A. phone book, starting, naturally, at the 'A' section. Aladdin was the first company I came upon."

Joey called the label's Eddie Mesner, who told him to come on down the next day for an audition. "[Mesner] heard me play, then he called in his wife. I played the same

few songs for her. They left the room for 10 minutes, and the guy came back alone and asked me if I wanted a contract. So I signed a record contract and a manager's contract and was unknowingly in with the sharks."

From his first record on, except for a 1955 Cal-West single, Joey was "Sonny Knight." "My cousin and I were working on a car. It was hot and we were drinking a lot of beer. We thought the name was a clever joke. I never thought that I'd have to live with it."

Aladdin issued "But Officer" and "Baby Come Back." When the royalties failed to appear, Sonny switched to Specialty Records. One release later, Specialty's Bumps Blackwell introduced him to the Morgans, Hite and Dorinda. They were songwriters and had a recording studio in their home. After a bit, Sonny and the Morgans worked up a song called "Confidential."

"I was disillusioned [by this point]," Knight recalled to liner-note writer Bill Millar. "I was working at a really bad club, A Bucket of Blood on Central Avenue. They had the front door open, and I could see the funeral home where my mother was lying in state and that was traumatic. My mother never wanted me to be a musician, and I thought I was letting her down . . . eventually, I thought, I don't have to spend the rest of my life doing this, and went into the studio."

The session Sonny debated attending produced his money-making moment. Unfortunately, two record companies, Viva and Dot, issued the track, and neither, according to Sonny, reported an accurate count on the number of disks sold. "The case was settled out of court, eventually . . . out of the whole thing, I got $2,100."

SONNY KNIGHT

Sonny Knight currently lives in Hawaii. Finally an author, his book *The Day the Music Died* was published under his God-given name by Grove Press in 1981.

JOE VALINO
GARDEN OF EDEN
(Dennise Haas Norwood)
Vik 0226
No. 12 *December 8, 1956*

"I had a record—a long time ago—Frank Sinatra heard it; and he blew me away," said Joe Valino, in an exclusive interview in July 1990. "I did 'Learning the Blues,' the original. That was my record, my first record. I was a kid; and it woulda happened . . .'"

Valino was born Joseph Paolino, in South Philadelphia on March 9, 1929, to a music-filled family. By six he was studying guitar, then piano and bass; at 11 he sang at a back-alley club called the Flamingo Cafe. Two years later he was on the road with the Marty Kent Band.

"I suffered a 'mishap' when I was young," Joe said. "It left me unable to sing or talk for three weeks. I promised myself that I was gonna sing as much as the Lord let me, for the rest of my life."

For four years he fronted his own four-piece; followed by stays as soloist with Buddy Fisher and Charlie Ventura. For a time, "Mr. Mood," as he became known was a soloist with the Woody Herman Band.

Valino's first recording was in 1950, with the Johnny Thompson Orchestra, "Shooting High," for Gotham. In 1953, he signed with Debut and issued "All the Things You Are," which was followed by Valino's most cherished recording, the noncharting "Learnin' the Blues" in '55. "Sinatra heard that one when I was working with him that summer at the 500 Club in Atlantic City. We got to know each other and he told me, 'You sing so great. I'm gonna remember your name. If I can do something for you, I'm gonna do it.' And he did it to me. I was in Detroit, when I got the call. Somebody called and said, 'Sinatra's recording your record, right now.'"

To repay the tribute, Valino covered Sinatra's "Not As a Stranger." Sales were mild. "Hidden Persuasion" followed with minimal sales. "Sinatra took that one, too," Joe said. "But, RCA heard of me and signed me up [to their subsidiary, VIK]. They had me come in to this Giselle MacKenzie session and cut two songs [his debut disk for the label, "The Four Seasons" b/w "Buckets of Love"]. They must have liked it 'cause I got my own session next, when I cut 'Garden of Eden.'"

Joe did a fine, fine skin-crawling crooning on "Garden of Eden," a tune of apples and lust. The take is built with "Bolero"—like tensions and what can only be called a semi-operatic ending. Joe Valino finally had his day. "I knew it would be a hit, even as I was recording it," said Joe.

The disk charted big in England and in regions throughout Europe. Follow-ups failed to maintain the momentum. VIK only issued "In the Arms of Love" and an EP named after the hit; no album. United Artist put out "Legend of the Lost," the title tune to the John Wayne-Sophia Loren flick (1957), and "God's Little Acre." Sales were negligible. There was a brief return to RCA for one single in 1959, "Everything I Touch Turned to Gold," and a single each for Philly's Crosley (Enrico Caruso's "Vesti La Giubba") and Jimmy DeKnight's Bandbox.

Years passed. Joe Valino worked the nightclubs. Finally an album, *Saint or Sinner*, was issued by Debut, in 1968. He also landed a bit part in Richard Grand's mini-budget flick about compulsive gamblers, *The Commitment* (1976).

"About 1980, I got hit with a heavy, heavy stroke and it took me four years to get myself back. Since then, I got two more. I've been blown away for years. Each time I get it going, it happens. When it's not a stroke, it's heart attacks and bypass surgery. I got to start a new album called *Atlantic City to McArthur Park* (1987). 'McArthur Park' was eight minutes and 15 seconds. I was pushing. . . . The day I wrapped it up, I went home and woke up stroked again. I'm trying to get myself together. It's this last round that got me. I'll get it back. I just won't stop. I'll just play the piano in the bars until I get my bearings back. . . . I'll sing again. I'm strong, thank God. I'm ready."

Debut Records released, *Joe's Atlantic City to McArthur Park*. I.M.C. pressed up copies of Valino's final 45, "Atlantic City."

Christmas Day 1996, within hours of its climax, Joe Valino died. He was at his mother's home in South Philadelphia when a heart attack claimed his life.

SIL AUSTIN
SLOW WALK
(Sil Austin)
Mercury 70963
No. 17 *December 22, 1956*

"I'm not as upset as some people think I should be," said Sylvester Austin (b. Sept. 17, 1929, Donellon, FL) in an exclusive interview. "If my career was startin' in these days, I woulda been a multi-millionaire. But, I ended up being one of the most recorded saxophonist of my generation. Thirty-two albums; probably more. I lost count. My stuff comes out in parts of the world I only hear about later on. I got to do things with strings and orchestras, the New York Philharmonic; all the voices I wanted, whatever. Mercury [Records] put everything at my disposal. They knew I was gonna happen; and hey, they paid me pretty well. It's been good."

Sil Austin was born to a family with little interest in music. "I was a maverick, from birth I guess. I'd always be listenin' to big bands on the radio and walk about in a haze hummin' tunes. . . .

"I was eight or nine when I got started; had this music teacher named Dominick. I got my first horn when I was 11; late cause I came from a poor family. It was just luck that I got any instrument. . . ."

When Sil was 13, his maternal uncle, George Hubert, who lived in New York City, came to St. Petersburg, Florida, where Sil and his mother now lived. "Now, he was a music lover, dug Coleman Hawkins and those guys. He told my mother, 'This boy's got potential. I'd like to take him back to New York and put him in a school and get him the proper training.' My mother didn't take to that well, but she did let me go."

Sil was given tutoring from reed instructor Joe Napoleon, brother to jazz pianist Teddy Napoleon, off-and-on for seven years. At his friends' insistence, 17-year-old Sil competed in a talent contest at the Apollo Theatre. Playing "Danny Boy," his favorite song, Sil won first prize and a two-week engagement at a local club—that gig matured into six months' work. Thereafter, he was in demand, playing sax with Roy Eldridge (1949), Cootie Williams (1949-1951), and Ray "Tiny" Bradshaw (1952-1954). The following year, Austin formed his own combo and recorded his solo debut, "Crossfire Part 1 & 2," along with a few other obscure sides, for Jubilee Records.

"'Tiny' Bradshaw had such a tight band. It was because of Bradshaw that I got to record my stuff. He was seeking hot saxophones, and I was one of the top men, at that point. I wrote stuff for him, including his hit 'Ping Pong.' Ella Fitzgerald did a scat on it; later giving me the nickname, 'Ping Pong.' Later, they got to calling me 'Slow Walk' Austin . . ."

In 1956, Sil was signed to the Mercury label. His finest singles, including the classic honky-tonk honker "Slow Walk," were cut in New York City with his usual assemblage of musicians: Mickey "Guitar" Baker (later one-half of MICKEY & SYLVIA), Clarence Collier (bass), Panama Francis (drums), Heywood Henry (baritone sax), Wallace Richardson or Kenny Burrell (guitar), and George Stubbs (piano).

"Now, it's hard to think of my 'Slow Walk' without thinking about Bill Doggett's 'Honky Tonk,' and I've talked to Bill about this. Our records got called rock-'n'roll. Now, we'd always played like the way we did. I was hanging out with Sonny Rollins and Jackie McLain. All we were doing was playing great horn. I was married at 19—had responsibilities—was nothin' I was gonna do but play horn; I knew it. I had to figure out how to make money with this band [Collier, Henry,

Stubbs, and "Foots" Sims (drums); sometimes Sonny Forrest (guitar)]. Exciting horn, honkin' horn, git-bucket horn is what kids wanted to hear, so I made sure I played more of that. They called it rock'n'roll. And the records sold."

In his follow-up 45s, Sil continued to work the frenzied-sax terrain he shared with Big Jay McNeely, Red Prysock, and Clifford Scott, but only "Birthday Party" (#74, 1957) and "Danny Boy" (#59, 1959) did well.

"Mercury had Clyde Otis, and David Carroll and these guys got together and decided, 'This guy's got such great tone, suppose we put strings and voices behind him.' Man, it changed my sound. They had strings from the New York Philharmonic, the Ray Charles Singers, and low and behold the sound sold. That's when they stopped concentrating on the 'Slow Walk' sound and on singles. I started doing theme albums—*Sil Austin Plays Pretty Melodies From Around the World, Sil Austin Plays Folk Tunes* . . . I didn't mind the change, because the albums were selling. All the honkers weren't gettin' much and I was gettin' paid pretty good. So, I played what sold."

When last noted, Sil Austin was living in Florida. On occasion, Sil has been known to pick up his horn and honk for Sew City, Jerri, Shelby Singleton's SSS International label and most recently Rounder Records.

"There's more Sil Austin coming. I'm not through. If I could get the right deal, I'd like to honk again."

VINCE MARTIN WITH THE TARRIERS
CINDY, OH CINDY
(Bob Baron, Burt Long)
Glory 247
No. 9 *December 22, 1956*

Critics reporting on a few of Vince's East Coast appearances at the South Boston or the Village Vanguard in the mid-to-late '50s noted that he was a "tall, personable," but "shy-appearing youngster." He was usually accompanied on two guitars and banjo by Alan Arkin, Bob Carey, and Erik Darling, THE TARRIERS. Midway through their act, Vince would come out and sing "Casey Jones," "So Long It's Been Good to Know You," and "Cindy, Oh Cindy," and then he'd walk off.

Arkin, Carey, and Darling were also present on Vinnie's vinyl excursion. "When we signed on with Phil Rose's Glory Records, they had another artist, Vince Martin," said Erik Darling in an exclusive interview. "Where he came from I will never know. They had 'Cindy, Oh Cindy,' that some New York pop writers had taken a Jamaican melody from and written some words for. Originally it went something like: 'Pay me, pay me, pay me my money down/pay me my money or go to jail.' We arranged it in a calypso style and sang behind this guy, Martin. That was issued first before any stuff we'd do; much to are chagrin. We wanted our record out ["Banana Boat"]. We didn't wanna sing with a Vince Martin. He wasn't a folksinger, in any manner or form. I mean, the last thing he knew anything about was folk music."

No one could have guessed it—though Erik and his buddies hoped it—but months later, the Tarriers would create their own momentous moment with "The Banana Boat Song."

Although Martin, with and without the Tarriers, appeared on a few other 45s, nothing further clicked.

Vince continued to work at a low-profile music career well into the '70s. ABC-Paramount and Elektra issued a few singles; Elektra even shipped an LP in 1964. In 1973, during the height of the singer-song-writer epidemic, Capitol made a last-ditch effort to revive Martin's flagging popularity with an album entitled, logically enough, *Vince Martin*.

JERRY LEWIS
ROCK-A-BYE YOUR BABY WITH A DIXIE MELODY
(Sam Lewis, Joe Young, Jean Schwartz)
Decca 30124
No. 10 *December 29, 1956*

Jerry was born Joseph Levitch, in a show biz family, in Newark, New Jersey, on March 16, 1926. His parents were often away performing in the Catskills on the "Borscht Circuit." During the summers, Jerry would join his mom and dad and their stage act, where he would sing a solo number. After one year of high school, Jerry quit to make the rounds of the booking agents. In between gigs, he would work as a soda jerk, shipping clerk, theater usher. By 18, when he married Patty Palmer, a vocalist with the Jimmy Dorsey Orchestra, Jerry Lewis was an experienced small-time stand-up comic, with a knack for impersonating big-time celebrities.

In 1946, Lewis met Martin—Dean Martin, a struggling vocalist and all-around entertainer. Their first appearance, as a team, at the 500 Club in Atlantic City, proved a tremendous success. Their basic bit involved Dean crooning and Jerry constantly interrupting, with much ad-libbing and the trading of insults and hurt feelings in the mix. By decade's end, Martin & Lewis were America's number one comedy team.

Before splitting in 1956, Dean and Jerry made a staggering array of flicks—17 money-makers; most notably, their debut *My Friend Irma* (1949), *That's My Boy* (1951), Scared Stiff (1953), and their last *Hollywood or Bust* (1956). Pursuing a solo career, Jerry continued to work his singular shtick—the benign fool,

with contorted facial expressions, silly slapstick, and something akin to a sympathy-inducing case of arrested development. As such, he created—sometimes producing, directing and scoring—*Cinderfella* (1960), *The Bell Boy* (1960), and most noted *The Nutty Professor* (1963); the latter most successfully refried in 1996 by Eddie Murphy.

Amidst all, Jerry Lewis found time to record semi-serious offerings, beginning the year of his break from Martin. His recording career was brief, but chart-altering when Jerry's reworked Al Jolson's 1918 hit "Rock-a-Bye Your Baby With a Dixie Melody." Only one other disk—his work-up of the 1927 Paul Whitman hit, "It All Depends on You" (#68, 1957)—his immediate follow-up, ever made *Billboard's* listings.

With increasing resistance to his films in the '70s and an awareness of a pain-killer drug addiction and worsening ulcers, Lewis regrouped, recouped, and eventually returned with his ever-intense attentions given to personal appearances, writing books—*The Complete Filmmaker* (1971) and *Jerry Lewis in Person* (1983)—and the perennial Muscular Dystrophy Telethon. In 1983, Jerry won critic-approval as an empty talk show host in Martin Scorsese's *The King of Comedy*.

In the '60s Jerry's son, Gary Lewis, went on to extensive teen fame with hits such as "This Diamond Ring," "Green Grass," and "Save Your Heart for Me."

IVORY JOE HUNTER
SINCE I MET YOU BABY
(Ivory Joe Hunter)
Atlantic 1111
No. 12 *December 29, 1956*

With a daddy preacher who played guitar, a mama who sang in a choir, a house full of instrument-abusing sibs, and a God-given name like Ivory, it was natural that Ivory Joe (b. Nov. 10, 1914, Kirbyville, TX) would take up the piano. He performed in school orchestras, sang in a church quartet, and after graduation, he and his combo, heavily influenced by Duke Ellington and Fats Waller, played the bars from Galveston to Port Arthur. In the '40s, Joe and his jumpers held down a radio program on KFDM in Beaumont, Texas. With the outbreak of World War II, Hunter dropped the band and hoofed it to the West Coast, where he worked the L.A. and San Francisco clubs.

In 1945, Hunter formed the Ivory label and pressed up some copies of his first record, "Blues at Sunrise" b/w "You Taught Me to Love." Accompanying him on the disk were the soon-to-be-famous Three Blazers (Charles Brown, Johnny Moore, and Eddie Williams). The disk sold well and was picked up for distribution by Leon Rene's Exclusive label. The following year, Hunter formed Pacific Records and, using top-drawer sidemen like Pee Wee Crayton, Wardell Gray, and Eddie Taylor, dashed off a series of now impossible-to-find waxings: "Ivory Joe's Boogie," "Pretty Mama Blues," "She's a Killer," "Jumpin' at the Dew Drop," "Boogie in the Rain," and "Big Wig."

In the fall of '47, Ivory Joe was so hot that King Records signed him up for what would prove to be a string of top-selling "race" records: "Don't Fall in Love With Me" (R&B: #8, 1948), "What Did You Do to Me" (R&B: #9, 1948), "Waitin' in Vain" (R&B: #5, 1949), "Guess Who" (R&B: #2, 1949), "Landlord Blues" (R&B: #6, 1949), "Jealous Heart" (R&B: #2, 1949), and "I Quit My Pretty Mama" (R&B: #4, 1950).

Ivory's first session for MGM produced "I Almost Lost My Mind" (R&B: #1, 1950), which many critics consider to be Hunter's finest outing. Although it topped the R & B charts and sold over a million copies, Hunter's classic was not even listed on *Billboard*'s pop charts. Six years later, Hunter's hymn would become a million-seller all over again, this time for the up-and-coming Pat Boone.

With two singles that sounded very much like "Almost"—"Since I Met You Baby" (#12; R&B: #1, 1956) and "Empty Arms" (#43; R&B: #2, 1957) b/w "Love's a Hurting Game" (R&B: #7, 1957)—Ivory Joe finally had major crossover success. Yet while he continued to record fine bluesy ballads and gospel-tinged country disks for Dot, Goldisc, Capitol, Smash, Veejay, Stax, and many other labels, Ivory Joe Hunter never made the pop or R & B listings after 1960.

Ivory's final album was issued early in 1974, *I've Always Been Country*. Shortly before his death, country entertainers—among them George Jones and TAMMY WYNETTE—sponsored a benefit for Ivory Joe at the Grand Ole Opry. In December 1973, Hunter began receiving treatment for lung cancer. He died in Memphis on November 8, 1974.

TARRIERS
THE BANANA BOAT SONG
(Alan Arkin, Bob Carey, Erik Darling)
Glory 249
No. 4 *February 9, 1957*

When Erik Darling (b. Sept. 25, 1933, Baltimore) was growing up in Canandaigua, New York, Burl Ives was his hero. Oh, to be Burl and roam the countryside, free of all concerns! Appearing before people to sing and strum truth seemed a great way to make money.

"My father was an artist and my mother too," said Erik Darling in an exclusive interview. "Painters. They encouraged me to do as I will." Erik found a loose gui-

tar, learned the chords, and by age 16, was singing Sunday afternoons in New York's Washington Square. In 1953, Darling joined a group of 19 singers, dancers, and actors that had been organized by Mary Hunter for New York's Theatre Guild's "Music Americana." Together they did 21 weeks of one-night stands.

With a flexible line-up made up of Dylan Todd, Don Vogel, Caroly Wilcox, Al Wood, and Bob Carey, Erik formed his own unit of traveling, soothsaying performers, the Tune Tellers. "We were acoustic and trying to be like the Weavers," said Erik. "We did a concert at the Circle on the Square, but nothing came of it. Eventually it became the Tarriers, with Bob, myself, Carl Calton, and Alan Arkin (b. Mar. 26, 1934, Brooklyn).

"We were just a part of this movement, centered in Washington Square. One of the tunes that was common place in the street was 'Tom Dooley.' It was a traditional murder ballad. I recorded a version of it—before the Tarrier thing got together—with Bob [Carey] and Roger Sprung as the Folk Say Trio. It was a 10-inch album for Stinson, with a couple of takes of Leadbelly and Woody Guthrie."

Dating from 1953 and Perry Como's hit "Pa-paya Mama," artists like Burl Ives, Harry Belafonte, the Fontane Sisters, TERRY GILKYSON, and Steve Lawrence had been making the charts with calypsoesque Caribbean-style tunes. Contributing to the blooming genre would be the Tarriers' debut disk, "The Banana Boat Song" and VINCE MARTIN's "Cindy, Oh Cindy."

"The Tarriers failed every recording audition we ever made," said Erik. "Carl didn't really mesh. With him, we failed a lot of auditions, until someone took us to this small record company on 47th Street. It was Glory Records, owned by Phil Rose, who went on to produce *A Raisin in the Sun*, that gave Sidney Poitier.

"Unbeknownst to us, Harry Belafonte had recorded 'The Banana Boat Song' on an album, about a year before us. When our record became a hit, RCA released his song as a single. They're like two different songs; from the same source, though. We had the larger hit, but in the long run, Belafonte's is the remembered one and, I think, the more interesting one.

"We'd accompanied this guy, Vince Martin, on this song, 'Cindy, Oh Cindy.' The record company wanted us to do it that way, but it would have been better for our career if they'd let us do that song, then 'The Banana Boat Song.' We'd be two-hit wonders, right."

Martin had one-hit with "Cindy, Oh Cindy," but neither he nor the Tarriers ever charted again, and the "calypso explosion" of the '50s petered out as rapidly as it had puffed up.

Very few copies were pressed of the Tarriers' self-titled album and the truly fine 45 "Those Brown Eyes." Within two years, the Tarriers were no more. "Alan really wanted to be an actor. He wasn't happy traveling

THE TARRIERS, WITH ALAN ARKIN (CENTER)

around singing. I mean, there wasn't college concerts yet, so we had to play in some miserable places. He left and Bob and I with Clarence Cooper recorded an album for United Artist in '59."

Bob Carey remained with the Tarriers—with the addition of ERIC WEISSBERG and Marshall Brickman, later of the Journeymen and screen credits shared with Woody Allen—recording with them well into the folk movement of the early '60s and the group's demise in 1964. Erik had stayed with the Tarriers through 1959, then toured and recorded with the legendary Weavers. In 1963, Erik Darling formed the Rooftop Singers with Bill Svanoe and Lynne Taylor (one-time jazz vocalist with Benny Goodman and Buddy Rich)—known the pop world over for "Walk Right In" and "Mama Don't Allow."

From the mid '70s on, Darling has concentrated on teaching music and sporadically recording solo albums. Alan Arkin had left the Tarriers in the late '50s to pursue a successful career on Broadway and in the movies, appearing as Sigmund Freud in *The Seven Percent Solution* (1976), and as a lovable, bumbling luster in Neil Simon's *Last of the Red Hot Lovers* (1972). He has twice been nominated for an Oscar—*The Russians Are Coming, The Russians Are Coming* (1967) and *The Heart Is a Lonely Hunter* (1969).

Arkin, however, never totally walked away from music. His group, the Babysitters—the Weavers' Lee Hays, Doris Kaplan, and Alan's wife Debra and brother Bob; with the sometime assistance of Eric Weissberg— has recorded at last count a half-dozen packages of tunes for tots.

JOY LAYNE
YOUR WILD HEART
(James Testa, Charles Sano)
Mercury 71038
No. 20 *February 23, 1957*

Although a mere junior attending Lyon Township High, Joy Layne (b. 1941, Chicago) seemed to be on the brink of a big-time career when "Your Wild Heart," her cover version of a single by THE PONI-TAILS, charted nicely. She had a searing range and the kind of one-two vocal punch that Brenda Lee was just about to unleash on "Dynamite" and "That's All You Got to Do."

Joy's dad was a construction worker but a household violinist and piano-picker as well. Mom was actively involved in local theater productions and her little 15-year-old's future. One day, Joy's mother took her downtown to see Mercury A & R man Art Talmadge. "She was bouncy and bright-eyed and carried her mascot, this squeaky toy dog Brownie," Talmadge recalled to *TV Radio Mirror*. Art already knew of this promising Poni-Tails platter, and after a quick audition, he had found the right singer to cover the wild number. Follow-ups included "My Suspicious Heart" and a cover of RANDY STARR's "After School."

Lennie LaCour, a multi-indie label owner (Lucky Four, Magic Touch, 620), talent scout, and recording artist, was the last person to record any tunes on Joy, in 1961. As Lennie revealed in an exclusive interview, "Her mother was her manager, and she had certain things that she didn't want Joy doing, like traveling and promoting her records. And that was the end of her career.

"She looked and sounded to me like Sandy Duncan. Everytime I see or hear Sandy, I think of Joy Layne."

MICKEY & SYLVIA
LOVE IS STRANGE
(Ethel Smith)
Groove 0175
No. 11 *March 2, 1957*

In 1950, while attending Washington Irving High School, SYLVIA Vanderpool (b. March 6, 1936, New York City) was spotted by a scout and given the chance to record some sides with Hot Lips Page for Columbia Records. "Chocolate Candy Blues," "Pacifying," and "Sharp Little Sister" were worldly numbers for a 14-year-old to handle. While these now-collectible records were critically lauded, they flopped commercially, as did the 78s she cut as "Little Sylvia" for Savoy and Jubilee.

In 1954, while Vanderpool was in the studio recording for the Cat label, she met prolific session guitarist McHouston "Mickey" Baker. Mickey (b. Oct. 15, 1925, Louisville, Kentucky) had been all over New York providing back-up licks for King, Okeh, and Savoy artists. Sylvia's Cat tracks failed to sell, and she approached Baker about guitar lessons. From this evolved the relationship that would produce a mammoth hit and the sexually suggestive rock and roll classic—"Love Is Strange," their sixth disk as a duet.

Incredible singles like "There Ought to Be a Law" (#47, 1957) b/w "Dearest" (#85) and "Bewildered" (#57, 1958) followed—but their act was always viewed as a novelty, a throwaway, and not one of this dynamite duo's disks ever captured a mass audience again.

In 1959, Mickey & Sylvia split. Baker signed on with Atlantic Records to cut jazzy items; Leiber & Stoller later teamed him with Kitty Noble for some obscure sides as Mickey & Kitty. Mickey and Sylvia soon patched up their "lover's spat" and returned to the stu-

MICKEY & SYLVIA

dios to produce some songs for their King-distributed Willow label and for RCA. "Baby You're So Fine" (#52, 1961) b/w "Lovedrops!" (#97) were not up to par, but they charted.

"That was Ike Turner playing on 'Baby You're So Fine' and on the follow-up 'He Gave Me Everything,'" Sylvia told *Blues & Soul's* Tony Cummings. "We returned the favor for Ike. In 1960, we'd recorded this song called 'It's Gonna Work Out Fine' but RCA didn't release it. So Tina Turner recorded it in 1961. I played lead guitar and Mickey did the spoken bits. It was a smash hit, of course . . . for Ike & Tina Turner."

In 1962, Mickey moved to Paris. Two years later, Sylvia married Joe Robinson and made some records as Sylvia Robbins for Sue and Jubilee. The couple set up the All Platinum Studios and a stable of record labels that eventually included Horoscope, Stang, Turbo, Vibration, and Sugar Hill. Sylvia went on to write several successful songs like "Love on a Two-Way Street" (a hit for the Moments in 1970 and Stacy Lattislaw in 1981), and to produce recordings for LINDA JONES, the Moments, SHIRLEY & CO., the SUGARHILL GANG, the Whatnauts, and Lonnie Youngblood.

Mickey has been playing sessions in France and elsewhere. He has recorded with the Coasters, Champion Jack Dupree, Willie Mabon, Sunnyland Slim, and TOMMY TUCKER. He has made nearly a dozen solo albums, and sporadically records duets with yet another "Sylvia," Monique Raucher. Baker is also well known to guitar students worldwide for his guitar-instruction books.

Sylvia, meanwhile, became a solo one-hit wonder in 1973 with her breathy recording of "Pillow Talk" (#3), which introduced her to a whole new generation of pop music fans.

JIMMY MCCRACKLIN
THE WALK
(Jimmy McCracklin)
Checker 885
No. 7 *March 10, 1957*

Legend has it that bluesman Jimmy McCracklin was annoyed by the poor quality of rock and roll records, and threw together what he thought was a dog of a disk to prove that rock consumers had no taste. "The Walk" strolled off with hit honors.

McCracklin was born James David Walker on a cotton plantation outside of Helena, Arkansas, on August 13, 1921. Jimmy's parents separated when he was young, and he moved with his mom to St. Louis, where he sang in the choir of his Baptist church. In his midteens, Jimmy and a cousin, John Henry Murrell, hopped a train to California. Their goal was to find boxer Archie Moore and to convince him to teach them all he knew about the sport.

Jimmy was yearning to become a professional boxer. In the late '40s, after a tour of duty with the Navy—where he won the title of All-American Light-Heavyweight Champion of the Military—he moved to San Francisco. A head-on car crash (in which Peter Morgan, brother of baseball's Joe Morgan, was killed) halted his boxing career. Shortly after, McCracklin turned his attention to singing, blowin' harp, and poundin' piano blues in Bay-area bars. Jim had been messin' with music for years; he had cut a number of singles for Globe, Excelsior, Courtney, Cavatone, Downtown, Trilon, and Modern, all before 1950. Nothing made the pop or R & B charts until Jim, on a dare and in disgust, wrote "The Walk" and lowered himself to the level of rock and roll.

"We were broke," said McCracklin to Howard A. Dewitt, *DISCoveries* magazine. The place was Chicago, the winter of '56. "I lived with the band in a hotel room. We had just enough money for food. It was a miserable time. I saw those black rock'n'roll guys like Chuck Berry write some early hits, and I knew I could make a successful record. I had lyrics and the music and knew what the white kids wanted. I had watched those kids dance, and I saw an opportunity."

To make ends met, Jimmy and band, the Blues Blasters, secured a gig at Rita's Lounge. "Rita's was a little but long club filled with black people. If you don't play good blues your ass is in a lot of trouble." Exactly at nine o'clock each night, a well-dressed smooth pair would dance into the club. "I'll never forget those folks, they'd just dance in slow like they were walking. They had style, grace . . . I knew I could write a song about those folks. . . ."

In January 1958, McCracklin and his Blues Blasters—Ray Cotton (drums), Horace Hall (bass), Big Johnny "Bird" Parker (sax), Lafayette Thomas (guitar)—had the song together and walked into a tiny do-it-yourself studio to record "The Walk." It took McCracklin three visits to Chess Records to convince the Chess brothers to take the tape.

"I was in a motel in Virginia and I got up one morning and turned on the radio. Damned if 'The Walk' didn't blast out at me. It had only been a few weeks since I dropped it off at Chess Records.

"Now, when 'The Walk' took off, Chess got in touch with me to record some more songs. They really promoted it, and I had finally broken into rock'n'roll." Trouble was, according to DeWitt, "'The Walk' was released without McCracklin signing a formal contract." Said Jimmy, "I didn't know how to protect myself. I didn't care, I just wanted a record out. I was on top of the world with a hit record. . . ." The Chess brothers refused to pay royalties to Jimmy McCracklin; in addition, a fictitious name—Bob Garlic—was added to the composition credits, as a means of snatching half of Jimmy's writing credits.

"I had a *Billboard* Top 10 hit and had been on 'American Bandstand,' and Leonard Chess told me there was no money. I knew I had to go else where. Chess cheated me." Jimmy and his Blues Blasters went to Mercury Records. "They didn't promote my records. . . ."

In the intervening years, Jimmy has written a couple of classic songs—"The Thrill Is Gone" and "Tramp"—and recorded some fine R & B numbers, some of which crossed over to the pop charts: "Just Got to Know" (#64, 1962), "Every Night, Every Day" (#91, 1965), "Think" (#95, 1965), and "My Answer" (#92, 1966).

Twenty-five years later—in 1983—after much leg and legal work, McCracklin got back what was his all along—the legal rights as sole author of "The Walk," with complete royalties henceforth. "Think of all that money I was cheated out of. Hell, I don't think 'The Walk' was ever out of print."

Jimmy McCracklin owns Budget Music and Sodium Publishing and continues to tour and to record for Rounder Records.

"I've been a lucky man," said McCracklin. "My wife and kids have been a hell of an inspiration. My willpower to go on comes from them. . . ."

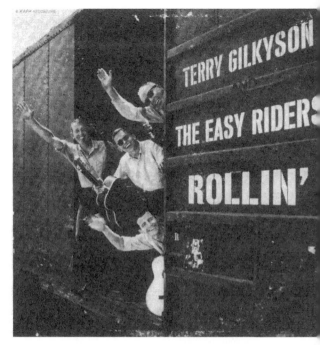

TERRY GILKYSON & THE EASY RIDERS
MARIANNE
(Terry Gilkyson, Frank Miller, Richard Dehr)
Columbia 40817
No. 4 *April 6, 1957*

Hamilton Henry "Terry" Gilkyson (b. 1919, Phoenixville, PA) was born in a stone house near the Schuylkill River. He attended the University of Pennsylvania as a music major until he grew bored with formal studies. During the summer of 1938, he traveled to Tucson, Arizona, to work on a ranch, hear genuine cowboy tunes, and learn how to play the guitar. He started singing in local watering holes, and sang folk songs over the Armed Forces Radio Service during the '40s. A decade later, Terry was humming and picking for Decca Records, recording numerous singles and a few LPs. Most notable among these waxings was a highly successful recording that Gilkyson cut with the Weavers, "On Top of Old Smokey" (#2, 1951).

By 1954, Terry had tailored and tuned an accompanying unit which he dubbed the Easy Riders. With Richard "Rudy" Dehr and Frank Miller, they roamed about the land performing folk favorites. T. G. and his Riders almost had a hit with an under-relished weirdie called "Yermos Nightmare, Yermo Red." The calypso-

flavored "Marianne" did what "Yermo" had barely managed to do—garner Gilkyson and his group a genuine folk hit.

For some reason, Terry immediately had his name pulled off all subsequent releases by the Easy Riders, and at some fuzzy point left the group entirely. Before his departure, he wrote or cowrote "The Cry of the Wild Goose" for Frankie Laine (#1, 1950) and Tennessee Ernie Ford (#15, 1950); "Greenfields" for the Brothers Four (#2, 1960); "Love Is a Golden Ring" for Frankie Laine (#10, 1957); and "Memories Are Made of This" for Dean Martin (#1, 1956) and Gale Storm (#5, 1956).

The Riders, meanwhile, carried on into the early '60s. Nothing further charted, but the group's ever-changing composition did allow a number of later music-makers an apprenticeship. Jerry Yester, a former member of the New Christy Minstrels who would move on to work with the Lovin' Spoonful and the Association, was an Easy Rider for a brief time, as was Doug Myres of Bud & Travis.

Terry is still of this earth, living a life of near though unintentional anonymity in Mexico. His son Tony has played bass for the rock group X; his daughter Liza is a folk artist with current LPs on Gold Coast Records.

JIMMY BOWEN WITH THE RHYTHM ORCHIDS
I'M STICKIN' WITH YOU
(Jimmy Bowen, Buddy Knox)
Roulette 4001
No. 14 *April 27, 1957*

Jimmy Bowen (b. Nov. 30, 1937, Santa Rita, NM), Wayne "Buddy" Knox, and Don "Donnie" Lanier all attended West Texas State College. Don Lanier played lead guitar, Buddy played rhythm guitar, and Jimmy— as Buddy told Jean-Pierre Chapados in *New Kommotions*—was "the worst bass player I have ever heard." They gigged at school functions and local night spots in Dumas and Amarillo as the Serenaders. "We started thinking we could take our Hank Williams sound, add a little Hank Ballard and some drums and it might amount to something," said Buddy to liner note writer Adam Komorowski.

"One night at a dance, this kid wanted to know if he could sit in on a cardboard box. He had a pair of brushes, and he played just a backbeat, and all of a sudden the floor was full of people dancing. Our whole sound changed right there. He was a little red-haired kid; Don Mills, our first drummer." A name change was needed; they became the Rhythm Orchids.

Early in 1956, Roy Orbison and his Teen Kings played the college. Jim and Buddy approached him about tips on getting on record. Roy told them of Norman Petty and his studio in Clovis, New Mexico. In April 1956, Oil man Chester Oliver financed the session with the intent of releasing "I'm Stickin' With You" backed with "Party Doll" on his teeny Blue Moon label. Such was not to be, but the boys did form their own label, Triple D—named after KDDD, the Dumas radio station the Orchids often performed on.

By this point Don Mills had departed being replaced by Dave Alldred a Clovis resident and sometime drummer with the Norman Petty Trio. Alldred would soon leave the Orchids to record with GERRY GRANAHAN as part of Dickie Doo & The Don'ts; known for "Nee, Nee, Na, Na, Na, Na Nu, Nu" (#40, 1958). Chico Hayak took over the vacated drum throne.

The response proved so hot for the double-sided disk that Phil Kahl, George Goldner, and Morris Levy reportedly formed Roulette Records just to distribute the Rhythm Orchids' record nationally. Seeing that airplay was evenly divided between the sides, and that each side featured a different lead singer, the Roulette bosses decided to split the disk in two, figuring that two hits would be better than one—"Party Doll" by Buddy Knox & The Rhythm Orchids eventually went to number one on the pop charts. "I'm Stickin' With You," with Bowen singing lead, was not quite as successful but still secured a spot in the Top 40.

With Kahl as their manager, the Rhythm Orchids played the Paramount in New York City, and appeared on "The Ed Sullivan Show."

Buddy went on successfully clicking for awhile with platters like "Rock Your Baby to Sleep (#17, 1957), "Hula Love" (#9, 1957), "Somebody Touched Me" (#22, 1958), and "Lovey Dovey" (#25, 1961). With "Rock Your Baby," Buddy was in the U.S. Army, stationed at Fort Hood, Texas, with Elvis. Serving his time in the Tank Corp, Buddy's slot in the Orchids was filled by Trini Lopez.

With HUGO & LUIGI the assigned producers for the New York sessions, Bowen's "Ever Lovin' Fingers" (#63, 1957), "Warm Up to Me Baby" (#57, 1957), and the maudlin "By the Light of the Silvery Moon" (#50, 1958) did moderately well, and for a few years, occasional releases bearing his name appeared on Crest, Decca, Capehart, Reprise, and his own Amos label.

By 1959, the Rhythm Orchids were no more.

While with Roulette, Bowen observed all studio activities, with the intent of becoming a producer. In the early '60s, Jim became a producer for the Chancellor label. In 1963, Bowen was asked to join Reprise Records, where he produced such acts as Sammy Davis, Jr., Dean Martin, JACK NITZSCHE and Frank and Nancy Sinatra. Jim moved to Nashville first in 1973 as president of Capitol's Opryland subsidiary, followed by stays as head of MGM country products and MCA's C & W Division; producing numerous hit recordings for the Bellamy Brothers, Glen Campbell, Crystal Gayle, MERLE HAGGARD, Reba McEntire, the Oak Ridge Boys, Waylon Jennings, JOHNNY LEE, Kenny Rogers, JOHN SCHNEIDER, George Strait, Conway Twitty, and Hank Williams, Jr.

Jim Bowen became vice-president and Nashville manager for Elektra/Asylum and is still considered a force in the music city. Early on, Donnie Lanier became Jim's assistant, a position he maintains to date. Buddy Knox resides in Canada, where he continues to sing of "Party Doll" and "Hula Love."

KEN COPELAND
PLEDGE OF LOVE
(R. Redd)
Imperial 5432
No. 12 *May 6, 1957*

The Mints were a local nightclub pleasure for the folks of Gainesville, Texas. Late in 1956 Joe M. Leonard, Jr., manager of radio KGAF and owner of the indie Lin label, approached Ken Copeland (b. 1937) and his group about cutting some tunes. Early the following year, "Busy Body Rock" was released (as by the Four Mints), but there was not much of a stir beyond the

Gainesville area. "Pledge of Love," however, was another story. Here was the type of song that was so innately appealing that almost any performer could have had a hit with it. When interest in the disk exceeded the ability of the lads at Lin to supply the stores with the side, a quick arrangement was made with Lew Chubb's Imperial label for national distribution. Speed was of the essence, for Mitchell Torok, Johnny Janis, accordionist Dick Contino, and a host of others were competing with nearly identical cover versions.

The initial pressings of "Pledge of Love" credited the disk's artist as "The Mints." As time progressed and the disk rose in popularity, Copeland, the group's lead singer, was given sole billing. Despite the competing covers—each which cut deeply into the potential sales of the Mints original—the Copeland-crooned "Pledge" managed to reach the number 12 position. But in all the uproar, Ken never established himself with the pop public as the singer of "Pledge of Love." Consequently, only three additional 45s by Copeland—"Teenage," "Someone to Love Me," and "Fanny Brown"—were issued before Copeland and his Mints returned to their local-level celebrity status.

Only years later, after Kenny had evolved into a "tel-evangelist," would he freely admit that all of this earthy success had left him sick, broke, overweight, and depressed. "Motorcycles, airplanes, and rock music were my life," he wrote in a biographical sketch for the members of the Kenneth Copeland Ministries. Five years after "Pledge of Love," Ken made his personal commitment to the teachings of Christ. In 1968, after attending Oral Roberts University, he and his wife Gloria formed their ministries in Fort Worth, Texas. Copeland's bio reports that he touches millions with his weekly and daily TV programs, TV specials, monthly magazine, teaching tapes, gospel recordings, and conventions.

BONNIE GUITAR
DARK MOON
(NED MILLER)
Dot 15550
No. 6 *June 10, 1957*

She was born Bonnie Buchingham on March 25, 1924, on a small farm in Auburn, Washington, 20 miles outside of Seattle. "I had four brothers and a sister; none cared much about music. Dad played violin," said Guitar, in an exclusive interview, "I wanted to play the clarinet. Some one in the band had already picked it, or—who knows—I coulda become Bonnie Clarinet."

Bonnie took an early interest in jazz, pop, and Irish folk tunes and made efforts to copy every note picked by her fav Nick Lucas. By age 16, Mrs. Buchingham was proudly taking her daughter around to the various area contests held at the movie houses—winning more times than she could recall. After graduation, Bonnie went out on the road with radio stars, the Arizona Wranglers. By 21, she was married and fronting her own band, a pop outfit, in L.A. Some demo recordings she cut for an aspiring songwriter got the attention of Fabor Robinson, in Malibu, California, owner of Fabor Records. Noting her talent, Fabor acquired her services as session guitarist, and soon she was learning the ways of being an engineer and producer. As such, in the mid-'50s she worked with DORSEY BURNETTE, THE DE CASTRO SISTERS, NED MILLER, and Jim Reeves.

Her debut solo single was "If You See My Love Dancing," a self-composed tune performed by just Bonnie and her guitar. Months later, while visiting her parents she received a call from Fabor. "'I've just received this song,' he said. 'I've worked it with Dorsey and others, and I can't seem to capture it. Will you come down and give it a listen.' I can tell you my exact words when I first heard 'Dark Moon.' I said, 'I'll give up my royalties and everything just to do this song.' I knew it was up for grabs and someone was gonna get it.

"I got it, but he took me at my word and I really did give up my royalties. It was one of the hardest things I ever put together. Ned [Miller] wrote it but we tried in maybe five or six different ways, in different studios before it came out right."

While Guitar's haunting take on "Dark Moon," a Ned Miller tune, would become her lone pop notable, she continued to rack up country hits into the early '80s. "After [her immediate follow-up] 'Mister Fire Eyes,' [#71, 1957] it just all fell apart for me having any further pop hits. Randy Wood [Dot Records' founder and owner] took my contract away from Fabor and had 'em put these big band productions on my records. 'Dark Moon' had just three instruments—two guitars and a bass."

In 1958, Guitar started a record label, Dolphin—within weeks relabeled Dolton—with a refrigerator dealer, Bob Reisndorf. and signed on the sensational sound-making services of the Fleetwoods, the Ventures, and DON ROBERTSON. Bonnie molded and produced the early Fleetwood hits and those by Seattle's Frantics and Little Bill & the Bluenotes. She recorded one solo single "Candy Apple Red" (#97, 1959), and with Robertson, an undercover disk, "Born to Be With You," as the Echoes (no relation to THE ECHOES, of "Baby Blue" fame). "I was getting too much attention, it seems," said Bonnie, "and Bob and I didn't get on—we were at each other's throats—so after a year and a half, two years, I left." Dolton was later sold to Liberty, now part of the EMI empire.

Bonnie has recorded for numerous labels (Radio, Dot, Dolton, RCA, Jerden, Fabor, Paramount, Columbia, ABC, MCA, 4-Star) and has done country A & R work for Dot and Paramount Records, session work for such as BILL JUSTIS, and obscure pop/rock productions for Dot and Dore. Several fine LPs (*Dark Moon*, 1957; *Two Worlds*, 1966) were issued through the '60s, though all of them are now out of print.

"I resigned, New Year's Eve, 1996," said Bonnie Guitar. "You just burn out. You go with the big labels, and you get lost with all the artists competing; go with a little label and you get more attention, but there's more crooks. . . .

"I'm blessed, though. I'm very grateful. It's 40 years later, and people still come up to me and say things like 'Your "Dark Moon," helped me; it touched me, when I was down.'"

MARVIN RAINWATER
GONNA FIND ME A BLUEBIRD
(Marvin Rainwater)
MGM 12412
No. 18 *June 10, 1957*

"Some people have it easy," said Marvin Rainwater to author Colin Escott. "They just walk up and everything just opens up. I don't know how hard they worked to do it, but no matter how hard I worked, it turned around the other way."

Part Cherokee, with Rainwater as his mother's maiden name, Marvin Karlton Perry (b. July 25, 1925, Wichita) took classical piano lessons as a child, until an accident left him minus a right thumb.

Perry kept writing songs, though. He majored in mathematics later taking pre-veterinary courses at Washington State University in Walla Walla, then worked with his father in an Oregon lumber camp. With the outbreak of World War II, he studied for two years as a pharmacist's mate.

On his return to civilian life, Marv worked as a tree surgeon and nearly got himself killed. "I was trying to write a song while cutting out the top of a tree," Rainwater told *Goldmine*'s Bill Millar. "I'd cut it off before I woke up and realized what I was doing." While hanging by his safety belt, some 75 feet above a slab of solid concrete, Rainwater re-evaluated his career goals. "That's when I quit tree surgery."

Perry picked up his guitar and with brothers Don and Ray, plus picker extraordinaire ROY CLARK, toured about "itty bitty clubs" in the Washington, D. C. area. A local studio owner named Ben Adelman heard something special in Marvin's rockabilly sound and recorded 50 of his songs; most of which have been issued—without Rainwater's approval—on budget labels like Spin-O-Rama, Crown, and Premier.

Red Foley heard one of Marv's reworked Hank Williams numbers, liked it, and offered him a spot on his "Ozark Jubilee" radio program. When Teresa Brewer and Justin Tubb covered Marv's self-penned "I Gotta Go Get My Baby" and outsold his own version, MGM president Frank Walker offered Rainwater a contract. "Albino Pink Eyed Stallion," "Tea Bag Romeo," "Hot and Cold," and then the hit happened. "Gonna Find Me a Bluebird"—proved a monster hit—though it did little to generate much moolah. Marvin struggled through two years of trying to find his niche. Despite a number one disk in the U.K. with "Whole Lotta Woman" (#60, C&W: #15, 1958), the following year, Marv was having a hard time consolidating his career.

"I didn't realize it at the time, it's not your first hit that's important, it's the second and third hits," said Rainwater to Escott, author *Tattooed on Their Tongues*. "The first hit just buys you a lot of hard work; it's the

MARVIN RAINWATER Sings WITH A HEART WITH A BEAT

NOTHIN' NEEDS NOTHIN'
LUCKY STAR
MY LOVE IS REAL
(Don't Be) LATE FOR LOVE
LOOK FOR ME
(I'll Be Waiting For You)
MOANIN THE BLUES

WHOLE LOTTA WOMAN
I DIG YOU BABY
DANCE ME DADDY
MY BRAND OF BLUES
GAMBLIN' MAN
BABY, DON'T GO

Before having throat surgery, Marv persisted in trying to make records for Warwick and Brave. After his recovery, he cut even better disks for Wesco, United Artists, and Warner Bros., but none of these ever charted, and most died quiet deaths. British tours in the mid-'70s led to the release of British-only LPs for Philips (*Marvin Rainwater Gets Country Fever*, 1972) and Westwood (*Especially for You*, 1976). Throughout the '80s, Germany's Bear Family label repackaged some of Marvin's finest rockabilly efforts.

With no labels showing any interest in a one-time country-rock man, Marv in 1988 issued *I'm Gonna Go Where the Livin' and Lovin' Is Good*, on his own Okie label.

Rainwater is still alive and kicking. "I think rock and roll makes you look younger and stay younger. I'm certainly not gonna stop. I'll be doing it till I'm bald-headed and lose all my teeth."

JODIE SANDS
WITH ALL MY HEART
(Bob Marcucci, Pete De Angelis)
Chancellor 1003
No. 15 *June 24, 1957*

Jodie Sands was a mainline pop vocalist from Philadelphia who sang in the tradition of Eydie Gorme, Giselle MacKenzie, and Kay Starr. But unlike these other songstresses, Jodie could sound like a sweet but sexually charged kid. Most of her songs had a seductive and slightly sassy Latin feel. Her solid seller was a cha-cha-like teen tune with plenty of "la-la-las" and a deep-voiced male chorus.

Her debut disk, "Love Me Always," had appeared on the tiny Teen label in 1955 only to reappear and disappear under the Bernlo logo months later. Bob Marcucci, who would later discover Fabian and Frankie Avalon, was one of the few who noticed the disk; when he formed his Chancellor company (reportedly with help from Dick Clark) in 1957, Jodie was his first signing.

Although Sands's "Sayonara (Goodbye)" was featured in the rock and roll flick *Jamboree* (1957), this follow-up to "With All My Heart" flopped. After some minimal action with "Someday (You'll Want Me to Want You)" (#95, 1958), Sands was forever absent from the airwaves and the charts. Up through the early '60s, numerous sides were issued by the Signature, Thor, Paris, and ABC-Paramount labels.

second and third hits where you make your money. Back then, I'd have a hit in some field or country and then move on to something else."

Reminiscing with *Goldmine* in 1980, Marvin noted that some miscalculations and misfortunes tripped up his career. Rainwater would appear in full Indian garb, a publicity ploy that he now feels typecast him. "It was my idea to start it," he told Escott, "but it wasn't such a good idea."

In 1958, Rainwater recorded his last Indian ode, JOHN D. LOUDERMILK's "The Pale-Faced Indian." It flopped, but reappeared at the top of the charts 10 years later by DON FARDON, relabeled "Indian Reservation." Two years later, the Raiders topped the charts with the tune Rainwater claims he and Marijohn Wilkin—uncredited and unremunerated—in part wrote.

That same year, Marvin lost near all his monies in an attempt to establish a country magazine, *Trail*. It closed after seven issues.

In 1959, he developed some vocal problems. "I didn't know it then but I had calluses on my vocal cords and should have quit for months. Instead, we'd spend hours and hours in the studio without ever getting anything decent. I felt bad for Jim Vienneau, the producer, 'cause he was really patient. One day I followed him out, and he was setting fire to a $20 bill. That gave me the message—he needed to spend his time with Connie Francis while MGM was burning money trying to cut a record on me."

JOHNNIE & JOE
OVER THE MOUNTAIN; ACROSS THE SEA
(Rex Garvin)
Chess 1654
No. 8 *July 22, 1957*
No. 89 *September 26, 1960*

Zelma "Zell" Sanders was always itchin' to be an entertainer. It never happened, but Sanders did become a
cult legend as the owner of the tiny J & S label and as a
mentor to numerous aspiring talents.

"She'd written a couple of songs when she was a
child, and she answered a couple of those ads in the
papers saying 'send us your song and we'll get it published,'" Johnnie Louise Richardson, Zell's daughter
and half of Johnnie & Joe, told *Goldmine*'s Aaron
Fuchs. "That was it. She was dedicated. And she liked
kids, too . . . [Later, when] she was working for the
Police Athletic League in Harlem in the 23rd Precinct,
she saw the talent, and it was just there on the street.
'Do you sing?' she'd ask them. 'Come on up to my
house.' They all got to know her around as the lady that
goes around grabbing groups."

One of those groups was the Hearts, which consisted of Hazel Cruchfield, Louise Harris, Joyce Weiss, and,
at various times, BETTY HARRIS and BABY WASHINGTON.
In 1953, Sanders placed the girls with Baton Records.
Disappointed with both the productions and the royalty statements issued by the label, Zell formed her own
label, J & S, the following year. She then issued singles
by Niecy Dizelle and the Machines, the Gospel Wonders, the Harptones, THE JAYNETTES, the Plants, and the
Pre-Teens.

"Rex [Garvin, a pianist/songwriter who lived next
door] brought Joe Rivers (b. Charleston, S.C.) up one
night, and said 'Hey, Miss Sanders, this is Joe Rivers and
we've been rehearsing some things,'" Richardson told
Fuchs. "'We want you to listen because we want to do a
thing together called 'Over the Mountain.' So, she listened and listened, and said 'I think it needs a little
something . . . I tell you what, Johnnie, you get over
there, and you sing with them.' I said, 'Oh no, do I have
to?' So she gave me that look that distinguishes between
mother and record manufacturer. So I knew I better get
over there and join them.

"At first they didn't want to do it with me. But when
we got into the studio, and we all listened, I guess it all
dawned on us, 'Hey maybe we got something here.'"

Issued on J & S, the disk almost immediately started to take off. Chess Records had picked up national
distribution on Johnnie & Joe's debut disk, "I'll Be
Spinning" (R&B: #10, 1957), and did the same for the
duos only mammoth mover. In addition to some fine
follow-ups shipped by J & S and Chess, and a recharting of "Over The Mountain' (#89, 1960), numerous

other Johnnie & Joe 45s appeared on ABC-Paramount,
Blue Rock, Gone, Masterpiece, Omega, and Tuff; most
notably, the immediate follow-up to "Over The Mountain," "My Baby's Gone On, On" (R&B: #15, 1957).

Personal appearances were rare, and tensions developed between the duo. Johnnie formed Dice, her own
short-lived label, and recorded the Avalons, the Click-
ettes, and the Premiers [not to be confused with the
L.A. group THE PREMIERS]. In the '60s, she turned away
from the biz to marry and to raise a family.

Ambient Sound resurrected the act in 1983. *Kingdom of Love*, their first and only LP, was issued, as was a
single, the album's title track. Neither generated more
than a cultish stir. Johnnie Louise Richardson died
from a stroke on October 25, 1988.

RUSS HAMILTON
RAINBOW
(Russ Hamilton)
Kapp 184
No. 4 *September 16, 1957*

Years before the Beatles got together, Ronnie Hulme
sailed out of Liverpool and into the ears and hearts of
teenage America. It was only a brief cross-cultural fling,
but Ronnie's "Rainbow" sold so darn well in the U.S.
that he garnered a gold record (signifying sales of over
1 million copies), becoming only the sixth British bloke
to do so.

Russ Hamilton, as he was known in the United
States, was born in 1934 in Liverpool. After some education, he worked for seven years in the costing office of
a metal box manufacturing company. For adventure,
Russ joined the Royal Air Force; during this stint he
acquired some decorations for activities in the Korean
War. On his return, it was back to the metal box manufacturing company.

"I'd met a girl in Blackpool when I was in the Royal
Air Force. I got infatuated," Hamilton told *Now Dig
This*, "and then we parted company. I went home that
night and I'd just bought a guitar. I got out my tape
recorder and I started singing. 'When the moon takes
the place of the sun in the sky. . . .' and the same night I
wrote 'Rainbow.' I took the tune to FRANKIE VAUGHN at
the North Pier in Blackpool, but he didn't want to
know about it. He missed out."

For continued adventure, Russ started singing and
strumming guitar at parties and clubs. In 1955, he
secured the first of a succession of jobs as a "red coat"
(sort of a singing waiter) at a summer camp, Butlins
Holiday Camps in Blackpool. A scout from Britain's
Oriole Records heard Russ sing while he was serving
and cleaning at the Ocean Hotel in Brighton. "I was suffering with a cold when we made the single and I hated

it," Hamilton said. "I wanted to do it again, but the people at Oriole said it was all right."

The name Ronnie Hulme didn't sound right to the powers at the record company. "The producer was walking down Hamilton Square in London and he thought it looked like a neat and clean place. I added Russ just off the top of my head, as it sounded American."

Listeners were touched by Ronnie/Russ sweetly and cheerfully singing of his wish to buy his little bird a rainbow, and, if he could scrape up enough, buy the moon itself. In England, "Rainbow" was not a hit. Teens weren't buying this ode—they wanted something with meat on it. Someone flipped the record over and found "We Will Make Love." To the surprise of many observers, the selection actually made it past the BBC censors, proof that Russ truly did sound like a lad who never had a lustful thought in his head.

All of his follow-up efforts, including "Tip Toe Thru' the Tulips"—later a consciousness-shakin' disk for TINY TIM—were given a pass by listeners in both the U.S. and Russ' homeland. By the time Hamilton got a good thrust on a tune, as in the thumping rockaballad "My Unbeatable Heart," his media moment had passed.

BOBBETTES
MR. LEE
(Heather Dixon, Helen Gathers, Emma Ruth Pought, Jannie Pought, Laura Webb)
Atlantic 1144
No. 6 *September 23, 1957*

These eight youngsters were attending P.S. 109 at the corner of 99th Street and Second Avenue in Manhattan in 1955. They met in the glee club, became after-school playmates, and started singing together as the Harlem Queens. Two years later, they were discovered by James A. Dailey when he spotted them on Herb Sheldon's local TV show. Dailey liked their sound, but not that god-awful name: "Sounded like some female motorcycle gang," he said. A sister of one of the girls had just named her baby Chantel Bobbette. Since there was already a "Chantels," the girls decided that they were going to be "The Bobbettes."

By the time Dailey took control of the group, there were five Bobbettes: baritone Heather Dixon (b. 1945), alto Helen Gathers (b. 1944), tenor Laura Webb (b. 1943), and the Pought sisters, alto Emma (b. 1944) and

The Bobbettes

JOE BENNETT
& THE
SPARKLETONES

soprano Jannie (b. 1945). One of the tunes they had been toying with was this ditty about a fifth-grade teacher that they did not exactly dig. Dailey brought the girls and their "Mr. Lee" song to Atlantic Records. The response was a positive one, but the company insisted that some of the negative comments about this Mr. Lee fellow would have to be deleted.

To the surprise of all, "Mr. Lee" sold 2,000,000 copies. "We didn't consider ourselves famous or even talented," Heather Dixon told *Goldmine*'s Jeff Tamarkin. "We were just singing. I think the record must have been out about six months before we said, 'Gee, we're on the radio and in the jukeboxes!'" For the next two years, Atlantic kept issuing new platters by the girls, but nothing clicked. When not busy touring or attending New York's Professional School for Children, they sang back-up for the Five Keys, IVORY JOE HUNTER, Clyde McPlatter, and JOHNNY THUNDER.

A few singles for Triple-X in 1960 almost restored the Bobbettes' momentum. In rapid succession, they charted: "I Shot Mr. Lee" (#52), "Have Mercy Baby" (#66) b/w "Dance With Me George" (#95), and "I Don't Like It Like That" (#72), their "answer" to CHRIS KEN-NER's "I Like It Like That."

Helen Gathers left the group in 1961, and the girls continued on as a quartet. The Bobbettes have yet to retire. "We have been singing together with the same four girls for 20 years," Dixon wrote years back in *Yesterday's Memories*. "And we will remain together for another 20, until we are old and gray, with one thing in our minds: that is to get one more gold record on the top."

JOE BENNETT & THE SPARKLETONES
BLACK SLACKS
(Joe Bennett, Irv Denton)
ABC-Paramount 9837
No. 17 *October 14, 1957*

History has finally granted rightful kingpin roles to Bo DIDDLEY and CARL PERKINS; someday even RONNIE HAWKINS will get a piece of the action. Unfortunately, Joe Bennett & The Sparkletones, one of the finest and raunchiest '50s rock bands, are hardly ever given a mention. Some may recall "Black Slacks," which a renegade oldies DJ will occasionally spin, but beyond that, Joe and the boys are largely forgotten.

They came together in the summer of 1955. Months later CBS talent scout Robert F. Cox caught their act, dug their cool sounds, and featured them on his local TV show. At the pinnacle of their popularity, Bennett and band ranged in age from 12 to 16. With Cox as their manager, the boys were soon on a nationwide tour, playing one-night stands in movie theaters.

They were all strict church-going boys, born and raised in Spartanburg, S.C. Joe, it's reported was the leader of the Church Youth Movement in his state. While other cats were meandering around the countryside boppin' mean licks, Joe and the fellows would drop everything come Sunday morn to attend a showing at the closest House of the Lord. By late '56, Cox had secured an audition in the New York City offices of ABC-Paramount Records. As legend would have it, they were "signed on the spot," with a recording session—the one that would produce "Black Slacks"—only hours later, at the Bell Sound Studios.

"Black Slacks," their first release, sold well and long, remaining on the *Billboard* charts for more than four months. The tune sported teenage expressions like "cool breeze," "crazy little mama," "hep cat," "cool daddy-o," and "rarin' to go." Joe (b. 1941, lead vocals and lead guitar), Wayne Arthur (b. 1943, stand-up bass), Howie "Sparky" Childress (b. 1945, second vocals, rhythm guitar), and Jimmy "Sticks" Denton (b. 1942, drums) appeared on Dick Clark's "American Bandstand," toured with the Alan Freed Rock & Roll Show, and even made the scene on Ed Sullivan's "r-r-really big show." Their 1957 follow-up, also an ode to tuff teenwear called "Penny Loafers and Bobby Socks," did fairly well, logging in at number 42 on the Top 100—not a bad showing.

Nothing with the Sparkletone name upon it, however, ever charted again. "Cotton Picking Rocker," "We've Had It," "Do the Stop"—despite being current collectibles—stiffed. Bennett and the Sparkletones broke up at this point, late in 1958; due to "the complex legal and economic ramifications involved in booking a group as young as the Sparkletones coupled with their decision to finish their education in a 'normal' environment," according to Steve Hoffman, liner-note writer for the act's 1983 "Best of" album.

Some of the band members and Bennett reassembled to record some sides for Paris Records in 1959. "Are You From Dixie" rocked, but the rest of the tracks leaned toward pop-puffery. Nothing was heard of the group until, in the belly of the folk-rock '60s movement, the Sparkletones name reappeared for one limp single, "Well Dressed Man."

"We hope our music will serve as a living reminder of growing up in the '50s," wrote the band on the liners of the '80s compilation. "We also hope that you enjoy the simplicity and good humor of the music as much as we have."

TUNE WEAVERS
HAPPY, HAPPY BIRTHDAY BABY
(Margo Sylvia, Gilbert Lopez)
Checker 872
No. 5 *October 28, 1957*

Frank Paul, a former bandleader and music director for off-Broadway shows, had acquired master recordings from the DuBonnett and Onyx record labels. By 1952, Frank was releasing some of these masters on a label he called Casa Grande, after his old Boston-based big band.

Nearby, Frank's brother-in-law ran a school that taught pattern-making for men's clothing. One of his students, Gilbert Lopez (b. July 4, 1934), had been singing with an *a cappella* group of relatives for about four months, so he pestered Frank to check out these "Tone Weavers," as they initially called themselves.

"I thought jeez . . . just another group," Frank recalled to *Goldmine*'s George Moonoogian. "So finally, one Sunday in October of '56, they were coming over to my brother-in-law's house in Medford, and I went over to hear them."

The group, based in Roxbury, Massachusetts, consisted of Lopez, a tenor, his sister and lead singer, Margo Sylvia (b. April 4, 1936), her husband and bass singer Johnny Sylvia (b. Sept. 8, 1935), plus Margo's cousin, obligato and opera student Charlotte Davis (b. Nov. 12, 1936). They played some tapes for Paul and sang some songs *a cappella*. When the Tone Weavers broke into a new tune that Margo and Gil had just written, "Happy, Happy Birthday Baby," "Paul jumped up and said, 'That's it! That's the one we're going to record!' I could then see its hit potential.

"I wrote that song for Donald Clements," Margo explained in an exclusive interview. "He and I had been an item. He was in the Sophomores and they'd recorded some of my songs; "He" and "I Get a Thrill." I had no musical training and when I'd sing as a child my mother would tell me to 'shut up.' I turned to poetry and quietly sang in my head. Donald and his group were the first to record my stuff. Just before his birthday, he told me he found a girl that had more going for her than I did. I felt I needed to write him something: 'Happy, Happy Birthday Baby/Although you're with somebody new/Thought I'd drop a line to say/That I wish this happy day would find me beside you . . .' The words came so easily. It was real."

Contracts were drawn up, Paul became their manager, and on March 7, 1957, the renamed Tune Weavers were ushered into Boston's Ace Recording Studio to record two tracks, "Happy, Happy" and its initial flip-side, "Old Man River." "That session—just two songs—took 18 hours to record. I was eight months pregnant. At one point—during the take that became the record—I thought I'd pass out." Once the promo copies got around, it took eight months before it became apparent that "Happy, Happy Birthday Baby" could be a big, big hit, and Paul made arrangements with Phil Chess to have the disk distributed on Chess' Checker subsidiary.

The response was phenomenal: sales eventually totaled 2 million copies. The Tune Weavers toured the nation, making stops at the Apollo Theatre, Dick Clark's "American Bandstand" and the Paramount Theatre, for a Alan Freed rock and roll show.

"I was a kid, a rock and roll fan, and I couldn't believe they paid us to sing," said Margo of her appearance on the legendary Freed show. "I stood in the wings with this wild beast in back of me. It was Little Richard, the most beautiful man I'd ever seen. He'd squeeze me and whisper, 'Aren't they wonderful.' I don't know who was performing; it was all unreal."

The following year, Charlotte dropped out of the group, and was replaced by another relative by marriage, William "Bucky" Morris, Jr., formerly of the G-Clefs, known for "Ka Ding Dong" (#24, 1956). The flipside of "Happy, Happy" began receiving heavy airplay. A marketing decision was made to pull "Old Man River" and release it as a separate single. Instrumentals, created by New Orleans keyboard wiz Paul Gayten were assigned to each release as "B" sides. An album and some nifty follow-ups appeared, but a major mistake was made. . . . "I Remember Dear" and Margo's compositions "I'm Cold," "There Stands My Love," and "Little Boy" all received zip in the way of airplay, and all bombed.

"Frank Paul got greedy. He was impressed with the sales that Chess Records was getting with us and violated the contract with them by having us record 'I Remember Dear.' He didn't give that disk and the others to Chess. He only printed 2,500 copies of each and almost no stores were able to get them."

The group also experienced some major problems when it came to compensation. "I wrote 'Happy' . . . and Gil paid $6 to copyright the song," Margo complained. "[As of December 1988], neither my brother nor I have received any money as artists. Corruption and greed are the reasons I stopped singing.

"It never got out of my system, though. To have made it so big while so young and then to have lost it— and not gotten the money—I've never gotten over it. You're talking to an endangered species. I'm frightened that I'll die before things are made right."

Margo and John have since divorced. Margo raised a family of six, pursuing an on-and-off again solo singing career. In 1989, Margo recorded again under the Tune Weavers name, singing all the harmony parts, on two singles—"Merry, Merry Christmas Baby" and "Come Back to Me" b/w "I've Tried"—for Bruce Patch's Classic Artists label.

Margo Sylvia died October 25, 1991, six months to the day after the interview for this book. Her fifth child, Mark Sylvia, went on to become a producer for Howard Huntsberry and Klymaxx.

John runs a TV and video store. Gil, who lives in San Francisco, became a mental health worker. Charlotte has been a Boston housewife. Donald Clements, the object of Margo's infatuation, is still living in Boston. Until the end, Margo and Donald kept in touch.

RAYS
SILHOUETTES B/W DADDY COOL
(Frank Slay, BOB CREWE)
Cameo 117
No. 3 *November 4, 1957*

Stanley "Bob" Crewe had been a male model and a less-than-successful teen idol. At a party in Philadelphia in the mid-'50s, he met a pianist named Frank C. Slay, Jr. Frank worked for Cameo Records by day and the British Information Service by night. The two hit it off, and talked of making their way in the world of pop music. Soon after, they formed a songwriting partnership and set up a little label called XYZ.

One night while riding the rails into Philly, Bob caught sight of a silhouette of two lovers in a warm embrace; the image stuck. Crewe told Slay of the incident, and one evening while shuffling papers for the Brits, Frank wrote the story line. Crewe created the chorus and thought up the title.

First tenor Walter Ford (b. Sept. 5, 1931, Lexington, KY), baritone Harry James (b. 1932), second tenor Davey Jones (b. 1931), and lead vocalist Harold "Hal" Miller (b. Jan. 17, 1931) were the Brooklyn-based Rays. Hal and Davey had recorded with the Four Fellows, whose 1955 R & B hit, "Soldier Boy," had peaked at number four.

When the Rays met the proprietors of XYZ, they had been together only a year or so. Chess had issued their "Tippity Top," but it had flopped. While doing his workaday chores at Cameo, Slay overheard the group's audition for the label. Cameo turned them down on the spot, but legend has it that Frank chased after them and signed them up with XYZ.

"Silhouettes" b/w "Daddy Cool" was a double-sided smash; number three on both the pop and R & B charts. For the next two years, Crewe and Slay put forth a number of goodies on their own XYZ and Topix labels, and, through a leasing arrangement, Cameo. Eventually, the persistence paid off, and the Rays returned to the airwaves with "Mediterranean Moon" (#95, 1960) and its copycat sister tune, "Magic Moon (Clair De Lune)" (#49, 1961)); the latter an adaptation of Claude Debussy's *Suite Bergamasque*.

"Listen, we're no One-Hit Wonders, said Hal Miller, in an all-to-brief exclusive interview. "'Silhouettes was a B-I-G hit! I was working for the city when it happened; and when we didn't get our money and we couldn't do it again, I went back to my job. I took 16 months leave, to give it a try. When it wasn't paying off, I returned to my job. That's it; story ended."

While the Rays failed to return, "Silhouettes" made the listings again—here and abroad—by Herman's Hermits and Cliff Richard; the flip side, "Daddy Cool" granted chartings for BONEY M and the Darts.

THURSTON HARRIS
LITTLE BITTY PRETTY ONE
(Robert Byrd)
Aladdin 3398
No. 6 *November 11, 1957*

"I pick 'em up and sell 'em," said Thurston Harris of his search for empty bottles in garbage cans. "Sometimes you can make enough to get by," *People* magazine's Patricia Freeman and Michael Small were told. "Sometimes you don't. I manage. Just some days I don't eat."

Thurston Theodore Harris (b. July 11, 1931, Indianapolis) began singing in church as a six-year-old member of the Canaan Crusaders. Years later, Thurston and brother William sang in the Indiana Wonders. After his return from military service, Harris started singing secular in a hometown joint named the Sunset Terrace. There, guitarman Jimmy Liggins—noted for his "Tear Drop Blues" (R&B: #7, 1948) and "Drunk" (R&B: #4, 1953)—caught Thurston's act. Liggins liked what he heard and hooked Harris up with his brother, Joe Liggins of "The Honeydripper" fame. "I toured with Joe around the Midwest for a while," Harris told *Goldmine*'s Jim Dawson, "and I came out West with him to Los Angeles. As soon as we got there, the band broke up."

Once in L.A., Harris allegedly went around passing himself off as the lead vocalist on the Five Royals' "Help Me Somebody" (R&B: #l, 1953), bluffing his way onto Hunter Hancock's popular R & B radio show and into talent shows. While appearing at the Club Alimony, Harris and a rag-tag group soon called the Lamplighters (Matthew Nelson, Willie Blackwell, and Leon Hughes, the latter an original Coaster) were spotted by Al Frazier. Drawn to their wildness and Thurs' voice, Al landed a recording contract for the group with Federal. The label released 13 Lamplighters singles between 1953 and 1956. Nothing charted, but all of these churners are now highly sought after disks.

On several occasions, Harris and the guys would have a falling-out. "[They] were too interested in wine,

women and dope," reported *Now Dig This'* Pete Bowen. After one of their break-ups, Thurston returned to Indianapolis. Variations of the Harris-less Lamplighters recorded as the Tenderfoots, the Sharps (backing Duane Eddy on "Rebel-'Rouser"), and still later as the Rivingtons—forever to be remembered for their delightfully idiotic "Papa-Oom-Mow-Mow." The Lamps reunited on a few occasions with Harris, and "Little Bitty Pretty One" was the result of one of these gatherings.

Thurston was released from a mental hospital the night before he and his Sharps (Al Frazier, John "Sonny" Harris, Matthew Nelson, and Carl White) recorded their moment of truth, "Little Bitty Pretty One"—actually a cover version of a song originally done by BOBBY DAY. Apparently, as Frazier told Bowen, "Thurston [had] gotten drunk and broke somebody's windows or something, and instead of calling the police they called the hospital."

"Little Bitty" made Thurston a star overnight; with stops on "American Bandstand," "The Ed Sullivan Show," and tours with Fats Domino, Buddy Holly, and the Everly Brothers.

"I didn't get nothin'," Harris told *People* of his bitter deal with the now-defunct Aladdin Records. "Nothin', you hear? Still not. They caught me when I was young and dumb and took advantage of me."

Thurston's follow-ups to "Pretty One" were as good, if not still better, than the hit, but sales were relatively paltry. "Do What You Did" (#57, 1958) and another Bobby Day cover, "Over And Over" (#96, 1958), charted, but "Be-Baba-Leba," "(I Got Loaded At) Smokey Joe's," "Runk Bunk," and other efforts slipped into obscurity without notice. Aladdin Records folded, and Thurston moved on to recording some one-off sides for Imperial, Dot, Cub, and Reprise. The last of these was issued in 1964.

Harris was homeless, moving between friends and relatives—for years. By the '90s, he was staying with his sister. "I'm lucky, I guess. I could be sleeping in cars and eating air like I used to when I quit music."

Jim Dawson interviewed Harris for *Goldmine* and produced a limited-release Harris EP in 1984. He reported that during the interview, Harris did not say much about those years, but that it was plain that there were a few hospitals and jails along the way, as well as a drug habit that he eventually shook.

Harris' dream—to "do it" once again. "I can still sing," he told *People*, "and I never stopped writing." "In a voice seasoned by malt liquor and Lucky Strikes," wrote the magazine writers, Thurston launched into a new tune, "Head of Lettuce," the tale of what drink had done to him. "I think it's gonna be a hit," said Harris.

On April 14, 1990, Thurston Harris died of a heart attack at his sister's place in Pomona, California.

SHEPHERD SISTERS
ALONE (WHY MUST I BE ALONE)
(Morty Craft, S. Craft)
Lance 125
No. 18 *November 11, 1957*

Not so very long ago, four sisters from Middletown, Ohio—blondes all—sang their way across this country. Martha, Mary Lou, Gayle, and Judy Shepherd performed at gatherings, niteries (as booze-houses were politely called at one time), and talent shows. Frequently, they would take top honors on the "Arthur Godfrey's Talent Scouts" TV show. Herbie Space noted their cheerful sound and invited the girls to fill a void in his band. A booking agent named Karl Taylor caught a glimpse of the act often referred to as the "LaLa Quartet" and put the sisters on a multinational U.S.0. tour.

On their return, a canny Morty Craft signed the Shepherd Sisters to Melba Records for a spunky but forgettable "Gone With the Wind." Craft next suited the quartet in his own number, "Alone (Why Must I Be Alone)," possibly the happiest heartacher to ever chart. The song, its arrangement, and those voices were so catchy that even those who noticed the girls' imprecise harmonies still liked it. The sisters worked the Nautilus Hotel in Miami, the Town and Country in New York, and the Barclay in Toronto. They were picked up by Mercury for a single or so—then in turn by MGM, Warwick, and United Artists Records—but nothing sold very well.

Finally, in 1963, the act passed through a watershed of sorts when they met someone who knew just how to make the best of the Shepherd Sisters' distinctive vocalizations. It was BOB CREWE who produced the sisters at their finest. Their Atlantic release "The Greatest Lover" had the feel of an innocent Shelley Fabares record, and their 20th Century Fox single "Finders Keepers" jumped out as if rendered by the livid EXCITERS. "Don't Mention My Name" staked out the number 94 slot on the Hot 100 in 1963, but it was all too late. The Shepherd Sisters time had passed.

BILL JUSTIS
RAUNCHY
(Bill Justis, Sidney Manker)
Philips 3519
No. 2 *December 16, 1957*

Little Billy (b. William E. Justis, Jr., Oct. 14, 1926, Birmingham, AL) and his family moved to Memphis when he was five. Father was an affluent roofing contractor; Mother was a concert pianist; under her influence and prodding, Bill took to tooting on the sax. In 1951, he formed his first dance band when he was 15. After gath-

BILL JUSTIS

ering some postgrad credits, he worked as the music director at Tulane University in New Orleans, and did choral arrangements for Arizona University. He moved to Memphis and married in 1954. Quite soon thereafter, Justis realized that extra money was needed. He kept dropping in on Sam Phillips's Sun studios, hoping to interest the legendary record man with his abilities.

"Justis, man, he was the first hip-talkin' cat that I ever heard," recalled Phillips in an interview with *Mean Mountain Music* magazine. "He'd repeatedly come by the studio at 706 Union and play these little dangle deals, 'Two Step,' 'Soft Shoe,' 'Be-Bop' . . . I never really took him seriously. I don't know why. I guess I thought he was a joke. I think everyone did. In my opinion, the guy's a genius. He's just been misdirected, all his life, until he cut 'Raunchy.'"

Phillips finally flagged and hired the cool dude with the honkin' sax to be his music director at Sun/Phillips. In that role, Bill arranged and led the studio bands for Elvis, Johnny Cash, Jerry Lee Lewis, and the rest. Legend has it that it was Justis who first labeled Lewis "The Killer." It was Bill, also, who "discovered" Charlie Rich in a bar singing ballads; and produced his biggest Sun-era disk, "Lonely Weekends."

"Bill would be around the studio all the time," said Phillips, "and I'd say, 'Now Bill, you've got to get raunchy sounding! Darn if he and [guitarist] Sid Manker [b. 1932, Memphis] didn't write a song and instrumentally put it down to become the biggest instrumental that was ever cut and out in the '50s.'"

"Raunchy"—initially titled "Backwoods"—proved highly influential; and was the first tune George Harrison ever learned to play. Cover versions by Billy Vaughn and ERNIE FREEMAN also sold well. A number of follow-up 45s were issued, but only "College Man" (#42, 1958) made the grade. After a dispute in March of 1960 involving charges of insubordination, Justis left Sun Records to do some production work for Sam's brother, Judd Phillips' label Judd—notably "Rockin' Little Angel"; for RAY SMITH—and to form his own short-lived label, Play Me. Not many did, and in the early '60s, Bill moved his services to RCA, and later to ABC-Paramount, Monument, Sound Stage, and Smash. As an arranger he worked with Brook Benton, Bobby Goldsboro, Roy Orbison, Bobby Vinton. Among his many other meanderings, Bill wrote the scores to the *Smokey and the Bandit* flicks.

Several LPs of increasing schmaltzy sounds appeared on Smash label. Both *Bill Justis Plays 12 Big Instrumental Hits* (1962) and *Bill Justis Plays 12 More Big Instrumental Hits* (1963) clicked, but with a more sedate audience.

Bill never got to right these later wrongs. The hip-talkin' honker died of a brief illness on July 15, 1982, at the age of 55.

Sid Manker, "Raunchy's" co-creator died of a heart attack on December 15, 1974. Sid who had studied design at the Academy of Art in Memphis, gave up the pursuit in the early '50s to play what he called "the starvation box," the guitar. He formed the Memphis Jazz Quartet, continued doing Sun sessions, but got hooked on heroin at about the time "Raunchy" hit.

"I was a full-fledged addict," Manker told the *Memphis Press Scrimitar*, in 1959. "From then on, it was three shots a day, seven days a week." In April 1960, Sid was placed in a penal farm for six months. Thereafter he worked at Axent Studios in Biloxi, Mississippi, until his death.

MARGIE RAYBURN
I'M AVAILABLE
(Dave Burgess)
Liberty 55102
No. 9 *December 16, 1957*

Margie, born in Madera, California, attended Hollywood High School. Later, she sang with Ray Anthony's Orchestra, toured with Gene Autry, worked the Frisco nightclubs, and had some singles issued locally on Alma and S & G labels—all before she was discovered by Norman Milkin, her future husband. Norm occasionally collaborated with Freddy Morgan on material for THE SUNNYSIDERS. Morgan, a banjo picker with Spike Jones and the City Slickers from 1947 to 1958, had created the Sunnysiders with Jad Paul—his replacement in Spike's band of music depreciators—as an outlet for his tunes. As a member of that group, Margie appeared on their lone hit, "Hey, Mr. Banjo." After the Sunnysiders tried more numbers with the banjo motif like "Banjo Pickers Ball" and "The Lonesome Banjo (In the Pawn Shop Window)," Margie went solo again.

"I'm Available" was sensuous, in a Patti Page-like manner. The tune was found by her hubby and was written by a young Dave Burgess, who a few years later would have a successful career as the leader of the Champs; know nationwide for "Tequila."

"Margie Rayburn was a frustrated singer. She always wanted to record. But I didn't want to record her," said Simon "Si" Waronker, founder of Liberty Records to author "Doc Rock" Kelley. "What were we doing? A 40-year-old woman. She would sing, but she had nothing unusual, nothing that means any thing. She came in one day with a tune called 'I'm Available.' But here was a woman of forty sounding like a little girl of 17 or 18. If you listen carefully, you will hear that there are only three men on that. Well, we weren't going to waste money . . . I did add a bass and a drum. It was cute.

"In those days, if an artist got a hit, he or she could go on tour. Margie was a little old, but she had a good figure, and with makeup, at a distance she could pass for a younger woman." After a three-month tour, Margie returned with the intent of cutting an album. Said Si to Margie, "'Don't do it . . . Margie, you don't know the business. You've earned about $70,000 or $80,000 on this record. Keep it, please!"

Standard contracts stipulated that the costs of future projects were to be deducted from royalties earned. To record Margie, $17,000 was spent. "We couldn't give it away. We even tried taking singles off of the album, to see if we could get some airplay. She never had another hit."

Despite her label-owners negative view of his artist, Margie went on to record a string of fine follow-ups—

"Smoochin'," "Try Me," and "Here I Am." Most of them were drenched in a delicious heavy echo and utilized multi-tracking to give her voice the same slinky and suggestive quality that "Available" had featured. Si was right about one thing—no subsequent efforts ever charted, and Margie last recorded in 1966.

That album—*Margie*—is now a collectible, valued at over $100 a copy.

ERNIE FREEMAN
RAUNCHY
(Bill Justis, Sidney Manker)
Imperial 5474
No. 4 *December 30, 1957*

Ernie Freeman was right there at the dawn of rock and roll. Next time you check out the classic Bill Haley flick, *Rock Around the Clock* (1956), be sure to take notice of the unimposing piano man tinkling in the shadows way behind the Platters as they warble "Only You." That's Ernie Freeman, the man behind a pile of California-born hits.

A little Freeman was born the morn of August 16, 1922, in Cleveland. Ernie took to the keyboards early and studied music at the university level. After his return from the service at the start of the '50s, Freeman worked the clubs playing light jazz and accompanying the likes of Dorothy Dandridge and Dinah Washington. In 1956, songwriter and producer Jerry Leiber discovered Ernie and used him as the pianist and arranger for his one-off rock and roll ensemble, Scooby Doo. Imperial Records got wind of Ernie, and enlisted his services as A & R man and recording artist.

For the next half-dozen years, Freeman recorded nearly 30 old fangled rockin' instrumentals. In 1957, Freeman covers of both Doc Bagby's "Dumplin's" (#75) and Bill Justis' classic "Raunchy" charted, as did three later disks—"Indian Love Call" (#59, 1958), "Theme From 'The Dark at the Top of the Stairs,'" (#70, 1960), and a version of "The Twist" (#93, 1962). These instrumentals usually featured Plas Johnson (sax), Irv Ashby (guitar), and a contingent of sticky strings.

In 1960, Percy Faith turned solid gold with the release of his mushy "Theme From a Summer Place." Freeman, in response, wrote, arranged, and produced an equally bathetic string-thing he called "Beautiful Obsession." Released under the name of "Sir Chauncey," Ernie's record sold well enough to chart (#89, 1960). Freeman and his usual session crew also hit pay dirt as both Billy Joe & the Checkmates—responsible for the coffee classic "Percolator (Twist)"—and "B. Bumble & the Stingers" when their recordings of "Bumble Boogie" (#21, 1961) and "Nut Rocker" (#23, 1962) made the big time.

Over the next two decades, Ernie's keyboard sounds, his arrangements, and/or his producing skills were used by Sammy Davis, Jr., Connie Francis, Dean Martin, Gene McDaniels, Sandy Nelson, Simon & Garfunkel, and Frank Sinatra, to name but a few. For 10 years, in his twilight career years, he was a music director for Reprise Records. Late in the '70s, Ernie Freeman retired and moved to Hawaii. On May 16, 1981, Ernie died of a heart attack.

HOLLYWOOD FLAMES
BUZZ-BUZZ-BUZZ
(J. Gray, Robert "BOBBY DAY" Byrd)
Ebb 119
No. 11 *January 27, 1958*

"The Flames originated in 1949, when we were all in our teens. We met at the Largo Theatre in Watts [in Los Angeles] at a talent show," Flames leader Bobby Byrd said in an article for *Yesterday's Memories*. "There were about 10 to 15 lead singers there, so the owner suggested that we get together to form several groups."

Byrd (bass) circulated and wound up with David Ford (tenor) and Willie Ray Rockwell (second tenor). After the show was over, the guys decided to remain together, and so the Flames were born. Curley Dinkins (baritone) was added, and the group started working the club scene. Success was definitely not an overnight operation: singles appeared on Selective, Specialty, Spin, Unique, and Recorded in Hollywood.

In 1953, Rockwell left to join Thurston Harris's group, the Lamplighters, and was replaced by Leon Hughes; Hughes left to sing with the Coasters, and was replaced in turn by ex-Platter Gaynell Hodge. That same year, the group signed with Aladdin; Dinkins left shortly thereafter, but only momentarily. His brief replacement was Curtis Williams (who moved on the following year to form The Penguins and write "Earth Angel"). After Aladdin, the Flames recorded more golden greats for the Lucky, Swingtime, Decca, Hollywood, and Money labels. The various companies released the group's records under an array of names—the Flames, the 4 Flames, the Hollywood 4 Flames, the Hollywood Flames, the Eddtides, the Jets, the Satellites, and the Tangiers.

"We were very popular all over Los Angeles, but we just didn't have a hit record," Byrd wrote. Hodge left in 1957, and his shoes were filled by Earl Nelson. Earl would later record as half of the Bob & Earl team (originators of the "Harlem Shuffle"), and also charted in 1965 as Jackie Lee. Like Hodge, Byrd also left the Flames in 1957, after waxing "Buzz-Buzz-Buzz."

"That was my song and Earl sang lead," Byrd explained. "I wrote and arranged it and the financing came from John Dolphin. He sold the song to Lee Rupe, who was the ex-wife of Specialty Records' Art Rupe, and the owner of Ebb Records.

"When the song became a hit, I found out I didn't have any publishing rights and only half the writer credit. Dolphin admitted he owed me $6, 000, but he was killed before I could get any of it."

Less than a year later, Byrd, recording as BOBBY DAY, got his just due when his "Rockin' Robin" (#2) b/w "Over and Over" (#41) became a double-sided smash.

The Flames would continue for another 10 years, with their line-up changing more rapidly than the seasons. Never again, despite flashes of high-quality music, would the group win its place on the pop charts.

Bobby Day died of cancer, on July 15, 1990.

SILHOUETTES
GET A JOB
(Silhouettes)
Ember 1029
No. 1 *February 24, 1958*

___

As a child Richard "Rick" Lewis (b. 1933, Philadelphia, tenor) received training in the arts at his neighborhood recreation center. From 1946 to 1949, he was a member of the Philadelphia All Boys Choir. During his army internship Rick performed with JESSIE BELVIN, THE PENGUINS' Curtis Williams and possibly THE HOLLYWOOD FLAMES' Gaynell Hodges as the Swords at the service club in Oxford. On his return to civilian activities in Philadelphia, in 1954, Rick joined the Parakeets—Ernie Banks, Benny Hart, James Jenkins—a pop act. For a while they played state fairs, carnivals, made the "Harlem Holiday Review" at the 81 Theatre in Atlanta; even toured Canada. When the promised money didn't come, the Parakeets flew.

In 1955, Rick was offered a position as the TURBANS' road manager. He accepted, but after a few tours and his mother's death, he returned to Philadelphia to tend to family needs and to singing; hooking up—as fate would have it—with the Gospel Tornadoes, baritone Earl Beal, bass Raymond Edwards, lead Bill Horton, and ex-Parakeet tenor James Jenkins. Jenkins, at this point, left the group to fill Lewis' slot with the Turbans. In 1956 at Rick's insistence these sacred singers went secular, changed their name to The Thunderbirds, and hammered out Rick's divine intervention, "Get a Job."

While appearing at the Uptown Theatre, the act attracted the attention of DJ, producer, and owner of Junior Records, Kae Williams. Williams really liked their ballad and intended "A" side, "I'm Lonely." Arrangements were made and in August 1957, the Thunderbirds were ushered into the Robinson Recording Laboratories at radio WIP. "Get a Job" was chosen

as the flip side. Rollie McGill was brought in to honk sax, and Earl dreamed up the group's new name, a cop on the title of THE RAYS runaway hit "Silhouettes."

"I'm gonna give you the story," said Rick Lewis in an exclusive interview. "It's been hushed too long. A distributor in town had connections with Ember Records in New York and Tony Mammarella and Dick Clark. He told them, 'This song's gonna be a hit. It needs national distribution, and I want you to play it. I'm gonna see that you all get half the publishing on this thing.' They said , 'No.' But after a deal was made with Al Silver at Ember, they went along with it."

Lewis maintains that is how "Get a Job" got its place on 'American Bandstand' and how without the act's consent they lost half of their publishing money.

"Get a Job" sold over a million copies, and still sells thousands every year. It was one of the first R & B singles to cross over into the pop/rock world and to simultaneously top both charts. Eventually, it became one of the most played and most memorable rock and roll recordings of all time.

"I have no idea how I came up with all that 'yip, yip' 'boom, boom' stuff," said Lewis, "other than the song demanded it. It was meant to be. When you sing *a cappella* as we did, you need something to fill out the song; and it just came to us. Now, the song came to me—not in Germany, like people say—but after I'm back from the service and sitting around collecting unemployment compensation. My mother said, 'What are you gonna do?' We had a piano, an upright laying around the house. I was playing music. She said, 'Get a job. You need to get a job. You get up in the morning and go out and get a job.' The song is so true, 'cause that is what mothers say. It hits everybody, 'cause we all know about needing to get it together."

The Silhouettes played the Apollo, toured with Sam Cooke and Clyde McPhatter, and made extensive Alan Freed and Dick Clark Caravan tours. Both the Tempos and the Heartbeats (soon to evolve into SHEP & THE LIMELITES) would record "answer records" to "Get a Job." The Miracles' very first disk was "Got a Job."

All of the follow-up songs were fine efforts, but all of them failed. "I Sold My Heart to the Junkman"— issued initially on Junior, then Johnny Vincent's Ace— was a classic and the groups finest ever. While the Silhouettes faded, the Patti LaBelle & The Blue-Belles name would establish itself with their frantic rendition of "Junkman" in 1962. History reveals that the voices heard on the disk were not those of the Blue-Belles, but actually those of THE STARLETS.

"You may not print this, but it's true. Kae Williams had the ability to become a threat to the dynasty being formed here by Dick Clark, Tony Mammarella, and [Cameo/Parkway Records'] Bernie Lowe. They knew that he couldn't go national unless he had the access to money—and he had no other groups happening but the Silhouettes, and there wouldn't be no money unless the Silhouettes had another hit. We went to New York in April of '58 to do the Saturday Night 'Dick Clark Show,' and they wouldn't let us introduce our second record. . . ." Lewis believes that a deal was cut whereby Al Silver's Ember label did not push the Silhouettes' "Heading for the Poorhouse," but another Ember Record, by a pseudo-group—"Op" by the Honeycombs. And in exchange of revenues lost, Clark and "American Bandstand" would heavily play the Honeycomb one-off disk.

"It hurt bad. We knew we had another hit," said Lewis. "And it was taken away from us. We still were doing tours. All that was missing was our charted record."

After the release of "Rent Man" in 1962, Horton and Edwards left the group, and were replaced by Cornelius Brown and John Wilson. Later in the same year, with the aid of Jerry Ragavoy—producer of Garnet Mimms, THE EXCITERS, and THE MAJORS—and VAN McCOY, the revamped Silhouettes recorded two singles—one on the Grand and one on the Imperial labels. Sales were poor, and the group called it quits in 1968 after the release (on the Goodway label) of their only album, *The Original and New Silhouettes—'58/'68 Get a Job*.

In the late '60s, Bill Horton recorded some sides with the Dawns and also had a few solo singles issued. *Working Hard*, the act's second overlooked LP was issued in 1982. The following year, the Silhouettes appeared in *Joey*, a generation gap flick starring James Quinn and Elisa Heinsohn. From 1986 through 1993, the Silhouettes, with all four original members, continued to make spirited appearances at rock and roll revival shows—on two occasions—Bill suffered a heart attack.

The Silhouettes' final curtain call was on November 6, 1993, in Beverley, Massachusetts. Lead singer Bill Horton died in Philadelphia, January 23, 1995. On March 4, 1997, Raymond W. Edwards—the bass man who rendered the immortal "yip, yip, yip, yip, yip, yip, yip, yip, boom, boom, boom, boom, boom"—died of prostrate cancer in Philadelphia. He was 74.

"Earl and I are doing fine, but there's not that much work for us to do anything. But, we did succeed in getting all our master recordings back and all our publishing back. We never got all the money. . . ."

CRESCENDOS
OH JULIE
(Kenneth R. Moffit, Noel Ball)
Nasco 6005
No. 5 *March 3, 1958*

"I've heard talk on this DALE WARD [a credible Elvis stylist who later charted with "Letter for Sherry"] being

THE CRESCENDOS

a member of our group. Well, absolutely not! And all those other guys that claim they were with us—Wanda Burt and this Clarence Wittenmeier; never met 'em," said George R. Lanuis in an exclusive interview. "Now, Janice Green is something. She wasn't one of the guys, but Janice was the female voice heard on 'Julie.'

"We were only together for a year. So, bogus groups started to use our name; ah, even while we were still together. I think, Ward was probably affiliated with our manager Noel Ball, possibly Ball sent him out with some others as us. Noel passed away, several years ago, so we'll never have the true story on that."

Lanuis, a Nashville realtor for much of his life, was the real thing, an original member and the lead vocalist on one of rock'n'roll's most cherished '50s classic, "Oh Julie"; and most assuredly one of the era's least known groups.

"The Crescendos were five guys. Besides myself, there was Tommy Fortner, Kenneth Brigham, Jimmy Hall, and my cousin Jim Lanuis. We're the originals. We're it. We met and formed the group while we were all attending Cumberland High in Nashville. In '57, we started doing talent shows and it was at one of these that this Nashville DJ [Noel Ball] recognized us. He took us to Nasco. And he gave us 'Oh Julie' to record. The label says Ball and Ken Moffit wrote it, but if the truth were to be known, it was Moffit's song.

"Our situation was like a lot of acts back then, a bunch of naive school kids being taken under the wing by individuals who took most of the profits. And we got the leavings. I still hear the record on the radio and sometimes they mention this Ward fellow. It's still in print, and we haven't gotten a royalty check since 1963; if I'm not mistaken. We traveled a year on 'Oh Julie,' which did sell a million and [for] which we didn't get the gold record. We did get to see it though, hanging on the wall at our manager's office.

"We didn't get incredibly wealthy. You might've guessed that. But, I do remember one royalty check for about $6,500 [per man]. That wasn't bad, then. Touring we made about $300, a piece, per week. And all expenses were paid. We toured with the 'Show of Stars.' With us were the Everly Brothers, Brenda Lee, Sam Cooke, LaVerne Baker, and I believe Frankie Valli and the Four Lovers.

"Probably the reason we broke up was we had burnt ourselves out. We were just out of high school and on the road for nine months, straight. And that will burn you out really quick. And then three of the boys went to college. Two of us got married. And all that makes it hard to get together. We were burnt and we had this bad taste in our mouths on how things had been handled. The rest of our records—there was only three more ["School Girl" b/w "Crazy Hop"; "Young and in Love" b/w "Rainy Days"; and some canned cuts for Nasco leased a few years later to Scarlet, "Strange Love" b/w "Let's Take a Walk"]. The rest—all of 'em—were by bogus groups. Our follow-ups probably didn't sell well 'cause we'd had it and had stopped traveling and promoting.

"We've all done really well, though. None of us went on any further in music. Nah. I'm in real estate. Ken's a doctor. Tommy's an architect-builder. Jim's an accountant. And Jimmy Hall has been working for years at Ford Motors."

Have you ever tried to go back, to make the rounds on the oldies circuit?

"No, we never did."

Are you still friends?

"Yeah. We all live within a 15-mile radius of each other."

Do you ever get together and harmonize?

"Nah."

George Lanuis, the Crescendos' lead vocalist, died in 1996.

EDDIE PLATT
TEQUILA
(Chuck Rio)
ABC-Paramount 9899
No. 20 *March 31, 1958*

Near zip is known about this Cleveland saxman. Eddie Platt did blow horn, and he did have a band that played local clubs and dances. When the Champs' "Tequila" heated up, Eddie and his guys burned rubber to a nearby recording studio to cop a cover. Eddie and the boys collected enough action on their instrumental version to hold down the number 20 position for a week. Their follow-up was another cover—this time of "Cha-Hua-Hua" by THE PETS. It didn't chart. No further releases were ever to bear the name of Eddie Platt, and never again was his name heard over the airwaves of this great nation.

JOHN ZACHERLE
DINNER WITH DRAC-PART 1
(Jon Sheldon, Harry Land)
Cameo 130
No. 6 *March 31, 1958*

"I was not allowed to see horror movies when I was a kid," said John Zacherle, the "Cool Ghoul," a moniker given him by friend and TV giant Dick Clark, in an exclusive interview. "So I spent a lot of Saturday afternoons with another poor sucker who couldn't go to the movies either. I didn't get to see *Dracula* and *Frankenstein* till after I was 37 or so and this TV ghoul."

Surely, John Zacherle (b. Sept. 26, 1918, Philadelphia) looked to be a highly unlikely candidate for the status of great ghouldom. He started legit earning a bachelor's degree from the University of Pennsylvania in English literature. During World War II, he served in the Army, eventually working his way to the rank of major. On his return, however, John reportedly looked about for what he considered a more relaxed profession, something with bite and depth, something intelligent, yet emotive. Yes, why not become an actor?

For years, he worked in local stock companies. "Action in the Afternoon" was a live sudsy TV cowboy show, broadcast daily over Philly's WCAU. "Now, things can go wrong with cows, guns and horses, live and all moving around," said John.

"Well, I played an undertaker, this one season. I put on these spats and a long black frock and left an impression, apparently. When RKO and Universal issued all these horror flicks, like 'Wolfman' and whatnot for TV, 'Shock Theatre' was created, with different 'horror hosts' in each major city; like Morgus in Baltimore and Marvin in Chicago.

"When WCAU launched their 'Shock Theatre,' someone at Channel 10 recalled my role in 'Action in the Afternoon' and I became Roland, the blood-drinking midnight emcee. They couldn't afford a second person on the show so I had a sack hanging on a meat hook; a creature named Gasport who moaned and groaned, and I would operated on him occasionally. Then my wife lived in a large box, you see, and all you could see of her was the stake that I'd move around once in a while to excite her."

The response was immediate. Ratings soared, Zacherle fan clubs were formed, personal appearances were demanded, and none of this madness was lost on the offspring of Cameo Records' president Bernie Lowe. "Bernie use to sit and watch the show with his little daughter," said John. "Some one sent us a limerick; others sent them, and it became a habit to do a crazy rhyme thing. Bernie got the brainstorm one night to have me come in and recite these lyrics and they'd put some funky music behind it." A session was arranged. Staff writers created some gruesome lyrical lines, while Dave Appel and his Applejacks (formerly known for "Mexican Hat Dance" and "Rocka-Conga") provided the legitimate rock accompaniment. "Dinner With Drac," a honkin' but decidely distasteful dish that featured a Dracula imitation from Zach, received enough airplay to plant this ghoul and his goons firmly in the upper reaches of the pop charts.

"I was in shock," said Zacherle. "I expected nothing from this foolery. The song was banned in England, however. I think that's a great mark of distinction. They had censorship back in those days. It was too gory or some such, so we had to change the lyrics and put it out a second time.

"Dick Clark had a Saturday night show with a Top Ten of the week, and I was on it and did a video-like an MTV thing—doing that song. Now, this is '58—oh so long ago, scary, really—had to be one of the first videos for a song. I was a very bad lip syncer, so it's fortunate that all those dancers were jumping around."

John moved his hobgoblin hosting to New York City and WABC. He fronted "American Bandstand"'s Halloween party in 1958, and for years thereafter.

In 1963, when "Bandstand" shifted to Saturdays only, Zach moved to WOR-TV to host a further run of horrors and whodunits. After "Dinner With Drac," several more singles—particularly, "Eighty-Two Tombstones," "I Was a Teenage Caveman," "Hury Bury Baby," "Hello Dolly"—and eventually a few LPs—*Spook Along With Zacherle* (1960); *Monster Mash* (1962); *Scary Tales* (1963)—were packed and pushed, but nothing much in the way of media attention was given to most of these artifacts.

In the mid-to-late '60s, John fronted a TV dance show in Newark, "Zacherle's Disco-Teen." Next, the ghoul moved over to radio, progressive rock radio WNEW in New York.

Numerous format and channel changes have transpired, but the near 90-year-old Zach is still going strong. Childhood fan, Howard Stern suggested him for WXRK, where he currently works weekdays, 7 A.M. to 10 A.M. In 1996, John Zacherle—now simply billed Zacherley—went back into the studios with a rock band to create a new album's worth, *Dead Man's Ball*.

LAURIE LONDON
HE'S GOT THE WHOLE WORLD IN HIS HANDS
(Traditional)
Capitol 3891
No. 1 *April 14, 1958*

A lad (not a lass) named Laurie London was born in London on January 19, 1944. When a wee one of 13, Laurie, with a high-pitched voice and no musical training, came to the forefront of pop consciousness when he auditioned for "London's Radio Show" and was given the opportunity to record a Geoff Love adaptation of an old gospel song. While the recording sold moderately well in his homeland, Laurie's tune, with a flash of fluke, resided in the coveted top spot on the Top 100 for four weeks. The disk became the most successful record by a British bloke in the U.S. in the '50s.

Whether it was Laurie's timing or the infectious feel the recording created that made London's big moment happen, we will never know. The flash of fame appeared so colossal that Laurie was allowed to leave school, and his dad, Will, gave up his sales management job to become the boy's manager. In fielding offers for his son's voice, Dad may have made a big mistake when he refused to let the 14-year-old travel to the States for a U.S. tour.

Neither Laurie nor his label had any idea what made this number so successful. Laurie went on to make more pop/gospel recordings—such as "Joshua," "The Gospel Train," and "I Gotta Robe"—for his label, and still more for Roulette Records, but nothing the little shaver ever recorded, even after his voice changed, came near to making *Billboard*'s charts.

Reports from England are vague, but it is reported that Laurie went on to a career working in the clothing industry in London.

RONALD & RUBY
LOLLIPOP
(Beverly "RUBY" Ross, Julius Dixon)
RCA Victor 7174
No. 20 *April 14, 1958*

In January 1958, young Beverly Ross, along with a black singing partner of 13 or 14 named Lee Morris, approached her manager, song plugger Arnold Shaw, later the author of a number of books on pop music history. They performed a catchy song Beverly had penned with Julius Dixon. Shaw flipped for the tune, called "Lollipop," and rushed Ronald and Ruby, as the duo would be called, into Associated Recording Studios. A demo was cut and packed within an hour. Before Shaw could have Lee's parents sign a recording contract for the underage lad, Archie Bleyer at Cadence Records had his Chordettes cover the song. The Chordettes were on a trail of hits ("Eddie My Love," "Born to Be With You"), and their version of "Lollipop" stole much of the sales and charting action from Beverly and her sidekick. The Mudlarks, a male/female British unit, started their career with their near chart-topping cover of "Lollipop." Their successive and successful Top 40 disks included a take on THE MONOTONES' "Book of Love" and "The Love Game."

"Lollipop" was not Ross' first shot at success. Born in 1939, the daughter of a New Jersey chicken farmer, she moved with her family to New York City while she was in her teens. Beverly wrote a number of songs for Bill Haley & His Comets, including "Dim, Dim the Lights." Shaw, who became her manager in the mid-'50s, convinced Columbia Records head (and prominent rock-hater) Mitch Miller to record some tunes that his client had penned.

Despite his scorn for rock and roll, Miller let Ross cut "Stop Laughing at Me" b/w "Head-lights," using full and hip rock accompaniment, but after generating some initial sparks, the platter sputtered.

Over the years, Beverly Ross has had substantial success as a songwriter, since artists like Lesley Gore ("Judy's Turn to Cry"), THE EARLS ("Remember When"), and Roy Orbison ("Candy Man") recorded her material. Reportedly, Bev owns her own recording studio and is involved in composing for the theater.

HUEY "PIANO" SMITH & THE CLOWNS
DON'T YOU JUST KNOW IT
(Huey "Piano" Smith)
Ace 545
No. 9 *April 14, 1958*

For many years now, Huey Smith, renowned New Orleans piano man, has been content with working his garden. Now a Jehovah's Witness and a strict Bible reader, Huey has long been embittered by the bad deals, the mistakes, and the way he feels his best material has been stolen from him.

Smith was born in the city's Garden District on January 26, 1934. His uncle played the piano, and Huey would imitate him. "I used to play till the neighbors used to bang on the walls for me knock it off," Huey told *Goldmine*'s Almost Slim. "When I was seven or eight, I began makin' songs up like 'Robertson Street Boogie.' My father used to give me money to take lessons every week. But I didn't go! I kept the money, and learned from my sister, who took lessons from the lady next door."

When he was 15, Huey met Eddie "Guitar Slim" Jones. "I had been fooling around with a friend of mine, Roosevelt Nettles, who played drums. One night I was coming home from Cohen [High School] and stopped over at Roosevelt's and there was this guy there with guitar. He was dressed in purple and yellow pants, a lime green shirt and a straw hat! Roosevelt said, 'He sounds just like Gatemouth Brown.' It was Guitar Slim." Smith made a living recording with Guitar Slim ("The Things That I Used to Do"), Earl King ("Those Lonely Lonely Nights"), Little Richard ("Tutti Frutti"), Lloyd Price and Smiley Lewis ("I Hear You Knockin'"). Ace Records released the first 45 under Huey's name— "Little Liza Jane"—when the core idea for Smith's earliest solo hit came.

"I was always trying to pick up catchy lines, and Chuck Berry had this line, 'I got rockin' pneumonia, sittin' down at a rhythm review,' and ROY BROWN had some line about 'young man rhythm.' So I started thinkin' about opposite lines like, 'kissin' a girl that's too tall.' We came up with 'Rockin' Pneumonia and the Boogie Woogie Flu' (R&B: #5, 1957) that night in the studio."

BOBBY MARCHAN, who was working as a female impersonator when he met Huey—and continues such activities—sang lead on this New Orleans classic, and joined Smith to form the Clowns. The idea was that Marchan would handle lead vocals, and Smith would write the tunes, play piano, and arrange. The line-up was liquid, but present during the band's hey day were Marchan, James Booker, Curly Moore (lead singer for most post-1959 recordings), Roosevelt Nettles, ROBERT PARKER, and even JESSIE HILL.

"Don't You Just Know It," Huey's next single, was a huge pop success. Gerri Hall, a perennial Clown and later one of Ray Charles' Raelettes, told John Broven in *Rhythm & Blues* that the tune's title came from an expression that Rudy Ray Moore, the Clowns' driver, was accustomed to saying. The Clowns hit the road in support of the disk, leaving a number called "Sea Cruise" behind in the can.

"In my mind, ["Sea Cruise"] was the one that was gonna throw me over the hump," Huey recalled. "But Johnny [Vincent] and FRANKIE FORD's manager Joe Caronna, liked it also. So Johnny came to me and said, 'Let Frankie do this.' I said, 'No way!' But Johnny said there was nothing I could do about it. It was coming out on Frankie."

The track was issued under Frankie Ford's name, with Frankie singing lead. Huey was livid. "I never got any royalties from Johnny. He kept sayin', 'It's comin', it's comin'.'"

When his contract ran out, Huey was gone, and so were the chartings. He continued recording for Imperial, Teem, Spinett, Instant, Constellation, and White Cliffs. Many times, his disks would appear under other names like Shindig Smith, Snuffy Smith, the Hueys, the Pitter Pats, and the Soul Shakers.

Smith worked where he could, even returning to the Ace label in the early '60s. Once he had recovered from a serious drinking problem, he turned to religion, working as a janitor in a drugstore and eventually turning to gardening. Huey "Piano" Smith has vowed never to perform again.

MONOTONES
BOOK OF LOVE
(Warren Davis, George Malone, Charles Patrick)
Argo 5290
No. 5 *April 21, 1958*

They were buddies living in the same housing project in Newark, New Jersey. They sang four-part harmony but were six in number; they called themselves the Monotones because, as one of the group told *Goldmine*'s Jeff Tamarkin, "the word means 'one tone' and we were so close, like one." Warren Davis, George Malone, Charles Patrick, Frank Smith, and the Ryanes brothers—John and Warren—started putting an act together in 1955. They had already done some singing together as part of their church choir—the same choir that included Cissy Houston, Dionne Warwick, and some of THE SWEET INSPIRATIONS.

In 1956, the Monotones were polished enough to appear on Ted Mack's "Amateur Hour": They won the first week, singing the Cadillacs' "Zoom," but lost the following week. Soon after, Charles' brother James joined the Kodaks, and this group's successful appearances at the Apollo spurred the Monotones to think more seriously of their careers. One day, as the group recalled to Tamarkin, "Charles heard [this] commercial ["You'll wonder where the yellow went/When you brush your teeth with Pepsodent"] on the radio. . . . He went home and got George and Warren and forged the song out of it."

They made a demo and took it around to all the labels in the area. Bea Casalin at Hull Records was impressed, and quickly arranged to get the group into Bell Sound Studios in New York City. "Book of Love" was initially released in December of 1957 on Mascot, a subsidiary of Hull Records. Within weeks, the response was too much for the little label to handle, and Argo Records picked up the disk for national distribution. The Monotones, meanwhile, were out having a ball on an extended tour with Bobby Darin and Frankie Lymon & The Teenagers.

No one gave a thought to putting a follow-up record together. By the time word came from the group's label to hustle home and record something, it was already May. The initial plan was for "Legend of Sleepy Hollow," written by Charles and his brother James, to be the next release; a few more months, however, were needed to get the eerie classic together. In the meantime, the label issued "Tom Foolery," but it failed to chart. Eventually, "Legend" was released, but by then, the group had lost its momentum. Only three more singles appeared before the group quietly disbanded. Members went off to marriages, the military, and regular jobs.

The Monotones still perform at oldies shows. The group has the same line-up as the day it was born, except for the Ryanes brothers—both John (d. May 30, 1972) and Warren have since died.

ART & DOTTY TODD
CHANSON D'AMOUR (SONG OF LOVE)
(Wayne Shanklin)
Era 1064
No. 6 *May 5, 1958*

Arthur (b. Mar. 11, 1920) and Dotty (b. June 22, 1923) Todd were born and raised in Elizabeth, New Jersey. It wasn't until a chance encounter in Providence, Rhode Island, in 1941 that they met and learned of their mutual interest in making music. At the time, Art was playing both guitar and banjo and studying music at Syracuse University; Dot had studied the piano, and was attending a business college. Before the year's end, Art and Dot shared the same last name, and before the decade's end, the twosome was performing together at clubs and hotels. RCA Victor issued some of their duets, which had sold well in Europe but which stiffed in the United States.

Art then happened on to what he thought was a neat number by the fellow who wrote "Jezebel" for Frankie Laine, Wayne Shanklin, called "Chanson D'Amour." Possibly with the successful sounds of Les Paul and Mary Ford in mind, Art and Dotty shaped and recorded their own mellow shuffle.

"One day this songwriter named Shanklin walked into our office and said, 'Lou, I got a master I did at Gold Star [Studios], and I've been turned down by six people,'" reported the co-owner of ERA Records, Lou Bedell, in an article for *Goldmine*. "I took it into this room and played it. The song was by this guy and his wife, from Rhode Island. I knew it was a hit. I asked Wayne what kind of deal he wanted. He said 'Give the artists four percent, give me $400 for the publishing, and it's yours.' I wrote him out a check right there.

"When Herb [Newman, the other owner of ERA] came back from the psychiatrist—where he went three times a week—he asked, 'Anything happen?' I said, 'Yeah, I just bought a master called 'Chanson D'Amour.' When I played it for him, he yelled, 'You paid $400 for this piece of shit?!'"

Within weeks the disk topped the mighty "Lucky Strike Hit Parade" and with near immediate sales of 650,000, the husband-and-wife act had their one and only crash into the nation's Top 10. The couple's next number, "Straight as an Arrow," whizzed by with bare a notice. For years, the two recorded Shanklin tunes and their own creations, but nowhere was that follow-up hit to be found.

When last spotted, the Todds were performing as a lounge act in the Las Vegas area. An album by Art, *I Love the Banjo*, is still in print on the GNP label.

VOXPOPPERS
WISHING FOR YOUR LOVE
(Sampson Horton)
Mercury 71282
No. 18 *May 5, 1958*

Officials at the Mercury label have confessed a complete ignorance of this one-charting act. But because the Voxpoppers' one-off EP had a picture sleeve, we can surmise that they were self-contained—playing guitar, bass, sax, accordion, and drums—and that they were five in number. The group from New York City cut guitar- and sax-dominated instrumentals like "Guitar Stroll" and "Stroll Roll," and sang group-harmony rockaballads like "Wishing for Your Love."

Presumably, the Voxpoppers' vinyl voyage began with a little-noted number called "A Love to Last a Lifetime." The tiny Poplar label issued the disk, backed with "Come Back Little Girl," just months before the group signed with Bill Lashley's Amp-3. "Wishing for Your Love" was their initial offering for the label. The response immediately moved Mercury to seek national distribution for the disk. Yet despite the group's striking success with "Wishing," only one further 45 ("Ping Pong Baby") and that rare EP appeared. A few years later, the Voxpoppers did manage to convince Morty

Craft at Warwick Records to release two now hard-to-find smoothies, "Helen Isn't Tellin'" and "In the Heart of Hearts."

RENATO CAROSONE
TORERO
(Renato Carosone)
Capitol 71080
No. 18 *June 2, 1958*

Nothing is known of Renato Carosone. Moments after Renato's sole intrusion into the U.S. charts, Julius LaRosa's cover version of this Mexican-sounding instrumental entered the *Billboard* listings (#21, 1958). "Torero" would be Renato's only contender and the last of the seven chartings for LaRosa, the Italian crooner familiar to TV viewers from his appearances on the popular program "Arthur Godfrey and His Friends."

VALERIE CARR
WHEN THE BOYS TALK ABOUT THE GIRLS
(Bob Merrill)
Roulette 4066
No. 19 *June 9, 1958*

Valerie was born in New York in 1936. A publicity pud from her label referred to her as a "normal girl" living "a normal schoolgirl's life." She attended the High School of Performing Arts and diligently studied to be a classical pianist. In her late teens, the lush lark decided to test her wings and flew to Boston, where she continued her musical studies at the Berklee School of Music. She studied voice with Lee Daniels and began singing at local nightclubs.

In 1956 or thereabouts, Valerie returned to New York to cut demo recordings for a music publisher. One number, "So Goes My Love," was brought to the attention of Roulette A & R men Hugo Peretti and Luigi Creatore. HUGO AND LUIGI signed her on the spot.

Valerie's first offering for Roulette was "You're the Greatest." Billy Scott happened to cover the tune at the same time, and his rendering (#73, 1958) overshadowed Valerie's. Next out of the hatch was "When the Boys Talk About the Girls," a teen-dipped tune that was to be Valerie's primo moment. Its pimple lyrics and clinky piano was enough to classify the disk as a rock and roll record.

Unfortunately for Valerie's career, much of her future work was packaged as lush-stringed, sophisticated, and adult. She never managed to click saleswise with the square market, and ended up losing forever her adolescent admirers.

VALERIE CARR

ED TOWNSEND
FOR YOUR LOVE
(Ed Townsend)
Capitol 3926
No. 13 *June 9, 1958*

"It's a dirty business," said Ed Townsend in an exclusive interview. "My follow-up record, 'When I Grow Too Old to Dream'—it hit the charts high (#59, 1958) and it disappeared just as fast. Some people have tried to explain that there was foul play somewhere. And back in those times, prejudice was more pervasive and covered over than it is now."

Anyone who has ever heard Ed Townsend sing must have asked himself at least once, "What happened?" With his second release and only hit, "For Your Love," Ed made it known that he was one of the finest ballad singers alive. How could such a talented individual have missed out on major stardom?

Townsend was born on April 16, 1929, in Fayetteville, Tennessee. Dad was a Methodist minister, and from early on, Ed was thoroughly involved in church affairs. He served as president of his church's youth council, and at 17, was elected leader of the International American Methodist Episcopal Youth Council. He majored in pre-law and education at Wilberforce University, and graduated from Arkansas State College. After teaching in a backwoods school for a year, Ed put in two years in Korea in the Marine Corps. It was while in the military that he found his calling.

"I was discovered in Korea, by Horace Heidt [creator of 52 Top 40 hits between 1937 and 1945]," said Townsend. "He was like a Lawrence Welk, with a big band and a television show, an amateur show. He was in Korea to entertain the troops. I was in the latrine, believe it or not, singing. This guy asked me 'How'd you like to sing for Horace Heidt?' I said, 'Man, this is ridiculous, I'm in the middle of a war zone.'"

The guy in question turned out to be Art Thoreston, Heidt's "forward man," who was the man with the responsibility of spotting potential talent. Townsend was then entered into Heidt's traveling amateur show, winning first place nine times and eventually becoming a permanent member of Heidt's wartime act. "I toured Japan with him," he said. "He had gotten permission from [General] McArthur for me to leave and come back to America. I was going on TV to be presented as this big find that they'd found in Korea and to become a regular on his TV show. . . . President Truman refused to grant my permission and I had to complete my tour of duty."

The abrupt move was not a career stopper. While turning the event over and over in his mind, the phrase, "That's the way the ball bounces" kept resurfacing. Townsend turned the line into a song; Nat "King" Cole recorded it, with the two thereafter becoming best friends. Said Ed with a grin, "I took the money I got from that song and got married."

On his return to the States, in 1954, Ed talked himself into hosting a local TV program in Los Angeles. In his off time, he had been composing tunes for Etta James, Gogi Grant, and Bull Moose Jackson. "I had to put food on the table, so that meant that I'd have to get one, two songs published a week. None of 'em became big or nothing. Eventually, I opened a small office and started Enceno Records. I recorded 'Tall Grow the Sycamore Trees' [issued by Dot, in 1957] and 'For Your Love' for my label and then managed to sell the master to the last one to Capitol."

Joe Zerga a V.P. at Capitol heard a demo and realized that Ed Townsend was no vocal fluff. With Zerga's help the tune was finished and issued. To this day, "For Your Love" is a gospelly golden great, a non-moldie oldie that should have created a mammoth career for Townsend. "When I Grow Too Old to Dream"—an old Glenn Gray hit from the '30s—was equally fine. The disk worked its way midway up the listings in the fall of 1958, then disappeared, along with a sizable portion of Townsend's visible career.

Over the years, he continued releasing records. "Stay With Me" and "Dreamworld" on Warner Bros. were two winners by any pop-esthetical standard. Mysteriously, neither they nor anything else sold very well. Not one to be stopped, Townsend as a writer and/or producer created gold for the Main Ingredients, the

Impressions, the Shirelles, Chuck Jackson, Maxine Brown, THEOLA KILGORE, and the R & B classic "How Can I Forget" for the late Jimmy Holiday. Townsend also wrote and produced Dee Dee Warwick's Grammy nominee "Foolish Fool," and Marvin Gaye's classic "Let's Get It On."

"I'm especially proud of the two albums I did with Nelson Riddle for Capitol, and 'I Love You,' and 'There Is No End' on Liberty," said Ed pausing, reflecting. "'If a Peanut Farmer Can Do It So Can I,' not my favorite record, but I've always believed if you try you'll get more out of life than if you don't. They can stop you from getting the prize, but not from winning."

Townsend's son David is a member of the band Surface, the highly successful trio known for four R & B number ones' "Closer Than Friends," "Shower Me With Your Love," "You Are My Everything," and "The First Time."

SHEB WOOLEY
PURPLE PEOPLE EATER
(Sheb Wooley)
MGM 12651
No. 1 *June 9, 1958*

Sheb has been around, done it all, and in some parts, he's more well known than his inclusion in this book might suggest. This Wooley critter has been a DJ, songwriter, music publisher, bandleader, scriptwriter, comedian, and TV and movie actor. And, of course, a singer—with numerous C & W chartings under not one, but two different names and personae.

He was born Shelby F. Wooley, part Cherokee, on a farm 12 miles outside of Erick, Oklahoma, on April 10, 1921. Shelby and his three brothers got on good with horses. In his teen years, he got to be something of a local rodeo star. Somewhere in this time frame, Sheb talked his pa into trading in his shotgun for a tattered guitar. Wooley practiced on the thing and formed his first band, the Plainview Melody Boys, while still attending high school.

Sheb worked as a welder in California, but soon discovered music—making to be the more satisfying. He and the Boys toured and did some radio programs. After World War II, Sheb set out on his own for Nashville with a sack of homemade tunes under his arm. "I spent about a year there," Wooley told *Now Dig This*. "I was pretty much starving. Eventually everybody heard my songs. Everybody seemed to like them. Ernest Tubb encouraged me and Eddie Arnold let me mow his lawn!" Soon, music folk like Jimmy Dean, Hank Snow, and others were recording his songs.

Wooley had some sides issued by Bullet and Bluebonnet, and in 1948, he started his long residency at MGM Records. One of his first efforts, "Peepin' Through the Keyhole, Watchin' Jole Blon," was a local hit in the late '40s. The idea for his biggie, "Purple People Eater," came from a throwaway joke that DON ROBERTSON told him. As Wooley told GOLDMINE's Larry Stidom, "[Robertson] said his son came home from school and asked him, 'Daddy, what has one eye, one horn, flies and eats people?' When he said he didn't know, his son told him, 'A one-eyed, one-horned people eater'; and I just took it from there."

"People Eater" made use of the speeded-up recording technique popularized by David Sevilles' "Witch Doctor," and later, by the squeaky Chipmunks. The record eventually sold more than 3,000,000 copies, and started a whole merchandising rampage. Kids and kooks alike wanted People Eater T-shirts, hats, horns, and even ice cream. But reportedly, when Wooley first approached MGM with the "Purple People" piece, they

SHEB WOOLEY

were less than enthusiastic about it. Sheb himself, after auditioning a number of tunes, even told the label's decision-makers, "It's nothing you wanna hear . . . it's the bottom of the barrel."

Other than a semiserious chart-topping C & W hit, "That's My Pa" (#51, 1962), pop fans didn't seem to want to hear Wooley singing anything but silly ditties. While Sheb has had numerous other chartings, most of these—"Hello Walls No. 2," "Almost Persuaded No. 2," and "Harper Valley P.T.A. No. 2"—were parodies created under the guise of an inebriated character Wooley called Ben Colder.

Describing the creation of "Ben Colder," Sheb told *Goldmine*: "It was 1963, I think, and MGM was holding a song for me called 'Don't Go Near the Indians.' I didn't get into town to record it, though . . . Rex Allen [did] and it was a smash. I told [MGM] I'd do one called 'Son, Don't Go Near the Eskimos,' and the name 'Ben Colder' seemed to go with the title."

Wooley has also worked wonders in Hollywood, appearing in nearly 50 flicks, such as *Rocky Mountain* (1950) with Errol Flynn, *Distant Drums* (1952) with Gary Cooper, *Giant* (1956) with James Dean, and *Rio Bravo* (1959) with John Wayne. His most notable movie role was that of whiskey-drinking killer Ben Miller in Gary Cooper's classic *High Noon* (1951). But Sheb Wooley is probably best remembered for his four-and-a-half year stay opposite Clint Eastwood as "Pete Nolan" on TVs western series "Rawhide."

Wooley, who lives in the Nashville suburb of Old Hickory Lane, is still working, writing scripts, and singing his silly, but occasionally serious, songs. "I'm not retiring. No way. I'm having too much fun."

GINO & GINA
(IT'S BEEN A LONG LONG TIME) PRETTY BABY
(Artie Zwirn)
Mercury 71283
No. 20 *June 23, 1958*

They were no Sonny & Cher. In fact, were it not for the fluke flight of their one tame tune, Gino (b. Aristedes/a.k.a. Harry) and Gina (b. Irene) Giosasi, the brother-and-sister team from Brooklyn, might only be known today for their tangential relationship to the hit "Sorry (I Ran All the Way Home)." Gino Giosasi and Artie Zwirn, Gino & Gina's manager, wrote the song for THE IMPALAS and hooked the youngsters up with MGM's Cub subsidiary.

The two Gs had a few more 45s issued by Mercury and by Brunswick. Gino, possibly in 1960 or so, tried for a solo bid with something called "Hand Clappin' Time." If the siblings had kept "Sorry" for themselves, their names might not be in this book.

JAN & ARNIE
JENNIE LEE
(Jan Berry, Arnie Ginsburg)
Arwin 108
No. 8 *June 30, 1958*

Jan Berry (b. Apr. 3, 1941, Los Angeles) and Arnie Ginsburg (b. early '40s) were members of the Barons, an informal all-male club based at L.A.'s University High—the same school that spawned the Beach Boys' Bruce Johnston, "Teen Beat" creator Sandy Nelson, and producer Phil Spector. One night, for kicks, the fellows trekked down to the New Follies Theatre at Fifth and Main. It seems that the feature of the evening was an overly endowed stripper named Jennie "The Bazoom Girl" Lee. Arnie and Jan were especially impressed. All the way home, they gestured and sang freely of the miss' mammoth mammaries.

"I was the predominant writer on that piece," Arnie told *Time Barrier Express*' Stuart Hersh. "I had the melody, and I think about two thirds of the words, before going up to Jan's house and working out the rest." The boys were determined not to let their feelings go unexpressed. In order to create an echoey shower-room effect, two tape players were set up in Berry's garage. "The track was actually recorded there in the garage on an old sort of out-of-tune piano; [the other parts] were overdubbed in one of the recording studios in Hollywood." Musicians heard on the disk include

ERNIE FREEMAN (piano), Rene Hall (guitar), and Jackie Kelso (sax).

A couple of Berry's buddies, the then—unknown duo of Lou Adler and Herb Alpert, successfully managed to get the dub placed on the Arwin label, reportedly then owned by Doris Day. All parties were surprised when the 45, with Arnie beating a cardboard box and singing nearly indecipherable lyrics, penetrated the nation's sacred Top 10.

But, according to Arnie, "I began to get disenchanted very quickly with entertainment . . . with the business and with the people. It didn't seem worth it. . . . It wasn't enough fun. Jan was a difficult person to deal with, and the people in the industry were not very 'neat.' They didn't seem very stable. . . . And it's hard to be an entertainer, a really hard thing."

Despite the tensions and Arnie's disenchantment, the duo did manage to tape enough for two more singles before their break-up: "Gas Money" (#81, 1958) b/w "Bonnie Lou" and "I Love Linda" b/w "The Beat That Can't Be Beat."

Arnie had one waxing issued by Arwin as by the Rituals ("Girl From Zanzibar" b/w "Guitarro") before leaving the music business for a career in commercial art and graphic design. Jan Berry found Dean Torrence, and with the help of the Beach Boys, Jan and Dean created almost the entire cross-fertilized genre of surfing/hot rod music.

JODY REYNOLDS
ENDLESS SLEEP
(Jody Reynolds, Delores Nance)
Demon 1507
No. 5 *June 30, 1958*

John Wesley Adams encouraged his young nephew Jody (b. Dec. 3, 1938, Denver) to take a poke or two at the family guitar while growing up in Mountain View, Oklahoma. Jody formed the Storms in 1952 with drummer Eddie Firth, guitarist Billy Ray, and bassist Noel Sutte, to play hops and barroom stops. When not gigging or boxing, Reynolds worked as a cotton picker, an insurance salesman, a miner, and a mortician's assistant.

After the boys had rocked and reeled their way through the western states for some years, a couple named Herb and Liz Montei, who had good ears and record-biz connections, encouraged Jody and his Storms to journey to L.A. and audition for Joe Green at the newly established Demon label. Green was duly impressed and rushed Reynolds—plus session players Al Casey (guitar), Howard Roberts (guitar), Ray Martinez (drums), and Irv Ashby (bass)—into Gold Star Studios to record some tracks. "Endless Sleep," a number Jody had been working on with George Brown

(who wrote under the pseudonym "Delores Nance"), was the first of three tunes taped that day. Only 20 minutes were needed to lay out "Endless."

The dusty disk is now a golden great, one of the finest of the "Death Rock" ditties to gather a mass audience (others include MARK DINNING's "Teen Angel," Ray Peterson's "Tell Laura I Love Her," the Shangra Las' "Leader of the Pack"). Aside from the immediate follow-up, "Fire of Love" (#66, 1958), none of Reynolds' half-dozen other Demon disks charted. Jody and his Storms persisted and blew through the '60s, disbursing singles for such labels as Sundown, Emmy, Smash, Brent, and Pulsar. The Storms finally got to show off their chops, recording a "Tarantula," a rocked out "B-movie"-like instrumental. Jody even duetted with a then-unknown Bobbie "Ode to Billy Joe" Gentry on one Titan single.

Reportedly, Jody Reynolds lives in Yuma, Arizona, where for a time he owned a guitar shop. He has shelved rock and roll in favor of "prospecting or building houses," according to *New Kommotion*'s Adam Komorowsky. His only solo LP appeared on Tru-Gems in 1978.

DANLEERS
ONE SUMMER NIGHT
(Danny Webb)
Mercury 71322
No. 7 *July 28, 1958*

Fresh out of the confines of a Brooklyn high school, good buddies Jimmy Weston (lead singer) and Johnny Lee (first tenor) were full to the brim with teen dreams of singing and success. In order to put together a hot-shot vocal group, they enlisted three of their mutual friends: Willie Ephriam (second tenor), Roosevelt Mays (bass), and Nat McCune (baritone). They practiced up a mite and approached Danny Webb; someone had fingered him as being the one in the know about making records (not much, though, on and making money). Danny groomed them, gave them a name (a variant on his own), and secured the Danleers their first recording contract with Bill Lasley's Amp-3 label.

For their first waxing, Webb supplied them with a jumper, "Wheelin' and A-Dealin'," plus what was to become one of summer radio's perennial classics, "One Summer Night." "We only had 45 minutes to record it," Weston told Krazy Greg, publisher of *Cat Tales*. The session actually belonged to someone else. We were booked in at the last minute. They were giving all the time to some young lady. I guess they thought it was her that was gonna be a big star."

"Summer" was such a scorcher that Mercury Records picked up the Danleers' recording contract from Amp-3. Mercury was the big time, and in 1958,

"One Summer Night" was one of the most thermal make-out tunes to be heard on rock and roll radio.

Unfortunately for Jim, John, and the rest, none of the other fine sounds they pressed in vinyl ever sold as well. "I Really Love You" was loosed, followed by "A Picture of You" and "I Can't Sleep"—but nothing sold well enough to even make *Billboard*'s "Bubbling Under the Hot 100" chart.

"It was all wrong—we were all young kids," said Jimmy. "We wanted to ROCK. But Danny was into that Platters thing and that wasn't making it for us. He was tellin' us that we would last longer singing that type of music. . . ."

After four stiffs, Mercury Records passed on issuing any more records by the group. Discouraged, the Danleers dispersed, but Jimmy Weston proclaimed that he was not ready to let the "Danleers'" name die. Webb brought in members of another group he was managing, the Webtones (a group so named as a variant on Webb's moniker) to fill in for the departed Danleers, and Epic Records gave the "new" Danleers a two-single spin. Record sales were as cool as a Klondike bar, and Epic politely showed the group the door.

Well into the mid-'60s, the Everest, Smash, and Le-Mans record labels gave the fluctuating mix of original members, Webtones, and fill-ins a shot at recording what culminated into a pile of fine doo-wop numbers. Good records all, they just didn't sell. Asked if he and the group got their fair share of the loot, Weston replied, "NOOOOO! NOOOOO! I tell ya man, the name Danny Webb is on 'One Summer Night' as writer. I wrote it, not him. But I was a young boy and Danny was such a sweet talker. I went along with it. At the time, I didn't think it was a big deal. I just wanted to sing; you understand?"

On July 23, 1988, the original Danleers sang together for the first time in nearly 20 years at the Westbury Music Fair on Long Island. Jimmy Weston continued to front the Danleers, with varying line-ups into the '90s. Jim died on June 10, 1993.

JOHNNY OTIS SHOW
WILLIE AND THE HAND JIVE
(Johnny Otis)
Capitol 3966
No. 9 *August 4, 1958*

Often referred to as "The Godfather of Rhythm & Blues," Johnny Otis (b. John Venotes, Dec. 28, 1921, Vallejo, CA) has worked in almost every realm of pop music—as arranger, publisher, musician (drums, vibraphone, piano), songwriter, DJ, producer, TV variety-show host, talent scout, record-company owner, and founder/frontman of the first "Rock 'n' Roll Caravan of Stars." His R & B revues gave artists like Hank Ballard, Etta James, Esther Phillips, and Jackie Wilson their first breaks. Johnny has also been a painter, sculptor, actor, politician, newspaper columnist, and, for nearly two decades now, a preacher.

THE JOHNNY OTIS SHOW

Otis had his first hit in 1946 with "Harlem Nocturne," a huge seller that, mysteriously, never charted nationally, pop or R & B. In 1950, nine of his recordings made *Billboard*'s R & B charts: "Double Crossing Blues" (#1), "Mistrustin' Blues" (#l) b/w "Mersey" (#3), "Cry Baby" (#6), "Cupid's Boogie" (#l), "Deceivin' Blues" (#4), "Dreamin' Blues" (#8), and "Wedding Boogie' (#6) b/w "Faraway Blues" (#6).

"I only had one pop hit," explained Johnny in an exclusive interview, "because in those days . . . there was a well-defined black show business, and the general pop/white-oriented market. My stuff was blues- and jazz-oriented, and my audience was black. . . . It wasn't until the mid-'50s that the music began crossing over to the pop charts. So back in the early days, I must have had 30 hits that I wrote or that one of my singers sang, but they were all called 'rhythm and blues' hits."

When Johnny signed with Capitol Records in 1957, they wanted him to create music that was "more tolerable to the white audience." He responded with "Willie and the Hand Jive," a pop monster sporting the now-classic "shave-and-a-haircut, two-bits'" beat. Johnny insisted that he had not lifted this bit from BO DIDDLEY.

"I was down South, after I'd had a few hit records, and saw a chain gang. Its a traumatic experience, seeing men in chains, under the shotgun, in the hot sun. Workin' on the railroad, they'd be called 'gandy dancers,' and their long metal hammers would go 'chung-y chung-y chung-chung, chung-chung'. . . . The next time I heard that beat, it was on a hit called 'Hambone' [Red Saunders & His Orchestra, 1952]. All that predates me and Bo.

"One day Bo was at my house—we both raised chickens and ducks, and I was giving him some—when he said to me, 'Motherf***er, what are you doin' takin' my song?' He said it half-jokingly. I said to him, 'You ever heard 'Hambone'? And he said, 'Shhh!'"

In the late '80s, there had been some talk of a major TV production company reviving Johnny's traveling revue as a weekly program. "The word is, I'm the Lawrence Welk of black music."

DOMENICO MODUGNO
VOLARE (NEL BLU DIPINTO DI BLU)
(Franco Migliacci, Domenico Modugno)
Decca 30677
No. 1 *August 18, 1958*

Franco Migliacci, a bunkie of Domenico Modugno, was inspired by the divine light of creation one day while peering at the back panel of a pack of cigarettes. At that instant, Franco had the idea to create a dreamlike song about a man with hands painted blue who flies through "blue painted in blue." Yes, it was quite an idea for a song, or so thought his buddy; Domenico drummed up the music, and together, they got the words just right.

The duo entered "Volare" in Italy's annual San Remo Festival of Music, where the flying blue man's tale was selected the best of the batch. Most Americans didn't know a hink about what this fellow was singing; some listeners figured that it must have something to do with love or a romp in the hay, because Domenico sure sounded happy. When the dust had settled, "Volare" had sold millions of copies and had won Grammys for "Best Male Vocal Performance," "Song of the Year," and "Record of the Year."

Domenico Modugno was born on January 9, 1928, in Polignano a Mare, Italy—"a bonafide descendant of gypsy royalty," proclaimed his record company. While no more than a tyke, Domenico ran away from home with 2,000 lire in his pocket to search out fame and fortune. He worked as a waiter and a factory worker, served a stint in his county's military, and enrolled in Rome's Experimental Movie Center, where one of his fellow students was a then-unknown Sophia Loren. Domenico won small parts in Italian flicks—notably the part of a balladeer in *Il Mantello Rosso* (1955)— wrote some tunes—"Ninna Nanna," "Lu Piscisnada" and "La Donna Riccia"—made radio appearances, and played Athos in a European TV takeoff on the Three Musketeers.

On three other occasions, Modugno won top honors at the San Remo Festival of Music. None of his vocal efforts, however, ever again successfully managed to cross the oceans. Not even his "Nuda," a sensitive song of a spiritual lad's lusty wish to embrace a naked damsel, sold very well. Try as he might to reconnect with his Muse while staring at a cigarette pack, Franco was never again to capture the magical touch of that flying blue man.

Domenico Modugno died on August 6, 1994.

ELEGANTS
LITTLE STAR
(Arthur Venosa, Vito Picone)
Apt 25005
No. 1 *August 25, 1958*

They were young, talented, and hungry. They met on the streets of Staten Island, New York, and found their name on the label of a whiskey bottle ("Schenley's, The Whiskey of Elegance"). After years of hard work, they successfully molded themselves into the group that created that smooth, unforgettable variation on Mozart's "Twinkle, Twinkle, Little Star." And still talented, hungry, and not so young, they would disappear. Like THE SILHOUETTES, THE HOLLYWOOD ARGYLES, and THE

SINGING NUN, the Elegants have the dubious distinction of hitting the number-one niche on the pop charts, then dropping out of sight entirely. Nothing they ever recorded again would even make the bottom most reaches of *Billboard*'s Hot 100.

In the mid-'50s, as the Crescents, lead singer Vito Picone (b. Mar. 17, 1940), baritone Carman Romano (b. Aug. 17, 1939), Ronnie Jones, and Patti Croccitto—all students at New Dorp High School in the Bronx—worked up a style and a repertoire impressive enough to convince Club Records to record and release one of Vito's compositions, "Darling Come Home." The record sold well locally, but since the group's average age barely broke 15, the Crescents were hardly able to tour behind "Darling Come Home" and generate any action. Pat soon left the unit to record as Pat Cordel, eventually working as a June Taylor Dancer and, still later, as a dare devil skydiver. Ronnie vanished in 1956; Vito and Carman searched about for replacements.

Bass singer James Moschella (b. May 10, 1938), second tenor Frank Tardogono, (b. Sept. 18, 1941), and first tenor Arthur Venosa (b. Sept. 3, 1939) joined up, and by early 1958, the Elegants were set. One of their songs, "Little Star," had been knockin' 'em dead at hops and talent shows. But word was out that a competing group called the Secrets [not to be confused with THE SECRETS of "The Boy Next Door" notoriety] were about to record "Little Star," so the Elegants auditioned the tune at a number of labels. Bea Casalin at Hull Records liked what she heard, signed them, and told them to start the song with that "Where are you, little star?" hook. Once the disk began its meteoric ascent, Apt, ABC-Paramount's new subsidiary, picked up the waxing for national distribution.

With "Star" atop the charts, the Elegants toured with Bobby Freeman, Jack Scott, and Dion & The Belmonts. For some now-forgotten reason, the group had no follow-up issued for nearly 18 months. By the time "Goodnight" was finally shipped, the Elegants were yesterday's news. "True Love Affair" and the half-dozen 45s that followed were quite good, but almost no one ever got the chance to hear them.

In 1981, the Elegants got it together for an album, their only album, *A Knight With the Elegants*, issued by Crystal Ball. Vito went on to record some solo singles, front groups with names like Bo Gest & The Legions and The Velvet Kite, became a car salesman, and in the late '80s became the manager of THE FORCE MD'S. When last noted, Art worked in construction and now owns a club in California. Carman owns a hair salon, Jimmy continues with the Manhattan Transportation Authority, and Frankie is retired

after years with New York's Department of Sanitation. Several times over the past few years, Vito has reassembled a vocal group, called them the Elegants, and played the "oldies" circuit.

PONI-TAILS
BORN TOO LATE
(Fred Tobias, Charles Strouse)
ABC-Paramount 9934
No. 7 *September 15, 1958*

Toni Cistone (lead vocals), Karen Topinka (low harmony), and La Verne Novak (high harmony) began singing together at Brush High School in Lyndhurst, Ohio. Discovered while performing at a benefit, they were introduced to a music publisher named Tom Illius. The girls showed him "Que La Bozena," a song that they had written; Tom liked the tune and the girls' voices. He offered to become their manager and to hawk their song around town.

Soon after, parental pressure forced Karen to quit the group; Patti McCabe replaced her. Point Records, a subsidiary of RKO Pictures, recorded the Poni-Tails singing "Que La Bozena" and another innocent number, "Your Wild Heart." The latter, the "A" side, was nearly a hit, but a young Chicago voice named JOY

THE PONI-TAILS

LAYNE beat the Poni-Tails to the punch with a successful cover version of the song.

After "Can I Be Sure" slipped from sight, Illius managed to interest Don Costa—later to arrange/produce for Paul Anka, Frankie Avalon, Dean Martin, Frank Sinatra; and found DCP Records—at ABC-Paramount in recording the girls. "Just My Luck to Be Fifteen" stiffed, but "Born Too Late" did as well as the trio of teens could have hoped. They appeared on "American Bandstand." They received fan mail and some spending money. And although their platter about an older boy has yet to be certified as a million-seller, "Born Too Late" is a rock and roll classic, a "girl group goldie," and a 'round-the-world turntable favorite.

For the next two years, the Tails tried their best to recapture that magic. Despite its suggestive title, "Seven Minutes in Heaven" (#85, 1958) was innocuous. "I'll Be Seeing You" (#87, 1959) was a rockaballad that went down well at hops as a "ladies' choice" number. Both charted, but that was about it for their recording success.

Toni, Patti, and La Verne never wrote anymore songs. The authors of their classic waxing did, however. Tobias wrote "Good Timin'"(a hit for Jimmy Jones, known also for "Handy Man") and "One of Us" (a hit for "the rage" Patti Page); Strouse wrote the music for *Bye Bye Birdie* and "Those Were the Days," the theme for TVs "All in the Family."

"The three years were fun," Toni told *Goldmine*'s Carlo Wolff, "but I just wanted to get out of the record business and get back to normal living." Each Poni-Tail married and settled down. Toni (Cistone) Costabile works at a high school in Shaker Heights, Ohio. La Verne (Novak) Glavic, a grandmother five times over, lives in Menor, Ohio, and works for a real estate agent. Patti (McCabe) Barnes died of cancer on January 17, 1989.

QUIN-TONES
DOWN THE AISLE OF LOVE
(Quin-Tones)
Hunt 321
No. 18 *September 15, 1958*

While his name never dangled on many a lip, Doc Bagby was a fairly successful organist and bandleader. More importantly, he was a man with a knack for finding and shaping potential hitmakers. For a brief spell in the late '50s, Doc set up the Red Top label in Philadelphia with Irv Nahan and Marvin Schwartz. During his stay with the label, he recorded the Students (not the Chess/Note group), the Sharmeers, Tony & The Twilights (later billed as Anthony & The Sophomores, noted for their "Play Those Oldies Mr. DJ"), a group assembled by Curtis Mayfield called the Kingsmen (not to be confused with THE KINGSMEN, known for "Weekend"), and the Ivy Tones.

The most successful and seemingly short-lived of all the Red Top recording acts was the Quin-Tones. Roberta Hayman and her back-ups—Phyllis Carr, Eunice Crist, Caroline "Cissy" Holmes, Ronnie Scott, and lone male Kenny Sexton—hailed from York, Pennsylvania. "The group started in 1957," explained Phyllis Carr, in an exclusive interview. "I was the last added. All of us attended William Penn Senior High; only a year separated us. We did shows around our hometown, playing teen halls, like the Odd Fellows Hall on Maple Street. We were the Quinteros then. I don't know why we changed our name.

"We were singing one night at a little dance. I had Sam Pendleton come in and hear us. He suggested that maybe we should talk to this DJ out of Harrisburg. Paul Landersman was his name. He was at WHGB, and was promoting dances held at the Nowhere Club and Dance Land. We did a show at the Nowhere, and he was impressed and said, 'If you stay with me, I'll have you on "American Bandstand" within a year,' which he did.

"He became our manager and had us record our first session [in February 1958] at the Reco-Art Studios in Philadelphia. We did four originals: 'Bells,' 'I Try So Hard,' 'The Stars,' and 'Please Dear.'" Through Landersman's radio connections, arrangements were made with a regional distributor for Chess Records to issue "I Try So Hard" (renamed "Ding Dong").

"It wasn't a big hit or anything," explained Carr, currently a caseworker with the Pennsylvania Department of Public Welfare, "but we did get to tour off that record. I remember clearly—and there's so much I don't remember as the years pass on—that we were seniors in the fall of 1957, so we had to ask our principal for permission to go out on the road, which he gave us. It was somewhere in the middle of the tour that we wrote 'Down the Aisle of Love.'

"Doc Bagby's band backed us. Our manager believed in 'The Aisle' so much he took it to Dick Clark. And somewhere in there, I understand, that 95 percent of our contract [reported by Phil Schwartz in the *Recorder* as "95 percent of the publishing royalties"] was sold to Dick Clark. They switched it over to Hunt [Records] and Dick Clark began playing it a lot. Of course, we didn't understand that, then. We made an appearance on his show that summer."

"Down the Aisle" was a "drag," that's a slow number with a beat, a "ladies' choice," a rockaballad. It was one of the best darn drags in rock'n'roll history. Reportedly, near a million copies were sold.

"People may not believe this but we've yet [as of the fall 1989] to receive royalties on that record. Never, not ever, did we get anything! I don't know what 800,000 copies would bring. I didn't even know till recently that many were sold. It's all so frustrating, so, so frustrating. We were just kids, too young, didn't know nothin'. We didn't know we had any recourse."

On August 28, 1958, they appeared at the Apollo Theatre with the Coasters, Olympics, Spaniels, and the group's rivals, the Chantels. "They had their hit with 'Maybe,' and we had ours, and we, and not they, received a standing ovation. . . . We never saw any money—and it took years to say this—but we got an experience that money can't buy."

"There'll Be No Sorrow" and a remake of Edna McGuff's 1952 R & B charter "Oh Heavenly Father" were issued each in turn, but sales were minuscule. No further recordings were ever issued by the Quin-Tones.

"By 1960, it was over. Roberta got married and whatever happens to groups happened to us. We had to make a living and just went our own ways."

Kenny Sexton joined the service, not to return to York. Scott lives in Arkansas, Sexton in San Diego. All of the others, but Roberta Hayman, who works in a hospital in Harrisburg, still reside in York. Caroline Holmes is a receptionist. Eunice Crist is involved in church activities.

All of the women, except Crist, are involved in the reformed Quin-Tones (with a line-up that includes Ron Webb and Phyllis's brother, Vance).

"In 1986, this DJ [Max Oates] called us out of Flint, Michigan, he said that he had been looking for the Quin-Tones for 25 years. I said, 'My gosh, we've been here all the time.'"

SHIELDS
YOU CHEATED
(Don Brunch)
Dot 15805
No. 12 *October 6, 1958*

The circumstances behind the Shields' "You Cheated" is, according to *Yesterdays Memories*' Dave Hinckley, "one of the most tangled stories ever to surround a hit record."

Most simply put, the Shields never existed. George Matola, the big cheese at Tender Records, heard this great little number called "You Cheated" by an Austin, Texas, group, the Slades. Matola reportedly had his good buddy JESSIE BELVIN toss together a one-shot group to do a quickie cover on the Slade's original. Everyone agrees that the lead vocalist on the track is Frankie Ervin. Frankie has identified the other Shields as Belvin (falsetto), Buzzy Smith (baritone), Johnny "Guitar" Watson (bass), and Mel Williams (second tenor). To complicate matters, Watson denies being involved. And to untidy the affair further, performers

like Tony Allan, Buster Wilson, and Charles Wright (later leader of the Watts 103rd Street Rhythm Band) claim to have been among the voices taped that night.

The Shields' cover version of "You Cheated" cheated the Slades out of most of the chart action; the Slades' original rendition (#42, 1958) never even broke into the Top 40. To promote the hit disk, something calling itself the Shields had to tour. The label hastily rounded up three guys to hit the road with Frankie Ervin.

For a follow-up, Nat "King" Cole's "Nature Boy" was dressed up and dished out. Ervin was reportedly present on this session, but beyond that, things get quite fuzzy. Hinckley has suggested that Belvin, Wright, "Pookie" Wooten, and James Monroe Warren might also perform on "Nature Boy." The voices on the Shields' third and last Dot release, "Fare Thee Well, My Love," could have been supplied by Belvin, Wright, Warren, Johnny White, and maybe even Chuck Jackson. As for "You'll Be Coming Home Soon"—released on Transcontinental and later Falcon Records—Tony Allan, a member of the various touring editions of the Shields, claims that he was on this recording with Tommy Youngblood, Charles Patterson, and David Cobb.

Regardless of which individual appeared on which record, none of these follow-ups to "You Cheated" sold more than a dribble. Collectors and pop historians may someday straighten out this cluttered pile of educated conjecture.

BOBBY DAY
ROCKIN' ROBIN
(Jimmie Thomas)
Class 229
No. 2 *October 13, 1958*

Bobby Day—born Robert Byrd on July 1, 1932—moved from Fort Worth, Texas, to Los Angeles in 1947. He would have only been 15 then, but claimed, in an interview with Jeff Tamarkin in *Goldmine*, that he came to town on a college scholarship. "In mathematics and music, I got straight As and one B, but I don't talk about that B."

School was out for good once Bobby, David Ford, Willie Ray Rockwell, and Curley Dinkins formed THE HOLLYWOOD FLAMES. The Flames recorded a slew of singles on labels like Selective, Specialty, Spin, Unique, and Recorded in Hollywood. Before they would finally click in a big way with Day's "Buzz-Buzz-Buzz," members would come and go, as would the names under which they recorded—the Flames, the 4 Flames, the Hollywood 4 Flames, the Hollywood Flames, the Eddtides, the Jets, the Satellites, and the Tangiers. Day left the group in 1957.

"Little Bitty Pretty One," penned by Bobby, was not his first record as a solo act; he had recorded as Bobby

Byrd as far back as 1955. Nor was "Little Bitty" his first 45 as Bobby Day—months earlier, Chess had released his "Come Seven" under that name. But "Little Bitty Pretty One" was a single that looked like it would be a solid hit. Unfortunately, competitors at the neighboring Aladdin label had THURSTON HARRIS cover Day's dazzler, and while Bobby's original reading did make the pop listings (#57, 1957), it was hardly the smash it could have been.

After a few forgettable follow-ups, Bobby came across the song of his life. "I was in tight with Leon Rene [a.k.a. Jimmie Thomas]," he told Tamarkin. "He called one night and told me about this tune he had and he thought we should do. So actually, 'Rockin' Robin' was his song, but we sort of had a little deal on this song. We used my group, which had been called the Hollywood Flames but was now called the Satellites. I told them how to sing the song. We were only recording on a one-or two-track in those days, so we couldn't make mistakes."

They didn't, and both sides charted. But in hindsight, perhaps it would have been better to have issued the "B" side, "Over and Over" (#41, 1958), separately. Day's next three singles, all released in 1959, did make the Hot 100, but only barely—"The Bluebird, The Buzzard, The Oriole" (#54), "That's All I Want" (#98), and "Gotta New Girl" (#82).

Bobby Day continued to record throughout the '70s, but nothing further ventured onto the listings.

Day soon joined forces with Hollywood Flame Earl Nelson as half of Bob & Earl. The act had chartings with "Don't Ever Leave Me" (#85, 1962) and the original "Harlem Shuffle" (#44, 1964); by 1964, Bobby Relf, a.k.a. JACKIE LEE, had replaced Day.

Bobby formed his own label, Birdland, and kept plugging away under various guises, as "Baby Face" Byrd, the Birds, the Birdies, the Daybirds, and the Sounds. His compositions, as recorded by other acts, were quite successful. "Little Bitty Pretty One" was a return-charter for Thurston Harris (#6, 1957), Frankie Lymon (#58, 1960), Clyde McPhatter (#25, 1962), and the Jackson 5 (#13, 1972); "Over and Over" was a hit for Thurston Harris (#96, 1958) and the Dave Clark Five (#1, 1965); and "Rockin' Robin" was a hit for THE RIVIERAS (#96, 1964) and Michael Jackson (#2, 1972).

And where has Bobby been all these years? After his own records failed to chart, he moved to Australia and New Zealand, remaining there for a lengthy spell.

Bobby Day died of cancer on July 15, 1990.

EARL GRANT
THE END
(Sid Jacobson, Jimmy Krondes)
Decca 30719
No. 7 *October 13, 1958*

Rock and rollers never gave more than a passing notice to Earl. Countless parents in the early '60s described Earl's style to their teenagers as "relaxing." A word like that was the kiss of death to any self-respecting hep cat, and boppers and rockers just couldn't understand. Man, it didn't have no beat; it wasn't blues, and it wasn't jazz, either. Nonetheless, Earl sold piles of plastic by tinkling the ivories and crooning, in a Nat "King" Cole style, all those standards only Mom and Dad could appreciate.

Born in Oklahoma City on January 20, 1933, little Earl took to playing the organ even before he set foot in kindergarten. When not touching the keys, Earl was blowing trumpet or pounding on drums. Earl's dad was a Baptist minister, and while still a mere tyke, the little one would perform at his pop's church services.

Earl went on to study at the Kansas City Conservatory of Music, the New Rochelle Conservatory, the University of Southern California, and Chicago's DePaul University. Thereafter, Earl became a music teacher. During World War II, while stationed as a soldier at Fort Bliss, Texas, he started his career as a singing organist in nearby nightclubs, signing with Decca Records in 1958.

"The End" was his first release and his only Top 40 hit. Five more singles did make the Hot 100, and two of Grant's albums sold well enough to place on the top pop albums chart. Earl was heavily heard on the "beautiful music" stations, showed up often on *Billboard's* easy-listening chart, and appeared in several motion pictures such as *Tender Is the Night* (1962), *Imitation of Life* (1959), and *Tokyo Night* (1959). While Earl's big moment on the charts may have passed by the late '60s, Decca Records never slowed down the flow of new releases. And bubbly Earl never cut back on his TV and nightclub appearances.

After a performance at the La Fiesta Club in Juarez, Mexico, on June 10, 1970, Earl Grant was killed in an automobile crash near Lordsburg, New Mexico.

ROBIN LUKE
SUSIE DARLIN'
(Robin Luke)
Dot 15781
No. 5 *October 13, 1958*

Robin (b. Mar. 19, 1942, Los Angeles) started playing guitar when he was only eight years old; within just as many years, he had written a sackful of songs, including a nifty number about his sister Susie. Starting in 1957, Robin co-starred on a local TV program with Kimo McVay. Not long after, someone in the biz brought the boy to the attention of Bobby Bertram, owner of Bertram International Records. Bertram did not care too much for "Susie Darlin," but was impressed instead with the 16-year-old's "Living's Loving You." Both tunes were recorded in Honolulu, Robin's hometown at the time, in a bedroom with the nearby bathroom functioning as an echo chamber. Percussion was created by Bertram wacking a box with a fountain pen. The crude disk received a lot of Hawaiian airplay. Luckily for Luke, Art and Dorothy Freeman, Cleveland distributors for the stateside Dot label, were honeymooning in Waikiki when they happened to hear Robin's record on the radio.

Dot Records then acquired the distribution rights to "Susie Darlin' " from Bertram International, and Robin Luke had a hit. "I bought it without ever hearing it," said Ron Wood, owner of the Dot label, on the CD liner notes to *The History of Dot, Volume 1*. "I had great faith in Art and would occasionally pick up on a record solely on the basis of the enthusiasm of the person who brought it to me."

Although Luke, Bertram, and Dot didn't give up the follow-up effort for a few years, almost no one in the U.S. even knows that the poor chap made another recording. His "A" sides included "Chicka, Chicka Honey," "Strollin' Blues," "Five Minutes More," "Make Me a Dreamer," "Bad Boy," "Everlovin'," "Poor Little Rich Boy," and a duet with Roberta Shore, "Foggin' Up the Windows."

Luke quietly left the biz in 1962, eventually receiving his Ph.D. from the University of Missouri. When most recently spotted, Robin Luke was a college professor in Norfolk, Virginia.

ROYALTONES
POOR BOY
(Mel, Mitchell, David R. Sanderson)
Jubilee 5338
No. 17 *December 1, 1958*

One of the best instrumental acts in all of rock'n'roll— the Royaltones never got the chance to make an album, or even see their works of pop art compiled in album form. Their material is long since out of print. Their individual names—as well as their collective moniker— are unknown but to those derisively labeled "record fanatics." To report that all is well and their excellent efforts have been rewarded would be a fabrication.

"I've worked behind and with many top-notch performers," said "Bob," David R. Sanderson to Noreen Kukkonen, writer for the *Leader Newspapers*. "Often, I'd be sitting back, watching them and say to myself, 'Some day I'm gonna be up there.'"

Bob was 58 when he died. The futuristic guitarist with the Royaltones—lone creator of their "Poor Boy"—died of a heart attack on June 25, 1994, at the Garden City Hospital, Dearborn Heights, Michigan.

Largely through his work with radio station WCXI, Bob had performed in concert with Johnny Cash and June Carter, Roger Miller and Johnny Paycheck, Tanya Tucker, Ricky Scaggs, and Conway Twitty. For years, Sanderson performed in his hometown haunts. In 1980, he began fronted his own touring band, the Porcupine Mountain Band. Sporadically singles would be issued—"Back on the Barstool Again," "I Know You're the Rain"; the later placed on *Billboard's* "Adult Contemporary" chart. His 1988 release, "Gettin' Down, Gettin' Together, Gettin' in Love," was given a positive review by *Cashbox*—"Top Single Pick." "It makes you feel good inside when you read your record review and it's among such names as Donna Fargo and Louise Mandrell," said Sanderson, at the time.

David Robert Sanderson was born in Cumberland City, in Tennessee, in 1936. Mama sang; Papa was a particularly good banjo picker. "I saw my dad playing various instruments as I grew up," he told Kukkonen. "I taught myself how to play guitar, but my main instrument was my voice." Before the Royaltones—ironically, an instrumental-only band—Bob got to record at least one single under his own name, a vocal, "Beauty" b/w "My Hands."

"They were all neighborhood kids," said Marilyn Sanderson, his widow, in an exclusive interview.

"George [Katsakis] and the Popoff brothers—Mike and Greg—were looking for a guitarist and a bass player, and they found Bob and Kenny Anderson. Most of 'em were still in high school; and this was about a year before they did 'Poor Boy,' about '57."

All had, what they called "fallback" plans, if their rock'n'roll dreams failed to materialize. Mike (b. 1941, piano) and Greg (b. 1941, drums), identical twins, were both enrolled in Fordson High; the former with plans of becoming an engineer, the latter felt the calling to become a physician. George "Kaye" (b. 1941, saxophone) had just graduated Fordson and was attending Ford Community College in Dearborn, as an music education major. School days were done for both Ken (b. 1939, bass) and Bob (guitar); the latter having dropped out of Wayne State University had plans to "study hairdressing"; the former education.

Initially, they were the Paragons—a previously utilized name and a moniker dropped by August 1958, when their manager Harry Nevins got them a recording contract with Jerry Blaines' Jubilee Records. "Poor Boy" was a hell-of-a rock-out. Sales were solid; airplay surprisingly strong for such a "dirty" instrumental. Either side of their divinely possessed follow-up—"Little Bo" or "Seesaw"—should have unalterably established the group name in rock history.

"I'm being very truthful," said Marilyn. "Their manager absconded much of their money." Adding to the misery, "Mel Williams" name was listed in the composers' credits. "Bob wrote 'Poor Boy' by himself, period. I have no idea who this Mel Williams is. It coulda been the producer or some other record company guy, with ideas of taking Bob's money."

After the chart-free double-sided classic "Seesaw" b/w "Little Bo," Bob, the brothers, Kaye and Kenny had "Flamingo Express" (#82, 1961), possibly their finest piece of musical madness, issued on George Goldner's Goldisc label. Goldner continued to release other Royaltone records despite their dismal sales. "Holy Smoke," "Lonely World," and "Yea Yea" appeared as late as the dawning of the "British Invasion."

"There was a payola scandal; then they went out on their own," said Marilyn Sanderson. "They traveled a lot. Bob was going to be signed by 20th Century Records; May '64. He got to come home for awhile, but just decided to never go back. He just didn't like the road anymore. George and Kenny formed the Peppermints, but they never got to record anything."

"George served some time in jail. I have no idea where the Popoffs disappeared to. Kenny Anderson died in an airplane crash; maybe 20 years ago."

Bob Sanderson's obituary in the Detroit News reported that he was especially proud that his "Poor Boy" was used in the TV series "Fantasy Island" and the rock flick *Let the Good Times Roll* (1973).

TEDDY BEARS
TO KNOW HIM IS TO LOVE HIM
(Phil Spector)
Dore 503
No. 1 *December 1, 1958*

When Phil Spector (b. Dec. 26, 1940, New York City) was nine, his father committed suicide. Engraved on the tombstone were the words: TO KNOW HIM IS TO LOVE HIM. Phil's mother picked up the pieces and moved with the family to L.A.'s Fairfax area. In his early teen years, Phil performed on acoustic guitar in talent shows and organized the Sleepwalkers, his first tentative group. He wrote bits of songs and studiously observed the goings-on at the Gold Star Studios on Vine Street in Hollywood.

Once he was ready to record, Phil formed the Teddy Bears—himself, Marshall Leib, Harvey Goldstein, and Annette Kleinbard (who later changed her name to Carol Connors). Leib and Kleinbard had frequented Phil's practice sessions in girlfriend Donna's garage, and it would be this quartet that would provide our pop heritage with one of its best-loved rockaballads.

"They'd been searching for a name left and right and couldn't come up with one," Goldstein (who soon left the group and became an accountant) told Mark Ribowsky in *He's a Rebel.* "Elvis' 'Teddy Bear' was a big hit at the time, so I casually mentioned at one of our bull sessions that we ought to name ourselves the Teddy Bears."

A demo of Spector's "Don't You Worry, My Little Pet" was cut at Gold Star and presented to the owner of Dore Records, Lew Bedell who signed the group. "Don't You Worry" needed a "B" side, though. Tacked onto the remaining minutes of that two-hour demo session that was supposed to produce something called "Wonderful Loveable You" was a hollow and haunting number Phil had written especially for Annette's voice. In two takes, "To Know Him Is to Love Him" was done.

"To Know Him Is to Love Him"—issued in demo form with only Phil on piano and a young Sammy Nelson (later billed, Sandy Nelson) on drums—soared up the charts, and almost immediately, wrangling of all sorts broke loose. Phil allowed his sister Shirley, to near everyone's displeasure, to become the group's manager. Spector disagreed on just what the Teddy Bears' follow-up should be.

The group quickly moved to Imperial. Arrangements were made to cut an album—a rare occurrence in these early days of rock and roll—and issued "Oh Why" (#90, 1959) b/w "I Don't Need You Anymore" (#98), the tunes that Bedell had refused to release.

The Teddy Bears Sing! LP sold poorly. A now-collectible Spector instrumental issued as by "Phil Harvey" called "Bumbershoot" also flopped. Two further

Teddy Bears singles, plus "Wonderful Loveable You" on Dore, barely scratched the bottom of the nation's charts.

In September 1960, Annette Kleinbard was seriously injured when her MG convertible tumbled down a mountainside. Several facial operations were required to reconstruct her features. When hospital visits were allowed, Phil reportedly never appeared.

As nebulous as they started, the Teddy Bears were now no more.

After a stay at UCLA as an anthropology major, Annette—now "Carol Connors—became a top songwriter. She wrote or co-wrote VICKI LAWRENCE's "The Night the Lights Went Out in Georgia," Billy Preston and Syreeta's "With You I'm Born Again," the Rip Chords' "Hey Little Cobra," BILL CONTI's "Gonna Fly Now" from *Rocky* (1976), and movie themes for *Falling in Love* (1980), *Sophie's Choice* (1982), and *Mr. Mom* (1983). Her music for *Rocky III* (1982) was nominated for two Academy Awards and a Grammy. Kleinbard has had a number of noncharting 45s issued sporadically under various names like Annette Bard, the Bompers, Carol Connors, and (with sister Cheryl and friend producer/songwriter Steve Barri) the Storytellers.

Marshall Leib formed the Marsh label, sang with the touring line-up of THE HOLLYWOOD ARGYLES, played second guitar on a number of Duane Eddy sides, and produced sides by the Everly Brothers and Timi Yuro. Leib was the music supervisor for such movies as *Macon County Line* (1974), ODE TO BILLY JOE (1976), and *Take This Job and Shove It* (1981).

Phil Spector? Well, that's a whole other story . . .

THE TEDDY BEARS WITH
PHIL SPECTOR (RIGHT)

BILLY GRAMMER
GOTTA TRAVEL ON
(Paul Clayton)
Monument 400
No. 4 *January 19, 1959*

Billy was one of 13 kids clamoring for attention. Born on a 40-acre farm in Benton, Illinois, on August 28, 1925, he was surrounded by stringed instruments and raised by a daddy who was a fiddle-playing coal miner. Pop spotted his son's musical abilities early and taught him what he knew. Bill, fascinated by the sounds and realizing that making music could possibly make him some money, soon picked up on playing the guitar, mandolin, and banjo.

Before serving in the Army, Bill played dances and local events; on his return from duty, he secured a spot on "Radio Ranch" (a program on WARL in Arlington, Virginia) and performed as a trusty sideman to country singers like Grandpa Jones, T Texas Tyler, Clyde Moody, and honky-tonker Hawkshaw Hawkins. In 1955, Bill became a regular on Jimmy Dean's daily TV show out of Washington, D. C. Two years later, "The Jimmy Dean Show" was picked up for national broadcast, and Billy was offered a contract with Monument Records.

"Gotta Travel On," a song based on a 19th-century British tune that had been adapted by Pete Seeger and the Weavers, hit the jackpot. The record was to become Billy's only major crossover record. The follow-up, however, did not do too badly—"Bonaparte's Retreat" (#50, 1959) and its flip side, "The Kissing Tree" (#60), both received extensive pop airplay, and both tunes charted on *Billboard*'s Hot 100.

Throughout the '60s, Grammer had minor hits on the country charts such as the curious "Ballad of John Dillinger," "Jesus Is a Soul Man," and "I Wanna Go Home" (the latter was covered by Bobby Bare as the pop and country monster hit "Detroit City"). All during this time, Grammer served as one of the busiest accompanists and session guitarists in Nashville.

Billy Grammer still tours and performs at the Grand Ole Opry. He no longer records or works sessions; his last album was *Grammer* (1977). Billy is also the originator and manufacturer of the Grammer flattop guitar.

BILL PARSONS
THE ALL AMERICAN BOY
(Bill Parsons, Orville "Bobby Bare" Lunsford)
Fraternity 835
No. 2 *February 2, 1959*

Bobby Bare has been managed by rock god-maker Bill Graham and called "the Springsteen of Country Music," been noted for the successful '60s merging of country and folk-rock, created the first C & W hit that utilized a horn section, and 30 plus years after his start-up fronted his own Nashville Network show; all while being held to a mere handful of nationwide Top 40 hits and one mystery record.

On April 7, 1935, Bobby Bare was born Robert Joseph Bare, in Ironton, Ohio. His family was musical, and he grew up pickin' and singin'. Money was tight, however, and Bobby's mother died when he was five years old. He went to work on a farm, and later in a clothing factory. Bob joined a country band that worked the night spots in Springfield. When he was 18, he picked up and moved to California, where, in 1956, he was discovered by the boys at Capitol Records. After three singles failed to spark much interest, the same folks turned him out.

When Bobby got his draft notice, he had to trek back to Ohio for his induction. There he met an old singing buddy named Bill Parsons (b. Sept. 8, 1934, Crossville, TN), who was just getting out the service and wanted to cut a record. Since Bare had some time to kill, he and Bill wandered over to Cincinnati, where they bought some studio time, some six packs and proceeded to knock out songs.

"We spent almost all of the three hours working on [Bill's] 'Rubber Dolly' thing, and we had at the most maybe 20 or 30 minutes," Bare told Bob Shannon and John Javna in *Behind the Hits*. "So I grabbed my guitar and said, 'Let me put this other song down before I forget it.'" The "other song" was a talkin' blues called "The All American Boy" that Bobby (alias "Orville Lunsford") and Bill proceeded to write together. The tune was a parody of Elvis' rise to fame and subsequent military conscription.

The recordings were sold to Fraternity Records; at this point, the label was erroneously informed that Bill Parsons was the singer on all the tunes. Months later, Bobby—at Fort Knox for his basic training—was shocked to hear his "All American Boy" on the radio. Even more of a jolt was the DJ's announcement that the record was by a new kid named Bill Parsons! By the time the error had been revealed, Bobby's baby was high atop the charts.

Fraternity issued one more Bare record as by "Bill Parsons," "Educated Rock and Roll." When Bobby was discharged, he returned to Fraternity, where he had a series of superb singles issued under his god-given name. A number of his country and pop records charted in the '60s and early '70s, most notable on the pop charts: "Shame on Me" (#23, 1962), "Detroit City" (#16, 1963), "500 Miles Away From Home" (#10, 1963), and "Miller's Cave" (#33, 1964). Bobby acted in the flick *A Distant Trumpet* (1964) and fronted his own TV series in the mid '80s.

The real Bill Parsons was given the chance by Star-day Records in 1960 to show his stuff. A couple of singles were issued—"Guitar Blues," and something called "Hot Rod Volkswagen." Nothing sold very well, and Bill returned to the quiet life in Wellston, Ohio.

REG OWEN
MANHATTAN SPIRITUAL
(Billy Maxted)
Palette 5005
No. 10 *February 9, 1959*

Eric Danlaney, Joe Loss, Jack Parnell, Ken Mackintosh, Ronnie Scott, and Reg Owen (b. ca. 1908, London)—what do these English folk all have in common? All of them are big-name bandleaders in their native nation, yet almost total unknowns in the U.S. Unlike his associates, however, Reg Owen did miraculously manage to crack the stateside charts with his reworking of composer Billy "Satin Doll" Maxted's spirited "Manhattan Spiritual."

Owen's life course was set when at 15 he contracted a serious attack of peritonitis. His father, in a get-well-quick gesture, gave his son a saxophone. While convalescing young Reg took to playing the instrument; an activity that has yet to cease. Instead of tending to his parents textile business in London, as his family had hoped, Reg joined the Royal Kiltie Juniors Band. The salary was a mere one pound per week—with free room and board—and lasted only a half year, but Reg now knew he had to make music. He studied sax with Benny Glassman, a member of Benny Goodman's orchestra, and attended the Royal College of Music.

In 1938, Owens formed his own outfit, the Local Gig Band, to make the rounds of the area's clubs. By 1940, Reg was fronting an eight-piece unit with a regular residence at the Montague Ballroom in Ealing. After a stay with Harry Roy's band, Reg joined the Royal Air Force. For his five years in the service, he wrote arrangements and played in the RAF Band. On the day of his discharge, Owens was asked to join the Ted Heath Orchestra, where he remained as sax man, arranger, and composer until 1955.

A car crash late in 1954, left Reg time for a life review. On his return, many months later, Reg Owen was determined to do his own music, and his way. With the aid of Belgian producer Jack Kluger, he made his first recordings fronting his own orchestra. At the time of his success with "Manhattan Spiritual," Owen was also creating music for the Cyril Stapleton Show Band and ABC-TV's "After Hours," hosted by Michael Bethine.

For the next few years, Palette Records issued his swinging, brass-blowin' disks, but nothing more caught the U.S. record-buying public's ear; "Obsession" briefly appeared in the homeland charts the following year. During the '60s, Reg did much of the arranging for the highly successful Knightbridge Strings; the group was known in the United States for their great numbers of easy-listening albums and its reworking of Johnny Ray's "Cry" (#57, 1959).

JESSE LEE TURNER
THE LITTLE SPACE GIRL
(Jesse Lee Turner)
Carlton 496
No. 20 *February 9, 1959*

Almost nothing is known about Jesse Lee. Born in the late '30s in Bowling, Texas, he had an Elvis-like quiver in his voice. "Teen-Age Misery" b/w "That's My Girl," his first waxing for Fraternity, sold miserably. The ducktailed kid next brought forth a tale about a sexually charged, alien beauty with "four arms, the better to hold you/Three lips, the better to kiss you"—sung in an Alvin Chipmunk-like voice. Like many a novelty number, it was cute the first time around but irritating after a few listens.

Jesse's immediate follow-up looked like two competing "A" sides, but both "Thinkin'" and "Baby Please Don't Tease' proved less than top-of-the-charts material. It was clear, however, that Jesse Lee did have some innate rockabilly ability; all the Texan needed was direction and some decent songs. His next outing, "Do I Worry (Yes I Do)" on the Top Rank label, was possibly his finest outing ever, but the record stiffed. Turner

was persuaded by the lads at the Sudden label to record an embarrassing turkey about mismatched "Elopers."

Moments before the arrival of the Beatles and the British Invasion, J. L. Turner reappeared, one last time, with two obscurities for GNP, silly creations by Sun Record producer Jack Clements, "The Voice Changing Song" and "The Ballad of Billy Sol Estes."

CHRIS BARBER'S JAZZ BAND
PETITE FLEUR (LITTLE FLOWER)
(Sidney Bechet)
Laurie 3022
No. 5 *March 2, 1959*

Chris Barber (b. Apr. 17, 1930, Welwyn Garden City, England) took up the trombone when a mere lad. Later, becoming quite proficient on the bass trumpet and the string bass, he attended the Guildhall School of Music. After a stay in Cy Laurie's band and an attempt at forming his own group, Chris joined Ken Colyer's band. In 1954, luck smiled upon him when Colyer reportedly "fired" the whole outfit and Barber took over.

With a repertoire that ranged from jug-band tunes to folk-blues to Duke Ellington numbers, Barber set up small units within his band to work up presentations of these various styles. One of these subgroups included Lonnie Donegan strumming guitar, Barber on bass, and a bloke beating a washboard. The resulting music, dubbed "skiffle," was a pleasantly crude blend of well-aged American folk, blues, and rock and roll. Barber's group cut an album in 1954, and two of these skiffle numbers were on it.

In response to the huge interest in skiffle, British Decca issued "Rock Island Line" and "John Henry" as a single, and with Lonnie's name prominent. Donegan up and left Barber's group and eventually became the most consistent hit-maker in Britain during the '50s. The simple arrangements and primitive musicianship required for playing skiffle encouraged thousands of young Brits to do likewise. Strongly influenced by skiffle-mania were four still-unknown lads named John, Paul, George, and Ringo.

Yet despite his influence on British popular music, Barber himself never charted much, not even in his homeland; "Petite Fleur" was one of only three such entries. While patching together a third LP, Chris got the notion to include a clarinet number. "I told Monty Sunshine [the group's clarinetist] to go away and think of something to do, and he came back the next day with Sidney Bechet's 'Petite Fleur,'" Barber explained to Sheila Tracy in *Who's Who in Pop Music in Great Britain*. "That album was released in 1957. Two years later, I hear we are number one in the German charts. 'With what?' I asked. 'We haven't got a single out. . . .'"

Once the band's sound had been supplanted by those of the Beatles, the Stones, and others, Chris refashioned the group into the Barber Jazz & Blues Band. An electric rhythm section was brought in that at times included Tony Ashton (later of ASHTON, GARDNER & DYKE, Pete York (later of the Spencer Davis Group), and, for a tour in the '80s, DR. JOHN.

Barber and the boys are still active. Teaching at Leeds Music College, Chris has also been working on his six-volume autobiography, to be published by the Black Lion Press.

BELL NOTES
I'VE HAD IT
(Carl Bonura, Raymond Ceroni)
Time 1004
No. 6 *March 9, 1959*

Back in the late '50s, Alan Fredericks was a rock and roll DJ on New York City's WADO. Like all good record-spinners, Al made appearances at teen dances. The Bell Notes were popular rockers with a sound that was slightly ahead of their time. "They were a local band from East Meadow who had worked with me at record hops," Fredericks told *Record Collectors Monthly*'s Don Mennie. "I took them to a Manhattan studio, produced this record ["I've Had It"], and sold it to Bob Shad, who had just started Time Records. It was a great success."

For their short spell together, the Bell Notes consisted of Carl Bonura (lead vocals, sax), John Casey (drums), Ray Ceroni (lead vocals, guitar), Lenny Giamblavo (bass), and Pete Kane (piano). With success momentarily theirs, they appeared on Alan Freed's TV show and toured with Frankie Avalon and Bobby Darin. Time Records rush-released a now hard-to-find EP and four high-quality 45s: "Old Spanish Town" (#76) b/w "She Went That-a-Way," "That's Right," "You're a Big Girl Now," and "No Dice."

In 1960, Fredericks brought the Bell Notes to Larry Utall's Madison label. After their cover version of Paul Chapman's "Shortnin' Bread" (#96, 1960), and the unnoticed "Friendly Star," the Bell Notes vanished.

THOMAS WAYNE
TRAGEDY
(Gerald Nelson, Fred Burch)
Fernwood 109
No. 5 *March 23, 1959*

Thomas Wayne Perkins was born in Battsville, Mississippi, on July 22, 1940. His older brother, Luther Perkins, was Johnny Cash's guitarist. While attending Elvis' alma mater, Humes High School, Perkins formed a

group with three girls called the De-Lons. Together, they worked up some numbers and approached Scotty Moore, Elvis' guitar man. Moore, a part-owner of the Memphis-based Fernwood label, swiftly produced some De-Lons sides: "You're the One That Done It," released nationally by Mercury Records, bombed.

Meanwhile, in Paducah, Kentucky, Gerald Nelson and his Escorts were tying down a take on something called "Tragedy." Early in 1958, Nelson and a buddy named Fred Burch dashed off this sad, sad ode of love lost. Tom Perkins and the fellows at the Fernwood label heard the Escorts' disk and dreamed up a cover version.

After Thomas appeared on "American Bandstand," his rendition of "Tragedy" rocketed to the top of the charts, and even became a hit later on for the Fleetwoods (#10, 1961). But the similar-sounding follow-up ("Eternally") and numerous other offerings failed to solidify Wayne's career. In the late '60s, he took a behind-the-scenes position with Audio Recorders in Nashville. Elvis recorded a song he had written: "The Girl Next Door Went a Walking."

Like brother Luther, he met his life's end at a young age—on August 15, 1971, Wayne was killed in a head-on car crash near Memphis, Tennessee. He was 31.

FRANKIE FORD
SEA CRUISE
(HUEY SMITH, Frankie Ford)
Ace 554
No. 14 *April 6, 1959*

"I have a quote for you on this 'One-Hit Wonder' thing," said Frankie Ford in an exclusive interview. "I'd like to go on record right here saying, whoever that disk jockey was that coined that phrase, well, he's a no-hit wonder! I mean, it can get rude. A jock did that to me one time in his introduction. I turned to him and said, 'Well then, you're a no-hit wonder. What have you ever done?' Some people have five records that sell a million each. Some sell none. I've had one that sold 30 million! And I've outlived that one record. I've been 38 years at this and it's still going. . . ."

Like it or not, Frankie Ford is mostly remembered and still eagerly sought out for that one disk, "Sea Cruise." Considering the fantastic acts (P.F. Sloan, the Pretty Things, and Billy Lee Riley) who have never had a hit and all the "superstars" (CARL PERKINS, BO DIDDLEY, and JIMI HENDRIX) who have managed to get one hit, Frankie has done alright.

FRANKIE FORD

Born Frankie Guzzo on August 4, 1939 in Gretna, Louisiana, Frankie was raised to be a performer. His mother started taking him to auditions early on. In time, Frankie was winning talent contests and guesting at local venues with Carmen Miranda, Ted Lewis, and Sophie Tucker. "Then, in August of 1952, I was on the 'Ted Mack Amateur Hour.' I won, but it was the last show of the season and I was never brought back."

In his high school years, Frank fronted the Syncopators. "They're still around," Frank says, "under a different name. Now, they're called Touch. And Buck Baker has still got them gigging. We started out in 1954 as a stock band, you know, playing stock arrangements; 'I'm in the Mood for Love' and the like. We were four horns and three rhythm players.... By the time I was a senior, we stopped the stock stuff and just played rock'n'roll.

"I was out working, one time, with Buck and the boys when this guy [Joe Caronna, then manager for Paul Marvin, Deluxe Records artist and a friend of Frankie's] came to me saying he'd like to talk to me about recording for Ace Records.... We met again at a rehearsal and about a month later he had me come in to Cosmo's to record 'Cheatin' Woman' and 'Last One to Know. That was my first record."

Backing Ford on the session were Huey Smith, Red Tyler, Frank Fields, Charlie Williams, and ROBERT "Barefootin'" PARKER. The Syncopators turned down the chance to travel with Frankie because of school and other job activities. To tour in support of the debut, Ford now formed a road band called the Skyliners, that included cousin Malcolm "Mac" Rebennack (a.k.a. DR. JOHN Creux, The Night Tripper). Frankie untangles the familial relationship between Ford and the good doctor, "Mac's grandmother on his mother's side and my grandmother on my father's side were sisters. Got it? I think that means that we're twice removed. Whatever that is.

"Now, 'Sea Cruise' was cut to be the follow-up to HUEY SMITH's 'Don't You Just Know It', but BOBBY MARCHAN, [then lead vocalist for Huey's group the Clowns] was leaving. The track was cut. It was to be Huey's new release. It was cut while I was in Philadelphia promoting 'Cheatin' Woman' and singing at the George Wood Show at the Uptown Theatre. When I got home, they said 'Well, let's try Frankie's voice on it.' Huey had heard me one night in a club and said, 'Hey, he sounds like Bobby.' So, I agreed and went into the studio, not knowin' the song. I still have the piece of paper that Huey had written the words on for me, misspellings and all.

"Now, we recorded it on this two-track Ampex. There was no punch-in. If you made a mistake it was just there. We did about 13 takes on 'Sea Cruise,' I think. On 'Roberta' the Clowns were actually in the studio. There was two microphones. I was on one and the four of them were on the other.

"My manager [then, Joe Caronna] and the owner of the label [Johnny Vincent] said, 'Huey, you don't need a release now. Let's put it out on Frankie.' And it was set, I was to be the new lead singer with his group, too. Contrary to the Monday morning quarter-backing, I was there when the agreement was made. Huey was to be listed as producer and as to what was his deal with Ace Records, I don't know.

"We're still friends. In a lot of books—including the first edition of *One-Hit Wonders*—it says that Huey was very displeased with me; and he was not, with me! We remained friends. We worked together and collaborated on a lot of compositions. And when things got as they did, we were instrumental in bringing him over to Imperial Records."

At first, "Sea Cruise" was issued only locally and the response was marginal. "Actually, it was 'Roberta' that was to be the 'A' side. Everyone liked it. I still have the original ads. Cosmo [Matassa] and I liked 'Sea Cruise.' I told them they should put out just one of the tracks and just put an instrumental on the back. That way we'd have two potential hits. I did suggest it, but they didn't listen to this 17 year old. So, 'Roberta' started happening and then the record got flipped, and we lost out on 'Roberta.'"

Asked when he first realized that he was about to have a hit record, Frankie answered, "I was coming back from somewhere in Mississippi, and I was sleeping in the back seat when I first heard it. I remember, I said, 'Oh yeah, they're playing "Sea Cruise."'" And someone in front seat said, 'No, it's not *they're* playing, it's Hose Allen on WLAC out of Nashville.' At that time, airplay on that station meant a lot of exposure. Then, Bill Randle at WERE in Cleveland picked it up. Bob Greene in Miami. And then Howard Miller in Chicago."

Frankie Ford never did join up with Huey's Clowns. He did have a couple of more rock'n'roll things in him, like the immediate follow-up "Alimony" (#97, 1959) and his last "B" side for the label, "What's Goin' On." Contrary to advice, Frank wanted to forge his own more mature style. "Yeah. You see, I was trained to do legitimate stuff. I write vocally. I was trained to be a crooner. I was getting a bit older and the trend then seemed to be going that way—you know, Bobby Darin, Bobby Rydell, and my good friend, Jimmy Clanton were going in that direction—so I recorded 'Time After Time" (Pop: #75, 1960) and "Chinatown"; stuff like that. I looked old enough and I could start working at the nightclubs, which was a lot better, believe me, than those rock'n'roll road tours."

After five singles and after receiving what Ford has previously referred to as "hilarious" royalty statements, Frank and his manager angrily walked away from Ace to form Spinett Records. With Huey, Mac, Robert Parker, and some others, Ford and Smith, still under contract with Vincent's company, recorded an obscure local favorite as Morgus and the Three Ghouls ("Morgus the Magnificent"). Earlier Frank and Huey had recorded as the Cheerleaders ("Chinese Bandits"), and Ford and his cousin as Frank and Mac ("True Love").

"Ace was getting so diversified and they weren't takin' care of their artists. Imperial gave me front money [reportedly $10,000] to go with them, and I took Huey with me." The first single, Frankie reports, actually made him more money than "Sea Cruise." "JOE JONES could talk himself into and out of any deal," explained Frankie. "He had cut 'You Talk too Much' for Roulette and then turned around and recorded it for Ric. When it started hittin' the charts on Ric, Roulette realized that they had the record, too. So, they slapped injunctions on each other. My producer, Dave Bartholomew, called and asked, 'Can you sound like Joe Jones?' I said, 'Yeah. Sure.' With the exception of one guy, we used the very same musicians that Joe had used. His was a turntable hit [#3; R&B: #9, 1960], but I sold a million on it [#87, 1960]."

Frankie Ford's career was basking in the midday sun when the malodorous mail arrived. "I was drafted! And I wasn't terribly pleased about that I mean, I had something going. When I got back to the States in 1965, it was all changed; the studio had moved. And sessions,

there used to be one or more a day. Now, there was zip; nothing was happening. It was bleak. But, I was determined. I was gonna keep on working. There's a lot of clubs in New Orleans and for years I worked them. Now, for the last 10 years [since 1980] I've been back on the road; did about a hundred shows last year."

In the '70s, thereafter, and right up through the present, Frankie Ford has recorded some hard-to-locate sides for White Cliffs, Doubloon, Paula, Cinnamon, ABC, Briarmeade, SYC, and Stardust. Some sides, as "Blue Monday" and "Whiskey Heaven" were darn near as good as "Sea Cruise." None, however, has charted.

Currently, Frankie and his firm Sea Cruise Productions manage such acts as the Dixie Cups, JIMMY ELLEDGE, Matt Lucas, Paula & Paula, Johnny Preston, TROY SHONDELL . . .

ROD BERNARD
THIS SHOULD GO ON FOREVER
(Bernard Jolivette, Jay Miller)
Argo 5327
No. 20 *April 13, 1959*

In the mid-'50s, Rod Bernard (b. Aug. 12, 1940, Opelousas, LA) was a DJ on KSLO in Opelousas, Louisiana. "Hot Rod," as his station called him, used to catch Guitar Gable and his singer King Karl (Bernard Jolivette) playing a number called "This Should Go on Forever" at their club dates. Karl had been announcing for a long spell that the swamp-pop song was set to be their very next disk.

"It really hit me as being one helluva song, "Bernard told *Goldmine's* Bill Milner, "and whenever I saw Karl, I'd ask him when it was coming out. He kept saying, 'Well, it's comin',' but it never did. Eventually, I went to his home and asked him if I could record it, and he taught me how to sing it."

Rod had started on radio one warm Saturday morn in 1950, when Dezauche's Red Bird Sweet Potatoes sponsored a talent search. Thereafter, Rod and his guitar would show up every Saturday to pick a quarter-hour's worth of Hank Williams songs and Cajun items. During his high school days in Winnie, Texas, he fronted a band that played tunes by local legends Bobby Charles, Johnnie Allan, and T. K. Hulin. In 1957, Jake Graffagnino, owner of Winnies music store, recorded a couple of sides on Bernard ("Set Me Free" and "Linda Gail") for his tiny Carl label. All this was a preamble to "Hot Rod"'s pop peak.

With King Karl's blessings, a promise from Floyd Soileau that he would issue "This Should Go on Forever" track on his newly-formed JIN label, and his band in tow, Rod went into the studio. Legend has it that it took so many efforts to get an acceptable take on the

DODIE STEVENS

tune that Bernard developed a nosebleed, and that for the last few takes (including the one eventually etched in vinyl), he was singing through a towel.

"Maybe that was the key," quipped Bernard to John Broven in *South to Louisiana.* "Maybe I should have kept singing with a towel around my face." Maybe— though Rod claims the offer was a good one—he should not have switched to the big-time Mercury label and started recording in Nashville. "Mercury had so many people like Brook Benton, Dinah Washington, and the Platters doing exceptionally well; they didn't need to spend money on me," Bernard explained to *Goldmine*'s Bill Milner.

After a string of sleepers on Mercury—including "One More Chance" (#74, 1959)—Rod enlisted in the Marine Corps. Since 1970, Bernard has lived in Lafayette, Louisiana, writing and producing commercials for KLFY-TV, occasionally releasing singles up until 1978. (Some of his Hall/Hallway sides featured the guitar and sax work of the young Johnny and Edgar Winter.) Five albums have been issued on such home-state labels as JIN, La Louisianne, and Crazy Cajun.

DODIE STEVENS
PINK SHOE LACES
(Mickie Grant)
Crystalette 724
No. 3 *April 13, 1959*

"He wears tan shoes and pink shoe laces/And a big Panama with a purple hat band"—Geraldine Ann Pasquale (b. Feb. 17, 1946, Chicago) was a mere miss of 12 when she first sang that song. "I didn't like that song, one bit," Geri Stevens (as she is now known) explained in an exclusive interview. "I thought it was dumb. I was really into rock and roll and R & B. I wanted rock, to do a 'Let's Have a Party' [Wanda Jackson] or 'Dynamite' [Brenda Lee]; something with guts to it. . . . Since I didn't feel I had anything to lose by doing it, I went ahead and recorded it, kept my fingers crossed and it was a hit."

Geraldine's folks had moved to the San Gabriel Valley when she was three. "My family was musical; Mother was a beautiful dancer and Dad had a wonderful voice, but neither got to do anything professionally. I think they lived vicariously through me. From four on I took sing and dancing lessons." At the age of eight, in 1954, Geri got to sing her first record—"Merry-Go-Round Go Round, " issued as by "Geri Pace," on Gold Star Records—on the "Art Linkletter's House Party" TV show.

Over the next few years, Geraldine performed at U.S.O. functions, veterans' hospitals, and on local television. Her vocal coach was secretary to Frankie Laine. "I got to appear on his show a few times, before that fated appearance on this local show called "Strictly Informal," hosted by Larry Finley. I was about 11 when Carl Burns, the president of Crystallette Records, happened to see the show. He called backstage to talk to my mom and dad. He wanted to know if I was available to do records. Of course, I was. So, he said he would search around for material and when the right thing came along, he would give me a call. We didn't hear from him for about a year and a half."

"Pink Shoe Laces" was "the right thing, " at the right time. "I was dubbed Dodie Stevens . . . and I didn't like it! Didn't like the song, didn't like the name. I look back on it now and it was really the first rap song. I talked all the verses and only sang the chorus." Three noncharting LPs— *Dodie Stevens* (1959); *Over the Rainbow* (1960); *Pink Shoe Laces* (1963)—were shipped. A few follow-up 45s made the pop listings from 1959 through 1961—"Yes-Sir-ee" (#79, 1959) b/w "The Five Pennies" (#89, 1959), "No" (#73, 1960), and "Yes, I'm Lonesome Tonight" (#60, 1960)—but the record game had pretty much run its course before Geri was out of her teen years.

Geri appeared in several films—*Hound Dog Man* (1959), with Stuart Whitmark and Fabian; *Convicts*

Four (1962), with Vincent Price and Ben Gazzara; and *Alakazam the Great* (1961), with Frankie Avalon. The latter was a full-length animated feature for which Geri did the voice of a DeeDee, Frankie's little girlfriend, a monkey!

"I gave it up. I was 16 when I got married. After about three years of a very active career, I was just through with it, I thought. I moved to Missouri, lived on a farm, and I had a baby when I was 19. I became an adult, real fast. Very shortly after her birth, I started feeling as though I wanted to do more. Being a housewife wasn't making it, and when I became a mother, I realized that wasn't making it, either."

Geri's marriage ended, and in 1966, Stevens resumed her singing career. After voice lessons and much daily practice, Geri contacted her old manager, who in 1972 arranged for her to be one of the two female voices in Sergio Mendes & Brasil '77; appearing on his LPs, *Live at the Greek* and *Primal Roots*. She went on to work some rock and roll revival shows, recorded with Raquel Welsh, Buddy Miles (*The Bicentennial Gathering of Eagles*); toured with Diahann Carroll, Loretta Lynn, Boz Scaggs through the *Silk Degrees* album; and for 12 years toured as a back-up singer for Mac Davis. In the '90s, as Geri Stevens, she has been touring with Fabian and her own company, "Dodie Stevens and The Pink Shoe Laces Review."

TRAVIS & BOB
TELL HIM NO
(Travis Pritchett)
Sandy 1017
No. 8 *April 27, 1959*

"Bob [Weaver] and I [both born in 1939] went to Jackson School together; played ball, baseball together," said Travis Pritchett, in an exclusive interview. "It was a grammar school, high school; the whole shot—a candy store across the street, dirt floor. Jackson, Alabama, was population 3,000; maybe four. It was a big town to us.

"We just found out that we liked to pick and sing a little bit. You know, music just became our thing. We worked it and everybody 'round said, 'Hey, you boys is good!' So, we gave it our best shot.

"One of those DJs over at WPBB [Jackson's hometown radio station] suggested that we go to Mobile to make a demo. There was this guy there that had a little sound studio; did commercials. We told him we wanted to do 'Dream,' the Everly Brothers' song, and put one of my originals on the flip. We started singing 'Tell Him No'—the first thing I ever did write—and he stopped us in the first verse. He had a big cigar in his mouth. This was Henry Bailey. Never will forget. He said, 'Are you boys interested in making a record?' I said, 'Hey,

like yesterday.' Then, he said, 'I can get you boys a recording contract . . . You boys is goo-oood.'"

Bailey introduced Travis and Bob to the Dubois brothers, Paul and Johnny, partners in what Travis called ". . . a little ole record company, named Sandy. They'd put out a lot before we show'd up, but no chart records. They had this guy Darrell Vincent, that had a song called 'Daddy's Goin' Batty.' He shoulda, but he couldn't make it, so he wound up committing suicide. He was a wild young guy that sounded like Jerry Lee Lewis. We'd figured if he couldn't make it, we weren't neither."

The Dubois boys recorded the duo in a garage in their hometown, Gulfport, Mississippi. Bigtime Dot Records' owner Randy Wood had a teenage daughter that by chance happened to hear "Tell Him No." "Fate would have it that way; no way else." explained Travis. "I hear it told that it stopped her in her tracks. She said, 'Daddy, this is a hit!' He said, 'I think you're right.'"

A deal was cut between the Dubois brothers and Dot, for the latter to distribute the disk nationally. "Two Cadillacs and $20,000," said Travis. "They got the Cadillacs and we got zilch. Man, oh man, we didn't know nothin'. We were just kids and our dads didn't know nothin' 'bout music. We got a cent and a half a record, a piece."

"Tell Him No" was rapidly covered by Dean and Marc (Mathis) on Bullseye Records. Their take on the tune went to #42, taking a good chunk out of sales away from the boys from Jackson, Alabama. "Some say we sold a million [copies]," said Travis. "Johnny [Dubois] looked me right in the eye and said 757,000. He's dead now, though; said he had to eat a lot of left over copies.

With Dot providing distribution, "Oh Yeah" "Wake Up and Cry," and "Little Bitty Johnny" were issued in rapid succession. Only the latter number did near anything—saleswise—when for one week, it occupied the number 114 slot on *Billboard*'s "Bubbling Under the Hot 100" chart.

"Gettin' that one hit was just like winnin' the lottery, I'd guess. We was in shock and we stayed in shock for five, maybe six years. 'Times we was gettin' $1,700 a night, a piece; not chicken feed. We had Cadillacs, the whole nine yards; the girls, you know, how that goes. . . ."

An album's worth of stuff was recorded, but never released. "They had quit trying on us," said Travis. "They'd made some bucks, and they were satisfied. It woulda meant puttin' more money into us."

Mercury Records issued a weird number by the duo, "The Spider & the Fly." Bigtop took a mild interest in Travis & Bob, but decided not to put out any singles.

"Now, Wesley Rose [owner of Hickory Records and Wesley-Rose Publishing]—who'd lost out on the Everly Brothers—offered us 10 grand if Bob and I would sign with him; put us on the Opry the next day. But,

Bob wouldn't cooperate. We split up. Bob went in the service; came back in '64. We tried again; traveled all over the South with MARK DINNING for six, seven months. There was just nothin' there...."

In the '70s, Travis gave it one more shot, recording "Hank's Hometown" for his own Red Eagle label. "It looked real big, for a little while...."

Bob up and disappeared. "Last I heard he was workin' at a door factory in Dearborn, Alabama." Travis, too, made a career change. "Got into insurance, worked myself up to district manager, then retired 'bout five years ago." Travis currently works as a bank guard in Mobile.

VIRTUES
GUITAR BOOGIE SHUFFLE
(Arthur Smith)
Hunt 228
No. 5 *April 27, 1959*

Good timing was not one of the Virtues' virtues. Created by Frank Virtuoso in 1946, nearly a decade before the official birth of rock and roll, the band waited 13 years for their first record and only hit, "Guitar Boogie Shuffle." By the time their classic cut was on the charts, the golden age of instrumentals (created in large part by acts like Johnny & The Hurricanes, Duane Eddy, and the Bill Black Combo) was just about done—and so was the band's low-keyed career.

Frank Virtue (b. Frank Virtuoso, 1927, South Philadelphia) began studying the violin at age nine, and in 1942 became interested in the guitar and stand-up bass. He continued his music studies at Temple University, where he was taught arranging by Bernard Morgan. In 1945, he enlisted in the Navy. With his musical background, he was given a position with the Regular Navy Dance Band—a unit that included Arthur "Guitar Boogie" Smith—stationed at Bainbridge, Maryland. A year later, Frank was discharged from the Navy to care for his father, who was suffering from cancer.

At this point, Virtue decided to form a group; billed the Virtuoso Trio and modeled on Nat "King" Cole's trio. Within months of their formation, Frank, Jimmy Bruno—who remained with the group throughout its 16-year career—and two others recorded "Limehouse Blues" and "Bye Bye Blues." Neither song was ever released. For the next 12 years, the unit stayed close to home, playing club dates and performing on local radio and TV programs. "We didn't want to travel, as we had plenty of work," said Virtue for the liner-notes for his *Collectables* CD. "In fact we were on the three main TV stations in Philadelphia and one minor one for over four years. We were appearing on the 'Grady & Hurst Plymouth-Chrysler Show' every Saturday." Then there

was the 'Tom Morehead Show' every day noon to 2 P.M. and the 'Plymouth Auto Show' twice a week. We also could be heard over WCAM in New Jersey." They played the area's Casablanca Club and Washington D.C.'s Casino Room and Blue Mirror. There longest gig was a stay at Chubby's "Home of the Stars," where the Virtuoso Trio accompanied Patti Page, Rosemary Clooney, June Christy and Don Cornell, Dick Haynes, and Savanah Churchill.

In 1958, Frank remembered a tune that his former Navy buddy Arthur Smith had created; and had chart success with in 1948. As he explained to *Goldmine*'s Robert Dalley, "I had Arthur Smith in my Navy Band, and I had heard his guitar boogie and liked it. I went one step further and made a rock record of it by using a different jazz ad-lib in between the boogie theme and adding a shuffle rock beat to it. Till this day, people tell me that the song was different enough that we should have had the original copyright to the song, but I felt as a friend I should give Arthur the writer's credit."

"We recorded the song in a private home using a Concertone two-track," said Virtue for the CD liner-notes. "I used a tape echo and produced the sound and later added a shuffle drum part. I was the engineer, musician, arranger... I played the lead on a Gibson L5 electric through an Ampeg amp."

After much searching for a label to issue his tape, Frank happened on to Sure Records, where the disk was issued late in 1958. The larger Hunt label reissued the 45 on May 4, 1959. In a wink, "Guitar Boogie Shuffle" shot to *Billboard*'s number five position. Eventually, 2 million copies were sold, but Frank (bass) and new crew—Jimmy Bruno (guitar), Dave Raplin (vocals, comic), John Renner (sax), and Joe Vespe (drums)—could never quite top that number, despite fine efforts like "Flippin' In," their immediate follow-up. With each successive record, the Virtues sounded more and more dated, almost pre-rock'n'roll, as if they were unearthing and releasing material recorded back in the early '50s.

"We did all kinds of crazy things," said Virtue. "Joe would go out into the audience and play on people's drinking glasses and chairs. One time he played on a woman's diamond ring and to everyone's embarrassment the stone broke! The thing must have been glass. Another time, on tour, we hired this second sax player, who had a wooden leg..."

Asked about the financial rewards of making a hit rock'n'roll record, Virtue said, "We were taken to the cleaners by the record companies."

In 1962, the year the band split up, the Virtues tried with some success to update their boogie with a twist beat. "Guitar Boogie Shuffle Twist" (#96) lasted a week on the charts before vanishing. Thereafter, Frank Virtue recorded seldom, though never again as the Virtues. His attentions turned to run the Virtue Recording Studio in South Philly where he produced "That's Life" for Gabriel & The Angels (#51, 1962), "Who Stole the Keeshka" for the Matys Brothers (#55, 1963), and "Hey There Lonely Girl" for EDDIE HOLMAN (#2, 1970).

"I will be recording and producing as long as I can," said Virtue. "Music is my life and that's the way I have always liked it."

Jimmy Bruno died sometime in the late '70s.

TOMMY DEE
THREE STARS
(Tommy Dee)
Crest 1057
No. 11 *May 4, 1959*

The music died, we've been told, at 1:50 A.M. on February 2, 1959. The small airplane carrying Buddy Holly, the Big Bopper, and Ritchie Valens crashed that morn. Numerous records were rush-released to commemorate rock and roll's loss; Tommy Dee's spoken-word tribute touched the heart.

Tommy (b. Thomas Donaldson, July 7, 1937, Vicker, VA) was a record-rider at KFXM in San Bernardino that fateful day. Raised in Boston, he had worked his virgin flight over the airwaves at KCLS in Flagstaff, Arizona. A short stint at KOFA in Yuma followed. It was during Tommy's first week on the Bernardino airwaves that Ritchie, Buddy, and the Bopper passed on to rock and roll heaven.

"I was on the air, when it happened," said Dee to writer Albert Leichter. "The bells went crazy on the teletype. 'What's this?' I started reading it. . . . I wrote the song, right on the spot; poured my heart out. 'No, it can't be true'. . . . My friend, next door, had a little Webco [tape recorder]. I just put it down as I wrote it, with just a strum of the guitar. He told me I should make a record on it. I told him all I meant for it to be was a tribute to play on my show."

The next day, with a change of mind, Dee went to American Music and Crest Records owner Sylvester Cross. As Dee recalls, "Cross said, 'Do you mind if Eddie Cochran records this song?' I said, 'No.' Within minutes Eddie and his manager Jerry Capehart were present. They listened to it. Eddie, in tears, said, 'Let's cut it right now.'" Cochran spent several hours in the studio, but as Dee put it, "It just didn't come off."

Paul Anka, George Hamilton IV, and Johnny Nash—a temporary trio that had been successful months earlier with "The Teen Commandments"—could not be gathered in time to record. At 9 P.M. six days after the crash, Dee was ushered into the Gold Star Studios in Hollywood. "They wanted a female voice on the record," said Dee. "Carole Kay—an act that American Music was working with—was chosen. I never met

her again. She got paid $50 for her part. She was a very important part of that record. Without her there wouldn't have been a record."

Dee, Kay and her vocal group, the Teen-Aires (a.k.a. Teen Tones) only got to practice the song one time before tapes rolled. There was no time to put together a flipside; an old demo by Kay and the group was put into service.

"I took an acetate back to the radio station," said Dee. "I gave it to the all-night man. 'Here's my new record,' I told him. 'Give it a play, if you get a chance.' I didn't have a radio in my car. I had a '47 Mercury; the radio was out. I couldn't even listen to it." The next morn when Dee returned to the station, orders for thousands of disks were waiting. Within a week, "Three Stars" was in the stores, only to leave moments later by way of sale.

Although Tommy Dee never considered himself a singer, he appeared on Dick Clark's "American Bandstand" three times and toured with Cochran and Conway Twitty; accompaniment was often provided by Gene Vincent's Blue Caps and sometimes by the Big Beats.

Said Dee, "My record was in the true sense of the word, a novelty record. I was in the right place at the right time. Everything fell in place."

None of Tommy Dee's numerous follow-ups to his monster moment—"The Chair," "Merry Christmas, Mary," "There's a Star-Spangled Banner Waving Somewhere," "The Ballad of the Drag Race," and "A Little Dog Cried"—received national notice. Tom went on to create tribute disks on the loss of Patsy Cline, Hawkshaw Hawkins, and Cowboy Copas in another plane crash ("Halfway to Hell") and for John F. Kennedy, "An Open Letter (To Caroline and John-John)."

In the '70s, Dee returned to the pop landscape with a noncharting controversial country classic, "Welfare Cadillac." Years later, he nearly pulled off a Hot 100 charting with an item called "Here Is My Love" (1981). Ah yes, persistence does count . . . sometimes.

Tommy Dee continued to work as a DJ, both in radio and for five years had a TV show in Bakersfield, California. Regulars on the program were MERLE HAGGARD and for $8 a program, BUCK OWENS. Currently, Dee is a Nashville-based talent scout.

Meanwhile, Carol Kay, now Carol Kaye, moved on to a successful career as a West Coast session guitarist and bassist. Her credits include studio work with the Beach Boys, Ray Charles, Joe Cocker, the Four Tops, the Monkees, Harry Nilsson, SONNY & Cher, the Supremes, the Temptations, and Stevie Wonder. Carol even made a brief appearance on FRANK ZAPPA's landmark *Freak Out* album. Her plucking sounds can be heard daily in the themes and musical backdrops of syndicated TV programs like "Hawaii Five-O," "Hogan's Heroes," "Ironside," "M*A*S*H," and "Mission Impossible." Her movie-soundtrack credits include *The Pawnbroker* (1965), *In Cold Blood* (1967), *Valley of the Dolls* (1967) *Butch Cassidy and the Sundance Kid* (1969), and *Airport* (1970). Carol Kaye has authored near a dozen music-method books, and into the '90s ran Gwyn Publishing in Monterey, California.

EDD BYRNES
KOOKIE, KOOKIE (LEND ME YOUR COMB)
(Irving Taylor)
Warner Brothers 5047
No. 4 *May 11, 1959*

Born in New York City on July 30, 1933, with the unhip moniker of Edward Breitenberger, Edd made the scene, like, weekly, on this tip-top TV trip, "77 Sunset Strip." As Gerald Lloyd Kookson III, the dad would lay wheels flat, perpendicular, and nowheres square at Dino's, a grease and bug-juice palace. You dig? Kookie was a skizzard with a comb, and had a thing for his hair and females with grooves to ride. Chicks were flippin' their wigs, saying that he was the utmost-like, dreamsville. Then, in 1963, the bubble burst—TV viewers were

weary of Edd and "kookie-isms!" like "piling up some Zs" (sleeping) and "a dark seven" (a depressing week).

Byrnes has admitted to being a reformed alcoholic. In 1988, while dedicating a drug and rehabilitation clinic in Maryland, he told a reporter for UPI: "It was hard to admit I had a problem when I still had money, property, prestige. How can I have a problem when I'm driving my new Mercedes, and it's paid for, and I have a house in Malibu?" Byrnes kicked the habit in 1983.

Edd had five good years with "77 Sunset Strip," but found it hard to shake his hip "Kookie" image once the series had been mothballed. He played some secondary roles in B-grade flicks (*The Secret Invasion*, 1964; *Beach Ball*, 1965) and moved to Europe, where he acted in spaghetti westerns like *Winchester per un Massacro* (1967) and *Ammazzo e Torno* (1967). He guested on TV shows like "The Hardy Boys" and "Police Woman," and appeared in *Wicked Wicked* (1973), *Stardust* (1975), and, with Frankie, Annette, and CONNIE STEVENS, *Back to the Beach* (1988).

Only four 45s, an EP, and one album were ever recorded by Byrnes. Aside from "Kookie, Kookie," which featured a duet with Connie Stevens, only the immediate follow-up—"Like I Love You," billed as by Edd Byrnes and Friend (actually JOANIE SOMMERS)—managed to chart nationally (#42, 1959).

HOT ROD ROCK
I DON'T DIG YOU, KOOKIE
SATURDAY NIGHT ON SUNSET STRIP
THE KOOKIE CHA CHA CHA

IMPALAS
SORRY (I RAN ALL THE WAY HOME)
(Artie Zwirn, Harry Giosasi)
Cub 9022
No. 2 *May 11, 1959*

"Well, the true story is there were three guys," Joe "Speedo' Frazier (b. Sept. 5, 1943) told *Goldmine*'s Wayne Jones. "Richie Wagner, Lenny Renda, and Tony Carlucci. [They] all used to meet at a candy store in Canarsie [a section in Brooklyn]. They were trying to get it together without much success. I was living in the same neighborhood, and I used to listen to them. One night, I offered to help them out."

Speedo was added to the Impalas lineup pronto, so that the group now had a black lead vocalist with three white back-up singers. The time was ripe for their big break. They were singing on the street corner one night when Artie Zwirn and Aristedes "Harry" Giosasi ("Gino" of the GINO & GINA act) happened by, liked what they heard, and invited the Impalas to their house to pick some material to do.

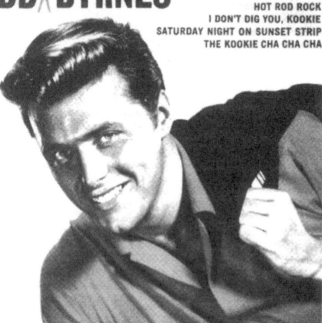

Artie and Gino offered the group a tune called "Sorry (I Ran All the Way Home)." The Impalas—so named for the speedy animal, not the popular Chevy—worked out an arrangement and brought the number to Alan Freed, who in turn set them up to audition for MGM Records. "Sorry," their debut disk on MGM's Cub subsidiary, ran all over the charts, sold a million-plus copies, and is currently one of the most requested rock and roll dusties on "Golden Oldies" radio stations, at high school reunions, and at nostalgia night spots.

The famous "uh-oh" mouthed at the beginning of the tune, Speedo reports was not intended, but was simply a knee-jerk utterance acknowledging that he had missed the cue given by Leroy Holmes, the producer and conductor of the session. Ah, the trivia never stops, but the hits. . . .

Four more singles and a one-off LP were issued on Cub. Only "Oh What a Fool" (#86, 1959) was given the slightest exposure. "Basically, I feel it was poor management on the part of the record company," recalled Frazier. "Our second release, 'Oh What a Fool', had 100,000 advance sales. We were in Chicago at the time, and received a telegram congratulating us that it looked like we had a second major hit . . . instead of the record company getting behind the record as they did with 'Sorry' . . . they figured 'Fool' would carry by itself. So, they just left it out there, and unfortunately it didn't carry itself."

After a final single for 20th Century in 1961, the Impalas hit the pavement. Lenny Renda went on to become a New York City police officer. Richard Wagner married his childhood sweetheart and moved to New Mexico, where he is a lineman with a telephone company. Tony Carlucci, according to Frazier, "simply disappeared."

None of the records billed to the Impalas on Checker, Corvet, or Hamilton, have anything to do with any members of the original group.

In 1980, "Speedo" Frazier resurrected the Impalas as a touring act; though one single, "My Hero" was issued by Red Boy. The '90s line-up includes John Monforte, Rick Shaw, and Randy Silver; the latter a former member of Vito & The Salutations.

FRANK POURCEL'S FRENCH FIDDLES
ONLY YOU
(Buck Ram, Ande Rand)
Capitol 4165
No. 9 *June 1, 1959*

The Platters were the most popular vocal group of the '50s; with Tony Williams up front, they soared. Who can ever forget "The Great Pretender," "My Prayer," and "Only You"? Buck Ram discovered the group, managed them, and penned the lyrics to some of the Platters' great ones, including "Only You."

Nearly five years later, Frank Pourcel (b. Jan. 1, 1915, Marseilles, France) stripped off the words to "Only You," and with a houseful of fiddles and a touch of some clinky rock and roll piano, brought Buck's ballad back as a lush instrumental. By the '80s, Frank's collective record sales are reported to have reached 15 million worldwide.

Frank studied at the Paris Conservatory during the day and played downtown jazz combo jive at night. Beginning in 1942, he arranged, composed, and led his string orchestra through piles of recordings. His disks have been available in the States for more than four decades, yet aside from his Platters platter, Pourcel is a virtual unknown. Not one of his "stringbeat," middle-of-the-road with a slight rock beat, albums has made *Billboard*'s top pop albums chart.

FIESTAS
SO FINE
(Johnny Otis)
Old Town 1062
No. 11 *June 15, 1959*

Sam and Hy Weiss operated their Old Town label out of a cloakroom in New York's old Triboro Theatre, on 125th Street and Third Avenue. One day, Hy overheard some guys singin' and horsin' around, and thereby discovered the Fiestas. "I heard them singing in the toilet next to my office," Weiss told liner-note writer Dan Nooger. "It cost me $40 to record 'So Fine,' that's all."

Another story has it that lead vocalist Tommy Bullock, tenor Eddie Morris, baritone Sam Ingalls, and bass Preston Lane—who had grown up together in Newark and had been singing together for about a year—went to Jim Gribble's hometown studios to cut a demo. Gribble was impressed, and it was Gribble [manager of the Classics, Passions, and Mystics] who supposedly brought the resulting disk to the attention of Hy Weiss.

Whichever of these two versions is the true story, Hy did realize that this bunch of rhythm makers had something special. "[They] were really a soul group, not a doo-wop group. They stood by themselves. There's a big difference between R & B and doo-wop, just like there's a big difference between doo-wop and rock and roll." The Fiestas' sound was gritty and delightfully crude, but their rough edges were possibly too much for '60s radio.

Weiss released many years' worth of capable follow-ups, trying to establish his group. But only "Broken Heart" (#85, 1962) managed to hold down a position on either the pop or R & B charts. After the Fiestas part-

ed company with the Old Town label in 1965, Tom left the group to record a few solo sides, as well as duets with Cleveland Horne as Tommy & Cleve. Randy Stewart, who later managed the Gypsies/FLIRTATIONS, joined the group.

The "Fiestas" name was kept alive through the '70s, with sporadic singles issued by Vigor, Respect, RCA, and Chimneyville.

PRESTON EPPS
BONGO ROCK
(Preston Epps, Arthur Egnoian)
Original Sound 4
No. 14 *June 29, 1959*

While stationed in Okinawa during the Korean War, Preston (b. 1931, Oakland, CA) learned how to play the bongos. He soon became adept at other percussive instruments as well. On his return from duty, he worked as a waiter, club manager, and gas-station attendant. At night, Preston would venture into the coffeehouses that dotted Hollywood. While playing in one of these pads, Epps was spotted by Art Laboe, a DJ on L.A.'s KPOP and the new owner of Original Sound Records.

"Bongo Rock" would be the first hit for Laboe's label. With the very next Original Sound release, Laboe would score again with another percussionist, Sandy Nelson, and the classic "Teen Beat" (#4, 1959). As for Preston, try as he did, he could not craft another chart-shaker. The first of his two LPs (*Bongo, Bongo, Bongo*, 1960; *Bongola*, 1961) did well—and his initial follow-up, "Bongo, Bongo, Bongo" (#78, 1960), did make the listings—but Preston began losing momentum. "Bongo in the Congo," "Bongo Rocket," "Bongo Boogie," "Flamenco Bongo," "Mr. Bongo" ... the public just lost interest. Not even Epps' last offering, "Bongo Rock '65," could garner enough sales to justify a continued career.

Many years later, Canadian producer Michael Viner put together a studio assemblage called the Incredible Bongo Band and returned Preston's pounder to the charts (#73, 1973).

In the early '70s, Preston toured and recorded with JOHNNY OTIS.

MYSTICS
HUSHABYE
(Doc Pomus, Mort Shuman)
Laurie 3028
No. 20 *June 29, 1959*

They grew up within blocks of each other and attended the same school in the Bensonhurst section of Brooklyn. For a brief time, bass Al Contrera (b. Jan. 8, 1940), baritone Albee Cracolici (b. Apr. 29, 1936), lead singer Phil Cracolici (b. Sept. 17, 1937), first tenor Bob Ferrante (b. 1936), and second tenor George Galfo (b. 1940) were street-corner singers, the Mystics—a name they literally drew out of a hat.

"We first went out and auditioned for a lot of record companies and didn't get anywhere," Contrera told *Goldmine* writer Wayne Jones. "So we figured we needed a demo record. We went up to the Broadway Recording Studio at 1650 Broadway and while we were doing this demo, Jim Gribble happened to be there. "Gribble was then managing the CLASSICS, THE FIESTAS, the Passions, and a young singer/songwriter named Paul Simon. (Paul sang back-up on "To Think Again of You," the "B" side of the Mystics' third single.) "Jim heard us, liked us, signed us, and introduced us to Laurie Records."

Laurie's founder, Gene Schwartz, commissioned the songwriting team of Doc Pomus and Mort Shuman to come up with something teenage for the group. "A couple of weeks later they came up with 'A Teenager in Love,'" said Contrera. "Laurie Records thought the song was so great they decided instead to give it to Dion & The Belmonts . . . they were established." Doc and Mort were asked if they could hammer out something else for the Mystics, something teenage, something that sounded like THE ELEGANTS' "Little Star." "So they went home and the very next day, we got a call that they had another song for us to do, which was 'Hushabye.'"

"Hushabye," the Mystics' first record, was a huge hit. "Don't Take the Stars," the follow-up, charted, but not well (#98, 1959). Even worse, the next four 45s failed to capture any attention. A cover version of the Harptones' "Sunday Kind of Love" would be the Mystics' last release for Laurie. "After that," Contrera noted, "we decided we had to get jobs."

All of the original Mystics except George Galfo found down-to-earth employment as engineers. Al Contrera, Albee Cracolici, and Phil Cracolici still perform under the name that they drew out of a hat decades ago. A comeback album and doo-wop delight called *Crazy for You* appeared on the Ambient Sound label in 1983.

PRESTON EPPS

FALCONS
YOU'RE SO FINE
(Willie Schofield, Lance Finnie, Robert West)
Unart 2013
No. 17 *July 13, 1959*

Eddie Floyd (b. June 25, 1935, Montgomery, AL) was black, Bob Manardo was white. They met in 1955 while working together in a jewelry shop in Detroit. After learning of each other's interest in what was then called "race music," they talked of forming a vocal group and began practicing together after work. Eddie (lead vocals) suggested they include a friend of his named Arnett Robinson (second tenor). Bob (first tenor) recommended Tom Shetler (baritone). Completing the line-up was a street singer, Willie Schofield (bass).

Luckily for the Falcons—a timely "bird" name that Arnett had proposed—Eddie's uncle,

Robert West, owned and operated a number of Detroit record labels (Contour, Kudo, Flick, LuPine, and Silhouette). After a quick listen, West offered to manage the group.

West got the group some club dates, plus a one-off release on Mercury Records in 1956. When Bob Manardo was drafted and Tom Shetler enlisted, two former members of the Fabulous Four-Lance Finnie (first tenor) and Four Top Levi Stubbs' brother Joe (lead vocals)—joined the Falcons. A month later, Arnett Robinson left and was replaced by Bonny Mack Rice (baritone), a former member of the 5 Scalders.

After a few highly-collectible false starts were issued, the gospel-gritty "You're So Fine," with a one-of-a-kind lead vocal by Stubbs, was let loose upon the world. Stubbs only remained with the group through 1960; his replacement, brought in by Schofield, was a young Wilson Pickett (b. Mar. 18, 1941, Prattville, Ala.). With "Wicked Pickett" front and center, the group entered the pop charts for the last time. "I Found a Love" (#75, 1962) was possibly the Falcons' greatest number but only a moderate pop-chart mover.

Willie Schofield was drafted. Floyd and Pickett were not always available, and finally, early in 1963, the group scattered. In an effort to keep the name alive and the money flowing, West, according to *Whiskey, Women and . . .*'s Marv Goldberg, took a group variously called the Ramblers or the Fabulous Playboys—comprising Johnny Alvin, James Gibson, Frank Holt, and Carlis "Sonny" Monroe—and renamed them the Falcons. This second unit carried on through the late '60s.

STONEWALL JACKSON
WATERLOO
(JOHN D. LOUDERMILK, Marijohn Wilkin)
Columbia 41393
No. 4 *July 13, 1959*

Stonewall Jackson was born in a railroad shack outside Tabor City, North Carolina, on November 6, 1932. His daddy, who named him after his great-grandfather (the famous Confederate general, Thomas Jonathan "Stonewall" Jackson), died when Stonie was but two. Papa Jackson was a logging train engineer who died of complications from a hernia, before Stonie was born; Mama, half Seminole Indian, married a violent man. Conditions were rough, with money hard to come by and a stepdad who would repeatedly beat him, one time leaving him for dead. Jackson played on an improvised, hand-me-down string box until '42 when he traded a tireless bike for a real guitar. At 14, Stonie left home to roam. First joining the Army with falsified birth certificate; then the Navy, where he was stationed on the U.S.S. *Kittywake*, which was a submarine rescue

STONEWALL JACKSON

ship. With a rigged up sound system, Stonie would play country tunes.

From 1954 to 1956, Stonie worked hard as a farmer and logger, saving up to go to Nashville and become a country star. Without any arrangements or recommendations, Stonewall drove his logging truck to the doors of the Grand Ole Opry, where he somehow wrangled an audition with Judge George D. Hay, the founder of the institution. The somber judge signed him on the spot, and Jackson made his first appearance on the Opry that night, November 3, 1956. The chances of managing such a move without a hit record, then as now, were next to nil. Two years later, Stonewall would have that hit.

Once he played the Grand Ole Opry, doors of opportunity opened, including those at Columbia Records. "Life Goes On," his first single, charted Top 10 on the C & W charts. The follow-up, "Waterloo," was a monster crossover hit, the most momentous recording of his entire career. Three more singles made *Billboard*'s Hot 100, and a few more charted big on the country listings. A quarter of a century ago, the hits stopped, but not Stonewall. In 1991, Stonie issued privately his autobiography, *From the Bottom Up*.

Things begin, things end. "Every puppy has his day," Stonewall sang, "Everyone must pay." How true, how true. And "Everyone must meet his Waterloo."

JERRY KELLER
HERE COMES SUMMER
(Jerry Keller)
Kapp 277
No. 14 *August 17, 1959*

Jerry Keller was born in Fort Smith, Arkansas, on June 20, 1937. When he was seven, he and the family moved to Tulsa, Oklahoma, where he became a member of the Tulsa Boy Singers, a choral group that toured the Midwest. In high school, he formed a secular quartet called the Lads of Note. Singing solo, Jerry won a talent contest organized by bandleader Horace Heidt (discoverer of ED TOWNSEND), and he fronted Jack Dalton's Orchestra for a while.

In 1956, Jerry moved to the city of glitz and garbage, New York. While dreaming of fame and fortune, he worked as a clerk for an oil company; he also studied singing, cut demos when he could, and appeared occasionally on local TV shows. But it was a Sunday meeting with Pat Boone on the steps of a church that opened that big door to secular stardom. Pat gave Jerry a list of individuals that might be able to help him. One of them, Marty Mills, was to be Keller's manager and his connection to Kapp Records.

Jerry's self-penned "Here Comes Summer" was apparently the 22-year-old's first waxing. For years afterward, whenever summertime was approaching, Jerry's joyous single would ride the turntables. Despite a massive tour of the U.K.—replacing the recently deceased Eddie Cochran—none of Keller's subsequent outings ever received much airplay; without hits, he was forced to move from Capitol to Coral to Reprise to RCA before chucking his career.

No Jerry Keller recordings are currently in print. Keller did continue penning tunes, though: his "Turn-Down Day" was a sizable hit for the Cyrkle in 1966, and his "Almost There" appeared in the 1964 flick *I'd Rather Be Rich* (a version by Andy Williams reached number 67 the same year). Keller made film appearances in *You Light Up My Life* (1977) and *If Ever I See You Again* (1978).

PHIL PHILLIPS WITH THE TWILIGHTS
SEA OF LOVE
(George Khoury, Phil "Phil Phillips" Baptiste)
Mercury 71465
No. 2 *August 24, 1959*

The year 1958 was a long one for John Baptiste, a frustrated guitar-playing bellhop. By day, he would move the luggage at the Chateau Charles in Lake Charles, Louisiana; by night, he would try to move a young girl named Verdie Mae.

PHIL PHILLIPS

"She'd not always be a lover, and I had my guitar, so I went and wrote this song, 'Sea of Love,'" reported Baptiste in an exclusive interview. "You see, she really didn't believe in me. But I felt if I could sing about it, a sea of love, you know, where it's quiet and peaceful, I could really show her how much I loved her and cared for her."

One day the gas-meter reader, making his usual housecall, overheard John practicing his ode of oceanic love. "He's the one that impressed on me that I really had something. He said, 'You're walking around with a million dollars in your hand. All you got to do is do something about it.'"

The meter man told John about George Khoury, a local record producer who had worked on Cookie & The Cupcakes' "Matilda" (#47, 1959). Khoury liked what he heard in John, and immediately brought him to Eddie Shuler's small Goldband Recording Studio. "We went in there, and I sung the song over and over again. We went back the next night, and the next, and over and over again we went on that tune, until we were sure that we got the cut on it."

John got some friends together and taught them how to sing the tune's haunting and seductive backing vocals. Shuler brought in a number of musicians, searching for the just-right sound which he eventually extracted from the Cupcakes. For reasons related to his interest in hypnosis, Khoury suggested that John make double use of his middle name, Phillip. By June 1959, John was "Phil Phillips," and "Sea of Love" was selling so well on Khoury's independent label that the record was leased to Mercury for national distribution. Within weeks, this eerie swamp tune was number two in the nation.

One-time gospel singer and bellhop Baptiste was never again to have another hit. Four more singles were released, but despite Clyde Otis' lush production—and back-up vocals by Brook Benton and the Jordanaires on several of these numbers—not one of them even came close to returning "Phil" to the charts.

Phillips never married Verdie Mae, the girl for whom he wrote "Sea of Love." "No, no, I sure didn't," he explained. "I married the right one, though, yes indeed. But ooh, it's a good thing I didn't marry that Verdie." He never got his hands on that million dollars. "I'm waitin' by the mail box, yet. I never did get my money. The only thing I did get off that record as an artist was $6,800."

Into the '90s, John has been a weekend DJ at KJEF in Jennings, Louisiana. He is the producer of the late '80s Fire Ants' rendition of his one hit. The Fire Ants are Rabbi, Shapina, Israel, Manedalisha, and Ethiopia Baptiste—five of his children.

In 1982, Del Shannon remade "Sea of Love" and charted at number 33; in 1984, the Honeydrippers—a one-off group consisting of Robert Plant, Jimmy Page, Jeff Beck, and Chic's Nile Rodgers—reached number three with their rendition.

An excellent Al Pacino-Ellen Barkin film thriller named for and including the rock'n'roll classic was released in 1989.

IVO ROBIC
MORGEN
(Paul Moesser)
Laurie 3033
No. 13 *September 21, 1959*

The only Ivo in all of pop-rock history was born near Zagreb, Yugoslavia, January 29, 1927. With plans of becoming a music teacher, Ivo Robic (pronounced *Eevo Robish*) studied the bass, clarinet, flute, piano, and saxophone at the local music conservatory. In 1948, he tried out for a dance orchestra as vocalist and was given the chance to begin making records. Great numbers of recordings, possibly 50 to 100 releases, were issued in his homeland before Ivo—who sings in English, French, German, Italian, and Spanish—had his one big moment on the U.S. charts. As a matter of fact, by the time "Morgen" came out, Ivo was one of Yugoslavia's top entertainers.

To those Top 40 radio listeners who didn't speak German, "Morgen" sounded like a bizarre love chant. With all the robust flair of a Swiss mountain climber, Ivo longingly implored "Morgen, Morgen" to do something we never knew. The title, however, is not a man's name, but the German word for "morning."

Ivo's next romp and last *Billboard* charting, "The Happy Muleteer" (#58, 1960), is probably just as innocent a ditty. After a few more singles, Ivo returned to being solely a homeland hero.

FLOYD ROBINSON
MAKIN' LOVE
(Floyd Robinson)
RCA 7529
No. 20 *September 28, 1959*

Floyd, born in 1938 and raised in the Nashville area, knew in his pea-pickin' heart that he was gonna grow up to be a music-makin' man. Before puberty set in, Floyd and his boys had a group called the Eagle Rangers. They would work the preteen hops, parties, and local radio programs. While in high school, Robinson and his Rangers had regular radio programs broadcast on Nashville's WLAC and WSM. When school days were through, Floyd made money and a name for himself providing back-up for touring country artists.

Floyd wrote tunes on the side and tried his best to have somebody to record them. JESSE LEE TURNER cut a rendition of Robinson's silly extraterrestrial love lyric, "The Little Space Girl" (#20, 1959). The gigantic sales success of such loony tunes as Betty Johnson's "Little Blue Man," David Seville's "Witch Doctor," and SHEB WOOLEY's "Purple People Eater" had created a nutty-novelty craze, so RCA ordered their scouts to find "The Little Space Girl"'s creator. Asked if he had any funny songs, Floyd sang "My Girl," a darling dinky about a strange boy and his emotionally damaged girlfriend. Chet Atkins and the big boys at RCA liked it, waxed it, and put something called "Makin' Love" on the "B" side. Someone discovered that the "B" side was better, and Floyd made the charts for his first and only time.

A self-titled album and many more teen-oriented 45s were issued. Some were quite interesting, like the Everly Brothers-influenced "Why Can't It Go On" and the hillbilly/surfer tune "Sidewalk Surfboard," but nothing sold too well. Not being one to quit easily, Floyd worked as an engineer on Duane Eddy sessions and continued to record novelty singles well into the '60s for Jamie, Dot, Groove, and United Artists.

her jazz LPs have crossed over to the top pop albums listings: *Nina at Newport* (1961), *Nina Simone in Concert* (1964), *I Put a Spell on You* (1965), and *Pastel Blues* (1965).

During the '70s, Simone turned her attentions to political issues. Tired of an America that she perceives as uncaring, she moved to France in the '80s. British audiences granted her a Top Five hit in '87 with the reissuance of "My Baby Just Cares for Me." She continues to record, but only sporadically.

BO DIDDLEY
SAY MAN
(Ellas "Bo Diddley" McDaniel)
Checker 931
No. 20 *October 26, 1959*

Bo Diddley, the legendary "Black Gladiator," was born Ellas Bates in McComb, Mississippi, on December 30, 1928. He was raised by his mother, a hard-core Baptist, and her cousin, Gussie McDaniel, who actually adopted him and gave him the "McDaniel" surname. The family moved to Chicago in 1935, where Bo started his musical training under the close watch of O. W. Frederick, music director of the Ebenezer Baptist Church. Frederick taught him violin; Bo's fellow pupil grew up to be jazz violinist Leroy Jenkins.

"I used to play all this funny music like Tchaikovsky," Bo confessed in an exclusive interview. "I wanted to play some jazz and get down, and everybody else is playing 'Drink to Me Only With Thine Eyes'! I found out later that I couldn't play blues. I could *not* play like Muddy Waters—I wanted to, but I just couldn't. I was cut out to be what I am, Bo Diddley."

At some point in the early '40s, Ellas picked up a cheap guitar and his nickname. He worked as an elevator operator, made circuit boards, drove a truck, and fought several bouts as a semi-pro boxer. All the while, Diddley and his band, the Langley Avenue Jive Cats (later named the Hipsters), played dives with names like the Sawdust Trail and Castle Rock; they also played street corners and passed the hat around. "We had a washboard and a guitar, and I was the man with the guitar. Roosevelt Jackson played the washtub, and Jerome Green [d. early '60s, "probably from alcohol"] shook the maracas, though he could play some tuba, too."

After a failed audition at Veejay Records, Bo tried Chicago's Chess/Checker label. "I just walked in there one day and asked [Phil and Leonard Chess] if they was makin' records. They told me, 'Yeah, what do you want?' I said, 'I wanna make a record.' They listened and liked this song, 'Uncle John' . . . They had me change the words, and that became my first record—'Bo Diddley' (R&B: #1, 1955) b/w 'I'm a Man (R&B: #1].'"

FLOYD ROBINSON

NINA SIMONE
I LOVES YOU, PORGY
(DuBose Heyward, Ira Gershwin, George Gershwin)
Bethlehem 11021
No. 18 *October 5, 1959*

She's a talented, bluesy woman with jazz influences, known the world over; a political activist, a pianist, a composer, a voice with a wallop. Yet Nina Simone has only made the nation's Top 40 once . . . and that was over 30 years ago.

She was born Eunice Kathleen Waymon, on February 21, 1933, in Tryon, South Carolina. Her parents were Methodist ministers, and she was surrounded by seven other sibs, all musical. She attended the Curtis Institute of Music in Philadelphia and the Juilliard School of Music in New York, starting her career as a piano accompanist. Her interpretation of "I Loves You, Porgy" from *Porgy and Bess* was one of her first recordings.

Simone has appeared at countless festivals, halls, and nightclubs, and has charted on numerous occasions on both the pop/rock and R & B listings. Her best-known singles include "Nobody Knows You When You're Down and Out" (#93, 1960), "Trouble in Mind" (#92, 1962), "Do What You Gotta Do" (#83, 1968), and "To Be Young, Gifted and Black" (#76, 1970). Many of

BO DIDDLEY

Diddley acquired an early rock and roll mystique, the result of the combined effect of his pounding, hypnotic beat, a menacing on stage presence, a slew of odd-shaped guitars, and an all-black outfit complete with Stetson hat and oversized turquoise ring. He had a string of R & B hits like "Diddley, Daddy" (R&B: #11, 1955) b/w "Pretty Thing" (R&B: #4) and "I'm Sorry" (R&B: #17, 1959) before crossing over to the pop charts with "Crackin Up' (#62, 1959).

"Say Man," his follow-up to "Crackin' Up," was an accident of sorts. As Bo explained in an article in *Record Review*, Leonard Chess and the recording engineer "had a tape recorder on, caught me and Jerome in the studio, clowning . . . pieced it together, took all the dirt out of it, and came up with 'Say Man.'"

Although he recorded a number of albums for the Chess brothers in the following years, only one of them (*Bo Diddley*, 1962) would find a large audience. He had three more pop clicks: "Road Runner" (#75, 1960), "You Can't Judge a Book by the Cover" (#48, 1962), and "Ooh Baby" (#88, 1967). Despite a brief cameo appearance as a pawnbroker in the Eddie Murphy-Dan Ackroyd movie *Trading Places* (1983), Bo kept a low profile throughout the '70s and '80s. But in the '90s, Bo was back, with the highly visible spots granted him in the Nike sneaker TV ads and his return to the record racks with new material cut for Triple XXX. The long awaited Bo book by Charles White, simply titled *Bo Diddley*, was issued in 1995.

"Nah, I ain't retirin'. I still got people out there looking for Bo Diddley. And I'm gonna go back to the roots with my next stuff, and get that '50s sound. I'm back up into the future."

MORMON TABERNACLE CHOIR
BATTLE HYMN OF THE REPUBLIC
(Julia Ward Howe, William Steffe)
Columbia 41459
No. 13 *October 26, 1959*

The Mormons have often been nicknamed "The Singing Saints," and vocal rejoicing has been a part of their religious practice since the formation of the Church of the Latter-Day Saints by Joseph Smith in 1830. The forerunner of the Salt Lake Mormon Tabernacle Choir, as it is officially known, was established on August 22, 1847, less than two weeks after Brigham Young and his hardy followers began setting up their base in Utah's Valley of the Great Salt Lake. Two years later, John Perry became the choir's first regular director.

Richard P. Condie (b. 1898, Springville, UT; d. Dec. 22, 1985), a graduate of the New England Conservatory of Music and a young tenor in many traveling opera-company productions, worked as the assistant conductor of the choir for 20 years before becoming the choir's 11th conductor in 1957, at the age of 59. The group had toured and recorded on numerous occasions: for one recording session, in 1910, the Columbia Phonograph Company used two mammoth horns, coupled directly to the recording needle and wax disk, to capture the rejoicing.

Condie had certain ideas about just how the choir should sound. He had grown up listening to Italian immigrants singing romantic old songs and wanted a sound like that for the choir. Many have since credited Condie with creating the "Tabernacle Choir sound."

In 1958, Condie and his 300-plus voices, with the frill support of Eugene Ormandy and the Philadelphia Orchestra, recorded one of the most memorable—and one of the strangest—entries on the charts, the "Battle Hymn of the Republic." Their rendition of this "oldie" from 1862 earned them a Grammy as "Best Performance by a Vocal Group."

The Mormon Tabernacle Choir has appeared on many TV programs, including "The Ed Sullivan Show"; an intercontinental satellite broadcast from Mt. Rushmore (1962); and NBC's coverage of the Statue of Liberty Centennial. More than 150 albums have been issued, and four of them—*The Lord's Prayer* (1959), *The Spirit of Christmas* (1959), *Songs of the North & South 1861-1865* (1961), and *The Lord's Prayer Volume II* (1963)—made *Billboard*'s top pop albums chart.

WINK MARTINDALE
DECK OF CARDS
(T. Texas Tyler)
Dot 15968
No. 7 *November 2, 1959*

Winston Conrad was born on December 4, 1934, in Bells, Tennessee. As early as 16 years of age, Wink, as he became known to his school chums, began making money with his mouth—first as a radio announcer, then as host of Los Angeles' "Teenage Dance Party" on KHJ-TV in 1959. That year, Dot Records chief Randy Wood spotted the young lad's face, heard that Wink voice, and placed him in a recording studio to recite his way into pop history.

"Deck of Cards," a remake of T. Texas Tyler's 1948 spoken-word tale (#21) of a lonely soldier's peculiar relationship with a pack of cards, was not Wink's first effort at singing (or talking) his way onto the charts. In 1954, Martindale had waxed a few sides for OJ Recordings. Nothing much happened with those, or with Wink's follow-ups to "Deck." Only "Black Land Farmer" (#85, 1961), a cover version of Frankie Miller's C & W hit, made the Hot 100.

While Wink's voice is no longer heard on pop radio, gobs of daytime television viewers have seen him on TV since 1978 as the host of the syndicated game show "Tic Tac Dough." In the fall of 1989, Martindale shifted to the Fox Network to host another game show, "Last Word," followed in the mid-'90s by "Debt," where contestants play to unload their debts.

ISLANDERS
THE ENCHANTED SEA
(Frank Metis, RANDY STARR)
Mayflower 16
No. 15 *November 16, 1959*

The Islanders were accordionist Frank Metis (keyboards, accordion) and New York dentist Dr. Warren Nadel (guitar, whistles), who for years was teen idol in-the-wings RANDY STARR.

Ever wonder what your dentist thinks about when he's yankin' teeth outa your face? For nearly a decade, Dr. Warren Nadel, an extractor with a 35-year history, dreamt up film fluff for Elvis. "Open wide," he'd said with authority. "Adam and evil . . . la, la, la, da, da . . ." he'd think to himself. Bizz, bizz went the drill. "That's kinda catchy," he'd mumble in the dungeon-like recesses of his professional mind. Bizz, bizz. "Nice beat, yes."

Near a dozen of Dr. Nadel's musical creations, such as "Kissin' Cousins" and "Almost in Love," were in Elvis' flicks. Others included: "Dayton" in *Paradise, Hawaiian Style* (1966), "Could I Fall in Love" in *Double Trouble*

(1967), and "Who Needs Money" and "The Girl I Never Loved" in *Clambake* (1967). In addition to the Elvis connection—and songs dashed for Jackie Wilson, George Hamilton IV, and the Kingston Trio; Connie Francis, Kay Starr, and Connie Smith—Nadel also has the distinction of being a "One-Hit Wonder", not once but twice and both times using a fabricated name.

Born in the Bronx, July 2, 1930, Warren took five years of violin lessons when he was just a tike. While working toward his D.D.S. at Columbia Dental School, he had started singing and writing folk songs. After graduation Warren served with the Air Force for two years earning the rank of Captain. Upon his discharge he walked into Republic Music with "Heaven High," a calypso that Nadel felt had the feel of success about it. Republic's Dick Wolf thought so too and brought Warren to the music publishing company's owner, Sammy Kaye. Sammy thought the kid had something about him that would make little girls shake and formed Dale Records, just to issue two of Warren's tunes.

"After School" sounded like Sonny James' hot item, "Young Love." "That was the idea," said Nadel in a recent interview with this writer. "Oh, not intentional; but Sonny James was the sound of that time. It was initially just a demonstration thing, but they felt it was good enough so it was put out as my first record."

The Board of Ethics branch of the America Dental Association "advised" Warren not to use his professional name. In compliance, Nadel appeared on Dick Clark's "American Bandstand" and toured with Buddy Knox, Charlie Gracie, and Frankie Avalon as "Randy Starr." "I really didn't like the idea of being a performer then. I was just interested in writing. I was afraid that performing would take too much time away from my practice." "After School" charted (*Billboard* "Top Pop": #37, 1957). JOY LAYNE, of "Your Wild Heart" flash-fame, covered it. A few more soured teen dream singles were issued by Dale ("Double Date" and "Sweet Talk and Sugar Kisses"), but nothing much sold that well.

In 1959, Warren met up with an accordionist named Frank Metis. Together they recorded exotic instrumentals like "The Enchanted Sea" as the Islanders and once again the dental doc was involved in a "One-Hit Wonder." "The Islanders was a studio-only orchestra. I played guitar [sometimes added guitar work was provided by Tony Mottola or Al Caiola] and did the whistling," says the good doc. "See, when I got out of the service I was about to open my practice, but I decided to go on a boat cruise first. The two strangers that were assigned to the state room I had booked were Frank Metis and as it happened Eddie Layton. Eddie, who has longtime been the New York Yankees organist, was then a name recording artist with Mercury Records."

While cruising the oceans the threesome got talking music and Metis and Nadel came up with some ideas

The 50s

for some exotic tunes in the style of Martin Denny's chart-buster "Quiet Village." "The Enchanted Sea" would be the lone hit for the Volkwein brothers' Mayflower label and the Islanders only find of buried treasure. "The band never toured under that name, and we were 'forbidden' to do any advertising." Excitedly, Warren adds: "We were named to both *Cashbox*'s 'Best Pop Studio Orchestra' list and as one of *Billboard*'s 'Most Promising Instrumental Groups' for that 1959. Santo & Johnny, Martin Denny, BILL JUSTIS, and Chet Atkins did record some of our songs." An impossible to fine long play and three follow-up 45s with teasing names like "Blue Rain," Tramp Streamer," and "Forbidden Island" sank from sight in shallow waters.

Frank Metis went on to become an arranger and did charts for George Shearing and DAVE BRUBECK. The doctor claims a few more "Randy Starr" singles were created during the early '60s. During all of this extracurricular activities Warren continued his dental practice. Warren has not returned to sing professionally and kept his dental practice in Manhattan until the mid-'90s.

ROCK-A-TEENS
WOO-HOO
(G. D. McGraw)
Roulette 4192
No. 16 *November 23, 1959*

Not much is known about these once-rockin' teenagers: Bill Cook, Paul Evans, Vic Mizell, Eddie Robinson, Bill Smith, and Bobby "Boo Walker" were from Virginia. They convinced the management of the tiny Doran record label to let them tape and release a couple of songs allegedly written by one "G. D. McGraw." A vocal number called "Untrue" was coupled with "Woo-Hoo," a wailing instrumental with one of rock's first midtune drum solos. This wild teen concoction featured searing guitar and sax work, topped off with a contagiously yodel-like "woo-hoo, woo-hoo" melodic line.

Once "Woo-Hoo" started receiving some positive notice, Morris Levy at Roulette acquired the rights to the disk's national distribution. An album was hastily assembled and released; sales were minimal, but the LP is now a highly sought-after item. Only one other Rock-a-Teens 45 is known to exist—the "Woo-Hoo"-styled "Twangy."

Only one member of these purveyors of rock and roll primitivism has been sighted on the musical landscape. Bill formed the Bill Smith Combo and had a few more well-tailored instrumentals like "Raunchy" released on Chess in the early '60s.

ERNIE FIELDS
IN THE MOOD
(Joe Garland, Andy Razaf)
Rendezvous 110
No. 4 *December 14, 1959*

Ernie had been tilling the fields for years and years before rock and roll discovered him. He was 54 years of age when his bottom-heavy revamping of Glenn Miller's "In the Mood" (#1, 1940; #20, 1943) found teen approval and bounced into the nation's charts.

Ernie Fields (b. Aug. 26, 1905, Nacogdoches, TX) was a pianist, trombonist, bandleader, and arranger. By the '30s, he was rooted in Tulsa and locally known for a band he fronted, the Territory Big Band. The act was discovered by John Hammond, in Kansas City, in 1938. Hammond encouraged Fields and the band to trek to New York City, where they toured and appeared at the Apollo Theatre. Beginning in the late '30s, he recorded for Vocation, Frisco, Regal, Bullet, Gotham, and Combo. Moving to Los Angeles in the mid-'50s, he found a comfortable if low-profile niche as an arranger for West Coast pop and rock sessions.

When Ron Pierce and Gordon Wolf formed the Rendezvous label in 1958, they enlisted Ernie to come up with some ideas for releases. "In the Mood," reportedly utilizing well-known sessioneers Rene Hall (guitar), Plas Johnson (sax), and Earl Palmer (drums), was the first of what would be a series of rockin'-good readings on big-band moldies like "Chattanooga Choo Choo," "12th Street Rag," "Charleston," "Castle Rock," "String of Pearls," and the "Hucklebuck."

Around this same time, Rendezvous Records struck it rich with "B. Bumble & The Stingers," a studio band comprising some of same session men as those on the Ernie Fields recordings. The Stingers are best remembered for stabs at the "classics" like Rimsky-Korsakov's "Flight of the Bumble Bee" (issued as the "Bumble Boogie," #21, 1961) and Tchaikovsky's "Nutcracker" (issued as the "Nut Rocker," #23, 1962). Reportedly, Fields was the keyboardist on a number of the Bumble/Stingers sides.

Ernie Fields died on May 11, 1997, in Tulsa, Oklahoma; he was 91.

THE NUTTY SQUIRRELS
UH! OH! PART 2
(Sascha Burland, Don Elliott)
Hanover 4540
No. 14 *December 28, 1959*

The Nutty Squirrels were the creation of Don Elliott and Sascha Burland. Working their "squirrels" like David Seville did his Chipmunks, Don and Sascha

SALT PEANUTS | DING DONG
ZOWEE | UH—HUH

DP-30

THE NUTTY SQUIRRELS

CREATED AND PRODUCED BY SASCHA BURLAND AND DON ELLIOTT

hanover
A DOUBLE PLAY HIGH FIDELITY RECORDING

THE NUTTY
SQUIRRELS

speeded up their scatlike voices to sound like the chat-terings of some hip little creatures.

Don Elliott (b. Oct. 21, 1926, Somerville, NJ) has been active on the jazz scene since the '50s. He has played mellophone, trumpet, and vibes with Benny Goodman, Buddy Rich, George Shearing, and Teddy Wilson. Elliott has his own 16-track recording studio, where he wrote and produced numerous radio and TV commercials during the '60s. He has composed for, and played in, Broadway shows like *A Thurber Carnival*, *The Happiest Man Alive*, and *The Beast in Me*; he has also supplied soundtracks to such films as *The Pawnbroker* (1965), *In the Heat of the Night* (1967), and *The Get-away* (1972).

In the '50s, Alexander "Sascha" Burland (b. Oct. 25, 1927, New York City) began producing, writing, and

working for TV and radio jingle sessions. Sascha was the creator of the theme song for "What's My Line?"

In 1959, the pair came up with the idea of having chipmunklike characters singing jazzy scat numbers. STEVE ALLEN and Bob Thiele had just formed Hanover-Signature Records, and were pleased pink to give it a try. "Uh! Oh!" was a hit, but a novelty hit at most, which meant that follow-ups like "Zowie" failed to excite enough record-buyers.

Despite successful records by the Nutty Squirrels, RAY BRYANT, Bill Evans, and Jack Kerouac, Allen and Thiele shut down Hanover-Signature in 1960. With the help of Columbia and RCA, Don and Sascha continued to work their nutty turf for another four years. None of these efforts fared well, and eventually the two returned to their previous endeavors.

THE 60s

LARRY HALL
SANDY
(Terry Fell)
Strand 25007
No. 15 *January 4, 1960*

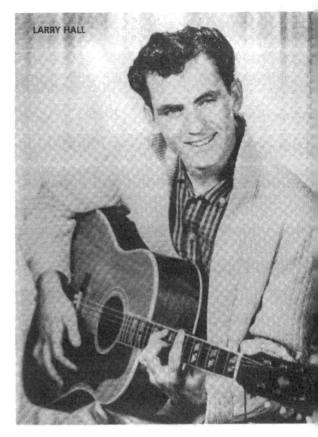

LARRY HALL

Lawrence Kendall Hall was born June 30, 1940, in Hamlett, Ohio, to Woody Hall and the former Toto Sizemore. Woody worked days at the Douglas Aircraft factory and nights plucked guitar with the Georgia Pickers; Uncle Bud "Cotton" Hall played with the Millie Pace Trio with Carole and Bob Sommers, brother and sister to Mary Ford, Les Paul's wife. Following in Pappy's footprints, Lawrence took to the guitar early on and in '57 won a talent contest sponsored by bandleader/Capitol Record executive CLIFFIE STONE.

"Not long after I won that," Hall explained to Collectable Records' Mark Marymont, "I was approached by Terry Fell, with a song he wrote called 'Sandy.' I knew it was a great song and wanted to record it."

For $50—using Les Paul's hand-me-down equipment and Bob Sommers's technical ability—Lawrence recorded the lusting moaner for his mythical dream queen. With copies pressed on his self-constructed Hot label, Lawrence and Mama Toto ran up and down the West Coast in their TR3 sportscar imploring DJs to add the disk to their play lists.

It was a great teen tune, and Larry sang it like he was smirking and twitching. The New York-based Strand label picked up distribution for the disk and acquired Hall's contract. Record number two was an early and forgettable Burt Bacharach item called "A Girl Like You." Unfortunately, by this point, someone had reached the boy, smoothed out his rough edges, and cleaned him up; he sung this cha-cha like a deboned Frankie Avalon.

For the next few years, Strand Records spared no expense with Larry, in Al Caiola and Jimmy Haskell to produce. The label secured hit songwriters like Billy Page (who would later create "The In Crowd") and the team of Aaron Schroeder and Wally Gold, who had written "A Big Hunk of Love" and "Good Luck Charm" for Elvis, "Because They're Young" for Duane Eddy, and "Fools Hall of Fame" for Pat Boone. An album—*Sandy and Other Larry Hall Hits*—now highly collectible, was issued. But, it was all for naught; after a few more singles for Gold Leaf, Larry checked out of the business.

"I was getting pretty discouraged," said Hall. "The '50s and '60s weren't a good time to be in the record business. It was hard to get any money out of the labels. They'd never tell you how many records you were selling. I tried to find out, but the culprits moved too much. They were too slippery."

After a time in the U.S. Marines, Lawrence returned to the business long enough to co-produce big hits for Terry

Stafford ("Suspicion," #3) and Dobie Gray ("The In Crowd, #13). Said Hall, "It was still hard to get any money. . . ." Within months of the hits, Lawrence and family moved to Oregon where they have remained operating a small cattle ranch in the Kings Valley area, near Corvallis. "I didn't get the money I had coming," Hall said, "but nobody can take away all those memories."

A year after "Sandy" charted, the tune's songwriter, Terry Fell, returned to the nation's play list when *Bobby Edwards's* "You're the Reason" (#11), which Fell co-wrote, became a country-rock hit.

MARK DINNING
TEEN ANGEL
(Jean Surrey, Red Surrey)
MGM 12845
No. 1 *February 8, 1960*

"I was born on August 17, 1933, on a farm near Drury, Oklahoma," Mark Dinning told *Record Exchanger*'s Bob Kinder. "Patti Page was once a babysitter for my sisters. She got her name from the Page Milk Company there.

My singing sisters were once known as the McDerring Sisters, because of the McCormick-Derring Tractor Company. It's odd how some of these people got their show business names."

Mark was born the last in a line of nine—five girls, four boys. His dad and his uncles were either ministers or evangelist singers. In the early '40s, three of his sisters were taken by brother Wade to the "Barn Dance Show" on radio KFH in Chicago, Ginger, Jean, and Louise soon dropped their tractor moniker in favor of their surname. As "The Dinning Sisters," they became quite popular with such disks as "My Adobe Hacienda" (#9, 1947), "I Wonder Who's Kissing Her Now" (#12, 1947), and the Oscar-winning "Buttons and Bows" (#5, 1948).

Meanwhile, little Mark milked cows and won first prize with his turkeys at a local 4-H show. His father had given him an electric guitar when he was 17, but this last of the Dinnings was determined to stay with what he knew best, farming. All that changed, however, once Mark and his guitar were assigned to an isolated military outpost in the Mojave Desert. "I was in the U.S.O. Club in Barstow, California, when I heard my first rock and roll record, 'Rock Around the Clock,' by Bill Haley & The Comets. I was 21 at the time, and when I got my discharge at 23, I decided to make music my career."

His successful sisters introduced Mark to star-makers like publisher Wesley Rose and Columbia Records' Mitch Miller; the latter had just that day signed Johnny Mathis and thereby was preoccupied. By 1957, however, Mark was a recording artist with MGM—but, for three years, an unsuccessful one. His sister Jean and her hubby, Red Surrey, had worked up a song they were sure was just right for the kid. The idea for "Teen Angel" had come to Jean via a 1959 magazine article by a DJ who argued that not all teens were dirty delinquents. According to Dinning, the article read: "I hear all the people putting down the teenagers of today: how rough and tumble they are, undisciplined, and how they're all a bunch of little devils. From my own experience, I happen to know quite a few teen angels." That last phrase stuck with Jean, who awoke one night from a nightmare to scribble down the lines to this classic death dirge.

"I didn't even think it was going to be a hit," Mark recalled. "They banned it in England because they considered it 'too bloody awful.' It was kind of a silly song, really; a girl going back for the ring and all that. It was a far-out, left-field teenage folk song that sold 3,500,000 copies."

Follow-ups were another story The next few releases did receive airplay and charted—"A Star Is Born (A Love Has Died)" (#68, 1960), "The Lovin' Touch" (#84, 1960), and "Top 40, News, Weather and Sports" (#81, 1961)—but eventually the records stopped, and the dust settled on Mark Dinning's career.

From 1962 through 1970, Mark moved through the South playing lounges either as a solo act, or in the company of his brother Ace. He began drinking heavily in the late '60s. "The Beatles really took us out. It was a blow to my ego and my wallet. . . . Groups were in and singles were out."

After appearing in a club in Jefferson City, Missouri, on March 21, 1986, Mark returned home, where he died of a heart attack.

SPENCER ROSS
TRACY'S THEME
(Robert Ascher)
Columbia 41532
No. 13 *February 22, 1960*

In the late '40s, Spencer Ross wrote arrangements for Gordon Jenkins and his orchestra, then arranged and led orchestral ensembles for both Bigtop and Columbia Records throughout the '50s and early '60s. One of Ross's sporadically issued singles caught fire in the winter of 1959. " 'Tracy's Theme'—limned by the silky sax of Jimmy Abato, an instructor at the Juilliard School of Music—had been the theme to a TV special called "The Philadelphia Story."

Before returning to his behind-the-scenes duties, Ross featured Abato on an album's worth of material, and on a pair of plush but long-forgotten follow-ups—"Theme for a Lonely Evening" and "Song for a Summer Night."

LITTLE DIPPERS
FOREVER
(Buddy Killen)
University 210
No. 9 *March 28, 1960*

If not for the heartache of producer Buddy Killen and the ethereal talent of Anita Kerr—unsung heroes both—"Forever" would not be.

Buddy was having a rough time coming to grips with a marital break-up; the summer of '59. "I'd close my office door, wanting to withdraw from other people," he wrote in his book, *By the Seat of My Pants*. "I'd sit down at the piano . . . a terrible-sounding piano, miserably out of tune, with half the keys missing. I could barely play the piano, but I would clumsily and slowly form three-note chords."

One day, Buddy hit a special chord and started humming. Jane Hines, his secretary noted it's extraordinariness; as did other office visitors. "Gee whiz," thought Killen, "if it's that good, I think I better make a demo on it. When Harold Sadler, a disgruntled Little

Rock, Arkansas, Chevrolet dealer, decided to start a record company [University] and approached Buddy about helping him cut some sides, Killen remembered that tune; "Forever" he called it. The session was for Smilin' Eddie Hill, a sometime singer and country DJ. With two songs in the can and 20 minutes to spare, Buddy showed his break-up ode to those studio musicians present: Floyd Cramer (piano), Hank Garland (guitar), Buddy Harmon (drums), Kelso Herston (guitar), BOB MOORE (bass), and the Anita Kerr Singers. Wrote Killen: "We made one false start and had time to make a final take and the session was over."

"Two by Four," an instrumental track, featuring Kelso Herston in the style of Duane Eddy was to be the top side. Within days, it was apparent that Buddy Killen and his buddy, the Chevy dealer, had a hit on their hands; a hit with the "B" side, "Forever." Dick Clark called Buddy saying he wanted the "group" to be on his "American Bandstand." Although others were assembled to tour as the Little Dippers (reportedly, Delores Dinning, Emily Gilmore, Darrell McCall, and Hunshel Wigintin) the actual voices heard on "Forever" were that of Anita Kerr and her behind-the-scene singers.

She was talented and ambitious, but no one could have guessed that Anita Kerr would become involved in—some claim—"possibly half" of all the records that came out of Nashville in the '50s and '60s.

She was born Anita Jean Grob on October 31, 1927, in Memphis. For 11 years, beginning at the age of four, she took piano lessons. While still in elementary school, she arranged songs for her church and formed the secular-singing Grilli Sisters to perform on her mother's radio programs on WREC. By age 14, she was a staff pianist at the Memphis station, and after graduation, she moved to Nashville to search out fame and fortune.

Anita made ends meet for several years by playing piano in local night spots. In 1949, she formed her first professional group with Dottie Dillard (alto), Louis Nunley (baritone), and Gil Wright (tenor). The Anita Kerr Singers/Quartet made radio appearances, and soon found that elusive cloud with the silver lining—studio back-up work.

For the next 10 to 15 years, the Anita Kerr Singers sang on piles of disks recorded in Nashville. To list all of their credits would be an encyclopedic task, but—to mention a mere sprinkling of acts—the Kerr Singers

THE LITTLE DIPPERS

accompanied Eddie Arnold, Chet Atkins, Brook Benton, the Browns, Perry Como, Floyd Cramer, Jimmie Davis, Skeeter Davis, Red Foley, Connie Francis, LORNE GREENE, Brenda Lee, Roy Orbison, and Jim Reeves.

Beginning in 1951, Kerr's groupings had the first of their very own disks issued by Decca Records. Over the next two decades, stacks of wax were shipped on several major labels. Surprisingly, none of these ever found positions on *Billboard*'s C & W singles charts. Kerr did briefly touch the pop charts as Anita & The So-and-So's with "Joey Baby" (#91, 1962).

Anita scored the Kate Jackson film *Limbo* (1972) and did well with a couple of albums in the late '60s (*The Anita Kerr Singers Reflect on the Hits of Burt Bacharach & Hal David* and *Velvet Voices and Bold Brass*). She also composed the music—with words and narration supplied by Rod McKuen—to seven LPs by the San Sebastian Strings & Singers.

"Forever" would make a One-Hit Wonder out of yet another—talking guitar picker PETE DRAKE and would extend the charting success of MERCY, known primarily for "Love (Can Make You Happy)."

CONNIE STEVENS
SIXTEEN REASONS
(Bill and Doree Post)
Warner Bros. 5137
No. 3 *May 2, 1960*

She was born Concetta Rosalie Ann Ingolia, in Brooklyn, on August 8, 1938. After dollin' up Monroe-style, platinum hair and all, and winning several talent contests, Concetta made a name change and a number of brief TV appearances ("The Bob Cummings Show," "Sugarfoot"). She also played innocent roles in teen flicks like *Young and Dangerous* (1957), *Rock-a-Bye-Baby* (1958), and *The Party Crashers* (1958).

While under contract to Warner Bros. Studios, Connie was chosen to appear opposite "77 Sunset Strip" star EDD BYRNES on "Kookie, Kookie (Lend Me Your Comb)," his much-ballyhooed debut as a rock and roll singer. Like the TV series itself, "Kookie" Byrne's vinyl venture was a winner.

Hoping to score again, "77 Sunset Strip"'s executive producer and other studio operatives quickly developed a TV series called "Hawaiian Eye"—according to Mike Bego of *Modern Screen*, an "island version of '77.'" Connie played Cricket Blake opposite two ever-vigilant and virile detectives, Lopaka (Robert Conrad) and Steele (Anthony Eisle). When not singing at the Hawaiian Village Hotel, Stevens would sashay about as a table-to-table photographer and snoop.

"Hawaiian Eye" ran from 1959 to 1963, and was a boob-tube hit. Like Edd Byrnes, Stevens was offered a shot at making a pop record. "Sixteen Reasons" was not bad for her label debut—unlike the insipid "Why Can't He Care for Me," a limited-release single she cut for ABC-Paramount in 1958. Four more 45s made the listings—"Too Young to Go Steady" (#71, 1960), "Why'd You Wanna Make Me Cry" (#52, 1962), "Mr. Songwriter" (#43, 1962), and "Now That You've Gone" (#53, 1965)—but by mid-decade, Stevens's recording career was almost history.

Connie has voyaged frequently on "The Love Boat," worked regularly on TV, and appeared in a number of movies: *Parrish* (1961), *Susan Slade* (1961), *Palm Springs Weekend* (1963), *Two on a Guillotine* (1965), *Never Too Late* (1965), *Way Way Out* (1966), *The Grissom Gang* (1971), *The Sex Symbol* (1974), *Scorchy* (1976), and in 1987 Connie was back with Edd Byrnes in the Frankie and Annette comeback *Back to the Beach*. The following year, she appeared on the noted TV production of "Bring Me the Head of Dobie Gillis."

Years later, Penny Marshall and Cindy Williams—recording as those lovable brewery bimbos, LaVerne & Shirley—recharted (#65, 1976) with their tender reading of Stevens's golden glory.

Following in the footsteps of Debbie Reynolds and Elizabeth Taylor, Stevens was also crooner Eddie Fisher's third wife—for a moment.

BILLY BLAND
LET THE LITTLE GIRL DANCE
(Spencer, Glover)
Old Town 1076
No. 7 *May 16, 1960*

Big Billy Bland is still around cooking up edibles. No longer actively performing, Billy now runs his own soul-food kitchen in New York City, dishing out fried chicken, black-eyed peas, and candied yams. A glance at the fine fellow's discography reveals the presence even then of a fowl fascination—"The Chicken Hop," "Momma Stole the Chicken," "Chicken in the Basket."

Bill Bland was born the youngest of 19, on April 5, 1932, in Wilmington, North Carolina. The Bland family was religious, and from early on, Bill was encouraged to sing his soul out. While still a student, he managed to cut the now-collectible "Mairzy Doats" for a small hometown label.

BILLY BLAND

Bland moved to New York at age 15, and quickly plugged into the nightclub scene. He was performing at the Baby Grand when Edna McGriff discovered him. Edna, who had charted with "Heavenly Father" in 1952, took him around town and got him booked at the Apollo Theatre and with the Lionel Hampton Band.

For two years, Billy was part of the 4 Bees, which had a string of failed singles on the Imperial label. After the unit buzzed off, he came to the attention of Hy Weiss, owner of the Old Town label. Hy thought well enough of Billy Bland to weather five years of only mildly successful singles, but in 1960, Bland made good on Weiss's expectations with the feeble but teen-targeted "Let the Little Girl Dance." While several of Bland's follow-up singles were more soulfully substantive, and three disks did chart on *Billboard*'s Hot 100 through 1961, nary a one ever again cracked the Top 40.

JEANNE BLACK
HE'LL HAVE TO STAY
(Joe & Audrey Allison, Charles Grean)
Capitol 4368
No. 4 *May 30, 1960*

Jeanne was born Gloria Jeanne on October 25, 1937, in Mount Baldy, California. Her singing ability was discovered while on a trip in the family car—her harmonizing with sister Janie in the back seat didn't sound bad at all. The girls were brought to the attention of CLIFFIE STONE, bandleader and executive at Capitol Records. Jeanne made many appearances on Cliffie's local TV program, "Hometown Jamboree," and eventually was given the chance to record an "answer record" to Jim Reeves's colossal C & W crossover hit, "He'll Have to Go."

An answer record takes the recognizable central idea or melody from what is usually a hit recording and places it in the heart and soul of a "new" song. The operating idea is that if the public liked it a whole bunch the first time and they still look a mite hungry, well then, they just may eat up the second offering, too. It doesn't always work: answer records to Buchanan & Goodman's "The Flying Saucer" and Ray Peterson's "Tell Laura I Love Her" stiffed badly.

Reaching the number four position, "He'll Have to Stay" was about as successful an answer record as has ever been made. An interesting new twist was added to the answer-record tradition when some mush-mouthed individual named Brumley Plunket came up with a response to Jeanne's number that was entitled "He'd Better Go."

Jeanne's visual presence was low key, and she sang in a pop-country style that was just beginning to be dubbed "The Nashville Sound." This style was not "real"

country and western music as the old folks knew it, but it wasn't rock and roll, either. Despite the protests of traditionalists, the Nashville country-pop blend did continue to pick up a following and grow in popularity.

Jeanne's career, however, just seemed to fade away. After "Lisa" (#43, 1960), Jeanne was rushed into the studio in the initial burst of heat generated by Elvis Presley's "Are You Lonesome Tonight?" An answer record, "Oh, How I Miss You Tonight," was concocted, but the public wasn't buying this time, or ever again.

RON HOLDEN
LOVE YOU SO
(Ron Holden)
Donna 1315
No. 7 *June 13, 1960*

When Ron Holden (b. August 7, 1939, Seattle) was 18 years old and en route to a stay in jail, he met the man who saved him from musical oblivion. Officer Larry Nelson had just finished fingerprinting Ron when he heard Holden's doo-wop echoing off the jailhouse walls. Nelson told Ron that he was about to quit the force, that he was thinking of doing something in the music field, and that Ron should look him up when he got out.

Holden and his Thunderbirds had been playing a teen sock hop that night. During a break, the guys in the band had taken a ride with a half-pint of I.W. Harper and what Holden described to *Goldmine* writer Steve Propes as "one of them funny little cigarettes." When the police pulled them over, Ron was the only one over 18.

Once free as a bird, Holden made plans to stop over at Officer Nelson's house. Nelson had decided to cut some tracks on Ron, and when Ron arrived at Nelson's home, there were microphones, a tape recorder, and a marching band waiting in the living room. For 20 hours, Holden and the kids in the band struggled to nail down what was to become Ron's big moment, "Love You So." To complicate matters, there was a barking dog in the house.

With the "perfect" take in the can, Nelson set up Nite Owl Records and pressed some copies. The disk started to take off locally, and Ron and Larry met with Ritchie Valens' discoverer, Bob Keane of Donna/Del-Fi Records. Keane, as Holden told *Goldmine*, "had a briefcase full of contracts, a big green cigar, and a pocketful of money. He said, 'We're gonna make this record a hit—now.' We said, 'Hey, now you're talkin', that's what we want.'"

Unfortunately, Holden's subsequent recordings for the Donna label made use of studio pros like keyboardist Rene Hall, sax-sensation Plas Johnson, drum legend Earl Palmer, and Darlene Love & her Blos-

soms—musicians who could never play, as Holden put it, "a little bit out of tune," like that marching band had done on "Love You So." Ron moved about cutting singles for Eldo, Rampart, Challenge, VMC, and Now. It's alleged that he even got the opportunity to record a one-off single (as half of Rosie & Ron) with Rosalie Hamlin of ROSIE & THE ORIGINALS, but nothing further charted.

For some years in the '70s, Ron Holden emceed at Art Laboe's Oldies but Goodies club in L.A.

Ron Holden died of unknown causes, in Mexico, January 20, 1997. Ron's Thunderbirds had reportedly been among the first bands to play Richard Berry's classic of the century, "Louie Louie." Ironically, Berry died just hours before his friend.

DANTE & THE EVERGREENS
ALLEY-OOP
(Dallas Frazier)
Madison 130
No. 15 July 4, 1960

Dante & The Evergreens' cover version of a number originally done by THE HOLLYWOOD ARGYLES was the most sanitized of the three chartings of the tune (the least successful version was by the Dyna-sores; a studio group with H. B. BARNUM and Jimmy Norman, the latter of "I Don't Need You No More" fame). Production was handled by a studio musician and an insurance salesman, Herb Alpert and Lou Adler respectively—both were just starting their careers in the music business, managing and producing Jan & Dean.

"We used to sing in the johns with Jan & Dean," said Dante Drowty to Gary Myers, author of Do You Hear the Beat. "We all grew up together. Actually, we got our break from Jan & Dean. Dean Torrence introduced us to Herb Alpert and Lou Adler. At the time, they were managing Sam Cooke and producing records for him and this great group, the Untouchables [reportedly, then with BILLY STORM as a member].

Lead vocalist Dante Drowty's (b. Donald Drowty, Oct. 5, 1939, Chesterton, IN) family had moved to Santa Monica, California, in 1956. It was while attending University High and later Santa Monica High that he met the rest of the group—first tenor Tony Joe Moon (b. Sept. 21, 1941, New York City), bass Frank "Frankie" Rosenthal (b. Nov. 12, 1941, Flushing, NY), and second tenor Bill Young (b. May 25, 1942, Santa Monica, CA).

No one is denying the existence of the L.A. Evergreens, but Alpert has claimed that the "group" heard on "Alley Oop"—though none of the follow-up recordings—is not Dante and peers, but himself, Adler, and some out-of-work studio singers. Adler has proudly proclaimed that "Alley Oop" was cut in one day, pressed the next, and received airplay on "American Bandstand" the following day.

Dante concurs with the latter boast. "Herb and Lou called us on a Tuesday night and wanted to know if we wanted to make a record the next night," said Drowty. "We made 'Alley Oop' on a Wednesday and were on the 'Dick Clark Show' in eight or nine days."

No one could of figured it, but largely due to this one-off creation the phenomenally successful A & M Records was born. ALPERT and MOSS, the label's co-founders—joined forces for the first time when as the Diddley Oohs they recorded "Hooray for the Big Slow Train," a blatant effort to jump on the short-lived "Alley Oop" fad.

Dante & The Evergreens toured frantically—with stops on the "Buddy Deane Show," hops for WINK MARTINDALE, even the Apollo Theatre. "We came back from our first tour so broke," said Drowty. "Herb [Alpert] sold me his '52 Pontiac for $50. . . ."

A few—way too few—equally fine or better 45s followed "Alley-Oop" in 1960—Howard Greenfield and BARRY MANN's "Time Machine" (#73) and "What Are You Doing New Year's Eve?" b/w "Yeah Baby" stirred some interest; "Da Doo" was put out without notice, as Madison Records shutdown it's operation. By year end—and the release of one highly sought-after LP—Dante & The Evergreens called it quits.

For the next few years, Dante continued to record some sides for Imperial. Some of these featured his own name, and some were credited to "Dante & His Friends." In 1965, Dante Drowty recorded a single as the Emerald City Bandits; returning the following year to Herb Alpert and A & M Records to wax his final outing, a remake of the Cadillacs' "Speedo."

In the mid-'60s, Tony Joe Moon went on to work as lead guitarist and conductor for Brenda Lee's band; writing such tunes as "The Water's Too Rough Tonight" and "More Than a Bedroom Thing."

Drowty went on to become a teacher in Japan, New Mexico, and Arizona and is involved in charity work for abused and disabled children through his American Music Project. A two-record EP, with eight cuts, is available through the Don Drowty Youth Foundation (P.O. Box 878, Paradise, CA 95969). Proceeds will go to help visually impaired children.

"It was kind of a Cinderella story. I had no idea how to save money. But when I tell someone I sang 'Alley Oop,'" said Drowty, "it gets me through the door . . . and I get to help children."

FENDERMEN
MULE SKINNER BLUES
(Jimmie Rodgers)
Soma 1137
No. 5 *July 11, 1960*

"Mule Skinner Blues" was an unlikely hit—a 30-year-old country tune about mules originally called the "Blue Yodel No. 8" and popularized in rural parts by the "Singing Brakeman," Jimmie Rodgers. Most peculiar, the record featured only a contorted vocal and two guitars; no bass, no drums, no other instrumentation.

Phil Humphrey and Jim Sundquist were both born in rural Wisconsin on the same day, November 26, 1937. Phil's hometown was Niagara; Jim's Stoughton. As fate would have it, 20 years later—almost to the day—they met at a beer party in Milwaukee. Musical noise was made by the drunk duo that night. Despite imparted joy, each went his separate way, only to meet by chance a year later when Phil, a truck driver for the Omar Bread Co., happened to see Jim's name on an apartment doorbell.

Now a unit—and one self-named for the brand of guitar they played—their first gig together was the Oats Bin in Stoughton; remuneration was all the beer they could consume—and possible $5, if the owner liked them. Phil had heard the mule skinner tune on an obscure bluegrass disk by Joe D. Gibson. Soon the number was a part of their swelling repertoire. A music fan and store owner named Bill Gregor suggested they drop down to his basement and record the mule tune on his VM tape recorder.

Enthused, Gregor took the result, a sparse, driving rendition of the "Singing Brakeman's" song, to Jim Kirchstein at Cuca Records. "Cuca didn't even have a studio," said Jim, to Gary Myers, author of *Do You Hear That Beat.* "With the money he got from 'Mule Skinner Blues' he bought a lot of equipment for a beautiful studio."

For several months the pair tried the hands-on approach to promoting their disk. "We had a trunk full of Cuca records and nobody would buy them," he said. "We had given up on it totally." Enter La Crosse, Wisconsin, DJ Lindy Shannon who played the track into the area's Top 10.

Taking notice were Amos and Dan Heilicher at Soma Records (Amos spelt backwards). The Heilicher brothers had the boys rerecord the raucous rocker at Vernon Bank's Kay Bank Studio in Minneapolis—the same locale where DAVE DUDLEY waxed his "Six Days on the Road" and the Trashmen later taped "Surfin' Bird." Despite signing with the brothers, Jim and Phil seemed to have paid the costs

of making their record. Soma contracts stated that for only $295 an artist could record two tunes, have them issued on Soma, and receive 350 45s, with an additional 150 disks going to DJs.

Sales were phenomenal—within weeks, the public seemed wild about mules. The tune, a bodacious boast about handling a mule, featured Jim and Phil's delirious whooping and their crackling guitars. The record rocked, and no one seemed to question just why these boys were so whipped up about a mule.

The Fendermen, with Johnny Hauser from La Crosse (drums) and Minneapolis man Den Dale (b. Dennis Gudim/bass), toured as an opening act for Johnny Cash and Johnny Horton. Their first big show was in Minneapolis. "When we walked out on stage," said Jim, "all that applause just hit us—10, maybe 20,000 people. It was the biggest thrill of my life." There

THE FENDERMEN

were appearances on "American Bandstand," even one at the Grand Ole Opry.

Problems, however, were noted almost immediately: No royalties were received from Soma. Phil and Jim, with Cuca's Kirchstein, brought a lawsuit against the label. A second and third single were released—to little response—and the now extremely collectible lone LP was held up near a year, due to the litigation.

Only months lapsed and the thrill was truly gone. "The last time I saw Phil Humphrey we were flipping a coin to see who was going to buy the turkey dinner as we said goodbye. We were in Minneapolis at the 600 Club. I wished him luck, and he wished me luck. We sat down, and we had a turkey dinner together and a couple of drinks. Then he went his way, and I went mine."

Phil picked up a Canadian band and recorded a few failed singles as Phil Humphrey & The Fendermen; later surfacing as a member of the inconspicuous Barbara Lee & The Kountry Kats. Jim immediately returned to Cuca recording the "Cocaine Blues" as Jimmy Sun & The Radiants; later as the Muleskinners, recording "Wolfman," "Galloping Paul Revere," and "Mule Skinner Blues '65."

Soma Records continued to issue disks with names that they hoped would successfully suggest the Fendermen still existed; the Embermen, Fenderbenders, Thundermen, Echo Men....

In 1968, Jim left the rock'n'roll world. "I was tired of being broke all the time and got a job at the Twin City Arsenal." In the '90s, he and wife Sharree perform gospel music together. "I don't drink anymore or smoke anymore or pop pills anymore. It's quite a sight to all these people that knew me before. when I could hardly stand up on the stage."

HOLLYWOOD ARGYLES
ALLEY-OOP
(Dallas Frazier)
Lute 5905
No. 1 *July 11, 1960*

Skip & Flip's cha-cha, "It Was I," had hit number 11 in 1959, and "Cherry Pie" had matched that position in 1960. But with their chart days apparently behind them, the "Flip" half of the team—Gary Paxton (b. Mesa, AZ—moved out of his place in Arizona and headed for Hollywood. When he arrived there, it was 2:00 A.M., and legend has it that the first gas station he stopped at was manned by Dallas Frazier. Dal's musical day had not come just yet—his songs "Mohair Sam" and "Elvira" were still to be conceived. He did tell Gary, though, that he was going to make it as a songwriter, and Paxton promised to look him up the next time he needed a tune.

In Hollywood, Paxton formed a music publishing "company"—Maverick Music, it's telephone number was the payphone at Happy's Chevron station, the corner of Sunset and Vine—with songwriter/producer/manager/full-time self-acknowledged eccentric Kim Fowley (creator of hits for B. Bumble & The Stingers, Paul Revere & The Raiders, the Rivingtons, THE SEEDS and THE MURMAIDS). Once settled, Paxton called on Frazier for a hit tune. Dallas came up with the tale of a cartoon caveman from way back named "Alley-Oop." As drummer and "Let There Be Drums" creator Sandy Nelson told Charlie Gillett in *The Sound of the City*, everyone present was sloshed on the day of the recording. The band was divinely sloppy, and "Flip" was so zonked that some soul had to hold him upright and aim him at the mike.

Apparently, this state of mind was nonconducive to memory formation since a dispute continues as to just who was present. Most reports credit Ted Marsh, Bobby Rey (sax), Deary Weaver (guitar), Gary "Spider" Webb (drums), Ted Winters, and, some claim, THE TEDDY BEAR's Marshall Leib (keyboards), though Paxton claims that this line-up (minus both Teds) was merely the touring group. Fowley adamantly maintains that those in presence were himself, Frazier, Nelson on garbage can and screams, Paxton's then-girlfriend ("Diane from Long Beach"), sometime dishwasher and "Skip" replacement Dave Martinez and JOHNNY OTIS bassist Harper Crosby, THE PENGUINS' Gayle Hodges on keyboards, and Olympics' session man Ronnie Silico on drums.

"We did the whole thing for $92, maybe $96," said Fowley to *Goldmine's* Steven Roeser. "We made the record, fed everybody, and still had money left over." Fowley took the disk around. No respectable labels were interested. "Everybody told us we were assholes," said Fowley, who decided to approach a Jehovah Witness preacher named Al Cavaland (produced Fess Parker/brief owner Cascade Records). The three together formed Lute.

Paxton's first 45 on Lute was "You're Ruining My Gladness"; the label credits read "Gary Paxton." "Alley-Oop" was likewise to be a solo single, until someone advised Paxton that he and "Skip" (Clyde Battin, an old University of Arizona buddy/one-time Tucson, Arizona, KMOP DJ) were still under contract to Brent Records. To avoid any legal hassles, Gary created the "Argyle" moniker. Why Hollywood Argyles? The recording studio was located at the corner of Hollywood Boulevard and Argyle Street.

An album, now nearly extinct, was released. It sold poorly, as did the group's remaining follow-ups (if you can locate it in a used lot, test-drive the Argyles' astonishingly primitive "Grumble"). Paxton formed a few record labels like Paxley and Garpax. The latter issued

Bobby "Boris" Pickett's perennial, "Monster Mash." Skip Battin went on to hippie haven playing bass for the Byrds, the Flying Burrito Brothers, and the New Riders of the Purple Sage.

"I just wanted to be in the music business," Paxton told *DISCoveries'* Peter Pittman. "I wanted to have hits, and I had hits, but I never got paid. Cavaland never paid us. We sued him, but I think he paid off our lawyers. . . ."

In more recent years, Paxton became a born-again Christian, issued some theological tunes, surfaced with a daily Nashville-based radio talk show, and wound up romantically linked to one Tammy Faye Bakker.

"Alley Oop" made a One-Hit Wonder also out of a Herb Alpert-Lou Adler group, DANTE & THE EVERGREENS (#15); though not for the Jimmy Norman-H. B. BARNUM studio-group, the Dyna-Sores (#59).

HANK LOCKLIN
PLEASE HELP ME, I'M FALLING
(Don Robertson, Hal Blair)
RCA 7692
No. 8 *August 1, 1960*

Hank, who was born Lawrence Hankins Locklin in McLellan, Florida, on February 15, 1918, was like a lot of pickers. When just a wee one, he learned the ways of the guitar and hit the talent contests. He also picked a lot of cotton, and during the Depression, he worked road projects for the government's Works Progress Administration. In the meantime, Hank played at clubs, barn yard parties, wherever he could.

In the late '40s, Decca and then 4-Star Records enlisted Hank to cut some country sides. His first Decca disk in 1949, "The Same Sweet Girl," proved a C & W winner (#8). A few others made the country charts, and Hank secured a regular slot on the "Louisiana Hayride" radio show. His popularity increased, and RCA signed Locklin to a long-term recording contract. Hank's "Geisha Girl" (#4) and self-penned "Send Me the Pillow You Dream On" (#5) charted big on the country listings and crossed over into the lower reaches of *Billboard's* Hot 100. But no one could have expected that his pure-country rendition of DON ROBERTSON's "Please Help Me, I'm Fallin'" would crash into the Top 10.

Because his follow-up singles were considered too conventionally country to garner airplay on the mainstream pop stations, none of Hank's successive releases did well on the pop charts. Country fans treated him much better, though not too many of his 45s ever climbed into the upper reaches of the C & W charts.

In the mid-'60s, Hank returned to live in his hometown, McLellan, where he was elected mayor in short course. In the '70s, he had his own TV program broad-

cast in Houston and Dallas. Hank still lives on his ramblin' Singin' L Ranch and occasionally ventures forth to sing some of his country tunes for the Plantation or Country Artist labels.

GARRY MILES
LOOK FOR A STAR
(Tony Hatch)
Liberty 55261
No. 16 *August 1, 1960*

James E. Cason, "Buzz," a.k.a. Garry Miles (b. Nov. 27, 1939, Nashville), began his career as an art student at Isaac Litton High in East Nashville. In 1956, a friend invited Buzz to the TV station, WSIX, where the local DJ, Noel Ball, hosted a show, "Saturday Showcase." In an exclusive interview, Buzz recalls, "Noel got a lot of people started down here, THE CRESCENDOS, DALE WARD . . . Once I saw the cameras, the lights, I got the bug, and there weren't no stoppin' me."

Buzz hung out at the station, thereafter, painting sets, pantomiming R & B songs with buddies as the Manhattans. "Noel would take his show on the road. There was this weird group, from East High, the Richard Williams Trio; a piano [Williams], accordion [Chester Power] and drums [Billy Smith]. I got Noel to let me really sing; told 'em I left my records at home. I sang 'Blue Suede Shoes,' with this trio. It was good and we decided to be a real group, the Casuals."

With Buzz on guitar, the Casuals recorded "My Love Song for You" b/w "Somebody Help Me"; issued in '57 on the tiny label Nu-Sound. Dot Records put out their "Hello Love." Sales were local-only, but strong enough to interest the powers that be in uniting the Casuals with the Everly Brothers. For 60 shows they provided back-up for the brothers—with the addition of Johnny McCreery (lead guitar) and Cary Potts (bass); later Wayne Moss replacing the former—followed by a 15-year run as accompanists for Brenda Lee.

"Now, I hung out with the Casuals for 'bout three years, but I always had my finger in other pots," said Buzz. "There was this studio above Tootsie's Orchid Lounge, Globe, that I met Bobby Russell at. He was trying to get a start; had this group the Impalas. . . ." We got writing together; did 'Tennessee' as the Todds for Paul Coin's Todd label. Later on Jan & Dean had something of a hit with it. Then, Bobby and I and Bergen White [noted arranger and studio member of Ronny & the Daytonas] did 'Popsicle' as the Todds. Jan & Dean were shadowing us and did alright with that one."

In the late '50s, Hugh Jarrett, an original Jordanaire rounded up Buzz, the Casuals' Richard Williams, and tunesmith Marijohn Wilkin [noted for "Long Black Veil," "PT 109," "Waterloo"] to form a vocal group. "He said, 'If we learn some original songs, Al Bennett will put us on Liberty. He figured, if we were gonna be on Liberty we ought to be the Statues. That way they can't expect no choreography . . . We did this Tony Bennett song, "Blue Velvet" (#80, 1960), with Snuff Garrett producing; one of the first hits that kid ever had. . . .

"Call came in this one morn, *Circus of Horrors* [1960], a British movie, was hittin' and causin' a stir. The song, 'Look for a Star,' was actually sung by Garry Mills. Snuff [Garrett, Liberty in-house producer] told me, 'We got to get this song on the streets fast; cut on Saturday, mastered/pressed on Sunday, and in the stores by Monday. I was 21 years old; petrified. This was to be my first solo; with Sy Waronker [label founder, co-owner] sittin' there, 18 players there. Snuff asked Sy, 'Whata we gonna call 'em?' Sy said, 'Hey, what's the other kid's name?' 'Garry Mills.' 'Call 'em, Garry Miles.' Nowadays, they'd be all over ya, with legal stuff; covering a guys record and covering his name, too. . . .'"

In addition to Buzz, that's Garry Miles, "Look for a Star" also made One-Hit Wonders out of the tunes' originator, GARRY MILLS, and DEAN HAWLEY; an event nearly without precedent in the annals of One-Hitdom.

After his moment passed, Buzz Cason had an EP—a four-cut packaged named for the hit—and a few more 45s issued as Garry Miles—"Dream Girl," "Love at First Sight." "Now, the Statues had broken up when 'Look for a Star' was a hit, because I was under contract as a member of a group, not as a soloist; and they were wanting some of the money for 'Star,'" Buzz adds.

About 1961, Snuff offered Buzz a job on the staff of Liberty Records, based in Hollywood. For the next three years, Cason was Snuff's assistant. "Leon Russell worked with me, and I produced the Crickets," said Buzz, "then Buddy Knox, and a bunch of hot rod records. . . . I did a lot of background vocals for Bobby Vee, Walter Brennan, Jackie DeShannon; ERNIE FREEMAN was doing all the arranging. They cleaned house, at Liberty, and fired everybody who worked with Snuff, in '64."

Buzz returned to Nashville to run BILL JUSTIS's publishing company, Tuneville Music. "Offbeat, but great musical mind, that Justis—through which I met Bucky [Marijohn's son John Wilkin] who already had 'Little GTO' as Ronny & The Daytonas. We wrote 'Sandy' and some others, when he was on this tour of Germany. The strings were cheaper over there, so we . . . recorded the Daytonas stuff there. With Buzz and Buck Wilkin as the prominent vocalists on the Daytona sides, it was decided to attempt a duet career as Buzz & Bucky. Nothing charted.

Recording as Buzz Cason, Jimmy cut a number of fine 45s through the '60s and the '70s for Don Lewis' Caprice, DJM, Mega, Monument, Warner Bros., Capricorn, and Elf, the latter owned by Buzz and Bobby Rus-

sell. Buzz and Bob, the latter then-husband to VICKIE LAWRENCE, set up a publishing company and built the still-functioning Creative Workshop Recording Studio in Nashville.

Cason discovered and produced the first two LPs for Jimmy Buffett and provided backup vocals for sessions for John Denver, Kenny Rogers, and Elvis. Alone—or in collaboration with such artists as Mac Gayden, Freddy Weller, Dan Penn, Leon Russell, or buddy Bobby Russell—Cason has written such tunes as "Popsicle," "Fantasy Island," "Bar Wars," and ROBERT KNIGHT's "Everlasting Love." "Me and Bobby wrote Dolly Parton's first 45 on Monument, 'Don't Drop Out.' It was good she listened and didn't do such.

"I'm still at it, tell folks. I've still got a group—have since the '80s—B.C. & The Dartz, an authentic slap-back rockabilly thing; got a couple albums—*An American Saturday Nite*, and *Rhythm Bound*—on my Track/America label. My studios are still here. And we've had Dolly, Buffet, Roy Orbison, DAVE LOGGINS, Olivia Newton-John, RANDY VANWARMER record at my place. I'm always lookin' for the next thing."

SAFARIS
IMAGE OF A GIRL
(Richard Clasky, Marv Rosenberg)
Eldo 101
No. 6 *August 1, 1960*

Sheldon Briar is currently a criminal attorney. Richard Clasky runs his own market research firm. Marv Rosenberg is Dr. Rosenberg, a psychologist with a hospital insurance company. The Safaris' former lead voice, Jim Stephens, is a sales manager at a bottled-water company. They are still friends, and they still sing together.

In the late '50s, Marv and Rich met at a party and quickly discovered that each had plans to become a rock and roll songwriter. "Ever since I was 11, I wanted to be a rock'n'roll star," said Marv to GOLDMINE's Randal C. Hill. "My father would say to me, 'You're wasting your time! Do something constructive.'" Neither Marv nor Rich wrote, read, or played music, but in a wink they had penned something called "Touch of Love." To flesh out the front of the group and warble the female sections of the tune, they rounded up Sandy Weisman.

The threesome grabbed the name "The Enchanters" and hawked their song to Orbit Records. Saleswise, "Touch"—arranged by Jimmie Haskell—didn't manage more than a twiddle. Sheldon Briar was added, and the gang relabeled themselves the Dories. With their new tune, "I Love Him So," they convinced producers Herb Alpert and Lou Adler—recently successful with the cover version of "Alley-Oop" by DANTE & THE EVER-

GREENS—to let them have another crack at the charts. Both "I Love Him So" and "A Lover's Prayer"—the latter, with vocal support supplied by Darlene Love & The Blossoms was issued as by the Angels on Adler and Alpert's Tawny label—stiffed as well.

Sandy married and took flight from the group, so Jim Stephens was brought in to sing lead. A local DJ introduced the group to the folks at Eldo Records. The first record for Eldo—a label allegedly part owned by JOHNNY OTIS—was "Image of a Girl," a doo-wop number with its origins in a spat between Marv and his girlfriend.

Marv's girlfriend, upset by his overinvolvement with music and under involvement with her, had asked Marv to choose between his music and her, then stormed angrily out of the room. Marv, thoroughly depressed, had flopped down on the girl's bed and thought to himself, "Why can't there be a girl to really love me for me?"

"Well, she had this really loud clock in her room, and there was a drip coming from the bathroom. That formed the beginning of the song. The rest just came to me . . . I wrote the whole thing in about five minutes." In two takes, with musician Bobby Rey—a recording member of the HOLLYWOOD ARGYLES—pounding on two ends of a wooden block to create that clocklike sound, "Image of a Girl," an atmospheric rock and roll moment, was created.

On the road to promote "Image," the Safaris encountered riots, terrible tours, hotel rooms with roaches, and a mere $25 per performance, per man. Worst of all, they reportedly received little in the way of remuneration for their colossal hit. "We each got a couple of thousand dollars," said Marv. "We were so young and naive. . . ."

After recording the follow-up, "The Girl With a Story in Her Eyes," Rich, Marv, and Sheldon left the group to acquire some college education.

"If we had been handled, we could have toured nationwide and been a much bigger success. We were young and pretty good looking; the lead singer had a great voice, and we had a hit record. . . ."

One further Safaris single—the Five Satins classic "In the Still of the Night," featuring Stephens and three friends—and a couple of Jim Stephens solo singles appeared, but nothing sold well enough to chart. Late in 1961, and then again in 1963, the original Safaris—minus Stephens, plus Lee Forester—came together to record two singles as the Suddens, but neither of these records caused much of a stir.

Nearly 30 years later, during the declining months of 1989, all of the original members reassembled in a high-tech studio to record a variation on their lone hit, "My Image of a Girl (Is You)." Given the state of pop music, no media took notice.

What became of that girlfriend that inspired Marv to create his classic number? "A month after the record hit, she called me and said, 'My mother and I are moving—would you be interested in buying the bed you wrote that song on?'"

DEMENSIONS
OVER THE RAINBOW
(Harold Arlen, E. Y. Harburg)
Mohawk 116
No. 16 *September 5, 1960*

Lenny Dell (b. Len Del Giudice/1944/lead vocalist) and Howie Margolin (b. 1943/baritone) sang together at Christopher Columbus High, in the Bronx, New York, as members of the Melody Makers, the school's premier choral group. Early in 1960, Len and Howie approached classmate Marisa Martelli (b. 1944/first tenor) about joining them in a pop group. Charles Peterson, for an instant, was the fourth member; followed by Len's "Uncle Phil," Phil Del Giudice (b. 1938/second tenor), a polished singer of opera and the classics.

The Demensions (with an E—usually—rather than the customary I, to catch the eye) were now complete. Lou Dell, Len's father, a professional musician, helped shape their sound, and when the time was right, brought them to Irving Spice at Mohawk Records.

Dreamy vocal-group remakes were hot in 1960. Early in the year, Dion & The Belmonts had clicked with Hal Kemp's 1937 hit "Where or When," and that spring, the Skyliners scored with their version of the Bing Crosby oldie from 1936, "Pennies From Heaven." "Over the Rainbow," first sung by Judy Garland in *The Wizard of Oz*, was a Top 10 hit for her in 1939—as were cover versions by Larry Clinton, Bob Crosby, and Glenn Miller—yet no one had touched the tune since then. With a slight rock and roll arrangement by Seymour Barab, Mohawk Records in April 1960 taped—at the dinky confines of the Dick Charles Studios—what would be the Demensions' lone note in the annals of pop history.

Other rockaballad remakes of oldie standards were soon dished up: "Zing Went the Strings of My Heart," "As Time Goes By," and "You'll Never Know." However, the only Demensions' follow-up to make the Hot 100 was their retake on Billy Eckstine's "My Foolish Heart" (#95, 1963). The Demensions' lone album was issued, but by this point, Marisa was ready to quit the group; Phil and Howie had already departed. At some point in the mid-'60s, Lenny Dell shelved the group name forever.

In the '80s the group name was revived when Len's friend Johnny Fast convinced him and Uncle Phil to round up Cathy O'Brien and with Johnny's membership make the oldies circuit.

Johnny Fast died in a car crash in 1990. Lenny continues to perform as a solo act in the New York area.

IVY THREE
YOGI
(Louis Stallman, Sid Jacobson, Charles Koppelman)
Shell 723
No. 8 *September 19, 1960*

The Ivy Three consisted of three students from Adelphi College in Garden City, New York. Hula hoops were hot, goldfish-gulping and Volkswagen-jamming were hip. When not engaged in such extracurricular activities or cramming for tests, Charlie (Koppelman) Cane, Don Rubin, and Artie (Berkowitz) Kaye would lift a glass or two and harmonize. Friends encouraged them, and one warm day, the trio walked into Shell Records at 1697 Broadway in Manhattan.

Shell Records had started with a dentist's bankroll and a street-smart songwriting team. Lou Stallman and/or Sid Jacobson had penned hits like "Treasure of Love" for Clyde McPhatter, "Round and Round" for Perry Como, and "Don't Pity Me" for Dion & The Belmonts. The day that the Ivy Three came in, Lou and Sid were constructing a novelty number based on the cartoon character Yogi Bear, then appearing on TVs "The Huckleberry Hound Show." Charlie kicked in his two cents, and the tune was done.

"Hush Little Baby," the non-novelty follow-up, was a flop. A few more silly singles like "Nine Out of Ten" and "Bagoo" were issued, but it was too little, too late.

Artie went off into the exciting world of insurance sales. While touring, Charlie had met Don Kirschner, founder of the successful Aldon Music, home for Gerry Goffin, Carole King, and Neil Sedaka. For Kirschner, he first functioned as a not-so prolific songwriter, then as head of the publishing house. In the mid-'60s Charlie and Don Rubin formed Koppelman-Rubin Productions and worked with/produced hits for Petula Clark, the Critters, Tim Hardin, Gary Lewis, Lovin' Spoonful, and the Turtles. Over the years, Charlie moved around—putting Barry Gibb with Barbra Streisand for a hit; Lionel Richie with Diana Ross for their smash, "Endless Love."

Late in 1986, Charlie discovered Tracy Chapman at Tufts University and not long after co-formed the Manhattan-based SKB Records: that's Stephen Swid, Koppelman, Martin Bandier, SKB Entertainment World, a globe-shaking entity that would make Charlie Koppelman a mogul—and phenomenally wealthy. In 1990, SKB completed its first full year of operations. With the

THE IVY THREE

stupendous successes of Vanilla Ice, Wilson Phillips, and Technotronic, SKB racked up well over $100 million in sales—a staggering sum for a new concern. Koppelman became CEO of EMI Records Group North America in 1991. As Bandier said to *Time*'s John E. Gallagher, "When people feel good, they buy records; when they are sad, they do the same."

As for Lou Stallman, he and co-producer Bobby Susser and an assemblage of studio players scored as THINK, in 1972 and again in 1974, with "Once You Understand," a noxious talkie.

JIMMY CHARLES
A MILLION TO ONE
(Phil Medley)
Promo 1002
No. 5 *September 26, 1960*

Jimmy Charles was born in Paterson, New Jersey, in 1942. As a preteen, he sang in church and at civic affairs. When 16, he entered a talent contest at the famed Apollo Theatre and won—not once, but for four straight weeks. Jimmy's uncle was impressed with the kid's abilities and took him to Phil Medley, a songwriter (known primarily for "Twist and Shout"), producer, arranger, and sometime recording artist.

Phil had a slow teen tune called "A Million to One" that he was looking to get waxed. He had Jimmy cut a demo, and presented it to Bill Lashley, the main cheese at Promo Records. Lashley signed Charles to cut the dirge, with a group called the Revellettes on back-up vocals, for his tiny label.

With odds something akin to a million to one, Charles's first outing on the Promo label rose to the top of the charts. The follow-up, "The Age of Love," charted fairly well at number 47, but none of the angst-ridden ballad-belters successive sides garnered more than a minor audience. In 1961, when he released "Just Whistle for Me," no one did.

LARRY VERNE
MR. CUSTER
(Fred Darian, Al DeLory, Joseph Van Winkle)
Era 3024
No. 1 *October 10, 1960*

"'Custard' happened, it hit, because it fit the perfect formula for comedy—tragedy, plus time," said Larry Verne, in an exclusive interview. "I didn't know that then, 'course. You gotta live awhile to figure that one.

"I wasn't no singer. I mean, I dabbled in it. I'd lose talent contests all over town. I really wasn't serious about nothin'. I had all kinds of jobs, after I served in

the Marine Corps.; truck driver, bartender, TV stuff as a stunt man for 'Zorro,' 'Circus Boy,' 'Range Rider,' 'Rin Tin Tin.'"

When Larry (b. Larry Vern Erickson, Feb. 8, 1936, Minneapolis) was discovered, he was a photographer's assistant. "The Balladeers, three fellows, Fred [Darian], Al [DeLory], and Joe [Van Winkle], had an office in the same building as the photo studio where I worked. 'Fact, their office was right across the hall. I got to know them and they mentioned this idea they had—it was no more than an idea. I'd throw in a line, once 'n while. So, one day, they said, 'Hey, we're gonna go down and make a dub on 'Custard.' Ya wanna come along?' I had nothin' to do, so I went down with 'em to Gold Star [Studios]. They laid down a basic rhythm track and said, 'Go in there; you do it.' It was a lot of ad-libbin' and 18 hours later we came out with a record."

As anyone who has heard the spoof on General Custer at Little Big Horn will attest, the disk is a slice of off-yonder-wall, dark humor. "They [Fred, Al, and Joe, the Balladeers] took it into their label, Del-Fi. Bob Keene, the owner [the man who discovered Ritchie Valens, the Bobby Fuller Four] gave 'em some advance money at first, but later passed on puttin' it out, saying he didn't think it was so funny.

"Then, back in the studio making a redubbing, a dub-down, Herb Newman [ERA Records founder] happened to be in the hallway and heard it. He says, 'What is that? I've gotta have that.' He snatched it up; signed me to a contract. We needed a flipside, so I joked 'round and ad-libbed this thing we called the 'Okefenokee Two Step,' a country boys take on 'The Madison.'"

Straightlaced folk weren't surprised, but nothing else Larry fooled with received nary a notice. "I did 'Mister Livingston' and this album full of Mister things and eight singles in addition. There was 'Abdul's Party,' 'The Speck,' 'Running Through the Forest,' and so many nondescript records that we did . . . 'The Porcupine Patrol' was misguided, and 'Charlie at Bat,' well Charlie was invisible, my alter ego. They were just sessions that we did, some released and some not."

When the records stopped in 1963, what became of Larry Verne? "I got into something I liked much better—I worked in motion picture business, set construction for 23 years; did [Sylvester Stallone's] *Tango and Cash* [1986] and *Rambo III* [1989], all three of the [Louis Gossett, Jr.] *Iron Eagle* flicks [1986, 1988, 1991]—hundreds of 'em. The last one I worked on was *Lost World, Jurassic Park 2*. I retired in February [1997]. Who knows, I got the guitar out and I've been writing a few tunes.

"You know, it stopped me when 'Custard' hit," said Verne. "I knew we had some funny lines, but I was just being a clown like I always am. It took me unawares, really. I was green as grass and by the time I figured which was up, I was down. I did Dick Clark 16 times, though; must be some kinda record for a guy with one hit.

"I still see Fred [Darian]. The Balladeers shut down after 'Custard' and Fred did a lot of club work and then got into real estate in the San Fernando Valley. Joe [Van Winkle] passed away a few years ago. And I worked on a lot of pictures where Al [DeLory] was scoring the film."

BOB LUMAN
LET'S THINK ABOUT LIVING
(Boudleaux Bryant)
Warner Bros. 5172
No. 7 *October 24, 1960*

Bobby Glynn Luman's dad—fiddle player, guitarist, and harmonica-honker extraordinaire—taught his boy (b. April 15, 1937, Nacogdoches, TX) to play country tunes. Bob was slightly interested, but liked baseball more. In high school, he also fronted a country band, singing his heart out like Webb Pierce and Lefty Frizzell. In his junior year, he tried out for the Pittsburgh Pirates. Whether he was picked up or passed on depends on whom you listen to, but either way, Luman never showed up at minor league camp.

Bob, you see, had seen Elvis and was quite impressed. "Man, I didn't believe it," Luman recalled to Paul Hemphill in *The Nashville Sound*. "This cat came out in red pants and a green coat . . . [and] started moving his hips real slow like he had a thing for his guitar. He made chills run up my back."

That was it for baseball and country music. Bob and his band switched to playing rock and roll, and in senior year, they won a talent contest sponsored by the Texas Future Farmers of America. In 1955, Imperial Records issued three classics—"Red Cadillac and a Black Moustache," "Red Hot," and "Make Up Your Mind Baby." Luman and buddy DAVID HOUSTON won a spot in the early rock flick *Carnival Rock* (1957). Capitol followed up with Bob's "Svengali," then Warner Bros. rush-released "Class of '59" b/w "My Baby Walks All Over Me" plus "Dreamy Doll." All of these disks were teenage dynamite, and represent Luman at the pinnacle of his form as a rockabilly artist—but none of them charted.

For the next record, Luman and the label leaders opted for a change of pace, and toned down the rock and roll energy. "Let's Think About Living" was a punchy protest piece: "Let's forget about the lyin' and the cryin'/The shootin' and the dyin'/And the fellow with the switchblade knife." None of Bob's immediate follow-ups, not even similar-sounding songs, charted pop or country.

A two-year stint in the military didn't help keep his name on teen's lips. On his return to civilian life in '63,

Bob hung up his rock'n'roll shoes, signed with Hickory, a country label owned by Wesley Rose and Roy Acuff. In August 1964, he became a regular member of the Grand Ole Opry. He toured and toured, eventually clicking with 39 singles on *Billboard*'s C & W listings, five of them in the Top 10.

In 1976, Bob was hospitalized for nearly six months for an operation on a blocked artery. After his release, Johnny Cash brought him back into a recording studio and produced Bob's penultimate LP for Epic, *Alive and Well*.

Bob Luman died of pneumonia on December 27, 1978, in Nashville. He was 41.

PARADONS
DIAMONDS AND PEARLS
(William Powers)
Milestone 2003
No. 18 *October 24, 1960*

"Songs came to me in dreams. And it all feels like that, now. Lifetime ago, or so," said William Ralph Powers the Paradons' tunesmith in an exclusive interview. "It was 1958. Just Bill Myers and myself at first; sittin' on a porch we thought up the name. He and I would run around together; thinking that we were Don Juans anyway—and Chuck Weldon and West Tyler ran around together—so we figured we'd be a pair of dons—Paradons.

"Now, Bill lived across the street; and we'd done some boys chorus stuff in school, sang in bathrooms, garages; like the normal doo-wop groups. By '59, we were all at Bakersfield High and things got serious. We did school dances, local clubs . . . ; did the Pike in Long Beach with WINK MARTINDALE—it's torn down, now—and the 'Cousin Herb' TV show, a country and western program. We sometimes played gigs and BUCK OWENS would be there. We're still in touch, though I haven't seen him in years since he got sick. We sang country, pop, rhythm & blues; whatever."

Milestone Records was set up by "the Delta Balladeer," Werly "Levi" Fairburn—to insiders, Jack Hammer—a one-time rockabilly contender from Folsom, La., Madelon Baker—producer of "the Skippy Hollywood Theatre" and a model groomed by General Mills in 1956 to be the next Betty Crocker, and possibly a few silent partners. Neither one of them wound up fulfilling those particular career dreams, but they did record some interesting vocal groups; such as THE BLUE JAYS, ROCHELLE & THE CANDLES, and the Paradons. Fairburn's initial plan had been to record C & W tunes when he happened onto Powers' group.

"Madelon and her folks owned the Big M, a publishing company, and the Audio Arts Recording Studio,

THE PARADONS

on Melrose near Western, in Hollywood. Werly heard us at some club and he was quite impressed." On January 23, 1960, Fairburn led Powers (b. June 10, 1942, alternated baritone, bass, 1st and 2nd tenor), Bill Myers (bass), Charles "Chuck" Weldon (1st and 2nd tenor), and West Tyler (alternated vocal roles) into Madelon and Jackson Baker's recording studio. That evening they dashed off "I Want Love"—the hit disk's "B" side—and possibly seven others, including "Diamonds and Pearls," a tune that not all members wanted to set to tape.

"No one wanted to record that tune," said Powers. "I had to argue with everyone. No one would listen to me. I was adamant, 'This is the song.' Round and round, we went; until they said, 'Alright, let's do it.' The song is now a classic—but where's my money. It's still selling to

this day. Five groups covered it, including THE TURBANS, but we had the hit. . . ."

"Diamonds and Pearls" had all the secret ingredients necessary to become a national Top 40 hit, and it sparkles to this day. In demand, the Paradons appeared on "American Bandstand," played the Apollo alongside Fats Domino, toured with the Five Satins and JOHNNY OTIS, and knocked 'em out at the Howard Theatre in Washington D.C. and the Palladium in L.A.

"It felt wonderful. The ride of my life. The limos. Wining and dining . . . but soon we found out—our agent was shady, contracts were fuzzy . . . These guys were making so much money, and they did not want us to get any of it."

Disputes arose—the wrong name appeared as writer of "Diamonds and Pearls," bickering set in as to what to release next and who's to sing what part and how; and most notably, very little money trickled down to the boys. "Bells Ring" was issued—months late. Without the groups consent, the Paradons were transferred to Warner Brothers for one 45, "Take All of Me"; followed after the group's break-up by "I Had a Dream," on Milestone. Unfortunately, for Powers and group, none of these all to few disks would make the listings.

Late in 1960, Powers left the group. Bill became Little Richard's road manager and worked for transsexual sensation Christine Jorgensen. Bill Myers died in 1992. West sold cars and worked the clubs as an R & B singer; he died in 1983—shot to death in a nightclub dispute. Chuck became an actor in TV and film; appearing in episodes of "Police Story," Alex Haley's noted series "Roots" and off-Broadway productions.

William Powers drifted into the culinary arts, becoming a noted chef and operator of his own restaurant, A Sure Thing Barbecue, in Long Beach. William has also produced TV commercials, anchored a cable TV program, and ran his own auto detail shop. Currently he operates Diamonds and Pearls Publishing in Fair Oaks, California.

"I never got the windfall from my creation," said Powers. "They got their cars, had parties, and they hid the money from us. I still haven't got my money, but I'm going to, though."

Madelon Baker went on to form the Audio Arts label and the discovery of the Incredibles and songwriting legend Jimmy Webb.

JOE JONES
YOU TALK TOO MUCH
(Joe Jones, Reggie Hall)
Roulette 4304
No. 3 *November 14, 1960*

"Joe had a big mouth—just like his song," DR. JOHN told *Blues & Soul* writer John Broven. "He talked his way into deals, and talked his way out just as quick. He had big ideas, and although Joe got his feet in the door, he had no talent to stay there."

Born on August 12, 1926, in New Orleans, Joe Jones attended the Corpus Christi Catholic and Booker Washington High Schools. He was drafted in 1942, and claims to have been the first black petty officer in the Navy; "handled mines, depth charges, that sort of thing," he explained to Broven. Joe played piano in the U.S. Navy Band, and on his return to civilian life, he formed his own group, the Atomic Rebops.

When ROY BROWN came to New Orleans in 1948 to record his "Good Rockin' Tonight," he used a good portion of Jones' band. Next in town was B. B. King. "He

told me he needed a piano player right away, so I played for him in New Orleans and I became his pianist, also his valet. I was driving and playing, then I became his assistant bandleader and was tuning his guitar up every night . . . I was writing the charts."

B. B. and Joe separated in 1954, and Capitol Records issued Joe's first single, "Adam Bit the Apple" b/w "Will Call." Three years would pass before his second single, "When Your Hair Has Turned to Silver" b/w "You Done Me Wrong," came and went. In between, Joe's band toured or did studio work for Ruth Brown, Jerry Butler, Dee Clark, and Shirley & Lee.

Things started to heat up when Sylvia Vanderpool of MICKEY & SYLVIA (and later, SYLVIA) fame, met Joe. "Sylvia was so impressed [with me] that when her date in New Orleans was over she flew back to record me on 'Every Night About Eight,' which she cut herself on her own money. She sang duet with me on another song, 'A Tisket, A Tasket' and she got me a deal with Roulette, then she was going to represent me as my manager."

The next recording session, produced by Harold Battiste, would yield "You Talk Too Much," or was it the next three sessions? Some confusion still exists. It seems that while under contract to Roulette, Joe recorded the tune for them, and that they rejected it, filing it in their

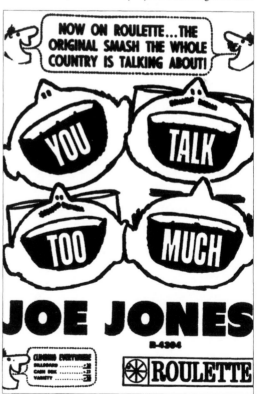

vaults. Believing that the tune would be a sure hit, Joe recorded the same number for Ric Records and possibly Flame Records.

Ric Records chief Joe Ruffino gave Jones $600 to hit the road and promote the disk. It all paid off—"You Talk Too Much" was a huge hit, in spite of the stiff competition provided by FRANKIE FORD's cover version (#87, 1960). But heated discussions developed between Ric and Roulette Records as to just who owned the rights to the master recording. Roulette secured the rights, so Ruffino rushed home to cut an answer record, "I Don't Talk Too Much," with the very same band and Martha Nelson's voice. It failed to fly, as did the few Joe Jones 45s that followed: "One Big Mouth," "California Sun" (#89, 1961)—which THE RIVIERA's covered and took to number 5 in 1964—and a dance number called "The Big Mule."

Joe Jones moved on to production work for Red Bird Records in the mid-'60s, most notably for Alvin Robinson ("Something You Got") and the Dixie Cups ("Chapel of Love").

MAURICE WILLIAMS & THE ZODIACS
STAY
(Maurice Williams)
Herald 552
No. 1 *November 21, 1960*

Maurice Williams's (b. Apr. 26, 1938, Lancaster, SC) sister is the one that got him interested in music. She taught him piano and soon he was chirpin' in a gospel group called the Junior Harmonizers. It was there that he met Zodiac-to-be Earl Gainey (tenor, guitar); both were students at Lancaster's Barr Street High School. Willie Jones (baritone), William "Bunchie" Massey (tenor, baritone, trumpet), and Norman Wade (bass), also Barr Street students, soon joined the pair in a secular group, the Royal Charmers (named after favs the Five Royals and the Charms). The Royal Charmers won a talent contest in 1955, and a Saturday morning hometown radio show over WLCM gave them exposure and a growing audience.

After numerous successful nightclub gigs, public parties, and a tour throughout the South, the Royal Charmers—with the addition of drummers Mac Badskins and Bob Robertson, seven in number—headed to Nashville in a beat-up bald-tired Chrysler to record for Ernie Young's Excello label. "Sweetheart Please Don't Go" b/w "Little Darlin'" credited to the Gladiolas, appeared in 1957; "Little Darlin'" went to number 41, but a cover version by the Diamonds (#2, 1957) became the cherished classic remembered by oldies fans the world over.

"Mr. Young told me somebody else wanted to record 'Little Darlin',' Maurice told *DISCoveries'* Stan Hardin, a one-time recording member of the Zodiacs. "At first I was against it, but Mr. Young gave me good advice—'Don't let your ego get between you and your money. You wrote the song. The more copies sold, the more money you make.' He was a very honest man. He could have bought the rights from me for peanuts." Excello released three more 45s by the Gladiolas— "Run Run Little Joe," "Hey, Little Girl," and "Shoop Shoop"—but not one nudged a notice.

When the group left Excello, Ernie Young retained the rights to the Gladiolas name. In their needed name change, Maurice told *DISCoveries*, "Our station wagon had broken down in Bluefield, West Virginia, and we were towed into a dealership. While the repairs were under way, we were looking at new cars in the showroom. Right there on the showroom floor was a German-made Zodia, a car about the size of a golf cart, and a group member Bobby Gore says, 'That's it! The Zodiacs! Maurice Williams & The Zodiacs.'" Under this moniker, Maurice and his group (minus Badskins and Robertson) briefly recorded for the Phil Gernhard's Cole and Selwyn labels. Massey and Wade left, and the group dissolved.

Maurice rebounded with a new and improved Zodiacs—Wiley Bennett (tenor), Henry Gaston (tenor), Albert Hill (bass guitar), Little Willie Morrow (drums), and Charles Thomas (baritone). After two singles on the Soma label, Gernhard—Lobo's manager and head of Big Tree Records—approached Al Silver at Herald about a little tune he, but not Maurice, believed in.

"I had never thought that much about 'Stay,'" *DISCoveries* was told. "In fact, I had thrown the lyrics in the trash. One night we were playing my demos and my girl's 10-year-old sister went crazy over 'Stay.' That changed my thinking."

The song was written by 15-year-old Maurice in 1953 within days of his creating "Little Darlin'; and written for the same never-to-be possessed dream girl. "She had to be in by 10 P.M.," he told Hardin, "and this one night I just didn't want her to leave. She argued that she would get into trouble. I tried to convince her she wouldn't, but she knew better and left. Like a flood, the words just came to me."

Silver liked "Stay," which would become the shortest number-one disk in pop history, but he told the group to sing the first word flat. "He said we were singing it too good," Williams recently told *Rolling Stone's* Parke Puterbaugh. "Man, we had cut this thing I don't know how many times, trying to get it right for him. When he said, 'Sing it flat,' that just pissed everyone off. I said, 'We couldn't care less how it comes out.'"

The outcome is history. Over the years, numerous other artists have had hits with their own readings of "Stay," among them the Hollies (1963), the Four Seasons (#16, 1964), Jackson Browne (#20, 1978), and Rufus & Chaka Khan (R&B: #3, 1978). Williams and the Zodiacs followed up with two singles that made the Hot 100—"I Remember" (#86, 1961) and "Come Along" (#83, 1961). Curiously enough, while the group's 1964 release of "May I" has been certified by the RIAA as a million-seller, the disk never appeared on either the pop/rock or R & B listings; though two years later Bill Deal & the Rondells would break the Top 40 with their rendition.

Despite an ever-shifting line-up over the years, Williams has never shut down the Zodiacs. When the times started a-changin', the Zodiacs did, too. Maurice told *Rolling Stone*, "we got Beatle wigs and had us a Beatle act! And when the hard rock came in, we started singin' hard rock, to keep workin'."

Maurice has outlived it all. His sides have appeared on Atlantic, Scepter, Sphere Sound, Vee Jay, Deesu, SeaHorn, 440/Plus, Veep, and his own R & M label. Maurice is currently living in Charlotte, North Carolina, and recording sporadically for Ripete Records.

In 1987, Maurice's "Stay" was included on the soundtrack of PATRICK SWAYZE's meteoric moment, *Dirty Dancing*. By decades end, Maurice Williams received a multiplatinum award for sales exceeding 8 million.

LOLITA
SAILOR
(Werner Scharfenberger, Fini Busch)
Kapp 349
No. 5 *December 19, 1960*

Lolita Ditta was born in St. Poelten, Austria, about 40 miles outside of Vienna. Until getting a chance airing over Radio Linz, Ditta was a children's nurse who sang mostly in her church choir on Sundays. The response to her radio debut was such that TV appearances, films, and the chance to make records were offered to her. One of the petite fraulein's first vinyl efforts was "Sailor."

A copy of the husky-voiced nurse's recording landed on the desk of the president of Kapp Records, Dave Kapp. Sensing something, Kapp released the record in the U. S. Despite its German lyrics, and with only a breathy monologue over one chorus in English, "Sailor" sold well enough to become the very first record sung in German by a female to reach *Billboard*'s Top 10.

Despite the higher probability back in the '50s of having a hit with a song in a foreign tongue, outlanders like ROCCO GRANTA, IVO ROBIC, and KYU SAKAMOTO never managed to explore the reaches of the Top 40 more than once. And holding to the tradition, Lolita's "Sailor" was her lone Top 40 success.

ROSIE & THE ORIGINALS
ANGEL BABY
(David Ponci)
Highland 1011
No. 5 *January 23, 1961*

Pictures on Rosie are a rarity so most fans don't know what she looked like. But from the sound of that high-pitched voice on "Angel Baby," Rosalie Hamlin was probably as thin as a barber's pole, with a 16-inch waist, two-inch-long eyelashes, and a stiff beehive hairdo up to there. Here was seemingly a sad, bad girl—or so us teen males hoped—who just needed a boy, a beer, and the submarine races, and everything would be all right.

In the late '80s, Rosie resurfaced with a new band, the L.A. Rhythm Section, and a story to tell. She was born July 21, 1945, in Klamath Falls, Oregon, raised in Alaska till age 11 when her family moved to San Diego. as a preteen she taught herself to play piano and to dash off songs.

In 1960, when 14, Rosie met four older guys with a future to mesh with hers. "They weren't yet a band called the Originals," she told *DISCoveries*' Ed Wittenberg. "They were just guys from the other side of town who played music with a couple of friends of mine." There was sax man Alfred Barrett, bassist Tony Gomez, guitarist David Ponci, lead guitarist Noah Tafolla, and drummer Carl von Goodat. Rosie and the boys rehearsed a few numbers, then approached Highland Records about recording some of their material.

History happened in an old airplane hanger converted into a studio of sorts in San Marcos, California. Rosie had scribbled the words to the unit's first and penultimate single as a poem in her notebook, then crafted a melody based on the chord changes to "Heart and Soul." She sings "Angel Baby" in one of the skimpiest voices to ever grace the *Billboard* charts, with the Originals pounding a sparse and primitive backdrop. At moments, the drummer seems to forget what track he's playing on, the record is flawed with flubs, and the sound quality of the recording is poor—but "Angel Baby" is undoubtedly one of rock and roll's greatest moments.

In explanation, Rosie told Wittenberg, "Alfred had to stay home that day to do the yard work for his parents. So, Tony who was the bass player had to play the sax line." To make matters, seemingly worse, Rosie had a bad cold. "We did it over and over. . . . We must have done 30-some takes; it was an all day deal."

Before the now-classic was even issued, the group disbanded; Rosie, in particular, was bothered that Highland Records had credited Dave Ponci as "Angel Baby"'s writer. "We were together only a summer, if even that," she told Wittenberg.

A follow-up, "Angel From Above," was put out by the label; then "We'll Have a Chance." Both went unnoticed by radio programmers and consequentially, the public. Jackie Wilson, however, did take notice, and introduced Rosie to his manager, Nat Taranapol. Nat got Rosie a recording contract with one of the big-time labels, his label, Brunswick Records. Aside from boyfriend Noah, the Originals were not part of the deal, and they apparently vanished from the face of this planet.

In place of the crudities the Originals had supplied were the lush strings and flubless instrumentation of the Dick Jacobs Orchestra; featuring the sax of legend Plas Johnson and keyboard great ERNIE FREEMAN. Two of Rosie's self-penned tunes, engulfed in the finest sounds money could buy, were issued as by "Rosie, formerly of Rosie & The Originals"; both failed miserably. An album appeared, but sales were minor league.

"The band on that album [*Lonely Blue Nights*] kind of swallowed me up," Rosie admitted to *Sh-Boom*. "They wanted to duplicate that 'Angel Baby' sound, but they were too professional. The saxophonist tried to get that off-key sound, and it sounded terrible—like he was trying to play off-key. Plus, the company didn't push the album. I think it was a tax write-off or something."

Two further solo singles were issued, but record-buyers' interest was apparently elsewhere. Brunswick set the girl free.

Rosie and Originals' guitarist Noah Tafolla were married for three and a half years. Their off-spring, Debbie and Joey, are full-grown; the latter is a guitar teacher. Rosie has remained in the music biz through all the years, with the exception of 1979 to 1983 when she was an art teacher in Colorado.

Kathy Young & The Innocents, of "A Thousand Stars," and bluesman Charles Brown recorded remakes of Rosie's ode. Her favorite rendition, however, is by John Lennon, produced by Phil Spector in the '70s and issued posthumously in 1986. On the *Menlove* album, John's voice can be heard: "This is one of my all-time favorite songs. . . . My love to Rosie wherever she may be."

Rosie and the Originals never received a penny from "Angel Baby," nor any of the other Highland recordings—until September 1994, when a financial settlement was reached and the masters of their recordings were returned to them.

"It looks like that song'll be around longer than I will," she told *Sh-Boom*.

CAPRIS
THERE'S A MOON OUT TONIGHT
(Al Striano, Joe Luccisano, Al Gentile)
Old Town 1094
No. 3 *February 27, 1961*

"I had just started to learn harmony," Mike Mincelli, first tenor (b. 1941) told *Record Exchanger*'s Art Turco

and Bob Galgano. "I went over to a friend's house [that of John Cassessa, bass (b. 1941)] one day. There was a song out then called 'Bermuda Shorts' by the Del Roys. I wanted this guy to sing the bass part, and he couldn't do it. Finally, he got it down, and I decided we would keep him. The other guys were picked up one by one. It took over a year."

By 1958, all the pieces had fallen in place—the line-up was complete with Mincelli, Cassessa, second tenor Vinnie Narcardo (b. 1941), baritone Frank Reina (b. 1940), and lead singer Nick Santo (b. Nick Santa Maria, 1941). All were from the Ozone Park section of Queens, New York, and in a shot at class, they named themselves after the large luxurious Lincoln Capri. Their big break came when they responded to an ad placed by two wanna-be producers. Present at the audition, though passed on, was an odd man and his ukelele, TINY TIM. "There's a Moon Out Tonight" was recorded at the Bell Tone Studios and finished in an hour. "We did ["Moon"] in three takes and they took the first one, it came out the best."

"There's a Moon Out Tonight" has a strange ending, technically known as a voice overlay: each Capri chants the tune's title in turn, but slows it down a little each time. After nearly three decades, this is still one of the most memorable endings in rock history. "I don't think it was intentional," Mincelli recalled. "It was one of the mistakes—there were a lot of mistakes on that record."

Planet Records picked up the rights to the release, but the disk bombed. By 1959, the Capris were no more. Mike married, Nick joined the Army, and the others went their separate ways.

What happened next was pure serendipity. In 1961, record fanatic Jerry Greene—later the owner of Collectables, the world's foremost 45 rpm reissue label—and a cartel of fellow collectors bought the "Moon" master for $200 and reissued it on red vinyl on their newly constructed Lost Nite label. Greene's group had been offered the publishing rights for $10, but passed; money was tight. Murray the K, a big-time Big Apple jockey, began riding the record like it had a satin saddle. Within six months, "There's a Moon Out Tonight" was such a smash that Lost Nite could no longer handle distribution, so Old Town Records provided the platter with national availability.

Although "There's a Moon Out Tonight" has yet to be certified as a million-seller, the Capris' musical monster still sells worldwide. Playing down the sales figures, each member was offered $265 in royalties. The band regrouped to tour and record four more singles, three of which charted: "Where I Fell in Love" (#74, 1961), "Girl in My Dreams" (#92, 1961), and their last waxing, "Limbo" (#99, 1962), an uptempo attempt for Mr. Peeke Records.

Nick left in 1963 to become a New York City police officer, Midtown Division; John and Vinnie, gone by 1965. There have been various reunions over the years. In 1982, Frank, Mike, and Nick reunited with Tommy Ferrara (formerly of the Del Satiⁱs) and Tony Danno (formerly of the Emotions) to record "There's a Moon Out Again, " an excellent '80s doo-wop treat for the Ambient Sound label. That year, the Columbia subsidiary issued "Morse Code of Love," the Capris first 45 in 20 years. In 1985, the Manhattan Transfer charted with the tune, retitled "Baby Come Back to Me" (#83, 1985).

The Capris continue to perform on the sidelines. Frank works as a traffic controller at New York's Kennedy Airport. As for the others: John fronts a hairpiece firm. Mike drives a school bus. Nick's retired, and Vinnie moves furniture.

BUZZ CLIFFORD
BABY SITTIN' BOOGIE
(Johnny Parker)
Columbia 41876
No. 6 *March 13, 1961*

Buzz was born Reese Francis Clifford III, on October 8, 1942, in Berwyn, Illinois. Buzz was hot on westerns and singing cowboys. Mom and Dad bought him a guitar, and the boy would stroll around the house pickin', grinnin', and makin' up the words to his own cowpoke tunes. As a high school senior, Buzz entered an amateur contest at the Morris County Fair in New Jersey, and clobbered the competition. Soon after some work as a stunt man, construction worker, and lifeguard, Columbia Records approached him to cut some recordings. The first, "Hello Mr. Moonlight," lived and died without notice. But his novelty number, "Baby Sittin' Boogie"— complete with goo-goo sounds from the producer's little kid— took off.

Buzz's tot tune was so catchy that it charted across the boards: pop/rock, C & W, and R & B. The follow-up, "Three Little Fishes," was another cutesy number, but neither this nor any further 45s would click. In the mid-'60s, while producing disks for ABC-Paramount and Apt, Clifford recorded some self-penned folk-rock sides for RCA. As the decade came to a close, he had a fine hippie-headed LP issued by Dot titled *See Your Way Clear*.

JORGEN INGMANN & HIS GUITAR
APACHE
(Jerry Lordan)
Atco 6184
No. 2 *April 3, 1961*

Jorgen Ingmann-Pedersen was born on April 26, 1925, in Copenhagen, Denmark. He took violin lessons, then acquired his first guitar at age 18. Two years later, he was playing jazz guitar in the style of Charlie Christian with his own quintet. Svend Asmussen, a noted homeland violinist, got wind of Ingmann and enlisted him in his band, where he remained for the next dozen years. In 1953, Jorgen got his first chance to create some solo singles. With Birthe Buch or Grethe Clemmensen (later Ingmann's wife), he also tried his hand with a sound modeled on the then-popular Les Paul-Mary Ford records.

In 1959, Jorgen's manager, Metronome Record Company head BENT FABRIC, arranged for the stateside Atlantic label to issue disks by Danish talent. Songwriter Jerry Lordan had a catchy tune for which he could dream up no lyrics. British instrumentalist Bert Weedon cut the first side on "Apache"; it drew little attention. The legendary Shadows worked up a rough and beat-bottom rendition that eventually outsold all versions worldwide, but that failed to chart in the U.S.

JORGEN
INGMANN

"Apache" was intended as the "B" side of Ingmann's self-penned "Echo Boogie," a number that he believed would establish him in America. His version of "Apache" featured guitar riffs that sounded like arrows whizzing by. When Fabric called in March 1961 to tell him that "Apache" was a hit, Jorgen could only respond with disbelief.

Jorgen Ingmann never toured the U.S. Promotion for his future releases, he charged, were minimal, and other than his initial follow-up, "Anna" (#54, 1961), nothing further sold well. Over the years, Jorgen has had sporadic homeland hits with "Drinamarch" and "Toy Balloons"; in 1963, he and his wife won the Eurovision Song Contest with their "I Love You."

In the mid-'60s, Ingmann became a head producer with Metronome Records. Gradually, he withdrew from public appearances due reportedly to bad nerves and alcohol problems.

KOKOMO
ASIA MINOR
(Jimmy "Kokomo" Wisner)
Felsted 8612
No. 8 *April 17, 1961*

James Wisner was born in Philadelphia, December 8, 1931. Both his mom and dad were self-taught piano pickers. "Mom played by ear, and Dad played by rote," explained Jimmy "The Wiz" Wisner in an all-to rare interview. "When they brought that piano home, I was eight or nine, and I discovered that I had this instant ability to play." Wisner became quite good and took an early interest in the serious stuff—jazz and the classics.

For 10 years, he was a classically trained at the Philadelphia Academy. By 1959, he was a Temple University psychology graduate and had formed the Jimmy Wisner Trio, composed of himself on piano, Chick Kinney on drums, and Ace Tsome on bass. The unit was playing the local clubs and had accompanied Mel Torme, Carmen McRae, Dakota Staton, and the Hi-Lo's. Their first album, *Blues for Harvey*, was just being released by a London Record subsidiary, Felsted Records, when an odd idea struck him.

The idea, as such, was sort of a rock'n'roll meets the masters. "We bought this old up-right piano for $50," said "The Wiz," "and painted the hammers with shellac to give it a sound in-between that of a 'tack' piano and that of a hard-harpsichord. I guess I was into sounds, even then.... This is at the RecoArt Studio, in Philadelphia. Now, we had only four string players, so to make it sound fuller we overdubbed them. I played this melody that I loved from the Grieg Piano Concerto."

The tune's title was easy, Wisner said. The now rockin' Grieg number was in the key of A minor and

when someone at the session called out "What key is it in?" the reply was "Asia Minor."

"We were turned down by 10 or 11 labels, so we put the thing out ourselves," said "The Wiz." A few weeks after Wisner had formed Future Records with a local record distributor, Harry Chipetz, and the records engineer, Amel Corset, "Asia Minor" became something of a local sensation. Only a few weeks more and Kokomo was a national item with a Top 10 hit.

"The first I knew something was happening was about a week after we put it out. I was doing this wedding and somebody came up to the band asking if anybody knew this song, 'Asia Minor,' by Kokomo. Records have always been a mystery to me. And this incident reinforced it. . . .

"I put Kokomo on the record label as a pseudonym because it was basically a rock'n'roll record, and I was a jazz man. I didn't want to tarnish my position in the community, but ironically the jazz guys that I knew really liked it the best."

To cover his I.D., Kokomo became a mystery. No photos were ever published of this self-imposed reclusive. No interviews were ever given. And no performances were ever held in support of "Asia Minor" or the Kokomo name. An album and three further singles—"Humouresque," "Like Teen," Journey Home"—were issued, but nothing ever again charted.

"I thought that was it, and I didn't see there being any reason to do anything more with the Kokomo thing," said Wisner. "From my point of view, I was a jazz artist." The Jimmy Wisner Trio's second album, *Apperception*, on the Chancellor label was issued in 1962.

"Little did I know then but, Kokomo was just the beginning," he said. "It was my first hit. And I've been in the music business now for near 40 years and have been involved in the creation of over 100 singles that charted."

As an arranger or producer, Jim Wisner worked with ALIVE AND KICKING on "Tighter, Tighter," Len Barry on "1, 2, 3," the Cowsills on "The Rain, the Park & Other Things," Spanky & Our Gang on "Lazy Day" and "Sunday Will Never Be the Same," Tommy James on "I Think We're Alone Now" and "Out of the Blue," THE INNOCENCE on "There's Got to Be a Word," THE SPOKESMEN on "The Dawn of Correction," Peaches and Herb on "Love Is Strange," MIRIAM MAKEBA on "Pata Pata," Jay & The Techniques on "Keep the Ball Rolling," Jerry Butler on "Mr. Dream Merchant," and CLINT HOLMES on "Playground of Your Mind."

In addition, Wisner has worked on recordings by Tony Bennett, Barbra Streisand, Carly Simon, Al Kooper, the Buckinghams, IGGY POP, and, yes, Brigitte Bardot.

"The Wiz" also co-wrote the Searchers' "Don't Throw Your Love Away," the Tymes' "Somewhere," Frankie Avalon's "A Perfect Day," and the theme for the

"Phil Donahue Show." He scored for the Robert Kennedy, Jr., documentary *The Last Frontier* and the movie *What's So Bad About Feeling Good?* (1968).

In addition to the creation of jingles and commercials for National Car Rental, IT&T, AT&T, and Burger King, Wisner's recent theater production, *Scrambled Eggs*, ran off-Broadway for two years at the Village Gate in New York. Of late, "The Wiz" has co-produced and arranged for Levon Helm, has been elected to the Board of Governors of NARAS, and is in anticipation of forming his own label.

Trivia fans: Wisner is also the organ-grinder heard on Freddy Cannon's "Palisades Park," the harpsichordist heard on Judy Collins's "Both Sides Now," and the pianist heard on Miriam Makeba's "Pata Pata."

"I've never performed as Kokomo," said the Wiz, "but it might be fun, to do the oldies shows; I'm certainly old enough. I could get a kick out of that. Maybe, Kokomo will return."

CATHY JEAN & THE ROOMMATES
PLEASE LOVE ME FOREVER
(Malone, Blanchard)
Valmor 007
No. 12 *April 24, 1961*

Steve Susskind (lead vocals, baritone) and Bob Minsky (bass) were in the same homeroom at Russell Sage High in Forest Hills, Queens. After discovering a mutual interest in singing, the duo competed in a talent contest at Forest Hills High, and came in second place—Paul Simon and Art Garfunkel, calling themselves Tom and Jerry, came in first. By 1959, Steve and Bob had formed the Roommates—so named because founders Steve and Bob were in the same homeroom in school—with second tenor Felix Alvarez and first tenor Jack Carlson. After much practicing, they spent $75 at the Associated Studios to make a demo of the Five Keys' classic "The Glory of Love." They hawked the number around to all the small labels they could locate, but no one was interested.

One night, while honing their skills in an apartment-building lobby, the Roommates were overheard by Gene and Jody Malis, owners of the new Valmor label; named for a furniture store across the street from the couple's apartment. The Malises became the group's managers and brought the guys down to Bill Lashley's Promo label. Lashley, who was momentarily hot with a one-off item by JIMMY CHARLES, released the Roommates' reworking of Kitty Wells' "Making Believe," but the single stiffed.

Noting the success that Kathy Young and the Innocents were having with their "A Thousand Stars," Jody Malis got the idea to package the Roommates with her new "discovery," Cathy Jean (b. Cathy Jean Giordano, Sept. 8, 1945, Brooklyn). The 14-year-old Cathy had already recorded a remake of Tommy Edward's 1958 hit "Please Love Me Forever"; Jody rounded up the Roommates and had them overdub a harmonized background onto the track. According to *Story Untold* writer Paul Heller, "The group was not enthused in taking a 'back seat' on somebody else's record. After hearing the playback, the group begged [the Malises] not to release it."

"They thought they were gonna launch two acts with one record," Cathy Jean recently told *Sh-Boom* magazine. "I didn't even get to meet the Roommates until we did a radio interview, after the record came out."

The disk was released on Valmor, and "Please Love Me Forever" became a rockaballad biggie. They toured with Ral Donner, B. Bumble & The Stingers, and aspiring teen idol Tony Orlando; lip-synced for Cousin Brucie, Dick Clark, and the rest. The dusty was a stone-cold smash. To reward the Roommates for their involvement in the well-received record, the Malises gave the group a free three-hour session at the Regent Sound Studio. That night, November 25, 1960, they laid down and packaged some of their finest stuff ever: "Band of Gold," "Glory of Love," and "My Foolish Heart." Unfortunately, none of their reworked standards—other than their take on "Glory of Love" (#49, 1961)—garnered much notice. Neither did any of Cathy Jean's follow-ups.

Before Valmor Records shut down in 1962, *At the Hop*, the lone and now highly collectible (estimated worth starts at $1,000) Cathy Jean & The Roommates album was issued. The Malises, still functioning as the group's managers, connected the Roommates to labels like Cameo, Philips, and Canadian-American. George Rodriguez was added making the unit a quintet. Cover versions of "Gee" and "Sunday Kind of Love" were waxed and shipped, but no one was buying. For the last time, the guys entered the studios to record "Someone to Watch Over You" never to be completed. It was the spring of 1965 when they parted, never to sing together again.

Cathy, likewise, had another whirl at it, but her few 45s for Philips failed to fly. She married and quit the music business. Her kids are now grown, and Cathy's back. As Catherine Jean Ruiz, she currently fronts an entirely new version of the Roommates and has hosted a Saturday-morning radio show on WNYG in Long Island, New York.

"For a long time I thought singing was something for the young; something you did before you got a real job," Cathy Jean told *Sh-Boom*. "But lately I've decided there's more to life than being a collection supervisor [for a New York bank]."

In 1991, the New York label Cure, issued on vinyl her first new single in near 30 years, "You Don't Have to Say You Love Me."

ECHOES
BABY BLUE
(Sam Guilino, Val Lagueux)
Seg-Way 103
No. 12 *May 1, 1961*

Harry Doyle (b. 1943), Tommy Duffy (b. 1944), and Tom Morrissey (b. 1943) were some Brooklyn-born'n'bred boys who liked to hang out and harmonize. They were calling themselves the Laurels when a friend of Duffy, Johnny Power, turned them on to "Baby Blue," a tune that Long Island High assistant principal Val Lageux and his music teacher Sam Guilino had handed him. Powers own group, Johnny & The Jokers, passed on the song to record their own "Do-Re-Mi Rock" for Harvard Records.

Meanwhile, the Laurels changed their name to the already overused "Echoes" name—a moniker yet to be used by BONNIE GUITAR & DON ROBERTSON on their lone pairing and 1961 charting "Born to Be With You." With funds from their own pockets, the guys cut a demo of "Baby Blue"—a slow, *a cappella* rendition. They brought the track to Jack Gold at Paris Records. Gold, who had formerly worked on recordings by THE TEMPOS (creators of the original "See You in September") and JOE BENNETT & THE SPARKLETONES, liked the group's gentle sound and that baby-talkin' tune. He took the tape back into the studio to add instrumental backing and speed up the tempo. To release the disk, he formed the SRG label (named after his newly-born son, Steven Richard Gold).

The initial response to "Baby Blue"—which the group misspells in the song as "B-a-b-by B-l-u-e"—was promising. A slightly larger independent label, Seg-Way Records, picked up the group's contract and the rights to the recording, and the Echoes had their first and only moment. A number of fine follow-ups were issued, but nothing else nudged the nation—not "Gee, Oh Gee," not their cover of Ersel Hickey's "Bluebirds Over the Mountain," not their moving remake of Brook Benton's "A Million Miles From Nowhere."

When last noted, in the mid-'70s, Tommy was still working with a new edition of the Echoes; Tom and Harry had a group called The Red Hook.

ERNIE K-DOE
MOTHER-IN-LAW
(Allen Toussaint)
Minit 623
No. 1 *May 22, 1961*

He's still a wild man, that Ernie K-Doe. Often dressed in iridescent apparel and huge gold rings, he'll jump about like a banshee during his unsettling sets, flippin' and trippin' and rippin' perfectly new suits. Even with an audience of 15 or less, Ernie K has been known to let loose. "I don't like to brag," he told Almost Slim, author of *Walking to New Orleans*, "but I still believe I can out-perform any man in show business. Ernie K-Doe can stop any show at the drop of a hat."

"Mother-in-Law" is possibly the finest record to ever emerge from the bubbling New Orleans scene of the early '60s, and Ernie performed it with conviction. "'Mother-in-Law'" wasn't a hard song to sing," he told Dave Hoekstra of the *Chicago Tribune*, "because my mother-in-law was staying in my house. I was married 19 years, and it was 19 years of pure sorrow. When I sang, 'Satan should be her name,' I meant that . . . Oooh, she was a lowdown."

The way Ernie remembers it, he literally found "Mother-in-Law" in an overstuffed garbage can: "Allen [Toussaint] had wrote it and thrown it away . . . I saw it in the garbage can and pulled it out. I looked at the words and said, 'Hey man, this is good. I want to do it.'" Other individuals, like the tune's creator, have disputed Ernie's tale.

He was born Ernest Kador, Jr., on February 22, 1936, in New Orleans, the ninth of 11 offspring. His dad was a Baptist minister. For unreported reasons, Ernie's aunt on his mom's side raised him, and religiously so. He sang in his father's New Home Baptist Church, and toured with gospel groups while still a student at Booker T. Washington High.

When he was 17, Ernie moved to Chicago, where he recorded his first solo and secular sides for United Records (none of the four cuts have been officially released). Back in New Orleans in 1954, K-Doe and his Blue Diamonds began playing neighborhood clubs and bars. Savoy Record's Lee Magid spotted the act at the Tijuana Club and set up a session for them: only one single ("Honey Love" b/w "No Money") was released, though Specialty ("Do Baby Do") and Ember ("Tuff Enough") also issued some K-Doe sides.

Minit Records was set up by Joe Banashak in 1960; Ernie's manager, Larry McKinley, was allegedly part-owner of the operation. "Mother-in-Law" was Ernie's third single for the fledgling label. It was Benny Spell-man—later noted for "Lipstick Traces" (#80, 1962) and the still later Rolling Stones revival "Fortune Teller"—who provided the tune's hook with his deep intonation, in all the proper places, of the long-drawed phrase "mother-in-law."

For the next couple of years, his 45s filed on to the charts—"Te-Ta-Te-Ta-Ta" (#53, 1961), "I Cried My Last Tear" (#69, 1961) b/w "A Certain Girl" (#71), and "Pop-eye Joe" (#99, 1962). Even the ones that didn't sell well were solidly-crafted, and are now highly collectible efforts. Eventually, his releases became fewer and farther between.

"Oh, Ernie K-Doe slipped up," Ernie admitted to Almost Slim. "But I have to believe that I'm going to the top. The only thing I know is singing and dancing. Ernie K-Doe is going back to the top. That's all there is to it."

SHEP & THE LIMELITES
DADDY'S HOME
(James Sheppard, William Miller)
Hull 740
No. 2 *May 29, 1961*

The Heartbeats (initially called the Hearts), Jim "Shep" Sheppard's first group, evolved from the friendship of four students at Woodrow Wilson High: second tenor Robbie Adams, first tenor Andrew Crump, bass Wally Roker, and baritone Vernon Seavers. It was 1953, and like many of the countless quartets working the New York City landscape, the Hearts would sing on street corners, in echoey school hallways, and in johns. One night, while the guys were rehearsing at Vern's house, someone tipped them off to some guy singing in St. Albans Park who was too good to be true. The group dashed to the park, where they found Shep. The five tried out a few numbers right there in the park. "Everyone blew their mind," is how Crump later described the occasion to *Big Town Review*'s Jeff Beckman.

By way of their neighbor, saxophonist Illinois Jacquet, Shep and the Hearts hooked up with Gotham/Network Records, an independent Philly label, and recorded "Tormented" b/w "After Everybody's Gone." Since a girl group had already beaten them out on the use of the "Hearts" name, they rechristened themselves the Heatbeat Quartet. The printer goofed, and the record label read: "The Heartbeats."

A frequent visitor to Vernon's neighborhood was Bea Casalin, a bookkeeper at Herald Records. Bea was preparing to leave Herald and start up her own label, Hull Records, so the Heartbeats did some recording for her in a Brooklyn basement: "Crazy for You," "Hurry Home Baby," "People Are Talking," and the classic "A Thousand Miles Away" (#53, 1957; #96, 1960). With the success of the latter platter, Bea sold the Heartbeats' contract to George Goldner's Rama label. Despite some truly great recordings and the broader audience assured by their new affiliation, only one other Heartbeats 45 made the charts—"Everybody's Somebody's Fool" (#78, 1957).

The Heartbeats began having internal problems. According to Roker, the group promised away too much of a percentage on their action; Shep was becoming intolerably bossy and drinking heavily, and musical differences arose. The end came in 1960, when Shep passed out at the microphone in Philadelphia. The Heartbeats disbanded. Andrew went on to become a psychologist. Rob is currently a teacher, Vernon is an electrical engineer, and Wally is working in the music business.

Two years later, Shep formed Shep & The Limelites with two former members of the Videos, Charles Baskerville (second tenor) and Clarence Bassett (first tenor). After two disks on Apt ("Too Young to Wed" and "I'm So Lonely"), Shep and the new crew found their slot in pop history with an answer record to the earlier Heartbeats number. "I felt, since 'A Thousand Miles Away' was a hit," Bassett told *Big Town Review*'s Mike Rascio, "why not write a song, relating to the guys coming home from the service, 'A Thousand Miles Away'? You know, 'Daddy's Home.'"

After the record peaked in the nation's Top 10, Shep became unmanageable. "[Shep] felt he didn't have to make the gigs anymore," Bassett recalled. "He was just too hard to get along with, so me and Charles gave it up."

The Limelites broke up, but the Hull label continued to issue 45s up through 1965. Five of these made the Hot 100 listings. Charles joined the Players; Clarence joined the post-prime Flamingos' line-up, and later sang with the Creative Funks.

Jim Sheppard was found dead in his car on the Long Island Expressway, on January 24, 1970—he had been beaten and robbed.

FARON YOUNG
HELLO WALLS
(Willie Nelson)
Capitol 4533
No. 12 *May 29, 1961*

Nora Jo Catlett of Clarksville, West Virginia, was 6 years old that day in September 1972. Nora stood in front of the stage at the Nathan Goff Armory, waiting for some country-music celebrity to add yet another autograph to her collection. Faron Young, self-proclaimed "Singing Sheriff," was performing onstage when he spotted little Nora. Several times Faron asked her to join him onstage, and several times Nora refused. Faron reportedly muttered a few choice words, walked offstage, grabbed little Nora, lifted her skirt, and spanked her repeatedly!

There ain't much old Faron Young ain't done. As one of the Top 10 all-time charting artists in country music, he's had dang near 100 singles on *Billboard*'s C & W charts; 42 have been placed in the Top 10. With more than 60 albums to his name, Young has sold roughly 30 million records.

"I've been around so long," Young told Joe Edwards of the Associated Press [in 1988], "that when I tell people I'm 56 years old, they laugh and say, 'And how many more?' The best thing is to say you're 75 and then they say, 'You look good for your age.'"

Faron (b. Feb. 25, 1932, Shreveport, LA) spent most of his early years on a dirt farm outside of Shreveport. He got his first guitar in grade school and spent hours figuring out how to play it, with a herd of cattle as his audience. At Fair Park High, he formed his first band to play school dances and local fairs. He attended Centenary College, until his growing popularity as a singer encouraged the young man to reevaluate his career goals.

While Faron was working as a shirt salesman for Sears, Roebuck & Co., some of his songs reached Webb Pierce. Webb didn't care much for the tunes, but took Young on the road to perform as a fill-in. Soon "The Singing Sheriff" was asked to join the "Louisiana Hayride" radio show (1951), to sign with Capitol Records, and, in 1952, to perform at the Grand Ole Opry. The country hits came almost immediately—a half-dozen crossed over on to the pop listings. Not one to till but one field, Faron even branched out into films, music publishing, and recording.

Faron has led a rough-and-tumble outlaw life-style. He shot up some light fixtures in a Nashville bar; been arrested repeatedly for reckless and drunken driving; indecent exposure—his wife divorced him on the grounds of physical abuse; and on one occasion, he allegedly threatened his wife and 16-year-old daughter with a loaded pistol, which he repeatedly fired into the kitchen ceiling.

As for that child-spanking episode, Young was arrested while leaving the county, on charges of assault and battery. The case has long been settled; Nora's family received $3,400 in damages.

In the '90s, Faron had retired from touring, suffered from emphysema, and, just before the end, undergone surgery for prostate cancer.

Faron Young died December 10, 1996, a day after he shot himself in the head at his home in Nashville. A suicide note said that he was depressed about his failing health.

Said wild honky-tonker Johnny Paycheck, to the *Chicago Sun Times*: "Faron gave me my first big job. He was big as life; enjoyed life. But he felt the industry had walked away from him after all that he had done."

CLEFTONES
HEART AND SOUL
(Frank Loesser, Hoagy Carmichael)
Gee 1064
No. 18 *June 19, 1961*

In 1955, lead singer Herbie Cox (b. May 6, 1939), bass Warren Corbin (b. 1939), first tenor Charlie James (b. 1940), baritone William McClain (b. 1938), and second tenor Berman Patterson (b. 1938) were students at Jamaica High School in Queens. They all started working for a student who was running for school president. "The idea of his campaign was to have singing slogans," Cox explained to *Bim Bam Boom*'s Bob Galgano. "The guys started singing in school and after the elections we just decided to stay together [calling ourselves the Silvertones]. After our smash success in the school election, we started doing gigs around the community."

David Ralnick, a schoolmate, approached the guys as a pseudo-manager, assuring them that his father and some friends had connections in the music business. Ralnick arranged recording auditions for the group. One of these was with George Goldner, the founder of legendary labels like End, Gee, Gone, Rama, and Roulette. Goldner rushed the Cleftones into the Master-Tone Studios. "You Baby You" (#78, 1956), their first offering, clicked, especially in local doo-wop circles. "Little Girl of Mine" (#57, 1956) did likewise. "Can't We Be Sweethearts," "String Around My Heart," and "Why Do You Do Me Like You Do," though quality outings, did not chart nationally.

"We went into a slump," Cox recalled. "[The company wanted] a production line of hits. They made no attempt to feed the artists new material. They made the next record almost exactly like your last record, [and] the public lost interest. We didn't realize what was happening."

Five years of persistence paid off, though. The Cleftones—now comprising Cox, Corbin, James, Gene Pear-

THE MARATHONS

son (baritone), and Pat Span (second tenor)—had their most successful recording effort in 1961 with a remake of Larry Clinton's 1936 chart-topping hit "Heart and Soul." Two subsequent remakes made *Billboard*'s Hot 100—Nat "King Cole's number one hit in 1946, "For Sentimental Reasons" (#60, 1961) and Paul Whiteman's number three hit in 1929, "Lover Come Back to Me" (#95, 1962)—but that was it for one of the era's finest vocal groups. Only a few more 45s were pressed.

After a final single issued on Ware in 1964 ("He's Forgotten You" b/w "Right From the Git Go"), the Cleftones lapsed into a period of inactivity. "We did stop performing for a couple of years, but we stayed together always as songwriters and maintained a very close relationship, personally," Cox told *Goldmine*'s Wayne Jones. "We've always been very good friends and still are."

Gene and Berman now work in law enforcement offices, Charlie works for IBM, and Herbie is a computer programmer.

MARATHONS
PEANUT BUTTER
(H. B. BARNUM, Cooper, Smith, Goldsmith)
Arvee 5027
No. 20 *June 19, 1961*

As the Vibrations, Don Bradley (bass), Carl Fisher (second tenor), Dave Govan (baritone), Jimmy Johnson (lead), and Richard Owens (first tenor) were hot stuff and in heavy demand in early 1961. Their delightful dance disk on the Checker label, "The Watusi," was a Top 40 item (#25). As THE JAYHAWKS, almost the identical line-up had made the nation's charts in 1956 with the original rendition of "Stranded in the Jungle."

Arranger/producer/tunesmith H. B. BARNUM (or possibly another hungry rep at the Hollywood-based Arvee label) offered the Vibrations some side line cash if they would moonlight their way through a sticky novelty number called "Peanut Butter." Neither Bar-

LITTLE CAESAR
& THE
ROMANS

num nor any of the vinyl pushers at Arvee expected "Butter" to spread its appealing way through thousands of American households, but it did.

However, since the Vibrations were under contract to Checker at the time, the success of "Peanut Butter" prompted the label to file a lawsuit against Arvee, and the Chess-Checker-Argo organization won the right to issue the single under its own logo. Arvee Records secured the rights to the "Marathons" name, and soon after released a highly-collectible LP and a follow-up single about an overly endowed vixen who should have known better than to wear a "Tight Sweater." (As a tasty tidbit of trivia, the "Sweater" songsmith was SONNY BONO.) This number did not sell well, and reportedly no Vibrations voices were present on this or any successive Marathon offerings.

LITTLE CAESAR & THE ROMANS
THOSE OLDIES BUT GOODIES
(REMIND ME OF YOU)
(Paul Politti, Nick Curinga)
Del-Fi 4158
No. 9 *June 26, 1961*

David Caesar Johnson (b. June 16, 1934, Chicago) began singing in church at a young age. After high school, "Little Caesar" joined the Air Force. While doing his time in Alaska, he formed the Northern Cru-

saders, a gospel group. Back in civilian life, Caesar sang with the Ivory-Tones.

In 1958, Caesar moved to Los Angeles and recorded with the Cubans—Early Harris, Johnny O'Simmons, Leroy Sanders, and a fellow remembered now only as Curtis. (Strangely enough, not one of these fellows was Cuban.) Johnson's next group, the Upfronts, featured Johnson, Harris, Sanders, and Bobby Relf —later claiming fame as half of Bob & Earl, creators of the original "Harlem Shuffle." The Upfronts cut two singles for Lummtone Records—"It Took Time" and "Too Late to Turn Around"—but neither one made any serious moves on the charts.

Caesar soon met a young tunesmith named Paul Politti, who had a tune in hand called "Those Oldies but Goodies." Bob Keene at Del-Fi/Donna Records wanted Johnson's group to do the number. Little Caesar & The Romans—Johnson, Harris, Sanders, ex-Cuban Johnny O'Simmons, and Carl Burnette—labored in the studio for six weeks. "Del-Fi didn't want the typical black sound," Johnson explained to *Goldmine*'s Rick Gagnon and Dave Gnerre. "They were looking for a white sound to reach the crossover audience."

"Oldies but Goodies" clicked, and is now considered an early rock classic. Little Caesar & The Romans toured with Jackie Wilson, Gary U.S. Bonds, and the Vibrations. "Here were five black dudes all dressed up in toga and sandals, wearing wreaths on their heads!" Caesar told *Goldmine*. "It was a good gimmick, but we

hated it at the time. Not only did we hate the togas, we hated the song, too!"

Weeks later, they were back in the studio to cut an answer to the Olympics' "(Baby) Hully Gully" called "Hully Gully Again" (#54, 1961). This would be their last charting. Their third disk, "Memories of Those Oldies but Goodies," looked like it was going to take off, but Johnson claims that the group and Keene were involved in a "financial dispute," and that Keene failed to adequately promote the record. Before Little Caesar *et al* disbanded, Del-Fi issued two more singles ("Ten Commandments of Love" and "Yoyo Yo Yoyo") and an LP entitled *Memories of Those Oldies but Goodies* (1962).

Caesar sang solo at various L.A. night spots throughout the '60s and early '70s, and reformed the Romans in 1975. For a six-month period in 1978, Rickie Lee Jones was even a member. "She could sing black, white, any style you wanted," Johnson recalled. The line-up has evolved considerably over the years, and as of 1988 included Johnson, Nathaniel Johnson (no relation), Laurie Ratcliff, and Larry Tate.

ARTHUR LYMAN
YELLOW BIRD
(Norman Luboff, Marilyn Keith, Alan Bergman)
Hi Fi 5024
No. 4 *July 24, 1961*

Arthur Lyman (vibraphone, piano, guitar, drums) was born in 1934 on the island of Kauai, Hawaii. After his father lost his eyesight in an accident, the family moved to the island of Oahu and settled in Makiki, a section of Honolulu. Following years of messing around with the marimbas and whatever instruments he could get his hands on, Lyman joined a downtown juice-bar jazz band. In the early '50s, Art worked with a group that would eventually become his primary competitor—the Martin Denny Trio.

Denny and his boys, with their bag of percussive toys and jungle calls, preceded Art in creating "exotic mood music." Denny would also precede his protege on the stateside charts: in 1959, a Martin Denny Trio instrumental, "Quiet Village," exploded, creating popular interest in the romantic and magical sounds of the rain forests.

By this time, Art—accompanied by Harold Chang (boobams, cocktail drums, ankle spurs, ass' jaw, bongo, conga, samba, xylophone), John Kramer (bass, bamboo flute, ukulele), Allen Soares (piano, celesta), plus nearly 50 instruments—was ready to roll. The group was holding down a gig in the Shell Bar at Henry J. Kaiser's Hawaiian Village Hotel when Lewis Amiel at Hi Fi Records approached them about recording some of their titillating tunes.

"Taboo," the title of Arthur Lyman's debut album and single (#55, 1959), clicked. While the Caribbean-flavored "Yellow Bird" was Lyman's sole excursion into the wilds of Top 40-land, Art and his sound explorers continued to perform and sell albums well into the '80s.

CHRIS KENNER
I LIKE IT LIKE THAT, PART 1
(Chris Kenner, Fats Domino)
Instant 3229
No. 2 *July 31, 1961*

According to Chris Kenner's booker, Percy Stovall, Kenner was not too professional a performer. "He couldn't sing, he couldn't dance, he dressed raggedy—he just stood there," Stovall told Almost Slim in *I Hear You Knockin.* "He would get so drunk he would forget the words to his song; they used to throw bottles at him." Despite problems of this sort, Kenner created some rock and roll perennials, cutting and canning some of the finest recorded examples of the New Orleans sound.

Chris was born Christmas Day in 1929, in Kenner, a suburb of New Orleans. He worked as a longshoreman and sang in a number of gospel groups, including the Harmonizing Four. In the '50s, Chris switched over to rhythm & blues. His first disk, "Grandma's House" b/w "Don't Pin That Charge on Me"—released on Baton Records in 1955—bombed. A few years later, the producer for Imperial Records, Dave Bartholomew, let Kenner have another crack at it. "Sick and Tired" (R&B: #13, 1957) turned out to be a big seller in New Orleans.

Kenner only made one other record with Imperial because label owner Lew Chudd didn't think he had much of a future. But the following year, Fats Domino covered "Sick and Tired" (#22, 1958) and sold a million copies. After a single for Ponchartrain ("You Can't Beat Uncle Sam" b/w "Don't Make No Noise") and one for Ron ("Life Is a Struggle" b/w "Rocket to the Moon"), Kenner had his moment.

"'Like It Like That' was a slang gimmick," Kenner told John Broven in *Rhythm & Blues in New Orleans.* "It was a good title and I tried to put a story to it. I worked on it a little while and got it together, you know. We didn't think it would be a hit record . . . I had it on tape at Allen Toussaint's house, and one day [Instant Records] Joe Banashak stopped by. He played him some old tapes, and that particular song Banashak liked." THE BOBBETTES, the Dave Clark Five, and Loggins & Messina liked it like that, too: each group charted with remade versions of Kenner's smash.

Chris received a Grammy nomination for "I Like It Like That," appeared on "American Bandstand," and toured with the Coasters, Gladys Knight & The Pips,

and Jackie Wilson. He continued to wax solid efforts like "Something You Got," a much-recorded disk, and in 1963 recorded his career crowner, the original version of "Land of a Thousand Dances" (# 77, 1963). Although most pop fans associate the tune with Wilson Pickett (#6, 1966), "Land" was also a hit for CANNIBAL & THE HEADHUNTERS (#30, 1965), Thee [sic] Midnighters (#67, 1965), THE ELECTRIC INDIAN (#95, 1969), and the J. Geils Band (#60, 1983).

As Kenner explained to Boven, the song ". . . actually came from a spiritual, 'Children Go Where I Send You,' and I turned it around. It was inspired by the dance tunes going around." Nowhere on the record does Kenner say anything about a "land of a thousand dances." But upon listening to the original master tape, *Goldmine*'s Almost Slim noted a 10-second introduction, snipped from the track at the last minute, that had Kenner calling out: "I'm gonna take you, baby/I'm gonna take you to a place/The name of the place is the Land of a Thousand Dances."

Chris's career came to a halt in 1968 when he was sent to the Louisiana State Penitentiary for statutory rape of a minor. On his release four years later, $20,000 in accumulated royalties was there for him. Almost Slim wrote that "in true Chris Kenner style, the money was exhausted within a month." Hep' Me Records issued two further singles, "You Can Run but You Can't Slip Away" and "We Belong Together."

Chris Kenner was found dead from heart failure in his rooming house on January 28, 1976—he was 46.

CURTIS LEE
PRETTY LITTLE ANGEL EYES
(Tommy Boyce, Curtis Lee)
Dunes 2007
No. 7 *August 7, 1961*

Curtis Lee (b. Oct. 28, 1941, Yuma, AZ) was a vegetable picker. Blue-eyed and blond, he sounded on his best days a mite like Bobby Rydell (on other days, he could sound more like a flat Fabian). In 1960, Ray Peterson, the teen crooner noted for that masterful piece of "death rock," "Tell Laura I Love Her," happened to catch one of Lee's sets at a Yuma nightspot. Curtis was hot that night, and Peterson liked what he heard enough to tip off Stan Shulman, his manager and with him owner of the Dunes label. Despite Lee's poor track record on the Warrior, Sabrina, and Hot labels, Shulman rushed the kid into the studios to cut "Special Love"; then a cover on KEN COPELANDS' "Pledge of Love." Like Lee's earlier sides, both disks nose-dived, as did another single, "D in Love."

In 1961, the production and songwriting team of Leiber & Stoller recommended to Shulman the dial-twiddling skills of an up-and-coming producer named Phil Spector. Up to this point in his career, Spector was known only for being a former member of THE TEDDY BEARS. Phil produced Ray Peterson's "Corinna, Corinne" for Dunes, then turned his attention to the hitless Curtis Lee.

Curtis had dashed off some tunes with an L.A. singer/songwriter named Tommy Boyce; the latter, later half of the successful duo of Boyce & Hart, creators of a numerous Monkees tunes. Spector listened to the rough outlines of the song and arranged to record "Pretty Little Angel Eyes" and some other numbers at the Mira Sound Studios, in the now defunct Hotel America on New York City's West 47th Street. Brought in to provide that catchy doo-woppin' background were the Halos, a recording act just an instant away from their own success with "Nag" (#25, 1961). "We came in and [Spector] gave us the lyric sheets and told us to do what we felt," Arthur Cryer of the Halos told Mark Ribowsky, author of *He's a Rebel*. "We stole all those 'bomps' and 'ha-ha-has' from the Spaniels and Cleftones."

"Angel Eyes" was a magnificent piece of rock and roll, as was the Spector-produced Lee and Boyce tune, "Under the Moon of Love" (#46, 1961). Soon afterward, Spector and Dunes Records parted company. Try as he did with C & W tunes, Del Shannon-like numbers, and fine material provided by Otis Blackwell and the team of Gary Geld and Peter Udell, Curtis Lee never again managed to get that "right" sound.

Curtis still lives in Yuma, and reportedly works in the construction business. His marginally successful follow-up tune, "Under the Moon of Love," went to the number one position in the U.K. when reworked by Showaddywaddy in 1977—more than a decade and a half later.

MAR-KEYS
LAST NIGHT
(Mar-Keys)
Satellite 107
No. 3 *August 7, 1961*

The Mar-Keys started out in 1957 as the Royal Spades. They all attended Messick High in Memphis, and all liked that funky black sound. Initially, the group consisted of Charles "Packy" Axton (tenor sax), Steve Cropper (guitar), Donald "Duck" Dunn (bass), Charlie Freeman (guitar), Terry Johnson (drums), and occasionally Jerry Lee "Smoochie" Smith (piano).

Estelle Axton and her brother, Jim Stewart—both bankers by day—had just set up a small make-shift recording studio in Brunswick, Tennessee. When the two ventured into the realm of record-making, they

THE MAR-KEYS

decided to name their label after those huge, thorny-looking golf balls that Cape Canaveral was blasting into space. Unfortunately, one immediate result of the success of Satellite, "Last Night" was the threat of legal action by a similarly-named California company, so Jim and Estelle quickly renamed their label "Stax Records" (Stewart + Axton).

The first few Satellite singles failed to lift off. Meanwhile, the Royal Spades—who in various configurations appeared on some of these early efforts—tightened up their chops playing sock hops, bars, and other venues, practicing every weekend in the primitive Stax studios in East Memphis. They backed up early Stax hit-makers like Rufus Thomas and his daughter Carla. But it was "Last Night," a deceptively simple, blues-riffin' instrumental worked up by those studio musicians, that established the trademark Stax sound—a sound that in its day was as unique, and nearly as influential, as Detroit's Motown sound.

"When we put it out, it exploded like nothing had ever exploded before," Estelle Axton told Peter Guralnick in *Sweet Soul Music*. "I'm telling you, I sold over 2,000 of it one by one over the counter [of Satellite's record store]. They certified a million on it eventually . . . I was so proud of it. I've never been so proud of a record in my life."

The tune reportedly evolved over a six-month period, and went through so many changes that the actual line-up of personnel present on the disk is in dispute. Guralnick has theorized that present for the session were probably Curtis Green (drums), Bob McGee (bass), "Smoochie" Smith, and a horn line-up comprising Packy, Gilbert Caples (tenor sax), and Floyd Newman (baritone sax). Yet it was the ever-evolving Royal Spades—Axton, Cropper, Dunn, Smith, and Johnson, plus Wayne Jackson (trumpet) and Don Nix (baritone sax)—who would tour and record as "The Mar-Keys."

Before the name was scrapped in the early '70s, several albums appeared, as did singles like "Morning After" (#60, 1961), "Pop-Eye Stroll" (#94, 1962), and "Philly Dog" (#89, 1966). Despite the act's success, internal frictions appeared almost immediately. Even by the end of 1960, Steve and Duck were off to join Booker T Jones and Al Jackson, Jr., in the label's second classic back-up unit, Booker T & The MGs. By 1965, Packy was fronting the Packers, a studio act that charted with a Mar-Keys knock-off called "Hole in the Wall" (#43, 1965). Nix went on to produce artists like Jeff Beck, Delaney & Bonnie, Albert King, Freddie King, and John Mayall.

Both Packy Axton and Charlie Freeman have since passed away.

ANN-MARGRET
I JUST DON'T UNDERSTAND
(Wilkin, Westberry)
RCA Victor 7894
No. 17 *September 11, 1961*

Considering her "sex kitten" image, one would have expected Ann-Margret on vinyl to come on like gangbusters, penetrate the charts, and leave American teens smoldering in her wake. RCA Victor certainly expected it, dishing her up as a curvaceous female Elvis who was going to make the label mucho dinero. On her early recordings, they garbed her in the dark soulfulness of Willie Dixon and Lincoln Chase, and subjected her to the teen vibrations of Gerry Goffin and Carole King.

Ann-Margret's lone Top 40 hit, "I Just Don't Understand," sported a mournful harmonica and possibly the earliest example of fuzz-tone guitar ever to be heard on the airwaves. It was a slinky, teasing number, and the follow-up, "It Do Me So Good" (#97, 1961), was no dog, either. Adolescent listeners could easily imagine little Annie on a zebra skin, gyrating and pleading,

ANN-MARGRET

120

"Close your lovin' arms around me, it do me so good." So much for a recording career: two fine rock and roll platters, and Ann-Margret was off to Hollywood, never to return to the charts again.

She was born Ann-Margret Olsson, the only child of an electrician, on April 28, 1941, in Valsjobyn, Sweden. At the age of five, she was brought to the U.S. and raised in various towns in Illinois. After a year attending Northwestern University and a well-noted spot on Ted Mack's "Amateur Hour," Olsson joined a combo and began making appearances at nightclubs.

In 1961, at the peak of her chart success, Ann was making her screen debut as Bette Davis' daughter in Frank Capra's *A Pocketful of Miracles* (1961). Following in rapid succession were *Bye, Bye Birdie* (1963) with Dick Van Dyke and Bobby Rydell, the Elvis flick *Viva Las Vegas* (1964), and the sleazy but sensational *Kitten With a Whip* (1964). She was nominated for an Oscar for both *Carnal Knowledge (1971)* with Art Garfunkel and Jack Nicholson and rock-extravaganza *Tommy* (1975).

She still sizzles, sings, dances, and makes movies such as *Middle-Aged Crazy* (1979) and *52 Pick-up* (1986)—she just doesn't do it on vinyl anymore.

DREAMLOVERS
WHEN WE GET MARRIED
(Don Hogan)
Heritage 102
No. 10 *September 18, 1961*

William "Pete" Johnson (lead), Tommy Ricks (first, second tenor, tenor lead), Cleveland Hammock, Jr. (second tenor), Conrad "Clifton" Dunn (baritone, lead) and brother James Ray Dunn (bass) had been holding tight a common dream since their first meeting on the streets of north Philadelphia in 1956. As the Romances they hung out on the sidewalks doo-woppin', practicing in the gym at Northeast High, and working occasional gigs. They were getting good and getting known. Before it happened though, it ended.

"Will and I had been at this park," said James Ray Dunn, in an exclusive interview. "We were just kids. Will was killed there. It was over a female. He was talking with this girl and her guy didn't like it. He was jealous and called him outside. I happened to be standing out there around the corner. They came outside, and he shot Will, five times. He died right there, bled to death. . . . The guy got six years in jail."

Morris Gardner (lead) was brought in. Out of respect, their name was changed. They were now the Dreamlovers, a name they picked off a Bobby Darin record. In 1960, perceptive ears at Len/V-Tone—a Philly-based company soon to be red hot with Bobby

Peterson discs and Bobby Parker's "Watch Your Step"—heard, liked, and gave the guys a triple shot at success with the issuances of "For the First Time," "Annabelle Lee" and shortly thereafter "May I Kiss the Bride."

"Buddy Caldwell was the owner," said Dunn. "He was a businessman here in Philly; owned an upholstering shop on Ridge Avenue. It was my brother's girlfriend who told us he had a record company. We just went down there with our guitarist [Donald Hogan] to see what it was about."

Don Hogan's involvement with the group has been clouded. "Ah, he was the only instrumentalist, still is, sometimes," said Dunn. "He'd write the songs. We'd write the arrangements. Actually, I guess, Donny was a member of the Dreamlovers. He sang lead on 'Annabelle Lee' and did the duet with my brother on 'For the First Time.' Don's had problems, but he still writes great songs for us."

None of the sought-after sides for Caldwell's little labels sold well, but neighboring Cameo/Parkway Records hired the Dreamlovers to provide back-up for a Chubby Checker recording session that would culminate in the creation of one of the biggest-selling singles in rock 'n' roll history.

"We had submitted a tape to Cameo. They liked what they heard and called us up. We went down to the label to record, as a group, or so we thought. But, they were more interested in dance-type tunes. We were more than that, but that was not what was selling. They weren't interested in ballads. What they had called us in to do was back-ups. We're the back-up on Chubby Checker's 'The Twist' and all of his hit recordings: 'The Pony,' 'The Continental,' all that. That was us. We backed Dee Dee Sharp, Lee Andrews, the Dovells, all of them. I'm the bass on their 'Bristol Twistin' Annie.' We didn't get rich, though," Dunn said. "You know, at that time we got a salary. You'd do so much per side and you'd get a check."

No need noting the dance discs gyrated and garnered money and a near-immortal status for Checker and the others. The Dreamlovers, meanwhile, wearied of the oohs and ahs, their nonentity status, and the lack of billing and the bread.

Nearby, Jerry Ross and Murry Wecht were forming Heritage Records and the offer was soon extended to the Dreamlovers to stand front and center again. "They had a few groups signed like the Strangers. We just wondered why no one was recording us." The label's first release, "When We Get Married," a Don Hogan composition, was the group's first moment in the bright sun. With a quiet simple styling that reminded aging listeners of SHEP & THE LIMELITES, "When We Get Married" was a delight. So were the follow-ups —"Welcome Home" and their remake of the Collegians' "Zoom, Zoom, Zoom"—but neither of these sold well.

The Dreamlovers charted with their next one, "If I Should Lose You," for End Records, but this was to be their last *Billboard* Hot 100 appearance. Fine and increasingly rare doo-wop recordings were made for Swan, Cameo, and even the big-time concerns—Columbia, Mercury, and Warner Brothers—but the doo-wop genre's time had passed. Younger ears wanted slick soul, not ghetto-street harmony sounds. The fellows tried their best to meet the needs of the moment with numbers like "The Bad Times Make the Good," but the public wasn't buying it.

Morris left the group in 1963. In 1973, after a one-off as "A Brother's Guiding Light" for Mercury, the Dreamlovers shelved the act.

"We got back together in 1980. So, it's been 17 straight years at reestablishing ourselves. But, we're still the same original group. There's Cleveland, Tom, my brother, myself, and Don Hogan, who's always got new songs when we ask him. We just celebrated our 41st year this last June 9th [1997]."

JARMELS
A LITTLE BIT OF SOAP
(Bert Burns)
Laurie 3098
No. 12 *September 18, 1961*

Bert Burns (a.k.a. Bert Russell, Russell Byrd) died of a heart attack years before he hit 40 and light years before he would run out of creative energy. He wrote "Twist and Shout," the Rolling Stones' "Everybody Needs Somebody to Love," and JANIS JOPLIN's "Piece of My Heart;" produced the Drifters, Lulu, the McCoys, Van Morrison, Neil Diamond; and headed Bang and Shout Records. Writing "A Little Bit of Soap," Bert created two One-Hit Wonders—the Jarmels and NIGEL OLSSON—and revived the career of a third, THE EXCITERS.

The Jarmels—lead vocalist Paul Burnett (b. 1942), tenor Earl Christiansen (b. 1940), bass Tommy Eldridge (b. 1941), baritone Ray Smith (b. 1941; no relation to the rockabilly wonder RAY SMITH), and tenor Nathaniel

Ruff (b. 1939) were all from Richmond, Virginia, and had been crossing paths for years. They attended the same church; they sang in the same glee club in school. They eventually became good friends, and in the late '50s decided to pull themselves together into a legitimate singing group. By 1960, they had traveled to New York City where they lifted the group name from a street sign in Harlem.

Jim Gribble, manager of the Passions and THE MYSTICS, happened on to the group, liked their material, and pointed them toward Bob and Gene Schwartz at Laurie Records. Although Laurie was well known as a doo-wop label, their artists were usually Italian (e.g. the Belmonts, the Del Satins), not black. Still, six singles in all were issued, all of them with a smooth racially integrated feel to them.

The Jarmels' debut disk, "Little Lonely One," was also a first 45 for Bobby Vinton; neither charting. The guys hit pay dirt with the Bert Russell (a.k.a. Bert Burns) tune, "A Little Bit of Soap." It cracked the Top 10, but nothing else the fellows ever waxed even brushed the Hot 100. "Soap" was loaded with magic, and over the years, The Exciters, Garnet Mimms, Paul Davis, Nigel Olsson, and Showaddywaddy all charted with their renditions of the Jarmels' original; the latter went Top Five in Great Britain in 1978.

When their recording contract with Laurie Records ended in 1963, the Jarmels returned to Virginia and apparently disbanded—for awhile. Reports are that Major Harris, later of the Delfonics and still later a suc-

cessful soul solo, was a practicing member of the group. No further records were ever released under the Jarmels name, though, in 1990 Burnett and Eldridge with new members—Carlton Hatch and Jimmy Smith—returned to making occasional appearances.

BARRY MANN
WHO PUT THE BOMP
(IN THE BOMP, BOMP, BOMP)
(Barry Mann, Gerry Goffin)
ABC-Paramount 10237
No. 7 September 25, 1961

Barry Mann's name is usually whispered with a reverence accorded very few. To mention Mann and not Cynthia Weil, his wife and songwriting partner of nearly 30 years, is next to impossible. Together, Mann and Weil composed some of the greatest rock and roll hits of all time. The list is long, and most are commonly known to even casual pop fans: "Blame It on the Bossa Nova," "Here You Come Again," "I Love How You Love Me," "Kicks," "Looking Through the Eyes of Love," "On Broadway," "Sometimes When We Touch," "(You're My) Soul and Inspiration," "We Gotta Get Out of This Place," "You've Lost That Lovin' Feelin'," and MAX FROST & THE TROOPERS' "Shapes of Things to Come."

He was born Barry Iberman, in Brooklyn, on February 9, 1939. In grammar school, Barry was introduced to a ukulele. He learned a few chords, but only a few—to this day, Barry maintains that he can barely read or write music. By age 12, Barry was pickin' and peckin' his way through pop songs that he would hear on the radio. With time and practice, he began writing his own little tunes.

After a year of architectural studies at Pratt Institute, Mann went to work for George Paxton's music-publishing firm; Paxton headed Coed Records, responsible for numerous hits for the Crests, Duprees, and Adam Wade. The Diamonds right off had a hit with Barry's "She Say (Oom, Dooby, Doom)," Steve Lawrence scored with "Footsteps," and Barry moved on to Aldon Music, headed by Al Nevins and Don Kirshner; the latter soon to find great fame with psuedo-groups, the Archies and Monkees.

"I was with them almost a year when I went to play a song for Teddy Randazzo [a big ballad singer and later producer of hits for Little Anthony & The Imperials], and I saw this girl who was writing with Teddy," Mann recalled to Joe Smith in *Off the Record*. "I presumed she was his girlfriend." She wasn't; it was Cynthia Weil, an aspiring actress/dancer/singer/songwriter. Mann and Weil married in 1961, and became an up-and-coming songwriting team. That year, Kirshner convinced Barry to record some of his own songs. An unforgettable nov-

elty record, "Who Put the Bomp" was Barry's third try. "I think a lot of people didn't get it," Mann told *Goldmine*'s Jeff Tamarkin. "They bought it because they dug the groove it was a piece of the times, a put-on of all the doo-wop records."

Barry has charted marginally a few times over the years, most recently with "The Princess and the Punk" (#78, 1976). His releases are sporadic, and range wildly in quality. If you get the offer, give a listen to his "Young Electric Psychedelic Hippy Flippy."

As composers, Barry Mann and his wife continued, creating in the late '60s and '70s, Dan Hill's "Sometimes When We Touch," Jay & The American's "Walking in the Rain," and B. J. Thomas' "I Just Can't Help Believing."

In 1987, Barry and Cynthia won the "Best Song of the Year" Grammy for "Somewhere Out There," featured in the animated film *An American Tail* (1986).

JOSE JIMENEZ
THE ASTRONAUT (PARTS 1 & 2)
(Bill "Jose Jimenez" Dana)
Kapp 409
No. 19 *October 2, 1961*

Jose was born in the fertile mind of Bill Dana in the cold winter of 1959. In a fit of creativity, Dana, the head writer for TVs "The Steve Allen Show," dreamed up this good-hearted Hispanic character who was to be the teacher in a one-off sketch involving a school for department-store Santas. The skit was so well received that "Jose" became a regular on Allen's show. Nightclub appearances, five fine-selling comedy albums, a hit single, and a spin-off TV turkey whizzed by like a fast-moving freight train.

Bill was born William Szathmary on October 5, 1924, in Quincy, Massachusetts. He graduated from Emerson College in 1950, and for the next few years performed as a stand-up comic in local watering holes and houses of laughter. Bill appeared in bit roles on TV programs with Imogene Coco and Martha Raye, and began writing gags for Don Adams. From 1956 to 1960, Dana was a behind-the-scenes writer for Steve Allen. After the Jose Jimenez character took on a life of its own, Bill cut some sides as Jose for the Kapp label. "The Astronaut," an "interview" with Jose, would be Dana's only Top 40 single, but all five of Jose's LPs sold well enough to place on *Billboard*'s top pop albums chart.

In the early '60s, Jose made regular appearances on "The Danny Thomas Show," and, for a season and a half, Bill's character had his own program on NBC. But with the rise of ethnic sensitivities in the late '60s, pressures were placed on Dana to put a stop to his characterization; some viewers looked on Jose's naivete as a racial put-down. In 1970, Dana "murdered" Jose, and a mock funeral was held in Los Angeles.

While lying low during much of the '70s, Bill returned to public view in the short-lived TV series "No Soap, Radio" (1982) and "Zorro and Son" (1983).

BOB MOORE
MEXICO
(Boudleaux Bryant)
Monument 446
No. 7 *October 2, 1961*

Bob Moore was born in the heart of country and western music, in Nashville, Tennessee, on November 30, 1932. As if answering a calling from the holy soil itself, Bob took to playing the bass fiddle, and after years of practice found himself laying down that bass foundation on countless C & W tours and recordings. As an accompanist, Bob toured the land with a young and wild Elvis Presley, country folkie Red Foley, and teen queens Connie Francis and Brenda Lee.

When not on the road, Bob jammed with Chet Atkins at the Carousel Club, becoming a lynchpin in what proved a successful informal grouping of sidemen—that included Floyd Cramer, Buddy Harman and BOOTS RANDOLPH—that repeatedly supplied the sounds for RCA and what was to become the "Nashville Sound."

In 1959, Monument Records main man Fred Foster noticed Moore's dual ability to take charge in the studio yet fit in well with almost any sound, and hired him to be the label's music director. Roy Orbison had just joined the Monument label, and it was Bob who created the plush and throbbing orchestral ambience of every one of those "Big 0" soap operettas. Foster liked what he heard, and decided to cut Moore loose to see what the kid could do as a solo act.

After a mildly successful initial release, "(Theme From) 'My Three Sons,'" Moore recorded "Mexico," an instrumental created by the most-noted Boudleaux Bryant ("All I Have to Do Is Dream," "Bird Dog," "Devoted to You," "Let's Think About Living," "Wake Up Little Susie". . .). In sound, Moore's lone Top 40 hit anticipated by a full year the style that would keep Herb Alpert's Tijuana Brass all over the charts for many years to come.

Throughout the remainder of the decade, Moore, on Monument and later Hickory, tried to keep up his charting momentum, with little success. An album entitled *Mexico and Other Great Hits* did sell well, but only on the strength of his big pop moment.

For a session man who played with rock an rollers like Elvis and Jerry Lee Lewis, Bob had a brassy yet tame sound on his solo sides. But listen to Jerry Lee Lewis' "What Did I Say?"—the pounding bass on that number reveals another, more primal side of Bob Moore. This is the Bob Moore found on records by CARL PERKINS, J. J. CALE, Moby Grape, Pearls Before Swine, Harvey Mandel, Kenny Rogers, Don McLean, and post-Righteous-Brothers' Bill Medley. Bob Dylan also made use of Moore's talents on the *Dylan* (1970) and *Self-Portrait* (1973) albums.

Somewhere in the '80s, Bob Moore quietly and unceremoniously retired from making public music.

TROY SHONDELL
THIS TIME
(Chip Moman)
Liberty 55353
No. 6 *October 23, 1961*

"I'm grateful for that one-hit," said Troy Shondell, in an exclusive interview, "but it's a shame that it had to be 'This Time,' 'cause I'm a high energy guy that likes to rock and that song gave people—for all time—the wrong impression about me."

Troy Shondell was born Gary Shelton, on May 14, 1944, in Fort Wayne, Indiana. For years, he worked hard, learning how to play the guitar, organ, drums, sax, and trumpet. In 1957, he was discovered by a manager to big band man Ted Weems. "Herb Gronower spotted me at this high school talent show," said Troy. "The girls reacted the way you'd want them to if you were looking for a deal. Anyway, he was impressed and

talked my parents into putting up the money to make a recording session in Chicago. Mercury Records put out 'My Hero,' from the operetta "Chocolate Soldier," but it got banned about everywhere cause of the lyrics, 'Come, come, I love you only.'"

Troy, under his God-given name, next recorded a wild Jerry Lee Lewis-like "Kissin' at the Drive-in," that proved a major Midwestern hit. Despite the success, a change of producer brought an end to his stay with the label. Troy left with Chuck Stevens to record with Alpine.

"My dad died. He was a big band leader and the one who mainly encouraged me. After he passed away, I thought it was all over. I went back to Fort Wayne to operate my parents' instrument repair business. A friend told me, 'You're too good. You ought to cut another record. I'll put the money up if you'll do it.' I took it around to every label in Chicago and was turned down by everyone. I told him, 'I'm sorry I've wasted your money.' He said, 'We'll just start our own company.'"

The song was Chip Moman's tear-jerking rockaballad, "This Time." (Moman was later to write "Luckenbach, Texas" and "Hey Won't You Play Another Somebody's Done Something Wrong Song".) The company became Gold Crest. And the name became "Troy Shondell." "I didn't want to be associated with all the tracks that Mercury still hadn't released on me so I changed Shelton to Shondell, but there was already a Chantells; and Troy Donahue was a popular actor. I figured I'd might as well go with the best."

When the disk was played on the radio, the local response was such that Liberty Records immediately picked up Troy's swamp-rock classic and released it nationally. Largely due to the support given the disk by Jim Lounsbury on his "Record Hop," "This Time" became a Midwestern monster and turntable perennial.

In the fall, Shondell entered the Valparaiso University as a music major. For years thereafter, he struggled to keep a music career going. Both sides of his follow-up, "Tears From an Angel" (#77, 1962) b/w "Island in the Sky" (#92), charted; ironically, these tunes seem rather lame in comparison to some of his later, but less successful 45s. Phil Spector produced "Na-Ne-No," a dynamite disk that featured a wall of echoey voices and the squeak of a doggy toy, but record-buyers passed on it. "That was cut back in the days when if something went wrong you had to do the whole thing over; and Phil used like take number 52," said Troy. "It took from 12-noon to 12-midnight to please him. Phil's kind of a strange guy. I'd never met him but a few hours before the session. And he said, 'Now take these songs and see what you think.' When he was ready, he'd never say what he didn't like just, 'Let's do this again.' It wasn't like he knew what he wanted; but that you'd have to find out what he wanted."

Troy's "Some People Never Learn" and "Little Miss Tease," for Everest, the latter a shaky Elvis knockoff, were likewise solid but overlooked efforts.

In the late '60s, Shondell moved to Nashville and made some country disks for TRX and Bright Star; notably, J. J. CALE's "Head Man." He became a songwriter for the publishing house of Acuff-Rose, and worked for ASCAP in the '70s. He never stopped recording, though: the Shondell name; in various spellings, appeared on, at the least, 14 different record labels.

Troy Shondell went to the top only once, but his impact on aspiring rockers was apparently significant. A young Detroit guitarist named Tommy James named his "Hanky Panky" group the Shondells; Jim Peterik, later of THE IDES OF MARCH, did the same with his first Chicago group; and when ROD BERNARD and rockabilly legend Warren Storm teamed up to record for the La Louisianne label, they called themselves the Shondells.

Since 1976, Troy Shondell has lived in Nashville, where he runs AVM Starmakers, a performance video and talent development company. His third album, *Vintage Gold*, was issued in 1996.

BOBBY EDWARDS
YOU'RE THE REASON
(Bobby Edwards, Mildred Imes, Fred Henley, Terry Fell)
Crest 1075
No. 11 *November 20, 1961*

Not much is known about Robert Moncrief (b. Anniston, AL). Reportedly, he was a member of the Four Young Men, a group of Alabamans with teen tunes like "You've Been Torturing Me" and "Sweetheart of Senior High." Between 1961 and 1963, the Four Young Men had some sides issued in rapid succession on Dore, Crest, and Delta. Bobby Edwards revived Tex Ritter's "Jealous Heart" in 1959 on Bluebonnet; the same record was reissued on the Manco label in 1962.

Bobby's "You're the Reason," with the Four Young Men in accompaniment, appeared in the fall of 1961. It was a choppy but melodically appealing country moaner. Cover versions that year by Joe South and HANK LOCKLIN shaved some of the chart momentum off Bobby's biggie, but his version still made the Top 10 on the C & W charts. Capitol Records invited the boy over to their stable, and dished up an incredibly derivative follow-up, "What's the Reason" (#71, 1962)—Bob's last pop placement.

Though Edwards continued recording throughout the late '60s, country-music listeners probably last noted his existence in 1963 with "Don't Pretend."

BARBARA GEORGE
I KNOW (YOU DON'T LOVE ME NO MORE)
(Barbara George)
A.F.O. 302
No. 3 *January 27, 1962*

Barbara (b. Aug. 16, 1942, New Orleans) was 19 when she was discovered by New Orleans recording artist JESSIE HILL of "Ooh Poo Pah Doo" (#28, 1960) fame. When Hill spotted her talent, Barbara had only been working the street scene for a few months; her musical background was the church. At an audition for Harold Battiste, head of A.F.O. (All For One) Records, Barb sang "I Know (You Don't Love Me No More)," a tune she had penned based on "Just a Closer Walk With Thee." Reportedly, Battiste was not too impressed with George's abilities, nor with the song. But Battiste badly needed material for his new label, so he reluctantly gave the go-ahead to record "I Know." Once it became apparent that George's catchy groove could become a national monster, Juggy Murray at Sue Records picked up the platter's distribution.

An album and only one further single by George appeared on the All For One label. Money, you see, had entered the picture. As Battiste told John Broven in *Rhythm & Blues in New Orleans*, Juggy Murray lured her to the Sue label with a fancy car and new clothes— and although Battiste urged Barbara to resist these temptations, "fatherly advice is no good when you're fighting Cadillacs and money." Barbara signed with Sue Records and cut a few more singles, but nothing sold very well. Shortly after the label switch, George, abandoned her singing career to pursue other activities.

In 1980, Barb made a brief come back attempt with a few 45s issued on the Hep' Me label. She currently resides in Raceland, Louisiana.

BRUCE CHANNEL
HEY! BABY
(Bruce Channel, Margaret Cobb)
Smash 1731
No. 1, *March 10, 1962*

Deep into the late '60s, Bruce managed to tour here and abroad on the strength of "Hey! Baby." Flashing a healthy sense of humor, Channel would often open for the Beach Boys or other big-time acts with the wisecrack, "And now, I'd like to do a medley of my hit."

Channel was born in Jacksonville, Texas, on November 28, 1940. Most of his youth was spent in nearby Grapevine, where his parents worked in a tomato-packing warehouse. Bruce's brothers played guitar; his father played the harmonica. A cousin showed him how to form a few guitar chords, and by his 15th year,

Channel had his own country band. They played youth centers, local bars, and, barns, even working the legendary "Louisiana Hayride's" radio show for six months.

"I wrote 'Hey! Baby' about 1959, with a good friend, Margaret Cobb," Channel recalled to Frank McNutty in *We Wanna Boogie*. "I had played the song in the clubs, although at the time [of the recording] I put more of an R & B feel to it. Somehow over the years, the song evolved." Originally taped in Fort Worth as a demo for producer/promoter Major Bill Smith, "Hey! Baby" featured DELBERT MCCLINTON on harmonica. Delbert's wailing accompaniment came from his band's local back-up work behind blues artists like Jimmy Reed.

Several more Channel singles charted—"Number One Man" (#52, 1962), "Come on Baby" (#98, 1962), "Going Back to Louisiana" (#89, 1964), and "Mr. Bus Driver" (#90, 1967)—and Bruce did manage to make a good living with his music for a few years. A non-charting stateside number, "Keep on," returned Bruce to Britain's Top 20 in 1968. But he never could locate that next big clicker.

Channel did, however, indirectly influence the next generation of rock and rollers when he toured England late in 1962 with McClinton. While Bruce was handling an interview, his harmonica man was backstage at the Castle in New Brighton, near Liverpool. McClinton got to talking with John Lennon, one-quarter of the opening act, the then-little-known Beatles. John was impressed with Delbert's harmonica style, and asked him if he'd show him how he did that "Hey! Baby" solo. A year later, John would play a similar harmonica break on the Fab Four's "Love Me Do."

For the time being, Bruce Channel is off the road. In the late '70s, he worked in Nashville as a staff songwriter with a music publisher. Sporadic recordings continued into the mid-'80s.

"It amazes me," Channel remarked to *Goldmine*. "People still come up to me and say 'I was in Pango-Pango or wherever and heard "Hey! Baby" And it amazes me that people would hear that record after so long. It's like the song never really died. It just keeps coming back."

named MR. ACKER BILK snoozed us with "Stranger on the Shore" and Kenny Ball and his band of trad-jazzmen gave us a reworking of a Russian tune originally called "Padmeskoveeye Vietchera."

To radio listeners in the U.S., this Russian number, with a banjo and horns all over it, seemed to come from out of, like, nowhere. In Kenny's merry ole England, jazz was then becoming immensely popular. Fans were split between the modernists, who were attuned to stateside hard bop and "cool jazz," and the traditionalists, who emulated the sounds of Dixieland and King Oliver. Ball and his boys represented the latter approach. Before British youth fell under the sway of American blues, R & B, and free-form jazz, Ball's tradmen would rack up 14 hit singles on the British pop charts.

Kenneth Daniel Ball was born May 22, 1931, in Ilford, Essex. After working at an advertising agency, and a brief stint as a salesman, Ball decided on a career as a professional musician. Before forming his own unit in late 1958, Kenny blew trumpet and harmonica with bands led by Sid Phillips, Eric Delaney, and Terry Lightfoot. The "King of the Skiffle," Lonnie Donegan, chanced on Ball's band in 1961 and set up an audition for the guys with Pye Records. While their first release, "Teddy Bear's Picnic," stiffed, the band's next 14 records all charted.

For a few years, Britain was a ga-ga about the tradjazz of Ball and his two main competitors, CHRIS BARBER'S JAZZ BAND and Mr. Acker Bilk. In the U.S., only Ball's fourth single, "Midnight in Moscow," broke the Top 40 barrier. Kenny had a way with dressing up nearly any tune in that New Orleans idiom, yet while his instrumental versions of "March of the Siamese Children" and "The Green Leaves of Summer" did make the Hot 100, American pop fans were, for the most part, unaccustomed to the sounds of trad-jazz—their attention was focused elsewhere.

New Orleans offered Kenny Ball honorary citizenship in 1963, and in so accepting, Kenny became the first British jazzman so honored. When last noted, Kenny and some configuration of his Jazzmen were still playing on British TV, radio, and in the clubs.

KENNY BALL & HIS JAZZMEN
MIDNIGHT IN MOSCOW
(Kenny Ball, Jan Burgers)
Kapp 442
No. 2 *March 17, 1962*

Nineteen sixty-two was the year a batch of non-rock-and-roll instrumentals paraded themselves all over the Top 40. Herb Alpert and his Tijuana Brass let loose with their mournful tribute to a "Lonely Bull," a clarinetist

BILLY JOE & THE CHECKMATES
PERCOLATOR (TWIST)
(Lou Bideu, ERNIE FREEMAN)
Dore 620
No. 10 *March 17, 1962*

The story of Billy Joe and his "group" is a mere blush in the grander tale of Lou Bedell.

He was born Louis Bideu, March 21, 1919, in El Paso, Texas. Lou attended Santa Barbara State College

for four years, then worked as a comedian in nightclubs and TV. For a time in 1954, settling into the Lew Bedell moniker, he fronted "The Lew Bedell Show" on WOR-TV in New York. The following year, he was on the West Coast working first for a publisher, Meadowlark Music, and then with cousin Herb Newman, forming the first of his L.A.-based record labels, Era.

Within months, Louis and Herb had acquired the label-free Gogi Grant and secured the pinnacle of her hits with "Suddenly There's a Valley" and the chart-topping "Wayward Wind." Over the next 3 years, before Herb's departure, the team scored repeatedly with One-Hit Wonders: RUSSELL ARMS' "Cinco Robles," Art & Doty Todd's "Chanson D'Amour," TONY & JOE's "Freeze."

"Herb's wife was mixing in our business," said Bedell in an article he wrote for *Goldmine* with Jim Dawson. "I wouldn't let my wife . . . so, I sure as hell wasn't gonna leave Herb's wife. Also, I was getting into rock'n'roll. Herb didn't want to foul up the label with rock'n'roll . . . So, we split up.

"About one out of every nine of our releases made the Top 50, thanks to [our national promotions man] George Jay. We were known as the Wonder Boys of Vine Street.

"Out of respect for Herb's father, who had raised me, I let Herb keep Era Records, and I went off and formed my own label, Dore Records, named for my son."

Era continued on with chartings by Donnie Brooks, the Castells and further One-Hit acts: JEWEL AKENS, DORSEY BURNETTE, KETTY LESTER.

Within months of forming Dore, again Lou had a lulu of a hit with THE TEDDY BEARS' "To Know Him Is to Love Him." But it was instrumentals—particularly those by Billy Joe & The Checkmates—that made Dore a notable collectors' item.

"I was Billy Joe, Billy Joe Hunter," said Bedell. "Now, for three years Ernie [FREEMAN, composer/keyboardist/producer] and I had this idea for a percolator song. One morning we had an earthquake and it woke Ernie up to this idea on just how to get this coffee sound on record. We went into Conway Recorders on Highland Avenue. The Baha Marimba Band was popular then, and Ernie figured he'd play the song on a marimba with chamois cloths on the mallets. Red Callender played stand-up bass; Rene Hall played guitar. The song wasn't really a twist, but the Twist was really big at the time, so we appended the word in parentheses to grab part of the market. When it became a hit, Joe Sarenceno [half of Tony & Joe] asked to go out on the road as B. J. Hunter. What the heck, I still get checks for that song."

For the next half-decade, "Billy Joe" and a roomful of sessioneers tried to reproduce the appealing inno-cence of that debut disk, with the rhythmic pulsations of a perky java pot. A string of singles, 14 in number, were insistently issued: "Rocky's Theme," "One More Cup," "The Chester Drag," "Claire de Looney," and "Voyage to the Bottom of the Sea"—all sold poorly.

Bedell never lost a beat and continued to chart with Ronnie Height's "Come Softly to Me," DEANE HAWLEY's "Look for a Star," the Superbs, the Whispers and Jan & Dean. In the '70s, tiring of the changing rock world, Lou turned to recording successful comedy albums by Hudson & Landry.

Still active in '95, Lou Bedell issued two CDs of Dore classics.

CORSAIRS
SMOKY PLACES
(Abner Spector)
Tuff 1808
No.12 *March 17, 1962*

The Corsairs were three brothers and a cousin from La Grange, North Carolina, that grew up and attended the same schools together. They were Jay "Bird" (b. July 14, 1942), James "Little Skeet" (b. Dec. 1, 1940), and Mose "King Moe" Uzzell (b. Sept. 13, 1939), plus cousin George Wooten (b. Jan. 16, 1940). They started singing together as members of the school glee club, performing at local gatherings and talent shows. Calling themselves the Gleems, they eventually made tracks to Newark, New Jersey, to audition for the record companies in and around the New York area.

One night early in 1961, the Gleems were playing in a smoky Newark nightclub. Abner Spector, a producer and big wheel at Tuff Records, was in the audience. Abner liked what he heard, and told the group that he wanted to record them as the Corsairs. The rest, as they say, is history—but a very sketchy history.

"Smoky Places," the Corsairs' second release, was a top-of-the-line neo-doo-wop goodie. Quality vocal-group numbers like this one were becoming increasingly scarce on the airwaves. (True, there were groups like the CLASSICS and the EARLS, but their days on the radio—and the charts—were numbered.) The Corsairs' follow-up, "I'll Take You Home," hit number 68 in 1962, and the singles kept rolling out: "Stormy," "Dancing Shadows," "On the Spanish Side," and "At the Stroke of Midnight." But regardless of who was credited on the disk as lead singer—"King Moe," Jay "Bird," or "Little Skeet"—not one of these well-arranged platters charted.

With time, the group's members did some weeding and seeding. Larry McNeil was added in 1965, the last year the group was known to exist. Just what happened to the Corsairs after this point is not known.

DON & JUAN

DON & JUAN
WHAT'S YOUR NAME
(Claude "Juan" Johnson)
Big Top 3079
No. 7 *March 17, 1962*

Claude Johnson, Alexander "Buddy" Faison, Bill Gains, Roy Hammond, and Fred Jones were boardwalk buddies who got together in Long Beach, Long Island, in 1956. If there was justice in the world these guys cut what should have been a monster hit. It was the spring of 1959, they were the Genies, and "Who's That Knocking," a fine, fine number that promised to be their proverbial master moment in the sun, inexplicably stalled at the number 71 slot on *Billboard*'s Hot 100. Shad Records shed them like a hound with fleas—with no follow-up 45, though subsequent outings for Hollywood Records and Warwick were likewise unsuccessful.

Three years later, Genie lead vocalist Claude and Roland Trone were working as house painters in an apartment building, singing as they slapped paint. A tenant with a refined ear told a friend, agent Peter Paul, about the duo, and once again, it looked like Claude Johnson would have another shot at a musical career. Paul piqued Big Top Records' owners Gene and Julian Aberbach, who also ran Hill and Range Publishing and a subsidiary label, Dunes. One of the earliest tunes laid out in the recording studio was this number Claude had been developing.

"It was common back then," Claude Johnson told *Chicago Sun-Times* writer Dave Hoekstra, "for everybody to ask 'What's your name?' And there was a girl I used to see in a grocery store that I wanted to meet. Finally, I told her I had seen her all the time and wanted to know, 'What's your name?' The idea just stuck with me."

This time, Claude ("Juan") saw a deserving record rocket into the ozone. "Magic Wand," the follow-up, peaked at number 91 in 1962, and that was it, even though 18 Don & Juan singles were released before the twosome called it quits in 1967. An interesting commercial failure was their "True Love Never Runs Smooth," a Burt Bacharach tune offered them prior to Gene Pitney's success with it.

Roland Trone died in 1982. Claude Johnson, 60, is back on the road again, touring with a new "Don"— sometimes Shorty Rogers of the Paragons; otherwise "Buddy" Faison, formerly a member of Claude's earlier group, the Genies.

SENSATIONS
LET ME IN
(Yvonne Baker)
Argo 5405
No. 4 *March 17, 1962*

The Sensations formed as the Cavaliers in Philadelphia in 1954. Lead singer Yvonne Mills and bass Alphonso Howell were half of the initial group. Before success was to be so kind as to let them in, nearly a decade would have to pass. Meanwhile, only months into the group's career, Atco Records sized up the appeal of the Cavaliers' female-lead doo-wop approach, and signed them to a multi-disk contract. Executives at the label considered the three guys and the coy-voiced gal something of a sensation, and changed the unit's name accordingly. Of the Sensations' many releases, "Yes Sir, That's My Baby" and "Please Mr. Disk Jockey" nearly caught a national audience. But after three years of Atco releases, Yvonne Mills settled down to being Mrs. Yvonne Baker, housewife and mother, and the Sensations disbanded.

Doo-wop started making an amazing resurgence in 1961; ethereal harmonies were popping up everywhere. Pointing to the success of groups like the Edsels, the Stereos, and the Marcels, Alphonso Howell urged Yvonne to join him in reforming the Sensations. She acquiesced, and Alphonso picked Kae Williams, a local DJ, to manage and record the new group. Filling out the ranks were baritone Sam Armstrong, a one-time voice with THE RAYS, and tenor Richard Curtain, an original member of the Hide-a-ways.

The Sensations' initial effort was the up-tempo "Music, Music, Music" (#54, 1961). With "Let Me In" and its contagious, nonsensical hook—"We-oop, we-oop, ooo-we-oop-we-ooo"—the group struck gold. "That's My Desire," credited to Yvonne Baker & The Sensations, charted (#69, 1962), but later releases did not. The group's moment of glory had come and gone (although Bonnie Raitt did include a remake of "Let Me In" on her 1973 album *Takin' My Time*).

Various gatherings of Sensations continued on, recording for Junior and later Tollie Records. Yvonne Baker attempted a solo career.

KETTY LESTER
LOVE LETTERS
(Edward Heyman, Victor Young)
Ers 3068
No. 5 *April 14, 1962*

Ketty was born Revoyda Frierson, on August 16, 1934, in Hope, Arkansas. Papa was a poor farmer, and Ketty was one of 15 siblings. After winning a scholarship, she moved to California to attend San Francisco City College as a nursing major. She sang in church and in the school choir, acting on the side in summer-stock productions. While performing at the Purple Onion, Ketty met country singer/comedienne Dorothy Shay. Dorothy, "The Park Avenue Hillbilly," had made the country charts in 1951 with "Feudin' and Fightin'," and helped make some record-business connections for Lester.

Four Preps alumnus (and later STANDELLS producer) Ed Cobb and Lincoln Mayorga were eager to record Ketty. Cobb tracked down just the right tune for her— "I'm a Fool to Want You"—and someone dug up Dick Haynes's 1945 hit, "Love Letters," for a flip side. "We recorded in a room over a garage," Ketty recalled to *DISCoveries'* Jon E. Johnson. "The piano, bass, drums, and guitar were all we had space for in the main room, and I had a little . . . well, it was like a toilet. I was forced to sing it in the toilet."

"I'm a Fool to Want You" b/w the sensuous-sounding "Love Letters" was released by Era Records. Once "Love Letters" proved to be a hit, an LP (*Ketty Lester*, 1962) was shipped by the independent, as were a pair of charting follow-ups, "You Can't Lie to a Liar" (#90, 1962) and "This Land Is Your Land" (#97, 1962). RCA released a few LPs and a number of singles, but nothing further attracted much of an audience. Elvis covered "Love Letters" in 1966, and took it to number 19. Before a momentary retirement to care for her son and her husband (who had suffered two heart attacks), Ketty cut some unsuccessful disks for the Tower and Pete labels.

Ketty had continued acting after college. In 1963, she even won an Off-Broadway Theatre Award for her role in the revival of *A Cabin in the Sky*. The producers of the TV show "Julia" noticed Ketty in an L.A. production of *A Raisin in the Sun* and offered her the lead role in the series that eventually starred Diahann Carroll. Numerous TV appearances on episodes of "The FBI," "Laugh-In," "Love American Style," "Marcus Welby, M.D.," and "Sanford and Son" followed. She co-starred in films like *Blacula* (1972), *The Terminal Man* (1974), and *The Prisoner of Second Avenue* (1975); was a cast member on the soaps "Days of Our Lives" and "Rituals"; and was a regular for four years on "Little House on the Prairie."

Mega Records approached Ketty about returning to the recording studio in 1985. "[They] actually wanted me to sing pop, but I said I wanted to make an album of Christian music. With the experiences that I've had . . . it could have only been the will of God that I have been able to help my husband the way have. So when [Mega] asked me if I would record again, I told [them] no, unless I could do at least the first one for Jesus." The label agreed and issued *I Saw Him* in 1985.

LARRY FINNEGAN
DEAR ONE
(Larry Finnegan, Vincent Finnegan)
Old Town 1113
No. 11 *April 21, 1962*

Johnny Lawrence Finneran was born in 1939 in New York City. With his brother Vinnie he studied and played guitar, piano, and drums, then made several radio and TV appearances. At Notre Dame College, he played a few dances, wrote songs, and listened to Del Shannon records.

In 1961, instead of cracking the books in his senior year at Notre Dame, John worked with Vinnie on a song derived from the familiar "Dear John letter" format. Once all the words had fallen into place and the melody felt just right, John recorded a demo, and walked the track into the offices of Hy Weiss' Old Town Records. Weiss—known for his successes with THE FIESTAS, ROBERT & JOHNNY and THE CAPRIS—waited not, and signed the boy on the spot. "Dear One" was issued in November 1961, with John's last name altered to "Finnegan." The response was incredible, as the up-tempo and country-flavored tune worked its way up the nation's pop charts.

Finnegan's follow-up flopped, as did a fine country number produced by session guitarist Billy Mure—of DADDY-O'S fame—called "Pick Up the Pieces." In 1964, John returned to the tried and true with "Dear One, Part Two": in the sequel, our hero gets the unfaithful hussy back. No one seemed to care, or even notice. Even Finnegan's tribute to Ringo Starr called "The Other Ringo" (based structurally on LORNE GREENE's "Ringo") failed to stir more than a few grains of interest.

In 1966, Finnegan moved to Stockholm to set up his own independent record label, Svensk-American. He returned in 1970 and died of a brain tumor on July 22, 1973.

JACK ROSS
CINDERELLA
(Jack Ross, E. Nemeth)
Dot 16333
No. 16 *April 28, 1962*

Nearly a year before Herb Alpert recorded "The Lonely Bull" and got hip to the commercial potential of Americanizing sounds from south of the border, Jack Ross cut and released "Happy Jose (Ching Ching)" (#57, 1962). Dot Records picked up the novelty instrumental for national distribution from the small Ramal label, and Jack almost had a Top 40 hit on his hands.

"Cinderella," the follow-up to "Happy Jose," was an entirely different affair—a comedy record. Ross, in this case, played a beatnik storyteller; in his hands, the familiar fairy tale was transformed into a jive-talkin', pig-Latin string of titillating innuendoes. Both disks were produced by Norman Malkin. The husband of MARGIE RAYBURN and founder of THE SUNNYSIDERS, Malkin wrote most of the selections for Ross' few recordings. Dot issued Ross' solitary album later in 1962.

Jack Ross (B. 1917) had been a trumpeter and orchestra leader throughout the big band era; he performed for 15 years at the Mark Hopkins Hotel in San Francisco, and later, at the Sahara Tahoe. Jack Ross died on December 16, 1982.

ERNIE MARESCA
SHOUT! SHOUT! (KNOCK YOURSELF OUT)
(Ernie Maresca, Thomas F. Bogdany)
Seville 117
No. 6 *May 19, 1962*

Ernie Maresca (b. Apr. 21, 1939, Bronx, NY) wrote or co-wrote God knows how many hits. He gave "Runaround Sue," "The Wanderer," "Lovers Who Wonder," and "Donna the Prima Donna" to Dion; "No One Knows," "A Lover's Prayer," and "Come on Little Angel" to the Belmonts; "Runaround" to the Regents; "Whenever a Teenager Cries" to Reparata & The Delrons; "Hey Jean, Hey Dean" to Dean & Jean; "Child of Clay" to Jimmie Rodgers; and piles of other enjoyables to the Del-Satins, the Five Discs, and Nino & The Ebbtides.

"I'm originally from the Bronx," Maresca told *Goldmine*'s Wayne Jones. "Dion lived on the next block. The Regents lived up the street. My block was Garden Street and 182nd Street. I grew up with guys like Guy Vallari of the Regents, so we used to all sing and start groups. I had cut a demo record on 'No One Knows' . . . Dion heard the demo and liked it, so he brought it down to Gene Schwartz at Laurie Records. That's how I got into it. That became the next record [for Dion & The Belmonts] after their 'I Wonder Why.'"

Ernie's chance to step out front and do his own thing happened as a direct result of the phenomenal success of "Runaround Sue," which Maresca co-wrote with Dion. Ernie admitted to *Goldmine* that he never liked the song, and never thought it would be a smash.

"In all honesty, we wrote 'Runaround Sue' around [Gary U.S. Bonds'] 'A Quarter to Three,' which was a big hit then. Laurie, at the time, was handling the distribution of the record. It's incredible: 'Sue' was more like a riff song, you know, with 'hep hep, bum de diddle it' . . . and it's not really a story"

Ernie wrote "Shout! Shout!" with a friend named Tom Bogdany. "I went around trying to get people to hear ["Shout! Shout!"] because I wasn't working exclu-

sively for Laurie at the time—I took it to Seville, which was just a tiny outfit . . . they had me rerecord it."

It doesn't take a critic's ear to hear echoes of "Runaround Sue" or "Quarter to Three" in Maresca's "Shout! Shout!" Released on Seville and distributed by London Records, the disk sold well and went Top 10. Follow-ups were something else altogether. "Mary Jane (You're a Pain in the Brain)" bombed, as did successive disks issued under names like Artie Chicago, the Desires, Foreign Intrigue, and the Hubcaps.

Ernie Maresca is still active with Robert Schwartz and the rest of the staff at Laurie Records, packaging seemingly endless compilations of that golden stuff from long ago.

"Shout Shout" returned to Britain's Top 20 in 1982 when rerecorded by Rocky Sharpe & The Replays.

MR. ACKER BILK
STRANGER ON THE SHORE
(Acker Bilk)
Atco 6217
No. 1 *May 26, 1962*

Mother was a church organist; Father was a Methodist preacher. And son Bernard Stanley Bilk (b. Jan. 28, 1929, Somerset, Avon, England) was serving three months in a brig in Egypt for sleeping on guard duty when he first discovered his love for the clarinet. "Acker" (slang for "buddy" or "mate") was just 18 then, and started playing to while away the sweltering evenings. After his army discharge, Bilk labored in a tobacco factory in Bristol, then worked as a builder's laborer and a blacksmith. The job was tough and dirty; a musician's life, he soon realized, might be a mite less demanding.

After a stay with Ken Colyer's jazz band, Acker formed his own Paramount Jazz Band in 1958. Two years later, Denis Preston, an independent producer, spotted Bilk, his ever-present bowler hat, and that trad-jazz band of his. Prior to his monster moment, Bilk and the band almost connected with their quiet, bluesy number, "Summer Set." Two years and a few more near-hits later, "Stranger on the Shore" appeared.

"Stranger"—recorded with the aid of the Leon Young String Chorale—was a tame instrumental, not a rock and roll record, and its staggering chart success took everyone in popdom by surprise. "Stranger" remained on the British listings for a whopping 55 weeks, eventually selling 4 million copies. Bilk, at this time, teamed with KENNY BALL and CHRIS BARBER for what proved a chart-topping album, *The Best of Ball, Barber and Bilk*. Acker also had the distinction of preceding the Beatles and the British Invasion acts as the first British artist to ever hit number one on *Billboard*'s pop charts.

Bilk repeatedly regained status on the British charts with such works as "That's My Home," "Frankie and Johnny" and most recently, in 1976, with "Aria." A continuing train of albums have been issued to moderate European success.

Acker Bilk remains an active musician. In addition to touring extensively, he has appeared in two Royal Command Performances (1978 and 1981) and has fronted his own British radio program, "Acker's 'Alf Our," on BBC's Radio 2.

In 1995, "Stranger on the Shore" received the Ivor Novello Award for "Most Performed Work."

RONNIE & THE HI-LITES
I WISH THAT WE WERE MARRIED
(Marian Weiss)
Joy 260
No. 16 *May 26, 1962*

In the early '60s, Stanley Brown (baritone), Sonny Caldwell (first tenor), Kenny Overby (bass), and John Witney (second tenor) were the Cascades, a Jersey City street-corner group in need of a lead singer. Their frontman had just been drafted, and without a replacement, the Cascades were sure to wash away. Witney, the group's organizer, happened to hear Ronnie Goodson singing in a class play at his school, P. S. 14. Before the day was out, Witney convinced the 12-year-old's parents to let Ronnie try out for their vocal group. Ronnie quickly fit in with the sounds the Cascades were making. Mike Amato, the Duprees' original lead singer, told Witney about Hal and Marian Weiss, some music buffs who might help the group make its mark. Marian had written some songs that publishers and record companies had turned aside, and was sure that she could tailor-make something hot for the Cascades. "I Wish That We Were Married" was her first offering, and it was a doozy.

A demo of the Cascades doing "I Wish That We Were Married" was taped and shopped around to various labels. ABC-Paramount Records passed on it, and so did Atlantic, but the ears over at Joy Records heard something in the demo, and quickly struck up a deal with the Weisses, Ronnie, and the group, now redubbed the Hi-Lites.

"I Wish That We Were Married" tore up the charts. Ronnie & The Hi-Lites hit the ceiling of pop success with appearances on "American Bandstand," shows at the Apollo Theatre, and tours with the Crystals and the Ronettes. Ronnie reportedly was even "the Loco-Motion girl" Little Eva's boyfriend for a time!

Not all stories of riches and fame end sadly or rapidly, but this particular one does. Weiss, in an interview with *Harmony Tymes* writer Joe T. Sicurella, com-

plained that Joy Records issued the wrong follow-up single: instead of "Send My Love," the label should have released the group's "natural" follow-up, something utilizing that marriage theme (namely, "What a Pretty Bride You'll Make"). The latter platter has yet to be released, while "Send My Love" stiffed.

A lawsuit between the Hi-Lites and Joy Records developed over a dispute as to just how many copies of "I Wish" were pressed. The Weisses set up their own label, Win Records, and issued several more Ronnie & The Hi-Lites singles—but nothing the group ever again recorded charted on the Hot 100.

One by one, the guys graduated from high school, separated, and sought out other careers. Sonny Caldwell became a computer programmer. John Witney is now a diesel mechanic. Ronnie Goodson died in his sleep on November 4, 1980.

JOE HENDERSON
SNAP YOUR FINGERS
(Grady Martin, Alex Zanetis)
Todd 1072
No. 8 *July 7, 1962*

Joe Henderson (not to be confused with the jazz saxophonist of the same name) was born in Como, Mississippi, around 1938. Shortly after, he and his family moved to Gary, Indiana, where Joe remained until he went off on his own to Nashville in 1958. Henderson's roots were in the Baptist Church, and over the next few years he performed with various gospel groups like the Fairfield Four.

In the early '60s, Henderson came to the attention of the disk dealers at Todd Records. Some initial waxings, such as the silky-smooth "Baby Don't Leave Me,"

133

sounded fine to those ears that managed a listen, but all of Joe's Todd sides failed to click—until "Snap Your Fingers."

"Snap Your Fingers," a catchy, hook-laden number with an uncanny Brook Benton sound, became Henderson's lone chart-shaker. A now-collectible album was released, and for the next two years, the Todd label issued a little pile of soulful sides. "Big Love" (#74, 1962), "The Search Is Over" (#94, 1962), and others were slick yet sincerely soulful. Apparently, these disks also sounded a little too much like the then-popular and well-established Brook Benton.

In 1964, the prestigious Kapp label, then Ric Records, gave Henderson a try at the charts, but he fared no better with these outings. Joe Henderson passed away in a Nashville hotel in 1966 at the young age of 36.

EMILIO PERICOLI
AL DI LA
(Guilio Rapetti, Carlo Donida)
Warner Bros. 5259
No. 6 *July 7, 1962*

When first sung by Betty Curtis, "Al Di La" became the 1961 winner of Italy's San Remo Song Festival. Over the next few years, more than 50 different run-throughs of the catchy tune would be recorded. Connie Francis (#90, 1963) and the Ray Charles Singers (#29, 1964) would both chart in the States with their renditions, but it was Emilio Pericoli's virile version that sold more than a million copies.

Pericoli was born in Cesenatico, Italy, in 1928. As a young man, Emilio trained to be an accountant. While at school, though, his appearances in local plays led others to encourage Emilio to study singing and acting. Although it was not until 1960 that he made his professional singing debut, Emilio had by that time secured some guest spots on Italian TV. Fleeting international fame came when Pericoli was approached to croon "Al Di La" in *Rome Adventure* (1962), a Troy Donahue/Suzanne Pleshette flick. Emilio continued to crank out the corn, but never again was he to have his way with American hearts and charts.

CLAUDE KING
WOLVERTON MOUNTAIN
(Merle Kilgore, Claude King)
Columbia 42352
No. 6 *July 21, 1962*

Claude is known to rural and urban folk alike for his tall tale of a dude's determination to possess a gal with "lips sweeter than honey" whom he's never met. Clifton Clowers, a mean mountain man "mighty handy with the gun and knife," has his daughter in storage on Wolverton Mountain, and there ain't no one gonna get her. The outcome of Claude and Clifton's confrontation is not revealed in the song's lyrics. "Wolverton Mountain" did typecast Claude as a "saga singer," but for the brief time that sagas were selling, King was the monarch of the mound.

Claude was born on a farm in Keithville, Louisiana, on February 5, 1923. There was no electricity, no gas, no running water. Before school bells were ringing for little Claude, his family moved to the wilds of Louisiana. "There was four of us brothers," said Claude to liner-note writer Colin Escott. "We'd have to swim seven creeks to get to school when the water was up." When 12, he bought his first guitar for 50 cents from a neighbor. He picked at the thing, but it was sports that was young Claude's passion. After high school, Claude spent a year with the Civilian Conservation Corps., training in metalwork and forestry.

He attended the University of Idaho on a baseball scholarship, but unfortunately, an arm injury snuffed his baseball dreams.

From college, Claude went to Shreveport where he turned to pickin' and singin' at local watering holes and on radio shows. Appearances on the "Louisiana Hayride" radio program led to unsuccessful recordings for the Gotham, Specialty, Dee Jay, and Pacemaker labels. At the behest of country star Johnny Horton, Columbia Records offered Claude a contract, and with his first release, "Big River, Big Man" (#82, 1961), King won a position on both the pop and country charts. The follow-up, "The Comancheros" (#71, 1961), did likewise. But with "Wolverton Mountain," a tune co-written with Merle Kilgore (country singer/later Hank Williams, Jr.'s manager) about a real man and real place in Arkansas, Claude King hit paydirt.

Popwise, Claude only had one more story-song in him—"The Burning of Atlanta" (#53, 1962)—and his reign on the C & W charts throughout the '60s had its downs and ups, but mostly the latter. During the '70s, though, his career began to stall. After six albums and a healthy run of C & W chartings, Claude and Columbia parted company.

Claude King continued to sing to this day of Clifton Clowers, and occasionally recorded country tunes. He turned up in a TV mini-series, "The Blue and the Gray" (1982) and obscure flicks like *Swamp Girl* and *Year of the Wahoo.*

Arkansas Governor Frank White declared August 7, 1981, as "Wolverton Mountain Day." Claude King died in 1983.

Clifton Clowers—the mean "Wolverton Mountain" man—died August 14, 1994. He was 102.

JOANIE SOMMERS
JOHNNY GET ANGRY
(Hal David, Sherman Edwards)
Warner Bros. 5275
No. 7 *July 21, 1962*

One of Sommers's LPs called her "The Voice of the Sixties." An overstatement, yes; but Joanie was the "Pepsi Girl," singing "Now it's Pepsi for those who think young" and "Come alive! You're in the Pepsi Generation." As *Goldmine*'s Frank Wright observed, she also sang, on "One Boy" (#54, 1960): "One boy to laugh with, to joke with/Have a Coke with . . ."

Born on February 24, 1941, in Buffalo, New York, Joanie moved with her parents to southern California in 1954. Soon after, she began singing with her high school dance band and later, with groups at the Santa Monica City College. Talent scouts for the newly-formed Warner Bros. label spotted her and signed her to a contract in 1959. Her first assignment was to replace CONNIE STEVENS singing opposite "77 Sunset Strip" celebrity EDD BYRNES. She appeared on a couple of "77 Sunset Strip" episodes, and added a breathy break to "I Dig You Kookie" on Edd's 1959 debut LP, *Kookie* (her name was misspelled on the record label as "Jeanie Sommers").

After "One Boy" (#54, 1960) and a number of non-charters, Joanie scored with "Johnny Get Angry." Who can ever forget those classic lines: "Johnny get angry/Johnny get mad/Gave me the biggest lecture I

ever had/I want a brave man/I want a cave man"? They don't make 'em like that anymore, and though Joanie tried hard with 45s like "Where the Boys Get Together," "Bobby's Hobbies," "Little Girl Bad," and "Big Man," she never managed to top her earlier record.

Joanie played opposite teen idol Rick Nelson in ABC-TVs "Stage 67" production of *On the Flip Side*, then retired to turn her attention to raising a family. Nevertheless, oddball 45s like "Trains and Boats and Planes" (1967), "Tell Him" (1968), "The Great Divide" (1968), and "Peppermint Choo Choo" (1977) were sighted well into the '70s.

Her career is not yet buzzin', but Joanie Sommers has since returned to the entertainment biz.

DON GARDNER & DEE DEE FORD
I NEED YOUR LOVING
(Don Gardner, Bobby Robinson)
Fire 508
No. 20 *July 28, 1962*

Donald Gardner was born and raised in Philadelphia. In 1952, with his school days behind him, Don and some neighborhood souls formed the Sonotones and cut some now-collectible disks for the Gotham and Bruce labels; sales, however, were zip. The Sonotones broke up, and for the next few years, Don and a quartet of musicians worked the Philly bars. Gardner had some solo sides issued on the Bruce, Deluxe, Kaiser, and Value labels.

During the '60s, the definition of a "commercial" R & B sound began to shift. Musical forms like the blues and doo-wop were fading in popularity; Ike & Tina Turner's hot and sweaty sound was selling a lot of records. In 1961, a keyboardist named Dee Dee Ford met Gardner, and together they taped a gutsy duet of "Glory of Love" for New York's KC Records. (The label sat on the sides until the duo's "I Need Your Loving" took off and stimulated the need for more gospel-influenced shouters.) For a handful of months—starting with "I Need Your Loving"—Don and Dee Dee had their sassy screams and screeches featured on AM radio. White boys and girls jumped all about. "Glory of Love" (#75, 1962) charted later in the year, as did Don and Dee Dee's official follow-up to "I Need Your Loving," "Don't You Worry" (#66).

Internal discord was not apparent—if the two were fussin', no one seemed to notice. By year's end, however, Don and Dee Dee separated. Before an unsuccessful one-off reunion in 1966, they each issued a few solo singles. Don did resurface briefly in 1973 on the R & B charts with a tune called "Forever," a duet with JEANETTE BABY WASHINGTON.

BARBARA LYNN
YOU'RE GONNA LOSE A GOOD THING
("Barbara Lynn" Ozen)
Jamie 1220
No. 8 *August 11, 1962*

A French-speaking Cajun, named in honor of Louisiana's Huey P. Long, Huey P. Meaux (b. 1929, Kaplan, LA) proved to be one heck of a barber, wheeler-dealer, label owner, and career-shaper. Huey P., who played drums in his daddy's band and with the piano-punching Moon Mulligan, handled numerous swamp-pop artists like JOE BARRY, ROD BERNARD, Freddie Fender, Roy Head, Jivin' Gene, Doug Sahm's Sir Douglas Quintet . . . and Barbara Lynn.

Fresh out of the Army, Huey worked as a DJ, for a mite—he'd mix a little 7-Up and bourbon, say whatever, and play Cajun music, or dang near anything else. He had some difficulties keeping the job, and his brother talked him into attending barber school. Huey opened a barber shop in Winnie, Texas, but continued to dabble in pop music.

"I got a tape from a guy in Beaumont," Meaux recalled to *Goldmine*'s Colin Escott. "It had been recorded over. This guy wanted to sell me an act by the name of T-Baby Green. In between the T-Baby cuts was this girl they had recorded over. It was knocking me o-u-t. It was reaching at the roots of my heart. I just wanted to meet that voice. I had a guy named Big Sambo recording for me [known in the deep South and the Midwest for his regional hit "The Rains Came"]. I played him the tape and said, 'Who's this?' He said, 'That's Barbara Lynn. If you want her, I'll get her.'

"So I keep cutting hair, and he came back around 6:30 with Barbara Lynn. She was about 15 or 16 [19, actually], I guess, and she limped a little because she had one leg longer than the other. I said, 'Barbara, if you'll pay the expenses for you and your mother, I'll meet you in New Orleans at Cosimo's studio. I'll pay for the musicians and the tape.' She went for it, and we recorded 'You'll Lose a Good Thing.'"

Goldmine's Almost Slim has reported a different version of these events. It seems that a late-night DJ named "Bon Ton" Garlow had a home studio for neighborhood kids to jam in. One of these participating youngsters was a left-handed guitar player named Barbara Lynn Ozen (b. Jan. 16, 1942, Beaumont, TX).

Barb had been pickin' piano since grammar school. "I was getting tired of that," she told Alan Govenor, author of *Meeting the Blues*. "Then I heard Elvis and decided that I wanted to do something odd," like being a lady guitar player. When Meaux happened on to her, Barb was leader of an all-girl band, Bobby Lynn & The Idols. "We'd do a lot of Elvis tunes, like 'Jailhouse Rock,' and I swung my instrument and we all wore pants."

As Garlow told Almost Slim: "I made a tape of her and took it to Huey Meaux. Huey listened to the tape and said, 'She's coming along, but I don't think she's strong enough yet' . . . The next time she was playing, I convinced Huey to come out and watch her lead a band. I picked Huey up and carried him to the Ten Acre Club outside of Beaumont. That's when he decided to sign Barbara Lynn."

Take your choice. Either way, Meaux recorded Lynn's "You're Gonna Lose a Good Thing," which Barbara had originally written as a simple poem when she was jilted at sweet 16. Six months after the session, studio boss Cosimo Matassa placed the disk with Harry Finfer's Philly-based Jamie label. While Barbara did have further local success, and did manage to chart with a steady stream of treats well into the '70s, the bluesy "Good Thing" would be her only Top 40 entry.

"I got married and that slowed me down," she told Govenor. "After the divorce I was able to purse my music more . . ." Barbara Lynn has still got a band and still hits the hard bars in Texas, Louisiana, Oklahoma. "I have faith, patience, and hope that things will break for me again."

In the mid-'90s, Barb signed with Bullseye Blues Records.

Huey P. made a cameo appearance in David Byrne's flick *True Story* (1986), testifying to the staying power of one self-named "Crazy Cajun."

CLAUDINE CLARK
PARTY LIGHTS
(Claudine Clark)
Chancellor 1113
No. 5 *September 1, 1962*

Born to a nonmusical family in Macon, Georgia, on April 26, 1941, little Claudine, from early on, took a liking to producing musical sounds. Her parents encouraged her, giving her guitar and organ lessons. After completing high school, she won a musical scholarship to Coombs College in Philadelphia, where she eventually received a B.S. degree in Music Composition.

While out on the dusty trail attempting to sell her wares, Claudine sang on a television program in Wilmington, Delaware. The TV spot was seen by Herald Records executive Al Silver, who offered Claudine the opportunity to record a couple of her tunes. "Angel of Happiness" bombed, as did her second effort for the Gotham label. Bob Marcucci's Philadelphia-based Chancellor label gave the lass her third crack at bat with "Disappointed" b/w "Party Lights."

"Disappointed," the intended "A" side, was a Marcucci-Russ Faith composition with a plush Jerry Ragavoy arrangement; it sounded almost like Carla

Thomas doing Brenda Lee's "I'm Sorry." But "Disappointed" didn't have a hit feel to it, so some DJ flipped the record to find this spontaneous, teen-alienation radiator, "Party Lights." Never again would Claudine implore and grovel like she did in this raunchy rocker. "I wanna, I wanna, I wanna," Clark moans, but "Momma just won't let me make the scene." Meanwhile, through her window, Claudine can see her friends next door partying it up, twistin', mashin', doin' the bop, and lawd knows what else.

The follow-up to "Party Lights" was a distasteful ditty called "Walkin' Through the Cemetery," complete with Claudine making creature sounds during the instrumental break. Months later, the powers that be decided to return Clark to her successful party theme. This time, in "Walk Me Home From the Party," Mama does let the poor girl go to that party and, of course, Claudine does find the right guy.

Sales were poor on both of these disks, so Clark next appeared on Swan Records under the billing "Joy Dawn"; her lone single under that moniker quickly sank from sight. Two records each were issued on the TCF and Jamie labels, but not many ears ever got to hear these, and Clark disappeared from public view. According to some reports, Claudine was off in the wilds writing a rock and roll operetta, or poetry, or plays.

When last heard from, Claudine Clark was in disguise as Sherry Pye. Her only release for Match Records: "Gimme a Break."

SPRINGFIELDS
SILVER THREADS AND GOLDEN NEEDLES
(Dick Reynolds, Jack Rhodes)
Philips 40038
No. 20 *September 22, 1962*

Mary (b. Apr. 16, 1939) and Dion (b. July 2, 1934) O'Brien—a.k.a. Dusty and Tom Springfield—grew up in Hampstead, London, singing with their parents in a rec room equipped with microphones and amplifiers. Dion worked as a bank teller, a stock broker, and an interpreter for the military. Mary, educated in British convents in High Wycombe and Ealing, worked as a clerk in a record store, a salesgirl in a department store, and even took jobs selling dustbins and toy trains. In the late '50s, Dion started folksinging with an ex-wine tester and ad man named Tim Field. Dusty, as Mary now called herself, was soon invited to join Dion and Tim in a Peter, Paul & Mary-type group.

The trio's name surfaced while they were practicing one warm spring day in an open field. In 1961, the Springfields auditioned for Philips Records and

THE
SPRINGFIELDS

secured a recording contract. Nearly a half-dozen of their singles rambled over the British charts before the Beatles even set foot in the United States.

"Silver Threads and Golden Needles" was an updated and electrified rendition of an early Wanda Jackson country hit. But before it peaked on the U.S. charts, Field had left and was replaced by Mike Hurst (b. Michael Longhurst-Pickworth). The group's initial stateside LP, 1962's *Silver Threads and Golden Needles*, sold well, and their follow-up single, "Dear Hearts and Gentle People," hit number 95 the same year. British mags like *Melody Maker* and *New Music Express* rated them the country's number-one vocal group for 1961 and 1962. Despite all the attention, the Springfields splintered in September 1963, after a performance at the London Palladium.

Mike Hurst went on to manage a folk club, work as a DJ, and produce some recordings, most notably Cat Stevens' early sides for the Deram label. Tom Springfield has been working as an arranger, has made some orchestral recordings, and wrote several hits for the Seekers. Dusty, the most successful ex-Springfield, launched her solo career in the fall of 1963. "I Only Want to Be With You" (#12, 1964), was the first in a best-selling line of ultra-fine lusties—"Wishin' and Hopin'" (#6, 1964), "You Don't Have to Say You Love Me" (#4, 1966), "The Look of Love" (#22, 1967), and onward through the '60s.

Dusty's singles stopped charting in 1970, and she kept a low profile throughout the '70s. Following a veiled admission to bisexuality, Dusty moved to the states in 1975. However, she returned to the public eye collaborating with the Pet Shop Boy's on their 1988 single "What Have I Done to Deserve This?" Homeland success continued with her rendering of the theme to the John Hurt/Bridget Fonda flick *Scandal* (1989), "Nothing Has Been Proven," and her 1995 album, *A Very Fine Love.*

BENT FABRIC
ALLEY CAT
(Jack Harlen, Frank "Bent Fabric" Bjorn)
Atco 6226
No. 7 *September 29, 1962*

Nineteen sixty-two was a goofy year. Two girls in Indiana standing two feet apart set some obscure record by tossing an ice cube back and forth 4,477 times before it melted. Some character baked up a 25,000-pound cake for the Seattle Fair. And a batch of instrumentals pervaded the airwaves of Top 40 stations. KENNY BALL and his band of jazzmen gave us "Midnight in Moscow." A trumpeter named Herb Alpert scored his first of a string of hits, a tune about a "Lonely Bull." A clarinetist

named MR. ACKER BILK presented us with "Stranger on the Shore." And a Danish pianoman named Bent Fabricius-Bjerre picked out a memorable melody called "Alley Cat."

Bent was born in Copenhagen on December 7, 1924, to a mom and dad who apparently knew just how to raise a multi-talented lad. In the wink of an eye, Bent was a musician and a teenage bandleader. Under his direction, Bent's boys made some of what are claimed to be Denmark's first jazz recordings. In 1950, Bjerre became head of Metronome Records. He played a mean piano, and for a while was the host of the Saturday-night Danish TV program "Around a Piano." In addition to working as A & R man for Metronome, he composed tunes under the pseudonym "Frank Bjorn."

"Alley Cat," a Bent creation, was a very innocent-sounding number. Its catchy melody moved over a lethargic bass pattern and faint percussion—the type of arrangement Bent would use on most of his stateside records. His *Alley Cat* album made *Billboard*'s top pop albums chart; strangely enough, the title track won a Grammy for "Best Rock and Roll Record" in 1962. Only one other Bent Fabric single, an instrumental entitled "Chicken Feed" (#63, 1963), appeared on the Hot 100.

FRANK IFIELD
I REMEMBER YOU
(Johnny Mercer, Victor Schertzinger)
Vee-Jay 457
No. 5 *October 13, 1962*

"When I was 13, I worked with a fantastic old fellow called Big Chief Little Wolf, who taught me all the intricacies of show business in the old-fashioned manner," Frank Ifield told Sheila Tracy, author of *Who's Who in Popular Music in Great Britain*. Frank (b. Nov. 30, 1937, Coventry, England) was a "spruker," a "roll over roll over," or what we in the Far West might call a "come-on man." His earliest of jobs, in other words, was to get people to lay their money down for traveling tent shows and circuses.

Frank's dad was an inventor and design engineer, and although the family was originally from England, most of Frank's youth was spent in Australia. It was in Sydney that he made his debut as a singer in 1950 at the Hornsby Pacific Theatre. Within a year, Frankie was making TV appearances and had recorded his first single, "Did You See My Daddy Over There?" More than 40 other disks were to follow over the next half-decade or so. By the end of his teen years, Frank Ifield was reported to be the hottest vocal item in Tasmania, New Zealand, and Australia.

Seeking to broaden his realm of influence, Ifield moved back to England in 1959, where under the tute-

FRANK IFIELD

lage of Norrie Paramor, he was quickly signed to Columbia Records. His countrified cover version of Carl Dobkins, Jr.'s, "Lucky Devil" established him in 1960. For the next six years, Frank could do little wrong: 15 singles charted in England. Three of these 45s—"I Remember You," "Lovesick Blues," and "The Wayward Wind"—topped the British listings; according to *New Music Express*, this was a first in British pop history. The only one of the trilogy to click in the States was "I Remember You," a remake of the Jimmy Dorsey hit from the Dorothy Lamour/Helen O'Connell flick *The Fleet Is In* (1942). Before being mothballed, Ifield's disk became the first record to sell a million copies in the U.K. alone.

Frank's stateside impact vanished as rapidly as the changing of the seasons. Although he did manage to place three other singles on the Hot 100 and four more on the C & W charts, not one could respark the nation's interest. Meanwhile, Ifield toured the remainder of the world, playing concerts and cabarets.

Frank is still very much a viable voice in England, where he was voted the "Best British Male Vocalist of the Year" for both 1981 and 1982 at the International Country Music Awards at Wembley.

CONTOURS
DO YOU LOVE ME
(Berry Gordy, Jr.)
Gordy 7005
No. 3 *October 20, 1962*
No. 11 *January 4, 1988*

"Now, 'Do You Love Me', let me tell ya, Berry Gordy told us, was intended for the Temptations," said Sylvester Potts, one of the still touring original Contours, in an exclusive interview. "We were in, rehearsing a song [with a then new and sixth member, guitarist Hugh Davis], 'It Must Be Love'; it became the B side to something. Berry was standing at the bottom of the stairs just watchin' us go through this song and he then interrupts us and says, 'Hey, I got a tune. I was suppose to do it on the Temptations, but they're late, so I'm gonna try you guys. It was 'Do You Love Me.' Now, I think it was just a psych-thing, though. He was psychin' us, makin' us hungry for it, you know. Think about it, can you imagine the Tempts doing 'Do You Love Me'?"

The appearance of the Contours' golden gospelish gripper in the flick *Dirty Dancing* in 1988 returned their name and the recording to the nation's Top 10; a feat matched by only a very few 45s. Together consistently, in some form, since 1970, the initial Contours took shape in the late '50s, in the Motor City.

"Joe Billingslea and Billy Gordon, the group's original lead singer, met in the service. Billy's gone now. I haven't seen him in a long time. He had a problem with, ah, drugs. When they got out of the service, they had this group, the Majestics. At the time, they were recording for a small company, Contour. That's how we later came up with our name.

"They put out one single ["Hard Times" b/w "Teenage Gossip"], then they tried for Lu Pine Records; sang 'em some songs. But, the label didn't want to sign 'em, just to use one of their songs with the Falcons. The guys said no, though. Hubert Johnson was the next to join. They changed their name to the Blenders, for a while. That's when Billy Hogg and me joined. I was the last one in.

"We became the Contours and went over to Motown, about 1960, and auditioned for Miss Ray and Berry [Gordy, Jr.]. She was his second wife and had this group the Rayber Voices. They'd do back-up on some records. BRIAN HOLLAND [a third of the famed writing/production team of Holland-Dozier-Holland] was in her group, too, for a while. She liked us, but Berry didn't. He said, 'Come back in a couple of years,' you know.

"We didn't know Hubert was related to Jackie Wilson. Hub said, 'He's my cousin.' But, we said, 'Ah Jackie Wilson! Yeah, sure, he's your cousin.' It turned out to be true. So, we went over to Jackie's house. He was good

friends with Berry. . . . And Berry wrote a lot of early things for Jackie, like 'Reet Petite.' Anyway, we sang the same exact songs that we had for Berry, for Jackie. He jumped up, says, 'Hold on, I got to make a phone call.' When he came back, he said, 'Go back to Motown.' We did and we did the same exact songs for Berry, again, and he signed us to a contract.

"Whole Lotta Woman" was issued on Motown. "It sold well locally, but our next one, 'The Stretch,' man, did nothin'! Berry next moved us over to his new label [Gordy]. We did 'Do You Love Me'; it hit, and we became the very first act to break that label. We even had the very first album issued by the company."

The Contours' "Do You Love Me" topped the R & B listings. The disk never charted in England, though months later a cover version by Brian Poole & The Tremeloes made the U.K. top spot. The tune saw chart-action for the Dave Clark Five in 1964 (#11) and FREE's Andy Frasier 20 years later (#84, 1984).

When the group came off the road to record their follow-up, Gordy dreamt up, on the spot, in the studio, "Shake Sherry" (#43); an intended topical take-off on the Four Seasons then world-topper, "Sherry." Every record released thereafter (but one: "You Get Ugly") made either *Billboard*'s R & B or pop charts; and all but one made both listings: "Don't Let Her Be Your Baby," "Can You Do It," "Can You Jerk Like Me," "That Day When She Needed Me," "First I Look at the Purse," "Just a Little Misunderstanding," and "It's So Hard Being a Loser." Considering their chart-tracking, very few singles were issued.

"We wanted to show people that we could not only dance but that we could sing," Billingslea has told researcher Dan Nooger. "But Berry said the ballads were too pretty to release because the public wasn't ready for that from the Contours. We were hot enough at the time that the public would have accepted anything from us in that particular groove."

"Like any other business that you're in," Potts said, "there's politics. Berry seemed to have his favorites, who he keep puttin' things out on constantly. We only had a single or two a year, put out. That's almost like not existing. A lot of people thought we'd broken up, long before we did. . . ."

Gordon was the first to leave, due to "drug problems". In 1964, Billingslea, Johnson, and Potts left. Potts later returned. Filling in were Council Gaye, Jerry Green, Joe Stubbs—the brother to the Four Tops' Levi Stubbs and formerly a member of the FALCONS and later a member of the Originals and ONE HUNDRED PROOF AGED IN SOUL—and lastly Dennis Edwards. The Contours officially disbanded in 1966 as their last charting and last single, "It's So Hard Being a Loser" dropped off the listing. Edwards joined the Temptations, as a replacement for David Ruffin.

In 1970, Billingslea and Potts revived the group name. Both have been a constant in the act since. Although no further recordings were ever issued—in the United States—the Contours have continued to tour and to hope for that one more shot at success.

"They didn't do no follow-up on us. Imagine, they just let it die after 'Do You Love Me' left the charts [for the second time]. See, Motown was going through some transition. It was bad timin' for us, but once, maybe, in a lifetime are ya gonna have a chance like this; you know, your very same record making the charts twice. They coulda put out an album of our unreleased stuff or put us back in the studio. But they were changing hands. It's too bad, really. We needed a follow-up record, then."

Besides Potts and Billingslea, the current Contours is composed of Charles Davis, Arthur Hinson, and Daryl Munlee. Billy Hogg is now a minister. Hugh Davis is said to be quietly working as a songwriter. Billy Gordon married Georgeanna Tillman, of the Marvelettes. Hubert Johnson died by his own hand on July 11, 1981.

In 1989, the group working with writer/producer Ian Levine recorded a new album for U.K. release-only; Motorcity's *Flashback*. "Face Up to the Fact" created quite a stir.

MIKE CLIFFORD
CLOSE TO CATHY
(Bob Goodman, Earl Shuman)
United Artists 489
No. 12 *November 3, 1962*

". . . His voice really rubs me the right way," said Mae West of Mike Clifford in the legend's last film—*Sextette* (1978).

"I've seen a lot of people go and come in the last 40 years," wrote Mike Clifford in a letter to the author. "In 1964, SONNY & Cher were my opening act! I toured with the Supremes, before their first hit; Mary Wilson wrote of me in her book, *Dreamgirls* . . ."

When five, Mike (b. Nov. 5, 1943, Los Angeles) started singing with a group of strolling sidewalk musicians on the island of Catalina, where his parents owned a summertime business. His father, Cal Clifford was a trumpet player with Tommy Dorsey, Stan Kenton, Paul Whiteman, and his own unit, the Cavaliers. Mike—who got the chance to perfect his performance with his dad's band—was making demos at the age of 15. The following year, he was greased up, suited, and crooning in nightclubs. Helen Noga, Johnny Mathis' manager, happened to hear Mike's singing and decided to manage him; she also introduced him to Mathis' label, Columbia. Mike's first few singles for Columbia were not bad teen idol tunes; the Paul Anka-supervised "Uh Huh" actually had raw and youthful energy.

Noga arranged for Mike to make his first of several appearances on "The Ed Sullivan Show," in 1961—an event that would cause him to miss his awaited high school prom and graduation. Bio materials report that Mike Clifford had his first major hit—a number-one charter, no less—that year with the Lawrence Welk-GEORGE CATES' tune "Bombay," in Venezuela. The success garnered the 18 year old his own TV special on the state-owned network, emanating from Caracas. On his return, Mike was ushered into the studios for a recording session for United Artist.

"Close to Cathy," as well as his debut LP, *For the Love of Mike*, were the result. His odes to girls like "Cathy" and "Joanna," though, were puffy pop, with leanings toward earlier times; definitely not the folder for diehard rock and rollers.

While "What to Do With Laurie" (#68, 1963) and "One Boy Too Late" (#96, 1963) did chart, the road as a recording artist got rougher for Mike. More records were made for Cameo, Sidewalk, America International, and Air Records; some reportedly popular in Argentina, Brazil, and Chile. Through it all, Clifford appeared often on "American Bandstand," made four tours with the Dick Clark Caravan and appearances on the Joey Bishop, Donald O'Connor, MIKE DOUGLAS shows; as well as repeat performances at such clubs as Mister Kelly's, the Hullaballoo Club and various Playboy Clubs.

In 1965, Mike Clifford made his acting debut opposite "Leave It to Beaver'"s Tony Dow and "Lassie's" Tommy Rettig in ABC-TV's short-lived soap series "Never Too Young." That same year, Clifford and Casey Kasem co-hosted the syndicated music show "Shebang," and appeared with 30-foot tall Tommy Kirk and Beau Bridges in the sci-fi silly *Village of the Giants* (1965).

For two years in the '70s, Mike played the dual role of Johnny Casino/Teen Angel—opposite John Travolta-Barry Bostwick—in the national touring company of the musical *Grease*. He sang "Love Will Keep Us Together" with femme fatale Mae West in her last flick, the Regis Philbin-Keith Moon-Alice Cooper extravaganza *Sextette* (1978); sang the love theme to Orson Welles' *Necromancy* (1972), and appeared in John Hurt's *Lord of the Rings* (1978).

And then there's the commercials he did—Inglenook Wine, MJB Coffee, Holloway Candies, and Ortho Mattresses.

"Right now, I have a part-time job, and I'm doing demos for songwriters," wrote Clifford. "Even though I only made $4,000 from 'Cathy'—and I'm obviously not a millionaire—I feel so lucky to have worked all over the world and known so many great people. All of my initial dreams have come true, as far as my career goes. Anything that happens after this is pure gravy.

"Music is a part of my life like breathing," said Mike. "As long as I still have a breath, I'll still be singing. I still enjoy it and do it every chance I get."

KRIS JENSEN
TORTURE
(JOHN D. LOUDERMILK)
Hickory 1173
No. 20 *November 3, 1962*

Kris Jensen was on his way to perform on Buddy Dean's TV program in Baltimore. He had what he felt was the hottest record of his career in his hands—"Big As I Can Dream," a song penned by Bob Montgomery, one-time singing and recording partner of Buddy Holly. "En route to the TV studio, we heard a bulletin on the radio that President Kennedy was shot in Dallas," Jensen told *Goldmine*. "By the time we got to the station, the Buddy Dean show was canceled for the day in order to cover the assassination. That was the last anyone heard of the record."

Kris was born Peter Jensen on April 4, 1942, in New Haven, Connecticut. As a little shaver, Pete was wild about the singing cowboys, Gene Autry and Roy Rogers. At age 16, he met Denise Norwood, a songwriter who had made good a couple of years earlier with JOE VALINO's rendition of her tune, "The Garden of Eden." For three years, they worked together, with Jensen recording Norwood's compositions in her home studio. Colpix Records released his "Bonnie Baby" in 1959, and Leader, then Kapp, issued a few singles each—but nothing much happened.

When Nashville music publisher Wesley Rose heard a demo album that Norwood was shopping around to various labels, he hooked Kris up with Hickory Records. Kris' first release on Hickory, "Torture," was a smash. The hypnotic tune had a slow, humping rhythm and a pleading Presleyesque vocal. For some reason, DJ Alan Freed was supposed to choose which cut would be the follow-up; Jensen insisted, to no avail, on his favorite disk, "Big As I Can Dream."

All of Jensen's later releases stiffed. White Whale released the good-timey "Good Pop Music" in the late '60s; A & M gave Kris his final outing in 1970 with a pre-JANIS JOPLIN cover of "Me and Bobby McGee."

Of all the teen idols that peopled the pop landscape before the arrival of the Beatles, Kris Jensen is considered one of the best. Tracking down his Hickory singles, or his (lone and highly collectible) *Torture* album, is not a bad idea.

JIMMY McGRIFF
I GOT A WOMAN, PART 1
(Ray Charles)
Sue 770
No. 20 *November 24, 1962*

Although James Harrell McGriff (b. Apr. 3, 1936, Philadelphia) was born into a musical family—his father was a pianist, his grandfather was a trombonist, and his brother played bass and drums—Jimmy wanted to be a policeman when he grew up. After a two-year stint during the Korean War in the U.S. Army as an MP and extensive study at the Pennsylvania Institute of Criminology, McGriff joined the Philadelphia police force.

It was not until McGriff heard jazz organist JIMMY SMITH playing a Hammond B-2 organ at a jam session that he began to reconsider his life's work. He had already toyed with the sax, violin, piano, and bass, playing the latter with Big Maybelle and in a number of bands; including those led by Charles Earland, Archie Shepp and Don Gardner (the Sonotones; later evolving into the pairing DON GARDNER & DEE DEE FORD).

Smith, who lived nearby in Norristown, offered to help McGriff with his organ playing. Jimmy left the police force, took lessons from Richard "Groove" Holmes, Milt Buckner, classical organist Sonny Gatewood and studied keyboards at Combe College in Philadelphia and New York's Juilliard.

In 1962, Juggy Murray signed McGriff to his New York-based Sue label. Jimmy's instrumental reading of Ray Charles' "I Got a Woman" clicked with jazz, rock, and R & B fans alike (R&B: #5). His style was jazzy, but danceable, and he continued to rack up Hot 100 chartings through the '60s with tunes like "All About My Girl" (#50, R&B: #15, 1963) b/w "M.G. Blues" (#95), "The Last Minute, Part 1" (#99, 1963), "Kiko" (#79, R&B: #79, 1964), and "The Worm" (#97, R&B: #28, 1968).

In the '80s, Jimmy saw a revival of interest in his recordings and tours; often in the accompaniment of Hank Crawford. Reportedly, his bluesy R & B-tinged etchings have been influential in the late '90s creation of "acid-jazz."

McGriff continues playing jazz organ to this day. As he has explained to Leonard Feather in the *Encyclopedia of Jazz*: "What I play isn't really jazz . . . it's sort of in between. Just old-time swing with a jazz effect."

MARCIE BLANE
BOBBY'S GIRL
(Henry Hoffman, Gary Klein)
Seville 120
No. 3 *December 1, 1962*

Marcie was no women's libber—all the poor little girl wanted to be in her whole darn life was "Bobby's Girl." Marcie, who was born on May 21, 1944, in Brooklyn, had just completed her home-economics classes and graduated from high school in June 1962. When Marv Holtzman, an A & R man from Seville Records, approached her about singing "Bobby's Girl," Marcie replied, "Sure." Teen girls could easily identify with Marcie's simple and stated wants, and bought up stacks of copies of "Bobby's Girl."

For the next few years, Marcie Blane continued to mine similar ground with "Little Miss Fool," "What Does a Girl Do?", and "Why Can't I Get a Guy?" They were all delightfully sweet but blatantly sexist singles. Male record collectors still play her demure disks, dreaming of her balloonlike bouffant and cherishing her singular sentiment.

By 1965, Marcie's name had disappeared from the record racks.

"[The music business] was impossible for me to deal with," Blane told *Goldmine*'s Bob Shannon and Jeff Tamarkin in 1989. "Everything changed. I felt very isolated and very lonely, and I decided not to continue. I couldn't. It was too difficult. I didn't feel comfortable in front of a lot of people, with everyone making a fuss. I didn't have the sense of myself I needed. It's taken all these years to be able to enjoy what there was."

Marcie Blane is currently married with two children and working as an education director at an arts theater in New York.

ROUTERS
LET'S GO (PONY)
(L. Duncan, R. Duncan)
Warner Bros. 5283
No. 19 *December 22, 1962*

At some point in the early '60s, there really was a legitimate group called the Routers, inspired by Dick Dale, "Father of Surfing Music." Mike Gordon has told record researcher Skip Rose that the original Routers consisted of Gordon, Lynn Frazier, Al Kait, Bill Moody, and some fellow he could only recall as Neil. Yet once this West Coast band hooked up with producer Joe Saraceno—half of TONY & JOE and producer of the Marketts, T-BONES—and Warner Bros., it seems that the Routers' line-up became markedly nebulous.

"Let's Go" (with the subtitle of "Pony") was a natural for the act's first 45, considering that a dance called the Pony was then something of a sensation. To capitalize on the enthusiastic response the disk received, the Routers' first LP, and the only one to sell in respectable quantities, was issued (*Let's Go With the Routers*, 1963). Even at this earliest of points in the Routers' flash flight to fame, many pop historians suspect that most of the

groups' members did not actually play on the Routers' records. Those who most likely did so were L.A. studio pros like Hal Blaine, Rene Hall, Plas Johnson, Sid Sharp, and future Walker brother, Scott Engel (a.k.a. Scott Walker).

More 45s and eventually more LPs were shipped by Warner Bros.; only "Sting Ray" (#50, 1963) managed to do well. In 1966, Jan Davis, a guitarist and regional charter with a biting instrumental called "The Fugitive," teamed up with the remnants of the Routers for a few RCA singles like "The Time Tunnel." And after a brief and largely undistributed outing on Mercury in 1973, the "Routers" name was boxed and buried.

TORNADOES
TELSTAR
(Joe Meek)
London 9561
No. 1 *December 22, 1962*

As a recording engineer, Joe Meek (b. 1933, Gloucester, England) did sessions for CHRIS BARBER'S JAZZ BAND, SHIRLEY BASSEY, Petula Clark, Lonnie Donegan, and FRANKIE VAUGHAN. Meek also wrote songs, and when one in particular was recorded by Tommy Steele, he took his royalties and opened his own studio and record label in North London—respectively, RGM Sound and Triumph Records.

To equip the studio with back-up musicians for recording sessions, Joe ran an ad in a London trade paper early in 1962. Five respondents were chosen: guitarist George Bellamy (b. Oct. 8, 1941, Sunderland, England), bassist Heinz Burt (b. July 25, 1942, Hargin, Germany), keyboardist Roger Lavern (b. Roger Jackson, Nov. 11, 1938, Kidderminster, England), plus two former members of Johnny Kidd's outfit, the Pirates—violinist/guitarist Alan Caddy (b. Feb. 2, 1940, London) and drummer Clem Cattini (b. Aug. 28, 1939, London).

Meek rehearsed the guys, tightened up their sound, and issued an unsuccessful debut 45, "Love and Fury." In 1962, when the U.S. launched the world's first communications satellite, Telstar, Joe was inspired to compose a commemorative instrumental featuring futuristic sound effects. The Tornadoes were on tour with Billy Fury, and Meek called them home. Legend has it that he managed to teach and tape the tune within 90 minutes.

British Decca acquired the rights, and London Records released "Telstar" in the States. The response was astounding. In a matter of weeks, the Tornadoes managed to do what no British group had ever done before—have a number-one hit in the U.S. The disk sold over 5 million copies worldwide. Numerous follow-ups were duly shipped, but only "Ride the Wind" (#57, 1963) charted, and while three more 45s clicked in the U.K., by year's end, the game was pretty much played out.

THE ORIGINAL TELSTAR THE SOUNDS OF THE Tornadoes

Burt was the first to leave, for a semi-successful solo singing career. Next went Bellamy, then Caddy, then Lavern. In 1965, Cattini, the last original Tornado, quit. Meek persisted and carried on the group's name with a completely new line-up, but with no further success. On February 3, 1966—eight years to the day after the death of Buddy Holly—he took his own life, with a shotgun.

As Bellamy complained to Fred Dellar, author of *Where Did You Go to, My Lovely?*: "Though ["Telstar"] made a fortune, somewhere in the link between Decca, Joe Meek, and ourselves, the money seemed to disappear. Certainly Decca paid all the royalties, there's no doubt about that. But we received very little—and when Joe Meek died, he was penniless. So you figure it out."

Bellamy recorded some solo singles for EMI, worked for a British publishing house, did studio sessions, and in 1971 formed his own SRT label. In 1975, he reassembled all the original Tornadoes except Caddy for one last effort as the New Tornadoes. Their remake of "Telstar" passed largely without notice.

Lavern now lives in Mexico, where he works in advertising. Cattini lives in north London and is a top-flight studio drummer. Burt lives in Southampton, where he has worked as a baker and a potato delivery man.

EXCITERS
TELL HIM
(Bert Russell)
United Artists 544
No. 4 *January 19, 1963*

Herb Rooney was born in 1941 and raised in New York City. Hankering for a better life, Herb and some of his buddies tried for years to get a break for their vocal group, the Continentals. Luck, however, was not on their side, and the group dispersed. With the Masters, Rooney got to record for Bingo Records, but sales were slow.

In 1962, Herb met what became the Masterettes, a sister group to the Masters—four singing, swinging high school juniors from Queens. Rooney thought that the girls—Brenda Reid, Carol Johnson, Lillian Walker, and Sylvia Wilbur—had a really hot sound. Their lone single, "Follow the Leader," for Lesage Records, flopped.

Sax man Al Sears referred Rooney and the girls to United Artist Records and production legends, Jerry Leiber and Mike Stoller. The duo concurred with Herb's assessment, and told Herb to stick around and sing bottom for the group, now redubbed the Exciters. Reportedly, Sylvia lost interest in the effort and dropped out of the group.

Before the year was out, the girls were out of school and the foursome's "Tell Him"—a Bert Russell (a.k.a. Bert Burns, author of "Twist And Shout" and a cover of a promising but inactive disk by Gil Hamilton (a.k.a. JOHNNY THUNDER)—was chugging up the charts. Listeners noticed not but it can now be revealed that Brenda, the lead vocalist, flubbed a number of lines and edits were made in the issued copy, along with a tape speed up to up the pitch and intensity.

Five more Exciters singles would place on the Hot 100: "He's Got the Power" (#57, 1963), "Get Him" (#76, 1963), the original version of the Manfred Mann hit "Do-Wah-Diddy (#78, 1964), "I Want You to Be My Baby" (#96, 1965), and a updated rendering of another Burns' composition, THE JARMELS' "A Little Bit of Soap" (#58, 1966).

In 1964, the Exciters switched to Roulette Records and recorded what may prove to be the first rock videos, made by an American group—one each for "Tell Him" and "He's Got the Power"—for Scopitone. Rooney and girls performed in Europe and the Caribbean, toured with Wilson Pickett, and opened for the Beatles. But after 1966 and a move to Burns' Bang Records, the media excitement died down to a dribble. Reid and Rooney—who had married in the '60s—continued to carry on whoopin' and hollerin', but in the '70s, Johnson and Walker quietly walked away from the Exciters, and were replaced by Skip McPhee and Ronnie Pace (both formerly of Mother Night). Tours of England brought the group a following on the northern soul circuit and a minor U.K. hit with "Reaching for the Beat" in 1975. Releases continued through the '70s on RCA, Elephant Y, Fargo, H & L, 20th Century, and Tomorrow—though billing shifted to "Brenda and Herb," reflecting the nature of the groups line-up.

Brenda and Herb are no longer together. Herb manages a cosmetic firm. The Exciters name carries on as a family tradition with Brenda fronting a unit composed

of offspring: Jeff, Tracy, Trisha, and sometimes Mark. Mark as "L.A. Reid" has produced and written for Young M.C., Eric B. and Rakim, Lisa Lisa, and Regina Belle.

By the turn of the decade, the act was recording for Ian Levine's Nightmare label as The Brand New Exciters.

JOHNNY THUNDER
LOOP DE LOOP
(Teddy Vann, Joe Dong)
Diamond 129
No. 4 *February 9, 1963*

"Like most everybody, I got my start in church and singing in high school," Thunder told this writer. "My friends got me into this. They told me I was good. I sang on street corners. And we'd just hang out half the night, till like one o'clock. Remember when that was late?"

None of Johnny's (b. Gil Hamilton, Aug. 15, 1941, Leesburg, FL) early group sides got recorded. "There wasn't that much of a recording industry down here then. It was the guys up north and on the West Coast who were doing all the records back in the '50s."

In 1959, Johnny headed up north in search of those recording opportunities. "I went to New York to work for the Drifters, as their lead singer. Ben E. King was getting ready to leave the group. Lacy Hollinswood was their road manager at the time. I had played football with him in high school. So, he use to tell me, 'You got to go to New York, man. You're great. You'd do good.' He kind of lied to me. So, I joined the Drifters for a few months and toured with them."

A few singles were issued under his God-given name for Fury and Capitol (the latter label even issued the original take on "Tell Him," which months later would be the EXCITERS biggie), but to make ends meet until he met his fate and Teddy Vann, Johnny had to do anonymous back-up singing sessions. "Teddy was a character. He was like the black Marlon Brando. We met by accident. Luther Vandeross, Dionne Warwick and others, and I were studio people. I just happened to be singing in the chorus, doing my back-up bit, trying to stay alive. And Teddy liked me and we did this "Don't Be Ashamed." We thought this was a good record. But we needed something to make the record bilaterally symmetrical . . . ," here John pauses to chuckle some to himself, "Ah, so we threw together this "Loop De Loop." We just made it all up as we went along; me and Teddy and his brother-in-law, Joey Dong. I was playing the drums, and they were feeding me words on scraps of paper. I just read what they handed me. It's sort of crazy, huh how things turn out. Teddy said it was a top-side song. The engineer came in and was gettin' to

mincing words about it. We all knew it was just a piece of garbage; all that is but Teddy. He said, 'You guys are crazy, it's a hit.'"

Thereafter, Thunder found himself being typecast. "It typecast me, boy did it ever. I met Bo Diddley and he said, 'I never seen nobody make a million dollars on nursery rhymes.' It's funny, but I wound up doing a lot of that simple stuff, like 'Ring Around the Rosey' (labeled "The Rosey Dance" #122, 1963) and "Everybody Do the Sloppy" (#67, 1965). That was Bert Burns' idea. I didn't want to do that. As a matter of fact, most of the records I did back in that era I didn't want to do. I didn't fight it so much because that 'Loop De Loop' hit, and I felt maybe I'd be lucky and hit it again, and then I'd get to do what I wanted to do."

Johnny did continue on making disks throughout the '60s for Diamond, Calla, and United Artist. Thunder is especially proud of his "Movin' and Shakin'" (issued on Vee Jay as by Gil Hamilton at the same time that he was on the charts with "Loop"), his only '70s effort for Arista, "Till the Waters Stop Running," and "I'm Alive" (#122, 1969). "That was my best. It was my first true rock effort and Bob Dylan in a *Rolling Stone* article said that it was the best record he'd ever heard."

Johnny Thunder still is actively performing and hopes to record some more hits, even flops, he adds, "Currently I'm working on a compilation LP. I'm not done yet, no-o-o."

NED MILLER
FROM A JACK TO A KING
(Ned Miller)
Fabor 114
No. 6 *February 16, 1963*

Most would have bet that it was not in the cards for Ned Miller. His voice was rough, sad, and old-timey, even to country ears. His "From a Jack to a King" had been recorded in 1957, and had sold poorly when released by Dot Records that year. Who could have figured that nine years later, this very same flop would be reissued and sell more than 2 million copies?

Ned was born Henry Miller in Rains, Utah, on April 12, 1925, and raised in Salt Lake City. His mother taught him how to play guitar, and by his teenage years, he was writing songs. Ned served three years in the Marines, and on his return, he studied two years under the G.I. Bill to become a pipefitter.

A pipefitter Ned may have remained, had BONNIE GUITAR not taken one of his tunes, "Dark Moon," to the Top 10 in 1957. Dot Records, Bonnie's label, was interested in just who this Ned Miller might be, and recorded his "From a Jack to a King." It bombed, and Ned returned to writing songs and pipefitting.

In 1962, Fabor Robinson, the owner of Fabor Records (where Ned had recorded the "Jack" track), decided to give the Dot disk another spin, and reissued the very same recording on his own label. To the surprise of all parties involved, even Robinson, the record sold its way into the Top 10.

Nothing that Ned ever recorded could match the success of his eerie incantation. In 1964, "Do What You Do Do Well" reached number 52 on the Hot 100, but Miller's big-name days were over. Ned tried throughout the remainder of the '60s to attain renown in the country field, but to little avail.

Ned Miller's current activities and whereabouts are not known. A lone album did appear on Plantation Records in 1981.

JOE HARNELL
FLY ME TO THE MOON—BOSSA NOVA
(Bart Howard)
Kapp 497
No. 14 February 23, 1963

Born in the Bronx, New York, on August 2, 1924, Joe Harnell studied at the Trinity College of Music in London and at Tanglewood, where for four years he studied under Leonard Bernstein, Aaron Copland, and Darius Milhaud. Once his education was complete, he became the conductor and arranger for Pearl Bailey, Marlene Dietrich, ROBERT GOULET, Peggy Lee, Anthony Newley, and Frank Sinatra. In addition to writing some piano preludes, chamber works, and art songs, Joe became the music director for many television programs, including "The Bionic Woman," "Cliffhangers," "The Incredible Hulk," and "The Mike Douglas Show." Recording for Columbia, Epic, Jubilee, Kapp, and Motown Records, Harnell has had more than a dozen albums issued.

The bossa nova—a sound, a style, and a dance—became a hot item in the winter of 1962. Following the release of Stan Getz & Astrud Gilberto's "The Girl From Ipanema," and preceding Eydie Gorme's "Blame It on the Bossa Nova" by a week or two, was Joe Harnell's instrumental, "Fly Me to the Moon—Bossa Nova." The tune eventually charted by five different artists, including LaVern Baker and Bobby Wommack. Harnell's follow-up, "Diane," pulled into the Hot 100 at the number 97 position for a week before vanishing from the land of pop culture.

Given Joe Harnell's musical background, he probably didn't mind being a One-Hit Wonder. After all, there were still all those TV shows to score, all those easy-listening albums to create, and all those Tin Pan Alley singers to conduct and arrange.

JAN BRADLEY
MAMA DIDN'T LIE
(Curtis Mayfield)
Chess 1845
No. 14 March 9, 1963

When she was about four years of age, Addie Bradley (b. July 6, 1943, Byhalia, MS) and her family moved to Robbins, a suburb of Chicago. Early on, her mother and father noticed she had a talent for singing. In 1961, Don Talty, manager of R & B guitarist PHIL UPCHURCH and owner of Formal Records, discovered Jan at a high school talent show. He had to wait two years, until Jan graduated, to get her parents' consent to become her manager and launch her recording career.

Through Upchurch, Talty got the Impressions' Curtis Mayfield to write some songs for her. "We Girls," Jan's debut disk and a Mayfield composition, sold well in Chicago, and garnered heavy airplay in the Midwest. There was something special to Jan's soft soul sound. "Sometimes as a singer it's not how well you sing," Mayfield told *Goldmine*'s Bob Pruter, "it's just that innocence or that certain something about the artist that makes a song appealing. Jan had that innocence in her voice."

After a few unsuccessful 45s, Jan recorded Mayfield's "Mama Didn't Lie," her big moment in Top 40-land. Perhaps if Mayfield had come up with more material for Jan to do, her career could have picked up some momentum. But as Bradley told *Goldmine*, Mayfield and Chess Records parted ways over a dispute concerning publishing rights.

Aside from the minor success of "I'm Over You" (#93, 1965), Jan Bradley was thence forth absent from the nation's pop charts. Talty produced a dozen more singles for Chess and for the small Adanti, Doylen, and Spectra Sound labels. But despite some fine Bradley-penned songs, guitar licks by Upchurch, and the occasional production wizardry of Billy Davis, nothing further clicked.

In 1970, Jan Bradley called it quits. She married, raised a family, returned to school, and earned an M.A. degree. She is now known as Janice Johnson, social worker.

CASCADES
RHYTHM OF THE RAIN
(John Gummoe)
Valiant 6026
No. 3 March 9, 1963

The Cascades were a self-contained band from San Diego, California. John Gummoe, the unit's spokesperson, lead vocalist/guitarist, and writer of their tip-top

n Bradley

tune, met pianist Eddie Snyder and the three Daves—bassist Stevens, saxophonist Wilson, and drummer Zabo—in the late '50s. By 1962, the group had developed a solid reputation for supplying smooth sounds for parties and dances. One night, while the guys were working their magic at a club called the Peppermint Stick, an executive from Valiant Records happened to catch their act. In late 1962, the label ushered Gummoe and the Cascades into Hollywood's Gold Star Studios to lay down "Second Chance" for their first 45. The platter stiffed, but "Rhythm of the Rain" rocked the pop and R & B (#7) charts.

The follow-up, "Shy Girl" (#91, 1963) b/w "The Last Leaf" (#60), proved to be a double-sided charter with airplay split between the two tunes. The Cascades switched to RCA and issued "For Your Sweet Love" (#86, 1963). Although the latter 45, and subsequent Cascades cuts, were solid efforts, the group to many sounded dated (and, with Beatlemania in full force, much too American) to record-buyers. Neil Young played guitar on their 1967 single for Smash, "Flying on the Ground." By 1969, only Dave Wilson remained from the original line-up.

ROCKIN' REBELS
WILD WEEKEND
(Phil Todaro, Tommy Shannon)
Swan 4125
No. 8 *March 9, 1963*

"I was a elementary school teacher; 30 years, now. I just retired [fall 1997]," said Paul Balon, the Rebels' (later billed the Buffalo Rebels, still later without their permission, the Rockin' Rebels) rhythm guitarist, in an exclusive interview. "If we'd got our money and another hit, I don't know if it woulda been the best thing. I've had a good life now, but I don't know if me and the Kippers [Jimmy and Mickey] woulda done so well, if things hadda happened different.

"Look, on that thing ["Wild Weekend"] I played three chords—think I knew five—and I didn't know why or how they were put together; didn't know anything. The drummer was the worst of us. We stunk! Listen close, our instruments weren't even in tune. If we could just record it again without the mistakes, it might be a nice stupid tune."

Paul Balon and Jimmy (lead guitar) and Mickey Kipper (sax) and Tommy Gorman (drums)—no bass—were the Rebels; hometown, Lackawanna, New York, just south of Buffalo. "We were together for about two years. This is '57, '58. I was going to a Timon Catholic High; raised in a restaurant. Filet mignon, lobster; didn't know what a hot dog was till I got married. My teacher, at Ruda's Music School introduced me to

Jimmy and his brother Mickey; raised by this Hungarian grandmother. Tommy was an orphan.

"In those days, local groups were able to put out records, by small companies and get played locally. They'd sell 5,000 copies—if lucky—and get work from it. This disk jockey named Tommy Shannon owned Mar-Lee with Phil Todaro. The label name had something to do with their girl friends; like Mary and Lee Ann, or so. Tommy Shannon had a theme song, and he was the weekend jock for WKBW, the Top 40 station in Buffalo. His theme went, 'Tommy Shannon Show/KB radio . . . things get better/we'll give you news and weather/Tommy Shannon Show.' The melody was what became 'Wild Weekend.'"

Writing credits were given to Phil Todaro, a local record producer and Tommy Shannon Buffalo jock with a night-time spot called "The Wild Weekend Show." The show's theme was reportedly previously recorded by a little known area act, the Russ Hallet Trio.

"Now this is '58 and Tommy [Shannon] was gonna have us do 'Red River Valley'; when he walked in on the session we were playing his theme as an instrumental, and he says, 'Record that.' We did; and we recorded 'Red River Valley,' but somehow that got to this other group and they [Johnny & The Hurricanes] recorded it and it became this big hit; exact arrangement as ours. Never figured that one out. . . ."

"Wild Weekend" was issued during the fall of 1959. "We did the local bandstands and got to do the Dick Clark Show, too," said Paul. "Clark asked me—live on the air—why call yourselves the Rebels? Being young and scared out of my gourd, I said, 'Cause Duane Eddy's our idol and we copied everything he does.' Very soon after someone told us the name had to be changed [Label credits then read, "The Buffalo Rebels"].

"They told us it sold about 100,000, the first time around; but they didn't give us any money so we were gone by the time it became a major hit in '62. Never got a penny, nope; not for the Mar-Lee record or the reissue—got nothin'. Tommy Shannon, then a Buffalo State art major, got a new Corvette. We're sure he got the money, but he denies it to today. We were babes in the dark woods. Tommy [Gorman] didn't have no one and the rest of our parents didn't know about the business; fact, my dad wanted me to go to college or work his restaurant. No one directed us, or much cared that we made music."

Only one follow-up—"Buffalo Blues" b/w "Donkey Walk"—was issued by Paul and the original group, before their attentions by necessity turned to the business of making a living. "That thing sold s-l-o-w, like at a walk. We never got paid, so we never went back," Paul said. "Another group promoted 'Wild Weekend,' as the 'Rockin' Rebels'; but the record was our record. Nothing was changed or rerecorded. They made up some-

thing for the flip side and a whole album of stuff was put out. The only thing on that album that is us, the Rebels, the Buffalo Rebels—is 'Wild Weekend.'"

"Wild Weekend" sold Top 10 and the public craved for Rebel-rockin' instrumentals. In order to flesh out an album for a long dead group, unknown musicians were rushed into Swan's studios to rework classics like "Whole Lotta Shakin' Going On," "Tequila," and "Telstar."

The Rockin' Rebels moniker was utilized for one further Hot 100 charting, a number called "Rockin' Crickets" (#87, 1963). The record was identical to an earlier release—also titled "Rockin' Crickets" (#57, 1959)—by a band known as the Hot-Toddys. These Toddy's were a legitimate Canadian unit—Port Colborne, Canada—that in the late '50s consisted of Terry Gibson (lead vocals), Vaughn Jonah (guitar), Garry Kelba (drums), Johnny "T-Bone" Little (bass), and Bill Pernell (sax).

"I never heard of that record," said Balon. "That was our follow-up, huh?" Apparently Shannon and Todaro were involved in the ownership of Shan-Todd label that originally issued the Hot-Toddys' "Rockin' Crickets." Three more Rockin' Rebels singles are known to have been issued, all without the participation of Paul and the original band.

Paul went to University of Buffalo; flunked out. Thereafter he went on the road with the Speedy Garfin band, worked steel mills, returned to college, graduated, married, and was a elementary teacher for 30 years. Paul retired in 1997. Mickey sold cars; Jimmy was an Army recruiter, stationed in Buffalo. The Kippers remained music makers, becoming regulars, as the Rebels, at Ciro's in Buffalo; later as the Kippers, a jazz bar band outfit. The brothers worked the area's theater pit and TV sessions. Tom "got into bad company" and his whereabouts for the last 30 years are unknown.

BILL PURSELL
OUR WINTER LOVE
(J. Cowell)
Columbia 42619
No. 9 *March 30, 1963*

Bill was born in Oakland and raised in Tulare, California. He learned to read music and play the piano before the age of five. After high school, he attended the Peabody Conservatory of Music in Baltimore on a composition fellowship. During World War II, Bill worked for three years as the official arranger for the Air Force Band in Washington, D.C. Once the war was over, Bill attended the Eastman School of Music in Rochester, where he received both B.A. and M.A. degrees and won the first Edward B. Benjamin Award in

composition. Bill, wife, and three little ones moved to a hillside house in Tennessee, where for years thereafter, he performed with the Nashville Symphony Orchestra and taught at Nashville's Vanderbilt University.

In 1962, Columbia Records signed Bill to a contract and sent him into the studio—with Grady Martin directing and BILL JUSTIS in the role of music arranger—to cut an album that would contain Pursell's haunting instrumental, "Our Winter Love." Never to chart again, Bill Pursell did not just vanish, however. Piles of singles and albums for the Dot, Epic, and Alton labels were issued. Bill continued teaching, as well as playing sessions behind Nashville's country pickers.

JOHNNY CYMBAL
MR. BASS MAN
(Johnny Cymbal)
Kapp 503
No. 16 *April 13, 1963*

Johnny Cymbal is best known for his 1963 doo-wop tribute hit "Mr. Bass Man." Few fans know that after numerous recordings—many under assumed names—Cymbal would return to the Top 40 listings in the late '60s with his recording of the million-selling "Cinnamon (Let Me In)," under the name of "Derek."

Two-time One-Hit Wonder Cymbal eventually turned his attentions elsewhere. He became the music director for the "Partridge Family" and the cartoon show "Catnooga Cats." He produced Gene Pitney and Mae West recordings, wrote tunes for Bette Midler, Reba McIntire, Terri Gibbs, and Elvis Presley. It was Presley who made a major hit out of Cymbal's "Mary in the Morning."

During his brief life-stay not much was written on Johnny Cymbal. "It's been said that I led a band at the age of seven. Now, that's a nice story," said Cymbal, who was born in Ochitree, Scotland, on February 3, 1945. "It didn't happen that way, but it's a nice story. . . . I mean, my life didn't start until I was about 13 or so when I saw this band in our town square [in Goderich, Ontario]. Only then did I get the idea of singing. And the next week, I was up there with them, ah, singing 'My Bucket's Got a Hole in It." That was my first song. After that I learned how to play the guitar some by watching this country show on TV."

In the late '50s, John almost got placed with Cameo-Parkway, but the label found out he lived in Canada and thought it would be too much of a hassle getting him around.

"The next year my folks moved to Cleveland, and I met this fellow through one of those song-poem things—you know, that you'd see in the backs of teen mags—that read 'We'll put your song to music. Send us your poems.' There was really something to it, and this guy liked me and brought me to this big DJ [at WWIN] in Baltimore, Jack Gale; who later became my manager. He had me sing at a hop that very night . . . The kids just went crazy. I just played guitar and it was the wildest thing I had ever seen. There happened to be a promotion man there and the next thing I knew I was signed to MGM and sent to Nashville to record."

"The Water Is Red" was his second release for MGM. "Yeah, yeah, it was tacky, wasn't it?" said Cymbal between choked laughter. In this 2 1/2-minute tale the girl of all of our dreams is eaten by a hungry shark. The record stirred some scattered radio action and some stomachs, too. "Jim Vinneau, my producer, had just done [Mark Dinning's] 'Teen Angel,' and he was convinced that death songs were the new thing. It didn't sell well enough so that was my last record for MGM. I thought, I was a has-been at 17."

Singles later, Cymbal again almost had a hit on Kedlen with the Bobby Vee-ish "Bachelor Man." "That was only a demo I made out in California," said Cymbal. "It wasn't suppose to be sold. I learned somebody also gave it to VeeJay, and they issued it, too. Now, I never saw any money on that one."

A switch to Kapp Records and John finally had his big moment with his first release, the self-penned "Mr. Bass Man." The tune with the throw-back sound was an up-tempo praise for that dwindling breed, the doo-wop bass man. "I had wrote this tribute song before I

was with the Kapp," he said. "I took it to New York. Columbia Records was interested, but it took them too long to decide, or something. The bass part on that record is done by Ronnie Bright. He'd been in the Valentines and the Cadillacs and was the bass guy you hear on Barry Mann's 'Who Put the Bomp?'"

For his follow-up, Johnny got himself into another tear-tumbler. "Teenage Heaven" (#58, *Billboard*'s Hot 100) told of all those eventual dead rock'n'rollers—Elvis, Ricky . . .—condemned to live out eternity locked in the bodies and minds of lusting teenagers. What a vision! Some radio stations rode this number like it had a satin saddle, others tossed it in the can. And again some sensitive stomachs were turned. "Ah, yeah, it was another dead and dyin' one," Cymbal said. "Course listening to it now it's, ah, all too real. Anyway, it failed to do it. So, again I was a has-been."

Kapp Records ran out of patience, and Johnny moved to Don Costa's DCP label, then switched to Columbia and Musicor ("I don't even remember that," said Cymbal. "I recorded for them, huh?"), and eventually he moved to the Amaret label. Nothing more charted. Cymbal's attention shifted to producing, writing, and occasionally appearing as a studio-only act—Johnny recorded some tracks as Milk for the bubblegum Buddah label. Milk soured, but not so for some sides Cymbal had issued as by "Derek" for Bang Records. John's co-written "Cinnamon (Let Me In)" returned him nearly to the Top 10 in 1968.

"I had just wrote 'Mary in the Morning,' probably the most successful song I've written," he said. "And I had the deal to produce Gene Pitney and some other acts. I did the vocals on 'Cinnamon,' but I thought, 'I can't go out on the road and produce these things as well.' So my brother Derek, who was a part of my band, at the time, went out as me. . . . At the time, there was three different Crystals and two different Drifters, so it seemed okay to have two different Dereks."

Other than the follow-up, "Back Door Man," which charted at #59 on *Billboard*, future Derek disks sold like duds. "The name had run its course," he said. "And my brother had gone out as me, as Derek, and hated it all. So, we were stuck without an act. By then, I was producing Mae West and the Partridge Family, so I just shelved the whole Derek idea."

Late in 1969, Johnny pulled some more name changes when he recorded as Taurus for Tower Records and then Brother John for A & M and . . . Months later, he struck up a relationship with Peggy Clinger, of the Clinger Sisters, a four sibling act that had appeared as regulars on the "Smothers Brothers Show." "They were to the "Smothers Show" what the Osmonds were to the "Andy Williams Show," Cymbal explained. "Peggy and I got together and wrote 'Rock Me Baby' for David Cassidy." For a few years, records were issued by Cymbal & Clinger.

Over the years, Johnny Cymbal continued to make public appearances, to be involved in production work, and every now and then reappeared with a new single. "I've lived in Nashville for the last decade, producing some things, but mainly I've been writing," Cymbal said. "I've had about 20 chart records on the country listings; things like "I'm Drinkin' Canada Dry" (the Burrito Brothers) and "Fire in the Sky" (the Wright Brothers). "I've been fortunate," he said. "People still remember my name. It's primarily due to 'Mr. Bass Man,' I know. And yes, Johnny Cymbal is my real God-given name."

Johnny Cymbal died of an apparent heart attack, on March 16, 1993 in Nashville. He was 48.

CHANTAYS
PIPELINE
(Bob Spickard, Brian Carman)
Dot 16440
No. 4 *May 4, 1963*

With only eight months of musical experience, Bob Spickard and Brian Carman created "Pipeline," possibly the best surfing song ever, and one of only two surfing instrumentals to ever reach *Billboard*'s Top 10.

Spickard (lead guitar) and Warren Waters (bass) were high school buddies. In the summer of 1961, they decided to learn how to play some instruments and become a surfin' band. In short order, fellow Santa Ana High School students Brian Carman (guitar), Bob Marshall (piano), and Bob Welch (drums) were enlisted.

"Pipeline" started out as a tough little dual-guitar idea that Spickard and Carman originally called "Liberty's Whip" and later "44 Magnum." But after seeing a surf flick about the notorious Hawaiian Pipeline, they named their tune "Pipeline." While playing a dance at the Big Bear, the Chantays were discovered by DJ Jack Sands, who offered to be their manager and get them a recording contract.

A few sides were cut at the Pal Recording Studio in Cucamonga, and Sands hawked the sounds around to the L.A. labels. No one nibbled except Bill and Jack Wenzel's Downey Record Company. The dinky label was buzzing with the mild surfin' success of the Rumblers' "Boss," and the Wenzels hoped that in securing the Chantays, they might continue their winning streak.

Within weeks of its release, "Pipeline" was a national hit and, as with the Rumblers disks, Dot Records stepped in to provide national distribution. An album was churned out, potential singles were cut and canned, but trouble was brewing. Promotion and touring by the group was limited, since the members were all full-time high school students. The guys fired Sands on the grounds that he was skimming too much off the top of the Chantays' earnings. Follow-up singles were issued—"Monsoon," "Space Probe," "Only If You Care"—but nothing charted or even appeared on *Billboard*'s "Bubbling Under the Hot 100" chart. After a three-month tour of Hawaii in the summer of 1964, the Chantays called it quits.

Bob Spickard joined his father-in-law's industrial equipment business. When last spotted, he was the president of the L & A Products Company. Brian Carman was last seen working at a musical instrument store in Anaheim, California. Bob Welch now works in a clothing store in Los Angeles. Spickard, Carman, and Welch still perform together on occasion as the Catalina Good Time Band. Rob Marshall plays part-time in a C & W band and is a school teacher in the Chico area of California. Warren Waters is reportedly a successful real estate broker.

THE CHANTAYS

ROCKY FELLERS
KILLER JOE
(Russell, Elgin, Medley)
Scepter 1246
No. 16 *May 18, 1963*

Frank "Killer Joe" Piro was the dancer who taught high society how to do everything from the Frug to the Watusi. They called him "Killer Joe" because he could out last anyone on the dance floor. For decades, the little guy did his stuff on both the big stage and the little screen. Mostly what he did was make the Manhattan rounds, hopping and bopping at all the glitzy parties and clubs. The Duke and Duchess of Windsor, and dance-floor damsel Luci Baines Johnson, were among his countless students

Poppa Feller (b. 1924) had a house full of sons and daughters, born and raised in Manila, the Philippines. His boys—Eddie (b. 1955), Albert (b. 1953), Tony (b. 1947), and Junior (b. 1945)—were musically inclined, and, beginning in 1959, they formed a group. Pop and his rockin' and rollin' Rocky Fellers made periodic stops in the States, appearing on "The Ed Sullivan Show" and other variety programs.

Nothing much happened with the Rocky Fellers' first sides for the Parkway label. But in 1963, the group recorded a little tribute tune to this peerless, pirouetting Piro. "Killer Joe" sold well; it was, however, a novelty number, much like the band itself. Once its newness turned stale, the Fellers and their disks faded from view.

"Killer Joe" Piro, however, danced on. Dorian Gray had nothing on Frank. Reportedly, he danced until he died on February 5, 1988.

DARTELLS
HOT PASTRAMI
(Doug Phillips)
Dot 16453
No. 11 *May 25, 1963*

With their first serving, the Dartells cut the mustard. Fried, boiled, and sauteed, "Hot Pastrami" was an enjoyably sloppy hit. Doug Phillips, leader of this group from Oxnard, California, claimed credit for writing this tune. But "Hot Pastrami" is actually a knock-off of an earlier number—"Mashed Potatoes," recorded in 1960 by Nat Kendricks, then James Brown's drummer.

The California kids were between 18 and 20 when their coach and manager, Tom Ayres, plucked them from out of the teen-scene clubs to audition for Buddy Jack at Arlen Records. Phillips (bass, vocals), Dick Burns (guitar), Gary Peeler (drums), Rich Peil (sax),

Randy Ray (organ), and Corky Wilkie (sax) whipped up a batch of the stuff they were successfully serving up at the nightspots. Most of these tunes were instrumentals in the tradition of the MAR-KEYS and Booker T. & The MGs.

Arlen Records decided to give the fellows a try, and wham, "Hot Pastrami." Dot Records picked up the national distribution when the "Pastrami" got hot, but nothing the band ever recorded thereafter got more than lukewarm. "Dance, Everybody Dance," the follow-up, checked into the charts at number 99 for a week, and then rightfully scurried for obscurity. A cover version of the Beau Marks "Clap Your Hands" interested almost no one, and the Dartells disbanded.

Doug Phillips formed another group in the late '60s called the New Concepts, and had singles issued on ABC-Paramount and Atco. In 1971, while fronting Cottonwood, Phillips and his band released *Camaraderie*, a hard-rockin' album for ABC. It is not known what became of the other members of the Dartells. There is some indication that a portion of the group remained intact to record several stray singles as a group called Rain.

BILL ANDERSON
STILL
(Bill Anderson)
Decca 31458
No. 8 *June 8, 1963*

"Whispering Bill," as he became known for his talkie singing style, was born James Anderson on November 1, 1937, in Columbia, South Carolina. In high school in Commerce, Georgia, Bill wrote songs, ran his own band, won talent contests, and worked as a DJ. He attended the University of Georgia's School of Journalism, all the while singing, writing, and winning contests. After graduation, Anderson became a sportswriter for the *DeKalb New Era* and a correspondent to the *Atlanta Constitution*.

In 1958, RAY PRICE recorded one of Bill's tunes, "City Lights," which went Top 10 on the country charts. Bill was given the chance to make some recordings for Decca Records; first out of the barn was "That's What It's Like to Be Lonesome." Throughout most of the '60s, Bill's voice or the results of his pen were hardly ever off the C & W charts. His duets with Jan Howard, and with Mary Lou Turner, also found a sizable country audience. ROY CLARK, ROY DRUSKY, MERLE HAGGARD, Jim Reeves, Connie Smith, Porter Wagoner, and Kitty Wells all had hits with Bill's tunes.

The Country Music Association named Anderson "Top Songwriter of the Year" from 1963 to 1965, "Top Male Vocalist of the Year" in 1963, and the creator of the "Record of the Year" ("Still") in 1963. Four other country hits by Anderson crossed over to the Hot 100 charts from 1962 through 1978. Bill also found the time to make appearances in minor movies like *Forty Acre Feud*, *Las Vegas Hillbillies*, *Country Music on Broadway*, and *The Road to Nashville*.

Bill Anderson has been recording for his own Whispering label, though his singles don't make the country charts like they did some decades back. Bill seems to spend most of his energy acting in soap operas and hosting various syndicated game shows like "Mr. and Mrs." and "Fandango." His autobiography, *Whispering Bill*, was published in 1989.

KYU SAKAMOTO
SUKIYAKI
(Hachidai Nakamura, Rokusuke Ei)
Capitol 4945
No. 1 *June 15, 1963*

The crash of a Japan Airlines 747 near Tokyo on August 12, 1985, claimed 520 lives, including that of Kyu Sakamoto. Kyu was one of only three Japanese artists (the other two are PINK LADY and the Yellow Magic Orchestra) to ever chart on *Billboard*'s Hot 100. "Sukiyaki" was the only record of the bunch to reach number one, and the only Hot 100 hit sung entirely in Japanese.

"Sukiyaki" was a tearjerker that had absolutely nothing to do with the Japanese taste treat. No, this was a tale of misery and desolation, as the translated lyrics indicate: "Sadness hides in the shadow of the stars/Sadness lurks in the shadow of the moon/I look up when I walk so the tears won't fall. . . ."

Kyu was born in 1941 in the industrial city of Kawasaki, the ninth child of a Tokyo restaurateur. In his teen years, he sang in jazz clubs, and was discovered by Toshiba Records in 1959 while fronting a group called the Paradise Kings. Kyu scored 15 homeland hits, made appearances in 10 movies, and was a regular on several radio and TV programs—all before recording "Sukiyaki" and the follow-up, "China Nights (Shina No Yori)" (#58, 1963).

Sakamoto's Top 40 moment was largely due to Louis Benjamin, then the head of England's Pye Records. While visiting Japan on business, Benjamin heard Kyu's ode and brought it home for his new artist, jazzman KENNY BALL, to record. The lyrics were dumped. Figuring that no one in the world would touch a tune with a title like "Ue O Muite Aruko" ("I Look Up When I Walk"), Benjamin decided to name the record after one of his favorite culinary delights. Ball's version eventually made the British Top 10. Meanwhile, in the States, Richard Osborne, a DJ at

KYU SAKAMOTO

KORD in Pasco, Washington, started playing and replaying Kyu's original rendition. The response was better than favorable, and the rest is history.

Before the sun set on Sakamoto's stateside success, his first and last LP—*Sukiyaki and Other Japanese Hits*, 1963—was packaged and pushed. Although satiation would set in all too soon, record-buyers snapped it up.

TOM GLAZER & THE DO-RE-MI CHILDREN'S CHORUS
ON TOP OF SPAGHETTI
(Tom Glazer)
Kapp 526
No. 14 *July 6, 1963*

Seeing that young Tom (b. Sept. 3, 1914, Philadelphia) took an interest in music, Mrs. Glazer encouraged him to sing in choirs and learn the basics on a number of instruments. After three years at New York's City College, Tom managed to earn a living playing tuba or string bass in jazz and military bands. By the '40s, Glazer turned to singing folk tales for children. From 1945 to 1947, he fronted "Tom Glazer's Music Box," a radio program over the ABC network. Later in the decade, he made singing or acting appearances on radio shows such as "Listening Post," "Theatre Guild on the Air," "True Story," and "We the People." He narrated Sweet Land of Liberty and wrote the score for the Andy Griffith-Patricia Neal movie *A Face in the Crowd* (1957).

From 1953 through 1967, Glazer recorded sing-a-long and folkie-flavored disks, his releases for the Young People's record label reportedly selling in the hundreds of thousands. While most who recall his name associate Tom with his parody of Burl Ives's "On Top of Old Smokey" (#10, 1952), Glazer has also had success as a songwriter, usually as a lyricist. He was involved in the co-creation of "Old Soldiers Never Die" for Vaughn Monroe (#7, 1951); "Pussy Cat" for the Ames Brothers (#17, 1958); "Skokiaan" for Ralph Marterie (#3, 1954) and the Four Lads (#7, 1954); "Till We Two Are One" for Georgie Shaw (#7, 1954); "Melody of Love' for Billy Vaughn (#2, 1955), the Four Aces (#3, 1955), and David Carroll (#8, 1955); and "More" for KAI WINDING (#8, 1963) and Vic Dana (#42, 1963).

ROLF HARRIS
TIE ME KANGAROO DOWN, SPORT
(Rolf Harris)
Epic 9596
No. 3 *July 13, 1963*

"The most famous Australian in the world," said Q magazine of Rolf Harris, in 1995. "Hey, I invented

ROLF HARRIS

tralian calypso. Instead of a donkey, I'll have a kangaroo in there somewhere."

Rolf's notoriety has rolled right along in England and Australia, where a number of his fractured follow-ups have charted. His 1969 reworking of a 1903 anti-war song "Two Little Boys" was reportedly the biggest-selling disk in the U.K. that year. In the late '60s, Harris had his own BBC-TV series, "Hey Presto, It's Rolf," and his own wildlife TV series, "Survival." In 1968, he received a royal accolade when he was awarded a medal from the Order of the British Empire, an honor he again received in 1977.

Rolf was the target for life-threatening threats in the early '90s. "I was touring in Australia," said Rolf to *Vox's* Ian McCann. "There was this TV show called 'The Money or the Gun.' I was asked to go on and do a musical item of some sort, and they asked me to do 'Stairway to Heaven.' I said, 'I don't know it' and they said, 'Well, you know of it,' and no, I didn't. I'd gotta be the only person in the world who'd never even heard of it, never mind heard it."

It was the policy of the program to every week have someone different do the tune. There'd been an operatic version, a folk-*a cappella* . . . and now with wobble board and didgeridoo (an oversized drone-making wooden pipe), Rolf Harris' one-of-a-kind rendering. "It was such a namby-pamby bloody dreadful song," said Rolf to *Q's* Tony Hibbert. An album, *Stairways to Heaven*—22 versions—was issued in Australia; Harris' cut dispensed as a single went Top Ten. Led Zeppelin fans thought it sacrilegious; Rolf fans went ga-ga.

Although, totally unknown to his American audience, Rolf operates as a "serious" painter. A 1992, British opinion poll asking a thousand Londoners to name a famous painter, found Harris mentioned by 38%; beating Michelangelo and Rembrandt. Harris's latest TV endeavor is "Animal Hospital," which reportedly attracts 11 million viewers per episode.

"I'm just a novelty-type guy doing weirdo bloody comedy. I'm bloody sorry that I've limited myself to being a weirdo comedy bloke," said Rolf, on his life's work, to Hibbert.

world music?," said Harris. "I suppose, in a way, I did. I pioneered world music, certainly."

Rolf (b. Mar. 30, 1930, Perth, Australia) was full of talent and eager to gain fame and fortune; won the junior backstroke championship, when 15 (an achievement he remains most proud of). At the age of 22, he moved to England and became a TV cartoonist and storyteller. He sculpted, painted, sang, and pounded musical instruments. In 1956, London's Royal Academy of Art held an exhibition of his art works.

Whenever he felt homesick, Rolf would visit the Down Under Club. It was there that he began singing his strange songs and "wobbling" in public. "Wobbling" is shaking a warped Masonite board to produce bizarre rhythmic sounds. It was in large measure this strange sound that sold the world on Rolf's kookie "Kangaroo" number; recorded in his bathroom with a tiny tape recorder and originally called "Kangalpso." In England, where the tune was a hit three years before its stateside embrace, the nutty need for record-buyers to create that sound at home became such that Masonite shipped out 55,000 warped boards.

"I liked [Harry Belafonte's] 'Hold 'Em Down,'" said Harris to *Wacky Top 40* authors, on the creation of his hit. "There was this line that went, 'Don't tie me donkey down there, let him bray, let him bray.' And I thought, That's good. I can change that and make it an Aus-

DORIS TROY
JUST ONE LOOK
(Doris "Doris Troy" Payne, Gregory Carroll)
Atlantic 2188
No. 10 *July 27, 1963*

Born on January 6, 1937, Doris Payne was raised in the heart of New York City and soul of Mount Calvary Church, where her daddy was the preacher. From childhood on, she sang in the church choir and became the lead in various offshoot church groups. In the '50s, she

worked as an usherette at the famed Apollo Theatre, joined a jazzy trio called the Halos (not to be confused with THE HALOS, known for "Nag"), recorded as the "Dee" half of a short-lived Shirley & Lee-ish Jay & Dee, and dashed off tunes in her spare time.

One of Doris's numbers, "How About That," made its way through the channels and was spotted by Dee Clark, who charted (#33, 1960) with his recording of it. Jackie Wilson and Chuck Jackson recorded some of her creations; Jackson and Solomon Burke sought her out to sing backup for their recording sessions. James Brown, after hearing her at a local nightclub, took an interest in Doris and walked her into Atlantic Records.

"Just One Look" was Doris's very first single. The record was solid in sound, with a gospel edge and just a touch of teen—catchy, powerful, and somehow hard to forget. The Hollies covered "Just One Look" and drove it deep into the British Top 10. Yet Troy's original did not even chart in the U.K., and her follow-up, "What'cha Gonna Do About It," did poorly here and only skirted England's charts.

Nothing more ever charted. Doris switched labels, first to Calla, then to Capitol Records. In 1969, she moved her body and soul to England to record some singles and an album for the Beatles' Apple label. Doris Troy featured a high-powered line-up of guest musicians; Doris co-wrote some of the songs with George Harrison, Ringo Starr, and Stephen Stills. In 1973, she won an immortality of sorts when she and Clare Torry sang back-up on Pink Floyd's *Dark Side of the Moon*.

Doris Troy still resides in London, still sings, still writes songs, still occasionally records tunes for British-only release—and still awaits that next and long-deserved hit.

CLASSICS
TILL THEN
(G. Woods, S. Marcus, E. Seiler)
Musicnote 1116
No. 20 *August 3, 1963*

Second tenor Johnny Gambale (b. Feb. 4, 1942), lead vocalist Emil Stucchio (b. Apr. 9, 1944), bass Jamie Troy (b. Nov. 22, 1942), and first tenor Tony Victor (b. Apr. 11, 1943) all lived on Garfield Place in Brooklyn. They met on the streets, messed around on the streets, harmonized on the streets, and echoed in the hallways and johns. By 1958, they were singing at hops and on shows in and around their turf. They were the Perennials, but Sammy Sardi, the comedian and emcee at the Club Illusion, couldn't pronounce their name, so he announced them as "The Classics" instead.

Louie Rotunda a friend of the group and member of the Passions, suggested the guys audition for the Pas-

sions' manager, Jim Gribble. After a listen, Jim was singing their praises to Roger Sherman of the dinky Dart label. Sherman signed the Classics up, and rushed them into the Bell Sound Studios on 56th Street, where they recorded three singles. "Cinderella" sold fairly well regionally, but "Angel Angela" and "Life Is but a Dream" (sold to Mercury Records) stiffed.

The Classics hooked up with Andy Leonetti, the manager of the Paragons, who was about to set up his own little label. "Till Then," a cover of the Mills Brothers' 1944 hit, was the Classics' first release for Musicnote. The group's success was short-lived, but sweet: the Garfield Park boys got to tour the country and stand on the same stage with the Dubs, THE SHELLS, and the Flamingos.

The follow-up, "P.S. I Love You," sold poorly. "The record didn't get much airplay," Emil Stucchio explained in an interview with *Bim Bam Boom* writer Steve Flam. "It was late 1963 and early 1964, and our style of music was going downhill. The English sound was in. The public didn't want to hear ballads." Two more singles were shipped, but failed to even smudge the lowest reaches of the charts.

Emil Stucchio has since become a transit policeman, John Gambale is a commercial artist, Jamie Troy has worked in the scrap-iron business, and Tony Victor had a seat on the New York Stock Exchange.

SURFARIS
WIPE OUT
(Ron Wilson, James Fuller, Robert Berryhill, Patrick Connolly)
Dot 16479
No. 2 *August 10, 1963*

Rhythm guitarist Bob Berryhill (b. 1947), lead guitarist Jim Fuller (b. 1947), bassist Pat Connolly (b. 1947), drummer Ron Wilson (b. 1945), and saxophonist Jim Pash (b. 1949) were looking for practice space when they found Dale Smallin. Dale, who had a small recording studio, became the Surfaris' manager and, with the help of parental funds, arranged a four-hour recording session at the Pal Studios in Cucamonga. "Surfer Joe" (#62, 1963) was to be the single; "Wipe Out" (originally called "Stiletto") was to be a flip side, so not much thought or time went into doing it.

Gimmicks at the beginning of tunes were, as always, a big thing. Someone simulated the sound of a crashing surfboard by breaking a wooden shingle; Smallin's "witch laugh" was added, Wilson worked up some drum breaks, and "Wipe Out" was cut and dried in two takes. Smallin pressed 100 copies of the disk on his own DFS label. "Surfer Joe" b/w "Wipe Out" came to the attention of Richard Delvy, the bass player with anoth-

er surf group, the well-established Challengers. Smallin gave Delvy the go-ahead to manufacture some copies of the disk using his Princess label. One of Delvy's pressings found its way to Dot Records, which issued the group's platter nationwide (fanatics, take note: the version of "Wipe Out" on the DFS label is a full 10 seconds longer than the Dot version).

While "Wipe Out" was to become one of the best-selling debut singles ever and one of the most cherished of all oldies, all was not well with the group, and there were soon lawsuits a-plenty. There were fishy goings-on in connection with the group's first and only LP for Dot, *Wipe Out*—the only Surfaris cuts on the album were "Surfer Joe" and "Wipe Out," but all the other tracks had Delvy's Challengers playing on them! The result was that the Challengers, and not the Surfaris, received performance royalties from the best-selling album. Delvy also managed to swipe publishing rights without the group members' permission. To top it all off, a group from Los Angeles brought suit against the fellows charging that they had the exclusive rights to the "Surfaris" name.

Once all the legal problems were ironed out, the group recorded some fine surf sounds for Decca, though their career was largely kaput. While only one other single made the Hot 100—"Point Panic" (#49, 1963)—the Surfaris churned out one high-quality single after another as well as five LPs; the last of the latter saw Ken Forssi—later of LOVE—replace Connolly. By the time the group formally signed with Dot Records in

1966 for the issuance of their last two singles, Berryhill, Connolly, and Fuller were gone.

The Surfaris have reformed on many occasions. In 1976, Berryhill, Fuller, and Pash recorded a greatest-hits album for K-Tel. In the spring of 1989, Fuller, Pash, and Wilson toured the nation, but Fuller had to leave the tour when he broke an arm. Ron Wilson—who once set a record for drumming endurance by playing nonstop for 104 1/2 hours, and who reportedly spent much of his life in poverty in Dutch Flats, California—died in May 1989 of a brain aneurysm.

Berryhill, a born-again Christian, has played with Christian groups and currently works as an instructor at an educational-opportunities center. Fuller was part of California groups like World War III and US, and was even a member of the SEEDS for a time. Pash (who was not present at the "Wipe Out" session) is a born-again Christian as well; he is also the inventor and manufacturer of the Gitsitar.

RANDY & THE RAINBOWS
DENISE
(Neil Levenson)
Rust 5059
No. 10 *August 24, 1963*

Initially the 12-year-old Safuto brothers, Dominick (lead) and Frank (first tenor), along with cousin Eddie Scalla and Rosalie Calindo, were "The Dialtones,"

responsible for the collectible cut, "Till I Hear It From You," issued on George Goldner's Goldisc. Later, while attending classes at Grover Cleveland High, the Safuto brothers met the Zero brothers, Mike (baritone) and Sal (second tenor), and their singing buddy Ken Arcipowski (bass). In 1962, with the addition of the Safuto's, the fivesome from the Queens became Junior & The Counts.

After six months of practice, they secured Fran Carrarie as their manager. Fran was friends with Neil Levenson, an aspiring songwriter who gave the group one of his tunes—"Denise." Levenson hooked them up with Bright Tunes productions, the creative front for the Tokens, known worldwide for "The Lion Sleeps Tonight," who produced the track and approached the Schwartz brothers, Bob and Gene, owners of Laurie/Rust Records.

"I don't know how it happened, but the Tokens came back to us and said you guys are now Randy & The Rainbows," said Mike Zero in an exclusive interview. "We hated the name . . . They insisted."

The rest is history—and unfortunately for this group of excited 16 year olds, Randy & The Rainbows could never again equal the phenomenal success of their debut single. The Hullabaloos, Jay & The Americans, and Jerry Lee Lewis recorded future songs by Levenson, though none charted.

The follow-up record was "Why Do Kids Grow Up?" "There was confusion," said Zero. "A lot of things were going on. We rehearsed it a certain way and it never seemed to come off right. It took too long to get it out. 'Denise' was already coming off the charts; . . . It came out just before President Kennedy was killed. That and the change in music. The Beatles were starting to happen."

"There was foot-dragging," added Vinnie Corella, a later member of the Rainbows. "The record company was at odds with the Tokens [the acts producers]. As a follow-up, the company was looking for something different. It took a while for the company, the producers, and the group to get in sync. Too much time lapsed."

"Initial record sales were such that, for a moment, it looked like it was going to be a bigger hit than 'Denise,'" said Zero.

"By the first of the year [1964], Neil [Levenson] was presenting us with tunes that had that British flavor," added Corella. "Except for the Beach Boys, Four Seasons, and Motown acts, it was getting really hard for any American act to get a break."

"Happy Teenager," a retake on THE ELEGANTS' "Little Star" and "Joy Ride" followed—none gave in to the sound of the future. "These were, for the time, high-tech records," said Zero. "We didn't lean toward the Beatles sound, but the sound wasn't dated. They were fat-sounding, dense records. It wasn't doo-wop either

that we were doing. We were on the cusp of a sound that could have happened."

The Rainbows continued to record sporadically for Eddie Matthews' Mike label—"Lovely Lies" and "Bonnie's Part of Town." In 1967, the group recorded "I'll Be Seeing You" for the Tokens' B. T. Puppy company.

Kenny left the Rainbows in 1968; Sal in '69. Thereafter, the Safuto brothers and Mike Zero with the addition of Vinny Corella performed continuously as Randy & The Rainbows and as Madison Street. Under the latter moniker, they recorded a pair of 45s—"Minstrel Man" and "Simple Love Song"—for Millenium by 1978. "In retrospect," said Zero, "we should have remained with the Rainbow name, rather than Madison Street. Both of those disks made Billboard's "Adult Contemporary" charts. It was the Rainbows who recorded them and there are people who want to get everything that we made that don't know that Madison Street is us."

In a continuing effort to contemporarize and make their music acceptable to a mass audience, Mike and the Safuto brothers worked the clubs as the hard rock outfit Them and Us. In 1978, the group Blondie had its first British chart success with "Denis," a sex-changed remake of "Denise." When the Rainbows played New York's Mudd Club later that year, Deborah Harry appeared asking for an autograph from the group.

In 1979, still as Madison Street, they recorded a disco thing, "Hey, Look Whose Dancin'" with Horace Hart, producer for the Village People and John Benitez, "JELLYBEAN," as "disco consultant."

It was 1982 when Mike, Vinnie, and the Safuto brothers returned to the studios as Randy & The Rainbows. Prior to the release of their first-ever LP, as merely "The Rainbows," the group had a Four Seasons medley disk issued by Fox-Moor. C'Mon Let's Go, an album of greased neo-doo-wop, with "Try the Impossible," was issued by Ambient Sound. Two years later, "Remember (Walking in The Sand)" and another package of harmony heaven, Remember were issued.

"We played in Washington, D. C., the Inaugural Balls for Reagan and Bush, the Bottom Line . . . We didn't just disappear," Zero said. "And we haven't been just sittin' on our hands, all these years. We're talking about something we love, as much as life."

Rainbow Records issued Silver and Gold in 1994, complete with new recordings produced by KOKOMO, Jimmy Wisner.

In the spring of 1990, group dissension split the act into two contingents, reportedly both are claiming the name Randy & The Rainbows.

KAI WINDING
MORE
(R. Ortolani, N. Oliviero)
Verve 10295
No. 8 *August 24, 1963*

Winding blew into the States in 1934. Born Kai Chresten Wilding on May 5, 1922, and raised in Aarhus, Denmark, Kai taught himself how to play the trombone during high school. At 18, Kai joined Shorty Allen's band. Throughout the '40s, Winding worked the big-band scene, playing and recording with Alvino Ray, Benny Goodman, and Stan Kenton. During the '50s, he appeared at Broadway jazz clubs, played with Charlie Parker, Charlie Ventura, Miles Davis, and formed various units with tip-top trombonist J. J. Johnson. Kai was in his artistic prime, winning various jazz polls, traveling the world, and producing records.

In 1962, Kai Winding was appointed musical director of the Playboy Club in New York City. Around this time, he started messing with mixing electronic instruments and more traditional ones. His *More* and *Mondo Cane #2* albums sold well; the title track from the former LP was Kai's lone pop hit. The tune was the theme from *Mondo Cane* (1963), an Italian documentary about some of the shocking peculiarities of Man. The beat and sound of "More" were just right for those young listeners still hungry for something that would remind them of THE TORNADOES' "Telstar."

In the '70s, Kai lead, co-lead, or sided with various units, including the Giants of Jazz with Dizzy Gillespie, Giant Bones with Curtis Fuller, and Lionel Hampton's All-Star Big Band. As the world moved into the '80s, Wilding slide into semiretirement; playing only when the urge hit.

Living in Spain, Kai Winding died on May 6, 1983.

INEZ FOXX
MOCKINGBIRD
(Charlie & Inez Foxx)
Symbol 919
No. 7 *September 7, 1963*

At the age of four or five, Inez (b. Inez Fox Fletcher, Sept. 9, 1942, Greensboro, NC) began singing years in the church choir. By age seven Inez and her two sisters were members of the traveling Gospel Tide Chorus.

"I told my mother at nine years old that I was going to be a big star," said Foxx to *Goldmine*'s Bill Carpenter. "She said, 'Well, if I can get enough money, I'm going to make sure I can send you to "The Ed Sullivan Show"

because I believe that you can win it'. . . I told her, 'Don't worry Mama, I'm going to be there, I'm gonna do it.' But I always believed it and God fixed it just by faith. And honey, He brought me through."

The family was financially poor and Mrs. Fox never got the money together, for her child. In 1953, Inez's beloved mother died of cancer. Beginning in 1956, Inez won her first contest singing secular music at the neighborhood bar. "$50! Fifty whole dollars, to the winner," said Inez, "I went down there, and they took me in through the back because I was too young to go in through the front. . . . That place was packed and that started it right there."

Inez and brother Charlie Fox (b. Oct. 23, 1939, Greensboro) began making music together when both were students at Dudley High. In the late '50s, Charlie moved to New York to make it writing tunes; Inez joined him. Almost every evening, she sang at Benny Goodman's and other Long Island clubs.

Two singles were issued as by "Inez Johnson," on the Brunswick label. "I didn't think my original name was all that great," said Inez. "When I was little, kids would always tease me and call me names like 'Foxy' and it irritated me." Both disks went largely unnoticed, and the label dropped her. Legend has it that Inez and Charlie and his three-string guitar then approached Sue/

Symbol label head Henry "Juggy Murphy" Jones in a Broadway restaurant and played him a nursery-rhyme novelty they had written called "Mockingbird." Juggy listened and liked what he heard, and by May 1963, the sound of that "Mockingbird" could be heard around the world. The sibling duo sounded much like Ike & Tina Turner—another one of Juggy's successful acts—but despite the vocal interplay between brother and sister, the label credited their debut disk—and several to follow—to only "Inez Foxx," with an extra 'X.'

Inez denies the much popularize tale, saying that WMJR DJ Herman Anderson introduced the sibs to Juggy. Whatever—"Mockingbird" went on to become one of the most cherished of all pre-Beatle rock'n'roll hits. Charlie claims sales of over 100 million copies; that's including sales of the tune as recorded by Peter, Paul & Mary, Dusty Springfield, plus Taj Mahal, THE BELLE STARS, Martha & The Vandellas, etc.

As it turned out Inez and Charlie reportedly saw little in the way of financial reparations for creating "Mockingbird." "Murphy displayed a keen ability to find a hit record," wrote Bill Carpenter. "Also, he seemed to have extreme difficulty with paying his artists royalties." Said Charlie, "He was a pretty nice fella, he just didn't like to pay out money . . . All I got out of it was a white Cadillac . . ."

King Curtis, Ike and Tina Turner, and others on Juggy label's sued for back money. So did Inez and Charlie. "When this lawsuit came up," said Charlie, "he went to get the car and wanted me to make the payments, so I said, 'Take it out of the royalties.' But he wanted to keep the royalties and have me pay for the car!"

Before the Sue/Symbol outfit folded, more Inez Foxx 45s were released: "Hi Diddle Diddle" (#98, 1963), "Ask Me" (#91, 1964), and "Hurt by Love" (#54, 1964). After their fifth single, Charlie was finally given equal billing on their releases and his own short shot at solo success. "Mulberry Bush" as by Chuck Johnson failed to chart. A change to Art Talmadge's Musicor/Dynamo chain managed to prolong the duo's career with their R & B audience.

The pair experienced extreme popularity in England where they were befriended by the Rolling Stones, toured with the Beatles, and accompanied by The Spencer Davis Group.

Inez and Charlie's final stateside pop charting—"(1-2-3-4-5-6-7) Count the Days" (#76)—appeared on Dynamo in 1968. At their new label, Luther Dixon—famed for his songwriting ("Soldier Boy," "Mama Said," "16 Candles") and production work with the Shirelles, Maxine Brown, and Chuck Jackson—became their producer, occasional co-writer, and eventually, Inez's spouse. "We stayed together for a while. It wasn't long. Our career's got in the way," Inez said. "He is a nice person." Charlie went on to produce a few acts; notably Gene

Pitney's "She's a Heartbreaker," with Inez providing an uncredited accompaniment. Luther and Inez wrote and the latter produced "I Love You 1,000 Times," for the Platters; their first Top 40 hit in years.

A few more Foxx 45s made the R & B listings before Inez called it quits in 1974—the same year that James Taylor and Carly Simon's remake of "Mockingbird" went to the number-five slot on the pop charts. Charlie had "retired" from the act in 1969.

According to a report by Bob Grossweiner in *Goldmine*, Inez and Charlie have "no interest" in ever returning to the world of rock and soul.

Said Inez, "Sooner of later, people get tired of you and you just lay low."

JAYNETTS
SALLY, GO 'ROUND THE ROSES
(Zell Sanders, Lona Stevens)
Tuff 369
No. 2 *September 28, 1963*

The girls came together in the Bronx, New York, in the mid-'50s, but the members would go and come and go; things were very iffy and liquid then. Mary Sue Wells, Ethel Davis, Yvonne Bushnell, and Ada Ray used to hang out with Zell Sanders, who was the entire staff of the Bronx-based J & S Record Company. Zell had this odd little number, "Sally, Go 'Round the Roses," when Abner Spector of Tuff Records came to town looking for some material and a girl group. The meeting of Spector, the fluid Jaynetts, and the mystifying lyrical ambiguity of Zell's "Sally" would culminate in the creation of a rock and roll classic.

Abner had been involved with acts like THE TUNE WEAVERS and The Corsairs. In an interview with *Goldmine* writer Aaron Fuchs, Johnnie Richardson (of JOHNNIE & JOE fame) described the "Sally" recording sessions and Abner's tendency to go a bit over the top in the studio. "He took them in the studio on a Friday, and they didn't get out of there until the next week. And he used everybody on that track. Anybody [including Buddy Miles and pianist Artie Butler] that came in the studio that week he would put them on. Originally, I think he had about 20 voices on that 'Sally.'"

The cost of that project alone, Richardson figures, was over $60,000—an unheard-of amount of money to spend on recording a pop single in 1963.

"Sally, Go 'Round the Roses" is a timeless wonder of a song, featuring an odd, hypnotic rhythm and soft voices seductively rising and falling. The lyrics seem to portray Sally in an alluring field of roses, catching an eyeful of her lover with another. But differing interpretations abound. Some listeners read the roses and the hushed throbbing of the music as expressions of a young woman's troubled acceptance of homosexuality. Others think that the song is about a religious experience, or possibly a mental breakdown. Still others remember "Sally" as nothing more than a silly nursery rhyme.

Zell and Abner are gone now, so we'll never know what it all meant, or even if "Sally"'s creators knew what it all meant. Abner never was able to concoct a follow-up with just the right ingredients. "Snowman, Snowman, Sweet Potato Noses" and "Keep an Eye on Her," produced in a Phil Spector-influenced style, yielded unsuccessful results. Some grouping of Jaynetts continued on with "Chicken, Chicken Crane or Crow" and "Who Stole the Cookie From the Cookie Jar?", both for Zell's J & S label. According to Richardson, Vernell Hill was also a recording member of the Jaynetts, and the lead vocalist on the "Chicken, Chicken" flip side, "Winky Dink," is none other than BABY WASHINGTON.

THE JAYNETTES

RAINDROPS
THE KIND OF BOY YOU CAN'T FORGET
(Jeff Barry, Ellie Greenwich)
Jubilee 5455
No. 17 *September 28, 1963*

Jeff Barry (b. Jeffery Adeberg, Apr. 3, 1938, Brooklyn) and Ellie Greenwich (b. Oct. 23, 1940, Brooklyn) met at a family gathering in 1944; both were mere tots. The Adeberg and Greenwich families were related by marriage. Jeff's family moved to Newark, New Jersey, where he listened to C & W; writing his first tune, "I Gotta Gun, I Gotta Pony, I Gotta Sweatheart Too," at the age of seven. Ellie's folks moved to Long Island, where while attending Levittown Memorial High, she wrote "The Moment I Saw Him."

In 1959, after he graduated Erasmus Hall High, served time in the U.S. Army and began studies at City College in New York, Jeff Barry—his self-created professional name—recorded his first disk, "Hip Couple," for HUGO & LUIGI at RCA. Ellie, now a student at Hofstra University and unaware of Jeff, likewise recorded one disk for RCA, "Silly Isn't It" b/w "Cha Cha Charming," as by Ellie Gaye. Neither 45 sold well.

Barry had just penned "Tell Laura I Love Her" (#7, 1960) for Ray Peterson, "The Water Is Red" for JOHNNY CYMBALL and was a songwriter with E. B. Marks, when Jeff and Ellie met again—Thanksgiving dinner at Ellie's aunt's house. Barry brought his wife; Ellie her accordion. As their relationship grew and Barry's marriage crumbled, Jeff included Ellie in his activities, paying her $15 a session to record some demos on his songs. A few more Barry records were issued, as were Ellie disks attributed to Ellie Gee & The Jets and "Kellie Douglas." Nothing clicked.

When she graduated from college in 1961, Ellie auditioned for a staff writing position with the production team of Leiber & Stoller. They hired her as a writer for Trio Music at $100 a week; soon Jeff was also with Trio, and together, Barry and Greenwich went on to compose some of the finest moments in rock and roll history: "Be My Baby," "Chapel of Love," "Da Doo Ron Ron," "Do Wah Diddy Diddy," "Hanky Panky," "I Can Hear Music," "Leader of the Pack," "The Look of Love," and "River Deep, Mountain High" . . . Meanwhile, Jeff recorded as "The Redwoods," for Epic and "The Spartans" for Web. Flops both.

The sale of most of their tunes involved the creation of a demonstration record, a demo-disk. At times, the demo sounded good enough for an interested record company to issue it as a finished product. Such was the case with Ellie and Jeff's previous "group" records and such was the Raindrops—actually just Ellie and Jeff handling all voices.

"We did this demo for a group called THE SENSA-TIONS," Ellie told Charlotte Grieg in *Will You Still Love Me Tomorrow*. "It was a song called 'What a Guy,' which we thought would be great for them. We made the demo, and the publishers said, 'This could be a record.' I said, 'What do you mean? There is no group.' But there had to be a group. So we released it as a record by 'The Raindrops' [after a record that Ellie loved, Dee Clark's 'Raindrops']. Back then, a lot of labels put out 'dummy groups.' We'd throw a few people together and have them go out and lip-sync the record. There really wasn't a 'Raindrops.'"

Group or not, the Raindrops charted with "The Kind of Boy You Can't Forget" as well as a string of others—"That Boy Joe" (#64, 1964), a cover version of THE MONOTONES' "Book of Love" (#62, 1964), and "One More Tear" (#97, 1964). "What a Guy," that song that the Sensations had turned down, went to number 41 in 1963. When the chartings stopped, the name was shelved.

"Jeff and I lasted as a writing team about as long as we lasted as a married team—a little less than five years," Ellie explained to Joe Smith in *Off the Record*. "We tried to write together right after we split up, but it was awful. We couldn't sit and write 'Baby, I love you' with divorce papers sitting right next to us."

When the marriage and the words stopped, Ellie, among other things, tried to create another demo-group, The Meantime—to little success—and to establish herself as a solo singer, remaking LILLIAN BRIGGS's "I Want You to Be My Baby"—likewise. A couple of LPs (*Ellie Greenwich Composes, Produces, and Sings*, 1968; *Let It Be Written, Let It Be Sung*, 1973) and some singles were issued. Thereafter, she turned to writing and singing jingles. Clarence Clemons and Ellen Foley have recorded her newer tunes, and she occasionally appears on record as a back-up vocalist, as she has done for Blondie, Deborah Harry, Cyndi Lauper, and BERNA-DETTE PETERS. In the mid-'80s, Greenwich was the subject of a Broadway production, *Leader of the Pack*. Behind-the-scenes, Ellie formed Hook, Line & Sinker, a jingle company, to write/produce/sing commercials for Clairol, Revlon, McDonald's, and Hebrew National Hot Dogs.

Jeff went on to produce hits for the Monkees and the Archies, producing all of the later albums and 45s; meaning, "Sugar Sugar," one of the most hated/loved tunes of all time. Barry went on to head Steed Records,

producing/sometimes writing disks for ILLUSION, Andy Kim and ROBIN MCNAMARA; to co-write/produce BOBBY BLOOM's "Montego Bay," numerous sides for the Persuasions, John Travolta, and the soundtrack to *The Idolmaker* (1980). Jeff Barry resides in semi-retirement in Bel Air, California.

In May 1991, Jeff Barry and Ellie Greenwich were inducted into the Song Writers Hall of Fame.

RAN-DELLS
MARTIAN HOP
(John Spirt, Robert Lawrence Rappaport, Steve Rappaport)
Chairman 4403
No. 16 *September 28, 1963*

The Ran-Dells, from Villas, New Jersey, were actually the Rappaport brothers, Bob and Steve (both b. 1943), and their cousin John Spirt (b. 1949). They are known to have only recorded three singles: "Martian Hop," "Sound of the Sun," and "Beyond the Stars." Their much-overlooked and -underplayed "Martian" novelty number featured a bass line that thudded like a flat tire under an ethereal falsetto. The tune told of the dynamic dancing abilities of hip Martians.

What became of Spirt and the brothers before and after their chart success is one of the murkiest mysteries in one-hitdom.

LITTLE JOHNNY TAYLOR
PART TIME LOVE
(Clay Hammond)
Galaxy 722
No. 19 *October 5, 1963*

"I'm a legend now," said Little Johnny Taylor, in an exclusive interview. "Thirty years now, but not too many people know that."

He was born Johnny Young, February 11, 1943, in Memphis. While still knee-high, Little John was asked to join the renowned Mighty Clouds of Joy—one-time home to BUNKER HILL—where he remained for half a decade. At 17, after a brief stay in the Stars of Bethel gospel group, John moved to Los Angeles to take up the life of a secular singer and harmonica man. "One song turned me 'round, Bobby 'Blue' Bland's 'I Smell a Whole Lot of Trouble,'" said Taylor. "I learned that and was a rhythm and blues man."

Little Johnny Taylor, as he renamed himself, worked the bars and let word of his music get around town. For a while in the late '50s, he was with the JOHNNY OTIS Show; making his first recordings about then for Hunter Hancock's Swingin' label. Sales were minimal, but scouts from the Berkeley-based Fantasy/Galaxy label took notice and offered him a contract. "You'll Never Need Another Favor" and "Part Time Love" were two of his earliest waxings for Galaxy; the latter, his big mainstream moment. "I had to beg 'em to let me record 'Part Time Love,' said Taylor. "It just fit me just right, but they didn't hear it. See, I had this girl I went with for five years and we broke up and she married this old 65 year old, and I was just this teenager, then, 18 when I cut it. I did that song for her, from my heart. She came and wanted me to take her back after that but it was too far gone."

Perennial favorites with R & B listeners are Taylor's "Everybody Knows About My Good Thing" (R&B: #9, 1971) and "Open House at My House" (R&B: #16, 1972). While pop listeners would get to hear little more by him—and would often confuse him with the more prominent Johnnie Taylor, of "Who's Making Love" and "Disco Lady" fame—Taylor, with his distinctive dry-voiced style, has maintained a loyal R & B following through the years. More than a half-dozen of his sides have made the black charts. In the '70s, Little Johnny would often do duets with his labelmate the late Ted Taylor (a cousin, according to Little John), who besides charting under this name charted as "Austin Taylor" with a rockin' regional hit, "Push Push," in 1960.

Little Johnny is still active, still recording, and most definitely still a contender for a second crossover hit.

SUNNY & THE SUNGLOWS
TALK TO ME
(Joe Seneca)
Tear Drop 3014
No. 11 *October 26, 1963*

Sunny Ozuna (lead vocals) and the rest of the Sunglows—Gilbert Fernandez, Alfred Luna, Tony Tostado, and the Villanueva brothers (Jesse, Oscar, and Ray)—met while attending the Burbank Vocational School in San Antonio, Texas. When they formed their act in 1959, they were Chicano rockers, but each member brought a unique musical influence to the total sound. Within the Sunglows were strong interests in the blues, country, Tex-Mex, mariachi, up-tempo polkas, and the swamp-pop leanings of JOE BARRY, ROD BERNARD, and Jivin' Gene.

In 1962, the group formed the Sunglow label, which had limited distribution. A positive response to the Sunglows' eclectic offerings came with "Golly Gee," possibly their initial single. For a time, Okeh picked up the disk for national dispersal. The following year, producer Huey "Crazy Cajun" Meaux—the Louisiana barber/eccentric known for his recording successes with

BARBARA LYNN and later Roy Head, Sir Douglas Quintet and Freddy Fender—had Sunny and crew cover "Talk to Me," a ramblin' rockaballad first popularized in the '50s by Little Willie John. The cut was swampy, pleasantly sloppy, and right on the groove.

Remakes of Tony Bennett's "Rags to Riches" (#45, 1963) and the Five Keys' "Out of Sight-Out of Mind" (#71, 1964) were similarly styled romps, and fairly successful ones at that. These platters appeared under the name "Sunny & The Sunliners," in order to distinguish the group's pop releases from the polka instrumentals that they were concurrently issuing under the "Sunny & The Sunglows" banner. One of these [pop] sax-soaked singles, "Peanuts," would reach number 64 in 1965.

Factions of the group, using a variety of names, continued to record for Disco Grande, Key Loc, and RPM. For a short period of time, the original unit also recorded as Los Stardusters.

MURMAIDS
POPSICLES AND ICICLES
(David Gates)
Chattahoochee 628
No. 10 *November 7, 1963*

Carol (b. 1948) and Terry (b. 1946) Fischer were sisters, and Sally Gordon (b. 1946) was a neighbor and a mutual friend. For a brief moment, they were the Murmaids from L.A. Daddy Fischer was a music arranger and director; Mama Fischer was the family's guiding light. Before the girls took off for college in the fall of 1963, Mrs. Fischer brought the teenage singers to the offices of Chattahoochee Record boss Ruth Conte.

Kim Fowley (a self-acknowledgedly bizarre and cultish personality/singer and producer/songwriter for B. Bumble & the Stingers, HOLLYWOOD ARGYLES, Run-

THE MURMAIDS

aways, SEEDS, WARREN ZEVON, early Paul Revere and later Byrds) was then Chattahoochee's in-house producer. Fowley had recently been handed a tune from the pen of future Bread frontman David Gates. The ditty was silly and sweet, an obvious vehicle for a wholesome trio like the Murmaids.

Once they had recorded "Popsicles and Icicles," the girls packed their bags and headed for college. But the disk became a huge success, and the label tried to extract more winners from the lasses. Apparently, Chattahoochee issued an unsuccessful single or two before the group splintered. As Murmaid members swam off toward a sea of obscurity, Cathy Brasher and possibly Yvonne Vaughn (who would each later attempt solo careers) were called in to be the Murmaids (of '66). Their folk-rockish "Go Away" was not a bad effort, but after that one release on Liberty Records in 1968, the group did just that.

LOS INDIOS TABAJARAS
MARIA ELENA
(Lorenzo Barcelata)
RCA 8216
No. 6 *November 16, 1963*

Surely one of the most unpredictable hits and strangest stories to arrive in the land of rock and roll is this tale of two Brazilian Indians named Natalicio and Antenor Lima. These brothers, born the sons of a Tabajaras Indian chieftain in the far-out jungles of Ceara, were said to have found a guitar laying about in the wild. The boys touched the strings and felt their bodies fill with a mighty, mighty magic.

ONE OF LOS INDIOS TABAJARAS WITH UNIDENTIFIED WOMAN (FROM "MARIA ELENA" SHEET MUSIC)

They trained themselves in the ways of this strange instrument, and traveled 1,200 miles to Rio de Janeiro to play their tribal folk songs for patrons and alcohol drinkers. A man calling himself an agent detected their presence, sized up their potential, and shipped them to Mexico to become schooled in the ways of Bach, Beethoven, and Latin American soul. The Lima brothers, who speak five languages in addition to their native Tupi, gave concerts in South America and began to pick up a following. RCA Records signed these keepers of the guitars to a contract, reasoning that the Lima brothers' tunes would sell well in their homeland. To everyone's surprise, someone at RCA ordered "Maria Elena," a remake of the 1941 Jimmy Dorsey hit, released in the United States.

Most astonishing about this disk is neither the level of musicianship nor its melody, but the ability of two dudes with no electric guitars, drums, bass, yells, overdubbing, feedback, or echo chambers to secure a stateside hit.

The current whereabouts of Los Indios Tabajaras are not known.

VILLAGE STOMPERS
WASHINGTON SQUARE
(Bob Goldstein, David Shire)
Epic 9617
No. 2 November 23, 1963

The Village Stompers were Dick Brady, Ralph Casale, Don Coates, Frank Hubbell, Mitchell May, Joe Muranyi, Al McManus, and Lenny Pogan—an eight-man band of Dixieland dusters. One was a music teacher by day, two had college degrees in music, and collectively, they claimed to have worked with almost every notable Dixieland jazz group of the period. Recording as Frank Hubbell & The Hubcaps, one subset of the Stompers had "Broken Date" issued on BOB CREWE's Topix label.

As the Village Stompers—named for Greenwich Village, their gigging turf in the Big Apple—they were arranged, produced, and "originated" by Epic staff artist Joe Sherman. Joe was known to the public at-large for creating such tunes as "Anything Can Happen Mambo," "Graduation Day," Perry Como's "Juke Box Baby," Nat "King" Cole's "Rambling Rose," and the theme for the Yvette Mimieux flick *Toys in the Attic* (1963). "Washington Square," the Stompers first 45 bright and buoyant horn blaster, was named after the large park smack-dab in the middle of the Village. Two of the next batch of 45s—"From Russia With Love" (#81, 1964) and "Fiddler on the Roof" (#97, 1964)—charted, and the unit's first LP, *Washington Square* (1963), sold well. The act—with ever changing line-up—recorded with such diversity as "Murmurio," "Haunted House Blues," and "Don't Think Twice It's Alright." Despite the lack of further success, the Village's dixie doodlers continued to record for the Epic label through 1967.

In '65, Sherman said of his invention, what he called "Folk-Dixie" music, "The Village Stompers are just beginning to explore the possibilities of Folk-Dixie's sound. We feel it's bound to be here as long as there is folk music and jazz."

THE SINGING NUN
DOMINIQUE
(Soeur Sourire)
Philips 40152
No. 1 December 7, 1963

In the spring of 1963, the bespeckled and rosy-faced Belgian nun Sister Luc-Gabrielle' (b. Janine Deckers, 1933) and a chorus of four other nuns from a convent in Fichermont, Belgium, recorded a dozen or so original tunes at the Philips studios in Brussels. Deckers' songs had been winners at youth retreats held at the monastery, and the order's elders wanted Philips Records to record and press up several hundred copies for the convent's own use. Big-wigs at the label, delighted with the simple, uplifting creations the good sister was offering, decided to test-market some of her recordings in Europe. An album released as by Soeur Sourire ("Sister Smile") sold well, so that *The Singing Nun* and a single, "Dominique"—Deckers' tribute to the founder of the Dominican order—were issued in the States.

The response was unbelievable. Both the album and single rocketed to the top of the charts and stayed there for weeks. The sister with the smile in her voice appeared on "The Ed Sullivan Show," and more singles were released—but interest in the sister's plaintive sound waned as quickly as it had waxed. One hundred thousand dollars was earned for her Dominican order.

"I'm not a singer who happens to be a nun. I am a nun who likes to sing," said Deckers to *McCall's*. "My missionary work is my life."

Abruptly in 1965, the singing stopped. The doors of the Convent of Fichermont closed to the outside world. Photographs and interviews with the sister were prohibited.

The following year, Sister Luc-Gabrielle left the convent. It was announced that the good sister would enter the world to sing—"with the full accord of her religious superiors," reported *McCall's*. "She will continue functioning as a Dominican nun, actively particularly in the world of arts and letters." The 31-year-old singer took up residence in a modest, fifth floor walk-up apart-

ment, in a small Brussels suburb near the Catholic University of Louvain, where she would continue her studies for a degree in religious-science.

To signify her changes, Deckers became Luc Dominique—Dominique for the founder of her order and Luc for the patron saint of artists. The woman label officials referred to as "Europe's Bob Dylan" attempted to continue her singing career—issuing in the States, *I Am Not a Star*—recording songs of her concern for the poor, the underdeveloped nations, the bomb, and, to the dismay of many church brethren, a poorly received pro-birth-control tune, "Glory Be to God for the Golden Pill."

As of her plans for the future, she said in the magazine, "I'm not sure yet what I'm going to accomplish—or how. . . . Maybe I'll marry a nice Dominican priest, and we'll have Dominican babies. It's not as unlikely as it sounds."

"I'm afraid some people may use me for their own ends," Deckers told *McCall's* Cynthia Grenier. "But, I'm prepared for it. And I do have God to sustain me. He'll make it easier."

Sister Smile, Jeanine Deckers—nee Luc Dominique, Sister Luc-Gabrielle, Sister Soeur Sourire, "the Singing Nun"—and her companion of 10 years, Annie Pecher, committed suicide in Belgium on March 31, 1985. Deckers was 52. The two women reportedly downed a massive amount of barbiturates with alcohol. Both it is alleged had been in despair after a center for autistic

children that they had founded was closed due to a lack of funds. The Belgian government had also been hounding Deckers for a large sum of back taxes.

ROBIN WARD
WONDERFUL SUMMER
(Gil Garfield, PERRY BOTKIN, JR.)
Dot 16530
No. 14 *December 14, 1963*

Robin was born Jackie Ward in Nebraska in the early 1940s; the family soon after moved to Los Angeles. As a young girl, Jackie loved to sing, to a few dismays. She went to school and did all those things people do when they are growing up. The pattern continued: she married, settled down, and started raising a family, but still she dreamed of making a niche for herself as a singer. Jackie recorded some demos, and the tiny Songs Unlimited label released "Lover's Lullabye." Dot Records took an interest and issued a single of hers called "Top 40 Blues" (credited simply to "Robin"). Both disks were poor sellers.

"We hired Jackie to sing the demo to 'Wonderful Summer,'" said the tunes co-writer Perry Botkin, Jr. to liner note writer Todd Everett. "It sounded so good, we decided to go for a master. We sped her voice up a quarter-tone on the track, so she sounded about 13 years old. It sounded like a Dot Record to us, so we went up

the street (from Gold Star Studios) to the label's office at Sunset and Vine and got Tom Mack, one of Randy's [label owner Randy Wood's] A & R men, to listen to it. We credited the record to Robin Ward, who was one of Jackie's three daughters. Jackie was so busy in the studios, she couldn't go out and promote it."

In the heart of the winter, Dot issued the Lesley Gore-like "Wonderful Summer." With the onset of spring, the label—with crossed fingers and pretzel logic—issued the similar-sounding "Winter's Here." No one bought the humor, and "Here" went nowhere. After a few more sides, Ward's public career dimmed.

"I knew it was a one shot," said Randy Wood, on the liners of *The History Of Dot, Volume 1.* "But I put it out anyway—it sounded good, and I liked Jackie, who worked on a lot of my sessions, very much."

Botkin, Jr. went on to One-Hit status as half of the duo—BARRY DE VORZON & PERRY BOTKIN, JR.—who created the "Nadia Theme (The Young and the Restless)." "Wonderful Summer's" other pen man, Gil Garfield, was with the late TV actor Bert Convy two-thirds of the Cheers, an act responsible for the noxious number "Black Denim Trousers (and Motorcycle Boots)."

CARAVELLES
YOU DON'T HAVE TO BE A BABY TO CRY
(Merrill, Shand)
Smash 1852
No. 3 *December 21, 1963*

In the early '60s, Andrea Simpson (b. 1946) and Lois Wilkinson (b. 1944) worked for a brokerage firm in London, their hometown. At office parties, after the rug had been rolled back and some folks had had a few, the girls would sing a few breathy numbers. Many a fellow employee thought the misses had the makings of stardom and encouraged them. Thereafter, Andrea and Lois spent many an after hour rehearsing and tightening up their tunes.

Late in 1963, the duo made a demo of something called "You Don't Have to Be a Baby to Cry" and brought it to the blokes at B.P.R. Records. The label lads liked the girls' wholesome style, and signed them up. With an eye to the sky, the young ladies named themselves after the Caravelle, a famous French airliner. Just weeks before the stateside Beatle Invasion, "You Don't Have to Be a Baby" landed on the nation's charts. Similar-sounding singles followed in the jet stream, but nothing nudged the masses to buy these Caravelle waxings.

With the failure of their folk-rocking "Hey Mama, You've Been on My Mind," Lois Wilkinson left the duo in 1966 for a solo career as Lois Lane and married bandleader Johnny Arthey. After a number of easy listening singles, Lois became something of a fixture on the BBC's "Light Programme" and "Radio 2" sessions, singing versions of pop hits, when the broadcast restrictions denied the use of prerecorded materials.

Against all odds, Andrea Simpson and a series of replacements have carried the "Caravelles" name into the '80s, but none of their sporadically released recordings have charted here or abroad.

THE SECRETS
THE BOY NEXT DOOR
(Johnny Madara, David White
[both members of THE SPOKESMEN])
Philips 40146
No. 18 *December 23, 1963*

Jackie Allen Schwegler (b. June 6, 1943, "high dum dee dummer"), Karen Cray Cipriana (b. June 16, 1943, lead), Carole Raymond McGoldrick (b. August 1, 1943, alto or bass), and Patty Miller (b. July 1, 1943, soprano) met at Cleveland's Shaw High in the early '60s. "I can't remember what we called ourselves in high school," said Karen to DISCoveries' "Doc Rock" Kelly. "You wanna know," adds Carole, "we always say it's a secret but really none of us remembers how we got the Secrets name." For a moment, they were the Sonnets. There they were on stage, 1963 and no name. "The pianist at the show," said Carole, "looked down at the piano and said, 'How about the Sonnets,' the brand of the piano." "We sang songs like 'Side by Side" and "September in the Rain," said Karen, "for the girls athletic club, the GAA, the friendship club . . ."

The girls went to school with Tom King, leader of the Starfires . . . later to become the Outsiders of "Time Won't Let Me" fame. Tom asked the four to do five Twist shows with his band accompanying. "Things happened surprisingly quickly after that," Karen said. "It was a fairy tale. We never expected anything like that to happen."

A talent promoter named Redda Robbins heard them at one of the gigs, and offered to take the girls under her wing. Robbins, who already represented Philips recording act Bocky & The Visions, coached them, dressed them, and lined up a meeting with Johnny Madara and David White, soon to-be members of THE SPOKESMEN; the latter recorded with Danny & The Juniors. They were affiliated with Mercury Records and the label was hot with Lesley Gore and THE PIXIES THREE and it's subsidiary, Smash, was having a protracted good time selling records by the Angels.

"They liked us," said Karen, "and immediately signed us to a recording contract. We went to Philadelphia to learn the songs and then we drove with them from Philadelphia to New York in two cars to cut the songs. It was all so fast."

Paul Anka was in the next studio, when they recorded "The Boy Next Door." That they found a distraction. Drummer BOBBY GREGG, saxman Buddy Lucus, and guitar renown Al Caiola (known for his recordings of "Bonanza" and "The Magnificent Seven") accompanied the girls through the mere 30 minutes allotted them to get the tune and its flip side recorded just right.

"Our lives got real exciting," said Carole. "The record company would set us up with a limo and a PR guy and we would go from hop to hop. We didn't have a band in those days, it was an all lip-sync show. . . ." They met Lou Christie, Vic Dana, Lesley Gore, and the rest. "We played the Palace Theatre in downtown Cleveland with Connie Francis . . . she was special, a very nice girl." "We were headlining over the Supremes at a series of hops in Detroit," added Jackie. "Two weeks later, it would have been reversed, but who needs to dwell."

Said Patty, "We always had chaperones. We were very square and never got to do anything."

Three more Philips singles—all breathy and bouncy, and all produced by the team of Johnny Madara and David White—appeared and quite quickly and unduly disappeared.

There were whispers that a few more singles were issued by the group; none not even the obscure Diana Ross rouser called "I Feel the Thrill Coming on" was made by this grouping of Secrets.

"We don't like to talk about the aspects of it all," said Patty, "but we got cheated. . . . We never made any money. Our manager made out fine on us." Carole added, "Our group wasn't really ready for show business when we first became successful. We were green . . . . Back at home, we still had to do the dishes."

Jackie and Karen fell in love and despite the Secrets being offered a continuation in their label contract and an offer to appear for 12 weeks at the New York World's Fair, the group split up in 1965. Carole and Patty, not wishing to shelf their music career, continued as the Memories, a duo, for about a year.

In the early '90s, all of the original Secrets regrouped to perform at their 30th High School Reunion. A limited production cassette with the tune "Never Too Old to Rock" was issued.

JOEY POWERS
MIDNIGHT MARY
(Artie Wayne, Ben Raleigh)
Amy 892
No. 10 *January 4, 1964*

Joey Powers was born in 1939 in Perry Como's hometown of Canonsburg, Pennsylvania. Apparently, the Powerses knew the Comos, for when Joey turned 20, Perry opened some doors and secured for Joey a job as

producer of NBC-TV's "John Hill's Exercise Show." After a brief stint there, Joey taught wrestling at Ohio State University. At some point, Powers must have opened his mouth and sung a song or two, since Como's label, RCA Victor, signed him to a recording contract in 1962. A few promising teen idol-type disks were issued, but nothing sold very well—not even a Fabian-like number by Hal David and Burt Bacharach, "Don't Envy Me".

Early in 1963, Joe met aspiring singer/songwriter/producer Artie Wayne. Artie (creator of "Mahzel [Means Good Luck]" and "At the Hop") had teamed up with Ben Raleigh (writer of "Wonderful! Wonderful! " and "Dungaree Doll") for a dirty little number called "Midnight Mary." Al Massler at Amy Records heard some preliminary demos and agreed to issue the tune. Of course, no one knew that Beatlemania was about to wipe out every single American teen idol with short hair.

"Mary" connected, but all of Joey's follow-up singles were swept away by the Fab Four's music. Before Artie Wayne joined Powers in the sea of oblivion, Liberty Records let him cut a single that asked the existential question: "Where Does a Rock and Roll Singer Go?" Ben Raleigh, who had written "Tell Laura I Love her" for Ray Peterson, went on to dream up "Love Is a Hurtin' Thing" and "Dead End Street" (both hits for Lou Rawls) as well as "Blue Winter" (a fan fav for Connie Francis).

TAMS
WHAT KIND OF FOOL (DO YOU THINK I AM)
(Ray Whitley)
ABC-Paramount 10502
No. 9 *February 22, 1964*

They were Floyd Ashton (b. Aug. 15, 1933), Horace Key (b. Apr. 13, 1934), Bob Smith (b. Mar. 18, 1936), and the Pope brothers, Charlie (b. Aug. 7, 1936) and Joe (b. Nov. 6, 1933). Each had personally known poverty and found relief in singing. In the late '40s, while still high school students, they came together with the predominant goal of escaping from the ghetto, from the deprivation, from the despair. They had no funds to attire themselves in flashy stage clothes. Multicolored tam-o'shanter hats were the best they could do; ergo their name.

They rehearsed, worked local clubs, and stuck it out for more than a decade before they approached Lowery Music, the music publishing and recording hub of rock'n'roll activity in Atlanta. The organization's big wheel, Bill Lowery, liked what he heard in Joe's gravel-throated leads and the unit's tight easy-going cohesiveness. Lowery assigned Joe South to produce them and to provide them with songs. The successful pairing

continued on for most of the group's recording career. "Untie Me," their first release charted, both pop (#60, 1962) and R & B (#12, 1962). ABC-Paramount Records took notice and picked up the group's contract from Harry Finfer's Arlen label.

At this point, the group's only personnel change took place when Ashton stepped aside for Albert Cottle, Jr. "What Kind of Fool" was their next single and their lone pop Top 40 charting. Five more singles occupied positions on *Billboard*'s Hot 100: ("You Lied to Your Daddy" [#70; R&B: #70, 1964]; "It's All Right" #79; R&B: #79, 1964]; "Hey Girl Don't Bother Me" [#41; R&B: #41, 1965]; "Silly Little Girl" [#87; R&B: #87, 1964]; "Be Young, Be Foolish, Be Happy" [#61; R&B: #26, 1968]). See, see, not all one-off hit-makers rapidly return penniless to the cauldron of obscurity. Persistence had paid off for the fellows from Georgia.

While the Tams never made the U.S. charts after the dawning of the new decade, they continued on a consistent basis to record fine releases for Lowery's 1-2-3, Capitol, and the Dunhill record labels. To the surprise of many, the reissuance of their 1964 "Hey Girl, Don't Bother Me" earned them a number one hit on the British charts in the summer of 1971. Two years later, Quality Records of Canada issued a new Tams EP, *Beach Music*; featuring a remake of THE SILHOUETTES' "Get a Job."

The group has been retracted from the bright spotlights of pop idolatry, but every so often, to the delight of their many fans, the Tams reappear with a new single or two on some small independent record company.

RIVIERAS
CALIFORNIA SUN
(Henry Glover)
Riviera 1401
No. 5 *February 29, 1964*

In the beginning, they were hungry teens, the Playmates, with a plan to play some "frat rock" hot rock 'n' roll, get some mates, and make enough moola to buy a machine like that 1963 Buick Riviera.

Bill Dobslaw was an "old man" of 21 but professed knowledgeable in the ways of the rock 'n' roll world. He knew Ral Donner, and this impressed Doug Gean (bass), Marty Fortson (vocals, rhythm guitar), Otto Nuss (organ) Joe Pennell (lead guitar), and Paul Dennert (drums)—all attendees of South Bend Central, in South Bend, Indiana.

"It was the fall of '62, we got together," said Otto Nuss, in an exclusive interview, "and got a start playing old-time country, rock'n'roll style, in this dance hall in LaPorte; eight dollars a night, per man. Marty's parents were square dancers and Bill [Dobslaw] owned this second-floor hall, the Tipton Terrace, 'bove a bar. It would hold about 300 kids; standing room only, after about six months. Everybody got to requesting [JOE JONES'] 'California Sun,' fact it got so requested each evening that Bill came up with the idea of going to Chicago and recording the thing."

In June 1963, Dobslaw, as the Playmates' manager, booked an hour of session time in Chicago's Columbia Recording Studios. In three takes, the guys had "California Sun" in the can. Also cut at the session was "Played On," the intended "A" side. Only a thousand copies were pressed on Dobslaw's Riviera label, and one of these found its way into the hands of a DJ named Art Roberts. Art liked the "California Sun" side, and rode the tune repeatedly on the mighty WLS.

After just three days of airplay, U.S.A., a small independent Chicago label, picked up national distribution on the Playmates' first waxing. ("Played On" was mysteriously pulled off the disk, so part of the group returned to the studio to tape an instrumental dedicated to record promoter, Howard Bedno: "H. B. Goose Step.") Considering the existence of another group named Playmates—known nationally for "Beep Beep" and "What Is Love"—a new moniker was needed. "We decided to name ourselves after the Buick Riviera," said Otto. "There was about 30 names to choose from and we had to be something; besides the Riviera was hailed as the car of 1963. . . . Never got one though. None of us did. You'll see our picture on the album with that '63 Riviera; but it was just a tease, a loaner."

Before Dobslaw even got the deal with Jim Golden and Bob Monico's U.S.A. for distribution, before "California Sun" had received much airplay and charted, Joe and Marty had enlisted in the Marines, on the "buddy plan." As Marty recalled to *Kicks* magazine, "I was in 'Nam getting shot at, and I heard the record. I thought, 'Oh man, you blew it.'" "California Sun" rocketed into the Top 10.

Filling in for Joe and Marty were Jim Boal (lead guitar), Willy Gaut (vocals, rhythm guitar) and on lead vocals, Bill Dobslaw. "He always wanted to be a rock star," said Otto. "We were a bunch of bananas, and he seized the opportunity. We were pretty much destroyed once Bill made himself lead vocalist.

"When you get what you're after, when the combination is just right, you can play on. We woulda probably been much hotter if Joe and Marty had stayed."

"California Sun" sold like hotcakes, but their debut album, *Campus Party*, and the follow-up, featuring manager Bill on vocals—"Little Donna" (#93, 1964) b/w "Let's Have a Party" (#99)—barely cracked the listings. Under parental pressure, another chunk of the Rivieras dropped out of the group to clean up their educational act. That left Bill, Doug, Otto, and various

THE RIVIERAS
LET'S HAVE A PARTY
U.S.A. 102
CALIFORNIA SUN · LITTLE DONNA

replacements to carry on with that crude but distinctive Midwestern surf 'n' party sound.

A cover of BOBBY DAY's "Rockin' Robin" held down the number 96 slot for a week in 1964, but later issuances did not do as well. *Let's Have a Party*, a highly collectible second album, was issued. Dobslaw struggled to keep the "Rivieras" name alive and a functional group together. Two singles—"Somebody New" and "Never Felt the Pain"—even appeared under the "Rivieras" name, utilizing local legend Bobby Whiteside and not one original member. Finally, in June 1965—slightly more than two years after the Playmates had come together—Doug, Otto, Jim Boal, and drummer Terry McCoy shut the group down.

"It just wasn't there at all," Nuss said. "We just didn't have that sound we use to have, the sound I wanted—the Rivieras sound.

"We got lied to throughout the whole thing. Bill [Dobslaw] was not very honest. We didn't get our money. There was shenanigans; with Bill sending out other groups as us. We were dumb, stupid, and naive. If we had wised up, learned 'bout copyrights, what not, they woulda had to pay us writers' fees and royalties."

Otto, Doug, and Marty reformed the Rivieras in 1980. In 1987, to commemorate their 25th anniversary they recorded 10 tracks for a vanity album sold at appearances.

PYRAMIDS
PENETRATION
(Steve Leonard)
Best 13002
No. 18 *March 14, 1964*

They had bald heads and were known as "the crazies of the surf scene." In the heat of the Beatle Invasion, the British press ran stories and referred to them as "America's answer to the Beatles." They were not to be, but the Pyramids did make an important contribution to the handful of never-ending summer classics annually activated by rock-radio programmers.

Willie Glover was a shy, poor, North Carolina-raised youth who moved to Long Beach, California, in the summer of 1961. Will would bring his guitar to school, keep to himself, and practice. Fellow Long Beach Poly

High student Skip Mercer approached Will, struck up a friendship, and suggested they form a group. After some shuffling of members, the line-up was set and the name was chosen. In addition to Mercer (lead guitar) and Glover (rhythm guitar), the Pyramids were Steve Leonard (bass), Ron McMullen (drums), and Tom Pittman (sax).

John Hodge approached the group, offering to manage the Pyramids as well as record them. With borrowed money, he hustled the guys into the Garrison Studios in Long Beach and cut two sides. Issued on Best Records, "The Pyramid Stomp" sold only a handful: airplay had been zip, and distribution was nil.

The Pyramids returned to playing school dances and record hops. Steve Leonard created a take-off on "Pipeline," an instrumental smash by THE CHANTAYS. The Pyramids recorded "Penetration"—originally entitled "Eyeballs"—as a "B" side to the otherwise forgettable "Here Comes Marsha." This time, Hodge managed to secure local airplay and national distribution with London Records. With an eye to a marketable gimmick, he convinced the guys to shave their heads, and invited the press to take snap shots. "Penetration" pierced the nation's Top 20.

The band was hotter than the noon-day sun. Stuffed in a station wagon with primitive sound equipment, the baldies moved about making TV appearances on "American Bandstand," "Hullabaloo," and "The Lloyd Thaxton Show"; they even snuck in a bit part in Frankie and Annette's third flick, BIKINI BEACH (1964).

Ironically, the Pyramids never received a penny for their chart-mounting moment in the sun. Glover, Leonard, and McMullen, in an interview with *Kicks*' writer Robert Dalley, charged that their trusted manager, John Hodge, had gathered up all the money for himself and lost it all in bad investments. Disgust and discord set in, and even though a few more highly collectible singles were issued, the Pyramids rapidly crumbled.

TOMMY TUCKER

TOMMY TUCKER
HIGH HEEL SNEAKERS
(Robert "Tommy Tucker" Higginbotham)
Checker 1067
No. 11 *March 21, 1964*

Tucker was born Robert Higginbotham in Springfield, Ohio, on March 5, 1933. He acquired his "Tommy Tucker" name while sitting on the bench during a high school football game. Some friend affectionately yelled at him, "Little Tommy Tucker's a real motherf***er." Robert thought the phrase was catchy enough to make a memorable moniker.

As "T. Tucker," he joined his first band, the Bob Woods Orchestra, in the late '40s, playing clarinet and boogie-woogie piano. The band worked the clubs in Columbus, Dayton, and Springfield. They were also called upon to back-up name acts like Big Maybelle, Billie Holiday, Little Willie John, and one harp player that would greatly influence Tommy Tucker—Jimmy Reed.

In 1955, Tucker formed the Dusters, a doo-wop quintet, with James Crosby, Dave Johnson, Clarence LaVille (from the old Bob Woods band), and Yonnie Peoples. Things looked hot when ARC Records redubbed them the Cavaliers, recorded them, and issued a single, "Ivory Tower." Soon after, Hudson Records brought the Cavaliers into the King Studios to cut "Please Don't Leave Me to Cry." When both 45s

failed to sell, the group disbanded. Tommy moved to Dayton, where for the next few years he worked a regular gig at the Harris Bar on 5th Street.

Johnny Smith, Tucker's manager, got the Hi, Atco, and Sunbeam labels to each record and release one Tucker single, but all three disks—"Miller's Cave," "Rock and Roll Machine" (as by Tee Tucker), and "My Blue Heaven"—fared poorly. However, once he met Herb Abramson (owner of the A-1 Studios and the Blaze, Festival, and Triumph labels), Tommy was set to score. With Jimmy Reed in mind, he took to the studios and cut a demo on "High Heel Sneakers," accompanied by Dean Young on guitar, Brenda Lee Jones on bass, and Johnny Williams on drums. Instead of asking Reed to record a polished version of the tune, Abramson, acting as Tommy's manager and producer, had Chess Records' Checker subsidiary issue the rough demo as a finished track.

The response was overwhelming and, unfortunately, unduplicable. After "Long Tall Shorty" (#90, 1964)—soon covered by the Kinks for their first LP—"Alimony," and further sides stiffed, Tommy returned to school. In the late '60s, he received a liberal-arts degree from the Thomas Edison College in New Jersey. He briefly returned to Chess for a few singles, and did a pre-Sinatra version of "That's Life" for Abramson's Festival label.

Tommy Tucker died of poisoning on January 22, 1982. Reports vary as to the precise cause of his death.

IRMA THOMAS
WISH SOMEONE WOULD CARE
(Irma Thomas)
Imperial 66013
No. 17 *May 16, 1964*

Irma Thomas was born Irma Lee in Ponchatoula, Louisiana, on February 18, 1941. Her parents moved to New Orleans when she was a baby. They lived in a rooming house behind the Bell Hotel. "That's where I really got interested in music," Irma told Almost Slim, author of *I Hear You Knockin'.* "The lounge in the motel had a jukebox, and I'd sneak off and listen to it every chance I'd get. I'd hear Clyde McPhatter and the Drifters, Joe Liggins, Lowell Fulsom, and Annie Laurie. My favorite record then was 'Ida Red' by Percy Mayfield."

Irma received her singing training on Sundays at the Home Mission Baptist Church. Her sixth-grade teacher entered her in a talent contest at the Carver Theatre, and she won first place singing Nat "King" Cole's "Pretend." But all was to stop when Irma became pregnant—a pregnant 14-year-old was not looked upon too highly in those days, and Irma felt like an outcast. She washed dishes for 50 cents an hour; her first marriage

ended. It was during her second marriage and the creation of two more children that Thomas started singing with bandleader Tommy Ridgely at New Orleans' Pimlico Club.

Ridgely hooked Irma up with Ron Records owner Joe Ruffino, who was immediately interested in recording her on something called "Don't Mess With My Man." "Don't Mess" (R&B: #22, 1960) was a solid-selling first outing. After a fine follow-up, "A Good Man," failed to fly, Thomas moved to Minit Records for some of her grittiest efforts ever—"Cry On," "It's Too Soon to Know," "It's Raining," and "Ruler of My Heart" (the latter was reworked by Otis Redding into "Pain in My Heart"). The Minit label had a family feeling to it: New Orleans artists like ERNIE K-DOE, JESSIE HILL, Aaron Neville, and Benny Spellman would often drop by and sing back-up on Irma's sessions.

In 1964, Minit was acquired by Imperial, a subsidiary of Liberty Records. "Wish Someone Would Care" was Irma's first single under this arrangement. In 1984, "Break-a-Way," the disk's flip side, would regally resurface as a hit for TRACEY ULLMAN. Three other Thomas 45s on Imperial—"Anyone Who Knows What Love Is (Will Understand)" (#52, 1964), "Times Have

IRMA THOMAS

Changed" (#98, 1964), and "He's My Guy" (#63, 1964) —made both the pop and R & B listings in 1964. A debut LP was packed and pushed, and Irma hit the road to tour behind her platters.

Irma's name may be familiar to rock and roll fans for another reason. The Rolling Stones took notice of Irma's soulful sounds, and quickly covered her unsuccessful follow-up to "Wish Someone Would Care"— "Time Is on My Side." The Stones' version was their first Top 10 disk (#6, 1964), although Irma was less than flattered.

"The Rolling Stones version was worse [than mine]," Irma declared to the *Chicago Sun Times*' Don McLeese. "I mean we won't say similar in their case—it was worse. English groups were on the rise at the time, and whether it was good, bad, or indifferent, they were English. It was beside the point whether or not they could sing." Irma told Bob Shannon and John Javna in *Behind the Hits* that with the success of the Stones' rendition, "I stopped doing it. I really liked that song, and I put my heart and soul into it. Then along comes this English group that half-sings it, and gets a million-seller."

Despite the creation of some high-quality product for the Chess, Roker, Fungus, RCA, and Maison de Soul labels, Irma never managed to replicate the success of "Wish Someone Would Care," though she did crack the R & B charts in 1968 with a cover of Otis Redding's "Good to Me" (R&B: #42). Irma Thomas has been active on the New Orleans club scene and the blues circuit ever since. Neighbors and faithful fans call her "The Soul Queen of New Orleans," and insist that she sounds every bit as good now as she did then. Into the '90s, Rounder Records has issued several LPs of new material.

DANNY WILLIAMS
WHITE ON WHITE
(L. Crane, B. Ross)
United Artists 685
No. 9 *May 16, 1964*

Throughout the pre-Beatles '60s, South African-born Danny Williams functioned as England's cloned answer to Johnny Mathis. From his very first Mathis-molded smoothie in 1961, "We'll Never Be This Young Again," through his chart-topping rendition of "Moon River" and his Top 10 tune, "Wonderful World of the Young," Danny could do little wrong with British audiences.

Williams, who was born in Port Elizabeth, South Africa, on January 7, 1942, had been singing professionally since his 13th year. While he was touring London with an African-based show called "The Golden City Dixies," record producer Norman Newell heard Dan's calming, crooning voice. Newell secured Danny a

recording contract with the HMV label, and in 1960, Williams and his family moved to London.

A pile of singles were issued before Williams managed to connect with an American audience. "White on White," a variation (possibly unintentional) on Bobby Vinton's "Blue on Blue" tale, was Danny's only stateside hit. His follow-up, "A Little Toy Balloon" (#84, 1964), made the Hot 100, but none of his successive releases did. Strangely, neither single was a hit with his homeland, where well into the '70s, he continued to work cabarets and concerts.

Danny Williams graced the British charts one last time in 1977 with "Dancing Easy," a reworked commercial jingle for a martini mix. He still continues to tour when the whim and the want are present. More recently, Danny has been breaking things up in his new career as a black-belt karate instructor.

REFLECTIONS
(JUST LIKE) ROMEO & JULIET
(B. Hamilton, F. Gorman)
Golden World 9
No. 6 *May 30, 1964*

Phil "Parrot" Castrodale (b. Apr. 2, 1942, Detroit), Ray "Razor" Steinberg (b. Oct. 29, 1942, Washington, PA), Tony "Spaghetti" Micale (b. Aug. 23, 1942, Bronx, NY), Danny Bennie (b. Mar. 13, 1940, Johnston, Scotland), and Johnny Dean (b. 1942, Detroit) were the Detroit-based Reflections, so named after Parrot caught the hot-shot reflection the group cast in the mirror of their rehearsal hall. Parrot, Razor, Spaghetti, and the rest were working record hops, school dances, and other social functions in 1963 when they were discovered by producer Jan Hutchens.

Hutchens liked the fellows' old-time doo-wop approach—they had a vocal style that was nearly extinct by this point in pop history—and lined up a recording session for the guys with the teeny-weeny Tigre label. The Reflections' first release, a cover of the Five Satins' "In the Still of the Night," charted in some Midwestern markets, including Chicago. Noting this response to the guys' throw-back sound, the Golden World label signed the group to a multi-record contract.

With their next release, "(Just Like) Romeo & Juliet," the Reflections secured their one and only sizable hit. Yet ironically, the group never even took the tune seriously.

"When I first heard [the song], I hated it," Tony Micale told *Goldmine*'s Stu Fink. "We thought it was a real bubblegum song, the words in it and all. So we would practice it every day to the point where we would mimic it. And by mimicking the song, we put in all the falsetto stuff. We did that as a joke, as a kind of payback: if they wanted to make it stupid, we'd really make it stupid."

The follow-up to "(Just Like) Romeo & Juliet," "Like Columbus Did," held down the number 96 slot on the Hot 100 for a week. "Poor Man's Son" also charted (#55, 1965), but six further Golden World releases stiffed. The problem: the group was now typecast by record-buyers, who expected the Reflections to replicate the sound of their big hit. "They wanted us to do that falsetto on most everything we did after that. We hated it, and we couldn't get any madder at a company than we were."

In 1966, the group switched to the ABC label for one rehash of their big moment ("Like Adam & Eve") and one effort at updating their sound ("The Long Cigarette"). The times were wrong or the approach wasn't right: nothing was coming together right for Spaghetti, Razor, Parrot, and the gang. In a last-ditch maneuver, the guys changed their name to the High and the Mighty—but their only single under their new identity, "Escape From Cuba," sputtered.

The Reflections carried on for years, playing college dates and clubs. Currently, Micale and Dean are playing in a Detroit-area band called the Larados.

PREMIERS
FARMER JOHN
(Terry Harris)
Warner Bros. 5443
No. 19 *August 1, 1964*

Very few Latino rock and roll bands, in the days before Santana, managed to successfully steal even a slight serving of the nation's auditory attention. Among the few such acts were the Blendells, the Midnighters, Cannibal & The Headhunters, and the Premiers.

The Premiers—George Delgado (guitar), Johnny Perez (drums), Larry Perez (guitar), Phil Ruiz (sax), Joe Urzua (sax), and Frank Zuniga (bass)—were East L.A.'ers through and through. Since they were building up a reputation on the southern California circuit as a knock-out band, producers Billy Cardenas and Eddie Davis made a special effort to check out their paces at the Rainbow Gardens in Pomona. Cardenas and Davis were impressed, and approached the guys about making some recordings. "Farmer John," a cover version of an old Don & Dewey number, was the first side issued on the local Faro label.

The unruly crowd sounds in the background give the impression that "Farmer John" was a live recording; the label even claims that the number was taped "live at The Rhythm Room in Fullerton, California." In actuality, Cardenas and Davis brought the band and a pile of friends into an old studio on Melrose Avenue. The friends were duly inebriated and instructed to whoop it up as if they were at a wild party (this bit of trickery became an increasingly common way to simulate the excitement of a live performance on record). When sales on "Farmer John" ballooned beyond the Hispanic community, Warner Bros. picked up the 45 for national distribution.

"Annie Oakley," the follow-up, flopped, and was the only other Premiers disk to receive national distribution. Thereafter, a few years' worth of now-hard-to-find, similar-sounding singles were issued on Faro. The band reportedly carried on working the southern California circuit for much of the '60s.

JELLY BEANS
I WANNA LOVE HIM SO BAD
(Jeff Barry, Ellie Greenwich [both members of The Raindrops])
Red Bird 10003
No. 9 *August 8, 1964*

The Jelly Beans were four gals and a guy from Jersey City. Alma Brewer, Diane Taylor, sisters Elyse and Max-

THE JELLY BEANS

ine Herbert, and Charlie Thomas were just high schoolers when they were discovered by manager-to-be Bill Downs. Bill knew producer Steve Venet, who brought the group to Red Bird Records. At Red Bird, the legendary recording [as THE RAINDROPS] and songwriting team of Jeff Barry and Ellie Greenwich were assigned the task of making the quintet into hit-paraders. "I Wanna Love Him So Bad" was the Jelly Beans' first release.

The girl-group sound was still hot. With Charlie's bass floppin' like a flat tire, and the girlies cheerfully chirpin' along, their disk sold close to a million copies. "Baby Be Mine" (#51, 1964), also penned by Barry and Greenwich, didn't do too badly, either. Things looked good for the Jelly Beans. There was talk of releasing an album, and some tracks were recorded; however, no LP and or subsequent singles ever appeared on Red Bird Records.

The following year, a lone 45 utilizing the group's logo was issued on the Eskee label.

JIMMY HUGHES
STEAL AWAY
(Jimmy Hughes)
Fame 6401
No. 17 *August 15, 1964*

Not everyone who has a hit, becomes a star, and makes some money wants to remain in the limelight. "I enjoyed performing, but I missed my family," Jimmy told Peter Guralnick in *Sweet Soul Music*. "When I quit, I didn't miss it one bit." After eight years of singing, recording, touring, and touring yet some more, Jimmy walked away from the entertainment game. What he has been doing to make a living since is not known, but most likely, he still sings Sundays in his church choir.

Jimmy Hughes was born in Florence, Alabama. From early on, he sang of God and His glory. By the age of eight, he was the lead singer in his choir. For years, he sang in various gospel groups, most notably the Singing Clouds, a group that often made local radio appearances. In 1962, while Hughes was working at the Robbins Rubber Company plant in nearby Leighton, a friend convinced him to drop by Rick Hall's Wilson Dam studio and audition on some sinful secular songs.

Hall, who had just produced ARTHUR ALEXANDER's "You Better Move On" (#24, 1962), taped several of Hughes' tunes and soon managed to lease "I'm Qualified" to the Philly-based Jamie/Guyden vinyl-pushers. Hall had the gut feeling that Jimmy could have a hit with "Steal Away," a dank, adulterous piece of business that Jimmy had written. After several labels declined to release the track, Hall decided to set up his own label, Fame.

Hall was right on the money—"Steal Away" was to become a solid Southern-soul single. "Try Me" (#65, 1964), "Neighbor, Neighbor" (#65, 1966), and "Why Not Tonight" (#90, 1967) all climbed on the pop charts. Still other singles clicked with the R & B audiences. But by the end of the '60s, Jimmy Hughes was burnt out on the whole scene, and walked away from it all, never to return.

JUMPIN' GENE SIMMONS
HAUNTED HOUSE
(R. Geddins)
Hi 2076
No. 11 *August 26, 1964*

"One day, I guess it was about 1954, I was visiting a cousin of Elvis Presley's," Simmons (b. 1933, Tupelo, MS) recalled to Randy McNutt in *We Wanna Boogie*. "I didn't know who Elvis was at the time, but somebody said he played the guitar, so I handed him one and he just smiled. He said, 'I only play for myself.' Personally, I thought the guy looked weird. Greased-back hair, tight pants, all that. Yeah, this guy was hipper than we country boys."

Weeks later, Elvis linked up with Sun Records, and Gene, not one to be left shakin' in the cold, asked the Pelvis to put in some good words for Jumpin' Gene at Sun Records. Sun issued one Simmons single, "Drinkin' Wine," but it went down the drain. With kind words, the guys at the label snuffed out Gene's hopes of having any more yellow-labeled Sun releases bearing his name. Fortunately, a good buddy and fellow one-off Sun recording artist, Ray Harris, got Gene a spot singing with the big-time Bill Black Combo. Hi Records, Black's label, issued a pile of sides with Jumpin' Gene's name on them, but nothing moved an inch.

Gene crossed paths with the man who would later become "Sam The Sham," Domingo Samudio. Dom had been doing a well-received Johnny Fuller R & B horror called "Haunted House" as part of his club set. Hi Records asked Gene to bring Samudio into the studio to wax the number, but Domingo refused, for some reasons now lost in the cracks of pop history. Hi was hot for the thing, so Gene offered to step in and record the contagiously inane tune.

Even though the British Invasion was in full force, Gene's Memphis ditty soaked up airplay time and creamed the charts. Follow-ups like "The Dodo" (#83, 1964), "The Batman," and "Keep the Meat in the Pan" did little to establish any momentum, however, and as the years rolled on, numerous 45s with Simmons' name on them sat around radio stations unplayed.

Gene was not deterred—well into the '70s, the lad from Tupelo continued finding record companies willing to give him one more shot. Nearly a dozen labels

issued Jumpin' Gene records. Some sold to country listeners; some were high quality but sold poorly anyway; and some just plain stiffed.

In the '80s Gene Simmons moved to Nashville, and currently works in music publishing.

JACKIE ROSS
SELFISH ONE
(McKinley, Smith)
Chess 1903
No. 11 *September 5, 1964*

When she was three, Jackie (b. Jan. 30, 1946, St. Louis, MO) began her singing career on Mom and Dad's radio show. Her parents were preachers and ran a church. "All of the big gospel singers at the time who would come to St. Louis, they would appear on the broadcast," Ross told *Goldmine*'s Robert Pruter. "I've been knowing Sam Cooke ever since I was just a little thing. Not only him but all the big groups. We knew them pretty well, because they would visit my parents' house for big dinners and everything."

Cooke and the family were especially close, and when Jackie's dad died in 1954, Sam encouraged the family to move to Chicago, where he could keep an eye on them. In 1962, Cooke, who had taken notice of Ross' singing abilities, won her mother's permission to record her for his Sar label.

"After the record, Sam wanted to take me out to California. But as much as my mother loved him, she said, 'No, I'm sorry, I can't let you take my 15-year-old child and continue to raise her out there.'" Her single, "Hard Time," failed to sell.

After winning a talent contest at the Trianon Ballroom, Jackie began touring with Syl Johnson's band. She was discovered at one engagement by Bill Doc Lee, a DJ on a gospel station owned by Leonard Chess of Chess Records. "Selfish One," Jackie's debut disk for Chess, was her only major charting on either the pop or R & B listings. Surely, her powerful "We Can Do It" and her cover of Evie Sands' "Take Me for a Little While" should have established her. Early in 1966, Ross left the Chess label after a royalty dispute.

"It was a big letdown for me after what they told me 'Selfish One' did not do. If I had all my old papers, I

could quote you a figure—but the amount of money I had gotten from it, it was just ridiculous."

After a couple of singles each for Brunswick, Mercury, and Jerry Butler's Fountain label, Ross found a half-dozen other labels to issue occasional singles with her name on them, but none of these attracted much attention.

JOE HINTON
FUNNY (HOW TIME SLIPS AWAY)
(Willie Nelson)
Back Beat 541
No. 13 *October 10, 1964*

Not much is known about Joe Hinton. He was born some time in 1929 and he died on August 13, 1968, in a Boston hospital of "natural causes." In between those two poles in life's continuum, Joe sang his guts out.

It was while singing with the Spirit of Memphis gospel group that Joe was discovered by Don Robey of the Duke and Peacock record labels. Robey persuaded Joe to sing of other things than Jesus. His first half-dozen singles elicited little response from pop audiences, but Robey had faith that something very real and urgent lived inside of Joe. More disks were waxed and shipped; "You Know It Ain't Right" (#88) and "Better to Give Than Receive" (#89) grazed *Billboard*'s Hot 100 in 1963.

Next out of the gate was "Funny (How Time Slips Away)," a Willie Nelson country/soul song that JIMMY ELLEDGE had charted with two years earlier (#22, 1962). "Funny" should have made Joe more accessible to the mainstream pop/rock radio listeners, but it didn't.

GALE GARNETT
WE'LL SING IN THE SUNSHINE
(Gale Garnett)
RCA 8388
No. 4 *October 17, 1964*

Gale was born on July 17, 1942, in Auckland, New Zealand. Dad was a carnival pitchman and a music-hall entertainer; consequently, the family moved around a lot. They landed in the U.S. when Gale was nine, moved about some more, and eventually settled in New York City. Dad encouraged her to find her place in the sun. By age 12, Gale was onstage, acting. When her father died, Gale left home to set her own place on the Lower East Side. In between bit parts, Garnett worked as a waitress and janitor. In her late teens, she got a role in a touring company of *The Drunkard*. Over the next few years, she made 60 acting appearances on TV episodes of "Bonanza," "Hawaiian Eye," and "77 Sunset Strip."

She also acted in stage productions of *Guys and Dolls*, *Threepenny Opera*, and *Show Boat*.

In her meager spare time, the exhausted youth wrote poetry and folk songs. Only three months before Gale walked into RCA Records with a pile of her compositions, she had made her singing debut in a Los Angeles coffeehouse. Label execs found her gravel-throated voice and material to be unique, and gave the go-ahead to record an album's worth of folkie things. "We'll Sing in the Sunshine" was the first single issued, and it was a winner. Garnett's feminist decree of eternal personal independence won a Grammy Award as "Best Folk Recording of the Year." But other than the immediate follow-up, "Lovin' Place" (#54, 1965), no other Garnett platters sold well.

It is not known what became of Gale Garnett. When her sun last shone, it was late in the '60s. Gale was backed by the Gentle Reign, an electric wall of hair, beads, and 12-string guitars. Two odd albums of acid-laced hippie happenings were unleashed by Columbia Records. Gale was definitely "far out" by this time.

HONDELLS
LITTLE HONDA
(BRIAN WILSON)
Mercury 72324
No. 9 *October 31, 1964*

Gary Usher is the number-one unsung hero of the sub-genre of rock and roll known as surf/hotrod music. Just as BRIAN WILSON and the Beach Boys were preparing to lay down the entire foundation for this California sound, Gary's uncle introduced him to Brian Wilson. Within days of their meeting, Usher and Wilson created "The Lonely Sea," which later appeared as a track on the Beach Boys' *Surfin U.S.A.* album. Over the years, Gary and Brian would co-write "In My Room," "We'll Run Away," and numerous others. Usher's solo surfer projects, released under his own name, all crashed on the shore.

Usher then picked up on the idea of fabricating groups by bringing together a clutch of musical friends in the recording studio to lay down his tunes as he saw fit. The finished product could then be sold off to various interested record companies and credited to whatever performers the label wished. Usher and his recording pack included (at various times) Chuck Girard, Joe Kelly, Richie Podolor, Ritchie Burns, Jan Berry, Glen Campbell, Bruce Johnston, Terry Melcher, and Brian Wilson. This aggregate of friends were thus the Four Speeds (with the lead vocals being handled by Dennis Wilson), the Super Stocks, the Wheelmen, the Revells, the Knights, the Ghouls, the Silly Surfers . . . and the Hondells.

With the immediate success of "Little Honda," the pressure was on to put together a touring version of the Hondells to take the hit on the road. Ritchie Burns, who was on the actual recording as a background singer, was enlisted to front a "Hondells." As the Hondells' first album was about to be released, a group still did not exist—for the photo on the LP's cover, Ritchie, who was working days as a bank teller, had three other tellers at his bank pose for the photos.

The Hondells were much more successful than anyone had imagined. There were tours, "The Dick Clark Show," "Shindig," and movies like *Ski Party* (1965), *Beach Blanket Bingo* (1965), and *Beach Ball* (1965). More singles were issued, including "My Buddy Seat" (#87, 1965) and "Younger Girl" (#52, 1966), the latter a cover of the Critters' hit.

By the seventh single, the touring company had rehearsed sufficiently to enter the recording studio. Randy Thomas, with folk-rock leanings, had sung lead on the JOHN SEBASTIAN tune "Younger Girl," and did likewise on their last Mercury release—BOB LIND's "Cheryl's Going Home." Usher and Burns took the "Hondells" name over to Columbia, and later to JIMMY BOWEN's Amos label, where a few more 45s were released. By then, however, the summer sun had set on the surf/hot-rod sound, and the group's efforts at folk-rock were generally unconvincing. In 1970, Usher packed up the Hondells' name and placed it into cold storage.

Gary Usher died on May 25, 1990.

LORNE GREENE
RINGO
(DON ROBERTSON, Hal Blair)
RCA 8444
No. 1 *November 7, 1964*

Born in Canada on February 12, 1915, Lorne had his first brush with music when 10 years old. His mother compelled him to study the violin, but a softball fall requiring many stitches soon spared little Lorne's family from the experience of further violin screeches.

It was an actor Greene wanted to be. He studied drama at Queen's University and won a fellowship to an acting school in New York City. In 1940, Lorne became a radio announcer for the Canadian Broadcasting Company, replacing Charles Jennings (father of ABC news anchor Peter Jennings). After a stint in the Canadian Army during World War II, Lorne returned to broadcasting and formed the Academy of Radio Arts.

To help radio announcers keep track of the time remaining in their programs, Lorne invented a stopwatch that counted backwards. While attempting to sell the gadget to an NBC executive, Greene crossed paths with television producer Fletcher Markle, who cast

Lorne in the first of many stage and screen productions. Between 1954 and 1958, Lorne made 12 movies. After a guest appearance on "Wagon Train," he was offered what soon became his most famous role—Ben Cartwright, in NBCs "Bonanza" series.

After the runaway success of a "Bonanza" Christmas album—featuring all the Cartwrights doing their stuff—RCA herded Lorne, Dan Blocker, Michael Landon, and Pernell Roberts back into the studio. For one of the ditties, Greene was handed a six-verse poem about some sheriff who saves the life of a gunfighter named Johnny Ringo. The record label apparently didn't know what it had until a Texas DJ started to play the life out of that "Ringo" cut.

For a full-grown Canadian cowpoke to have a number-one hit with a talkie-style country song is hard to believe, but Lorne Greene did it. (Of course, the fact that the tune's title was also the name of one of the members of the hottest sensation in the entertainment world at the time—the Fab Four—did not exactly hurt record sales.) Lorne recorded seven albums and many

LORNE GREENE

more singles, but he charted only one more time, with a religious talkie titled "The Man" (#72, 1965).

In 1973, after "Bonanza" went to rest in TV Boot Hill, Lorne starred in two other series, "Griff" and "Battlestar Galactica." On September 11, 1987, just prior to filming the resurrected "Bonanza" series, Lorne Greene died of respiratory failure from pneumonia in Santa Monica, California.

NASHVILLE TEENS
TOBACCO ROAD
(JOHN D. LOUDERMILK)
London 9889
No. 14 *November 7, 1964*

Not one of these underrated artifacts from the British Invasion had even set foot in Nashville—they were all from Weybridge, Surrey—nor was any one a teen at the time. And in no way were these root-rockers playing C & W. They were darn good, though, at their special blend of good old rhythm 'n' blues.

The Nashville Teens convened in 1962 when Ramon "Ray" Phillips (vocals, bass, harmonica) and Arthur Sharp (vocals), members of two local rival groups, decided to join their musical juices. Michael Dunford (guitar), Roger Groom (drums), John Hawkes (keyboards), and Pete Shannon (bass) completed the original line-up. The

unit spent most of 1963 in Hamburg, Germany, at the now legendary Star Club—backing Jerry Lee Lewis for several months. When they returned to England, BO DIDDLEY recruited them for his European tour. Mickey Most—a singer with Bo's opening act, the Minutemen—convinced the teens that he was something of a producer and that he could get them on a label.

Most took the Teens into the studio as part of a one-off deal to record "Tobacco Road," a tune that Sharp had heard while working in a record shop. By this point, Dunford and Groom had left, so the group consisted of Phillips (b. Jan. 16, 1944, Tiger Bay, Wales), Sharp (b. May 26, 1941, Woking), Hawkes (b. May 9, 1940, Bournemouth), and Shannon (b. Aug. 23, 1941, Antrim, Northern Ireland), plus two new members—guitarist John Allen (b. Apr. 23, 1945, Albans) and drummer Barry Jenkins (b. Dec. 22, 1944, Leicester).

"Tobacco Road" was a major chart invader on both sides of the Atlantic. Unfortunately, for their follow-up, the Nashville Teens chose to remake another (and much less appealing) JOHN D. LOUDERMILK (a.k.a. JOHNNY DEE) tune—"Google Eye," a folkie tale about an unfortunate trout. The disk went nowhere in the States. The group made a few minor movie appearances (*Be My Guest*, 1965; *Gonks Go Beat*, 1965; *Pop Gear*, 1965), but visa restrictions limited the Teens to a tour of only New York State. Further singles—and there were a few peculiar ones over the next year or two—failed to cap-

THE NASHVILLE TEENS

italize on the group's talents. At this point, the Teens' tale becomes fuzzy to both fans and pop historians.

By 1966, members started their flight. Jenkins joined the Animals. Hawkins left to work with Spooky Tooth, the Strawbs, and Renaissance. Dunford went on to record with Renaissance. Sharp left in 1972 for a desk job alongside Don Arden at Jet Records. By the early '70s, only Ray Phillips remained from the original line-up; when last spotted in the mid-'80s, he was fronting a new edition of the Nashville Teens.

J. FRANK WILSON & THE CAVALIERS
LAST KISS
(Wayne Cochran)
Josie 923
No. 2 *November 7, 1964*
No. 92 *December 22, 1973*

"Last Kiss" was one of those short love stories about a guy, a girl, and a car crash. The tune, based in part on a true incident, was written by blue-eyed soul singer Wayne Cochran. Wayne, whose own vocal performances inexplicably never cracked the Hot 100, was a wandering Georgia boy who had been screaming his guts out for years in an effort to bring home the bacon. In the early '60s, he lived in a $20-a-month shack on Route 1941. It was a main drag, so over the years he witnessed more than one gory car accident. One night in 1964, three couples in a Chevy Impala were killed after crashing into a flatbed truck. With this tragedy as his inspiration, Cochran penned "Last Kiss."

Gala Records took an interest in Wayne's dirge and offered him a chance to record it. Locally, sales of the disk were promising enough for Syd Nathan to sign Cochran to the King label. Another rendering of the ode was waxed, but, according to Cochran, Nathan did not like the teen-death tune and failed to adequately promote the single. Hundreds of miles away fate would strike . . .

"We're the longest rockin' band in the world," said Sid Holmes, Jr., lead guitarist/manager for more than 40 years with the Cavaliers, in an exclusive interview. "We ain't never stopped; never will."

Sid got the band together in the spring of 1955, in San Angelo, Texas. The boys—Alton Baird (vocals), Carroll Smith (upright bass), Ron Stovall (drums)—and Sid would play the bars, West Texas theaters, and make appearances on the "Louisiana Hayride" with Johnny Horton. "We flipped over the original Sun recording stuff; Bill [Black], Scotty [Moore], Elvis. That was our influence," explained Sid.

"We got offered a deal to record one record; over in Dallas. A banker had heard us, liked us, and got this deal with Jay-Gee Records in New York." "Crazy Guitar" sold well locally. Baird soon joined the military and San

Angelo DJ Jerry Naylor (b. Jerry Naylor Jackson) filled the slot as the Cavaliers' vocalist. When Buddy Holly died, the Crickets called on Naylor to do what he could as Holly's replacement.

Over the years, Sid remained a constant; the line-up changed often. In the early '60s, the group moved to Memphis where Sid's sister Sylvia Holmes was a D.J. at WHHM and a member of Elvis' nightlife scene. Sid recorded some with Bill Black, accompanied FRANKIE FORD and THOMAS WAYNE in concert; jammed with Ace Cannon. In 1962, with the band broken and homesick, Sid returned to San Angelo to restart the Cavaliers.

As a three-piece, Sid, Lewis Elliott (bass), and Bob Zeller (sax) packed them in, playing "Happy Hour" at Tiny's. "They told me, 'Man, you all need a singer.' Someone said they knew this guy getting discharged. So, I went and picked him up at the base, nearby [the Goodfellow Air Force base]. We tried him out that night. Everyone in the band, said 'No way.' I overruled them, thinking this guy had a recording voice."

J. Frank Wilson (b. Dec. 11, 1941, Lufkin, TX) was the guy. "We got popular so fast with him singing with us, that we got booked six months at the Dixie Club, the hottest spot 'round. Man, we were doin' the Blue Note club in Big Spring, in Midland, the Rock & Roll Club . . . and it was there that we met 'em, Sonley Roush. Strange man, he was; lived with his ma, had no money, always request this one song from Frank. He's the one introduced us to 'Last Kiss.' I didn't think anything good 'bout the song; still don't today."

Sonley, who was buddies with Ron Newdoll owner of the tiny Accurate Sound studio, made arrangements for J. Frank and the Cavaliers to record a duplicate of Wayne Cochran's tune. "Everybody was beat, man, worn-out, when that thing was cut," said Sid. "They did 64 takes on that damn song. Sonley and I got into it . . . and I left. Lewis stayed; Zeller was gone. They had to pay this piano guy, Jim Wynne, $100—that was all he ever got for the record—to play the session. Rowland Atkinson was there; Buddy Croyle played badly on my guitar with my amp. Gwen Coleman sang back-up; had to leave to go to attend church. I believe they double-tracked her voice."

Sonley persuaded Tamara Records and then LeCam Records to issue "Last Kiss"; with Jay-Gee eventually picking up the disk for national distribution via its Josie label. As luck would have it, the remake was to become a flash hit . . . but all was not well.

"'Last Kiss' was the very worst thing that could happen to Frank. He had problems. He didn't need all that. Frank had hit his head bad when 10, and he never was right again. He just couldn't handle it. One day he was playin' a dang joint; next day up there with the Beatles. . . . It all went to his head, and he thought he was a superstar.

"After three damn jobs, the Cavaliers quit him. Frank had gone ape-shit—sex, booze, up all night. He couldn't handle it; and Sonley couldn't keep him together, or keep up.

"Sonley's driving, falls asleep, and they had a wreck; at a slow speed head-on into an 18-wheeler. It killed Sonley and busted Frank all up. Understand the records going up the charts. When he appeared on 'American Bandstand' Frank was on crutches."

While Lewis Elliot reformed the Cavaliers with lead vocalist James Thomas—both still carrying the Cavaliers name into the 21st Century—J. Frank Wilson and Josie Records continued to use the Cavaliers name, with assorted session musicians. That year, in addition to the Texans' successful debut album and their Top 10 tune, a reworking of DORSEY BURNETTE's 1960 hit "Hey Little One" charted at number 85. Over the years, a number of other disks by J. Frank appeared on the April, Charay, LeCam, and Sully labels. In 1971, a hard-to-find LP appeared on Dill Pickle; in 1974, a rerelease of "Last Kiss" made number 92.

"All his stuff was bad. Bad bands, bad material, bad arrangements . . . It's sad, though," said Holmes. "Frank never could get his lost fame outta his head. He drank beyond the limit, DWI's, married eight times . . . worked in a nursing home and as a cook on a rig outta Houston. His health got worse. . . ."

J. Frank Wilson died on October 4, 1991, in Lufkin, Texas. He was 48.

What are one-time Cavalier members doing?: Lewis and Thomas continue the Cavaliers name; as did Sid Holmes with a competing Cavaliers group between '72 and '87. Sometime member Ed Logan recorded with the Memphis Horns. Bobby Wood, a touring member, injured in the crash that took Sonley's life, made the C & W listings with "That's All I Need to Know" (#46, 1964) and for years worked sessions. Jerry Naylor charted near a dozen singles on the C & W listings; fronted the award-winning radio series "Continental Country," in the '70s.

A slightly modified rendition by WEDNESDAY, a Canadian pop unit fronted by Mike O'Neil, made the Top 40 during the winter of '73.

HONEYCOMBS
HAVE I THE RIGHT?
(Howard Blaikley)
Interphon 7707
No. 5 *November 14, 1964*

Annie "Honey" Lantree (b. Aug. 28, 1943, Hayes, Middlesex, England) was a hairdresser and a drummer. In 1962, she worked at a small salon in Edgeware, North London, under the supervision of former skiffle gui-

tarist Martin Murray (b. Oct. 7, 1941, London). Marty still took a whack at his ax every now and then, and despite the pleasure of doing numbers on heads full of hair, he still had an itch to form a group and play beat music.

To that end, Marty ran an ad in a music paper, which was promptly answered by guitarist/keyboardist Alan Ward (b. Dec. 12, 1945, Nottingham). Friends introduced Marty to lead vocalist/pianist/guitarist Denis d'Ell (b. Denis Dalziel, Oct. 10, 1943, London), and Honey recommended her brother John (b. Aug. 20, 1940, Newbury, Berkshire) for the slot of bass player. The line-up was set, and a name was chosen: "The Sherabons."

By mid-'63, the group was garnering favorable notices at the local pubs. Songwriters Ken Howard and Alan Blaikley (collectively known under the pseudonym "Howard Blaikley") offered to manage the band and hooked them up with independent producer Joe Meek. Joe had worked wonders with Mike Berry, Lonnie Donegan, Johnny Kidd & The Pirates, and especially THE TORNADOES. Soon the Honeycombs (a moniker created from taking Annie's nickname plus Honey and Marty's occupation as "combers"; others claim Pye Records' managing director Louis Benjamin had a thing for Jimmie Rodgers's record "Honeycomb") were stomping near the top of charts with their debut disk, Blaikley's "Have I the Right?"

The only stateside LP (*Here Are the Honeycombs*, 1965) sold well, and follow-up 45s were quite appealing. (Oddly enough, the album's liner notes misidentified the Honeycombs as "The Sherations.") However, someone shipped the group off on a tour of France, Australia, and New Zealand. Because they were away from their home turf for so long, the Combs failed to chart with their next batch of singles. On the group's return, Murray, having injured himself by falling off a stage, dropped out and was replaced by Peter Pye (b. July 12, 1946, London).

On February 3, 1967, Joe Meek, the Honeycombs' producer and guiding force, fatally shot himself in the head. No further records were issued by the group. Denis d'Ell departed for a lackluster solo career.

The Honeycombs' managers and songwriters, Howard and Blaikley went on to create a string of sounds for the Herd, Gary Wright, IAN MATTHEWS and his MATTHEWS SOUTHERN COMFORT, Phil Collins' Flaming Youth, and the British quintet of Dave Dee, Dozy, Beaky, Mick & Tich. They are currently involved in writing musicals for London's West End stage and working as in-house composers of theme music for the PBS series "Masterpiece Theatre."

THE HONEYCOMBS

ROBERT GOULET
MY LOVE, FORGIVE ME (AMORE, SCUSAMI)
(V. Pallavicini, S. Lee, B. Mescoil)
Columbia 43131
No. 16 *January 2, 1965*

Robert was born Stanley Applebaum on November 26, 1933, in Lawrence, Massachusetts, and raised in Edmonton, Canada. He sang in church choirs and with local orchestras before winning a scholarship to the opera school of the Royal Conservatory of Music in Toronto. There he studied acting and singing, making many theater and TV appearances. In 1954, he came to New York City to try his luck at Broadway, but nothing panned out, so for four months he sold stationery in Gimbel's department store. Returning to Canada, he won a leading role in the CBCs production of *Little Women.* Numerous other theatrical productions then followed.

Stanley's transformation into "Robert Goulet" occurred when he was cast as Sir Lancelot—opposite Richard Burton and Julie Andrews—in the Broadway production of *Camelot.* Columbia Records offered the saccharine singer a contract, and for many years

Goulet's easy-listening LPs graced *Billboard*'s top pop albums chart.

Before "My Love, Forgive Me," Robert Goulet did manage to chart with a recording of "What Kind of Fool Am I?" (#89, 1962); his follow-up to "My Love," "Summer Sounds" (#58, 1965), also made the Hot 100. He continues to appear on TV variety programs, and in musical productions like *Brigadoon, Carousel,* and *Kiss Me Kate.*

JULIE ROGERS
THE WEDDING
(Joaquin Prieto, Fred Jay)
Mercury 72332
No. 10 *January 2, 1965*

Rogers was born Julie Rolls on April 6, 1943, in London. She took piano lessons as a child and began her professional career as a cabaret singer in the early '60s. After completing school, she became a secretary; she also worked as a dancer in Spain and as a stewardess on a slow ship to Africa. Still a teen and still wanting to sing easy-listening material, Julie auditioned for bandleader Teddy Foster. With the band, Julie made her radio debut in 1962 on the BBC Light Program's "Music With a Beat." During one of her engagements with Foster, Mercury A & R man Johnny Franz heard her belt a few. Franz told the boys at Mercury about the girl; contracts and songs were quickly arranged.

After unsuccessfully covering the Platters' "It's Magic," Rogers waxed "The Wedding," an Argentine tune that had made two earlier chart appearances—for the Chordettes (#91, 1956) and for June Valli (#43, 1959). June's rendition, however, became a perennial. For years thereafter, whenever young lovers tied the knot, some wedding guest would inevitably beseech the reception band to play the sugary strains of this song. By the time the recording had aged but 10 years, sales had totaled 7 million copies worldwide.

Julie Rogers continued exploring that queasy (and decidedly unhip) easy-listening terrain. "Like a Child" (#67, 1965) and her "Hawaiian Wedding Song" sold fairly well in the U.K. After an LP and a few more stateside singles, Rogers' name, but not "The Wedding," faded away into oblivion.

DETERGENTS
LEADER OF THE LAUNDROMAT
(Paul Vance, Lee Pockriss)
Roulette 4590
No. 19 *January 9, 1965*

Paul Vance and Lee Pockriss had been writing pop songs together for years. In the late '50s, they penned

"Catch a Falling Star" (Perry Como), "What Is Love?" (The Playmates), and "Itsy Bitsy Teenie Weenie Yellow Polka Dot Bikini" (Brian Hyland). Columbia Records let them make a stack of silly singles as Lee & Paul. Only "The Chick," their nutty number of 1959 about a beatnik chicken and his electric guitar, ever earned a notch on the Hot 100.

Ron Dante (b. Carmine Granito, Aug. 22, 1945, Staten Island, NY) was working for Don Kirshner's Aldon Music, recording demos for staff songwriters like Burt Bacharach, Carole King, Neil Sedaka, and Vance & Pockriss. In 1964, the latter duo worked up a parody of the Shangri-Las' chart-topping "Leader of the Pack." Dante and a couple of Brooklyn boys—Danny Jordan (Vance's nephew) and Tommy Wynn—were recruited to cut a quickie demo on this "Pack" parody. A few minor changes were made, sound effects were added, and Morris Levy at Roulette Records issued the demo as by "The Detergents."

The response was immediate and favorable. Dante toured with the group for a few months, but eventually was replaced by Phil Patrick and Danny Jordan's cousin, Tony Favio. A half-dozen follow-ups were issued, of which only a James Bond-inspired novelty number, "Double-O-Seven" (#89, 1965), was mildly successful. Before they disbanded, the Detergents appeared with Nick Adams and Rose Marie in Morey Amsterdam's flaky flick, *Don't Worry, I'll Think of a Title* (1966).

Danny, who had recorded clean teen tunes for the Climax, Leader, and Smash labels, returned to his staff songwriter position at Columbia's Screen Gems, and

THE DETERGENTS

later produced HOT BUTTER's 1972 hit, "Popcorn." Dante, plus session singer Toni Wine, became the voices for the Archies (of "Sugar Sugar" fame); Dante was also, in multi-tracked form, all the voices in THE CUFF LINKS. In the '70s, Ron worked as a session singer for Melissa Manchester and Valerie Simpson; recorded as the Webspinners, Dante's Inferno and under the Ron Dante name; did numerous commercial jingles; and formed a lengthy personal and professional relationship with Barry Manilow.

LARKS
THE JERK
(Don Julian)
Money 106
No. 7 *January 16, 1965*

The Larks—or the Meadowlarks, as they were first called—were an L.A. unit formed in 1953 by Don Julian (lead vocals, tenor), who tapped the vocal talents of his fellow high-school choirmates. The original crew included Ronald Barrett (tenor), Earl Jones (baritone, bass), and a later member of THE PENGUINS, Randy Jones (bass). Cornell Gunter, of the Flairs and later the Coasters, took an interest in the guys and introduced them to the Bihari brothers at Modern/RPM. A few singles were waxed and shipped, but nothing caught on. Barrett dropped out of the group.

While daydreaming in a warm bath, Julian wrote a nifty number called "Heaven and Paradise." With Earl, Randy, and a new tenor, Glen Reagan, Don approached Dootsie Williams, owner of the DooTone/Dooto label. In a flash, Dootsie knew the group had put together a doo-woppin' classic. "Heaven and Paradise," "Always and Always," and a number of other disks were issued. Members came and went; Don and his gang recorded for a while as the Medallions, backing up Vernon Green.

A decade passed. Don Julian had managed to have some further singles released under various names, but none of them sold very well. Then Don happened on to a new dance in his sister's front room. "I went over to my sister's; the kids were dancing to Martha & The Vandellas' 'Dancin' in the Street,'" Julian recalled to *Goldmine*'s Steve Propes. "I said, 'Hey, what's that you're doing?' One of the kids said, 'The Jerk.' I asked her what it was, and she said, 'If you don't know how to do it, come on, I'll teach you.'"

Don dashed home, wrote up some lyrics, and reassembled his Larks/Meadowlarks. (At this point, the "Meadowlarks" name was used to refer to the vocal group's back-up musicians; "The Larks" referred to the singers themselves.) The Larks now consisted of Julian plus two L.A. lads, Charles Morrison and Ted Waters.

Once "The Jerk" appeared on the Money label and started climbing the charts, all the majors rushed in to stomp out their own Jerk tunes and hopefully grab a piece of the action. Before the dust had settled, Bob & Earl ("Everybody Jerk"), THE CAPITOLS ("Cool Jerk"), Clyde & The Blues Jays ("The Big Jerk"), THE CONTOURS ("Can You Jerk Like Me?"), the Dukays ("The Jerk"), the Miracles ("Come on and Do the Jerk"), Jackie Ross ("Jerk and Twine"), and a mess of other acts had worn the craze out. There seemed no need for Don and his duo to keep jerking: it had all been said and done. Consequently, the Larks' follow-ups, "Soul Jerk" and "Mickey's East Coast Jerk," and two further albums— *Soul Kaleidoscope* (1966) and *Superslick* (1967)—sold poorly.

ALVIN CASH & THE CRAWLERS
TWINE TIME
(Andre Williams, Verlie Rice)
Mar-V-Lus 6002
No. 14 *February 20, 1965*

Alvin Cash and his eight brothers and sisters attended Sumner High in St. Louis; fellow classmates included Luther Ingram, Billy Davis (later of the Fifth Dimension), and Annie Mae Bullocks—a.k.a. Tina Turner. "I used to sit behind Tina and kick my knee in her butt all the time," Cash confessed to *Chicago Sun-Times* writer Dave Hoekstra. "She'd turn around and say 'Alvin Cash, would you cut that out! . . .'"

Around 1960, Alvin (b. Alvin Welch, Feb. 15, 1939, St. Louis) formed a song-and-dance act with three of his brothers, Arthur, George, and Robert, then aged 8 to 10. "I danced pretty good in school," Cash told *Goldmine*'s Robert Pruter, "and I wanted us to be the world's greatest dance act—tap, soft-shoe, flash, all of it." As the Crawlers, they did their stuff in town and across the river in East St. Louis. In 1963, Alvin trekked to Chicago to see if his act could cut a record.

Andre Williams (who had scored an R & B hit in 1957 with "Bacon Fat") was a producer and talent scout for George Learner's One-derful/Mar-V-Lus/M-Pac labels. Williams had caught the Cash brothers' bit, and approached Alvin about yelling some lines on a new dance disk that he was planning called "The Twine." Cash came in with the Nightlighters, a band he was touring with at the time. This back-up unit subsequently changed its name to the Crawlers, and later, to the Registers.

"Twine Time" was a pleasantly crude instrumental with an unstoppably funky groove; sales of the disk came close to a million. Flush with solo success, Cash shelved his brothers' dance act and continued to cash in on dance disks: "The Barracuda" (#59, 1965), "The Penguin," "The Philly Freeze" (#49, 1966), "Alvin's Boo-Ga-Loo" (#74, 1966), "The Boston Monkey," "The Charge," "The Creep," and "Keep on Dancing" (#68, 1968). Alvin even recorded a number of Muhammad Ali tributes: "Doin' The Ali Shuffle," "Ali-Part 1 & 2" and the hard-to-find *Alvin Cash Does the Greatest Hits of Muhammad Ali* (1980).

The years have passed, but Alvin is still dancin'. Over the years, he has had bit-part appearances in 1978's *The Buddy Holly Story* (as a member of the Five Satins) and in a number of black action flicks like *Black Jack* and *Peetie Wheatstraw, The Devil's Son-in-Law*. Obscure disks with titles like "You Shot Me Through the Grease" and "Funky Washing Machine" still find their way into a handful of record stores.

Alvin Cash currently lives above a pool hall in Chicago, and works as the head of promotion for Triple T Records.

AD LIBS
THE BOY FROM NEW YORK CITY
(John Taylor)
Blue Cat 102
No. 8 *February 27, 1965*

J. T. Taylor was born and raised in Morristown, New Jersey, and later attended the Bordertown Military College. During the '30s and '40s, J. T. played clubs, bars, and music houses, sitting in with the band that supplied the sounds for Martin Block's "Make Believe Ballroom" radio program. In the '50s, J. T. moved to Jersey's Hudson County and started teaching. One night in the late '50s, a street-corner group of doo-woppers caught his ear—the Creators, consisting of Johnny "Angel" Allen, Danny Austin, Chris Coles, Hughie Harris, and Jimmy Wright.

J. T. offered the guys some advice, gave them some songs, and took them down to the dudes at Diamond Disks. Diamond cut a few tunes and leased the tracks to the tiny T-Kay label. "I'll Never Do It Again" sold very little, but Philips Records waxed two more Creators singles. These collectible disks also made a poor showing.

One warm day, while sipping wine and thinking about a woman, J. T. got this notion for a number to be called "The Boy From New York City." Taylor rounded up the Creators, now known as the Ad Libs, and had them record a demo of the song. Hughie and Danny were the only original Creators left; filling in the vocal gaps were Norm Donegan, Dave Watts, and Mary Ann Thomas.

A club owner brought the demo to the renowned production team of Leiber & Stoller who signed the group to their new Blue Cat label. Taylor's tune hit the spot, but the Ad Libs' 45s that followed—fine

THE ADLIBS

efforts like "He Ain't No Angel" and "I'm Just a Down Home Girl"—never matched the appeal of "The Boy From New York City." Before moving to the Karen, Philips, and Share labels, the Ad Libs recorded the highly collectible "New York in the Dark," for A.G.P. and Eskee.

As the '70s drew to a close, J. T. Taylor and the Ad Libs were still working hard at locating another hit. In 1981, Manhattan Transfer took a remake of "The Boy From New York City" into *Billboard*'s Top 10; two years later, a new Ad Libs single, "Spring and Summer," appeared on the group-owned Passion label.

JEWEL AKENS
THE BIRDS AND THE BEES
(Barry Stuart)
Era 3141
No. 3 *March 20, 1965*

His mama had her heart set on getting a girl child. Jewel was to be her name. Ma didn't get no daughter, but the baby got the name just the same. "Nobody bothered me about that though," said Jewel Akens, in an exclusive interview. "It must be cause I'm a jewel, you see."

Akens (b. Sept. 12, 1940, Houston, TX) almost never got to record "The Birds and the Bees." "I had to wait three years for that song. You see, when I first meet Herb Newman [Era Records owner] he said, 'I like your voice. It's got a commercial sound. Come back in three years.' I said in my head, 'Three years!' Well, believe it or not, three years later I'm knockin' on his door. He said, 'I'm ready.'"

By this point, Jewel already had an extensive music history. At age 11, Jewel was singing in church. "I used to live next door to this blues house . . ." said Jewel. I'd hear all these guys pick and sing. My daddy didn't want us listenin' cause he was real religious—but you couldn't help but hear it. The first thing I ever remember singing is 'Wintertime Blues,' Lester Williams, it was by. I loved that so much I wrote a blues when I was nine, called 'Raining Blues.' My Mama used to say, 'One of these days you're gonna be a star, you're gonna be something.' She was sick, bad, and before she passed away, she said, 'If I don't make it, I want you to go to California and be a star.'"

In 1949, his family was uprooted and moved to L.A. In his teens years, he sang with the Four Tunes and later with a friend named Eddie Daniels; the Four Dots were formed. Someone introduced them to Jerry Capehart, Eddie Cochran's manager, songwriter, and confidant. The Dots cut a single for Freedom Records in 1959 and Akens and Daniels, recording as Jewel & Eddie recorded several sides for Jerry's Silver and Capehart labels; notably, "Opportunity." Rumors have persisted that Eddie Cochran's guitar can be heard on these collectible singles. "Yeah, Eddie did the music on that; just the music. We were good buddies, close friends. He played on all my stuff I recorded for Crest. I also did some background sessions for John Ashley, this pretty boy actor, who was in some movies like *Hot Rod Gang*. . . .

"As the Four Dots, we also did something called 'Don't Wake Up the Kids,' that came out on Liberty. That was like a regional hit, in about 1960."

For Imperial, in 1961, Jewel and probably Eddie and possibly some reconstituted Dots calling themselves the Astro-Jets recorded one of the finest and now one of the hardest to find double-sided neo-doo-wop delights, "Boom a Lay" b/w "Hide & Seek."

When Newman gave the go-ahead sign to Jewel, Akens was fronting yet another group, the Turn-arounds. Newman recorded them on a song called "Ain't Nothin Shakin'" and asked them to sing back-up behind Jewel on a tune Newman's 12-year-old son had written about those birds and bees and things. Akens and the group disagreed over the song's merits, the label credits, and split up.

"I knew it was a hit . . ." Akens said. I sang it for my wife and anybody I could find. And they'd all say, 'It's cute.' I worked on the melody and the four or five different arrangements we went through. We even tried bird whistles, but that didn't work."

The lyrics were pre-teen, but there was an underlining thrusting, hypnotic rhythm that was definitely post-pimples. "Yeah. Yeah. Well, you see, I was getting ticked by the 27th take," Akens added, "that's why there's those heavy accents in parts of the song like on 'Let me tell ya 'bout the birds and . . .'"

As directed, Akens went back into the studios to record more in that nursery rhyme vein. The immediate issuance, "Georgie Porgy," (#68, 1965) sold fair in parts of the country. "I never liked that thing," said Jewel. Nothing further charted. He toured with the Monkees, recording—what he considered to be his finest recordings—cover versions of THURSTON HARRIS' "Little Bitty Pretty One," ARTHUR ALEXANDER's "You Better Go Now" and the Monkees' "I Wanna Be Free."

In 1973, Jewel co-produced the critically-acclaimed *Super Taylors*, a duet album of Southern soul by Ted Taylor and LITTLE JOHNNY TAYLOR (no relation). Two years later, American International Artists issued Akens' remake of Sam & Dave's "When Something Is Wrong With My Baby."

"I've been lucky," he said. "And a lot of that probably has to do with my being versatile. I've been able to make a living with my music, performing and touring, all these years. Depending on where I'm booked, I sing old standards, or rock'n'roll hits, even country. I've no complaints. I'd like to get another hit, though. And every now and then, I do get tired of 'tellin' about the birds and the bees' but life's been good to me."

SHIRLEY BASSEY
GOLDFINGER
(Leslie Bricusse, Anthony Newley, JOHN BARRY)
United Artists 790
No. 8 *March 27, 1965*

Life was not easy for young Shirley Bassey. She was born the youngest of seven on January 8, 1937, in Tiger's Bay, a working-class section of Cardiff, Wales. When Shirley was two, her dad died. Listening to the tunes on the radio, she taught herself how to sing and dreamed of being a star on the stage. In her teens, to help her family get by, Shirley worked in an enamel factory; all the while, friends would coax her into singing at parties and push her to audition for show biz parts.

Shirley's first professional gig came with her assignment to a chorus line in a touring British show, *Memories of Al Jolson*. After her appearance in the 1956 revue of *Such Is Life*, Bassey was signed to a Philips recording contract. Early the following year, "Banana Boat Song,"

a cover of the stateside Harry Belafonte/TARRIER's hit, became the first of more than two dozen British hits. While "Goldfinger," the stirring theme from the third James Bond thriller, was Shirley's lone Top 40 hit on these shores, a few follow-up 45s did make the Hot 100, including a full-bodied version of the Beatles' "Something" (#55, 1970) and yet another Bond theme, "Diamonds Are Forever" (#57, 1972).

Voted the "Best Female Entertainer" of 1976, by the American Guild of Variety Artists; the following year she received the Britannia Award as "Best Female Solo Singer in the Last 50 Years." In 1981, Shirley announced her retirement, but "Bassey the Belter," the "Tigress of Tiger Bay" has yet to stop. Most odd among her recent musical adventures—the pairing with Yello in 1987 for "The Rhythm Divine."

A bountiful bunch of Bassey LPs are still in print, and Shirley is still a top-draw attraction in the theaters and nightclubs of Europe.

SOUNDS ORCHESTRAL
CAST YOUR FATE TO THE WIND
(VINCE GUARALDI, Frank Werber)
Parkway 942
No. 10 *May 8, 1965*

British producer John Schroeder had been noticing with dismay that teens were just not appreciating the sounds of big orchestras with Sousa horns and glockenspiels. This rock and roll music, it seemed, was raucous and lacking in hummable melody. Schroeder's ambition was to rectify the situation by creating what he described, in the liner notes to Sounds Orchestral's only album, as "a better music . . . nearer to the understanding of the younger generation, keeping within commercial boundaries and retaining a teenage, yet adult appeal."

To shape such music, Schroeder enlisted pianist Johnny Pearson—BBC producer, radio personality, and arranger for the likes of Cilla Black, Connie Francis, and SHIRLEY BASSEY. Schroeder brought in drummer Kenny Clare and not one, but three bass players—Pete McGurk, Frank Clark, and Tony Reeves. The band laid down a sound bottom that teen ears would like, but that adult ones could tolerate—"Cast Your Fate to the Wind," a remake of the VINCE GUARALDI TRIO's instrumental pop-jazz hit of 1963, was Sound Orchestral's first effort at tailoring a "better music" for teens. To the surprise of many, the disk took off, eventually cracking the Top 10. The follow-up, an update of the Andy Williams/Eddie Heywood hit "Canadian Sunset," appeared in the summer of 1965, and scraped onto the Hot 100 at number 76.

GLENN YARBROUGH
BABY THE RAIN MUST FALL
(Ernie Shelton, ELMER BERNSTEIN)
RCA Victor 8498
No. 12 *May 22, 1965*

The Limeliters were quite successful in their day—one of the prime components in the '50s revival of folk music in the U.S. From 1959 to 1963, all 10 of this folk trio' s LPs made healthy in roads on to *Billboard*'s top pop albums chart. The group played all the big New York night spots like the Village Vanguard, Mr. Kelley's, and the hungry i. They appeared with Shelly Berman, Mort Sahl, and George Shearing. While only "A Dollar Down" made the pop charts (#60, 1960), the Limeliters were one of the hottest campus and concert acts of the entire hootenanny/folk revival period. Burn-out and the British Invasion ended all that.

Lou Gottlieb, Alex Hassilev, and Glenn Yarbrough parted company in 1964. Al and Lou continued on as the Limeliters for a spell, with Ernie Shelton filling in for Glenn. Months later, Yarbrough had his big moment with a Shelton number picked as the theme for the Steve McQueen/Lee Remick flick *Baby the Rain Must Fall* (1964).

Numerous Yarbrough albums followed—three featuring lyrics totally created by Rod "Dor" McKuen (half of the comedy team BOB MCFADDEN & DOR)—but his only other Hot 100 item came in 1965 with the folk-rockish "It's Gonna Be Fine" (#54). Glenn, you see, was big, bulky, and balding, and did not look like your hip and happening hoodoo. RCA packaged him as a lawn-tending family man: no problem there, only during the '60s this image began waning in fashionability. Change was a-blowin' in the wind.

Glenn Yarbrough (b. Jan. 12, 1930, Milwaukee/guitar, vocals) began his musical career at the age of eight, as a featured vocalist at Grace Church in Manhattan. His soaring soprano won him a scholarship to the St. Paul School in Baltimore. In his late teens, wanderlust struck, so he hiked around Canada and Mexico before settling down with ancient philosophy texts at St. John's College and, later, the New School for Social Research in New York City.

For post-Socratic fun, Glenn sang folk songs. His discovery in the mid-'50s by the owner of Chicago's Gate of Horn quickly led to a career on the coffeehouse circuit. For awhile, Yarbrough and Alex Hassilev (b. July 11, 1932, Paris/guitar, banjo, vocals), an aspiring actor, owned their own coffeehouse in Colorado Springs called the Limelite. While the two were playing together at the Cosmo Alley Club in L.A., Lou Gottlieb (b. 1923, Los Angeles/bass)—a Ph.D. who had studied music under Arnold Schoenberg, was sometime arranger for the Kingston Trio, and a former member of the Gateway Singers—appeared. In 1959, the three formed the Limeliters.

As of the mid-'90s a reconstituted Limeliters has been touring and recording albums for GNP Crescendo and Folk Era Records. Glenn is the only original member involved; the others now include Lou Gottlieb's son Tony and Mike Settle, formerly of the Kenny Rogers's fronted First Edition.

HORST JANKOWSKI
A WALK IN THE BLACK FOREST
(Horst Jankowski)
Mercury 72425
No. 12 *July 10, 1965*

Horst Jankowski was born on January 30, 1936, in Berlin. During World War II, his father was killed, and he and his family were driven out of the city. He later returned and attended the Berlin Conservatory of Music, where he studied the contrabass, tenor saxophone, trumpet, and piano. At 16, Jankowski met the popular European singer/dancer CATERINA VALENTE, who engaged him in a two-year tour of Africa, France, and Spain. On his return, he frequently worked with Valente through 1964 and also did some arranging

HORST
JANKOWSKI

and composing for the German orchestra of Erwin Leha.

With his own jazz combo, Horst started performing on the Berlin nightclub circuit, and from 1957 on, a number of various German polls voted Horst the top jazz pianist in Germany. Beginning in 1960, he worked as a freelance orchestra director/arranger for such renown acts as Miles Davis, Ella Fitzgerald, Benny Goodman, Gerry Mulligan, and Oscar Peterson. He also began experimenting with various combinations of conventional instruments and the human voice, much as RAY CONNIFF was doing in the States.

With the Beatles, the Stones, the Dave Clark Five, the Byrds, the Yardbirds, and Dylan all in their prime—and all over the charts, airwaves, and teen mags—it seems incredible that Horst could muscle his way onto the pop charts with a melodic piano-voice-orchestra thing originally called "Eine Schwarzwaldfahrt." But he pulled it off, and the LP featuring the aria even made the top pop albums chart in the U. S.

Another easy-listening lulu, "Simpel Gimpel" (#91, 1965), appeared on the Hot 100 for a week; several more albums, and many more singles, flowed forth. The saccharine jazz-pop of Horst Jankowski is occasionally heard even to this day on "Beautiful Music" radio stations across the land.

Reportedly, Horst Jankowski died in his homeland, sometime during the late '80s.

IAN WHITCOMB & BLUESVILLE
YOU TURN ME ON (TURN ON SONG)
(Ian Whitcomb)
Tower 134
No. 8 *July 17, 1965*

"I was brought up stiff-upper-lip English; I had to be reserved, and performing was considered vulgar," said Ian Whitcomb to *Sh-Boom*'s Joel Sanoff. "But I was dying to be vulgar."

Ian (b. July 10, 1941, Woking, Surrey) acquired an unsavory reputation for punching out people, like that cop who called him "punk" and that one-legged bloke who called him "lady." This Britisher washed ashore with the Beatle Invasion, yet he preferred Jerry Lee Lewis and Little Richard to the Fab Four. Bred in an upper-class setting, Ian was attending Dublin's Trinity College when his record became a national novelty.

Throughout his younger years, Whitcomb listened avidly to rock and roll, this "devil music" from the States. Not only that, but he practiced piano-banging those satanic songs; fronting Warren Whitcomb's Bluesmen, later Bluesville, M.FG. During the summer of 1963, 22-year-old Ian took a trip to Seattle to visit a cousin. Once there, he tested his facility on the ivories in several coffeehouses around town. The following year Whitcomb returned in search of an American record company.

After hearing a crude demo of Whitcomb and his group Bluesville (rhythm guitarist Deke O'Brien, drummer Jan McGarry, lead guitarist Mick Molloy, harp/sax man Barry Richardson, and bassist Gerry Ryan) Jerry Dennson—owner of the Jerden label responsible for the Sonics, the Kingsmen's "Louie Louie," and some early sides by Paul Revere & The Raiders—signed Ian up. First out of the stall was "This Sporting Life," which Capitol's Tower subsidary soon picked up for national distribution. It was a mini-sized charter (#100, 1965). But no one could have predicted what would come next.

"I was visiting this lady in Seattle," Whitcomb recalled to *Goldmine's* Bill Guarneri. "I was at her house romancing her with my British accent . . . We were sort of doing heavy petting, when she suddenly said, 'Ian, your accent is turning me on.' I'd never heard this phrase used this way before. I thought it was very graphic and started using it in songs."

At first, Whitcomb used the catchy line in his Jerry Lee Lewis styled rendition of "Memphis." Noting the positive audience response, he slowly developed the expression into a whole number. "No Tears for Johnny," a Dylanesque protest song against the Vietnam War, was slated as his follow-up single to "This Sporting Life." At the end of the recording session, there was time to spare, so Ian recorded "You Turn Me On." Tower picked that number as the "A" side, much to Ian's disgust: "I was just depressed, really depressed. I thought it was junk."

Nonetheless, rock and rollers bought piles of Ian's "junk." He appeared on TV shows like "Shindig" and "American Bandstand," and toured with the Beatles, the Stones, and other British Invasion acts. *Sixteen* magazine awarded Ian the "Gee Gee Award," for "most promising new singer of 1965." On one of these package tours, Whitcomb slugged a program director, which he alleges led to his singles being blacklisted from airplay by the station and its affiliates. Others report that Ian was in a boil about his lack of repeated singles successes and went off into the sunset in a huff.

Yes, despite numerous follow-ups, including "N-E-R-V-O-U-S!" (#59, 1965), Ian seemed pegged as a novelty act; one "turn on" tune was all American record-buyers needed.

Ian Whitcomb is still a very busy man. He now lives in California and has issued nearly a dozen LPs, most of them featuring eccentric ragtime romps like "They're Parking Camels Where the Taxis Used to Be," "Charlie's a Cripple (You Know)," and "Yaaka Hula Hickey Dula." He has taught film and pop music courses at the University of Southern California, worked as a DJ on

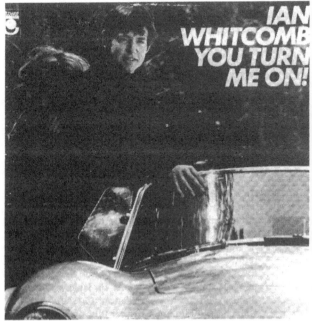

Pasadena's KROQ and L.A.'s KCRW, written a few books (most notably *After the Ball*, scored a Las Vegas revue (*DooDah Daze*) and Mae West's *Sextette*, composed music for the movie *Bugs Bunny, Superstar* (1975), and scripted the PBS TV special "Tin Pan Alley"

"Today, you could never get the break that I had," said Ian to *Sh-Boom*. ". . . My record cost $25 to make and started out as a local hit in Seattle. Today, you've got to be signed up to a major corporation . . ."

Bluesville quietly split from Whitcombe following his first U.S. tour. After much parading around Ireland and England, the band evolved into the homeland faves Bees Make Honey.

BARRY MCGUIRE
EVE OF DESTRUCTION
(Philip F. Sloan, Steve Barri)
Dunhill 4009
No. 1 *September 25, 1965*

As songwriters for Lou Adler's Trousdale Music, P. F. Sloan and Steve Barri had cranked out surfin' songs (what Sloan referred to as "formula stuff") for Jan & Dean, the Rip Chords, and their own pseudo-groups—the Fantastic Baggies, the Life-guards, the Rally Packs, the Street Cleaners, The Rincon Surfside Band, and Willie & The Wheels. All that changed in 1965, when Adler, hoping to influence Sloan's writing, handed him an early Bob Dylan album.

"After I heard that LP, I started writing by myself again," Sloan recalled in an exclusive interview. "The first songs that I wrote outside the partnership [with Barri], I wrote in one night—'Eve of Destruction,' 'Take Me for What I'm Worth,' 'The Sins of the Family,' and 'This Mornin'.'

"I went up [to Trousdale Music] and played them 'Eve of Destruction' and the rest, and they didn't like the songs. They thought they were awful—you know, 'that's not hit material, forget it.' Then one afternoon, Barry McGuire came to see them for material. He was a big star at the time. They played him all the hip things of the day that they had, Sloan-Barri formula stuff. I was sittin' alone in the corner, watchin' the business go down. [McGuire] came over, saw this depressed young kid playing guitar by himself, and said, 'What's the matter? You got any songs to play me?' I played 'Eve of Destruction,' and boom! 'That's the one,' he said. He hugged me and said, 'You're what I've been looking for.'"

Barry McGuire was born in Oklahoma on October 15, 1935. He first came to prominence as a minor actor in the TV series "Route 66" and with Barry Kane, as Barry and Barry, recorded an album and single for the tiny Horizon label, but it was McGuire's role in the formation of Randy Sparks' New Christy Minstrels that brought the gravel-throated folkie his first notice. Barry wrote and sang lead on "Green, Green" (#14, 1963), the group's biggest hit. The same year, the Kingston Trio successfully recorded Barry's "Greenback Dollar" (#21, 1963). By 1965, Barry was ready to strike out on his own, and "Eve of Destruction" would be his first solo single.

Adler had Sloan and Barri taped McGuire's rough vocal over the instrumental backing track, for Barry to use as a guide in creating the final version. But one radio station got hold of the unfinished record and began playing it; when "Eve of Destruction" was released, it was the rough mix that Sloan and Barri had slapped together late at night.

According to Sloan, a number of radio stations banned the disk. "The record company had never seen anything like it. They were actually happy. When every major market refused to play it, that's when the label decided to really push it. I hear some DJ in Ohio or somewhere in the Midwest play 'Eve of Destruction' every hour on the hour. It was number one there in, like, no time. That's what broke it nationally."

"Eve" became such a major hit that THE SPOKESMEN quickly recorded and charted with a response record, "Dawn of Construction."

Barry's *Eve of Destruction* LP (1965) sold well, though only two more of his subsequent singles— "Child of Our Times" (#72, 1965) and "Cloudy Summer Afternoon (Raindrops)" (#62, 1966)—ever made the listings. McGuire made a few movie appearances, joined the Broadway production of *Hair*, introduced the Mamas and Papas to Dunhill Records, and toured for awhile with a spiritual group called The Agape Force. In the early '70s, Barry was half of a duo with Eric "Dr" Hord, a Mamas and Papas' sideman. Their delightful album *Barry McGuire and the Doctor* bombed . . . and Barry walked away from secular music. He is now a born-again Christian living in Waco, Texas, and recording gospel music sporadically for specialty labels like Myrrh and Word.

Phil "Faith" Sloan (b. Phillip Gary Sloan, 1944, New York City) went on to create/co-create an enormous number of hit songs for Herman's Hermits, Jan & Dean, the Turtles, Johnny Rivers, and the Grass Roots. Before a reclusive phase in the mid-'70s, P. F. recorded his own versions of "Eve of Destruction," "This Is What I Was Made For," and some of his other tunes. These appeared as now-collectible singles, and on four hard-to-find albums (*Songs of Our Time*, *12 More Times*, *Measure of Pleasure*, and *Raised on Records*).

In 1990, Sloan rewrote "Eve of Destruction"—and Barry McGuire reappeared to record the tune. The media took no notice . . . but in November of that year, P.F. performed at the annual National Academy Of Songwriter's convention, receiving a standing ovation.

SONNY
LAUGH AT ME
(Sonny Bono)
Atco 6369
No. 10 *September 25, 1965*

They met in November 1962, in a little coffee shop on Hollywood Boulevard in L.A. Sixteen-year-old Cherilyn Sarkisian LaPierre was just sitting with some friends, goofing off. Sonny, a promo man for Philles Records, was married and had a daughter. Their meeting that night would change their lives, and the couple would quickly move on to influence folk-rock as well as countercultural fashions like hippie wear and long hair.

Salvatore Phillip Bono was born in Detroit, on February 16, 1935, the youngest of three. Mama called him "Sonny," and the name stuck. His family moved to Inglewood, California, when he was seven years old. At 16, Sonny quit school to become a grocery store clerk. Within a few years, he was married to Donna Rankin and the father of Christy. Late at night, he would practice at the piano, scribble lyrics, and dream of pop stardom. He worked as a waiter, assembly-line worker, butcher's assistant, and truck driver.

Bono started out assisting Harold Battiste, who was the A & R man at Specialty Records. "His personality was contagious," Battiste told J. Randy Taraborrelli,

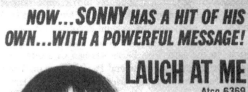

NOW...SONNY HAS A HIT OF HIS OWN...WITH A POWERFUL MESSAGE!

LAUGH AT ME
Atco 6369

Arranged and Produced by: SONNY BONO
A YORK-PALA Production
Chez, Greene/Brian Stone

THE SHINDIG PICK OF THE WEEK!
Watch Sonny perform it August 11

WHY CAN'T I, BE LIKE ANY GUY
WHY DO THEY TRY TO MAKE ME DUM, SON OF A GUN
WHAT DO THEY CARE, ABOUT THE CLOTHES I WEAR
WHY GET THEIR KICKS FROM MAKIN' FUN
THIS WORLD GOT A LOT OF SPACE
AND IF THEY DON'T LIKE MY FACE
IT AIN'T ME THAT'S GOIN' ANYWHERE
SO I DON'T CARE
THEN LAUGH AT ME
IF THAT'S THE FARE I HAVE TO PAY TO BE FREE
THEN BABY, LAUGH AT ME
AND I'LL PRAY FOR YOU
AND I'LL PRAY FOR YOU
AND I'LL DO ALL THE THINGS
THAT THE MAN UPSTAIRS SAYS TO DO
I'LL DO 'EM FOR YOU, I'LL DO 'EM FOR YOU
IT'S GOTTA START SOMEPLACE
IT'S GOTTA START SOMETHING
I'LL MAKE THAT OTHER CHEEK MINE,
AND MAYBE THE NEXT GUY, THAT DON'T WEAR A SILK TIE
HE CAN WALK BY AND SAY HI, SAY HI, INSTEAD OF WHY
LAUGH AT ME

| Current
SONNY & CHER
Smash:
I GOT YOU BABE
Atco 6359 | JUST RELEASED!
SONNY & CHER's
FIRST LP
LOOK AT US
Atco LP 33-177 | |

 ATCO RECORDS · 1841 Broadway   New York, New York 10023 (212) PL 7-6306

the author of *Cher*. "Sonny had style; man, the cat had boundless energy and ambition . . . There were dozens and dozens of cats in Los Angeles like Sonny . . . most of whom ended up back at the grocery store baggin' food for old ladies. Not this guy."

Before long, Sonny was songwriting ("Koko Joe," "She Said Yeah," and "Tight Sweater" for THE MARA-THONS) and producing for Specialty: Wynona Carr, Don & Dewey, Larry Williams. In 1959, "Wearing Black," Bono's first solo effort, was issued by the label as by Don Christy. By then, he had left Specialty to buy into/become involved with/set up small labels like Fidelity, Go, Name, Rush, and Sawmi. He issued singles as Don Christy, Sonny Christy, or Ronny Sommers.

Late in 1962—after co-writing the classic "Needles and Pins" with JACK NITZSCHE—Bono was hired by Phil Spector to be a promo man, A & R rep, and sometime percussionist for his Philles label. Sonny's lanky new girlfriend was soon doing sessions, as a back-up singer. Bob B. Sox & The Bluejeans, the Crystals, Darlene Love, the Ronettes . . . what legendary acts and tracks Spector was recording, and what a sound! Spector became Sonny's idol, and he learned a lot about producing from watching Spector at work in the studio.

With "I Got You, Babe," written and produced by Sonny, Sonny & Cher became an overnight sensation in

1965. Their golden disks feature a suspiciously Spector-like "Wall of Sound" technique. Together they dominated the Top 40 charts in 1965: "Baby, Don't Go," "Just You," "But You're Mine," "What Now My Love" They appeared in movies—*Good Times* (1966) and *Chastity* (1968)—had their own successful CBS-TV show (1971-74), and divorced in 1974.

Sonny recorded only a few solo sides after his semi-serious, partially autobiographical "Laugh at Me"—which was later reworked by MOTT THE HOOPLE, for its debut LP—charted. These included "The Revolution Kind," "Pammie's on a Bummer," "Misty Roses," and one LP.

The bubble burst, as all bubbles must. Sonny went on to appear in commercials, in "B" flicks (in particular, the John Waters flick *Hairspray* [1988]), and on reruns of "Fantasy Island" and "The Love Boat." In 1988, Sonny was elected mayor of Palm Springs, California; followed by an election to Congress in '94.

CASTAWAYS
LIAR, LIAR
(James J. Donna)
Soma 1433
No. 12 *October 23, 1965*

"Where did you get that stuff? No, no, none of us were wrestlers. None of us were even baseball players," says Roy Hensley (b. December 31, 1947, Ridgefield, MN), the Castaways rhythm guitarist in reference to an earlier *Goldmine* piece.

"We were not fraternity brothers out to make a buck," adds Dennis "Ludwig" Craswell (b. June 5, 1948, Ridgefield, MN) the group's drummer. "People never really knew who we were. They never even asked! So consequently whenever anybody wrote anything about us they just pulled it outta the air."

Let's set it straight, right here, right now.

"Look, the nucleus of the band, that's Denny Craswell, Dick Roby [bass], and myself [Roy Hensley] went to school together. . . . It was 1962, and we had this other guitar player at the time, but he left and we got Bob Folschow [and for a short while Jim Donna (keyboards)]. All of us had musical training, and we each played in the school band. We got involved with this guy Ira Hilecker and his partner, Dick Shapiro. Ira's father was Amos and Soma, the label they had was Ira's pop's name spelt backwards, get it?

"'Liar, Liar' was our first recording, as a group. Actually, we only recorded it because we couldn't get into any of the main rooms [clubs and night spots] in town. . . . Everybody else, it seemed, had a record on the radio. So, we got together and said, 'Sure, we'd like to make an extra 50 bucks a night and maybe get into

those rooms.' We approached Ira, and he signed us to a one-record contract. That was 'Liar, Liar', and it took off, and we subsequently never got into playing those rooms we had recorded the record for; we were too busy traveling the country."

"I think Soma was kind of a toy for Ira," adds Craswell, later a drummer with Crow yet another "One-Hit Wonder" act. "Now a regular label understands that you've got to have more product, but they had us on the road touring and doing TV and then when it was too late they say, 'Hey, you guys need another record.' We didn't know what was suppose to be done. We just did as we were told.

"You know, when 'Liar, Liar' was like #13 in *Billboard* we didn't have a record contract. We could've signed with anybody, but we didn't know any better. We were only like 15 years old."

Soma had quickly shipped one other disk, "Goodbye Baby" (#101, 1965), but then nothing. Finally after more than a year, the group was signed to Dunwich Productions and Fontana. Two non-charting 45s ("Walking in Different Circles" and "What Kind of Face") were issued by the latter label. Both bombed.

"The momentum was gone," Hensley adds. "After that we had our own company for a while. Tonna Records. . . . We released a number of singles on that label. There was "Peace of Mind," "Hit the Road Jack," and, ah . . . frankly, I can't think of the other ones. Hey, I've had people come up to me with Castaway records that I didn't even know were released. . . ."

"Yeah, it's nice that everybody wants our old records," says Craswell, "but we'd like to get something new going. . . . We could've had more hits if we had someone to direct and support us."

191

"But, we've never stopped," adds Hensley. "The Castaways have been in some kind of form or another ever since. . . . Occasionally we'd tour and then that *Good Morning Vietnam* (1987) [which included their notable both in the flick and on the soundtrack] came out and we got some offers we could not refuse. Agents were calling from all across the country, and we appeared in Chicago with the Mamas & Papas and did some shows with Brian Hyland and Del Shannon . . ."

"We'd like to get an interest in the string of hits that we could have had, if only we had pursued it," says Craswell.

"We've all kept active," Hensley breaks in. "We've done some session jobs and played under different names, for awhile. Currently, we're working on getting an album released. We're label shopping. It's all new stuff . . . and everyone's back in the group but Jim [currently being replaced by Al Olivera (keyboards)] . . . and we're ready, this time. . . ."

GENTRYS
KEEP ON DANCING

(Allen A. Jones, Willie David Young)
MGM 13379
No. 4 *October 30, 1965*

"We started in 1963. We were all in Treadwell High School," said Gentry guitar man Larry Raspberry to *Goldmine*'s Randal C. Hall, "except Pat [Neal], the bass player. He was a man, 27, 28; married, worked for the railroad." Besides Larry and Pat, the initial Gentrys were composed of Bruce Bowles (vocals), Bobby Fisher (sax, piano, guitar), Jimmy Hart (vocals), Jimmy Johnson (trumpet, organ), and Larry Wall (drums. They came in third place in the Mid-South Fair Talent Competition; got better and appeared on Ted Mack's "Amateur Hour," and won top honors at the Memphis Battle of the Bands.

In 1964, producer Chips Moman signed the Gentrys to his newly formed Youngstown label. "Little Drops of Water" sold less than modestly. "When we cut our second record, it was the only time I had sung 'Keep on Dancing,'" said Raspberry. "It was done as the flip side, so there was nothing to be lost with my not having a good voice. It took about 35 minutes from the time we decided to cut it until Chips said, 'That's the take.' Our version ran only 1 minute 30 seconds—too short even for a "B" side—and Chips taped the beginning over and stuck it at the end. It sounds as if the song starts all over again . . ." The planned top-side was "Make Up Your Mind," but when the hastily dashed and patched "B" side showed some sparks, Moman contacted MGM's Jim Vienneau, who acquired the waxing for national release.

Like many one-shot Top 40 moments, "Keep on Dancing" was a fluke hit; what the industry calls a "throwaway." A group called the Avantis—three black guys who modeled themselves after the Isley Brothers, and who had toured with, and befriended, the Gentrys—had recorded the original version of "Keep on Dancing" for the Chess subsidiary Argo. "We very much changed 'Keep on Dancing' from the way the Avantis did it," said Raspberry, "but did keep the words and the background vocal part. Their version was much like the Isley Brothers' 'Twist and Shout,' midtempo, like a cha-cha."

Everybody was surprised at the Gentrys' early success. "We were young kids," Raspberry said, "and not great musicians. We didn't know anything about tuning drums . . . or how to make things really sound good . . . Chip wanted us to be competitive with the musicians being recorded in Nashville, and yet here he was with kids 17 years old who couldn't play worth a darn."

Despite it all, the Gentry name returned to the national listings several more times. "Spread It on Thick" (#50, 1966) and "Everyday I Have the Blues" (#77, 1966) sold moderately well. Fisher and Johnson were gone by this point; Larry Butler was brought in from Nashville to play organ. Three further 45s appeared on MGM; three more on Bell, before what remained of the Gentrys broke up in 1970.

"Our world broadened, when 'Keep on Dancin'' hit," Raspberry said. ". . . Then—bam—we opened for Jerry Lee Lewis, the Beach Boys, Paul Revere; did 'Shindig,' 'American Bandstand' twice, 'Where the Action Is' least twice . . . We were a one-hit act."

Hart, singing lead with a completely new line-up—consisting of Dave Beaver (keyboards), Mike Gardner (drums), Steve Speer (bass), and Jimmy Tarbutton (guitar)—revived the group's name for three chartings on the legendary Sun label: "Why Should I Cry" (#61, 1970), "Cinnamon Girl" (#52, 1970), and "Wild World" (#97, 1971). This version of the Gentrys also recorded for Capitol and Stax.

Jimmy Hart went on as the "Mouth of the South," to become a successful wrestling manager with the World Wrestling Federation. Rick Allen resurfaced in as a later addition of the Box Tops. Bruce Bowles is a sales rep at a Memphis radio station. Bobby Fisher is a civil engineer with the city of Memphis. Jimmy Johnson is a physician. Pat Neal works for the railroad and moonlights with local country bands. Larry Wall is a promo man with Columbia/Epic Records. Raspberry formed a hard-rock band called Alamo that recorded one self-titled LP for Atlantic in 1970; he has since fronted the High-Steppers for at least four albums.

In 1971, "Keep on Dancing" produced by JONATHAN KING, became the first homeland major hit for the Scottish group the Bay City Rollers.

JONATHAN KING
EVERYONE'S GONE TO THE MOON
(Jonathan King)
Parrot 9774
No. 17 *November 6, 1965*

Kenneth King (b. Dec. 6, 1944, London) was right and proper when he was a lad. He was attending Trinity College in Cambridge when he came upon this scruffy bunch of beat musicians called the Bumblies. It was through the Bumblies that King met some execs at British Decca Records—in particular, a Ken Jones, who encouraged the youth to try his hand at writing some hip songs. One of the first of these was the hodgepodgy "Everyone's Gone to the Moon." At the time, everyone liked it, but no one seemed to really understand it. Nonetheless, King's thing became a worldwide hit, and can now be heard ad nauseam in the rear of baby boomers' aging minds.

King was never a great rock and roll singer, but then again, he never claimed that he was. After the success of "Everyone's Gone," King issued further flakies, charting in the States with only one other single, "Where the Sun Has Never Shone" (#97, 1966). But more importantly, this upright lad became the assistant to Sir Edward Lewis, head of Decca's London office. At Decca, and later at his own U.K. Records label, King discovered and produced acts like the Bay City Rollers, Genesis, Hedgehoppers Anonymous, the Kursaal Flyers, and 10cc, to name but a few.

Jonathan also has the distinction of appearing on the British charts under more guises than any other bloke in all of popdom. In addition to eight further homeland chartings under the "Jonathan King" moniker, King had hits under pseudonyms like Father Abraphart and The Smurps ("Lick a Smurp for Christmas"), Bubblerock ("Satisfaction"), 53rd and 3rd ("Chick-a-Boom"), 100 Ton and a Feather ("It Only Takes a Minute"), Sakharin (a heavy-metal version of "Sugar Sugar"), Shag ("Loop Di Love"), Sound 9418 ("In the Mood"), The Weathermen ("It's the Same Old Song"), and possibly untold others. Other less successful King personae include Nemo, the Piglets, Robin Jack, Saccharine, and St. Cecilia.

From 1979 through 1980, King hosted a radio talk show over New York's WMCA. He has written *Bible Two*, an anti-drug novel; hosted "Entertainment USA" and "A King in America" for the BBC; made regular appearances on "Top of the Pops"; and continues to work as a prolific newspaper columnist, an independent producer, and recording artist. In 1993, King established his own music business publication, *Tip Sheet*.

SILKIE
YOU'VE GOT TO HIDE YOUR LOVE AWAY
(John Lennon, Paul McCartney)
Fontana 1525
No. 10 *November 27, 1965*

England's Silvia Tatler (lead vocals) and her mates—Ivor Aylesbury (guitar), Kev Cunningham (bass), and Mike Ramsden (guitar)—were specialists in traditional folk music and fellow students at Hull University. They met during the summer of 1963, and a couple of years later Beatle-man Brian Epstein sought them out, signed them up for management, and connected them with Fontana Records.

Silkie's debut single, "Blood Red River," sold poorly. For their second disk, Epstein got John Lennon, Paul McCartney, and George Harrison to accompany and produce "You've Got to Hide Your Love Away," a remake of the Beatle song from the *Help!* soundtrack. The three Beatles never again tangled with Silkie, and Silkie consequently never again received much of a hearing. For a while, the group toured England, but visa problems prevented them from playing throughout the U.S. They released an album and two more 45s, one of which was "Born to Be With You" (a remake of BONNIE GUITAR and DON ROBERTSON's minor hit as the Echoes; no relation to THE ECHOES, known for "Baby Blue"). Although "Born to Be With You" had all the markings of a mini-hit, it wasn't, and Silkie eventually unraveled.

"LITTLE" JIMMY DICKENS
MAY THE BIRD OF PARADISE FLY UP YOUR NOSE
(N. Merritt)
Columbia 43388
No. 15 *December 4, 1965*

Nineteen sixty-five was the 50th anniversary of the first nude scene ever in a motion picture (Annette Kellerman in *Daughter of the Gods*). The same precious year, someone set a world record by baking a loaf of bread that weighed 20 pounds and measured 20' 5". Disposable paper dresses were being sold in cans for two bucks. And a 4' 11" old-timey country singer with a Stetson and glittery stuff all over his duds treated radio listeners to such lyrical significa as "May an elephant caress you with his toes/May your wife be plagued with runners in her hose."

"May the Bird of Paradise Fly Up Your Nose" was the pinnacle of Jimmy Dickens's career. It would be his last major C & W hit and his only appearance on *Billboard*'s Hot 100. In 1983, the little guy with the tall hat was voted into the Country Music Hall of Fame.

LITTLE JIMMY DICKENS

He was born Jimmy Cecil Dickens, the youngest of 13 in Bolt, West Virginia, on December 19, 1925. After a stay at the University of West Virginia, Jim started hawking his vocal talents as "Jimmy the Kid," on numerous radio stations. While doing a radio spot for WKNX in Saginaw, Michigan, Dickens met Roy Acuff, who liked the kid's chops and offered him a guest spot on the Grand Ole Opry. The Opry outing opened doors for Jimmy, who was quickly signed to a contract with Columbia Records. Country toppers like "Out Behind the Barn," "A-Sleeping at the Foot of the Bed," "Hillbilly Fever," and "Take an Old Cold Tater and Wait" followed.

In May 1989, Little Jimmy and his long-time manager Richard Davis walked away from a plane crash that totaled Davis' airplane. While not as active as he used to be, "Little" Jimmy Dickens still performs and occasionally waxes wares.

WONDER WHO?
DON'T THINK TWICE
(Bob Dylan)
Philips 40324
No. 12 *December 25, 1965*

Pop fans did not have to wonder long: the sound on the record was so distinctive that recognition was nearly instantaneous. Call them Tubular Tinsel, the Barbies,

the Sewer Rat Stinkers . . . no name alone could disguise one of the biggest pop groups of the '60s.

By 1966, the Four Seasons had reached the apex of their musical success. The group had sold more than 50 million records; nearly everything the Seasons released at this time would chart, and usually quite well. The group was saturating the radio with hit after hit. Thus was born The Wonder Who?, a bogus group that was fabricated as a drain for excess Four Seasons recordings.

Frankie Valli and the others had originally cut "Don't Think Twice" as part of a tribute album to Bob Dylan. The LP never materialized, and Frankie never could get his lead vocal just right. But the number was appealing in an oddball way, so the powers that be at the Philips label saw fit to issue it. To avoid competing with themselves and denting the sales action on other Seasons sides, another name had to be concocted. There was already the Who, the You Know Who Group, and the Guess Who, so why not a Wonder Who?

To the surprise of many, including the Seasons themselves, "Don't Think Twice" nearly cracked the Top 10. Two more records were issued by Philips under the "Wonder Who? name—"On the Good Ship Lollipop" (#87, 1966) b/w "You're Nobody Till Somebody Loves You" (#96, 1966), and "Lonesome Road" (#89, 1967). To further confuse fans, record collectors, and radio programmers, Veejay (the Seasons' previous label) did a mini-issuance of the Season's remake of LITTLE JOE & THE THRILLERS' "Peanuts" as by the Wonder Who?

BARRY YOUNG
ONE HAS MY NAME
(THE OTHER HAS MY HEART)
(Eddie Dean, Dearest Dean, Hal Blair)
Dot 16756
No. 13 *January 1, 1966*

Barry was a Dean Martin impersonator and a darn good one. Unless DJs made special efforts to stress that this was not the "lush one," listeners would probably assume that "One Has My Name" was yet another musical monster from Dean Martin, who was making a momentous return to the charts. Unfortunately for Young, the scam got old fast. None of his follow-ups for the Dot, Columbia, or Hooks Brothers labels measured more than zip on the popularity polls.

"One Has My Name" was a much-covered country number that went back more than four decades—it was a hit for cowpoke star Eddie Dean (also the tune's co-writer) in 1948, for Jimmy "The Melody Kid" Wakely the same year, and for the old piano pumper, Jerry Lee Lewis in 1969.

STATLER BROTHERS
FLOWERS ON THE WALL
(Lewis DeWitt)
Columbia 43315
No. 4 *January 8, 1966*

These boys are neither Statlers nor brothers, but they are the undisputed kings of country group harmony. The Statlers won the Country Music Association's "Group of the Year" award for every year between 1972 and 1977, and again in 1979 and 1980. More than 70 of their singles have made *Billboard*'s C & W charts, and a dozen of their LPs have made contact with the top pop albums listings. Their 1975 "Best of" compilation has reportedly sold more than 2 million copies, and is still in print. Since 1970, the Statler Brothers have been throwing an Old-Fashioned Fourth of July Celebration in Staunton, Virginia, that in the mid-'90s has been drawing more than 90,000 people, making it the largest annual country-music festival in the world.

Bass singer Harold Wilson Reid (b. Aug. 31, 1939, Augusta County, VA), tenor Lew C. DeWitt (b. March 8, 1938, Roanoke County), and baritone Philip E. Balsley (b. Phillip Elwood, Aug. 8, 1939, Augusta County) started singing together in 1955 at the Lyndhurst Methodist Church in Staunton. They were the Kingsmen, gospel groovers with a unique sound, but in 1958, they went their separate ways. Two years later, they reorganized, adding a lead singer—Harold's younger brother Donald Sydney Reid (b. June 5, 1945, Staunton).

Their big break came in 1963, when the group met Johnny Cash backstage at Watermelon Park in Berryville, Virginia. Cash eventually added the boys to his traveling show, let them appear on his TV show, and soon introduced them to the bigwigs at Columbia. Soon Columbia signed the singing act, which had switched over to secular music. For nearly two years, their vinyl issuances vanished without much notice. Columbia was about to cut the Statlers loose when Cash snuck them in on one of his recording sessions to cut "Flowers on the Wall." This nonsense number about languishing love won two Grammy awards—the Statlers were voted "Best New Country Group," and their smash won "Best Contemporary Performance by a Country Group."

"I really shouldn't be saying this to a professional journalist," Harold once admitted to *Country Music*'s Patrick Carr, "but we just ain't got no hook. We're patriotism and nostalgia and Mom and apple pie, and that's it. What more can you say? We're the Bland Brothers."

Where did the "Statler Brothers" name come from, anyway? As Harold told Rick Marschall in *The Encyclopedia of Country and Western Music*, "We could just as easily have become the Kleenex Brothers." You see, when holed up in a shabby hotel and in need of a new name, one of the brothers happened to notice a box of Statler facial tissues.

Between 1965 and 1993, the Statler Brothers have received more than 80 awards, from the American Music Awards, Country Music Awards, Country Music News . . . 70+ singles have won positions on *Billboard*'s country charts; four such 45s have garnered the number one slot: "Do You Know You Are My Sunshine" (1978), "Elizabeth" (1983), "My Only Love" (1984), "Too Much on My Heart."

The Statler Brothers' line-up has remained the same for all these years, except for the departure of Lew DeWitt in 1982 for reasons of ill health. Lew went on to record one solo album, *On My Own*. His replacement was Jimmy Fortune (b. Lester James Fortune, Mar. 11, 1955, Newport News, VA). Currently, the Statlers host their own show on the Nashville Network. Lew DeWitt died from Crohn's disease on August 15, 1990.

KNICKERBOCKERS
LIES
(Buddy Randell, Beau Charles)
Challenge 59321
No. 20 *January 22, 1966*

They were the first American group to successfully capture on vinyl a sound so vibrant and similar to the Beatles that some still believe that "Lies" was yet another Fab Four 45.

There was Beau Charles (b. Oct. 21, 1944, Bergenfield, NJ/guitar), Buddy Randell (b. Bill Crandall, Nov. 9, 1941, Dumont, NJ/sax, vocals), Jimmy Walker (b. 1940, Brooklyn, NY/drums, vocals), and Johnny Charles (July 3, 1943, Bergenfield, NJ/bass), and they had the sound down; but not the look.

"There wasn't a time my brother and I weren't into music," said Beau Charles in an exclusive interview. "I started taking guitar lessons in '58, and by '59 Johnny and I were playing in the bands that played the high school dances. By 1960, we named ourselves the Supremes . . . We played VFW's and sock hops. It was *American Graffiti* time.

"Now, Buddy was a famous guy. We'd heard of him long before he joined us. He was this wild guy—from a neighboring town—that could play all this down-on-your-knees sax stuff. He was a good musician; had been in the Royal Teens, co-wrote 'Short Shorts' . . ."

After "Big Name Button" and a few 45s, Buddy left the Teens to join the Vikings. After a few gigs, Buddy joined the Supremes. "I had just graduated high School, when Buddy joined in the fall of '62. We became the Knickerbockers; the name for Buddy's street in Dumont, New Jersey. . . . For awhile there was also Skip Cherubino (drums) and Red Brown (organ)," Beau added.

By the spring of 1963, the line-up came together around the Charles brothers, Buddy, and Jimmy Walker. "Jimmy—what a big fat voice. He could sing, though we weren't interested in what he was doing at the time. He'd been in this rockabilly outfit, the Castle Kings. He'd been in the Rockin' Saints, too . . . Neither had recorded anything, and he was ready for a change; and we were it.

"We played this place—the Village Inn—in Glens Falls, New York, for three months; lived above the hall, and we got tight. . . . It was here at the University Twist Palace in the spring of '64 that we met Jerry Fuller," Beau said. Jerry, who would later write "Young Girl" and "Lady Willpower," was an aspiring teen idol recording artist with the Gene Autry-established Challenge Records. The Knickerbockers were a cover band, quite good at imitating the Beatles; and Jerry took notice. With his assistance, the group was signed to the label.

Their initial singles, "Bite, Bite Barracuda" and "Jerktown," did not sell very well. Neither did an oddball and now highly-collectible debut album, *Sing and Sync-Along With Lloyd: Lloyd Thaxton Presents the Knickerbockers.* The LP made use of a gimmick called "Trick Track": when any one of five different cuts could be heard. For example, the listener might hear "Hully Gully," "It's Not Unusual," or the Knickers' fine rendition of "I Wanna Hold Your Hand."

"I don't even have a copy of that thing," said Beau. ". . . I never did figure it out; making it is all kind of a blur, now. Lloyd's niece did vocals on that . . . It was a nepotism thing."

"Lies," the third Knickerbockers 45, was filled with so much energy, so many Beatle vibes that it could not be denied hit status. "Me and Buddy came home one night from playing the Excelsor House; couldn't sleep. We deliberately tried to write something like the British Invasion; wrote it in less than an hour. We demoed it at Variety Arts in New York; Jerry like it and asked me to rearrange it. Bruce Botnick, who went on to do the Doors, engineered it, when we recorded it at Sunset Sound in LA. Things weren't right so we took the master track up to Leon Russell's house in Hollywood Hills. Jerry knew Leon, and Leon had this great little studio. . . . It was just a four-track and we did our vocals there; with me adding my guitar part again, distorted though through this beat Fender amp. This could have gave it that meaty feel that people refer to; still have that amp . . .

"One, two takes, that was it. We had it. Things were so simple then," said Beau.

Within weeks, "Lies" was to be heard everywhere. "KRLA played it and the phone lines filled up; 20,000 copies sold in two days. We were all over the trades and teen magazines. . . . One station played us for a week without identifying us. Listeners thought we were the Beatles. . . ." The confusion helped, immediately—though later the association would hurt.

Within weeks, the Knickerbockers were invited to be a regular on Dick Clark's daily broadcasted "Where the Action Is." "We were on like every other day; in the studio cutting stuff, always. The pace was wild, but it was a mistake . . . Dick Clark was tight with the buck. It was good exposure, but in the long run it hurt, 'cause if we had toured we would have made a lot more. We only got a nominal amount—scale money. After six, eight months, they didn't pick up our option and went with this other group, the Robbs. They had the look, long hair, handsome guys," said Beau.

Their follow-ups, "One Track Mind" (#46, 1966) and "High on Love" (#94, 1966), did not chart as well as expected. "Leon produced most of our *Lies* album, but we should have probably recorded the voices again at his home studio, 'cause something was missing. Everybody around us thought they knew what a hit was. Dave Burgess [member of the Champs, of 'Tequila' notoriety], [label head] Joe Johnson, and Jerry Fuller had a major impact on what we were allowed to record. It was frantic, trying to find that next hit," Beau adds.

More than a half-dozen further 45s were issued in rapid succession, but not one of them even flirted with the charts.

"We got bad press, 'cause we could sound like anybody. We were versatile. They called us a copy band and that hurt. . . . But, I suspect what hurt most . . . we didn't look the part. . . . Eventually, it hit that we'd have to change our wardrobe. . . . We finally got hip quick . . . but by then not many noticed," said Beau.

Problems arose with Challenge Records. "They were sending us some real garbage to record, and it got to the point where we weren't speaking. We couldn't sign with anybody else, and they won't let us go. . . . We were managed by the record company. We were sunk," said Beau.

Buddy was the first to leave. "About '67, he had an emotional breakdown, of sorts; his wife left him. Then Bobby Hatfield had Jimmy fill in for Bill Medley in the Righteous Brothers. John and I hired some others and carried on; recording some stuff for George Tobin [composer of DEREK's 'Cinnamon']."

In 1970, the Knickerbockers were signed to Motown's MoWest subsidiary. Due to contractual difficulties with Challenge the one album—produced by Bob West, composer of "I'll Be There"—issued by the group was credited to Lodi. The following year, Buddy sang lead on an obscure one-shot 45 by a group called Blowtorch. "Come and Get It" was the tune—almost no one did.

Beau went on to create station IDs, commercials for KFC, Figaro, local banks; recording off-camera vocals for the "Kojak" TV series and flicks *Across the Great Divide* (1977), *The Laughing Policeman* (1974), and

Grease (1977). John runs a catering business. Buddy, a born-again, sings for the Lord and works a "9-to-5." Jimmy lives in Napa Valley; sings the blues, works as a freelance musician.

The Knickerbockers reformed in 1990 to play gigs at Charles' Place in Del Ray, Florida.

"It was great; we were kids again," said Beau, "but we had to play the bills. We stay in touch . . . and if the chance offers itself—we're here and tight."

JACKIE LEE
THE DUCK
(Earl "Jackie Lee" Nelson, Jr.)
Mirwood 5502
No. 14 *January 22, 1966*

Jackie Lee was born Earl Lee Nelson, Jr., on September 8, 1928, in Lake Charles, Louisiana. He was raised in California, where he sang in his church's choir. On and off again, from 1957 until their demise in 1967, Earl sang with THE HOLLYWOOD FLAMES. That was Earl up front, singing lead on their "Buzz-Buzz-Buzz" b/w "Crazy." That was Earl, recording rock-bottom soul singles with Bobby Relf as half of Bob & Earl, featured on "Harlem Shuffle" (#44, 1964). And that was Earl

singing back-up on BOBBY DAY'S "Rockin' Robin" b/w "Over and Over" as a member of Day's Satellites.

Jackie Lee—not to be confused with the Philly-based Jackie Lee who charted in 1959 with "Happy Vacation"—was just one of many names that Earl has recorded under; other aliases were Earl Cosby and Earl Nelson & The Pelicans. In the '70s, Earl recorded an album for Warner Bros. under the guidance of his old buddy Barry White. For this effort, Barry dubbed Nelson "Jay Dee." A single pulled from that one and only Jay Dee album made the R & B listings: "Strange Funky Games and Things" (#88, 1974).

Explaining his one-off dance hit as Jackie Lee, Nelson told *Soul* magazine: "I didn't create the dance. I saw kids doing it, and I wrote the song. Some people at Mirwood Records liked it and said, 'Great, we'll put the name "Jackie Lee" on it.'"

Earl has continued to record under various guises, making the R & B listings twice more as Jackie Lee with "African Boo-Ga-Loo" (R&B: #43, 1968) and "The Chicken" (R&B: #47, 1970).

MIKE DOUGLAS
THE MEN IN MY LITTLE GIRL'S LIFE
(Eddie Dean, Mary Candy, Gloria Shayne)
Epic 9876
No. 6 *February 5, 1966*

For a while, Mike was the hottest host on daytime television. According to *TV Guide*, his impact was such that "dishes go unwashed and shirts remain unironed when Mike Douglas comes on." In 1967, his syndicated program was piped over nearly 200 channels and viewed by close to 6 million glassy-eyed housewives. That year, he won an Emmy Award for "Outstanding Daytime Performance."

Douglas was born Michael Dowd, Jr., in Chicago, on August 11, 1925. Mom encouraged him to open his mouth and let that voice out, which he did at all the family gatherings. In his teen years, he became a singing master of ceremonies aboard a cruise ship that bobbed about Chicago's shoreline. After his involvement in World War II and a spell at Oklahoma City College, Mike's big break happened. For five years, beginning in the mid-'40s, he got the chance to sing with Kay Kyser and his Kollege of Musical Knowledge, on radio, record, and TV. Mike even sang lead on Kyser's number-one hit, "Ole Buttermilk Sky" (1946).

In 1950, Kyser called it quits, and Mike's career floundered for a period. For awhile early in the '50s, Mike appeared as vocalist on the Dumont Network's "Music Show" and hosted a daytime variety show in Chicago, "Hi-Ladies"; in the late '50s, Mike was the featured vocalist on the NBC-TV program "Club 60,"

broadcast live and in color from the Windy City. In 1961, he started up the Cleveland-based TV program that would eventually capture the hearts of daytime viewers everywhere; four years later, Epic Records signed Mike up to create mood music for his millions. "The Men in My Little Girl's Life" was one such mellow moment, and his lone Top 40 hit.

In 1980, Group W Broadcasting abruptly dropped Mike in favor of John Davidson, whose youthful appeal was expected to draw in an even larger audience. Mike continued as the program's producer until its demise in 1982.

T-BONES
NO MATTER WHAT SHAPE (YOUR STOMACH'S IN)
(Sascha Burland)
Liberty 55836
No. 3 *February 5, 1966*

Liberty Records was quite hot with the surfing/hot rod sounds of Jan & Dean, and moved quickly to churn out similar products by groups like the Eliminators, the Zip-Codes, and the T-Bones. Nothing charted, but apparently the T-Bones were successful enough to be allowed to wax not one, but three drag-race LPs—*Boss Drag* (1964), *Boss Drag at the Beach* (1964), and *Doin' the Jerk* (1965).

By the time album number four was out the door, the T-Bones consisted of Danny Robert Hamilton (b. Spokane, WA) on guitar, Joe Frank Carollo (b. Leland, MS) on bass and drums, and Tommy Clark Reynolds (b. New York City) on drums and steel drums. Hamilton had worked sessions for Chad & Jeremy, Jerry Lee Lewis, the Marketts, Johnny Rivers, Ronny & The Daytonas, and the Ventures. Carollo had been playing bass and drums since his early teens, and had majored in music at Mississippi's Delta State College and Los Angeles City College. Reynolds had made and played steel drums in Bermuda.

The T-Bones' fourth LP (*No Matter What Shape*, 1966) was produced by Joe Saraceno, half of the teen duo TONY & JOE—who handled similar duties for the Marketts, THE ROUTERS, the Sunshine Company, and the Ventures—and featured a contagious number created by Sascha Burland (half of THE NUTTY SQUIRRELS) for an Alka Seltzer commercial. Hoping to cash in on the cover-a-jingle craze, the T-Bone organization did their best with Chiquita Banana and Nabisco ditties; only the latter disk, "Sippin' and Chippin'" (#62, 1966), placed on the pop charts.

After two more LPs, Dan, Joe, and Tommy shelved the "T-Bones" name to become Hamilton, Joe Frank & Reynolds. The trio scored hits like "Don't Pull Your

Love" (#4, 1971), "Fallin' in Love" (#1, 1975), and "Winners and Losers" (#21, 1976). They remained a viable force in pop music for much of the '70s.

Reynolds had also been a member of a group called Shango, and left Hamilton, Joe Frank & Reynolds in 1972; although the act's releases continued to use the Hamilton, Joe Frank & Reynolds name until July 1976. He is currently a minister in Texas. Dan Hamilton died on December 23, 1994. He was 48.

DAVID & JONATHAN
MICHELLE
(John Lennon, Paul McCartney)
Capitol 5563
No. 18 *February 12, 1966*

"David" was Roger Greenaway (b. Aug. 23, 1942, Southmead, England); "Jonathan" was Roger Cook (b. Aug. 19, 1940, Bristol, England). Both dropped out of school at the age of 15 and worked their way through the world of everyday jobs. In 1965, the Rogers began songwriting together as fellow members of a Bristol group called the Kestrels. One of their tunes, "You've Got Your Troubles," was a hit for the Fortunes, and soon Petula Clark, Freddie & The Dreamers, and other artists were approaching the duo for songs.

Beatles producer George Martin heard one of the team's demos and offered to record them in the style of pop duos like Chad & Jeremy and Peter & Gordon. "Michelle" was David & Jonathan's initial release, and their only stateside charting. British fans responded even more warmly to the duo's follow-up, "Lovers of the World Unite," but after that, even in their homeland, all future recordings failed to spark much interest.

By mid-'68, Cook and Greenaway had shelved the "David & Jonathan" *nom de plume* to concentrate on composing, jingle-writing, and session work. In addition to creating another biggie for the Fortunes ("Here Comes That Rainy Day Feeling Again") and hits for both the New Seekers ("I'd Like to Teach the World to Sing") and the Hollies ("Long Cool Woman"), Cook and Greenaway wrote the tunes that eventually made One-Hit Wonders out of WHISTLING JACK SMITH ("I Was Kaiser Bill's Batman"), EDISON LIGHTHOUSE ("Love Grows"), WHITE PLAINS ("My Baby Loves Lovin'"), and CAROL DOUGLAS ("Doctor's Orders"). In 1971, the British Songwriters Guild voted Cook and Greenaway "Songwriters of the Year."

Cook and Greenaway also wrote or performed commercials for Allied Carpets, British Gas, Typhoo, and Woodpecker Cider. They reportedly dreamt up the entire "It's the Real Thing" ad campaign for Coca-Cola.

A studio group called Blue Mink jelled into a decade-long rock and roll ride for Roger Cook and co-

vocalist MADELINE BELL. In 1970, Blue Mink's "Melting Pot," an ode to racial harmony, nearly topped the British charts, yet neither Blue Mink nor any of Cook's solo outings managed to find much of an audience in the States. Roger Greenaway, meanwhile, has recorded with Edison Lighthouse, THE PIPKINS, White Plains, and a sprinkling of other lesser known pseudo-groups.

In the mid-'70s, Cook and Greenaway parted company. Cook has since moved to Nashville, where he continues to dash off songs. In 1983, Greenaway was appointed chairman of the British Performing Rights Society, and has since cut down on his composing.

BOB KUBAN & THE IN-MEN
THE CHEATER
(John Mike Krenski)
Musicland 20001
No. 12 *March 12, 1966*

The lyrics to "The Cheater" prefigured ironically in the fate of lead singer "Sir" Walter Scott, who met an untimely end at the hands of his wife and her lover.

"We were putting together the In-Men again," Bob Kuban recalled in an exclusive interview. "This was 1983. We had formed the band in 1964, and the 20th anniversary was coming up. Wally was excited about the idea . . . He'd been on the road a long time, and was planning on being home for the Christmas holidays. He left his home in his jogging suit and running shoes to get a battery for his car, and nobody ever saw him again—he just vanished, two days after Christmas . . . Three and a half years later, in April of '87, they found his body stuffed in a cistern."

The assistant prosecuting attorney for the case determined that Wally Scott (real name: Walter Notheis) had been tied up and shot in the back execution-style, and Scott's wife and her lover were indicted for murder.

In 1963, when Kuban (b. Aug. 1940, St. Louis) and Scott first met, Bob was a high-school teacher who played drums for weekend wedding gigs, and Wally was lead singer in a group called the Pacemakers. Bob recruited Wally for a band he was putting together that included Pat Hixon (trumpet), Greg Hoeltzel (keyboards), Mike Krenski (bass), Ray Schulte (guitar), Harry Simon (tenor sax), and Skip Weisser (trombone). Almost immediately, Norman Weinstoer had the Bobby Kuban Band record for his Norman label, but neither "I Don't Want to Know" nor "Jerkin' Time" charted.

A friend of Weinstoer, Mel Freedman, heard the band and "The Cheater" (which, in its original form, was written in the first person, as "Look out for me, I'm the cheater"). Freedman had some connections in New York with Bell/Amy Records, and promised the group that if they went with him and his Musicland Records, they would get some national distribution. "The Cheater" was the first Bob Kuban & The In-Men single released under this arrangement. Two albums and two 45s—"The Teaser" (#70) and "Drive My Car" (#93)—appeared in 1966. Scott, Hoeltzel, Krenski, and Schulte spun off and recorded as the Guise. Kuban recruited replacements, and cut two further singles on the Musicland label—"Harlem Shuffle" and "The Batman Theme." In 1970, one final disk appeared on Reprise, "Soul Man" /w "Hard to Handle." The Guise never got off the ground, so after an attempted solo career, Scott returned to the band for a brief period.

Kuban currently leads a band under his own name. But where are the In-Men of "The Cheater" fame now? "Greg's a dentist, Harry's a school teacher, Pat's a computer programmer, Skip's out in Vegas and has been working as a bartender, and Mike's been working with McDonald Aircraft. We're all still in contact with each other," said Kuban.

In 1975, The Bob Kuban Brass recorded an album entitled *Get Ready for Some Rock & Soul* for Norman Records. In the late '80s, the same label issued two 45s—"Everybody's Gonna Have a Party" and "Triple Shot of Rhythm & Blues."

BOB LIND
ELUSIVE BUTTERFLY
(Bob Lind)
World Pacific 77808
No. 5 *March 12, 1966*

"Who was I then? An abrasive unpleasant coward whose talent, face it, was hopelessly midgelike when stacked against his good fortune," wrote Bob Lind for the liners of his *Best of . . .* CD ". . . If there's anything positive to say about me in those days, it would be that I loved what I was doing, loved the passion and drama of words; loved this music . . ."

Robert Lind was born in Baltimore (b. Nov. 25, 1942). His mother remarried when he was five years old. "We lived everywhere," said Lind, in an exclusive interview. "My [step-]father was in the Air Force and we traveled all over. When you're always moving . . . you look for ways of beating the loneliness and playing records just wasn't enough. My family wasn't much into music other than my younger sister, Fiddlin' Annie Lind, now the best fiddle player in Texas (with the Isaac Payton Sweat Band). She had a num-

ber-one record in Houston, with 'Cotton-Eyed Joe' (in the early '80s)."

During his teens at Aurora High, Lind joined Jerry Valdez and his three-chord Moonlighters; later fronted Bob Lind and the Misfits. Later, he enrolled in the theater-arts program at Western State College in Gunnison, Colorado. "All I did was play music, there," said Lind. "I'd check my watch and it'd be time for class, and I'd say, 'F**k it.'" After three years of study, he flunked out and moved to Denver, where he worked the folk houses for a year.

Al Chapman, at the Analyst Coffee House, taped one of Lind's sets so he could take the tape around to the labels. "World Pacific [a jazz label and subsidiary of Liberty] was the first record company that I went to," said Lind. "I gave him my tape, Dick Brock [label president], and he listened and he signed me. I thought, 'Whoa, this is easy! Man, this is great! All you got to do is go to a company and get a deal.' I had no idea that people work at it for years and maybe never get a deal."

Lind signed with Metro Music; before his first disk was even issued, acts were showing an interest in Bob's material. Weeks before the release of "Elusive Butterfly," the label issued "To My Elders With Respect," a release that Bob Lind himself was unaware of until recently; "terrible song," said Bob.

"SONNY [Bono] was gonna produce me, but he got too busy, and JACK NITZSCHE and I hit it off—both of us like to drink and do drugs—so he was with me from the start; took me in, let me live at his house. 'Elusive Butterfly' was one of the first songs we cut; the one I had the least faith in, probably because it had five verses and we had to cut three out. 'Butterfly' came to me after I was up all night. It was started when the sun was coming up . . . I was on the border. . . . The words are about the magic of the quest, the thrill of searching, even when that which is sought is hard to see."

Nearly every tune that would eventually account for Lind's cult status—"Elusive Butterfly," "Truly Julie Blues," "Mister Zero," and "Cheryl's Goin' Home"—was recorded at that first session, for Lind's first LP, *Don't Be Concerned*. Nitzsche was producing and arranging the swirling, haunting strings; Leon Russell on piano. A host of artists would record Lind's material—the Blues Project, Cher, ADAM FAITH, Marianne Faithfull, Noel Harrison, Nancy Sinatra, the Turtles, the Yardbirds' Keith Relf.

Both sides of Bob's follow-up single, "Truly Julie Blues" (#65, 1966) b/w "Remember the Rain" (#64), charted marginally. Lind recorded another high-quality and similarly-styled LP, *Photographs of Feeling* (1966), but inexplicably it never made the listings. None of Lind's successive 45s fared well, either. To make matters worse, Verve/Folkways got hold of some old tapes of lesser material from Lind's Denver days that he cut for Bandbox Records, and (without permission, apparently) with accompaniment added, issued in album form *The Elusive Bob Lind*.

"My career was pretty much down the toilet by this time," wrote Lind. "I was hanging onto sanity by my teeth." It was January 23, 1967, Bob's last recording session for World Pacific. Recording the unreleased "I Fall to You," Bob fell down. "My strongest memory of this record session is that when I put my vocal on, I was so drunk, I literally fell off the stool. I wasn't hurt . . .

Lind then went off into the deserts of New Mexico to retire. He reappeared briefly in 1971, with a single, "She Can Get Along," and a critically acclaimed LP for Capitol, *Since There Were Circles*. In the '80s, *Goldmine* researcher Steve Eng reported that all was well: Bob was writing short stories, plays, and even a novel (*East of the Holyland*). One of Lind's plays, *The Sculpture*, had won the California Motion Picture Council's "Bronze Halo" award.

"What is remarkable about that period is that I survived it," wrote Lind, on the liner notes. "Why am I alive when so many of my contemporaries are not. We all drank and drugged our way through the same shadowy L.A. night world, kept the same breathless hours, fought the same ghosts, and nodded to one another's blurry images on the periphery of our own thin thread existences."

DEON JACKSON
LOVE MAKES THE WORLD GO ROUND
(Deon Jackson)
Carla 2526
No. 11 *March 19, 1966*

"I would cringe every time the song came on the radio," Deon Jackson told *Goldmine* writer Bill Dahl. The distasteful song? Deon's big musical moment, "Love Makes the World Go Around."

Deon Jackson was born on January 26, 1946, in Ann Arbor, Michigan. As a child, he studied clarinet and drums, and while a high school student, he formed a vocal group. The Five Crystals tried out for a spot with Tamla Records and Maximillian. Nothing clicked until 1962, when producer and publisher Ollie McLaughlin—the man responsible for producing the initial hits for Barbara Lewis, Del Shannon, and soon THE CAPITOLS—caught Jackson and group singing their hearts out at a school concert.

"When we first meet Ollie, we didn't know about his standing in the music business," said Jackson in an exclusive interview. "We just knew him as this disk jockey with the 'Scoop Scobby Dooby Show.' He came out to a lot of our rehearsals . . . He was just going after this Detroit group—the Capitols—when he picked me

to work with. I wished that we coulda stayed together, but Ollie could see that while I was the youngest, I was the one most serious about music. The others didn't always show up and they weren't contributing. I was the only one writing."

Ollie became Deon's manager, and in the mid-'60s he recorded two singles on Jackson that were issued on Atlantic Records—both bombed. Jackson, meanwhile, had dashed off that hated number and, unhappy with the results, had tossed it aside. "I wrote that song when the United States was in a riot, said McLaughlin, "from Detroit to Florida, California to New York City. It was a result of the Civil Rights movement. It happened one . . . very sun shiny morning. My sister was singing in the kitchen and I thought, 'Jesus, all this stuff going on around me; ah, the world needs more love. Although all this crap was happening around me, our dear God can make a beautiful day anyway.' Three or four minutes and the song was done."

Eventually, Deon did record a demo of "Love Makes the World Go Round" and sent it off to his manager. The song was recorded with buddy Edwin Starr present and with Thelma Hopkins and Joyce Vincent—the

female portion of Dawn—providing vocal accompaniment. The demo sat around for another year until Ollie released it. Once available to the public, "Love Makes the World Go Round" sold like no one would have believed.

"All of a sudden, I get this call from Ollie," said Deon. ". . . I had forgotten all about the song. Ollie said, 'You realize you've got a hit record.' I didn't know what he was talking about. He mentioned the song. and I just sat back, shocked. . . ."

While "Love Takes a Long Time Growing" (#77, 1966) and "Ooh Baby" (#65, 1967) were respectable follow-up efforts, everything else Jackson released for the remainder of the decade sank from view.

His proudest moment happened in 1969. "I was invited to the Command Performance before the King of Portugal; the 'Ball of the Century.' It was an all-celebrity deal. This King had spent some three or four million dollars getting the cast—Frank Sinatra, the Supremes, King Curtis, THE SWEET INSPIRATIONS, Ike & Tina Turner . . . It was something any entertainer would want to be a part of."

Shortly afterward, Deon turned away from the record biz, and for much of the early '70s tickled the keyboards in New York City nightspots like Nathan's and Matt Snell's. Thereafter, Deon moved his base of operations to Chicago, where for the past 20+ years he has touched the ivories to Nat "King" Cole, Johnny Mathis, and Frank Sinatra tunes. People in the know still ask Jackson to play "Love." "It kinda gets to me to do it," Jackson told Dahl. "But I do it."

With a back log of self-penned tunes just sitting around on Deon's dresser way too long, Jackson got the itch and with his new group Sunlight returned to the studios in the early '90s. Nothing has surfaced yet.

"The record companies are looking for a sure thing," said Jackson. "Now, what does a sure thing look like, sound like? I don't know. They tell me if after five seconds they see dollar signs, its a hit. I'm finding it hard to get listened to. I'm not gonna stop, though."

ROBERT PARKER
BAREFOOTIN'
(Robert Parker)
Nola 721
No. 7 *June 18, 1966*

Robert Parker (b. Oct. 14, 1930, Crescent City, LA) is remembered for one disk, one dance, one slim slice of time. But in addition to his mid-'60s hoofer hit, Parker packed more than 20 years with other musical quests.

In the '40s and '50s, Parker and his sax ran the house band at the Tijuana Club in New Orleans, backing performers like Ray Charles, Guitar Slim, CHRIS

KENNER, and Little Richard. For several years, Parker was a member of Professor Longhair's Blue Scholars, and appeared on their celebrated "Mardi Gras in New Orleans" single. As a session saxophonist, he appeared on disks by New Orleans artists like Jimmy Clanton, ERNIE K-DOE, Fats Domino, FRANKIE FORD, Joe Tex, IRMA THOMAS, and HUEY "PIANO" SMITH. Parker was also a member of the back-up band for Huey Smith's Clowns for a number of years.

In the '60s, Robert was touring with Eddie Bo and Percy Stovall. "We worked a show in Tuskegee, Alabama, where all the kids piled their shoes in the corner to dance," Parker told *Goldmine*'s Almost Slim. "We joked about it in the band and thought it might be a good gimmick for a tune." Once he had sketched out the tune, Parker brought the ditty to Wardell Quezergue, an arranger for Nola Records. When the foot-floppin' 45 took flight, Robert left his job as an orderly at Charity Hospital.

At one Apollo Theatre appearance, Parker, prodded by the MC, pulled off his shoes for his performance. "I went on stage and the crowd went nuts," Parker recalled. "I started doing that every night and it worked great."

Nola Records released an album of attractive New Orleans numbers. Follow-up singles were crafted to zero in on the barefoot theme—there was "Happy Feet," then "Tip Toe" (#83, 1967)—but it was all over quickly. Nola filed for bankruptcy. Parker later recorded unsuccessfully for the Island and Silver Fox labels.

In the '80s, the folks at Spic 'n Span made use of "Barefootin'" in one of their TV ad campaigns; Pete Townsend included a cover version of the tune on a live album in 1986. Robert Parker still works as a session sax man and still continues to make occasional appearances at festivals and oldies shows.

SHADES OF BLUE
OH HOW HAPPY
(Charles Hatcher)
Impact 1007
No. 12 *June 25, 1966*

One of the biggest mysteries in the history of One-Hit-dom is the Shades of Blue. What little was known was offered by Edwin Starr (a.k.a. Charles Hatcher), creator of their hit "Oh, How Happy."

"I wrote 'Oh How Happy' while in the service in Germany [1960-62]," said Starr, in an interview with *Soul Survivor*'s Richard Pack. "Golden World had one white act on its books at the time—THE REFLECTIONS. I told Ed Wingate [the label's owner] that we needed another white act on the label . . . So I found this group of Italian-Americans and took them to Golden World

to see Ed, who said, 'Get that group out of here! I don't want no more white groups!' So instead, I gave the record to a good friend of mine, Harry Balk, and his Impact label. It was a monster."

Who exactly were these "Shades of Blue"? Starr seemed unable to recall.

"A mystery, I've been told that," said Shades of Blue's lead vocalist Nick Marinelli, in an exclusive interview. "I don't get it, we've always been here . . . I've never left the business. For awhile, I produced the 'Bozo the Clown Show' . . . ."

Now for the "true" story: "The Shades of Blue got together when I was in eighth grade, 'bout '61," explained Marinelli. "We were the Domingo's then. I sang lead and was at Emerson Junior; Bob Kerr (baritone) Ernie Dernai (1st tenor), and Dan Guise (baritone) were at Bentley High. We were all from the Lovina area, 'bout 30 miles northwest of Detroit.

"It was rural . . . but we were all impressed by the doo-wop groups, the Miracles, Temptations, Marcels. We'd hang out . . . and harmonize; got good and started doing assemblies and dances . . .

"When I got to college . . . Dan decided to give it up. He disappeared and Bob and Ernie went to Farris State College, miles away. We'd only get together on weekends, but at this time we got to know Tony MiCale, Ray Steinberg, and the guys in THE REFLECTIONS. They were all from Lovina and . . . Ray's sister, Linda, was in one of my classes."

Sister Linda filled the slot vacated by Dan. Her brothers' group, the Reflections caught one of the Shades appearances, and suggested that the group go to Ed Wingate's Golden World Studios to do some demo work. "We got to be studio rats," Nick continued. "One time Edwin Starr happened to be there; so was this independent producer John Ryse [produced Newbeats], who liked our blue-eyed soul sound. Edwin said he had a few songs that we could kick around. He had the title, and we bounced around some melodies and between the five of us, we wrote 'Oh, How Happy.' We never got the [songwriter's] credit, 'cause we were 19 years old and stupid naive kids. That became a thorn, later."

Ryse who renamed them—and continues to claim ownership of the Shades of Blue moniker—had taken the master to Harry Balk's Impact label. ". . . By May when school ended, it was on the charts. It just blew us away . . . We knew we had to get some management, get a band together, hit the road. . . . Right out of the bag, we were on the road for a year."

There was local stops, TV, the Dick Clark Caravan and charting follow-ups in "Lonely Summer" (#72) and "Happiness" (#78). "It was reality check time," said Nick, "when we did the Caravan with the Rascals and Paul Revere & The Raiders. They talked of these fantastic royalty checks, and we're going like, 'What royalty checks? We soured. 'Wait a second,' we thought, 'we're making really good money on the road, but we're getting ripped off here.'

"By late '69, music had taken a big change with psychedelic stuff and acid rock and it wasn't our bag. We tried to look more mod . . . but by late '69 we decide to let it fade away."

In 1977, Nick gathered Bob, Ernie, and Linda back into a studio. Four cuts were laid down, "but," said Nick, "the heart wasn't in it."

Nick worked for years as an automobile designer and currently as Nick Allen performs what he calls "positive country," that's country with a gospel message. "Ernie's had various jobs," said Nick. "Bob was the hippy of the group; . . . and he's still in the ozone. Linda, left Bob, and got married again and is living on the East Side of Detroit."

CAPITOLS
COOL JERK
(Donald Storball)
Karen 1524
No. 7 *July 2, 1966*

Each of the guys had been singing for as long as they could remember. In 1962, lead vocalist/drummer Samuel George, guitarist Donald Storball, and three others got their act together and presented Detroit producer Ollie McLaughlin—the man responsible for producing initial hits for DEON JACKSON, Barbara Lewis, and Del Shannon—with a number called "Dog and Cat." McLaughlin liked the ditty, and cut it for his Karen label. It flopped, and the Capitols—originally billed The Three Caps—returned to their workaday worlds. Four years later, George, Storball, and a new Capitol—pianist Richard McDougall—returned to McLaughlin's little label with an up-tempo dance number called "Cool Jerk." Again, Ollie liked what he heard and cut the track for his label. Like never before and never since, the Capitols danced into the nation's Top 10.

The group returned to McLaughlin's offices on many more occasions with fast numbers and dance disks like the "Afro Twist" and the "Patty Cake," but America wasn't buying it. While tracks from their lone album indicate that the Capitols were quite capable of fine ballads as well as get-down bluesy bits, the group got pegged as an upbeat rug-cuttin' group. McLaughlin believed in the Capitols—only after eight failed singles did the guys and Ollie call it quits.

Donald Storball is currently a Detroit policeman. Richard McDougall's whereabouts and activities are unknown. Samuel George died in an "altercation" on March 17, 1982.

SWINGIN' MEDALLIONS
DOUBLESHOT (OF MY BABY'S LOVE)
(Don Smith, Cyril E. Vetter)
Smash 2033
No. 17 *July 2, 1966*

"We had recorded the song several times," explained Medallions leader John McElrath in an exclusive interview. "We tried all different arrangements and tempos, but it wasn't going anywhere. We decided to pick up and go to another studio, Arthur Smith's [the guitarist/composer of THE VIRTUES' "Guitar Boogie Shuffle" and ERIC WEISSBERG AND STEVE MANDELL's "Dueling Banjos"]. We said, 'Look, let's set this up just like we're live, playing on stage.' We called in the roadies, our friends, and people from off the streets to make noise with us, to party with us; . . . It worked: we did 'Double Shot' in one take. The song was originally recorded in Columbia, South Carolina, in the early '50s, by Dick Holler & The Holidays; it was a cult number, a beach number."

The Swingin' Medallions were first formed in 1962 in the tiny town of 96, South Carolina. By the mid-'60s, the Medallions line-up was John McElrath (keyboards), Jimbo Doares (guitar), Carroll Bledsoe (trumpet), Charles Webber (trumpet), Brent Forston (keyboards, sax, flute), Steven Caldwell (sax), James Perkins (bass), and Joe Morris (drums).

Dave Roddy, the DJ at Birmingham's WSGN who broke "Double Shot" locally, suggested that the group add the "Swingin'" prefix to their moniker. Just before the release of "Double Shot," Dot Records issued the group's poor-selling debut single, "I Wanna Be Your Guy."

Follow-ups to the "Double" disk were hard to launch. "'She Drives Me Out of My Mind' [#71, 1966] charted real good. And we did real well with our remake of BRUCE CHANNELS' 'Hey! Baby.' But we had to go back to college or we'd be drafted, so we couldn't devote ourselves to the music as much as we wanted to."

By 1970, the band started falling apart. McElrath started up his own studio in Greenwood, South Carolina; Brent Forston and Steven Caldwell had already split from the group in 1967 to record as the Pieces of Eight for A & M. Some labels bearing the "Pieces of Eight" name also tagged the group as "The Original Swingin' Medallions."

McElrath has kept the "Swingin' Medallions" name active—"We actually played more in 1989 than we did in all of the '60s." McElrath is the only original Swingin' Medallion touring under that name, but each year, from 1983 onward, all of the original members reunite for a one-off concert in Atlanta.

According to McElrath, Jimbo is currently an accountant, Carroll is a sales representative for Zenith,

Charlie is a captain with the South Carolina Law Enforcement Department, Brent is a lawyer, Steve is the president of a computer firm, James is with Eastern Airlines, and Joe is an executive with the Sonoco Paper Company.

STANDELLS
DIRTY WATER
(Ed Cobb)
Tower 185
No. 11 *July 9, 1966*

The Standells, formed in Los Angeles in the early '60s, reportedly chose their name because they would stand around a lot in their agent's office waiting for work. More than a half-dozen trial disks were issued on Linda, MGM, Vee Jay, and Liberty The latter label even issued a now-rare LP, *The Standells Live at PJ's.*

By 1966, when the group came under the influence of producer, writer, and one-time Four Preps member Ed Cobb, their much fluctuating line-up—that had once included drummer Gary Leeds, later "Gary Walker" of the Walker Bros.—had solidified. It was drummer Dick Dodd (former Mouseketeer and one-time member of the Bel-Airs), bassist Gary Lane, keyboardist Lawrence Tamblyn (brother of actor Russ Tamblyn), and guitarist Tony Valentino that recorded "Dirty Water."

"I wrote the song when I was in Boston," Cobb told *Blitz*'s Mike McDowell. "I was with a girl. We were walking along the Saint James River and two guys tried to mug us, but they ran away. So when I got back to the hotel, I wrote [the] song . . . .

"The group hated the record so much that they refused to do it! So they just fluffed through it every time. . . . Nine months later it was a smash."

Larry's memories of the events are different. "We recorded it in Armin Steiner's little studio up in a garage," Tamblyn told *Goldmine*'s Robyn Flans. "'Dirty Water' was just an idea, more or less, with lyrics that Ed Cobb brought to us and said 'See what you can do.' Tony came up with the beginning riff, and we all kind of put our ideas into it. All that chanting that Dick does [at the beginning]—'I'm gonna tell you a story/I'm gonna tell you about my town—Dick made up on the spot."

This seminal garage band was extinct within two years of the release of "Dirty Water." On the band's first tour in support of the release, Gary Lane left the group to become a plumber, and was replaced by Dick Burke. The response to the Standells' immediate follow-ups, "Sometimes Good Guys Don't Wear White" (#43, 1966) and "Why Pick on Me" (#54, 1966) was quite good. But by the release of "Can't Help but Love You" (#78) and their appearance in the American-International flick *Riot on Sunset Strip* in the fall of 1967, the Standells were in disarray. "They had all these rhythm and blues

musicians in there, ..." Tamblyn told *Goldmine.* "Ed Cobb said, 'This is the Standells; you aren't the Standells.'"

Dodd remained with Cobb and the Tower label for a solo album, *The Evolution of Dick Dodd*, and a few failed singles. Despite threats from Cobb, Tamblyn and Valentino—along with a young Lowell George, later of FRANK ZAPPA's Mothers of Invention and Little Feat—continued for a brief period to perform live as the Standells. In the mid-'80s, Tamblyn and Valentino formed their own indie label, Telco. Despite a few Standells reunions in 1986, the creators of "Dirty Water," one of rock and roll's raunchiest perennials, are together no more.

SYNDICATE OF SOUND
LITTLE GIRL
(Bob Gonzalez, Don Baskin)
Bell 640
No. 8 *July 9, 1966*

Bassist Bob Gonzalez, keyboardist/guitarist John Sharkey (b. June 8, 1946, Los Angeles), lead singer/saxophonist Don Baskin (b. Oct. 9, 1946, Honolulu), lead guitarist Larry Roy, and drummer John Duckworth (b. Nov. 18, 1946, Springfield, MO). were the San Jose-based Syndicate of Sound; students at Camden High, initially billed the Pharaohs. The group played at the San Mateo Teenage World's Fair "Battle of the Bands" and won first prize—free recording time with Bob Keen's Del-Fi Records, home of the hits by RON HOLDEN and LITTLE CAESAR & THE ROMANS.

A Syndicate single, "Tell the World," was issued in small quantities by Del-Fi, and illegally reissued on the Scarlet label. Garrie Thompson, who would later become the group's manager, wanted to issue something on his Hush label and asked the group if they had anymore original material on hand.

As Sharkey told *RPM*'s Don Rogers, "We didn't have very much, but we had gotten wind of THE LEAVES 'Hey Joe' . . . We were already into the Byrds and that kind of stuff, so we just made something up. We didn't even have the words till the day we went in to record. . . ."

It was January 9, 1966, when the group and Garrie entered Leo de Gar Kulka's new Golden State Recorders in San Francisco. In liner notes for *The History of . . .*, Baskin has said, "I had no idea how I would interpret it ['Little Girl'] vocally. It didn't really work putting a melody on top of the changes we had, so we agreed I'd

do it without a melody, but with attitude." Divinely sloppy, and created on the spot, "Little Girl" had a raw garage/punk sound.

Initially issued on Hush, Bell Records acquired the national distribution. As the record broke, members elbowed out Larry Ray, for a more sedate guitarist Jim Sawyers. Brian Epstein offered the act a slot on the Beatles summer tour; management, without, notifying the guys turned Epstein down. They toured exhaustively, appearing on Clark's "Bandstand" and "Where the Action Is," and opened for James Brown at the Cow Palace.

For a follow-up, the Syndicate of Sound dreamt up "Rumours" (#55, 1966), a much smoother number. "Bell gave us three weeks and $1,500 to come up with an album," said Baskin.

Two more Bell releases rang no bells. Duckworth was drafted; replaced by Carl Scott, of the San Jose Bees. JOHN PHILLIPS' asked the band to play the Monterey Pop Festival; they turned it down when told it was a free gig.

Capitol Records tried the group on for size for a lone single. Buddah Records issued two Syndicate sides. The first of these, "Brown Paper Bag" (#73, 1970), did mildly well. But the crude group sound of "Little Girl" could not be coaxed again, and internal problems beset the Syndicate. Sharkey left the group; Gonzalez was gone, and Sawyers rejoined the Otherside.

The Syndicate of Sound name kept playing concerts and club dates into the early '70s, but no further records were issued after the Buddah releases in 1970. John Sharkey is currently teaching music for a living, and reports having recorded a few solo albums. John Duckworth left the military and refurbishes homes. Don Baskin was spotted in the mid-'80s playing bars with a C & W band. Bob Gonzalez manages a furniture store. And here and there, Jimmy Sawyer still plays rock and roll.

RAY CONNIFF
SOMEWHERE, MY LOVE
(P. F. Webster, M. Jarre)
Columbia 43626
No. 9 *August 13, 1966*

A creator of mood music, and one of the founding fathers of easy-listening music, Ray Conniff was born in Attleboro, Massachusetts, on November 6, 1916. Ray's mother was a piano player, and his father was the leader and trombonist of the local Attleboro Jewelry City Band.

Under his father's instruction, Ray quickly learned how to play the trombone, and formed his own band while still in high school. He soon became mesmerized by the different nuances and moods he could conjure

up with instruments. Excited about these possibilities, Ray sent away for a mail-order arranging course and taught himself the basics.

Graduating in 1934, Ray moved to Boston and played with a number of bands—Bunny Berrigan, Bob Crosby, Harry James, Artie Shaw—then studied at Juilliard. While serving in the military during World War II as an arranger with the Armed Forces Radio Service, he worked with Meredith Wilson and Walter Schumann.

After years of analyzing music and radio jingles, Ray felt confident that he had discovered the secret of just what it takes to make a hit record. "One day, something hit me," Conniff told Joseph Lanza, author of *Elevator Music*. "In 80 percent of the records, either the song or the background score had recurring patterns . . . You could call it a ghost tune behind the apparent one."

In 1953, he approached Columbia Records exec Mitch Miller with his brilliant idea; Miller played along. Conniff dreamt up an arrangement for big-band vocalist Don Cherry, whose career was in a downslide. Ray's arrangement of "Band of Gold" pole-vaulted Cherry to the top of the heap once again.

Miller rewarded Ray with a position at Columbia as an arranger, conductor, and recording artist. Conniff's first album, 'S Wonderful, was a heavy hitter, and eventually sold more than 500,000 copies. Over the next decade, 27 albums with the Conniff name became full-blown successes. Apparently, Ray and his Ray Conniff Sound (that often included Billy Butterfield, Al Caiola, and Doc Severinsen)—and four male/four female voices becking with do-doos and da-da-daas—could do no wrong. Throughout the '60s, it was hard to listen to a or "mood music" radio station without hearing that signature sound.

As an arranger for others, Conniff produced an impressive array of smashes for Frankie Laine, Johnny Mathis, Guy Mitchell, Marty Robbins, and Johnny Ray. During the summer of 1966, Conniff grafted his unique sound on to a theme from *Doctor Zhivago*, "Somewhere, My Love." Ray had charted on the Hot 100 three times earlier, and would do so once more during his career, but the eerie theme would be his only Top 40 hit.

Throughout the '70s, Ray Conniff remained active with Columbia Records. Many of his albums have never gone out of print and are still available.

In reply to jazz buffs and big band purists who criticized Ray throughout his protracted career, Conniff said to Lanza: "Instead of playing trombone solos that other musicians like, I made an about-face and wrote my arrangements with a view to making the masses understand and buy my records . . . I could have gone on as I did with the big bands and be a little over the heads of the general buying public, but this is a better way to go."

NAPOLEON XIV
THEY'RE COMING TO TAKE ME
AWAY, HA-HAAA!
(Jerry "Napoleon XIV" Samuels)
Warner Bros. 5831
No. 3 *August 13, 1966*
No. 87 *September 1, 1973*

Jerry Samuels had a seemingly normal background and upbringing. He was born in 1938 in New York City. He became a recording engineer at the Associated Studios, writing songs on the side. One of his compositions, "The Shelter of My Arms," became a huge hit for Sammy Davis, Jr. (#17, 1964).

Two years later, however, Jerry was in a different mind set. With the nub of a nutty number in his craw, Samuels booked himself an hour and a half of studio time. He brought in a drum, a tambourine, and this idea for a "tune" called "They're Coming to Take Me Away." Jerry beat his instruments and recited the composition with an ever-increasing feverishness. It was a bizarre novelty song about a man who suffers an emotional setback when his beloved pooch leaves him.

"It popped into my head, and I thought it was funny," said Samuels to authors Bruce Nash and Allan Zullo. Nine years earlier, Samuels had spent eight months in a psychiatric hospital. "We always made fun of our experience. Later, when I did the record, I knew it wouldn't offend mental patients. . . . I would have laughed at it if I had heard it when I was in the hospital."

George Lee, an executive at Warner Bros., heard Jerry's waxing and issued it immediately. A name was needed for the label. "I picked XIV—Napoleon XIV—because I liked the way the Roman numerals looked together." Because the platter could be perceived as poking fun at the mentally ill, the negative response to it was substantial: within days, most radio stations pulled it from their playlists. The sales response, however, was strong—in less than a week, 500,000 copies had been purchased. "Take Me Away, Ha-Haaa!" became the fastest-selling record in Warner's history—and the only Top 40 single to feature the same song recorded backwards on the flip side!

In support of his new career, Jerry formed a rock and roll band and performed in a mask as Napoleon XIV. Warner issued an LP full of like-minded ditties: "I Live in a Split-Level Head," "Marching Off to Bedlam," "I'm in Love With My Little Red Tricycle." The latter was released as Nap's follow-up. Both the single and the album were soon discontinued.

In 1973, Napoleon XIV's rereleased rendition of "They're Coming to Take Me Away, Ha-Haaa!" returned to the charts (#87). Samuels maintains that he has only performed the tune once in public and that

any such sightings are completely bogus. "The first and only time that I sang the song in front of a live audience, I felt I was being laughed at. That was very hard for me to take."

Some say that Jerry Samuels operates a talent agency in Philadelphia that specializes in supply entertainment to senior citizen facilities.

Years after the dust settled, TINY TIM recorded a convincing rendition of "They're Comin'"—a disco version.

TOMMY MCLAIN
SWEET DREAMS
(Don Gibson)
MSL197
No. 15 *August 20, 1966*

In the mid-'60s, Tommy McLain played bass with Clint West and the Fabulous Boogie Kings, a hot band known throughout South Louisiana. Floyd Soileau, the big cheese at Jin Records, had been cutting regionally successful tracks on some configurations of the band ever since the label's inception in 1958. Clint and some of the guys had laid out numbers like "Jail Bird" and "Take a Ride" as Bob & The Veltones.

McLain, striking out on his own, cut a swamp-pop rendition of Don Gibson's country classic, "Sweet Dreams." He had a few hundred copies pressed, and tried to persuade local record stores to stock his disk. The proprietor of the Modern Record Shop in Alexandria, Louisiana, was soon reporting to Soileau that McLain's vanity pressing was selling quite well. When Floyd realized that McLain was in Clint West's band, which was already under contract to the Jin label, he had Tommy re-record "Sweet Dreams" for his Jin label, and used the uncredited Boogie Kings as back-up.

Soileau had a gut feeling that there was something wrong with McClain's rendering, according to John Broven's *South to Louisiana*, so he shelved the disk for several months. McLain pestered him about the release date until he finally issued the lopsided, slip-slidin' "Sweet Dreams." When soaring sales of the 45 outstripped Jin's ability to manufacture and distribute, arrangements were made with Jamie Records to create MSL. The new Jamie-distributed company would be owned by Soileau, Harold Lipsuis, and Huey P. Meaux.

Tommy McLain failed to find a successful follow-up. Covers of Ray Charles's "Sticks and Stones," Bobby Charles's "Before I Grow Too Old," and the Righteous Brothers' "Try to Find Another Man" fared well only regionally.

McLain is still active in the Texas and Louisiana regions with his band Mule Train. An album and a few singles appeared on the Starflite label in 1979.

LOS BRAVOS
BLACK IS BLACK
(Tony Hayes, Steve Wadey)
Press 60002
No. 4 *October 1, 1966*

As Mike & The Runaways, Mike Kogel (b. Apr. 25, 1945, Berlin), Miguel Vicens Danus (b. June 21, 1944, Palma de Mallorca, Spain), Manolo "Manuel" Fernandez (b. Sept. 29, 1943, Seville, Spain), Pablo "Gomez" Samllehi (b. Nov. 5, 1943, Barcelona), and Antonio Martinez (b. Oct. 3, 1945, Madrid) had a heap of success in Spain. Some observers claim they were the numero-uno groupo in their homeland. One of the representatives at Decca's branch office in Spain sent some copies of the group's recordings to England. There, Decca's Ivor Raymonde—a producer who had worked wonders for Dave Berry, Billy Fury, Dusty Springfield, Marty Wilde, and others—detected a Motown-ish British Invasion sound in the grooves. Raymonde flew to Madrid with a pile of British songs. After hearing Mike & The Runaways' magical rendition of "Black Is Black" (a tune penned by two blokes from the village of Hoo, England), Ivor invited the group to join him in London for a recording session.

"Black Is Black" was their first release as Los Bravos.

In support of this disk, Antonio (guitar), Manuel (organ), Miguel (bass), Pablo (drums), and (lead vocals, guitar) toured feverishly. Despite their considerable talent and effort, their follow-ups were not successful. "I Don't Know" charted in the U.K., but only "Going Nowhere" (#91, 1966) and "Bring a Little Lovin'" (#51, 1968) made the listings in the U.S.

Mike Kogel did return to the charts for a brief moment in 1972 as Mike Kennedy with an album and a single, "Louisiana" (#62).

COUNT FIVE
PSYCHOTIC REACTION
(Kenn Ellner, Roy Chaney, Craig Atkinson, Sean Byrne, John Michalski)
Double Shot 104
No. 5 *October 15, 1966*

They only recorded one album and six singles, but Count Five are still spoken of reverently and adored worldwide. "Psychotic Reaction" is a '60s-weekend radio staple; used by movie-makers as a time- and tone-setter, as in *Drugstore Cowboy* and *Less Than Zero*.

Rolling Stone in the '90s referred to Count Five as the premiere "psychedelic garage band." "A garage band, well, that we were, said Sean Byrne, the groups' primary songwriter and vocalist, in an exclusive interview. "Psychedelic, I don't know where they get that . . . . We were clean college students, we didn't do drugs; none of us . . . 'Psychotic Reaction' is just about a love that's gone bad. Okay?"

Five teens from San Jose, California—Kenn Ellner (b. 1948, vocals, harmonica), John "Sean" Byrne (b. 1947, vocals, rhythm guitar), Craig "Butch" Atkinson (b. 1947, drums), Roy Chaney (b. 1948, bass), and John "Mouse" Michalski (b.1949, lead guitar)—donned Dracula capes and formed the group in the aftershock of the British Invasion.

"... It was Roy and John who first got it together in '65, with a drummer named Skip Cordell and this piano guy, Phil Evans," said Byrne. "... I came over one time when they were practicing, and Roy let me use his guitar. We were the Squires, then. We played local school dances and this club called What's lt."

Soon, Phil Evans was gone. "It was a real hassle hauling a 100 pound piano around." Then Skip was gone. Kenn's neighbor was Butch Atkinson. "He could play like Michael Clarke of the Byrds, and we had been writing these Byrd-like things, so he fit right in; ..."

At this point, they became Count Five. Their big breakthrough came by way of a lawman—Lt. Robert Podesta. He ran a youth club weekends at a place called the Cinnamon Tree. "Once we got connected with the Cinnamon Tree things got smooth. We were so big

Cinnamon Tree things got smooth. We were so big there that they did a full length painting of us on the wall; capes and all. Primarily, we had girl fans . . . And 'Psychotic Reaction' stood out as everyone's fave," said Byrne.

Kenn's dad was the band's manager. He was sure that "Psychotic" was a hit to be. "He told us that he was gonna get us a record contract in six months and that within a year we'd have a hit on the charts. And that's just what happened," Byrne adds.

While playing an opening spot for the Dave Clark Five in San Jose, Kenn's dad approached KLIV DJ Brian Lord. Lord liked the act and got them an audition for Irwin Zuckner's Double Shot Records. "Lord got us the shot at it. Six record companies turned us down; Capitol twice. 'There's something missing,' they said." Zuckner signed the group and waved "Psychotic Reaction" as their first release. The flip side—"They're Gonna Get You"—was an ode to that terrible place, the barber shop. The reaction was immediate—though short-lived.

Once on the charts, Zuckner and crew were wanting an album's worth of stuff fast. "We had some originals, but they wanted a lot. They had us holed up in a

hotel, in L.A., solely to create new material. This one time we were sittin' around and Mr. Ellner yells out, 'Their coming down over to listen to what you got. What've you got?' We had nothin.' So we faked something on the spot, where I hit these chords and sang 'Some nights I'm alone . . . Some nights I'm alone" Hal [Winn, the producer] comes in and says, 'I like it.'" It became "The Morning After" ["B" side to their second single, "Peace of Mind"].

"Things just didn't turn out right for us," says Byrne. The *San Jose News* reported and Byrne confirmed that the band was offered a million dollars to tour, but turned it down to continue their educations.

"We were young. What did we know," said Byrne. "We didn't get any support, or direction. The success caught us off guard . . . We figured that the engineer, arranger, and producer didn't know their asses from a hole in the ground. They wouldn't let us get controlled feedback or to develop our sound. When we weren't looking, they changed everything. They actually changed the tapes. Even 'Psychotic Reaction' got messed with . . . None of us liked the album."

Within 18 months, Mouse and Ron were gone; replacements were temporary and from the SYNDICATE

OF SOUND. By the close of '68, Count Five were reduced to none.

Due to unrelenting interest, The Count Five—all original members—in 1986, reformed for their high school's 20th anniversary reunion. An album, *Psychotic Reunion: Count Five Live!*, was cut and issued in 1993. Plans for future recordings and touring are in the works.

NEW VAUDEVILLE BAND
WINCHESTER CATHEDRAL
(Geoff Stephens)
Fontana 1562
No. 1 *December 3, 1966*

Geoff Stephens (b. Oct. 1, 1934, New Southgate, England) taught French, English, and religion. In his spare time, he would spin 78s and search junk shops for those high-speed acetate jewels from the '20s and '30s. After dashing off mini-skits for the BBC and a brief twirl in the world of advertising, Geoff went to work for a London music publishing firm. There, in his own cubicle, he dreamed up successful songs for British acts like the Applejacks and Dave Barry. One day, while staring at a photo of Winchester Cathedral on the wall, Geoff was inspired to scribble an unforgettable melody. Still in the heat of passion, Stephens organized a recording session, and with a megaphone to his mouth, crooned the tale of a poor lad whose girlie had left him heart-broken beneath that Gothic structure.

"Winchester Cathedral" quickly became an international item, and even won a Grammy for "Best Rock and Roll Record" in 1966. A Geoff-less debut album went Top Five and sold a million copies. Since a New Vaudeville Band did not actually exist, and since Stephens had no desire to tour singing and dancing this tune, a vaudevillian unit had to be built swiftly from scratch. Alan Klein, who liked to call himself "Tristram, Seventh Earl of Cricketwood," was recruited to work the megaphone. At the core of the new construction was drummer Henri Harrison (b. June 6, 1943, Watford, Hertfordshire) and what had once been an R & B group called Cops 'n' Robbers. On keyboards was Stan Heywood (b. Aug. 23, 1947, Dagenham, Essex); on bass, Neil Korner (b. Oct. 6, 1942, Ashford, Kent); on trombone, Hugh "Shuggy" Watts (b. July 25, 1941, Watford, Hertfordshire); on guitar, Mick Wilsher (b. Dec. 21, 1945, Sutton, Surrey); and on French horn, saxophone, and trombone, Robert "Pops" Kerr (b. Feb. 14, 1943, London), and ex-member of the Bonzo Dog Doo-Dah Band.

The immediate follow-up, "Peek-a-Boo" (#72, 1967), charted in the U. S.; a few others did likewise on their native turf. Nothing further was to save this pseu-

do-group from their impending stateside obscurity. Their descent, however, was slowed by a year's stay at the Aladdin Hotel in Las Vegas. In the '70s, after a three-year tour of Canada, the not-so-new Vaudeville Band returned to England and the cabaret circuit.

Remnants of the band, fronted by Henry Harrison, occasionally are spotted romping through the oldies. "Pops" Kerr reappeared in the '80s fronting Bob Kerr's Whoopie Band. Geoff Stephens went on to penning hits for THE FLYING MACHINE ("Smile a Little Smile for Me") and CAROL DOUGLAS ("Doctor's Orders"). In 1972, Wayne Newton garnered his last hit with Stephens's "Daddy Don't You Walk So Fast."

MUSIC MACHINE
TALK TALK
(Thomas Sean Bonniwell)
Original Sound 61
No. 15 *Jan. 14, 1967*

Sean Bonniwell (b. 1940, San Jose, CA) was the founding father and leader of the Music Machine, one of the most loved—if least played—garage bands of the '60s. Sean, now a born-again Christian, is quietly living in Lindsay, California, where he and his wife run a small engraving shop. His income from those masterful Music Machine sides totaled $7,000; his songwriter's royalties are less than $100 [as of the late '80s]. To free himself from a contract with Warner Bros., Sean sold off the group's name and the rights to all of the group's recordings to producer Brian Ross—reportedly, for the paltry sum of one dollar!

Sean's mother was a ballerina; his father was a military man and a trumpet player. Sean started his own music career in a folk trio, the Noblemen, and learned how to play guitar. After a stint with the Wayfarers (and three albums for RCA), Sean gathered together drummer Ron Edgar and former GALE GARNETT bassist Keith Olsen to create a Beatle-influenced band, the Raga-muffins.

After several months of practice, the Ragamuffins evolved into the well-oiled Music Machine, five strong: Bonniwell, Edgar, Olsen, Mark Landon (guitar), and Doug Rhodes (keyboards). For their concert appearances, each member dyed his hair black, dressed in an all-black outfit, and mysteriously wore one black glove. "I wanted to make a statement that was rebellious, but not for the sake of rebellion," Bonniwell explained to *Goldmine*'s Jeff Tamarkin. "It was for the sake of a unified image."

While the Music Machine was playing a bowling alley, producer Brian Ross discovered the act. He plunked down $150 to tape demos on "Talk Talk" and "Come on In," quite a bargain in those days. Art Laboe

THE MUSIC MACHINE

at Original Sound—a label primarily known for instrumental hits by Sandy Nelson, PRESTON EPPS, and the Incredible Bongo Band—offered to issue some sides, the first of which was "Talk Talk." "I wrote the song in about 20 minutes while I was waiting for my girlfriend to get ready," Bonniwell revealed. "I just sat down with the guitar and wrote it. All the good ones happen like that. I wrote it in '65, so it laid around for a year."

The Music Machine began dismantling itself even as the single was mounting the charts. Sean was at loggerheads with Laboe about which record to issue as the follow-up to "Talk Talk"; Bonniwell wanted to put out "Hey Joe," which no one had recorded yet. In addition, the group was growing resentful of Bonniwell's bossy ways. They recorded the (*Turn On*) The Music Machine LP (1967) in one intense 10-hour session, but the strain was beginning to show.

A few more 45s trickled into circulation, and one even charted—"The People in Me" (#66, 1967). Bonniwell secured a contract with a big label, Warner Bros., but no Machine men stuck around long enough to enter a studio again. He renamed the group Bonniwell Music Machine and used session players for several singles and an LP, *Bonniwell Music Machine* (1967).

During the '70s, Bonniwell dropped out of the music scene and tuned in to a variety of psychedelic experiences. "I made a practice of getting out of my body," he told *Rolling Stone*'s David Fricke. "I became very good at it." During his more grounded moments, Sean hosted an astrology radio program ("The Sun Sign Report") in Charleston, South Carolina; wrote a movie and music review column for *The Charleston*; trained Arabian horses; and made a brief appearance in the flick *Swamp Thing* (1982).

Keith Olsen has become the most visibly successful ex-Machine member. As a record producer, Keith has worked with the Babys, Russ Ballard, Kim Carnes, Fleetwood Mac, Foreigner, THE GRATEFUL DEAD, Heart, and Santana.

SENATOR BOBBY
WILD THING
(Chip Taylor)
Parkway 127
No. 20 *February 4, 1967*

Finally, the full story on Senator Bobby, rock and roll's Robert F. Kennedy impersonator. What follows are extracts from an exclusive interview with the man behind this bizarre version of "Wild Thing," Chip Taylor, one-half of the folk-rock duo JUST US. Taylor (b. James Wesley Voigt, 1940, Yonkers, NY) is a country-rock singer and the songwriter responsible for classics like MERRILEE RUSH & THE TURNAROUNDS' "Angel of the Morning," the Hollies' "I Can't Let Go"—and the Troggs' "Wild Thing."

"My brother Jon [Voigt, the actor] had gone to school with Dennis Wholey. This one day, Dennis and I met on a bus; it was the fall of 1966. We were just kidding around when he started telling me about this guy he knew [Bill Minkin] who did all these impersonations—Chet Huntley, the Lone Ranger, Murray the K. Without thinking, I just said, 'Well, why don't we bring him in the studio and just fool around, and do 'Wild Thing' as if it was SENATOR EVERETT MCKINLEY DIRKSEN [who had recorded a spoken-word tribute to "Gallant Men" in 1966]?

"I went into the Mirasound Studios. I had this demo track, the original demo track that the Troggs had sent me, doing 'Wild Thing.' We had the guitar on this one channel, and we used that channel with a vocal overdub by this guy, Bill Minkin. We had Bill do one side imitating Robert Kennedy, and the other, doing Everett Dirksen.

"When the single took off, we just went back in with Minkin and a bunch that Dennis had assembled, called the Hardly Worthit Players [Wholey, Steve Baron, and Carol Morley], and did this straight-ahead comedy LP [*The Hardly Worthit Report*, 1967] as a follow-up. 'Wild Thing' surprised us all, and so we went and did one other single, a take-off on Donovan's 'Mellow Yellow' [#99, 1967; a "duet" as by Senator Bobby & Senator McKinley], but that was it."

Minkin has moved on to public relations firms and ad agencies, where he has created industrial videos for such firms as McGraw-Hill and Nabisco. Bill has also written comedic material for Sandy Baron and Dave Astor, and during the '60s made stand-up appearances at night spots like New York's Scene.

Baron has written TV scripts as well as pop and folk songs for publishers like April/Blackwood and Wild Indigo. Steve was a folksinger and played at New York's Bitter End and Gaslight Cafe. More recently, Taylor reports, he has worked as an independent television producer in Nashville.

Morley was active in the '60s, playing the theater scene in Newport, Rhode Island, and Provincetown, Massachusetts. Carol also did TV commercials for Cascade Soap and Rival Dog Food.

Wholey was a TV talk-show host (WNDT) and DJ (WBAI-FM) in Baltimore. Dennis also emceed a late-'60s quiz show ("The Generation Gap," 1969) and functioned as a radio director for the NBC Radio Network, later he was a host of a PBS late-night talk show.

BLUES MAGOOS
(WE AIN'T GOT) NOTHIN' YET
(Ronald Gilbert, Ralph Scala, Michael Esposito)
Mercury 72622
No. 5 *February 11, 1967*

The Blues Magoos, New York City's first psychedelic experience, took shape in 1964 around the core of lead singer/guitarist Peppy Castro (b. Emil Thielhelm, June 16, 1949), bassist Ronnie Gilbert (b. Apr. 25, 1946), and Ralph Scala (b. Dec. 12, 1947). In 1964, guitarist Mike Esposito (b. 1943, Delaware) and drummer Geoff Daking (b. 1947, Delaware) joined up, and the group started playing in Greenwich Village. Before the Magoos (originally spelled "B-l-o-o-s Magoos") developed a marketable persona, they waxed a few rare and righteous singles for Verve/Folkways ("People With No Faces" b/w "So I'm Wrong and You're Right") and Ganim ("Who Do You Love').

By the time their second 45 for Mercury was out, the Blues Magoos had gone psychedelic. These boys were literally wired: whenever they performed, their outfits would flash on and off. As Castro told *Goldmine's* Lydia Sherwood, "Our concept really started after we had played the Night Owl for a while. People began freaking out and turning on. In those early days of drugs, when people were really expanding, we were more conceptual, more psychedelic."

The Blues Magoos' first album, *Psychedelic Lollipop* (1966), was certainly "conceptual": the cover featured Peppy and his mind-bent bandmates in multi-colored threads, superimposed on a far-out background of swirly goo. They opened the LP with their anthem, "(We Ain't Got)

Nothin' Yet"; weirded out with an extended rave-up on JOHN D. LOUDERMILK's "Tobacco Road"; and eerily sang that "Love Seems Doomed" (LSD). Their second LP, *Electric Comic Book* (1967), included an electric comic-book insert, the moving "Albert Common Is Dead" (ACID), and their follow-up single to "Nothin' Yet" —"Pipe Dreams" (#60, 1967) b/w "There's a Chance We Can Make It" (#81). *Basic Blues Magoos* (1968) sported a cover version of the Moves' "I Can Hear the Grass Grow" plus a number called "Subliminal Sonic Laxative."

"By our third album, we had leased a house in the Bronx on University Avenue, and we did home recording," Peppy recalled. "Our music room was done in black light and strobe. The cops would come over because people would complain that there were strange flashing lights. We literally had the police walk in the house and wham, we'd hit the strobes, and they'd go for their guns! . . . We were stoned all the time then."

The Blues Magoos drifted apart, and in 1969, Peppy and an entirely new Magoo constituency signed with ABC-Paramount for two albums. Castro then departed to act in the Broadway production of *Hair*. After a year there, he and two other cast members, Billy and Bobby Alessi, formed a pop unit called Barnabye Bye. Two LPs later, Peppy was part of the short-lived Polydor recording act Wiggy Bits. Finally, in 1981, Peppy Castro—with Doug Katsaros and Dennis Feldman—returned to the playlists and the Top 40 charts as a group called BALANCE, with "Breaking Away" (#22, 1981). Thereafter, Peppy's name has appeared as tunesmith on songs cut by Cher and Kiss.

BOB CREWE GENERATION
MUSIC TO WATCH GIRLS BY
(Tony Velona, Sid Ramin)
Dyno Voice 229
No. 15 *February 11, 1967*

For years, Bob Crewe seemed to be able to do no wrong. Everything he touched turned to gold—gold records. . . .

"Music to Watch Girls By" was born as jingle music for a mid-'60s Diet Pepsi ad campaign. Crewe, a studio veteran, best known for his production and songwriting work with the Four Seasons, thought the tune was catchy enough to record as a pop single for general release. He swiftly assembled a studio full of session musicians to play seven brass instruments, three saxes, three guitars, a piano, drums, timpani, and a xylophone as the Bob Crewe Generation.

Although none of the Generation's subsequent musical musings approached the popularity of "Music to Watch Girls By," Crewe's crew did do well with their *Music to Watch Girls By* (1967) LP and a follow-up single entitled "Birds of Britain" (#89, 1967). More than a decade would pass before Bob—as a recording artist—would bounce back with "Street Talk" (#56, 1976), issued under the acronym B. C. G.

Bob was born Stanley Robert Crewe on November 12, 1937, in Bellville, New Jersey. During the '50s, Crewe moved to Detroit, then to Philadelphia, recording numerous puffy/teen-idol sides for the BBC, Jubilee, Spotlight, Vik, U.T., Warwick, and ABC-Paramount labels. Some of his later efforts were quite solid; "Sweetie Pie" and "The Whiffenpoof Song" (#96, 1960) almost connected.

In Philadelphia, Crewe took up painting, modeled for magazine ads, and dabbled in interior decorating. In 1953, he struck up a friendship with a piano-playing Texan named Frank Slay, Jr. Together, Crewe and Slay wrote and arranged songs, set up the XYZ label, and did some independent production work. One of their earliest successes was the double-sided 1957 smash "Silhouettes" b/w "Daddy Cool" by THE RAYS. Before parting ways in the early '60s, the team of Crewe and Slay worked on disks by Billie & Lillie, Freddie Cannon, and Dickie Doo & The Don'ts, to name but a few.

Bob Crewe is best known to rock and roll fans for his instrumental role in shaping the phenomenal career of the Four Seasons. From the group's release of "Bermuda" in 1961, through 1967, Bob produced all of their recordings. With one of the Seasons, Bob Gaudio, Crewe also co-wrote many of the group's most memorable musical moments—"Big Girls Don't Cry," "Let's Hang On," "Rag Doll," and "Walk Like a Man."

Before success stalled, Crewe went on to form music publishing companies, record labels (Crewe, Dyno Voice), and to produce or write for such artists as the Eleventh Hour, Lesley Gore, the Highwaymen, Ben E. King, La Belle, Oliver, DIANE RENAY, Mitch Ryder & The Detroit Wheels, NORMA TANEGA, Disco Tex & The Sexolettes, and Frankie Valli.

To observers, Bob Crewe could do no wrong and had it all. One over-the-edge day in 1974, Bob walked into his den where all his gold records filled the walls—floor to ceiling—and flew into a rage. "I took them all off the wall, went out onto the terrace, and pounded all the gold records into a ball with a sledge hammer and threw it down into a ravine," said Bob to *Rolling Stone*'s Rob Tannenbaum.

The incident stirred Crewe to realize that he needed help. "Fun had become the first three letters in the word funeral," he said, of what had been a long bout with booze and drugs. "I decided it was time to cool it."

To all, Bob Crewe had it all; alone with himself, he felt hollow and undeserving. "My father was a hard-working man, and here I was making big bucks on music, and fun and games."

He spent a year sobering up. In 1977, a serious car accident laid him up for six months, followed by three years of intense physical therapy. In 1980, Bob met Martha Friedman, author of *Overcoming the Fear of Success*. With her assistance, he overcame what he felt was a tremendous writer's block. "I used to complain to her that I couldn't come up with great, fabulous, tremendous ideas, and she would say, 'Cut the crap and write ordinary.'"

Crewe now spends time painting and sculpting. He continues to write "ordinary" and with Sugar Loaf's Jerry Corbetta formed C. C. Trax, a talent development outfit.

SPYDER TURNER
STAND BY ME
(Ben E. King, Elmo Glick)
MGM 13617
No. 12 *February 11, 1967*

What a memorable song! Most people, if asked who had a hit with "Stand by Me," would respond with the name of Ben E. King, who recorded the original rendition of the song (#4, 1961; #9, 1986). Others might mention cover versions by John Lennon (#20, 1975) and Jerry Lee Lewis' cousin MICKEY GILLEY (#22, 1980). Poor Spyder; no one but a hard-core record buff would know that Spyder Turner's novelty working of this classic was also a chart-shaker. And worse yet, Spyder didn't even like the record.

"It was never intended to be used as a record," Spyder told *Blues & Soul*. It was only an audition tape of Turner doing impressions of how Jackie Wilson, David Ruffin, Billy Stewart, Smokey Robinson, and Chuck Jackson might have handled the song. "[MGM] felt it was good enough. I didn't agree. I didn't like it, but I wanted a [record] deal, so I went on ahead and did a 'B' side for them." Spyder's nutty number sped up the charts like nothing he would ever again create.

Spyder was born Dwight Turner in Beckley, West Virginia, in 1947. After some years of moving about, his family settled in Detroit. In his teen years, Dwight sang in glee clubs and in various doo-wop groups. By the mid-'60s, he and his eight-piece band, the Nonchalants, were working the watering holes around town. After the band split up, Annie Gellen—host of "Swing Time," a TV show out of Lansing, Michigan—arranged for Spy to submit the above-mentioned audition tape to MGM Records.

Turner's immediate follow-up, "I Can't Make It Anymore," scraped by at number 95 in 1967, but further releases fared poorly. For the next decade, Turner worked primarily behind the scenes, managing acts and trying to write songs. When Rose Royce successfully recorded his "Do Your Dance" (#39, 1977), Spyder approached Whitfield, the group's label, about letting him have one more crack at stardom. However, none of his numerous efforts in the late '70s and '80s (for both Whitfield and Polydor) have done well.

"CANNONBALL" ADDERLEY
MERCY, MERCY, MERCY
(Joe Zawinul)
Capitol 5798
No. 11 *February 25, 1967*

Julian "Cannonball" Adderley—one of the few jazz musicians to appear with regularity on the pop chart—was born in Tampa, Florida, on September 15, 1928. Because he had such a huge appetite, his friends nicknamed him "Cannibal," later corrupted to "Cannonball." While still in high school, the alto saxophonist formed his first jazz combo. After graduation, he became a band director at Dillard High for two years, served in the military, led a few Army bands, and gigged with Oscar Pettiford. In the late '50s, he began attracting critical attention for his work with Miles Davis and John Coltrane.

Cannonball and his brother Nat formed their own funky unit in 1956. At various times, pianists such as Barry Harris, Victor Feldman, Bobby Timmons, and Joe Zawinul (a founding member of Weather Report) passed through the band. Multi-instrumentalist Yusef Lateef and flutist Charles Lloyd also played with Cannonball's group. Present at the "Mercy" sessions were Nat Adderley (comet), Joe Zawinul (piano), Sam Jones (bass), and Louis Hayes (drums).

Seldom does a jazzman manage to attract a large pop audience with his recordings, but Cannonball's soulful sounds made the Hot 100 listings five times in all, from 1961 through 1970. His instrumentals were rooted in jazz, but always had an engagingly bluesy backbeat.

Cannonball Adderley died on August 8, 1975, in Gary, Indiana. He was only 45 when he suffered a massive stroke.

CASINOS
THEN YOU CAN TELL ME GOODBYE
(J. D. LOUDERMILK)
Fraternity 977
No. 6 *March 11, 1967*

"The original group was called the Capris, and we go way back to the '50s," said Gene Hughes, lead singer for the Casinos, in an exclusive interview. "We were doin' hops for disk jockeys and THE CAPRIS came out with

'There's a Moon Out Tonight.' I knew we had to change our name; didn't wanna. This jock [Bob Smith, WCPO] just getting back from Las Vegas, jokingly said, 'Why don't you call yourselves the Casinos?'"

They had been singing on street corners in Cincinnati since 1958, when mere high schoolers and greasers. "There was myself and my brother Glen, Ray White, and J. T. Sears; never learned his first name. It was strange, though, cause they'd be another two, three guys that were in and out of the group. So there was also Pete Noble, Roger West, and Joe Patterson.

"We sang a lot of clubs, like the Lookout Club and the Beverly Hills in Cincinnati . . . and the Playboy circuit; had this local TV show for a while, 'Five a-Go-Go.' Now, we were a vocal group initially, then we decided to add a band. That's when we had Bob Armstrong [organ] come in; Bob Smith [bass], and Mickey Denton [guitar]. Ray [White] played drums. Eventually, changes came on us and there was just me, Armstrong, Mickey, Ray, and Smith; the ones who actually recorded 'Then You Can Tell Me Goodbye.' When the hit came, all the guys came back and went on the road with us; that's nine pieces, and that's all but J. T., who had died in this car crash in '63."

The Casinos recording history begins in 1961 when on the road they had met teen idol Carl Dobkins, Jr.— then known for "My Heart Is an Open Book" and "Lucky Devil"—"He had his own label—Name Records—and let us record this thing we had written called 'Do You Recall.' That was like a regional hit for us; as was "That's the Way" and "Too Good to Be True," that we had out on [record distributor Tommy Wills'] Terry Records. We were able to play the area clubs like we were a hit act; all while the rest of the country knew nothing about us."

Harry Carlson of the Cincinnati-based Fraternity label liked their sounds and gave them another chance. "We'd record stuff and license it out to labels. At the same session we did 'Then You Can Tell Me' we did 'Moon River' . . . Then Harry [Carlson] put out three things by us before the hit. "Right There Beside You" had this Beatle sound, but it didn't happen.

"I had heard this song 'Then You Can Tell Me Goodbye,' performed by Johnny Nash on WLAC, the 'John R [Richbourg] Show.' His version was never a hit, so we started doing it at the clubs; for years. . . . So, while we were in the studio at the King Studios in Cincinnati, cutting this instrumental [King Curtis'] 'Soul Serenade,' for a disk jockey, we used the time to cut 'Then You Can Tell Me.'" The JOHN D. LOUDERMILK tune was a musical throw-back, a beautiful slow-paced crawler, but it also sounded collegiate and choral, like something the Association would do, and ergo hip.

"Everybody says, 'What a great idea [doing 'Then You Can Tell Me']; what a great arrangement . . .' It was luck; luck and perfection. . . . We were comfortable with it. There was nothing to it. . . . Luck. Work hard; and sometimes the luck happens."

Premier Talent signed the act for managerial representation. Tours were a constant—opening for the Beach Boys, Turtles, the Dick Clark Caravan . . . and then . . .

The record was a smash. Things looked bright as the morning sun for the squeaky-clean crew from Cincinnati. Critic Earl Wilson congratulated the guys on their "normal look." Follow-up 45s appeared—on an assortment of labels well into the '70s— but with the exception of the immediate follow-up, "It's All Over Now" (#65, 1967)—penned by Don Everly—not a one gained more than a glance.

"Harry [Carlson] and I—well, it was the only argument we every had. He followed the hit with 'It's All Over Now'—and as I told him, that song didn't have our sound. It was just to be an album cut, then on the way back from a gig I heard it on the radio—announced as our next single—and I knew it was all over."

Wrong song, yes, but possibly worse—the Casinos didn't look the part. With nary a short hair out of place and no jeans and peace signs, Gene and his Casinos were deviates. The look was of a Sunday morn choir, a gathering of Young Republicans.

"In 1968, I went to Nashville and recorded some solo things for United Artist. We'd worked hard for that hit record, but there was the strain. 'Can't speak for the rest, but I was burnt out. The group remained in Cincinnati, playing gigs. But it didn't last all that long. I was the lead singer—and I don't mean that egotistically—and without me, the sound, it didn't happen. I blame me more than them. I needed a rest. By '70, we got back together."

Gene Hughes lives in Nashville and still performs. The "Casinos" name is alive and can be seen annually in Cincinnati's "WORS Shows," the World's Oldest Rock Stars.

"I've no regrets. It was wonderful. And Harry [Carlson] treated us right. We're one of the few acts that got our money. If anything, Harry probably gave us more money than he shoulda. When he retired, he handed me our tapes; said, 'They're all yours. do what you can with them.'"

"Then You Can Tell Me Goodbye" had returned to the C & W charts in 1968 with Eddie Arnold and in 1996 with Neal McCoy.

BUFFALO SPRINGFIELD
FOR WHAT IT'S WORTH
(Stephen Stills)
Atco 6559
No. 7 *March 25, 1967*

On May 6, 1997, Buffalo Springfield was inducted into the Rock 'n' Roll Hall of Fame. The group never sold millions of records, never had a number-one hit, and never earned a gold, or even a platinum record. But, Buffalo Springfield is legendary . . .

"'For What It's Worth,' that's what people know of us," said RICHIE FURAY to *Goldmine*'s John Einarson. "It's the anthem of the '60s because it summed up the feelings of the '60s, the restlessness. . . ."

These seminal folk-rockers were originally known as the Herd, until someone spotted, on the back of a parked steamroller, the name "Buffalo Springfield." The initial inspiration for the band seems to have come from guitarist Steve Stills (b. Jan. 3, 1945, Dallas), a member of the New York-based Au Go Go Singers. With the latter group's break-up, Stills headed for L.A. Once there, he phoned a fellow ex-Go Go, Richie Furay (b. May 9, 1944, Dayton, OH), asking him to come out and play rhythm guitar for a new group he was thinking of forming.

Legend has it that on April 6, 1966, Stills and Furay, while stuck in a traffic jam, spotted a black hearse with Canadian license plates. On closer inspection, Stills identified the driver as guitarist Neil Young (b. Nov. 12, 1945, Toronto), a member of the Squires— whom Stills had met in Canada. In Young's company was a fellow Canadian, bassist Bruce Palmer, formerly with Capitol of Canada's Jack London & The Sparrows. "The most remarkable karmic event ever," said Palmer to *Goldmine* of the synergistic meeting.

Now all that the new supergroup needed was an extraordinary drummer. For a moment, that seat was filled by Billy Mundi, later of the Mothers of Invention and Rhinoceros. Enter Dewey Martin (b. Walter Dwayne Midlkiff, Sept. 30, 1952, Chesterville, Canada), formerly of the Dillards and the Modern Folk Quartet. Martin had worked in Nashville with FARON YOUNG and Patsy Cline; recorded a half dozen 45s with Sir Raleigh & The Coupons.

"The very beginning was the best," said Furay. "The original five of us, as far as I'm concerned had the magic. There was a connection that cannot be put into words. We were all so different, and yet we were all made to make that music at that particular time."

After a seven day hold-up in the dingy Hollywood Center Motel—compliments of their momentary manager Barry Friedman—Buffalo Springfield became the house band at L.A.'s Whiskey a Go-Go, where they were soon spotted by SONNY & Cher's ex-managers, Charlie Green and Brian Stone. "The first week at the Whiskey was absolutely incredible," said Stills to John Einarson, co-author of *For What It's Worth*. "That's when we peaked and after then it was down hill."

Personality frictions built into the very make-up of the band. "The Buffalo Springfield was Steve's band," said Furay. "He was the heart and soul of the band. Steve was the leader, always." Other's didn't see things that way; in particular, Neil Young.

Meanwhile, Green and Stone secured a recording contract for the guys with Atco—featuring an unheard of $12,000 advance. Although it was a fine track, not many people picked up on the group's debut single, Young's "Nowadays Clancy Can't Even Sing." "Unfortunately," said Greene, "'Clancy' was too sophisticated for AM radio. When 'Clancy' bombed, we all panicked," said Furay. "We really began to have communication

BUFFALO SPRINGFIELD

problems and grew further and further apart."

The follow-up was a Stills number inspired by an altercation on Sunset Strip on November 12, 1966 near Pandora's Box, when tensions peaked between teens and the community's businesses. "For What It's Worth," featuring Neil Young's sinister-sounding lead guitar, brought the group immediate fame as well as a national following.

Their first album, *Buffalo Springfield* (1967), had included "Clancy" and this biggie, but had not sold well, despite favorable reviews; with the success of "For What It's Worth," the LP took off.

"The band was that first album, and it was never captured again," Furay told Einarson. "After that it started to fall apart."

"We were still looking for the commercial single," said Furay, "and it never happened. 'Bluebird' didn't do very well and 'Rock and Roll Women' did even worse. This was all a big let down for us. Had maybe a hit single appeared, it may have been a different story."

By the release of their second album (*Buffalo Springfield Again*) in late 1967, Palmer was gone, having been deported for a visa violation. He was replaced by Jim Fielder—session man for FRANK ZAPPA and Tim Buckley and later a member of Blood, Sweat & Tears. Young, departed briefly, and Doug Hastings with the Daily Flash stepped in. Young soon returned, Hastings left, and the group's recording engineer, Jim Messina—a future member of Loggins & Messina and former member of the Jesters—took over bass and vocal duties for Fielder.

With internal dissension and acrimonious exchanges everpresent, Buffalo members rarely were spotted in the same recording studio together. "Every guy had his songs, his studio time, and his frame of mind," said Martin to the author. In order to finish the LP, Furay and Messina shifted through tapes left behind, applied overdubs, and brought in sidemen, as steel guitarist Rusty Young. By the end of 1968, Buffalo Springfield's final package, *Last Time Around*, was issued—posthumously. Their last appearance was at the Long Beach Sports Arena, on May 5, 1968.

Stills joined ex-Byrd David Crosby and ex-Hollie GRAHAM NASH in the formation of Crosby, Stills & Nash—later Young would also join the act. Young set up a multi-decade solo career with his back-up band, Crazy Horse. Furay and Messina formed Poco, forged a solo career and occupied the SOUTHER, HILLMAN, FURAY BAND; while Martin made a vain effort to keep the "Buffalo Springfield" name alive with three new members. This pseudo-version of the group never recorded, and Dewey embarked on an unsuccessful solo career.

"We were good, even great," said Young. "When we started out, we thought we would be together forever.

But we were just too young to be patient, and I was the worst."

EASYBEATS
FRIDAY ON MY MIND
(Harry Vanda, George Young)
United Artists 50108
No. 16 *May 20, 1967*

The Easybeats met and merged at a youth hostel in 1963 in Sydney, Australia. Guitarist George Young (b. Nov. 6, 1947, Glasgow, Scotland) joined forces with lead singer "Little" Stevie Wright (b. Dec. 20, 1948, Leeds, England); bassist Dick Diamonde (b. Dec. 28, 1947) and lead guitarist Harry Vanda (b. Mar. 22, 1947), who had both moved to Australia from their native Holland; and drummer Gordon "Snowy" Fleet (b. Aug. 16, 1945, Liverpool), who had played with the Mojos, and who picked the "Easybeats'" name.

By 1964, the Easybeats were a scruffy-haired band playing at a Sydney club called The Beatle Village. A talent scout named Mike Vaughn caught one of their shows, and recommended them to J. Albert & Son, the label that issued the first of the beat group's many 45s, "For My Woman." Nothing much happened until "She's So Fine," their next Australian release: it topped the homeland charts, and the follow-up, "Wedding Bells," went Top 10. Yet George and the rest were not pleased with the results.

"That's when all the bullshit started," Young told Greg Shaw, editor of *Who Put the Bomp*. "With that track, we tried to be commercial. It paid off, but wasn't as big as we thought it could have been. We decided then that we wanted to get out of Australia." Before leaving for England, three more collectible singles were issued—"Sad and Lonely and Blue," "Make You Feel Alright (Woman)," and "Come and See Her."

Once on British shores, the Easybeats recorded an irresistibly pulsating track with a Beatle-esque yet rough-edged feel. "Friday on My Mind" was a slice of working-class rock and roll, and remains a classic here-comes-the-weekend party platter. According to George, that was the beginning of the end—the band was pressured to come up with another "Friday," and a U.S. tour was hastily arranged. Snowy dropped out, to be replaced by Tony Cahill.

"By that time, the band was really stoned most of the time, and we had been at it for a fair while. When everybody else was getting in to it, we were trying to get out of it. The general lethargy of the band was due to dope, plus there were contractual hassles popping up, and we still weren't making any money. Then we found ourselves exclusively signed to more than one record company! To this day [late '70s], we're still involved in lawsuits."

THE EASYBEATS

in Australia. Snowy Fleet has taken over his family's construction company. Stevie Wright conquered a dreadful heroin problem; as he admitted to *Rolling Stone*, "[it] was devastating, going from the stardom of the Easybeats to sweeping floors."

PARADE
SUNSHINE GIRL
(Jerry Riopelle, Murray MacLeod, Smokey Roberds)
A & M 841
No. 20 *May 27, 1967*

Jerry Riopelle was born more than a half-century ago in Detroit, and his family moved to Arizona shortly thereafter. He relocated to California more than 25 years ago, but he is Arizona's favorite pop artist—his obscure disks sell by the thousands there. "Other guys [like me] who didn't get that break have to quit the business and get into selling pharmaceuticals or something," Riopelle told Steve Clow of the *Los Angeles Herald*. "The best thing is that I get to do what I like to do, and that's write and play the music and make records. It's nice to go to Arizona and play the star."

Riopelle was the first and only producer hired by the legendary Phil Spector in the early '60s, when the "Wall of Sound" man was planning to develop a stable of in-house producers for his Philles label. Jerry played piano and sang back-up on sessions for the Righteous Brothers, the Ronettes, and Ike & Tina Turner. He produced "Things Are Changing," a song for the U.S. government in the '60s (with Spector and Brian Wilson) that encouraged kids to stay in school.

Over the years, Jerry's songs have been recorded by Rita Coolidge, Kenny Loggins, and Meatloaf. He has been an A & R man for A & M Records, and has recorded nine LPs for labels like Capitol, ABC, and his own Little Eskimo label. Jerry has also produced, in Spector-like fashion, collectible disks for Clydie King, Ramona King, the Lornettes, Shango, Bobby Sheen (of Bob B. Soxx & The Bluejeans), Sugar 'n' Spice, Nino Tempo & April Stevens, and Bonnie & The Treasures.

After releasing just a handful of fine stateside singles and two albums—*Friday on My Mind* (1967) and *Falling Off the Edge of the World* (1968)—the Easybeats called it quits in 1969. Harry Vanda and George Young have since moved on to become Australia's top producers (AC/DC, Rose Tattoo, JOHN PAUL YOUNG), and have recorded under pseudonyms like Paintbox, Tramp, Moondance, the Band of Hope, Flash & The Pan, Grapefruit, and the Marcus Hook Roll Band. Young's two younger brothers are AC/DC's Angus and Malcolm Young.

Tony Cahill later joined the Australian quintet Python Lee Jackson (whose 1972 release "In a Broken Dream" featured Rod Stewart guesting on lead vocals). Dick Diamonde reportedly retired to New South Wales

Early in 1967, Riopelle, Murray MacLeod, and Smokey Roberds went into a studio as Parade. "Sunshine Girl," with its light, West Coast hippie feel, was a big success. The five high-quality follow-ups—"She's Got The Magic," "Frog Prince," "I Can See Love," "A.C.D.C.," and "Laughing Lady"—were not.

"I'm the guy in *One Trick Pony*," Riopelle lamented. "Oh, Paul Simon wasn't thinking about Jerry Riopelle when he made the movie, but he was thinking about a guy who has good songs, but never became famous. That's me."

WHISTLING JACK SMITH
I WAS KAISER BILL'S BATMAN
(Roger Greenaway, Roger Cook)
Deram 85005
No. 20   *June 3, 1967*

Whistling Jack Smith never existed. There had been a Whispering Jack Smith, though—a British recording artist who half-talked and half-sang his way through tunes because of a World War II injury. Not a soul who bought "I Was Kaiser Bill's Batman" suspected that Whistling Jack Smith was a total fabrication. Even knowing this would not have made much difference: the song and the artist had silly names, the tune had an infectious little melody, and the dingy disk was disturbingly different from anything on Top 40 radio at that time.

A fog surrounds the actual conception of Jack the whistler. Was it the uncredited producer of the session, or the tune's conceivers—the songwriting/recording team of Greenaway and Cook (a.k.a. DAVID AND JONATHAN—who dreamed up the idea? Possibly the whole episode was a spur-of-the-moment studio fluke. We do know that the song features the Mike Sammes Singers, a then-popular TV group, plus some session musicians.

Once copies of "I Was Kaiser Bill's Batman" began flying off the shelves, a Jack Smith had to be located for making personal appearances. Billy Moeller (b. Feb. 2, 1946, Liverpool)—brother of Tommy Moeller, lead singer for UNITFOUR PLUS TWO—agreed to play the role of Jack Smith and tour behind the single. He had been recording for British Decca as Coby Wells, and his disks under that name had not exactly been burning holes in the charts.

When Whistling Jack's magic moment had passed, Billy Moeller returned to being Coby Wells and, later still, recorded under his God-given name. Poor fellow: even under three different pseudonyms, he was unable to place another disk on the charts in the United States or the United Kingdom.

JON & ROBIN & THE IN-CROWD
DO IT AGAIN A LITTLE BIT SLOWER
(Wayne Thompson)
Abnak 119
No. 18   *June 24, 1967*

Jon and Robin Abnor were a husband-and-wife team from Dallas. SONNY & CHER were fabulously popular at this time, and other duos were hopping on the folk-rock bandwagon. Jon & Robin's slightly suggestive hit single (pressed on yellow vinyl, an unusual practice back then) was produced by rockabilly legend Dale Hawkins of "Susie Q" fame, as was "Do It Again"'s follow-up, "Drums" (#100, 1967).

One other Jon & Robin 45 charted—"Dr. Jon (The Medicine Man)" (#87, 1968). Thereafter, Jon worked alone and with studio players as Jon & The In-Crowd, Jon Abnor, H. Rabon, Jon Howard, Jon Howard Abnor, and the Abnor Involvement. Wife Robin even had a solo try as (naturally) Robin. Most of these offerings eluded critical notice with the greatest of ease.

The Abnors reportedly owned Abnak Records, the label of a group called the Five Americans that racked up a number of pop hits—"I See the Light" (#26, 1966), "Evil Not Love" (#52, 1966), and "Western Union" (#5, 1967). Herein lay the source of the financial wherewithal that allowed Jon and Robin to prolong what otherwise might have been more truncated careers.

FIFTH ESTATE
DING DONG! THE WITCH IS DEAD
(E. Y. Harburg, Harold Arlen)
Jubilee 5573
No. 11   *July 1, 1967*

"I was taking advantage of senior class privileges, skipping a study hall and taking a nap under a grand piano in the empty school auditorium," explained Don Askew to *DISCoveries*' Joseph Tortelli, "when I was aroused by 'The Charge of the Light Brigade.' This guy, Wayne Wadhams had come down to play and—not noticing me—had begun."

Such was the meeting in Stamford, Connecticut, in 1964, of Stamford High's aspiring wordsmith and poet and "Wads" Wadhams, a keyboard pro known in the region for his pipe organ recitals and the beginning of a relationship that would culminate in the Fifth Estate. Said Askew, "Once I got out from under the piano, I got to talking about songs and groups and lions in the street. Some spirit whispered in my ear, 'Wayne's got the music, you've got the words.'"

Together they created "Nothin Is, but Thinking Makes It So," "Oh Baby, You Exceed the Norm," and "Talking Macbeth Blues"; all yet to be issued. Soon

Wads, on fuzz organ and electric harpsichord, and Don, on nonlinear thoughts, were surrounded by mandolin and fuzz guitar picker D. Bill Shute, guitarist Rick "Ric" Engler, an ex-member in a surf band, the Galaxies, bassist Doug "Dick Duck" Ferrar (plus kazoo, electric clarinet, violin, vocals), formerly of a competing surf unit, the Chicanes, and a drummer/maraca man with jazz-leanings, Ken "Furvus" Evans—soon, they were the D-Men.

"We played intense rock'n'roll," said Evans. "It was heavy rock for the time." Within a month, the D-Men had a manager in Kevin Gavin; two months further, Gavin had the boys signed to Veep, a United Artist subsidiary. All but Don Askew acquired new "D" names: Wayne hid beneath the Dwayne persona, Rick became Don; Ken, D'Arcy; Doug, Duke; and Bill, D.Wm. "It was really magic," said Doug/Duke. "I was 16 years old when we went into the [A & R] studio, and the other guys weren't much older. We just sat in the studio and whipped off these tunes."

"Don't You Know" and "I Just Don't Care" got little in the way of charting, but were teen-approved by those who got to hear them. An International Fan Club was formed and in March 1965, the D-Men appeared opposite Peter & Gordon and CANNIBAL & THE HEADHUNTERS on NBC-TV's "Hullabaloo." "After the curtain closed, the place was mobbed," said Doug/Duke. "People were trying to rip our clothes off . . . it was like with the Beatles . . . and I wasn't much out of junior high school."

Kapp issued a folkie-flavored single; it, too, flopped. Before 1965's end, Chuck Legrow was added, as vocalist; and the group became the Fifth Estate. Red Bird, founded by George Goldner and legends Leiber & Stoller, signed the act for a lone single, "Love Is All in the Game." With time on their side, Wads and Askew wrote tunes for the Two People, Brothers Four, and Highwaymen; and the group recorded commercials for Ocean Spray, Proctor & Gamble, and McGregor, a clothier. Years' end saw the disappearance of Legrow and manager Gavin.

With basement tapes in hand—20 tracks that they had recorded in Wads' basement—the band approached Bill and Steve Jerome, producers of the Left Banke's "Pretty Ballerina." "They were impressed, but not enough to make a commitment," said Doug/Duke. "Then we returned with 'Ding Dong! The Witch Is Dead.' It really blew their socks off. They thought it was a great idea."

Recording the old tune was born during a Christmas party bet. Askew had advanced a theory that any song properly presented could become a hit. One partyer doubted it and challenged him to a wager, 'Bet your group can't get a hit with a song from The Wizard of Oz.'

"At the time, I was studying Renaissance dance music," said Wads. "I felt there was no more purely entertaining music; it seemed delightfully, bubbly, and simple. I thought, 'Why not use it?'" Wads embellished "Ding Dong" with the Bouree from *Terpsichore*, a collection of dance songs by 17th-century composer Michael Praetorious.

As "Ding Dong" hit, summer vacation was at hand and the band stuffed in a station wagon and made the best of it—with appearances at the Red Rooster in Pittsburgh, Surf Ballroom in Clearlake, Iowa, and the Wedgewood Village Amusement Park in Oklahoma City.

"We did a tour with Gene Pitney," D. Bill/D.Wm. told *Goldmine*'s Tom Bingham. "There were a bunch of other groups, too; the Happenings, THE MUSIC EXPLOSION, THE EASYBEATS. Anyway, that was a real taste of rock and roll stardom. I figured, 'I don't want to do this anymore!' That was enough of that." D. Bill didn't have much of a choice anyway—he was drafted. And after a total of seven more Jubilee 45s, all issued as by "the Fifth Estate"—including "The Mickey Mouse Club" and "Heigh Ho" from the Walt Disney animated *Snow White*—and a noncharting LP (*Ding Dong! The Witch Is Dead*), the group broke up.

"The straw that brought the whole camel down," said Wads, "was when I heard our version of 'The Parade of Wooden Soldiers' on the radio. The Jeromes had hired studio musicians and singers to do the whole thing, and it went out on Jubilee with our names on it. Outraged, I called and was informed that the label owned our name, and they could issue anything they wanted. . . ."

On D. Bill's return from the service, he married and settled into a life as a teacher. In the mid-'70s, D. Bill formed the Green Linnet record label with Lisa Null and folkie Patrick Sky. D. Bill and Null have collaborated on a few LPs; notably *The Feathered Maiden & Other Ballads and American Primitive*.

Group members continued for awhile working as session musicians for advertising jingles and other artists. Wads and Askew wrote tunes as "Sal Paradise" and "Harry Krishna," respectively. Wads—whose rearranged "Candid Camera" theme was utilized by Alan Funt for years—reportedly graduated from Dartmouth, receiving further degrees from MIT and Harvard in nuclear physics and English. He's alleged to have gone on to teach recording techniques at the Berklee College of Music, run the Orson Wells Cinema in Boston, and done unsung independent production work.

"The record company wanted more novelty tunes, and that's all they wanted from us," said Wads to Tortelli. "Once we had the hit with 'Ding Dong' all they could think of was . . . novelty songs."

"I see "Ding Dong" as a bit of fun that backfired. . . . We had worked and prayed for a hit for over three years," said Askew. "And then had our dreams shattered by our answered prayer."

Fifth Estate's second album was never issued; Jubilee went bankrupt in 1969.

EVERY MOTHER'S SON
COME ON DOWN TO MY BOAT
(Wes Farrell, Jerry Goldstein)
MGM 13733
No. 6 *July 8, 1967*

For five years, Dennis (b. Nov. 22, 1948) and Larry "Lar" Larden (b. Aug. 10, 1945) had been a two-guitar folk duo, working clubs and pubs in New York's Greenwich Village. Much like fellow folkies the Lovin' Spoonful and The Mamas & The Papas, they went electric. It was early in 1967 when a mutual friend introduced the brothers to a New York University dental student, keyboardist-to-be Bruce Milner (b. May 9, 1943).

"I was a Cabana Boy at this beach club, on the shore, in Brooklyn, that my parents went to," explained Dr. Bruce Milner in an exclusive interview. "God, you know how many years ago? . . . It was the Dovell Cabana Club, in Sheepshead Bay, Brooklyn. It was '65, and I was in this *a cappella* group—no name; sang '50s stuff. Larry and Denny were hired to walk around and serenade. We had a mutual friend and without thinking we

decided to get together as a group. Against my family's wishes, I went out and bought an organ."

The threesome hit it off, and by year's end, two theater majors, drummer Christopher "Chris" Augustine (b. Apr. 25, 1941) and bassist Schuyler "Sky" Larsen (b. Feb. 19, 1947), were added. Chris had acted in New York's Shakespeare Festival and the American Playwrights' Festival in Maine; since the age of 11, Sky had been making money in TV commercials. All the guys were New York—born and bred, and each of them looked as squeaky clean as the boy next door.

During this time, the group was approached by Peter Leeds. "Leeds was impressed, saw himself as a manager, and wanted to get involved with us," said Milner. "Later, he was involved in an off-track betting scandal. He didn't do right by us; had power of attorney and when the royalties came, he kept them. He was a cheerful, confident guy; maybe he managed others. He was dashing, a ladies' killer."

Leeds connected them with noted songwriter/producer Wes Farrell. Wes, who had written "Boys," "Come a Little Bit Closer," and "Hang on Sloopy," signed them to his Senate Record Productions and cut 12 sides on the band. Included at Wes' suggestion was a cover version of the Rare Breed's bubble-gummy "Come on Down to My Boat."

Industry legend has it that five major labels grappled to acquire the rights to the Sons sounds. MGM won, and hastily issued the *Every Mothers' Son* album and "Come on Down to My Boat." Image-constructing ads—playing on the boys' natty neckties and closely cropped hair—depicted Every Mothers' Son as cheerful, clean, courteous, friendly, healthy, kind, and loyal. Their "Boat" single cruised up the charts, and the future looked bright for this wholesome bunch.

During the "Summer of Love," at a outdoor festival in Berkeley, they played alongside JANIS JOPLIN and Jefferson Airplane. "I went out on stage in this white suit," said Milner. "I had to be the only guy in Berkeley wearing a suit and tie to this thing!

"Right there from the start, they packaged us. We weren't really that 'squeaky clean,' as you say. It was Peter's package; Peter's idea that we wear . . . straight-looking clothes. The name—Peter's idea—it came from Shakespeare's 'Midsummer's Night Dream.' Now, this got old fast—especially for Denny and Larry . . . after San Francisco. We just didn't want to do it anymore."

As so often happens, instant success created instant dissension within the group. Rather than follow Leed's lead and Wes's

paternal advice, the Larden boys decided to produce and record their own tunes.

"Larry and Denny were more interested, it seems, in putting out their own material. I always felt if we had just listened to Wes, we could have followed things up better than we did," says Milner.

Three further 45s made *Billboard*'s Hot 100, but each one sold more poorly than its predecessor. By 1969, the group was relegated to playing small halls, high school hops, and hole-in-the-wall clubs.

"We wound up playing a senior prom in Connecticut in 1969," Milner said. "It was embarrassing; playing for drunks. That was the last time we played together."

Dennis Larden continued to rock and roll. In addition to supplying back-up vocals for Keith Moon's *Two Sides of the Moon* (1975) album, Dennis, for much of the '70s, played guitar for Rick Nelson's Stone Canyon Band. Sky Larsen is a bus mechanic in Pennsylvania. Chris Augustine was spotted in the late '70s as a contestant on "The Dating Game."

Dr. Milner still gives thoughts to his rock'n'roll days. "I don't have one thing from those days; not one tape, no photos, no TV clips, anything. I'm looking, but I can't find anything; yet people remember us fondly. As for the guys—I never speak to them, but I would love to get together just for one night and play. Just for one show; I dream about it sometimes."

MUSIC EXPLOSION
A LITTLE BIT OF SOUL
(John Carter, Ken Lewis)
Laurie 3380
No. 2 *July 8, 1967*

"Volcanic, eruptive, explosive, . . ." the publicity puds at Laurie Records spared no superlatives in their claims for these manipulated music-making teens from Mansfield, Ohio. Per those puds, the Music Explosion were to be the next great thing to overwhelm the fickle rock and roll *haut monde*.

Before their destruction, they did leave humanity with "A Little Bit of Soul," in hindsight a mammoth moment in the audio annals of vinyl popdom.

"If there's a beginning to this story, it was when "Tudor" [Don Adkins] and I became friends," said Rick Nesta in an exclusive interview. "We were neighbors. This is Mansfield, Ohio, 1963. We became basketball buddies; hung out together. His family was from West Virginia; Dad played guitar, but not a lot. So, guitars were around. One day he played this riff. . . . It was cool. He got serious about playing. I figured, I should, too. Before long we were playing in bands."

Just as the Beatles were beginning to happen, Tudor and Rick got their first act together. "The line-up keep

changing, because of the draft, but it started to get good in '63," said Nesta. "There was me [rhythm guitar], Tudor [lead guitar], Jim Pfayler [keyboards] and Tim Corwin [drums], both [later] of the Ohio Express, and Jim Gibson [bass]. We were the Kings' English. Then, as bands go, someone gets mad at someone and they went off to be Sir Timothy & The Royals, later the Ohio Express, and me and Tudor became the Chosen Few, then the Music Explosion."

In addition to Tudor and Rick, the Explosion was Burton "Butch" Sahl, a folkie guitarist turned bass and keyboardist, a ultra-young kid named Dave Webster (replaced after the initial "Little Bit of Soul" session by Bob "Avery" Tousignant), and an "old guy," a vocalist named Bob Hallenbeck. "Bob got drafted, and we came across this band, the Lost Children. Fabulous. Their singer was Jamie Lyons, real animated, tremendous voice, genius with working girls; a Mick Jagger. He had all the moves. We told him to ditch the band and to join us. We played a few Stones tunes and he joined."

By 1966, the Explosion had a statewide following playing gritty Rolling Stone-like tunes. Andy Apperson, a business associate of the aspiring production team of Jeff Katz and Jerry Kasenetz, spotted the act and encouraged the guys to scrape up some money and venture to New York City for an audition.

"We went. It was the summer of '66; just graduated from high school. Jeff and Jerry took us to this little rehearsal studio," said Nesta. "Nothin' fantastic. A rented room. Heck, we were living cheap; had two, three hundred dollars and all of us were set to live and eat on it for two weeks. So, we had nothin'; they had nothin'. They had us play what we knew; saying 'Keep playing till we say, "Next."' We went through 20 songs. They liked 'The Little Black Egg' alot; had us play it three times. The Nightcrawlers had had a local hit with it, but we played it with more grip and a 12-string."

Jeff and Jerry gave them some demos to study and practice; among them "A Little Bit of Soul." "It was written by these two guys in the Ivy League," said Nesta. "It was a folk version, sung like a 'Puff the Magic Dragon,' with a flat-top guitar. It was a chordy song; nothin' special. Tudor or Burton—one of 'em—came up with this riff. Jeff and Jerry liked it, and we cut four sides."

With BOBBY BLOOM present, Ritchie Cordell playing keyboards, the Explosion recorded quickly at the A-1 Sound Studio on 8th Avenue. When there were no takers on the first release, "Little Black Egg" was issued on Katz-Kasenetz's Attack label. The disk was a big regional hit; encouraging Kapp Records to acquire and issue the original by the Nightcrawlers; which scored on *Billboard*'s Hot 100 (#85, 1967).

"A Little Bit of Soul" was a hard sell initially. "Laurie Records issued it, but reluctantly," said Rick Nesta. "They didn't figure it for a hit; but Jeff and Jerry really

hustled it. It sold well locally, again, but nothing nationally. We had this meeting at my house and Jerry said they had done all they could. He did have some friends out in California in radio and he said 'Well, if you guys give me the funds for a plane ticket, I'll go out there and give it a last shot.'"

The band did scrounge up the money; and the record did click first in L.A., then Phoenix. All was oh so well in paradise; but only for what in the course of life is an instant. "Here's the rub," said Nesta, "'Beg, Borrow and Steal' was to be our follow-up. We'd been doing it; great song. Rare Breed had recorded it. Jeff and Jerry wanted us to put our name on the record. They didn't want to rerecord it. We said, 'No way.' They told us they'd give us part of the action if we'd find a band to tour with 'Beg, Borrow.' That's when we thought of Sir Timothy and that's when they became the Ohio Express. They were really quite a good band; but were treated really just like a touring group. They never got to record as they should have."

"Sunshine Games" charted marginally (#63, 1967). "It never translated well from the studio to the car radio. It lost something. Jeff and Jerry—Super K Productions—were always pushing for us to go the bubble-gum route, and we wanted to be more gritty and do mystical things. Now, while we're on the road they wanted Jamie to come in to put his voice on these prerecorded tracks. When we asked them, they'd say, 'It's nothing just a project.' Then they'd put out whatever they wanted without the rest of us even being involved. It was their way of doing things . . . it was getting away from us . . . it was the beginning of the end."

The Explosion returned to the listings once more, but few noticed. As part of "The Super Guys," Jeff and Jerry's Kasenetz-Katz Singing Orchestral Circus, billed "the world's first all rock orchestra"—a composite act comprised of the Explosion, 1910 Fruitgum Band, the Ohio Express, Professor Morrison's Lollipop, and the Shadows of Knight; plus dancers and strobe lights—they performed at Carnegie Hall in a two-hour "rock vaudeville" show in June of 1968. As such they hit it big with "Quick Joey Small" (#25, 1968). an album and further 45s were issued, though the act's name was changed to Kasetz-Katz Super Cirkus when contractual problems arose between the assembled groups.

"The last performance of Music Explosion was this high school in Akron. It was January 1969 and Avery and I were the only guys left. Tudor was drafted; Jamie was gone. Burton quit; he didn't like the guys that were being brought in to fill the spaces. Jerry came up to me said, 'We're puttin' a new record out—"Gimme, Gimme, Good Lovin'"—with you guys and callin' it Crazy Elephant. We're just gonna go with it and make what we can with it; that's that.' That was a polite way of firing a guy."

As directed, what was left of the Explosion—minus Nesta—toured as Crazy Elephant. Laurie Records issued a few sides with Jamie and a studio group as the Jamie Lyons Group. In 1973, Jamie returned with a one-off album and a real group, The Capitol City Rockers, but the Rockers fizzled fast. In 1991, Nesta and all of the original Music Explosion reformed—with the exception of Avery—for local gigs and nostalgia shows.

BILL COSBY
LITTLE OLE MAN (UPTIGHT–EVERYTHING'S ALRIGHT)
(Sylvia Moy, Stevie Wonder, Henry Cosby)
Warner Bros. 7072
No. 4 *October 14, 1967*

A phenomenon . . . Bill Cosby. What's left? He was the production seer and "acting" head of the house on one of TV's biggest blockbusters, the top-rated NBC sitcom "The Cosby Show." He is one of TV's most sought-after commercial pitchmen—he has plugged away for Coca-Cola, Ford, E. F. Hutton, Jell-O, Kodak, and Texas Instruments. He is also a pack-'em-in stand-up comedian, with a 1988 asking fee of $250,000 a night; a TV star with a history ("I Spy," "The Bill Cosby Show," "The New Bill Cosby Show," and "Cos!"); a successful author (*Fatherhood*, *Time Flies*); a movie star (*Uptown Saturday Night*, *California Suite*, *Hickey and Boggs*, *Leonard Part 6*); and a whole lot of fun.

Time magazine has noted that solid-gold Cosby has dominated the media like no star since the days of Lucille Ball and Milton Berle. His earnings for 1987 were estimated at $57,000,000, making him at that point the highest-paid entertainer on the face of the earth. Perhaps no performer in history has or ever will be as successful as Bill Cosby, but in terms of Top 40 success, Bill is but a one-hit wonder.

In terms of album sales, Cosby was the hottest comedian of the '60s: his first seven comedy albums, recorded from 1965 to 1968, were all million-sellers. Three of these LPs even went platinum—*I Started Out As a Child* (1965), *Wonderfulness* (1966), and *Bill Cosby Is a Very Funny Fellow, Right!* (1966). "Little Ole Man," a novelty number based on a Stevie Wonder tune, was his only single to crack the Top 40. Cosby's funny-boned follow-ups, though less successful, still made the Hot 100 listings: "Hooray for the Salvation Army Band" (#71, 1967), "Funky North Philly" (#91, 1968), "Grover Henson Feels Forgotten" (#70, 1970), and "Yes, Yes, Yes" (#46, 1976).

"When you're younger," Cosby told *Time*'s Dan Goodgame, "you want to be sure that by the time you're 80 years old, you can sit on the park bench and look back and say, 'Man, I did it all. I didn't miss a thing.'"

HOMBRES
LET IT OUT (LET IT ALL HANG OUT)
(Bill Cunningham)
Verve Forecast 5058
No.12 *November 18, 1967*

Hombre roots date back to the '50s and Cover Records in Memphis. "My father was one of the Sun artists that didn't fit in," said B. B. Cunningham, the Hombres keyboardist, eldest brother to the Box Tops' Bill Cunningham, in an exclusive interview. "He was variously Buddy Cunningham or Buddy Blake. His 'Right or Wrong' was the release just before Elvis's 'That's All Right.' Daddy was an Eddy Arnold-like singer, a big band singer and Sun didn't make many records of that sort. After that he did some recording in Chicago and came back and set up a studio. It was there that I got toyin' around with sounds."

B. B. (b. Blake Baker Cunningham, 1942, Panama City, FL, vocals, keyboards, bass) got the chance to have six singles issued by his daddy's label in the late '50s. "We was B-B. & The Six O'Clock Boys. We did 'Scratchin' and 'Trip to Bandstand,' rockabilly stuff. I couldn't get enough Sun Records. I was there in the studio when CARL PERKINS was recordin' 'That's Right.' That stuff was hotter 'an a pistol. . . . They was puttin' black music on white kids, and we was diggin' the rhythm."

For a while B. B. was an accompanist for Jerry Lee Lewis; latter he served time in the Air Force. In 1964, John "Bucky" Wilkin was having success with a pseudo-group, a studio creation called Ronnie & The Daytonas. In a Nashville studio, Bucky, Buzz Cason (a.k.a. GARRY MILES), and tunesmith Bobby Russell (wrote "Honey," spouse to VICKIE LAWRENCE) were creating surf music—"Sandy," "Bucket T," "G.T.O."

"Buck elected to go to college, so a touring Ronnie & The Daytonas group was needed. BILL JUSTIS [Buck's producer] approached Ray Brown, president of National Artist Attractions, about putting this group together. Ray picked Jerry [Lee Masters, an ex-sideman for Charlie Rich, Jerry Lee Lewis (b. 1940, Little Rock, AK, bass)], and he found this Memphis High guy, Gary [Wayne McEwen (b. 1944, Memphis, TN, guitar)]. And there was also Lee Corneau (drums) and Jimmy Vincent (keyboards), for awhile. I took Vincent's place when he dropped out for the service in '65. Shortly after, Lee left and we found this Southside High guy, Johnny [Will Hunter (b. 1942, Memphis, TN)] drummin' in a local club, the Rebel Room; playing with Wayne Jackson and some of the other Memphis Horn/MAR-KEYS characters.

"You wouldn't figure it, but the times were great. I loved that surf music. It was much different than my Jerry Lee Lewis and rockabilly background, but it was energetic; specially "California Bound," and "Little G.T.O."

B. B. and the road version of the group got to record a portions of things as Ronny & The Daytonas, "Hey Little Girl," "All American Girl" . . . But as the road crew got better and better it got frustrating.

"I'll tell ya how it happened; how the Hombres came about . . . Memphis is located in a tri-state area," said B. B. "You got Arkansas across the river, Mississippi to the south, and Memphis being in Tennessee—you got three states close. In Arkansas you can get mixed drinks, so that's where the hot spot clubs were;

THE HOMBRES

just across the river. In Memphis—in the '60s—you couldn't get it; you'd 'brown bag it,' if you could. So, there was this Mexican restaurant over there called Pancho's and Lewis Jack Bergman had entertainment in the club behind—the El Toro Lounge. It was there we played when we weren't on the road. 'Course we weren't makin' more than a $120 a week, but it kept us hot for the next road jobs. We didn't mind workin' for that money 'cause it kept us honed up; we kept our chops.

"The road gigs as the Daytonas was gettin' played out. This is late '66 and the hits weren't happenin' anymore. Ray suggested that when we toured again through Bay Town, Texas, we meet with this producer, Huey P. Meaux. He liked our stuff and said he wanted to sign us to a production agreement. So, we were now able to get away from the Wilkin stigma and gettin' to be our own group. We did five, six, seven songs for him and 'Let It All Hang Out' was one of 'em."

"Let It Out (Let It All Hang Out)," the band's first release and only chart-chumper, was a verbal collage of profound nonsense, featuring a lead vocal that sounded like a funked-up Dylan with a face full of marbles.

"Yeah, it was, wasn't it now," said B. B., the song's creator. "I had the title of that 'un in my mind; my 'back pocket,' we called it. This friend in the service was always sayin' that phrase. He didn't invent it neither, it was just in the wind. What prompted me to write it was Dylan playing on the radio. We heard 'Subterranean Homesick Blues' and realized right there that Bob was really putting these kids on. Shit, man, this junk don't mean anything. I said, 'Hell, we can do that.' Well, we were on the road and ridin' so long, we were giddy. I was noticin' this sewer plant with a wide-lipped curb and a no parkin' sign, then, Joe's Hot Dog stand, and a billboard for Gillette. . . . Put it all together: 'No parking by the sewer sign/hot dog, my razor broke.' Hell, the first verse. After that we realized we didn't need to look at nothin', stuff in our heads was comin' faster than we could write it down."

Against the will of Cunningham and the rest of the boys, Meaux and the record company figured it was best to continue to issue silly singles. Subsequent singles and cuts bore titles like "It's a Gas," "Am I High (Boy, Am I High!)," "Mau, Mau, Mau," and "Take My Overwhelming Love and Cram It Up Your Heart." Sales were miserable. A lone album, bearing a cover photo of the Hombres posing as *bandoleros* in a garbage dump, was released and quickly dropped from sight. Shortly after, the Hombres did likewise.

"We were evolving into a good vocal group," said B. B. "That Daytona run was good practice for us, and we *woulda* liked to compare ourselves with the Association. Now, maybe we weren't there yet; though we thought we were. We wanted to come back with something strong and more serious. We woulda had a good shot at it if they'd put out this thing called 'The Prodigal.' It woulda made us legitimate, as a group. Things weren't to be, you know . . .

"I'm not gonna say, I'm sorry I ever wrote it, ever sang it. It's just different and different is a good tool to get ya in the door; as long as ya don't stay that different, or people will think ya just a novelty."

A second album was record, containing more serious, more Association-like songs, but the label passed on issuing the package. The Hombres lasted until the end of 1969, when B. B. and Jerry Lee went into audio engineering; Gary joined the sheriff's department, and Johnny returned to the clubs. B. B. joined Stan Kessler at Sounds of Memphis; later with Rick Hall's 1, 2, 3, Independent Recorders in California. There, B. B. worked sessions for Mac Davis and "discovered" Juice Newton. Currently, B. B. is part-owner of Audio East in Memphis, a 24-track facility. Jerry Lee recording in Muscle Shoals worked sessions for Clarence Carter and Bob Seger. At the Criteria Studios, he worked with the Bee Gees; later becoming the main A & R man at Malacco Records. In the early '80s, Gary became a Baptist minister. In 1976, Johnny Will Hunter died of a self-inflicted head wound.

Larry Raspberry, of THE GENTRYS, encouraged the Hombres to reform in 1991 for Jerry Lee Lewis's birthday party.

ROBERT KNIGHT
EVERLASTING LOVE
(Buzz "GARRY MILES" Cason, Mac Gayden)
Rising Sons 705
No.13 *November 18, 1967*

Robert's (b. Apr. 24, 1945, Franklin, TN) mother died giving birth to his stillborn twin brother. She had been a musician who played various woodwind instruments in local bands; Robert's father taught music at the Tennessee State University. Young Robert took trumpet lessons and sang as a soprano in the Franklin High School choir. When his voice broke, he teamed up with some friends—Pete Hollis, Neal Hopper, Richard Simmons, and Kenny Buttrick—and formed a vocal harmony group, the Paramounts.

On a vacation to New York City in the late '50s, Knight met Jimmy Breedlove, formerly the lead voice for the Cues. Jimmy reportedly introduced the group to Noel Ball—a Nashville TV jock, sometime producer at Dot Records, possible songwriter involved with THE CRESCENDOS and DALE WARD, and manager of ARTHUR ALEXANDER and JOE HENDERSON. Dot issued at least three singles: one by the Paramounts ("Free Me" successfully covered on the pop charts by Johnny Preston), two as solo efforts by Robert. Nothing matched the musical needs of the nation, so the group dispersed.

As a chemistry major, Knight attended Tennessee State University and sang on evenings with the Fairlanes—Daniel Boone and James Tait. In 1967, Bobby Russell (hubby to VICKIE LAWRENCE and Buzz Cason (a.k.a. GARRY MILES) owners of the Rising Sons label, heard the group giving their all at a Nashville night spot. Buzz's buddy Mac Gayden offered to manage and record Knight as a solo act. "Everlasting Love," Robert's first release, clicked like nothing he would ever again record; becoming even a bigger hit the following year in the U.K. for Love Affair (a beat group that featured keyboardist Morgan Fisher, later of MOTT THE HOOPLE) and seven years later in the States, for Carl Carlton (#6, 1974). Yet another seven years and "Everlasting Love" lived again as a Top 40 duet for REX SMITH and Rachele Sweet (#32, 1981). Of a small pile of similar-sounding singles, only two other Knight singles placed on Billboard's Hot 100.

"He should have been a bigger act," said Buzz Cason in an exclusive interview. "I guess we blew it. We maybe didn't cut the right kind of stuff with him. We had him do 'Blessed Are the Lonely' [#97, 1968], then 'My Rainbow Valley'—actually a number one in England, for Love Affair; the same act that covered his 'Everlasting Love.' He may have had another charting record, with 'Isn't It Lonely Together' [#97, 1968]. My memory is fading on me.

"I do remember that, he was hard to record and it became a chore, and we just backed off on him. They liked him over in England and five years later, he got a Top 10 hit with an old cut ['Love on a Mountaintop'] and then 'Everlasting Love' went Top 20 again! He toured over there and could have been big; but he didn't want to leave his job and pick up his family and move there. If he had, he could've been a giant act. Talented guy, that Robert Knight."

When last noted, Knight was a chemist involved in research. He occasionally performs, and releases a single sporadically. Gayden went on to become a member of Area Code 615, record three solo albums, and has been involved in Nashville session work for Hoyt Axton, J. J. CALE, Dave Davies, Kris Kristofferson, DAVE LOGGINS, Tracy Nelson, and Pearls Before Swine. Cason formed the ELF label and the Creative Sound Workshop Studios with Bobby "Honey" Russell; wrote "Popsicle," the English lyrics to KYU SAKAMOTO's "Sukiyaki"; produced the Crickets, Freddy Weller, among others; provided back-up vocals to scads of disks by Bobby Vee, John Denver, and Elvis, and was a studio member/songwriter of Ronny & The Daytonas.

MIRIAM MAKEBA
PATA PATA
(Miriam Makeba, Jerry Ragavoy)
Reprise 0608
No. 12 *November 25, 1967*

Miriam Makeba (b. Zensi Makeba, Mar. 4, 1932, Johannesburg, South Africa) has had more than her fair share of trials and tribulations. In her 1988 autobiography, *Makeba: My Story*, she details her exile from South Africa (1960), several bouts with cancer, the death of a daughter, five marriages (among her husbands were HUGH MASEKELA and Stokely Carmichael), and 11 car crashes. She also describes being blackballed by the music industry following her 1968 marriage to black radical Stokely Carmichael.

Miriam's parents were of the Xhosa nation; she was born in Prospect Township. For eight years, she received a musical education through the Methodist-sponsored Kilmerton Training School in Pretoria. Miriam sang in school and church choirs, and toured in the late '50s with the 11-man Black Manhattan Brothers musical revue. A bit part in an American documentary, *Come Back Africa* (1959)—as a singer in a *shebeen*, an illegal club where blacks are served alcohol—brought Makeba international attention, even though she only sang two numbers in the movie. Concert engagements were soon lined up in Venice, London, and the U.S.

Steve Allen and Harry Belafonte befriended Miriam, becoming her mentors. Reviewing her performance at New York's Village Vanguard, *Newsweek* dubbed her "easily the most revolutionary talent to appear in any medium in the last decade." She recorded one successful album after another: *The World of Miriam Makeba* (1963), *The Voice of Africa* (1964), *An Evening With Belafonte/Makeba* (1965), *Miriam Makeba in Concert* (1967), and *Pata Pata* (1967). "Pata Pata" was issued as a single, and its success took many people by surprise.

"The song 'Pata Pata' was a turning point because it was a hit," Makeba told the *Chicago Tribune*. "I didn't understand why that one became so popular, because it's one of my most insignificant songs. And here I have songs that I think are very serious, and people remember 'Pata Pata.'"

The next year, Miriam followed up "Pata Pata" with "Malayisha" (#85, 1968). She married Stokely Carmichael, the controversial black-power activist, with disastrous consequences. "My marriage to Stokely didn't change my life—it just made my career disappear in [the U.S.] and England! I don't know why people did that to me.... I married him, and then all my contracts were canceled."

Miriam has never stopped singing her mixture of traditional and jazz-influenced pop, nor has she cur-

tailed her political activities. When South Africa was still under apartheid, she had made four appearances before the United Nations to testify against South Africa's racial policies. After a 20-year vinyl hiatus in the U.S., she released *Sangoma*, an album of sacred tribal songs, in 1988.

VICTOR LUNDBERG
AN OPEN LETTER TO MY TEENAGE SON
(Victor Lundberg)
Liberty 55996
No. 10 *December 2, 1967*

At the time of his cultural impact, Victor Lundberg was the owner of a company that specialized in creating radio and TV ads. Hippies were growing their hair everywhere; flower power was in full bloom; there was talk of a generation gap. Who better to address this social situation but someone with the credibility of an ad man? Are you buying this? Someone did. Lundberg's "Open Letter to My Teenage Son" was a pin-headed narrative with advice and optimism and more advice. Some people obviously needed reassurance and snapped up what Lundberg was hawking—"Open Letter" became one of the fastest-selling spoken-word disks in recording history.

Victor was born in 1923 in Grand Rapids, Michigan. He created his own advertising company, worked for five years in the Psychological Warfare Department (aptly enough) during World War II, and became an announcer and newsman at various stations in Grand Rapids, Tulsa, and Phoenix. After his "Open Letter to My Teenage Son" found a soft spot in the wallets and heads of mass America, Lundberg tried to package an entire LPs worth of ninny narratives that would address other important social topics. His marketing stratagem, however, had run its course.

ROSE GARDEN
NEXT PLANE TO LONDON
(Kenny "KENNY O'DELL" Gist, Jr.)
Atco 6510
No. 17 *December 30, 1967*

Rose Garden sprouted in Parkensburg, West Virginia. Diana Di Rose had been a fan of beat poetry, the sounds of bongos, and the aroma of espresso. She performed at such New York night spots as the Bitter End and the Night Owl, and appeared on TV's "Hootenanny." Just how they all came together is not known, but by the end of 1966, Di Rose was part of a band named after her. Rose Garden consisted of Diana Di Rose, drummer Bruce Boudin (b. 1946), bassist/pianist

William Fleming (b. 1949), guitarist James Groshong (b. 1947, Los Angeles), and lead guitarist Johnny Noreen (b. 1950, Los Angeles).

The following year, Di Rose and her Garden group ventured to L.A. to improve their lot and, if possible, get recorded. As luck would have it, they met Charlie Greene and Brian Stone, two hip and hungry hot-shot producers. Greene and Stone were doing studio work for BUFFALO SPRINGFIELD, DR. JOHN, the Daily Planet, the Rising Sons, and a whole horde of other '60s acts.

"Next Plane to London" was an innocent period piece from the pen of Kenny Gist, Jr., who grazed the Top 40 in 1967 as KENNY O'DELL with a peace-and-love single entitled "Beautiful People." With seemingly little effort, "Next Plane" landed on the charts. An album and "Here Today," a Byrds-like follow-up, were quickly pressed. Neither sold well, but it didn't matter: Rose Garden's season had passed, and the group disbanded.

JOHN FRED & HIS PLAYBOY BAND
JUDY IN DISGUISE (WITH GLASSES)
(JOHN FRED, Andrew Bernard)
Paula 282
No. 1 *January 20, 1968*

"We just started out as a bunch of guys that liked black music," said John Fred in an exclusive interview. "Parents didn't like it, but we did. They didn't like us neither; . . . but we didn't care none."

John Fred Gourrier (b. May 8, 1941, Baton Rouge, LA) had been listening to "Sugarboy" Crawford, Smiley Lewis, and the Spiders since he was knee-high. He started his first band—the Playboys, so named for his favorite reading material, *Playboy*—in 1956 at the age of 15; the idea was to work the weekend dances, make some money, and have fun. Three years later, Sam Montel spotted John and his Playboy pack and signed them to his Montel label.

"In 1959, we went down to Cosimo's Studio in New Orleans and recorded 'Shirley' with Fats Domino's band," said John. "That day, Fats was recording 'Whole Lotta Lovin' and 'Little Coquette.' After he got through recording that, I just went right in with his band. We didn't expect nothin'. We just wanted to make records to get more jobs."

"Shirley" charted at number 82. After Montel issued several more singles and the band toured up north and appeared at one of Alan Freed's rock and roll shows at the Brooklyn Paramount Theatre, John—who was the son of Fred Gourrier, one-time third baseman for the Detroit Tigers—decided to put his career on hold while he attended Southern Louisiana College on a basketball scholarship. When he graduated in 1964, John formed a new Playboy Band and cut

THE ROSE GARDEN

a remake of bluesman John Lee Hooker's "Boogie Chillun" for the En-Joy label.

When "Boogie Chillun" began attracting some sales action, En-Joy chief Rocky Robin approached Stan Lewis at the Shreveport-based Jewel/Paula record complex about national distribution. Soon afterward, Fred and his Playboys moved over to Lewis' labels.

"Stan put us with Dale Hawkins [rockabilly legend, known for "Susie Q"] first, but soon let me do pretty much what I wanted," Fred explained. "I got to produce the band. Andrew Bernard, our sax player, did most of the arrangements. We burned. We got some hot cuts put out before 'Judy' got us typecast."

The members of the Playboy Band at time of the recording of "Judy in Disguise' were saxophonist Andrew Bernard (b. 1945, New Orleans), bassist Harold Cowart (b. June 4, 1944, Baton Rouge, LA), keyboardist Tommy "Dee" DeGeneres (b. Nov. 3, 1946, Baton Rouge), trumpeter Ronnie Goodson (b. Feb. 2, 1945, Miami), percussionist Joe Miceli (b. July 9, 1946, Baton Rouge), guitarist Jimmy O'Rourche (b. Mar. 14, 1947, Fall River, MA), and trumpeter Charlie "Spinn" Spinosa (b. Dec. 29, 1948, Baton Rouge).

"Judy in Disguise (With Glasses)" was the group's 16th single. "We were playing in Florida, and all the girls at that time had these big sunglasses. One of the

guys was hustling this chick. She took off these glasses, and she could stop a clock. I said, 'That's it.' That's what gave me the idea." That, and the Beatles' "Lucy in the Sky With Diamonds," said Fred.

Where did John Fred and Andrew Bernard, the song's writers, pick up "Judy"'s bizarre/psychedelic references to "lemonade pies" and "cantaloupe eyes"? "At the time, 'The Monkees' was on TV, and the show's sponsor was Yardley and Playtex," Fred recalled. "I was sitting there and writing words while the TV was on. And they said something like 'Cross your heart with a living bra.' I just wrote that down, too. We first called it 'Beverly in Disguise,' but it just didn't flow, you know."

"Judy" was a weird one, but what a hit—it stayed perched atop the charts for two weeks straight. Though Fred and his Playboy Band tried to repeat the trick, only their immediate follow-up, "Hey, Hey Bunny" (#57, 1968), managed to make the national listings.

"Everytime we put out another record, they'd go, 'Oh, man, this ain't no 'Judy in Disguise.' Well—shit no, of course it wasn't. Paul McCartney told me, 'That's the most unique song I've ever heard.' It wasn't a great song; it was a great record," Fred explained.

"It was problems. We didn't get much promotion and what we did got us miscast. Man, people who did not know of our history thought we were some novelty act; then that album cover made us look like some drum and bugle corp. Here we were doin' tight Wilson Pickett.... We were a white R & B band. We wanted to do what was happening, but didn't get the chance to show our roots. We got cast and put on tours as this bubble-gum thing that we weren't."

In 1969 John and band were signed to Uni. "Uni was gettin' hot. They signed three acts at once—me, Neil Diamond, and Elton John. One of us got lost. Actually, I shoulda stayed with Stan Lewis [Jewel/Paula]."

Fred remained a full-time music-maker until 1976, when he became the vice president of Deep South Records. There, he wrote commercials and did some production work (one notable project: IRMA THOMAS' Safe With You album). Currently, he runs John Fred Music and the Sugarcane record label. In the '80s, he retooled the Playboy Band for performances throughout the South. In the '90s, Fred organized and recorded with the Louisiana Men, a trio comprised of himself, ex-CHASE vocalist G. G. Shin and ex-Uniques vocalist JOE STAMPLEY. Playboy bassman Harold Cowart went on to play bass with the Bee Gees for 10 years and later sessioned for Kenny Rogers, Dolly Parton, and Barbra Streisand.

Fred adds, "'Judy in Disguise' was a once in a lifetime thing. You can never cut anything like it again. That song was us, but we were so much more and most people never got to know that side of us. Hey, what can I say, that song is gonna outlive me."

HUMAN BEINZ
NOBODY BUT ME
(Rudolph Isley, O'Kelly Isley)
Capitol 5990
No. 8 *February 3, 1968*

In 1963, before the Beatles altered planetary history, by appearing on "The Ed Sullivan Show," what was to become the Human Beinz was beginning to gel in The Old Barn bar in Youngstown, Ohio. Members came from bands with names like Dick Nard & The Imperials and Bill Davids & The Rockets; the later outfit made a footnote in rock history when they were utilized in the studio on THE EDSELS' "Rama Lama Ding Dong." At $10 a night per man—stationed at The Old Barn bar but appearing at Mickey's Bar and The Cove and near anywhere—the band line-up came together about the time they preceded the Shadow of Knight in recording the garage classic "Gloria."

On that session and thereafter, the group initially called the Premiers—no relation to THE PREMIERS, known for "Farmer John"—was Dick "Richard" Belly (b. 1947, lead vocals, lead guitar, harmonica), Joe "Ting" Markulin (b. 1946, rhythm guitar), Mel Pachuta (b. 1946, bass), and Gary Coates (drums). "We lost out [to the Shadows of Knight]," said Mel to DISCoveries' Robert Hanley. "The studio was on the fourth floor and we had to haul all our equipment up there. No elevator, nothing! We paid for the studio time and even paid for the records. And, damn, it took them like six months to get us the records." By then the Shadows were high atop the charts with "Gloria."

As the Human Beingz (with a "g") Mel and the rest rapidly recorded remakes of Dylan's "The Times They Are A-Changin'" and Crispian St. Peter's "Pied Piper" for the tiny Pittsburgh-based Gateway label. "We were working Youngstown, Pittsburgh, a lot of Michigan, and even the Chicago area," said Mel. "By '66, the owner of Elysian [Records] wanted to be our manager and to back us. He took us to Cleveland to record [the Yardbirds'] 'Evil Hearted You' b/w [the Who's] 'My Generation' and [THE LEAVES'] 'Hey Joe' b/w 'Spider Man.' 'Evil Hearted' sold pretty well; but 'Hey Joe' didn't do much. From there, we got noticed and got the chance to go with Capitol Records. Gary had left to join the service just before the Elysian session, so we had this new drummer Mike Tateman [b. 1947] by the time we did 'Nobody but Me.'"

It was Tommy Shannenberger, a sales rep with Capitol Records that spotted their singles at the Plaza Record store in Boardman, Ohio, who altered the label about the promising act; later becoming the Human Beinz' manager. "The black stations picked up on 'Nobody but Me' fast," said Mel. "They thought we were black! When they realized we weren't, they dumped it.

THE HUMAN
BEINZ

But by that time the white stations heard it, and it started getting some play there. It was slow moving, but it kept building and building."

With their first 45 for Capitol, and an unimaginatively titled album, *Nobody but Me*, the Beingz were the Beinz. "Belly had came up with the name, and we spelled it with a 'z' to be a little bit different—Beingz," said Mel. "But when we cut 'Nobody but Me' Capitol left off the 'g.' All the records were pressed before we realized it, and it was too late. But when we played anywhere, we put the 'g' back it."

In promoting the 45, they opened for Mitch Ryder & The Detroit Wheels, Paul Revere & The Raiders, Gary Puckett & The Union Gap, and Neil Diamond. "We opened for him in New York, when he was in his 'black period.' He'd sit back stage by himself before going on, and not say a word to anybody."

After a one-off appearance in Japan and a tour with the Beach Boys, Belly announced he was quitting. Shannenberger bought in a then unknown Joe Walsh.

The future James Gang/Eagle star practiced with the band but was put out when Belly decided to remain . . . but only for what would prove to be a moment. "Dick quit for good, then I left the group," said Mel, "and that was it. Ting tried to keep it going, but it was Dick [Belly] that had the voice."

Following their retread of the Isley Brothers' "Nobody but Me," the act only got to release a dusting of Bobby "Blue" Bland's "Turn on Your Love Light" (#80, 1968) and "Everytime Woman." A more psychedelic *Evolution* was issued and retracked. "Without Dick's voice, it was over. 'Hold on Baby' was only released in Japan and it went to number one, but Capitol wasn't about to push a record in the U.S. without a group to promote it."

All of their Capitol sessions took place at the Cleveland Recording Company. John Hanson was there in the studio at the time, and offered his vague memories about the group in an exclusive interview. "I remember the session. The boys were after some kind of sound,

and nobody there knew just how to help them get it. I remember they wanted to multi-track and use feedback, and nobody knew how to handle them. They did have that big hit, so all wasn't lost—right?"

To coincide with the chart success, Gateway compiled their early singles for an album issued as by the Human Beingz and the Mammals. Mel Pachuta has been working the lines at General Motors in a Cordstown, Ohio, plant, performing on the side with his Ohio Boardline Band. "Ting" Markulin put together a group billed the Human Beinz, to record "Nobody but Me"/"Mony Mony" for 3C Records in 1987. Mike Tateman has been spotted selling boats, in Florida. Dick Belly went off to no-one-knows-what in Boulder, Colorado.

"There's talk of us getting together for a reunion," said Mel, "but the only way I'd go back is if Dick Belly comes back from wherever."

LEMON PIPERS
GREEN TAMBOURINE
(Paul Leka, Shelley Pinz)
Buddah 23
No. 1 *February 3, 1968*

They were almost history before they made it. Their 1967 single, "Turn Around, Take a Look," had stiffed badly. Had they not accepted bubble-gummy Buddah Records offer to record one more tune—of the label's choice—the Lemon Pipers (once known as Ivan & The Sabres) would now be remembered by very few people.

Shelley Pinz got the idea for "Green Tambourine" from a newspaper article about a British street musician who would play a number of instruments while seated in front of his receptacle of donations—a tambourine, filled with green. Producer/writer Paul Leka—later to work his winning ways with STEAM, Harry Chapin, The Left Banke, and REO Speedwagon—added the music to Pinz's piece, and before long, the boys at Buddah were excited about the song's hit potential. But first, someone had to persuade the Lemon Pipers to learn it and to get it down on vinyl.

"It was a strange meeting," Leka recalled to Fred Bronson in *The Billboard Book of Number One Hits*. "I played the song on an upright piano they had, and asked [the group] what they thought. They were more into psychedelic songs. They went into the other room, and came out and said they really didn't like the song. I said, 'I don't know if I should say this—you're being dropped from the label. Bob Reno and Neil Bogart [then the president of Buddah] are determined to record this song. You're gonna be dropped if you don't record this.'"

The band—all raised in Oxford, Ohio, except Britisher William Albaugh—acquiesced. Albaugh

(drums), William Bartlett (lead guitar), Ivan Browne (lead vocals, guitar), Reg G. Nave (a.k.a. R. G. Nave, keyboards, green tambourine, fog horn, toys), and Steve Walmsley (bass) entered the Cleveland Recording Studios, where they waxed "Green Tambourine," the *Green Tambourine* album, and a couple of unmemorable sides: "Rice Is Nice" (#46, 1968) and "Jelly Jungle (Of Orange Marmalade)" (#51, 1968). *Jungle Marmalade*, a second and final—though more adventurous LP, appeared in 1968. Sales were sparse; the Pipers were perceived as disposable bubble-gum on the basis of their lone chart-mover.

Guitarist Bill Bartlett would reappear years later as the leader of RAM JAM.

PAUL MAURIAT
LOVE IS BLUE
(Andre Popp, Pierre Cour)
Philips 40495
No. 1 *February 10, 1968*

No one expected fireworks and bliss from the union of Paul Mauriat and an innocent item called "*L'Amor Est Bleu*" ("Love Is Blue"). In 1967, the tune was selected to represent Luxembourg at the annual Eurovision Song Contest. Vicky Leandros sang the number at the festival, where it came in fourth; on record, even recorded in 19 languages, it sold only mildly. No instrumental had topped the American charts in more than five years, and no born-in-France single had ever reached number one on the pop charts. In short, no one expected Mauriat's mood music to pillage the charts, but the dulcet ditty did.

Born in 1925, Paul Mauriat grew up in a house full of music. When he was four years old, Mom and Dad taught him how to have his way with a piano. At the age of 10, when his family moved to Paris, he enrolled in the Conservatoire. And by his 17th year, Paul was leading an orchestra and touring Europe's concert halls. He soon found a nice niche arranging, conducting, and producing artists like Charles Aznavour and himself. In 1962, under a pseudonym (Del Roma Mauruit) Paul co-wrote "Chariot" a major European hit for Petula Clark. The following year—retitled "I Will Follow Him"—the ditty topped the U.S. charts by Little Peggy March.

There is no indication that Paul conceived of "Love Is Blue" as anything more than just another track for his *Blooming Hits* album. The tune remained at the top of the charts for five weeks, as did the LP which featured the song and reportedly eventually totaled sales of 2 million copies. Two further singles, "Love in Every Room" (#60, 1968) and "Chitty Chitty Bang Bang" (#76, 1969) later appeared on *Billboard*'s Hot 100.

GENE & DEBBE
PLAYBOY
(Gene "Gene" Thomas)
TRX 5002
No. 17 *April 13, 1968*

Gene Thomas was born on December 28, 1938, in Palestine, Texas. In his early 20s, he gathered a youthful C & W following with his self-penned rockaballads "Sometime" (#53, 1961) and "Baby's Gone" (#84, 1964). In 1967, while a staff songwriter at the Acuff-Rose music-publishing house, Gene met an aspiring country singer from Nashville named Debbe Neville. Gene had some new SONNY & Cher-type tunes that he thought could make Gene and a female sidekick into a lucrative pop act. Debbe agreed to give the songs a shot, and singer/songwriter Don Gant, before his days with THE NEON PHILHARMONIC, produced the sessions.

"Go With Me," their first folkie-flavored 45, charted at number 78 in 1967, and was followed by "Playboy." Gene & Debbe's future looked bright; they appeared on TV shows and made the nightclub rounds. Later in the year, their third single, "Loviin' Season," reached number 81 on the Hot 100, but only briefly. Nothing the duo recorded would ever sell as well as these disks. Gene returned to his staff position at Acuff-Rose, and Debbe disappeared into the wilds of anonymity.

SWEET INSPIRATIONS
SWEET INSPIRATION
(Dan Penn, Spooner Oldham)
Atlantic 2476
No.18 *April 27, 1968*

It all began in Newark's New Hope Baptist Church, where Emily "Cissy" Houston, her nieces Dee Dee and Dionne Warwick, and the sisters Judy (a.k.a. Judy Clay) and Sylvia Guions (a.k.a. Sylvia Shemwell) became members of the Drinkard Singers. Before evolving into the Sweet Inspirations, the group recorded traditional gospel for RCA.

"Growing up, mine was a pretty narrow road," Cissy Houston—perhaps best known to younger pop fans as the mother of Whitney Houston—recalled to Gerri Hershey in *Nowhere to Run*. "Now I had been brought up strict, to think that all of it, rock and all, was the devil's music. But if God gives you a gift, if he gives you a voice, well, I don't think He's gonna discriminate on how you best put it to use. But I didn't always feel this way. Not at all . . . I suffered a great trauma when I went over [to singing pop music]. But I had three children to raise."

Over the course of the '60s, after some personnel changes, the Drinkard crew became one of the finest—

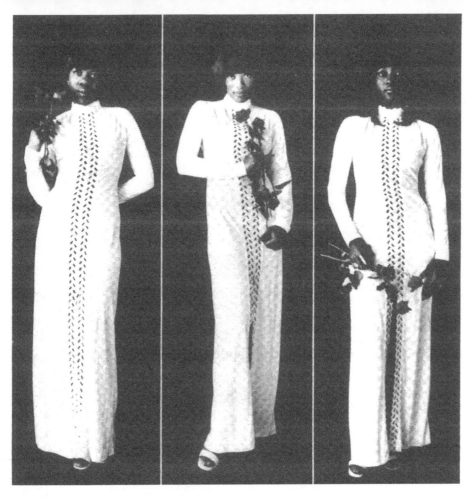

THE SWEET
INSPIRATIONS

and most recorded—back-up vocal groups in the business. Little did they suspect as much when Cissy, Sylvia, Estelle Brown, and Myra Smith did their first secular studio work behind Ronnie Hawkins and a group later known as The Band. For six years, the girls labored behind the scenes spicing and enticing the best performances out of acts such as WILLIAM BELL, Maxine Brown, Solomon Burke, Neil Diamond, Aretha Franklin, Wilson Pickett, and Dusty Springfield. It was Jerry Wexler at Atlantic Records who dubbed them "The Sweet Inspirations" and gave them the opportunity to record their own effort.

"A lot of girls got into doing that kind of session work," Cissy told Hershey. "But once we got it together in the Inspirations, well, nobody could touch us. Except maybe the Blossoms."

Elvis, beginning in 1968 and throughout his much-publicized comeback, constantly drew upon the Sweet Inspirations' vocal talents for his nationwide extravaganzas and Vegas shows. But as soloists—out front and on their own—the Sweets clicked on the Top 40 with only one 45, a tune dashed off by Dan Penn and Spoon-

er Oldham. A few other disks, appearing before and after their big moment, did stir up some chart action— "Why (Am I Treated So Bad)" (#57; R&B: #36, 1967), "Let It Be Me" (#94; R&B: #13, 1967), "To Love Somebody" (#74; R&B: #30, 1968), and "Unchained Melody" (#73; R&B: #41, 1968)—but Cissy and the others never achieved a sustained stardom.

Cissy left the group in 1970 to tour with Darlene Love and Dee Dee Warwick as back-up singers for Dionne Warwick, and soon thereafter, tried her way with a solo career. "Be My Baby" (#92; R&B: #31, 1971) has been her only Hot 100 entry to date; though "Think It Over" (R&B: #32, 1978) and a few others made the R & B listings. In 1981, Myrna resurfaced as co-writer of many of the songs on Beach Boy Carl Wilson's lone solo LP (*Carl Wilson*). Myrna and Sylvia continued on as sessionists, recording a few disappointing solo projects during the '70s; Estelle's position was filled by Gloria Brown, later Pat Terry.

In 1994, Estelle, Myrna, and Sylvia reunited for a series of concerts, including a tribute to Elvis.

BLUE CHEER
SUMMERTIME BLUES
(Eddie Cochran, Jerry Capehart)
Philips 40516
No. 14 *May 4, 1968*

The first truly American heavy-metal band, Blue Cheer was excessive in every way—with their hair length, the volume of their music, and their guitar solos. Their name came from a particular strain of LSD then in vogue. From behind their towering wall of Marshall amps, Blue Cheer, in the words of their manager, could "play so hard and heavy they [made] cottage cheese out of the air."

The *Sturm und Drang* started in Boston in 1967. Bassist Dick Peterson (b. 1948, Grand Forks, ND) was dissatisfied with the off-the-wall psychedelic music that his band, Group B, was playing. He wanted to do more stripped-down and heavier material, so he quit Group B. Dick located lead guitarist Bruce "Leigh" Stephens through a newspaper ad; several drummers came and went before Paul Whaley, a friend of Dick's and a member of a group called Oxford Circle, completed the thunderous trio.

After moving to San Francisco, the band was spotted by Abe "Voco" Kesh. "Voco was a DJ at KMPX, the first real FM underground station," Peterson told *Goldmine*'s Geoff O'Keefe. "Most blues people at the time were saying, 'Oh, man, this [Blue Cheer] is trash. These guys are so loud. Look at the dwarfs.' But Voco liked it. So we went into the studio and we did a tape of 'Summertime Blues,' 'Doctor Please,' and 'Out of Focus.' We gave it to Voco and asked him to play it on his station. He did, and people went nuts! We were getting play every hour. We didn't even have a contract or an album or anything."

That state of affairs changed, and quickly Philips Records signed Blue Cheer to a contract and issued their debut cut—the trio's take on Eddie Cochran's "Summertime Blues." Their debut album, *Vincebus Eruptum* (1968), hit number 11 on the top pop albums chart; their next three LPs—*Outsideinside* (1968), *New! Improved! Blue Cheer* (1969), and *The Original Human Being* (1970)—did not sell quite as well. The group's career momentum stalled when a follow-up suitable for AM radio was not forthcoming.

Meanwhile, personnel problems began to develop. Peterson and Whaley fired their lead guitarist, briefly replacing him with Randy Holden, member of the Other Half. Holden soon departed, so guitarist Bruce Stephens and keyboardist Ralph Burns Kellogg, both formerly of Dot Records' Mint Tattoo, stepped in. That crucial follow-up, "Just a Little Bit" (#92, 1968), was finally pulled from Blue Cheer's second LP—but for many radio programmers, it was a case of too little, too late. This was Blue Cheer's last charting single. Kak guitarist Gary Yoder replaced Stephens and soon Whaley was gone (replaced by Norman Mayell), and so was their trademark sound.

"Those [first] three albums were all done during tours, and we just burned ourselves out," Peterson admitted. "[By 1970] I was the only original member left. . . . I was just fulfilling contracts. I was so frustrated with Blue Cheer and everything that was happening around it . . . I wanted to get away."

After the release of one more album (*Oh! Pleasant Hope*, 1971), minus still more members, Peterson shut down the band to become a baker. Paul Whaley was spotted in the mid-'80s making pizza in San Francisco. Bruce Stephens, who is now married to Peterson's ex-wife and works as an electrician, recorded one solo LP (*Watch That First Step*) in 1982. Ralph Kellogg is a producer and owner of the Radio Tokyo Studios. Leigh Stephens, who currently runs a thoroughbred horse ranch in California, issued two solo albums, one LP as part of Silver Metre, and two albums (with the accompaniment of Bruce Stephens) as part of Pilot (not PILOT, of "Magic" fame).

In 1979, and again in 1984, Peterson formed a new Blue Cheer band. Megaforce Records released an album, *The Beast Is Back . . .* , in 1985, but soon the group was extinct again. Dick joined Motown's Foxtrot. In 1990, a package called *Blitzkrieg Over Nuremberg* brought the Blue Cheer name back to some lips—notably appreciators of the Seattle grunge guitar sound.

HUGO MONTENEGRO
THE GOOD, THE BAD AND THE UGLY
(Ennio Morricone)
RCA Victor 9423
No. 2 *June 1, 1968*

Hugo was born in 1925 and raised in New York City. He attended the city schools, and after a two-year stay in the Navy where he arranged for Service bands, graduated from Manhattan College. Montenegro was for some years the staff manager for André Kostelanetz, the conductor for Harry Belafonte sessions, and (starting in 1955) a purveyor of easy-listening music. None of Hugo's mellow recordings—such as *Bongo's and Brass*, *Pizzicato Strings*, and *Montenegro and Mayhem*—made the top pop albums chart until the release of *Original Music From "The Man From U. N. C. L. E."* in 1966.

Montenegro moved to Los Angeles to do film work, eventually creating and conducting the scores for Otto Preminger's *Hurry Sundown* (1967) and *The Ambushers* (1968), Elvis' *Chario* (1969) and the John Wayne flick *The Undefeated* (1969). In 1967, he undertook what he

thought would be his last project for RCA—*Music From "A Fistful of Dollars" & "For a Few Dollars More" & "The Good, the Bad and the Ugly."*

Hugo wanted the album to be different and hip. After studying a number of rock and roll disks, he brought electric guitars, a full set of drums, and an assortment of oddball instruments into the studio. On the title track to the final entry in Sergio Leone's "spaghetti western" trilogy, Montenegro used an electric violin (the only one then in existence, played by Elliot Fisher), a piccolo trumpet (played by Manny Klein), an ocarina (played by Arthur Smith, writer of THE VIRTUES' "Guitar Boogie Shuffle" and ERIC WEISS-BERG & STEVE MANDELL's "Dueling Banjos"), and an electronic harmonica (played by Tommy Morgen). The whistler was Muzzy Marcellino, noted for his extensive blow job throughout John Wayne's *The High and the Mighty* (1954). The tune's distinctive grunting was actually Hugo himself, mumbling nonsensical syllables in Italian.

Hugo Montenegro died of emphysema on February 6, 1981, at the age of 55.

FOUR JACKS & A JILL
MASTER JACK
(Marks)
RCA 9473
No. 18 *June 8, 1968*

Here today, gone tomorrow—Four Jacks & A Jill was a fivesome that fit that cliche all too well. One hit, one other Hot 100 charting, two singles, and two albums, and these South Africans were never to be heard from again.

Their eerie "Master Jack" was a bizarre little item, and not just because of its folklike, sucked-clean-and-dry instrumentation. This Jack fellow is apparently a teacher of some mysterious insights that lead singer Glenys Lynne thanks him for imparting. In the song, she repeatedly tells him, "It's a strange strange world we live in, Master Jack," and announces she is leaving him, probably never to return. Glenys sings all of this as if she has experienced ontological reality, has been transformed forever, and is not very happy about the whole matter.

Not content to rest on the despair created by their big moment, the unit that seems to have taken its name from a lackluster 1942 Ray Bolger flick created an ode to an equally wise old "Mister Nico" (#96, 1968). Nico's place of business is about to be torn down in the name of progress, and Glenys laments that no one cares. With Clive Harding (bass), Till Hanamann (guitar), Bruce Barks (guitar), and Tony Hughes (drums) providing a starkly shallow backdrop to this tale, "Mister Nico" sounds like the onset of an existential vacuum.

Formed in the heart of the British Invasion in 1964 as the Nevadas, the Jacks decided to freak out and grow their hair long. Once their new look was in place, the guys became the Zombies (no relation to the legendary English group of "She's Not There" and "Time of the Season" notoriety). At one of their performances, they met their "Jill," Glenys Lynne. She with the angst-ridden voice convinced the fellows that only she should be the one with the long hair. The Four Jacks trimmed their locks and secured a recording contract, soon garnering a homeland hit with "Timothy."

On their post-"Jack" and post-"Nico" recordings, the group seems to have found philosophical grounding: all of a sudden, Four Jacks & A Jill sounded upbeat, the instruments sounded gayer, and their lyrics were less profound. While their popularity continued in South Africa, further success in the U.S. thoroughly eluded them.

FRIEND & LOVER
REACH OUT OF THE DARKNESS
(Jim Post)
Verve Forecast 5069
No. 10 *June 22, 1968*

"I met Cathy in Edmonton, Alberta, at this state fair in the summer of '64," Jim Post (b. Oct. 28, 1939, Houston), the male half of Friend & Lover, recalled in an exclusive interview. "She was a dancer; I was with a folk group, the Rum Runners, on a Canadian tour. When we got there, I saw this wonderful woman jumping off a balcony and two other dancers catching her, and then she flipped five or six times across the stage."

Chicago-born Cathy Conn soon quit her acrobatic activities in order to marry Post. When she began pining for the stage shortly afterward, Jim started teaching her to be a singer. After much practice, some demo tapes, and a few discouraging gigs in awful clubs, the husband-and-wife act landed both a manager and a recording contract as Friend & Lover. A Joe South production of "If Tomorrow" b/w "A Town Called Love" was issued by ABC-Paramount, but sales were minimal, so the label let Jim and Cathy slip away. They played a Playboy Club in Atlanta, toured with the Buckinghams,

and even opened for Eric Clapton's Cream on their last United States tour.

"We went to MGM/Verve and saw Jerry Schoenbaum and said we wanted to sing for him. He said, 'I only take tapes, 'cause I don't want to be impressed by the way you look.' So I said, 'Good, turn around and look out the window.' We sang this song—probably only the fourth thing I had ever written—called 'Reach Out of the Darkness.' He liked the idea."

"Reach Out" was inspired by Post's experience at a New York love-in. "People were throwing flowers; this was before cops knew that the kids were probably tripping on acid. 'Reach out of the darkness, and you might finda friend/Freak out in the darkness' . . . Wow, man! If you listen, you'll hear one of us singing 'freak out in the darkness' while the other is singing 'reach out of the darkness.' They mixed it way down, but it's in there."

Despite the huge success of "Reach Out," Verve issued only two other Friend & Lover singles—"If Love Is in Your Heart" and "I Wanna Be Free"—plus an album. According to Post, the label "thought and acted like we were a one-record group; that's the way they treated us." Columbia Records offered the two some $222,000 to sign, but Verve wouldn't release Jim and Cathy from their contract. Once they were free, though, they recorded a couple of 45s ("People Stand Back," "Hard Lovin'") as Jim & Cathy for a Chess Record subsidiary, Cadet. Sales of the Cadet sides were next to nil; their career on a downslide, Jim and Cathy divorced.

Jim Post has gone on to record numerous albums for the Fantasy, Mountain Railroad, Flying Fish, and Freckle labels (the title of his Freckle effort: *The Crooner From Outer Space*). Since 1988, Post has been promoting *Galena Rose*, a one-man play that he wrote and produced. Reviews have been quite favorable.

RICHARD HARRIS
MACARTHUR PARK
(Jim Webb)
Dunhill 4134
No. 2 *June 22, 1968*

In 1993, syndicated columnist Dave Berry asked his readers to tell of their most hated song. The winner—writer Jimmy Webb and "singer" Richard Harris's "MacArthur Park."

If Webb had gotten his way, the tasted tune would never have gotten into Harris's mouth. Jimmy's oblong ode was intended to be a 22-minute cantata that he wanted recorded by the Association. The opus was to fill a side of an LP and be sliced into singles. "I set up a meeting with Jimmy and the Association, and he played the cantata for them on the piano," said producer Bones Howe to authors Bruce Nash and Allan Zullo. "It was a

wonderful piece of music. After he left, the group met with me and said, 'Any two guys in this group could write a better piece of music than that.'"

In 1967, Richard and Jimmy became fast friends; with the former inviting the later to trek with him to Ireland to hit pubs. Back in Harris's London abode, Jimmy played his yet to be recorded tunes; among them "MacArthur Park." "He went for it immediately," said Webb to Nash and Zullo. "He must have had some kind of premonition. He fastened on that song and wanted to record it. At the time, I though, 'How adventurous and ambitious of him.'"

Richard Harris (b. Oct. 1, 1932, Limerick, Ireland)—who had never recorded a single before—was educated at the Sacred Heart Jesuit College and trained in drama at the London Academy of Music and Art. He made his acting debut in 1956, and his first film appearance two years later in *Alive and Kicking* (1958). He acted in many notable flicks, including *The Guns of Navarone* (1961) and *Mutiny on the Bounty* (1962), but attained international notoriety with his role in *This Sporting Life* (1963). He received an acting award from the Cannes Festival for his performance, and was nominated for an Oscar. Four years later, Harris played King Arthur in the film version of *Camelot* (1967).

Do inquiring minds still want to know? It has been near 30 years since we first heard of this poor cake that was left out in the rain: "I don't think I can make it/'Cause it took so long to bake it/And I'll never have the recipe again, oh, no." Richard Harris' seven-minute singing sensation seemed so sincere and ever so impassioned. But what was this tune all about?

"The song is about a girlfriend of mine," songwriter Jimmy Webb (creator of the more fondly remembered "Up Up and Away" and "By the Time I Get to Phoenix") told Joe Smith in *Off the Record*. "You associate a place with a person. You spend a lot of time there with that person, and when the relationship ends, you do a lot of thinking about that place. That's what 'MacArthur Park' is all about. I used to go there [to a park at the end of Wilshire Boulevard in Los Angeles] and have lunch. That's where the cake comes from. 'Sitting in the park on a bench eating cake.' The image is, the rain comes, and the whole thing is going, or melting, and then it's gone."

Okay, one of the pop world's perplexing mysteries has been solved, and right from the horse's mouth. Sometimes things are much simpler than they seem.

Harris, not primarily known for his vocal chops, did manage to sustain a recording career of sorts with more Webb creations like "The Yard Went on Forever" (#64, 1968), "Didn't We" (#63, 1969), and "My Boy" (#41, 1972). He also recited his way through best-selling spoken-word albums like *Jonathan Livingston Seagull* (1973) and *The Prophet by Kahlil Gibran* (1974). His

post-popdom screenwork includes *A Man Called Horse* (1970), *Cromwell* (1970), *Robin and Marian* (1976), *The Cassandra Crossing* (1977), *Gulliver's Travels* (1977), *Orca* (1977), *Tarzan the Ape Man* (1981), *Triumphs of a Man Called Horse* (1982), *Martin's Day* (1984), *The Return* (1988), *Mack the Knife* (1989), and *The Field* (1990), for which he was nominated for an Oscar.

As for Jimmy Webb's little cake, the drenched dessert reappeared on the Hot 100 via renditions by Waylon Jennings (#93, 1969), The Four Tops (#38, 1971), and Donna Summer (#1, 1978).

Legend stands that Richard and Jimmy had a falling out after "MacArthur Park"—which Harris unconscionably sings as "MacArthur's Park," from begin to end—became a hit. The actor promised the tunesmith his Rolls Royce if the record went Top 10. After the disk peaked at number two, Harris is reported to have offered Jimmy a different Rolls Royce. Jimmy was ticked, wanting what was promised, and the two ceased to communicate for years.

PEOPLE
I LOVE YOU
(Chris White)
Capitol 2078
No. 14 *June 22, 1968*

Success comes too late for some. Such was the case with the Zombies, the British group that originally wrote and recorded this powerful gem in 1965. By the time the group crashed the Top 10 with "Time of the Season," the Zombies were no more. Jeoff Levin (guitar/vocals)—fresh out of the country-leaning Pine Valley Boys, a group that included David Nelson later with New Riders of the Purple Sage renown—surrounded himself with Larry Norman (vocals), Gene Mason (vocals), Albert Ribisi (keyboards), Robb Levin (bass), and Denny Friedkin (drums). The San Jose sextet cut a demo of the two-year-old Zombie flop, and in a wink, Capitol packed and shipped a finished version.

Any pop fan who had heard the Zombies creation, with all of its soul and polish, must have wondered how People's version could have outstripped the original in popularity. People never again made the Top 40, or even the Hot 100. Capitol issued three more singles, Paramount released four, and in 1971—with the issuance of "Chant for Peace" on Polydor—People apparently called it quits.

Ironically, each of People's successive post-Capitol sides was an artistic improvement over its predecessor. By the time the group switched over to the Paramount label, the unit had developed a tight sound and moved beyond its previously limp arrangements. Not many people were listening, however, and People's third and

For the next two years, Cliff made audition tapes for a producer named Jimmy Rogers. In the company of Benny Williams (bass), Bobby Tucker (lead guitar), and Tommy Soul (drums), Nobles hooked up with producer Jesse James and Phil-L.A. Records. The second release for the label, "Love Is All Right," was a tight, soulful item fleshed out with brass sounds from future members of MFSB. On the flip side was the filler—"The Horse"—which was nothing more than "Love Is All Right" with Cliff's vocal track scraped off. Cliff does not play an instrument, so in effect, Cliff was not even on what became his only Top 40 moment. A Florida DJ played the wrong side of the record, and within a week, 10,000 copies of "The Horse" were sold in Tampa alone.

Two more instrumentals credited to "Cliff Nobles"—"Horse Fever" (#68, 1968) and "Switch It Only" (#93, 1969)—followed, but Cliff's voice was yet to be heard, again. After "The Horse" galloped up the pop listings, Rogers compiled some pre-"Horse" tracks as an album for Moonshot Records called *Pony the Horse.* Although Nobles sings on only three of the cuts (none of which show the man in his best light), record collectors to this day will pay more for this elusive album than for Cliff's own LP, entitled (naturally) *The Horse.*

"This Feeling of Loneliness," featuring the voice and the billing of Cliff Nobles, did reach and make a moderate placement on the R & B charts in 1973 (#42).

last album, *There Are People and There Are People,* remains a sought-after collector's item.

CLIFF NOBLES & CO.
THE HORSE
(Jesse James)
Phil-L.A. 313
No. 2 *June 29, 1968*

No one—not the tiny record label, not Cliff, not even Cliff's mama—could have figured that this "Horse" thing was going to be a big hit. Heck, the tune was what's called in the recording profession a throwaway. Not that the recording was not done with the finest of care and enthusiasm, but "The Horse" was an instrumental intended as the flip side of a single. Poor Cliff—his one big moment, and he doesn't appear anywhere on this contagious little number!

Cliff was born in Mobile, Alabama, in 1944. From early on, he sang in the church choir, and before his move to Philadelphia in 1965, Cliff was already quite well known in his hometown as a gospel singer. Within months of this move, Nobles was signed to Atlantic Records; he cut three singles, but each one fell on deaf ears.

MERRILEE RUSH & THE TURNABOUTS
ANGEL OF THE MORNING
(Chip Taylor)
Bell 705
No. 7 *June 29, 1968*

"The day I wrote 'Angel,' I was fooling around with some chords for about three or four hours," Chip Taylor told Bob Shannon and John Javna in *Behind the Hits.* "But nothing came out. So I took a little break, and still nothing came out. Then all of a sudden, out of nowhere, came 'There'll be no strings to bind your hands, not if my love can't bind your heart.' I said, 'What the hell is that? That is beautiful'. . . . Within 10 minutes I'd written the whole song."

Chip is legendary for his oddball C & W solo albums; for compositions like "Wild Thing," "I Can't Let Go," and "Step Out of Your Mind"; and for his part in the folk-rock duo JUST US. Taylor had penned "Angel of the Morning" for Evie Sands, one of rock and roll's unsung singing sensations. "Angel," issued on the

Cameo label, was going to make her a star. The record company, however, went bankrupt, and Evie's single died along with it.

Seattle-born Merrilee Rush had been taking piano lessons since she was knee-high. After 10 years of classical training, the 13-year-old joined a local band called the Aztecs, then assembled the first of her bands, Merrilee & Her Men, a year later. ("She played piano and sang like wild," hometown DJ Pat O'Day wrote in the liner notes to her first solo album in 1968.) In 1962, Merrilee joined Tiny Tony & The Statics, recording for the Seafair/Bolo labels and playing clubs, hops, and dives.

Merrilee was soon fronting a new group, the Turnabouts, which consisted of bassist Terry Craig, drummer Pete Sack, guitarist Carl Wilson, and saxophonist Neil Rush. After catching one of their performances, Paul Revere set up a managerial relationship with Merrilee and company; featured them on Raiders' tours; had them booked as a semi-regular act on Dick Clark's "Happening '68" TV program; and secured a production deal for them with Tommy Cogbill and Chips Moman. Bell Records issued "Angel of the Morning," and it became that million-seller Evie Sands would never see.

Despite two fine follow-ups—"That Kind of Woman" (#76, 1968) and "Reach Out" (#79, 1968)—Merrilee was unable to consolidate a high-profile career. Recordings bearing her name surface sporadically; she returned to the Hot 100 in 1971 with "Save Me" (#54). In 1982, the resurrected Liberty label issued a long-overdue solo album.

As for the Turnabouts: Carl formed White Heart (later shortened to "Heart") with sisters Anne and Nancy Wilson. Pete became a real estate broker and currently resides in Tacoma, Washington. Neil lives in the Portland area and runs a floor-covering company; Terry lives and works in L.A. as a studio musician.

In 1981 country-pop singer Juice Newton returned Chip's eerie tune to *Billboard*'s Hot 100, where it peaked at number four.

TINY TIM
TIP TOE THRU' THE TULIPS WITH ME
(Al Dubin, Joe Burke)
Reprise 0679
No. 17 *June 29, 1968*

"I'm the only living artist, probably the only celebrity in the world, who actually is able to duplicate the sound of Byron G. Hardin. He was Thomas Edison's favorite singer in 1902," quoth the not-so-tiny but still very much Tiny Tim to *Record Collector's Monthly*, in 1986. Tim was quite a character, then as for all his life, six foot-one, with his unruly hair, prominent nose, loud clothes,

childlike and seemingly asexual demeanor, ratty-looking shopping bag, ukulele, wavering falsetto—and that featherheaded song (initially popularized by Nick Lucas in 1929), "Tip Toe Thru' the Tulips With Me."

Tiny Tim seemed to sprout up fully formed from nowhere; his past is rather sketchy. As Herbert Khaury (b. possibly Apr. 12, 1930, New York City), he used to perform in the '50s, but was booed quite often. Apparently, audiences failed to understand that "the spirits of the singers whose songs I do are living within me," as Tim explained to *Rolling Stone*'s Jerry Hopkins.

In the mid-'60s, as Darry Dover, Larry Love, later Tiny Tim (a name given him by an agent for midgets), Tim played to increasingly receptive crowds in Greenwich Village coffee-and-bongo spots like the Fat Black Pussycat Cafe. Rowan and Martin's "Laugh-In" and Johnny Carson's "Tonight Show" brought him national exposure; he starred with Paul Butterfield, The Electric Flag, and BARRY McGUIRE in the hippie-era film *You Are What You Eat* (1968). His televised wedding to his true love, 17-year-old "Miss Vicki" (Victoria May Budinger), took place December 17, 1969 on "The Tonight Show," as 35 million viewers watched in wonderment. Their daughter was named Tulip, and they split up in 1977.

"It's important for me to see myself the way others see me—as a freak, a curiosity," said Tim to the *Chicago Sun Times*' Jeff Zaslow. "All of us have to look honestly at ourselves."

The immediate follow-up to Tim's "Tulip" tune was "Bring Back Those Rock-a-Bye Baby Days" (#95, 1968). "Horribly done," groaned Tim to *Record Collector's Monthly*. "Don't mean a thing that it made the Hot 100. . . . 'Hello, Hello' [Tiny's fourth single] was also horribly done. I'm an artist who needs a sketch, and needs time to complete his work. That song was first done in 1922, by Lee Morse . . . I did it in August of 1968 when I was in Las Vegas and when that horrible album *Concert in Fairyland* came out. It wasn't produced by Warner Bros., it was recorded six years before. The owners wanted $25,000 from Warner Bros. to withhold the release, and they refused to pay. It was old studio tracks with a canned audience, and it had 100,000 buyers. That's what killed me in the phonograph business."

Reprise, the Warner Bros. subsidiary, dropped Tim in 1971. Recordings thereafter, were issued but only sporadically and on labels with limited distribution. Some of these, if you can find them, are quite interesting, such as: "I Saw Elvis Presley Tiptoeing Through the Tulips," "Am I Just Another Pretty Face?", "I'm Gonna Be a Country Queen," and "The Hicky on Your Neck." Again in the '80s, he made appearances on TV talk shows, "acting" in the gory slasher flick *Blood Harvest* (1986), working rock and roll revival shows, and touring with Alan C. Hill's Great American Circus.

"Remember it's better to be a has-been, than a never-been," said Tiny to Zaslow, in 1984, when appearing with a boxing kangaroo in a one-night stop in Ottawa, Ill. "It's okay. Whether you're a flash in the pan, like me, or whether you last longer at the top, at least you know you accomplished something. I can go to any library 10 years from now and read the tons of publicity I received. It was wonderful to have been there once."

Added Tim: "People can humiliate you, only if you let them. . . ."

By the '90s, Tiny's situation had improved. "I think this is my 39th comeback," Tim quipped to the paper's Patricia Smith. "I've been trying to record for years." His turn to the alternative scene seemed promising, in a novel way. A new generation gave listen to his workings with the Brave Combo, the New Duncan Imperials and in particular, his redo of AC/DC's "Highway to Hell." "It started out kinda wobbly, but I sold 900 copies in the first week, and that's more than I've sold in 20 years. Who knows? Maybe my future is in heavy metal."

Tiny Tim, who had a history of heart trouble—and was told he might only have a year or two to live—was stricken at a benefit for the Women's Club of Minneapolis. He died of cardiac arrest, Nov. 30, 1996. Tim was 64; possibly 74, or somewhere in between. His widow, Susan Khaury, told the Associated Press that he had just cut short "Tulips" and had told her he was not well. She was trying to help him back to their table when he collapsed. "I don't think he had time to feel pain," she said. "He died singing 'Tiptoe Thru' The Tulips,' and the last thing he heard was applause, and the last thing he saw was me."

SHORTY LONG
HERE COMES THE JUDGE
(Billie Jean Brown, Suzanne DePasse, Frederick "Shorty" Long)
Soul 35044
No. 8 *July 6, 1968*

Shorty was born Frederick Earl Long in Birmingham, Alabama, on May 20, 1940. As a teenager, he listened attentively to the mellow JOHNNY ACE and the wails of Little Willie John, sang at the Birmingham Baptist Church, was tutored by Alvin "Shine" Robinson and the "Father of the Blues," W. C. Handy—he could play piano, organ, drums, guitar, trumpet, harmonica. Before moving to Detroit in 1959, Shorty—so named due to his height, or lack there of; he was 5' 1"—worked as a local DJ, toured for nearly two years with the Ink Spots, and played keyboards at a club called the Old Stable. Some now-collectible sides were issued on the Valley, Tri-Phil, Harvey, and Anna labels.

When Berry Gordy acquired the Tri-Phil/Harvey/Anna family of labels, he also picked up Shorty's contract. "Devil With the Blue Dress On," a self-penned piano boogie complete with a bluesy guitar break, was Shorty's first single for the Motown organization and the debut disk for Gordy's Soul label. This "Devil" did not chart, though years later it proved to be a monster hit for Mitch Ryder & The Detroit Wheels (#4, 1966). "Function at the Junction" (#97, 1966) and "Night Fo' Last" (#75, 1968) did stir up some action before Shorty scored with "Here Comes the Judge," a novelty tune based on a PIGMEAT MARKHAM comedy skit.

After two unsuccessful follow-up 45s—and only two albums—Shorty Long and his friend Oscar Williams drowned on June 29, 1969, during a mishap in Ontario, Canada, when a freighter flooded their fishing boat. Shorty's funeral held on July 2 was attended by Stevie Wonder, who after the service laid his harmonica on Long's coffin.

HUGH MASEKELA
GRAZING IN THE GRASS
(Philemon Hou)
Uni 55066
No. 1 *July 20, 1968*

Hugh Ramapolo Masekela was born in Wilbank, South Africa, on April 4, 1939, the son of a famous sculptor. Hugh's grandmother raised him until school age. He attended missionary schools, and learned how to play the piano by age seven. When he was 13, Hugh saw Kirk Douglas in *Young Man With a Horn* (1950), the film biography of Bix Beiderbecke. His future appeared to him with crystal clarity—within a year, he had his first trumpet.

Masekela played in the Huddleston Jazz Band, until the group's leader—a priest and anti-apartheid advocate, Father Trevor Huddleston—was deported. Hugh formed the Merry Makers of Springs. In 1958, he played in the orchestra for the road company of the opera *King Kong*, which starred MIRIAM MAKEBA (his wife from 1964 to 1966). Thereafter, he toured with the Jazz Epistles (reportedly the first black band to record a jazz album in South Africa), Dollar Brand, and Miriam Makeba.

In 1959, British orchestra leader John Dankworth arranged for Hugh to receive a scholarship to the Royal Academy of Music in London; the following year, Harry Belafonte lined up a four-year scholarship for Hugh at the Manhattan School of Music. In 1965, Masekela formed his own band and started recording on his own label, Chisa. A number of his instrumental albums, then leased to MCA's Uni label, sold quite well—*Hugh Masekela's Latest* (1967), *Hugh Masekela Is*

Alive and Well at the Whisky (1968), and *The Promise of a Future* (1968). In addition to topping the charts with "Grazing in the Grass," Hugh made the pop listings with "Up, Up and Away" (#71, 1968), "Puffin' on Down the Track" (#71, 1968), and "Riot" (#55, 1969). His duet with Herb Alpert, "Skokiaan," registered at number 87 on the R & B charts in 1978.

As for the tune by which Masekela is best remembered, "It was all very contrived," he told *Rolling Stone*'s Gordon Fletcher. "It happened because I came along about the time Herb Alpert was making it big with his 'South American sound,' so MCA figured that they would make me into a black Herb Alpert. I did it but it wasn't what I wanted—I wanted the fulfillment of playing something that was me."

Less than a year later, Floyd Butler, Jessica Cleaves, Harry Elston, and Barbara Jean Love—the Friends of Distinction—did a vocal rendition of "Grazing in the Grass" that went Top 10 on both the pop and R & B listings (#3; R&B: #5, 1969).

PIGMEAT MARKHAM
HERE COMES THE JUDGE
(Billy Jean Brown, Suzanne DePasse, Frederick "SHORTY" LONG)
Chess 2049
No. 19 *July 27, 1968*

The late Dewey "Pigmeat" Markham (b. 1904, Durham, NC) began performing in 1917 in Southern carnivals and medicine shows. He would dance and do a comedy bit with George Wilshire, his buddy and straight man of many years. In the late '20s, Markham and Wilshire came to New York City, making appearances at the Apollo and Alhambra theaters.

For years, Pigmeat would appear "under cork," that is, he would perform with burnt cork applied to his face (a variation of black-face). After World War II, Markham and other vaudevillians ceased to employ this device. Many of Pig's plentiful fans were surprised to see that he was just as dark without the cork as he had been using.

He traveled the 'race circuit' with blues legend Bessie Smith and appeared on burlesque bills with Milton Berle, Eddie Cantor, and Red Buttons. By the 1950s, Pigmeat was one of black America's most successful acts.

Before his death in December 13, 1981, Pigmeat traveled the world, and made numerous TV appearances on shows like "The Tonight Show," "The Ed Sullivan Show," and "Rowan and Martin's Laugh-In."

"Judge" was born of a reoccurring gag line, Markham made on the latter TV program.

STATUS QUO
PICTURES OF MATCHSTICK MEN
(Francis Michael Rossi)
Cadet Concept 7001
No. 12 *August 3, 1968*

For almost three decades now, Status Quo has been dishing out three-chord bone-crunching music, and there's no end in sight. Critics have consistently dismissed the band's trademark sound as low brow and monotonous, but Status Quo has acquired a legion of British fans who don't want them to ever stop playing, though the guys have tried. At the end of their 1984 European tour, and prior to their appearance at the Band Aid concert (1985), members declared that after more than 20 years it was, indeed, all over. But after many such announcements, Status Quo usually returns in their tried and true form to the British charts.

Despite the group's sole appearance on the U.S. Top 40 with "Pictures of Matchstick Men"—an early and atypically psychedelic pop platter—main man Mike Rossi and his rockers have racked up more than 40 U.K. hits (surpassing the Rolling Stones, the Beatles, and the Hollies), making them one of the most successful British groups in rock history. Half of these singles went Top 10, and every Status Quo album issued in the U.K. since 1974 has made the British Top 5.

Guitarist Francis Michael Rossi (b. Apr. 29, 1949, London), bassist Alan Lancaster (b. Feb. 7, 1949), and guitarist Alan Key met in their school orchestra in the spring of 1962. All were 12-year-olds with a desire to make some music, and for a while, they played together as a traditional jazz combo. Keyboardist Jess Jaworski replaced Key, drummer John Coghlan (b. Sept. 19, 1946) stepped in, and the group's sound began leaning toward rock and roll.

In 1965, the Spectres, as they were now known, started gigging around holiday camps outside London. Jaworski dropped out, and his spot behind the organ was filled by Roy Lynes. The Spectres signed to the Piccadilly label and issued three singles—"I (Who Have Nothing)," "Hurdy Gurdy Man," and "We Ain't Got Nothin' Yet." All of them sank without a trace, as did a single credited to Traffic Jam entitled (aptly enough) "Almost but Not Quite There."

By 1967, the group, now called Traffic Jam, was working mostly as a back-up band for Madeline Bell, Tommy Quickly, and a miscellanea of touring U.S. rock and rollers. Steve Winwood of Traffic reportedly complained about the similarity of the guys' new name to his own outfit's moniker. To avoid any possible legal problems, Rossi and Traffic Jam became Status Quo.

Then guitarist Richard Parfitt (b. Richard Harrison, Oct. 12, 1948, Woking, Surrey) joined the group, and Status Quo recorded "Pictures of Matchstick Men."

Before that bashin'-boogie trademark style had fully evolved, Lynes quit the band. Several similar-sounding follow-ups were cut and canned: "Ice in the Sun" (#70, 1968), "Technicolor Dreams," and "Black Veils of Melancholy."

The group persisted on a pile-driving path through the '70s and '80s. Coghlan retired in 1982, and their line-up has shifted repeatedly over the years, with Rossi and Parfitt as the mainstays. At various times, keyboardist Andy Bown, bassist John Brown, ex-Original Mirrors guitarist Pete Kirchner, and ex-Climax Blues Band drummer Jeff Rich have been touring and/or recording members. Toward the end of the decade, Status Quo went through some label changes; releases are now more sporadic, and sometimes are not even issued in the States.

In October 1991, Status Quo made history—being entered into the *Guiness Book of World Records* for completing four charity concerts in four different British cities in a 12-hour period. "Come on You Reds," a single cut with league football champions, Manchester United, returned the group to the top of the U.K. charts in 1994. The group and their head-banging brand of boogie still prevail.

MASON WILLIAMS
CLASSICAL GAS
(Hank Snowball)
Warner Bros. 7190
No. 2 *August 3, 1968*

At Oklahoma City University, Mason Williams (b. July 24, 1936, Abilene, TX) studied mathematics and music. After classes, he played guitar and sang in folk clubs, briefly joining up with the Wayfarers Trio. Following a stint in the Navy, Mason took up folksinging full-time. At a coffeehouse in L.A., he met the Limeliters' GLENN YARBROUGH, who introduced him to Tommy Smothers. Mason and Tommy became good friends, and eventually shared an apartment together.

Williams joined the Smothers Brothers' back-up band, penned tunes for the clean-cut but controversial duo, and even wrote some comedy material. Johnny Desmond, GALE GARNETT, the Kingston Trio, and Claudine Longet recorded some of his compositions. Esther and Abi Ofarim's cover of his "Cinderella Rockefeller" topped the British charts, and Longet's work on Mason's marvel in 10/4 time, "Wanderlove," was a sizable seller in Singapore.

By the release of "Classical Gas"—which he described to *Goldmine* as "half flamenco, half Flatt & Scruggs, and half classical"—Williams was a writer for "The Smothers Brothers Comedy Hour," the highly-popular TV program. Before the brothers' boob-tube

demise and Mason's departure from the show in 1969 for other creative endeavors, Williams won an Emmy for "Outstanding Writing Achievement for a Variety Show." "Classical Gas," his three-minute classic, garnered three Grammys: "Best Instrumental Arrangement," "Best Contemporary-Pop Performance," and "Best Instrumental Theme."

Over the next year, Warner Bros. did a rather brisk business of selling Williams' mongrel music. His first three LPs—*The Mason Williams Phonograph Record* (1968), *The Mason Williams Ear Show* (1968), and *Music by Mason Williams* (1969)—were all best sellers. A few of his singles dotted the lowest reaches of the Hot 100— "Baroque-a-Nova" (#96, 1968), "Saturday Night at the World" (#99, 1969), and "Greensleeves" (#90, 1969).

Mason periodically pops up in the record racks on one label or another. In the meantime, he is certainly not idle. He has had, at last count, seven books published, including such tomes as *The Mason Williams Reading Matter* and *The Bus Book*, and he writes material for Glen Campbell, Petula Clark, Pat Paulsen, Andy Williams, and the brothers Smothers. For a period in the early '80s, he was the headwriter for NBC's "Saturday Night Live."

AMBOY DUKES
JOURNEY TO THE CENTER OF THE MIND
(TED NUGENT, Steve Farmer)
Mainstream 684
No. 16 *August 24, 1968*

"I started playing guitar when I was about six or seven years old," wrote Motor City Madman and chief Amboy Duke TED NUGENT in a self-penned piece for *Hit Parader*. "I got an acoustic guitar from my aunt, and was highly influenced by Elvis, Ricky Nelson, and James Brown songs that I'd heard on the radio. I took about two years of guitar lessons in Detroit at the Royal School of Music. Learned the basics and got into boogie-woogie and honky-tonk. I did my first professional performance when I was 10, at the Detroit State Fair Grounds for the Polish Arts Festival. And I was a sensation."

Detroit-born Nugent (b. Dec. 13, 1948) also formed his first band at age 10, The Royal High Boys. "It was just me and a drummer named Tom Noel," Nugent told *DISCoveries'* Allan Vorda. "The band's name came from this shirt that all greasers wore. We wore it, too, 'cause we were cool. We ended up getting a bass player and that became the nucleus of the Lourds." The Lourds quickly attracted a local following, and even opened a sold-out show in Detroit with the Supremes and the Beau Brummels. (The band's only recorded tracks, three in number, are currently available on a compilation LP called either *Long Hot Summer* or *Friday at the*

THE AMBOY DUKES,
WITH TED NUGENT
(SECOND FROM LEFT)

Cafe a Go Go.) But all that ended when Ted's father accepted a phone-company job in Chicago; the family moved there in 1965.

Once in Chicago, Nugent (lead guitar) formed a group with Greg Arama (bass), Steve Farmer (rhythm guitar), Dave Palmer (drums), and Andy Soloman (keyboards). As Ted explained to Vorda, the "Amboy Dukes" name came from a Detroit R & B band that had recently broken up. "I thought it was a cool name and when I moved to Chicago, I decided to use the name.

Obviously, I learned much later there was a street gang in the '50s from Perth Amboy, New Jersey. And there was this famous novel about the gang called *The Amboy Dukes*, but I've never read it. . . . That's how the original Detroit group got the name."

With graduation behind him, Ted moved his group to Detroit. There, they competed with a budding bunch of local talent like Bob Seger & The Last Heard, Tim Tam & The Turn-Ons, The Rationals, and The Wanted for a recording contract. Mainstream Records, wowed

244

by Nugent's Hendrixlike guitar pyrotechnics, signed the guys and issued their self-titled debut album in 1968. The LP largely eluded public attention, but their quickly-pressed second outing, *Journey to the Center of the Mind* (1968)—plus the 45 of the title cut—were successful enough to launch Ted's rock and roll career.

"When we put out 'Journey to the Center of the Mind' in 1968, it had that pipe collection on the front cover and I didn't have the faintest idea what those pipes were all about! Everybody else was getting stoned and trying every drug known to mankind; I was meeting women and playing rock and roll. I didn't know anything about this cosmic inner probe. I thought 'Journey to the Center of the Mind' meant look inside yourself, use your head, and move forward in life."

How could the obviously drug-related connotations have escaped him? "I have never smoked a joint. I have never done a drug in my life. I've never had a cigarette in my mouth. I don't drink. . . . I watched incredible musicians fumble, drool, and not be able to tune their instruments. It was easier to say no than to say, 'Hey, gosh, that's for me.' I've seen my fellow musicians die."

Nugent's indignant anti-drug stance shaped the short careers of his Dukes. John Drake, a later member, was fired partly due to his inability to meet rehearsal schedules. Also removed was Steve Farmer, whom Nugent described as a brilliant and creative thinker but who was "so high and so irresponsible you couldn't get from point A to point B with him." As for Greg Arama, "heroin took over and I had to get rid of him" (Greg is reportedly deceased). And Drake's replacement, Rusty Day? "He insisted on doing LSD together as a band; after I fired him, he was machine-gunned to death because of a bad drug deal.

"There never really was a break-up of the Amboy Dukes. It just got to be such a revolving door mentally with the musicians. I also took a break in 1973. I was so upset internally. I felt like a baby-sitter! I also acted as a road manager—I used to book the band; I used to maintain all the equipment; I used to change the oil in the cars."

By album number four—*Survival of the Fittest—Live* (1971)—the band was billed as "Ted Nugent & The Amboy Dukes." The following year, the artist credit for their *Call of the Wild* album read simply "Ted Nugent." The Amboy Dukes officially disbanded in 1975, at which time Nugent signed a contract as a solo artist with Epic Records.

According to Ted, John Drake is now a car salesman. Steve Farmer is a conservationist planting trees in Oregon. Robbie LaGrange is a realtor in San Diego, and Andy Soloman is "doing commercials in Philadelphia."

In 1989, Nugent formed the Damn Yankees with Styx's TOMMY SHAW, Night Rangers' Jack Blade, and Michael Cartellone. The act has been quite successful with the Top 10 self-titled album and several singles; notably "High Enough" (#3, 1990), "Where You Goin' Now" (#20, 1992), and "Silence Is Golden" (#62, 1993) from the Jean-Claude van Damme flick *Nowhere to Run* (1993).

BARBARA ACKLIN
LOVE MAKES A WOMAN
(Eugene Record, William Sanders, Carl Davis, Gerald Sims)
Brunswick 55379
No. 15 *August 31, 1968*

Barbara Acklin (b. Feb. 28, 1944, Chicago) came from a musical family. Her grandma was blues singer Asa Eskridge; her cousin was keyboardist/arranger Monk Higgins. Mom and Dad were attuned and hip, so they encouraged Barb to sing her soul out. By age 11, she was a featured vocalist in the choir of the New Zion

BARBARA ACKLIN

Baptist Church. While still a student at Dunbar Vocational High, Acklin sang secular at night spots on Chicago's South Side. When Barbara graduated, Monk Higgins got her a job as a secretary with St. Lawrence Records, where he worked as a producer and recording artist. "When somebody would come in to record and they needed a background singer, I would run in the back and sing," Acklin told *Goldmine* R & B editor Bob Pruter. Monk recorded one single on her as "Barbara Allen," but it fizzled.

Higgins then moved his base of operations to Chess Records, and Barbara followed. At Chess, she sang back-up for Fontella Bass, Etta James, MINNIE RIPERTON, and Koko Taylor. In 1966, Barbara obtained the job of secretary/receptionist for Carl Davis at Brunswick Records, and began writing songs on the side.

"I kept asking Carl to record [me]," recalled Acklin, "and he kept saying 'I will, I will, just keep on writing.' I wrote a tune with another person [The Five DuTones' David Scott, of "Shake a Tail Feather" notoriety] called 'Whispers,' and Jackie Wilson heard the tune and really liked it. He recorded it, and after it became a big hit for him, he told me, 'If there is anything I can do for you, let me know.' I said, 'You tell Carl I want to record!'" Three weeks later, Barbara was in a recording studio. Her first two singles flopped, but a duet with Gene Chandler called "Show Me the Way to Go" (#30, 1968) did moderately with the R & B crowd. Then "Love Makes a Woman" appeared and soared into the Top 40. A number of follow-up solo sides—among them "Am I the Same Girl," later a British hit for Swing Out Sister—and duets with Chandler placed fairly well on *Billboard*'s R & B charts—but none of them could duplicate the success, or recapture the charm, of "Love Makes a Woman."

Disappointed by her lackluster chart showings, Acklin left Brunswick in 1973 and signed with Capitol Records. Over the next few years, three singles and an album—*A Place in the Sun* (1975)—were issued by Capitol. Of these 45s, "Raindrops" (R&B: #14, 1974) sold the best, but these would prove to be her last disks to date. Later in the '70s, Acklin stepped out of the spotlight. "I went out on the road with Tyrone Davis as a back-up singer. Everybody thought I was nuts, but it was a way of staying in touch with the business without a deep involvement."

In 1979, Barbara parted company with Capitol and joined the Chi-Sound label the following year, but no records were released. In the '80s, Barbara Acklin was spotted in the role of road manager for Ike Turner's occasional "Tina" fill-in Holly Maxwell. Barb, also, continues a writing partnership with the Chi-Lites' Eugene Record, that resulted in major hits with "Have You Seen Her" and "Stoned Out of My Mind."

JEANNIE C. RILEY
HARPER VALLEY P.T.A.
(TOM T. HALL)
Plantation 3
No. 1 *September 21, 1968*

Before writing that song about the small-town widow who would arouse local ire for her free-thinking ways, her short skirts, and sexy ways, TOM T. HALL was a traveling DJ and a $50-a-week songwriter. Hall has claimed that Johnson, the heroine of "Harper Valley P.T.A.," was an actual woman whom he had seen as a schoolboy in Carter City, Kentucky. The tune's vocalist, Jeannie C. Riley, was a secretary and a sometime demo singer. Within two weeks of its release, almost 2 million copies of "Harper Valley P.T.A." had been sold, and much had changed for Tom T. and Riley.

Jeannie Carolyn Stephenson (b. Oct. 19, 1945, Anson, TX) grew up dreaming of being a big-time country singer. After graduating from high school and marrying Mickey Riley, her childhood sweetheart, Jeannie convinced her hubby to do what all aspiring country stars do—move to the center of the country-music action. Once in Nashville, Mickey found work in a filling station, while Jeannie struggled as a secretary at Jerry Chesnut's Passkey Music Company. In her spare time, she cut demos for the Wilburn Brothers, Johnny Paycheck, and the folks at Little Darlin Records. She would call home often and tell here mama that someday this little girl would make it big.

Shelby Singleton, Jr., the maverick producer who had acquired Sun Records from the legendary Sam Phillips, was sitting on what he thought would be a sure hit. All he needed was a singer with the right appeal to pull off the tasty nugget about Southern hypocrisy. Then Singleton heard that voice—that of Jeannie C. Riley—on a demo she had made. On the night of July 26, 1968, after Riley had ripped though "Harper Valley" in just one take, she called her folks in Texas and told them that she had just cut a million-seller. Having heard this type of exciting news before, her mother responded with skepticism.

But Jeannie was on the mark this time—sales of her single eventually reached 6 million copies. She became an overnight star, bought a purple Cadillac, polished up her image, and weeks later appeared in a mini-skirt and boots on "The Ed Sullivan Show." She made the rounds of TV talk shows, and won a Grammy in 1968 for "Best Female Country Vocal Performance." Other plaques were presented, photos taken, and concerts given. *The Harper Valley P.T.A.* LP, naturally, sold in massive quantities. A couple of "Sin City"-type tunes made the C & W listings in 1969 and several of her follow-up disks made the Hot 100—"The Girl Most Likely" (#55; C&W: #6, 1969), "There Never Was a Time"

(#77; C&W: #5, 1969), "Oh, Singer" (#74; C&W: #4, 1971), and "Good Enough to Be Your Wife" (#97; C&W: #7, 1971).

All was not well, however. "I wanted to change the image," Riley told Bob Gilbert and Gary Theroux in *The Top Ten.* "I wanted to build a more wholesome image and convince people that I'm not like the heroine of 'Harper Valley P.T.A.' I was just tellin' a story in those songs, but I soon found out people thought that's what I was really like."

A decade after charting, *Harper Valley P.T.A.* (1978) was turned into a successful flick starring Nanette Fabray and Barbara "I Dream of Jeannie" Eden as the sexy widow, Mrs. Johnson. In 1981, Eden repeated the role in the NBC TV show of the same name. Fanny Flag played the part of her friend and ally; George Gobel, the town's main man Mayor Otis Harper.

Things began to unravel for Jeannie, though. As the singer admitted in her autobiography—*From Harper Valley to the Mountain Top* (1981)—she [started] drinking heavily, and her marriage to Mickey Riley ended. The C & W hits slowed to a trickle in the mid-'70s, then stopped altogether in 1976. But by then, Jeannie was a born-again Christian, singing and recording gospel songs.

Mickey and Jeannie remarried in 1976. Her career continues on—being divided between gospel and country recordings.

DON FARDON
INDIAN RESERVATION
(JOHN D. LOUDERMILK)
GNP Crescendo 405
No. 20 *October 5, 1968*

The Sorrows of Coventry, England—home of rugby and the Rolls Royce—were one of the best beat groups around in 1965. Their lead singer, Don Maughn, remembered his mother holding him in bomb shelters during the Nazi blitz; Maughn sang with pain even when singing of love. The Sorrows' "Take a Heart" grazed the British charts and was released in the U.S. on the Warner Bros. label. Despite the Sorrows' haunting and atmospheric sound, none of this futuristic unit's singles ever again charted in England. Early in 1967, the group came apart.

Miki Dallon, the group's manager, was also a songwriter, producer, record company executive, and sometime RCA recording artist. Miki had plans for the Sorrows' mournful 6-foot 6-inch vocalist: he renamed Maughn "Don Fardon" and had him record cover versions of "The Letter" and "Indian Reservation," encasing the soulful lad in both bubblegum and easy-listening settings.

Despite a misconceived orchestral accompaniment, Don's reworking of JOHN D. LOUDERMILK's 1963 lament for the Cherokee Indians, "Indian Reservation," touched home. Paul Revere & The Raiders had a huge hit with it two years later, but "Indian Reservation" was Fardon's only notable release in the U.S. He did have a British hit even before his stateside success, however: "Belfast Boy," a tale of talented, but troubled football player George Best. Five years later, Fardon popped up on the Hot 100 with "Delta Queen" (#86, 1973).

Over the years, Don Fardon continued his relationship with Miki Dallon and his Young Blood label. In 1974, Capitol released a brassy rendition of the Kinks' "Lola." Decca/MCA toyed with the idea of Don recording a prepubescent cover version of CRAZY ELEPHANT's hit, "Gimme Gimme Good Lovin'." Both Don and his manager have recorded solo versions of the classic Sorrows single, "Take a Heart," but nothing much happened with either reworking. (The Sorrows' original rendition and their lone album, 1965's *Take a Heart*, are highly sought-after by American and European record collectors.) When last spotted, Fardon was singing bubblegum material, his vocal talents constricted by antiquated orchestral arrangements.

O'KAYSIONS
GIRL WATCHER
(Buck Trail, Wayne Pittman)
ABC 11094
No. 5 *October 5, 1968*

In 1954, at the tender age of eight, Donny Weaver (lead vocal, bass) started singing around the house. A decade later, a neighborhood guitar man named Jimmy Hennant (b. 1947) joined Donny in making joyful noise. Over the next few years, other O'Kaysions-to-be would join the duo to sing praises of the Lord: Bruce Joyner (drums), Wayne Pittman (guitar), Jim Spidel (sax), and Ronnie Turner (trumpet). Beginning in 1960 as the Kays, they played gospel and, later, country music in the coastal areas of their home state, North Carolina.

By the spring of 1968, they were the secular-singing O'Kaysions, and they had recorded a leering lyric about ogling babes for the peewee Northstate label. Local DJs, appreciating that bird-watching was a popular pastime for their listeners, rode the number as if it had a satin saddle. Sales of the single outpaced the little label's ability to produce the merchandise fast enough, so ABC picked up distribution and gave the O'Kaysions their lone Top 40 moment.

Success was a wearout, said the tune's co-writer Wayne Pittman to the *Washington Post.* "It all went so fast; and it's hard to describe it other than saying it was hard work. Day to day, it was a lot of hard work, because we had to do a lot of promotion of the record. Driving all over the country, flying all over the country. A lot of one-nighters."

Despite the promotion and a few further releases, featuring Donny Weaver's raspy voice, only the immediate follow-up to "Girl Watcher"—"Love Machine" (#76, 1968)—managed to chart. An album was casually tossed together; as Pittman admitted to the *Washington Times*, it was this careless attitude, plus the group's lack of direction, that brought an end to the O'Kaysions. "You had the hippie generation and acid rock, and music was going in crazy different ways. There was no one voice [within the band] saying 'this is the way we should go." The O'Kaysions broke up in 1968.

Wayne is currently fronting a new version of the O'Kaysions. They are working the highways, byways, and backwater bars of the Carolinas, where even now, worn-out copies of "Girl Watcher" can be found on jukeboxes.

THE O'KAYSIONS

CRAZY WORLD OF ARTHUR BROWN
FIRE
(ARTHUR BROWN, Vincent Crane)
Atlantic 2556
No. 2 *October 19, 1968*

"Crazy world" may be a marked understatement when it comes to describing the realm that Arthur Brown inhabits even to this day.

Believe it or not, the genesis of "Fire" as well as Brown's pioneering rock theatrics (i. e. moving stage, outlandish costumes, hideously-painted face, and helmeted head ablaze) was Brown's deep involvement with . . . philosophy! "Ah, philosophy will never touch reality," Brown mused to *Blitz*' Allan Vorda. "It always describes it. It's an idea of what reality is. But reality isn't an idea."

Arthur Wilton was born on June 24, 1944, in Whitby, Yorkshire. He studied philosophy and law at both Reading University and Yorkshire University, and reportedly was a school teacher when the Who's Pete Townshend offered him the chance to act out his deepest and darkest dreams. For years, Brown had been soaking up the sounds of Sinatra, Elvis, Delta blues, New Orleans jazz, Scottish folk tunes, and classical music. Brown and his band— keyboardist Vincent Crane and drummer Drachian Theaker—were indulging in their special brand of musical and visual lunacy at the underground UFO Pub when Townshend spotted the act. He persuaded his manager, the owner of Track Records, to record The Crazy World of Arthur Brown (in 1989, Townshend even included a cover version of "Fire" on his *Iron Man* album).

"Fire" was Brown and company's first release, and their only charting single here or abroad. Success came upon them too fast—constant touring, plus the ingestion of large amounts of mind-altering substances, took a hefty toll on the band. As Brown told the *Chicago Tribune*'s Dave Hoekstra, Crane was dosed with LSD at a party: "For a long number of years, he never came back. He talked in numbers for a day and a half. He had to return to England for mental attention." Drachian Theaker "used to kick his drums offstage during an act; he would run by hotels, pressing his vital parts against the windows! After that, we became unmanageable."

Yes, after that, the Crazy World blew apart. Crane and his tour replacement, Carl Palmer, formed Atomic Rooster; Palmer would later join Keith Emerson and Greg Lake in EMERSON, LAKE & PALMER. Theaker, after a stint with Arthur Lee's LOVE, worked as a percussionist with the Scottish Symphony Orchestra, and now tours Europe with a traveling band of Indian artists.

And Brown? Well, Arthur has been keeping busy with an unusual project or two. After three LPs of increasingly electronic excursions with a new outfit, Kingdom Come, Brown did studio work with Alan Parsons, appeared in the Who's *Tommy* (1975) flick, had some obscure solo albums issued in Europe on the Gold label, and spent some years recording and touring with the technologically-attuned Klaus Schulze. Not one to remain rooted in any one reality for too long, Brown lived in the late '70s in Burundi, Africa, where he reportedly taught music history and directed the Burundi National Orchestra. In the '80s, Arthur took guitar lessons from King Crimson's Robert Fripp, then moved to Austin, Texas, to form a keyboard-based band. When the latter activity proved unfulfilling, he formed a carpentry and painting concern with ex-Mothers of Invention drummer Jimmy Carl Black.

Did the flaky flavor of "Fire" typecast Art Brown as a nut and a novelty act? "Yeah, it was like that. They just thought I made fun records. Most of them still do. I look at it as being extremely lucky, however. Here I am, 20 years after [now nearly 30 years after] I've had a hit, and I'm still in line to get a big record deal. In between, I've been making albums. I've got 15 out, and they vary between sheer electronic, industrial electronic, and electronic synthesizer."

The pending "big record deal" of which Brown spoke was said to possibly involve Jack Bruce, Peter Gabriel, Carl Palmer, Alan Parsons, and African juju man King Sunny Ade. Release was slated for 1990; nothing of the sort has been spotted in the states. Currently available via Blue Wave Records is a collaboration with Jimmy Carl Black entitled *Brown, Black, and Blues*. There is also an anti-nuclear Arthur Brown LP, *Requiem*, available on the Republic label. "It's not something with a heavy message," Art explained to Fred Dellar in *Where Did You Go to, My Lovely?* "There's a conversation between an ant and a cockroach who meet after the world's blown up."

JIMI HENDRIX
ALL ALONG THE WATCHTOWER
(Bob Dylan)
Reprise 0767
No. 20 *October 19, 1968*

James Marshall Hendrix's death on September 18, 1970 dealt a stunning blow to rock and roll fans the world over. An unusually innovative musician, he single-handedly rede-

fined the role of the electric guitar in rock music, inventing a sonic vocabulary still drawn upon by rock guitarists to this day. This psychedelic voodoo child and father of Heavy Metal was also a One-Hit Wonder.

More than a hundred LPs of his music have been issued; many of them were issued posthumously and consist of unauthorized live recordings, studio outtakes, and the like. Several of them have made *Billboard*'s top pop albums chart: *Are You Experienced* (1967), *Axis: Bold as Love* (1968), *Electric Ladyland* (1968), *Smash Hits* (1969), *Band of Gypsies* (1970), and *The Cry of Love* (1971). Yet despite Hendrix's superstar status, his success with Top 40 audiences was limited to but one 45—and it is not, as many would guess, "Purple Haze" (#65, 1967).

Jimi's version of "All Along The Watchtower"—originally penned by one of his heroes, Bob Dylan—was a performance of which the guitarist was especially proud. With the Experience (Mitch Mitchell and

Noel Redding), Jimi made the Hot 100 with five other 45s: "Foxy Lady" (#67, 1968), "Up From the Skies" (#82, 1968), "Crosstown Traffic" (#52, 1968), "Freedom" (#59, 1971), and "Dolly Dagger" (#74, 1971).

LEAPY LEE
LITTLE ARROWS
(Albert Hammond, Mike Hazelwood)
Decca 32380
No. 16 *December 7, 1968*

Even when he was a mere tike, Leapy Lee could not keep from bounding, bouncing, frolicking, and making other bodily movements. He was born as Lee Graham to an apparently normal set of parents on July 2, 1942, in Eastbourne, Sussex, England. From early on, this was a frisky squirt with diverse interests. Before terminating his school career at the age of 15, Lee had already done some preliminary work toward becoming an actor and a rock star. Once out of an educational setting, however, money was an issue, and he worked a year or so in a factory.

Leapy's group, with a name now long lost to time, became professional and played about the town. Leapy billed himself as an entertainment manager and searched out clients, worked as an antiques dealer, wrote songs, performed in plays such as *Sparrows Can't Sing* and *Johnnie the Priest*, and acted for a year in *Large As Life*. Not a bloke to sit on his laurels or even sit still, Lee even opened up a bingo hall in London's Shepherd's Bush.

While pursuing all these activities, Leapy also found time to make recordings for the Cadet and Decca labels. Before the Kinks' Ray Davies became internationally known for his songwriting abilities, Lee, noting Ray's talents with words, cut a version of Davies' "King of the Whole Wide World." The disk bombed, much like every recorded effort Leapy ever issued save his good-timey "Little Arrows." This cutesy tune about Cupid and his missiles of love has not worn well, has probably irritated more listeners than it has tickled, and consequently, is rarely heard on oldies radio stations.

Lee persisted in expelling records, like a cover version of Christies' "Yellow River" and "Little Yellow Aeroplane," well into the '70s. Nothing ever again charted on the Hot 100.

"Waywardness proved his undoing," it is written in *The Guinness Encyclopedia Book of Popular Music*. Reports are that Lee was in a bar with actress Diana Dors and her hubby Alan Lake and became involved in an altercation with a knife. Leapy was arrested, charged, and served jail time. Upon his release, his former manager Gordon Mills employed him occasionally as a producer. By the '90s, Lee was off singing in bars in Majorca, Spain.

RENÉ & RENÉ
LO MUCHO QUE TE QUIERO
(THE MORE I LOVE YOU)
("René" Ornelas, "René" Herrera)
White Whale 287
No. 14 *January 4, 1969*

At 14, René Victor Ornelas (b. Aug. 26, 1936, Laredo, TX) sang and played trumpet in his father's band, the Mike Ornelas Orchestra. But a few years later, rock and pop music would gain entry to his soul. In high school, two René's and two Juan's—René Ornelas, René Herrera (b. Nov. 1935, Laredo, TX), Juan Orfila, and Juan Garza-Gongora—formed the Quarter Notes, a vocal quartet patterned after the Four Aces and the Four Lads, who were hot at the time.

"We toured all over and got to make some records for Deluxe and Dot," René Ornelas recalled in an exclusive interview. "It was hard back then being a Latin act. The things we had to do! We had hits in the Spanish community, and the Top 40 stations took notice, but we couldn't come in the front door—it had to be through the back or the side door."

After 10 years together, the Quarter Notes broke up in 1962. The two René's, however, stayed together and recorded as a duo for another decade. "We did a lot of records, made it to Dick Clark's "Caravan of Stars," and toured with the Beach Boys and the Grass Roots. But we couldn't get away from our roots: we'd put a Latin song on one side and a pop-rock song on the other. We couldn't get away from it.

"Herrera quit in '72. For a while, I picked up a couple of guys to sing harmony with. I was the lead singer, always. I tried to keep on touring and recording, and I still used the 'René & René' name. As long as there were two of us and the sound was there, the people didn't care."

For a spell in the early '70s, René retired from performing. He wrote songs or did arrangements for Herb Alpert, Vikki Carr, PETER NERO, Trini Lopez, Jose Feliciano, and Lawrence Welk. He earned a teaching degree and tried to teach for a few years, but missed singing and was soon back in action. During the last few years, Ornelas has been performing under the moniker of René René. "That way they'll only expect one of us, right?"

If you look, they're out there—more than 30 albums with either the "René & René" or "René René" name. René Ornelas is most proud of his 1989 effort, *El Gallito Enamorado*, for JB Records.

DEREK
CINNAMON
(George Tobin, JOHNNY CYMBAL)
Bang 558
No. 11 *January 11, 1969*

"Derek" was an alias briefly assumed by singer/song-writer JOHNNY CYMBAL. After his 1963 hit "Mr. Bass Man," Johnny recorded five years' worth of flopped 45s, so he needed a new, untarnished, and heavily hip name to represent his case to the American people. Yes, out of all the silly pseudonyms in the world, "Derek" was chosen.

"I had just written 'Mary in the Morning' [a Top 40 hit for Al Martino]," Johnny explained in an exclusive interview. "It was probably the most successful song I've ever written. And I had this deal to produce Gene Pitney and some other acts. I did the vocals on 'Cinnamon,' but I thought, I can't go out on the road and produce these things at the same time. So my brother, who's really named Derek and who was part of my band at the time, went out as me—he did the road work. Hey, there were three different touring versions of the Crystals, and two different versions of the Drifters, so it seemed like a good idea to have two different Dereks."

"Cinnamon," a self-penned bubblegum tune, outsold even "Mr. Bass Man," but except for "Back Door Man" (#59, 1969), future releases under the Derek persona bombed.

On March 13, 1993, Johnny Cymbal died of a heart attack.

BROOKLYN BRIDGE
WORST THAT COULD HAPPEN
(Jimmy Webb)
Buddah 75
No. 3 *February 1, 1969*

Johnny Maestro (b. John Maestrangelo, May 7, 1939, New York City) shook the charts with the Crests on such golden oldies as "Sixteen Candles" (#2, 1959), "Six Nights a Week" (#28, 1959), "The Angels Listened In" (#22, 1959), "Step by Step" (#14, 1960), and "Trouble in Paradise" (#20, 1960). When internal dissension and a decline in popularity set in, Johnny was pruned from the Crests. Groomed as a teen idol, he had solo hits with "Model Girl" (#20, 1961) and "What a Surprise" (#33, 1961), but by 1962, the times they were a-changin'.

Maestro tried to reform the Crests and cut more teen-dream disks. In the mid-'60s, when all else had failed, he joined what remained of the Del Satins: Les Cauchi (b. 1945) and Fred Ferrara (b. 1945). The Del Satins had never clicked on the national listings, but they did have a solid reputation on the East Coast, and they had backed up ERNIE MARESCA and Dion on a number of their chart-toppers.

One night in 1968, the Del Satins appeared in a Battle of the Bands on Long Island. One of the contending

BROOKLYN BRIDGE

acts was the Rhythm Method, a coed seven-member unit fronted by the husband-and-wife team of Tom Sullivan (b. 1946) and Carolyn Wood (b. 1947). After the contest was over, both groups exchanged words of praise, and later that night, discussed the possibility of merging into one big group.

By April 1968, the two had indeed become one—a conglomeration of 11 members. The line-up featured Maestro (lead vocals), Les Cauchi (vocals), Fred Ferrara (vocals), Tom Sullivan (sax), Carolyn Wood (organ), Artie Cantanzarita (drums), Shelly Davis (trumpet, piano), Mike Gregorio (vocals), Richie Macioce (guitar), Jimmy Rosica (bass), and Joe Ruvio (sax). When word got around that these musicians were considering forming so huge a performing entity, someone exclaimed, "That is going to be as easy to sell as the Brooklyn Bridge." All members agreed that there was the name for them.

Buddah Records caught the Brooklyn Bridge's act at the Cheetah, then the ultimate in hip Big Apple clubs. *Brooklyn Bridge* (1969), an album of pop and jazz-inflected numbers, was quickly produced by Wes Farrell—known for his work with EVERY MOTHER'S SON, Jay & The American's & The McCoys—packaged, and shipped. With the group's second single, a cover version of a Fifth Dimension tune written by Jimmy Webb—creator of RICHARD HARRIS' "McArthur Park" —"Worst That Could Happen," the Bridge had found their groove. A second LP (*The Second Brooklyn Bridge*) was released in 1969, and a string of follow-up singles made the Hot 100: "Blessed Is the Rain" (#45, 1969) b/w "Welcome Me Love" (#48), "Your Husband—My Wife" (#46, 1969), and "You'll Never Walk Alone" (#51, 1969).

In the early '70s, the group shortened its name to Bridge, and by mid-decade, the members had shrunken to a quintet. Maestro led a version of his pop-rock band through the '80s, and Bridge is reportedly still performing.

TAMMY WYNETTE
STAND BY YOUR MAN
(Tammy Wynette, Billy Sherrill)
Epic 10398
No. 19 *February 1, 1969*

Virginia Pugh is one of the most successful female country singers of all time. Don't let her inclusion in this book fool you—Virginia Pugh, a.k.a. Tammy Wynette, has made *Billboard*'s C & W listings on more than 60 occasions; 20 of these singles reached the coveted number-one position. For three consecutive years, Tammy was named the Country Music Association's "Vocalist of the Year" (1968-1971) .Her *Tammy's Great-*

est Hits (1969) album and her lone crossover pop hit are considered, respectively, the best-selling album and best-selling single by a female in the entire history of country and western music!

"The First Lady of Country Music" was born in Itawamba County, Mississippi, on May 5, 1942. Her father died when she was a few months old; her mother moved to Birmingham, Alabama, to work in an aircraft factory, leaving little Virginia with her grandparents until the end of World War II. There, she fiddled with her pa's old instruments. She married at 17 and produced three little ones.

To add to her earnings as a Birmingham beautician, Virginia sang in local night spots, and from 1963 to 1964, was the featured vocalist on WBRC's early-morning TV program, "The Country Boy Eddie Show." After some appearances on Porter Wagoner's syndicated TV show, Virginia made the usual Nashville record-company rounds. Hickory, Kapp, and others turned her down; Epic's Billy Sherrill, however, thought he heard something special. With "Apartment No. 9" (C&W: #44, 1967), her very first record, Tammy Wynette, as she henceforth was to be known, proved Billy Sherrill oh so right.

Tammy Wynette has been married five times; her union with country legend George Jones (1968-1975) proved fruitful in the form of numerous duet hits, but the Tammy-George merger, like the three marriages before it, ended in "D-I-V-O-R-C-E" (#63, 1968). This country queen has withstood some disastrous marriages, ill health, numerous home fires, threats on her life, and even a kidnapping. Wynette's autobiography, *Stand by Your Man*, was made into a 1981 TV movie starring Annette O'Toole.

ARBORS
THE LETTER
(Wayne Carson Thompson)
Date 1638
No. 20 *April 5, 1969*

Brothers Ed and Fred Farran from Grand Rapids, Michigan, crossed paths with Scott Herrick of East Lansing, Michigan, at the University of Michigan, where all three were students. Ed was studying zoology and biology, Fred, aeronautical and mathematical engineering, and Scott, industrial engineering. In their spare time, the guys discovered their mutual interest in singing and their vocal compatibility. Scott's twin brother Thomas dropped out of Michigan State to join the others as the Arbors, so named after Ann Arbor, the location of the University of Michigan campus.

In 1965, after the silky-smooth group had established a local reputation, Mercury Records showed an interest in signing them. "Anyone Here for Love" was their only release; it bombed, and the boys were let go. Despite their singing talents, by 1966, their sound seemed antiquated and definitely un-British. Their appearance was all-too-wholesome and thus unhip. Yet the success of groups with similar images, such as the Association and the Vogues, won the act a final shot at stardom. Date, a Columbia Records subsidiary, released a small heap of 45s by the Arbors before their moment in the sun. Only their easy-listening but psychedelicized rendition of the Box Tops' chart-busting "The Letter" would receive national Top 40 acceptance.

After their lukewarm career had cooled, the Arbors moved their base of operations to Chicago, where they set themselves up in the jingle business. For years, they were reportedly making in the six figures singing master-works like "It's the real thing," "In the valley of the jolly, ho, ho, ho," and "You deserve a break today."

BUBBLE PUPPY
HOT SMOKE & SASAFRASS
(Roy E. Cox, Jr., William Rodney Prince)
International Artists 128
No. 14 *April 19, 1969*

BUBBLE PUPPY

Bubble Puppy was discovered performing in Houston, at the Love Street Light Circus, a hippy haunt; three floors of fevered light flashes, smoke, and guitar screams. No alcohol served; "heads" would lay on the floor on cushions and experience, man, what the group's groping groupies called "hard rock with a soft touch."

Named for the Centrifugal Bumble Puppy kiddie game in Aldous Huxley's *Brave New World*, they were a hot and heavy herd of good ole boys from San Antonio, Texas, and thereabouts. Members—although mere teens—had histories with the Buckle, Strawberry Shoemaker, and the Bunch. Composed of Roy L. Cox, Jr. (bass), David Fore (drums), Todd "The Kidd" Potter (guitar), and Rod Prince (guitar), the psychedelic punksters (originally known as the Bad Seeds—with Fabulous Michael—45s were put out on J-Beck; later New Seeds; still later, the Willowdale Handcar) were signed in 1968 to the tiny Texas-based International Artists label—owned by Kenny Rogers' brother Leland; home of the Lone Star State's decidedly dusted Rory Erikson & Thirteenth Floor Elevators.

"We played some acoustic stuff for Ray Rush [the label's producer] and he said, 'You guys are gonna be bigger than the Beatles," said Rod Prince, in an exclusive interview. "Apple Records almost picked us up—Peter Asher [the producer/manager half of Peter & Gordon] wanted to sign us—but we couldn't get out of our contract with International Artist."

The members of Bubble Puppy looked like Dixie-fried and drugged flower children in the photo on their debut album, *Gathering Promises*. "Hot Smoke & Sasafrass," the lead cut, featured near-nonsensical hippy-dippy lyrics, but is arguably one of the finest flakies ever to be created by a one-off act. "The idea for the song came from the 'Beverly Hillbillies," said Rod. "We were on the couch, watchin' [at the Bubble Puppy mansion, in Bel-Aire, Texas] when Granny said something like, 'Hot smokin' sassafras, somebody drank my moonshine!' It wasn't suppose to be 'Hot Smoke and,' but 'Hot Smokin'.' We had this killer track, no lyrics. It knocked me over, when I heard that line; so now there was words everywhere."

A year's worth of singles was issued, but not one disk packed the charge or the magic of that silly "Sasafrass" song. In 1970, the International Artists label

experienced deep difficulties; a second album remained in the can, never to be issued. Prince, Potter, and the rest had been touring with Steppenwolf. Nick St. Nicholas, bassist with Steppenwolf, convinced Bubble Puppy to sign on with the folks at ABC Records and to let him produce an LPs worth. *Demian*—a name of a Herman Hesse novel, much as Steppenwolf's moniker —a self-titled album of heavenly heaviness and frilly folk was issued and quickly passed over. The group disbanded after one mini-Texas tour.

"Those times were better than any drug," said Rod, of the "Hot Smokin'" days. "Our entire lives were music, then. We nearly starved, but our music gave us a dream to live with. Our stuff was the only real and sane place in my live. If I didn't play even for a day, I'd be filled with doubts and would drift off to brood."

Rod went on to work for the Presidio Theatre, as janitor, then projectionist. Todd played with Bob Weir in the Filler Brothers. Rod and Todd later formed and recorded as Sirius. David recorded with Endle St. Cloud for International Artist, Potter St. Cloud for Mediarts, D-Day for A & M.

In 1984, all the original members of Bubble Puppy reunited in Austin; recording a live version of "Hot Smoke & Sasafrass" for a European compilation LP, *Live At The Continental Club*. A long-awaited second Bubble Puppy album, *Wheels Go Round*, appeared in Europe only on One Big Guitar in 1987.

Bubble Puppy, with all founding members intact, continue to voyage into the 21st century, to venture where no Bubble Puppy has gone before.

CRAZY ELEPHANT
GIMME GIMME GOOD LOVIN'
(Joey Levine, Ritchie Cordell)
Bell 763
No. 12 *May 3, 1969*

The story of Crazy Elephant appeared in a *Cashbox* article. According to *Cashbox*, a Welsh newspaper called *Mining News* had mentioned the hard-rock activities of a group of coal miners who would dig by day and play rock and roll by night. *Cashbox* also described how Neville Crisken, a London nightclub owner, read this human-interest item and rushed to Wales to check out this crew. Upon his arrival, Crisken descended "18,372,065 feet beneath the surface" and signed the blokes on the spot. When *Mining News* inquired if the group was any good, Crisken was quoted as saying, "Who cares? All the publicity about how I discovered them will guarantee their first album a million dollars in sales."

A fanciful tale indeed—especially since the *Cashbox* article was a complete fabrication. The story apparent-ly was planted by publicity people: Crazy Elephant was actually a studio creation courtesy of veteran bubblegum-meisters Jerry Kasenetz and Jeff Katz.

Leading the studio group that actually laid down the sounds for "Gimme Gimme" was a former lead singer of the Cadillacs, Richard Spencer, and songwriter, Third Rail member Joey Levine, who was the voice of REUNION and several of the disks bearing the name Ohio Express and KASENETZ-KATZ SINGING ORCHESTRA CIRCUS.

The unit that toured as Crazy Elephant consisted of five New Yorkers: ex-MUSIC EXPLOSION Bob Avery (drums), Ronnie Bretone (bass), Hal Hing (credited with "[doing] various things as the feeling moves him"), Larry Afuer (a.k.a. Larry Lafuer, lead vocals, organ), and someone named "Jethro" on flute, sax, guitar, bass, and percussion.

EDWIN HAWKINS SINGERS
OH HAPPY DAY
(Edwin R. Hawkins)
Pavilion 20001
No. 4 *May 31, 1969*

The Edwin Hawkins Singers were 42 strong and originally known as the Northern California State Youth Choir. They were formed in 1967 by Betty Watson and Edwin Hawkins (b. Aug. 1943, Oakland, CA) to represent their Berkeley church, the Ephresian Church of God in Christ, at a youth congress that summer in Washington, D.C.

In 1968, anticipating the next congress in Cleveland, the choir commissioned Century Record Productions to record one of their performances. A thousand copies of "Oh Happy Day" were pressed and sold to family and friends; one copy of the group's spirited vanity pressing fell into the hands of Tom Donahue, former owner of Autumn Records and the future "father of underground radio." "Big Daddy" Donahue began riding the record on his program on San Francisco's KSAN, and the response was incredible. Neil Bogart of Buddah Records flew in and acquired the national distribution rights, the State Youth Choir was renamed, and the sounds of God's gospel were on the nation's charts again.

The Edwin Hawkins Singers toured the States and abroad, appearing at churches and colleges, on TV, and in concert halls. Dorothy Morrison, the lead voice on "Oh Happy Day," left the group for a solo career within minutes of the tunes charting—in the coming years, several of her sides ("All God's Children Got Soul," "Spirit in the Sky," "Border Song") would appear on the Hot 100 and R & B listings. In 1970, the choir would revisit the Top 10 as back-up singers on Melanie's "Lay

Down (Candles in the Wind)" (#6). Three of the Hawkins crew's albums—*Let Us Go Into the House of the Lord, Children (Get Together),* and *I'd Like to Teach the World*—sold well, but the choir's success was fading rapidly.

By 1980, the core of the Hawkins Singers consisted mainly of family members: brothers Edwin (keyboards), Daniel (bass), and Walter (keyboards); sisters Carole, Freddie, and Lynette; cousin Shirley Miller; nephew Joe Smith (drums); and Walter's wife, Tremaine (lead singer).

The Edwin Hawkins Singers are still touring, and currently record for the Birthright label; the most recent release is *Give Us Peace* (1987).

MERCY
LOVE (CAN MAKE YOU HAPPY)
(Jack Sigler, Jr.)
Sundi 6811
No. 2 *May 31, 1969*

Jack Sigler, Jr., was born in Tampa, Florida, in 1950. In high school, while playing in the school band, Jack decided to stuff the Sousa and form a rock and roll unit with some fellow band members. In almost no time, the group, Mercy, was gigging at local dances. In 1968, Jack went off to the University of Southern Florida.

Mercy's line-up shifted a bit at this point, but soon settled down to include Sigler (guitar), Ronnie Caudell (guitar), Rodger Fuentes (drums), Buddy Goode (bass), Debbie Lewis (organ), Jamie Marvell (guitar), and Brenda McNish (piano).

George Roberts, a Hollywood producer, came to Tampa with Lou Chaney, Jr., to film *Fireball Jungle.* Jack's father was good friends with the movie mogul, and recommended that Roberts catch his son's act. The producer liked one Mercy number called "Love (Can Make You Happy)," so the tune was recorded and included in *Fireball Jungle*—only the film was never released.

Not overly discouraged, Mercy managed to place their gooey Steve Alaimo-Brad Shapiro production with Sundi, a small independent label. After months of airplay and some chart action in the Miami area, Warner Bros. stepped in and acquired the disk for national distribution.

"Love (Can Make You Happy)" proved to be an unrepeatable smash. Mercy's immediate follow-up was "Forever," a well-worn Buddy Killen number to which the late PETE DRAKE and THE LITTLE DIPPERS owe their One-Hit Wonder status. Mercy managed to chart with their retread (#79, 1969), but the platter would be their final notable—only one more single is known to have been released. Jack, Jr.'s interest apparently turned elsewhere, and the "Mercy" name was shelved.

NEON PHILHARMONIC
MORNING GIRL
(Tuppy Saussy)
Warner Bros. 7261
No. 17 *June 7, 1969*

The Neon Philharmonic was a two-man studio act; a project, if you will. Tuppy Saussy, keyboardist/arranger /conductor, had the words and music for what he called a "phonographic opera"; Don Gant had the voice. Both were based in Nashville, well-versed in the ways of music-making and both were under the sway of the new psychedelic sounds and lyrical freedom of the Beatles and Beach Boys.

Tupper was the product of a prominent Georgia family of lawyers, leaders, and painters. His 1962 LP *Discover Tupper Saussy* featured pop piano tinkling and strings and was pronounced a critical success by DAVE BRUBECK. Three years later, Tuppy was in Nashville creating jazzy interpretations of a Walt Disney flick, *The Swinger's Guide to Mary Poppins*. In 1968, he arranged and conducted several sides for MICKEY NEWBURY.

The chronological order of Don Gant's life is vague, but there are numerous scraps of detail. It is known that Don had given pop singing a try in the early '60s; Colpix issued some solo sides. He was also a member for a moment, with producer/singer/songwriter Norro Wilson, of an Everly Brothers-type duo. Nothing momentous happened, but Don Gant kept on writing songs (co-wrote "Cry Softly, Lonely One" with Roy Orbison), worked day jobs with the Acuff-Rose and Tree International music-publishing houses, and sang back-up for artists like JOHN D. LOUDERMILK, Don Gibson and Mickey Newbury.

Over the years, Gant produced recordings for Bobby "Blue" Bland, Jimmy Buffett, GENE & DEBBE, Lefty Frizzell, Ferlin Husky, the Newbeats, and Eddie Raven. He was director of ABC-Dunhill Records, and served as president of the Nashville chapter of the National Academy of Recording Arts & Sciences. At the time of his death, he was the head of Don Gant Enterprises and a board member of the Country Music Foundation. Don was 44 when he died on March 6, 1987.

"Morning Girl," recorded with a chamber-sized gathering of musicians from the Nashville Symphony Orchestra, was a surprise smash. The tune was a melodic hodge-podge, an extract from a larger work, *The Moth Confesses: A Phonograph Opera*, released as the act's debut album. Their label, Warner Bros., trumped the album as the logical successor to The San Sebastian Strings/Rod McKuen opus *The Sea*.

The immediate follow-up, "No One Is Going to Hurt You," sank like a stone. "Heighdy-Ho Princess," did receive a scattering of airplay (#94, 1970). Warner Bros. released the act's self-titled album and five more

singles, but the Neon Philharmonic's magic moment had passed.

To this day, a cult following surrounds this "group" of pop-rockers. Over the years, Donald and Tuppy had returned to the studio twice to revive their Neon project: the result was two limited-release singles, "Annie Poor" (for the TRX label) and "So Glad You're a Woman" (for MCA).

According to liner note scribe Andy Zax, Tuppy left the world of music to become a playwright, ad man, illustrator; eventually turning his energies to politics and anti-tax activism. In 1980, he published a manifesto, *The Miracle on Main Street: Saving Yourself and America From Financial Ruin*. "A few years later," writes Zax, "he fled the Feds and went underground; as of this writing [1996], he remains at large, his whereabouts unknown."

SPIRAL STAIRCASE
MORE TODAY THAN YESTERDAY
(Pat Upton)
Columbia 44741
No. 12 *June 14, 1969*

The Sacramento-based Spiral Staircase had been working the varnish off of their tootsies for half a decade before they received their first and only national notice. For years, they paid their dues in hometown liquor holes and tacky Reno/Tahoe lounges. When SONNY KNIGHT discovered the Spirals at a Las Vegas gig, they consisted of Pat Upton (lead vocals, guitar), Harvey Kaye (organ), Dick Lopes (sax), Vinny Parello (drums), and Bobby Raymond (bass).

Sonny liked their stuff, and approached their manager about cutting some sides on the group for Columbia Records. Upton's brassy "More Today Than Yesterday," the Spiral Staircase's second single, was a shiny success. Two follow-ups charted—"No One for Me to Turn To" (#52, 1969) and "She's Ready" (#72, 1970)—and their future seemed bright.

Horns were hot at that point in pop history: Chicago (Transit Authority) was waiting in the wings, and Blood, Sweat & Tears was invading the Top 10. Unfortunately, Spiral Staircase could not re-create their record's sophisticated brass arrangements in a live setting, since they didn't blow their own horns. Pop fans were sticklers for authenticity: a brassy band had to have brass, simple as that.

Abruptly, the end was at hand. Nothing further made of vinyl and stuffed in a sleeve by this band ever made the charts again.

Well into the '90s, Pat Upton has been working the oldies circuit, singing again and yet again, possibly more than ever: "More Today Than Yesterday."

DESMOND DEKKER & THE ACES
ISRAELITES
(Desmond Dacris, Leslie Kong)
Uni 55129
No. 9 *June 28, 1969*

It was Bob Marley who convinced a young Jamaican named Desmond Dacris to approach Leslie Kong, owner of Beveley's Records. Marley and Dacris both worked in the same welding shop. Marley had his dreams of pop success and would soon achieve his own triumph, but it was Dacris (a.k.a. Desmond Dekker) who got there first—he became the first successful reggae artist in the U.S. and Europe. "Israelites," his personalized portrait of the Biblical Exodus saga, was Desmond's only charting in the States. Jamaica and England responded strongly to his rhythms, providing him with a string of popular singles in those regions.

Dekker (b. July 16, 1942) grew up in Kingston, Jamaica. In his teens, he worked the streets as an amateur performer. By 1962, knowledgeable natives were calling Desmond "King of the Blue Beat." From 1963 through 1969, he won the Golden Globe award as Jamaica's top vocalist. Starting with his initial release ("Honor Your Father and Mother"), his Kong singles repeatedly made the Jamaican listings. By 1967, English ears were beginning to take notice of Dekker's reggae rhythms—"007 (Shanty Town)" nearly made the Top 10 over there. (A cover version of this tune appeared on the seminal stateside reggae album *The Harder They Come*.)

Besides "Israelites" and "007," Desmond secured British chartings with "It Miek"(1969), "Pickney Gal" (1970), a rendition of Jimmy Cliff's "You Can Get It If You Really Want" (1970), and "Sing a Little Song" (1975). Unfortunately, Dekker's career slowed to a halt soon after Leslie Kong, his producer and mentor, died of a heart attack in 1970.

Stiff Records signed Dekker up at the height of the British rock-steady/ska revival in 1980. Two LPs followed: *Black and Dekker* (1980) and the Robert Palmer-produced *Compass Point* (1981).

SONNY CHARLES & THE CHECKMATES, LTD.
BLACK PEARL
(Phil Spector, Toni Wine, Irwin Levine)
A & M 1053
No. 13 *July 5, 1969*

SONNY CHARLES (b. Charles Hemphill, Sept. 4, 1940, Fort Wayne, IN, lead vocals, keyboards), Marvin "Sweet Louie" Smith (b. Sept. 25, 1940, Fort Wayne, drums), and Bobby Stevens (b. Sept. 6, 1939, Fort Wayne, lead vocals) grew up together, played together, and attended the same Fort Wayne, Indiana, high school. In 1958, they started performing together as the Checkmates, Inc., playing blues, rock, and light jazz. In the '60s, Bill Van Buskirk (b. Feb. 7, 1941, Fort Wayne, bass) and Harvey Trees (b. June 14, 1940, Aitkin, MN, guitar) were added, making the group multi-racial. The guys had one 45 issued in 1963 on the Chicago-based I.R.P. label and then were sidetracked for a few years by military service; but on their return, the group's persistence paid off with gigs throughout the Midwest and ultimately, Las Vegas.

While working the Pussycat A Go-Go, a late-night desert resort where the stars would stop by, the Checkmates were spotted by Nancy Wilson. She offered to manage the group, so a deal was struck the next morning; Wilson handled the Checkmates for several years. Under her direction, they appeared at swanky venues like Caesar's Palace, the Coconut Grove, and the Copa. In 1966, Wilson secured a recording contract for them with Capitol Records, but "Do the Walk," "Mastered in the Art of Love," and a critically acclaimed LP (*The Checkmates Live in Las Vegas*) failed to sell.

Meanwhile, the legendary Phil Spector, after a two-year hiatus, was ready to return to the studio. His deal with A & M called for him to produce some sides on the Checkmates. Their A & M debut, "Love Is All I Have to Give" (#65, 1969)—penned by Stevens and Spector—almost clicked. Their second effort, "Black Pearl," is considered one of Spector's finest productions.

All, however, was not bliss. The billing on "Black Pearl's" label read "Sonny Charles & The Checkmates, Ltd.," and Bobby Stevens, a founding member and co-lead singer, was not pleased. "Proud Mary" (#69, 1969)—credited to "The Checkmates, Ltd. featuring Sonny Charles" and also produced by Spector—and a hastily assembled album, reportedly budgeted at $450,000, were released. As "Sweet Louie" Smith told *Black Stars*, the album "didn't make us a dime." Further recording plans fizzled, and in 1970, the Checkmates split up.

The group has since reformed, separated, reformed, separated. . . . For a while, they had their own record label (Rustic), their own TV production company (Associated Video Artists), and their own L.A. night spot (The Club). In 1976, Bobby and "Sweet Louie" returned the Checkmates, Ltd. to the R & B charts with "All Alone by the Telephone" (#97) for Polydor. Sonny Charles had a solo hit in 1983 on the Highrise label with "Put It in a Magazine" (#40; R&B: #2). Following this solo charting, Sonny reported returned to the fold . . . for awhile.

ZAGER & EVANS
IN THE YEAR 2525 (EXORDIUM & TERMINUS)
(RICK EVANS)
RCA 0174
No. 1 *July 12, 1969*

Denny Zager, born and raised in Wymore, Nebraska, was a member of the local Eccentrics when he chanced on Lincoln, Nebraska, native Rick Evans in 1962. Denny stumbled onto Rick at a talent contest at Wesleyan University, and offered him the guitarist slot in his band. Rick accepted and joined the Eccentrics, but left in 1965 to form his own group of giggers, the DeVilles. As the '60s drew to a close, Denny and Rick, equally disenchanted with their respective group situations, formed a folkie duo.

Rick was eager to try out "In the Year 2525," a futuristic fable of depressing proportions he had dashed off in 30 minutes. Since 1964, the darn thing had been collecting dust in his dresser drawer. Denny agreed to perform the tune, but clearly wasn't happy about it. "I didn't go nutty over the song," Zager confessed to Fred Bronson in *The Billboard Book of Number One Hits*. "It really wasn't the style I wanted to do." But wherever they sang the song, audiences seemed to like it.

Rick convinced Denny to travel to Odessa, Texas, where they taped the tune and pressed up a thousand copies on Truth Records to sell at concerts and hand out to local radio stations. Someone over at RCA heard the disk and signed Rick and Denny to a recording contract. "In The Year 2525" darted to the pinnacle of the pop listings, where it remained for six weeks, eventually selling more than 5 million copies. Nothing the Nebraskans ever again recorded managed to muscle more than minimal attention. "We tried everything to come up with that second hit, but it never happened," Zager lamented to Daniel Mills of the *Washington Times*. "A lot of groups climb their way up very slowly. They get a mediocre hit, then a little bigger hit, and then they get a super-big hit and just stay in the limelight. But we were misfortunate enough to have a monster right off the top. What do you do to top it?"

In the year 1970, Zager quit the duo. Despite the parting, RCA continued releasing their materials; most non-notably: *Food for the Mind* (1971). Denny now lives in Lincoln, where he makes string instruments,

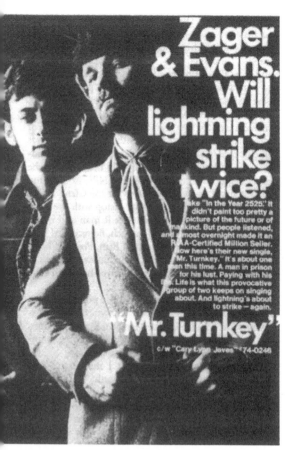

Zager & Evans. Will lightning strike twice? Take "In the Year 2525." It didn't paint too pretty a picture of the future or of mankind. But people listened, and almost overnight made it an RIAA-Certified Million Seller. Now here's their new single, "Mr. Turnkey." It's about one man this time. A man in prison for his lust. Paying with his life. Life is what this provocative group of two keeps on singing about. And lightning's about to strike — again.

"Mr. Turnkey"
c/w "Cary Lynn Javes" 174-0246

teaches music, and continues to perform country-type tunes in local clubs. Rick Evans lives in Arizona and works as a real estate broker, occasionally writing songs.

WINSTONS
COLOR HIM FATHER
(Richard Spencer)
Metromedia 117
No. 7 *July 19, 1969*

As a recording act, the Winstons began and ended in 1969. They are remembered for one song, their first disk and a Grammy winner for best R & B song, "Color Him Father."

The band was born in the late '60s in Washington, D.C. Richard Spencer was the leader, singer, songwriter, and tenor sax man. G. C. Coleman, their drummer, had been a Motown sessioneer and a member of the Marvelettes' touring band. Lead guitarist Quincy Mattison had been with Arthur Conley's band when the Otis Redding protegé was on the charts with "Sweet Soul

Music." Rich, Quincy, and G. C. had all played with Otis Redding. Ray Maritano, the Winstons' alto saxophonist, had attended the Berklee College of Music and played in the U.S. Air Force Band. Keyboardist Phil Tolotta doubled on lead vocals, and bassist Sonny Peckrol completed the line-up.

The Impressions discovered the band, took them out on the road as their back-up players, and eventually gave them a solo spot on the tour. Spencer's ode to the ideal dad—protective, kind, and loving—came to the attention of the Atlanta-based Metromedia label. "Color Him Father" was the Winstons' first 45, and it struck a chord with both pop (#7) and R & B (#2) listeners. In just months, the Winstons faded from view, leaving in their wake only two known 45s—"Love of the Common People" (#54, 1969) and "Birds of a Feather"—plus a lone LP named after their hallowed hit.

JOE JEFFREY GROUP
MY PLEDGE OF LOVE
(Joseph Stafford Jr.)
Wand 11200
No. 14 *July 26, 1969*

Little can be pieced together about Joe Jeffrey and his flash flight into and out of fame. He was a Buffalo, New York-based boy who had been playing the local bar circuit. Someone, possibly Jerry Meyers at Stone Gold Productions, took a liking to him and booked studio time at Cleveland's Audio Recording Studio and, later, at Chip Moman's American Sound Studio in Memphis. "My Pledge of Love" seems to have been Joe's first recording.

Following "My Pledge of Love" were three more singles—"Dreamin' Til Then" (1969), "Hey Hey Woman" (1969), and "My Baby Loves Lovin'" (1970)—plus an album, *My Pledge of Love*. Despite glowing liner notes on the latter supplied by DJ Sandy Beach, who favorably compared Joe's effort with the Beatles' *Sgt. Pepper*, Joe's moment had come and gone by the end of 1969.

ROY CLARK
YESTERDAY, WHEN I WAS YOUNG
(Charles Aznavour, Herbert Kretzmer)
Dot 17446
No. 19 *August 2, 1969*

By the time he was 11, Roy Linwood Clark (b. Apr. 15, 1933, Meherrin, VA) was already a hell of a country picker. His family had moved to Washington, DC, where his father was working as a computer programmer. Hester Clark had been a tobacco farmer by day, but played guitar five nights a week in a local country/bluegrass

band. The house was always full of music: there was a ukulele, a mandolin, a banjo, and Ma's piano. Before Roy's grammar school days were done, Hester Clark had taught his son everything he knew about stringed instruments; Roy started sitting in on some of his dad's gigs. In 1951 and 1952, Clark won two consecutive National Banjo Championships. The second win awarded him an appearance at the Grand Ole Opry.

Back in D.C., Clark tried out for the St. Louis Brown's baseball club, won a string of boxing matches, and—in his spare time—played at local bars. Eventually, he was offered a job as back-up guitarist for an up-and-coming country singer, Jimmy Dean. Roy appeared on some of Dean's ABC-TV spots, and then secured a similar slot with "The George Hamilton TV Show."

Clark's early recorded efforts were issued on the Four Star, Debbie, and Coral labels. After working as the lead guitarist for MARVIN RAINWATER and Wanda ("The Female Elvis") Jackson, Jackson's manager hooked Roy up with Capitol Records. The pairing was quite fruitful, producing C & W hits like "Tip of My Fingers" (1963), "Through the Eyes of Love" (1964), and "When the Wind Blows in Chicago" (1965).

Numerous country hits followed once Clark switched over to the Dot label in 1968. His flashy guitar and banjo licks adorned tunes that ranged in style from easy-listening to hard-core bluegrass; "Yesterday, When I Was Young" was representative of much of his material, and just happened to be that one single that crossed over to the Top 40. He continues to rack up hit after country hit, with more than 50 of his 45s scoring on the C & W charts.

Roy has made many TV stops on talk and variety shows. But perhaps he is best known for his long-running appearances as co-host (with Buck Owens) of country music's answer to "Laugh-In," "Hee Haw." He also guested as "Cousin Roy" and (in drag) as "Big Mama Halsey" on "The Beverly Hillbillies."

Clark performs over 250 shows a year; he was reportedly the highest-paid country concert star between 1969 and 1971. He also works the Las Vegas scene, and has occasionally hosted "The Tonight Show." In 1973, the Country Music Association named Roy Clark "Entertainer of the Year."

CHARLES RANDOLPH GREAN SOUNDE
QUENTIN'S THEME
(Robert W. Lorbert)
Ranwood 840
No. 13 *August 2, 1969*

Charles Randolph Grean, to those in the know, wrote "the novelty song of the 20th century." Phil Harris

recorded it, "The Thing"—the tall tale of a mere male and his find of an incredible "thing" on the beach—became one of the blockbuster hits of 1950. Grean arranged/conducted Nat "King" Coles' "The Christmas Song," Vaughn Monroe's "Riders in the Sky" and for a few years with Steve Shoals headed RCA's pop division—but remains a shadowy behind-the-scenes legend.

Charles Grean (b. Oct. 1, 1913, New York City) was a music major for two years at Wesleyan University. For a decade, Grean played bass with various orchestras and combos; fronting his own dance band in the mid-'30s, and working the cruise ships. In the early '40s, he gained a spot playing bass with the NBC house band and freelanced as a copyist; often for the Glenn Miller and Artie Shaw Orchestras. After a stop with the Kraft Music Hall, Grean became an A & R man and music conductor with RCA Victor. As such, he recorded with Eddie Arnold, Perry Como, Elton Britt, Pee Wee King, Freddie Martin, Dinah Shore, Hank Snow, the Sons of the Pioneers ... For awhile Grean played bass with Chet Atkins' group, the Country All-Stars.

Grean managed and was married to pop lark/multi-hit artist Betty Johnson; best known to pre-baby-boomers for "The Little Blue Man," a tall tale of a short, cute, though annoying, stalker that our heroine, Johnson, eventually throws out a highrise window.

"I think my mistake was that I met Betty," said Grean to *DISCoveries'* Mike Streissguth. "I fell in love with her, started working with her exclusively, and just sacrificed everything else that I had ever done. . . . You can't work together and be married. You can't separate it. If something goes wrong, it affects your marriage, not only your business relationship."

Grean reports he started all over again, copying lead sheets for Trinity Music, "working for peanuts," and doing a lot of Muzak, ". . . a hack job where you go in and do 10 arrangements in three hours, just grind them out." In 1966, Grean became head of the New York office for Dot Records; "discovering" the musical side of Leonard Nimoy. "I knew this guy was gonna be hot," Grean told *DISCoveries*. "He didn't have to do anything. He said, 'I can do something. I sing a little bit and play guitar.' I said, 'Fine. Send me a tape.' He sent me a tape, and he doesn't sing that well, kind of moos . . ." Four Nimoy albums—Star Trek convention staples—were issued and Grean was eager for the next happening.

On June 26, 1966. something new appeared under the sun—"Dark Shadows," a Gothic daytime drama, complete with a ghost, werewolves, haunted houses, and a 200-year old vampire, Barnabas Collins (played by Jonathan Frid). Grean's daughter Lorin drew her dad's attention to the creepy tummy-turner. With blessings from Dan Curtis the shows creator, Grean issued an album's worth of the serial's crispy sounds; billing the affair "nostalgic modern music."

Robert Cobert, who wrote and arranged "Quentin's Theme"—originally written as a waltz for Dan Curtis's TV production of "The Strange Case of Dr. Jekyll and Mr. Hyde" (1966)—for the December 1968 series appearance of the ghostly character of Quentin Collins (played by David Selby, later the illegitimate son Richard Channing on "Falcon Crest"), went on to chart big with his own album, *Original Music From Dark Shadows* (#18, 1969).

Grean's follow-up was "Josette's Music Box." "Even went into business with a guy, and we made music boxes and sold them, mail order," said Grean. "This music box had some musical power!"

Charles Randolph Grean continues to labor in the dark shadows, coping and scoring background music for soaps, movies, and variety shows.

In January 1991, a more sexually explicit and considerably more gory prime-time remake of "Dark Shadows," with no original cast members, appeared for a two-month run.

TONY JOE WHITE
POLK SALAD ANNIE
(Tony Joe White)
Monument 1104
No. 8 *August 23, 1969*

"They don't know if I'm black, white, country or rock," said Tony Joe in a publicity handout. In a pigeon-holed world that can be a problem of success-impeding proportions. Astute critics have dubbed White's funky country-blues style "swamp rock," but "swamp soul" might be a more accurate label to bare.

Tony Joe White (b. July 23, 1943)—who was affectionately billed "the Swamp Fox" by French press—was born in Goodwill, Louisiana, and raised in Oak Grove, Louisiana, a town near the borders of Arkansas and Mississippi, in a community that he described to *Blues & Soul* as "[thriving] around one cotton gin and three stores." The youngest of seven children, Tony Joe—born part-Cherokee—spent much of his youth picking cotton and listening to the rest of the family playing tunes.

"I didn't care much about music when I was growing up," White recalled to Irwin Stambler in *The Encyclopedia of Pop, Rock, and Soul.* "I heard it all the time. My daddy played every kind of instrument you could think of. But I was much more interested in baseball." All that changed in Tony Joe's late teens, by which point he was roaming the region playing in country-rock bands. "The first group I had was called Tony and the Mojos. We wore blue-speckled smoking jackets and played a lot of bars around home. Another outfit was called Tony & The Twilights."

Tony and his Twilights migrated to Texas in the mid-'60s, but then splintered. White stayed on in Corpus Christi, working the bars as a solo act. In 1968, he took that obligatory trek to Nashville to make the rounds of the publishers and record companies. Combine Music signed him on as a songwriter, and one of his demo disks found its way to the offices of Monument Records. A variety of now-rare singles ("Georgia Pines," "Watching the Trains Go By," "Soul Francisco") were issued before Tony Joe hit paydirt with "Polk Salad Annie"; all of these sides were produced by BILLY SWAN.

White did make the Hot 100 on three other occasions, with "Roosevelt and Ira Lee" (#44, 1969), "Save Your Sugar for Me" (#94, 1970), and "I Get Off on It" (#79, 1980). In the early '80s, he picked up a minor following with watered-down country material for Columbia Records. "Mama Don't Let Your Cowboys Grow Up to Be Babies" (1980), "The Lady in My Life" (1983), and "We Belong Together" (1984) all made the C & W charts—an interesting development, considering Tony Joe's distaste for the genre. "I listen to most things as long as they've got guts and soul," he told *Blues & Soul.* "I just can't stand Cajun music at any price, same goes for country. Now, blues I like."

TONY JOE WHITE

In addition to recording, White has written notable numbers for Ray Charles, George Jones, Roy Orbison, Hank Williams, Jr.; and charters for Brook Benton ("Rainy Night in Georgia"), Dusty Springfield ("Willie and Laurie Mae Jones"), and Elvis Presley ("For Old Times Sake," and "I've Got a Thing About You Baby"). Four of his tunes were included in Tina Turner's 1989 watershed album *Foreign Affair*, including "Steamy Windows (#39, 1989). The same year, Tony Joe formed his own Swamp label to issue *Closer to the Truth*, followed by 1993's *Path of a Decent Man*.

The last tune Conway Twitty would ever put voice to was Tony Joe's "Rainy Night in Georgia," dueted with Sam Moore—the Sam of Sam and Dave—for the genre-crossing rhythm, country, and blues album.

YOUNGBLOODS
GET TOGETHER
(Chester Powers)
RCA Victor 9752
No. 62 *September 2, 1967*
No. 5 *September 6, 1969*

"Come on people now/Smile on your brother/Everybody get together/Try and love one another, right now." Classic lines indeed. "Get Together" was jangling 12-string folk-rock, message music, and—as faithful fans will attest—the Youngbloods at their very best.

Jesse Colin Young (b. Perry Miller, Nov. 11, 1944, New York City) was a moderately successful folksinger with two LPs under his belt—*Soul of a City Boy* (1964) and *Youngblood* (1965)—when he met a fellow folkie and former bluegrass picker from Cambridge named Jerry Corbitt (b. Tifton, GA). When in town, Jesse—who lifted his name from Wild West figures Jesse James and Cole Younger and Grand Prix race car driver Colin Younger—would drop in on Jerry, and the two would jam for hours, exchanging harmonies.

Beginning in January 1965, the two began gigging on the Canadian circuit as a duo (eventually, as the Youngbloods, Young would play bass, and Corbitt would play lead guitar). Corbitt introduced Young to a bluegrass boy named Harmon Banana (b. Lowell Levinger, 1946, Cambridge, MA). "Banana" was handy with the banjo, mandolin, mandola, guitar, and bass; he had played in both the Proper Bostoners and the Trolls, and knew of a fellow tenant in his building who could flesh out the band. Joe Bauer (b. Sept. 26, 1941, Memphis), an aspiring jazz drummer with experience playing in society dance bands, was at first quite unmoved by Banana's offer to perform in a rock and roll outfit, but soon gave in.

Once the line-up was set, Jesse Colin Young & The Youngbloods, as the group was then known, began building a solid reputation from their club dates. (Early demo sides recorded in 1965 were later issued by Mercury on the *Two Trips* album.) Their first gig had been at Gerde's Folk City in Greenwich Village; months later, they were the house band at the Cafe Au Go Go and had snagged a recording contract with RCA Records. Jesse, though, was not too satisfied with the label. "Nobody [at RCA] was really mean or anything; everybody was just kind of stupid," he explained to *Rolling Stone*. "They never knew what to make of us, and tried to set us up as a bubblegum act . . . they never knew what we were, and never knew how to merchandise us."

The arrangement did produce one solid success in "Grizzly Bear" (#52, 1967). Several classic albums followed—*The Youngbloods* (1967; later retitled *Get Together*), *Earth Music* (1967), and *Elephant Mountain* (1969). When that paean to universal brotherhood, "Get Together," first appeared in the Summer of Love, it did not sell too well (#62, 1967). But two years later—after the National Council of Christians and Jews used the song as their theme song on radio spots—the track was rereleased and cracked the Top 40.

The Youngbloods recorded a few more albums, then split up. In an interview with *Crawdaddy*'s Peter Knobler, Jesse ascribed the legendary act's break-up to a conflict over one of his tunes, "Peace Song."

"I played ["Peace Song"] the night I wrote it during the recording session for *Rock Festival* at the Fillmore, and the people just went crazy, they loved it! And the next night the guys played on it, and I didn't dig it. I thought [their playing] detracted from the power of the song. . . . For the first time since the band had been together, I said, 'I want to do this alone.' Also, Joe [Bauer] said, 'That's not Youngblood music, that's you; I don't want that on the Youngbloods album, and it hurt."

According to Young, tensions within the Youngbloods came to a head a year later. "Banana came to me and said, 'Joe thinks that there's some musical value to the ["Peace Song"), some musical direction.' I said, 'Musical direction? Screw off!' . . . It made me think, what am I doing in this band?"

The group's final LPs were *Ride the Wind* (1971), *Good and Dusty* (1971), and *High on a Ridgetop* (1972). Corbitt, who had left the Youngbloods in 1971, became a producer (Charlie Daniels, Don McLean) and cut two LPs on his own (*Corbitt* and *Jerry Corbitt*). Bauer made one solo record (*Moonset*) and, with Banana, recorded as Banana & The Bunch (*Mid Mountain Range*) and Noggins (*Crab Tunes*). Jesse, the Youngblood with the highest profile, established the solo career he apparently always wanted. No hit singles so far (not even "Peace Song"), but albums like *Light Shine* (1974), *Songbird* (1975), and the live *On the Road* (1976) have sold well. *Perfect Stranger* was issued in 1982; six years later, *The Highway Is for Heroes*.

THE
YOUNGBLOODS

In 1984, Banana reappeared with a band, the Bandits. Soon after, he dropped out of the music biz to run a hang-gliding shop.

ELECTRIC INDIAN
KEEM-O-SABE
(Bernard Binnick, Bernice Borisoff)
United Artists 50563
No. 16 *September 27, 1969*

"Bernie Binnick [co-founder of Swan Records] had this idea for a sitar instrumental," Frank Virtue (formerly of THE VIRTUES) told Tony Cummings in *The Sound of Philadelphia*. "It was around the time all the kids were into that Indian stuff. So he got together a bunch of musicians, a lot of the guys who're in MFSB now, and they put down this sitar thing called 'Keem-O-Sabe.' It was like funky Indian music. They leased the tape to United Artists Records. It was a gimmick, but it was a stone smash."

This "group" recorded an album's worth of similarly inane instrumentals (*Keem-O-Sabe*, 1969) and even did an Indian-flavored cover version of the overly recorded and charted (CHRIS KENNER, CANNIBAL & THE HEADHUNTERS, The Midnighters, Wilson Pickett; later J. Giels Band) "Land of 1,000 Dances" (#95, 1969) as a follow-up 45. But pop fans wearied quickly of Electric Indian's brand of auditory cotton candy.

MOTHERLODE
WHEN I DIE
(William Smith, Steve Kennedy)
Buddah 131
No. 18 *October 11, 1969*

Motherlode was part of a short-lived, big-time burst in the Canadian rock scene. Nineteen sixty-nine was the year that the Guess Who opened the door for a "Canadian Invasion," and before the door closed, more than a dozen northern acts ran up and down the U.S. charts:

MOTHERLODE

Edward Bear, Five Man Electrical Band, Lighthouse, the Poppy Family, the Stampeders, THE BELLS, OCEAN, and, of course, Motherlode—not to mention Gordon Lightfoot, Joni Mitchell, and Anne Murray.

Before Motherlode came together in London, Ontario, Steve Kennedy had been blowing barroom sax for almost a decade. In the mid-'60s, Kennedy and Dougie Riley had been members of the R & B-oriented Silhouettes (not to be confused with THE SILHOUETTES, of "Get a Job" fame) and Eric Mercury & The Soul Searchers. When Kennedy (sax, harmonica) first hooked up with Kenny Marco (guitar), Wayne "Stoney" Stone (drums), and William "Smitty" Smith (keyboards), Motherlode was a Top 40 cover band working at the Image Club. Dougie brought the group to the attention of Mort Ross at Revolution Records, and Motherlode was soon asked to create some original material for the label.

As soon as Buddah Records boss Neil Bogart heard Motherlode's first Revolution single, "When I Die," he issued the tune on his stateside label. The situation looked bright as the soulful single cut its way up the charts. But business hassles developed, and before the year was even over, Motherlode was no more. Their debut album sold fairly well, but the follow-up single, "Memories of a Broken Heart," did poorly.

In 1971, Kennedy, Marco, and Stone formed a new group, Dr. Music, and issued several unsuccessful singles. In 1973, "Smitty" Smith assembled a new Motherlode and recorded an LP for Buddah, *Tuffed Out*. The album died without notice.

Over the years, Ken Marco has recorded with the King Biscuit Boy Band and Crowbar; he has also worked sessions for David Clayton-Thomas, Ten Wheel Drive's Genya Ravan, and the Ozark Mountain Daredevils. "Smitty" Smith has played on albums by Blood, Sweat & Tears, Bob Dylan, RICHIE HAVENS, The James Gang, Billy Joel, DAVE LOGGINS, Robert Palmer, and the Pointer Sisters.

CUFF LINKS
TRACY
(Lee Pockriss, Paul Vance)
Decca 32533
No. 9 *October 25, 1969*

"I had two different singles in the Top 10 at the same time under two different group names and nobody seemed to notice," Ron Dante, lead singer for the Archies and multi-tracked voice of the Cuff Links, told *DISCoveries'* Gary Theroux. "I couldn't believe it, 'cause

my voice sounded the same. The same week that 'Tracy' entered the Top 10, 'Sugar Sugar' was the number-one record in the country. I even had a third record out as the Pearly Gate ["Free," 1969]. It was yet another of my ghost groups."

Ron Dante was born Carmine Granito, on Staten Island, New York, on August 22, 1945. When he was 11 years old, he fell out of a tree, and learned how to play the guitar as he recuperated. A year later, he was fronting the Persuaders, a junior-high band made up of fellow classmates. By 1963, Carmine was working as a "runner" for an accounting firm, and he would drop by 1619 Broadway (the famed Brill Building) to knock on doors in hopes of selling off some of his songs.

Don Kirshner hired Carmine as a staff songwriter for Kirshner's Aldon Music and renamed him "Ron Dante." When Tony Orlando, Kirshner's top demo-maker, left to pursue a solo career, Ron was called in to fill the void. In that capacity, he cut background tracks for Neil Diamond, Jay & The Americans, Andy Kim, and The McCoys. He also did demos for songs that would eventually be recorded by the Animals, Ronnie Dove, Gene Pitney, and the Vogues.

In 1965, one of Dante's demos was issued as THE DETERGENTS—"Leader of the Laundromat," a parody of the Shangri-Las' "Leader of the Pack," was a smash. Four years later, Ron sang lead on the Archies' "Sugar Sugar" (#1, 1969). At that time, he was struggling to establish a solo career, but decided to do some singing, songwriting, and producing for the cartoon group. " I did the singing for the Archies, yes, but I didn't want to become a star from that. I just wanted to earn some money to pay some rent. When those records first hit the charts, I just hid."

As for the Cuff Links, "Tracy" was a song that a friend handed to Dante. Ron agreed to record it, so he overdubbed his vocal tracks to sound like a group of singers. He refused to tour behind it because he was "in a ghost-group phase." But he did consent to doing just one album (*Tracy*, 1969). "When the royalty check came in, Paul Vance called me up and said, 'Well, are you ready for the next album?' I said, 'What next album?' I told you I was going to do just one LP and that's it. Now where's my money?'"

Ron did get his money and Vance did get a second Cuff Links album, but not with Dante's involvement. Called in to substitute was Rupert Holmes, the arranger on the group's first LP and later quite a successful singer/songwriter in his own right.

Ron Dante has never stopped, or, as he claims to have, never even slowed down. In addition to doing jingles (for Coca-Cola, Coppertone, Dr. Pepper, Pepsi, Kentucky Fried Chicken, and Lifesavers), he has worked as a record producer (Irené Cara, Cher, LADY FLASH, Barry Manilow), as a producer of plays (*Duet for*

One, *Whose Life Is It, Anyway?*), and as co-producer of the Fats Waller revue *Ain't Misbehavin'*. Dante has had solo recordings issued by Almont, Music Voice, Musicor, Columbia, Dot, Mercury, Kirshner, Scepter, Bell, RCA Victor, Handshake . . . whew! As a continuation of his ghosting activities, Ron has recorded as Bo Cooper, Dantes Inferno, Ronnie & The Dirtriders, C. G. Rose, and the Webspinners. Ron Dante was also, for a brief time, the publisher of the *Paris Review*—reportedly, he acquired the literary journal from George Plimpton by beating him in a billiards match.

GARLAND GREEN
JEALOUS KIND OF FELLA
(Josephine Armstead, Garland Green, Maurice Dollison, Rudolph Browner)
Uni 55143
No. 20 *November 1, 1969*

Garland Green, the 10th in a brood of 11, was born on June 24, 1942, in Dunleath, Mississippi. When he was 16, he moved to Chicago to attend Englewood High, and later worked at the Argo Corn Starch plant. Garland had been singing and swinging since his early years in the Mississippi Delta region. While performing at a community recreation center, he was discovered by one of Chicago's barbecue kings, Argia B. Collins. Argia, who had a mess of barbecue houses and marketed Mambo Bar-B-Que Sauce, sponsored Garland, sending him to the Chicago Conservatory of Music.

While attending the Conservatory, Green worked the black club scene on the South Side. One night while he was singing in Chicago's Sutherland Lounge, Melvin Collins and Josie Jo Armstead—the husband-and-wife owners of the Gamma/Giant labels—happened to be in the audience. "I really liked Garland's voice," Armstead, a one-time Ikette, explained to *Soul Survivor*'s Robert Pruter. "There was that pleading quality that I knew that women would just love. I was with Melvin and I told him, 'I believe I can get a hit on him.'"

"Jealous Kind of Fella" was a telephone talkie tune: Garland calls his girl and apologizes for the jealous rage that caused him to "hit that guy last night." Droves of females snapped up the record. About a third as many went for his follow-up, which mined the same vein—"Don't Think That I'm a Violent Guy" (R&B: #42, 1970). Though none of his successive singles made the Hot 100, eight of them (nine if you count the rerelease of 1974's "Let the Good Times Roll" in 1975) charted on the *Billboard* R & B listings, right up through 1983.

SMITH
BABY IT'S YOU
(Burt Bacharach, Mack David, Barney Williams)
Dunhill 4206
No. 5 *November 1, 1969*

Before her bluesy rock days, Gayle McCormick (b. Nov. 26, 1948) attended Pattonville High in St. Louis and sang high soprano with the Suburb Choir, a 150-voice unit that performed annually with the St. Louis Symphony. In 1966, fronting a foursome she met while enrolled in a music class—the Chevels, named for a hip Chevy—Gayle and group played the hops, became regulars at "Chain of Lakes Splash Party", and waxed a few singles—released as by Gayle McCormick & the Klassmen—for Musicland U.S.A. "Without You" and "Mr. Loveman" were passed over with little national fanfare. In late 1968, the Smiths, a disintegrating L.A. band, came to town touring behind a Columbia single, "Now I Taste the Tears." Most of the Smiths' members had departed, and replacement players were needed.

"The Klassmen were being strongly promoted by KXO radio, the rock station in St. Louis; especially by Johnny Rabbit, the number one DJ," said Gayle, in an exclusive interview. "Jerry [Carter (bass)] and Rich [Cliburn (lead guitar)]—what was left of the Smiths—needed a band to back them for their appearances in town, and Ernie Cummings, our drummers' dad and our manager, was a go-getter. He pushed for it, and we got to back them."

With thoughts in her head that "these guys are big-time, L.A. and on their way," Gayle left the Klassmen and St. Louis—with Jerry and Rich—in order to continue promotion on the 45. "When we got to L.A., we put an ad in the musician's union paper and started playing the Rag Doll," said Gayle, "with Bob Evans, the drummer and Larry Moss, the keyboards. We were now a five piece and Smith."

Right from the start, the heart and soul of the new grouping was McCormick. She was only 20 years old that day in 1969 when out of the blue, dimming stars Del Shannon and Brian Hyland stopped in to wet their whistles at the Rag Doll, a San Fernando Valley bar. Smith had only been together a month or two, but Shannon loved what he heard.

"Del was real excited about the group. I mean, maybe he saw us as a financial thing or a way to advance his career, but he said, 'Hey, this is want I want to do. . . . Come out to the house; I got some songs for you. 'Baby It's You' was one of 'em. It had always been a favorite of mine, by the Shirelles; not the Beatles version."

Once at Shannon's home, with the roomful of recording equipment, Del showed them the outlines of the song; working with them until he got the sound just the way he heard it in his head. "I don't know if he had

this vision that it would be a hit, or what," McCormick said. "But, using the Rag Doll as the spot, he had [Atlantic Record's] Ahmet Ertegun come in to hear us. He wanted to alter this sound that Del had worked up, so we didn't go with Atlantic. He had Liberty, Decca, then Steve Barri, Jay Lasker, the president and Joel Sill, wives and all, from ABC-Dunhill. It was like an immediate celebration. It was electric, and unreal. Within nine months, we were doing 'Ed Sullivan,' the 'Mama Cass Show,' and 'Red Skelton'—and he never had rock groups on—and had this Top five record."

The tale gets foggy from this point on. Even Gayle's not clear as to why, but before even a second 45 was needed, Del was gone. "I think it was a business decision; [the label] just wanted to do their own thing, with Joel [Sill] producing and Steve [Barri] sweetening," said Gayle.

"Take a Look Around," a fairly tough follow-up, sold well (#43, 1970), but with the release of *A Group Called Smith*, their debut LP, Jerry and Rich were, as Gayle phrased it, "released." "We were incurring conflicts, within the group—personal—and they didn't receive any royalties from the hit or the album that they played on." Brought in were Al Parker (lead guitar) and Jade Hass (bass).

"The group thing was about through," said Gayle. "All this nit-picking; with nobody getting on. We were promoting 'What Am I Gonna Do' [Smith's third and penultimate 45], when Larry quit, then Bob; so there's just Gayle McCormick and two guys that weren't in the original group. I didn't feel that I had any control either, so I told 'em, 'I'm a goner, too.' They got some girl to finish the tour." *Minus Plus*, a second album was pieced together.

Gayle McCormick carried on for a while with lone solo releases on Dunhill, MCA, and Fantasy. "I got lost," said Gayle. "With each album, I got further away from the Smith sound. I think people expected more of a gritty sound. By the last stuff, I was being produced by this guy who was doing Dianne Carroll . . .

"But I could have only gone on for only so long—my voice would have been gone if I had carried on. I wasn't born to be a professional singer. It wasn't meant to be more than it was. One of the guys—I ain't sayin' who—said, 'It's a good thing that we only had one hit, . . .' cause I liked drugs too much. It woulda killed me."

Gayle works for Sears, in St. Louis. Rick lives in the wilds of Oregon, phoneless; Bob owns a refurbishing company in North Ridge, California; Larry runs a construction company in Tulsa and plays organ in a Pentecostal Church. Jerry's whereabouts are unknown.

As for Gayle's first group: The Klassmen, in 1970, traveled to L.A. in search of success. No such luck; no further 45s. Their saxman, five foot-six and blond, Jimmy Koerber, went on to work with Ike & Tina Turner.

FLYING MACHINE
SMILE A LITTLE SMILE FOR ME
(Tony Macauley, Geoff Stephens)
Congress 6000
No. 5 *November 22, 1969*

In the winter of 1966, Danny "Kootch" Kortchmar and Joel O'Brien were members of a hot band called The King Bees. They had a contract with RCA and several biting rhythm rockers in release. Crowds loved them, and their sound, rock and roll with an R & B edge, was ahead of its time. The problem was, no one was buying their records.

Kootch had grown up with a skinny depressive kid named James Taylor. As the Bees bit he dust, Kootch, O'Brien, and Taylor went into the studios and cut some sides for JUST US members, producer/writers Al Gorgoni and Chip "Wild Thing" Taylor; the latter author of MERRILEE RUSH's "Angel of the Morning" and creator of SENATOR BOBBY. One single credited to "The Flying Machine" ("Rainy Day Mary") was issued on Rainy Day Records in the summer of 1967. Nothing much happened, and James Taylor flew to England to see if he could interest the Beatles' Apple label into recording "Carolina in My Mind" and some of his other folky material.

This short-lived unit is the group that many people think recorded "Smile a Little Smile for Me." They didn't. After "Smile" was a huge hit, Gorgoni, Chip Taylor, and others repackaged these early James Taylor recordings with the "Flying Machine" name prominently featured on the album cover, hoping to trick record buyers into thinking that this was the second album by the "Smile" group. For the most part, the ruse worked.

The Liberators from Rugby, England, had been playing together since 1964. Reg Calvert, the manager of the Fortunes, stumbled upon the Liberators, hooked them up with British Decca, dressed them up in pink sportcoats, and renamed them Pinkerton's Assorted Colours. In their motherland, Barrie Bernard (bass), Dave Holland (drums), Samuel Kempe (vocals, autoharp), Tom Long (guitar), and Anthony Newman (guitar) had a huge hit with their first release, "Mirror, Mirror." Their follow-ups did poorly, and by the late '60s, the Pinkertons needed a change. Many record collectors believe that this was the Flying Machine that recorded "Smile a Little Smile for Me." Wrong again.

Songwriter/producer Tony Macauley had written "Smile a Little Smile for Me" with Geoff Stephens; the composer and voice of THE NEW VAUDEVILLE BAND, heard on "Winchester Cathedral." Experienced music men that they were, Tony and Geoff just knew they had a hit on their hands. Using studio musicians, and possibly the lead vocal of Macauley himself, a recording was quickly made. "Smile" was never a chart wonder in England, but for what seemed like an eternity in the U.S., the tune was played on Top 40 stations.

When "Smile" exploded on the stateside landscape, a touring version of The Flying Machine was needed, so the remaining pieces of the Pinkertons—Anthony Newman, Samuel Kempe, Stuart Colman, Steve Jones, and Paul Wilkinson—were invited to fill the bill. "Baby

Make It Soon" (#87, 1970)—a cover of a MARMALADE tune—was the pseudo-group's follow-up.

Shortly afterward, and miles outside the proverbial spotlight, The Flying Machine crashed and burned on the isle of perishable pop platters. Surviving the crash was Dave Holland, who reappeared in the '80s playing drums in Shakin' Steven's band; and Stuart Colman, soon a noted BBC radio announcer and the producer of disks for the Blasters, the Inmates, Jets, Cliff Richard and in 1986, Little Richard.

STEAM
NA NA HEY HEY KISS HIM GOODBYE
(Gary DeCarlo, Dale Frashuer, Paul Leka)
Fontana 1667
No. 1 *December 6, 1969*

Steam came from Bridgeport, Connecticut. As the Chateaus, Gary DeCarlo (drums), Dale Frashuer, and Paul Leka (piano) recorded some failed 45s in the early '60s for Coral and Warner Bros. As time moved on, they separated but kept in touch. Paul became a tunesmith with Circle Five Productions. In 1968, Leka met Shelley Pinz; the couple wrote and produced THE LEMON PIPERS' "Green Tambourine" in addition to other Pipers numbers.

The following year, Leka was working at Mercury Records. Gary DeCarlo, his old Chateau buddy, had convinced the label's A & R man, Bob Reno, to let DeCarlo record some solo sides. With Paul producing, four numbers were quickly canned. Reno liked the tracks, and thought that each would do well issued as an "A" side. To fill up the "B" side of the first single, Paul and Gary were sent back into the Mercury Sound Stu-

dios to cut a throwaway flipside. Dale Frashuer stopped by the studios that night and suggested using a 1961 ballad from the trio's Chateau days called "Kiss Him Goodbye." "I said we should put a chorus to it, "Leka told Fred Bronson in *The Billboard Book of Number One Hits.* "I started writing while I was sitting at the piano going 'na, na, na, na, na, na, na, na . . .' Everything was 'na na' when you didn't have a lyric."

To the great surprise of all involved, the powers-that-be at the label decided to release "Na Na"—". . . an embarrassing record . . . an insult," in Leka's opinion—as the "A" side on Fontana, a Mercury subsidiary. Since no one wanted credit for creating the tune, a name for this nonexistent group had to be concocted. Steam—now there's a name that sounds nebulous. Gary's solo singles, which Leka and Reno had preferred to "Na Na," were eventually issued as by Garrett Scott, but not one even charted. Steam's "Na Na," however, sold more than a million copies, and has been for years the unofficial anthem for the Chicago White Sox.

Paul assembled a Steam band to tour in support of the studio creation: Jay Babins (guitar), Ray Corries (drums), Mike Daniels (bass), Hank Schorz (keyboards), Bill Steer (vocals), and Tom Zuke (guitar) were all from the Bridgeport area. When an album was needed, Gary was approached, but refused to return to the studios. Before Steam went the way of all water vapor, more singles appeared, but only one made the charts—"I've Gotta Make You Love Me" (#46, 1970).

Sarah Dallin, Keren Woodward, and Siobhan Fahey—Bananarama—returned "Na Na Hey Hey Kiss Him Goodbye" to the U.K. Top 10 in 1983; Fahey, wife to DAVID A. STEWART, is 1/2 of SHAKESPEARE'S SISTER. Four years later, THE NYLONS brought Leka's "embarrassing" ditty back to the U.S. Top 20.

the 70s

CROW

CROW
EVIL WOMAN DON'T YOU PLAY YOUR GAMES WITH ME
(Larry Weigand, Dick Weigand, Dave Wagner)
Amaret 112
No. 19 *January 10, 1970*

Crow frontman Dave Wagner began taking bass lessons in 1964. Within months, he was a plucking bassist for the Aardvarks. Early in '66, Dave changed groups—joining Joker's Wild; a Beatlesque band so named for the Brian Hyland hit.

Meanwhile, across town, responsible for nurturing the Trashmen, Gestures, and THE CASTAWAYS (and eventually Prince, MORRIS DAY, Jimmy "Jam" Harris, and Terry Lewis) were brothers Larry (bass) and Dick Weigand (guitar). Active in sound production early on, the brothers formed the Knights in '61; and with future Castaway guitarist Lonnie Knight, the Rave-Ons, in '63.

When in 1966, both the Rave-Ons and Wagner's Joker's Wild came under the managerial hand of David Anthony Productions, things got the shake-up and the "best" members of each act were merged, becoming South 40.

Before their precarious perching as Crow—Wagner, the Weigand brothers, Dave "Kink" Middlemist (organ), and Harry Nehls (drums)—South 40 worked as a Twin Cities bar band with their hard-edged R & B. One album, *Live at the Someplace Else*, and two singles were issued locally and in limited numbers by Metrobeat. South 40's big break came when they won first prize in a talent contest sponsored by the National Ballroom Operators Association in Des Moines, Iowa, in September, 1968—a recording session with Columbia Records.

Before the session, a name change was in order. Why Crow? "Well, a crow is a funky bird," explained Kink for liner-note writer Jim Oldsberg. "It's a scavenger, a nasty, hard-hitting kind of bird and our music is kind of that way. Also, it's a short name; one that's easy to remember."

On January 31, 1969, Kink, the brothers, and the rest appeared as scheduled at the Columbia Recording Studios in Chicago. Five tunes, including "Evil Woman," were taped. After listening to their demos, Columbia passed on the group. Unbeknownst to Crow, Bob Monaco, co-owner with Bill Traut of the Chicago-based Dunwich/Amaret labels, was present at the Columbia session. Monaco felt the bird band had

270

something special to offer rock and roll listeners; Traut didn't. Nearly a year passed before. Traut caved in to his partner's insistence.

In the spring of 1969, Crow was flown to Chicago to record a number of tracks, including what was to become their lone hit, "Evil Woman Don't You Play Your Games With Me." By this point, Nehls had departed and was replaced by Denny "Ludwig" Craswell, formerly of the Castaways and Blackwood Apology. The line-up was now complete. Both Atlantic and the tiny Amaret label were now bidding for the group's services. "Of course we wanted to go with the bigger company of the two," said Wagner to Oldsberg, "but nobody listened to us. In a matter of months, it turned out to be the biggest mistake we ever made. . . ."

Amaret issued "Time to Make a Turn" as the first single. Quickly it sank into oblivion. Label heads suggested issuing "Evil Woman" as the next release, but seasoned with overdubbed horns. The band balked at the idea, but the label lads went ahead and did the deed anyway. "Amaret decided to add horns to get more of a 'Chicago' sound like the Buckinghams. They had their own thoughts as to how to make our music sound better," said Wagner. "The bottom line was; if we didn't have the horns in it, they weren't going to put it out. That plucked our strings."

"Evil Woman"—with horns—became a national notable, but Crow disliked the "horrible" horns and refused to duplicate the sound in their live performances. By years end, Crow had opened or headlined at the Whiskey a-Go-Go and both the Fillmore East and West

Two follow-ups charted, "Cottage Cheese" (#56, 1970) and "Don't Try to Lay No Boogie Woogie on the King of Rock & Roll" (#52, 1970). Before the Crow crashed, four LPs of material were quickly issued.

"We were becoming more and more disillusioned with Amaret by the day," said Wagner. "We fought with them (particularly Kenny Myers who ran Amaret) over our artistic direction." Elektra Records showed an interest in acquiring Crow, but reportedly Amaret refused to let the act leave with the rights to the Crow name. "We were so tangled up in financial bullshit," said Wagner, "that I think we lost focus as to why we were really there—for the music."

Feeling there was no way of disengaging the group from the financial and managerial malaise, Wagner left Crow in 1971. The band carried on for a half year with vocals provided by Mick Stanhope, former of White Lightning. Their final gig—June 26, 1971—was a benefit for Rapid City, South Dakota, flood victims, held at Coffman Memorial Union on the campus of the University of Minnesota.

Dave Wagner recorded a poor-selling solo album for Amaret Records; Denny Craswell returned to Minneapolis, where he now owns a recording studio with former band mate Bob Folschow of the Castaways.

Beginning in 1983, Wagner revived the Crow name, which continues into the present as a touring act; though no other original members are involved.

SHOCKING
BLUE

Said Wagner, "I fully attribute the collapse of Crow to a bunch of kids not knowing anything about the business. . . ."

SHOCKING BLUE
VENUS
(Robby van Leeuwen)
Colossus 108
No. 1 *February 7, 1970*

Dark-haired, brown-eyed, and lovely lead singer Mariska Veres (b. 1949) is the daughter of Lajos Veres, internationally known gypsy violinist. "I really enjoy myself when I'm performing," she once told *Hit Parader*. "I love to smile. And I am very happy when people smile back at me." As a little girl, the half-Hungarian/half-German Mariska accompanied her father on the piano. She later played in garage bands.

Shocking Blue was a Dutch group founded by lead guitarist/sitarist Robby van Leeuwen (b. 1944). Robby had been a member of the Motions, one of Holland's leading beat groups, whose their lone stateside album, *Electric Baby* (1968), is quite sought after by vinyl collectors. In 1969, he lured drummer Cor van der Beek, bassist Klaasie van der Wal, and lead singer Fred de Wilde away from their band (Hu & The Hilltops) to form Shocking Blue. Pink Elephant Records signed the group and issued their first disk, "Lucy Brown Is Back in Town," which went to number 21 on the Dutch Top 40.

While attending a party given to honor Golden Earring's first chart-topping homeland single, van Leeuwen spotted Mariska, then singing with the Bumble Bees, the evening's entertainment. That night, legend has it, Fred de Wilde was asked to leave Shocking Blue, and Mariska was asked to join. The group's next single, "Send Me a Postcard Darling," charted in Holland.

When "Venus," their third single, was clocking in at number three on the Dutch listings, American record producer Jerry Ross was there to sign Shocking Blue-plus the George Baker Selection and THE TEE SET-to a U.S. distribution deal via his Colossus label. Considering the odds, it's incredible that all three Dutch acts charted in the States with their debut disks. Baker's "Little Green Bag" (#21, 1970) and "Paloma Blancia" (#26, 1975) both went Top 40, as did the Tee Set's "Ma Belle Arnie" (#5, 1970).

Despite her multi-charms, Veres and her band hit the American airwaves with only two more singles, "Mighty Joe" (#43, 1970) and "Long and Lonesome Road" (#75, 1970), the former a global million-seller. Ross continued to issue Shocking Blue sides in the States, although 45s like "Never Marry a Railroad Man" usually did better overseas. The group's lone stateside LP, *The Shocking Blue* (1970), sold a respectable number of copies. In 1974, Shocking Blue disbanded, allegedly due to quarrels over van Leeuwen's inability to craft another "Venus."

In the mid-'70s, Robby resurfaced with a folk-and jazz-inflected unit called Galaxy Inc. He also produced some solo sides on Veres. Neither projects garnered much global notice. In 1984, Shocking Blue reunited for two shows in a Back-to-the-'60s festival. Two years later, the strains of "Venus!" were once again permeating the nation's airwaves-a rerendering by Bananarama (#1, 1986) all the way to the top of the charts.

EDDIE HOLMAN
HEY THERE LONELY GIRL
(Earl Shuman, Leon Carr)
ABC 11240
No. 2 *February 21, 1970*

With more than 30 years of recording history behind him, Eddie Holman is still best remembered for his soulful, falsettoed/sex-changed recycling of Ruby & The Romantics' big-time smoothie from 1963, "Hey There Lonely Boy."

Eddie was maneuvered toward a musical career not long after the third day in June 1946, when he was born in Norfolk, Virginia. As a child performer, he appeared in Off-Broadway theaters as Little Eddie; was a regular on NBC-TV's "The Children's Hour." Minor releases appeared on Leopard and Ascot. He trained in the ways of sounds at the Victoria School of Music and Art in New York City, and later attended Cheyney State College in Philadelphia. While in Philly in 1965, Eddie connected with Parkway Records and won himself his first Top 20 R & B charting with "This Can't Be True" (#57, 1966). Another Parkway single, 'Am I a Loser" (#17), rode onto the R & B listings before the record label collapsed.

After a brief stay with Bell, Eddie hit his stride with ABC Records and arranger/producer Peter DeAngelis. Pete dressed Eddie's high-pitched voicings in the sticky-sweet strings of the Philadelphia Symphony Orchestra; the very same organization utilized by MFSB. The first DeAngelis-Holman collaboration, "I Love You" (R&B: #30, 1969), was a fruitful one, but their second creation, "Hey There Lonely Girl," went almost to the pinnacle of popularity.

"[Peter] recommended I do the song," Holman told *Goldmine*'s Stu Fink. "I really didn't want to do it. The only reason I did is because my wife asked me to-and that's a very good reason."

A rerelease of "Don't Stop Now" (#48, 1970) b/w a take on the Skyliners' sorrowful "Since I Don't Have You" (#48) was a double-sided mini-success, both in pop and R&B; years later, Eddie's voice would once again grace the pop charts with "This Will Be a Night to Remember" (#90, 1977). In 1974, Holman's smash was rereleased and soared to the Top 10 in England.

Sometime in the '80s Eddie became a born-again Christian and studied for a degree in theology. He recorded noted gospel releases such as *United*, "Holy Ghost" and "Give It All to the Lord." Eddie was still going strong through the '90s with secular recordings on the GSF, Silver Bird, and Salsoul labels, as well as on his own Philly-based Agape label.

TEE SET
MA BELLE AMIE
(Hans Van Eijck, Peter Tetteroo)
Colossus 107
No. 5 *March 14, 1970*

The Tee Set hailed from Delft, a tiny town in the Netherlands best known for its blue-and-white earthenware. When American pop producer Jerry Ross met these Dutch darlings, the Tee Set consisted of Pete Tetteroo (vocals), Dill Bennink (guitar, flute, banjo), Joop Blom (drums), Franklin Madjid (bass), "Heavy" Hans Van Eijck (keyboards), and a bonafide British guitarist Ray Fenwick. Due to work permit irregularities, Ray was soon absent from the group; only to appear later as a member of the Spencer Davis Group. Weeks earlier, Ross had stumbled onto Holland's SHOCKING BLUE, and in anticipation of a "Dutch Invasion," he signed up the Tee Set, a unit he had detected in a discotheque in Zurich, the George Baker Selection, and a host of other Dutch acts. While Shocking Blue, the Tee Set, and the George Baker Selection did score some stateside success, other notable Dutch acts—such as the Mob and Kannibal Komix—never dented a chart. By the end of 1970, the Dutch Invasion was essentially over.

The Tee Set had first assembled in 1966; their debut disk, "Early in the Morning," was a homeland hit. Many of their singles sold well in Denmark, Luxembourg, and other European rock regions. "Heavy" Hans, who had studied piano and composition at the Royal Conservatory, wrote tunes that were covered by the Spencer Davis Group and Germany's legendary Rattles. Lead singer Tetteroo recorded solo material concurrently with the group's platters; "Red Red Wine" was a winner in Holland. A handful of U.S. follow-ups to "Ma Belle Amie" appeared, including the charting "If You Do Believe in Love" (#81, 1970) and the tasty "She Likes Weeds"-the last song the Tee Set ever recorded.

JAGGERZ
THE RAPPER
(Donnie Iris)
Kama Sutra 502
No. 2 *March 21, 1970*

The Jaggerz were a hard-working Pittsburgh bar band formed in the mid-'60s. At the moment of their flash flight to fame, the Jaggerz consisted of keyboardist/trumpeter Thom Davis (b. Duquesne, PA), guitarist/bassist Benny Faiella (b. Beaver Falls, PA), drummer/bassist Billy Maybray, drummer Jim Pugliano, trombonist/bassist, Jimmy Ross (b. Aliquippa, PA), and lead singer/guitarist Dominic Ierace (b. 1943, Ellwood City, PA). Their individual roots dated back to the pre-Beatle years and bands with names like the Silvertones, the Starliners, and Donnie & The Donnells; the latter, long-time regulars at Dominic's dad's place, Lou's Tavern.

Joe Rock—manager of Jimmy Beaumont and the Skyliners, known to oldies fans for their perennials' "Since I Don't Have You" and "This I Swear"—discovered the Jaggerz in a saloon one night. The story goes that without much effort, he convinced Kenny Gamble and Leon Huff, later kingpins in the creation of the "Philadelphia Sound," to record the guys for the Gamble label. The resulting 1969 album (*Introducing the Jaggerz*) and several singles (notably "Baby I Love You," with Maybray singing lead) stiffed. Rock next approached Kama Sutra, brandishing one of Dominic's songs in particular. True, "The Rapper" has not aged with its colors flying, and is not a heavily-requested oldie, but at the time, "The Rapper" was a stone-cold smash.

Later sides such as "I Call My Baby Candy" (#75, 1970) and "What a Bummer" (#88, 1970) did not do as well. Five years later, Wooden Nickel Records gave what remained of the Jaggerz another go-round in the studios, but the results were worse than could be expected.

Dominic Ierace, the group's voice and main tunesmith, changed his name to Donnie Iris. For a while, Iris was a member of WILD CHERRY and later half of Iris & Taylor with MCA artist B. E. Taylor. His subsequent solo career—with the co-writing skills of ex-Cherry Mark Avsec—produced a string of Hot 100 chartings from 1980-1985 and several LPs on MCA. Don Gavin (guitar/bass) and Robert Peckman (bass), both post-hit members of the Jaggerz went on to One-Hit status with "Dancin' Man," as Q. For years, Jimmy Ross has been a member of eternally touring Skyliners.

EDISON LIGHTHOUSE
LOVE GROWS (WHERE MY ROSEMARY GOES)
(Tony Macaulay, Barry Mason)
Bell 858
No. 5 *March 28, 1970*

"I never figured on being a musician," said Tony Burrows, lead singer for Edison Lighthouse, the Brotherhood of Man, and three other One-Hit Wonders—the man who fronted more One-Hit Wonder acts than anyone. In an exclusive interview, Burrows says, "I just fell into music. I was old enough to do National Service in the Army. I was 16; which I did with David "Roger" Greenaway, John "Roger" Cook [both halves of DAVID & JONATHAN fame], Jeff Williams [and Roger Maggs, who dropped out of the group in '63]. We were all in the same ranks; all knew each other from school days and we just got together in the army and [beginning in 1958] started singing as a vocal group. We entered a couple of talent contests, in which we won. We got on television; all while in the army. And it all developed from there. It was never a conscious decision. . . ."

Tony (b. Apr. 14, 1942, Exeter, England), Jeff, and the two Rogers recorded for Donegal and Pye as the Kestrels; there were no major hits. One of their publicly passed-over sides was the Beatles' "There's a Place," a tune Burrows claims was given to them by the Fab Four. "We toured with the Beatles in England till about '65. It was the most extraordinary time; the likes not seen before or since. We'd go on directly before them on

the bill and it wasn't a good place to be, 'cause they were all waiting for the Beatles. . . . It was a great time to be alive; all was absolutely mad. . . . That time is locked in my memory. . . .

With the break up of the Kestrels in the mid-'60s, Burrows recorded a solo LP as Tony Bond (à la James Bond, which due to problems with the producer was withheld from release until 1965) and soon after joined the Ivy League. The League's back-up for touring was the Jaybirds, later relabeled TEN YEARS AFTER.

Later, as a member of the psychedelic Flowerpot Men, Burrows had a British hit in 1967 with "Let's Go to San Francisco." Flowerpot follow-ups failed to sufficiently freak people. With a decade of barrooms and ballrooms behind him, Tony called it quits and returned to what promised to be a sedate life with his wife and daughter. But writer/producer Tony Macaulay—composer of THE FLYING MACHINE's "Smile a Little Smile for Me" and the Fifth Dimensions' "(Last Night) I Didn't Get to Sleep Alone"—needed a session singer to bring to life a bubblegummy tune called "Love Grows (Where My Rosemary Goes)," so he approached Burrows.

"Love Grows" was dashed off in 40 minutes in his London apartment, with Macaulay playing guitar, said co-author Barry Mason—creator of "Delilah," "Here It Comes, Again," "Kiss Me Goodbye"—to liner-note writer Gordon Pogoda.

Once "Love Grows" and the Edison Lighthouse name were on the charts, Macaulay faced the same problem that had plagued every packager of studio groups: finding a band that would tour under the moniker on the label. After auditioning 35 or more acts, Macaulay settled on guitarist Ray Dorsey (b. Feb. 22, 1949, Berkshire), guitarist Stuart Edwards (b. May 18, 1949, Kent), bassist David Taylor (b. Oct. 7, 1950, High Wycombe), and drummer George Weyman (b. May 18, 1949, Kent). Together, these musicians had been appearing as the Greenfield Hammer. A few more Edison Lighthouse 45s were issued, but after the mild success of "It's Up to You Petula" (#72, 1971), the Edison Lighthouse name was retired; Dorsey and the rest of his crew reverted to being Greenfield.

For Tony Burrows, Edison Lighthouse was only one of many such studio-created groups for which he provided the lead voice. Tony worked with the Brotherhood of Man ("United We Stand"), WHITE PLAINS ("My Baby Loves Lovin'"), and THE PIPKINS ("Gimme Dat Ding") for their 1970 hits.

"Things got especially confusing this one night, when I went on 'Top of the Pops' as three of the groups. With 'Top of the Pops,' if you had a hit, they'd contact the record companies and say 'Can I have you on the show?' So, I got three invites this one week. Now, they weren't aware that I was actually singing lead on three different group records that were on the charts at the same time. . . . Between each song, I'd change clothes right there off to the side of the set. After the program, the producer came over to me and said, 'Tony, the word has come from above that you are not to be used anymore.' I said, 'What are you talking about?' He said, 'The word is that people are going to think that this is a con.' Quite honestly, I released some solo records after that—this hurt—and I couldn't get a play on the BBC for two years. This was frustrating. It was never as blatant as 'We ban you; you're not to be used, ever,' but records with my name didn't appear to be getting played."

Macaulay was so impressed with Burrows' vocal abilities and at the singer's insistence that he signed him to a solo contract with Bell Records. Two years' worth of 45s issued under Tony's own name did so poorly that in 1974, Burrows returned to working sessions. His only *Billboard* Stateside charting as Tony Burrows, "Melanie Makes Me Smile," peaked at number 87 in 1970.

"I finally got to record one solo album, as Tony Burrows, but it was never released. That was about the time that the BBC was blackballing me. It was finished, but it has yet to see the light of day. *The Lost Tony Burrows Album*, I would love to see that freed, someday."

As a member of THE FIRST CLASS, yet another pseudo-group of studio players, Burrows mounted the charts for a final Stateside time when the Beach Boys-esque "Beach Baby" nearly topped the *Billboard* pop charts, in 1974.

"Not as White Plains, Edison Lighthouse, or any other '70s group have I ever toured the United States. . . . I would have liked to. Fact, I never toured England with any of those groups. At times I've felt bad, particularly with Edison Lighthouse, because that decision to tour or not was taken away from me. 'Love Grows' was suppose to be a solo record—my record—but the producer and writer Tony Macaulay was coming off a bad experience with a solo artist. . . . I agreed only to do television appearances, but never work live with a band. And he agreed. And made it a group record. That one bites at me, a bit."

Three other Lighthouse 45s were issued in the U.S.; none charted though it is noteworthy to mention that for 15 years, Burrows never knew of the existence of his act's immediate follow-up, "She Works in a Woman's Way." "Ehh, you learn something new every day," he said to his informant, *Goldmine*'s Guy Aoki.

The seemingly tireless Tony Burrows continued to do demos for Vanity Fair and PAPER LACE and session work for artists like Elton John, Tom Jones, Engelbert Humperdinck, Alan Price, Cliff Richard, Chris Spedding, and KIKI DEE. Tony's voice is also heard on the initial "I'd Like to Teach the World to Sing" Coca Cola commercial.

Of note, the accompanying female voices on "Love Grows" were those of the recording act Sue & Sunny, (a.k.a. Sandra Stevens and Heather Winkland), the girls likewise revisited and heard on the Brotherhood of Man's "United We Stand."

"I'm still at it, writing, producing, and singing commercials and doing voice-overs," said Burrows. "I do have a band [more so than not called Fraud Squad] that's name keeps a-changing; though there is talk of putting it together as White Plains. I'm not sure, I may be a little too long in the tooth for it."

FRIJID PINK
THE HOUSE OF THE RISING SUN
(Alan Price)
Parrot 341
No. 7 *April 4, 1970*

When Motor City pop music is discussed, Berry Gordy's Motown empire springs to mind quicker than a hungry hound after a cheese-and-sausage pizza. "Detroit" might conjure thoughts of Bob Seger, self-proclaimed "Motor City Madman" and ex-AMBOY DUKE TED NUGENT, John Sinclair's MC5, and IGGY POP's psychedelic Stooges. Somewhat of the latter ilk-although neither as gifted nor as well known-was Frijid Pink (when the band members were asked what the name meant, they replied "cold excellence"). Frijid Pink's hopped-up and fuzzified cover version of the Animals'

FRIJID PINK

1964 classic was their brief magical moment in pop music.

Organized in Detroit in the late '60s, the band initially consisted of lead screamer Kelly Green and high school buddies Gary Ray Thompson (lead guitar) and Thomas Beaudry (bass). Drummer Richard Stevens and keyboardist Larry Zelanka were recruited from a pool of local talent. All too soon, these Pinkmen were under contract with Parrot and ravaging the charts with their third single. "Sing a Song for Freedom" (#55, 1971) and "Heartbreak Hotel" (#72, 1971) followed their smash, but the next three 45s sold poorly. Whether the band might have developed into a top-flight act is unknown, for in 1972 most of the group's original core members departed.

In 1972, with Stevens and Zelanka remaining, Pink reorganized, signed with MGM's Lion subsidiary, and issued the *Earth Omen* album and two singles, all to little avail. In 1975, with only Stevens present, another reorganization generated a final but pedestrian package for Fantasy, *All Pink Inside.*

As the sun sets on the little house that Frijid Pink built, some remnants of the act have continued to tour into the late '90s.

NORMAN GREENBAUM
SPIRIT IN THE SKY
(Norman Greenbaum, Erik Jacobsen)
Reprise 0885
No. 3 *April 18, 1970*

Mention his name and as surely as the letter B will forever follow A, pop music fans mention "Spirit in the Sky," and little else. "Spirit" wasn't Greenbaum's only charting, or arguably even his best creation, but "Spirit in the Sky," with sales scaling the 2 million mark, is now and henceforth a rock classic, on 'round the clock "oldies" radio rotation, with a trail of appearances in Hollywood flicks, from *Miami Blues, Wayne's World II*, MAID TO ORDER through the recent ozone-oozer, *Apollo 13*.

"That song of mine, I hear it all over the place," says Norman Greenbaum, ever so slowly, in a flat, but twangy monotone. "It helped and destroyed me in the same moment. With that success, I failed. . . . It was such an influential song, I was never able to satisfy people with anything else I did. I never was able to write another song that could measure up to 'Spirit.' It was just too special. And it was a fluke; certainly it wasn't me. I'd spent my career doing acoustic things; before and after. With that song I stepped outside my side and something took me over."

It was in high school that Norm (b. Nov. 20, 1942, Malden, MA) first picked up a guitar and started picking and singing. "From the start, my love was for the country-blues and old timey stuff that I heard the folkie types playing in the coffeehouses in the Boston area," says Greenbaum. As a student at Boston University, he worked the city's bongo parlors and java joints. In 1966, after years of this scene, Norm put together what might be one of the first psychedelic bands; at the least, the world's first psychedelic jug band. Greenbaum, Jack "The witchdoctor" Carrington, Evan Engber, and ballerina-wanna be Bonnie Zee Wallach—collectively known as Dr. West's Medicine Show & Junk Band—would rub, whack, or blow on such objects as a washtub, whiskey jug, Taiwan finger piano, Tibetan temple block, and their favorite, a 1949 Buick bumper bracket.

"It had to be a '49 Buick bumper bracket," Greenbaum adds. "We tried others, even a '50 Buick bracket. There's no comparison, believe me; none at all. On stage, we'd paint our faces and our clothes and had a light show; these projectors would throw these wild colors all over our bodies."

The primary influence? "It was Jim Kweskin's Jug Band, though we can't blame them for what we were doing. We were probably the only jug band into psychedelics. This is all before the Summer of Love, which I missed; must've been off on some gig."

Go Go Records caught the act, the other worldly persona and the oddball tunes like "Weird" and "The Egg Plant That Ate Chicago"; issued as the band's first single. "Egg Plant" peaked on the *Billboard* Hot 100 at #52. Their follow-up, "Gondoliers, Shakespeares, Overseers, Playboys, and Bums," failed to make a chart showing.

"What that one is all about; you got me," says Greenbaum. "Frankly, I don't know if I ever knew what it was about. I can tell you that, it had nothing to do with Bob Dylan. It was the last song that I wrote that long. I had a mentor that told me, 'Kid, you got to keep it short.'"

Months later, despite the charting success of "The Egg Plant" song, the band split up.

Norm moved to the City of Angels, and after some aborted efforts to reconstruct a jug band, he went solo. He was discovered by Eric Jacobsen while playing "Hoot Night" at the famed Troubadour; Jacobsen was then producing the Lovin' Spoonful and Sopwith Camel. Reprise issued Greenbaum's solo debut, the Jacobsen-produced *Spirit in the Sky* album, containing "Spirit," and such stand-outs as "Marcy" and "Skyline." Despite warnings by record company heads that the "Spirit" was too controversial and that religious records don't sell worth a dink, "Spirit in the Sky" became the fastest selling 45 rpm in Warner Brothers history. Overnight, Norman Greenbaum was a rock star.

"I have different stories, but I'll tell you the most popular one," says Greenbaum, in preparation for the tale of the making of the "Spirit in the Sky." "Believe it or not, that song was due to Porter Wagoner. He used to have a half-hour TV show out in L.A., at one time. About 20 minutes into the show he'd religiously do a religious song. This one time, he had this huge stained glass backdrop. Breath-taking, it was. And he did this song about a man who lived deep in the mountains, who hadn't been to church in 20 years. He'd been out there with his mule panning for gold, when it hit him that he needed to go back to church; one more time. So, he made it all the way into town—with his mule, you understand—went through the gate and up to the church. And there was a sign, that read: 'The preacher is on vacation.' It floored me. I fell down; plus Porter was wearing those really great clothes from Nudies. I knew then that, God almighty, I needed a religious song. I didn't want to get weird about it, but it took me months and months to get that song together. Finally, it came together; my version of a spiritual."

The colossal success of the single surprised everyone, including Norm, who did not have a touring band ready to take advantage of the disk's popularity. Momentum was lost when his immediate follow-ups— "Canned Ham," a track on Norm's second album, *Back Home Again*, peaked at #46 and "California Earthquake," #93—charted only moderately.

"'California Earthquake' did okay, but ultimately it didn't go anywhere," Greenbaum told *Creem*'s Ed Ward. "I sat back, and I said, 'Well, I'm not a rock and roller. I got money—f*** it.' And I went into the dairy business." With 45 cows, Norm and his wife marketed their Velvet Acres Goat Milk in health food stores in Berkeley and Marin County.

With the aid of legendary string man Ry Cooder and Fritz Richmond, an alumnus in the Kweskin Jug Band, Norm put together his third and last solo album, the acoustic and country-bent *Petaluma*. He excitedly planned to tour in support of the effort, but divorce proceedings soon left him in a funk. According to Jacobsen, Greenbaum's wife got the farm, and when spotted in the declining '70s, Norm was "living in a reconditioned chicken coop."

"One day I stopped doing music," says Greenbaum. "I got frustrated and for quite awhile I just didn't do it; until last year (1995)."

Norm refers to the unissued "Day They Sold Beer in Church" as "sort of a follow-up to "Spirit." "I was under such pressure to follow 'Spirit' that one day I just got silly and moody and it all came together; all these thoughts that were just up there and out there. 'Beer in Church' is good. It needed to be released."

"You know, they used 'Spirit' in a commercial for American Express," says Greenbaum. "They did a kind of neat thing with it visually, with this huge airplane headin' up high. It gave me a lot more faith in American Express; but they still won't give me a card. They gave me money for using it, but not the Gold Card."

MICHAEL PARKS
LONG LONESOME HIGHWAY
(James Hendricks)
MGM 14104
No. 20 *April 18, 1970*

With an eye to the success of *Easy Rider*, NBC constructed a TV series about a youth, his motorcycle, and the search for the meaning of life. Each week for a year, America watched stone-faced, alienated Jim Bronson as he moved about meeting faces and places and doing his thing, man. While the series—"Then Came Bronson"—was warm, Mike had MGM Records issue his "Long Lonesome Highway." When the series left the scene, so did Mike's singing career.

Born a truck driving man's son, on April 4, 1938, in Corona, California, Michael's real life was much like that of Jim Bronson. As a teen, he left home and took up odd jobs trying to get a fix on his place in the universe and a spot on the mammoth movie screen. During the '60s, he guested as off-beat characters on TV shows like "The Asphalt Jungle," "Bus Stop," and "The Detectives." In 1966, Mike played the nudie role of Adam in John Huston's *The Bible*. Other movie roles followed: *The Happening* (1967), *The Private Files of J. Edgar Hoover* (1977), *The Evictors* (1979), *The Return of Josey Wales* (1986), *The Hit Man* (1991), *Caged Fury* (1990); the latter he co-associated produced. In 1980, he did some episodes for a TV pilot called "Reward." The program was to be about an alienated cop. But alienation was no longer hip, and the series was shelved. For two seasons—the fall of '85, through the spring of '87—Parks was the brother of Jeff Colby, the main player in the "Dynasty" spinoff series "The Colbys."

MARMALADE
REFLECTIONS OF MY LIFE
(W. Campbell, T. McAleese)
London 20058
No. 10 *May 9, 1970*

Marmalade was formed in Glasgow, in 1961 when two aspiring guitarists, "Junior" Willie Campbell (b. July 24, 1946, Glasgow, Scotland) and Pat Fairley (b. Apr. 14, 1946, Glasgow), met in Glasgow. Pat and Junior recruited vocalist Dean Ford (b. Thomas McAleese, May 31, 1947, Airdrie, Scotland), vocalist/bassist Graham Knight (b. Dec. 8, 1946, Glasgow), and soon-to-depart drummer Raymond Duffy. Before Marmalade's sight and sound jelled, the unit was named the Gaylords. They quickly became quite popular in Scotland, and were voted the country's top group from 1964 to 1966.

Duffy left, and Alan Whitehead (b. July 24, 1947, Owestry, England) was whacking the skins by the time the group decided to move to London. Once settled there, they redubbed themselves Marmalade for a show-stopping appearance at the 1967 Windsor Jazz Festival. After a successful Thursday-night residency at the famed Marquee Club—where the Yardbirds, the Animals, and the Rolling Stones first earned their reputations—England's CBS label signed the group to a recording contract.

From 1968 through 1976, Marmalade could do little wrong with British fans. Almost a dozen of their singles became U.K. hits, and more than half of these reached the Top 10 (a cover of the Beatles' "Ob-La-Di, Ob-La-Da" sold a million copies). Ten albums were released throughout Europe, yet the moody "Reflections of My Life" was the band's only excursion into the hallowed halls of stateside hitdom. Before Marmalade's success soured, "Rainbow" (#51, 1970) and "Failing Apart at the Seams" (#49, 1976) caused minor U.S. chart disturbances.

As of the early '90s, an edition of Marmalade was still actively working the London bars. A solid self-titled LP appeared in the U.S. on G & P Records in 1982, produced by Junior Campbell. By this point, Graham Knight was the only original member present. Ex-Poet, Hugh Nicholson, Junior's replacement, would later chart in the States with the Elton John produced group Blue. Junior had left the fold in 1972 to attend the Royal Academy of Music, to jingles and film music, and to record with something called Fishbaugh Fishbaugh Zorn. He went on to cut a few solo albums and to score Top 20 slots in England with two singles, "Sweet Illusion" and "Hallelujah Freedom." After a Sunday paper's expose of the members' sex life on the road, Dean Ford exited in 1974, did sessions for the Alan Parsons Project, and recorded an unsuccessful solo album; reportedly, he now works as a house painter in Los Angeles.

IDES OF MARCH
VEHICLE
(Jim Peterik)
Warner Bros. 7378
No. 2 *May 23, 1970*

Jim Peterik (lead vocals, guitar) was a mere 13 in the summer of 1964, when he and some buddies—students at Piper Grade School in Berwyn, Illinois—formed the Renegades. "Larry Millas was in the audience when we played this 4th of July celebration," said Peterik, in an exclusive interview. "He came by and told me, 'You know your band really stinks. But you're really good, and I got this band, the Shy Lads . . .'" After Larry persisted, Jim checked out the band and within moments was a member, with Millas (rhythm guitar, vocals), Bob Bergland (guitar, sax), and Bob Erhart (drums); later replaced by Mike Borch.

"'If I join,' I told them, 'that name has got to go,'" As the Shondels—no reference to TROY SHONDELL, as alleged—they played Beatles tunes and recorded a one-off single, "No Two Ways About It" b/w "Like It or Lump It," for the Epitome label.

Paul Sampson, the owner of The Cellar—a converted warehouse known for featuring the Shadows of Knight, Saturday's Children, the Little Boy Blues, H. P. Lovecraft, and other area garage bands—liked the spunky Shondell sound enough to let the guys play there as regulars. The catch was, they had to appear as Batman & The Boy Wonders.

"We agreed," said Peterik, "but when we showed up to play, we took the stage dressed liked everybody else in the audience. Sampson had to make up some kind of excuse for us, saying that our capes and masks were at the cleaners! It was our first experience with rock and roll hype."

Thoroughly displeased with the Batman concept, the Shondells—now high school students, studying Shakespeare—renamed themselves the Ides of March (for the first disk, misspelled "I'des") after the day of Julius Caesar's assassination. Larry's mom persisted and got the act signed with Parrot Records. Their debut, "You Wouldn't Listen" (#42, 1966), became a major Midwestern hit; but because their labelmates were Tom Jones, Them, and the Zombies, listeners thought these infectious I'des were British. "Our manager and the label said, 'Hey, you got to go along with the charade.' So, for awhile, we had to put on these English accents," said Jim, "and we had to wear these really strange wigs, not because of the English thing, but because our school had this rigid dress code."

"Roller Coaster" (#92, 1966) charted modestly, but three other 45s for Parrot failed to connect nationally. Recast as a horn band—with Ray Herr (vocals/utility man, various instruments), John Larson (horns), and Steve Daniels (horns); soon replaced by Chuck Somar—the Ides switched to Kapp for a 45, then Warner Bros; "Vehicle" was their second single.

"The idea for the song," Peterik explained, "came from the stereotype [of the] dirty old man, cruising the streets in his black sedan and enticing little girls by offering them candy. Also, I had this lab partner, Bill, kind of a doper, and he showed me this anti-drug pamphlet that depicted the drug pusher as a 'friendly stranger.' So, I put those things together and came up with 'Vehicle.'"

"Superman" (#64, 1970), basically a remodeled "Vehicle," was a way to do a similar follow-up. Label heads warned the Ides were being pegged as a horn band or jazz-rockers; something no longer cool and on the way out. The following year, another sound change was made with the folk-flavored "L.A. Goodbye" (#73, 1971). When another 45 flopped, the group was let go. With the addition of the blind pianist Dave Arelano, the group moved to RCA for several not so financially successful albums and singles.

"Our major problem was we were recorded so young; caught, you could say, before we developed a style of our own," said Jim. "Most artists hit it when they're 25 or so. We were doing the British thing when I was 13. We became a blotter of everything that was out there. We went from British Invasion, to horn rock, to Crosby, Stills and Nash, to country rock. And, frankly, nobody knew where we were."

They played their last set before screaming teens in the gymnasium of their alma mater, Morton West High, one November night in 1973.

Bergland became an accountant. Borch joined a group called M.S. Funk. Herr appeared in various local acts, such as the Orphanage, Scott & Stevens, and Showboat. Larry Millas and John Somar got together in 1974 with Tom Dooley of the Cryan' Shames in order to form the Ides/Shames Reunion. Thereafter, Millas became an engineer and part-owner of Chicago's Tanglewood Studios.

Dating back to 1971, Peterik had been writing tunes for CHASE. When the Ides split, Jim, who had been appearing with the band and appeared on their third and last LP, was considering joining Chase. Bill Chase and three other members were killed in a plane crash on August 9, 1974.

Peterik went on to do some solo sides for Epic; notably "Don't Fight the Feeling." For awhile he fronted the Chi-Rhythm. With Gary Smith, Frank Sullivan, Marc Roubay, and Stephan Ellis, Peterik charted repeatedly throughout the '80s as Survivor—with soundtrack hits like "Eye of the Tiger" (#1, 1982) for *Rocky III*, "The Moment of Truth" (#63, 1984) for *The Karate Kid*, and "Burning Heart" (#2, 1986) for *Rocky IV*. When Survivor took a hiatus in the early '90s, Peterik with original members—Bergland, Borch, Larson, Millas—plus Scott May (keyboards) and Dave Stahlberg (trombone) reformed the Ides of March. New packages continue to be issued, *Ideology* (1992), *Age Before Beauty* (1997).

WHITE PLAINS
MY BABY LOVES LOVIN'
(Roger Cook, Roger Greenaway)
Deram 85058
No. 13 *June 27, 1970*

"I played in the Ivy League for a few years," said Tony Burrows, lead voice for White Plains, in an exclusive interview. "I was on 'Funny How Love Can Be,' which was a minor hit over here, in the States. I had replaced John Carter in the group, and he was the voice of their bigger hit, 'Tossin' and Turnin'' [(#87, 1965)]. Then I went on to the Flowerpot Men—Flower Pot, it was called in America. Potty idea it was, really. It was not the best thing for us to lumber ourselves with a name like that cause when flower power disappeared so did the band. It was that band that evolved into White Plains—the first of my big-time bands, in my homeland; second or third over here in the States. But it was at this time, 1970, that I'd decided that I'd had enough, enough of the traveling, and to stick to working in studios; of course this is when it just happened that my voice became accepted and the hits happened.

"Dick Rowe at Decca, head of the A & R at [British] Decca, said, 'Hey, we got all these [Flower Pot] tracks [cut in 1969] in the can, can we release them.' I said, 'Sure,' and Dick came up with the name White Plains [the name of an actual place, a suburb in New York State]. And the very first record—"My Baby Loves Lovin'"—was a hit, so the band was back together again—though not with me."

Besides Burrows, White Plains was to be a one-off grouping of Robin Shaw, Pete Nelson, Neil Landon—all sometime members of Edison Lighthouse—and British sessioneers, singers, writers, producers David "Roger" Greenaway and John "Roger" Cook. Recording as DAVID & JONATHAN, Cook and Greenaway had secured their own niche as One-Hit Wonders in the U.S. with a cover of the Beatles' album track "Michelle" (#18, 1966). More importantly, the two Rogers were formidable songwriters, who alone or as a duo, throughout the '60s and '70s, penned hits for artists like CAROL DOUGLAS, THE ENGLISH CONGREGATION, the Fortunes, the Hollies, the New Seekers, WHISTLING JACK SMITH, and Tony Burrows' other frontings, THE PIPKINS and EDISON LIGHTHOUSE.

Burrows, the one-time member of the British charting Ivy League and White Plain earlier incarnation the Flowerpot Men, had previously, earlier in 1970, found further successes with two other pseudo-groups, the Brotherhood of Man and Edison Lighthouse. Still further studio-only creations by the Pipkins ("Gimme Dat Ding") and FIRST CLASS ("Beach Baby") were to follow shortly.

"The melody for 'My Baby Loves Lovin' came in about 30 minutes," said Burrows, "except for the middle eight bars, which came later. . . . The song was like an after-thought, the last song cut at this session. We'd already cut four songs and 10 minutes were left. We did the song in one take; and that was it."

White Plains' immediate follow-up to "My Baby Loves Lovin'" was "Lovin' My Baby," which charted at number 82 in 1970. Nothing further issued in the United States even so much as hinted at hitdom, though British record-buyers were much more receptive—nearly half a dozen more pop puffs by White Plains left their marks on the U.K. charts, including a Top 10 cover of Bobby Sherman's "Julie Do Ya Love Me."

BLUES IMAGE
RIDE CAPTAIN RIDE
(Frank Konte, Carlos Pinera)
Atco 6746
No. 4 *July 11, 1970*

They were high school friends, all born and raised in Tampa, Florida—percussionist Manuel Bertematti (b. 1946), drummer Joe Lala, and lead singer/guitarist Carlos "Mike" Pinera (b. Sept. 29, 1948). Beginning in the mid-'60s, they performed together at local functions. It wasn't, however, until after they graduated, and after Joey had worked for a while as a barber, that the three-some met bassist Malcolm Jones (b. Cardiff, Wales) and the idea of a Latin-like blues band became a reality. Malcolm was a pro, had spent 10 years in bands in Wales, and was now settled in the States as the DJ for an underground radio program called "The London Scene."

They toured about the East Coast, and even touched down in Europe, presenting their evolving blues blend. For a while, they ran a psychedelic hangout in Tampa called Dino's. Keyboardist Frank "Skip" Konte (b. Canyon City, OK)—Alaskan-raised philosophy dropout, and one-time welder and sign-painter—joined early in 1968. By year's end, the group was based in New York City, where they ran a club in a converted bowling alley called The Image. Besides offering their own performances, the Blues Image booked acts like the Mothers of Invention, the Lovin' Spoonful, and Cream.

Reps from Atlantic Records spotted the troupe at the Whiskey-a-Go-Go in 1968. A first album, *Blues*

BLUES IMAGE

Image, was issued in 1969; it was quickly followed by *Open* (1970). *Open* featured what would become the group's singular single of significance, "Ride Captain Ride." But with success came dissension: Pinera left to join IRON BUTTERFLY, so singer Dennis Correll and guitarist Kent Henry were brought in. Before the name was shelved, and some of the members drifted into a band called Manna, one more LP—*Red, White and Blues Image* (1971)—was patched together.

In the early '70s, Pinera and Bertematti recorded with the New Cactus Band. Thereafter, Mike recorded with Ramatram, his own Thee Image, and in the early '80s, with Alice Cooper. After a few solo efforts, he appeared in the '90s on an attempted comeback album for TINY TIM. Jones moved to England, where he did studio work with Pink Floyd's Syd Barrett and the Soft Machine's Kevin Ayers. Konte has since recorded with Brooklyn Dreams, Cold Blood, and Three Dog Night.

Lala has hardly been out of the studio limelight, having played with artists like the Bee Gees, Jackson Browne, Harry Chapin, John Cougar Mellencamp, Crosby, Stills, Nash & Young, RICK DERRINGER, SOUTHER-HILLMAN-FURAY BAND. . .

FIVE STAIRSTEPS
O-O-H CHILD
(Stan Vincent)
Buddah 165
No.8 *July 18, 1970*

Clarence Burke, Sr., a Chicago police officer, had been stabbed and shot twice in the line of duty, and considered himself fortunate to be alive. He was the father of five when an idea struck him. Mrs. Burke had been lining her offspring up on the couch and teaching them to sing along with TV commercials and pop records. Stepping back to view them, she remarked, "They look just like stairsteps." In 1965, when the quality of the harmonizing had improved, Papa entered his brood in a contest at the famed Regal Theatre. They sang, danced, and walked off with first prize.

While shopping in a neighborhood grocery, Papa boasted about his kids to Fred Cash, a guy he knew from way back. What he didn't know was that Cash was now a member of the Impressions. Cash offered to set up an audition for the Five Stairsteps with his boss, Curtis Mayfield. Curtis liked what he heard, and before long, the group—which consisted of guitarist Clarence, Jr. (b. May 25, 1949), guitarist James (b. Sept. 19, 1950), guitarist/drummer Dennis (b. 1952), bassist Kenny (b. Sept. 28, 1953), and Alohe "Lannie" (b. 1948), the group's eldest and the only female—was an overnight success.

"You Waited Too Long" (#16, 1966), the flip side of their first release for Windy C, did well with R & B listeners, like nearly every disk right up until their double-sided monster masterpiece, "O-o-h Child" b/w "Dear Prudence." Up until this point, they billed themselves as "America's First Family of Soul." Thereafter, things changed.

Mr. and Mrs. Burke eventually had 11 children. The group's line-up fluctuated constantly. Little Cubie (b. 1966) was added: he would make sounds, prance, and wet his pants. Pop even slapped the bass and sang lead. But more threatening to the group's credibility were their unsuccessful forays into pop and rock, which created internal conflicts about musical direction.

Before the family group splintered in the early '70s, the Stairsteps provided session support to recordings by Quincy Jones, Stevie Wonder, and Billy Preston. In 1976, with the aid of Preston—who Kenny had toured with for much of 1974—some members regrouped for an album, *Second Resurrection*, and a few singles for George Harrison's Dark Horse label. "From Us to You" (#10) did quite well on *Billboard*'s R & B listings, but the revised edition was short-lived.

In 1980, Clarence, Dennis, James, and Kenny returned as The Invisible Man's Band with a R & B Top 10, "All Night Long" (#9); minor R & B chartings continued into the mid-'80s. Kenny (now spelled "Keni") left to forge what seemed a promising solo career: to date, he has had three albums issued and only a few mild R & B chartings: "Let Somebody Love You" (#66, 1981) and "Risin' to the Top" (#63, 1983).

As a bass player, Keni has recorded with Peabo Bryson, the Emotions, the Four Tops, Gladys Knight & The Pips, Smokey Robinson, Eugene Record, Diana Ross, Sly & The Family Stone, Bill Withers . . . as a producer, his work includes efforts for THE JONES GIRLS, O'Jays, the Whispers, and the Whitehead Brothers.

PIPKINS
GIMME DAT DING
(Albert Hammond, Mike Hazelwood)
Capitol 2819
No. 9 *July 18, 1970*

"It all came about like this, explained Pipkin co-lead Tony Burrows in an exclusive interview, Roger Greenaway and I were doing back-up vocals for Freddie & The Dreamers, for an album, a children's story, *Oliver and the Underworld*, that Freddie [Garrity] was doing a soundtrack for, that they didn't know how to approach. The song was actually about a conversation between a pianola and a metronome. . . . So Albert [Hammond, the tunes co-writer] said, 'Have you got any ideas,' and Roger and I just came up with these two silly verses. Eventually, the record company decided that this was probably single's material and released it. It was a hit; surprised me. Freddie was upset, it was the only song on the album that he didn't sing himself."

Greenaway provided the falsetto, the pianola's part; while the metronome was given voice by Burrows who utilized what he called his "hairy caveman" or "throwaway, spoken, bass-crook."

"We did some television promotion, on 'Top of the Pops,' dressed as clowns—Sssh!—so that no one would know who we were," added Burrows. Then, they asked us to do more songs, and to do them in that vein. Now, we knew it was a one-off thing. But we gave them the Coasters' 'Yakety Yak,' which worked well as an original by them; but it flopped [by us]."

The Pipkins session was assembled by producer John Burgess. During the '60s, John had helped create hit disks for Freddie & The Dreamers, Manfred Mann, Peter & Gordon, and ADAM FAITH. Soon after "Gimme Dat Ding," Burgess would do it again and assemble yet another studio group, THE ENGLISH CONGREGATION.

Burrows (b. Apr. 14, 1942, Exeter, England) was a one-time member of an evolving assortment of British groups, the Kestrels, who toured with the Beatles; the Ivy League; and the Flowerpot Men. Burrows' voice pops up quite frequently in '70s pop history footnotes for his work with numerous successful studio-only units. Earlier in 1970, Burrows had sang lead on "Love Grows (Where My Rosemary Goes)" by EDISON LIGHTHOUSE, "United We Stand" by the Brotherhood of Man, and "My Baby Loves Lovin'" by WHITE PLAINS. Post-Pipkins, he would reemerge with "Beach Baby," a 1974 hit for FIRST CLASS. Less notoriety would be accorded his offering as Kincade, Domino, Touch, Magic, and the West End Boys.

David "Roger" Greenaway (b. Aug. 23, 1942, Southmead, England) and Burrows had both been members in the Kestrels. Greenaway, with yet another Kestrel, John "Roger" Cook went on to become One-Hit Won-

MIGUEL RIOS

times, living in the country, and being very enthusiastic. . . . We're all silly inside at times. And that's an okay place to be."

MIGUEL RIOS
A SONG OF JOY
(HIMNO A LA ALEGRIA)
(Orbe-W. De Los Rios)
A & M 1193
No. 14 *July 18, 1970*

Family and friends say that Miguel (b. 1944, Granada, Spain) started singing when he was six. Two years later, he was a member of his school choir. Once his school days were behind him, he formed a rock group that worked the local bars. A record man with Hispavox Records let the lad cut some sides for the homeland market. "El Rio," "Vuelvo a Granada," "Yo Solo un Hombre," and "El Cartel" all proved winners; with Rios being allegedly elevated to the status of "the pop star" of Spanish youth. At this juncture, Miguel was offered the shot at doing a commemorative number, with composer/arranger Waldo De Los Rios (no relation), for the bicentennial of Beethoven's birth. De Los Rios and someone named Orbe had concocted a mammoth production of a portion of the last movement of Beethoven's Ninth Symphony, complete with a huge chorus and a host of instruments.

After Ludwig's immortal melody worked its way through the world's pop charts—with massive sales registered in Holland, Poland, Italy, France . . . and throughout all of Central America—other adaptations, as "Himno a la Alegria" (another slicing of the last movement of Beethoven's Ninth) fell on worn ears and Miguel's popularity returned to that of being merely a homeland hero.

The following year, Waldo returned to *Billboard*'s listings with his own pop treatment, "Mozart's Symphony No. 40 in G Minor K 550, First Movement" (#67, 1971). His album, *Sinfonias* (#53, 1971), also sold well. On March 28, 1977, Waldo De Los Rios died.

ders in the States as DAVID & JONATHAN—in the successful tradition of Chad & Jeremy and Peter & Gordon—with their George Martin-produced remake of the Beatles' "Michelle." Thereafter—together or apart—Greenaway was responsible for much jingle-writing, session-work, and composing; notably "Here Comes That Rainy Day Feeling Again," "I Was Kaiser Bill's Batman," "Doctor's Orders," and "I'd Like to Teach the World to Sing"—to name but a few. In 1983, he was appointed the Chairman of the British Performing Rights Society.

"Gimme Dat Ding" was an Albert Hammond and Mike Hazelwood composition commissioned for a British TV series. "I obviously had children in mind," explained Hammond to Martin Aston of Q magazine, "but I love rhythmic things, like American novelty songs. The story I wrote was of a little boy and his grandfather clock which had lost its memory, who meet various types of machinery on their odyssey, like the Angry Drain, the Clockwork King, the Underdog, the Mighty Dictaphone, even. One was a metronome who has lost his 'ding,' so he can't tell his beloved friend the pianola if it's playing a waltz in 4/4, 7/8. . . ."

Albert had scored in 1968 as a member of the MAGIC LANTERNS ("Shame Shame") and would have later pop success in the States with "It Never Rains in Southern California" (#5, 1972) and "I'm a Train" (#31, 1974).

"It was a stupid song, wasn't it? I like it though," added Hammond, "because it reminds me of very good

PACIFIC GAS & ELECTRIC
ARE YOU READY?
(Charlie Allen, John Hill)
Columbia 45158
No. 14 *August 1, 1970*

Not well known, they were a long-haired experiment in tolerance and love. That's how Frank Cook, the band's drummer, has described Pacific Gas & Electric: "We think of PG & E as not just a music group, but a brotherhood," Cook explained in the liner notes on the group's first album. "We've found that if there is a bad karma going down between any members of the group, the music does not fall together." Eventually, the inevitable "bad karma" was the band's downfall.

Formed early in 1968, at the peak of the San Francisco peace + love phenomenon, the band consisted of Charlie Allen (lead vocals), Tom Marshall (guitar), Glenn Schwartz (guitar), Canned Heat alumnus Frank Cook (drums), and Brent Block (bass); soon replaced by Frankie Petricca. "A Jew, a Christian, a black, a greaser, and a WASP" was Cook's description. "Five more different and divergent personalities could not be conceived of."

In 1969, Bright Orange Records issued an album of their blues- and gospel-influenced rock sounds, *Get It On*. Months later, Columbia Records took great notice of the thunderous applause the act received for their four performances at the optimistically titled First Annual Miami Pop Festival. The event was a success in generating revenues, good vibes, and a Columbia contract for PG & E. It would, however, be the last of such a three-day affair (December 28-30, 1968) in the state.

A truncated-for-radio version of "Are You Ready?" (featuring the vocal assistance of famed session singers, the Blackberries—Vanette Fields, Clyde King, Shirley Matthews, Lorna Willard) from the brotherhood's second Columbia LP (*Are You Ready?*) proved to be a winner. While a few other 45s—"Father Come on Home" (#93, 1970), "Thank God for You Baby" (#97, 1972)—gathered some interest, and a fourth LP (*PG & E*, 1971) sold fairly well, all was not well within the fold. Guns were drawn and shots fired after a gig at the Cat's Eye, a reported redneck room in Raleigh, North Carolina. The band's lead guitarist swore off drugs, found God, and unwittingly had the group barred from Canada when at the border en route to Toronto's Electric Circus, he confessed to his former drug habit. Various personnel changes resulted and "bad karma" was now pervasive. After their final effort, *The Best of PG & E*, Pacific Gas & Electric, in the words of one record-company rep, "went the way of all rock and roll flesh."

Glenn Schwartz, the born-again who could not lie to the Canadian border guards, went on to work with the James Gang. Petricca hung up his ax for commodity trading at Chicago's Mercantile Exchange. Explained Petricca, to *Chicago Sun Times* writer Leslie Baldacci, of his radical career change: "The hours are different, the situation is different, but the excitement is the same." His eight-year-old son Luke was recently shown a video of the band in action. His reaction: "You know Dad, that was awesome."

And Charlie, he did resurrect the band's name for a one-off album (*Pacific Gas and Electric, Starring Charlie Allen*) on Dunhill in 1973. No other original brothers were in attendance. Charlie Allen died on May 7, 1990, at the age of 48.

ALIVE AND KICKING
TIGHTER, TIGHTER
(Tommy James, Bob King)
Roulette 7078
No. 7 *August 8, 1970*

"I should have recorded that—it was my song," said Tommy James, the undisputed bubblegum king, in an exclusive interview. "But, I'll tell ya, I decided that [at that point] I had taken it as far as I could take it. I was a burn-out. Matter of fact, I played Montgomery, Alabama, and that's when it happened—I conked out on stage. I just wasn't interested in doing anything anymore."

Alive and Kicking was a late '60s Big Apple-based band fronted by two vocalists, Pepe Cardona and Sandy Toder. They played the Bitter End, the Electric Circus, and momentarily were considered a happening band. Pepe, Sandy, and the rest—Vito Albano (drums), John Parisio (guitar), Bruce Sudano (organ), and Thomas "Woody" Wilson (bass)—were brought to the attention of Tommy James by what seems on first glance a rather complex lineage.

"Get this," said Pepe, in an exclusive interview, "Sandy's brother was married to this girl, see, who became our manager and her best friend was Tommy's wife. So, she got Tommy to come down and see us. At the time, in the late '60s there was these Hullabaloo clubs, and he came to this out of the way one in Brooklyn. Man, he loved us and decided then to give us this song. At first it was 'Crystal Blue Persuasion.' That was nice, but then he changed his mind saying, 'Don't worry, I'll write something else for you guys, 'cause I want this one.' It was disappointing 'cause we had worked it up, the vocals and all, and here he comes and says 'No, I'll write you another one.'"

James did come through and wrote and produced "Tighter, Tighter," with an arrangement by Jimmy Wisner (a.k.a. KOKOMO, of "Asia Minor" fame), for the group. And while James' career would experience something of a second coming after his reported "break-down" and break-up of the Shondells (with the charting of "Draggin' the Line" [#4, 1971], "I'm Comin' Home" [#40, 1971], and "Nothing to Hide" [#41, 1971]), Alive and Kicking died after the issuance of one LP (*Alive 'n Kickin'*) and a few faulty Tommy James-less 45s, "Just Let It Come" (#69, 1970) and "Good Ole Lovin' Back Home."

Pepe was asked why the group didn't get James to write them some more tunes: "Well, we were real cocky.

I'll tell ya, we thought we were really it and that 'Tighter, Tighter' was too bubblegum. We were really long-haired and doing all original material, and we wanted to go into more heavy rock. Tommy felt we ought to come out with something along the lines of 'Tighter.' We didn't want to do it, so then Tommy didn't want to record us anymore.

"We did three singles and that one LP and broke up just after that last single. They didn't even put our names on the back of the album! It was terrible. We finally had to break up, just to get away from Morris Levy [owner of the Roulette label].

"I lost track of Sandy. For a long time after, she was trying to make it on her own. She did a little off-Broadway and a play, but I lost contact. In 1976, I reformed the group with Vito Albano and Woody Wilson [included in the line-up are Richie Incorvaia [bass] and Steve Spagis [guitar]. We're still doin' it, five nights a week in the New York area. Basically, we do covers [of current hits], but we each have our own projects. Like, I've got this remake of 'Tighter, Tighter' that I'd like to get released."

John Parisio recently resurfaced in the Lynch Boys Band; Bruce Sudano, who married Donna Summer, has had some solo sides issued in the '80s by Millennium and has experienced some success with his trio, Brooklyn Dreams. Dueting with Summers, the act went Top 10 with "Heaven Knows" (#4, 1979).

Twenty years after reforming—almost 30 years after that lone hit—Pepe, Vito, and Woody still work the Big Apple bars, and ache for that next deal, that next disk.

ERIC BURDON & WAR
SPILL THE WINE
(Howard Scott, Morris Dickerson, Harold Brown, Charles Miller, Lonnie Jordan, Sylvester Allen, Lee Oscar Levitin)
MGM 14118
No. 3 *August 22, 1970*

"Mother Blues," a Memphis Slim tune, was the last music to ever to be executed by JIMI HENDRIX. Jimi was depressed, holed up in his London apartment for months. The night of September 17, 1969, buddy Eric Burdon pursued Jimi to check out his new band, War, and to jam a tune or two. Later that evening, he would take nine sleeping pills.

As lead singer of the Animals, Eric Burdon (b. May 11, 1941, Walker-on-Tyne, England) had helped create some of the finest R & B-based British Invasion records. After a string of hits like "House of the Rising Sun," "Don't Let Me Be Misunderstood," "It's My Life," and "We Gotta Get Out of This Place," Eric discovered LSD and led his New Animals through a psychedelic love-and-peace phase. Gentler and softer singles followed: "San Francisco Nights," "Monterey," "Anything." In 1968, Burdon announced that the album *Love Is* would be the group's final record, and soon dropped out of sight.

Meanwhile, an early incarnation of War—a group called either the Creators, the Romeos, or Senior Soul—was cutting unsuccessful sides. When Eric ran into them in L.A. in 1969, the band, redubbed Night Shift, consisted of percussionist Sylvester "Papa Dee" Allen (b. July 19, 1931), drummer Harold Brown (b. Mar. 17, 1946), bassist B. B. Dickerson (b. Aug. 3, 1949), keyboardist Lonnie Jordan (b. Nov. 21, 1948), saxophonist Charles Miller (b. June 2, 1939), and guitarist Howard Scott (b. Mar. 15, 1946).

"We were playing in North Hollywood with Deacon Jones, the football-player-turned-singer," Harold Brown recalled to *Rolling Stone*. "One night we were sitting around waiting for the star to arrive. He never did show up, but Eric Burdon and [harmonica virtuoso] Lee Oskar [b. Mar. 24, 1948, Denmark], a musician from Copenhagen, did. Lee got up there, and we started doing this shuffle, it must have lasted about 40 or 45 minutes. . . . When it was over, everybody's mind was blown."

In his autobiography, *I Used to Be an Animal, but I'm All Right Now*, Eric reports that he was penniless, when the proposed union of he and the Night Shift happened—living on a Hollywood hill with a girlfriend named Caroline, who sold psychedelic pillows door-to-door. "She was hawking her wares in Beverly Hills when she met two guys who said they wanted to manage me."

They were Far Out Productions, the Gold Dust Twins, Jerry Goldstein and Steve Gold, "an ex-CPA and one-time stand-up comedian," who at the time was selling pop posters out of his office. "They were ruthless and vicious," wrote Burdon, "one brain with two mouths."

The day after the jam, Eric invited Night Shift over to Goldstein's pad in Benedict Canyon. Burdon offered the guys co-billing if they would work for him as his back-up band. They agreed; Goldstein and Gold, renamed the band War. "The deal," Burdon explained, "was I'd give them talent and they'd give me the tools I needed to move forward as an artist."

"We started doing road shows with Eric—and I mean road shows in the real sense of the word. We took seven band members plus our road manager, and a trailer on the back of a '66 Ford station wagon that was knocking before we even left California. We did that for two years."

Eric Burdon & War crafted a soulful mix of Latin, funk, and jazz. Success finally materialized with "Spill the Wine" and its follow-up, "They Can't Take Away Our Music" (#50, 1971). Their collaboration generated two best-selling albums, *Eric Burdon Declares War* (1970) and *The Black Man's Burdon* (1970), but problems with the MGM label beset the group.

"Right to this day [1973], I haven't seen any kind of statements or money from MGM," Brown complained. "Steve [Gold] decided that he wasn't going to let MGM have us, especially since they already had Eric all tied up. So we became the first group in the history of the record business to get a gold record who wasn't signed to a record company."

During a 1971 European tour with the group, an exhausted Burdon departed. Steve Gold negotiated a contract for War with United Artists, and later that year, they released *War*. Burdon appeared in the flick *The Comeback* (1978), as a fading rock star; teamed up with Jimmy Whitherspoon for an album and with the German rock band Fire Engine for another poor selling LP; and moved into the '90s in what proved a low-keyed solo career. Meanwhile War scored on the charts with 45s like "Slippin' Into Darkness," (#16, 1972), "The

ERIC BURDON & WAR

World Is a Ghetto (#17, 1973), "Cisco Kid" (#2, 1973), "Low Rider" (#1, 1975), and "Why Can't We Be Friends?" (#6, 1975).

In 1976, MCA Records issued _Love Is All Around_, a collection of Burdon & War outtakes and leftovers.

ROBIN MCNAMARA
LAY A LITTLE LOVIN' ON ME
(Jeff Barry, Robin McNamara, Jim Cretecos)
Steed 724
No. 11 _August 22, 1970_

Not much is known about this Robin fellow. He was one of the original cast members of _Hair_, and one of the longest-lasting members, too. We don't know when or where he was born, what he did before becoming a hairy guy, or what he has done since. But while he was a hairy guy, he met songwriting legend Jeff Barry—half of the RAINDROPS—who was starting up a new record label—Steed, which would later succeed with Andy Kim and ILLUSION—and in need of talent. Together, they grooved and groomed nearly a dozen tunes. "Lay a Little Lovin' on Me" was one of those creations. A lot of the brothers and sisters bought that record, and it almost smoked its way into the establishment's Top 10.

In support of the disk, Rob toured with his group, the Exiles—Buzzy "Buzz Ball" Cornelison (pianist), Mark Davenport (drums), Bernie Falconer (organist), Billy Luxon (trumpet), Jimmy Pennington (lead guitar/bass), Jimmy Sokley (vocals). Crowds responded well to their rendering of "The Flesh Failures" and "Beer Drinkin' Man." "Got to Believe in Love" (#80, 1970)—a follow-up recorded with the cast of _Hair_—sold only a few copies; "Hang on in There Baby" sold less, and Rob and, not that much later, Steed Records rode off into the sunset.

ASSEMBLED MULTITUDE
OVERTURE FROM TOMMY (A ROCK OPERA)
(Pete Townsend)
Atlantic 2737
No. 16 _August 29, 1970_

Thomas Coleman Sellers (bass, keyboards) was born and raised in Wayne, Pennsylvania. Back in Wayne 39 years later, on March 9, 1988, Tommy died in a freak fire in his parents' home. His career saw him labor as an arranger, producer, songwriter, singer, and musician. At death's door he was full of promise.

In the mid-'60s, Tom became involved with ex-SPOKESMEN John Madara's production company as a songwriter. Madara matched, then long-haired, Sellers

up with Daryl Hall, Jim Helmer, and Tim Moore. They all recorded together as Gulliver. Madara placed an album of these winnable and now—rare tracks with Elektra. Nothing much happened, and by year's end, the group was no more.

The Assembled Multitude was a spur-of-the-moment studio conception, concocted at the Sigma Sound Studios in Philadelphia. Sellers rounded up some of what would later become the One-Hit MFSB—as he had done months earlier when he arranged/produced/wrote ELECTRIC INDIAN's "Keem-O-Sabe"—and slapped together some orchestrated reworkings of a theme from the Who's _Tommy_ album, Crosby, Stills, Nash & Young's "Woodstock" (#79, 1970), and a medley of jewels from "Jesus Christ Superstar" (#95, 1971).

When the Assembled concept had worn itself out, Tom dismantled the Multitude and returned to the studios to produce sessions for Eric Anderson, Chubby Checker, Millington, Essra Mohawk, SILVER, and the Righteous Brothers.

During the mid-'70s, Sellers worked in New York City for Radio Band of America, composing and arranging radio and TV commercials. During his career, he garnered four Clio awards, was affiliated with six gold records, and two Grammy nominations. With high hopes, just prior to his death, he had formed his own production company, Tom Sellers Productions.

MUNGO JERRY
IN THE SUMMERTIME
(Ray Dorset)
Janus 125
No. 3 _September 12, 1970_

Ray Dorset (vocals, guitar, casaba, feet) was born March 21, 1946, in Ashton, England. For years, Ray played any kind of music that might put food on his table. In 1968, "Mungo" Dorset was a member of a starving London-based progressive-pop band called Camino Real. Their future looked bleak, when out of the blue, things took a turn for the worse. The band's bass player walked off, and Dorset sacked the drummer—but replacements couldn't be found in time for a gig at Oxford University.

Ray and his diminished Camino cluster, bassless and drumless, nonetheless put on a fine show. Dorset, piano man Colin Earl (b. May 6, 1942, Hampton Court, England), and a washboard player named Jo Rush explored the terrain of their new musical turf as The Good Earth Rock & Roll Band. Before he left the group, Rush turned them on to the sounds of Leadbelly, Willie Dixon, and Britain's banjo-beating skiffle king, Lonnie Donegan.

MUNGO JERRY

appeared on an on-again off-again basis well into the '80s, but nothing sold worth a darn. Eventually, a despondent Dorset dissolved the band name. Solo efforts are sporadic; Jo, Colin, and Paul formed the King Earl Boogie Band. In the late '80s, Ray with ex-Fleetwood Mac-man Peter Green and Vincent Crane, formerly of THE CRAZY WORLD OF ARTHUR BROWN, were a recording unit called Katmandu.

ERNIE
RUBBER DUCKIE
(Jeffery Moss)
Columbia 45207
No. 16 *September 26, 1970*

Since childhood, Jim Henson (b. Sept. 24, 1936, Greenville, MS) had been fascinated by puppets. With glee, he followed the adventures of Edgar Bergen and Charlie McCarthy as well as the "Kukla, Fran & Ollie" characters. While a senior in high school, he had a TV program on a local Maryland station. While attending the University of Maryland as a theater student, Jim and his future wife, Jane Nebel, presented a series called "Sam and Friends" over WRC-TV in Washington.

In the late '50s and early '60s, Jim and his Muppets (a combination of marionettes and puppets) made TV commercials and appeared on "The Perry Como Show," "The Ed Sullivan Show," and "The Tonight Show." In 1965, Jim, who had begun experimenting in film, was nominated for an Academy Award for his short *Time Piece*. Beginning in 1967, Jim became affiliated with the Children's Television Workshop. By the fall of 1969, the company was ready to unveil "Sesame Street," a groundbreaking program for preschoolers destined to become what Alex McNeil, author of *Total Television*, has called "the most important children's show in the history of television." Central to this success were Jim's Muppets—Big Bird, Cookie Monster, Bert, Ernie, Grover, and Oscar the Grouch. In addition to teaching children the alphabet and numbers, Jim presented beguilingly informative skits and songs. One of these told of the joyous relationship between a mite Muppet and his "Rubber Duckie." Jim Henson is the voice of the innocent and mischievous song's star, Ernie, as well as KERMIT THE FROG and the game show host, Guy Smiley. Over the years, a number of spin-off albums have been issued. Only one other Muppet, however, has earned the distinction of placing a tune on the nation's Top 40

A "goodtime"/jug band/country-blues sound was coming together. Banjo-picking and jug-blowing Paul King (b. Jan. 8, 1948, Dagenham, England) and the bass-bashing Mike Cole were soon added to the roll call. A magazine plea for a manager garnered the group sometime-producer Barry Murray. After Mungo Jerry successfully opened for Traffic and the GRATEFUL DEAD at London's Hollywood Music Festival, Murray was able to secure a contract for the group with England's Dawn label. "In the Summertime" was their debut disk, and the first of what would total a towering 10 Top 40 45s in their homeland. In England, they were a pop phenomenon; pundits talked of "Mungo-mania" and publicity hand-outs labeled them "The New Beatles."

"What we're about," Dorset said to a *Circus* interviewer, "is everybody getting up and jumping about. We just want everybody to be happy." Yet Americans soon wearied of jumping up and dancing. Singles and albums chock full of cheerfully cheesy Mungo shuffles charts—Kermit the Frog, with "Rainbow Connection" (#25, 1979).

The tremendous success of "Sesame Street" spawned other Muppet vehicles, "The Muppet Show," "Fragile Rock," and numerous flicks, among them: *The Muppet Movie*, in which he starred and produced (1979), *The Great Muppet Caper*, in which he directed and acted (1982), and *Teenage Mutant Ninja Turtles*, for which Henson provided the designs for the assorted creatures (1990).

Jim Henson passed away on May 16, 1990, from pneumonia. He was 53 years old. His mammoth Muppet enterprise was acquired by the Disney company; operations are run by his son, Brian. His daughter Lisa is a film executive. Jim's legacy continues to be seen in 80 countries, in addition to the United States.

FREE
ALL RIGHT NOW
(Paul Rodgers, Andy Fraser)
A & M 1206
No.4 *October 17, 1970*

Guitarist Paul "Koss" Kossoff (b. Sept. 14 , 1950, London) and drummer Simon Kirke (b. July 28, 1948, Shropshire, England) were unhappy playing in a band called Black Cat Bones. When they happened to catch a glimpse of lead singer Paul Rodgers (b. Dec. 14, 1949, Middlesbrough, England) fronting Brown Sugar, they knew he would fit into a new band they were hoping to create. A mutual friend introduced the three to 15-year-old Andy Fraser (b. Aug. 7, 1952, London), then playing bass in John Mayall's Bluesbreakers. Andy was not keen on the jazzy direction that Mayall was moving toward, and agreed to drop by and jam with the other three.

"We were just a bunch of kids who loved rock and roll and the blues," said Kirke to *Circus'* Andy Secher. "When we got together, the oldest of us was 20, and while that might have been the reason we had a great deal of inner turmoil, it also helped us sacrifice just about everything for that music."

The British blues institution Alexis Korner gave the guys the name "Free" and walked them into Island Records and a contract. The band's first two LPs—*Tons of Sobs* (1968) and *Free* (1969)—passed by both U.K. and U.S. audiences without much notice. Album three, *Fire and Water* (1970), contained something just too fine to be ignored by anyone, even by those who only listened to Top 40 radio. "All Right Now" had a pulsating, electric sound, packed with

blues power and rock excitement. Rodgers was gritty, the riff was contagious, and Kossoff's guitar was hot.

"There was a purity to what we were doing that was very special," Kirke explained. "We weren't that concerned with making hit records, and we weren't jaded by the industry—we just wanted to keep everything as simple as possible."

Highway (1971), their next LP, offered "Stealer" (#52, 1971) as a single. The boys would never make the stateside pop/rock 45 listings again, though British fans would later rechart the group name with takes on "My Brother Jake," "Little Bit of Love," and "Wishing Well."

Free ran its course. Their label packaged a live set (*Free Live*, 1971). Rodgers went off and formed Peace; Kossoff formed Toby. Both efforts were short-lived. Kossoff then rejoined Kirke to record an instrumental LP with Tetsu Yamauchi and John "Rabbit" Bundrick called *Kossoff Kirke Tetsu and Rabbit* (1971).

The original band members reunited for one explosive occasion and a resulting album, *Free at Last* (1972). Fraser departed, then Rodgers dropped out. Rabbit and

FREE

Tetsu functioned as replacements for the band's last effort, *Heartbreaker* (1973). Rodgers and Kirke formed Bad Company and carried on for another decade or more. Fraser joined the Sharks and later fronted his own Andy Fraser Group; Rabbit recorded with Pete Townsend and toured with the Who; Tetsu joined Rod Stewart's Faces.

Paul Kossoff, possibly the group's most talented individual and certainly one of rock's most distinctive guitarists, formed Back Street Crawler (later billed Crawler), but died on March 19, 1976, of a drug-induced heart attack on an airplane en route to New York City.

In 1984, Rodgers with ex-Yardbird/Led Zeppelin guitar extraordinaire Jimmy Page and ex-URIAH HEEP drummer Chris Slade formed THE FIRM, for two LPs. Then Rodgers and ex-Faces/Who drummer Kenny Jones formed The Law.

R. DEAN TAYLOR
INDIANA WANTS ME
(R. Dean Taylor)
Rare Earth 5013
No. 5 *November 19, 1970*

Born in 1939 in Toronto, little Dean set his sights on becoming a country singer. Rock and roll didn't officially exist yet, but when it did, Dean was ready. In 1960, under the influence of Jerry Lee Lewis, Taylor recorded a rough tune entitled "At the High School Dance." A Canadian label, Parry Records, released the rocker and at least two follow-up singles. The kid must have been ripe and on to something, because in 1964 Mala Records in the U.S. decided to pick up his second single, the two-year-old "It's a Long Way to St. Louis," for release.

Between 1965 and 1973, Taylor occasionally released singles on Motown's VIP and Rare Earth labels. From Motown's point of view, Dean was Brian Holland's protege, present primarily to co-write hit songs like "Love Child" and "I'm Living on Shame" for the Supremes, as well as "I'll Turn to Stone" and "You Keep Turning** Away" for the Temptations. Taylor has claimed that he was "shafted" by the label when songs that he wrote were listed on the label as the creations of others.

"[Holland-Dozier-Holland] were building up an image as a production team which they succeeded in doing, and they were stingy in letting any of the glory go," R. Dean told Sharon Davis, author of *Motown: The History*. "They used to pay me cash for whatever I wrote and left my name off. I co-wrote "You Keep Running** Away," "Standing in the Shadows of Love" and "Seven Rooms" for the Four Tops, and "Love Is Here and Now

Your Gone" for the Supremes, but I didn't get my name mentioned."

R. Dean also worked as part of the Clan and the Corporation production teams. These gatherings, comprising Taylor, Jeffery Bowen, Marc Gordon, Hal Davis, Freddie Perren, Deke Richards, and Frank Wilson, were called in to fill the void at Motown when the Holland-Dozier-Holland songwriting team and production company walked out on the label.

With all the pressure to keep the Hitsville production line rolling, not much attention was apparently given to the production work-up Dean was preparing for some of his self-penned tunes. One of these, "Indiana Wants Me," was the tale of a critter on the lam for murdering a fellow who says something foul about the critter's lady. Dean followed this vacuous ode with three more mournful situations that each charted the lower reaches of the Hot 100. The last one, "Taos New Mexico" (#83, 1972), is about a poor thief serving time in the Big House, feeling sorry for himself.

Shortly after this last release, Taylor separated from the Motown empire to set up Jane Records, and issued one single, "Bonnie." No one is known to have actually heard this record, or to know what it is about. A few years later, another 45 surfaced on the Farr label, only to vanish without a trace. Apparently, Dean had served his time in the spotlight, and neither Indiana nor any of the other 49 states wanted him any longer.

Brits, however, consider R. Dean something of a Motown legend and have so honored the lad with three more Top 40 hits in 1974: "There's a Ghost in My House," "Window Shopping" and "Gotta See Jane"; the later had clicked earlier, in the summer of 1967.

As to his limited success, R. Dean told Davis: "Brian Holland wanted to break me as a white artist with Motown, but he kept trying to make me sound black, recording me in the wrong keys and such. That's why I'd never got anywhere."

ONE HUNDRED PROOF AGED IN SOUL
SOMEBODY'S BEEN SLEEPING
(Greg Perry, General Johnson, Angelo Bond)
Hot Wax 7004
No. 8 *November 14, 1970*

Clyde Wilson was born in Walhall, South Carolina, on Christmas morning, 1945. By 1954, he and his family were living in Detroit. Clyde, along with Wilbert Jackson, were signed by Harvey Fuqua to his HPC label as the Two Friends. Fuqua, former lead singer of the Moonglows, would later give the Spinners the opportunity to record their debut disk, and would also be the main force behind New Birth, Sylvester, and the NITE-LITERS. Unfortunately for Clyde and Wilbert, Fuqua's magic did not work well for them: "Just Too Much to Hope For" was a flop.

Years later, Don Davis invited Clyde to record for his Wheelsville/Groovesville/Groove City labels. Davis suggested that Clyde become "Steve Mancha." Clyde acquiesced, and shortly after, the Mancha man made the R & B charts with "I Don't Wanna Lose You" (R&B: #34, 1966) and "Don't Make Me a Story Teller" (R&B: #34, 1967).

When Clyde's contract ran out, the Motor City souls at Holland-Dozier-Holland's newly established Hot Wax/Invictus complex enticed Clyde to join a Four Tops-ish unit to be called Aged in Soul; second pressings of their debut read: One Hundred Proof Aged in Soul. The original line-up included Clyde, Eddie Holiday (a.k.a. Eddie Anderson), and Joe Stubbs (brother of the Four Tops' Levi Stubbs, and a veteran of THE FALCONS and THE CONTOURS). Before disagreements and mutiny set in, the Aged in Soul singers recorded "Too Many Cooks (Spoil the Soup)" (#94; R&B: #28, 1969) but hit the big time with "Somebody's Been Sleeping"—written in part by General Johnson, who wrote "Patches" for Clarence Carter and was the lead vocalist with both the Showmen and the Chairmen of the Board. Two other raunchy recordings clicked with pop/rock listeners: "One Man's Leftovers (Is Another Man's Feast)" (#96; R&B: #37, 1971) and "Driveway" (R&B: #33, 1971). Soul fans went for "90 Day Freeze (on Her Love)" (R&B: #34, 1971) and "Everything Good Is Bad" (#45; R&B: #15, 1972).

It was just as the "Sleeping" single topped out that the original group folded. Clyde then reformed the group with guitarist Ron Byowski, percussionist Dave Case, drummer Darnell Hagen, and bassist Don Hatcher. Both "90 Day Freeze" (R&B: #34, 1971) and "Everything Good Is Bad" (#45/15, 1972) sold quite well, but successive 45s failed to even chart. In 1973, the group's name was shelved, and Steve Mancha returned to being Clyde Wilson, a gospel singer and producer for Heavy Faith Records.

BOBBY BLOOM
MONTEGO BAY
(Jeff Barry, Bobby Bloom)
L & R/MGM 157
No. 8 *November 28, 1970*

Shortly after Bobby Bloom's career had blossomed and seemingly withered, he was killed by a gun shot to the head. A small derringer lay next to his body. Bloom and his male roommate were visiting Bloom's girlfriend, Linda Karakehian, at her West Hollywood apartment. According to the sheriff's report, Bobby went off into the bedroom. A lone shot was heard.

BOBBY BLOOM

Bobby was born in New York City in 1946. By age 13, he was making efforts to play drums, guitar, and piano. "I always knew I wanted to be a performer," he told *New Spotlight* magazine. "I wasn't sure that I could do it. I knew that I could write songs and produce records, but only other people could tell me if I was good enough."

Bloom's essentially behind-the-scenes 15-year musical career began in 1961, when he had two unsuccessful but now quite collectible singles with his group, the Imaginations, that were released for the Music Makers label. His craft germinated in the mid-'60s when—in various affiliations with John Linde, Peter Andreoli, Vinnie Poncia, Jr. (the latter two members of THE INNOCENCE, THE TRADEWINDS, the Videls), and the legendary Jeff Barry (half of THE RAINDROPS)—he got the big break—to write tunes, produce records, and work as a sessions singer.

Bobby filled in for THE MUSIC EXPLOSION's lead vocalist on one of their last recordings, "Where Are We Going." He co-wrote Tommy James's "Mony Mony," the 1910 Fruitgum Company's "Indian Giver" and was also the voice for Captain Groovy and His Bubblegum Army on their lone and quite forgettable number, "The Bubblegum March."

On several occasions, Bobby had tried to establish himself as a solo act; in 1967, he recorded some blue-eyed soul for Kama Sutra. The only single released, "Love Don't Let Me Down," stiffed, as did the 1969 White Whale release, "All I Wanna Do Is Dance."

In 1970, bubblegum producers Joey Levine (the lead voice heard on REUNION's "Life Is a Rock") and Artie Resnick formed L & R Records. Bloom's first release for the novice label was the culmination of his efforts—"Montego Bay" finally made Bobby Bloom a household word.

At the peak of Bobby's meteoric rise, he was asked by *Hit Parader*'s Alan Smith about his new found fame. "The traveling is okay, but it's lonely. I travel on my own. . . . Being married wouldn't help, anyway, I'm not ready for that kind of responsibility. I've tried to ease the travel schedule . . . but right now, I've got to promote Bobby Bloom."

The Staple Singers' cover version of "Heavy Makes You Happy," a tune he co-authored with Jeff Barry, made the Hot 100 in February 1971. Two more Bloom singles and a couple of sides from the 1967 Kama Sutra sessions also charted on the Hot 100 before Bobby's sudden death on February 28, 1974.

"I think music should make people forget their troubles," he told *New Spotlight*. "Montego Bay, in Jamaica, is probably my favorite place in the whole world. It's magical. The music is very special, very happy . . . just the kind of thing to make you feel great to be alive. And that's what I like. Rather than sing about how rotten things are, I'd rather sing about a way that things could be better."

PRESIDENTS
5-10-15-20 (25-30 YEARS OF LOVE)
(Tony Boyd, Archie Powell)
Sussex 207
No. 11 *December 26, 1970*

None of their former labels, nor usually knowledgeable industry heads, could tell us much about the Presidents. While they did sell some records, they received scant coverage in the media. So here is what little could be gleaned: Tony Boyd, Archie Powell, and Billy Shorter were from Washington (others insist that they were from Philadelphia). Before their limited success on Sussex, they had recorded for Hollywood (1968) and Deluxe (1969-1970, with "Gold Walk," "Which Way," and "Lover's Psalm"). Possibly, they are the same Presidents that recorded for Warner Bros. in 1961. Some have claimed that they sang "Pots & Pans" for Mercury the following year, though the Chi-Lites' Marshall Thompson has told this writer that the latter disk was his group incognito.

Only four 45s are known to have been issued by the group while on Sussex; all successfully made the R&B charts: "For You" (#45, 1970), "Triangle of Love (Hey Diddle Diddle)" (#5, 1971), "The Sweetest Thing This Side of Heaven" (#30, 1971), and their monster-sized moment, "5-10-15-20." Mysteriously, Archie, Bill, and Tony reappeared on a Columbia charting—"On and Off (Part 1)" (R&B: #41, 1972)—as Anacostia. Presumably, the Presidents no longer exist, though as Anacostia, they did continue to have numerous disks issued by Columbia (1972-1975), MCA (1977), Tabu (1978-1979), and possibly Roulette (1984).

RAY PRICE
FOR THE GOOD TIMES
(Kris Kristofferson)
Columbia 45178
No. 11 *January 2, 1971*

Ray Nobel Price (b. Jan. 12, 1926, Perryville, TX) grew up on a farm, served in the Marines, and attended the North Texas Agricultural College in Abilene with plans to become a veterinary surgeon. Ray, however, had been moonlighting—singing under the guise of "The Cherokee Cowboy" at school events—and beginning in 1948, he appeared on the "Hillbilly Circus" radio show on KRBC. The response was better than he had hoped, so the next year, he joined KRLD's "Big D Jamboree" in Dallas. School days were done.

The program received some network coverage, and soon Price was recording for Bullet, singing on the Grand Ole Opry, and hanging around with the country legend Hank Williams. Their styles were similar, and often, when Williams was under the weather and unable to perform, Ray would fill in. Months before Hank's death, Price earned his first country charting with "Talk to Your Heart" (#3, 1952), followed by "Don't Let the Stars Get in Your Eyes!' (#4, 1952). Upon Hank's death, members of Williams's Drifting Cowboys became Price's band, the Cherokee Cowboys.

For years, Ray successfully worked the honky-tonk genre. His C & W hit songs are in some cases even well-known to pop/rock fans: "Release Me" (#6, 1954), "If You Don't Somebody Else Will" (#8, 1954), "Crazy Arms" (#1, 1956), "My Shoes Keep Walking Back to Me" (#1, 1957), "City Lights" (#1, 1958), "Heartaches by the Number" (#2, 1959), "Under Your Spell Again" (#5, 1959), and "Make the World Go Away" (#2, 1963). In all, more than 100 of his 45s have made *Billboard*'s C & W listings, and Ray is still going strong.

But 1967 marked a major turning point for Price, pundits claim. The more perceptive detected his future leanings as early as 1964, in "Burning Memories" (C&W: #2, 1964). Ray abandoned his Texas stylings, scrapping the fiddle, the steel guitar, and all the other instrumental touches that rural folk considered "authentic" country. Great numbers of violins—whole symphonies, it seemed—were added, as Ray over-hauled his repertory.

"For the Good Times" is a fine example of Ray's middle-of-the road phase. Eventually, he or his staunch public tired of this easy-listening syrup, so Price recorded gospel for the Myrrh label before semi-retiring to his Golden Cross Ranch in Texas. He recorded a duet album with Willie Nelson, acted in Clint East-wood's *Honkytonk* Man (1982), and recently returned on record, full-circle, to his honky-tonkin' ways. Ray and his Cherokee Cowboys—a band that at times has included Johnny Bush, Buddy Emmons, Willie Nelson, Roger Miller, and Johnny Paycheck—are now back playing that authentic country music.

In 1989, Ray open up his own theater in Branson, Missouri. Four years later, he was nominated to the Country Music Hall of Fame, but lost out to his former band member, Willie Nelson.

LYNN ANDERSON
ROSE GARDEN
(Joe South)
Columbia 45252
No. 3 *February 13, 1971*

A big year for Lynn was 1966. She was named the California Horse Show Queen at the state fair and was offered a contract with Chart Records. A good dozen country chartings would result from the latter.

Lynn Rene was born the daughter of country singer Liz Anderson, on September 26, 1947, in Grand Forks, North Dakota. By the mid-'60s, Liz was having C & W Top 10 hits like "I'm a Lonesome Fugitive," and little Lynn was showing signs of following in Mom's line of endeavor. None of her mother's waxings, how-ever, would approach the magnitude of Lynn's cover of Joe South's "(I Never Promised You A) Rose Garden." Even the *Rose Garden* album has sold over a million copies.

Lynn cut the South tune shortly after marrying songwriter-producer Glen Sutton and moving to Sutton's base of operations, Columbia Records. From the sales of "Garden" sprouted a Grammy—"Best Country Vocal Performance, Female"—plus the Country Music Association's "Female Vocalist of the Year" award.

"['Rose Garden'] was perfectly timed," Anderson explained to Joe Edwards of the Associated Press. "We were just coming out of the Vietnam years, and a lot of people were trying to recover. The song's message was that you can make something out of nothing. You [can] take it and go ahead."

Five more of Lynn's singles made the Hot 100, and several more charted on the C & W listings. In the mid-'70s, Sutton and Anderson divorced. In 1978, Lynn married Louisiana oil man Harold Stream III and retired from performing to concentrate on horse riding; a life-time interest that has garnered Lynn 100 trophies and 600 ribbons. Four years later, that marriage over, Lynn Anderson was back in the music-business saddle again. She appeared in an episode of "Starsky and Hutch" and starred in an NBC "Movie of the Week: Country Mile." "I am the Annette Funicello of country music," she declared. "Music is in my blood and bones—I ain't done yet."

Of late, Lynn can be spotted pitching the merits of a certain phone-in psychic hotline.

WADSWORTH MANSION
SWEET MARY
(Steve Jablecki)
Sussex 209
No. 7 *February 27, 1971*

Here lies what must be considered the archetypal One-Hit Wonder act. These period-appropriate but grubby-looking boys seem to have no recorded history. The bubblegummy "Sweet Mary" appears to be their very first recording. Two other 45s ("Michigan Harry Slaught" and "Nine on the Line") and an LP (*Wads-worth Mansion*, 1971) of similar sounds were issued, went nowhere, and the band all but disappeared. No revivals, no lineage—nothing turns up.

All of their known music was recorded in late 1970 at Hollywood Sound Recorders. Producing were Jim Calvert and Norm Marzano. Wadsworth's line-up, per their minimal liner notes, consisted of the Jablecki brothers, Mike (drums, percussion, vocals) and Steve (keyboards, lead vocals, guitar, percussion), plus Wayne Gagnon (lead guitar, handclap, cowbell) and John Poole (bass, vocals, percussion).

JANIS JOPLIN
ME AND BOBBY MCGEE
(Kris Kristofferson)
Columbia 45314
No. 1 *March 20, 1971*

Joplin was found in a room at Hollywood's Landmark Hotel, on October 4, 1970, with puncture marks in her arm. Her death was ruled an accidental heroin over-dose. She was the premier white blues singer of the '60s, a gutsy but vulnerable tough-mama icon from Texas, an overnight sensation, and yes, literally a One-Hit Wonder.

JANIS JOPLIN

While every album that featured Joplin—*Big Brother & The Holding Company* (1967), *Cheap Thrills* (1968), *I Got Dem Ol' Kozmic Blues Again Mama!* (1969), *Pearl* (1971), *Joplin in Concert* (1972), *Janis Joplin's Greatest Hits* (1973), *Janis* (1975), and *Farewell Song* (1982)—sold well enough to grant her superstar status, only the posthumous release of "Me and Bobby McGee" (penned by her ex-lover, Kris Kristofferson) managed to make the nation's "hit parade." Four other 45s did make the Hot 100, though: "Kozmic Blues" (#42, 1969), "Cry Baby" (#42, 1971), "Get It While You Can" (#78, 1971), and "Down on Me" (#91, 1975).

SAMMI SMITH
HELP ME MAKE IT THROUGH THE NIGHT
(Kris Kristofferson)
Mega 0015
No. 8 *March 27, 1971*

She was born Jewel Fay Smith, August 5, 1943, in Orange, California. Her family moved often; before she

dropped out of school at 11 she had lived in Oklahoma, Texas, Arizona, and Colorado. At 12, she was singing nightly in smoke-filled bars.

"I've been singin' as far back as I can remember, and there's always been music around me," saucy-voiced Sammi Smith, recalled in an exclusive interview. "While other kids were out doin' stuff, I'd be staying home, singin' or listenin' to records by Dinah Washington and Louis Prima and Keely Smith—not country music. I got into country proper a long time later. When I was 12, I started doin' pop standards with the big bands, but I also sang with some rock bands."

At age 15, Sammi was married and soon with four children. While Sammi was fronting a country unit in 1967 in Oklahoma, bassist Marshall Grant—half of Johnny Cash's back-up band, the Tennessee Two—spotted her and convinced Sammi to take the Greyhound to Nashville. There, Johnny Cash hooked her up with his label, Columbia. Some moderately successful singles were issued, like "So Long Charlie Brown, Don't Look for Me Around" (C&W: #69, 1968).

Two years later, Columbia terminated their contract with Smith. "What happened next was, I was playing the Alley in Nashville, and the chairman of the board of Mega [Records] kept harassin' me—sayin' that he wanted to have me be the first artist with this new label. Finally, I did go ahead and sign with 'em. The label, I found out later, was actually formed as a tax write-off, and I wasn't supposed to have a hit record!

"Trouble for them was that once my album [*He's Everything*, retitled *Help Me Make It Through the Night*] came out [in 1971], DJs were playin' 'Help Me Make It Through the Night' and there was no stoppin' it. They had to issue it as a single." More than 2 million copies have been sold since. The song was awarded two Grammies—"Best Country Vocal Performance, Female" and "Best Country Song"—and was named the Country Music Association's "Single of the Year" (1971). "Help Me" was also used on the soundtrack of John Huston's flick *Fat City* (1972).

While Smith has made the pop listings on only one other occasion, with "I've Got to Have You" (#77; C&W: 13, 1972), she became affiliated with Waylon and Willie's "Outlaw Movement" of the '70s and has been near continuously on the C & W charts with songs like "Then You Walked In" (#10, 1971) and "Today I Started Loving You Again" (#9, 1975). She has had more than 40 charting C & W singles.

Nicknamed "Girl Hero" by Waylon Jennings, Sammi moved to Globe, Arizona, in 1975 to adopt three Apache children and to live on the San Carlos Apache Reservation. Smith, part Kiowa-Apache and a direct descendant of the famed chief Cochise, has continued to crusade for the rights and conditions of the Apache Indians.

"There are those who sell a million records and as quickly as it happens, it's gone—I was one of those," Sammi noted. "But I knew I was gonna always sing whether it was for $10 a night or in the big time. I've forfeited makin' the Top 10 cause I've always felt I would only do songs I wanted to do."

BREWER & SHIPLEY
ONE TOKE OVER THE LINE
(Mike "Brewer," Tom "Shipley")
Kama Sutra 516
No. 10 *April 10, 1971*

Mike Brewer and Tom Shipley were both talented musicians, but when they are remembered at all, it is for that one song.

"People are always asking, 'Geez, what was the meaning of it? Was it a drug song?'" Mike Brewer said in an exclusive interview. "I always look 'em in the eye and ask 'em, 'Come on, have you ever been one toke over the line; done one hit too many?' Yeah, it's about any drugs, or anything that you push too far. A toke seemed apropos at the time. And at that time, I'd had one too many

hamburgers, one too many Holiday Inns, one too many nights on the road: toots, tokes, everything."

Both Mike Brewer (b. 1944, Oklahoma City) and Tom Shipley (b. 1942, Mineral Ridge, OH) had a folk-music history, five or more years apiece, preceding their union in 1966. Each had worked the coffeehouse circuit and the college stops on his respective turf. After Tom graduated from Baldwin Wallace College in Berea, Ohio, he and his new bride moved to California, then Toronto, and even lived in a tent on a Hopi Indian reservation before settling in Los Angeles. There, Shipley worked as a duo with Tom Mastin and signed a songwriting contract with Good Sam Music, an affiliate of A & M Records. Mastin grew tired, and disappeared.

Luckily for Brewer and Shipley, their paths crossed one smoggy Los Angeles night. Immediately, they began writing together and recording demos for Good Sam Music. In 1968, A & M issued their incomplete tracks as an album (*Down in L.A.*) without permission, so the duo actively sought out a firm recording contract. Kama Sutra obliged. "One Toke Over the Line," with Mark Naftalin on keyboards and GRATEFUL DEAD's Jerry Garcia on pedal steel guitar, was the opening cut from their second Kama Sutra LP, *Tarkio* (1971).

BREWER & SHIPLEY

"The song came about by chance, in a dressing room, one night," Brewer recalled. "We'd had one too many and just broke into song. We were just kiddin' around, not tryin' to write a song or anything. Neil Bogart [the founder of Buddah and later Casablanca Records] heard us do the number as an encore, at a show. He said it was a natural and had to be our next single."

Over the next couple of years, a few more countrified albums appeared, and two more singles—"Tarkio Road" (#55, 1971) and "Shake Off the Demons (#98, 1972)—won positions on the Hot 100. Mike, Tom, and their families lived on a farm outside of Kansas City. Into the '80s they continued to tour, to eat hamburgers, and to stay at Holiday Inns.

Michael Brewer's 1983 release, *Beauty Lies*, received favorable reviews. Shipley, meanwhile, turned his attention to working as a studio engineer; most successfully on Joni Mitchell's albums *Dog Eat Dog*, *Chalk Mark on the Rainstorm*, and *Night Ride Home*.

BELLS
STAY AWHILE
(Ken Tobias)
Polydor 15016
No. 7 *May 1, 1971*

The Bells started ringing when folksinger Jacki Ralph (b. Surrey, England) first met vocalist Cliff Edwards (b. Montreal) in 1965 at a ski resort in Montreal. Jacki was performing there, and Cliff was a skier with an interest in forming a rock and roll band. Edwards had noticed local drummer Doug Gravelle (b. Montreal) playing at a bar; Doug liked the idea of joining Cliff, his sister Annie, and Jacki in a group, and Cliff rounded up Mickey Ottier. For five years, they worked the Montreal club scene as the Five Bells. In 1968, Polydor signed them to a recording contract—a few singles were moderately successful on a local level.

By 1970, the success of groups like the Guess Who and MOTHERLODE laid the foundation for a "Canadian Invasion"; more and more Canadian groups were tempted to try their luck in the States. Guitarist Charlie Clarke, bassist Mike Waye, and keyboardist Denny Will joined the Bells. (Annie Edwards, an interim member and Cliff's wife, left the group to have a child.) Polydor issued a debut album and began a publicity campaign in the U.S., where the band started to tour.

"Fly Little White Dove Fly" (#95, 1971) made an mild showing, yet the slinky, sexy "Stay Awhile" was a much bigger hit. Their lone stateside moment was penned by Canadian folkie/recording artist Ken Tobias, a songwriter latter utilized by Anne Murray. The Bells' follow-up, "I Love You Lady Dawn" (#64, 1971), did fairly well. But over the course of the year, dissension set in, and by the end of 1971, Denny Will and Jacki Ralph were gone. They were replaced by keyboardist FRANK MILLS (later of "Music Box Dancer" fame) and singer Jackie Edwards, Cliff's sister.

A second album and more singles were issued in the States—all to no avail. Cliff developed a local following for a solo career in the '70s and early '80s; Jacki retired to the quiet life in Vancouver.

BUOYS
TIMOTHY
(Rupert Holmes)
Scepter 12275
No. 17 *May 1, 1971*

"'Timothy' is not about cannibalism," said Florence Greenberg, owner of Scepter/Wand Records in an exclusive interview. "The writer . . . assured me it was about a mule, or something. Frankly, I don't know of the record. It must have been done in the office without me. I can't remember the thing at all. I must have been out of the country . . .to let that thing out."

Cannibalism! Surely a song about the bodily consumption of a poor fellow named Timothy would not be tolerated on the top reaches of *Billboard*'s Hot 100. A call to Rupert Holmes—the tune's creator, and previously a writer/arranger for artists like the Drifters, the Platters, and Gene Pitney—seemed in order.

"The Buoys were from Wilkes-Barre, Pennsylvania, and were so named to conjure images of cleanliness, you know, like Lifebuoy soap. Michael Wright, a junior engineer at Scepter Recording Studios, discovered them. Mike and I were buddies, so he came to me for advice. He really liked the group and wanted to record them, but he told me that Scepter didn't take the group seriously. I said, 'I think you should record a song that will get banned—that way, you can take the Buoys to another label and say 'This is the band that everyone is talking about.' Mike asked me if I could write something that would get the group banned.

"I wasn't going to write about drugs, and everything that could be said on the air about sex had been said already. At the time, I was working on an arrangement of '16 Tons' for Andy Kim, and in this kind of 'Proud Mary' guitar groove. In the other room there was this TV on. The show was 'The Galloping Gourmet' with Graham Kerr. I started singing the lyrics: 'Some people say a man is made out of mud/A coal man is made out of muscle and blood/Muscle and blood and skin and bones.' I thought, 'God, that sounds like a recipe.' I said, 'Yeah, muscle and blood and skin and bones: bake in a moderate oven for three hours. That's it! Cannibalism and mining.

THE BUOYS

"I just turned out this story song about three boys who were trapped in a mine. And when they're pulled out, there's only two of them left. They don't know what happened to the third one, but they know that they're not hungry anymore!"

The Buoys—which consisted of Fran Brozena (keyboards), Chris Hanlon (guitar), Gerry Hludzik (a.k.a. Joe Jerry, bass), Bill Kelly (lead vocals), and formerly of Glass Prism, Carl Siracuse (drums)—gathered in the studio. Rupert played piano on the track. Bill Kelly sang lead. Scepter issued the disk and no one noticed, not even the label, for 14 months. A part-time promo man at the company finally took it into his own hands to drum up interest in the disk, particularly on college stations—in short order, gatherings of the "Timothy for Lunch Bunch" were being reported in university tabloids.

"The label copped out on the cannibalism," said Holmes. "They started this rumor that Timothy was actually a mule, so it wasn't so bad for these survivors to eat him. I was offended at the very idea of this pure defenseless mule being eaten. To this day, people come up and ask me, 'Was Timothy a mule?' I tell them, 'No, he was a man—and they ate him.'"

The group formed in the summer of 1964 in Wyoming, Pennsylvania; they were first the Escorts, then the Moffets. When Bill Buchanan, DJ at WBAX in Wilkes-Barre, became their manager, they were rela-

beled the Buoys. Their line-up changed some. With the brief addition of Bob O'Connell (keyboards) in 1969, the Buoys got the chance to affiliate with Michael Wright and to record for Scepter.

The Buoys followed their Top 40 hit with other tall tales of death and what not. There was "Give Up Your Guns" (#84, 1971), about a Tex/Mex showdown, followed by "Bloodknot," about some reform-school ritual. Both were written by Rupert, who likewise penned most of the tunes for the Buoys' 1971 *Portfolio* LP. After Scepter folded in 1972, the Buoys and Rupert signed with Polydor, where two further singles were issued ("Don't Try to Run" and "Liza's Last Ride"). Holmes, however, wrote neither of these numbers and neither was noticed by the media, even a mite. One final effort, "Don't Cry Blue"—produced by Michael Kamen of the New York Rock and Roll Ensemble—was put out by Ransom in 1977. With an ever-changing line-up, the Buoys name carried on into 1987.

Rupert Holmes continued writing, producing, and arranging. He also launched a solo career that eventually led to chart success—with singles like "Escape (The Pina Colada Song)" (#1, 1979) and "Him" (#6, 1980), and the *Partners in Crime* (1980) album. His 1986 Broadway musical, *The Mystery of Edwin Drood*, won five Tony Awards, including "Best Musical." The following year, the Jets topped the Adult-Contemporary charts with his "You Got It All."

In 1978, Bill Kelly and Gerry Hludzik resurfaced as Jerry Kelly with a album on Epic, *Somebody Else's Dream*; two years later, as Dakota and a self-titled LP on Columbia Records, they worked as the opening act for Queen's "The Game" tour. A second album was issued in 1984. Dakota called it quits in 1987. Kelly and Hludzik had success as producers of JIMMY HARNEN's "Where Are You Now?" Both continue as tunesmiths; two Hludzik compositions have been cut by the Oak Ridge Boys.

Incredibly, it is reported that the Buoys' follow-up flop, "Give Up Your Guns," became a Top 10 hit in Holland in 1979, after extensive use in a tire commercial.

OCEAN
PUT YOUR HAND IN THE HAND
(Gene MacLellan)
Kama Sutra 519
No. 2 *May 1, 1971*

Before the righteous vision hit them, they were Leather and Lace, like, a hippie band. According to Greg Brown, the band's keyboardist and vocalist, he and this dude, lead guitarist Dave Tamblyn, came together as a weekend group in the summer of 1970, the year of the birth of *Jesus Christ Superstar*. Greg brought in clear-voiced Janice Morgan, who would sing up-front on Ocean's only Top 40 hit; his booking agent, meanwhile, was on the lookout for other guys to gig with. "Primarily, we were searching for a bunch of people that we would like," Greg told Ritchie Yorke in *Axes, Chops, and Hot Licks*. "Ocean is more of a people thing than anything else."

Jeff Jones and Chuck Slater were located to fill in on bass and drums, respectively. Canadian Arc Records signed Ocean to a contract, put them in a studio, and told them to do their stuff. Never to be known for their song-creating abilities, the group decided to cover singer-songwriter Gene MacLellan's "Put Your Hand in the Hand." (Months before, Anne Murray had sold a million copies of her cover version of MacLellan's "Snowbird.")

With the success of NORMAN GREENBAUM's delightfully confused "Spirit in the Sky" and George Harrison's "My Sweet Lord," it looked to Greg like the world was ready for religious pop-rock songs. "I wouldn't say that we feel strongly about the religious angle of the song," Greg explained to Yorke. "We were concerned that it might give the group a gospel image."

Unfortunately for the group, that is just what the record did. Top 40 radio will take to a spiritually inclined tune every now and then, but not even when Jesus was a superstar and great numbers were under a Godspell could an act sing the praises record after record and get away with it. Three follow-up singles, all

ecological or religious in theme, did chart in the lower reaches of the Hot 100. Thereafter, Ocean remained a Canadian happening.

When last heard from, the brothers and sisters, except for Slater (who committed suicide sometime in the '80s), were living together on a farm in Markham, about 30 miles outside of Toronto. The main building is, like, a 100-year-old log cabin, man.

DADDY DEWDROP
CHICK-A-BOOM (DON'T YA JES' LOVE IT)
(Janis Lee Guinn, Linda Martin)
Sunflower 105
No. 9 *May 8, 1971*

The "original" Daddy Dewdrop was Dick Monda. Publicity handouts from Dick's long-deceased record label would have us believe that he was born in Cleveland in 1952. Reportedly, at the ripe age of 19, Dewdrop turned to music, and was hired as a songwriter and producer for a CBS cartoon series, unveiled for the fall of 1970, "Sabrina & The Groovy Ghoulies." "Sabrina, the Teenage Witch," as the show was soon billed, had been introduced on the successful "Archie's Show." The publicity releases fail to mention Monda's previously unsuccessful waxings for Verve and Moonglow.

"Chick-a-boom, Chick-a-boom/Don't Ya Jes' Love It"—it was fluff, all right, but catchy to the ear, for a spin or two. As performed by the Groovy Ghoulies on the Saturday-morning cartoon show, this novelty number began attracting much notice. In an effort to beat out the Ghoulie "group's" release of the tune for RCA, Dick Monda assembled a studioful of sessioneers, whom he called the Torrance Cookers (Larry "Boom Boom" Brown, Tom "The Hen" Hensley, Bill "Ma Brutha" Perry, and Steve "Atom Bomb" Rillera). They ran through many other noxious numbers like "John Jacob Jingle Heimer Smith" and "Abracadabra Alakazam."

More efforts at public-pleasing pabulum appeared under the "Daddy Dewdrop" name, but fared poorly. In the late '70s, another Daddy Dewdrop surfaced with more 45s, but none of these efforts—not even "Nanu Nanu (I Wanna Get Funky With You)"—received much of a response.

P.S. The Groovie Ghoulies—without Sabrina—moved into the Horrible Hall, where they continued making weekend musiclike noises on ABC, through September 1976. Word is that Dickie "the Drewdrop Daddy" Monda was involved. Sabrina was later reunited with Archie and crew on "The Archie Comedy Hour" and "The New Archie Sabrina Hour." In the fall of 1977, she resurfaced with her own series again, "Super Witch."

RICHIE HAVENS
HERE COMES THE SUN
(George Harrison)
Stormy Forest 656
No. 16 *May 22, 1971*

Richie Havens (b. Jan. 21, 1941, Brooklyn) was born into a large musical family, the eldest of nine children; his father was a piano player. His turf was the Bedford-Stuyvesant section of Brooklyn. "Kids who didn't have jobs or who didn't finish school ended up singing together," Havens told *Frets'* Mark Humphreys. "That's what I was doing when I was 13. In the '50s, everyone did that to stay out of trouble. There was nothing else to do.

"When I first started playing the guitar, it wasn't for myself; it was because I sang with *a cappella* groups. I had a girlfriend who had two younger brothers, 11 and 13. They had a little group, and they were dynamic. I used to do rehearsals with these kids, and a friend loaned me a guitar. This was the time of the hootenannies in Greenwich Village, so I took the kids over there. They killed everybody . . . I wasn't really into jumping up on anybody's stage and singing by myself. But once I started fooling around with the guitar, it was fun. And I started doing hootenannies [about 1960]." To support himself, Richie drew portraits, and also worked for a florist and Western Union.

Havens developed a distinctive style, which has been preserved for all time in the *Woodstock* (1970) film footage: eyes shut, a sawing, thrashing guitar attack, and the unorthodox use of his thumb in chord fingering. Albert Grossman, Dylan's manager, discovered Richie at the Cafe Wha? in the Village. Richie recorded a few LPs worth of demo materials for the Douglas International label (none of which was issued until fame found Richie) before switching to Verve-Folkways, and later, Stormy Forest, for the creation of his most noted work. He appeared at the Newport Folk Festival (1966), then the Monterey Pop Festival (1967), the Isle of Wight Pop Festival (1968), and finally, the Woodstock Festival (1969).

"I opened the [Woodstock] Festival," Havens told *Goldmine's* Bob Grossweiner. "I was supposed to be fifth. I said, 'What am I doing here? No, no, not me, not first!' I had to go on stage because there was no one else to go on first—the concert was already two-and-a-half hours late. Everyone was at the Holiday Inn seven miles away and couldn't get to the stage because the one back road they thought they could take was completely blocked.

"My impression was that there were over a million people there. It was a completely unique experience. No one expected it. 'Freedom' [Havens's peak performance, featured in the film] was written right there on the stage; it had never been sung before! It was spontaneous . . . I was alone on stage for two-and-a-half hours before any of the other performers came."

Shortly after "the event of the century," Havens issued his rendering of George Harrison's "Here Comes the Sun." "I thought it was one of the happiest songs I could sing," wrote Havens, for a "Best of . . ." compilation. "It was a hopeful song, and I was singing a lot of songs that were not so hopeful, but were explaining our problems. So, I thought, 'This is a release for me, a song I could feel good about and other people could feel happy about. It projected the fact that, in any case, it's gonna be all right.'"

Havens never became a successful singles artist, but his large collection of LPs sold well throughout the '70s—albums such as *Richard P. Havens, 1983* (1969), *Alarm Clock* (1971), and *Richie Havens on Stage* (1972). Richie branched into acting, in the '70s, appearing in the stage production of the Who's *Tommy* (1972), the filmed version of *Catch My Soul* (1974), and co-starring with Richard Pryor in *Greased Lightning* (1977). As an activist, he was responsible for founding the Natural Guard, a national hands-on teaching vehicle for kids to learn of man's effect on the environment, and the co-founding of Northwinds Undersea Institute, an oceanographic museum located on City island in the Bronx.

His relaxing, reassuring voice can be heard daily in commercials for McDonald's, AMTRAK, Budweiser, and the Cotton Association of America. In January 1993, Havens aided the ushering in of the Clinton presidency by performing at the Earth Ball, an inaugural event sponsored by Renew America.

Currently living in New York City, Richie continues to perform and record, and is also a sculptor.

TIN TIN
TOAST AND MARMALADE FOR TEA
(Steve Groves)
Atco 6794
No. 20 *May 29, 1971*

Tin Tin consisted of two Steves, surnamed Groves (guitar, bass, mellotron) and Kipner (keyboards, bass). In the late '60s, both blokes walked out on group affiliations in their native Australia to form what was intended to be a successful songwriting partnership. After cranking out a number of tunes, the Steves recorded some demos and moved to London.

With a stack of psychedelicized Beatles-like records cut and canned, the Down Under dudes approached fellow Australian Maurice Gibb of the Bee Gees. Gibb liked their stuff, particularly an item called "Toast and Marmalade for Tea." For some long-forgotten reason,

the guys named themselves after Tin Tin, a Belgian cartoon character. Atco Records released the disk, and a sizable chunk of the Western world concurred with Maurice's thumbs-up assessment. "Marmalade," produced by Gibb, oozed onto the charts. The follow-up, "Is That the Way" (#59, 1971)—also produced by Gibb—struggled with the lower reaches of the Hot 100, but "Talkin' Turkey" and other singles stiffed.

By the close of 1973, each Tin Tin member had gone his own way. Groves found security in obscurity. Kipner resurfaced in the late '70s with an album and some singles for Elektra and RSO. Kipner has also done session work for George Benson and ex-Hollie Allan Clarke. A number of his tunes have charted as recorded by other acts—in 1984, Chicago clicked with his "Hard Habit to Break" (#3), and Olivia Newton-John had success with his "Physical" (#1, 1981) and "Twist of Fate" (#5, 1984).

BEGINNING OF THE END
FUNKY NASSAU—PART 1
(Ralph Munnings, Tyrone Fitzgerald)
Alston 4595
No. 15 *July 17, 1971*

The Beginning of the End was one of the few Caribbean acts at the time that managed to tickle American's fancy. Essentially, the Bahama band was a brothers act—Rafael "Ray" Munnings (vocal and organ), Frank "Bud" Munnings (drums), and LeRoy "Roy" Munnings (guitar)—augmented by Fred Henfield (bass) and the Funky Nassau Horns: Ralph Munnings (tenor sax), Nevill Sampson (trumpet), and Kenneth Lane (tenor sax). They cut some tracks in Miami for the fledgling Alston label. The very first release was their big one, "Funky Nassau." Rafael sang from his stuffings, the beat swirled, the brass blasted, and in a three-month period, America bought a bargeful of the Munnings' "junkanoo" sound.

Bud, Ray, Roy, and the rest hung in there long enough to lay down some sunny album tracks and a few singles with names like "Come Down Baby" and "Monkey Tamarino." But their monster moment was indeed the beginning of the end. According to *Goldmine*'s Robert Pruter, one executive at the Alston label quipped: "They had one helluva lot of talent—problem was, they just didn't trust Americans."

By 1974, Henry Stone's Alston label had been folded into TK Productions, and the Beginning of the End was history.

CYMARRON
RINGS
(Eddie Reeves, Alex Harvey)
Entrance 7500
No. 17 *August 7, 1971*

Producer Chips Moman had something of an open-door policy at his American Recording Studios in Memphis. One promising day in 1969, Rick Yancey (b. 1948) walked through that door. Yancey, who was born and raised in Memphis, had drifted in and out of music and likewise Memphis State University. That morn, Rick approached Moman with some self-penned songs. "Chips listened, didn't like the songs, and hired me," Yancey joked on the liner notes to Cymarron's lone album. For a year, Rick hung around the studios, working on recording sessions and trying to write that smash hit.

Looking for some action, Sherrill Parks (b. 1948, Jackson, TN), a guitarist and sax player from Tennessee, dropped by the studios. Rick and Sherrill hit it off, and soon talked of constructing a group to cut some hit records. Rick suggested the addition of Richard Mainegra (b. 1948, New Orleans) to the group that was to be named after a local TV Western series, "Cymarron Strip." Richard had co-written some songs cut by Gary Puckett and Skeeter Davis, had recorded with the Phyve, and had made some unsuccessful solo singles for Scepter Records.

Cymarron's sound resembled the mellow folkie emissions of Crosby, Stills, Nash & Young and America. Moman, agreeing that the blend of their voices was quite good, gave the group a pile of tunes to practice, and arranged for some top session musicians to flesh out Cymarron's acoustic instrumentation. Sweet and bouncy, "Rings" scaled the pop listings and nearly creased the Top 10. Nothing more, however, charted. At least three more singles were issued before the fellows decided to branch off into other endeavors.

Later in the decade, Rich Mainegra made appearances on albums by Doug Kershaw and some pre-Fleetwood Mac sides for Billy Burnette.

TOM CLAY
WHAT THE WORLD NEEDS NOW IS LOVE/ ABRAHAM, MARTIN AND JOHN
(H. David, B. Bacharach, D. Holley)
Mowest 5002
No. 8 *August 14, 1971*

Tom Clay was a substitute DJ, with a three-week assignment at L.A.'s KGBS. Using his own funds, he created a narrative collage that combined snatches of speeches by John Kennedy, Robert Kennedy, and Martin Luther King, Jr., with sound effects and recordings of little children attempting to define terms nebulous terms like "prejudice." Gene Page arranged the period piece, and the Blackberries (the line-up, at this point, in their career: Oma Drake, Jessie Smith, and Clydie King) supplied the vocal backdrop.

Tom told *Zoo* magazine that the hope was to "get across the idea that what we need now is love . . . we're up to our armpits in hate and war and killing." The children's redeeming voices were added as an after thought. The tone of the initial tape was negative. "There was no hope in it," he told the magazine, "so I added some little girls at the beginning and the end, giving their definitions of hate, bigotry, and segregation. Not knowing about such things, they symbolized children everywhere."

Clay spun the disk on his radio program; though he had no plan to ever issue the piece as a record. All that changed when Motown mastermind Berry Gordy, Jr., heard the DJ's sociopolitical statement, and soon issued a shaved version on Gordy's Mowest label. The timing was right, and Clay found himself with a national audience.

Asked about the recording's success, Clay said at the time, "Nothing's really changed. Right now I'm drawing $65 a week in unemployment, and they tell me that in a few weeks I could be a millionaire. Well, I did go to Martioni's restaurant in Hollywood and blew $23 on a meal for two, which is kind of extravagant for me, but the money thing doesn't really excite me.

"I'm not looking for money. It isn't what I want, I've had it. I've had my big Cadillac. My Lincoln. I've made my $50,000 a year, and I've made $10 a year. I've paid my dues, and I can look in the mirror and say with total honesty that I don't give a damn about becoming a millionaire.

"I suppose what I want, what every other human being wants . . . to be wanted and appreciated and loved, and money can't love me."

Follow-ups such as "Whatever Happened To," a rambling reminiscence about sugar sandwiches wolfed when young, sold little.

Clay was relieved of his duties at WJBK in Detroit, when it was learned that he had accepted $6,000 from several independent record companies to push their music.

Tom Clay died on November 11, 1995; he was 66.

JEAN KNIGHT
MR. BIG STUFF
(Joe Broussard, Ralph Williams, Carrol Washington)
Stax 0088
No. 2 *August 14, 1971*

"Mr. Big Stuff" was to be the hit of her life. "It was unbelievable," said Knight of that peak moment, to author Marc Taylor. "I almost had to pinch myself to see if it was real. . . . I went everyplace, all across the country, and just about every major city in the country.

Jean Knight was born Jean Caliste, in New Orleans, on January 26, 1943. During the early '60s, she sang on weekends in small clubs. Her first recordings date back to some sessions for legend, Cajun king, self-proclaimed nut Huey Meaux; there were two disks for his Jetstream label and three for his Tribe operation. By 1970, she had hooked up with Wardell Quezerque, a noted New Orleans arranger and producer who had started out as a trumpet man in Dave Bartholomew's band. (Wardell had fronted bands like the Sultans and the Royal Dukes of Rhythm and arranged the Dixie Cups' "Chapel of Love" and ROBERT PARKER's "Barefootin'"; DR. JOHN had even played piano for him at one point.) Jean Knight worked for Quezerque as a back-up singer on his sessions.

Quezerque had made arrangements with Tommy Couch and Wolf Stevenson of Malaco Productions to record some sides at their studio in Jackson, Mississippi. On May 17, 1970, he brought Jean, King Floyd, and a number of other acts down to Jackson for a one-off Saturday afternoon session. Knight taped "Mr. Big Stuff," and King Floyd did his "Groove Me." Both waxings would eventually rocket to the top of the R & B charts.

Present in the studio was tunesmith Albert Savoy. "He said, 'Jean, everybody knows you're flip and sassy,'" said Jean to Taylor, author *A Touch of Classic Soul*. "'Just approach the song like you're sacking a guy out.' It felt right, so I just took it and went with it."

Initially, no one was interested in leasing the sides from Quezerque. Couch and Stevenson resolved the situation by forming Chimneyville Records to release the King Floyd track. Once "Groove Me" became a huge pop hit (#6, 1971), a number of labels began bidding for Wardell's other Saturday afternoon sides, Knight's "Mr. Big Stuff" included.

"Big Stuff," picked up by the Stax label, was a smooth shaker and, once released, a big money-maker. Why not work that groove again? The follow-up, "You Think You're Hot Stuff" (#57, 1971), did fair. "That song wasn't my idea," said Knight. "When you're a fresh star like that, it's not much say you have. Everybody's got everything programmed for you. Stax had a really good song for me called 'Cold, Bold and Ready.' It was hot and I was fired up to do that song, but when I got back from New Orleans, Wardell said, 'No,' they had their own songs. It was a bad move."

The next two singles for the Stax label flopped, then Stax folded. Without a label, Jean Knight continued gigging on weekends locally and attended nursing school. Some singles were issued by Staff, Dial, Chelsea, Open, Ola . . . .

In 1981, Jean's recording career was revived when a song she had waxed for Isaac Bolden's Soulin' label—"You Got the Papers (But I Got the Man)" (R&B: #56, 1981), an answer disk to Richard "Dimples" Fields and Betty Wrights' "She's Got the Papers on Me"—was picked up for national release by Cotillion and nicked the R & B charts. Her tasty cover of Rockin' Sidney's Zydeco zinger "My Toot Toot" (#50, 1985) was promising.

In 1986, Heavy D & The Boys made the charts with their remake of Knight's "Mr. Big Stuff." "It woke me back up [my career]," said Jean. "That always brings attention back to the person who actually did it." In 1994, Spike Lee made use of Jean's recording in his flick *Crooklyn*.

When not working as a nurse, Jean Knight still performs in the New Orleans and Gulf Coast area. Quite probably, we've yet to see the end of Jean's soulful sounds.

UNDISPUTED TRUTH
SMILING FACES SOMETIMES
(Norman Whitfield, BARRETT STRONG)
Gordy 7108
No. 3 *September 4, 1971*

Joe Harris, the only constant member of this ever-evolving group, was born and raised in Detroit. "I came out of the Brewster Projects, along with Martha & The Vandellas, Diana Ross, and Mary Wilson," Harris told *Blues & Soul*'s Denise Hall and Tony Cummings. "In high school, I was involved with Little Joe & The Moroccos. We had been competing against the Spinners in a series of talent shows and finally we were the ones to win."

A 1957 release entitled "Bubblegum" on the Bumblebee label bombed, and the group disbanded. After some college, Harris and Richard Street (later a member of the Monitors and the Temptations) formed the Peps and had a series of unsuccessful disks issued on Thelma and D-Town. Joe left for the Ohio Players and was their lead vocalist for a year in the late '60s. "I co-wrote and produced most of their first album for Capitol, but found myself hooked up with a bogus production deal." After a short stay in Canada with the Stone Soul Children, Harris returned to Detroit and met Norman Whitfield, a top-flight producer-writer for Motown and later, head of Whitfield Records.

Whitfield (then on a hot streak with million-selling productions on Marvin Gaye, Edwin Starr, and the Temptations) wanted to put together a new act to feature his abilities. Undisputed Truth was Joe Harris plus the Delicates—Billie Rae Calvin and Brenda Joyce Evans, who had been singing back-up sessions for the Four Tops and the Supremes.

"Smiling Faces Sometimes" was a sure hit. To the dismay of the Temptations, Whitfield pulled it off the Temps' *The Sky's the Limit* LP and gave it to the Undisputed Truth for their second single. While a cover of "Papa Was a Rolling Stone" (#63, 1972) and several other increasingly funkified Undisputed Truth 45s cracked the pop and R & B listings, "Faces" proved to be the group's only Top 40 showing.

After the marginal success of "Law of the Land" (R&B: #40, 1973) from the LP of the same name, Billie and Brenda left the group. The Magictones (Tyrone Berkley, Tyrone Douglas, Virginia McDonald, and Calvin Stevens), a Motor City bar band, was brought in to back Harris as the "new, higher-than-high, cosmic 'Truth.'" This reworked group's sound was more rock-oriented, and obviously influenced by JIMI HENDRIX and Sly Stone. Truth also took on an overtly theatrical image: silver faces, flashing sequins, and towering white afros.

Before the temporary demise of Truth in the late '70s, Harris and Whitfield fired the entire line-up and shelved the freaky fashions. Among the members of the last incarnation were Melvin Stuart, Marcy Thomas, Hershel "Happiness" Kennedy, and Chaka Khan's sister and former member of the Glass Family, Taka Boom (a.k.a. Yvonne Stevens), who has had a couple of R & B hits during the late '70s/early '80s; notably "Night Dancin'" (R&B: #20, 1979).

In the late '80s, Harris and another line-up of Undisputed Truths reassembled for some recordings for the U.K.-based Motorcity label. Billie Calvin, an original Truth and songsmith on the Rose Royce hit "Wishing on a Star," likewise has been recording for Motorcity.

On reflection, Whitfield, Truth's producer/creator told Sharon Davis, author of *Motown—The History*: "The Truth represented a challenge to me. People were saying Motown had become stagnant so I set about making a new group with completely new ideas. But my efforts for the Truth were all in vain because the company simply was never into what the group meant. As a company, they developed a lack of respect for what people were doing for them, and they lost their sense of direction."

MAC & KATIE KISSOON
CHIRPY CHIRPY CHEEP CHEEP
(Harold Stott)
ABC 11306
No. 20 *October 2, 1971*

Jerry "Mac" Kissoon and his younger sister Kathleen were born in Port of Spain, Trinidad. The Kissoon family moved to England in the late '50s. Mac did some solo singing and eventually joined a couple of West Indian youths, Lance Ring and Pauline Sibbles, in the Marionettes. After Katie joined the group, a number of singles produced by Britain's '50s pop star Marty Wilde were issued in Europe by Pye. In 1965, while still a member of the group, Katie, recording as Peanuts, covered the Bonnie & The Treasures hit-free classic "Home of the Brave." That same year, the siblings also recorded a few girl-group sides with the Rag Dolls. None of these charted in England or the States.

Years later, freed of all solo and group alignments, Mac and Katie finally scored in the U.S. with their bubblegum number, "Chirpy Chirpy Cheep Cheep"— reportedly a well-veiled anti-war tune. While years of follow-ups charted on the continent, the Kissoons returned to oblivion in the States. "Sugar Candy Kisses," "Don't Do It Baby," and other cute pop-soul numbers became big U.K. sellers in the mid-'70s.

Katie is still a pop performer. She has toured and recorded with Van Morrison and Roger Waters, and has made 45s for the Jive label.

DENISE LASALLE
TRAPPED BY A THING CALLED LOVE
(Denise LaSalle)
Westbound 182
No. 13 *October 30, 1971*

Born in LeFlore County, Mississippi, on July 16, 1939, Denise Craig had early childhood ambitions of becoming a fiction writer. At age 15, after moving to Chicago to live with her brother, Denise was delighted when *TAM*, a magazine of black culture, bought one of her stories. Only rejection slips followed, but Craig (who changed her name to "LaSalle" in order to sound French) was not one to be defeated easily.

Denise turned to songwriting, and in 1968, she started recording for Billy "The Kid" Emerson's Tarpon label. Neither "A Love Reputation" nor its follow-up, "Count Down," charted. In 1969, she set up her own production company, signed artists, wrote tunes for them, and recorded them in Willie Mitchell's Memphis studio. That same year, she also met her husband-to-be, Bill "Super Wolf" Jones, then a DJ on Memphis' WDXI.

While she was hitless herself, Denise produced R & B hits like Bill Coday's "Get Your Lie Straight" and the Sequins' "Hey Romeo." Magazine editors had turned down her writing, but now LITTLE MILTON, ANN PEEBLES, and others were seeking her out and recording her tunes. Encouraged by her behind-the-scenes success, Denise walked into a recording studio to lay down some tracks with her voice up front. "Heartbreaker of the Year," released on her own Crajon label, did not chart, but Westbound Records signed her, and one of

DENISE
LASALLE

the tracks from her first session secured her a place in rock and soul history.

"Trapped by a Thing Called Love" caught a large audience, hit number one on the R & B charts, and gave Denise the hellfire-loving image she has to this day. A sassy, gritty singer, Denise told a *Blues & Soul* reporter that she likes her music "mean, down-home, and funky." The flip side of "Trapped" was the suggestively-titled "The Deeper I Go the Better It Gets." Trailing that ditty by a year was 'A Man Sized Job" (#55, 1972), on which Denise informs her former lover that he "left his job half done" and that she's now with a younger dude. Her next release continued the theme: in "What It Takes to Get a Good Woman," she sings that "You can't start out a loverman and wind up being a sleeper."

Denise has said that despite her racy innuendoes, she is ladylike and a feminist of sorts.

"Maybe it isn't the kind of stereotype of femininity that women have been tagged with. And maybe it isn't that sweet delicate, fragile, gentle image of womanhood that a lot of people still envision. But it's a new side of women—it portrays a strength that has never been portrayed before. Women aren't just housewives any longer . . . they are out there fighting and standing up

for their rights. That's the kind of woman that Millie [Jackson] and I are portraying—the woman of today who won't be no doormat."

Denise's R & B charting continued into the mid-'80s. Reportedly, she owns and runs radio WFXX in Jackson, Tennessee.

FREE MOVEMENT
I'VE FOUND SOMEONE OF MY OWN
(Frank K. Robinson)
Decca 32818
No. 5 *November 13, 1971*

History doesn't reveal just how they came together, nor just how and why they fell apart so rapidly. All we know is that they were six kids from all across the country who met in Los Angeles in 1970. Only Josephine Brown and Godoy Colbert had any musical background. Godoy, the oldest, had sung professionally in the Afro Blues Quintet, the Pilgrim Travelers, and the Pharaohs; Josephine had received training from her gospel-singing father and had been a member of the Five Bells of Joy. The others in Free Movement were Cheryl Conley, Jennifer Gates, and the Jefferson brothers, Adrian and Claude.

After rehearsing for a few months, Free Movement made a demo and shopped it around town. Decca Records liked what they heard and quickly issued "I've Found Someone of My Own" as a single. Six months later, when the pop/soul single charted, the group had already changed their allegiance, having signed with Columbia Records. An album—named after the hit— was quickly issued. Kal Rudman, columnist with *Record World* magazine, in his assessment of the Fifth Dimension-like group could barely control his excitement: "There is no question in my mind that this album will become one of the top sellers of the year and that this group will undoubtedly win all the polls as the 'hot new group discovery' of the years 1971-72." The LP barely broke into the *Billboard*'s Top 200 Albums (#167). Two more singles were released. "The Harder I Try (The Bluer I Get)" (#50, 1972) did so-so, and then—silence.

FREDDIE HART
EASY LOVING
(Freddie Hart)
Capitol 3115
No.17 *November 20, 1971*

Freddie Hart: what a man, what a life. No way could it have been easy. Born one of 15 children in Lockapoka, Alabama, on December 21, 1933, Freddie ran away from home when seven years of age. To survive, he picked cotton, washed dishes, laid pipeline, worked in sawmills, steel mills, and on oil rigs. At age 14, Freddie passed himself off as being of proper age, and enlisted in the Marines, where he saw action on Iwo Jima, Okinawa, and Guam. On completing his tour of duty, Freddie, always a physical-fitness advocate and possessor of a black belt in karate, became a self-defense instructor at the Los Angeles Police Academy.

Barely 20, Hart met C & W honky-tonk legend Lefty Frizzell. Lefty took the kid under his wing, put him in his band, let him sing some songs, and walked him into Capitol Records in 1953. It would be six years before Hart would have his first major C & W hit with "The Wall" and another decade before nearly the whole world would hear of Freddie and his "Easy Loving." The self-penned tune eventually sold more than a million copies and garnered the Country Music Association's "Song of the Year" award for both 1971 and 1972.

"Pretty Sex, that's what I like to put across in my songs," Freddie told *Country Music*'s Joan Dew. "'Easy lovin', so sexy lookin'" . . . that one line says it all. I almost took it out of the song."

While Hart never again managed to cross over onto the pop/rock charts, he continued for much of the '70s

to claim top-five C & W positions with recordings that included "My Hang-up Is You," "Got the All Overs for You," "If You Can't Feel It, It Ain't There," and "Hang on in There Girl." In addition to recording as a solo artist, Hart has been composing tunes for more than 30 years, some of which have been successfully waxed by other country performers. His "Loose Talk" has been covered more than 50 times.

Freddie Hart is reportedly a very wealthy man. He owns a trucking company, raises fruit and cattle, and runs a school for the handicapped. While his popularity in country circles has declined of late, Freddie still records honest, honky-tonkin' material for the small Brylen label.

LES CRANE
DESIDERATA
(Max Ehrmann, Fred Werner)
Warner 7520
No. 8 *December 4, 1971*

Not much is known about where he came from or even where he went to, but the San Francisco born'n'bred TV talk-show host Les Crane (b. 1935) annoyed plenty of people in the mid-'60s with his sandpapery communication style. ABC had set up "The Les Crane Show" to compete against NBC's "Tonight Show." The attempt, like similar efforts today, was short-lived—Crane's show nose-dived into oblivion within four months. The successor to the Crane program was billed "Nightlife," which featured a different guest host each week. Within months, Crane was back as regular host; the obligatory sidekick was wordsmith Nipsy Russell. Les was finally dethroned in April 1967 when the show was converted into "The Joey Bishop Show," with sidekick functions for the next quarter decade being supplied by Regis Philbin.

Four years later, the sometime DJ had a Top 10 hit with a reading of Max Ehrmann's 1906 poem, "Go Placidly Amid the Noise and Haste." (Ehrmann had died 27 years earlier.) The groundwork had been laid a year earlier. In 1970, ex-Nice drummer Brian Davidson's group Every Which Way had utilized Ehrmann's words for a song on their only album; that same year, King Crimson, thinking the poem was an ancient document, had also used it, in an ad for their *Lizard* album.

The Crane dubbing did garner a Grammy for "Best Spoken Word Recording" of 1971, but, to no one's surprise, Les never charted again. The follow-up, "Children Learn What They Live," was heard'n'heeded by few.

Crane was married to Tina Louise, the long cherished movie star Ginger Grant in the inane but perennially favorite TV series "Gilligan's Island."

JONATHAN EDWARDS
SUNSHINE
(Jonathan Edwards)
Capricorn 8021
No. 4 *January 15, 1972*

Jonathan Edwards has been jotting down catchy lines for a quarter of a century, but remains remembered solely for those he dashed off for "Sunshine," his Vietnam War-era hit: "He can't even run his own life/I'll be damned if he'll run mine."

Edwards was born on July 28, 1946, somewhere in Minnesota. His father worked for the FBI, and at the age of six, Jon and the family moved with the old man to Virginia. He auditioned for the Ice Capades, was arrested for racing bulldozers, and in the pre-Beatles '60s formed a redneck bluegrass band, the Rivermen. Over the years the name, the personnel, and the overall sound of the group changed: they were the St. James Doorknob, then Headstone Circus, and finally, the heavy and blues-influenced Boston-based Sugar Creek (Edwards, Gary Gans, and the McKinney brothers, Malcolm and Tod).

Peter Casperson heard Sugar Creek's top-quality sounds at a one-nighter and approached the guys about becoming their guiding light and manager. The group agreed, and Casperson set the band up with Metromedia Records. Sugar Creek's self-titled album was a musical winner, but fared poorly saleswise, so the band split up in 1970.

Jonathan signed on as a singer-songwriter with Phil Walden's Capricorn label. "Sunshine," a hastily composed tune from his first solo album, connected with pop listeners. The single and the album sold in healthy quantities, but nothing further charted.

Edwards has provided back-up services for Jimmy Buffett and EMMYLOU HARRIS and still sporadically records and tours for a loyal following. In 1984, he recorded a bluegrass set with Seldom Scene. By decades end, Jon was traveling as a member of the road-show version of *Pumpboys and Dinettes*.

"I do this joke on stage where I tell 'em I got to ride around in a limo for an hour and a half," says Edwards of his brief touch with stardom, to David Mills, of *The Washington Times*. "I wish I knew then what I know now. I would have taken a lot more advantage of the situation than I did. I would have tried to parley that initial success into something bigger. But I was young, and I didn't care . . . I was just happy."

HILLSIDE SINGERS
I'D LIKE TO TEACH THE WORLD TO SING
(IN PERFECT HARMONY)
(William Backer, Billy Davis, Roger Cook, Roger Greenaway)
Metromedia 231
No. 13 *January 15, 1972*

Producer Al Ham is a collection of moments in pop music history, a personable man with stories and snapshots. At what now seems like the dawn of rock and roll, he was functioning and in top form—long before producers were given a second glance, label credits, or much else (like money). He was a bass player and arranger for Tex Beneke, Artie Shaw, and Glenn Miller.

As a producer with Columbia Records, he worked throughout the '50s for acts like Tony Bennett, Rosemary Clooney, RAY CONNIFF, Percy Faith, Erroll Garner, the KIRBY STONE FOUR, Johnny Mathis, and Mitch Miller (on his "Sing Along With Mitch" albums). He also produced the original cast recordings for *My Fair Lady, Gypsy, West Side Story,* and *Bells Are Ringing.* In the intervening years, Ham has scored films like *Harlow* (1965) and *Stop the World, I Want to Get Off* (1966); arranged and composed commercials for Breck, Gillette, and McDonald's; and both handpicked and groomed a number of vocal units, the most successful of these being the Hillside Singers.

"I was the arranger and producer, and they were my group," Ham recalled in an exclusive interview. "I formed them explicitly for the purpose of making that record. In fact, it was our idea—Jack Wiedinman was the president of Metromedia—to do this cover version of a Coca-Cola jingle. We got the permission from the ad agency, BBDO, to record it." The New Seekers muscled in on the Hillside Singers' action with their own version of the jingle (#7, 1972) and eventually outsold—and outcharted—Ham's Hillsiders.

The Hillside Singers was composed of Ham's daughter Lori; his wife, Mary Mayo; Ron and Rick Shaw; and a group called the Good Life (Frank, Bill, Laura, and Joelle Marino). Ham assembled the unit, worked up an arrangement, and made the record. The disk took off, and the Hillside Singers recorded two LPs before the downslide began.

"It was bad timing, or bad luck, but by the time we had that hit, they wanted to kill the [Metromedia] label, if you can imagine that. We went through the motions with our albums and our touring, but by the time the last LP was out, the label was defunct." The Hillside Singers are still active—"it's been pretty much an ongoing thing, all these years, but obviously it's not been as active as we'd like it."

Mary Mayo, once a New York nightclub singer and Capitol recording artist, has since died. Ron Shaw, a later member (with DON WILLIAMS) of the Pozo Seco Singers, has since gone on to C & W fame, charting nearly 10 times. His most notable country winner was "Save the Last Dance for Me" (#36, 1978).

APOLLO 100 FEATURING TOM PARKER
JOY
(J. S. Bach)
Mega 0050
No. 6 *February 26, 1972*

Tommy Parker (b. Newcastle-on-Tyne, England, multi-instrumentalist) was playing the piano at age six. By his teens, he was successfully performing at local jazz clubs.

In the '60s, he did some production or session work with the Animals, Jimmy James & The Vagabonds, and the Mark Leeman Trio.

Apollo 100 was Tom's idea. The so-called group comprised Clem Cattini, Vic Flick, Z. Jenkins, Jim Lawless, and Brian Odgers, among others. Their "Joy" was an adaptation of Bach's "Jesu, Joy of Man's Desiring." While Parker had a hundred such instrumentals up his sleeve, the public took a lean liking to his version of "Mendelssohn's 4th (2nd Movement)" (#94, 1972), and passed on all subsequent Apollo flights; including a remake of the TORNADOS' "Telstar." Apollo 100 drummer, Clem Cattini, had been a member of the original Tornados, as well as Colin Hicks and his Cabin Boys.

Once the Apollo concept was scrapped, Parker joined the Doggerel Bank as a keyboardist for their two mid-'70s albums on the Charisma label. Tom has also done some production work for Marc Ellington, Gerry Rafferty, Chris White, and STATUS QUO.

CLIMAX
PRECIOUS AND FEW
(Walter Nims)
Carousel 30055
No. 3 *February 26, 1972*

Sonny Geraci, the voice of "Precious and Few," got his start in a forgotten high school band in Cleveland, in the pre-Beatles '60s. "By 1965, I was wanting to make a record and get the girls," said Sonny Geraci in an exclusive interview. "There was this local band called the Spitfires, that had made some records that needed a vocalist. They were old, older than I—22, 23—and tired of the game and didn't care to make anymore records. In there was Tom King and he and Chet Kelley had this song 'Time Won't Let Me.' I knew it was great, so I pushed . . . finally at $40 an hour, we recorded just that one song in three hours at Cleveland Recorders."

With Capitol Records taking an immediate interest and "Time Won't Let Me" as their first single, the Spitfires were set for the ride of their lives. Three of the five heard on the record were gone by the time of the disk's release. "Our manager spotted this sign that said, 'Outsiders keep out!' It was now a new band, so we figured we needed a new name . . ."

As the Cleveland-based Outsiders, Sonny (b. 1947, Cleveland) and the rest had the charts sewed up. "Time Won't Let Me" (#5, 1966), "Girl in Love" (#21, 1966), "Help Me Girl" (#37, 1966), and their remake of the Isley Brothers' "Respectable" (#15, 1966)—what Baby Boomer can forget them? They toured constantly, and three of their four LPs sold well—*Time Won't Let Me* (1966), *The Outsiders Album 2* (1966), and *Happening 'Live'* (1967).

"That was our big year, 1966, but it was all over for us," said Geraci. "By the end of the year, our manager had a Porsche; we didn't. We could see that we weren't getting our money, and it just tore us apart." One by one members dropped out and the hits stopped. Sometime in 1968, Sonny and guitarist Walter Nims left what remained of the Outsiders. "We want to go to Los Angeles, and I just wanted to stay out of it and get my life back. When your always out on tour, it's hard to form a relationship with a girl; or even to think."

Six months of normality and Sonny was itchin' again to do music. After some starts and stops, Sonny, Walt, and a ever-changing line-up found a positive response from Marc Gordon, manager of the Fifth Dimension and founder of Carousel Records (soon relabeled Rocky Road Records, due to legal threats from a similarly named company). "Changes," the first release by Sonny and Walt was billed as by the "Outsiders." The initial response was favorable, but Tom King and others in the original Outsiders voiced a complaint and the disk was reissued as by Climax.

"I can't recall where the idea for the group's name came from," said Sonny. "And I got a good memory, too. Probably I should've just put my name on the records." "Hard Rock Group," accredited to Climax, failed to sell nationally, but the follow-up, Walt's "Precious and Few"—with a line-up that included Geraci, Nims, Robert Nelson (drums), Virgil Weber (keyboards), and Steven York (bass, harmonica)—did what no other Climax cut would ever do—charted Top 10. Numerous poorly-distributed disks were tried (and trampled) over the next several years. "Life and Breath" (#52, 1972) and their one LP (Climax, #177, 1972) were only marginal successes.

"When 'Rock and Roll Heaven' [later a reworked hit for the Righteous Brothers] didn't make it, I just decided to stop for awhile." Tired of performing in Cleveland bars, Sonny married in 1982 and became a father, a born-again Christian, and a salesman of siding and replacement windows.

In the late '80s, Sonny found a new personal manager, reformed and modified an Outsiders/Climax group, and was musically active on a part-time basis. With the release of Sonny Geraci on the Verge in 1997, Sonny was back to rock'n'roll full time.

Nims, who has experienced a string of bad health and lives on the East Coast, continues to write tunes. Weber went on to membership in a later edition of the Grassroots. In his post-Climax career, York—at various times a member of East of Eden, Manfred Mann's Chapter Three, Vinegar Joe—has become a top-notch session bassist, having recorded with Joan Armatrading, Graham Bond, THE CRAZY WORLD OF ARTHUR BROWN, DR. JOHN, Marianne Faithfull, Charlie Musselwhite, and others.

T. REX
BANG A GONG (GET IT ON)
(Marc Bolan)
Reprise 1032
No. 10 March 4, 1972

Marc Bolan never did pick up a following in the States like he did in England. Most American rock fans have little idea of just how big a star this seminal glam-rocker was in the U.K. At the height of Bolan's powers (1971-1974), his T-Rex concerts could generate a level of hysteria not seen since Beatlemania. Before Bolan's death in 1977, he had sold 37 million records—surpassing the combined sales in England of all products issued by JIMI HENDRIX and the Who.

"The people in the business think I've had a cold spell since 'Bang a Gong,' whereas in reality I've been selling loads of records all over the world," Bolan explained in 1974 to Rock's Alan Betrock. "But if you're not hot in their country, they think you've had it. I admit that I should've approached America differently after 'Bang a Gong' was a hit here. I should have come over and followed it up, but we were just so busy all over the rest of the world, we didn't have time."

Guitarist Marc Bolan (b. Mark Feld, July 30, 1947, London) attended the same primary school as British pop singer Helen Shapiro and Procol Harum's Keith Reid. At 15, he was a male model. His early rock career had him signed with British Decca for a few solo singles as Toby Tyler, Marc Bowland, and finally, as Marc Bolan. Briefly, in 1967, he was a member of the proto-glam-rock group John's Children.

In 1968, drawing on percussionist Steve Peregrine-Took (b. July 28, 1949, London), his own considerable imagination, and imagery from J. R. R. Tolkien's The Hobbit, Bolan assembled Tyrannosaurus Rex. Starting with their debut album, My People Were Fair and Had Sky in Their Hair but Now They're Content to Wear Stars on Their Brows, the duo played acoustic instruments and dressed in flower-power threads, beads, and headbands. Bolan's mystical lyrics spoke of unicorns, gnomes, impish forest folk, and fairies.

Gradually, Bolan added more electric sounds to his recordings; Unicorn (1970), a half-acoustic and half-electric set produced the act's first charting "Ride a White Swan" (#76, 1971). By LP number five (A Beard of Stars, 1971), Took had taken leave. His replacement was Mickey Finn, a former rocker from Hapash & The Coloured Coat. Also added were bassist Steve Currie (b. May 21, 1947, Grimsby) and drummer Bill Legend (b. Bill Fifield, May 6, 1944, Essex). Subtracted were a number of letters from the group's name: they became simply "T. Rex."

"The [British] press have never been off my back, ever," Bolan complained. "With a few exceptions I've

T. REX, WITH
STEVE TOOK AND
MARC BOLAN

never had a good review for anything." Not that it mattered: T. Rex racked up 11 singles on the British Top 10 from 1970 to 1973, including four number-one disks.

While T. Rex only made the U.S. Hot 100 on one other occasion, with "Telegram Sam" (#67, 1972), the act gathered a growing stateside following and had two best-selling albums—*Electric Warrior* (1971), which featured "Bang a Gong," and *The Slider* (1972). *Tyrannosaurus Rex (A Beginning)* (1972) and *Tranx* (1973) also did well.

In 1973, the Bolan-mania was captured on film by Ringo Starr, as director, in a semi-documentary, *Born to Boogie*. At this moment, homeland fans got fickled as they are apt to do, and his stardom waned.

"I was living in a twilight world of drugs, booze, and kinky sex," Bolan told *Rolling Stone*. In an effort to avert his descent, Bolan in 1975 left his wife and England for America. With a remodeled T. Rex band and the punk rockers the Damned in support, Bolan made a last dash effort. *Dandy in the Underworld* was passed over.

On September 17, 1977, Bolan perished in a car crash near Putney Common, England. Behind the wheel was girlfriend Gloria Jones, creator of the original version of SOFT CELL's "Tainted Love." Steve Peregrine-Took and Steve Currie died in 1980 and 1981, respectively.

CHAKACHAS
JUNGLE FEVER
(William Albimoor)
Polydor 15030
No. 8 *March 25, 1972*

Fiction is often stranger than truth: a case in point is the story of the Chakachas. Fiction has it that these guys were led by a mysterious Gaston Boogaerts, who would paint raw chickens and other assorted livestock. Gaston and the group, including a conga-beating beauty named Kary, supposedly appeared in an Italian movie, introduced the Twist to much of the continent, and had a European hit called "Eso Es El Amor" back in 1958. Quite a strange little story.

In truth, the musicians were six Belgian studio players, married and middle-aged. They cut "Jungle Fever" and some other sides, then walked off into the sunset. Polydor Records issued "Jungle Fever," and to the surprise of many, it took off. To tour behind the record (always a problem when studio groups have hits), the label located a New York Latino group called Bario to pose as the Chakachas. Chee Chee Navarro, Felix Tollinchi, Eddie Perez, Paul Alicia, Eddie Babato, and Frankie Malabe did record some further albums and singles as the Chakachas, but nothing ever budged from the basement. Eventually, Chee Chee and the guys reassumed their original name.

MALO
SUAVECITO
(Richard Bean, Abel Zarate, Pablo Tellez)
Warner Bros. 7559
No. 18 *May 6, 1972*

Malo was a Latin-rock group from San Francisco front-ed by Carlos Santana's brother, Jorge. Formed in the early '70s, this short-lived conglomerate included vets from a number of top-notch Bay Area rock and Latin acts. Guitarist Jorge Santana (b. June 13, 1954, Jalisco, Mexico), guitarist Pablo Tellez (b. July 2, 1951, Grana-da, Nicaragua), and lead singer Arcelio Garcia, Jr. (b. May 7, 1946, Manati, Puerto Rico) were former mem-bers of the Malibus. Trumpeter/trombonist/flutist/sax-ophonist Roy Murray, drummer Richard Spremich (b. July 2, 1951, San Francisco) and guitarist Abel Zarate (b. Dec. 2, 1952, Manila, Philippines) had been in a unit called Naked Lunch. Trumpeter Luis Gasca (b. Mar. 23, 1940, Houston) and keyboardist Richard Kermode (b. Oct. 5, 1946, Lovell, Wyo.) had worked together in JANIS JOPLIN's Kozmic Blues Band (Gasca had also played with Count Basie, Woody Herman, and Mongo Santa-maria). Percussionist Raul Rekow (b. June 10, 1944, San Francisco) had been with Soul Sacrifice, and percus-sionist Leo Rosales (b. San Francisco) had performed with the Escovedo Brothers and Soul Sauce.

Shortly after pulling their numbers together, Malo (Spanish for "bad") met with David Rubinson, one of the area's name producers and managers. Rubinson—who shaped the sounds of ELVIN BISHOP, the Chambers Brothers, and Moby Grape—arranged for the group to be signed to Warner Bros. "Suavecito," from the unit's self-titled first album, would be their lone chart entry. Each of Malos four albums sold well, their debut LP best of all.

For reasons now lost in time, Malo splintered in 1974. Richard Kermode toured and recorded with Betty Davis. Luis Gasca went on to play with George Duke, Mother Earth, and Van Morrison, also cutting solo sides for Fantasy Records. Kermode, Gasca, Raul Rekow, and Pablo Tellez provided support for Carlos Santana. Jorge Santana had a few solo disks issued, and has appeared as a guest artist with the Fania All-Stars.

COMMANDER CODY & HIS
LOST PLANET AIRMEN
HOT ROD LINCOLN
(CHARLIE RYAN, W. S. Stevenson)
Paramount 0146
No. 9 *June 3, 1972*

Piano-plunking Commander Cody—George Frayne IV (b. July 19, 1944, Boise, ID)—was raised in Brooklyn and on Long Island. His interests were serious indeed: art, painting, and sculpture. At the University of Michi-gan in Ann Arbor, George sidelined in such bands as the Amblers, Lorenzo Lightfoot, and the Fantastic Surf-ing Beavers. But it was while seeking out some Strohs at an Ann Arbor bar that Frayne conceived what would become the Lost Planet Airmen's trademark sound.

"This was 1966," the Commander told *Sound Trax* writer Martin Porter, "and they had this stack of BUCK OWENS records on sale. I had never heard anything by him . . . I picked up one of the records, the one with 'Act Naturally' and also this number 'Tiger by the Tail.' And I got turned on by that . . . [here was] stuff that nobody had ever heard before. And it even had a 'yahoo!' in there somewhere. That's what northern hippies always like about country music—that 'yahoo!', that knee-slappin.'"

The first version of Commander Cody & His Lost Planet Airmen was formed in 1966. (The Comman-der's name is of dual origin: "Commando Cody, Sky-marshall of the Universe" a '40s radio serial; later adapted for the silver screen and a line in Coleridge's "The Ancient Mariner.") Ultimately, a regrouped and seemingly ever-changing organization fronted by Frayne and lead guitarist/vocalist Bill Kirchen (b. Jan. 29, 1948, Ann Arbor, MI) was firmly planted in San Francisco. Their best-known line-up was of this period, and included "Buffalo" Bruce Barlow (b. Dec. 3, 1948, Oxnard, CA) on bass, Steve "The West Virginia Creep-er" Davis on pedal steel, Lance Dickerson (b. Oct. 15, 1948, Livonia, MI) on drums, Billy C. Farlow (b. Decatur, AL) on harmonica and vocals, Andy Stein (b. Aug. 31, 1948, New York City) on fiddle and sax, and John Tichy (b. St. Louis) on guitar and vocals.

The band quickly developed a substantial reputation among partyin' people of all persuasions, playing a hodgepodge of Texas swing, boogie-woogie, and rocka-billy. They became known as the first hippie country band—genuine synthesizers of flagrant flower-power and country-roots music. They would sing everything from truck-driver tunes and corny country ballads played tongue-in-cheek to jump numbers from the '40s.

"When it hit, we weren't ready for it," the Comman-der recalled. "We were on the road at the time and they called us and said that they thought 'Hot Rod Lincoln' [a remake of a 1960 novelty hit for country man JOHN-NY BOND and pre-rockabilly CHARLIE RYAN] was gonna be a hit. I said, 'What?' And, you know, what you gotta do next is come up with something of equal quality right away. We went right back into the studio and re-did [the Andrew Sister's 1941 hit] 'Beat Me Daddy Eight to the Bar' [#81, 1972] to follow it up. It should have been a good follow-up, but for some reason it wasn't."

While only making marginal inroads with two fur-ther 45s—a remake of Tex Williams's 1947 C & W

COMMANDER CODY & HIS LOST PLANET AIRMEN

chart-topper "Smoke! Smoke! Smoke! (That Cigarette)" (#94, 1973) and a take on Roy Hamilton's shooter "Don't Let Go" (#56, 1975)—Cody and his Airmen did sell plenty of LPs: *Lost in the Ozone* (1971), *Hot Licks, Cold Steel and Trucker's Favorites* (1972), *Country Casanova* (1973). All was to end, however, when the band broke up in 1976.

The Commander had a few solo efforts issued in the late '70s by Arista (*Rock 'n' Roll Again* and *Flying Dreams*)—both featuring the vocal assistance of Nicolette Larson—a 1980 LP for Line/Peter Pan (*Lose It Tonight*), and has since continued with a spin-off band, the Moonlighters, (which also included Barlow and Kirchen). Venting his serious side, Commander has gained acclaim as a painter, exhibiting in galleries worldwide. A book of his paintings, *StarArt* was published in 1979.

Buffalo Bruce had a pair of LPs issued in the '70s (*Lovin' in the Valley of the Moon* and *Desert Horizon*) and has done session work for Bette Midler, Steve Miller, and DAVID SOUL. For a while, both Barlow and Dickerson were members of Roger McGuinn's post-

Byrd group, Thunderbyrd. Dickerson has played with Hoyt Axton, David Bromberg, the New Riders of the Purple Sage, Link Wray, and Mitch Woods and His Rocket 88s. Kirchen has appeared on NICK LOWE's *The Impossible Bird* and toured in the mid-'90s with the ex-Rockpile man. Andy Stein was involved in the National Lampoon films and had a jazzy LP (*Gold Places*) issued in 1987 on the Stomp Off label. Farlow has had some obscure solo singles issued.

The Commander and Billy C. reformed the Lost Planet Airmen in the '90s.

ROYAL SCOTS DRAGOON GUARDS
AMAZING GRACE
(John Newton)
RCA Victor 12304
No. 11 *July 1, 1972*

After 300 years of togetherness, the Royal Scots Greys Band dissolved in July, 1971. Shortly after, though, members of the Greys joined the Prince of Wales Dra-

rately, 20 pipes were piping, and 10 drums were drumming; eventually, more than 7 million copies were spinning. With that kind of success, "The Day Is Done"—the Guards' follow-up 45—couldn't help but be a royal disappointment.

MOUTH & MACNEAL
HOW DO YOU DO
(Henry van Hoof, Hans van Hemert)
Philips 40715
No. 8 *July 22, 1972*

The Mouth (Willem Duyn)—so named because he was always running off with it— and Maggie MacNeal (Sjoukje Van't Spijker) teamed up in 1971 after both artists' solo releases bombed. Mouth happened to hear a tape of Maggie's at the Phonogram Studios in Amsterdam. He approached producer Hans van Hermert about arranging a meeting with MacNeal. Frustrated with her failed single, MacNeal agreed to a coupling with the gravel-throated Duyn. Recorded in English, "Hey Love You," their first release, did well regionally. "How Do You Do," their second single, sold incredibly well internationally. Eventual sales in the U.S. alone exceeded a million copies.

Willem Duyn was born in 1942, in Haarlem, Netherlands. For years, he worked as a construction worker, and played drums on evenings and weekends in a jazz combo, the Holland Quartet. Willem joined the more pop-oriented Jay-Jays in 1968. Not content, he moved on to spinning records at a radio station, opening up his own nightclub, and, in 1970, fronting a beat group, Speedway. The latter configuration achieved some success, and Duyn was becoming known as something of a Dutch Joe Cocker. After the group splintered, he cut some solo sides. Mouth's cover of the Shangri-Las' "Remember (Walkin' in the Sand)" failed to generate sales.

Maggie MacNeal was born in 1951, also in the Dutch city of Haarlem. When 18, Maggie studied classical singing for three years before quitting school to join up with a pop group. A local DJ liked her stuff and arranged an audition with the Philips label. Her first release, a cover of Motown classic "I Heard It Through the Grapevine," flopped.

It was at this point that Mouth and MacNeal came together for their mini-moment on the American airwaves. Never again were they able to interest stateside ears to buy their solo or duet recordings—four singles

goon Guards, the 3rd Carabineers. Together, this new formation became the Royal Scots Dragoon Guards, a bagpipes-and-drums military band. Within months of this new alliance, they made a series of recordings; Rev. John Newton's 1779 classic, "Amazing Grace," was one of more than 30 tunes that were taped. When the album, *Farewell to the Greys*, received some BBC late-night airplay and a positive response, RCA issued the timeless tune as a single.

Record sales were truly phenomenal—at its peak, the Royal Scots record was selling 70,000 copies a day. Pipe Major Tony Crease and company became the first group to ever sell a million copies of a record with the bagpipe as the predominant instrument. More accu-

and two albums were issued in the U.S.—though in the Netherlands, their popularity continued. In 1974, they crashed the U.K. Top 10 with "I See a Star," the tune they utilized in representing Holland in the Eurovision Song Contest.

GODSPELL
DAY BY DAY
(John-Michael Teblak, Stephen Schwartz)
Bell 45210
No.13 *July 29, 1972*

It was designed to be a two-act rock musical based upon the Gospel according to St. Matthew. *Godspell's* original conceiver, and later the author of the like-titled book, was one John-Michael Teblak, a Carnegie Tech student who created the work as a requirement for his master's program. Music and new lyrics were furnished by Stephen Schwartz (b. Mar. 6, 1948, New York City). Stephen was a recent Juilliard graduate and co-author, with Leonard Bernstein, of the English text for Bernstein's *Mass*, the commissioned work for the opening of the John F. Kennedy Center for the Performing Arts. *Godspell* debuted at Stephen's alma mater, the Carnegie-Mellon Institute in Pittsburgh; its Big Apple opening took place at the Cherry Lane Theatre on May 17, 1971 (the better-remembered *Jesus Christ Superstar* opened a few months later).

Original cast members, decked out in colorful clown costumes and facial make-up, included Lamar Alford, Peggy Gordon (co-writer with Jay Hamburger of "By My Side"), David Haskell (as John the Baptist and Judas), Joanne Jonas, Robin Lamont (lead vocalist on "Day by Day"), Sonia Manzano, Gilmer McCormick, Jeffrey Mylett, Stephen Nathan (as Jesus), and Herb Simon. Despite the musical's near-blasphemous touches (like the portrayal of Jesus as having a clown's red nose and wearing a Superman T-shirt with striped overalls), most critics were liberal in their praise. Five singles from the cast recording were issued, but none were noticed save the rousing "Day by Day." The original soundtrack album sold well.

After 2,124 performances, *Godspell* was temporarily tucked away. It was revived in 1976 and ran for over 500 performances on Broadway at the Broadhurst Theatre. A filmed adaptation, directed by David Greene, appeared in 1973.

The cast of the London production, which stayed at Wyndham's Theatre for near three years, featured Julie Covington, DAVID ESSEX, Marti Webb, and Jeremy Irons. In Los Angeles, in 1993, *Godspell-Now*, a reinterpretation in the light of the city's 1992 riots was offered.

Schwartz has experienced more composer/lyricist success with *Pippin, The Magic Show, The Baker's Wife,* and *Children of Eden.* In 1995, he collaborated with Alan Mencken on the score for the Walt Disney flick *Pocahontas.*

DEREK & THE DOMINOS
LAYLA
(Eric Clapton, James Beck Gordon)
Atco 6809
No. 51 *March 27, 1971*
No. 10 *August 5, 1972*

"This business devours so much of your time. You don't know if you're doing the right thing or the wrong thing—or even who you are!" Having said this (according to Irwin Stambler's *Encyclopedia of Pop, Rock, & Soul*, Eric Clapton and the rest of Cream—Jack Bruce and Ginger Baker—split up in mid-1968. The strain of playing loud and long night after night had taken its toll: Clapton needed to recuperate, and sought the lower profile offered by Blind Faith and an equally short-lived group, Derek & The Dominos.

The Dominos were Jim Gordon (b. 1945, Los Angeles) on drums and (on "Layla") piano, Carl Radle (b. 1942, Oklahoma) on bass, and Bobby Whitlock (b. 1948, Memphis) on keyboards and vocals. All of them had worked with Leon Russell and Delaney & Bonnie, and they backed Clapton on his first solo album (*Eric Clapton*, 1970). Eric and the Dominos gathered in the fall of 1970 at Atlantic's Criteria Studios in Miami. No one knew it, but only one studio album—*Layla and Other Assorted Love With Songs* (1970)—would result from these Eric Clapton sessions.

The Allman Brothers' Duane Allman (b. Nov. 20, 1946, Nashville) became a major contributor to the album and something of a pseudo-member, later making limited personal appearances with the band. Producer Tom Dowd had told Duane of the impending sessions; work was already underway when he arrived. "Eric knew me, man, greeted me like an old friend," Allman told Irwin Stambler. "He said, 'Come on, you got to play on this record'— so I did. We'd sit down and plan it out, work out our different parts . . . Everybody contributed. Most of it was cut live, no overdubbing—and it was all done in 10 days."

Commenting on the loose atmosphere, Bobby Whitlock told Gene Santoro columnist with *The Nation*, "Tom [Dowd] couldn't believe it, the way we had these big bags laying out everywhere. I'm almost ashamed to tell it, but it's the truth. It was scary, what we were doing, but we were just young and dumb and didn't know. Cocaine and heroin, that's all—and Johnny Walker."

"When we finished it," said Dowd to *Rolling Stones'* Robert Palmer, "I felt it was the best goddamn album I'd been involved with since *The Genius of Ray Charles.*

DEREK & THE DOMINOS, WITH ERIC CLAPTON (FAR RIGHT)

But we couldn't get the goddamn thing ["Layla"] on the air; couldn't get a single out of it. Nothing. I kept walking around talking to myself for a year. Now, suddenly, it's a national anthem."

Their label was only to issue three singles. A Phil Spector-produced version of "Tell the Truth" (a hopped-up variation on the album version) missed the charts entirely. "Bell Bottom Blues" made the lowest reaches of the Hot 100 (#91, 1971). Finally, within weeks of the "Bell Bottom" release, a truncated version of "Layla" was issued—inspired by Clapton's unrequited love for Patti Harrison, George Harrison's wife. It managed only a mild showing on the charts, number 51.

"Layla" is often considered a pinnacle in Clapton's career, and is a much-requested (and much-performed) part of his live set even today. The tune features soaring slide guitar from Duane Allman—Clapton even reported at one time that Allman plays all the electric guitars on the track—and a piano section composed by Jim Gordon. In 1972, the song was reissued, this time in its entirety—all 7 minutes and 10 seconds of it; becoming possibly the longest Top 10 tune in rock'n'roll history.

The group received a critical drubbing during its tour in 1972. "By the end of the tour, the band was getting very, very loaded, doing way too much," said Clap-

ton to *Rolling Stones'* Robert Palmer. "Then we went back to England, tried to make a second album, and it broke down halfway through because of the paranoia and the tension. And the band just . . . dissolved. I remember to this day being in my house, feeling totally lost and hearing Bobby Whitlock pull up in the driveway outside and scream for me to come out. He sat in his car outside all day, and I hid."

Surviving tracks from the planned second album appeared on Clapton's *Crossroads* compilation. To fill the commercial void, a half-hearted live LP for RSO, *Derek & The Dominos in Concert*, appeared in 1973. With the Dominos fallen, Clapton went into hiding. He did some session work and appeared at 1971's Concert for Bangladesh, but was otherwise out of public view. Clapton had acquired a serious heroin habit—it was reported— due to a deep depression from the sudden death of Duane Allman, and from what he perceived as a lack of public acceptance for Derek & The Dominos.

Time has treated "Layla" as a gem; life has extracted a price.

Jim Gordon—co-writer with Clapton of "Layla"—was convicted of murdering his mother and has been imprisoned since 1984. Jim had a long history of music-making, beginning with Frankie & The Jesters in Hollywood in the early '60s; followed by a slot in TV's

"Shindig" house band, stays with Delaney & Bonnie, Leon Russell's Mad Dogs and English Men, SOUTHER, HILLMAN, FURAY BAND. He also had a lengthy and tortured history of living with a foreign voice in his head—his mother's voice; attempted suicides followed as did 14 self-inflicted stays in psychiatric hospitals. On the night of June 3, 1983, Jim killed his 76-year-old mother with a hammer and knife. He has been diagnosed with paranoid schizophrenia and was found guilty of second-degree murder; receiving a 16-year-to-life sentence. Reportedly, Jim no longer hears her voice.

Duane Allman died in a motorcycle crash in October, 1971. Carl Radle died of alcohol poisoning in 1981.

ARGENT
HOLD YOUR HEAD UP
(Rod Argent, Chris White)
Epic 10852
No. 5 *August 26, 1972*

Although vast sums of money were offered, Rod Argent and his fellow Zombies refused to reunite for even one show. Surely, Rod and Paul Atkinson, Colin Blunstone, Hugh Grundy, and Chris White would want to have a second shot at stardom. Since the Zombies' break-up,

PEOPLE had unearthed "I Love You" (#14, 1968), an obscure "B" side. And both "Time of the Season" (#3, 1969) and the *Odessey* [sic] *and Oracle* (1969) album was suddenly a stateside smash.

But alas, such was not to be. Once the pressure for a Zombies reunion had abated, Rod Argent (b. June 14, 1945, St. Albans, England) set to work launching a self-named group. The unit's first album, *Argent*, appeared in 1970, and featured Argent, lead singer/guitarist Russ Ballard (b. Oct. 31, 1947, Waltham Cross, England), bassist Jim Rodford (b. July 7, 1945, St. Albans), and drummer Bob Henrit (b. May 2, 1945, Broxbourine). Ballard and Henrit were both ex-members of the UNIT 4 PLUS 2 and ADAM FAITH's back-up band, the Roulettes.

Neither *Argent* nor *Ring of Hands* (1970) sold in sizable amounts, though Three Dog Night did all right with Ballard's "Liar" (#7, 1971), a cut from the first album. The band toured America, with stops at both Fillmores, the Whiskey-a-Go-Go, the Kinetic Playground, and the Boston Tea Party. The audience response was favorable and growing.

With the issuance of *All Together Now* (1972) and its lead single, "Hold Your Head Up," Argent had found a niche, though they seemed to notice not. "Tragedy," the group's follow-up cut, was similarly dense and hook-ridden and should have charted; it did in England.

ARGENT

Months later, a much more self-indulgent *In Deep* (1973) was released.

A year later, Ballard left the fold to start his solo career. Russ has since written for FRIDA, ACE FREHLEY, and RAINBOW. He also penned "You Can Do Magic" for America (#8, 1982), and had his own solo success with "On the Rebound" (#58, 1980) and "Voices." His replacements in Argent were guitarist John Grimaldi (b. May 25, 1955) and guitarist John Verity (b. May 2, 1944). A double-live set, *Encore-Live in Concert* (1975), was issued while the band attempted their regrouping. Two more LPs followed—*Circus* (1975) and *Counterpoint* (1975)—but these were marred by Rod's pseudo-classical pretenses. When Grimaldi left the group in 1976, Rod folded his band up.

Verity, Rodford, and Henrit remained together as Phoenix for two unsuccessful LPs. Verity has fronted a band named after himself; Rodford has since joined the Kinks; Henrit joined G. B. Blues & Company, and is now involved in musical-instrument retailing. Argent had his first musical, *Masquerade*, staged at London's Young Vic Theatre. He has worked sessions (Colin Blunstone, the Hollies, CHRIS REA, Andrew Lloyd Webber, the Who), had two jazz-oriented LPs issued (*Moving Home*, [1978]; *Ghosts*, [1982]), and has recently lent his name to a chain of keyboard shops. In 1985, Rod briefly reformed a group under his own name for a charity appearance. As a producer, he has experienced some success with Tanita Tikaram and jazz artist Barbara Thompson.

In 1992, Kiss revived what should have been Argent's second Top 40 charting, Ballard's "God Gave Rock'n'Roll to You," an FM turntable hit from the *In Deep* album.

SAILCAT
MOTORCYCLE MAMA
(John Wyker)
Elektra 45782
No.12 *August 26, 1972*

Sailcat was never a group per se. They were more of a happening that, well, happened to find one good soft-shoe song. Their lone self-titled album indicates that "officially" Sailcat comprised two guitar pickers named Court Pickett and John Wyker. They had been hanging around the Muscle Shoals, Alabama, recording scene, and had picked up some influential friends, like Clayton Ivey (bass), Chuck Leavell of the Allman Brothers (keyboards), and Pete Carr (guitar)—a producer, songwriter, and later one-half of LEBLANC & CARR. All of these sessioneers and two others played on the tracks. And all of the aforementioned (with the exception of Leavell) contributed to writing Sailcat's tunes.

"Motorcycle Mama" was a fluke hit from Sailcat's debut LP. When a follow-up was needed, all returned to the Widget Studios to cut something called "Baby Ruth." Sales were slow, to say the least. Their swan song, "She Showed Me," came next. In light of the disk's poor showing, the "Sailcat" name was shelved, and the loosely knit aggregation directed their energies elsewhere.

In 1973, Court Pickett had a solo album issued by Elektra.

DANIEL BOONE
BEAUTIFUL SUNDAY
(DANIEL BOONE, R. McQUEEN)
Mercury 73281
No. 15 *September 16, 1972*

Like many other young lads, Peter Stirling was given piano lessons. At age 13, while laid up with an illness, the Britisher took to strumming a guitar; three years later, he was playing in the Beachcombers. In 1963, just as the world was being overtaken by Beatlemania, Peter was a member of a pop group named the Bruisers, who had a medium-sized hit in England with "Blue Girl." The group was not part of the British Invasion, and after a few more singles on Parlophone, the Bruisers disbanded.

In 1965, Stirling began his career as a session musician with songwriter Les Reed, and reportedly played on many Tom Jones sessions (including the one that produced "It's Not Unusual"). The Merseybeats and Kathy Kirby were among the first artists to record Peter's early songwriting efforts. Larry Page—producer of the Troggs and founder of Page One and Penny Farthing Records—took a demo Stirling had created on "Daddy Don't You Walk So Fast," sweetened the thing with strings, credited the track to "Daniel Boone," and released it on his Penny Farthing label. The recording made the Top 20 in the U.K., but Wayne Newton's cover rendition stole some of Stirling's glory by making the Top 10 stateside.

Peter's moment, however, was at hand. The very next release was the infectious and bouncy "Beautiful Sunday." The world could not get enough of this tune; but the world also did not take kindly to any future recordings Peter ever made, either as Daniel Boone or as Peter Lee Stirling. By July, 1972, Pete's high point had sold a million copies worldwide. Two years later, producer Page rereleased the recording, and sales continued. Two more years passed, and "Beautiful Sunday" was picked up as the theme song for a popular Japanese TV program. Another million copies were sold, and the tune remained number one on the Japanese charts for four months—reportedly becoming one of the top-selling records in Japanese pop history.

HOT BUTTER
POPCORN
(Gershon Kingsley)
Musicor 1458
No. 9 *October 21, 1972*

ARLO GUTHRIE

Hot Butter was Stan Free, a session keyboardist and Moog synthesizer player. As a Moog man, Stan had provided behind-the-scenes synth sounds to rock, pop, and semi-classical works. Over the years, he had sound-seasoned recordings by John Denver, ARLO GUTHRIE, and even Arthur Fiedler's Boston Pops. Not counting a few forgettable solo sides for the Amy label in the mid-'60s, Stan's catchy "Popcorn" was his first front-line outing. Although the instrumental was momentarily appealing, in a humbly hummable way, its allure diminished with each hearing.

In an attempt to forestall the inevitable satiation with Stan's quirky sounds, Steve Jerome, Bill Jerome, and Danny Jordan (formerly with THE DETERGENTS) at MTL Productions had Stan "Moog-ize" former hits with distinctive melodies. BILLY JOE & THE CHECKMATES' "Percolator," THE CHANTAYS' "Pipeline," JORGEN INGMANN's "Apache," and EDDIE PLATT's "Tequila" were all issued as singles, but not one found a receptive audience.

ARLO GUTHRIE
THE CITY OF NEW ORLEANS
(Steve Goodman)
Reprise 1103
No.18 *October 28, 1972*

"I was going to be a forest ranger," said folk legend Woody Guthrie's son Arlo, to *DISCoveries'* Jeff Tamarkin. "I had absolutely no intention of being a professional musician. I am not a social animal. I do not enjoy the company of large amounts of people most of the time. I'm much better off with trees . . ."

For a brief period in the late '60s, Arlo was America's favorite folkie. Many fondly recall the classic lines—"You can get anything you want/At Alice's Restau-rant"—from "Alice's Restaurant," the rambling 18-minute saga about his arrest for littering in Stockbridge, Massachusetts, on Thanksgiving Day in 1965. Not only did that offense allegedly render Arlo ineligible for the draft, but it also launched his career. "Alice's Restaurant" became the core of his same-titled 1967 debut LP and served two years later as the flaky foundation for Arthur Penn's film of the same name.

Arlo (b. July 10, 1947, Coney Island, NY) was born the eldest son of Woody and his wife, Marjorie. People like Bob Dylan, Ramblin' Jack Elliott, Cisco Houston, and Pete Seeger were always dropping by and playing music together. When he was three, Arlo danced and blew his harmonica for Leadbelly. A few years later, his mother, a former Martha Graham dancer, taught him the workings of the guitar. He attended private schools and, for a while, a college in Billings, Montana.

In mid-'65, Arlo started working the East Coast coffeehouse circuit. He toured Japan with Judy Collins, and on his return in 1967, he presented the initial work-up on "Alice's Restaurant Massacre" at the WNYC Folk Song Festival. Warner Brothers representatives noted the ode and wanted the song, and bad. Was Arlo surprised? "Nobody in their right mind would ever think that an 18-minute monologue would, first of all, be on a record," Tamarkin was told, "let alone be played on the radio in an era when a song over two-and-a-half minutes didn't stand a chance of being played.

"Frankly, I don't even feel that it has anything to do with me anymore—it became bigger than me."

After his first album, a number of highly-praised LPs followed: *Arlo* (1968), *Running Down the Road* (1969), *Washington County* (1970), and *Hobo's Lullabye* (1972). Some of Guthrie's most popular numbers included "Coming Into Los Angeles," a song about dope-smuggling that Guthrie performed at Woodstock; the deliciously vicious anti-Nixon number, "Presidential Rag"; an Arab-Israeli political commentary, "Children of Abraham" . . . and that Steve Goodman train tune, "The City of New Orleans."

Arlo is still active on the music scene. During the '70s, he toured and recorded with Pete Seeger. He frequently performs for causes like the anti-nuclear and ecological movements. But Guthrie rarely sings of Alice and the restaurant these days. As he told an interviewer in the late '70s: "'Alice,' it's just too long. I forgot it about four or five years ago. I'm trying to learn it again, but . . . I got the first part down, the garbage down. I'm just workin' on the trash part now."

In 1997, on the eve of the 30th anniversary of "Alice's Restaurant," Arlo rerecorded the tale for Kock Records. Guthrie continues to run his label Rising Son Records, with his son keyboardist/producer Abe, and to publish a newsletter *Rolling Blunder Review*. [Arlo Guthrie can be reached at his official Web site, ArloNet (http://www.clark.net/pub/arlonet/arlonet-main.shtml).]

DANNY O'KEEFE
GOOD TIME CHARLIE'S GOT THE BLUES
(Danny O'Keefe)
Signpost 70006
No. 9 *November 4, 1972*

Danny O'Keefe, who wrote many portrait pieces that others would popularize, is primarily remembered for his lone, lazy lingering in Top 40-land. "Good Time Charlie's Got the Blues" was no party platter, but a poignant vignette of an abandoned Charlie, his pills, and his pain. "It was about a good friend of mine," O'Keefe told *Rolling Stone*'s Judith Sims. "He's a very mellow, beautiful friend who was going through heart attacks and it was rough [back in 1968]. It was a rough period for me, too."

Danny grew up in the small town of Wenatchee, Washington. Papa was a lawyer, an insurance adjuster, and, by Dan's pre-teen years, a dying man. "My grandmother put me into a military school in St. Paul. That was for the first two years of high school." About the time of his dad's death, O'Keefe began writing poetry and hanging out in the area's coffeehouses. After a short stay at the University of Minnesota, he returned to his hometown to attend Wenatchee Valley College. "In the winter when I was 20, I stayed there being lonely and crazy, starting to take drugs and playing guitar. I did it for a release, not seriously trying to do anything except to get some of the stuff inside out."

In the mid-'60s, O'Keefe was seriously injured in a motorcycle accident that involved extensive surgery and years of recovery. During this time, O'Keefe was encouraged to continue writing. By 1966, he had some songs and a band, later labeled the Bandits. A musical buddy introduced them to Jerry Dennson, who had recorded IAN WHITCOMB, the Sonics, and early sides on Paul

Revere & The Raiders. (Dennson also discovered the Kingsmen of "Louie Louie" fame.) A few O'Keefe singles (like "That Old Sweet Song") and a Bandits 45 ("Little Sally Walker") were issued on Dennson's Jerden label, but no great wealth and popularity were to follow. As Calliope, the Bandits band had singles issued on a variety of labels (Epic, Jet Set, Shamley) and an LP (*Steamed*, 1968) on Buddah, but again, nothing quite clicked.

Charlie Greene and Brian Stone—who supervised the careers of BUFFALO SPRINGFIELD, Bob Lind, and SONNY & Cher—spied O'Keefe palling around with a group called Daily Flash, and managed to convince Atlantic Records' Ahmet Ertegun to record him as a singer-songwriter solo act. "Good Time Charlie" was included on Danny's debut album; the tune was recorded on four or five occasions before everything was deemed just right.

A few follow-ups nearly cracked the Hot 100 ("The Road," "Angels Spread Your Wings") and two LPs sold well—*O'Keefe* (1972) and *Breezy Stories* (1973). But Danny never managed to solidify a mass audience for his story songs. Jackson Browne, Judy Collins, Waylon Jennings, B. W. STEVENSON, and even Elvis have recorded his material.

In the mid-'80s, O'Keefe had an album (*The Day to Day*, 1984) and single ("Along for the Ride") issued by Coldwater Records. Thereafter, for awhile, he was a member of the Seattle Helps the Hungry configuration that issued "Give Just a Little" as a 45 on the DJ label.

CHI COLTRANE
THUNDER AND LIGHTNING
(Chi Coltrane)
Columbia 45640
No. 17 *November 18, 1972*

Born in Racine, Wisconsin, on November 16, 1948, Chi began her classical piano studies at the age of seven. She sang in her church choir, and at the age of 12 gave her first public keyboard performance. By high school graduation, Chi was singing in the bars and hot spots of the Badger State. She attended Salter School of Music in Los Angeles for two years, and led the first of her bands. Shortly after, she moved to the Windy City and formed the Chicago Coltrane.

While working the club scene, Chi caught the attention of talent scouts for Columbia Records. Contracts were signed, arrangements were made, and songs were recorded. Upon hearing her debut/self-titled album, a critic for the *San Francisco Chronicle* wrote: "Miss Coltrane has two things going for her beyond talent—an engrossing urgency in her voice and a distinctive presence and beauty . . . She is, all in all, the most impressive new girl singer."

CHI COLTRANE

The verdict given by most listeners, however, was quite different. With the exception of her lone tuffy, "Thunder and Lightning," Chi's LP featured only humdrum hoofers. The package did place modestly on *Billboard*'s top pop albums chart (#148, 1972), and "Thunder" rumbled the airwaves, but lightning did not strike twice for Chi. A second album, *Let It Ride* and follow-up 45s like "Go Like Elijah," "You Were My Friend," and "Who Ever Told You" sank from sight with nary a spin.

Before her disappearance, Coltrane spoke through a publicist: "Listen to my lyrics—my songs tell more about me than anything I could ever say."

DELEGATES
CONVENTION '72
(Nick Cenci, Nick Casel)
Mainstream 5525
No. 8 *November 18, 1972*

"The Delegates were myself and two other principals," Tampa DJ Bob DeCarlo explained in an exclusive interview. "One was Nick Cenci. The name might ring a bell with some because a long time ago, he was involved in a record distributorship in Pittsburgh called Co & Ce. He also had a label [bearing the same name] and handled Lou Christie and, early on, the Vogues. The other guy was his partner, Nick Kousaleous [a.k.a. Nick Casel]. They would handle Motown and some other labels in the tri-state area.

"We played golf together, all three of us. And we'd been kicking this idea around for a long time. It seemed no one had done a break-in record [wherein a narrative is intercut with excerpts from then-current hits] in a long, long time, and here was this convention. So, we decided to do it. I brought over a bunch of singles from KQU, where I worked, and we sat in my kitchen and wrote it.

"Cenci set out to sell it. He must have visited all the offices he could. Buddah, Motown—no one wanted to press it. Then Mainstream, the jazz label, comes up and says 'Sure, let's do it.' It was a shock, like 'Really, you will?' Cenci had 10,000 copies pressed, and it started to take off in Parkersburg, West Virginia.

"I worked at KQU, one of the big pop stations and an ABC affiliate, at the time. They thought it smacked of payola if they played the tune, so they didn't . . . But it made the Top 10, and without any airplay, on WLS in Chicago, another affiliate. And we got no play in New York. But wherever it was played, it sold well. It was a cute record."

When "Convention '72" hit big, the Mainstream label issued a now-rare but low-grade album that included Nick Casel lisping his way through "My Way." "I have one of the few copies of that thing," continued DeCarlo. "It was a whole album of crap, that's what. It stunk to high heaven . . . but, the label called for a follow-up LP." Bob's station forbade him to be involved with the project, and recording funds were in short supply. "They wanted us to pay the costs of producing that thing, so you can believe me when I say, we put nothin' into it; it sucked.

"We were sued by everybody, for copyright infringement. We called up Dickie Goodman [creator of the break-in genre], and he said use whatever you want and let them sue you. It don't mean nothin'. Eventually, everyone dropped their suits."

An obscure follow-up single, "Richard M. Nixon—Face the Issues, Pt. 1 & 2," appeared under the "Delegates" name, but DeCarlo has denied any knowledge of its existence. Almost as quickly as they appeared, the Delegates vanished into pop oblivion.

Bob DeCarlo was born January 9, 1941, in New York City. "I went to college, Penn State. I was gonna be an actor, but I got dragged into spending a lot of time working at the campus radio station, WDFM. Before I knew which way my life was going, I was a DJ. I went to WMAJ in Providence, R.I.; next WICE, where I worked my way up from all night man to program director." Into the '90s, Bob worked the morning drive time on WUSA, an "adult contemporary" station out of Tampa, Florida.

BRIGHTER SIDE OF DARKNESS
LOVE JONES
(Randolph Murph, Clarence Johnson, Ralph Eskridge)
20th Century 2002
No. 16 *February 3, 1973*

Ralph Eskridge, Randolph Murph, and Larry Washington met at Calumet High on Chicago's South Side in 1971. Anna Preston, a one-time entertainer and mother of a houseful of music-makers, became their manager, music director, and body-and-soul shaper. She added 12-year-old Darryl Lamont to the group to give them a touch of Jackson Five/teen-appealing bubblegum soul.

After the group had played a few talent contests and successful gigs, producer Clarence Johnson cut a demo on the trio and rushed it over to 20th Century's new president, Russ Regan, the man responsible for the DANCER, PRANCER & NERVOUS phenomenon. Russ liked what he heard, and "Love Jones" became the group's first record. "Jones," a slang expression for addiction, was a string-infested talkie thing that surprised many folks when it mounted the upper reaches of *Billboard*'s pop charts.

Overnight, the teens were a full-grown success, but only momentarily. En route to a "Soul Train" TV guest appearance, a dispute of some sort took place, and the record company fired three-quarters of the group; only Lamont remained. The group had already recorded an album's worth of material; after its release, and three more singles, 20th Century dropped them.

Both parties wrangled in court over who—management and the record company, or the fired parties—owned the rights to the group's name. The courts eventually ruled in favor of the former.

Clarence Johnson hired Jesse Harvey, Nate Pringle, and Arthur Scales to fill in the vocal void behind Lamont. A one-off single for his Starve label was issued, but on release, it sank from sight. Later that year, 20th Century decided to pick up on some Johnson-produced sides by the new Brighter Side (Harvey, Pringle, Scales, and newcomer Tyrone Stewart). For whatever reason, 20th Century renamed the group the Imaginations; two albums and a batch of nifty singles were shipped, but nothing ever charted—pop or R & B.

In the late '70s, Darryl Lamont and Randolph Murph reformed Brighter Side of Darkness. Apparently, the rightful owners of the group's faded moniker no longer cared whether anybody used the name or not. Lennie LaCour's Magic Touch label released one final single, "He Made You Mine," in 1978.

TIMMY THOMAS
WHY CAN'T WE LIVE TOGETHER
(Timmy Thomas)
Glades 1703
No. 3 *February 10, 1973*

"I was born in Evansville, Indiana, on the 13th of November, 1944," Timmy Thomas told *Blues & Soul*. "By the time I was 10, I was playing organ at my father's church. I always had a good ear for music. I was one of 12 kids and most of them were into music, but I guess I pushed a little harder."

Timmy formed his first band in high school. In 1962, he won a scholarship to attend the Stan Kenton Jazz Clinic. There he studied with CANNONBALL ADDERLEY, Donald Byrd, and Woody Herman. "When I got a scholarship to attend Lane College in Jackson, Tennessee, I started messing with a lot of the dudes who were into a soul thing. I started getting session work with Stax, and I played on a lot of Stax/Volt Records. I played with the MAR-KEYS, filling in when Booker T took leave."

Thomas also worked as a house musician for Bobby Russell's and Quinton Claunch's Goldwax label. Timmy's keyboards accompanied James Carr, Percey Milem, Spencer Wiggins, and O. V. Wright. Impressed with his abilities, Russell and Claunch let Thomas, with the aid of Willie Mitchell's band, record two solo singles—"Have Some Boogaloo" and "Whole Lotta Shakin' Goin' On." Neither gathered much notice.

When Goldwax shut its doors, Tim returned to college to complete his musical studies. In 1970, he moved to Miami, took a teaching position with Florida Memorial College, and opened a lounge in the beach area. Thomas would often provide entertainment at his bar. One tune in particular was getting quite a reaction. Once all the wrinkles were ironed out, Thomas walked "Why Can't We Live Together" into Henry Stone's offices at TK Records.

"Why Can't We" has got to be one of the most memorable of all hits from the '70s—and one of the simplest. With its cheesy organ, a rhythm box ticking out a metronome beat, and Timmy sincerely sobbin' about peace, love, and the brotherhood of man, the disk was effective and sold several million copies. The follow-up, "People Are Changin'" (#75, 1973), did fair; in all, 13 of his singles made the R & B listings from 1973 to 1984, with "Gotta Give a Little Love (Ten Years After)" (#80; R&B: #29, 1980) also scoring on the Hot 100.

Until TK Records went under in 1980, Tim provided back-up services for K. C. & The Sunshine Band, Betty Wright, and others. In 1984, prior to her groundbreaking hit "Smooth Operator," the Nigerian-born Sade tastefully worked up a rendition of Timmy's tune. Into the '90s, Thomas ran his lounge and recorded for Gold Mountain Records.

HURRICANE SMITH
OH, BABE, WHAT WOULD YOU SAY?
(Hurricane Smith)
Capitol 3383
No. 3 *February 17, 1973*

Born in northern England in 1923, reportedly to a family of gypsies, little Norman Smith began messing with instruments as diverse as the drums, piano, vibes, trombone, and stand-up bass. As a young adult, he held down gigs as a jazz trumpeter for years. With the offer of an eventual apprenticeship as a recording engineer, Norman went to work as a "gofer" in 1955 at EMI's legendary Abbey Road studios. One of his first shots at being a full-fledged engineer came with the FRANK IFIELD session that produced "I Remember You" (#5, 1962).

Norman was present as the engineer on June 6, 1962, when the Beatles auditioned for George Martin. "I couldn't believe what louts they looked with their funny hair cuts—they didn't impress me at all," Smith said in Brian Southall's *Abbey Road*. Impressed or not, Smith engineered nearly all the Beatles sessions through *Rubber Soul* and *Revolver*. In the late '60s, Norman was given the chance to produce Pink Floyd, a bizarre new group named after Georgia bluesmen Pink Anderson and Floyd Council. From Pink Floyd's earliest singles—such as "Arnold Layne," the tale of an undergarment-stealing transvestite—through many of their albums, it was Norman Smith who attempted to manage the occasionally chaotic Pink Floyd sessions.

Smith had always secretly wanted to be a pop star. He had written something called "Don't Let It Die," and one day when things were not going too well at a Floyd session and all the band members had left for a break, Norman taped the song. When noted producer Mickie Most (Animals, Jeff Beck, Donovan, Herman's Hermits, NASHVILLE TEENS . . .) overheard the recording session, he encouraged Norman to release the disk himself rather than approach John Lennon with the song, as Smith had intended.

Naming himself after the title character in a 1952 Forest Tucker-Yvonne de Carlo flick, Norman "Hurricane" Smith, at age 49, had his first British Top 5 hit with "Don't Let It Die" in June 1971. His follow-up, the charming "Oh, Babe, What Would You Say?" made Hurricane a genuine pop star—at least for a moment or so.

"The melody [was] happy and simple," he told *Rolling Stone*'s Pete Gambaccini. "It was the producer in me that designed the lyric to recapture almost the era I grew up in. It's almost a true story of my life. I would go to a ballroom, but I was so shy I couldn't even ask someone to dance. I'd walk home imagining a romance when I'd never even reached first base. 'Oh, Babe' was about those fantasies."

By the time the follow-up—"Who Was It?" (#49, 1973)—and at least one more single were released, Norman had retired his "Hurricane" character and was breeding race horses in Surrey, England. He has, however, popped up blowing trumpet on various pop projects, like the first Teardrop Explodes album in 1980. He works as a free-lance producer, and did production work on Wings alumnus Denny Laine's albums.

KING HARVEST
DANCIN' IN THE MOONLIGHT
(Ronald Altback)
Perception 515
No. 13 *February 24, 1973*

The members of King Harvest came from diverse musical backgrounds. Tony Cahill (bass) had played with the EASYBEATS, done some session work with R & B shouter Willie Mabon, and, with David Montgomery (drums), had played on underground classic Python Lee Jackson's *In a Broken Dream* (1970). Davy "Doc" Robinson (keyboards, trombone) had recorded with United Artist act Boffalongo. Ron Altback (keyboards), the band's prime writer, had a heavy leaning toward the Beach Boys, ballads, and jazzy musical structures. Completing the line-up were Sherman Kelly (keyboards), Rod Novack (sax), and Ed Tuleja (guitar).

Terry Phillips' Perception label had been unsuccessful in the realm of hit-making. When Phillips heard of

KING HARVEST

the sounds that Altback and his Big Apple-based band were creating, he quickly offered them a recording contract. "Dancin' in the Moonlight," a Boffalongo track revamped with jiggly keyboards and tight vocal harmony, appeared as the group's debut single. To the dismay of the more hard-rockin' faction within the group, "Dancin'" cracked the charts. Harvest was promptly pegged as a "lite" group, a purveyor of pop puffery.

"A Little Bit of Magic" (#91, 1973) and later releases sold poorly, and members came and went. In 1976, with the aid of Beach Boys Mike Love and Carl Wilson, a reconstructed band—featuring Altback, Novak, Robinson, and Tuleja—was signed to A & M. Their lone self titled album died shortly after birth.

Ed Tuleja did some session work on Dennis Wilson's 1977 solo album. Ron Altback and Doc Robinson joined Mike Love in the creation of his CELEBRATION band, which did the soundtrack to the film *Almost Summer* (1978), a mindless synopsis of the end-of-term frolics.

DEODATO
ALSO SPRACH ZARATHUSTRA
(Richard Strauss)
CTI 12
No. 2 *March 31, 1973*

Deodato was born Eumire Deodato Almeida on June 21, 1942, in Rio de Janeiro, Brazil. Deo is a self-taught musician who can work his way with the keyboard, bass, or guitar. He made his professional debut in

Brazil accompanying Astrud Gilberto and won honors for a composition, "Spirit of Summer," at a Rio song festival.

In 1967, Deo started making connections with musicians and producers in the U.S. By 1970, he was involved in studio work with Roberta Flack, Bette Midler, Wes Montgomery, and Frank Sinatra. Three years later, Deo was in the spotlight with his truncated though funky instrumental rendition of Richard Strauss' "Also Sprach Zarathustra," a.k.a. the theme from Stanley Kubrick's *2001: A Space Odyssey*. The track won a Grammy for "Best Pop Instrumental Performance." His scoring abilities were thereafter made use of for TV programs, specials, and movies.

Deodato has recorded numerous albums for CTI, MCA, and Warner Bros., and produced Kool & The Gang from 1979 to 1982 and in '89 DEXY MIDNIGHT RUNNER frontman Kevin Rowland's debut solo album.

LOUDON WAINWRIGHT III
DEAD SKUNK
(Loudon Wainwright III)
Columbia 45726
No. 16 *March 31, 1973*

"I'd like it if people knew about a lot of other songs, instead of, 'Oh, yeah, that's the guy that wrote '"Dead Skunk,'" remarked Loudon Wainwright to *DISCoveries'* Rush Evans. "But on the other hand, it created some opportunities for me and gave me some exposure, and it was kind of fun . . . I feel pretty good about it."

Loudon (b. Sept. 5, 1945, Durham, NC) was born into a noted lineage. He is a direct descendant of Peter Stuyvesant, the renowned Dutch sovereign and first governor of New Amsterdam (New York). His grandfather was an insurance magnate, and his father(Loudon Wainwright II) was a journalist for *Life* magazine. Loudon III attended a private school in Middlebrook, Delaware—the very same Episcopalian boarding school that was the setting for the film *Dead Poets Society* (1989). When he was 16, he made his folksinging debut at the Coffee Gallery in San Francisco's North Beach.

Loud had attended the Carnegie Mellon Institute in Pittsburgh with the intention of becoming an actor. The romance of the open road hit, however, and Loud was soon hitchhiking across the land. He was in San Francisco in 1967 for the Summer of Love. It was after this experience and upon his return to the East—and assorted gigs in Greenwich Village houses like the Gaslight—that Wainwright, like his father before him, put words to paper.

In 1970, Atlantic Records signed him in the hopes that he would turn out to be "the next Dylan." Critical response was enthusiastic; two starkly bitter albums were issued by the label, followed by three more accessible works for Columbia. The first of these Columbia LPs (*Album III*) included Loud with a countrified back-up band and that song. "I wrote 'Dead Skunk' in 15 minutes as an answer to those who kept saying I was too intellectual," he told *Crawdaddy*'s Rob Patterson. A

DEODATO

dozen more Loudon Wainwright III LPs have been issued, two of which sold reasonably well—*Unrequited* (1975) and *T Shirt* (1976).

Over the years, Loudon has taken periodic pot-shots at the music business. There was "The Grammy Game," which recounts a dream Loud had about winning the cherished statue, complete with the standing ovation and the mumbled, humbling speech: "I'd like to thank my producer and Jesus Christ." Most recently, there was "T.S.D.H.A.V.," a cut on Loud's *Therapy* (1989). The lines go: "This song don't have a video/Use your imagination/Forget about the radio/They won't play it on the station."

"I have some bitterness about the Biz," he told *DIS-Coveries*, "but who doesn't? . . . I consider myself very lucky to be doing something that I really like to do."

Loudon has also found an outlet playing various roles on TV ("M.A.S.H.," as Captain Spaulding), the stage (*Pump Boys and Dinettes*), and the silver screen (*The Slugger's Wife*, [1985]; *Jackknife*, [1988]).

VICKI LAWRENCE
THE NIGHT THE LIGHTS WENT OUT IN GEORGIA
(Bobby Russell)
Bell 45303
No. 1 *April 7, 1973*

Vicki Lawrence, to most anyone with a soft heart for TV comedy, is known for her appearances on "The Carol Burnett Show" and her own short-lived spinoff series, "Mama's Family." Legend has it that a young Vicki was pestered by her mother to write to Carol Burnett; she told the comedy star just how much she resembled her, and just how much it would mean to her little heart if they could meet, even if just for a moment. Burnett's secretary supposedly spotted this plea among the hordes of fan mail and brought it to Carol's attention. And, yes, a meeting was arranged and consummated. Different tale-tellers describe the actual meeting in various ways, but the gist is that at that moment, Vicki was discovered.

Lawrence, born on March 26, 1949, in Inglewood, California, had been preparing for show business nearly all of her days. As a child, she had studied ballet and tap dancing and had taken lessons on the piano and guitar. In college, she performed with various folk groups, and three years prior to meeting with Burnett, Vicki joined a singing group, the Young Americans. A journalist reviewing a concert by the group mentioned Lawrence's resemblance to Burnett. Vicki sent the clipping to Burnett, and reportedly was quite surprised to receive a return phone call from her, suggesting that Vicki audition for a role in Carol's upcoming TV series.

Vicki became a regular member of the cast. In 1969, while filming an episode, she met songwriter ("Honey," "Little Green Apples") and husband-to-be Bobby Russell. A few years later, when Russell had a fact-based, murder-out-of-passion song turned down by Cher, he looked to his wife to record the number. She did so, and the results were pleasant enough, but no one in his or her right mind expected "The Night the Lights Went Out in Georgia" to sell as well as it eventually did. Two more Lawrence disks, "He Did It With Me" (#75, 1973) and "The Other Woman" (#81, 1975), made the Hot 100, but Vicki never again waxed anything that approached the contagious popularity of her murderous ode.

In 1976, Vicki Lawrence won an Emmy for her protracted work with Carol Burnett—"Outstanding Continuing or Single Performance by a Supporting Actress in Variety or Music"—and closed the door on her pop-music career. None of her recordings are currently in print, but almost every day, somewhere on the planet Earth, Vicki's likeness can be spotted in syndicated reruns of "The Carol Burnett Show" and "Mama's Family."

To insure permanence in the western world's collective unconscious, Vicki returned to TV-land in the fall of 1987 as host of the daytime version of "Win, Lose, or Draw," one of the few game shows to be fronted by a woman. The evening and syndicated rendition of the show was hosted by Bert Convy, 1/3 of THE CHEERS (#6, "Black Denim Trousers," 1955). For two years, beginning in 1992, her hour-long "Vicki" show survived the talk show jungle.

LOU REED
WALK ON THE WILD SIDE
(Lou Reed)
RCA 0887
No. 16 *April 28, 1973*

"The apostle of rock nihilism" or "the king of decadence," as he has been dubbed, will readily acknowledge that he hasn't had a hit single since "Walk on the Wild Side," his 1973 ode to the gender-bending Andy Warhol crowd. "I haven't even tried to duplicate it," Lou Reed told *Revolution*'s Roy Trakin. How a controversial cut such as "Wild Side"—with its reference to "giving head"—ever snuck past the nation's censors, is not known.

Reed has been in the public eye quite a bit. His appearance at the 1986 Amnesty International concert, the Greenspan compilation LP, and TV commercials

LOU REED

for Honda and American Express card, have all increased his visibility among young rock fans. His album, *New York* (1989), like a fair number of his earlier works, had received critical praise, but hadn't yielded that second big hit. Reed also collaborated with John Cale in 1990 to compose and perform *Songs for Drella*, a musical tribute to Andy Warhol.

He was born Louis Firbank on March 2, 1943, to an upper-middle-class family in Long Island, New York. By age 14, Lou was opting for a life of rebellion and rock and roll. He played guitar in garage bands with names like the Jades, Pasha & The Prophets, the Shades, and the Eldorados. He attended Syracuse University but dropped out; dabbled in journalism and acting; and worked for a number of years as a staff songwriter and ghost artist for Pickwick Records. As such, Lou wrote hot rod and surfing songs, recorded as the Beach Nuts, and almost had a local hit as the Primitives with "The Ostrich."

In 1964, Reed teamed up with John Cale and Sterling Morrison, and came under the guiding hand of multimedia artist Andy Warhol. With the addition the following year of Maureen Tucker, they became the Velvet Underground, stark minstrels of urban decay, drugs, and the perverse. During the reign of flower power and LSD-stoked utopianism, the Velvets were proto-punks, crafting music that depicted the sleazy underbelly of the Beat Generation and the evolving counterculture. Their albums sold only marginally at first and their time was short, but the influence of their sound and attitude on today's rock music was profound.

With the release of the group's *Loaded* in 1970, Lou called it quits, dropping out of music and working at his father's accounting firm in Long Island. The following year, Reed returned to the scene with the release of *Lou Reed*, the first of now nearly 20 albums, all of which have charted on *Billboard*'s top pop albums listings. Each album, fans will attest, has its distinctive direction and style, and each is peopled by a predictable assortment of bizarre characters: the speed freak, the trashy biker, the killer, and, yes, the elder rock statesman.

JUD STRUNK
DAISY A DAY
(Jud Strunk)
MGM 14463
No. 14 *May 19, 1973*

On one of his last eclectic albums, Jud referred to himself as "a semi-reformed, tequila-crazed gypsy." He was born Justin Strunk, Jr., on June 11, 1936, in Jameston, New York; he died in a plane crash on October 15, 1981. People were just getting to know and appreciate who

JUD STRUNK

this story-telling, banjo-picking, folkie-cum-country man was.

He was raised in Farmington, Maine. While in second grade, he won first prize at a community hall talent contest playing spoons and tap dancing. In his teens, he recited poetry in nearby clubs and sang. For a while, he toured as a "one-man show" for the United States Armed Forces. Not many noticed, but he appeared in the off-Broadway production of *Beautiful Dreamer*.

In the '70s, Jud moved west to California, where he would do his personalized entertaining on local TV programs. For a couple of years (1972-1973), he was a regular on "Laugh-In." His records, when you could find them, were always a little different. He'd sing of amnesia, describe Howard Hughes' permanent plot on this planet, read patriotic poetry, or recite verse about an old man's undying love for his long-departed wife. Some of his stuff made minor motions onto the pop and country listings—"Next Door Neighbor's Kid" (C&W: #86, 1973), "My Country" (#59, 1974), "The Biggest Parakeets in Town" (#50, 1975), and "Pamela Brown" (C&W: #88, 1976). But only "Daisy a Day" was a box-office smash.

SKYLARK
WILDFLOWER
(Dave Richardson, Doug Edwards)
Capitol 3511
No. 9 *May 26, 1973*

Skylark was a fleeting fling for Bonnie Jean Cook, DAVID FOSTER, and their fluctuating fraternity. Bonnie Jean and David had been members of RONNIE HAWKINS' Hawks before they hatched a scheme to start their own band in the early '70s. Based in Vancouver, Canada, Cook (lead vocals) and Foster (keyboards) rounded up some hometown help from Donny Gerrard (lead vocals), Carl Greaves (percussion), Duris Maxwell (drums), Norman McPherson (guitar), and Steven Pugsley (bass).

After six months of rehearsals, Capitol of Canada took an interest in the group. Little did the label know that the band's days were numbered. By the time Skylark's self-titled LP was released, Greaves, McPherson, and Pugsley were ex-members. After the group's first 45 flopped, Windsor's CKLW took a protracted airtime interest in a tender track called "Wildflower."

Reportedly, internal tension's resulted from the swelling success of "Wildflower," a tune written by a studio musician and a Victoria police officer. Follow-up 45s failed to fly, and by the time their second and last album was recorded, the only Skylarks remaining were Donny Gerrard and the Fosters (David had married Bonnie Jean Cook by this time).

In addition to doing session work with Eric Carmen, Donovan, and Yvonne Elliman, Donny Gerrard had a solo charting in 1976 with his Greedy release, "Words (Are Impossible)" (#87). Carl Greaves experienced homeland hits with "Hey Radio" and "Baby, Hang Up the Phone." Duris Maxwell resurfaced in the '70s as a member of Doucette, and in the '80s drummed for the Powder Blues Band.

David Foster has been a member of groups like Airplay, Attitudes, Fools Gold, Highway, and later, the Average White Band; Attitudes went Hot 100 in '76 with "Sweet Summer Music" (#94). His "Love Theme From St. Elmo's Fire," the successful title take from the 1985 Rob Lowe-Demi Moore flick clicked Top 20. Foster has also racked up an incredible list of session credits, having played keyboards for PATTI AUSTIN, George Benson, Kim Carnes, Chicago, Earth, Wind & Fire, Hall & Oates, Michael Jackson, Gladys Knight, Little Feat, Lynyrd Skynyrd, the Pointer Sisters, and both George Harrison and Ringo Starr—to name but a few. In 1993, Foster produced Color Me Badd's rendition of "Wildflower."

FOCUS
HOCUS POCUS
(Thijs van Leer, Jan Akkerman)
Sire 704
No. 9 *June 2, 1973*

They were a Dutch group whose goal was to perform a fusion of rock, jazz, and even the classics. Drummer Hans Cleuver, bassist Martin Dresden, plus classically-trained founder/frontman Thijs van Leer (b. Mar. 31, 1948, Amsterdam) on organ and flute, banded together in 1969. Focus developed a strong local reputation backing Cyril Havermans, Robin Lent, and other Dutch singers. They soon added guitarist extraordinaire Jan Akkerman (b. Dec. 24, 1946, Amsterdam) and worked as the pit band for the Dutch production of *Hair*. There they would often include amplified arrangements of pieces of work by Bartok and Rodrigo. In 1971, Polydor issued *In and Out of Focus*, an LP of their music-merging meanderings. Two years later, after Focus' touring and charting success in England and in the States, Sire Records would reissue the album.

By the time of the recording sessions for *Moving Waves* (1973), Cleuver and Dresden were gone. Their replacements were bassist/singer Cyril Havermans and drummer Pierre Van der Linden (b. Feb. 19, 1946), who had played with Akkerman in one of his former groups.

If Focus is recalled at all by Top 40 listeners, it is for that near-novelty number, "Hocus Pocus," with its yodels, yelps, and manic guitar runs. But there was more to the band than just this song, or so believed the devotees of Focus' progressive sounds who liked to flow with the group's long, stylized improvisations. It was this following that snapped up offerings like *Focus 3* (1973), *Live at the Rainbow* (1973), *Hamburger Concerto* (1974), *Dutch Masters* (1975), *Mother Focus* (1975), and *Ship of Memories* (1977).

Havermans left the fold in 1971, and was replaced by bassist Bert Ruiter (b. Nov. 26, 1946). Van Der Linden departed in 1973; his replacement was former Stone the Crows drummer Colin Allen, who himself was replaced but two years later by David Kemper.

Havermans had his own LP (*Cyril*) issued in 1973 by MGM. Numerous solo efforts were issued by van Leer during the '70s—*Introspection* (1972), *O My Love* (1975), *Nice to Have Met You* (1978). Akkerman, who left Focus in 1976, has gone on to create a fairly successful and critically acclaimed solo career, with albums like *Profile* (1973), *Tabernakel* (1974), and *Jan Akkerman* (1978).

Focus' last recorded work seems to have been the much-anticipated *Focus Con Proby* (1978), which involved the addition of vocal sensation P. J. PROBY and Akkerman's fill-in, Phillip Catherine.

In 1985, Akkerman and van Leer regrouped for a one-off reunion album; five years later all members of the line-up that created "Hocus Focus" gathered in a Dutch television studio for a special about the group.

SYLVIA
PILLOW TALK
("Sylvia" Robinson, Michael Burton)
Vibration 521
No. 3 *June 9, 1973*

While Sylvia did share a huge hit as the feminine half of MICKEY & SYLVIA, her solo singles would be issued for nearly a quarter of a century before Syl managed to crack the pop and R & B charts on her own.

Born Sylvia Vanderpool on March 29, 1935, in Washington, DC, she was discovered at a function at Washington Irving High in 1950. Sylvia was but 14 when she recorded hot numbers like "Chocolate Candy Blues" opposite the trumpet of Hot Lips Page. More bluesy sides appeared on Savoy, Jubilee, and Cat, as by Little Sylvia. In 1954, she teamed up with McHouston "Mickey" Baker, her guitar teacher and New York sessioneer supreme. With their sixth duet, "Love Is Strange," the duo captured the imaginations of rock and rollers worldwide. Follow-ups inexplicably failed to generate a similar response, and in 1959, Mickey & Sylvia split. While the two assayed a number of reunions and many recordings during the '60s, only "Baby You're So Fine" (#52, 1961) b/w "Lovedrops" (#97), released on their Willow label, managed to gain any chart action.

In 1964, Sylvia married Joe Robinson. The couple have since established the All Platinum Studios and numerous labels like Horoscope, Stang, Turbo, Vibration, and Sugar Hill. Over the years, Sylvia has produced recordings for LINDA JONES, the Moments, SHIRLEY & CO., THE SUGARHILL GANG, the Whatnauts, and Lonnie Youngblood. Her hit compositions include "Love on a Two-Way Street," "Sexy Mama," and "Shame, Shame, Shame," a tune she wrote for her friend Shirley Goodman, half of the legendary Shirley & Lee and the lead vocalist for Shirley & Co.

After years of recordings under the names of Sylvia Vanderpool, Little Sylvia, and Sylvia Robbins (for Sue and Jubilee in the early '60s), Robinson finally cracked the charts on her own, as Sylvia, with the breathy and self-penned "Pillow Talk." "I thought it'd be right for Al Green," Sylvia told *Blues & Soul*'s Tony Cummings. "I

cut the song and put my voice on it to show Willie Mitchell [Al Green's producer] how it might be good for Al. But they turned it down, so we decided to release my version."

Other than a duet each with the Moments and Ralph Pagan—and the initial follow-up to "Pillow Talk," "Didn't I" (#70, 1973)—subsequent Sylvia sides have not found niches on the pop/rock airwaves. Nearly a dozen of her singles, however, have placed on the R & B charts; "It's Good to Be the Queen" (R&B: #53, 1982), an "answer" disk to Mel Brooks' "Good to Be the King." In the mid-'80s her son Joey made the R & B listings with several 45s as a member of the West Street Mob.

With the mammoth success of her Sugarhill label—with its rap roster of Grandmaster Flash, Melle Mel,

and the Furious Five—Sylvia Robinson continued in the biz into the late '80s, when Sugarhill was absorbed by the colossal MCA. As an artist, she records only sporadically.

CLINT HOLMES
PLAYGROUND IN MY MIND
(Lee Pockriss, Paul Vance)
Epic 10891
No. 2 *June 16, 1973*

"In a sense, 'Playground' hurt me," Clint Holmes told Bob Gilbert and Gary Theroux in *The Top Ten*. "It branded me as a novelty singer . . . We recorded another song in the similar vein, which I did not want to do. It was called 'Shiddle-ee-Dee' and the very title tells you what the song was like—a bomb."

Born in Bournemouth, England, on May 9, 1946, Clint was raised in Farnham, New York. Holmes showed an interest in music while quite young, and his mother, a former British opera singer, encouraged him and acted as his first vocal coach. While in high school, Clint had his own pop band, and majored in music at Fredonia College. After a stay in the service as part of the Army Chorus, Clint began playing nightclubs in Bermuda and the Bahamas. One night, the successful songwriting team of Paul Vance and Lee Pockriss happened onto his stage act. After Clint's performance, they approached him with some tunes they hoped he might record—in particular, "Playground in My Mind."

Clint was not ecstatic about recording the ditty, but was impressed with their credentials. Paul and Lee had composed Perry Como's "Catch a Falling Star," THE CUFF LINKS' "Tracy," THE DETERGENTS' "Leader of the Laundromat," and Brian Hyland's "Itsy Bitsy Teenie Weenie Yellow Polka Dot Bikini," to name but a few. The fact that the tune would require a little boy's goo-goo gaa-gaa babblings (supplied by Paul Vance's son Phillip) didn't help, Clint agreed to give it a shot. Upon the issuance of the disk, certain regions of the country took an immediate liking to "Playground," but it was nearly a year before the nation began buying up skids full of Clint's "Playground." Lightning need not always strike twice, however, and all of Clint's future singles on Epic Records stiffed—as did his years and years of releases on the Buddah, Atco, and Private Stock labels. Nothing, but nothing Clint recorded seemed to ever recapture the pulse of pop America.

Clint Holmes is still carrying the torch of hope and making the nightclub circuit. "I'm trying to create a new image, which is why I don't do that song in my act anymore. 'Playground' was an excellently-made record, but it could have been almost anybody singing it; therefore, it was not a career-making record. It didn't bear the stamp of Clint Holmes. I think that's why, even today, a lot of people remember the song but not the fellow who sang it."

NEW YORK CITY
I'M DOIN' FINE NOW
(Thom Bell, Sherman Marshall)
Chelsea 0113
No. 17 *June 23, 1973*

John Brown, Claude Johnson, Tim McQueen, and Eddie Schell were high school buddies with a history of singing that goes way back. John had chirped with the Five Satins (1957-1960) and the Cadillacs, also filling in for the Moonglows. Just prior to N.Y.C.'s big moment, John and the others recorded a lone single for Buddah Records as "Triboro Exchange," after the bridge linking three of New York City's boroughs. The record did little, but Chelsea Records man Wes Farrell liked the group just the same. (Wes wrote tunes for the Shirelles, Jay & The Americans; produced disks by the Cowsills, EVERY MOTHER'S SON, the Partridge Family, Tony Orlando & Dawn.) He convinced the fellows to change their name to the more memorable "New York City"; they acquiesced.

Wes Farrell persuaded Philly magic man, producer/arranger Thom Bell (produced and wrote for Delfonics, Detroit Spinners, TEDDY PENDERGRASS, Stylistics) to cook up some instrumental tracks for the chaps to lay some vocals on. With four in the can, Thom sent for New York City. "The session was so easy, so relaxed," lead vocalist Tom McQueen reported to *Blues & Soul's* Tony Cummings. "Everybody just mellowed out down there and when we finished we knew we had a hit." "I'm Doin' Fine Now" was one of the tracks, and it did real fine. McQueen's self-penned "Make Me Twice the Man" (#93, 1973) and "Quick, Fast, in a Hurry" (#79, 1974) did all right, but nothing further charted.

Trivia buffs, take note: the back-up band that toured with New York City was called the Big Apple Band; two of its members were Nile Rodgers and Bernard Edwards, both former members of the Apollo Theatre's house band and future founders of Chic, arguably the hottest band of the disco era.

In 1992, the Pasadenas' rerecording of "I'm Doin' Fine Now" topped the U.K. charts.

DR. JOHN
RIGHT PLACE, WRONG TIME
(Mac Rebennack)

Atco 6914

No. 9 *June 30, 1973*

Malcolm "Mac" John Rebennack, Jr. (b. Nov. 21, 1940, New Orleans) grew up in a world full of music. "There was this white baby grand Kimball piano in our house," Mac recalled in an exclusive interview. "My sister, who was, like, 10 years older, would have musicians over rehearsing. My uncle John could play, and the family was near always getting together for these jam sessions. Then there was my aunt named Odetta who used to play the boogie-woogie piano; I learned some from her as a little kid.

DR. JOHN

"I also had some friends that used to work around my father's [appliance] store, like Al Johnson. He taught me how to play another kinda boogie. I took guitar lessons formally. I studied maybe two, three years under studio cats like Walter ["Papoose"] Nelson, Ralph Montell, and Paul and Al Bowman. I think that's what got me accidentally working as a studio cat. Now with the piano, I learned more from watchin' people like Professor Longhair and Huey "Piano" Smith."

By the mid-'50s, Mac was doing sessions for Ace, Edd, Ric, and Specialty, among other New Orleans labels. He toured in the back-up bands for Jerry Byrne, Professor Longhair, Joe Tex, and for his second cousin, Frankie Ford. He also began producing and arranging sessions for other recording acts. In 1962, Mac moved to the West Coast and studio activity with Sonny Bono, H. B. Barnum, and Phil Spector. His work with Spector included some of the legendary "wall-of-sound" sessions.

"I liked that they were using a lot of New Orleans cats and that they'd combine some funk with their sound. But when I first saw this deal of using five piano players and six guitarists—even though they added echo and stuff to get a new sound—I was under the impression they was paddin' the payroll. I didn't realize they was doin' this 'cause it was the sound they dug."

While working a Sonny Bono session, Mac got the chance to book for himself some otherwise unused studio time. With the help of producer Harold Battiste, Jessie Hill, and others, Rebennack came up with a heady musical concoction and a voodoo persona that he called "Dr. John Creaux, The Night Tripper." Bono heard the tracks and sold Atco on issuing the *Gris Gris* album in 1968 as a one-off deal. The music was a mix of Creole chants and West Coast psychedelia; the visuals were equally offbeat. Mac's Night Tripper was a self-proclaimed "Grand Zombie," complete with witch-doctor robes, weirdly feathered headdresses, and— later airbrushed from the cover photo—a finely-rolled marijuana joint.

Two more similarly styled LPs— *Babylon* (1969) and *Remedies* (1970)— followed before the good doctor, aided by Mick Jagger and Eric Clapton, recorded *The Sun, the Moon & Herbs* (1971). The next year's *Gumbo*—a more straightforward affair and a salute of sorts to his New Orleans roots—sold even better. Gradually, the Grand Zombie was accruing a following; all he needed was a hit single to consolidate his base. With "Right Place, Wrong Time"—a funky track cut with the Meters/Neville Brothers as accompanists—Dr. John found it.

"After we did the *Right Place* album [1973], they more or less demanded that I do something real commercial. We tried to do a couple of tracks commercial for 'em, but we really wanted to do something fresh that no one else was doin'. So we got into experimentin', so they weren't knocked out with it when it wasn't super-commercial."

The Doctor went on to make a number of largely one-off albums for Columbia (*Triumvirate*, a 1973 collaboration with Mike Bloomfield and John Hammond), United Artists, DJM, Horizon, and Street Wise. He appeared at the Band's 1976 farewell concert (*The Last Waltz*) and recorded two albums of solo piano music for the Demon (1982) and Clean Cuts (1988) labels.

Mac Rebennack was involved in a serious car crash late in 1988. Ribs were broken, but the Doctor is now back on the road—and back on the record racks. His *In a Sentimental Mood* (1989) topped *Billboard*'s Traditional Jazz album chart; winning the "Best Jazz Vocal Performance, Duo or Group" category of the 32nd Annual Grammy Awards. Three years later, his *Goin' to New Orleans* garnered the "Best Traditional Jazz" Grammy.

The hyper Doc appeared on tribute albums for THE GRATEFUL DEAD (*Dedicated*) and tunesmith Doc Pomus (*Till the Night Is Gone*), contributed to *Put on Your Green Shoes*, for the Earth Island Institute and Save the Children, and provided piano for *The Simpson's Sing the Blues*. In 1990, *Bluesiana Triangle*, a jazz set with David "Fathead" Newman and Art Blakeley was issued; followed by a live set with CHRIS BARBER (*On a Mardi Gras Day*) and in 1995, by *Afterglow*, a big band tribute to music of the '40s.

No longer is he clad in robes and glittery whatnot. It's tweed suits, or tuxedos and top hats, but the sounds remain as fresh as ever. *Under a Hoodoo Moon*, John's autobiography, co-written with Jack Runnell, was published in 1994.

STORIES
BROTHER LOUIE
(Errol Brown, Anthony Wilson)
Kama Sutra 577
No. 1 *August 25, 1973*

Lead singer Ian Lloyd (b. Ian Buonconciglio, 1947, Seattle) and keyboardist Michael Brown (b. Michael Lookofsky, Apr. 25, 1949, Brooklyn) were introduced by their fathers, two old friends who had worked together for years as session violinists. Ian had been singing for

STORIES

years and had attracted local notice recording as Ian London. Michael had played with his group the Left Banke: their success included "Baroque rock" items like "Walk Away Renee" (#5, 1966) and "Pretty Ballerina" (#15, 1967).

The two seemed to click and agreed to set about forming a Beatlesque band. They recruited New Yorkers Steve Love (guitar) and Bryan Madey (drums) and located an interested record company in Kama Sutra. A self-titled album and a single—"I'm Coming Home" (#42, 1972)—followed. Success was immediate. The second LP, *About Us* (1973), also did well, but primarily because of the inclusion of an afterthought, "Brother Louie." This tune about a black girl and her white boyfriend had been a British hit for Hot Chocolate in 1973. Once issued as Stories' second single, the group's whole world changed.

"All of a sudden," Lloyd explained to *Triad*'s Russel Wiener, "we had a big hit with a song that did not represent our music and the direction we were trying to go in. I didn't think it would affect me that much, but it did. Consequently, I decided that I had to remove myself from that, so that I could come back and show what I really can do."

Lloyd did remain with Stories for one more album—*Traveling Underground* (1973)—but Brown left immediately. Bassist Kenny Aaronson (b. Apr. 14, 1952, Brooklyn) and keyboardist Ken Bichel (b. 1945, Detroit) stepped in to fill the void. This new group made the Hot 100 with "Mammy Blue" (#50, 1973) and "If It Feels Good, Do It" (#88, 1974). Before their short story ended, Madey moved on, and was replaced by Rick Ranno, later of Starz fame.

Lloyd has since recorded some sorely-overlooked solo albums and has done studio work for Foreigner, Fotomaker, and Peter Frampton. Brown next formed the Beckies, yet another Beatles-like band. Love reappeared in the early '80s in Landscape. Madey, after a two-LP stay with the Earl Slick Band, reportedly provided accompaniment for Peggy Lee. And Aaronson remained busy; first as the frontman for Dust, then as co-founder (with Carmine Appice's brother Vinnie) of Axis. Bichel has since worked sessions for Hall & Oates, Billy Squier, ex-MOUNTAIN Leslie West, and RICK DERRINGER.

B. W. STEVENSON
MY MARIA
(B. W. Stevenson, Daniel Moore)
RCA Victor 0030
No. 9 *September 29, 1973*

His trademark was a stovepipe hat and an expansive amount of hair, beard, and belly. He was shy, afflicted with stage fright, but quite a drinker. He also had a for-midable voice that was rarely heard "unpackaged." Jan Reid, author of *The Improbable Rise of Redneck Rock*, considered him in a league with Texan "outlaws" (long-haired country-music rebels) like Waylon Jennings and Willie Nelson. Reid even dedicated a chapter in his book to this chap, dubbing him "The Voice."

Louis C. Stevenson was born in Dallas, on October 5, 1949. In his teen years, he worked in bar bands. He attended North Texas State in Denton on a voice scholarship, transferring to Cooke County Junior College. He joined the Air Force, and not too long afterward, played the clubs in Austin.

Reid, who spent an evening at Stevenson's spread with multiple six-packs, reported that "The Voice" was a singular talent capable of singing "understated, gut-wrenching, back-woods blues." Yet few listeners ever heard that side of the big man: RCA signed him early in his career, called him B. W. (short for "Buckwheat"), and positioned him, against his wishes, as a pop-country singer.

In mid-'73, B. W. almost had his break-through hit with "Shambala" (#66, 1973). But he was beaten to the punch by Three Dog Night's hugely successful cover of the tune, so RCA needed another disk to issue. Fortunately, Stevenson and songwriter Daniel Moore had just worked up a similar-sounding number called "My Maria." It was catchy, and finally the company had their hit, plus a successful LP, *My Maria* (1973).

Other albums and singles were tried, but B. W.'s limited fame faded. He was only 38 when he died on April 28, 1988.

BYRON MACGREGOR
AMERICANS
(GORDON SINCLAIR)
Westbound 222
No. 4 *February 9, 1974*

Byron (b. Gary Mack, 1948, Alberta, Canada) was the news director of CKLW radio in Detroit when his brief rub with national notice paid off. MacGregor had heard a winning editorial broadcast on Canadian radio by GORDON SINCLAIR about those mighty but maligned minions to the south, "The Americans," and decided to read the opinion piece himself over the air. Listener response was overwhelming—the station was swamped with calls. Not much coaxing was needed to get the newsman into the recording studios of Armen Boladian's Detroit-based Westbound Records. The disk became an instant but one-off smash.

Byron MacGregor died on January 3, 1995 at age 46.

TOM T. HALL
I LOVE
(Tom T. Hall)
Mercury 73436
No. 12 *March 2, 1974*

Tom T. Hall has been called "the Nashville Storyteller" and "the Mark Twain of Country Music." Hall's songs are vignettes of intriguing characters and offbeat situations. Tom has written of a visit with a dying girlfriend ("Second Hand Flowers"), of the aftereffects of a mining disaster on a small community ("Trip to Hyded"), and of the would-be star who insists that his next record will be his big one ("Homecoming").

You need not be a die-hard country-music fan to have heard many of Tom T. Hall's tunes. JEANNIE C. RILEY's "Harper Valley P. T. A." (#1, 1968) is a landmark Hall hit. You might have caught DAVE DUDLEY's performance of the anti-war anthem "What Are We Fighting For" (C&W: #4, 1966), or Hall's own voice on both "Old Dogs, Children, and Watermelon Wine" (C&W: #1, 1973) and "The Year That Clayton Delaney Died" (C&W: #l, 1971).

Hall (b. May 25, 1936, Olive Hill, KY) was born in a log cabin, and into poverty. His father, the Reverend Virgil L. Hall, was a lay preacher, a worker in a brick factory, and the owner of a battered old Martin guitar. Tom took an interest in the instrument and repaired it. The year after his mother died, when he was 14, Tom quit school to work in a graveyard, a funeral home, and later, a clothing factory.

Within two years, Hall had himself a band of bluegrass pickers called the Kentucky Travelers. They played local dates, and made radio appearances on WMOR in Morehead, Kentucky. When the band broke up, Hall remained at the station as a DJ for five years before joining the army. On his return to civilian life in 1961, he moved around, filling various DJ slots. Tom would work in the evenings with a band called the Technicians, all the while sketching out songs based on characters he observed.

In 1963, JIMMY NEWMAN recorded Hall's "DJ for a Day" (C&W: #9, 1964); the following year, Dave Dudley cut his "Mad" (C&W: #6, 1964). Tom moved to Nashville in 1964 to work as a staff writer, and soon other country artists were approaching him for hits: Bobby Bare, ROY DRUSKY, Flatt & Scruggs, Burl Ives, STONEWALL JACKSON, and George Jones. With the phenomenal success of "Harper Valley P.T.A.," Hall was offered a recording contract with Mercury Records. And despite the lone Top 40 charting of "I Love," Tom T. has racked up more than 60 C & W chartings, including "Ballad of Forty Dollars" (#4, 1969), "Me and Jesus" (#8, 1972), "That Song Is Driving Me Crazy" (#2, 1974), and "I Like Beer" (#4, 1975).

When Hall's career cooled in the late '70s, he took some time off to do book reviews for the *Nashville Tennessean* and write books—*How I Write Songs . . .* , *Why You Can*, *The Storyteller's Nashville*, *The Laughing Man of Woodmont Coves*, and *Acts of Life*. He also hosted the syndicated "Pop Goes the Country" TV variety show.

TERRY JACKS
SEASONS IN THE SUN
(Jacques Brel, Rod McKuen)
Bell 45432
No. 1 *March 2, 1974*

Terry Jacks was born in 1945 in Winnipeg, Manitoba, Canada, and grew up in Vancouver. When Buddy Holly died, Jacks was moved to buy a $13 guitar, and joined a rock and roll band soon afterward. "I was the worst in the group," Terry admitted to Ritchie York in *Axes, Chops, and Hot Licks*. "So I decided to write some songs in the hopes that they'd keep me. The only trouble was, they expected me to sing them, too." As the Chessmen, the band waxed a number of locally successful singles.

When the Chessmen made an appearance on Canadian TV's "Music Hop," Terry met 18-year-old Susan Pesklevits, a folkie from Vancouver. The two soon pooled their resources, becoming husband and wife and forming a group called Powerline; later with guitarist Craig McCaw, Winkin' Blinkin' and Nod, and finally a quartet, the Poppy Family. The soon successful act first jelled in the winter of 1966 at a tiny coffeehouse in Blubber Bay, British Columbia. The idea was that Sue would sing and Terry would work behind the scenes—writing, arranging, and producing.

When "Which Way You Goin' Billy?"—the "B" side of the Poppy Family's third single—hit big all over North America (#2, 1970), Jacks was caught off-guard. "'Billy' was cut for only $125. . . . It was simple music, simple lyrics." When the follow-up, "That's Where I Went Wrong" (#29, 1970), charted, Terry called it quits. "I went fishing for two or three months. . . . The pressure was incredible." Terry and Sue split up as well: "We'd been together 24 hours a day for almost four years, and it was just too much."

During the Poppy Family's travels, Jacks had met and befriended Al Jardine of the Beach Boys. In late 1972, Jardine called Terry to L.A. to produce a Beach Boys session. Jacks suggested they record a tune by Belgian poet-composer Jacques Brel written in 1961 and originally entitled "Le Moribond (The Dying Man)." The tune was taped and completed. When the Beach Boys nixed the idea of releasing the track, Jacks returned to Canada and, with guitar legend Link Wray, recorded his own version of what was to be called "Seasons in the Sun." Terry received permission to rewrite

TERRY JACKS

the reflective tale's final verse in order to lighten up the song.

"I was out on the golf course with a friend of mine, Roger," said Terry to author Barry Scott, of his initial need to create the "Seasons" song. "He said, 'I'm not going to be around much longer.' I said, 'What are you talking about?' He replied, 'The doctor says I'm only going to be alive another six months.' I couldn't believe it . . . He wasn't kidding. Roger died of leukemia four months later. It must be terrible to have to tell your best friend and your father—and Roger had a little girl—that you're going to die. Terrible. So I rewrote the words to 'Seasons of the Sun,' about a young person dying."

But four seasons came and went before Terry decided to form Goldfish Records to release his mournful masterwork. "It sat in my basement for about nine months," he said to Scott. "I probably never would have released it. . . . I made it as a piece of art, as a picture I needed to paint. . . ."

The initial response was staggering: "Seasons" became the biggest-selling single in Canadian history. Worldwide record sales eventually totaled 11,500,000 copies.

Terry met the French legend/tune's creator Jacques Brel shortly before his death from cancer in 1978. "He told me he wrote the song in Tangiers, in a whore-house," said Terry to Scott. "He said it was written about an old man who was dying of a broken heart because his best friend had been goofing around with his wife."

A few more follow-up 45s were issued—"If You Go Away" (#68, 1974) and "Rock 'N' Roll (I Gave You the Best Years of My Life)" (#97, 1974)—but then Terry seemed to drop out of sight entirely.

It wasn't until 1990 that Terry Jacks, in an oldies concert in Boston, performed for the first and only time "Seasons in the Sun" in the United States.

Into the mid-'90s, Jacks continued to live on a large estate in Vancouver. His Goldfish label sporadically releases records, including singles by his ex-wife, Susan Jacks. However, Terry is through with being a performer.

DAVID ESSEX
ROCK ON
(David Essex)
Columbia 45940
No. 5 *March 9, 1974*

His given name was David Albert Cook (b. July 23, 1947), and he grew up in London's tough East End, the son of a docker. "It was the poor part of town," said Essex in an exclusive interview. "School I went to was lousy; a waste of time. Soccer's what got my interest. By 13, though, I knew music was what I wanted to be involved in. Joe Morello [a mainstay with DAVE BRUBECK] was my hero, so I wanted to be a jazz drummer. That didn't turn out, but I went on to play with some blues bands, like Mood Indigo. By 15, I was touring all about. We were the Everons, cause we were never off. We tried to be authentic and black; which means we starved a lot and got thrown out of pubs for being so depressing."

The archetypal blokes with the big cigars and shiny cars pulled the lad aside, said he'd go far, that he'd be made into a star. "It sounded like quite a good idea to me," Essex told *Creem*'s Richard Cromelin. "So I went off with them. . . . I had nothing, so I thought, 'Well, they must know what they're doing.' They'd come up with a song, and I'd sing it, and it'd come out and not do a thing."

Essex had 10 disks issued prior to his Grammy nomination for "Rock On." All were, as he described them, ill-conceived. David might not have even had the opportunity to cut his most remembered record were it not for *Daily Express* theater columnist Derek Bowman, his manager. In the late '60s, at Derek's behest, David began taking voice and dance lessons, and tried out for some parts in plays. "There I was, off on the stage. I didn't know anything about it. I'd never seen a play. . . . It was all a bit of a fluke."

But theater did save his floundering musical career. He played the lead in *The Fantasticks*, and in 1971, he earned rave reviews as Jesus in the London production of *Godspell*. The following year, he starred as rags-to-riches '50s rocker Jim MacLaine in the film *That'll Be the Day*. At the request of producer David Putnam, David wrote "Rock On" for the flick's freeze-frame ending.

"It was a strange record," said David. "I wanted to do something different, intriguing; the mid-section was meant to be like an Indian mantra. Lyrically, I wanted it to feel like what it was like to be a working class boy in the U.K. in the '50s. Though I wanted it to have a '70s sound. Odd though, Putman thought it was too weird, so it didn't get to make the film; though it made number one worldwide."

Essex went on to inspire teenybopper hysteria in his homeland. While only his immediate follow-up—"Lamplight" (#71, 1974)—made the listings in the States, 20 further offerings charted in England. "I had no idea 'Rock On' would be a hit," said Essex. "Even more, I've had 25 Top 30 things in Great Britain, and it hasn't stopped. . . ."

David Essex continued his stage and film work. He appeared with Ringo, Dave Edmunds, and EDD BYRNES

in *Stardust* (1975), and in the late '70s, played Che Guevara in the London production of *Evita*. He starred with Beau Bridges in *Silver Dream Racer* (1980), and in 1987, he portrayed Fletcher Christian in his own stage project, *Mutiny*. In 1988, he wrote the theme for the TV sitcom "The River"; which he starred in. Next Dave played the part of an evil Spanish Duke in *Shogun Mayeda* (1990) with Christopher Lee. In the early '90s, Essex was appointed "ambassador" for the charitable organization Voluntary Service Overseas.

"It woulda been nice to have been successful in America," said Essex. "I don't know why, but I've never worked in America . . ."

Essex rewrote and rerecorded "Rock On" in the early '90s. It's release and that of such charmers as "Missing You," "The Sun Ain't Gonna Shine Anymore," and his last 13 albums have not been made available in the United States.

"It is upsetting, that as an artist—I take things seriously—and people in certain parts of the world don't get the chance to buy or even to hear my new things. A lot of the world, I'd imagine, don't even know I'm still creating."

Michael Damian, star of TV's "The Young and the Restless," returned "Rock On" to the *Billboard* charts in 1989; outselling Essex's original and peaking in the number-one position. Damian's take was included in Piper Laurie's *Dream a Little Dream* (1989).

CLIFF DEYOUNG
MY SWEET LADY
(John Denver)
MCA 40156
No. 17 *March 23, 1974*

Cliff DeYoung was the lead vocalist with Clear Light, an early Los Angeles folk-rock band. In addition to De-Young, the mid-'60s unit comprised Doug Lubahn (bass), Mike Ney (drums), Ralph Schuckett (keyboards), Bob Seal (guitar), and Dallas Taylor (drums). They impressed Paul Rothchild, the big cheese at Elektra Records who went on to produce the Doors. And for two years, Clear Light dazzled the Sunset Strip scene with their psychedelicized/folkie repertory. Rothchild ordered up one critically acclaimed debut—and departure—album, plus a lone single, "Black Rose." Nothing charted, and the band folded.

Lubahn is still very much alive and active. He went on to do session work for the Doors, Dreams, JOHN PHILLIPS, and Billy Squier; in the '80s, he was a member of the group Riff Raff. Taylor, in addition to being a member of Crosby, Stills, Nash & Young and of Stills' Manassas outfit, has recorded with Buddy Guy, Sammy Hagar, GRAHAM NASH, and Stephen Stills. Most prolific

of the Clear Light crew has been Ralph Schuckett: his keyboard services have been used by late-legend David Blue, James Cotton, the Four Tops, Hall & Oates, and Carole King, to name a few. As for Cliff DeYoung, he became an actor.

DeYoung was born in Los Angeles, on February 12, 1946. Shortly after Cliff's fling with Clear Light, Hollywood beckoned. In addition to his TV work in the short-lived "Sunshine" series (1975), the "Centennial" (1978) mini-series, and the "King" and "Robert Kennedy and His Times" made-for-TV flicks, Cliff has appeared in films like *Harry and Tonto* (1974), *Blue Collar* (1978), *The Hunger* (1983), *Protocol* (1984), *F/X* (1985), and *Glory* (1989), *Flashback* (1990).

DeYoung's return to the disk world in 1974 was confined to a solo album and a year's worth of singles—among them, his "Sunshine" spinoff, "My Sweet Lady."

MOCEDADES
ERES TU (TOUCH THE WIND)
(Juan Carlos Calderon)
Tara 100
No. 9 *March 23, 1974*

The Amezaga sisters—Amaya (b. Feb. 18, 1947) and Izaskum (b. Apr. 17, 1950)—are the voice of Mocedades. They were born and raised in Bilbao, Spain, as were guitarist Roberto Amezaga (b. Apr. 21,

1948), bassist Javier Barrenechea (Dec. 16, 1946), and keyboardist Carlos Uribarri (b. Oct. 10, 1944). Guitarist Jose Urien was born in Madrid, on January 7, 1949. Together they are the sweet-sounding Mocedades.

Their initial North American release, "Eres Tu," caught pop fans by surprise. The sound was delicate, folk-flavored, and mysterious. Juan Carlos Calderon, the tune's composer, told Al Clark, *Rolling Stone*, "The song was already written for Mocedades to record some time before it was chosen for Eurovision [Song Contest in 1973]. Originally, it was two different pieces which somehow fitted together and built up to something, and in the course of doing so it became apparent to me that the construction was sufficiently similar to that of a hymn to benefit from having a choral sound, which was simply achieved by double-tracking the six voices."

For a brief spell, the group basked in the limelight. Mocedades's follow-up 45, "Dime Senor," went nowhere. While their debut disk has been their only stateside success, the group still has a sizable following with its predominantly Spanish-speaking audience.

It's ironic, thought Calderon, that "Eres Tu" was issued in America in English by Mocedades, as well as Eydie Gorme, and that both versions failed. "It's curious," said Calderon, "but singers always sound more convincing in their own language.

"When people ask me what the success of the record means, my instinctive reply is: 'As a Spaniard, everything; as Juan Carlos Calderon, not much.'"

SISTER JANET MEAD
THE LORD'S PRAYER
(Arr. by Arnold Strals)
A & M 1491
No. 4 *April 13, 1974*

Mead was born in 1938 in Adelaide, Australia. At 17, she became a member of the Sisters of Mercy Convent. During the '70s, when youth-oriented masses were common, Sister Mead and a unit she called her Rock Band provided music for a weekly rock mass at the Adelaide Cathedral. Her music also began attracting attention via her weekly radio program.

In 1973, Sister Janet was asked to make some recordings that would be distributed only to churches and schools. Australia's Festival Records became interested, and they decided to use her version of Donovan's "Brother Sun, Sister Moon" for her first record. The "B" side of the single was reserved for a modern-age rendition of the prayer that Jesus taught his disciples nearly two millennia ago.

Within months, 2 million copies of "The Lord's Prayer"—which featured an earthy bass line, ominous fuzz-tone, plushly uplifting strings, and an ethereal lead vocal—were sold. Sister Mead donated all of her royalties to charity. She continued recording for Festival Records, and at least one further single was issued in the United States—"Take My Hand."

Sister Janet Mead

MFSB & THE THREE DEGREES
TSOP (THE SOUND OF PHILADELPHIA)
(Kenny Gamble, Leon Huff)
Philadelphia International 3540
No. 1 *April 20, 1974*

To those in the know, like Philly arranger Bobby Martin, MFSB stood for "Mother F***in' Son of a B****." But if you asked any one of the group's members what the initials stood for, he or she would reply, "Mothers, Fathers, Sisters, Brothers." Cute.

For years, this 30-plus crew of session musicians, the house band at Philadelphia's Sigma Sound Studios, were crack accompanists. In the guiding hands of Kenny Gamble and Leon Huff, the founders of the Philadelphia International label, MFSB created and embodied "TSOP," "The Sound of Philadelphia," and together they cranked out an assembly line of hits.

On virtually every disk recorded in the late '60s and '70s by Archie Bell & The Drells, Jerry Butler, the Intruders, Harold Melvin & The Blue Notes, the O'Jays, Billy Paul, Bunny Sigler, and the Three Degrees, odds are that the back-up band present is MFSB. Prior to the release of their own charter, an assorted crew of Mothers-to-be created "The Horse" as Cliff Nobles & Co., "Keem-O-Sabe" as The Electric Indian, "United (Part 1)" as the Music Makers, "Overture From Tommy (A Rock Opera)" as The Assembled Multitude, an instrumental version of Sly & The Family Stone's "Family Affair" as the Family, and a number of obscurities as the Locomotions and the Men From Uncle.

At the time of "TSOP," MFSB included Ronnie Baker (bass), Roland Chambers (guitar), Bobby Eli (bass), Kenny Gamble (piano), Norman Harris (guitar), Ron Kersey (guitar), Vince Montana (vibes), Lenny Pakula (organ), Larry Washington (percussion), Earl Young (drums), Zach Zachary (sax), and Don Renaldo (conductor, contractor for the horns, reeds, and strings). The Three Degrees co-credited on the disk—singers Sheila Ferguson, Valerie Holiday, and Fayette Pinkney—had their own hit at the end of 1974 with "When Will I See You Again" (#2, 1974).

"A practice that jocks were into [some years back] was finding a little-known or forgotten record with a special quality and using it as a theme song," Don Cornelius, creator of TV's long-running "Soul Train," explained to Bob Gilbert and Gary Theroux in *The Top Ten.* "Whenever I did a [radio] show, I would open and close with my personal theme, which was 'Hot Potatoes' by King Curtis." When Cornelius premiered 'Soul Train' on TV, an instrumental theme was needed, but arrangements to use Curtis' tune fell through.

"People in music were just starting to hear about the show when I happened to run into Kenny Gamble in New York. We really hit it off, and I mentioned that I wanted to do a special song for the show." Months later, Cornelius had his new theme—but not for long. The immediate popularity of the number compelled Gamble and Huff to back out of the deal with "Soul Train" and offer the disk to the record-buying masses.

Some follow-up 45s placed well on the R & B listings, particularly "Love Is the Message" (#85; R&B: #42, 1974) and (minus the Three Degrees) "Sexy" (#42; R&B: #2, 1975). Several of MFSB's LPs also sold in large quantities.

MIKE OLDFIELD
TUBULAR BELLS
(Mike Oldfield)
Virgin 55100
No. 7 *May 11, 1974*

"I suppose the first things I liked were by the Beatles, really," Mike told *Guitar Player*'s Stefan Grossman and Tom Mulhern. "After that, I started liking Bert Jansch and John Renbourn, when I was 10 or 11. [About then] I started playing on a 6-string acoustic guitar that my father gave me." By all reports, Mike (b. May 15, 1953, Reading, England) was a precocious kid. By age 14, he and his sister Sally were Sallyangie, a recording act; their *Children of the Sun* (1968) album sold only moderately. Oldfield fronted a unit called Bearfoot before joining ex-Soft Machine founder Kevin Ayers' band, the Whole Wide World, as a bass player. The teenager remained with Ayers for three albums and accompanying tours.

"[Thereafter] I did occasional jobs. I was adapting the play *Hair* for six months or so, and I played a couple of gigs with Alex Harvey. Then I was introduced to composer David Bedford and Richard Branson [who were just starting Virgin Records], who spent about a year making up their minds about whether to take 'Tubular Bells.'" For some time, Mike had been feverishly working up his "Bells" idea on a borrowed tape recorder. He approached five record companies with the demo, and met with five rejections.

Once Virgin was up and running, Mike was generously allowed a year's time in the Manor Studios in Oxfordshire. There, he single-handedly taped some 80 tracks using 28 different instruments. He expanded the layers of sound exponentially, dubbing and over-overdubbing hundreds of times. The result was the Grammy-winning ("Best Instrumental Composition") "Tubular Bells," a singular 49-minute fusion of riffs and fragments from rock, folk, and classical themes. These musical elements had been melded to form a musical collage that, some claim, anticipated the meditative sounds of New Age music.

In a talk with Karl Dallas of *New Musical Express*, Mike described his creation in relation to his life at the time: "There was one point where I suppose you'd say that I had a nervous breakdown . . . I just went mad for a few weeks. I was incredibly frightened all the time, about being alive, and the only thing that gave me any comfort was playing the guitar. I had to invent a mood that was totally opposite to what I was feeling."

Both the *Tubular Bells* (1973) album and an edited version of the single were runaway best-sellers. That year, Oldfield's opus was used as the theme for *The Exorcist* (1973). While none of his later 45s placed on the U.S. charts, the reclusive Oldfield continues to create music—reportedly, in darkened, late-night, solitary studios. His more popular albums include *Hergest Ridge* (1974), *Ommadawn* (1975), *QE2* (1981), and *Five Miles Out* (1982).

MIKE OLDFIELD

MARVIN HAMLISCH
THE ENTERTAINER
(Scott Joplin)
MCA 40174
No. 3 *May 18, 1974*

From the time of his first encounter with the piano, Marvin (b. June 2, 1944, New York City)—the son of a Vienna-born accordionist—was a marvel with it. By the age of seven, he was the youngest student ever admitted to Juilliard. In 1963, while working at a summer camp, Hamlisch met Liza Minnelli and her mother, Judy Garland, who performed one of his first creations at the London Palladium. Lesley Gore soon recorded his "Sunshine, Lollipops and Roses" (#13, 1965) and "California Nights" (#16, 1967).

A chance meeting with movie producer Sam Spiegel at a Broadway party opened the door to cinematic success. Sam liked the kid's compositions, and hired him to create the theme music for Burt Lancaster's *The Swimmer* (1968). Marvin moved to Hollywood and was asked to compose scores for Jack Lemmons' *The April Fools* (1969) and *Save the Tiger* (1973); Woody Allen flicks, *Take the Money and Run* (1969) and *Bananas* (1971); the Oscar-nominated "Nobody Does It Better" for the James Bond vehicle *The Spy Who Came in From the Cold* (1977), and "The Girl Who Used to Be Me" for *Shirley Valentine* (1989). Marvin scored three Neil Simon comedies, *Chapter Two* (1979), *Seems Like Old Times* (1980), and *I Ought to Be in Pictures* (1982); the Academy Award-winning *Ordinary People* (1980); *Pennies From Heaven*, in collaboration with Billy May; and the ASCAP-awarded *Three Men and a Baby* (1987).

In 1974, Marvin became the first individual to win three Oscars in one night: one for "The Way We Were" (with co-writers Alan and Marilyn Bergman), another for the score to the Barbra Streisand-Robert Redford classic *The Way We Were* (1973), and another for his adaptation of rag-time master Scott Joplin's music for *The Sting* (1973). Two years later, the score for his first Broadway musical, *A Chorus Line* was pelted with awards: the Pulitzer Prize for Drama, a Tony Award for the score, a Tony and New York Drama Critics Award for best musical, among others. *A Chorus Line* closed in March 1990, after a run of 6,137 performances—the longest-running show in Broadway history. Album sales totaled near 1.5 million copies sold.

In 1979, Hamlisch returned to Broadway with *They're Playing Our Song*, with lyrics by Carole Bayer Sager. The musical dealt with the rough relations between two in-love songwriters; allegedly based on the liaison between Hamlisch and Sager. Other productions included *Jean Seberg*, *Smile* and a score to Neil Simon's *The Goodbye Girl*, starring Bernadette Peters.

Other Hamlisch scores include *Frankie and Johnny* (1991), *The January Man* (1989), and *Missing Pieces* (1983). In 1994, Marvin Hamlisch appeared in London, conducting the orchestra for Barbra Streisand's first British concert.

WILLIAM DEVAUGHN
BE THANKFUL FOR WHAT YOU'VE GOT
(William DeVaughn)
Roxbury 0236
No. 4 *June 29, 1974*

Once upon a time, there was this record operation in Philadelphia called Omega Sound. Omega had an unusual method of working: they would seek out talent, then charge the artist to be recorded. William DeVaughn was a songwriting guitarist from Washington, DC, who had a hankering to be a singing star. Will noted Omega's ad in a music publication and sent the company a demo of some tunes he had hammered out. "They said they'd record me if I paid for a session," DeVaughn explained to *Blues & Soul's* Tony Cummings. "That would cost me $1,400. I went home and managed to raise $900. We were able to scrape by on that, and I went down to Sigma Studios."

As producer Alan Felder recalled to Cummings, "We did the session real quick, with the guys feeling it as they went along. It wasn't mixed properly; the whole thing was done quickly and cheap." Weeks later, Rox-

DAVE LOGGINS

PAPER LACE

bury Records picked up "Be Thankful for What You've Got," and it sold in huge amounts—nearly 2 million copies had flown off the shelves. But DeVaughn lost interest in the music business shortly after his big hit—he became a Jehovah's Witness.

"By the time the record was number one, [William] was going door-to-door in Washington, handing out pamphlets," the single's producer, John Davis, told *Blues & Soul.* "That's why the album, which was recorded after, was all religious. William didn't feel he could put the two things together. He'd come into a club to do a gig, and instead, he'd tell people, 'You're crazy, you shouldn't be in here, you shouldn't be drinking, you shouldn't be chasing women!'"

DeVaughn's follow-up, "Blood Is Thicker Than Water" (#43, 1974), nearly floated into the Top 40. One other single is known to exist; soon William returned to the void.

DAVE LOGGINS
PLEASE COME TO BOSTON
(Dave Loggins)
Epic 11115
No. 5 *August 10, 1974*

Dave was born on November 10, 1947, in Mountain City, Tennessee, the son of a country fiddler and a cousin to Kenny Loggins. Like mockingbirds and moonshine, music was everywhere. After sowing some oats and a short stay at East Tennessee State University, Dave trekked to New York City in search of a music

career. MCA Music signed the lad to create tunes for them, but nothing much happened.

In 1972, the Vanguard label took an interest in Loggins' musings and dished out a disappointing debut LP, *Personal Belongings.* In a Denver coffeehouse, a member of Three Dog Night heard Dave's "Pieces of April." As covered by the Dog band, Loggins, the writer, had a Top 20 hit. Epic Records stepped in and ordered a helping of Dave's acoustic numbers. The plaintive "Please Come to Boston" was culled from his *Apprentice (in a Musical Workshop).* While Dave Loggins's disks continued to be issued well into the '80s, his "not really rock/not wholly country" style has left him with a very small audience.

PAPER LACE
THE NIGHT CHICAGO DIED
(Mitch Murray, Peter Callander)
Mercury 73492
No. 1 *August 17, 1974*

Paper Lace rewrote a piece of history in 1974 when they sang about a showdown between Al Capone's goons and Chicago's men in blue. Their bubblegummy voices maintained that 100 officers died one mythical night in a big gun battle on Chicago's non-existent East Side. By evening's end, the forces of truth and justice triumph by either killing or arresting all the vermin, and the Windy City lived happily ever after.

Formed in Nottingham, England—known for its lace, hence the band's name—Paper Lace started up in

339

1969 with lead singer/drummer Phil Wright (b. Apr. 9, 1948, Nottingham) and bassist Cliff Fish (b. Aug. 13, 1949, Derbyshire). Within the next few years, lead guitarist Michael Vaughn (b. July 27, 1950, Sheffield) and guitarist Chris Morris (b. Nov. 1, 1954, Nottingham) joined. For a while, they were the house band at a club called Tiffany's in Rochdale. Several TV appearances garnered the group the attention of the production/songwriting team of Mitch Murray and Peter Callander. By this point, a third guitarist, Carlo Santanna (b. June 29, 1947, outside Rome, Italy), had joined the group.

Murray and Callander auditioned the unit, liked what they heard, signed them to their Bus Stop label, and gave the fellows a tender teenybop tune, "Billy, Don't Be a Hero." "Billy" became a number-one British hit but, to the group's dismay, Bo Donaldson & The Heywoods—a Cincinnati septet—covered the song in 1974 and took it to the top of the charts in the U.S. Paper Lace's thunder was not stolen, however, with "The Night Chicago Died," another Murray-Callander creation. A third Murray-Callander piece, "The Black-Eyed Boys" (#41, 1974)—an ode to a gang of super-bad motorcyclists who come to town to make rock and roll—made the Hot 100.

Someone whispered in the group's collective ear that they might make a better deal with some other record company; the guys reportedly walked out on their contract, and little has been heard of them since. Supposedly, there was a fourth single, "The Himalayan Lullabye"—and Paper Lace did show up for a duet billing with the Northingham Forest on a fairly successful British hit called "We've Got the Whole World in Our Hand"—but Paper Lace died one night in 1974.

JOHNNY BRISTOL
HANG ON IN THERE BABY
(Johnny Bristol)
MGM 14715
No. 8 *October 5, 1974*

"I got into show biz by accident, pure accident," Bristol told *Blues & Soul*'s Tony Cummings. "I'd joined the Air Force in the '50s. I was born in Morgantown, North Carolina, but was stationed near Detroit. In the force I met a guy named Jackey Beavers. We found we both dug singing and formed a duo, called ourselves Johnny and Jackey."

The two servicemen did a couple of local shows and were spotted by Gwen Gordy (the sister of Motown mogul Berry Gordy and the wife of Harvey Fuqua, leader of the Moonglows). Gwen signed the guys on to her Tri-Phil label and issued four regional winners. Johnny would later recycle two of these—"Someday

We'll Be Together" and "Do You See My Love (For You Growing)"—for the Supremes (#1, 1969) and Junior Walker (#32, 1970), respectively.

By 1960, the doo-wopping duo separated. Jackey returned to Georgia, where he has since had a number of poor-selling sides issued on Mainstream, Sound Stage 7, Warner Bros., and others. As for Bristol: "After I starved a little, I got involved with the Motown situation. I knew Lamont Dozier—he was Lamont Anthony for a while, when he was with Harvey [Fuqua]—and he helped me get in there."

At Motown, Bristol was Fuqua's assistant and soon husband to Iris Gordy. For six years, the pair wrote and produced some of the finest Motown moments: "Ain't No Mountain High Enough," "My Whole World Ended," "Twenty-Five Miles," "Pucker Up, Buttercup," and "Yester-Me, Yester-You, Yesterday."

In 1973, Johnny moved to Columbia Records. There, as an in-house producer, he worked with Buddy Miles, O. C. Smith, and Boz Scaggs, among others. But it was a shot at a singing career that he wanted. Columbia turned down his request to cut some sides himself. MGM, meanwhile, agreed to let the music vet have his chance.

"Hang on in There Baby" was to be the first single to bear his name as lead singer. "When I heard the final thing, I flipped! You see, after I'd finished putting down the vocal tracks, H. B. BARNUM and I had spent a lot of time 'sweetening'—getting the strings and the girl chorus integrated into the sensuous feeling I wanted. I just broke up when I caught the final mix . . . sometimes you can tell a new recording's a hit . . . with 'Hang on in There Baby,' I could taste it."

Johnny has had some mighty R & B chart-movers and a couple of best-selling albums. In the mid-'70s, Bristol turned to producing and writing for Tom Jones, Johnny Mathis, and Tavares; in the '80s, he returned to Motown to produce the Four Tops' "I'm Ready for Love." He charted in duet form with AMII STEWART, "My Guy, My Girl" (R&B: #76, 1980), a composite of the Mary Wells and Temptation tunes. Nine years later, Johnny recorded a few stand-out singles for Ian Levine's Motor City label; particularly, "Keep This Thought in Mind." In the '90s, Bristol switched to Whichway Records.

FIRST CLASS
BEACH BABY
(John Carter, Jill Shakespeare)
UK 49022
No. 4 *October 5, 1974*

"I once heard this interview with BRIAN WILSON; . . ." said an excited Tony Burrows, First Class co-lead vocalist, in an exclusive interview. "They played this promotion copy of First Class for him and he said, 'I have no idea who that is, but it is definitely a West Coast American record.' I can't forget it. That's one of the nicest things that was ever said to me."

The First Class was presented as an actual group. Liner notes to their debut LP claimed that the "group" was comprised of Tony Burrows, John Carter, Del John, and Chas Mills as vocalists. Instrumental accompanist—and proclaimed members—were Clive Barrett (keyboards), Spencer James (guitar), Eddie Richards (drums), and Robin Shaw (bass); the latter a former member with Burrows in WHITE PLAINS and sometime member in the Flowerpot Men.

No such group existed. And all vocals were provided by John Carter and Tony Burrows.

First Class was the brainchild of producer/songwriter/singer John Carter. During the early '60s, John, long-time buddy Ken Lewis, and future Yardbird Jimmy Page were members of Carter-Lewis & The Southerners. The group had a minor British charting with "Your Mama's Out of Town" before they—Page-free—evolved into the Ivy League. The League, while successful in England, never notched much of a charting in the States—and eventually evolved into the Flowerpot Men.

Tony Burrows—England's premiere session singer and pseudo-group member—was Carter's replacement in the Ivy League and was later with the Flowerpot Men. Burrows had such pseudo-entities as EDISON LIGHTHOUSE, the Brotherhood of Man, White Plains, and THE PIPKINS; not to mention under his own name and that of Tony Bond (a la James Bond) and as Domino, Touch, Magic, Kincade, and the West End Boys.

Pseudo-member Chas Mills participated in session work for Long John Baldry, Alan Price, and Al Stewart; briefly a member, with Burrows, in yet another, the Goodies.

"Beach Baby" was written by Carter and wife Jill Shakespeare and was not intended to be a Beach Boys tribute or sound-alike. "My original concept mix had the effect of a radio being tuned in at the beginning," said Carter to liner-note writer Gordon Pogoda, "and every station it tuned to was playing a Beach Boys record. The record company [JONATHAN KING's UK label] got cold feet at this, so it was cut out. When I remixed the album, I went back to the original idea, except this time every station was playing 'Beach Baby.'" Listen close to the track—as it fades THE CHANTAY's "Pipeline" can be heard.

First Class did chart on the Hot 100 with their next two singles, "Dreams Are Ten a Penny" (#83, 1974) and a remake of Ivy League's homeland hit "Funny How Love Can Be" (#74, 1975). Nothing thereafter was noticed—though two more albums were recorded;

only one issued—and in 1976 the pseudo-group was dismantled—though later reassembled when their recordings returned to the charts in Holland. A First Class "group" was together as recent as 1985.

John Carter—known for "Sunday and Tea," "Can't You Hear My Heartbeat," and THE MUSIC EXPLOSIONS' "Little Bit O' Soul"—continued to write tunes and went on to form a much less successful studio unit, Ice.

Aside from his continued studio work with pseudo-groups, Burrows cuts TV commercials, sang in a duo with Stephanie Desykes as Heart to Heart, produced such acts as New Horizon and Sunny (his accompanist on Edison Lighthouse), and has provided session singing for Elton John, Tom Jones, Engelbert Humperdinck, and an uncredited accompaniment of DAVID SOUL on "Don't Give Up on Us." Burrows performs locally, with The Fraud Squad. In 1995, he and Neil Landon toured Germany as their "real" group, the silly and psychedelic '60s Flowerpot Men.

Nothing further, with Tony Burrows involved, ever made the United States charts.

REUNION
LIFE IS A ROCK (BUT THE RADIO ROLLED ME)
(Norman Dolph, Paul DiFranco, Joey Levine)
RCA Victor 7559
No. 8 *November 16, 1974*

"There's a Reunion philosophy," Paul DiFranco, the pseudo-group's co-writer and co-producer, revealed to *Rolling Stone's* Ian Dove in 1974 when 'Life Is a Rock' was a chart-rider. "We're in the business to make happy, funny records, and I think right now it's important for the music to stay happy...."

"Life Is a Rock" was placed under the production abilities of bubblegum veteran Joey Levine, who co-penned "Chewy, Chewy," "Gimme, Gimme," "Yummy, Yummy, Yummy" . . . Levine was also one-third of the Third Rail.

"Life Is a Rock" lay on the shelf for two years. DiFranco and his co-writer, Norman Dolph, meanwhile had little success as Reunion with 45s like "Smile" and "Just Say Goodbye," so they approached Joey about working up a bubble-bit on "Life Is a Rock."

"What happened was this—see, Mark Bellac [an associate of the songwriters] and I had gone to school together—best friends—written together, and hadn't seen each other in three, four years," said Joey Levine in an exclusive interview. "He got in touch with me, with this song. I loved it; thought it was great, but I told 'em that the record they cut with it was really missing the mark. I'd love to just spruce it up; cut the record. . . . They said, 'Cut it.' It's [recorded at] the Hit Factory. That's me singing lead, with the group Reunion—really just Mark, me, Tommy Faye, and his wife were there; just some guys from Long Island; friends of Mark. Called it Reunion 'cause it's me and Mark gettin' back together as pals. . . .

"Once fixed, I felt so good about 'Life Is a Rock,' I went to Clive Davis at Arista and this fellow at RCA and both started bidding for it. I chose RCA cause I figured they were more equipped to make it happen."

"The machine-gun vocal delivery," explained DiFranco," is a result of no rehearsing whatsoever; the key was to read the lines rapidly and not to memorize them at all. . . ."

"Immediate hit. Right to the top. Four weeks," said Levine. "No group, so no tour; right. They wanted me to cut an album, but it would like just eat up the royalties. I figured it was just a novelty idea. . . ."

Follow-ups to the group's biggie included "Disco-Tekin'" and "They Don't Make 'Em Like That Anymore"—but, as Joey figured, Reunion's moment seemed to have passed. Neither charted.

"That fast-talking style, I did, is evident in a lot of commercials, other records. It lives; got a lot of energy, ya know . . . ," said Levine.

Joey was born in Queens and attended Bayside High School and Queens College. "Moved into New York; started makin' records," added Joey. "First thing I did was as Joey Vine, 'Hercules.' I was 16; it stiffed. 1967. Met K&K [Jeffery Kasenetz and Jeffrey Katz, "fathers of bubblegum music"] when I was hot with stuff with Arnie Resnick; writing for Aaron Schroder, Hudson Bay Music . . . wrote with Jeff Barry [half of THE RAINDROPS], Kenny Young . . . It was in the Brill Building and a song called 'Try It'—written by me and Mark Bellac—was done by the STANDELLS; an underground record 'cause it was considered risque. K&K had their Ohio Express do it; only clean. They heard my demos and asked me and Artie to write some stuff. We came up with 'Yummy, Yummy, Yummy.' I cut the track; they asked me to put a lead vocal on. Me singing. Neil Bogart [then Cameo Record head] heard it, said 'You're not taking that guy off it.' Before I even knew it, I heard it on the radio. Didn't believe it. First of the Top 10 hits nobody knows I did. I felt shitty 'bout it, but did most of their [Ohio Express] lead vocals. . . . Artie and I had a record company, L&R; BOBBY BLOOM's "Montego Bay" was on it. Had another, Earth Records; Life, too. WIND was on it; Tony Orlando's thing. Rare Earth sued. . . ."

Asked how he felt being a founding daddy of "bubblegum music," Levine replied, "People missed it, bubblegum was meant to be tongue-in-cheek, 'cause the lyrics were risque. . . .

"That's how I got into the business I'm in now. They told me the stuff I wrote sounds like commercials. First one I wrote was 'Sometimes I feel like a nut'; still on the air. I'm a big, big jingle guy now. . . ."

BILLY SWAN
I CAN HELP
(Billy Swan)
Monument 8621
No. 1 *November 23, 1974*

Billy (b. William Lance Swan, May 12, 1944, Cape Girardeau, MO) grew up listening to his uncle play the saxophone. At 14, he learned to master the drums, later teaching himself organ, piano, and guitar. By 1959, Swan worked in a band fronted by area plumber Mirt Mirley called The Rhythm Steppers; their "Lover Please" single, a Swan song, bombed ignobly. "Bill Black took it to Clyde McPhatter," Swan told *Rolling Stone's* Chet Flippo, "who didn't like it but went ahead and cut it." Clyde's recording of "Lover Please" (#7, 1962) became a huge pop hit. It also earned Billy a nice chunk of change—"I figured show business was the easiest thing in the world."

Swan moved to Memphis, and later to Nashville, doing whatever he could to make it in this "easy" biz. He chauffeured for Webb Pierce, and lived in a hearse for awhile. While staying with Travis Smith, Elvis's uncle, Billy tended the gate at Graceland. In Nashville, he worked as a recording assistant at the Columbia Records Studio. Initially, he was a janitor—a position he later passed to Kris Kristofferson—but by 1966, Billy was signed to Monument Records as a recording artist and producer. Over the next few years, Swan would produce TONY JOE WHITE's first three albums and White's hit single, "Polk Salad Annie" (#8, 1969).

Eight years of solo efforts had yielded no chart action for Billy Swan on either the pop or country listings. While waiting for that big hit, Swan wrote songs for Bill Black's Combo, worked as a road manager for country acts like Mel Tillis, and played guitar in Kris Kristofferson's band. For a time, Billy was even a member of Kinky Friedman's Texas Jewboys band. Finally, it happened.

In 1974, Kristofferson bought Swan a compact RMI organ as a wedding gift. "My wife had one of these little electric drummers, so I was just sitting at the organ and . . . started playin' chords, and pretty soon the words came out. I did it in two takes and didn't even overdub the vocals—just stood up and played the organ and sang." The song was "I Can Help." And while Billy has yet to have another pop hit, 15 of his 45s have chalked up positions on *Billboard's* C & W chart. His studio skills have appeared on recordings for Barefoot Jerry, Harry Chapin, and T-Bone Burnette.

In 1986, Swan, ex-Eagle Randy Meisner, and ex-Bread members James Griffin and Rob Royer briefly formed a band called Black Tie. *When the Night Falls,* its debut album, was issued by Bench Records.

JIM WEATHERLY
THE NEED TO BE

(Jim Weatherly)
Buddah 420
No. 11 *November 23, 1974*

James Dexter Weatherly (b. Mar. 14, 1943, Pontotoc, MS) was an All American quarterback for Ole Miss. Jim chose songwriting over pro football, the story goes. Jim Nabors hired him to tour with him; RAY PRICE recorded about 50 of his tunes; LYNN ANDERSON, Brenda Lee, BOB LUMAN, and Gladys Knight & The Pips (to name but a few) also etched some of his creations in vinyl. Knight, in particular, has been quite successful with her renditions of Weatherly's "Midnight Train to Georgia" (#1, 1973), "Neither One of Us (Wants to Be the First to Say Goodbye)" (#2, 1973), and "Best Thing That Ever Happened to Me" (#3, 1974).

As a performer, Weatherly cut his teeth on some obscure sides in 1965 for 20th Century Records. After a layoff, he returned in the early '70s with a contract to RCA. Nothing seemed to gel until those Pips platters peaked, at which point Jim moved over to Buddah Records, Gladys Knight's post-Motown home. While only his "Need to Be" collected a following of easy listening fans, Jim did manage to stir up some C & W interest in the mid-to late '70s. He has had half a dozen country chartings to date, including "I'll Still Love You" (#87; C&W: #9, 1975) and "All That Keeps Me Going" (C&W: #27, 1977).

"Every song I compose is a personal statement," he told *The Guinness Encyclopedia of Popular Music.* "My music tells how I feel, what I believe, and what I see. I try to tell all of it in an intimate, subtle way."

KIKI DEE BAND
I'VE GOT THE MUSIC IN ME

(Bias Boshell)
Rocket 40293
No. 12 *November 30, 1974*

Freddie Matthews was a British textile worker. Every night, he would come home and find his daughter Pauline (b. Mar. 6, 1947) singing the daylights out of some "Top of the Pops" tune. Freddie did what most proud papas do—he entered his little 10-year-old in a talent contest, which she won. In her teens, while working days in her sister's beauty shop, she began singing with local dance bands.

"The determination to sing has always been with me," Kiki Dee told Mick Patrick, the editor of *That Will Never Happen Again*, ". . . At 16, I knew that my voice was the only thing that could get me free—get me away from the environment that I was born in." Her reputa-

KIKI DEE

tion grew. Someone suggested that she make a demo and send it to record companies. One found its way to songwriter Mitch Murray, later to be known for such sterling staples as "I'm Telling You Now," "How Do You Do It," and "The Ballad of Bonnie and Clyde."

At Murray's insistence, Fontana signed Pauline, now known as Kiki Dee, to a contract in 1964. Over the next five years, numerous singles and an LP—*I'm Kiki Dee* (1968)—were issued. Murray produced the latter, as well as many of her singles, but nothing charted in her homeland. In the late '60s, Liberty and World Pacific issued some of these sides in the States, but all of them went without notice.

In 1969, Kiki became the first and only British white female signed to the Tamla/Motown label. *Great Expectations* and a few 45s were shipped, but sales were low. Disillusioned and frustrated with the business, Kiki headed for Africa and Australia, where for the next few years, she worked the cabaret circuit.

Upon her return, John Reed, the former head of the Motown label in England, got in touch with her. Reed, who was now Elton John's manager, introduced the two. Elton offered to sign Dee to his newly established Rocket label. "I've Got the Music in Me," her third release for Rocket Records, brought Pauline Matthews pop success. (The single credits "The Kiki Dee Band," actually a studio group; for touring purposes, the band included the tunes of songwriter/keyboardist Bias Boshell, bassist Phil Curtis, guitarist Jo Partridge, and drummer Roger Pope.)

A few other 45s cracked the Hot 100—"How Glad I Am" (#74, 1975) and "Once a Fool" (#82, 1976). "Don't Go Breaking My Heart" (#1, 1976), a one-off duet with Elton, brought the two to the top of the pop charts in both England and the U.S.

Several of Kiki's albums sold well, but Dee left the Rocket label in the late '70s. Only one further album, *Angel Eyes* (1986), has appeared since her 1981 release, *Perfect Timing*.

In 1984, Kiki played a leading role in a London West End staging of *Pump Boys and Dinettes*, opposite former Manfred Mann vocalist Paul Jones and Johnny Cash's daughter Carlene Carter. In 1989, she played the part of Mrs. Johnson in a British production of *Blood Brothers*.

While no plans exist to return to recording, Kiki told *Q* magazine in the early '90s: "When you've been recording since you were 17, it becomes a habit."

Kiki has continued to sporadically provide back-up vocals for Elton John and the Alan Parsons Project.

"I have a problem explaining my career," she told *Q*, "because it starts to sound negative. But everything is in good shape now. I had a serious illness, which helped me reassess what I'm doing. I'm very optimistic at the moment, and I don't regret anything I've done."

CARL DOUGLAS
KUNG FU FIGHTING
(Carl Douglas)
20th Century 2140
No. 1 *December 7, 1974*

Carl was born in Jamaica, raised in California, and attended college in London. He had intended to become an engineer and work in his family business. Friends, however, heard him sing and encouraged him to stop in at London's Two I's Coffee Bar. At lunch hour, the java joint offered an open mike to any takers. After a few performances, Carl was asked to front the all-white Big Stampede.

Beginning in 1964, Big Stampede waxed soul singles for Strike, Okeh, United Artists, and Columbia. "Crazy Feeling" almost did something; "Nobody Cries" sounded like a chart-stalker. Various names were assumed and discarded, different styles were tried—but nothing

clicked. Carl toured Europe with a band called Explosion, and for a while was a member of the British band GONZALES.

Biddu, who would chart in 1975 with the theme to the Jennifer O'Neill flick *Summer of '42* (1971), was an Indian-born producer in need of a singer for a London session. A friend of his, New York songwriter Larry Weiss, had a new tune he needed to have recorded. (Weiss had previously hit paydirt in 1967 with "Mr. Dream Merchant" for Jerry Butler, and would strike again in 1975 by penning "Rhinestone Cowboy" for Glen Campbell.) Biddu, having worked with Douglas on the theme song for the Richard Roundtree flick *Embassy* (1972), presented Carl with Weiss's number, "I Want to Give You My Everything."

Once Douglas had recorded the song, a flip side was needed, and Carl offered one of his own compositions—"Kung Fu Fighting." "Fu" was intended as little more than a filler: reportedly, only 10 minutes of studio time were used in creating this lightweight number. But the commercial timing was right—fu flicks were everywhere. Once the record company loosened its promotional arsenal on the "B" side, Carl had his huge hit. "Fu" even became the first 45 from England to top *Billboard*'s R & B charts. Before his disappearance, Carl managed to milk the kung fu theme for one more single, "Dance the Kung Fu" (#48; R&B: #8, 1975).

Three years later, Carl returned to England's Top 30 with "Run Back." A smattering of recordings were made for Blue Mountain and Landslide. Thereafter, little has been heard from the martial arts music man.

CAROL DOUGLAS
DOCTOR'S ORDERS
(Roger Cook, Roger Greenaway, Geoff Stephens)
Midland International 10113
No. 11 *February 8, 1975*

Since her teen years, Carol Douglas (b. Apr. 4, 1948, Brooklyn) had been making commercials and playing small roles on TV; she also performed on the silver screen, in minor roles. She appeared in the off-Broadway production of *Moon on a Rainbow* with James Earl Jones and Cicely Tyson. During the early '70s, Carol also worked the revival circuit as a member of the CHANTELS. In 1974, she began her solo singing career and a four-album association with producer Ed O'Loughlin.

"Doctor's Orders," Douglas' disco dinger, was culled from her debut LP. The tune was written by songwriting pros Roger Cook, Roger Greenaway, and Geoff Stephens, and was a U.K. Top 20 tune previously for Sunny (a.k.a. Sunny Leslie, half of the recording duo Sue & Sunny). Geoff had dashed off hits for Wayne

Newton and THE FLYING MACHINE, and was both creator and lead singer of THE NEW VAUDEVILLE BAND's "Winchester Cathedral." Cook and Greenaway had recorded as DAVID & JONATHAN, and were the writers behind successful 45s by EDISON LIGHTHOUSE, the English Congregation, WHISPERING JACK SMITH, and WHITE PLAINS.

Follow-ups have continued to appear for Carol Douglas into the '80s, but only "A Hurricane Is Coming Tonight" (#81, 1975) managed to chart. Her continuing recordings included takes on Abba's "Dancin' Queen" and the Bee Gees' "Night Fever." Carol still lives in New York City, is the mother of three, and in the late '80s recorded for 20th Century Records.

POLLY BROWN
UP IN A PUFF OF SMOKE
(Gerry Shury, Phillip Swern)
GTO 1002
No. 16 *March 15, 1975*

In 1970, producer and tunesmith John MacLeod, who had dreamed up some successful disks for the Foundations and THE FLYING MACHINE, wrote what he believed to be a sure-fire hit. To realize it just as he heard it in his cranium, he fabricated a group consisting of blue-eyed soul singer Polly Brown, Maggie Farren, and four guys. MacLeod coached them in rehearsal, placed them in the studio, and, for unknown reasons, called them Pickettywitch, after a Cornish village. After their debut single, "You Got Me So I Don't Know," stiffed, "That Same Old Feeling" (#67, 1970) went Top 10 in England and charted modestly in the States. After two more homeland hits—"(It's Like a) Sad Old Kinda Movie" and "Baby I Won't Let You Down"—and a fallow two years, Pickettywitch was parked and junked.

For a brief spell in 1974, Polly was singing in blackface as Sarah Leone with a British reggae romper named Tony Jackson. Billed as Sweet Dreams, Brown and Jackson charted in both the United States (#68, 1974) and England with "Honey Honey." Jackson had previously sang in Paul Young's band and did some sound-alike Levi Jean ads. By year's end, the duo was done, and Gerry Shury and Phillip Swern were entrusted with writing material for Polly to record solo. "Up in a Puff of Smoke," with Brown doing her best Diana Ross impersonation, was her initial solo waxing. It clicked in the States, but flopped in England. All other vinyl ventures by the white chick named Brown who sang black failed to ignite record buyers' interest.

A revived Pickettywitch made the music circuit in the mid to late '70s, sans the now reclusive Polly Brown.

SWEET SENSATION
SAD SWEET DREAMER
(D. E. S. Parton)
Pye 71002
No. 14 *March 22, 1975*

Sweet Sensation was a soft-soul band from Manchester, England. They were a struggling pub unit working the local circuit when, in 1974, they happened upon a 15-year-old tenor named Marcel King. "I used to work in this delicatessen, but they fired me for messing about," King told *Blues & Soul.* "I was always singing when the customers were in. This guy that worked there with me introduced me to Leroy [Smith], and he took me to where the group was rehearsing. When I started singing, they all fell out laughing. They said it was because I was so ugly! After that, I hung around with them all the time, and I just sort of joined."

Before the addition of little King, Sweet Sensation consisted of Junior Daye (vocals), Roy Flowers (drums), Barry Jackson (bass), Vincent James (vocals), St. Clair Palmer (vocals), Gary Shaughnessey (guitar), and Leroy Smith (keyboards). With Marcel now on board, young girls screamed, shouted, and threw kisses whenever "Ugly" and the boys hit the stage. Taking note of this ruckus, Decca Records made some demos, but nothing came of them. Pye Records signed them and issued "Snow Fire," but still no action.

Next up was the soulful and pretty "Sad Sweet Dreamer," which topped the charts in England. Sweet Sensation's follow-up, "Purely by Coincidence," did nearly as well, but only in their homeland. The group recorded a self-titled album and possibly a single or two more.

In 1976, Marcel King left the band that considered him ugly, for a solo career. Numerous recordings have been issued in Europe for Wanted, A & M, Factory, and Debut.

In 1989, the group's name returned to the Top 40. This Sweet Sensation, also from the U.K., is an entirely new outfit—all three are most certainly of the female persuasion.

SHIRLEY & COMPANY
SHAME, SHAME, SHAME
(SYLVIA Robinson)
Vibration 532
No. 12 *March 29, 1975*

Shirley Goodman (b. June 19, 1936, New Orleans) was working as a switchboard operator at Playboy Records in L.A. With access to a WATS line, she would call her old pal SYLVIA regularly to chat—the two had met when they were both touring the country with their respective R & B acts, MICKEY & SYLVIA and Shirley & Lee. During one of these exchanges, Sylvia asked Shirley to come on down and take a shot at recording a Sylvia composition called "Shame, Shame, Shame."

The "Company" portion of this entry's name—and the male vocalist on this disco-driven ditty—is Jesus Alvarez (b. Dec. 28, 1951, Havana), an aspiring singing sensation and Cuban refugee. Originally, the legendary Hank Ballard—composer of "The Twist," "Finger Poppin' Time," etc—was supposed to sing along with Shirley Goodman, but for some reason, Hank couldn't make it. Jesus had written some tunes and created some demos for Sylvia Robinson and her All Platinum/Sugar Hill/Stang/Vibration stable of labels. Nothing was released, but a couple of labelmates did take an interest in Jesus; the Moments recorded a few of his songs.

Shirley (Goodman) & Lee was a long-lived R & B duo that started when Eddie Mesner at Aladdin/Philo Records teamed Shirley up with Leonard Lee in 1953. "I'm Gone" (R&B: #2,1953) launched the act nicknamed "Sweethearts of the Blues" and best remembered today for "Let the Good Times Roll" (R&B: #1, 1956) and "Feel So Good" (R&B: #2, 1955).

"Mesner thought that this was a cute little thing, to make people think that we were sweethearts," Goodman told Blues & Soul's Norbert Hess, "because with all the records that we recorded, it was like a story. From 'I'm Gone' we did 'Shirley Come Back to Me,' then we did 'Lee's Dream' and 'The Proposal'. . . ."

Shirley and Lee parted in 1963. She moved to Los Angeles, but Lee stayed in New Orleans, reportedly completing college and working for the government. He died of a heart attack on October 26, 1976. They reunited only once over the years—for Richard Nader's Rock'n'Roll Revival in New York, in 1972.

Shirley Goodman, meanwhile, cut some solo 45s and a few team efforts issued as by Shirley & Alfred (with Brenton Wood, of "Gimme a Little Sign" fame), Shirley & Jessie (with JESSIE HILL, of "Ooh Poo Pah Doo—Part 1"), and Shirley & Shep (with songwriter Maurice Rodgers). She sang back-up for Jackie DeShannon, SONNY & Cher, DR. JOHN, and the Rolling Stones (on Exile on Main Street). In the '70s, Shirley became a PBX operator, a Girl Friday, and a switchboard operator before hooking up with Sylvia for her Top 40 moment.

Following "Shame," the Shame, Shame, Shame LP (1975), and a few minor-league R & B hits, Shirley Goodman once again drifted away. Today, she lives in New Orleans, and confines her singing to spirituals. "I've written a few hymns, and I'd really be interested in recording them," she recently told Goldmine's Almost Slim. "Gospel is what's in my heart now."

MINNIE RIPERTON
LOVING YOU
(Minnie Riperton, Richard Rudolph)
Epic 50057
No. 1 April 5, 1975

My mother graduated from Rust College in Mississippi," Riperton told Goldmine's Robert Pruter. "She was an English major, and she couldn't find a job when she moved from the South to the North; so guess who ended up scrubbing somebody's floors? She studied voice and sang, and my sisters, everybody in my family studied music, piano, or something."

Minnie Riperton (b. Nov. 8, 1947) was born on the poor side of Chicago, the youngest of eight. When she was 10, her mother signed her up at the Lincoln Center. "When I started [singing], my voice teacher, Marion Jeffery, taught me about breathing . . . Then we got into songs. They were classical, mostly. We did a show tune every now and then, but it was operas and operettas mostly. I studied until I was 16, but I got swayed off my path once I got a little rock and roll dangling in front of my eyes."

Representatives for the Gems, a success-seeking Chess group, spotted her performing in the Hyde Park High School A Cappella Choir. One of the Gems was leaving the group, and a replacement was needed. Minnie joined, but was soon forced to make a major decision. "My teacher wanted to put me in the Junior Lyric Opera, but I was offered to go on tours and things [with the Gems] and God, I couldn't pass that up." Unfortunately, not many record-buyers took a shine to any of those girlie-group Gems disks, nor did many people snap up Riperton's initial solo flight, "Lonely Girl" (issued against her wishes as by Andrea Davis).

Numerous critics have considered the output that followed as Riperton's artistic peak. With Sidney Barnes, Mitch Aliotta, and an ever-changing configuration of studio characters, Minnie recorded six albums (the best-known: 1968s Rotary Connection and Aladdin) and several singles as part of the Rotary Connection. The Rotary Connection concept, born of Marshall Chess' intention to update the Chess label, was to create something unheard of before and since—psychedelic soul. The group would roll out revamped versions of "Lady Jane," "Soul Man," or "The Weight."

The Connection came apart in 1970. Minnie moved to Gainesville, Florida, to raise her family and to retire. It was Stevie Wonder who coaxed her back, first with the offer of a position in his Wonderlove group, and later with the offer of a solo contract with Epic. Wonder produced Perfect Angel (#4, 1974), from which a third and most soaring single, "Loving You," was pulled. Despite Minnie's vocal talents (including a five-octave range) and choice material, only one other 45 made the pop listings—"Inside My Love" (#76, 1975). Her LPs, however, continued to sell—*Adventures in Paradise* (#18, 1975), *Stay in Love* (#71, 1977), *Minnie* (#29, 1979), and *Love Lives Forever* (#35, 1980). She also had a string of successes on the R & B listings, most notably her postmortem singles: "Memory Lane" (#16, 1979), "Lover and Friend" (#20, 1979), "Here We Go" (#14, 1980).

Riperton died of cancer at Cedar-Sinai Medical Center in L.A., on July 12, 1979; she was 31. The night before her death, Stevie Wonder visited Minnie. Reportedly, she said, "The person I was waiting for has arrived, and everything will be all right now."

PHOEBE SNOW
POETRY MAN
("Phoebe Snow" Laub)
Shelter 40353
No. 5 *April 12, 1975*

PHOEBE SNOW

"An undeniable virtuoso" (*Musician*), "one of the most versatile" (*Creem*), "one of the most gifted voices of our generation" (*Rolling Stone*)—these are just a few of the critical accolades that have been bestowed on vocal stylist Phoebe Snow. Raised in Teaneck, New Jersey, Phoebe Laub (b. July 17, 1952, New York City) played piano and guitar as a child and teenager. Friends of her mother—folk players like Woody Guthrie, Cisco Houston, Leadbelly, and Pete Seeger—used to drop by regularly. Her musical endeavors took a serious turn in the late '60s. She was very shy—"to the point of being mortified to have to look at people," she once confessed to *Downbeat*—but nonetheless, she began performing folk, pop, jazz, and bluesy numbers in Greenwich Village nightclubs.

In 1972, while working a hootenanny at the Bitter End, Phoebe was spotted by Doni Airali, a rep for Leon Russell's Shelter label. Two years passed before the release of her self-titled debut album on Shelter, but once it came out, the response was immediate and overwhelming. *Phoebe Snow* (#4, 1974)—featured guest appearances of jazz giants Zoot Sims and Terry Wilson—made the Top 10 on *Billboard*'s top pop albums chart, and went gold. It also generated what would become her only hit to date—"Poetry Man."

By the time Columbia released her second album (*Second Childhood*, #13, 1976) two years later, life had become complicated. There were record-company lawsuits when Phoebe left Shelter; tense family relations; a separation and ultimately, divorce; and, most crippling, the birth of a severely brain-damaged daughter, Valerie, in late 1975.

"Once I woke up to the realities of the situation, I knew my world was shattered," Snow told Edward

Kiersh in *Where Are You Now Bo Diddley?* "It was rock-bottom time. I just gave up on myself, emotionally and professionally."

For a while, new LPs were issued on a regular basis: *It Looks Like Snow* (#29, 1976), *Never Letting Go* (#73, 1977), and *Against the Grain* (#100, 1978). The albums were well-crafted and sold well, but not quite as well as her initial output. Phoebe was also finding herself typecast by the style of her first LP.

"I was taking a backseat to whoever was producing my albums," Snow admitted to *Illinois Entertainer*'s Joan Tortorici Ruppert. "I never said, 'Hey, this is what I want to do,' and everybody started thinking I was a jazz singer. And it's obvious when I do live shows that I'm not just a jazz singer. I like to rock out."

She told the *Chicago Tribune*'s Chris Helm, "Rock is something I've always wanted to do, and no one would have ever believed it . . . . Everybody said, 'You're this, because your first record happened that way.' I really didn't know who I was [then], so I let everybody else intimidate me and tell me who I was musically."

Other than a one-off LP for Mirage (*Rock Away*, [#51, 1981]), Phoebe kept a low profile throughout the '80s. She did jingles for Bloomingdale's, General Electric, Stouffer's, and Salon Selectives to support herself. In 1989, she came forward and told the music press that she just wanted to rock and roll. That year's release on Elektra, *Something Real*, marked her professional comeback.

In the early '90s, she was performing with DONALD FAGEN's New Rock and soul Revue; appearing on the disk *Live at the Beacon* (1991). By the mid-'90s, Phoebe was appearing sporadically in a gospel formation with Mavis Staples, CeCe Peniston, and Thelma Houston.

SAMMY JOHNS
CHEVY VAN
(Sammy Johns)
GRC 2046
No. 5 *May 3, 1975*

Little Sammy was big on Elvis, and at the impressionable age of 10, he got a hold of his first guitar and started shakin' and strummin'. Later, someone noted the teenager's twitches and music-like sounds, and placed him in a group of fellow Charlotte, North Carolina, youths that wanted to make rock and roll. The Devilles, as they were known, cut several singles for the Dixie label and had something of a local hit with their tune "Makin' Tracks." Sam aged 10 years with the Devilles before he opted for a change and embarked on a folk-like solo career.

A bigwig from the newly forged General Recording Corporation happened to catch a Sammy Johns performance, signed him to the label, and installed him in Atlanta's Sound Pit Studio with session pros like Jim Gordon, Buddy Emmons, Jim Hom, and James Burton. Larry Knechtel, one-time member of Duane Eddy's Rebels and the keyboardist for Bread at the time, produced this 1973 session. Released were two singles that went nowhere fast; the third, "Early Morning Love" (#68, 1974), was a teasing male fantasy with a folkie feel and countrified pedal-steel guitar underpinnings.

The follow-up to "Early Morning Love," "Chevy Van," gave vent to a more galvanic male fantasy. "Chevy Van" tells of a sweet young thing, who shyly asks you to please make love to her. You obediently oblige her request and take her in your big, fully-rigged machine to a tiny town far away from it all, whereupon the virginal goddess walks off in bare feet. Now here was a tune that Sammy clearly could not top!

The next single, "Rag Doll" (#52, 1975), was a chaste and sad ode. Sammy, it seemed, had spent his creative juices. In 1977, he switched to Warner Bros., and made some recordings for Real World Records. But never

again would his name or his fantasies grace the *Billboard* charts.

Hollywood was not unmoved by Sammy Johns' "Chevy Van" premise: within months of the recording's penetration of the Top 10, an inane movie called *The Van* (1976), featuring Danny DeVito and some nymphets, was quickly tossed together. Sammy was asked to concoct a soundtrack album that would flesh out the concept, but both the film and the album were a bust.

ACE
HOW LONG
(Paul Carrack)
Anchor 21000
No. 3 *May 31, 1975*

A quarter of a century ago, a beat group called the Action were a hip and happening part of the swinging London scene. Alan "Bam" King (b. Sept. 18, 1946, London) had been a member of that fading memory. Over the years, Action went through a number of transformations. During the flower-power era, they were the bottom-heavy Mighty Baby. Remnants of that unit evolved into Clat Thyger, then Ace Flash & The Dynamos. When guitarists Phil Harris (b. July 18, 1948, London) and "Bam" King from the latter grouping merged with keyboardist Paul Carrack (b. Apr. 22, 1951, Sheffield) and bassist Terry "Tex" Comer (b. Feb. 23, 1949, Burnley, Lancashire) from Warm Dust, Ace Flash became simply Ace. With the addition of drummer John Woodhead, Ace eventually developed a reputation as a top-notch London pub-rock outfit.

After a year on the pub circuit, Ace was picked to be the opening act for a planned Hawkwind tour. John Anthony—who had done production work for Genesis, Van Der Graaf Generator, and Lindisfarne—happened to catch one of the band's performances, and offered the guys a chance to record some sides. At about this time, Woodhead departed to join the Sutherland Brothers & Quiver. He was replaced by Fran Byrne (b. Mar. 17, 1948, Dublin), formerly of Rockhouse and Bees Make Honey.

Carrack, who was angered by Woodhead's ill-timed departure, wrote "How Long" and dedicated it to the drummer. Surprisingly, this smoothie became Ace's lone Top 40 hit. For *No Strings*, Ace's third and final album, Byrne was banished and Woodhead was allowed to return to the fold. Unable to consolidate their initial success, the band with the rootsy history ceased operations in 1977.

For an album in 1977 and a few good miles, Byrne, Comer, and Carrack served as a large part of Frankie Miller's back-up band. In the early '80s, Byrne and King

became ingredients in the little noted Juice on the Loose. Most visible and remunerative have been the recent rumblings of Paul Carrack. After his prized 1978 stay with Mel Collins' Retainers, Carrack joined Roxy Music for two years and two albums (*Manifesto, Flesh and Blood*). Session work for the Undertones and John Hiatt followed. For a blink, Carrack was a member of Squeeze (singing on "Tempted"), Carlene Carter's band, and NICK LOWE's Noise to Go. In the '80s, Paul has had a few major hits as a soloist, and several as the voice of Mike + The Mechanics.

JESSI COLTER
I'M NOT LISA
(Jessi Colter)
Capitol 4009
No. 4 *June 21, 1975*

Jessi was born Miriam Johnson on May 25, 1947, in Phoenix, Arizona. Daddy was an inventor/race-car builder, and Mama played piano/preached as a Pentecostal minister. By the age of 11, Miriam was an accomplished church pianist and accordion player. Just five years later, she met guitar icon Duane Eddy, through her sister's hubby (Sun Records producer/sometime singer) Jack Clements; they were married shortly thereafter. They toured the world, with Duane delivering twangy sounds all around. Duane's producer, Lee Hazlewood, taped some tracks on Eddy's wife, releasing the sides as by Miriam Eddy on the Jamie and RCA labels. Nothing much became of her records, and by tour's end in 1968, the couple's split was official.

At one of her recording sessions, Miriam met former Buddy Holly accompanist and C & W "outlaw" Waylon Jennings. The attraction grew, and in 1969, Miriam Johnson became Miriam Jennings. To make a new start, she changed her name to "Jessi Colter" after her great-great-grandfather, Jesse Colter, who had been a buddy of Jesse James. In the following years, Jessi sold solid country sides, had C & W duet hits with her man—most notably "Suspicious Minds" (#2, 1976), "Wild Side of Life"/"It Wasn't God Who Made Honky Tonk Angels" (#10, 1981)—and wrote successful tunes for Eddie Arnold, Anita Carter, Don Gibson, Nancy Sinatra, and DOTTIE WEST.

In 1974, Jessi switched to Capitol Records and released *I'm Jessi Colter*, produced by Waylon. Her anguished "I'm Not Lisa" earned two Grammy nominations and secured a mammoth but momentary pop/rock audience. The follow-up, "What's Happened to Blue Eyes" (#57; C&W: #5, 1975) b/w "You Ain't Never Been Loved (Like I'm Gonna Love You)" (#64, 1975), was a Hot 100 holder, but these would be Colter's last crossovers. Two years later, Jessi made an appearance on the colossally successful and genre-shaping *Wanted! The Outlaws* album, which also featured Waylon, Willie Nelson, Tompall Glaser, and was to become the first country album to be certified platinum; sales by 1985 reached 2 million.

In 1985, Jessi recorded a gospel album as Miriam Johnson and *Rock and Roll Lullabye*, a package of Chip Moman-produced standards, for the tiny Triad label. "Jessi Sings Songs From Around the World for Kids," a hour-long home video featuring international kiddie faves like "London Bridge" and "Old King Cole" was issued in 1991.

MAJOR HARRIS
LOVE WON'T LET ME WAIT
(Bobbie Eli, Vinnie Barrett)
Atlantic 3248
No. 5 *June 21, 1975*

Major's brother is famed tunesmith Joe Jefferson, known for the Spinners' "Mighty Love," "One of a Kind (Love Affair)," and standard "Love Don't Know Nobody"; his cousin, Norm Harris, "the Philly Guitar," was a member of MFSB and recorded with THE LARKS, FIRST CHOICE, BUNNY SIGLER . . .

Harris—christened Major as his father and his father before him—was born in Richmond, Virginia, on February 9, 1947. His grandparents were vaudevillians, his father was a professional guitarist, and his mother was leader of the church choir. During the late '50s, Major recorded with the Charmers and claims that he was a member of Frankie Lymon's Teenagers. In the early '60s, he joined THE JARMELS. Both acts had peaked, but Harris says that he recorded with the latter group and later cut some solo singles for the Jarmels' label, Laurie Records. Later in the decade, Major was called upon to front the Philly Groove act Nat Turner's Rebellion, which resulted in a few unsuccessful 45s. Between 1971 and 1974, Harris was a member of the Delfonics, and with his assistance, the group had their last pop chartings, "Tell Me This Is a Dream" (#86; R&B: #15, 1972) and "I Don't Want to Make You Wait" (#91; R&B: #22, 1973).

In 1974, Major passed an audition as a solo act for W.M.O.T. Productions. He made an album for Atlantic

MAJOR HARRIS

Records, and while his first single (issued as by the Major Harris Boogie Blues Band), "Each Day I Wake Up," flopped, "Love Won't Let Me Wait" fared much better (R&B: #1, 1975). Several other smooth-talkin' singles did well on the R & B charts. Two years later, even these R & B hits stopped.

Harris has been appearing as a member of the reconstituted Delfonics.

ROGER WHITTAKER
THE LAST FAREWELL
(R. A. Webster, R. Whittaker)
RCA 50030
No. 19 *June 21, 1975*

Roger's father was a grocer from Staffordshire, England. In 1929, on the advice of a doctor, he moved to East Africa, where Roger was born March 22, 1936. As a child, Roger took to singing in the school choir and plucking a guitar made for him by an Italian prisoner-of-war. Two years of military service in the Kenya Regiment turned young "Whittle" into a performer. "Stuck in the bush camps for months on end meant we had to make our own entertainment," Whittaker explained to Sharon Tracy in *Who's Who in Popular Music in Britain.* "Before I knew it, I was standing on a make-shift stage, guitar in hand, having enormous fun developing into a second Elvis."

On his return from the wilds, he attended the University of Capetown in South Africa and the University of Bangor, Wales, where he acquired a Bachelor of Science degree. Before closing the books on his interests in zoology and bio-chemistry, Whittaker got the chance to record an independently funded single for charity. Despite some chart successes for Fontana Records as Rog Whittaker on the continent, Roger remained an unknown in the U.K. until the end of the '60s and the release of his self-penned "Durham Town (I'm Leavin')." Five more of his easy-listening 45s found their way on to the British pop listings in the '70s. The last of these, aptly titled "The Last Farewell," was to be his only introduction to the American Top 40. Sales figures have totaled 11 million.

In 1986, Whittaker returned to the British Top 10 with "The Skye Boat Song," a duet disk with Des O'Connor. Roger, who currently lives in Essex, England, continues to tour for his devoted following. His many middle-of-the-road LPs still sell fairly well, thanks, in part, to those late-night-TV mail-order commercials.

PILOT
MAGIC
(David Paton, Bill Lyall)
EMI 3992
No. 5 *July 12, 1975*

In the early '70s, vocalist/keyboardist/sometime flutist Billy Lyall (b. Mar. 26, 1953, Edinburgh, Scotland) was the head engineer at Edinburgh's Craighall Recording Studio. It was there that he met again with bassist Dave Paton (b. Oct. 29, 1951, Edinburgh) and drummer Stuart Tosh (b. Sept. 26, 1951, Aberdeen), two frequent ses-

sion players. Billy and Dave had for a moment been involved in an initial formation of what would become the Bay City Rollers, then a mere Beatles cover band. In 1973, the three decided to form a rock and roll group, and derived the unit's name from the initial letters of each surname (Paton, Lyall, Tosh). No one noticed at the time that there was already a recording act named Pilot. No matter—that BLUE CHEER spinoff crashed after a lone album.

Early in 1974, the threesome created some demos and took them around in search of a record deal. Attracted by their Hollies-like harmonies and Sgt. Pepper styling, EMI took a bite and ushered the guys into the Abbey Road studios in London. Alan Parsons, the studios long-time engineer, was given the task of producing Pilot's first product. The Beatle-esque "Magic" and the follow-up, "Just a Smile" (#90, 1975), were both pulled from the band's self-titled LP. These disks charted extremely well in the U.K., as did two other 45s. Overall, the group seemed to fare better in England than in the States: "January," their third U.S. single, was number one over there but only reached number 87 (in 1976) over here.

Before Pilot bailed out, guitarist Ian Bairnson (b. Aug. 3, 1953, Shetland Isles) was added to the group's line-up. By their third album, *Morin Heights* (1976), Pilot was a fairly accomplished outfit. An unsuccessful fourth LP, *Two's a Crowd*, appeared in the States on Arista in 1977, but by this point—and for the remainder of the '70s and part of the '80s—Pilot (minus Lyall) was absorbed into the Alan Parsons Project. Each ex-Pilot person did session work: most notable is Tosh's late '70s studio stint with 10cc. Lyall, meanwhile, had a solo album (*Solo Casting*, 1976) released on EMI, became a member of the short-lived Runner, guested on ALI THOMSON's first two albums and joined the short-changed Dollar. Billy Lyall died in December 1989.

VAN MCCOY
THE HUSTLE
(Van McCoy)
Avco 4653
No. 1 *July 26, 1975*

He died young—of a bad heart, they say. Like Bobby Darin, whose fate was similar, Van started early and maintained a pace fueled with an unusual drive and motivation.

While a sophomore, pianist Van McCoy (b. Jan. 6, 1944, Washington, DC) got some of the singers in the Dunbar High glee club to join him in forming a Frankie Lymon & The Teenagers-style group called the Starlighters. Although they bombed at their high school talent contest, they eventually became good enough to literally impersonate Frankie Lymon & The Teenagers at John Brown's Farm, a club near Harpers Ferry, West Virginia. Before breaking up, the band waxed three singles for the End label and briefly replaced one member with Marvin Gaye.

McCoy went on to release some fine solo material that caught the attention of Florence Greenberg at Scepter/Wand Records. Greenberg hired McCoy as an all-around studio hand, A & R man, songwriter, and assistant to producer Luther Dixon. In this capacity, Van would soon contribute to the success of Chuck Jackson, the Shirelles, and Dionne Warwick.

Van became a part-owner, with Larry Maxwell, of Maxx Records, and began producing disks for Gladys Knight & The Pips. Subsequent production/writing credits included the Drifters, Aretha Franklin, Jay & The Americans, the Marvelettes, IRMA THOMAS, Bobby Vinton, and Jackie Wilson. During this period, Columbia attempted to make a solo singer out of Van. His own offerings were disappointing, considering the brilliance of his work for other artists. Nothing with his name on it sold, not even singles he recorded as the Sound City Symphony.

"It was all exhausting . . . I needed more time," McCoy told Blues & Soul's Tony Cummings. "The whole thing was so hectic, like I was working seven days a week." Under doctor's orders, Van took a short rest. Then he was back, writing, arranging, and producing.

"When I wrote 'The Hustle' I'd never even been to a disco to see the dance. What happened was that David Todd, who's one of the top DJs in the New York discos, came to me and told me about this new dance. I got a couple of girls to do the Hustle for me in the office so I could get the rhythm right, and I wrote the tune. Pretty hard to believe, huh?

"It's tough to have to follow a record like 'The Hustle.' It sold 10 million copies and was a complete accident—how do you top it? It changed my life." It also won a Grammy as "Best Pop Instrumental" of 1975, and was to become (according to The New York Times)"the biggest dance record of the '70s." Van had a point: what may be the best-selling disco disk of all time was going to be a tough act to follow.

Van quickly dispatched LPs like Disco Baby (1975), From Disco to Love (1975), and The Disco Kid (1975), plus a few more dance singles that made the Hot 100— "Change With the Times" (#46, 1975), "Night Walk" (#96, 1976), and "Party" (#69, 1976). But by the decades end, he was ready for a change. "Disco has played an important role in the development of my career," he told Billboard. "But I am seeking greater versatility. I do not want to be forever locked into the image of the 'disco kid.'"

Before his death in Englewood, New Jersey, on July 6, 1979, Van McCoy did manage to make musical moves in other directions. He wrote the scores for Cicely Tyson's made-for-TV movie "A Woman Called Moses" (1978) and Mae West's Sextet (1978).

BAZUKA
DYNOMITE—PART 1
(Tony Camillo)
A & M 1666
No. 10 August 2, 1975

Bazuka was a studio disco group assembled by producer Tony Camillo. Prior to creating this short-lived hit, Tony had worked with the Persuasions and Gladys Knight & The Pips. "Love Explosion," Bazuka's follow-up to "Dynamite," just barely made the R & B listings (#92, 1975), but "Police Woman," "(C'est) Le Rock," and a string of other dance-floor riffers stiffed.

In the mid-'70s, Camillo teamed up with producer/manager Bob Marcucci, star-maker for Frankie Avalon and Fabian, to form Camillo/Marcucci Productions. As disco maneuvered into the '80s, Camillo reactivated the Bazuka name for a few obscure things for Venture Records.

GWEN MCCRAE
ROCKIN' CHAIR
(CLARENCE REID, W. Clarke)
Cat 1996
No. 9 August 2, 1975

Gwen was born in Pensacola, Florida, on December 21, 1943. Reportedly, in 1969, she met a soused sailor named George McCrae. Gwen at first resisted his charms and told the so-and-so to get lost. A few weeks later, Gwen and George were married, and shortly thereafter, became a recording act for Henry Stone's TK label. Their debut, the country war horse—the tune that rendered ROY DRUSKY a one-time winner—"Three Hearts in a Triangle," died a dreadful death.

George, who had a history of crooning with locals like the Jivin' Jets and an outfit called the Atsugi Express, was then handed a tight-tailored junkanoo jumper entitled "Rock Your Baby." The tune had been written specifically for Gwen, but George's spouse turned it down flat. Little did Gwen know that the number would go on to sell millions, help launch the discomania of the mid-'70s, and become the very hub of her hubby's series of hits. Some writers have written that George's meteoric rise to pop stardom hastened the demise of the couple's marriage.

After the success of "Rock Your Baby," Gwen was less reluctant when offered the similar-sounding "Rockin' Chair," her lone pop crossover hit to date.

Over the years, a number of her soul singles have modestly mounted the R & B listings. Before George's death from cancer on January 24, 1986, George and Gwen secured a minor R & B charting with their final 45 as a duo, "Winners Together or Losers Apart"(#44, 1976).

AMAZING RHYTHM ACES
THIRD RATE ROMANCE
(Howard Russell Smith)
ABC 12078
No. 14 *September 13, 1975*

Howard Russell Smith (lead vocals, guitar, harmonica) and Butch McDade (drums) grew up in and around Lafayette, Tennessee. Beginning in the early '70s, the two played together in a succession of bands. They met Jeff Davis (bass) and Danny Kennedy (guitar) in 1972 and formed a foursome to work bashes and bars in Alabama and East Tennessee. When the offer came for Davis and McDade to join JESSIE WINCHESTER's touring band, they accepted and began calling themselves the Rhythm Aces. The "Amazing" tag was added in 1974 when the two accompanists left Winchester to form—along with Smith, Barry "Byrd" Burton (guitar, steel

guitar, dobro, mandolin), and Billy Earheart III (keyboards)—a group that would play all kinds of music: old-timey, bluegrass, R & B, country, gospel, whatever.

The Amazing Rhythm Aces were brought into a studio in Memphis by Knox Phillips, the eldest son of Sun Records legend Sam Phillips. James Hooker (piano), who played on the group's first session, joined the line-up. The Aces' *Stacked Deck* (1975)—from which "Third Rate Romance" was drawn—and their next three LPs were all recorded at Sam Phillips's Recording Studios. The Amazing Rhythm Aces had only two more Hot 100 chartings—"Amazing Grace (Used to Be Her Favorite Song)" (#72, 1976) and "The End Is Not in Sight" (#42, 1976)—but single after single made the country charts. "The End Is Not in Sight" even won a Grammy for "Best Country Vocal Performance" of 1976.

All six of their LPs sold well, but management problems began to plague the band. Their penultimate album, *Amazing Rhythm Aces* (1979)—featuring guest appearances by Joan Baez, Tracy Nelson, and the Muscle Shoal Horns—first appeared on ABC, but was soon withdrawn and reshipped on Columbia when their contract changed hands. Another label switch followed: their final LP, *How the Hell Do You Spell Rhythm* (1980), was issued by Warner Bros.

Russell Smith has become a solo artist with Capitol Records. A few of his singles, like "Three Piece Suit" (#53, 1988) and "Betty Jean" (#49, 1988), have had success with the C & W crowd. Russ has also had country artists like George Jones, Mel McDaniels, and Conway Twitty record some of his tunes.

In 1986, Bill Earheart joined Hank Williams, Jr.'s back-up unit, the Bama Band. A number of Bama Band 45s have clicked, most recently "Real Old-Fashioned Broken Heart" (C&W: #69, 1989).

MORRIS ALBERT
FEELINGS
(Morris Albert)
RCA 10279
No. 6 *October 25, 1975*

Legend has it that one sunny day, when Morris was a mere lad of five in Brazil, he snuck up on the family keyboard and plucked out "I Wish You Love" entirely by ear. Well, Mom and all the other kinfolk encouraged him to be a musician. At 14, Morris Albert Kaisermann had his own band, the Thunders. Two years later, Albert became a solo act and began making a reputation for

MORRIS ALBERT

himself at the local night spots. After graduating high school, he came to the United States to attend Columbia University as a phonology major, but soon returned to his native Brazil to pursue a career in music. In 1975, Morris Albert had his international moment in the sun with one of his own creations, "Feelings."

For nearly eight months, this lounge-lizard classic remained on the Hot 100. At first, it sounded harmless enough—a touch of Bread, a pinch of Fleetwoods-like harmonizing, and that ethereal melody. Soon, millions of people were singing "whoa, whoa, whoa" along with Morris. The *Feelings* album flew off the shelves, and Albert became a pop sensation—until, thanks to airplay ad nauseam, radio listeners grew weary of his sentiments. Morris's follow-up, "Sweet Loving Mary" (#93, 1976), was no chart-buster.

In 1985, a Federal District Court in Manhattan found that more than 80 percent of "Feelings" had been plagiarized from "Pour Toi," a 1956 composition by French composer Louis Gaste. A settlement of $500,000 was awarded to Gaste. Morris continues to live and perform in Sao Paulo, Brazil. Word is that he is understandably reticent to record anything of his for the American market.

PETE WINGFIELD
EIGHTEEN WITH A BULLET
(Pete Wingfield)
Island 026
No. 15 *November 29, 1975*

Pete was born in England, May 7, 1948. Early on, he was mesmerized by American black music. Wingfield was educated at Sussex University, where he wrote R & B articles and published his own fanzine called *Soul Beat*. "Graduated, I did," said Pete in an exclusive interview. "Get that in there; whole band [Jellybread] did...." Pete played keyboards in college bands like the Cossacks, Pete's Disciples, and then Jellybread. The latter group (named after a cherished Booker T & The MGs instrumental)—consisting of Wingfield, bassist John Best, drummer Chris Waters, and guitarist Paul Butler. When Jellybread crumbled, Pete joined the Keef Hartley Band for the 1972 session that produced the *Seventy Second Brave* album.

Pete formed the studio-only Olympic Runners in 1974 with producer and Blue Horizon Records chief Mike Vernon on harmonica and percussion, DeLisle Harper on bass, Joe Jammer (ne Joseph Wright) on guitar, and Glen LeFleur on drums. For the remainder of the decade, Wingfield and company churned out a pile of pumped-up 45s and five LPs. The band never cracked the stateside pop listings but did have a string of R & B chart-makers from 1974 to 1976 with insistent titles like "Do It Over" (#72, 1974) b/w "Put Your Money Where Your Mouth Is" (#72, 1974), "Grab It" (#73, 1975), "Drag It Over Here" (#92, 1975), and "Party Time Is Here to Stay" (#97, 1976).

"There's talk of reviving the name, reissuing the first two, three albums on CD," said Wingfield, "but not the band itself.

In 1975, Pete got an offer from Island Records to do a solo platter. "I got naked and did this album [billed, *Breakfast Special*, in the U.S.]; understand, it's not that I did this hit and they let me do an album. I played grand piano, Hammond organ, clarinet, melodica, mellotron, synthesizer, stylophone, and made the tea. All the voices are mine, though I don't have the greatest voice. On 'Eighteen With a Bullet,' I pitched the bass voice in the wrong key, and we had to speed up the tape, slightly.

"'Eighteen,' I wrote years before—about '72—with the Dells in mind. Our paths didn't cross, and they never got to know of it; though I understand Pookie Hudson & The Spaniels do the song, currently." "Eighteen" was a nostalgic number with double-entendre lyrics. Stranger than fiction—on November 11, this first Wingfield single hit number 18 on the Hot 100 chart—with a bullet.

"The next single didn't do anything, I know that. 'Bubbling Under' it was called. . . . Then, there was another one—my personal favorite. . . . That flopped. Boom, it went. Ah, 'Scratchy 45s,' about the glories of New Orleans rhythm & blues. I made a second album—*Love, Bombs and Dizzy Spells*—but they wouldn't let me release it, here, there, or anywhere. . . ."

Waxing no further waves, Wingfield returned to the shadows. Pete has toured as a back-up pianist and singer for Maggie Bell, the Zombies' Colin Bluestone, Van Morrison, and as music director for the Everly Brothers. Pete has recorded with Bloodstone, the Chimes, the Hollies, B.B. King, FREDDY KING, Lightnin' Slim, Memphis Slim, IAN MATTHEWS, NAZARETH, Al Stewart, Jimmy Witherspoon . . . Beginning in the early '80s, his attention turned to producing: THE BELLE STARS, DEXY'S MIDNIGHT RUNNERS, Hot Chocolate, THE KANE GANG, Alison Moyet, THE SUGARHILL GANG, and Mel Brooks.

In the mid-'80s, , Pete found time to create the pseudo-group Band of Gold, responsible for the "Love Songs Are Back—Medley" (#64, 1984), containing tasty tid-bits from "Have You Seen Her," "Betcha by Golly Wow," "You Make Me Feel Brand New."

In 1993, Pete Wingfield enjoyed his biggest production success with the Proclaimers' Top Five shaker, "I'm Gonna Be (500 Miles)."

"The only other thing with just my name on it—I did a one-off thing for Richard Vernon, Mike's bro . . . It was a spoof thing, 'They All Came Back,'" said Pete.

"About all the former hit-makers?" I asked. "No, no, no such thing. It was about records that we've all heard too many times. They all came back, you know."

LEON HAYWOOD
I WANTA DO SOMETHING FREAKY TO YOU
(Leon Haywood)
20th Century 2065
No. 15 *December 13, 1975*

"I was born [Feb. 11, 1942] and raised in Houston, Texas, and I grew up listening to people like Muddy Waters, Jimmy Reed, and Roy Brown," Leon Haywood told *Blues & Soul's* Denise Hall. "My parents got me a piano when I was about three. I didn't care nothin' about singing in those days. When I was about 14, I played with a professional group. I can't recall their name, but we played a lot of local gigs."

For a while, Leon accompanied Guitar Slim (of "The Things That I Used to Do" fame) and Clarence Greene. He moved to L.A. and eventually managed to hook up with saxophone legend Big Jay McNeeley. In 1962, the honkin' horn man arranged for Leon to record his first disk, an instrumental for Swingin' called "Without a Love." "It did pretty well, sold about 100,000. Anyway, I didn't make no money out of it."

Leon joined Sam Cooke's band as a keyboardist. Months later, super-soul-singing Sam was dead. "You're All for Yourself" and "The Truth About Money," Leon's solo efforts, were issued by Fantasy. "The truth about money," Haywood quipped, "was there wasn't any."

Magnificent Montague, a wheeler-dealer DJ in L.A., got Haywood his next contract and first chart ride, but reportedly at quite a price. "She's With Her Other Love" (#92, R&B: #13, 1965) made the airwaves and the listings all right, but since Imperial made the deal directly with Montague, he received all the royalties and Haywood never got a cent. To add insult to injur*y*, the label spelled his name "Leon Hayward."

Before finally finding his niche and working it raw, Leon cut some more sides set up by Montague. "One of the guys [Charles "Packy" Axton of THE MAR-KEYS; son to Stax Records co-owner Estelle Axton] who played on a lot of the Stax things was in L.A., and Montague got him together with me and a bunch of the other musicians and cut a record that had that 'Memphis Sound.'" The instrumental, "Hole in the Wall" (#43, R&B: #5, 1965), was credited to "The Packers." Haywood also did sessions with Dyke & The Blazers and recorded with Kenny Gambles and Thom Bell's Romeos.

Finally, in 1974—after many singles for Decca, Capitol, and Atlantic (not to mention some earlier sides for Fat Fish, Galaxy, and his own Eve-Jim)—Leon struck gold at 20th Century Records. In addition to hitting the big time with his sexually suggestive "I Wanta Do Something Freaky to You," Haywood has made the R & B chart more than 20 times.

"The success hasn't really changed me," said Haywood to *Blues & Soul*'s John Abbey of his single hit "I Wanta Do Something Freaky." "The biggest change for me will be financial. For first time, my bank manager really loves me!"

Leon continues into the '90s as an executive/producer with Edge Records.

WING & A PRAYER FIFE AND DRUM CORPS
BABY FACE
(Benny Davis, Harry Akst)
Wing & Prayer 103
No. 14 *March 6, 1976*

The Wing & A Prayer Fife and Drum Corps was nothing more than a temporary studio venture. Stephen Scheaffer and Harold Wheeler had just set up a label with a national distribution network supplied by the Warner Communications conglomerate. Disco was the rage; Steve and Harry had a smart idea, and rounded up a heap of Big Apple sessioneers. The twosome's scheme was to take stiff standards and, with the assistance of David Horowitz, violate them with that insistent disco beat.

Seven such songs were cut: "The Charleston," "Eleanor Rigby," and, yes, "Baby Face," a number one charter for Jan Garber in 1926. Perched atop the repetitious churning were the voices of Vivian Cherry, Arlene Martell, Helene Miles, and Linda November. The fife blowers were Lew Delgatto, Louis Manni, and Gerald Nielwood. On sticks and skins were Roy Markowitz and Andrew Smith.

"Baby Face" became an instant sensation with disco devotees. Nothing further charted, but before Steve and Harry's Wing & A Prayer crashed, *Babyface Strikes Back*, another LP of pulsating oldies, was dispensed.

CLEDUS MAGGARD &
THE CITIZEN'S BAND
THE WHITE KNIGHT
(Jay Huguely)
Mercury 73751
No. 19 *March 13, 1976*

Now, Cledus can't be that boy's real name, you say? You're right as night ain't day. See, Cled is really Jay Huguely (b. Quicksand, KY), a one-time Shakespearean actor turned ad man. Yup, Cledus Maggard was just an idea gone loco. One day while working at an ad agency in Greenville, South Carolina, Jay got this joltin'

notion to do a novelty number around the then-hot CB (citizen's band radio) craze. Jay got some jingle men to give him a hand, and poof! There it was, "The White Knight." Some copies were pressed and circulated. "I figured the agency would be giving these away as Christmas presents for the next 20 years," Huguely told Jeannie Sakol in *The Wonderful World of Country Music*. Mercury Records got wind of the effort, and decided to distribute the disk worldwide.

For the remainder of the decade, Mercury kept shipping Cledus's comedic, country corn pone. "Kentucky Moonrunner" (#85; C&W: #42, 1976), "Virgil and the $300 Vacation" (C&W: #73, 1976), and "The Farmer" (C&W: #82, 1978) managed to tickle some funny bones.

NAZARETH
LOVE HURTS
(Boudleaux Bryant)
A & M 1671
No. 8 *March 13, 1976*

Pete Agnew (bass), Dan McCafferty (lead vocals), and Darrel Sweet (drums) were all born in Scotland. They played in various local bands and met during the '60s as members of the Shadettes, which was a junior version of Cliff Richards' Shadows. When fellow Scot Manny Charlton (guitar) joined the guys in 1969, they changed their name to Nazareth, after the first line of the Band's "The Weight" ("I pulled into Nazareth . . ."). In 1971, the band moved to London and then secured a record deal.

"Our recording career started off strangely," Agnes told *International Musician*'s Ed Nash. "We were just knocking about playing 'covers.' And when we did our first album, it was a case of leaving our full-time jobs and being told to get in the studio . . . We hadn't really made up our mind about what we wanted to be musically, either. We were torn between being a heavy rock band or playing the more subtle kind of stuff we enjoyed listening to. We never actually listened to hard rock—we just enjoyed playing it."

Nazareth has been pounding away in a semi-heavy metal vein ever since. While only their make of the Everly Brothers classic "Love Hurts" and "Holiday" (#87, 1980) made the United States charts, a solid dozen tracks made the British listings. Their popularity has always been greater in Europe than in the States, though nearly every LP released domestically through the early '80s made the top pop albums chart. The Nazareth specialty seems to be pile-driving cover versions of subdued folkie fare like Joni Mitchell's "This Flight Tonight," Bob Dylan's "The Ballad of Hollis Brown," and, of course, "Love Hurts."

While their releases are fewer in number, Nazareth apparently is still seeking an ever-larger following. Guitarist Zal Cleminson (b. May 4, 1949, Glasgow), formerly of the cultish Sensational Alex Harvey Band, was also a Naz man from 1978 to 1980; in 1982, guitarist Billy Rankin and ex-SPIRIT keyboardist John Locke were added to the group. Locke left after the release of *Snaz*, a long-awaited double live album.

Following the self-title swan song for A & M in 1989, Nazareth remained label-free until their homeland revival three years later with *No Jive*.

LARRY GROCE
JUNK FOOD JUNKIE
(Larry Groce)
Warner Bros. 8165
No. 9 *March 20, 1976*

Where did this junk-food junkie come from? Before his fleeting success, Larry (guitar, mandolin) plus his sidekicks—Berke McKelvey (bass) and the Currence brothers, Jimmie (banjo, fiddle) and Loren (guitar, fiddle, mandolin)—were working the backwoods bar circuit. Groce had recorded four LPs of folkie things on tiny labels like Peaceable and Daybreak, albums that were so poorly distributed that even Larry may not be aware of them.

Larry Groce was born in Dallas on April 22, 1948. Attending W. H. Adamson High School at the same time as Larry were future music-makers Michael Murphy, Ray Wylie Hubbard, and B. W. STEVENSON. With school behind him, Larry and guitar moved about the states singing folk music and rhyming tales. (Walt Disney's Vista label issued his "Winnie the Pooh for President" as a single.) Early in the '70s, Groce went to work for the National Endowment for the Arts and West Virginia's Arts and Humanities Council. Larry was sent to the Appalachian Mountains in West Virginia to teach songwriting. It was there that wild imaginations aided him in coming up with his one and only hit. Recorded before a live audience at a guitar shop, McCabe's, in Santa Monica, "Junk Food Junkie" touched a repressed nerve.

"I was raised on junk food. Dallas, my hometown, is home to Dr. Pepper and Fritos," said Larry, in a publicity handout from the record company. "My big weakness is Peanut Paddies, a candy type thing only made in Texas. My dad is a connoisseur of them, like fine wines."

Warner Brothers picked up the tune for national distribution, but there was a fear in the air that some of the major makers of the junk would take offense and pursue a legal recourse. "I was in the publicity department at Warner, and they were worried because they heard that local outlets of McDonalds and Kentucky Fried Chicken had put some heat on the local stations to drop the song from their playlists," said Groce to authors Bruce Nash and Allan Zullo. "Although there were a few local franchises who were upset with the song . . . the home offices understood that every time their name was mentioned good things happened."

As the *Junk Food Junkie* album attests, Groce and his cohorts were capable of creating some pleasing rural sounds, but the label felt the record-buying public wanted more novelty numbers. Warner Bros. issued follow-up singles with titles like "Big White House in Indiana," "The Bumper Sticker Song," and "Turn on Your TV," all to little avail.

Larry Groce still resides in a 120-year-old farmhouse outside of Philippa, West Virginia. Larry still sings some, and writes a little, too. In the late '80s he hosted "Mountain Stage," a national radio show. He proudly notes that he starred in a low-budget, video store-only flick, *Paradise Park* (1991). "It's a humorous story of a trailer park in West Virginia," said Groce. "I play a teacher who lives there and everyone is an oddball, but me."

Asked about his goals in life, Larry told a publicist, "I'm on the search for the ultimate junk food, one with no natural ingredients whatsoever."

JOHN SEBASTIAN
WELCOME BACK
(John Sebastian)
Reprise 1349
No. 1 *May 8, 1976*

His lone solo charting outsold anything by his former group, the Lovin' Spoonful, becoming the second biggest selling single of 1976.

"They said 'Write the theme song,' John Sebastian told *Rolling Stone*'s Patrick Snyder. " I said, 'What's the title?' and they said, 'Kotter,' and I said, 'Gimme a chance!' So I read the original treatment and wrote 'Welcome Back,' and the next week, they made that the show's title. Then, a few weeks later, some network guy had a flash of brilliance—'If we call it "Welcome Back," it'll sound like a nostalgia show. So we should call it "Welcome Back, Kotter."' I wrote it in 15 minutes. Generally, they're hits if you write them fast."

Sebastian ought to know—he was the principal songwriter and de facto leader of the Lovin' Spoonful. The Spoonful created a string of '60s chestnuts: "Do You Believe in Magic?," "You Didn't Have to Be So Nice," "Daydream," "Summer in the City," "Nashville Cats."

JOHN SEBASTIAN

He was born John Besson Sebastian, son of a classically trained harmonica player (b. Mar. 17, 1944, New York City). He hung out with poets and folkies in Greenwich Village. John played music with the Even Dozen Jug Band and Mama Cass Elliot's Mugwumps; recorded, as accompanist, with Eric Andersen and Judy Collins. After a trek for truth to study with Lightnin' Hopkins, John returned to the Village to form with Steve Boone, Joe Butler, and Zal Yanovsky, the Lovin' Spoonful. Sebastian also scored two flicks—Woody Allen's *What's Up, Tiger Lily* (1966) and Francis Ford Coppolla's *You're a Big Boy Now* (1966)—and tunes for the Broadway show *Johnny Shine*.

The Spoonful sound was magical, but their success evaporated amongst drug bust, bickering, and a hippie boycott. "I'm glad the group broke up when it did," Sebastian told Bruce Pollock in *When the Music Mattered*, "because the alternative is sort of playing in cheesier and cheesier entertainment parks, as a lot of famous groups going down the tubes do. So, instead of cashing in on the downfall and taking the slow road, we just pulled the plunger."

John was off on a solo career that got an early boost at the Woodstock festival. He was not scheduled to appear, and his tie-dyed, dazed-hippie routine was the result of a healthy dose of LSD. The crowd response was enthusiastic, though Sebastian remains "sorry that the highest visibility performance I've ever given was one where I was smashed beyond belief."

In the recording world, Sebastian was headed for an even bigger bummer. MGM wanted his initial solo issued as a Lovin' Spoonful record. Sebastian balked, and signed with Reprise, who agreed to issue the same material under his own name. Eventually, the disk in question—*John B. Sebastian* (1970)—was released on both labels at the same time! To make matters worse, MGM, in what John claims was either an act of vindictiveness or an effort to cash in on his Woodstock appearance, released a half-finished, poorly-recorded live LP *John Sebastian Live* (1970).

Disenchanted, John moved into a tent outside an apartment complex run by his friend, Cyrus Faryar. Sebastian stayed for two years. "I did a crazy year of cocaine, and then I said, 'Oh my God, I'm not funny anymore . . .' It was about 1974 when I really said to myself, 'Okay, you're going to have some slim years as far as recording goes, so you better go where you can work.'"

After three albums for Reprise, John Sebastian hit the East Coast college circuit, where he often performs to this day. "Welcome Back," unfortunately, was his sole hit; nothing further was issued for 17 years! Of late, John has been engaged in work for a Canadian animation firm, writing a kiddie book of tunes for children's TV shows, "Strawberry Shortcake" and "The Care Bears," and supplying the music for a musical based on E. B. White's classic *Charlotte's Web*. John also wrote the music to the NBC-TV production of "The Jerk II" (1984).

John refuses to be a part to any proposed reformation of the Lovin' Spoonful. In 1994, he formed J-Band, a jug band, which has made appearances on Garrison Keillor's radio review, "The Prairie Home Companion."

ELVIN BISHOP
FOOLED AROUND AND FELL IN LOVE
(Elvin Bishop)
Capricorn 0252
No. 3 *May 22, 1976*

"For 99 percent of the people," blues guitarist Elvin Bishop explained to *Guitar World*'s Bill Milkowski, "if

ELVIN BISHOP

you don't have a record, you're not on the radio ... you don't exist. For some reason, I never felt much pressure to make a record. I lead a pretty full life. Got a real nice home, nice wife, nice kid, ..."

As for the "Pigboy Crabshaw" persona often flogged by critics, Bishop told *Relix*'s Clark Peterson: "What's wrong with being a good old fella? I didn't see a TV until I was 12. I was born and raised on a farm outside Tulsa, and I'd seen a lot more chickens and pigs than people."

Despite his hayseed image, Elvin (b. Oct. 21, 1942, Tulsa, OK) was a bright kid. It was while studying physics at the University of Chicago on a National Merit Scholarship that he fell under the mesmerizing sway of the blues. "There must've been 40 blues clubs that were just hoppin' every night, all over the South Side and the West Side," Bishop recalled to Milkowski. "Needless to say, I got swept up by the scene."

Elvin hooked up with a young harmonica-player named Paul Butterfield. The two worked parties as a duo, backing up blues greats like Magic Sam, Junior Wells, and Hound Dog Taylor. In 1965, Bishop and Butterfield formed a blues band that became quite popular in Chicago. The Butterfield Blues Band, featuring the lead-guitar work of Mike Bloomfield, succeeded in bringing the authentic blues (by white kids, no less) to middle-class rock and folk fans. For three classic albums—*The Paul Butterfield Blues Band* (1965), *East-West* (1966), and *The Resurrection of Pigboy Crabshaw* (1968)—the band purveyed its unique brand of electric blues. When Bloomfield left after the second album, Bishop moved into the lead-guitar chair.

In the late '60s, Bishop left Butterfield, moved to the Bay area, and led his own group. A few LPs were issued on the Epic, Fillmore, and Capricorn labels. Two singles—"Travelin' Shoes" (#61, 1974) and "Sure Feels Good" (#83, 1975)—as well as two albums—*Let It Flow* (1974) and *Juke Joint Jump* (1975)—did well. But it was not until 1976 that Bishop won the major portion of his audience. "Fooled Around and Fell in Love," featuring vocals by future Starship singer Mickey Thomas, sold beyond all expectations.

"I wrote that song four or five years earlier," Bishop told *Creem*'s Tom Dupree, "and I never was able to sing it well enough, and there was nobody singing in my group who could do it to my satisfaction until Mickey tried it. It was just a throw-in on the last album. We needed a little bit more time filled."

A few more singles and albums followed, but by 1980, Elvin was nowhere in sight. He resurfaced in 1989 with *Big Fun* on Alligator Records, assisted by DR. JOHN. Releases thereafter have been sporadic.

PRATT & MCCLAIN
HAPPY DAYS
(Norman Gimbel, Charles Fox)
Reprise 1351
No. 5 *June 5, 1976*

They started early and were persistent in their pursuit, but talent is also of some importance. Three months on the charts and they were history. Viewers of the phenomenally successful Ron Howard-Henry Winkler TV show, "Happy Days" would endure their voices for a much longer time, however.

Truett Pratt (b. San Antonio, TX) sang as a youngster in the choir. But in high school, it was a rock band that grabbed his interest. Jerry McClain's (b. Pasadena, CA) daddy was a man of the cloth, so it's no surprise to learn that Jerry also started out singing for the Lord.

In the mid-'60s, Jerry met up with Michael Omartian. Michael would one day do production work for folks like Cher, Christopher Cross, Dion, RICHIE FURAY, Jermaine Jackson, TOM JOHNSTON, Rod Stewart, Donna Summer, and ROGER VOUDOURIS. Together, Jerry and Mike formed the American Scene and recorded a single or two for Dot Records. In 1970, Omartian went off to make those hit records for others. Before leaving, he introduced Jerry to Truett. These two were part of a group called Brotherlove, did studio back-up work, and made TV and radio commercials.

As Pratt & McClain, Truett and Jerry made an LP and some 45s for ABC/Dunhill, but it wasn't until Michael Omartian and Steve Barri signed the act to Warner Bros. that their ship came in. They were chosen to record a tune that would replace the theme song for the "Happy Days" TV show. Once Bill Haley's "Rock Around the Clock" had been pulled as the series' theme in favor of the marketable Pratt & McClain substitute, the brass ring was theirs.

Follow-ups were few and flops all, save Pratt & McClain's remake of Mitch Ryder's "Devil With the Blue Dress On" (#71, 1976). Their second and last known LP, *Pratt & McClain Featuring "Happy Days,"* appeared in 1976.

BRASS CONSTRUCTION
MOVIN'
(Randy Muller, Wade Williamston)
United Artists 775
No. 14 *June 26, 1976*

Our roots go back to the Gershwin Junior High in Brooklyn," the Guyana-born Randy Muller (keyboards, flute, percussion, vocals) told *Blues & Soul*'s John Abbey "My original roots were South American music, but as soon as I got to the States in 1963, I started being

exposed to R & B, jazz, rock and roll, everything. In 1967, I formed a quartet in school—me, Wade Williamston [bass], Larry Payton [drums, vocals], and Jessie Ward, Jr. [sax, vocals]—and we played a few school dances, youth clubs, things like that."

Two years later, Morris Price (trumpets, vocals) and Wayne Parris (trumpets, vocals) were added, and the growing group became the Dynamic Soul. Sandy Billups (vocals, conga), Michael "Mickey" Grudge (sax, vocals), and Joseph Arthur Wong (guitar) joined up in the early '70s, and the Brass Construction line-up was complete.

With the aid of Jeff Lane, their manager and the producer for B. T. Express (a group that frequently worked with Muller and Brass Construction), a unique sound was forged. "Two Timin' Woman," Brass Construction's debut single on Lane's Dock label, failed to sell, largely due to a lack of distribution. Follow-up

tapes cut at the Ultra-Sonic and Groove Sound Studios, however, found their way into the hands of the people at United Artists. Brass Construction's self-titled album was a big seller, and featured an unusual mixture of strings, horns, and fuzz guitar.

"Until ['Movin'] hit, we had a regular gig at a disco in New York, the Adonis," Muller recalled. "Then, all of a sudden we were stars!" While "Ha Cha Cha (Funktion)" (#51; R&B: #8, 1977) was the only other disk to cross over to the pop/rock listings, Brass Construction did go on to rack up over a dozen R & B hits and sell an impressive quantity of albums.

While no Brass Construction tracks have dusted the listings since the mid-'80s, Randy Muller has continued as a producer for B. T. Express, Iris, Gamet Mimms, Motivation, and the Spider's Webb, and was the brain behind such Big Apple funkers as First Circle, Funk Deluxe, and Skyy. In 1988, Randy formed the

Plaza label and put together a new group, BC Underground.

That same year, a number of the Brass Construction's chartings were remixed and reissued in Europe on the Syncopation label. "Movin'" returned once again to Britain's Top 30 in 1988.

STARLAND VOCAL BAND
AFTERNOON DELIGHT
(Bill Danoff)
Windsong 10588
No. 1 *July 10, 1976*

Lead singer Kathy "Taffy" Danoff of the Starland Vocal Band explained to *Rolling Stone* just how "Afternoon Delight" was conceived. "[My husband] Bill wrote it after having lunch at Clyde's in Washington, DC. It seems Clyde's has a menu called 'Afternoon Delight' with stuff like spiced shrimp and hot Brie with almonds. So Bill ate it . . . [then] explained to me what an 'Afternoon Delight' *should* be."

Oh sure, it was naughty, but nice. Conservative AM radio stations played it and consumers bought it up by the million. The group was awarded Grammys for "Best Arrangement for Vocals (Duos, Group or Chorus)" and "Best New Artists of the Year." Their *Starland Vocal Band* (1976) album sold well, and later 45s charted modestly—"California Day" (#66, 1976), "Hail! Hail! Rock and Roll" (#71, 1977), and "Loving You With My Eyes" (#71, 1980).

These Mamas & Papas clones were given a six-week CBS summer replacement TV show—a major shot at stardom. "Major mistake," said keyboardist/guitarist Jon Carroll (b. Mar. 1, 1957, Washington, DC). "To make a long story short, it was a bad show, and we knew it early on." The show did feature, as a comedy regular, one David Letterman. The Starland Vocal Band remained together through 1980, issuing predictable musical products.

Taffy (b. Kathleen Nivert, Oct. 24, 1944, Washington, DC) and co-lead singer Bill Danoff (b. May 7, 1946, Springfield, MA) had been working the DC music scene for some years before their meteoric rise. During the late '60s, Bill was the light and sound man at the Cellar Door. It was there that he met Chad Mitchell Trio member John Denver. Danoff slipped Denver some of his songs, and a friendship grew. Later, Bill and Taffy wrote "Take Me Home, Country Roads," a colossal hit for John. Years later, after the Danoff's recorded failed efforts as both Fat City (*Reincarnation* [1969]; *Welcome to Fat City* [1971]) and as Bill and Taffy (*Pass It On*; *Aces*), Denver returned the favor by signing the duo to his Windsong label. "Afternoon Delight" was the first single for Windsong.

Jon Carroll has continued to write songs. In 1982, he was particularly successful when Linda Ronstadt had a hit with his "Get Closer" (#32, 1982). Jon and the Starland Vocal Band's fourth member, singer Margot Chapman (b. Sept. 7, 1957, Honolulu) have since married. Bill and Taffy have since separated, though they have reappeared as Fat City during the late '80s in Washington, DC.

THIN LIZZY
THE BOYS ARE BACK IN TOWN
(Phil Lynott)
Mercury 73786
No. 12 *July 24, 1976*

Thin Lizzy was known for its well-crafted lyrics, hard-rock rills, raised fists, and anger. "The aggression is what I love," said Phil Lynott, the charismatic frontman and bass anchor of Thin Lizzy, in an exclusive interview conducted shortly before his death in 1986. "I get that feeling whenever I hit the stage. I'm sure I'd be locked up for doin' something if I didn't have rock and roll. It quiets me and we quiet the kids. I love that black leather, it feels so lovely on the skin . . . The power pose is to show I'm black, black Irish. The fist is the black power salute. I have to do it—I don't know, I hit the stage, and I'm in another world."

The only constants in the group's decade-plus history were lead singer/bassist Lynott (b. Aug. 20, 1951, Dublin) and drummer Brian Downey (b. Jan. 27, 1951, Dublin). "We go back to being school kids together, and had this thing called the Black Eagles," Lynott explained. "We'd cover the hit records, do some soul hits, and Elvis things, too." Phil and Brian separated briefly: Phil joined Garry Moore in Skid Row, and Brian played with Sugar Shack.

In 1969, Lynott and Downey formed Orphanage with guitarist Eric Bell (b. Sept. 3, 1947, Belfast), a one-time member of the legendary Van Morrison group, Them. Orphanage scored a hit in Ireland with their single "Morning Dew." In 1970, one of Decca Records' A & R men scouted the group out and signed them up. Thin Lizzy's first (and self-titled) album appeared in 1971, and by the next year, the band had moved to London to launch a successful worldwide career.

After their third album, Eric Bell dropped out and returned to Ireland. A number of fine musicians drifted in and out of the band over the years: John Cann, Andy Gee, Scott Gorman, Gary Moore, Mark Nauseef, Brian Robertson, John Sykes, Midge Ure, Darren Whaton, and Snowy White. In 1976, Thin Lizzy broke through in both the United States and U.K. with the *Jailbreak* album, which yielded "The Boys Are Back In Town." From that point on, the group racked up 16 hits in the U.K., including Top 10 smashes like "Waiting for an Alibi" and "Killers on the Loose." In the States, nine Thin Lizzy albums made the listings, but only "Cowboy Song" (#77, 1976), their immediate follow-up to "The Boys Are Back in Town," managed to make the Hot 100.

In 1978, Phil recorded *Solo in Soho*, his first solo album, and fronted Greedy Bastards with Garry Moore, Jimmy Bain, and Gary Horton. He continued to work both with Thin Lizzy and on his own throughout the '80s, until the band broke up in 1983. "No way, no way, at all am I gonna let Thin Lizzy die. It's just on hold," said Lynott.

In a last interview, Lynott said of his future: "I'm takin' it to the natural conclusion. I'm just gonna chase my imagination . . ." On January 4, 1986, Phil Lynott died of heart failure and pneumonia, complications from a drug overdose.

KEITH CARRADINE
I'M EASY
(Keith Carradine)
ABC 12117
No. 17 *August 7, 1976*

Keith, son of character actor John Carradine (the "Bard of the Boulevard," so labeled due to his habit of reciting Shakespeare while wandering the avenues), half brother of David Carradine (played Kwai Chang Caine, the soft-spoken martial arts-drifter in ABC TV's "Kung Fu"), and brother of Robert Carradine (acted in the *Revenge of the Nerds* series) was born in San Mateo, California, on August 8, 1949. He studied drama at Colorado State University and won a role in the L.A. production of *Hair* (1969-1970). Keith has appeared in films like *McCabe and Mrs. Miller* (1971), *Welcome to L.A.* (1977), *The Duelists* (1977), *Pretty Baby* (1978), *The Long Riders* (1980), *Southern Comfort* (1981), and *The Moderns* (1988). In Robert Altman's *Nashville* (1975), Carradine, in the role of a corrupt rock star, sings his own composition, "I'm Easy," which won an Academy Award for "Best Song." Way into the '80s, Keith continued his attempts to bore his way back into the pop charts, but all of his efforts to date have been fruitless.

Keith Carradine's daughter is actress Martha Plimpton, noted for her appearance in controversial commercials for Calvin Klein jeans and such flicks as *The Mosquito Coast* (1985) and *Parenthood* (1990).

VICKI SUE ROBINSON
TURN THE BEAT AROUND
(Pete and Gerald Jackson)
RCA 10562
No. 10 *August 14, 1976*

"I've paid my dues," Robinson told *Soul*'s Duane Folke. "I come from a very mixed background: my father, who is black, was an actor, and my mother, who is white, was a folksinger. She sang with famous folksingers like Woody Guthrie and Pete Seeger. When I was eight, I sang at the Philadelphia Folk Festival with my mother—I had to stand on a crate to reach the microphone."

Vicki (b. 1955, Philadelphia) grew up in Harlem, studying acting and dancing at New York's Neighborhood Playhouse. At 16, she appeared in the original Broadway production of *Hair*. She acted in Scott Fagan's rock musical *Soon* and played Mimi Farina in a production of *Long Time Coming, Long Time Gone*. She portrayed a frizzy-haired hippie in the Lloyd Bridges flick *To Find a Man* (1972), and had a bit part in Robert Mitchum's *Going Home* (1971).

VICKI SUE ROBINSON

Robert Stigwood noticed Vicki and landed a part for her in the original Broadway production of *Jesus Christ Superstar*. This led to a trip to Japan to model, sing commercials, perform with the Sadistic Mica Band, and record an album with Itsuru Shimoda. On her return to the Big Apple, Vicki worked as a waitress and a salesperson, and for *Ms.* magazine.

Next, Robinson formed a rock band with Wendy Simmons, and was discovered by Walter Schwartz, who in turn made arrangements for RCA to record Vicki. The disco-fied "Turn the Beat Around" was the first single from Robinson's debut LP, *Never Gonna Let You Go*; she was only 21 when her big hit bounced onto the charts. "Daylight" (#63, 1976) and "Hold Tight" (#67, 1977) cracked the Hot 100, but "Turn the Beat Around" remains the pinnacle of Vicki Sue Robinson's jam-packed life in the world of performance—thus far.

WILD CHERRY
PLAY THAT FUNKY MUSIC
(Robert Parissi)
Epic 50225
No. 1 *September 18, 1976*

Guitarist/lead singer Rob Parissi (b. Steubenville, OH) was laid up in a hospital in 1970. His bandmates came by to pay him a visit. "As they were getting ready to leave," Parissi recalled to Bob Gilbert and Gary Theroux in *The Top Ten*, "one said, 'Hey, we don't have a name for our band.' So I held up this box of cough drops, . . .

and said, 'You can call it this,' and pointed to the words 'wild cherry.' They liked it, and I hated it. I said, 'Are you serious?'"

In 1972, Terry Knight, manager of Grand Funk Railroad and head of the Brown Bag record label, heard Wild Cherry and had the guys cut some singles. A few years later, Jeff Barry produced "Voodoo Woman," an obscure 45 for A & M. None of these numbers gained much notice.

Soon the original Wild Cherries scattered. Parissi sold all of his equipment and became a manager of some steakhouses. Our tale could have ended here, but the gnawing itch for pop success got the best of Rob. He reformed Wild Cherry with musicians from the Steubenville, Ohio, area: keyboardist Mark Avsec, guitarist Bryan Bassett, drummer Ronald Beitle, and bassist Allen Wentz.

While playing Pittsburgh discos, the group made a discovery that would lead to their moment in Top 40-land. "We played too much rock, I guess," Rob explained, "because people came up to us and said, 'Play that funky music.' In the dressing room, I told the guys that we had to find a rock and roll way to play this disco stuff. Our drummer said, 'Well, I guess it's like they say, "you gotta play that funky music, white boy."' I said, 'That's a great idea.'"

Parissi crafted a number around the phrase, and the band went into a studio to record "Play That Funky Music" and a cover version of the Commodores' 1974 hit, "I Feel Sanctified." The latter was meant to be the "A" side. Fortunately, Mike Belkin and Carl Maduri at Sweet City, a Pittsburgh-based production company, suggested that "Funky Music" should be the unit's first single for Epic Records.

"Funky" sold more than 2 million copies and won the group two Grammy nominations, for "Best New Vocal Group" and "Best R & B Performance by a Group or Duo." A number of Hot 100 heavies followed: "Baby Don't You Know" (#43, 1977), "Hot to Trot" (#95, 1977), "Hold On" (#61, 1977), and "I Love My Music" (#69, 1978). Wild Cherry's first three LPs—*Wild Cherry* (1977), *Electrified Funk* (1977), and *I Love My Music* (1978)—were healthy sellers as well.

"After that, we started to overproduce our records," Parissi admitted, "and that's probably why we never had another major hit. A lot of that was my fault, striving to sound different. We cut our [fourth and] last album in February 1979, and then just kind of fell apart."

Rob Parissi currently lives in Mingo Junction, Ohio, and works as a morning DJ at a station in Wheeling, West Virginia. "My bags are packed," he told David Mills of the *Washington Times*. "All I need is material. I'd like to get just enough hits . . . to build a catalog and be visible for a while—to know that I was there long enough for people to remember who the hell I was."

Parissi and crew have not returned to the media-driven forefront, though, in 1988, a hard rock outfit from Riverside, California, named Roxanne relodged Wild Cherry's moment in the charts (#63). This reappearance was followed three years later by white-rapper Vanilla Ice's Top 10 showing with "Play That Funky Music" (#4, 1991).

SILVER
WHAM-BAM (SHANG-A-LANG)
(Rick Giles)
Arista 0189
No. 16 *October 2, 1976*

Singer/guitarist John Batdorf was entranced with the sounds of country-rock from the moment of its birth. In the late '60s, Batdorf met up with Mark Rodney. Both were situated in Los Angeles, and fans of Crosby, Stills & Nash. For five years, starting in 1971, the Atlantic, Asylum, and Arista labels issued unsuccessful singles and albums featuring the dudes acoustic music. Rodney, discouraged by the critical and commercial drubbing, dropped out of sight.

Batdorf bounced back in 1976. John had met keyboardist Brent Mydland at an Eric Andersen recording session, and the two agreed to join forces. Guitarist Greg Collier, bassist Tom Leadon, and drummer Harry Stinson were added to form Silver, a country-rock outfit. Tom Sellers—a member of Daryl Hall's '60s group Gulliver—who had produced the final Batdorf & Rodney album, was brought in for Silver's first and only album; Sellers had produced hits for THE ELECTRIC INDIAN and THE ASSEMBLED MULTITUDE.

"Wham-Bam," an atypically pop-oriented number, clicked, unlike Silver's two subsequent singles. By year's end, Batdorf and company were finished. Stinson went on to play with the Shot in the Dark band and to do session work for Jay Ferguson, Peter Frampton, Juice Newton, and the Pointer Sisters. Mydland, for several years, has been with THE GRATEFUL DEAD.

WALTER MURPHY & THE BIG APPLE BAND
A FIFTH OF BEETHOVEN
(Arranged by Walter Murphy)
Private Stock 45073
No. 1 *October 9, 1976*

Walter was born in New York City in 1952. At the age of four, he was taking piano lessons from Rosa Rio, an organist for radio soap operas. By the time he entered the Manhattan School of Music, Murphy was quite proficient on the keyboards, and was writing arrangements for Doc Severinsen's "Tonight Show" orchestra. After graduation, Walter entered the world of advertising, writing jingles for Lady Arrow, Korvette's, Revlon, Woolworth's, and Viasa Airlines. After a spell of concocting B-grade movie scores for made-for-TV flicks like "The Savage Bees" (1976) and "The Night They Took Miss Beautiful" (1977), Murphy approached Major Records with disco-fied Christmas tunes. A few singles like "DiscoBells" were issued.

Early in 1976, Murphy acted on what he described to Bob Gilbert and Gary Theroux in *The Top Ten* as a "crazy idea to take symphonic music and combine it with contemporary rhythm." The idea was not totally new: B. Bumble & The Stingers clicked with a rockin' take on Tchaikovsky's "Nutcracker Suite," Tom Parker's APOLLO 100 had hit paydirt in 1972 with "Joy," a pseudo-rock rendition of Bach's "Jesu, Joy of Man's Desiring." With Walt playing nearly every instrument, a demo tape of some disco-styled classical works was made. Larry Uttal at Private Stock Records took an interest. An album's worth of the stuff was cooked up—again with Murphy playing nearly every instrument. Label men informed him that a group name was needed—ergo, The Big Apple Band; a name already being utilized. The bouncy Beethoven number was released as a single, and Walter Murphy had his one moment in the sun. The album, *A Fifth of Beethoven*, peaked at number 15 on the "Top Pop" album charts. Similar treatments of Gershwin's "Rhapsody in Blue" and Rimsky-Korsakov's "Flight of the Bumble Bee" (#44, 1976, billed as "Flight '76") met with much less enthusiasm.

When last observed, Walter Murphy was with MCA Records. His take on the "Theme From E. T. (The Extra

Terrestrial)," featured in the Steven Spielberg flick, charted at number 47 on *Billboard*'s Hot 100 in 1982.

Financially fortunate is Walt for when his tune peaked in popularity, he signed a seemingly fluff contract giving the rights to his song being included in the soundtrack to a low-budget disco flick. That flick, *Saturday Night Fever* (1977), clicked big, with soundtrack sales totaling 25,000,000. Analysts wager that Murphy need never earn another dollar.

RICK DEES & HIS CAST OF IDIOTS
DISCO DUCK (PART 1)
(Rick Dees)
RSO 857
No. 1 *October 16, 1976*

Rigdon Osmond Dees III has made money for years as a "personality" DJ—and as Rick Dees, the man behind a string of nutty novelty numbers.

Rick attended North Carolina University, specializing in radio and TV studies. His first spot was at WBGB, in his hometown of Winston-Salem, North Carolina. As the "move-'em-out" morning man on WMPS in Memphis, Dees devised an array of wacky promotions. Reportedly, he holds some sort of world record for whipping up the largest fruitcake (3,000 lbs.), jelly doughnut (300 lbs.), and lollipop (150 lbs.).

"I was working out in a gym in Memphis when disco was coming out," Dees explained to Fred Bronson in *The Billboard Book of Number One Hits*, "and I also worked in a club called Chesterfield's, telling jokes and spinning records. The more I played the songs, the more I knew it might be time for a disco parody. One of the guys who worked out in the gym did a great duck voice, and I remembered a song called 'The Duck' [by JACKIE LEE] back in the '60s, so I said, how about a 'Disco Duck'?"

Dees went home and tossed the idea around for an afternoon. Three months later, he walked the idea into Fretone Records, a small label owned by Estelle Axton, founder of the Stax organization. "Actually, they thought I was an idiot," Dees told Bob Shannon and John Javna in *Behind the Hits*. "I went into the studio with a bunch of song ideas, all of them warped. First, I hit them with my song about Elvis exploding, 'He Ate too Many Jelly Doughnuts.' And later, 'Disco Duck.'" First out of the stall was an item called "The National Wet Off." It bombed, but that darn "Disco Duck" didn't: once it became popular throughout the South, RSO acquired the track for national release.

Everywhere one went, that quacker could be heard—except in Memphis, where rival stations refused to play the disk and where Rick's own WMPS forbade Dees from spinning it. "I talked about it on my morning radio show," Dees told Bronson, "and the station manager came in and said, 'We think that's a conflict of interest—you're fired.'"

WHBQ-AM, his former station's chief competitor, swiftly hired Rick. Dees later transferred to KHJ in Los Angeles and has since moved to KIIS-FM, the top radio station in the City of Angels; where he plays "the best of the eight-dees and nine-dees." Rick has hosted TVs "Solid Gold," for a season, ABC's late-night series "Into the Night," for a moment, and currently appears on an internationally syndicated Top 40 countdown radio program for the United Stations.

As for follow-ups, Rick Dees still finds the time to issue amusing musings like "Dis-Gorilla" (#56, 1977), "Big Foot" (1978), "Barely White," and "Eat My Shorts" (#75, 1984) b/w "Get Nekked."

BARRY DEVORZON & PERRY BOTKIN, JR.
NADIA'S THEME (THE YOUNG AND THE RESTLESS)
(Barry DeVorzon & Perry Botkin, Jr.)
A & M 1865
No. 8 *December 12, 1976*

There is quite a history to this eerie melodic movement called "Nadia's Theme." DeVorzon and Botkin originally conceived this instrumental number for a film, *Bless the Beasts and Children* (1972). It was titled "Cotton's Dream" and featured on the movie's soundtrack, then basically forgotten. A staffer involved in the production of a new TV daytime soap, "The Young and the Restless," acquired the rights to the Barry and Perry piece. Renamed in honor of the tube tearjerker, the work went on to become the most recognized theme in all of soapdom.

During the 1976 Summer Olympics, ABC-TV used the soap theme during playbacks of the gymnastic feats of Romania's 14-year-old Nadia Comaneci. The response was so great that A & M Records issued the number as a single. Two competing albums appeared in 1976—one issued by A & M and the other by Arista—the title for both was *Nadia's Theme (The Young and the Restless)*; both albums sold well. Another DeVorzon-Botkin instrumental, "Bless the Beasts and Children" (#82, 1977), followed before Barry and Perry quietly returned to their former behind-the-scenes music careers.

Barry had been involved in the music biz for quite a while before his big moment. RCA Victor (1957-1959) and Columbia Records (1959-1961) issued some of his teen-idol sides. With Botkin arranging, DeVorzon and two others, as BARRY & THE TAMERLANES, created a momentary stir on the pop charts with their debut single, "I Wonder What She's Doing Tonight" (#21, 1963).

Reportedly, Barry headed Valiant Records, was involved in the success of THE CASCADES and managed and eventually married singer/songwriter SHELBY FLINT. In 1960, Perry was a member with Gil Garfield and rockabilly legend Ray Campi of in the McCoy Boys, and cut one 45, "Our Man in Havana."

Over the years, DeVorzon and Botkin have each worked as an arranger, producer, and writer for Valiant, Warner Bros., and A & M.

In 1983, a California jury awarded Barry $241,000 in damages against A & M because the label had failed to credit DeVorzon as the co-writer of "Nadia's Theme" on first pressings of the single.

DAVID DUNDAS
JEANS ON
(David Dundas, Roger Greenaway)
Chrysalis 2094
No. 17 *January 29, 1977*

David Dundas is an aristocrat, born in 1943 in Oxford, England, the son of the Marquess of Zetland. He sang with a skiffle band in high school, but it was acting that captured his adolescent attention. He spent three years in drama school, bummed around France, and wound up in bed with Judy Geeson. Figuratively speaking, that is: an intimate scene with Geeson in the Deborah Kerr-David Niven flick *Prudence and the Pill* (1968) was the peak of David's acting career.

Before mothballing this phase of his existence, Dundas joined the Royal Shakespeare Company for a few performances. "I was really a committed actor," Davy told *Melody Maker*. "I used to be quite good, but I gradually became worse. Mentally, it's a precipitous way of living, and though I did some plays and television things, they got worse until I decided I wanted to get into music."

David turned to the world of advertising and jingle-writing. "Jeans On" was, in effect, one long commercial for Brutus Jeans, and the ad itself was conceived by Dundas. To flesh out the ditty, a jingle-juggling comrade, producer, and songwriter, Roger Greenaway half of the singing team DAVID & JONATHAN and co-writer of hits for THE ENGLISH CONGREGATION, Fortunes, New Seekers, THE PIPKINS, WHITE PLAINS. . . .

"I like doing jingles because if you get a good one, it's a sort of musical theater, like a mini-film," Dundas explained. "The ultimate [now] is to get good songs and a good band together . . . This isn't going to be a one-off thing."

Two unremarkable and never to chart albums were issued. Dave did return to his homeland listings with a second hit, "Another Funny Honeymoon." Thereafter, another career change seemed in order: writing scores for the silver screen. Dundas has supplied the musical seasoning to *Dark City*, a British flick, *Withnail and I* (1986), and *How to Get Ahead in Advertising (1989)*.

DAVID SOUL
DON'T GIVE UP ON US
(Tony Macauley)
Private Stock 45129
No. 1 *April 6, 1977*

Born in Chicago, on August 28, 1943, the son of a Lutheran minister and diplomatic advisor to the U. S. State Department, Davey Solberg moved about quite a lot when he was small. In the '60s, Dave dropped out of college to become a folksinger. He apparently developed a sizable reputation, since he soon landed work as the opening act for the Byrds and the Doors. He was also aware that you needed a gimmick to be noticed in the world of music. To this end, Dave sent a photo of himself in a ski mask to the William Morris Agency. They took the bait, and so did Merv Griffin, who eagerly had David perform as "The Covered Man" on his TV program a good 20 times. MGM Records released some singles, but none of them charted.

Dave removed his covering and a casting director, noting his fair-haired ruggedness, offered him a slot

opposite Bobby Sherman in the role of his younger brother, on the TV series "Here Come the Brides." A brief stay with the "Owen Marshall, Counselor at Law" series, starring Lee Majors, followed before Soul signed on with Paul Michael Glaser to star in his biggest small-screen success, "Starsky and Hutch." Playing hip bachelor/detective Ken "Hutch" Hutchinson on this teen-centered cops and robbers show, David Soul became visible and popular.

Again, he tried to hawk his vocal wares. Private Stock Records provided the medium and the songwriter, British tunesmith Tony Macauley, who created and produced all of Dave's U.S. chart entries.

"Going in With My Eyes Open" (#54, 1977) and "Silver Lady" (#52, 1977) were solid follow-ups, and did extremely well in England. About the time Detective Ken was asked to turn in his badge, Dave also shut down his recording activities. No one has yet confirmed rumors that Soul has been seen performing with a certain ski mask at semi-seedy coffeehouses as "The Covered Man." David did, however, go on to appear in two more TV series in the mid-'80s— "Casablanca," as cafe owner Rick Blaine and "The Yellow Rose," with Cybill Shepherd—and his likeness has been seen in such TV movies as "Salem's Lot," "Rage," and "World War III."

In 1989, Dave played the part of Wes Grayson in the short-lived NBC series "Unsub."

WILLIAM BELL

WILLIAM BELL
TRYIN' TO LOVE TWO
(William Bell, Paul Mitchell)
Mercury 73839
No. 10 *April 30, 1977*

He was born William Yarborough on July 16, 1939, in Memphis, Tennessee, just a few blocks from where Stax Studios would eventually set up shop. William attended Booker T. Washington High and was a member of the Central Baptist Choir. While still in school, he formed the Del Rios with Harrison Austin (tenor), David Brown (bass), and Melvin Jones (baritone). They won second prize in a talent contest and signed a recording contract with Les Bihari's Meteor Records. "Alone on a Rainy Night" was shipped, but quickly sank from sight, so the Del Rios disbanded. As a solo artist, Bell worked for two years at the Plantation Inn before joining Phineas Newborn's band in the late '50s as a vocalist.

"I was studying to be a doctor, but during the summer of 1961 I went to New York with Phineas on a job, and I started writing a few songs," Bell told *Goldmine*'s Almost Slim. "When I got back to Memphis, Chips Moman, who was a local producer/songwriter [creator

of TROY SHONDELL's "This Time"], asked me if I wanted to do a session for a new label called Stax. I had nothing to lose."

Four songs were recorded that day; the country-soul classic "You Don't Miss Your Water" (#95, 1962) became a heavy southern hit, and the largest chart-mover in Stax's brief history. The response convinced Bell to bury his medical ambitions. Before Bell rocked the pop and R & B listings with his "Tryin' to Love Two," he had a slew of gritty Stax singles grease the pop and R & B charts in the late '60s: "Share What You Got" (R&B: #27, 1966), "Never Like This Before" (R&B: #29, 1966), "Everybody Loves a Winner" (#95; R&B: #18, 1967), "A Tribute to a King" (#86; R&B: #16, 1968), "I Forgot to Be Your Lover" (#45; R&B: #10, 1969), and "My Whole World Is Falling Down" (R&B: #39,1969).

William Bell has also had success singing duets with Janice Bullock, Mitty Collier, Mavis Staples, Carla Thomas, and Judy Clay. Bell wrote the bluesy "Born Under a Bad Sign," Albert King's signature tune, and he was the one who introduced Booker T. Jones, his church's organist, to Stax.

In 1986, Billy Idol reworked Bell's "I Forgot to Be Your Lover" into his Top 10 hit, "To Be a Lover."

Currently, Bell and his manager operate the Peachtree and Wilbe record labels, as well as the Bel-Wyn Management company. Recordings are sporadic.

BILL CONTI
GONNA FLY NOW (THEME FROM "ROCKY")
(Bill Conti, Carol Connors, Ayn Robbins)
United Artists 940
No. 1 *July 2, 1977*

William Conti was born April 13, 1942 in Providence, Rhode Island. Bill's father was an accomplished pianist, and piano lessons was a must for the boy. He majored in piano and composition at Louisiana State University, and earned a master's degree at Juilliard School of Music in New York.

In the mid-'60s—under the influence of Hugo Weisgall, his composition instructor at Julliard—Conti moved to Rome, where he directed the Italian version of *Hair,* wrote the music to *The Garden of the Finzi-Continis* (1971)—winner of an Oscar as "Best Foreign Language Film"; and arranged, composed, and conducted other creations such as *Liquid Subway, Candidate for Killing,* and *Bloom in Love.* In 1972, Bill and wife returned to the United States to score *Harry and Tonto* (1972), starring Art Carney, and Sylvester Stallone's *Rocky* (1976). The soundtrack went to number four on *Billboard*'s top pop albums chart. Conti has since scored Stallone's *Rocky* sequels II, III, and V, *F.I.S.T.* (1978) and *Paradise Alley* (1978), and other films such as *An Unmarried Woman* (1978), *The Karate Kid* (1984), *Baby Boom* (1987), *Broadcast News* (1987), *For Your Eyes Only* (1981)—which garnered Conti his second Oscar nomination for his co-authored title tune, and *The Adventures of Huck Finn* (1993). He received an Academy Award for his music to the adaptation of Tom Wolfe's *The Right Stuff* (1983). Bill has also written the themes for a number of TV series: "Dallas," "Dynasty," "Falcon Crest," "Lifestyles of the Rich and Famous," and "Cagney & Lacey."

In 1995, Bill Conti was given the Golden Soundtrack Award for his lifetime achievements by ASCAP.

ALAN O'DAY
UNDERCOVER ANGEL
(Alan O'Day)
Pacific 001
No. 1 *July 9, 1977*

"There was a local hit on the radio called 'He Did Me Wrong, but He Did Me Right' by Patti Dahlstrom," Alan O'Day told Fred Bronson in *The Billboard Book of Number One Hits.* "In that song, she used the word 'undercover.' I thought it was a neat idea. I've always loved things about angels, too, so the words came together." O'Day's own "Undercover Angel," a hypnagogic, spacey tune with sexual undertones, shot to the top of the charts.

Alan was born in Hollywood on October 3, 1940. As a tot, he'd tap on a tiny xylophone until Ma and Pa turned him loose on a piano. Spike Jones was his favorite—that is, until he saw *Blackboard Jungle* (1955), with Sidney Poitier, those delinquent teens, and that "Rock Around the Clock" noise provided by spit-curled Bill Haley. Thereafter, while attending Coachella Valley Union High School, O'Day played in rock and roll bands with names like the Imperials, the Renees, and the Shoves.

While working at a $1.50 an hour job at a nearby recording studio, Alan met Sidney Goldstein, who liked the kind of tunes that Alan was knocking out and signed him on as a writer for his Viva Music publishing firm. O'Day eventually wrote tunes for Cher, Dobie Gray, and Bobby Sherman, and had several of his numbers popularized by Helen Reddy ("Angle Baby") and the Righteous Brothers ("Rock and Roll Heaven").

ALAN O'DAY

In 1977, Ed Silvers, the president of Warner Bros. Music, gave Alan the chance to record some of his songs—Warner had recently purchased Viva, and was launching a new label for its own staff songwriters. Alan O'Day was the first artist to record for Pacific Records, and "Undercover Angel" was the first thing he etched in vinyl.

Despite the tune being banned by numerous radio stations, America ate up "Undercover Angel," but no second helping was called for. Alan O'Day tried hard to re-entice listeners, rapidly writing of "Soldiers of Fortune" and "People Who Talk to Themselves," but the verdict was in and Alan was strongly encouraged to leave the media via the back door and pronto.

HOT
ANGEL IN YOUR ARMS
(Terry Woodford, Clayton Ivey, Tom Brasfield)
Big Tree 16085
No. 6 *July 16, 1977*

"The whole thing was an accident," Gwen Owens told Leonard Pitts, Jr. of *Soul* magazine. "None of it was planned at all. We accidentally happened to be from three ethnic backgrounds [Gwen is black, Cathy Carson is white, and Juanita Curiel is Mexican], we accidentally happened to choose the material we chose on our album, which accidentally happened to be commercial."

Cathy (b. Oct. 7, 1953) and Gwen (b. June 19, 1953) met in the early '70s in Los Angeles while auditioning for Wolfman Jack's "Shock & Rock" tour. They won the slot and became Sugar & Spice (not to be confused with the '60s recording act of the same name). By 1976, they were making appearances on BILL COSBY's show, which brought them to the attention of the folks at Big Tree Records. Juanita (b. Feb. 25, 1953) was added to the group, and Sugar & Spice became Hot. An album was cut in Muscle Shoals, Alabama, with "Angel in Your Arms" issued as their debut single. "Angel," with its catchy chorus, catty but coy lyrics, and slick pop styling, clicked with both pop/rock (#6) and R & B (#29) listeners. For a week of Sundays, Hot was hot. But then even the sun, they say, is cooling at a frightening pace....

Over the next two years, a pile of 45s and three LPs were released. "The Right Feeling at the Wrong Time" (#65; R&B: #58, 1977) and "You Brought the Woman Out of Me" (#71, 1977) made respectable showings, but nothing further made it to *Billboard*'s charts.

PETER MCCANN
DO YOU WANNA MAKE LOVE
(Peter McCann)
20th Century Fox 2335
No. 5 *August 6, 1977*

Peter McCann, a Connecticut native, sang in barbershop quartets and liked Cole Porter plus other tunesmiths from the '30s and '40s. In 1971, while attending Fairview University on a glee club scholarship, Pete hooked up with the critically underrated, folk-rockin' Repairs. The group was produced by Andrew Loog Oldham—noted for his managing/production work with the Rolling Stones—and recorded two highly sought-after LPs for the Motown subsidiaries Rare Earth and Mowest. Despite the high quality of their sound and material, neither album sold well enough to justify the group's continued existence.

In 1973, after the Repairs had proved unsalvageable, McCann joined the staff of ABC Music Publishers. Nothing much happened until Pete suggestively applied his voice to his self-penned (and banned in Bismarck, ND) "Do You Wanna Make Love." Meanwhile, Jennifer Warnes, a former actress and lead player in the Los Angeles production of *Hair*, had a Top 10 hit with a McCann composition, "Right Time of the Night" (#7, 1977). For a brief period, each of McCann's songs shared positions on the *Billboard* pop listings.

Warnes' "Right Time" proved to be the start of a sizable string of hits, the most prominent of which was to be "Up Where We Belong" (#1, 1982), her duet with Joe Cocker. McCann has yet to rechart.

MERI WILSON
TELEPHONE MAN
(Meri Wilson)
GRT 127
No. 18 *August 20, 1977*

Born in Japan and raised in Marietta, Georgia, Meri played piano, cello, and flute from childhood. In the mid-'70s, after graduating from Indiana University as a music major, Meri began singing and playing Anne Murray and Crystal Gayle type tunes in night spots; supplementing her work as a daytime Dallas jingle singer. "Telephone Man," a novelty number laden with cognitively inviting innuendoes, was her first record.

"I swore for years that I'd never admit in public that I dated the telephone man, but the truth is, yes I did," said Meri to Bruce Nash and Allan Zullo, authors of *The Wacky Top 40*. "So I wrote a silly song about it. I shouldn't say anything more about him because I'm happily married—but not to the telephone man." The "Telephone" tune would eventually be produced by a

duo with One-Hit Wonder pasts of their own—
BOOMER CASTLEMAN, marginally known for "Judy Mae"
and BLOODROCK's Jim Rutledge, of "D.O.A." note. They
had met at a demo session arranged by famed country
producer/writer Allen Reynolds; nothing came of the
recordings made that day.

For a mere $228 Meri and the boys recorded "Tele-
phone Man," in a Dallas video studio.

"I didn't see the likelihood of this song becoming a
hit, and I didn't realize how unique the song was," said
Meri. "Boomer took it to 17 record companies, and
they all scoffed at the song and said, 'no way.' And
Boomer told me, 'Don't worry. We'll create our own
label and put it out.'"

Acting as Meri's manager, Boomer dropped copies
of "Telephone Man" at radio stations all across the state
of Texas.

"I was in a Dallas store when I heard 'Telephone
Man,'" she said. "I was shocked. So Boomer and I kept
calling the radio stations, acting as typical listeners and
asking them to play the song again and again."

Soon GRT picked up the disk for national distribution and a hit was made.

"Midnight in Memphis" and other successive singles, failed to reignite. An album titled *Telephone Man
a.k.a. First Take* was issued before her departure from
the nation's footlights.

Currently, Meri Wilson is a choral director at a high
school in Atlanta. Evenings she sings with a jazz grouping called the Hotlanta Jazz Singers. Meri adds: "It was
fun to have a hit record, but in my heart I was really disappointed that I couldn't have had a real piece of music
out there."

RAM JAM
BLACK BETTY
(Huddie Ledbetter)
Epic 50357
No. 18 *September 3, 1977*

Ram Jam's main man, guitarist Bill Bartlett (b. 1949)
complained to *Illinois Entertainer's* Don Case that civil-
rights groups like NAACP and CORE were calling for a
boycott of "Black Betty." "[They say that] 'Black Betty'
is considered an insult to black womanhood, but that's
a lot of hogwash. Leadbelly [Huddie Ledbetter] was
black, and he wrote all of the lyrics. No blacks that I've
talked to find the song offensive."

Despite the protest, "Black Betty" became a Top 40
hit. Nonetheless, as Bartlett noted, ". . . Just over 40 percent of all rock stations [would] not play it due to the
boycott."

Ten years earlier, Bartlett had been the lead guitarist
with THE LEMON PIPERS, known the globe over for their

bubblegummy and allegedly drug-drenched "Green
Tambourine." "Well, I must admit I still hate that song
as much now as I did then," Bill told Case. "But the idea
of playing in such a band no longer bothers me—after
all, Joe Walsh was with the Ohio Express at the same
time."

After the Lemon trip soured, Bill went into semiretirement, and passed the time by soaking up the sounds
of Albert Ammons, James Burton, Cliff Gallop, and
Leadbelly. One of the tunes he happened across was
Leadbelly's "Black Betty." Bill cut a demo of the
song and left his Ohio farm for New York City.
Through a series of coincidences, Bartlett met the
brains behind the bubblegum phenomenon, Super K
Productions, Jerry Kasenetz and Jeff Katz. Jerry and Jeff
immediately spotted the hit potential of the old Leadbelly tune.

For their brief duration, Ram Jam was composed of
Bartlett, bassist Howie Arthur Blauvelt (an ex-member
of an early Billy Joel/United Artist unit, the Hassles),
drummer Pete Charles, and lead singer Myke Scavone,
a fellow that Bill met hitchhiking on the New Jersey
turnpike. Two LPs—*Ram Jam* (1974) and *Portrait of an
Artist as a Young Ram* (1975)—were released, and only
two other 45s—"Keep Your Hands on the Wheel" and
"Pretty Poison"—are know to have been issued.

In the spring of 1990, a remixed version of the tune
charted Top 20 in Britain as by The American Ram Jam
Band.

FLOATERS
FLOAT ON
(Marvin Willis, Arnold Ingram, James Mitchell, Jr.)
ABC 12284
No. 2 *September 17, 1977*

Fame did not float in gently for this act; it ran fleet of
foot. In an instant the Floaters were big-time; in another they weren't. Charles Clark (first tenor), Larry Cunningham (second tenor), and brothers Paul (baritone)
and Ralph Mitchell (lead) were born and raised in
Detroit. As the pre-teen Junior Floaters, they danced
and lip-synched their way through local gigs until, 13
years later, they were discovered by Arnold "Brimstone"
Ingram, James Mitchell, Jr., and Marvin Willis of the
Detroit Emeralds. Brim, Jim, and Marvin arranged for
the Floaters to open for the Emeralds tour, and hooked
them up with ABC Records. Once ABC signed the
group up, Ingram, Mitchell, and Willis wrote, produced, and arranged the tunes for the Floaters' debut
album. "Float On," extracted from that first album, sold
well, but no future product could match that feat.

"It was a refreshingly different sound, at the time,"
Cunningham told *Blues & Soul*. "And because 'Float

On' was our first record, it became a burden—one that we still haven't gotten off our backs. Now, don't get me wrong—without it, we'd be nowhere today. And hundreds of groups would give their lives for such a record! I think the mistake we made afterwards, though, was to try to better 'Float On.' And it can't be done."

The group has remained afloat. "As long as we can keep a good stage show together we can continue to work," Larry Cunningham told *Black Star*'s Frederick Douglas Murphy, "whether we have another hit record or not."

SANFORD/TOWNSEND BAND
SMOKE FROM A DISTANT FIRE
(Sanford, Townsend, Stewart)
Warner Bros. 8370
No. 9 *September 17, 1977*

Aspiring songwriters Eddie Sanford (keyboards, vocals) and Johnny Townsend (lead vocals, keyboards) met in Los Angeles in the mid-'70s and decided to form a band. John was an old pro, having played in the mid-'60s psychedelic group Dead Sea Fruits. He had also done session work, most notably with Loggins & Messina and Steve Harley & Cockney Rebel. With seasoned studio players like Otis Hale (guitar, woodwinds), Roger Johnson (guitar), Jim Varley (bass), and Jerry Rightmer (drums), the Sanford/Townsend Band was complete. Expectations were high. For their first LP, the two writers had a bag full of tunes, Jerry Wexler and Barry Beckett as producers, and access to the famed Muscle Shoals recording studio.

"Smoke From a Distant Fire," the catchy opening track on their debut album, was a very 70s-sounding moment. Two other less-inspired LPs—*Duoglide* (1977) and *Nail Me to the Wall* (1979), minus both Wexler and Beckett—followed, as did several singles. Nothing gathered much notice, and the band folded in late 1979. Sanford has since worked as a back-up for Michael McDonald; Townsend was a charter member in Cher's short-lived hard-rock experiment, Black Rose, and later did studio work for LAUREN WOOD.

DEBBY BOONE
YOU LIGHT UP MY LIFE
(Joe Brooks)
Warner Bros. 8455
No. 1 *October 15, 1977*

Like it or not, "You Light Up My Life," composed by Joe Brooks—a one-time $500,000-a-year advertising man —spent more time at number one than any song since Guy Mitchell's 1956 hit "Singing the Blues." It garnered

DEBBY BOONE

a Grammy Award for "Song of the Year," one for Debby Boone as "Best New Artist of the Year," and an Academy Award for "Best Original song" of 1977. "Light" eventually sold more than 5 million copies worldwide, making it the biggest-selling record of the year and the biggest-selling single in Warner Bros. history.

Born Deborah Anne Boone—the third daughter to Shirley and Pat Boone and granddaughter to country staple Red Foley—in Hackensack, New Jersey, on September 26, 1956, Debby was surrounded from birth by the sounds of music. During her teen years, Debby and her three sisters toured state fairs, theaters, and revivals with their parents. The Boones—Cherry, Lindy, Laury, and Debby—cut some white-soul singles for Motown and later for Warner Bros./Curb, but none of these efforts sold well, so each clan member moved onto other interests. Debby still wanted to pursue music. MIKE CURB—producer, anti-drug crusader, and future lieutenant governor of California—obliged, offering her the title song of a low-budget Columbia Picture.

Deb has had a few modest pop chartings—"California" (#50, 1978) and "God Knows" (#74, 1978)—and a few major country successes—"My Heart Has a Mind of Its Own" (#10, 1979), "Free to Be Lonely Again" (#14, 1980), and "Are You on the Road to Loving Me Again?" (#1, 1980)—but has yet to find another "Light" in her life. She is married to Gabriel Ferrer, the son of actor Jose Ferrer and jazz/pop singer Rosemary Clooney. In the late '80s, Deb decided to do acting instead. She resurfaced in 1990 as Maria in a Broadway stage revival of *The Sound of Music*.

RONNIE MCDOWELL
THE KING IS GONE
(Ronnie McDowell, Lee Morgan)
Scorpion 135
No. 13 *October 22, 1977*

Ronnie McDowell's unique talent in the world of Top 40 pop is that he is—or was—an Elvis impersonator, and one of the best. Ronnie told *Country Music*'s Kip Kirby that following a session, Presley producer Felton Jarvis told him, "Lord, son, I only wish Elvis had been able to sing that good." McDowell's ability to reproduce the sounds of the legendary one brought him overnight success, screaming hordes, a healthy hit, and a stigma.

He was born in Fountain Head, Tennessee, 30 miles outside of Nashville. While in the Navy in 1968, Ronnie started writing songs and singing "sound-alikes"; his Elvis medley always brought the house down. On his return to civilian life, McDowell headed to Nashville in hopes of peddling his songs and finding his fortune. ROY DRUSKY, Jean Sheppard, Billy Walker, and others would record his tunes, but Ronnie continued working as a commercial sign painter.

In the mid-'70s, McDowell wrangled a job as a clean-up boy at the Chart and Scorpion labels. He cut a sound-alike record of Roy Orbison's "Only the Lonely" in 1976, but the disk stiffed.

When Elvis died, Ronnie and a friend, Lee Morgan, quickly penned a homage to the King. At first, no one was interested in doing a tribute single, so McDowell bankrolled a recording session himself and shopped the acetate around to Nashville radio stations. Within hours, phone lines were lighting up; within weeks, Ronnie was appearing at Los Angeles's Palomino Club and on "American Bandstand," "Midnight Special," and "Solid Gold."

"It was frightening," McDowell recalled to Kirby. "People were coming to my concerts in droves, but they were really comin' to see Elvis. . . . Sometimes I could not hear a note I was singing." A few more ersatz-Elvis platters made the country listings, but Ronnie soon wearied of the gimmick. "I was losing my identity. I wanted to sound like myself, . . . but everyone else wanted to hear another Elvis. I felt like I was beating a dead horse. I knew I had to get away from it or it would destroy my career."

Ronnie has successfully broken free of what he has called "the Elvis thing," and gone on to major C & W success. More than 30 of his singles have made the country listings In the late '80s, Ronnie teamed up with Conway Twitty for a remake of "It's Only Make Believe" and Jerry Lee Lewis to cut his tune "Never too Old to Rock'n'Roll."

And while he occasionally reaches into his sound-alike tool kit—as he did for the short-lived "Elvis" TV series in 1989—McDowell feels that he is finally his own man.

In the mid-'90s, Ronnie has slowed down, turning the limelight over to his son, Ronnie Dean McDowell, a member of Six Shooter.

PAUL NICHOLAS
HEAVEN ON THE SEVENTH FLOOR
(Dominic Bugatti, Frank Musker)
RSO 878
No. 6 *November 26, 1977*

A performer of stage, screen, and vinyl, Paul Nicholas (b. Paul Beuselinck, Dec. 3, 1945, Peterborough, England) launched his show biz career at the age of 16—pounding piano as "Paul Dean" with wild man Screaming Lord Sutch & The Savages. Three years later Paul was making recording efforts as "Oscar." In 1967, he landed a role in the London cast of *Hair*, which he followed with the title role in *Jesus Christ Superstar* (1972) and a brief stay in the cast of *Grease*.

Nineteen seventy-five was a big year: Nicholas appeared with ANN-MARGRET in *Tommy*, with ROGER DALTREY in *Lisztomania*, and with EDD BYRNE, DAVID ESSEX, and ADAM FAITH in *Stardust*. RSO Records offered to record some sides; the resulting "Reggae Like It Used to Be," "Dancing With the Captain," and "Grandma's Party" were smash singles in England. Only "Heaven on the Seventh Floor," however, found its way onto the stateside radio waves. A few more 45s were issued, but nothing further garnered any airplay.

Before Paul Nicholas' disappearance—in the United States—from the world of high visibility, he starred in *Nutcracker* (1982), *The World Is Full of Married Men* (1979), and *Sgt. Pepper's Lonely Hearts Club Band* (1978).

In his homeland, Paul has been acting dramatic and light comedy roles on TV. Through the '80s, and into the '90s, he has appeared on British stages in productions of *Barnum, Blondel, Cats, Charlie's Girls*, and *The Pirates of Penzance*. In 1993, he appeared in the West End revival of *Grease*; followed two years later by *Singing in the Rain*.

HIGH INERGY
YOU CAN'T TURN ME OFF
(IN THE MIDDLE OF TURNING ME ON)
(P. Sawyer, M. McLeod)

Gordy 7155

No. 12 *December 24, 1977*

Linda Howard, Michelle Martin, and Barbara and Vernessa Mitchell were born and bred in Pasadena, Ca. The Mitchell sisters began singing in church, writing songs when pre-teens, and joined choral groups and theater productions. In 1976, fresh out of Blair High School, the gals entered Pasadena's Bicentennial Performing Arts Program. While rehearsing an act of original songs, skits, and dances in the program's auditorium, word reached the teen queens that Gwen Gordy, the sister of Motown Berry Gordy, Jr., had caught a glimpse of their act and wanted them to stop by to audition. Gwen, who had helped shape the Supremes, was immensely impressed with the newly named High Inergy, a packed act that one mag rag would proclaim: "The Miss American Teenagers of Soul." Gwen and sidekick, Gwendolyn Joyce Fuller, became the girls'

managers, molders, and stage door mamas. Together they groomed the gals with tested tips on hair care, makeup, and poise.

"We're creating a young, fresh image for the girls," Gordy told *Circus*' Daisann McLane. "Nothing sexy, just modest young ladies . . . We build artists . . . there's more to being a star than just musical ability and talent. If their heads are in the right place, and they listen, they can go to the stars."

Dinah Shore introduced them to the show business elite at a function at the Century Plaza Hotel. And soon, the suggestively titled "You Can't Turn Me Off (in the Middle of Turning Me On)" was issued. High Inergy's debut disk was to become their first and only major moment on the nation's pop charts. Inexplicably, only the group's immediate follow-up—"Love Is All You Need"—placed well on *Billboard*'s R & B listings (#89; R&B: #20).

Problems arose almost immediately. Only months into their career, Gordy off-handedly referred to her discovery as "the New Supremes." "I do think that the group can be even stronger than the Supremes," J. Randy Taraborrelli reports her as saying in *Motown:*

HIGH INERGY

Hot Wax, City Cool & Solid Gold. The author noted that James Turko, Mary Wilson's attorney, took exception to the line of promotion: "It doesn't make any sense to bring in a new group and push it like that unless that means you're gonna move the old one out."

After the release of their second LP (*Steppin' Out*) in 1978, High Inergy became a trio when Vernessa, the act's lead vocalist, left the group—reportedly because she felt the material she was singing went against her religious beliefs. Seven of their remaining singles made the R & B listings. None, however, made the Top 40. After the release of *Groove Patrol a*nd their 1983 appearance on Motown's 25th anniversary special, High Inergy called it quits. Shortly after, Barbara Mitchell signed a contract with Capitol Records.

RANDY NEWMAN
SHORT PEOPLE
(Randy Newman)
Warner Bros. 8492
No. 2 *January 28, 1978*

He received a death threat during a tour stop near the site where Martin Luther King, Jr. was assassinated. Not all individuals came to appreciate Randy Newman's "Short People" as a "joke," or as "a humorous statement against prejudice."

"'Short People' was the worst kind of hit anyone could have," Randy Newman (b. Nov. 28, 1943, Los Angeles) told Joe Smith in *Off the Record*. "It was like having [SHEB WOOLEYS'] 'Purple People Eater.' I'd try to watch a ball game and the band would play the song and the announcers would make jokes about it."

As a recording artist, Newman is a cult figure; as a writer, he has achieved substantial success. His early songs were recorded by a number of artists, including Ray Charles, Joe Cocker, Judy Collins, Art Garfunkel, Harry Nilsson, Peggy Lee, the Animals' Alan Price, Linda Ronstadt, NINA SIMONE, Ringo Starr, Barbra Streisand, and Three Dog Night.

"My music has a high irritation factor," Randy told *Rolling Stone*'s Timothy White. "I've always tried to say something. Eccentric lyrics about eccentric people. Often it was a joke. But I would plead guilty on the grounds that I prefer eccentricity to the bland."

Newman recalled to *Keyboards*' Gil Podolinsky, "I started taking piano lessons when I was six or seven. At 11 or 12, I got into studying theory, harmony, and counterpoint. I wanted to be a film composer, because I was influenced by what my uncles [Lionel (conductor of Fox orchestra), Emil (scored John Wayne flicks), and the late Alfred Newman (winner of nine Academy Awards for scores such as *Anastasia, Airport, Camelot,* and *The King and I*)] were doing. So I studied with

Mario Castelnuovo-Tedesco for about four years, and then went to UCLA and studied with George Tremble—a good man; . . . I started writing songs at 16, and I took them to a publisher [Metric Music, then a subdivision of Liberty Records], and they signed me up. I did that for about eight years before I recorded myself in '67 or '68."

The reaction to Newman's first album, a self-titled effort for Warner Bros., was what one might call underwhelming. His second LP—*12 Songs* (1970)—brought a little more notice; it contained "Mama Told Me Not to Come," a major hit for Three Dog Night.

Album number three—*Randy Newman: Live* (1971)—was the first to reach the top pop albums chart. To this day, Randy continues to issue critically acclaimed records; his best-selling LPs include *Sail Away* (1972), *Good Old Boys* (1974), *Little Criminals* (1977), *Trouble in Paradise* (1983), and *Land of Dreams* (1988). He has also written evocative film scores such as the Oscar-nominated *Ragtime* (1981), *The Natural* (1984), and *Parenthood* (1989).

Randy's "I Love Los Angeles" became something of an area anthem, thanks largely to a video created by cousin Tim Newman, the man responsible for catchy ZZ Top video vehicles.

Newman co-wrote the script and several songs for the film *Three Amigos* (1986). His guest appearance as "the Singing Bush" went largely unnoticed. In the mid-'90s, Randy's updating of Goethe's *Faust*, "Randy Newman's Faust," toured the circuit to mixed reviews.

SANTA ESMERALDA
DON'T LET ME BE MISUNDERSTOOD
(Bennie Benjamin, Sol Marcus, Gloria Caldwell)
Casablanca 902
No. 15 *February 18, 1978*

Leroy Gomez was born and raised in Cape Cod, and became proficient on the sax, guitar, and flute at an early age. Nineteen seventy-three was his year: Elton John made use of Leroy's sax sound on *Goodbye Yellow Brick Road*, and Gomez toured with Tavares. He had moved to Paris and started working the cabaret scene when Nicolas Skorsky and Jean-Manuel de Scarano of Fauves-Ruma Productions approached him about performing as lead vocalist for a proposed studio group to be called Santa Esmeralda.

Four tunes were recorded. Don Ray, who had assisted in arranging and mixing a hit for CERRONE and would do the same for LOVE AND KISSES, did the disco arrangements on two Gomez originals and on two British Invasion classics, "Gloria" (Them) and "Don't Let Me Be Misunderstood" (the Animals). Gomez's vocals were soulful, and even the pulsating background was more musically appealing than the usual disco drone. "Don't Let Me Be Misunderstood" was issued as a 45, and an album of the same name also shipped. Both the single and the LP fared well on the charts—even rock fans enjoyed that hypnotic beat.

"House of the Rising Sun," another Animals hit, was the choice for a follow-up single. Unfortunately, neither Don Ray nor Leroy Gomez was involved in the project. Jimmy Goings was brought in to do lead vocals. "House" (#78, 1978) was a Hot 100 item, and the *House of the Rising Sun* (1978) album sold well. Once Gomez was gone, so was the chart activity. Three more LPs were released before Casablanca shelved the "Santa Esmeralda" name.

SAMANTHA SANG
EMOTION
(BARRY GIBB, Robin Gibb)
Private Stock 45178
No. 3 *March 18, 1978*

One thing I always have to make clear to people who only know me from . . . my association with BARRY [GIBB] and his brothers—I am not a Bee Gee girl," Sang declared to *Vibe*'s Kit Lachatte. "I have been a performer for most of my life. My parents were performers. I love working with the Bee Gees. I love singing their songs. But what they have always wanted for me was that I was a success. And that means being able to stand on my own feet."

Australian Samantha Sang was an experienced vocalist—having sung on the radio as eight-year-old "Cheryl Gray" and having performed with her warbling parents—when she met Barry Gibb at the age of 16. He suggested that she record some material he had been concocting. Samantha recorded Gibbs's "Don't Let It Happen Again," but it flopped. A single or two was issued in the States that same year, but not until "Emotion" did Americans hear from Sang again.

With the Bee Gees on top of the charts with their disco gyrations, Sam approached Barry about lending her another number. Within an hour's time, Gibb brothers Robin and Barry shaped up a smoothie with more than a morsel of Bee Gee mystery magic encased therein. On "Emotion," Samantha's and Barry's vocals blended together so well that it was impossible to tell who was breathing and panting those passionate words. With Gibb at her side, Sammi sounded like a virile Bee-Gee-ette.

"You Keep Me Dancing" (#56, 1978) and "In the Midnight Hour" (#88, 1979) did not have Barry's participation, nor did any of Sang's successive singles. The *Emotion* LP sold well, but never again would Sammi crash the charts.

LEBLANC & CARR
FALLING
(Lenny "LeBlanc," Eddie Struzick)
Big Tree 16100
No. 13 *April 1, 1978*

By the time they met in 1968, Floridians Lenny LeBlanc (b. June 17, 1951, Leominister, MA) and Pete Carr (b. Apr. 22, 1950, Daytona Beach, FL) were both accomplished musicians. Carr had been a member of Hourglass with Paul Hornsby and Duane and Gregg Allman. When the Glass shattered, Carr (guitar, bass) and LeBlanc (guitar) trekked to Cincinnati in search of session work. Pete subsequently moved to Muscle Shoals, Alabama, where he became a guitarist with the Muscle Shoals Sound Rhythm Section; he wound up producing and performing on the SAILCAT sessions that resulted in "Motorcycle Mama." Lenny likewise relocated to Muscle Shoals following the disbanding of his recording act, Whalefeathers.

By 1976, each musician had solo albums issued by Big Tree, but listener response was less than enthusiastic. The following year, the old friends joined forces for their lone Top 40 hit. *Midnight Light* produced three back-to-back charting singles: "Something About You" (#48, 1977), "Failing," and "Midnight Light" (#92, 1978). However, all was not well. The duo had a falling out. In support of their hits, the LeBlanc-Carr Band toured, but minus Pete Carr. No follow-up LP was ever issued.

Lenny LeBlanc placed two solo singles on *Billboard*'s Hot 100—"Hound Dog Man (Play It Again)" (#58, 1977) and "Somebody Send My Baby Home" (#55, 1981)—and has worked recording sessions for Dobie Gray, Delbert McClinton, Roy Orbison, and the mysterious Swamp Dogg. In 1979, Pete and two former members of the LeBlanc-Carr Band, Thom Flora and Steve Nathan, recorded as Boatz for Capricorn Records. Word in the '90s is that Lenny has turned to performing and session work for Christian acts. Carr remained incredibly busy as a studio musician, playing on albums by Jim Capaldi, Kim Carnes, Joe Cocker, Art Garfunkel, Millie Jackson, Paul Kossoff, Wilson Pickett, Johnny Rivers, Boz Scaggs, Bob Seger, Paul Simon, Cat Stevens, Rod Stewart, and Travis Wammack, among others.

PATTI SMITH GROUP
BECAUSE THE NIGHT
(Patti Smith, Bruce Springsteen)
Arista 0318
No. 13 *June 24, 1978*

Her interest in rock and roll began when she first heard Little Richard's "The Girl Can't Help It." Well, by the mid-'70s Patti Smith was bashing out guitar feedback, copping Keith Richards stances, and screaming out raw poetry laced with surreal images.

Patti Lee Smith was born in Chicago on December 30, 1946; was raised in Pitman, South Jersey; and grew up "shy, sickly and creepy lookin'," per her self-penned press bio. She took an early interest in the Bible, prayer, art, and literature—in particular, the works of William Burroughs and French poet Arthur Rimbaud. In the '60s, she attended Glassboro State College in New Jersey. With savings earned while working in a New Jersey factory, Patti and her sister Linda tripped to Paris, where Smith studied art and worked the roadways as a musician with a street troupe of poets, singers, and fire-eaters. Back in New York, she attended Brooklyn Art College and befriended photographer Robert Mapplethorpe, who took her in for a stay in his Chelsea Hotel apartment.

The next several years were productive. Patti co-wrote a book of plays (*Mad Dog Blues*); performed with Sam Shepard in *Cowboy Mouth*, a one-act play she co-wrote with the renowned playwright and actor; had her first book of poetry (*Seventh Heaven*) published; and wrote articles and reviews for *Creem* and *Rock*. Her poetry readings at St. Mark's Church in lower Manhattan began attracting a sizable following. On February 10, 1971, Patti invited Lenny Kaye to accompany her

THE PATTI SMITH GROUP

readings on his electric guitar; by 1973, keyboardist Richard Sohl had been added, and the Patti Smith Group was born. This avant-garde aggregation recorded "Piss Factory" b/w "Hey Joe," a one-off, limited-release 45 (1,600 copies) for Mer Records.

Bassist/guitarist Ivan Kral and drummer Jay Dee Daugherty soon climbed aboard. An engagement at New York's CBGB caught the attention of Arista Records head Clive Davis, who signed the Patti Smith Group in 1975. *Horses* (1975), the band's debut album—produced by former Velvet Underground member John Cale—sold well beyond expectations. *Radio Ethiopia* (1976) followed, but no tracks were issued as singles.

On January 23, 1977, Smith suffered a near-fatal accident when she fell off a stage in Tampa, Florida, and broke her neck. After a year's recuperation, Patti and her group returned with *Easter* (1978) and "Because the Night," a single written with Bruce Springsteen. In 1979, after the *Waves* LP and two further 45s—"Frederick" (#90, 1979) and a revamping of the Byrds' "So You Wanna Be a Rock'n'Roll Star"—the Patti Smith Group quietly dissolved.

Sohl and Daugherty pursued solo projects. Kral formed his own group, the Eastern Bloc, while Kaye helped produce SUZANNE VEGA's *Suzanne Vega* (1985) and *Solitude Standing* (1987) albums. Patti married Fred "Sonic" Smith, founder of the militant MC5 and the Sonic Rendezvous.

In 1986, Patti started work on a comeback album. Three years later, her *Dream of Life* album appeared. The sound was strikingly calm and peaceful, compared to her previous work; critics differed in their assessments. "People Have the Power," the only single extracted, did not chart.

"I view my absence from the business as a sabbatical—a nine-year study period of Positive inner strengthening," Smith told *The Music Express.* "I've been using my time in a very disciplined way, writing my first novel and a bunch of short stories—being a good mother, wife, and concerned citizen."

"Sonic" Smith died in 1994. Patti made her return to TV on May 18, 1996 in Fox's "Saturday Night Special." *The Cruel Sea*, a book of poems, was published that year.

ERUPTION
I CAN'T STAND THE RAIN
(Donald Bryant, ANN PEEBLES, Bernard Miller)
Ariola 7686
No. 18 *July 8, 1978*

"What we really want to develop is a real kind of British soul music," explained Lintel in an interview with *Blues*

& *Soul*. "[We] could be the Beatles of soul music!" Ah, but that was not to be. After Eruption's debut single, Lintel became a pop memory.

For a brief period, however, Lintel (lead vocals), Precious Wilson (lead vocals), Eric Kingsley (drums), Horatio McKay (keyboards), and the Petrineau brothers, Gregory (guitar) and Morgan (guitar), were England's Eruption, a bottom-heavy funk/dance unit. They were Jamaica-born and London-based and bred. Early in 1976, after three months of rehearsals, the band's manager entered them in the RCA-sponsored "Soul Search"—Eruption grabbed top honors.

One of "Soul Search"'s judges, Philly record producer Billy Jackson, approached the band to cut some sides for RCA's Ariola subsidiary. Eruption's factory-fresh debut "Funky Love" failed to chart, but "One Way Ticket" and "I Can't Stand the Rain" (a reworked version of ANN PEEBLES's 1973 hit) were smashes in England, both going Top 10. Only the latter disk made the United States pop listings.

About this time, someone must have whispered "solo career, solo career" in Precious Wilson's ears, for in a wink, she was gone. So ends our tale of fickle fame. Eruption ceased to emit, and aside from the limited success of "I'd Be Your Friend" (R&B: #40, 1986), Precious Wilson still hopes to hit the big time.

STEVE MARTIN
KING TUT
(Steve Martin)
Warner Bros. 8577
No. 17 *August 12, 1978*

A former "wild and crazy" stand-up comedian and current maestro of comic invention on the big screen, Steve Martin has earned accolades from audiences and critics alike.

These days, Martin is primarily an actor and screenwriter. The list of his cinema credits is long: *The Jerk* (1979), *Pennies From Heaven* (1981), *Dead Men Don't Wear Plaid* (1982), *The Man With Two Brains* (1983), *The Lonely Guy* (1984), *All of Me* (1984), *The Man With Two Brains* (1984), *Roxanne* (1987), *Planes, Trains, and Automobiles* (1988), *The Three Amigos* (1988), *Dirty Rotten Scoundrels* (1989), *Parenthood* (1989), *My Blue Heaven* (1990), *L.A. Story* (1991), and *Father of the Bride* (1991).

Steve has also made comedy records like *Let's Get Small* (1977), *A Wild and Crazy Guy* (1978), *Comedy Is Not Pretty* (1979), and *The Steve Martin Brothers* (1981). Rarely has the Martin been found in the 45 format. Among the latter efforts are "Grandmother's Song" (#72, 1977); "King Tut," given a full-production treatment on an early "Saturday Night Live" show; and the sadistic "Cruel Shoes" (#91, 1979). All of these are worth near as much of a listen, as his flicks a view.

TOBY BEAU
MY ANGEL BABY
(Danny McKenna, Baide Silva)
RCA 11250
No. 13 *August 12, 1978*

Balde Silva and the guys were just a happy Texas bar band until star-maker Sean Delaney came to town. Sean—was a producer for Kiss and the force behind the heavy-metal Starz—offered to transform Balde and company into big-time celebrities. He whisked the group off to the Big Apple, instructed them to create original material, and then shipped them to England to record their eponymous debut album. RCA issued the *Toby Beau* LP and the syrupy "Angel Baby" as the first 45. The catchy, countrified number clicked, and image-makers at Aucoin Management were off and running. First Balde and the boys were packaged as young Texas toughs; later, they were cutey-pies with cactus in their teeth. While "Then You Can Tell Me Goodbye" (#57, 1979) (formerly a major hit for THE CASINOS) and "If I Were You" (#70, 1980) made the Hot 100, Toby Beau

never managed to come up with anything potent, and never shook their staid, tumbleweed persona.

Balde Silva (vocals, guitar, harmonica), Danny McKenna (guitar), Ron Rose (guitar, banjo, mandolin), Rob Young (drums), and Steve "Zip" Zipper (bass) had been classmates, all born and raised in the Rio Grande Valley. The band formed in 1975 and was named after a shrimpboat that one of them had spotted on the Gulf of Mexico.

McKenna quit during the band's first recording session. By the time of their third LP in 1980, only Balde remained.

WALTER EGAN
MAGNET AND STEEL
(Walter Egan)
Columbia 10719
No. 8 *August 26, 1978*

Walter Egan (b. July 12, 1948, Jamaica, NY) grew up in Forest Hills, New York, though he is usually thought of as being a genuine Cal State soft-rocker. In the early '60s, Walt fronted the Malibooz, a surf band. Things were looking promising for Walt (guitar, bass, vocals), Dennis "Ace" Lopez (bass), Chris "Golden Rule" Mur-

Walter Egan

ray (vocals), Tom "Sparkle Plenty" Scrap (drums), and John "Z" Zambetti (guitar, vocals). They played at the New York World's Fair in 1964 and issued "Goin' to Malibu," an impossible-to-find single.

During the psychedelic era, Walt and his band became Sageworth. With Annie McLoone as a co-lead singer in the band, Sageworth edged toward country-rock; Gram Parsons and EMMYLOU HARRIS even recorded some of Egan's songs; notably "Hearts on Fire." Next up, Walt toured with Kaleidoscopes' Chris Darrow and formed Southpaw with Jules Shear and Stephen Hagen. Reportedly, it was Emmylou who encouraged Walt to give up the East Coast for those Golden State waves he had been singing about years back.

Once situated in Los Angeles, Egan joined a group called the Wheels. A scout for Columbia Records caught their act, and singled out Walter for a solo recording contract. Lindsey Buckingham and Stevie Nicks were brought into support and co-produce Egan's *Fundamental Roll* (1977) album, which yielded "Only the Lucky" (#82, 1977). Buckingham also produced a second release, *Not Shy* (1978), from which "Magnet and Steel" was culled. The similarity of Egan's sound to that of Fleetwood Mac, plus the presence of Buckingham and Nicks on his recordings, led to Walter being unjustly pegged as a Fleetwood Mac clone.

Two more charts items—"Hot Summer Nights" (#55, 1978) and "Fool Moon Fire" (#46, 1983)—followed, as did three more LPs. Both Randy Meisner ("Hearts on Fire," 1981) and Night ("Hot Summer Nights," 1979) had success with remakes of Egan songs.

In 1981, Walter combined the old and the new Malibooz to cut some exciting surf sounds for Rhino Records. With boss sounds like "The Fluorescent Hearse," "The Lonely Surfer," and a remake by the original band of "Goin' to Malibu," *Malibooz Rules* is worth a look-see. *Wild Exhibitions*, Walt's final album was issued and passed over in 1983.

CHRIS REA
FOOL (IF YOU THINK IT'S OVER)
(Chris Rea)
United Artists 1198
No. 12 *September 16, 1978*

In the U.K. 27 charted tunes bear Rea's name; his *Road to Hell* album (1989) went quadruple-platinum in the homeland alone. *Water Sign* (1983) went Top 20 in Denmark, Belgium, Norway, Sweden, France, Germany, Holland . . . Two years later, *Shamrock Diaries* scored in most of the same countries, plus Australia, Japan, and New Zealand.

Chris Rea does not sell well in the States. The reason, explained Rea to Danny McCue, *The Music Paper*:

his visits here are seldom. "The danger of touring America is that you can't tell your bedroom in St. Louis from your bedroom in Milwaukee . . . That sounds like prison to me and a high price to pay for inflating your ego and your bank account."

In addition to being seldom heard, Rea feels he is misperceived by Americans. "This single ["Fool"] which I wasn't particularly happy with became a massive hit," said Rea to McCue. ". . . In the end, I finished up virtually having a breakdown, and three years later if you mentioned Chris Rea's name, the reaction was, 'Leave him. he's a failure.'"

"The English Springsteen," as Chris Rea (b. Mar. 4, 1951, Middlesbrough, England) has often been labeled by the British press, is of mixed mind about having a hit recording in America. "Fool," a tune he wrote for his sister, came from his debut LP, *Whatever Happened to Benny Santini?*, produced by Gus Dudgeon. However, Chris was not pleased with this overorchestrated and, in his view, misconceived album (although it did sell 1 million copies in the United States alone). A few years later, Columbia Records allowed Rea a free hand in their Chipping Norton Studios in Oxfordshire, England. Chris referred to the resulting album, *Tennis* (1980), as "my first album—one that sets the record straight." Neither the LP nor any of the singles pulled from it have sold much in the United States.

In the five years preceding his One-Hit Wonder status, Chris worked as a musician on the pub and concert circuit fronting Magdelene, later relabeled the Beautiful Losers, after a Leonard Cohen novel. David Coverdale of Deep Purple, later Whitesnake, was once a member of the Beautiful Losers, designated by *Melody Maker* as the "best new band of the year." Magnet Records soon signed a recording contract for Rea's solo services. The "miscast" *Benny Santini* was the initial result.

In the '80s, Chris continued to record, with substantial success, in his homeland. "Whatever Happened to Benny Santini?" (#71, 1978) was issued in the States as his follow-up to "Fool." Four further singles have charted in the United States, most notably, "Diamonds" (#44, 1979) and "Work on It" (#73, 1989). Odds are that Rea will maintain his one-hit status. "I don't want anything that much that it would mean I wouldn't get to see my daughter's face for six months," said Rea to McCue.

JOHN PAUL YOUNG
LOVE IS IN THE AIR
(Harry Vanda, George Young)
Scotti Brothers 402
No. 7 *October 14, 1978*

J. Paul was born in Glasgow, Scotland, in 1953, and his family moved to Australia when he was a tot. Left to his own devices, he played around with the family accordion and tinkered with the piano. He served a five-year apprenticeship as a sheet-metal worker, and toward the end of this workout, John began playing music in local watering holes, with a band called Elm Tree.

Producer Simon Napier-Bell—who had ventured into recording studios with acts like the Yardbirds and Marc Bolan (of T. Rex fame)—had a sure-shot hit song in his hands called "Pasadena," and needed a vocalist. Reportedly, Napier-Bell spotted Young doing one of his gigs and offered to record him. John Paul accepted, and though the tune did zip in the States, it made the British Top 10. Other disks placed on the Aussie charts, and Young won a slot in the Australian production of *Jesus Christ Superstar*.

A few years prior to his big moment with a composition by Harry Vanda and George Young—founding members of THE EASY-BEATS—John Paul had a moderate stateside success with "Yesterday's Herd" (#42, 1975); eight Top 20 singles and two Top 20 albums followed in his homeland.

J. Paul formed the All Stars, a touring band comprised of members of the Aztecs, Dingoes, Sherbert, and the Bee Gees band. Only one other John Paul Young single made the Hot 100 listings: "Lost in Your Love" (#55, 1979). His last known recording, *One Foot in Front*, was issued on IC, a German label in 1983.

NICK GILDER
HOT CHILD IN THE CITY
(Nick Gilder, James McCulloch)
Chrysalis 2226
No. 1 *October 28, 1978*

In 1961, Nick Gilder (b. Nov. 7, 1951, London) moved with his family to Vancouver, Canada. Nicky soon started singing with a group called Throm Hortis. They won a talent contest, worked in some clubs and high schools, and attracted the attention of several record labels.

In 1971, Jim McCulloch, lead guitarist with Rasputin, asked Gilder to join his own group. As Sweeney Todd—named for the "demon barber of Fleet Street"—they performed throughout Vancouver with high visibility, i.e. with garish make-up, hideous clothes, flashpots, and a smoke machine. By 1976, some Sweeney Todd 45s for London Records, in particular the Gilder-McCulloch song "Roxy Roller" (#90, 1976), had begun to receive major attention. Reportedly, a second version of the song charted by Sweeney Todd, just

months later; this time with Bryan Adams supplying the lead vocals.

At about this point, Nick and Jim abandoned Sweeney Todd and moved to Los Angeles; Gilder then signed a contract with Chrysalis Records, and the twosome collaborated on Nick's solo projects. "Hot Child in the City" really clicked—2 million copies were eventually sold. Speaking of "Hot Child," Gilder told *Rolling Stone* magazine: "I've seen a lot of young girls, 15 and 16, walking down Hollywood Boulevard with their pimps. Their home environment drove them to distraction so they ran away . . . It hurts to see that so I tried writing from the perspective of a lecher—in the guise of an innocent pop song."

"Here Comes the Night" (#44, 1978) and "Rock Me" (#57, 1979) as well as Nick's second and third albums—*City Lights* (1978) and *Frequency* (1979)—have sold well.

ALICIA BRIDGES
I LOVE THE NIGHTLIFE (DISCO 'ROUND)
(Alicia Bridges, Susan Hutcheson)
Polydor 14483
No. 5 *December 23, 1978*

Alicia is not saying how old she is (shhh! July 15, 1953), though she does freely admit to being born and raised in Lawndale, North Carolina. After working in a bank and pushing goods at Sears, Roebuck, Bridges began her singing career in Zachary Ridge, a heavy rock band that played accompaniment for strippers in burlesque houses.

The disco staple "I Love the Nightlife" was not Alicia's first or last recording, but it certainly looked like it. "Nightlife" was a Grammy nominee for "Best Song of the Year." Her follow-up, "Body Heat" (#86, 1979), was less successful. Further recordings were issued by A.V.I. and Second Wave to nary a smidgen of notice, let alone success. Reportedly a second album was issued by Polydor, called *Play It As It Lays*; pressings were so few in number that 20 years have passed with this writer spotting nary a copy.

"Since I turned to guitar one Sunday, music has been the most important thing in my life," Alicia told Bret Primack of *Grooves*. "There are people I love and care about, but music is the moving force . . . I live it, and I am dedicated to it."

Alicia Bridges's whereabouts are unknown.

ACE FREHLEY
NEW YORK GROOVE
(Russ Ballard)
Casablanca 941
No. 13 *February 3, 1979*

When Paul "Ace" Frehley (b. Apr. 27, 1951, the Bronx, NY) walked away from Kiss, they still were one of the hottest and most influential rock and roll bands in the world. Nearly all of their albums had gone double platinum, and their concerts were sell-outs. Their memorabilia—posters, T-shirts, concert books, and all the rest—was still raking in m-i-l-l-i-o-n-s.

"At the end of my stay with Kiss, even playing live had become something of a drag," Frehley confessed to *Hit Parader*'s Winston Cummings. "The fun had gone out of it for me. I realize now that it was my health that was making me feel that way, because once I got my life straightened out, the only thing I wanted to do was get in front of people and play."

Ace Frehley left the band in 1983, and spent the next four years battling a drug habit. He bounced back with three hard-rocking, fairly-well-reviewed LPs on Atlantic/Megaforce—*Frehley's Comet*, *Live + 1*, and *Second Sighting*—and commands a cultish following of aging metal-heads and Kiss fans.

Frehley started playing guitar at 13. "Once I played an electric guitar I was hooked," Frehley told *Guitar Player*. To make a living, "I drove a cab, and I worked in an upholstery place. I was a mailman, an art student, you name it, I did it."

Peter Criss, Paul Stanley, and Gene Simmons had already formed Kiss (then called Rainbow) when Ace was enlisted in 1972. "They advertised in the *Village*

Voice. At the time, I was unhappy with the group I was with, and I just thought I would try an audition. We worked out pretty good, and they said, 'We can't give you a definite answer today' . . . They called me back and said, 'Come back and jam with us again.'"

"Look, I don't expect this band [Frehley's Comet] to ever be as big as Kiss was," Frehley told *Hit Parader*. "That was a once in a life time experience which is still very near and dear to me. But I'm happy as I've ever been."

In February 1996, Kiss successfully reformed with all original members, in full rock drag—"Bat Lizard" (Gene Simmons), "The Cat" (Peter Criss), "Star Child" (Paul Stanley), and "Space Man," Ace Frehley.

CHERYL LYNN
GOT TO BE REAL
(Cheryl Lynn, David Paich, DAVID FOSTER)
Columbia 10808
No. 12 *February 17, 1979*

Cheryl Lynn is a big woman, but critics have also noted that she is hugely talented.

"You know what is projected on television," Lynn told *Black Star*'s Gerrie E. Summers. "We never saw the large-sized woman until a few years ago. Now we have the JENNIFER HOLLIDAYS and Nell Carters—we have more of the Cheryl Lynns."

Delbert Langston believed in her. He was her manager and boyfriend, and arranged for Cheryl to audition for TV's "The Gong Show."

"I guess Delbert got tired of me singing in church and thought I could do more. He begged me to audition, and I argued because I was kind of shy. I didn't like being in front of people because I was inhibited. I've never liked being in front of the guys because I didn't want them snickering."

Cheryl Lynn Smith (b. Mar. 11, 1957, Los Angeles) met Delbert Langston at Washington High in Los Angeles. Del was forming a group called Happy, Free, and Easy, and needed a girl's voice—he found one in Cheryl Lynn (a.k.a. Lydia Smith). They remained together for a few years, doing gigs whenever and wherever. Finally, in 1976, Langston set Cheryl up with auditions for "The Gong Show" and for the national touring company of *The Wiz*. She was accepted for both, and while waiting for the "Gong" episode to air, Lynn subbed for three months as the Wicked Witch of the West.

"[When the show aired], I got a call from Chuck Barris' production company," Lynn told *Soul*'s Leonard Pitts, Jr. "He says, 'You're gonna be a star overnight. We've never gotten a response like this for anybody on 'The Gong Show.'"

Producer Bob Johnston brought her to the attention of the powers at Columbia Records. Once they viewed the 90-second "Gong" spot, she was signed to the label. Her self-titled debut album and single, "Got to Be Real," were instant successes. Over the years, she has followed through with "Star Love" (#62; R&B: #16, 1979), "Shake It Up Tonight" (#70; R&B: #5, 1981), and "Encore" (#69; R&B: #1, 1984). Her string of R & B hits is impressive: 16 singles on the listings through 1988, including a duet with Luther Vandross, on a remake of the Marvin Gaye-Tammi Terrell tune "If This World Was Mine" (R&B: #4, 1982).

IAN MATTHEWS
SHAKE IT
(Terence Boylan)
Mushroom 7039
No. 13 *February 17, 1979*

He has told *Rolling Stone* that he's known primarily as a rebel. Outside of his faithful cult following, however, singer-songwriter Ian Matthews is known mostly for his smoothwork with the Fairport Convention and his namesake band, MATTHEWS SOUTHERN COMFORT. Both of his former groups were at the peak of their creative and pop powers when Ian left them.

He was born Ian McDonald in Lincolnshire, England, in June, 1946. He began attracting notice playing guitar and singing with a teenage R & B band called the Rebels. "The Drifters, the Coasters, that's what I latched onto," Matthews told *Rolling Stone's* Byron Laursen. "I must have sounded so dumb." Next, Matthews tried playing surf music in a Deram recording act called the Pyramid. One single was issued, "Summer of Last Year."

In 1967, Ian was asked to join the original Fairport Convention (for three albums). "I've never really been a folkie," he explained to *Guitar Player*. "When I joined Fairport Convention, they weren't a folk band, . . . They were doing their own interpretations of mainly American material; they'd do songs by the Byrds and Tim Hardin. That's the nearest we came to folk music." All was to change, however, when Sandy Denny was admitted into the fold, and the group's direction veered toward Celtic allusions and medieval English balladry. "That was when I really became disillusioned with the band."

Ian left in 1969 to form his own group, Matthews Southern Comfort, with Carl Barnwell (guitar), Ray Duffy (drums), Mark Griffins (guitar), Gordon Huntley (pedal-steel guitar), and Andy Leigh (bass). Three country-folk-rockin' LPs followed; with the success of a take on Joni Mitchell's "Woodstock" (#23, 1971), Ian was gone, though two other singles from Matthews Southern Comfort's *Later That Same Year* album made

the Hot 100: "Mare, Take Me Home" (#96, 1971) and a cover of Neil Young's "Tell Me Why" (#98, 1971). Huntley and the rest carried on as Southern Comfort for three more LPs before disbanding in 1972.

Since his departure from the Southern Comfort band, Ian has carried on as a soloist for most of the time with a loyal following. There have been occasional one-off projects with groups like Plainsong (*In Search of Amelia Earhart*), the Hi-Fi's, and the Mallards. Critics have praised Matthews for his tasteful and folk-tinged interpretations of songs by Jackson Browne, Carole King, RANDY NEWMAN, Tom Waits, and Neil Young. A few of these solo efforts sold well: *Tigers Will Survive* (1972), *Valley Hi* (1973) (produced by ex-Monkee Mike Nesmith), and *Stealin Home* (1978). Only one of the many singles taken from these albums has been a Top 40 hit: producer/singer/songwriter Terence Boylan's "Shake It." In reference to his big moment, Ian said to *Rolling Stone* that "I don't think I did anything different. I guess it's my reward. After all, I've been doing exactly what I want for . . . years."

Ian Matthews—currently an A & R director at the Windham Hill label—continues to record albums, though sporadically.

BOBBY CALDWELL
WHAT YOU WON'T DO FOR LOVE
(Bobby Caldwell, Kettner)
Clouds 11
No. 9 *February 24, 1979*

Bobby Caldwell has inhabited two distinct musical worlds. Those who have written about him usually praise one side of him and totally ignore the other. Rock and rollers, after all, don't usually mess with songs that sound like they could have been on the *Saturday Night Fever* soundtrack. How is it possible for Bobby Caldwell to make hard-rock records with Johnny Winter and RICK DERRINGER one day, and sing well-baked disco ballads the next?

Born in Manhattan on August 15, 1951, Bobby pulled together his first group, the Rooftops, during his teens. At 19, his new group, Katmandu, recorded an album for Mainstream Records. The LP didn't sell well, but it did catch the attention of Little Richard, who hired the band to be an opening act for his Las Vegas appearances. Caldwell left the group months later and joined up with Johnny Winter's band.

After a live album with Winter, Bobby joined ex-IRON BUTTERFLY bassist Lee Dorman for an album with Dorman's Captain Beyond. He moved on to ex-McCoy Rick Derringer's band for the *All-American Boy* (1971) album, then played alongside ex-Yardbird Keith Relf in the short-lived Armaggedon. One highly collectible album later, Bob vanished, but not for long. He reappeared on later albums by Derringer, Winter, and Captain Beyond, also making scads of TV commercials and recording tracks and the theme for Walt Disney's "New Mickey Mouse Club."

After 20 years in the shadows, Bob stepped out with a solo release on Cloud Records, a T.K. subsidiary. Could this be the same Bobby Caldwell? With its smooth veneer, "What You Won't Do for Love" sounded like something a tipsy George Benson might have recorded. The ballad fared well, even though it surprised listeners who were more familiar with the hard-rockin' Caldwell. Two follow-ups, both in a similar vein—"Coming Down From My Love" (#42; R&B: #28, 1980) and "All of My Love" (#77; R&B: #67, 1982)—made the Hot 100, and a few more singles placed on the R & B listings.

"I think that my album [1978's *Bobby Caldwell*, which featured "What You Won't Do for Love"] is nice," Bobby told *Soul*. "You can listen to it over and over again, but I know there is nothing there that really sticks its foot up your ass."

Caldwell switched recently to MCA Records, where he continues to work the terrain created by his lone Top 40 hit. Bobby has also become known for his songwriting abilities—Roy Ayers, Peabo Bryson, Natalie Cole, Roberta Flack, CHERYL LYNN, and Dionne Warwick have all recorded his compositions. Pete Cetera and Amy Grant topped the pop charts in 1983 with Bob's "The Next Time I Fall."

In the late '90s, Bobby starred in the theatrical production *The Rat Pack*, in the role of Frank Sinatra.

BELL & JAMES
LIVIN' IT UP (FRIDAY NIGHT)
(LeRoy "Bell," Casey "James")
A & M 2069
No. 15 *April 21, 1979*

Florida native LeRoy Bell and Casey James from Portland, Oregon, met in a Philly-based band called Special Blend. Their band broke up, but Bell & James stayed together and formed a songwriting team.

LeRoy's uncle was Thom Bell, the producer/arranger/tunesmith for Gamble & Huff and their renowned "Sound of Philadelphia." Bell (drums, guitar) & James (guitar, bass, keyboards, synthesizers) were hired by Uncle Bell's Mighty Three Music company to write songs and create demos. Elton John, L.T.D., MFSB, Maxine Nightingale, the O'Jays, Freda Payne, Gladys Knight & The Pips, and the Pockets all recorded some Bell & James tunes. A sprinkling of their disco ditties appeared in the Jonathan Winters flick *The Fish That Saved Pittsburgh* (1979).

At about this time, executives at A & M Records heard one of their demos, and offered the duo a recording contract. Instant success was theirs: "Livin' It Up," Bell & James' debut disk, went solid gold. Weeks later, Elton John repeated the feat with his rendering of their "Mama Can't Buy Me Love." A few more weeks, and their popularity was on the wane. Before the onset of their obscurity, three more 45s graced the middle reaches of the R & B chart through 1980.

AMII STEWART
KNOCK ON WOOD
(Eddie Floyd, Steve Cropper)
Ariola 7736
No. 1 *April 21, 1979*

"I've never bought a disco record in my life," Amii Stewart told *Record Mirror*'s Paul Sexton. "And I don't want to buy one. When I go home and close the door, I don't want my brains to be blown out." A peculiar comment indeed, considering that Amii's "Knock on Wood," her one and only international chart-topper, was one of the hottest disco disks of 1979.

Amy Stewart was born in 1956 in Washington, DC, the daughter of a top-secret Pentagon man. As a child, she was given music and dance lessons. She attended Howard University, but left to work with the D.C. Repertory Dance Company, where she studied ballet and modern dance. In 1975, she joined the Miami cast of *Bubbling Brown Sugar* and, soon after, the Broadway cast. Amii also appeared in *The Return of the Pink Panther* (1975), *King Kong* (1976), and the Muhammad Ali story, *The Greatest* (1977).

Stewart's big break came in 1977, when one of her old dance instructors, bringing *Bubbling Brown Sugar* to London, picked Amii to not only join him as assistant director but also play one of the lead roles. The part offered Amii the opportunity to show off her vocal abilities on "I Got It Bad" and the title tune. Sitting in the audience one night was songwriter/producer Barry Leng, who was looking for a female to cut a demo on a tune that he and his associate Simon May had written. Amii agreed to give the song a whirl. The demo turned out so well that Leng and May walked the tape into the offices of Hansa Productions. "You Really Touched My Heart" was released, and sold fairly well in Europe.

Peter Meisel, Hansa's part-owner and controller, suggested that Amii cover one of his '60s favorites, Eddie Floyd's "Knock on Wood," for her next single. Disco or not, Stewart initially seemed to like the idea. "Pete went in and did the track," Stewart told *Blues & Soul*, "and when I heard it, I just flipped out! In fact, I asked him what I was supposed to sing since the track sounded so good just as it was."

The disk was a knockout with both pop (#1) and R & B (#6) audiences worldwide. An altered, appended, and equally discofied cover of the Doors' classic "Light My Fire/137 Disco Heaven" (#69; R&B: #36, 1979) followed, and sold fairly well. A year later, Amii dueted with JOHNNY BRISTOL on a reworking of Mary Wells/the Temptations' "My Guy/My Girl" (#63; R&B: #76, 1980), which was a moderate success.

In 1984, Amii had a Top 10 in the U.K. with "Friends." "The track" is totally different from anything I've ever done, thank God," Stewart told Record Mirror. "You can't spend your life singing songs like 'Knock on Wood.'" The following year, however, Amii's "Knock on Wood" was remixed and recharting in England. A few more albums have been issued, with limited success.

Amii Stewart lives in Italy, where she continues to work the cabaret scene.

FRANK MILLS
MUSIC BOX DANCER
(Frank Mills)
Polydor 14517
No. 3 *May 5, 1979*

"Maybe 'Music Box Dancer' will be it, but I don't think so, because I'm not going to quit, "Mills told *Music Scene* magazine. "I would rather think that my 'Moon River' isn't too far around the corner."

Frank Mills was born in 1943 in Toronto and grew up in Verdum, Quebec. For years, he studied piano, theory, composition, and arranging and when alone, trombone. After leaving Montreal's McGill Conservatory of Music in 1965, Mills sold industrial gases and real estate, spent three months with the Sirocco Singers; eventually joining THE BELLS. They recorded a few of his tunes, but by 1970, Frank wanted to go it alone and do his stuff his way. A first-off single, "Love Me, Love Me Love" (#46, 1972), made the United States pop listings; follow-ups like a cover of Rick Nelson's "Poor Little Fool" charted in his homeland. A hard to find debut album, *Seven of My Songs (Plus Some Others)*, was issued in 1971.

By 1974, Frank Mills was without a record label. For a long time, he had been stifling his aspirations to create easy-listening mood music for the older, more sedate crowd. He publicly praised the MOR orchestral strains of Bert Kaempfert and particularly JAMES LAST, and proposed creating soothing sounds of this nature. When all the record labels turned him down, Mills paid out of his pocket to have an album of these Muzak-like smoothies made. Years later, someone noticed with a tingle the pleasing piano puffery of the "Music Box Dancer" album track. In the midst of the disco phenomenon, Polydor boldly reissued "Music Box Dancer"

and that five-year-old album to an enthusiastic response.

Frank Mills still plays music for an audience he has described as "the totally forgotten." Numerous albums have been issued into the '90s—notably *Christmas With Frank Mills and Friends* (1992)—most, however, are not released in the United States.

INSTANT FUNK
I GOT MY MIND MADE UP
(YOU CAN GET IT GIRL)
(Kim Miller, Scotty Miller, Raymond Earl)
Salsoul 2078
No. 20 *May 12, 1979*

Raymond Earl (bass) and the Miller brothers, Kim (guitar) and Scotty (drums), met in the mid-'60s in their hometown of Trenton, New Jersey. They formed the Music Machine (not to be confused with the similarly titled One-Hit Wonder act) and shopped their sounds around for three years before an up-and-coming vocal group named the TNJs hired them as a backup band. The Newark label issued a few promising sides by the TNJs in the late '60s, but nothing monumental happened, so Ray and the brothers moved their base of operations to Philadelphia in 1971.

A chance meeting with BUNNY SIGLER led to a job as Sigler's back-up band and a recording contract with Gamble & Huff's TSOP. Sigler had the guys assume the "Instant Funk" moniker and encouraged them to flesh out their sound with the addition of Dennis Richardson (piano) and Charles Williams (percussion). Some funkified 45s and an album, *Get Down With the Philly Jump*, were issued in the mid-'70s, all to little avail; Bunny and the band departed from the label.

While with TSOP, Instant Funk was also a studio band for Archie Bell & The Drells, Evelyn "Champagne" King, the O'Jays, and Sigler. After Bunny connected the group with Salsoul Records, they continued working sessions for the likes of Double Exposure, Loleatta Holloway, the Love Committee, and the Salsoul Orchestra. For their first album on the Salsoul label, George Bell (second guitar), James Carmichael (lead vocals, percussion), Larry Davis (trumpet), Johnny Onderline (sax), and ex-Ritchie Family member Eric Huff (trombone) were added to the group. *The Instant Funk* (1979) album was released, and the opening cut, "I Got My Mind Made Up," was issued as a single. "I Got My Mind" got the nation funkin' again. The 45 held down the R & B chart's number-one slot for three weeks. The LP even made the top pop albums chart. Eight other follow-up singles charted on the R & B listings through 1983—notably, "Witch Doctor" (#35, 1979) and "No Stoppin' That Rockin'" (#32, 1983)—

INSTANT FUNK

but nothing further found favor with the nation's pop fans. Two years later a last known single was issued by Pop Art Records, "Tailspin."

RANDY VANWARMER
JUST WHEN I NEEDED YOU MOST
(Randy Vanwarmer)
Bearsville 0334
No. 4 *June 16, 1979*

Randy was born Randall Van Wormer on March 30, 1955, in Indian Hills, Colorado—a town with a gas station, a post office, a trading post, and 2,000 souls. Randy's folks were Fundamentalists and disallowed many activities, including listening to rock and pop music. When Randy was 12, his dad died in a car crash;

his mother moved the family to a fishing village near Cornwall, in England.

While attending St. Austell College, Randy took to playing the guitar and began making demo tapes. Familial restrictions apparently were lifted, because Vanwarmer soon began singing songs in secular clubs and night spots.

In 1979, Randy moved to Woodstock, New York, and signed with the town's label, Bearsville. "Just When I Needed You Most," a Vanwarmer composition, was delicate, easily digestible, and a huge hit.

After "Whatever You Decide" (#80, 1970) and "Suzi" (#55, 1981), and an album—"Warmer" (#81, 1979)—Vanwarmer's career cooled. A few passed over LPs were released in the early '80s. Few critics noted the appearance, late in 1988, of Randy's warm release on 16th Avenue Records, *I Am*. The disk featured two tracks that placed on the country charts—"I Will Hold You" (#53, 1988) and "Where the Rocky Mountains Touch the Sun" (#72, 1988). *The Vital Sparks* (1994) seems to have only been issued in Canada.

REX SMITH
YOU TAKE MY BREATH AWAY
(Bobby Hart, Stephen Lawrence)
Columbia 10908
No. 10 *June 23, 1979*

Rex Smith was born on September 19, 1956, in Jacksonville, Florida. After a series of moves, Rex's family settled in Atlanta. He played in bands (as did his older brother, Michael Lee Smith of Starz) and got involved in amateur theater productions.

In the mid-'70s, Smith moved to the Big Apple to give up rock music and become an actor. Before these dreams firmed up, David Krebs and Steve Leber, a couple of hot-shot music managers, convinced Rex to front a hard-rock combo comprising Lou Van Dora (guitar), Lars Hansen (guitar), Mike Ratti (drums), and Orville

REX SMITH

Davis, formerly of the Capricorn recording act Hydra. Krebs and Leber called the boys Rex. Two albums' worth of raunchies were issued by Columbia Records, but sales were nil, despite the photos of would-be teen heartthrob Smith on the LP covers.

In 1979, Rex landed the lead in "Sooner or Later," a made-for-TV movie about a rock star who lusts for a pre-teen fan. "You Take My Breath Away," from the soundtrack, was shipped as Rex's first solo side. The album and the single clicked, but aside from "Everlasting Love" (#32, 1981), a one-off duet with Stiff Records' act Rachel Sweet, Rex's chart-topping days were over.

For a season (1981-1982), Rex was Andy Gibb's replacement as co-host, with Marilyn McCoo, of TV's "Solid Gold," then starred in a short-lived series, "Street Hawk." The two-month series was so named for the super-charged cycle Smith rode often at speeds of 300 miles an hour.

In the late '80s, Rex appeared in the cast of the CBS-TV soap opera "As the World Turns." Smith performed in, and sang the title tune to, *Headin' for Broadway* (1980), and also starred in the Broadway and East Coast productions of *Grease*. With Linda Ronstadt and Kevin Kline, he worked in both the Broadway and film renditions of *The Pirates of Penzance* (1983).

ANITA WARD
RING MY BELL
(Frederick Knight)
Juana 3422
No. 1 *June 30, 1979*

Anita Ward (b. Dec. 20, 1957, Memphis) was always interested in music. While attending Rush College in Holly Springs, Mississippi, she sang in their *a cappella* choir and with the Rush Singers, who appeared on an album with Metropolitan Opera star Leontyne Price.

While Anita worked days as a substitute elementary-school teacher, her manager sent photos, bio sheets, and demo tapes out to record companies. FREDERICK KNIGHT, president of Juana Records, agreed to record some tunes with Ward.

Fred had a tune in his head that he had hoped to place with 11-year-old Stacy Lattisaw. "It was then a teenybopper type of song, about kids talking on the telephone," Knight told Bob Gilbert and Gary Theroux in *The Top Ten*. "Ring My Bell" had to be rewritten, but once

Freddie did so, and once Anita moved her way through the suggestive romp—which featured Knight playing a synthesized drum—the record became a stone-cold smash, topping both *Billboard*'s pop and R & B charts.

"'Ring My Bell' was almost an accident," Ward recalled to *Cashbox*. "When we went into the studio, we had no intention whatsoever of cutting a disco number. We were down to our last number in the studio, and we realized that we needed something up tempo." Anita was not even enthusiastic about her hit. "I am not really a disco queen," she told *Blues & Soul*. "You see, I'm basically just a naive, shy little church girl. I don't smoke and I don't drink." Ward had never even been to a disco when her bell-ringer was reverberating off the walls of countless dance halls.

Ward's first album, *Songs of Love* (1979), was a huge seller. Before year's end, one more single and another, tamer LP were issued. Only the single, "Don't Drop My Love" (#87, 1979), sparked a mild interest. It is quite possible that Anita made no further recordings.

MCFADDEN & WHITEHEAD
AIN'T NO STOPPIN' US NOW
(Gene "McFadden," John "Whitehead," Jerry Cohen)
Philadelphia International 3681
No. 13 *July 21, 1979*

They met as kids in a North Philly ghetto. While in high school in the '60s, Gene McFadden (b. 1948, Philadelphia), John Whitehead (b. 1948, Philadelphia), Alan Beatty and possibly Lloyd Parkes—later a member Harold Melvin & The Blue Notes—formed the Epsilons. Legend has it that one morn, while Gene was standing on a street corner holding some Otis Redding records, Otis's bandleader noticed and asked him if he would like to meet the "Southern Soul King." That evening, the Epsilons got to sing for Redding, who asked the boys to join his Revue. Gene, John, and Alan remained in the entourage for a year before tiring of the one-nighter grind.

"We told Otis that we [were real tired and] wanted to go home," Whitehead told *Blues & Soul*'s John Abbey. "Otis said he wanted us to stay because he had a song he wanted us to record—but we were adamant and we just said we were too tired so he would have to get somebody else. So he did! He brought in Arthur Conley and they cut that song, 'Sweet Soul Music.' The worst thing was that we didn't end up going home, and we sang the backgrounds for Arthur."

Only weeks later, Otis was dead. Gene and John returned home. Al Beatty left the group. With their new member, James Knight, and a new group name, Talk of the Town, McFadden and Whitehead approached Kenny Gamble and Leon Huff, then

heads of the newly established Philadelphia International label. After a few Talk of the Town singles flopped, John was relegated to the position of chief mailboy. Gene was unemployed.

One night in desperation, while sitting at a kitchen table in a Philly project, they wrote "Back Stabbers." "I told Gene to come to work with me 'cause we were gonna show that song to Huff," John told *Soul*'s J. Randy Taraborrelli. "So we were standing at the elevator door in front of Huff's office. I knew he'd have to go to the bathroom. When he did come out, he went to the soda machine, and I followed him all the way, reading the lyrics." By the time Whitehead got to the chorus, Huff was sold on the song's potential. The rest, as they say, is history. "Back Stabbers" became the O'Jays' first R & B chart-topper and Philadelphia International's first gold single.

McFadden and Whitehead went on to write and/or produce some of the biggest chart-movers, playing a seminal role in the development of the "Philadelphia Sound." Archie Bell, the Intruders, Harold Melvin & The Blue Notes, Melba Moore, Teddy Pendergrass, Lou Rawls—all recorded tunes by the duo.

"I guess that after 22 gold records, 2 platinum albums, and 2 Grammy nominations, we simply felt we wanted to do something for ourselves," Whitehead told Abbey. Seeking to gain some of the public acclaim that they had been dispensing to others, McFadden and Whitehead walked into the studios as recording artists; "Ain't No Stoppin' Us Now" was their debut disk. Nary a thing stood in their way—'Ain't No Stoppin'" scaled the pop charts and hit number one on the R & B listings, eventually selling 2 million copies. The McFadden & Whitehead album went gold.

Unfortunately, only McFadden & Whitehead's "I Heard It in a Love Song" (R&B: #23, 1980) came anywhere near to being as popular, although "I've Been Pushed Aside" (R&B: #73, 1980) and "One More Time" (R&B: #58, 1982) were solid efforts. In 1984, the duo rerecorded the tune as "Ain't No Stoppin' (Ain't No Way)" for Sutra.

After serving some time in jail for tax evasion, John Whitehead returned to the R & B charts as a solo act with "I Need Money Bad" (#50, 1988). He is the father of Johnny and Kenny, who recorded for Philadelphia International as the Whitehead Brothers. Gene McFadden went on to work with Willie Collins, Gloria Gaynor, Freddie Jackson, Melba Moore, and Beau Williams.

DAVID NAUGHTON
MAKIN' IT
(Dino Fekaris, Freddie Perren)
RSO 916
No. 5 *July 21, 1979*

Dave Naughton is primarily an actor and a dancer, and only a sometime singer. Born on February 13, 1951, and raised in Hartford, Connecticut, he received a degree in English literature from the University of Pennsylvania and studied acting at the London Academy of Music and Dramatic Arts.

Naughton's big break came in the late '70s, when he sang and danced in a series of mini-musical Dr. Pepper commercials. The spots caught the attention of the casting director of an upcoming TV series, "Makin' It," to be based on the film *Saturday Night Fever* (1977). Dave had the honor of playing the John Travolta role. To beef up the connection with the movie, the producers used Bee Gees music, gave John's sister Ellen Travolta a small part, and brought in the film's producer, Robert Stigwood, for "technical" input. Two months later, ABC pulled the plug on the series.

"Makin' It" was used as the theme for the TV series and used in the flick *Meatballs* (1979). Despite the massive response, only a few more efforts were issued before Dave turned his full attention to being an actor.

Naughton has since had roles in two other TV series, "At Ease" and "My Sister Sam," and starred in the films *An American Werewolf in London* (1981), *Hot Dog . . . The Movie* (1984), *Kidnapped* (1987), *Overexposed* (1990), and *Steel and Lace* (1990).

Dave's older brother is actor James Naughton, known for his supporting roles in *The Paper Chase* (1973) and *The Glass Menagerie* (1987).

PATRICK HERNANDEZ
BORN TO BE ALIVE
(Patrick Hernandez, Herve Tholance)
Columbia 10986
No. 16 *September 28, 1979*

Patrick Hernandez's name is forever linked to his then unknown but briefly contained back-up singer—Madonna Louise Ciccone, Madonna.

Pat's Spanish dad had been a big-band guitar player; his Austrian/Italian mom had been a singer. With that kind of background, it would seem nearly impossible for the young man (b. 1949, Guadeloupe, France) not to have developed an interest in music.

From 1963 through 1966, Hernandez attended school in England, where the pervasive audio backdrop was the Beatles sound. Patrick took notice. He later moved to Paris and decided to give singing a try. After more than a decade of getting by on the bar circuit with a succession of rock bands, Hernandez met "the Two Jeans," Jean Van Lieu and Jean Claude Pellerin who—acting in the dual roles of producers/managers gave the lad the chance to tape some songs, in particular a vibrant, dancey thing that he and Herve Tholance had written called "Born to Be Alive."

The response was awesome. The disk topped or nearly topped music charts in Australia, Brazil, Canada, Mexico, and a number of countries in Europe. "Born to Be Alive" it is reported by author Christopher Andersen, *Madonna: Unauthorized*, became an international hit, "grossing more that $25 million."

In support of this tremendous success, the record label and the two Jeans searched for talented bodies to flesh-out Hernandez's world tour. Madonna, in response to an ad in a trade publication, attended the New York audition. "Van Leiu and Pellerin were so impressed with her passionate delivery that they offered to bring her to Paris and mold her into a star," wrote Andersen. It's disputable how much work she put into the "Patrick Hernandez Show" before her departure from the two Jeans three months later. "I kept saying, 'When are you going to do something with me?' And they were busy with Patrick," said Madonna to the author.

Madonna most likely did travel with Hernandez's trek to Tunisia. About Madonna, Hernandez is quoted by Andersen as saying, "She once told me, 'Success is yours today but it will be mine tomorrow.'"

NICK LOWE
CRUEL TO BE KIND
(Robert IAN GOMM, Nick Lowe)
Columbia 11018
No. 12 *September 29, 1979*

He has worked with top-notch groups, written great songs, and recorded treasured tracks, but it's his producing skills that have earned him his major success.

Bassist/guitarist Nick (b. Mar. 24, 1949, Woodchurch, Suffolk, England) grew up listening to Elvis and dreaming of making ethereal rock and roll. The son of a Royal Air Force officer, he learned guitar and organized a few bands with his school chum, guitarist Brinsley Schwarz. They were the Sounds 4 Plus 1, Three's a Crowd, and—with the addition of keyboardist Bob Andrews, keyboardist Barry Landerman, and drummer Pete Whales in 1965—the Kippington Lodge. The band made some inroads and in the following year recorded five failed singles for Parlophone.

NICK LOWE

Pete and Barry dropped out in 1969, drummer Billy Rankin was added, and the group renamed itself after their lead guitarist—Brinsley Schwarz.

Brinsley acquired a riotous reputation and became the centerpiece of the blooming British pub-rock scene. They briefly appeared in DAVID ESSEX's *Stardust* (1974) flick and performed on the soundtrack to David Bowie's *Ziggy Stardust* (1983, filmed in 1973. Brinsley Schwarz labored for half a decade, creating critically lauded but commercially unsuccessful albums that featured a number of Lowe compositions.

The Schwarz boys split up in March, 1975. After cutting sardonic glam-rock sides as the Disco Brothers ("Let's Go to the Disco") and the Tartan Horde ("Bay City Rollers We Love You"), Lowe began playing what would become his most winning role—that of producer. Over the years, he has produced recordings for his wife (and Johnny Cash's step-daughter) Carlene Carter, Paul Carrack (formerly of ACE and later of Mike + the Mechanics), Huey Lewis's Clover, Elvis Costello (every album up through 1981's *Trust*), the Damned, Dave Edmunds, the FABULOUS THUNDERBIRDS, Dr. Feelgood, John Hiatt, Michael Jupp, the Kursaal Flyers, GRAHAM PARKER & The Rumour, the Pretenders ("Stop Your Sobbing"), and Wreckless Eric. He was present for the famed "Live Stiff"/Stiff Records packaged tour of 1977. And for a while—with Billy Bremner, Dave Edmunds, and Terry Williams—Lowe was a member of the short-lived but incredibly promising Rockpile.

All the while, Nick recorded solo singles, sporadically issuing LPs and EPs. Only "I Love the Sound of Breaking Glass" (from his first album, 1978's *Pure Pop for Now People*) and "Cruel to Be Kind" (a remake of one of his early "B" sides) made any major dents in the British charts, and only the latter would do likewise in the States. His "I Knew the Bride (When She Used to Rock and Roll)" (#77, 1986), credited to Nick Lowe & His Cowboy Outfit and produced by Huey Lewis, marked his return to *Billboard's* Hot 100.

In 1992, Nick and buddies Ry Cooder, John Hiatt, and Jim Keltner formed Little Village, a surprisingly overlooked supergroup. The loose-knit band folded but Lowe remains as busy as ever—sporadically issuing solos and producing Katydids, the Rain, and others. Possibilities remain slim that Nick Lowe will remain a dweller in the Hall of One-Hit Wonders.

After 30 years in the biz, Lowe let it slip, in '96, that he had crept into millionaire status—largely due to the inclusion of CURTIS STIGERS' work-up of his "(What's So Funny 'Bout) Peace, Love and Understanding" included in the flick *The Bodyguard* (1992).

SNIFF 'N' THE TEARS
DRIVER'S SEAT
(Paul Roberts)
Atlantic 3604
No. 15 *September 29, 1979*

___

Sniff 'n' The Tears was the realization of a British rock-er named Paul Roberts. Paul wrote and shaped all of the group's songs, sang lead, played guitar, created the album covers, and—when not otherwise occupied—painted. His reputation in Europe is more for his art-work than for his musical abilities: exhibitions of his paintings have been held in Amsterdam, London, Milan, and Paris.

The predecessor of this peculiarly named act was Ashes of Moon, put together by Roberts in 1974. He eventually dismantled the band, but some demo tapes had been made that found their way to drummer Luigi Salvoni. Roberts, meanwhile, had left for France to con-centrate on painting for three years. Upon Paul's return, Luigi convinced him to put aside his palette and give rock and roll another spin.

Chiswick Records was interested in the venture. Luigi rounded up bassist Chris Birkin, guitarist Mick Dyche, keyboardist Alan Fealdman, and guitarist Loz Netto—the first official Sniff 'n' the Tears line-up. *Fickle Heart* (1979) and "Driver's Seat" (released domestically on Atlantic) followed, and both albums fared well. Reviewing *Fickle Heart*, *Billboard* compared the band to

the Dire Straits and proclaimed their debut album as heralding "a new age of music that will hold up long after the last dance has ended."

By the time *The Game's Up* (1980) appeared, only Roberts, Dyche, and Netto remained. Roberts and an entirely new group recorded *Love Action* in 1981. The latter remains Sniff's last stateside recording. Both albums are intriguing, well-crafted works that are well worth a listen.

IAN GOMM
HOLD ON
(Ian Gomm)
Stiff/Epic 50747
No. 18 *October 27, 1979*

___

For four of the band's five years, Ian Gomm (b. Mar. 17, 1947, Ealing, England) was a member of Brinsley Schwarz with Bob Andrews, NICK LOWE, Billy Rankin, and Brinsley Schwarz himself. "The Brinsleys were inti-mate, alright," Gomm told *Trouser Press'* Dave Schulps. "They not only worked together but lived communally in the same house, families and all. Ugh, it was awful . . . It had nothing to do with the music, nothing to do with the group. Everybody's personal life just became jum-bled together. Maybe if we'd split into separate flats we might still be together today. That, plus our never being able to break through commercially, finished the group."

Gomm left the group, depressed, and lazed around. In the meantime, Andrews and Schwarz achieved some success backing GRAHAM PARKER in the Rumour; Lowe went on to establish himself as a top-notch producer.

In the mid-'70s, Gomm revived him-self. Hanging out at the 16-track Foel Stu-dios near Welshpool in Wales, Ian learned the technical side of recording from Buzz-cocks/Stranglers producer Martin Rush-ent. Ian produced some sides for the Stranglers, Van Der Graaf, Plummet Air-lines, Alex Korner, and the bagpipe-blow-ing Second Battalion of the Scots Guard.

"I wanted to do something with my hands, to erase my mind of what had gone before," said Gomm to Steve Clarke, the *New Music Express*. In his off-time, he compiled some solo demos. "I took them around and got rejected by everyone," Gomm lamented to Schulps. "It's the old story, but even worse. I'd go into the offices and they'd say, 'Face it, Ian, not only are the tunes awful, but you can't even sing. Why bother? Get a day job.' I began to think they might be right." Only months before the release of *Gomm With the Wind* (1979) and "Hold On"—one of those "awful tunes"—Ian's mom took him aside and told him to stop all of this rock-and-roll nonsense and get a real job.

Intermittent singles have been shipped and three further albums have been offered—the most recent, *Images* (1986)—but Gomm has yet to reestablish a foothold on the charts.

M
POP MUSIC
(Robin Scott)
Sire 49033
No. 1 *November 3, 1979*

M is Robin Scott, a former art school student and folksinger from England. Hard to believe, you say? Once you have heard his hit single, it is difficult to imagine that Scott ever did anything other than commune with computers and noise-making techno-toys.

Press releases claim he grew up like a regular lad in London, managed a couple of groups, wrote a few songs—most notably the "French Elvis" Johnny Halliday— and even set up a small-time record label: Do It Records. Before collapsing, his label would discover Adam Ant, then a man with an Ant band.

In 1978, Rob moved to Paris, produced the Slits and a few French bands and conceived of his bizarre, electro notions. The act was called M, after the signs all over the city that announce the Paris Metro. A first single, "Moderne Man," failed as did "Cowboys and Indians," a 45 he had issued as by Cosmic Romance.

"I was looking to make a fusion of various styles which somehow would summarize the last 25 years of pop music," Scott told Fred Bronson in *The Billboard Book of Number One Hits*. "Where as rock and roll had created a generation gap, disco was bringing people together on an enormous scale. That's why I really wanted to make a simple, bland statement, which was 'All we're talking about basically [is] pop music.'"

Three different versions of "Pop Music" were shaped and taped. There was an R & B rendition; a funky burner à la James Brown; and the punchy, three-minute opus that we all have come to know. His hit-containing debut LP, *New York-London-Paris-Munich* (1979)—featuring the voice of Betty Vinchon and Roogalators' bassist Julian Scott—sold well in the States. While M's three immediate follow-ups charted in the U.K., none of these 45s made the *Billboard* listings. *The Official Secrets Act*, M's second album, featured Level 42's Mark King.

Robin has collaborated on a pair of albums with actor Ryuichi Sakamoto (he appeared in the 1983 flick *Merry Christmas, Mr. Lawrence*) and the keyboardist of the Yellow Magic Orchestra. In 1985, Scott recorded an album in London entitled *The Kiss of Life*, under his God-given name.

A 1989 remix of "Pop Music" returned M's name to some European charts; and Britain's Top 15.

FRANCE JOLI
COME TO ME
(Tony Green)
Prelude 8001
No. 15 *November 17, 1979*

France Joli (b. 1963, Dorion, Montreal) hit the ground running. As a tot, she would lip sync while jumping rope with a microphone. She was encouraged to take drama, dance, and voice lessons; at age four, she was performing professionally. By 11, France was so busy doing local radio, TV spots and commercials, that her parents let her drop out of school to pursue her career.

Two years later, Joli sought out Canadian recording artist/teen idol Tony Green. After one of his sets, she followed a bunch of excited teenyboppers backstage. "They went backstage to get Tony's autograph," she told *Cashbox*. "I went backstage to audition."

As Tony Green recalled to *Cashbox*, "She showed up with a couple of Barbra Streisand albums and had the nerve to sing a duet with the record." Apparently, Tony was impressed: he eventually became France's manager—succeeding Mama, Michelle Joli, wrote some songs for her—including her lone looper, produced her first recordings, and got the girl her first recording contract.

"Come to Me" was the 16-year-old's virgin vinyl voyage, and it charted fairly well on both *Billboard*'s pop and R & B (#36) listings. Despite the rapid fire of subsequent releases, however, Joli retains one of the lowest profiles in all of one-hitdom; this all despite the fact that she continued to record well into the '80s, often for Epic—a major label.

Joli appeared and won guest slots on the Bob Hope, Merv Griffin, and Dinah Shore TV shows; played the Riviera Hotel in Las Vegas with Peaches & Herb and in 1982 performed at Radio City Music Hall with the Commodores.

"I'm starting young and have a lot of time," Joli explained to *Variety*'s Andy Nulman some years back. "If I fail, I have a lot of time to make it up. And if I don't make it now, I have more of a chance to make it later."

J. D. SOUTHER
YOU'RE ONLY LONELY
(John David Souther)
Columbia 11079
No. 7 *December 15, 1979*

John David Souther was born in Detroit but raised amid the tumbleweeds in Amarillo, Texas. In the late '60s, J. D. became fast friends with a fellow Motor City man named Glenn Frey. Both had independently trekked to Los Angeles to pick and sing. As the Long-branch Pennywhistle, the duo recorded an album for Amos Records in 1970. In attendance on that session were session-playing legends: James Burton, Ry Cooder, Larry Knechtel, and Doug Kershaw.

Soon after, Frey wandered off to become a founding member of the legendary Eagles. J. D., meanwhile, dashed off tunes, a number of which were recorded by sometime girlfriend Linda Ronstadt and Bonnie Raitt. In 1972, Asylum, Linda's label, took an interest in Souther and released a self-titled album. Critics liked the disk, and commented that the boy showed much promise.

In 1974, David Geffen, Asylum's main man, applied his negotiating abilities to creating a country-rock supergroup along the lines of Crosby, Stills & Nash. RICHIE FURAY had helped form Poco and had played with BUFFALO SPRINGFIELD. Chris Hillman had been in the Byrds, the Flying Burrito Brothers, and Stephen Stills's Manassas. The Souther-Hillman-Furay Band's self-titled album was a big seller, as was Furay's fluffy "Fallin' in Love" (#27, 1974). But after a disappointing second album, the group called it quits in 1976.

Over the years, J. D. has continued to record coolly received albums. The Orbison-esque title tune from his third LP, *You're Only Lonely*, was a monster mover, but follow-ups have failed to sustain the Texan's career. The Eagles, however, have had hits with versions of his "Best of My Love," "New Kid in Town," and "Heartache Tonight." As a session singer, Souther has backed up KARLA BONOFF, Jackson Browne, Christopher Cross, Joni Mitchell, RANDY NEWMAN, the Outlaws, and WARREN ZEVON to name a few. "Her Town Too," a duet with James Taylor, hit all the right notes and heights (#11, 1981). Souther also made acting appearances on the "Thirtysomething" TV series.

THE 80s

ROGER DALTREY

STEVE FORBERT
ROMEO'S TUNE
(Steve Forbert)
Nemperor 7525
No. 11 *February 23, 1980*

When White's Auto Parts Store in Meridian, Mississippi, went out of business in 1976, Steve Forbert (b. 1955), their warehouse man and truck driver, found himself out of a job. With Dylan dreams dancing in his head, Steve hopped a train for Greenwich Village, singing and strumming his guitar on street corners and in the echoey confines of Grand Central Station. After a bit more practice, Steve began working the folk haunts and opening for New Wavers like the Talking Heads and John Cale.

Danny Fields, the Ramones' manager, soon arranged for the talent police at Nemperor Records to give a listen to "the new Dylan in town." Critical acclaim greeted Forbert's, first LP, *Alive on Arrival* (1978). "Romeo's Tune"—dedicated to the memory of Supreme Florence Ballard—came from Steve's second album, *Jackrabbit Slim* (1979). Sales on the "Romeo"

STEVE FORBERT

number surprised nearly everyone who had an inkling of who or what Steve was trying to be. Two more LPs were issued to a shrinking following, and in 1982, the big boys at Nemperor Records showed the lad from Meridian the back door.

Steve Forbert bounced back in 1988. While fronting the legendary Crickets at a Buddy Holly tribute in New York City, he was spotted by Garry Tallent, who recommended him to the powers at Geffen Records. Later in the year, Tallent, a member of Bruce Springsteen's E Street Band, produced Forbert's first release for the new label, *Streets of This Town* (1988).

Steve returned to recording in 1992 with the critically praised *The American in Me*; and three years later with *The Mission of the Crossroad Palms*.

Without knowing it, MTV viewers have probably seen Steve as Cyndi Lauper's tattooed boyfriend in her video "Girls Just Want to Have Fun."

TERI DESARIO WITH K. C.
YES I'M READY
(Barbara Mason)
Casablanca 2227
No. 2 *March 1, 1980*

Teri DeSario had gone to school with Harry Wayne Casey, that's dance king K. C. of K. C. & The Sunshine Band. They had been teenage friends, both later claimed. Neither knew then that their paths were destined to cross years later to re-create a one-off classic—a disco-dancin' reworking of Barbara Mason's "Yes, I'm Ready."

Once school days were behind, the woman from Hialeah, Miami, took to the streets playing recorder and harp in an undisclosed Renaissance band. Teri then tried folksinging, but by 1976 was settled into a local jazzy/pop unit called Abacus, with husband and horn man Bill Purse. Purse friend and recent Bee Gee co-producer Albhy Galuten gave the band a listen. A demo tape was made, which Galuten took back to a French recording studio where the Bee Gee brothers were laying down tracks. Barry Gibb, intrigued by Teri's vocal assets wrote her a tune, "Ain't Nothing Gonna Keep Me From You," and placed the proper calls getting her a contract with Casablanca Records.

"Ain't Nothing," her first 45 from her debut album, *Pleasure Train*, charted (#43, 1978), but Teri was not pleased. "My first recording experience was pure hell," she told *Billboard* magazine. "I had a lot of bad feelings about that first record."

Wanting a musical change and wanting to get out of Miami, Teri was linked up with her old school chum, K. C., to produce something to her liking. "I was skeptical. It took awhile to trust," said DeSario. "Also, I was scared because he has a distinctive sound and my sound is so different."

K. C. also experienced a case of nerves. "I was scared because Teri wanted to come to Los Angeles to do the album," said Casey, who has done most of his production work in Miami. "I was also afraid that, because of her bad experience before, she wasn't going to believe in me and it wouldn't work."

By accident and while en route to their first recording session, "Yes I'm Ready" became a duet. "We originally picked out the song for Teri, and we were singing it on the plane to Los Angeles," K. C. explained. "Everyone on the plane liked it so we decided to leave it that way and do it the same way in the studio."

"Moonlight Madness" (#80, 1980) and a retreading of Martha & The Vandellas' "Dancin' in the Streets" (#66, 1980) were issued to a modicum of attention, before the mainstream limelight dimmed on Teri's career.

"I'm not going to follow trends anymore," Teri told *Billboard*. "You lose your creativity when you follow trends. I'm just going to pick out the songs which I like best and not be afraid to do different kinds of arrangements. It'll be a little more fun."

CHARLIE DORE
PILOT OF THE AIRWAVES
(Charlie Dore)
Island 49166
No. 13 *May 3, 1980*

Charlie Dore was born and raised in London. She went to drama school, acted in a repertory company in Newcastle, and even did a brief stint on the TV series "Rainbow." With a voice like EMMYLOU HARRIS, she burst onto the British pop scene in 1977 with a band called Prairie Oyster. One of the seven drummers who made his way through the group's line-up was Pick Withers, later of Dire Straits. Charlie's Oysters played city-bred country music at a time when England was embroiled in the punk-rock assault, so the group's gigs were few and far between.

Prairie personnel kept wandering in and out of the band—by the time scouts from Island Records had opted to record the act, Prairie Oyster—then billed Back Pocket—had perished. Nevertheless, the label signed Charlie, and assigned Bruce Welch of the Shadows and Alan Tarney of the Tarney-Spencer Band to produce Dore's disk. Part of the *Where to Now?* (1979) album was recorded in Nashville, with ex-Cricket Sonny Curtis—author of "The Mary Tyler Moore Theme"—among the stellar session crew.

"Pilot of the Airwaves," Charlie's tribute to DJs, was her first 45 and so far, the only track of hers to make the pop charts. "Fear of Flying," the follow-up single (U.K. debut single), crashed ignobly. The next year, Charlie changed labels and musical direction: *Listen!* (1981), her Chrysalis debut, was easy-listening music.

A career change in order, Charlie co-starred with Jonathan Pryce and Tim Curry in Richard Eyre's *The Ploughman's Lunch* (1984); thereafter appearing in several homeland TV shows, "Hard Cases" and "South of the Border." Since 1990, Charlie, as a member of the comedy team of Dogs on Holiday, has been a resident act at the Hurricane Club in London.

As a songwriter, Dore has placed material on Celine Dion's *The Colour of Love* album, had a Top 10 each in the United Kingdom and the United States; respectively, Jimmy Nail's "Ain't No Doubt" and Sheena Easton's "Strut." In 1995, Charlie Dore returned to recording, with the release of *Things Change*.

LIPPS, INC.
FUNKYTOWN
(Steven Greenberg)
Casablanca 2233
No. 1 *May 31, 1980*

Lipps, Inc. (pronounced "lip-synch") was the brain child of Minneapolis native Steven Greenberg. Decades before the idea struck, little Stevie began coaxing sounds out of a multitude of instruments. By age 15, he was pounding drums in the Diplomats and later, the Storm Center. Five years later, with feverish dreams of stardom, Steve tripped to Los Angeles with a box of demos. No one paid much attention, and a dejected Greenberg caught a Greyhound home. Over the next eight years, he worked for a traveling party service, tried to set up an entertainment-production company, and sang as part of a duo (with Sandy Atlas) in brass-rail bars and dives.

After tiring of that scene, Steve resolved to make another major move on fame and fortune. With designs on integrating disco and R & B, Steve created a tune called "Rock It." A demo with him on nearly all the instruments was quickly cut, pressed, and promoted all over town. Minneapolis's KFMX rode the number, and Steve reapproached the music moguls in Los Angeles. This time, Casablanca commissioned an album. Tinseltown sessioneers were rounded up, and Steve recruited Cynthia Johnson to front his project. Cynthia had played sax since she was eight, had been 1976's Miss Black Minnesota, and, when discovered by Greenberg, was a police department secretary singing on weekends with a group called Flyte Tyme. (Flyte Tyme would later evolve into that punchy Prince satellite, The Time.)

"Funkytown" was one of but four tracks on Lipps, Inc.'s debut album, *Mouth to Mouth* (1980). After "Rock It," the first single, stiffed, the danceable "Funkytown" was issued. No one, not even Greenberg, expected this anachronistic disco ditty to sell 2 million copies and become a huge pop and R & B (#2) hit. For a follow-up, a remastered version of "Rock It" (#64, 1980) was issued, and stirred a little interest on its second time out. Three more R & B chart entries appeared, but "Rock It" was the last sighting of Lipps, Inc. on the pop listings.

In 1983, after three albums and a handful of failed singles, Johnson left Greenberg's unit to raise a daughter. Margaret Cox and Melanie Rosales have since taken her place.

GARY NUMAN
CARS
(Gary Numan)
Atco 7211
No. 9 *June 7, 1980*

GARY NUMAN

Some souls claim that Gary Numan (b. Gary Anthony James Webb, Mar. 8, 1958, Hammersmith, England) was an innovative and exciting figure on the techno-pop landscape. Then there are those listeners who considered this mascara-faced alien to be nothing more than a KRAFTWERK-influenced, David Bowie clone.

Right from the start, Gary dreamed up his own tunes. "I had to write my own songs," he told *Hit Parade*'s Janel Bladow. "I couldn't play anybody else's." He joined his first band in 1977 when he was 19—per his report, they threw him out on his ear. For a moment, he was a member of Meanstreet. Soon after, he auditioned and was accepted as a member of the Lasers; within a year, Numan—the self-proclaimed "Valerium"—was in charge, and renamed them the Tubeway Army.

The Tubeway Army issued a couple of punk-styled singles ("That's Not It" and "Bombers") on the Beggar's Banquet label before Gary was struck by inspiration. While the group was recording their *Tubeway Army* (1978) album, Gary started fiddling about with some studio synthesizers. The resulting sounds—icily soulless, robotic noises—seemed to him to be a perfect match for the lyrics of alienation, despair, and desolation that he was crafting. The rest of the group, except for bassist Paul "Scarlett" Gardiner, disagreed with this musical direction and walked out, later forming the Station Bombers. To complete the LP, drummer Jess "Rael" Lidyard, Gary's uncle, was enlisted in the revamped Tubeways.

"Are Friends Electric"—credited to the Tubeway Army, and extracted from the group's second album, *Replicas* (1979)—was a big British hit. The Tubeway Army moniker was then tossed aside. "Cars"—from Numan's *The Pleasure Principle* (1980) LP—was Gary's only appearance on the United States charts, but went to number one in the U.K. By the end of 1985, Gary had racked up 15 British hits. He and his strange-looking sidemen toured the States complete with smoke machines, throbbing fluorescent lights, frigid demeanors, and dead-pan vocals. Americans were not all that interested—two albums later, with *Telekon* (1980) and *Dance* (1981), Gary's career on these shores began to vaporize.

"I've got a very big fear of being a has-been," Numan admitted to *Trouser Press*' Jim Green. "I'm getting out of it before I get too involved to get out of it. I have to face not being famous anymore."

In 1981, Gary Numan announced his retirement. The following year, he attempted to fly his single-engine Cessna around the world. Gary was arrested in India on suspicion of spying; charges were later dropped. Numa Records was formed by Gary in 1984 (closed in 1987); its first release was Paul Gardiner's last recording, "Venus in Furs"—Gardiner died of a drug overdose, just prior.

398

Despite retirement, Numan has continued to record, tour, and chart in his homeland. With Dave Clark Five's Mike Smith, Gary wrote music for Rodman Flender's flick *The Unborn* (1990). Gary continues to perform for charities as The Whales Fund and The Royal Society for the Prevention of Cruelty to Animals. Gary has charted in his homeland in duet with Shakatak's Bill Sharpe, as vocalist with Radio Heart, and with his bassist, the late Paul Gardiner.

In 1996, Gary's "Cars" was utilized for a Carling Premier TV ad, generating enough interest for the 17-year-old tune to return to the British Top 20.

ROCKY BURNETTE
TIRED OF TOEIN' THE LINE
(Rocky Burnette, Ron Coleman)
EMI-America 8043
No. 8 *July 26, 1980*

His nephew is Billy Burnette, a mid-'80s addition to the Fleetwood Mac line-up. And his father and his uncle were, respectively, Johnny and DORSEY BURNETTE, co-pioneers in the development of rockabilly music. Johnny and Dorsey plus Paul Burlison were Memphis' Rock 'n' Roll Trio, a unit that from 1953 to 1957 crafted classic rockabilly singles like "Tear It Up," "Train Kept A-Rollin'," "Hush Hush," and "Lonesome Train."

Eddie Cochran, Gene Vincent, and Elvis were often over at the house when Rocky (b. Jonathan Burnette, June 12, 1953, Memphis) was small, so music was all around when he was growing up. Jon was even nick-named after his relatives' favorite musical style; as was his nephew Billy—ROCK a BILLY. Despite the family tradition, Burnette attended college with dreams of being a football player, and studied theater, cinematography, and the Bible. He had written some tunes as a teen, and worked briefly for the Acuff-Rose music-publishing outfit—the Osmonds and David Cassidy recorded a few—but it was not until the '70s and the completion of his education that Rocky sought to record his songs.

After a failed affair with Curb Records, Rocky traded songwriting credits for studio time to cut "Clowns From Outer Space." The flip side was "Tired of Toein' the Line"—a tune Rocky claims he effortlessly dashed off in 20 minutes time. EMI issued the 45 in Europe, and later, it met with success in the United States. The album featuring the track, *The Son of Rock 'n' Roll* (1980), sold well, and the future looked bright.

Nothing to date—and a number of sides have been issued by EMI, Goods, and KYD—has managed to regain a chart footing for this self-proclaimed son of rock and roll. Last spotted, Rocky was fronting the New Rock 'N' Roll Trio, featuring Tony Austin, Johnny Black,

brother to Elvis's original bass player the late Bill Black and Paul Burlison, guitarist with his father's band. Late in 1997, Rocky was a guest vocalist on Burlison's debut solo album.

S.O.S. BAND
TAKE YOUR TIME (DO IT RIGHT) PART 1
(Harold Clayton, Sigidi Abdullah)
Tabu 5522
No. 3 *August 16, 1980*

It all began in 1977, in a bar in Atlanta. Jason "T. C." Bryant (keyboards, synthesizers, lead vocals), Billy R. Ellis (saxophone) (who had played with Billy Preston, Otis Redding, and NINA SIMONE), James Earl Jones III (drums), and Mary Davis (lead vocals, keyboards) were the house band at a jumpin' night spot called Lamar's Regal Room. Milton Lamar took an interest in the outfit, and in short order became their manager. The group played Top 40 tunes, ballads, and jazzy jams, and alternately called themselves Santamonica or the Sounds of Santa Monica.

Local publicist Bunnie Jackson Ransom hooked the band up with Clarence Avant, president of Tabu Records. By this point, Santamonica had expanded to include Willie "Sonny" Killebrew (saxophone, flute) (who had worked with Millie Jackson, Gladys Knight, Johnny Taylor, and the Ohio Players), John Alexander "Skin" Simpson III (bass, keyboards), and Bruno Speight (guitar). Avant signed the act, and changed their name to "The S.O.S. Band," the acronym variously interpreted as standing for the Sounds of Success, the Sound of the South, or Satisfaction on Stage.

"Take Your Time (Do It Right)," the S.O.S. Band's funk-flavored premier platter, became a number-one R & B record, eventually selling 2 million copies. The S.O.S. (1980) album was also a healthy seller, and went gold, as did both *On the Rise* (1983) and *Sands of Time* (1986). In all, 17 of their 45s have placed on the R & B listings through 1987. Yet in spite of all this success, "Take Your Time" remains the group's only foray into pop Top 40-land.

Jerome "J. T." Thomas (drums) replaced James Earl Jones III in 1981; the same year, Abdul Raoof (trumpet, flugelhorn, congas) was added. In 1987, Davis left the fold for a solo career; ex-Reach vocalist Pennye Ford filled her shoes. Ford is the daughter of Gene Redd, Sr., James Brown's long-time producer. R & B chartings continued for the restructured S.O.S. into the early '90s.

FRED KNOBLOCK
WHY NOT ME
(F. Knoblock, C. Whitsett)
Scotti Brothers 518
No. 18 *August 23, 1980*

BENNY MARDONES

J. Fred Knoblock was born and raised in Jackson, Mississippi. He first gained notice in the mid-'70s playing in a rock unit called Let's Eat. For six years, Let's Eat labored. Shortly after country acts began recording some of his tunes, Fred managed to convince the folks at the Scotti Brothers label that he had the makings of a country-rock star. "Why Not Me" was a successful effort—yet while Knoblock continued to appear on the C & W charts, staging a follow-up on the pop listings was another matter entirely. "Let Me Love" was neglected by pop programmers, but Fred did score with "Killin' Time" (#28, 1981), a one-shot collaboration with former Miss California TV actress Susan Anton ("Baywatch," and short-lived "Cliffhangers," "Mel and Susan," and "Presenting Susan Anton").

In the mid-'80s, Fred Knoblock teamed up with Thom Schuyler, Jr., and Paul Overstreet. As Schuyler, Knoblock & Overstreet (a.k.a. SKO), they started their string of C & W hits with "You Can't Stop Love" (#9, 1986), "Baby Got a New Baby" (#1, 1987), and "American Me" (#16, 1987). Overstreet left the fold, and Craig Bickhardt joined. The group's new name? Schuyler, Knoblock & Bickhardt, naturally.

ALI THOMSON
TAKE A LITTLE RHYTHM
(Ali Thomson)
A & M 2243
No. 15 *August 23, 1980*

While little Ali (b. 1959, Glasgow, Scotland) was struggling to learn his multiplication tables, his big brother Dougie was blasting his bass in the British beat group the Alan Bown Set. After this group's break-up in the early '70s, Dougie joined his fellow Bown buddy John Helliwell in the band Supertramp. Encouraged by Dougie's example, brother Ali started singing and playing piano in local bands. In the mid-'70s, he moved to London, took a job with Mountain Records, and tried his hand at composing. Gary Wright crashed the stateside Top 10 charts in 1976 with his cover of Thomson's "Dream Weaver." Wright would return to hitdom in 1982 with yet another Thomson tune, "Really Wanna Know You."

Ali moved to California to join his brother, who set up an audition for him with A & M Records. "Take a Little Rhythm," a mellow McCartneyesque number, was featured on Ali's debut album. Scads of souls thought the record was yet another puffball from ex-Beatle Paul. "Little Rhythm" sold big. Another track, "Live Every Minute" (#42, 1980), made the Hot 100, another album appeared, and not a whisper has been heard from Ali Thomson since.

BENNY MARDONES
INTO THE NIGHT
(Benny Mardones, Robert Tepper)
Polydor 2091 / Polydor 889368
No. 11 *September 6, 1980*
No. 20 *June 3, 1989*

Benny was raised in a small factory community of 1,200. "I never took a voice lesson because I've always wanted to stay as raw and real as I can," he told a *Billboard* interviewer. "And besides, in Savage, Maryland, the only records people have are police records." By age 11, Mardones was imitating Elvis at county fairs and sock hops. In his teens, he left Savage to work the South fronting different bar bands.

By the mid-'70s, Benny was working in New York as a songwriter. Private Stock Records took an interest and issued his first LP, *Thank God for Girls* (1977). Although the album featured David Bowie guitarist and Ian Hunter sidekick Mick Ronson and Humble Pie drummer Jerry Shirley, it stiffed. The label soon folded, but by then, Polydor had signed Mardones up.

Both "Into the Night" and the LP featuring it—*Never Run, Never Hide* (1980)—were, according to Benny, a lot of fun to record. "But that was where the fun stopped," Mardones revealed to interviewer Barry Alfonso for a Curb Records hand-out. "I was starting to slide into a world of drugs and fast living and just being crazy. Everything lost perspective for me, and I was very disheartened by the record company [Polydor]. I worked real hard, but when *Never Run, Never Hide* didn't sell, it broke my heart.

"In '82 and '83, I was in a self-destructive mode, flying back and forth coast-to-coast like it was a big party. Then it finally ended. I woke up one morning in '85, and I'd lost everything.

"Back around 1973, I met Elvis backstage, and he autographed a photo for me. Well, when I was broke after my first success with 'Into the Night,' that Elvis photo and a bed were about all I had left. I didn't have food in my refrigerator; everything from diamonds to equipment was sold and gone. They were shutting my phone off the next day—I was penniless. Somebody offered me $2,500 for that Elvis photo, and I said, 'No . . . if I die tomorrow, at least they'll find me with this.' That was the day my life turned around."

Benny moved in with a friend in Syracuse and kicked his dependency on drink and drugs. He worked whatever gigs he could find, cutting a couple of independent LPs—*Unauthorized* (1985) and *American Dreams* (1988)—and awaiting his rediscovery. In 1989, a Phoenix DJ began playing "Into the Night" as if it were a new ballad. Other area stations picked up on the song, and soon Polydor reissued the dusty disk. It made the Top 40 charts, making Mardones the only '80s artist to have a hit twice with the same record.

Whereabouts of the extremely talented Benny Mardones: unknown.

LARRY GRAHAM
ONE IN A MILLION YOU
(Sam Dees)
Warner Bros. 49221
No. 9 *September 20, 1980*

Before his teen years, Larry Graham (b. Aug. 14, 1946, Beaumont, TX) had taken tap dance lessons, learned to play the piano, guitar, harmonica, and drums, and fronted his own vocal group. His father was a guitarist, and his mother was Dell Graham, a lounge singer. By the time he was 10 years old, little Larry was playing bass, accompanying his mother at nightclubs in San Francisco. They would play standards like "Ebb Tide" and "Time After Time"—audiences loved it.

One night, Larry was forced to play with a "thumpin' and pluckin'" style on the bass to fill in for a missing drummer. Sylvester "Sly" Stewart, a local DJ, overheard Graham and asked him to join his Family Stone. Larry accepted and stayed with the legendary Sly for six years.

Shortly after his departure, Graham restructured Patryce "Chocolate" Banks's Hot Chocolate band into a hot soul outfit, GRAHAM CENTRAL STATION. Five funky albums and more than a dozen R & B hits later, Larry dismantled the Station and started singing in a much mellower, lounge-lizard style. "One in a Million You" was a million-seller, a number-one record on the R & B listings; his subsequent croonings, including a guest appearance with Fire Fox (produced by Ollie Brown, half of OLLIE & JERRY) and a duet with Aretha Franklin, have graced those charts on several occasions into the late '80s.

"Actually," Graham told *Black Star*'s Lisa Collins, "the singing that I'm doing was the style of singing I was doing before I joined up with Sly and went off into that funk bag. It just took me a little while to get back around to where it all started."

JOHNNY LEE
LOOKIN' FOR LOVE
(Wanda Mallette, Patti Ryan, Bob Morrison)
Full Moon 47004
No. 5 *September 20, 1980*

Johnny Lee Ham (b. July 3, 1946, Texas City, TX) was raised on a dairy farm in Alta Lorna, in East Texas. While milking the cows, Johnny Lee would listen to rock and roll—"I thought country music was too twangy then," he told *Country Style*. In the early '60s, he and some of the guys at Sante Fe High formed Johnny Lee & The Road Runners. After his school days were done, Lee joined the Navy and toured Vietnam on a guided missile cruiser; four years later, home safe and sound, he began bumming around California, undecided about his life's vocation.

Having decided to pursue the field of music, Johnny Lee met country star MICKEY GILLEY, one of his heroes in 1970. As Johnny recounted to *Country Style*: "I said 'Mickey, do you remember me? I was on the Larry Kane TV show in Galveston with you.' Well, that was an outright lie, of course, but Mickey was busy, you know, and he wanted to be nice, so he said, 'Uh . . . yeah, yeah, I think I do remember you, but I can't remember what you did on the show.'" Lee laid it on thick, then asked Gilley if he could sit in with his band. The audience response was encouraging, and after a few more appearances at Gilley gigs, Mickey asked Johnny to join his outfit full time. When Mickey opened his legendary Gilley's Club (billed as "The World's Largest Honky Tonk") in Texas in 1971, Johnny Lee worked there as an opening act and trumpeter in the house band. Nine years later, when the cameras were there to record the goings-on for John Travolta's *Urban Cowboy* (1980) flick, Lee was still Mickey's right-hand man.

Ham had already charted with a few C & W notables, like his remakes of Bing Crosby's "Red Sails in the Sunset" (#22, 1976) and Rick Nelson's "Garden Party" (renamed "Country Party," #15, 1977). But it was "Lookin' for Love," a cut from off the *Urban Cowboy* soundtrack, that clicked big. Lee also met a wife-to-be in the film, Charlene Tilton ("Lucy Ewing" on TV's "Dallas").

Ham remained on a roll for a few good years. Three cuts from his *Lookin' for Love* (1980) LP—"One in a Million" (#1, 1980), "Pickin' Up Strangers" (#3, 1981), and "Prisoner of Hope" (#3, 1981)—were C & W winners, and "Bet Your Heart on Me" (#54; C&W: #1, 1981) made the pop charts as well.

Johnny Lee's marriage to Charlene ended in divorce, but his disks remained active on the C & W airwaves through 1986. Gilley's is gone, but Ham had left Gilley in 1981 to front his own band—the Western Union Band—and to open up his own club nearby—Johnny Lee's. He set up the Johnny Lee Pro-Am Golf Tournament to aid the Home of Guided Hands, a charity for the mentally handicapped, and for a season sang the theme tune for the Cybill Shepherd-DAVID SOUL TV series, "The Yellow Rose." Alas, all that is past. "I lost everything except my talent," Lee recently told Joe Edwards of the Associated Press. "I never saw a dime."

Lee's autobiography, *Lookin' for Love*, was published by Diamond Books in 1989.

DEVO
WHIP IT
(Mark Mothersbaugh, Jerry Casale)
Warner Bros. 49550
No. 14 *November 15, 1980*

Devo was different, avant-garde, and definitely a noncommercial entity of stellar proportions. "We were a devolving three-prong attack," says Jerry Casale, the act's bassist and co-founder with keyboardist-guitarist Mark Mothersbaugh, in an exclusive interview. "We had a devolving look, a sound, and the answers. Devo was an all-out assault on nothingness."

First spotted in the mid-seventies, Devo was perceived as an alien entity, faceless and bone-chillingly cool. "In a six-week period in our initial deformation, we had descended to this look that stuck on us," said Casale. "We wore paper yellow suits with paper 3-D eyewear. Put five guys in such and the look was of uniformity. We were replaceables, totally alike, yet different from the abyss."

Later Devo would further their visual decline into pseudo J.F.K.-Reagan wigs (Devo-dos), flowerpot hats (energy domes), and toilet-seat collars.

Their movements on stage were jerky, their sounds sterile, convoluted, industrial. Devo "singing" was at great effort emotionless, though tension was ever present. "We were not musicians," Casale explained. "We were users of instruments."

Devo lyrics were apocalyptic jabs at contemporary society, with asides to lust and contorted sexual activities. "We were students and humans—angst-ridden—and had steeped ourselves in Nietzsche and Ronald McDonald and punk science."

Devo handouts and album inserts propagated an ambitious philosophy. Mankind, Devo declaimed, had finally reached the omega point and all was now falling apart, devolving. "We were spuds devolving from a long line of brain-eating apes," added Casale.

Fans became Devotees. Their sizable though never mainstream numbers are now—nearly two decades later—devolving, though Casale assures there is an ever-dutiful cluster of cult cling-ons that are vigilant for new and further devolved Devo product and performance.

The Devo tale dates back to the dark mid-70s and Akron, Ohio, a town Casale describes as "industrial, gray, hideous—culturally, a black hole. Nothing inside of nothing."

Casale and Mothersbaugh met at Kent State University, where both were aspiring visual artists. "We were doing more or less what we wanted visually, using a lot of printing techniques," he said. Soon there were five spudsters—added were Jerry's brother Bob Casale (keyboards, guitar) plus Mark's brother Bob Mothersbaugh (lead guitar) and Alan Myers (drums). Their outlandish get-up and tongue-in-cheek musical approach accrued notice; they played in Cleveland and at New York's CBGB's, then relocated to Los Angeles. IGGY POP spotted Devo's act and brought them to the attention of the proper authorities, David Bowie and Brian Eno; the latter produced the group's debut album.

Two swell-selling singles were issued on Devo's own Booji Boy label, including a strangely syncopated version of the Rolling Stones' "Satisfaction." Warner Bros. signed the band in the hopes of capturing a mutated mainstream audience for Devo's quirky music.

Said Casale, "Warner Bros. had this attitude: 'Okay, you guys are totally bizarre. We don't get it, but somebody does. Do what you want. Hang yourself.'"

Despite the S&M connotations, "Whip It"—a cut off *Freedom of Choice*, their third LP—received a massive amount of airplay and a lone gold disc. Two other mainstream bids—"Working in the Coal Mine," a herky-jerky remake of the Lee Dorsey classic, and "Theme From Doctor Love"—followed. But all was not well with the mating of the nine-to-five surface world and these robotic spuds.

"We frightened normal people," says Casale. "There was this strong reaction. Radio hated us. We didn't fit the demographics." In 1985, after seven albums, Warner Bros. dropped the group.

Capitol Records subsidiary Enigma revived the act in 1987. Before the label's demise in 1990, Devo issued three further album adventures. More recently the act has returned to live performances and has been recording for Rykodisc, both as Devo and their alter-ego Dove the Band of Love, a strictly mundane Muzak-making concern.

"What could be more devoluted than our becoming a Muzak band?" asked Casale. "Like the Bible, devolution is basically an extended joke. One man's doughnut is another man's death."

ROGER DALTREY
WITHOUT YOUR LOVE
(Billy Nicholas)
Polydor 2121
No. 20 *November 29, 1980*

"Hope I die before I get old . . ." screamed Roger Daltrey, 30-plus years back as the voice of the rock revolution called the Who. He didn't . . . die and for years has warred with himself as to just what to do about it. "Who wants to make albums for juveniles? Not me," said Daltrey, one of the most distinctive voices in rock history, to *Music Express*. "Just because you're 45 doesn't mean you can't get out there and groove."

Roger (b. Mar. 1, 1944, London) grew up in a working-class neighborhood of London's Shepherd's Bush. At 12 years of age, Roger began making music on guitars he had constructed himself. Three years later, he was expelled from the Action County Grammar School. "I was a school rebel," Daltrey explained to Dave Marsh in *Before I Get Old*. "Whatever they said do, I didn't do. I was totally anti-everything. I was a right bastard, a right hard nut . . . Rock and roll was the only thing I wanted to get into."

With Reg Bowen on rhythm guitar, Daltrey formed a band, the Detours. He worked days in a sheet-metal shop, and weekends and nights the group played weddings, bar mitzvahs, and company gatherings. For two years, he envisioned himself as a guitarist, but then shelved the instrument to become the group's lead singer. About this time, John Entwistle and Pete Townsend, former members of the rival Scorpions, were invited to join the Detours. Before long, the band evolved into the Who, one of the biggest and most explosive rock acts of all time.

By 1973, Roger, like the other Who men, was looking to step outside the confines of the band and try some solo projects. *Daltrey* (1973), his well-received solo debut, was produced by ADAM FAITH and featured songs by a then-unknown Leo Sayer. Leo's "Giving It All Away" (#83, 1973) gave Daltrey his first and biggest British hit. Once outside the blaring sounds of the Who, Roger toyed with ballads and softer songs. "Without Your Love" was his fifth Hot 100 entry but remains his only Top 40 moment. Nearly all of his LPs have sold well, especially *Ride a Rock Horse* (1975), *One of the Boys* (1977), *McVicar* (1980), *Best Bits* (1982), and *Parting Should Be Painless* (1984). As an actor, Daltrey has appeared in *Tommy* (1975), *Lisztomania* (1975), *The Legacy* (1979), and *McVicar* (1980).

In 1984, Roger appeared in a TV adaptation of John Gay's *The Beggar's Opera*, followed by a run in the BBC children's series, "Buddy." The success of the latter culminated in *Buddy's Song* (1991), a movie spinoff of the series starring CHESNEY HAWKES as the aspiring teen star and Daltrey as his pop, a burned out Buddy Holly-obsessed dad.

"I don't have any illusions anymore," said Roger Daltrey to *Rolling Stone* magazine's Mick Brown. "The illusion that rock'n'roll could change anything—I don't believe that. That the Who was this strange machine that could do anything—I don't believe that. I've changed. Who would have ever thought that I'd end up saying I want to be an all-round entertainer? But that's what I want to be.

"I miss the Who very much, but it's over for good now, and you can't live in the past. I've got my own life to get on with."

KORGIS
EVERYBODY'S GOT TO LEARN SOMETIME
(James Warren)
Asylum 47055
No. 18 *December 27, 1980*

Before there were the Korgis, there was Stackridge (originally the Stackridge Lemon). Jimmy Warren (bass, guitar, vocals) and Andy Davis (b. Andrew Cresswell-Davis, drums, guitar) were members of this eccentric British configuration, which recorded mutant melodies and loony lyrics about characters like Marzo Plod, Percy the Penguin, and Dore the Female Explorer. Stackridge was a colorful art-rock ensemble with an esoteric reputation and a cult following to match. Fans would bring dustbin lids, rhubarb stalks, and a variety of unmentionables to the group's participatory concerts. Finally, in the late '70s, Warren, Davis, a manic man named "Mutter" Slater, and the other band members called it quits.

But before normalcy could grab hold of Warren and Davis, the twosome made demos of their off-beat tunes at a friend's house with the support of the Short-Wave Band (possibly comprising guitar/violinist Stuart Gordon and keyboardist Phil Harrison). After hearing material like "Young 'n' Russian," "Dirty Postcards," and "Mount Everest Sings the Blues," the Asylum label issued a now-rare *Korgis* (1979) album.

The following year, *Dumb Waiters* (1980), yet another package of palatable but peculiar pop product, appeared. Asylum shipped "Everybody's Got to Learn Sometime," one of the act's more conventional numbers. The response was such that Davis left the group.

It's alleged that a few other singles and possibly two albums were issued—in Europe only—and that Warren operating alone carried the Korgis banner on into the mid-'80s. By 1990, Davis returned from who-knows-where to take his rightful place opposite Warren and a new bloke named John the Baker (guitar, keyboard, vocals) for a new album and an time-altered version of their lone-one, "Everybody's Got to Learn Sometime." During the summer of 1993, the act that had never given a public performance quietly toured a town or two.

DELBERT MCCLINTON
GIVING IT UP FOR YOUR LOVE
(Jerry Williams)
Capitol 4948
No. 8 *February 21, 1981*

Playboy once described Delbert McClinton as "the best white R & B rock and roller in the world." For more than 30 years, Del has been playing foot-stompin' blues for the boys in the bars. McClinton has also been around some rock greats and participated in creating some of popdom's most treasured tracks, including BRUCE CHANNEL's "Hey! Baby," on which he played the harmonica.

"I spent a lot of nights in beer joints," Delbert told *Grooves'* Janel Bladow. "It's what I know. I love women, and I love it when they run out on you. It inspires me. 'Damn, I thought I had it by the balls, I had this woman—now, I see she's gone.' Women ought to leave more often."

Delbert McClinton (keyboards, harmonica, vocals) was born in Lubbock, Texas, on November 4, 1940, and raised in Fort Worth. The son of a railroad man and a beautician, Del bought himself a $3.50 F-hole Kay guitar in his teens and performed for the first time at the Big "V" Jamboree in 1957. While driving a truck, he worked with his brother in a weekend band they called the Mellow Fellows. "There were four guitars, no bass, a sax, and a drummer," Del told Randy McNutty. "None of us could play."

Gradually, the Mellow Fellows sharpened up and evolved into the Losers, the Bright Side, the Acme Music Company, and finally the Straitjackets—the house band at Jack's Place, a rowdy roadhouse outside Ft. Worth. There, Del and the fellows backed all the blues legends that came to town: Bobby "Blue" Bland, BUSTER BROWN, Lightnin' Hopkins, Howlin' Wolf, B. B. King, Joe Tex, Big Joe Turner, T-Bone Walker, Sonny Boy Williamson, and McClinton's idol, Jimmy Reed. Reed's wailing harp on "Honest I Do" had encouraged Del to pick up the harmonica in the first place.

Starting in 1960, McClinton and his Straitjackets recorded singles—under names like Mac Clinton and Del McClinton—for various labels owned by Major Bill Smith. McClinton also did some session work for the Major, backing Paul & Paul and Bruce Channel. It was while touring England with Channel that Del met John Lennon at the Castle Club in New Brighton. John, as the tale goes, asked McClinton how he got those

DELBERT MCCLINTON

sounds out of his harmonica. Results of the encounter were to appear as Lennon's harmonica break on "Love Me Do."

Upon his return, McClinton cut a great number of sides with Ronnie Kelly as the Ron-Dels, but only one made the pop charts—"If You Really Want Me to I'll Go" (#97, 1965). Tiring of the bar dates and failed 45s, Del moved to Los Angeles in 1970 and hooked up with hometown buddy Glen Clark. As Delbert& Glen, the duo recorded two country/soul LPs, *Delbert and Glen* (1972) and *Subject to Change* (1973); one track, "I Received a Letter" (#90, 1972), was a mild success.

The twosome parted company, and Del returned to Ft. Worth, where a local promotion man brought him to the attention of ABC Records. *Victim of Life's Circumstances* (1975), *Genuine Cowhide* (1976), and *Love Rustler* (1977) featured a critically lauded blend of country, blues, and R & B. Then came two albums for Capri-

corn—*Second Wind* (1978) and *Keeper of the Flame* (1979)—and two more for Capitol, *The Jealous Kind* (1980) and *Plain' From the Heart* (1981). The former included Del's lone Top 40 hit, "Givin' It Up for Your Love"; the latter featured "Shotgun Rider" (#70, 1981).

The 1989 release of *Live From Austin* on Alligator Records marked Delbert's return to the music business, after an eight-year lay-off. The disk was nominated for a "Best Contemporary Blues" Grammy. McClinton is now something of a cult rocker, with a stable and strong following of fans. The albums continue to turn heads and sell some—not platinum or gold, but enough. In 1991, he won a Grammy—"Best Rock Performance by a Duo or Group With Vocal"—for his duet with Bonnie Raitt, "Good Man, Good Woman." Two years later, he and Tanya Tucker received a Grammy nomination for their duet, "Tell Me About It."

TIERRA
TOGETHER
(Leon Huff, Kenny Gamble)
Broadway 5702
No. 18 *February 21, 1981*

Tierra is a Latino band born and based in the barrios of East Los Angeles. The group's founders and core components are Rudy (guitar, vocals) and Steve Salas (lead vocals, trombone, timbales), music vets with a combined history of more than 60 years in the biz.

The brothers started when knee-high. "We were two kids imitating Mexican trios and singing in Spanish before we could even speak Spanish," Steve told Damon Webb in the *L.A. Supplement*. Under the care of Eddie Davis (producer of CANNIBAL & THE HEADHUNTERS and THE PREMIERS), they recorded a number of singles as the Salas Brothers in the early '60s. In 1964, they joined an instrumental combo variously called the Jaguars and the Percussions. As the house band at Los Angeles's El Monte Legion Stadium, the Salases had the opportunity to provide back-up services for the Coasters, the Olympics, and the Righteous Brothers.

In the late '60s, the brothers formed Six Pak, later to be renamed Maya. The group consisted of Max Carduno, ex-Jaguar Anthony Carroll, and three former members of Thee [*sic*] Midnighters: Jim Espinoza, Danny Lamont, and George Salazar. A Six Pak single was issued by the Gordo label. In 1970, the Salases' producer started working with a Latin-rock band called El Chicano, and as auxiliary members, Rudy and Steve appeared on a number of their disks. Reportedly, Steve sang lead on El Chicano's "Brown Eyed Girl" (#45, 1972).

Tierra, phase one, was created by the Salas brothers in 1972. In addition to Kenny Roman (drums), Dave Torres (keyboards), and Rudy Villa (sax), the group included Conrad Lozano (bass), later a member of Los Lobos. Before the group split, the *Tierra* (1974) album for 20th Century and a single for the Tody label were released.

Phase two began in the late '70s. After a salsa-orientated LP for Salsoul, the Salas brothers and the revamped Tierra—Andre Baeza (percussion), Steve Falomir (bass), Joey Guerra (keyboards), Phil Madayag (drums), and Bobby Navarrete (reeds)—developed a jazzy/R & B/Latin-tinged sound and switched over to Neil Bogart's Boardwalk label. The boys from the barrios finally hit paydirt with "Together," a remake of the Intruders' 1967 R & B hit.

A few more albums and singles were shipped, including "Memories" (#62, 1981) and "La La Means I Love You" (# 72, 1981), the latter a cover version of the Delfonics dusty. With Bogart's death, the Boardwalk label has ceased to exist. Reportedly, the Tierra name continues to play on, with some singles being issued in the late '80s.

YARBROUGH & PEOPLES
DON'T STOP THE MUSIC
(ALISA PEOPLES, Lonnie Simmons, Jonas Ellis)
Mercury 76085
No. 19 *April 11, 1981*

They first met when she was four and he was six. Calvin Yarbrough and Alisa Peoples shared the same piano teacher. Since Cal and Al lived in the same area of Dallas, their parents sent them to a neighborhood church, where they became soloists in the choir.

For years, Alisa and Calvin went their separate ways, attending different hometown colleges. Afterward, Peoples joined the 9-to-5 world; Yarbrough played in bars around town with units like Grand Theft. Charlie, Robert, and Ronnie Wilson—later known as the Gap Band—happened to catch a Grand Theft performance, and offered Cal a back-up vocal spot on a Leon Russell tour they were set to work. When the tour was over, Calvin returned to Grand Theft and local engagements. In 1977, Alisa showed up at a gig and sang a song or two with the band. The result was good-time, danceable music magic.

The Gap Band was burning up the R & B listings, and Yarbrough had them give a listen to the act. The Wilson brothers in turn recommended Yarbrough & Peoples to their manager and producer, Lonnie Simmons. After two years of delays, Yarbrough & Peoples' debut album, *The Two of Us* (1981), was issued to critical acclaim and healthy sales. "Don't Stop the Music," a pop hit and a number-one R & B item, was only the beginning: eight more singles made the R & B listings, including "Don't Waste Your Time" (#48/1, 1984) and "I Wouldn't Lie" (#93/6, 1986). Mysteriously, the R & B hits and all recordings stopped by 1987.

In the early '80s, Calvin and Alisa solidified their relationship with quietly exchanged wedding vows.

TERRI GIBBS
SOMEBODY'S KNOCKIN'
(Ed Penny, Jerry Gillespie)
MCA 41309
No. 13 *April 25, 1981*

Terri (b. Teresa Fay Gibbs, June 15, 1954, Grovetown, GA), who has been blind since birth, first started playing with her parents' piano when she was three. Family members would say the music was in her genes; her great-grandpa had started the tradition of all-day gospel sings in Georgia. In her teens, she played the keyboards regularly in church and school, winning talent contests and performing locally. A false start happened in 1962 when Terri happened on to Chet Atkins who encouraged the then 18 year old to come to Nashville. Nothing came of the venture and Gibb returned to Augusta. From 1973 to 1975, she was a member of the Sound Dimension, but left that group to form her own unit for an extended gig at Augusta's Steak and Ale Restaurant. Gibbs plugged away there for five years, doing 50 songs five nights a week, three sets a night.

All the while, Terri made and distributed demo tapes, hoping someone would take notice. Jim Foglesong, president of MCA's Nashville operation, kept an eye on Terri for most of her stay at the Ale house. On the liner notes to her first album, *Somebody's Knockin'* (1981), Foglesong wrote: "It wasn't until earlier this year . . . when [independent producer/songwriter] Ed Penny played some things and told me of his belief in Terri's talent, that it seemed to make sense for us to sign her to MCA, with Ed as her producer."

A masterful move, hindsight would surely say: the timing was perfect. Penny and Jerry Gillespie supplied Gibbs with an alluring country-blues number, "Somebody's Knockin'," and before long, *Music City News*, *Record World*, and the Country Music Association were all over Terri, showering her with awards and nominations for her debut effort.

Aside from one pop follow-up, "Rich Mary" (#89, 1981), Terri has been most visible on the country listings. She has rocked out with "Baby I'm Gone" (#33, 1983) and "Tell Mama" (#65, 1983), stalled with "Somedays It Rains All Night Long" (#45, 1982), and tried to knock off her major moment with "Ashes to Ashes" (#19, 1982).

By 1983, the chartings had dried up. Over the next two years, she tried recording for Phonorama, then Warner Brothers, but things weren't right. Terri signed with Word Records and returned to gospel music in 1986. *Turn Around* was her debut. "Promised Land," "Comfort the People" and "Unconditional Love" charted Top Five on the Contemporary Christian singles charts in 1988.

GROVER WASHINGTON, JR., WITH BILL WITHERS
JUST THE TWO OF US
(Bill Withers, William Salter, Ralph MacDonald)
Elektra 47103
No. 2 *May 2, 1981*

"My mother used to sing in church choirs in Buffalo, and my father used to play saxophone and has an extensive collection of jazz 78s," said Grover to author Irwin Stambler. "Now, my brother Michael is the organist for a gospel group in Buffalo called the Varsons. My brother Darryl is a drummer who's played with the likes of Angela Bofill, Gato Barbieri, Charles Earland, Grove Holmes, Jimmy Owens, and myself. We came out of the ghetto, but despite that fact, and despite Buffalo's cold winter climate, the city had a warm creative atmosphere . . ."

"When I left home, I found myself playing piano one night, saxophone another, and bass the next. I played behind everything from groups to snake charmers," Stambler was told. "I did just about everything but play in a burlesque house."

"In the early '70s, CTI really filled the gap," said Grover to Steve Ivory, *The Music Paper*. "Pop was over here, jazz was over there . . . Creed Taylor was an innovator then, with all the easy listening jazz things. I guess he started making a little money, and that's usually when the problems start.

"I just wanted to get these record companies off my ass. . . . I ended up setting up interviews and autograph sessions myself. I was doing their job and mine."

Grover told Stambler, "I don't like categories. I like to keep it as low key as possible. We try to communicate with our audience by playing the widest spectrum of music possible, not playing down to our audience, but trying to play what they want to hear, and play something that they can think on."

When "Just the Two of Us" happened, Withers—noted for such '70s staples as "Lean on Me," "Use Me," and "Ain't No Sunshine"—was suffering from his own label problems. "I was locked out," said Withers in an exclusive interview. "My record company [Columbia] was big and WHITE. They didn't know what I was wanting to do, and when some of my stuff didn't sell as well as they figured it should have, I was locked out of recording. Helping Grover out, I got to get back into a studio . . . Nobody woulda figured it, but we hit it big."

Three years later, Withers—whose solo hits had stopped—charted again with "The Name of Love" (#58, 1984), assisting percussionist/bandleader Ralph MacDonald.

DOTTIE WEST WITH KENNY ROGERS
WHAT ARE WE DOIN' IN LOVE
(Randy Goodrum)
Liberty 1404
No. 14 *June 27, 1981*

"I'm a survivor," said West, mid-year 1991, to *Music City News* writer Robert K. Oermann. "You can knock me down, but you better have a big rock to keep me there."

Nineteen-ninety one was her worst year. Dorothy Marie Marsh West divorced her third husband, Alan

Winters. A financial catastrophe—due largely to what she called "bad management"—forced foreclosure on her home outside of Nashville; citing over a million dollars in debts, she filed Chapter 11 bankruptcy. In June, 1991, much of her property was sold off to satisfy those debts. To her embarrassment, an "Entertainment Tonight" crew reported the event worldwide. In July, she was injured in an auto accident while driving to Opryland for a performance.

Weeks later, on August 30, again en route to the Opry, Dottie was in another car accident. A stranger, 81-year-old George Thackston, in an apparent effort to get West to the famed hall at Opryland, crashed his vehicle. Dottie's liver was ruptured. Three operations were performed at Vanderbilt Medical Center in an extensive effort to save the singer's life. She died on September 4. She is survived by four children from her marriage to steel guitarist Bob West; among them is the country star, in her own right, Shelly West. Sons Mo and Dale are rock drummers; daughter Kerry is a sound engineer.

"While some people sang words," said Kenny Rogers to the Associated Press, "she sang emotions."

Said TAMMY WYNETTE, "She paved the way for so many of us . . . us girls."

Dottie West was born the youngest of 10, on October 11, 1932, on a farm outside of McMinnville, Tennessee, in a village called Frog Pond. Pelina, her mom, gave her a guitar when she was seven. In the late '40s, when in seventh grade Dottie wrote her first tune, "Frog Pond Boogie." After high school she enrolled as a music major at Tennessee Technological University in Cookeville. It was there that she met fellow student and steel guitar player Bill West. The couple eventually married in 1952 and moved to Cleveland, where Bill worked days as an engineer.

On weekends, Dottie and Bill performed on a local TV show. Her first recordings for Starday, beginning in 1952, failed to gather much attention. After Jim Reeves successfully charted with a take on her tune "Is It Me," RCA Victor signed West in 1963. A string of C & W hits followed; most notably her self-penned "Here Comes My Baby," recipient of a Grammy for "Best Country & Western Performance, Female." That year, Dottie West was made a member of the Grand Ole Opry.

In 1968, Dottie appeared in the movies, *Second Fiddle to a Steel Guitar* and *There's a Still on the Hill*. Duets with Jimmy Dean, Don Gibson, and Jim Reeves made the C & W listings. "Country Sunshine," in 1973, proved to be her career peak; becoming a Coca Cola commercial, winning the prestigious Clio advertising award, and receiving two Grammy nominations. For years thereafter, Dottie was to fans "the Country Sunshine Girl."

Dottie and Kenny Rogers began a duet relationship in 1977, when by accident Kenny happened into one of West's first recording sessions for her new label, his label, United Artist. "Every Time Two Worlds Collide," their first pairing, topped *Billboard*'s country charts in 1978. Dottie and Kenny continued their respective solo ventures, but rejoined the following year to record "Anyone Who Isn't Me Tonight," winner of the Country Music Association's "Vocal Duo of the Year" award.

The pop world learned of the West-Rogers pairing in 1981, when the C & W number-one "What Are We Doing in Love" became the first disk by West to ever become a national Top 40 pop hit. Dottie would never make *Billboard*'s pop charts again; though Dottie and Kenny would have yet another Top 20 C & W pairing, "Together Again."

In 1983, at age 51, West became a member of the touring company of "The Best Little Whorehouse in Texas," and appeared in a revealing spread for *Oui* magazine. That year she married her sound man, Al Winters, 23 years her junior.

Country chartings became a rarity. She signed with the tiny Permian record company. Little was heard of Dottie until 1991.

Dottie West is fondly remembered for aiding the careers of numerous songwriters and singers. Kris Kristofferson wrote "Help Me Make It Through the Night" while hanging out at her house, eating her homecooked meals. Eddie Rabbit received her encouragement; as did her then bass player Steve Wariner and Larry Gatlin.

"If it had not been for Dorothy Marie, Larry Wayne would've probably been a bad lawyer somewhere in Houston," said Larry Gatlin (nee Larry Wayne Gatlin) to the Associated Press.

LEE RITENOUR
IS IT YOU
(Lee Ritenour, Eric Tagg, Bill Champlin)
Elektra 47124
No. 15 *June 27, 1981*

"Captain Fingers," as Ritenour is known to friends and fans, is a top-of-the-line session artist, arranger, composer, and fusion-funkin' guitar virtuoso. Claims about his prolificness vary wildly. At the more imaginative end of the spectrum, pro-Rit forces affirm that "Fingers" has appeared on more than 3,000 albums. More conservative estimates place the number at closer to 200. Regardless of which is the proper count, Lee has graced recordings by a host of pop artists, including George Benson, Stanley Clarke, Natalie Cole, George Duke, Aretha Franklin, Herbie Hancock, Peggy Lee, Kenny Loggins, Johnny Mathis, Diana Ross, Carly Simon, Paul Simon, Barbra Streisand, and Steely Dan.

Lee (b. Jan. 11, 1952, Palos Verdes, CA) first picked up the guitar at the age of eight. He progressed swiftly on the instrument: by age 12, he was playing with a 19-piece orchestra. A year later, Rit laid down some guitar lines on a yet-unreleased JOHN PHILLIPS solo album. He attended the University of Southern California and studied with guitar greats Joe Pass, Howard Roberts, and classical guitarist Christopher Parkening. In 1975, he settled into the Los Angeles session scene.

Ritenour's picking can be heard on the soundtracks to such flicks as *Saturday Night Fever* (1977), *The Champ* (1979), and *An Officer and a Gentleman* (1982). Nearly half of his numerous albums have placed on *Billboard*'s top pop albums chart. "Is It You" and "Cross My Heart" (#69, 1982), both featuring vocals by Eric Tagg, are Lee's lone crossover pop successes.

In the late '80s, Rit signed with GRP Records; recording solos and with Don Grusin as Friendship. In the '90s, with Nathan East, Bob James, Harvey Mason, Lee has put together some jazz/funk/soul albums as *Fourplay*. His 1993 tribute to Wes Montgomery, *Wes Bound*, topped *Billboard*'s jazz chart.

JOEY SCARBURY
THEME FROM "GREATEST AMERICAN HERO" (BELIEVE IT OR NOT)
(Mike Post, Stephen Geyer)
Elektra 47147
No. 2 *August 15, 1981*

Little Joey first won acclaim from his peers with his Elvis impersonation at a kindergarten show-and-tell session. His parents knew the tike had something, and they would constantly enroll Joey in talent contests. Joey (b. June 7, 1955) was raised in Thousand Oaks, California, and discovered by singer-songwriter Jim Webb's father. Webb senior walked into the furniture store where Scarbury's mother was working, and heard her praising Joey's singing abilities.

Jim Webb brought the 14-year-old into a recording studio in 1968 to cut a track on his tune "She Never Smiles Anymore." The record bombed, but Joey was now a professional. Over the years, Scarbury recorded for the Reena, Dunhill, Lionel, Bell, Big Tree, Playboy, and Columbia labels. He had one minor Hot 100 item, "Mixed Up Guy" (#73, 1971), but that was all. Everyone agreed that the kid had talent, so how come no hit records?

To support himself, Joey did back-up vocals for Loretta Lynn and sang on various recording projects run by producer Mike Post. Mike enlisted him to sing the theme to an upcoming ABC-TV series, "The Greatest American Hero," starring Stephen J. Cannell (the son of Bill Williams and Barbara Hale of "Kit Carson"

and "Perry Mason," respectively). The series about a bumbling superhero carried on for two years, but Joey Scarbury's visibility in the record industry did not last quite as long. The follow-up single, "When She Dances" (#49, 1981), would be Scarbury's last chart showing.

After his separation from Elektra, Joey recorded a single or two for RCA. Nothing much happened. When last spotted—in the late '80s—Joey was playing second base for the Thousand Oaks softball league.

JOHN SCHNEIDER
IT'S NOW OR NEVER
(Aaron Schroeder, Wally Gold)
Scotti Brothers 02105
No. 14 *August 15, 1981*

Born on April 8, 1954, in Mount Kisco, New York, John came to the nation's attention as young Bo Duke on TV's "The Dukes of Hazzard." Besides John, the popular program featured Waylon Jennings' voice as the narrator and that 1969 Dodge Charger, known as "General Lee."

After practicing night and day, recording an obscure children's album in 1977, and spending three years crunchin' cars and watchin' girls jiggle on the show, John geared up for a career as a pop singer with country leanings. "It's Now or Never," a remake of Elvis' operatic plea, was a monster moment, but smaller and smaller numbers bought his later offerings. "Still" (#69, 1981), "Dreamin'" (#45, 1982), and "In the Driver's Seat" (#72, 1982) still found their way into plenty of teenage girls' bedrooms.

No longer a Duke or a pop crooner, John has continued his acting career, occasionally appearing as "Larry Lamont" in the day-time soap "Loving," and has even branched out into directing and screenwriting. His movies include *Dream House, Happy Endings, Gus Brown and Midnight Brewster, Eddie Macon's Run, Fine White Line, Stagecoach*. He sings straight country these days, and quite successfully, too: 17 of his singles have made the C & W listings; four topped the charts—all this despite the perception by many country DJs that John was not the real thing, a r-e-a-l country singer, and consequently was often the target for a broadcast boycott. His final C & W Top 10 hit was in 1987, "Love, You Ain't Seen the Last of Me."

In 1990, Schneider returned to the little screen in the short-lived ABC series "Grand Slam." Four years later, John returned in the syndicated "Heaven Help Us," as an apprentice angel, sent back to Earth to help persons in need.

ROYAL PHILHARMONIC ORCHESTRA
HOOKED ON CLASSICS
[Various classical composers]
RCA Victor 12304
No. 10 *January 30, 1982*

The Royal Philharmonic Orchestra (RPO), like the London Philharmonic (LPO) before it, was formed by Sir Thomas Beecham (b. 1879, St. Helens, Lancashire, England), in 1947. Under his baton, the RPO became associated with the annual Glyndebourne opera season in Sussex. Sir Beecham became known for his advocacy of new and unusual music. His greatest achievement in this capacity was popularizing the then-little-known works of Frederick Delius.

Under the leadership of Louis Clark (b. Birmingham, England), the RPO has continued to experiment with its repertoire, performing pieces that are generally associated with the pop or jazz realms. Clark has done arrangements for the Electric Light Orchestra, and his crew has recorded with Deep Purple, Glen Campbell, and B. B. King and the CRUSADERS.

"Hooked on Classics," a disco-fied medley of classical themes, has been the RPO's only Hot 100 spot to date. Three similar LPs have sold quite well—*Hooked on Classics* (1982), *Hooked on Classics II* (Can't Stop the Classics) (1982), and *Hooked on Classics III (Journey Through the Classics)* (1983). The RPO's concept also kicked off 45s like "Hooked on Big Bands" (#61, 1982) and "Hooked on Swing" (#31, 1982).

BUCKNER & GARCIA
PAC-MAN FEVER
(Jerry Buckner, Gary Garcia)
Columbia 02673
No. 9 *March 27, 1982*

While diligently researching the subject one night in a local bar, Jerry Buckner (keyboards, vocals) and Gary Garcia (guitar, vocals) came up with the idea of writing a tune about their favorite video game. They sketched out their "Pac-Man Fever" concept to record producer Arnie Geller. Upon further reflection, however, Jerry and Gary decided to nix the number, but Geller urged the duo to go ahead with it.

Arnie had the right instincts; though every major label and then some . . . rejected it. "I still got the letters like, 'Thanks . . .but . . .' and 'It doesn't sound like a hit,'" said Buckner in an interview with authors Bruce Nash and Allan Zullo. Not one to take a number of no's for an answer, Arnie formed his own BGO label and issued the novelty number. The response to the ditty (com-

plete with actual Pac-Man gobble sounds, recorded off a machine in a crowded deli) was phenomenal. (Listen close, said Buckner, you can hear a patron actually ordering a sandwich in the background.)

Columbia Records acquired the rights to national distribution, and the pair was promptly dispatched to research more video-game material. An album was needed, and fast; within four weeks the label-heads wanted that product on the streets and in the stores. Novelty items like "Hyper-Space," "Ode to a Centipede," "Golly Berserk," and "Foggy's Lament" were duly conceived, cut, and issued on Buckner & Garcia's debut album, *Pac-Man Fever* (1982). Follow-up efforts such as "Do the Donkey Kong" and "E.T. (I Love You)," however, failed to chart, but Jerry and Gary got their thrill of a lifetime when they appeared on Dick Clark's "American Bandstand." "[Dick Clark] did a little pre-interview with us first and when he asked us some questions, we just stared at him. He said, 'Guys, you're going to have to talk if this is going to work.'"

Jerry and Gary had first met in high school in Akron, Ohio. Each had their own band; Jerry, the Rogues and Gary, the Outlaws. "We both had the same dreams and desires. Akron used to be a big industrial town with rubber factories and after graduation most guys worked for those folks. We wanted to get out of that life." And music was to be the way. In the '70s, the guys, then based in Atlanta, got there start writing jingles for radio commercials.

The pair has since returned to producing and writing. Jerry and Gary were responsible for Steve Carlisle's TV theme "WKRP in Cincinnati" and Edgel Groves's C & W charter "Footprints in the Sand" (#42, 1981). Recording as Willis "The Guard" & Vigorish, the twosome made the pop listings with the seasonal single "Merry Christmas in the NFL" (#82, 1980), a nutty number about Howard Cosell as Santa. In 1986, Anne Murray scored well on the country charts with Jerry's "On and On."

BOB & DOUG MCKENZIE
TAKE OFF
(Kerry Crawford, Jonathan Goldsmith, Mark Giacommeli, Rick Moranis, Dave Thomas)
Mercury 76134
No. 16 *March 27, 1982*

Okay, so they were a couple of lovable bozo losers, eh? Still, these burpin', beer-swiggin' McKenzies in flannel shirts and toques parlayed their let's-poke-fun-at-the-Canadians routine from TVs "SCTV" comedy series into a hit single, a top-selling album (*Great White North*), a one-off book, and a full-length movie which they co-wrote and co-directed, *Strange Brew* (1983).

In real life, Bob and Doug McKenzie were Canadians Dave Thomas and Rick Moranis, respectively. Dave acquired an M.A. degree, then worked as a Canadian Broadcasting Company scriptwriter. He also appeared in Toronto stage shows as half of a comedy team with "SCTV"'s Catherine O'Hara. Rick, who went to grade school with RUSH's Geddy Lee (the vocalist featured on "Take Off"), earned $3 an hour as a teenager writing gags and glib jibs for tongue-tied Toronto DJs. Four years later, he hosted his own all-night program, also doing stand-up comedy at local clubs and cabarets.

Dave—whose brother is IAN THOMAS of "Painted Ladies" (#34, 1974) fame—in the late '80s worked his own Canadian syndicated series, "The Dave Thomas Show." But Rick has moved on to become quite the hot item in Hollywood. In 1989 alone, he appeared in three major releases: *Ghostbusters II*, *Parenthood*, and *Honey, I Shrunk the Kids*. His earlier film appearances include *Ghostbusters* (1984), *Streets of Fire* (1984), *The Wild Life* (1984), *Brewster's Millions* (1985), *Little Shop of Horrors* (1986), and *Spaceballs* (1987). *Honey, I Shrunk the Kids* has sprouted two successful sequels—and the end may not be in sight.

BERTIE HIGGINS
KEY LARGO
(Bertie Higgins, Sonny Limbo)
Kat Family 02524
No. 8 *April 17, 1982*

In the early, pre-Beatles '60s, drummer Bertie (b. 1946, Tarpon Springs, FL) had a hometown band called the Romans. Besides Bert, there was guitarist Bob Clever, singer Lane Langfort, bassist Joe Pappalardi, and guitarist Ronnie Schwartz. With the help of Tommy Roe and his producer Felton Jarvis, the band toured the world and crafted some fine rock and roll.

"Felton discovered [the Romans] in Florida," Tommy Roe explained in an exclusive interview. "He really liked them and wanted to produce them. I was working in England a lot then, and we thought a good way to get them some recognition was to change their name slightly [to the Roemans] and have them tour with me. Felton would record them with me and as a separate act. They became quite popular in the States and had several singles on ABC, but they never did catch on nationally."

In 1968, the Roemans played the last of their one-nighters. Once the glory and the royalty checks were gone, Bertie returned to Tarpon Springs. He took to playing guitar, writing songs, and checking out old movies. Bert met Beverly Seaberg, and the two fell in love.

"I lived with [Bev] a long time," Higgins told Bob Shannon and John Javna in *Behind the Hits*. "We used to watch old movies on the weekends, and to us, the Bogart and Bacall romance was a phenomenal one." When the couple split up, Higgins was hurt. Inspired by the Bogie-Bacall flick *Key Largo* (1948), he penned what would be his only Top 40 hit "as a plea for her return. And she did."

When last sighted, Bertie and Beverly were still together, perhaps sharing "Just Another Day in Paradise" (#46, 1982).

LE ROUX
NOBODY SAID IT WAS EASY
(LOOKIN' FOR THE LIGHTS)
(Tony Haselden)
RCA Victor 13059
No. 18 *April 17, 1982*

They took their named from the Cajun/French term for the gravy base used to make gumbo, that Southern favorite. Jeff Pollard, the group's leader, pointed out to *Cashbox* the aptness of the moniker for a unit that could play "a little bit of this and a touch of everything." On their first two albums, the band was actually called Louisiana's Le Roux.

Pollard (lead vocals, guitar), Bobby Campo (trumpet, flugelhorn, flute, congas), Tony Haselden (guitar), Leon Medica (bass), David Peters (drums), and Rod Roddy (keyboards) met while working sessions at the Studio in the Country in Bogalusa, Louisiana. In this capacity, they accompanied Clarence "Gatemouth" Brown, Clifton Chenier, and the Nitty Gritty Dirt Band, among others.

"We had a lot of things that we wanted to do," Pollard explained. "Everybody wanted to express themselves musically. Backing up someone else is good because it keeps your chops in shape, but if you don't get the opportunity to get out and play what you want to play, that can stifle what you do."

Once the boys had a couple of albums' worth of their own material ready, William McEuen, the Dirt Band's manager, offered to represent them. Capitol

Records issued three LPs: *Louisiana's Le Roux* (1978), *Keep the Fire Burning* (1979), and *Up* (1980). Each one sold moderately well, as did "New Orleans Ladies" (#59, 1978), but the group was still groping for that chart-topper. Two years later, Le Roux signed with RCA and scored big with the moody "Nobody Said It Was Easy" from the *Last Safe Place* (1982) album.

Despite Hot 100 listings with "The Last Safe Place on Earth" (#77, 1982) and "Carrie's Gone" (#81, 1983), nothing further has cracked the Top 40. Following their fleeting encounter with success, Le Roux experienced a major shake-up in their internal workings; both Bob Campo and the group's lead voice, Jeff Pollard, left the unit. Replacements included guitarist Jim Odom and lead singer Fergie Frederiksen. Fergie, however, has since been spotted in Toto's evolving lineup. To date, only one other album—*So Fired Up* (1983)—has been issued by RCA.

GREG GUIDRY
GOIN' DOWN
(Greg Guidry)
Columbia 02691
No. 17 *May 1, 1982*

"I want to be a viable artist, one with lots of hits, but one who can sell LPS, too—mass acceptance is what I'm definitely going for," Greg Guidry told *Circus'* Charley Crespo in 1982.

Greg was born in 1950, in St. Louis, Missouri. By kindergarten, he was singing in the family's gospel group at church and at local functions. In his teenage years, Greg took piano lessons, wrote touching tunes, and played with local rock bands. His big break came in 1981, when he sang back-up on the Allman Brothers' album, *Brothers of the Road*. Gradually, acts such as the Climax Blues Band, Robbie Dupree, and England Dan & John Ford Coley recorded Greg's songs.

Over the Line (1982) was Guidry's debut album. His lone looper, "Goin' Down," did quite well for a novice. However, the follow-up 45, "Into My Love" (#92, 1982), went largely unnoticed. The potential momentum was lost forever and not much has been heard or seen of this singing songsmith since.

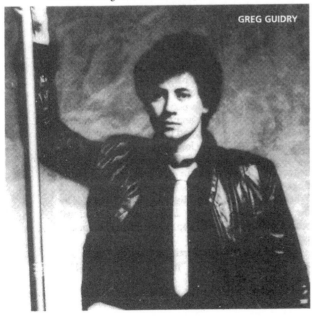

GREG GUIDRY

CHARLENE
I'VE NEVER BEEN TO ME
(Ron Miller, Ken Hirsch)
Motown 1611
No. 3 *May 22, 1982*

Charlene D'Angelo was born on June 1, 1950, in Hollywood. In 1976, the Motown moguls happened upon

this angelic miss and arranged for her to work with their short-lived Prodigal subsidiary and the Ron Miller-Ken Hirsch writing team. Tunes were hatched and patched, and before long, an album of smooth, country-flavored Charlene songs was gathering dust in radio stations and cut-out bins across the land. As a countrypolitan singer, D'Angelo was not considered the real thing by C & W purists; she was also neither a rock'n'roll, nor a soul singer. Easy-listening music might be the most apt description of her specialty.

After three Hot 100 singles on Prodigal, "I've Never Been to Me" (#97, 1977) appeared and fared as poorly as its predecessors. Charlene dropped out of the music business. Then, five years later, Scott Shannon, a Tampa DJ, reintroduced the disk to the airwaves. To meet the swelling demand for the single, the Motown brass resigned Charlene—who was discovered working as a shop clerk in Ilford, Essex, England—and hustled her into the studio to re-record "I've Never Been to Me." (In order to underscore the tune's feminist sentiments, a metaphysical spoken segment was added to the middle of the song.) The record became a smash success.

Months late, "Used to Be" (#46, 1982), a duet with Stevie Wonder, was issued, but nothing much has been heard from Charlene since. A final album, *Hit and Run Lover*, was issued in 1984 before Motown again dropped Charlene from its recording roster.

DAZZ BAND
LET IT WHIP
(Reggie Andrews, Leon "Ndugu" Chancler)
Motown 1609
No. 5 *July 17, 1982*

Nearly 30 years ago, alto saxophonist Bobby Harris started playing with a jazz combo in his hometown of Cleveland. By the early '70s, he was appearing around town in a hot four-piece jazz-fusion band, Bell Tele-phunk. When not with his Bell bunch, Bob would often hang out and jam with the house musicians at the Kinsman Grill. Eventually, the two groups merged into one dance band called Kinsman Dazz ("dazz" being short for "danceable jazz"). Some demos were made; 20th Century Fox signed up the group and shipped about a half-dozen singles. "I Might As Well Forget About Loving You" (R&B: #46, 1979) and "Catchin' Up on Love" (R&B: #33, 1980) sold promisingly with R & B listeners. Motown offered the group a contract. They accepted, shortening their name and reworking their line-up to include Steve Cox (keyboards), Pierre DeMudd (trumpet, flugelhorn, vocals), Eric Fearman (guitar), Sennie "Skip" Martin III (trumpet, vocals), Kenny Pettus (percussion, vocals), Isaac Wiley, Jr. (drums), and Michael Wiley (bass).

"Let It Whip," a number-one R & B hit, was the first single pulled from the Dazz Band's *Keep It Live* (1982), its third album. "Joystick" (#61, 1984) and "Let It All Blow" (#84, 1984) were also pop-charters. While "Whip" remains Dazz's only Top 40 intrusion, Harris' outfit continued to rack up funky R & B hits through 1988, 20 of them in all.

In 1988, after a short stay with Geffen Records, Harris and his funksters shortened their name again, this time to simply "Dazz." They then recorded for RCA. Fearman, Martin, and Wiley, Jr., are gone; lead singer Jerry Bell, keyboardist Keith Harrison, and producer and ex-Pleasure guitarist Marlon McClain have been added to the roster.

SOFT CELL
TAINTED LOVE
(Ed Cobb)
Sire 49855
No. 8 *July 17, 1982*

"We thought if we were really lucky, we'd scrape into the Top 75 in Britain," Marc Almond—the lipsticked, mascaraed, and earringed half of Soft Cell—quipped to *Rolling Stone*'s Steve Ponds. "We didn't think anything would happen over here [in the United States]."

Almond (b. Peter Marc Almond, July 9, 1956, Southport, Lancashire, England) and multi-instrumentalist David Ball (b. May 3, 1959, Blackpool, Lancashire, England) met in 1979 at Leeds Art College. "I used the art school facilities for doing performances, writing songs, and making films," Marc explained to *Creem*'s Chris Salewicz. "One day I heard a lot of noise coming from the sound room. I checked it out and found Dave working away in there. He wanted a vocal side to what he was doing. So basically our Fine Arts courses consisted of forming Soft Cell."

Both knew what they were after: "People were using electronics in unfeeling, robotic ways," Almond told Ponds. "But Dave got these rich, warm, moody sounds. Exciting and slightly dirty sounds." Their first gig was a Christmas party at a local nitery. Months later, the duo found a guiding light and manager in a former brick-layer named Stevo. This 19-year-old ran Some Bizarre, a small label distributed by Phonogram. "Memorabilia," Soft Cell's first single, sold fairly well. But the follow-up—a throbbing techno-pop remake of Gloria Jones' (whose boyfriend was T-REX's Marc Bolan) little-known '60s soul classic, "Tainted Love"—really shook things up. Not only was the tune—written by ex-Four Preps' Ed Cobb; prod/manager of THE STANDELLS—a number-one hit in England, but it stayed on *Billboard*'s Hot 100 chart for nearly a year!

Hughie Feather, a friend and designer, built a white padded cell with pink and blue neon bars for the duo to perform in. All of England's "New Romantics" loved Soft Cell's musical approach. Eight more singles charted in the U.K., but none did anything in the U. S. However, *Non-Stop Erotic Cabaret* (1982), *Non-Stop Ecstatic Dancing* (1982), and *The Art of Falling Apart* (1983) were respectable sellers in the United States.

By 1984, Almond had grown weary of the Soft Cell concept, and went off to record a slew of successful projects. Even while a Soft Cell-lite, Marc had recorded as the pundit-approved Marc and the Mambas (nee Marc and the Willing Sinners). Once Cell-free, Almond embarked on the unknown, recording the dark *Mother Fist and Her Five Daughters* (1987) and the far-fetched, a one-off chart-topping duet with vocal-powerhouse Gene Pitney, "Something's Got a Hold of My Heart." In 1992, Marc revived the little-remembered David McWilliams charter, "The Days of Pearly Spence."

Ball, meanwhile, issued a solo album, *In Strict Tempo* (1983), worked with Psychic TV and Jack The Tab, and teamed up with Richard Norris (ex-Fruitbats, Mr. Suit, Innocent Vicars) as Grid. Totally unknown in the United States, Grid has issued a number of praised products and become homeland-known for its remixes for the Art of Noise, Brian Eno, Happy Mondays, and the Pet Shop Boys.

KARLA BONOFF
PERSONALLY
(Paul Kelly)
Columbia 02805
No. 19 *August 7, 1982*

Karla, born on December 27, 1952, and raised in Los Angeles, was inundated with music lessons when she was growing up: piano, then violin, clarinet, and finally, in the thick of her teen years, guitar. When 16, Karla

and sister Lisa formed a twosome to pick 'n' sing at the Troubadour's Monday-night hootenannies. In 1969, Bonoff met Linda Ronstadt's bass player, Kenny Edwards. Kenny was between jobs with Linda, and approached Karla about forming an acoustic group with him, session singer Andrew Gold, and songwriter Wendy Waidman. As Bryndle, they recorded a yet-unreleased album. Only one highly sought-after single, "Woke Up This Morning," was issued in 1972. After playing the folkie circuit for a bit, Bryndle broke up, and Bonoff returned to the Troubadour hoots.

Kenny Edwards had introduced Karla to Linda Ronstadt. On her 1976 *Hasten Down the Wind* album, Ronstadt recorded three of Bonoff's moody musings: "Someone to Lay Down Beside Me," "If He's Ever Near," and "Lose Again." Columbia Records decided to give Karla a spin, and a critically acclaimed debut disk was issued late in 1977. Over the years, more LPs and a stash of singles have been released; "Personally" was pulled from her *Wild Heart of the Young* (1982) album. LYNN ANDERSON, Nicolette Larson, and Bonnie Raitt have also recorded Bonoff's tunes. "I Can't Hold On" (#76, 1978), "Baby Don't Go" (#69, 1980), and "Please Be the One" (#63, 1982) were Karla's additional Hot 100 items.

Word is that Karla continued her involvement with music into the early '90s; *New World*, the last known album, was issued by Goldcastle in 1988.

SYLVIA
NOBODY
(Kye Fleming, Dennis W. Morgan)
RCA 13223
No. 15 *November 20, 1982*

As a teen, Sylvia Kirby Allen (b. 1957, Kokomo, IN) gained some notoriety doing pencil sketches of the country stars that would happen by Indiana's Little Nashville Opry concert hall. By high school graduation, Syl was sure that she, too, wanted to be a country queen. In 1976, with school behind her and an *a cappella* tape in her hand, Sylvia headed for Nashville and stardom—but like the perennial horde of other aspiring Loretta Lynns and Dolly Partons that flock to Music City each year, Sylvia had to settle for a less glamorous clerical job at Pi-Gem, a music publishing house.

Fortunately for Allen, her boss was Tom Collins, who was then producing CHARLIE PRIDE and BARBARA MANDRELL. Sylvia typed the letters and answered the phone but successfully persuaded Collins to let her make demo tapes and sing back-up for Mandrell, Ronnie Milsap, and Dave & Sugar. In 1977, Sylvia got the chance to tour as a back-up singer for Janie Fricke. Finally, in the summer of 1979, after a failed audition for a replacement slot in the country grouping Dave & Sugar, RCA signed her up as a solo artist. "You Don't

Miss a Thing," her debut disk, made the C & W charts, as did a hefty heap of follow-up singles. In 1983, the Academy of Country Music voted Sylvia "Female Vocalist of the Year."

While "Nobody" is the Hoosier's only pop/rock hit, Sylvia had a continuous string of country chartings through 1987. Growing weary of the touring necessary to maintain her country popularity, Sylvia retired from performing in the late '80s. Attention turned to songwriting and hosting her own cooking specials on TNN, "Holiday Gourmet," and guest hosting for Lorianne Crook on TNN series "Crook and Chase." As Sylvia Hutton, she returned to performing in 1992.

PATTI AUSTIN WITH JAMES INGRAM
BABY, COME TO ME
(Rod Temperton)
Quest 50036
No. 1 *December 4, 1982*

"Ask anyone in the business," wrote a journalist with *Blues & Soul*, "it's never been a question as to whether Patti Austin would make it big league. It's always only been a question of when!"

Patti Austin was born August 10, 1948; possibly somewhere in California. Some reports say that her dad was a jazz musician. Most bios mention that at age three or four, Quincy Jones—possibly a friend of her father's—became her godfather. At about this time, Patti's parents had gotten the lass backstage at the Apollo Theatre to meet and audition for Dinah Washington. Impressed terribly, Washington let Patti sing "Teach Me Tonight" at her show, that evening; in the key of B-flat. The band botched up the number and Patti stopped them cold and had the big band do it right.

"Sure, I was precocious," said Austin to *Blues & Soul* magazine. "I was schizophrenically precocious, because I was doing a TV show every evening for a year and a half without the rest of the kids in my class even knowing about it. I always had to keep my two lives separate."

A TV appearance with Sammy Davis, Jr., won the little one a slot in the stage performances of *Lost in the Stars* and *Finian's Rainbow*. When nine, in 1957, Quincy took Patti on one of his European tours. Following a tour with Harry Belafonte and Phyllis Diller, when 16, and a win with Quincy at a Brazilian song competition, Patti Austin had her first single issued by Coral Records. Her first R & B charting happened in 1969, with the United Artist release "The Family Tree" (#45, 1969).

There were spots on the "Tonight Show," "Dean Martin Show," "David Frost Show," but the hits failed to happen. Patti's attentions were turned to the lucrative world of jingles and back-up singing. Her session cred-

its include work with George Benson and Billy Joel, Paul Simon, Frankie Valli, Joe Cocker, and Roberta Flack. In the '80s, Patti recorded with the Blues Brothers, the Marshall Tucker Band, and Steely Dan.

Austin's breakthrough happened with her work with mentor Quincy Jones's *The Dude*; the title cut garnered a Grammy in 1982. As a featured vocalist, Patti had appeared on Quincy's successful "Razzamatazz," the previous year. After three moderate seller albums for CTI—which involved much heartache for the singer and financial litigations—Patti was signed to Quincy's new Quest label and given a R & B hit with "Do You Love Me" (#24, 1981), followed by a duet with James Ingram on "Baby Come to Me." Her major pop moment was to become the theme for the TV tummy-turner "General Hospital."

One other matching of Austin and Ingram (with both artists receiving equal billing)—"How Do You Keep the Music Playing?" (R & B: #3, 1983)—from the Goldie Hawn-Burt Reynolds flick *Best Friends* (1982), won the pair an Oscar nomination. Patti ventured on with theme tunes for more movies, the John Travolta-Olivia Newton-John bow-wow *Two of a Kind* (1983), and Pauline Collins's uplifting *Shirley Valentine* (1989).

Patti has been paired with soul legend Jerry Butler and Narada Michael Walden, for a R & B charting each—"In My Life" (#92, 1983) and "Gimme, Gimme, Gimme" (#39, 1985)—and has had a few major R & B solo's in "Honey for the Bees" (#24, 1985) and "The Heat of Heat" (#13, 1986). Other matchings include Patti's appearance with Michael Jackson on "It's the Falling in Love," Tom Browne's "The Closer I Get to You," and a take of "Love Light," with Japanese koto player Yutaka Yokokura.

"No matter how long it takes to make it," said Austin, "it really does happen overnight. It's all about reaching a new and totally different level of success."

James Ingram continues his near 20 year R & B chartings; notably with "Just Once" (#11, 1981), "Yo Mo B There," with Michael McDonald (#5, 1983), and "The Secret Garden (Sweet Seduction Suite)" (#1, 1990), a communal release featuring Quincy Jones, AL B. SURE!, El Debarge, and Barry White.

TONI BASIL
MICKEY
(Nicky Chinn, Mike Chapman)
Chrysalis 2638
No. 1 *December 11, 1982*

What do you say about a woman who is practically the most influential choreographer of popular music?" asked Bette Midler of *Dancemagazine's* Kevin Grubb.

TONI BASIL

"This is someone who found street dancing before anyone knew what it was and successfully commercialized it. She taught David Byrne how to move. Anthony Tudor wrote her fan letters. She pretty much discovered DEVO. She's helped provide Bowie with an identity. Her style has been ripped off by so many other choreographers . . . It's about time she got her due."

"The Dance Queen of Rock," as she was deservingly dubbed, claims to have been born Antonia Basilotta in 1950, in Philadelphia. The family moved around quite a bit: her dad was big-band leader Louis Basil, and her mother was an acrobatic dancer. When the relatives got together, there was often quite a commotion in the house.

"It was an amalgamation of acrobatics and comedy," Basil explained to *Dancemagazine*. "They would jump through hoops with their names on them, and my mother and my uncle would do a tap/boxing dance where she beat him up . . . I also had an aunt . . . [who would] put her leg around her neck and hop around like a contortionist, or lie on a table while my two uncles grabbed her legs and spun her around in circles. Really! That's my roots."

She moved to Los Angeles to become a dentist, but after completing her studies at Laughton Dental School, Toni turned to the world of dancing. She started by doing choreography for seminal TV shows like "Hullaballoo" and "Shindig." Once in the industry,

Toni met Brian Jones of the Rolling Stones, Peter Fonda, and Dennis Hopper. She was at Hopper's when *Easy Rider* (1969) was conceived, and found herself playing a "spaced-out chick" in the flick. Her later movie appearances include *The Cool Ones* (1970), *Five Easy Pieces* (1970), *The Last Movie* (1971), *Greaser's Palace* (1972), *Mother, Jugs and Speed* (1976), *Hey Good Looking* (1982), and *Slaughterhouse Rock* (1988). As a choreographer, she worked on the famed *T.A.M.I. Show* (1964), Elvis's *Viva Las Vegas* (1964) and *Girl Happy* (1965), the Monkees' *Head* (1968), and Bette Midler's *The Rose* (1979). She has also devised dance moves for groundbreaking tours and videos by such acts as David Bowie, Devo, Melissa Manchester, George Michael, Bette Midler, the Pointer Sisters, Linda Ronstadt, David Lee Roth, the Talking Heads, and Tina Turner.

In the early '70s, Toni became involved with South Los Angeles's street-dancing scene and formed the Lockers (a.k.a. The Campbell Lock Dancers), a dance troupe. Moonwalkers and break-dancers are what we might call them now, but Toni and her team were way ahead of their time. Before breaking up in 1975, the Lockers opened for Sly Stone and Frank Sinatra, also appearing repeatedly on "Saturday Night Live."

As for her musical moment, "Mickey" was not Basil's first foray into pop/rockdom. Her recording history dates back to 1966 and two singles for A & M, "Breakaway" and "I'm 28." "Mickey"—originally titled "Kitty" and unsuccessfully recorded by a group called Smile—was cut in 1980 as a pre-MTV music video, but Chrysalis passed on the record and its cheerleader concept until the overseas success of "Mickey" prompted the label to reconsider. The single, which was a definite disco/new wave hybrid, eventually sold 2 million copies.

To date, Toni has had only two other pop platters released—"Shoppin' From A to Z" (#77, 1983) and "Over My Head" (#81, 1984). Her debut album, *Word of Mouth* (1982), which included music contributions provided by Devo and was also available as a "video album," went gold, but after her second album—*Toni Basil* (1984)—failed to generate much in the way of revenue, Chrysalis Records let her go. Early in 1988, she signed with Island Records.

MUSICAL YOUTH
PASS THE DUTCHIE
(Jackie Mitoo, Lloyd Ferguson, Fitzroy Simpson)
MCA 52149
No. 10 *February 26, 1983*

Freddie Waite had been the lead vocalist in the Techniques, a successful Jamaican reggae band. He moved his family to Birmingham, England, in the late '70s. Having spotted talent in a friend's offspring, Freddie encouraged the father to let him give the boys music lessons. Kevin and Michael Grant (then ages 9 and 11, respectively) were schoolmates of Waite's own two sons, Patrick (age 12) and Junior (age 13). Before the year was out, Waite had them all whipped up into a fairly decent band.

For the next few years, Kevin (guitar), Michael (keyboards), Junior (drums), and Pat (bass) made local appearances as the Cultural Music Workshop Youth. Freddie sang lead with the group (since he was a small fellow, nobody seemed to notice the age discrepancy). A homemade single—"Political" b/w "Generals"—was recorded and shopped around; one of the copies found its way to John Peel, a big-time DJ on the BBC. Peel, impressed with the group's unique blend of reggae and pop, repeatedly played the disk on his show.

Charlie Ayre, an A & R man with MCA Records, suggested that Freddie replace himself with someone more age-appropriate. After the addition of 14-year-old Dennis Seaton and six months of rehearsals, MCA was ready to release Musical Youth's *Youth of Today* (1982) LP and what would become one of the best-selling singles in British pop history. "Pass the Dutchie" was an old reggae hit that had been updated by the Mighty Diamonds as "Pass the Kutchie." But since a kutchie is a marijuana jar and the musicians were all underage, the explicit drug references were toned down with the reinsertion of the word "dutchie" (a stewpot).

Irene Cara, Michael Jackson, Donna Summer, and Jody Watley guested on the group's second album, *Different Style!* (1983). Musical Youth's popularity and record sales remained high in the U.K. through the mid-'80s. "She's Trouble" (#65, 1984) made the United States pop charts, and two 45s appeared on the R & B listings, but none of their subsequent offerings have met with tremendous success.

"I hope the band will go a long way," Michael Grant told *Rock & Soul*. "People that think we're puppets or a one-hit wonder are wrong."

Musical Youth split up in 1985, with Dennis attempting a solo career, with the aid of his own band XMY. Efforts to reform the outfit ended February 18, 1993, when Patrick Waite—who had turned to the life of crime—died of "natural causes," while awaiting a court appearance on drug charges.

FRIDA
I KNOW THERE'S SOMETHING GOING ON
(Russ Ballard)
Atlantic 89984
No. 13 *March 26, 1983*

She was born Anni-Frid Synni-Lyngstad on November 15, 1945, in the little iron-export town of Narvik, Norway. At the age of 10, Frida made her first stage appearance in a talent contest, and a few years later she was fronting a local dance band. In 1967, she moved to Stockholm, became a local celebrity on a TV program called "Hyland's Corner," and met rock-and-roller and husband-to-be-Benny Andersen. Up to this point, Frida had been a singer in what she described as a "traditional" mold, influenced by the likes of Ella Fitzgerald and Peggy Lee. "Benny was responsible for molding my musical taste toward more 'today' sounds," she told *Billboard* in 1979.

Benny had already seen success as front-man of the Hep Stars and as half of the duo Bjorn & Benny, with Bjorn Ulvaeus. Sides by each of these acts were issued in the United States, but to only minimal notice. It was not until Benny, Frida, Bjorn, and Bjorn's wife AGNETHA FALTSKOG became Abba that the entire world responded with overwhelming acceptance. In each year of its existence, the group reportedly earned more for the Swedish economy than the entire Volvo car-and-truck operation.

After numerous awards, hit singles, and LP chartings, Abba quietly retired in 1981. Frida and Benny were divorced in 1982. The following year, with Phil Collins producing, Frida recorded what would be the first of two albums, *Something Going On* (1982); *Shine* would follow in 1984. "I Know There's Something Going On," written by Russ Ballard—an ex-member of ADAM FAITH's Roulettes, THE UNIT FOUR PLUS TWO and ARGENT—featuring Collins's pounding drums, remains Frida's only solo hit to date.

"I'd become stuck in a part working with Abba," she explained to *Record*'s Mark Mehler. "Benny and Bjorn do all the writing; you sing the way they want you to.

419

Now I'm using my voice in a new, tougher way. I'm singing out. I'm not so afraid of giving it a little more from down here."

DEXY'S MIDNIGHT RUNNERS
COME ON EILEEN
(Kevin Rowland, Jim Paterson, Kevin Adams)
Mercury 76189
No. 1 *April 23, 1983*

In England, they were stars for three years. They had 10 hits in their homeland; four of these went Top 10. Only three LPs were issued while Dexy's Midnight Runners were the rage, but with each album a new image was utilized, and a new group was needed to accompany the volatile Kevin Rowland.

Dexy's Midnight Runners were a Birmingham-based band. Lead singer/guitarist Rowland (b. Aug. 17, 1953, Wolverhampton, England) was the brains behind the operation. He and Al Archer had initially started in the music world as New Wavers in Lucy & The Lovers and another group called the Killjoys. The latter issued one single on Raw Records, "Johnny Won't Get to Heaven," in 1977. Then it was over, and the two were off to plan phase one of Dexy's Midnight Runners, a name they apparently derived from "dexedrine," a widely-used amphetamine.

At this point, the Runners were a soul band dedicated to the sounds of American acts like Sam & Dave and James Brown. They had a "look" that can best be described as straight out of Martin Scorsese's *Mean Streets*. They were tough, and their horn-filled music definitely ran counter to popular trends. Parlophone Records issued *Searching for the Young Soul Rebels* (1980) and three singles; their R & B-drenched sound sold well.

All the band members then left—except for Rowland and trombonist Jimmy Paterson—due to disagreements over the group's musical direction and which songs to issue as singles. A new Runners line-up—Billy Adams (guitar), Mickey Billingsham (keyboards), Brian Maurice (alto sax), Paul Speare (tenor sax), Steve Wynne (bass), and ex-Secret Affair Seb Shelton (drums)—created *Too-Rye-Ay* (1983), and the chart-topping "Come on Eileen." In dungarees and street-urchin garb, this revamped unit added an Irish-folk tinge to their hard-edged soul style via a fiddle section. "The Celtic Soul Brothers" (#86, 1983) was a moderate mover of a follow-up.

Predictably, by the third LP, *Don't Stand Me Down* (1985), there was another shift in the group's sound, and everyone left save Rowland. Dexy's new image was described by Ira Robbins in the *Trouser Press Record Guide* as "conservative pinstripes," and the music itself deemed "a torpid snore."

DEXY'S MIDNIGHT RUNNERS

Kevin resurfaced three years later. His solo LP *The Wanderer* and its accompanying singles charted neither here nor in England. In 1990, Kevin announced the reformation of Dexy's Midnight Runners. The same was promised again in 1993.

AFTER THE FIRE
DER KOMMISSAR
(R. Ponger, Falco)
Epic 03559
No. 5 *April 30, 1983*

Apparently, After the Fire is now little more than scattered ashes. Nothing has been heard from the foursome from East London and Essex since *ATF* (1982), the stateside album that featured a solitary hit single, "Der Kommissar" (translation: "government official").

Before the Fire flickered out, they consisted of ex-Yes/FLASH Peter "Mr. Memory Banks" Banks (synthesizer), Pete King (drums), Andy Piercy (lead vocals, bass), and John Russell (guitar). They all met in the post-punk late '70s. An EP issued on Rapid, their garage label, caught the attention of the big-money wielders at British CBS. The ATF sound was lacking in extended solos, flash, and pomposity, but CBS liked the group's respect for traditional Anglo-rock, their Beatles-like energy, and the splashes of Yes, Genesis, and 10cc that colored their music. This was a band that corporate types could appreciate, and maybe market.

Three fairly well-received LPs were issued in England from 1979 to 1982 before the CBS label's American affiliate saw fit to release *ATF*, a compilation of the more "commercial" sides from the British album releases. "Der Kommissar" was an English-language version of a song by German artist Falco, the fellow known for the Wolfgang Amadeus Mozart tribute, "Rock Me Amadeus"; the single, the album, and a follow-up 45, "Dancing in the Shadows" (#85, 1983), all sold well. Reportedly, After the Fire disbanded shortly thereafter.

As with the seasons, a restructured After the Fire returned when original member Andy Piercy reactivated a clone of the group for touring purposes, in the late '80s; it was billed as ATF.

THOMAS DOLBY
SHE BLINDED ME WITH SCIENCE
(Thomas Dolby, J. Kerr)
Capitol 5204
No. 5 *May 14, 1983*

"I think it's the most meaningless song I've ever written," Thomas Dolby, the techno-pop geek behind "She Blinded Me With Science," told *Creem*'s Michael Goldberg. "It's about a sort of fuddy-duddy old scientist who gets obsessed with his lab assistant. When I made that song, it was with the thought in my head that . . . people were finding my music too demanding and that maybe I should let loose and make a record that was basically nonsense like everything else on the charts. And it's just a sad reflection on the state of things that it was that successful."

He was born Thomas Morgan Dolby Robertson, in Cairo, Egypt, on October 14, 1958. His father was an archaeologist, so little Tom's travels to and from obscure terrain were constant. He was in and out of boarding schools and piano lessons. When he could, he would tinker with ham radios and electronics, and soon developed interests in film production, meteorology, and computer programming. Dolby dropped out of formal schooling in order to putter with a four-track tape player, and he took his homemade synthesizer to the streets of Paris, where he played Dylan tunes and passed the hat.

With his homemade PA system, Tom began traveling with several New Wave acts, mixing for the Fall, the Members, the Passions, and the U.K. Subs. In short order, Dolby become known to his peers as something of an electronics whiz. He recorded with the Thompson Twins, SW9, and Low Noise; joined Bruce Woolley & The Camera Club, producing their *English Garden* (1979) LP; and toured with Lene Lovich, writing and producing her European mini-hit, "New Toy."

After recording a few singles for Armageddon and Happy Birthday Records, Dolby formed his own EMI-distributed Venice in Peril label, issuing his first album—*The Golden Age of Wireless* (1982)—plus two British hit singles, "Europa and the Pirate Twins" and "Windpower." During this time, he also guested with his keyboards on LP projects by Joan Armatrading, Def Leppard, Andy Partridge's Fallout Club, Foreigner, and M. With the release of his "most meaningless song," Dolby was in public demand, and began performing as a one-man music-making entity—complete with computers, keyboards, tape machines, and video slides.

Thomas' *Blinded by Science* (1983), *The Golden Age of Wireless* (1983), and *The Flat Earth* (1984) albums all sold well, as did "Europa and the Pirate Twins" (#67, 1983) and "Hyperactive" (#62, 1984). Dolby continued to work sessions for the likes of Adele Bertel, Malcolm McLean, Joni Mitchell, Prefab Sprout, and Whodini. He appeared at the 1985 Grammy Award ceremony with Herbie Hancock and Stevie Wonder; played keyboards for David Bowie's "Live Aid" performance; and created the movie scores for *Gothic* (1986) and *Howard the Duck* (1986). Recording as Dolby's Cube, he and funkmaster/FUNKADELIC frontman George Clinton have cut a few singles together.

Dolby's fourth album, *Aliens Ate My Buick* (1988)—and "Airhead," his first 45 in four years—appeared in 1988. The LP featured the unlikely musical aid of small screen spectacles Ed Asner and Robin Leach. In 1992, his *Astronauts and Heretics* was issued. When last spotted, Thomas was newly married to "Dynasty" star Kathleen Beller.

KAJAGOOGOO
TOO SHY
(LIMAHL, Nick Beggs, Kajagoogoo)
EMI-America 8161
No. 5 *July 9, 1983*

At the start of the '80s, Kajagoogoo started a trend in England called Googoomania. Thank goodness for the waters that divide us: by the time these weird-lookin' pretty boys made it to the States, their number-one GooGoo was preparing to be gonegone.

In 1980, four guys from Leighton Buzzard, Hertfordshire, England—Steve Askew (guitar), Nick Beggs (bass), Stuart Croxford Neale (keyboards, synthesizers), and Jez Strode (drums)—formed Art Nouveau, renamed two years later the Handstands. They played Steely Dan and other off-beat fare in clubs and cabarets. LIMAHL (real name: Chris Hamill) placed an ad in *Melody Maker* describing himself as "good-looking, talented . . . and looking for four guys with the same qualifications." The Handstands responded, and before long, everyone agreed that some kind of musical magic was happening. A chance encounter with Duran Duran keyboardist Nick Rhodes led to a meeting with the folks at EMI, and soon Rhodes and Duran producer Colin Thurston were walking Kajagoogoo into a recording studio.

As for their bizarre name, Nick Beggs told Debbie Geller of *Record*: "It's like something a child would say. When people say it, they can't quite pronounce it but once they know it, they can never forget it."

"Too Shy" was the first single pulled from Kajagoogoo's debut album, *White Feathers* (1983). A half-dozen singles would eventually chart in Britain. But in 1983, just as extensive plans had been made to spread Googoomania to the land of the free and the home of the brave, Limahl left the band to go solo.

Both Kaja (the "googoo" portion of their moniker was dropped with Limahl's departure) and Limahl continued their respective careers. Stateside, neither—aside from Limahl's one-off clicker, "Never Ending Story," from the movie of the same name—has managed to reconstruct a winning arrangement of sights and sounds. In the late '80s, Beggs formed a gospel group, Iona; shut-down by 1993, when he became an A & R man for Phonogram Records.

TACO
PUTTIN' ON THE RITZ
(Irving Berlin)
RCA Victor 13574
No. 4 *September 3, 1983*

Taco Ockerse (b. 1955, Jakarta, Indonesia) was born of Dutch parents. His grandfather was a professional pianist and artist in Indonesia. After settling in Hamburg, little Taco studied body movement, dance, and theater, and was acting in musicals by the mid-'70s. In 1979, he played Chino in a German remake of *West Side Story*. The following year, Mr. T—in tails and talcum—was working night spots with his own group, Taco's Bizz. A portion of his act involved updating nostalgic numbers like the Irving Berlin evergreen "Puttin' on the Ritz."

Late in 1981, with the aid of arranger/multi-instrumentalist Werner Lang, Taco cut "Puttin' on the Ritz"—a 1930 chart-topper for Harry Richman—and other reworked oldies for his debut LP, *Taco After Eight* (1983). Nearly a year passed before Taco's tune was tasted by the German public. "I tried everything [including acting out the song as part of a computer music program at a department store] to get it going," Taco told *Cashbox*. Finally, Germany, Austria, Yugoslavia, and a number of other countries took a transitory liking to Taco's take on Berlin's timeless tune.

To date, "Cheek to Cheek" and similar auditory excavations have fared poorly.

FRANK STALLONE
FAR FROM OVER
(Frank Stallone, Vince DiCola)
RSO 815023
No. 10 *October 1, 1983*

Frank Stallone (b. Jul. 30, 1950, Philadelphia), as his name would suggest, is the younger brother of Sylvester Stallone, the mammoth movie-maker. The Philly kid began dashing off lyrics when a mere lad of 14. After high school, Stallone moved to New York City to share an apartment with his brother, an aspiring actor. Years of odd jobs (like selling shirts in

Bloomingdale's) and singing stints in seedy clubs followed before Frank's group, Valentine, got a shot at recording an album's worth of material. The debut disk sold poorly, and Valentine split up.

Frank continued with his vocalizing and garnered a big break singing *a cappella* in Sly's first *Rocky* flick (1976). "Case of You" (#67, 1980), a single on the Scotti Brothers label—written by Joni Mitchell and produced by Harry Nilsson—was Frank's first chart dent. Perspiration and persistence paid off three years later when Stallone's "Far From Over"—an extraction from the soundtrack of *Staying Alive* (1983), Sly's athletic sequel to *Saturday Night Fever*—was issued as a single. Before he vanished—the following year—Frank made the listings for a moment with "Darlin'" (#81).

"No one gave me anything, I had to submit the songs like everybody else," Stallone insisted to *Cashbox* . . ."Just tell people to listen to [my stuff], to give me a fair chance—just give it a good listen and don't judge me by my brother. We're two different people."

BIG COUNTRY
IN A BIG COUNTRY
(Big Country)
Mercury 814467
No. 17 *December 3, 1983*

"Big Country is not punk, New Wave, heavy metal, progressive, or pop," Stuart Adamson, the group's lead singer/guitarist and frontman, remarked to *Creem*.

Some critics heard traces of Celtic folk tunes in Big Country's music, and many pop pundits put the group in a class with the Alarm and U2. And on an auditory landscape of synthesizer washes and electronic rhythm machines, the bagpipe-like droning of Big Country's twin lead guitars defiantly stood out.

Adamson (b. Apr. 11, 1958, Manchester, England) was raised in Dunfermline, Scotland, and schooled in Scottish folk music. "There would always be folks around on Friday and Saturday night, after the pubs had shut," he told *Record*'s Adrian Thrills. "There would be guys up there playing guitars, bagpipes, accordions, and fiddles, so some of the things I write go right back to then."

He began writing songs when he was 12. From 1977 to 1981, Stuart played in a punk group with Eddie Jobson called the Skids. Virgin Records issued five albums, and nine of the Skids' singles charted in England (none of these were released in the United States). When the group split up, Jobson went on to form the Armoury Show, and Adamson returned home to Scotland.

Dunfermline—the burial place of seven Scottish kings—is also where the British Navy docks its nuclear submarines. Guitarist Bruce Watson (b. Mar. 11, 1961, Ontario, Canada) was scrubbing out those subs when he met Stuart. Both were ready to form a band, but it had to be something different. Together, Stuart and Bruce developed a distinctive twin-guitar sound beneath a community pool hall. When they felt ready, they took Big Country out on the road in support of Alice Cooper. Disappointed with the response, they disbanded, and the two returned to the basement for further practice.

Chris Briggs—an A & R man with the British Phonogram label who had worked with ABC, Def Leppard, and Dire Straits—knew of Adamson from his Skids days and invited him and Watson to London to record some demos. Briggs hooked the twosome up with drummer Mark Brzezicji (b. June 21, 1957, London) and bassist Tony Butler (b. Feb. 13, 1957, London). The four had met earlier: Mark and Tony had played with Simon Townsend's On The Air, an act that had once opened for the Skids.

When Briggs located them, Mark was doing TV jingle sessions, and Butler had briefly played bass for the Pretenders.

"Something just clicked," Adamson recalled to *Rolling Stone*'s James Henske. "It was magic right from the start." Briggs signed the group on the spot, and ushered Big Country into a studio with producer Chris Thomas. The resulting album was *Harvest Home* (1982), a disappointing effort that nonetheless attracted critical attention. Producer Steve Lillywhite was brought in, and with the second LP, *The Crossing* (1983), everything jelled. The album went gold in the United States, and featured "In a Big Country" and "Fields of Fire" (#52, 1984).

Big Country had an extended run of British and European hits. *Wonderland* (1984), *Steeltown* (1984), and *The Seer* (1986) followed, but except for "Wonderland" (#86, 1984), no other Big Country sides ever again appeared on the American pop listings.

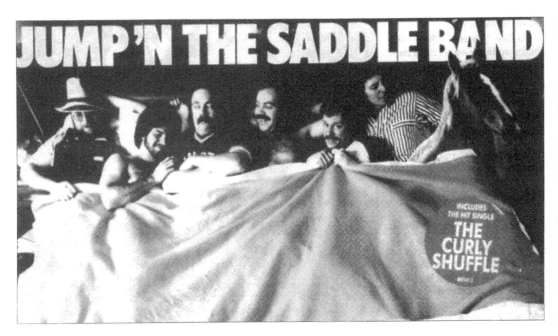

PETER SCHILLING
MAJOR TOM (COMING HOME)
(Peter Schilling, David Lodge)
Elektra 69811
No. 14 *December 24, 1983*

Some have called him a shameless Bowie impersonator, a charge based on the thematic similarity of "Major Tom" to Bowie's 1973 hit, "Space Oddity." "It's definitely not from Bowie, except the title, and the figure of Major Tom," Schilling declared to *Melody Maker*'s Paul Rider. "I was inspired to write the song by a film in 1968 called *Danger on the Moon*, with Gregory Peck."

Schilling (b. Jan. 28, 1956, Stuttgart, Germany) grew up listening to the Beatles and the Stones. He took up playing folk guitar, served in the army, and upon his return, worked for some music publishers and WEA Records. Some of his tunes were recorded by others; a few singles bearing his own name were shipped. In 1981, Peter became friends with a guitarist and the co-writer of many of his tunes, Armin Sabol. Schilling's debut LP, *Error in the System* (1983) —featuring his much-panned but entertaining hit—was first issued in Germany, and did not appear in the United States until nearly a year later.

Peter still continues to record, though sporadically, and has shown his skills at pessimism and electric protest with such items as "The Noah Play" and "Silent Night." The latter is worth a holiday listen. "I hate that Christmas song," Schilling told *Illinois Entertainer*'s Jeff Tamarkin. "I'm glad that my version got some negative reaction from some Christians because I want to say to them that it's not a holy night and a silent night; everything is not well."

JUMP IN THE SADDLE BAND
THE CURLY SHUFFLE
(Peter Quinn)
Atlantic 89718
No. 15 *January 21, 1984*

"There hadn't been a novelty hit like 'The Curly Shuffle' for 10 years," Saddle Band man T. C. Furlong said in an exclusive interview. "You know why it was a hit, even though it started on a basement label with no distribution? It was genuine. It was a tribute to Curly and the Three Stooges, and we meant it."

T. C. (steel guitar, electric guitar) and Pete Quinn (lead vocals, harmonica) formed a country bar band in 1974 with Jack Burchall and Don Bains. For three years they were Rio Grande, until Bains and Burchall quit and took the name with them. T. C. and Pete added Barney Schwartz (guitar) and Ann Schwartz (bass), changed their repertoire slightly, and began calling

themselves the Jump 'n The Saddle Band. The line-up fluctuated: Vince Dee (drums, vocals), Don Sternberg (fiddle, guitar), and Tom "Shoes" Trinka (sax) joined up, then Sternberg departed. He was briefly replaced by Dan Parks (fiddle, guitar), who then left to work with Dickie Betts and Mel Tillis.

"We came up with this 'Curly Shuffle' song. Pete just brought it into a rehearsal—we knew it was good. So we recorded it and put it out as a single [the first for both the band and Chicago's Acme Recording Studio label] and it was literally passed around from radio station to radio station.

"Atlantic had heard what a hot item the single was. They picked up its distribution and signed the band and asked us to make an album. It was all over, one, two, three. We did the *Jump 'n The Saddle Band* [1984] LP and one more single.

"We walked into a production meeting with the president of Atlantic Records and the head of A & R. 'Curly Shuffle' is on the charts, but they don't even know the name of the band. They were introducing us around as the Curly Shuffle Boys. So the president sits down with us and says, 'What have we got here? The Three Stooges? Fine. You guys are the creative geniuses—come up with a Marx Brothers song.'

"We told 'em we did 'Curly' as a homage; it would be impossible to manufacture another one. So he says, 'Here's what you're gonna do: You're gonna do BENNY BELL's "Shaving Cream."' So we did record 'Shaving Cream' big-band style, but Atlantic hated it and wouldn't issue it. I don't think they liked our last verse. The last line of each verse goes, 'I stepped in a big pile of . . . shaving cream, shaving cream.' Well, we changed the last verse to 'Atlantic wanted us to record a hit/We sent them a big pile of . . . shaving cream, shaving cream.' They had no sense of humor. We alienated the company, but at that point, we didn't give a . . . shaving cream.

"They put out 'It Should Have Been Me' from the album, and that was it for the band. We're still active and on the circuit—no records and no more tapes, though."

SHANNON
LET THE MUSIC PLAY
(Chris Barbosa, Ed Chisholm)
Mirage 99810
No. 8 *February 25, 1984*

When success struck her like a bolt of lightning, Brenda "Shannon" Greene (b. 1958, Washington, DC) was a Brooklynite and a student at York University. She was majoring in accounting with a minor in music, and had taken years of formal voice and dance lessons. A few of her music professors insisted that she give music-making a serious try. When 20, in 1978, Shannon joined the New York Jazz Ensemble as their vocalist. Through this experience she met jazz drummer Lenny White—formerly with Miles Davis, Return to Forever; later the Jamaica Boys, responsible for the E.U., hit "Da' Butt"—and a soul group, Brownstone. While with the latter group some recordings were made, reportedly due to the efforts made by Lenny; one of them "Let the Music Play." Shannon had no idea that her name was going to appear on the label. Emergency Records with a belief in her talents, looks, and that contagious song issued the disk as an extended play during the fall of 1983.

"I always knew that it was possible," she told *Billboard*, "but I didn't know if I wanted to do it so soon." Mirage, a subsidiary of Atlantic Records, acquired her contract and the rights to "Let the Music Play." It was a huge hit, a catchy pulsating thing, surely just the first outing for a major new artist. "Give Me Tonight" (#46, 1984) and "Do You Wanna Get Away" (#49, 1985) were her sole Hot 100 chartings, but a groovy little pile of Shannon 45s continued to place on *Billboard*'s R & B listings through 1986: "My Heart's Divided" (#48, 1984), "Stronger Together" (#26, 1985), "Urgent" (#68, 1985), and "Prove Me Right" (#82, 1986).

Only her debut album—*Let the Music Play* (1984)—struck pay dirt. *Do You Want to Get Away*—the second and apparently last Shannon album—was quietly put out in 1986. The singer's disappearance is completely inexplicable.

NENA
99 LUFTBALLONS
(Joem Fahrenkrog-Peterson, Carlo Karges)
Epic 04108
No. 2 *March 3, 1984*

In 1980, lead singer Gabriela Susanne "Nena" Kerner (b. Hagen, W. Germany), drummer Rolf Brendel, and keyboardist Uwe Fahrenkrog-Peterson were members of a fairly successful band called Stripes. Their self-titled CBS LP was selling decently in West Germany when the three Blondie proteges decided to split for the bright Berlin bar scene. With the addition in 1982 of bassist Jurgen Demel and guitarist Carlo Karges, both ex-members of a band called Odessa, Stripes became the nouveau Nena. Months of rehearsals and banging around Berlin passed before the band was invited into a recording studio. An innocent-sounding tune, "Nur

Getraumt," was extracted from their first Nena album; both the LP and the 45 did quite well.

"99 Luftballons," a pseudo-nuclear-protest song, was the next Nena number issued. A disk jockey at Los Angeles's KROQ-FM took a liking to the tune and ran it so often that the group's label decided to release the song in the United States. Despite the 45s chart-topping success and healthy sales of *99 Luftballons* (1984), Nena's later releases have slipped by without even mini-notices in the United States.

KC
GIVE IT UP
(Harry "K.C." Casey, Deborah Carter)
Meca 1001
No. 18 *March 17, 1984*

In 1978, the times were a-changin' again, and the musical tastes that moved the nation's feet on the disco dance floor were shifting, too. Also present was some friction between the T. K. label and the two founders of KC & The Sunshine Band—Harry Wayne Casey (KC) and Rick Finch, popularizers of that funky, up-beat party music called the "Sunshine Sound" or "Miami being lax in promoting their current output.

Despite the chart-topping success of the group's "Please Don't Go," KC, Finch, and the Sunshine name moved over to Epic Records early in 1980. Over the next few years, two LPs—*The Painter* (1981) and *All in a Night's Work* (1982)—plus a spray of singles were issued. Nothing charted in the United States, and the two Sunshine boys separated. Casey issued *Space Cadet* (1982), his first solo album, though he had already made the Hot 100 dueting with TERI DeSARIO on Barbara Mason's '60s hit "Yes, I'm Ready" (#2, 1980) and Martha & The Vandelas' "Dancin' in the Streets" (#66, 1980).

In January, 1982, Harry Casey was seriously injured in a head-on car crash. All feeling was lost on one side of his body as the result of nerve damage, and he spent over a year recuperating and learning to walk again.

Meanwhile, "Give It Up," an extract from *All in a Night's Work*, rose to the number-one slot in England. When Epic refused to issue the single in the United States, Casey negotiated an end to his contract and formed his own Meca label. "Give It Up" was quickly released in the United States as a KC solo. It did quite well, but to this date, it remains the only solo effort by the former dance king to make the listings.

KC has referred to his music simply as "the happy sound." Its roots, he has freely admitted, are to be found in a form of Bahamian pop music called junkanoo, which he first heard at CLARENCE "Blowfly" REID's wedding in January, 1973. "[The Junkanoo Rhythm Band] played all these percussion instruments," KC told *Circus.* "They were pounding steel drums and gut-covered instruments and clanging cow-bells and blowing whistles. The vibrations were just unbelievable." Within months of Reid's wedding, Rick Finch and KC had forged their westernized work-up of that Bahamian pop style. Starting with "Get Down Tonight," nearly everything the two recorded from 1975 to 1980 made the pop charts.

TRACEY ULLMAN
THEY DON'T KNOW
(Kristy MacColl)
MCA 52347
No. 8 *April 28, 1984*

Tracey Ullman (b. May 25, 1959) was born in the London suburb of Hackbridge. Her father died when she was six. "We had it hard," Ullman explained to the *Chicago Sun Times*' Ernest Tucker. "But we did everything for a laugh." Her mother encouraged her to sing, to dance, to mimic. She attended the Italia Conti School for four years, but claims she was expelled. Soon

in productions of *Grease, The Rocky Horror Picture Show*, and *Elvis*. In 1981, at the tender age of 21, she received the London Theatre Critics Award for her performance in the improvisational play, *Four in a Million*. This led to the BBC series "Three of a Kind," which established her as a TV star in Britain.

In rapid succession, Tracey appeared in Paul McCartney's *Give My Regards to Broad Street* (1984); played the part of Alice Park, the beat bohemian, in the Meryl Streep flick *Plenty* (1985); and recorded *You Broke My Heart in 17 Places* (1984), her first pop effort. Three singles from that '60s-sounding LP made the British charts. Thus far, only Tracey's retooling of IRMA THOMAS's "Breakaway" (#70, 1984) has managed to join "They Don't Know" on *Billboard*'s stateside Hot 100. "I made that [album] as a lark, really," Ullman told *Spin*'s Glenn O'Brien. "I can't hold a note or hold a tune and it was good fun. But it was a joke that became successful. It was the old Midas touch. I was doing everything. When I go into a record store, I always look for it in the bargain bin."

In the meantime, Ullman made her United States TV series debut in April, 1987, in "The Tracey Ullman Show," one of the first series on the Fox network and one of its best. Critics have cheered, and the industry itself has decorated the vehicle with five Emmy nominations. Paula Abdul provided the choreography; FUNKADELIC's George Clinton, the theme song. As the

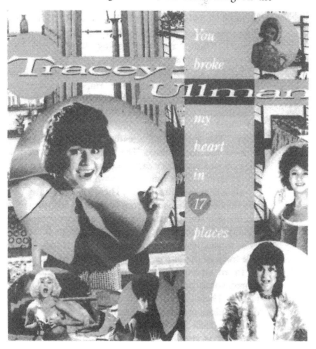

series ended in September 1990, Matt Groening, the creator of an animated segment of her show called "The Simpsons," was given his own series. Ullman appeared with Kevin Kline in the comedy *I Love You to Death* (1990). Her HBO special "Tracy Ullman—Takes on New York," garnered an Emmy for "Outstanding Individual Performance in a Variety or Music Program."

OLLIE & JERRY
BREAKIN' . . . THERE'S NO STOPPING US
("Ollie" Brown, "Jerry" Knight)
Polydor 821708
No. 9 *August 4, 1984*

They met seemingly countless times on tours and at recording sessions. Both Ollie Brown (drums, vocals) and Jerry Knight (bass, guitar, vocals) were born and raised in Detroit, and both eventually found themselves caught up in the Ray Parker, Jr., success story. They played for a while in Parker's Raydio, and Jerry—who had previously recorded as the bass man in Bill Withers band—even sang lead on the group's chart-shakin' debut, "Jack and Jill" (#8, 1978).

In the early '80s, Jerry repeatedly made the R & B charts as a solo act; notably, "Overnight Sensation" (#17, 1980) and "Perfect Fit" (#16, 1981). His tunes were successfully recorded by such acts as Atlantic Starr, PHILLIP BAILEY, George Duke, and the Whispers. Ollie, meanwhile, played drums for Lamont Dozier, Michael Henderson, Lenny Williams; worked and produced sessions, most notably for PATTI AUSTIN, Howard Hewett, Klique, and the Rolling Stones; and had recorded one LP as a soloist named Ollie Baba.

In 1983, Brown was conferring with Polydor's Russ Regan—the man behind "The Happy Reindeer"—when the offer was made to work up material for the breakdancing flick, *Breakin'* (1984). "They asked me to get started on this fast," Ollie told *Billboard*'s Steve Ivory. "The movie had already been shot, and they showed me the footage. The first thing one of the dancers said was 'They can't stop us.' I introduced that line to Jerry, and he went crazy with it."

Ollie & Jerry's "Breakin' . . . There's No Stopping Us" was the first single issued from Polydor's platinum-selling *Breakin'* soundtrack (1984). "Actually, we were writing that song about us," Knight admitted to *Billboard*. "The music business is full of hardships. It may be the title track of the movie, but we can relate to it."

In an attempt to do it once again, Ollie & Jerry scored some tracks for *Breakin' 2: Electric Boogaloo* (1984). Their title tune took off (R&B: #45, 1984), as did the film's soundtrack album.

With such an extensive history—together and alone—it is startling to report, but neither Ollie or Jerry has been observed anywhere on the musical landscape since 1985.

SCANDAL FEATURING PATTY SMYTH
THE WARRIOR
(Holly Knight, Nick Gilder)
Columbia 04424
No. 7 *September 22, 1984*

Zack and Patty met in 1982. They argued. Guitarist Zack Smith (b. Westport, CT) had played with Dee Murray and Davey Johnston, Elton John's sidemen. In 1982, Zack had a Big Apple-based band called Scandal, a unit that would eventually consist of bassist Ivan Elias, keyboardist Benji King, and drummer Frankie LaRocka. But something was missing, and that something, Zack surmised, was the presence of a female. After they auditioned 80 or more promising presences, someone suggested Patty Smyth. The audition took so long to set up and was so poorly planned that Zack and Patty's first meeting turned into a heated argument.

Patty (b. June 26, 1957, New York City) was a hard-as-nails rocker who had grown up in Greenwich Village. Her mother was a club manager. "Backstage was my home," Smyth told *Creem*. "I was a little kid hanging around while JOHN SEBASTIAN, Dylan, and the BLUES MAGOOS went out to have their say."

PATTY SMITH
OF SCANDAL

Once the yelling subsided, Patty passed her audition, and the female-fronted Scandal was ready for the world. They toured with Hall & Oates, John Cougar Mellencamp, and the Kinks, and cut the five-tune *Scandal* (1983) EP for Columbia. The group's first two singles—"Goodbye to You" (#65, 1982) and "Love's Got a Line on You" (#59, 1983)—came from what was to become the largest selling mini-album in Columbia Records history. *The Warrior* (1984), the unit's first and only full-length LP, was a huge success, as was the title track (#7, 1984)—written by NICK GILDER and Holly Johnson of SPIDER; later DEVICE. The two immediate follow-ups—"Hands Tied" (#41, 1984) and "Beat of a Heart" (#41, 1985)—just missed the nation's Top 40 hit parade.

Meanwhile, all was not well within the hell-raisin', hard rockin' group. Zack disappeared, saying he wanted to write and produce. Patty married punk rocker Richard Hell, for awhile, had a child, and seemed to wave bye-bye to the world of rock and roll.

After three years, the label shipped *Never Enough* (1987), Patty's debut solo effort, plus a stack of 45s. The waxings presented a mellower woman and met with mixed reviews. In 1992, Patty did strike back with two major hits, "Sometimes Love Just Ain't Enough" (#2), which featured vocal assistance from Don Henley, and "No Mistake" (#33). "You can't keep doing the same things when you get married and have a family," Patty Smyth told Dennis Hunt of the *Los Angeles Times*. "You have to slow down. You have to be responsible. You can be crazy if you only have yourself to worry about. I can't be that way any more."

DENNIS DEYOUNG
DESERT MOON
(Dennis DeYoung)
A & M 2666
No. 10 *November 11, 1984*

It began as one of those seldom-fulfilled, teen-dream long shots in 1963 in Roseland, Illinois. "John Panozzo [drums] and his brother Chuck [bass] lived across the street from me," said Dennis DeYoung (keyboards, vocals) to *Chicago Soundz's* Joe Ziemba. "We'd always hung around together and played whatever gigs we could get—it was a big deal when we got to do a college dance." They were called the Tradewinds. In 1968, once the threesome was attending Chicago State University and had added fellow student Johnny "J. C." Curulewski on lead guitar, they were simply TW4.

By 1970, Jim "J.Y." Young (guitar) was added, a demo record was cut for RCAs Brian Christian, and Bill Traut—a major force in the forging of '60s Chicago groups like the American Breed, H. P. Lovecraft, and the Shadows of Knight—offered to sign TW4 to his

RCA-distributed Wooden Nickel label. But first they would have to change their name to something a bit more hip, like "Styx." (According to Greek mythology, Styx is the river that dead souls are ferried across to reach Hades.)

In rapid succession, Wooden Nickel issued *Styx I* (1972) and *Styx II* (1973). Both albums met a lukewarm response, but the latter LP did include what would become the first of 13 Top 40 hits. Following "Lady" (#6, 1975), Styx—with DeYoung as lead singer—switched to A & M and clicked with such pop-radio memorables as "Come Sail Away" (#8, 1978), "Babe" (#1, 1979), "The Best of Times" (#3, 1979), and "Mr. Roboto" (#3, 1983). Styx toured to sold-out concerts and scored big with albums like *The Grand Illusion* (1977), *Pieces of Eight* (1978), *Cornerstone* (1979), *Paradise Theatre* (1981), and *Kilroy Was Here* (1983). Of their 14 LPs, 27 million copies were sold in all; 4 went triple platinum, 2 double platinum, and 1 gold.

"After *Kilroy*, we decided to do a live album and then to take some time off," DeYoung, the group's primary songwriter, told Joe Ziemba. "After 14 albums in 12 years, it was time to pursue other things . . . time for a period of growth." J.Y. Young, TOMMY SHAW (b. Montgomery, AL; Curulewski's replacement as of 1976), and DeYoung have since pursued solo careers, the latter two with some success. In addition to his "Desert Moon" and the LP from which it was pulled—*Desert Moon* (1984)—DeYoung has appeared on the Hot 100 with "Don't Wait for Heroes" (#83, 1984), "Call Me" (#54, 1986), and "This Is the Time" (#93, 1986), the latter from *The Karate Kid Part II* (1986).

Dennis's solo career was shelved in 1990 when he and Young and the Panozzo brothers, minus Shaw—then a member of Damn Yankees with TED NUGENT—plus ex-Shanghai/formerly billed SPIDER Glen Burtnick reformed Styx. Major hits, "Show Me the Way" (#3, 1990) and "Love at First Sight" (#25, 1991), followed.

JACK WAGNER
ALL I NEED
(Cliff Magness, Glen Ballard, David Park)
Qwest 29238
No. 2 *November 24, 1984*

In the early '80s, Rick Springfield—"Dr. Noah Drake" on one of TV's most successful and longest running soap operas, "General Hospital"—had a string of hits: "Jessie's Girl," "I've Done Everything for You," "Don't Talk to Strangers" . . . Near concurrently, Jack Wagner (b. Nov. 3, 1959, Washington, MO) broke into *Billboard's* Top 40 with "All I Need," becoming the second and only other cast member of "General Hospital" to be successfully passed off as a genuine rock'n'roller.

The idea was that Wagner, as "Frisco Jones," would front this imagined band Riff Raff. Beginning in December, 1983, Jack was Frisco. He had the poses. He walked that walk. Girls liked it. Kelly Ross, musical consultant to ABC daytime television, noted the potential in Jack's voice and alerted the legendary producer/composer Quincy Jones. With little interruption, Quincy got Wagner into a recording studio with a couple of sidekicks, Cliff Magnus and Glen Ballard, and tracks were laid down.

Young females, in particular, bought his "All I Need" in massive quantities; but not so for his "Lady of My Heart" (#76, 1985), "Too Young" (#52, 1985), "Weatherman Says" (#67, 1987), though all charted. Thereafter his attentions seem to have drifted back to acting, with some golf on the side.

His prime interest when growing up in small town Missouri was sports; in particular, golf. At 19, he found himself way-laid and pursuing a career in acting. A big break came with his being added to the cast for the cable soap "A New Day in Eden." For a moment there was a role in the CBS perennial "Knots Landing," that he filled.

In the '90s, Jack had the good fortune to be included in the casts for both "Santa Barbara" and "Melrose Place," the latter as "Dr. Peter Burns."

PHILLIP BAILEY WITH PHIL COLLINS
EASY LOVER
(Phillip Bailey, Phil Collins, Nathan East)
Columbia 04679
No. 2 *December 8, 1984*

"He's the greatest singer ever," said famed producer and Chic man Nile Rodgers (David Bowie, Madonna, Diana Ross, and others) of Phillip Bailey, to *Musician.*

Bailey (b. May 8, 1951, Denver, CO) is largely known for his chart-storming soul/funk sensations cut with Earth, Wind & Fire, the act he entered as a co-vocalist and percussionist in 1971. Maurice White, one-time Chess Records session drummer and Ramsey Lewis Trio member, formed EWF initially as the Salty Peppers in 1969. The act— named for the three elements in Maurice's astrological sign—went through numerous line-up shuffles. But Phillip was there through hit after hit: "Mighty, Mighty," "Shining Star," "Sing a Song," "Getaway"—13 years in the shadow.

In 1983, George Duke produced Phillip's initial solo effort, *Continuation* Sales were moderate. A year later Bailey met Collins, and his world changed.

"If I had known Phil [Collins], I probably wouldn't have asked him to work with me," said Bailey to Allan Barra of *Musician.* "I didn't own any Genesis records or Phil Collins records. . . . "

"Whose idea was it to marry Phillip to Phil for an album is not known, though the union produced Bailey's most successful *Chinese Wall* and "Easy Lover," one of the '80s' most distinctive dusties.

Of the classics creation, Bailey said, "Nathan [East, the sessions bassist] and Phil [Collins] were playing around with a riff on the piano, but it was very Los Angeles slick, smooth changes. So I went up to Daryl and said [winking], 'Whatever you do, put a fuzz box on it.' I was going around singing 'Choosy Lover' over the piano chords. After working on it all day, we put a rough version of it down on tape. The next day we said, 'Let's check it out so we can go in and record it.' When we heard it, we realized there was nothing wrong with it. We tried doing it again, but we kept the original.

"Then Phil said, 'You've written the words, you may as well sing some.' I said [hesitation], 'Okay,' So we worked it out as a duet. Then after we'd sung it, he said, 'We've got to do a video.' I said, 'Ehh, yeah, okay'—a little bit reluctantly, because I'd just done some singing with Clapton and Atlantic Records was saying, 'Don't sing anymore or people are going to get fed up with your voice.' Needless to say, I didn't listen.

"People started suggesting shit about the lyrics that's not even there," Bailey said. "They said, 'We won't play any records by a guy who talks about an easy lover.' Then you ask, 'Did you listen to the lyrics?' It's almost a parallel to Proverbs, Chapters six and seven, and how the man goeth after the woman as an ox goes to slaughter. When I read the lyrics, I reflected back to those passages. But it seems like some of these Christian folks got nothing else to do but sit at home and pick."

In response, numerous stations yanked Bailey's gospel album, *The Wonders of His Love,* from their play lists.

Phillip Bailey had only limited success thereafter. Only "State of the Heart" (R&B: #20, 1986) has charted well on the R & B listings.

GIUFFRIA
CALL TO THE HEART
(Gregg Giuffria, David Glen Eisley)
MCA 52497
No. 15 *January 5, 1985*

Gregg Giuffria is no quitter.

For nearly a decade he was the atmospheric key-boardist for the flamboyant Los Angeles-based hard-rock glam-boys Angel. Despite ample musical talent and the visual appeal of their white satin stage drag and cutesy drummer Edwin Lionel "Punky" Meadows, Angel sold massive quantities of concert tickets, but not enough records. In 1981, Angel crashed.

With the passage of a few good years, the angst of Angel flew again as Giuffria (pronounced: *Je-free-ah*).

Gregg and vocalist David Glen Eisley, guitarist Craig Goldy (ex-Rough Cutt), drummer Alan Krigger (sessions: Beach Boys, Doobie Bros., Ike & Tina Turner), and bassist Chuck Wright (ex-Quiet Riot) created a demo for Camel Records' head Bruce Bird. Bird had previously been affiliated with Angel and on May 2, 1985, upon hearing the act's demo signed the boys on the spot.

"Call to the Heart" was pulled from their fast-assembled self-titled debut album. "It was 'cinema rock,'" explained Eisley to *Cashbox*. "Very big and euphoric, *Star Wars*; yet at the same time real and down-to-earth." After a tour in support of their lone hit, Goldy left the fold to join Driver, later Dio; Wright disappeared into the studios for session work; replaced respectively by Lanny** Cordola and David Sikes. "Lonely in Love" (#57, 1985) and "I Must Be Dreaming" (#52, 1986) charted. The departures, however, delayed the release of *Silk and Steel* until late 1986; months later Giuffria was without a label.

Not content to be dead, and with the aid and advice of Kiss' Gene Simmons, Giuffria became the RCA act the House of Lords. Soon Eisley and Krigger were gone, replaced by vocalist James Christian (ex-Canata) and drummer Ken Mary (ex-Alice Cooper). Before their break-up in the early '90s, two stateside and a Japanese-only album were issued to a less than mild response.

Gregg is reportedly at work on some yet to be revealed project.

MIDNIGHT STAR
OPERATOR
(Bo Watson, Reggie Calloway)
Solar 69684
No. 18 *January 12, 1985*

Brothers Reginald "Reggie" and Vincent "Cino-vincent" Calloway got their start beating garbage pails, pans, and pots in Cincinnati, Ohio. "We were very imaginative kids," said Reggie to *It's Hip* magazine. "Grandmother had an old piano, which we'd play every now and then. Then in high school, we joined the choir. . . ." The soon-to-be multi-instrumentalists played around separately in a succession of semi-pro bands; Reggie cooked with the Mad Dog Fire Department and the little-noted Motown Masters. By the early '70s, the two brothers and a third bro, Greg, were one act, Sunchild, a jazz-funk unit that often accompanied Sonny Stit.

In 1976, while attending Kentucky State University, Cino-vincent (trumpet, trombone, keyboards, flugelhorn) and Reggie (trumpet, flute, keyboards) formed a self-contained techno-funk unit, Midnight Star with fellow students—Jeffery Cooper (lead guitar, keyboards), Kenneth Gant (bass, vocals), Melvin Gantry (lead vocals), Barbara Lipscomb (lead vocals), Walter

GIUFFRIA

Simmons (saxophone, keyboards, percussion), and Bo Watson (lead vocals, keyboards).

Midnight Star worked a lot of gigs in Ohio and Kentucky until the opportunity arose to perform in New York City. Once there they were soon spotted by Dick Griffey at Solar Records. Once signed, Midnight Star cut hit after R & B hit. "I've Been Watching You" (#35, 1981), "Hot Spot" (#35, 1982), "Freak-a-Zoid" (#2, 1983), "Wet My Whistle" (#8, 1983)—all charted well on *Billboard*'s R & B Top 40, before the release of "Operator," their lone crossover hit.

"We often look around for concepts that relate to day-to-day life and figure out how we can make a twist on it," explained Reggie of the thinking behind the creation of "Operator." "Almost every day you're talking to an operator or you get disconnected or you dial a wrong number. It was before sampling, so we recorded an actual operator and used it in the record."

"We're seriously interested in becoming the premier Pop/R & B self-contained group," said Lipscomb to *Billboard*'s Steven Ivory, when the R & B hits seemed never-ending. "Let's face it, there's a void since Earth, Wind & Fire slowed down."

Black radio continued its affair with Midnight Star, but all was not well within the group. Members were bothered that the continued success of labelmates, such as the Whispers, Shalamar, and Lakeside diminished the attention that Midnight Star received. More irking to members was the outside success Reggie and Cinovincent were garnering with their production work for DEELE, Klymaxx, and others.

Before Reggie and Cino-vincent departed the big name R & B unit in 1988 to become CALLOWAY, numerous Midnight Star albums were successful and a dozen plus singles had charted on *Billboard*'s R & B listings, notably: "Headlines" (#3, 1986), "Midas Touch" (#7, 1986). Thereafter, Midnight Star remained a chart-shaking R & B act into the early '90s.

FRANKIE GOES TO HOLLYWOOD
RELAX
(Pete Gill, William Johnson, Mark O'Toole)
Island 998705
No. 67 *April 7, 1984*
No. 10 *February 2, 1985*

Banned in Britain, by the BBC for being "obscene," was "Relax" and its accompanying video, shot in a gay bar. Their high-gloss magazine, *And Suddenly There Came a Bang*, was banned from the racks by the National Graphic Association, for being "peppered with swear words" and drawings of "kinky sex acts between humans and animals."

Frankie Goes to Hollywood was upsetting to many, dismissed by fewer people and idolized by the youthful multitudes.

"The best thing: discovering the works of Marquis de Sade with a partner of your choice," read an ad for one of Frankie Goes to Hollywood's singles. The response was outrage, be it righteous or delicious. "We would like to take this opportunity to confirm that we do not agree with the Marquis de Sade's thoughts that sex while killing someone is the ultimate orgasm," explained Frankie frontman Holly Johnson to *Melody Maker*, "preferring in this instance to agree with Wordsworth when he talked of 'the pleasure that there is in life itself.'"

They were Britain's pop sensation of 1984. The land was engulfed in a Frankiemania, in a sea of "Frankie Says . . ." T-shirts, with slogans racing the range from politics to seamy sex. "Relax"—a messaged groaner reeking of the joys of relaxed sex—became the biggest-selling single ever in Britain.

For one album, a few singles, several months—until the appearance of Wham! and its George Michael, the next sensation of the year, Holly and his horde were the royalty of ruffle.

They were a Liverpool band formed in the hot months of 1980. Holly Johnson (b. William Johnson, Feb. 19, 1960, Khartoum, Sudan, vocals) had been a member of Big in Japan and had a few solo singles—"Yankee Rose," "Hobo Joe"—put out prior to his meeting up with Peter "Pedro" Gill (b. Mar. 8, 1964, drums), Nash Nasher (b. Brian Nash, May 20, 1963, guitar), Marc O'Tool (b. Jan. 6, 1964, Liverpool, bass), Paul Rutherford (b. Dec. 8, 1959, Liverpool, vocals). Rutherford had recorded the song "Mein Kampf," as part of the Spitfires.

Legend has it that their cumbersome name came from a caption under a photograph of a young Frank Sinatra; or possibly from a headline in a Liverpool paper for home grown FRANKIE VAUGHAN. Despite their act that one critic described as "a leather-bound bordello of punk funk," two years were spent before record companies took notice of Frankie. When they did—Arista and Polygram turned the "sensation of '84" down flat. Ex-BUGGLES Trevor Horn and rock journalist Paul Morley signed the act in a flash in 1983, when their ZTT label was formed. "Relaxed"—their debut—became an overnight happening.

Much as the Sex Pistols went #1 in Britain while suffering a BBC radio/TV ban, so too Frankie Goes to Hollywood. Censorship seemed to help matters. For a solid month the disk was top-of-the-charts; 2 million copies were sold. The openly homosexual orientation of vocalists Holly and Paul seemed to add to their curiosity value.

"Two Tribes," their follow-up was a chilling six-minute funker dealing with nuclear arms and the prospect of global annihilation—complete with a voiceover, taken from government papers, instructing listeners on how to dispose of dogs, grandparents, and other loved ones who have fallen. A GODLEY & CREME produced video featured a fist-fight between look-alikes for then-President Ronald Reagan and the Soviet Union's Chernenko.

"Two Tribes" and Frankie's next single "The Power of Love" topped the U.K. charts, making the act only the second act in British pop history to have their first three singles become number one. All the while some Americans took notice, but aside from "Relax" none of these shenanigans translated into massive record sales.

After the release of their double-album, *Welcome to the Pleasure Dome*, for the 1984 holiday season, Frankie Goes to Hollywood experienced homeland difficulties. A few singles did not chart as well as expected, *Liverpool*, their second album stalled, and in 1987 FGTH called it quits. So ended the tale of the most short-lived headline-garnering Brit-band since the Sex Pistols.

Holly attempted a solo career, won a lawsuit against ZTT Records, and early in the '90s discovered that he was HIV-positive. In 1994, he published *A Bone in My Flute*, his autobiography. "Legendary Children," an isolated solo single, followed.

HAROLD FALTERMEYER
AXEL F
(Harold Faltermeyer)
MCA 52536
No. 3 *April 13, 1985*

A private soul is Harold Faltermeyer; a behind-the-scene music-maker responsible for successful disks, though disks bearing others' names. Harry's a West German born arranger, keyboardist, producer, and songwriter. For years he was a protege of GIORGIO MORODER, playing keyboards on many of the Italian-born composer's productions. Faltermeyer arranged and performed on the scores for the Richard Gere-Lauren Hutton flick *American Gigolo* (1980), Brad Davis' *Midnight Express* (1978), and Tom Cruise's *Top Gun* (1986). "Axel F" was a piece of background scoring that Harry had created for Eddie Murphy's *Beverly Hills Cop* (1985). The title being a play on Murphy's characters name, "Axel Foley."

Faltermeyer is responsible for composing the music for such as the theme for the flick *Fletch*, "Bit by Bit," Glenn Frey's "The Heat Is On," Donna Summer's "Hot Stuff," and Bob Seger's "Shakedown." Before returning to his back stage work, Harry made a duet recording with Patti LaBelle, and another with Steve Stevens.

MARY JANE GIRLS
IN MY HOUSE
(Rick James)
Gordy 1741
No. 7 *April 27, 1985*

It was the punk-funk priest who came up with the concept that would become the Mary Jane Girls. Rick James, the bead-braided, wild man from Buffalo, New York, who in 1981 signed on Cheryl Ann "Cheri" Bailey, Candice "Candi" Ghant, Joanne "JoJo" McDuffie, and Kimberly "Maxi" Wuletich to be his alter-ego, his female companions to his Stone City Band. Also, the Los Angeles-based girlie group was meant to compete with his arch rival, Prince and his Vanity/Apollonia 6.

"He put the group together, produced and arranged the material," said JoJo to *Creem*'s Roy Trakin. "The concept was totally his. He had sketches of how he wanted each girl to look, how he wanted us to dress."

The name JoJo explained to *Black Beat*'s Matthew Pearson, Jr., ". . . can mean two or three different things. It can mean marijuana. It can mean the Mary Jane candy or the T-strap patent-leather shoes for little girls. With us, it means femininity. It's a girl's name and it means female. Something nice and sweet."

Each was to be alluring but unique in presentation—there was JoJo, the streetwise female Rick, a Buffalo-born, ex-record store clerk; Candi, all sultry and sophisticated (formerly an accountant and school teacher from Detroit); Pittsburgh Maxi, the leather-queen with suggestions of kinkiness; and Cheri, the girl next door.

"At first I couldn't get into it," said JoJo to *Creem*. "but it's funny, once you get into your clothes and lock into your character, it comes out. After awhile it gets easy."

Only two albums would be issued before the Mary Jane Girls project was shut down, in 1986. Black radio loved near every single the lasses laid down.

"Candy Man" (R&B: #23), "All Night Long" (R&B: #11), and "Boys" (R&B: #29) did well in England and *Billboard*'s R & B charts. "In My House" went to #3 on the R & B listings.

In explanation of "In My House," JoJo said: "It's like guys always want you to come to their house. Right? We're just turning that around. We just being honest females. How many women have dreamt of doing the same thing? We're taking that desire to its extreme."

By album two, in 1984, Cheri was gone for a promised slot in a newly forming RCA group, which would be followed—she hoped—by a solo career. Her replacement was disco-diva Patti Brooks' daughter and weight-lifting trainer, 19-year-old Yvette Marine, "Corvette," the valley girl, rich with polka dots, braids, and whatnots.

Creem's Trakin asked the women if they minded being Rick James' "3-D House of Slave Chicks," after all it's all just some Little Annie Fanny cartoon, right?

"I prefer to call it serious fun," responded JoJo. "Serious in the sense it's a career and fun in the sense we're doing things ladies don't normally do . . . We won't go quite so far as nudity, though."

On Rick: "He's a very, very sensitive man," said Corvette. "He's not at all what people think of him. sometimes, he's shy and quiet. Then, he'll be loud and boisterous. He's got a good sense of humor. Often, he'll have us on the floor."

Their last single, a remake of the Four Season's perennial "Walk Like a Man" (R&B: #91, 1986), appeared in the Ted Danson flick *A Fine Mess* (1986).

LIMAHL
NEVER ENDING STORY
(Giorgio Moroder, Keith Forsey)
EMI American 8230
No. 17 *May 4, 1985*

As lead singer with KAJAGOOGOO—known in the United States for its Top 5 charting with "Too Shy" in 1983—Limahl had been for a brief moment in the forefront of a growing pop movement labeled by the British pop press "Googoomania." Born Christopher Hamill, in Wigan, England, on December 19, 1958, Limahl (an anagram of his surname), a record collector and sometime piano-picker, won a slot in the Kajagoogoo band in 1981 when members responded to his ad in *Melody Maker* that described himself as "good-lookin, talented . . . and looking for four guys with the same qualifications." A half-dozen singles with Limahl in attendance charted in England. With the success of "Too Shy" plans were constructed to spread "Googoomania" to the United States. Limahl—for reasons as yet unknown to the annals of history—up and quit, and the group reduced to "four guys with the same qualifications" carried on with limited homeland success as Kaja.

Limahl, a flamboyant performer and dear friend of BBC pop presenter Paul Gambaccini, hoped to duplicate the international success as a soloist. *Don't Suppose*, his debut album charted in the States, though the initial singles—"Only for Love" and "Too Much Trouble"—failed to gather much notice. All that changed for a moment with the release of "Never Ending Story," the theme tune from the West Germany flick (1984) of the same name. Mysteriously, however, Limahl's work-up on the GIORGIO MORODER opus was to be one of his parting efforts. No further albums are known to have been issued and ever so quickly, the one-time "Googoo" man was absent from the media, here and abroad.

PAUL HARDCASTLE
19
(Paul Hardcastle, Coutourie, J. McCord)
Chrysalis 42860
No. 15 *June 22, 1985*

Paul Hardcastle (b. Dec. 10, 1957, London) has been called a putterer, a back-room boy—a studio genius. As a teenager, he worked in a hi-fi store, as a salesman and dabbled with tape recorders and synthesizers. Of his musical training nothing is known, but by the early '80s he was touted as something of a keyboard wiz. Signed to DJ Charlie Gillet's Oval Records, Paul recorded some disks with Direct Drive and with Derek Green as the funky First Light. He formed his own Total Control

label in 1983 and the following year charted in the States with "Rainforest" (#57, 1985), a tune originally created for a British television special on the hip-hop and breakdance scene.

Moved by a documentary about the Vietnam conflict, Hardcastle created "19," a hypnotic scratch disk that utilized actual news reports from the era. The recording—titled for the average age of the American soldiers in Vietnam and issued to coincide with the 10th anniversary of the war's end—topped the charts in 13 countries, including the U.K. The follow-up, "Just for the Money," was based on what has come to be called the "Great Train Robbery" and boasted the voices of actors Bob Hoskins and Sir Lawrence Olivier. Neither it nor any further Hardcastle records have charted in the United States.

Before "retiring" to his home studio in Essex, in the '90s, Paul scored some homeland success with "Papa's Got a Brand New Pigbag," as Silent Underdog, wrote a "Top of the Pops" theme tune, "The Wizzard," and moved into production/remixing for such acts as the BELLE STARS, Ian Dury, LW5, Third World, and the last ever single from THIN LIZZY's Phil Lynott, coincidentally titled "Nineteen."

While retired, Paul has resurfaced under pseudonyms such as Beeps International, Def Boys, Jazzmasters, and beginning in 1992, with Jaki Graham, as Kiss the Sky. Hardcastle formed Fast Foward Records in 1990 and has written the theme music to two BBC series, "Supersense" and its sequel "Lifesense."

GODLEY & CREME
CRY
(Kevin Godley, Lol Creme)
Polydor 881786
No. 16 *August 17, 1985*

"We're not in the music business," proclaimed Lol Creme to *Musician*'s Scott Isler. "We left it in 1976, and we haven't taken it seriously since."

Kevin Godley (b. Oct. 7, 1945, vocals, drums) met Lol Creme (b. Sept. 19, 1947, vocals, guitar) on a playground in 1960. Both, born and raised in Manchester, England, soon got involved in a pre-professional band called the Sabres. Their paths crossed again in art school. "I was playing Dracula, and we were after a hunchback," explained Godley to Chris Helm, *Illinois Entertainer*. "Lol auditioned, and guess who got the part. We've been friends ever since, but it's always been a very work-based thing."

The visual arts would become a major component of their lives later, but in the mid-'60s, with art school behind, "beat music," the Beatles, the Stones and the rest, were calling. Godley played in the Mockingbirds with Graham Gouldman, another Manchester mate. By 1969, Godley and Creme had a single as Frabjoy & Runcible Spoon. The disk collected dust in store record bins. The following year, with Eric Stewart—formerly with Wayne Fontana & The Mindbenders—Godley and Creme recorded "Neanderthal Man," as HOTLEGS.

Explaining the situation, Stewart told *Goldmine's* Gary Theroux, "We came up with this thing called 'Neanderthal Man.' It was really just a drum experiment, not intended for a single or anything. and at the time we were looking for a name for our new band. We had this really, really foxy secretary there. What was her name? Gilmore. Yeah, Pam Gilmore. She used to wear these little leather hot pants, and we used to call her 'Hotlegs.'"

Surprising everyone, "Neanderthal Man" became a major hit. When Gouldman—a tunesmith for the Hollies, Yardbirds and Herman's Hermits—joined Hotlegs and no further hits could be gotten, the foursome renamed themselves 10cc. They recorded Richie Vallens's "Donna" and "Rubber Bullets." "The only person we thought could handle it was JONATHAN KING," said Stewart, "who'd just started his own label, U.K. We gave him a ring that night and he flew down the next morning. He heard 'Donna,' thought it was great, and we signed a deal with him. On the day he flew down to sign the contracts, he told us about a dream he'd had. It was a group onstage, with the logo over them that said: '10cc—The Greatest Group in the World.' We said, 'All right. Let it be us. We'll be 10cc.'"

10cc were clever mixing pop hooks and harmony with art rock entanglements, and it worked to the tune of numerous hits and several hot seller albums.

By 1976, Godley and Creme were ready to check out on making music. "We were becoming a little restricted by the confines of the band," Godley told Helm. "We had to take time off to start working on the Gizmo [an electric guitar-like synthesizer] which we had promised ourselves we would do. And that grew into the monstrosity called *Consequences*."

Consequences was a concept album to show off the abilities of this Gizmo gadget and to tell nothing less than "The Story of Man's Last Defence Against an Irate Nature." "They turned their back on huge success," said their manager Harvey Lisberg to the *Guiness Encyclopedia of Popular Music*. "They were brilliant, innovative—and what did they do? A triple album that goes on forever and became a disaster." An edited version was eventually issued to a similar minimal amount of sales.

They had a few homeland chartings prior to their one stateside hit, "Cry." "We were stunned," said Godley to Helm, upon learning "Cry" was a hit. "We had drifted away from the studio for awhile. It inspired us to go back and do more recordings."

Other recordings—such as *L* and *Freeze Frame*—would follow over the years, but it is with videos that the two, kiddingly self-billed 5cc, would make their duo mark. It all started in the late 70s with some visual ideas they had for one of their popular U.K. singles, followed by a request from Steve Strange of Visage to do a video for him. "From that point it all snowballed," said Godley. "It opened up a whole new world. They just kept coming, and we found ourselves with an entirely new career."

Among their works are Herbie Hancock's "Rockit," the Police's "Every Breath You Take," Duran Duran's "A View to Kill," and FRANKIE GOES TO HOLLYWOOD's "Two Tribes;" plus various video views for Culture Club, Elton John, GRAHAM PARKER, Ringo Starr . . .

"We have a nonstyle," said Godley to *Musician*. "We rarely do a literal video or tell a story. Instead, we try to give each song an atmosphere without destroying any images you may have already for yourself."

Besides the videos the duo have found time to publish a book, *The Fun Starts Here*—a behind-the-scenes look at rock—and to produce recordings for the Boomtown Rats, Mickey Jupp, and others.

"We haven't got an act," said Godley to the *Illinois Entertainer*. "We haven't got a direction we're going in. We like almost everything."

JAN HAMMER
MIAMI VICE THEME
(Jan Hammer)
MCA 52666
No. 1 *September 21, 1985*

Jan Hammer was born April 17, 1948, in Prague, Czechoslovakia. He performed with Miroslav Vitous while attending high school, won a music competition in Vienna, when 18; attended the University of MUSE Art in Prague, as a music composition major. With a music scholarship at the Berklee School of Music in Boston and a interest in becoming a jazz pianist, Hammer left his native land in 1968, just prior to the Russian invasion. A semester later, he dropped out to become pianist/composer/arranger for Sarah Vaughan. By the early '70s, Jan had relocated to Greenwich Village where he struck up a musical alliance with John McLaughlin that evolved into the celebrated jazz-rock fusion act the Mahavishnu Orchestra.

After three prized albums, McLaughlin temporarily disbanded the act and Hammer was off to create jazz-rock recordings with Stanley Clarke, Al Di Meola, Jerry Goodman, and Carlos Santana. Among his most noted collaborations were those with Jeff Beck, *Wired* (#16, 1976) and *There and Then* (#21, 1980). Jan fronted his own group, Hammer, for two LPs, made an album with

Journey guitarist Neol Schon and another with jazzman John Abercrombie, before turning much of his attention to creating accompaniment music for TV and the movies.

In 1983, he was commissioned to score his first flick, the Carrie Snodgrass-Lesley Ann Warren *A Night in Heaven.* "Matching music to film is something I never studied," Hammer told *BAM*'s Bill McIlvaine. "The only real education I got was working with John Avildesen, the director of *A Night in Heaven.* That was the best school, because he's one of the best at editing. He showed me a lot about how to focus on a scene, who to focus on, whether to focus on the character or the emotion, or the mood or atmosphere. After that, you just follow your instincts."

A year later, Hammer was introduced to producer Michael Mann, a man with a new TV project: "Miami Vice." "I clicked instantly with the look and the feel of the show," he told *Billboard*'s Brian Chinn. Hammer scored the pilot and when NBC picked up on the series, he was asked by Mann to create about 20 minutes of new music per episode.

DAVID FOSTER
LOVE THEME FROM ST. ELMO'S FIRE
(David Foster)
Atlantic 89528
No. 15 *October 5, 1985*

"I don't know if I have the goods. People tell me that they think I could do it," said David Foster to *Billboard*'s Paul Grein, about the odds on his establishing himself as a big-time, hit-making performer. "I think I could do it, but you don't know . . . I know that I could do it musically, but I don't know if I'll be interesting enough . . . Maybe, people will see me on TV and go, 'That's the guy? Forget it.'"

David Foster (b. mid-'40s, Victoria, British Columbia) has had quite an impact on pop music, even without the solo career he sorely wants. It was he who produced Whitney Houston's take on Dolly Parton's "I Will Always Love You," the biggest charting record in history—annihilating all contenders and remaining the number one tune in the nation for 14 weeks.

As a producer/songwriter, David has been responsible for huge hits by Chicago, DeBarge, JENNIFER HOLIDAY, Kenny Loggins, CHERYL LYNN, Olivia Newton-John, Kenny Rogers, Boz Scaggs, the Tubes. . . . In less than a decade, the man gathered 20 Grammy nominations, ranging from "Record of the Year" to "Best Rhythm & Blues Song." Incredible, also, is his list of session credits, as keyboardist: PATTI AUSTIN, George Benson, Kim Carnes, Earth, Wind & Fire, Hall & Oates, Michael Jackson, Gladys Knight, Little Feat, Lynyrd

Skynyrd, the Pointer Sisters, and both George Harrison and Ringo Starr—and that's naming but a smidge.

It was fleeting, but Dave Foster has known success as a performer. With school behind, he joined the Teen Beats in the mid-'60s; then the Strangers and toured England. For awhile he and his future wife, Barbara Jean Cook, were members of RONNIE HAWKINS' Hawks. In the early '70s, the couple decided to strike out on their own. Barb and Dave were big for a instant as SKYLARK, when "Wildflower" went Top 10 across the North American continent. Thereafter, Dave worked as a session musician and as a member recorded with— Airplay, Attitudes, Fools Gold, Highway, and even, the Average White Band; Attitudes went Hot 100 in '76 with "Sweet Summer Music" (#94).

"If I've reached them as a record producer and as a songwriter," he told Grein, "I can reach them as an artist."

Foster has the hunger to fill a void. "That void of playing your songs on the piano with an orchestra around," said Foster to *Billboard*, "that void was filled in the '60s by Burt Bacharach and Henry Mancini, but it's wide open now. I think I could be the guy to fill it."

Dave wants renown bad; and if the Bacharach-Mancini void cannot be his, he wants to make it in the movies. "I've always wanted to score a love story, but those kind of films aren't being made anymore. That's the kind of film I'd like to make. If I can't find one to score, I'd like to go out and try to make one. Music-making and film-making have a lot in common . . ."

Acting as his own best-kept cheerleader, he told Grein, "I think I'm ready to grow again. When I was a hot studio musician, that's right when I made the move to be a record producer, and when I was a hot record producer, that's when I made the move to be an artist. That must mean if I become a hot artist, I'll want to make the move into films."

His "Love Theme From St. Elmo's Fire," the title take from the similarly labeled Rob Lowe-Demi Moore flick (1985), however, would prove Dave's lone hit.

In 1993, Foster produced Color Me Badd's rendition of his one-off happening as Skylark, "Wildflower."

SCRITTI POLITTI
PERFECT WAY
(Green Strohmeyer-Gartside, David Gamson)
Warner 28949
No. 11 *October 26, 1985*

As it was conceived in Leeds, England, in 1978, Scritti Politti was to be an avant-garde punky band with a proudly-proclaimed political agenda. Core member and resident intellectual "Green" Strohmeyer-Gartside (b. June 22, 1956, Cardiff, Wales, vocals, guitar) was a young communist with a mission—the destruction of the corporate record industry. Green encouraged listeners to throw off the yoke of artistic oppression; create your own music, was the Scritti Politti call.

Enacting their agenda, Green and the initial Scritti Politti—art students all: Nial Jinks (bass), Matthew K. (b. Matthew Kay, keyboards), and Tom Morley (drums, programming)—played the punk palaces, produced pamphlets on record making and manufacturing, and formed their own label, St. Pancras. Two EPs and "Skank Bloc Bolognia," a lone single were issued before fate moved in. While driving through Wales in support of the Gang of Four, Green, who reportedly had "overindulged in drugs," suffered a "nervous collapse," and "heart complaints."

To recuperate, Green retired to his parents' home in Cardiff; other members scattered. Kay and Morley regrouped with Gartside in the fall of 1981 for a single for the independent Rough Trade label. By year's end, both were gone—as were, seemingly, much of Gartside's professed propaganda.

"The biggest change was the one from wanting to really work against popular conceptions of what pop music was to wanting to work with them," explained Gartside, soon after, to Stephen Padgett, Cash Box. "I went into pop music because it was a perverse thing to do it. It was putting two fingers up at what was expected of you in post-punk Britain."

Scritti Politti was now to be Green and a loose ring of players—Joe Cang (bass), Mike MacEvoy (keyboards), and Jamie Talbot (sax)—who had been gathered for Songs to Remember, the act's initial album. Featuring "Asylum in Jerusalem" and "Jacques Derrida"—an ode to the French philosopher—the package of pop, reggae, and jazzy experimentations was well-received by the critical community; becoming Rough Trade's best charting album to date, in the U.K.

In celebration, Green excused all members and signed to a still larger label, Virgin Records. In 1985, after three years of perspiration and possible procrastination, Gartside—with the assistance of David Gramson (guitar) and Fred Frith (drums)—returned under the Scritti Politti moniker with Cupid and Psyche. "Stunning," said pundits; "ethereal," said others. A series of homeland hits followed; these included "Wood Beez (Pray Like Aretha Franklin)," "Absolute," and "The Word Girl (Flesh and Blood)." "Perfect Way," Green's solitary stateside mover, scored only a modest U.K. charting.

Another three year absence followed before Green's Scritti Politti name returned in 1989 with Provision; containing the massive British hit "Oh Patti (Don't Feel Sorry for Loverboy)." Later that year, Gartside would chart with a "Boom! There She Was," featuring the help of ROGER—Roger Troutman of Zapp fame.

While largely absent from view, Miles Davis, Madonna, and Chaka Khan have recorded Scritti Politti songs; most notably, Davis' take on "Perfect Way" on Tutu, one of his final albums. Green has achieved a modicum of success at home remaking the Beatles' "She's a Woman"—featuring reggae rocker Shabba Rank—and Glady Knight & The Pips' "Take Me in Your Arms," aided by Jamaican star Sweetie Irie.

Scribes have lambasted him for his seeming sell-out to mainstream techno-pop. "The point of what I'm doing," said Green to Musician's John Leland, "is realized by the people who buy my records. They are the point. And if it's a succession of 15-year-old girls who don't have any interest in French writers, I still don't think they're missing it."

Where is Green Strohmeyer-Gartside now? "I've gone where a lost cause can be found," wrote Green, on the last line to "Oh Patti."

CHARLIE SEXTON
BEEN SO LONELY
(Charlie Sexton)
No. 17 December 14, 1985

"I figure I'm young an' I'm gonna do it right the first time, not like all these other assholes," said a 17-year-old Sexton to a British rock journalist.

"I'd like to see Charlie Sexton become a big star," wrote Bob Dylan on the liners for his Biography compilation, "but the whole machine would have to break down right now before that could happen."

He's one precocious guitarist . . . been called the "Boy Wonder," "the Anointed One" . . . "destined for major stardom, if he survives the hype." Given his looks, unfortunately, Charlie has also been labeled "The Most Likely to Succeed Billy Idol." Rail-skinny, full-lips, high cheekbones, androgynous sensuality can only get you so far. With "Been So Lonely" and Pictures for Pleasure, his debut album in 1985, Sexton got heavy rotation on MTV, picture displays in teen mags, and a stigma—"teen idol," ergo talent-free. It's this misperception that has keep Charlie Sexton from the stream of hits his talent would seem to warrant.

Encouraged by his rockabilly-loving Mama, Charlie (b. Aug. 11, 1968, San Antonio, TX) got his first guitar at age four. "But I didn't start to play seriously till I was eight," said Sexton to Creem. "At eleven, I started to play in front of people [accompanying cult country rocker Joe Ely]. They thought I was like a trick dog for a while. Then I went on tour at 13 . . ." He had his own recording contract with MCA at 17; been in various groups, toured with Ely and the Clash, and recorded with Bob Dylan, Don Henley, Ron Wood (on the film soundtrack to Easy Street), Keith Richards. . . .

Charlie's initial single and album each went Top 20; follow-ups have performed otherwise. A self-titled package released in 1989 failed to place in *Billboard*'s Hot 100 albums. For awhile, Charlie played with brother Will—from Will and the Kill—locally in Mystic Knights of the Sea. In 1990, while working up material at the Austin Rehearsal Complex (ARC) for an attempted comeback, Charlie met up with the late Stevie Ray Vaughn's rhythm section, Double Trouble —Chris "Whipper" Layton (drums) and Tommy Shannon (bass)—and Doyle "Doyle Two" Bramhall II (guitar, vocals)—son of Doyle Bramhall, drummer with Stevie Ray's brother Jimmy's band, THE FABULOUS THUNDERBIRDS—to form the Arc Angels. Their self-titled debut—produced by Little Steven van Zandt— was roots rock and gritty; winning critical acclaim and moderate sales. The band, however, shut down in 1994. In 1995, Sexton resurfaced fronting the Charlie Sexton Sextet; issued was *Under the Wishing Tree*, with tunes co-authored by Tonka K.

Creem had asked the 17-year-old Sexton what he figured he'd be doing when 30 (1998), "I'll probably be ridin' skateboards and playin' with Barbie Dolls."

JELLYBEAN
SIDEWALK TALK
(Madonna)
EMI American 8297
No. 18 *December 21, 1985*

Jellybean, the Manhattan club DJ/remixer/producer, was born John Benitez, the son of Puerto Rican parents, November 7, 1957, in the Bronx, New York. His nickname was bestowed by his sister, when he was 10. The inspiration was his initials, J. B. and the common saying, "Do you know what I mean, Jellybean?"

"I really loved music. I would spend any money I had on buying records," said Jellybean to Mary Campbell, the *Chicago Sun Times*, of his formative years. "When friends had parties, I was asked to be the disc jockey because I had the records. One day a woman asked how much I would charge to do her daughter's 'Sweet 16' party. I realized somebody would actually pay me to do something I'd been doing free."

Jellybean auditioned and got his first job in 1973 DJing at Charlie's, an uptown dance club. Within a year, he was one of the most in-demand spinners in the Big Apple, working such spots as the Fun House, Studio 54, and Xenon. It was his experimenting, his adding percussion tracks onto songs, and splicing elements from one song to another, that got him the shot at remixing dance disks.

Jellybean was asked to remix Irene Cara's "Flashdance (What a Feeling)" and Michael Sembello's "Maniac." The response was more than just positive; both reworked disks went on to top *Billboard*'s dance charts." "It snowballed," he said. "The first three, four years, I've been involved with 60 Top 20 and 20 No. 1 records."

The total figure of successful Jellybean remixes to date is yet to be tallied. It's known that he did have his way with tracks by David Bowie, Hall & Oates, Whitney Houston, Billy Joel, the Pointer Sisters, and the Paul McCartney/Michael Jackson pairing, "Say, Say, Say."

"There's no secret to it," said Jellybean to *Cashbox*'s Ethlie Ann Vare. "I go to clubs and watch people dance. I listen to what they're dancing to. I see how the DJ programs. I look at the bar business."

At one of his DJing dates, Jellybean met Madonna. It was the Fun House and Run-D.M.C. were making their debut. She hired him to remix her first dance hit, "Holiday," and soon to produce "Borderline," "Crazy for You" and "The Gambler." Their relationship was said to have lasted until just after the issuance of *Like a Virgin* in 1984.

The next career move was for Jellybean to produce recordings by vocalists that he had discovered; that would appear under his name. First out was a five-song mini-album called *Wotupski!?!*, which featured an unreleased Madonna song, "Sidewalk Talk." The vocalist was Katherine "Katt" Buchanan.

As "Sidewalk Talk" moved up the charts, he signed a contract with Warner Bros. Records calling for the Jellybeans Productions logo to appear on releases by four new artists a year for the next two years. Under the agreement, the first release was Jocelyn Brown's R & B charter "Love's Gonna Get You" (#38, 1986).

"What I'm trying to do," he said to *Cashbox*, "is create a club record that can also get on radio."

Subsequent albums, bearing his name, bore *Billboard*'s pop chartings for Steven Dante and Niki Haris. The Jellybean name did return to *Billboard*'s pop Top 40 once more—"Who Found Who" (#16, 1987)—but the disk was billed as a duet, with co-billing being given to Elisa Fiorillo, a winner on TV's "Star Search."

Jellybean Benitez went on to produce film soundtracks for *Spaceballs* (1987), *The Principal* (1987), *Carlito's Way* (1993) and *The Shadow* (1994).

"It's all an adventure for me," said Jellybean to Campbell of his future. "What inspires me the most is trying something new and learning how to do something. The worst thing that can happen is I would fail. That wouldn't be so bad."

BALTIMORA
TARZAN BOY
(Naimy Hackett, Maurizio Bassi)
Manhattan 50018
No. 13 *January 11, 1986*
No. 51 *March 27, 1993*

"In Italy, it's like I can't walk the streets anymore," explained Baltimora to *Cashbox* of his fame. "Through Europe, girls run after me in the streets, run after me in their cars, pulling bits and pieces off me."

Concealed under his God-given name—Jimmy McShane (b. May 27, 1957)—Baltimora roamed his home turf of Londonderry, Northern Ireland, a self-acknowledged unknown and underfed performer. With the '80s dawn, he moved first to London, naming himself after a tune by his audio goddess—NINA SIMONE. "I started off as a dancer in Ireland, but once in England I went to stage school, where I studied music, dance, and acting. On the side I was doing session work, and I met up with Dee D. Jackson, who had a smash hit with 'Automatic Lover,' [a British Top 10 in 1978]. I did a European tour with her as back-up singer/dancer. The last few dates were in Italy. I just freaked out. I didn't know what was going on. I thought that they were still into that old 'O Sole Mio' bit." Instead, Baltimora found the underground. "It was all high energy; everything was happening."

Soon he was to meet composer/producer Maurizio Bassi and lyricist Naimy Hackett. Together they introduced the former Jimmy McShane into leopard skins, makeup, and the Baltimora persona. "For someone in my type of music—which is disco dance music—you can't just stand behind a microphone and not move; that's boring."

"Tarzan Boy" went Top Five in the U.K. "Success in England was like a 'Lassie Come Home' sort of thing," said the transformed one. "It was very immense."

In addition to the moderate attention given his follow-up—"Living in the Background" (#87, 1986)—Baltimora's signature tune was utilized in a Listerine TV commercial and hand-picked for the flick *Teenage Mutant Ninja Turtles III* (1993)—causing a rekindled interest and recharting of "Tarzan Boy" (#51, 1993).

SLY FOX
LET'S GO ALL THE WAY
(Gary Cooper)
Capitol 5552
No. 7 *February 15, 1986*

Gary "Sly" Cooper and Michael "Fox" Camacho were a contrived duo, assembled by British producer Ted Currier. The latter had learned of Sly—then affectionately known as "Mudbone"—through his session work with George Clinton and his Parliament/FUNKADELICS organization. Previously, he had drummed for Bootsy's Rubber Band, Mtume, and Sly Stone. Fox, meanwhile, had been bar-hoppin' with an unnamed *a cappella* outfit.

Currier deliberately integrated the Caucasian Fox with the African-American Sly, in the hopes of creating a marketable black-white pop hybrid. "It was intentional," explained Sly to *Melody Maker*'s Simon Reynolds. "The philosophy is to bridge the gap." Music is music, according to Sly, and there in reality is not a gap. But since people act as if there is such a divergence, the plan was to give the public a black-white musical marriage.

As for the party pumpin' droner "Let's Go All the Way": "The song was intended as a positive statement," said Sly, the tune's writer. "What I wanted to re-create was factory sounds, the noise of a machine compressing things, y' know . . . boom shwack, boom shwack. Most people think it has a . . . er . . . sexual connotation. That's cool, we like to leave it up to the listener's interpretation."

Sly and Fox were presented as clean-cut, wholesome, and health conscious. Journalists were told that their preferred beverage was water and that they were filled with a faith in the Lord. Their "Don't Play With Fire," a follow-up, advises to "go to church with Mama/Take a part in Sunday School."

"We just like to thank *you* and all your readers," said Sly to Reynolds, "and say that we hope that whatever you do in life, you'll *go all the way*."

FORCE M.D.'S
TENDER LOVE
(Jimmy Jam, Terry Lewis)
Warner 28818
No. 10 *March 1, 1986*

They got their start in 1977 working for tips *a cappella* doo-woping, rappin', impersonating, break dancing, throwing karate punches . . . in Times Square, on the Staten Island Ferry, and in New York City's Washington Square Park. Lee "Jessie D" Daniels (b. 1962), Charles Richard "Mercury" Nelson (b. 1963), Trisco Pearson (b. 1961) and the brothers Lundy, Steve "Stevie D" (b. 1962) and Antonio Maurice "T.C.D." (b. 1961) boast that they could gather an average of $400 a day by performing that way. "Whenever the guys needed money, we hit the street to perform," Trisco told *Black Beat*'s Ken Simmons.

In the early '80s, they met Vito Picone, lead vocalist with the ELEGANTS, who became their manager. Soon after they settled on the name Force M.D.'s; the M.D.

was short for Musical Diversity—Force stood for the expression of the struggle they felt growing up in Staten Island. By late 1983, they came to the attention of *Dance Music Report* publisher and Tommy Boy Record mainman Tommy Silverman, thanks to a sharp-eared DJ, Mr. Magic.

"Let Me Love You" (R&B: #49, 1984), their debut single, started what was to become a long list of R & B chartings. "Tears" (R&B: #5, 1985) went Top Five; "Itchin' for a Scratch" (R&B: #13, 1985) from the Mario Van Peeples flick *Rappin'* (1985) charted Top 20. Their biggest hit to date followed a brief association of Tommy Boy with Warner Bros. when the group got to sing the smoothie "Tender Love" in the all-rap Sheila E/Fat Boys flick *Krush Groove* (1985). Sometime MORRIS DAY sidemen/Grammy-winning Jimmy Jam and Terry Lewis had written and produced the tune specifically for the Force M.D.'s.

By 1987, their 10th year together, "T.C.D.," "Stevie D," and the rest were cash register-hot and well-appreciated—"Love Is a House" (#78) also topped *Billboard*'s R & B listings; "Touch & Go" (R&B: #10) did nearly as well; the New York Music Awards named them "Best Vocal Group," the Rhythm & Blues Awards voted them "Most Promising Group." And a chance meeting with the "Material Girl" in the Big Apple's Cadillac Bar—complete with an impromptu audition—won them a slot on Madonna's "Who's That Girl" Tour.

Jessie D" had left the act for a solo career in 1987. "Mercury" Nelson died of a heart attack, March 10, 1995. The R & B hits became less frequent and their chart placements less notable, but Force M.D.'s continued on well into the '90s.

"Too many people think that we are a rap group," said Stevie "D" to Simmons. "We want everyone to know that we are 100% singers, who can also rap."

BOYS DON'T CRY
I WANNA BE A COWBOY
(Brian Chatton, Nico Ramsden, Nick Richards, Jeff Seopardi)
Profile 5084
No. 12 *May 17, 1986*

It was looney. "I wanna be a cowboy/And you can be my cowgirl/My name is Ted/One day I'll be dead. . . ." It was rendered deadpan. Lead singer/keyboardist Nick Richards claims the whole idea was to sound as banal as possible. Okay, that being successful, now what?

"We want to prove we're a real band, not just a one-off with a novelty record and quick success," said Richards to *Billboard*'s Jim Bessman. "We're certainly not that at all. Basically we're rock musicians with very good pedigrees, and it's important that we do not get

typecast because of 'Cowboy,'" added fellow keyboardist Brian Chatton.

"It was done as a joke," Richards further explained to the *Chicago Sun Times*' Dennis Hunt. "The whole thing was done in the studio in 12 hours. We just decided to do something as silly as possible—something that made us laugh. We never thought anyone else would find it funny."

As to the sexy cowgirl heard on the disk: "She's not one of the boys. She's the drummer's girlfriend. She [Heidi Lea] was just hanging around the studio when we were doing this. She sounds just right. But I don't think you can build a career on what she does on the single," said Richards to Hunt.

Nick Richards had recorded in the days pre-Boys Don't Cry as a solo for RCA and had done session work for Sad Cafe, Judy Tzuke, and Roy Wood. In 1984, Richards teamed with Chatton, a session man for Jon Anderson, Phil Collins, Meatloaf, and MIKE OLDFIELD. Added were ex-Sad Cafe drummer Jeff Seopardi, former Camel and CHRIS REA guitarist Nico Ramsden, and bassist Mark Smith.

The group initially recorded for Richards's Legacy label and named themselves such because "it makes the group hard to categorize, " *Billboard* was told.

Nick Richards, the co-owner of London's Maison Rouge recording studios, which is noted for its work with EMERSON, LAKE & PALMER, Level 42, and the Psychedelic Furs, was well aware that there were those who didn't like the tune—even when it rested high on the charts. "I can live with that," he told Dennis Hunt. "My wife hates it."

An album baring the single's title was issued. "Cities on Fire" flopped, as did other concerted attempts.

FABULOUS THUNDERBIRDS
TUFF ENUFF
(Kim Wilson)
CBS Assoc. 05838
No. 10 *May 24, 1986*

Once they were the best gutsy, bar-scarred, rootsy rockin', party-provoking band working the circuit. For a decade the Fabulous Thunderbirds toured unrelenting. "Tuff Enuff" sold massive . . . in a flash, it seemed, they were no more.

"When I was about 13," said T-Bird guitarman Jimmie Vaughn to Bill Dalton, *Illinois Entertainer*. "I was trying to play football one day and I broke my collarbone. I was home for about two months and this friend of my dad's gave me a guitar and said, 'Why don't you try playing this; it won't hurt you.'"

Soon, Jimmie (B. Mar. 20, 1951, Dallas, guitar) got good and earned his way playing cover versions in bands with names like the Chessmen and the Swinging Pendulums. In 1974, Jimmie, vocalist Lou Ann Barton and drummer Otis Lewis put together the Fabulous Thunderbirds. Soon Barton and Lewis were gone; replaced by drummer Mike Buck (b. June 1, 1952), harp man/vocalist Kim Wilson (b. Jan. 6, 1951, Detroit), and bassist Keith Ferguson (b. July 23, 1946, Houston).

"I met Jimmie at a place called Alexander's," explained Wilson to Alan Govenar, author of *Meeting the Blues*. "Jimmie was playing in a band called Storm, and Stevie [Ray Vaughn, Jimmie's brother] asked if I could sit in, and they said, 'No.'" Stevie and Kim got up during Storm's break and jammed something the crowd dug. A month later, Jimmie gave Kim a call saying 'You played alright. Let's do something.'"

Before this encounter, Kim figures he worked with near 20 bands; including workouts with Jimmy Reed and Muddy Waters. It was while providing accompaniment for the latter that the T-Birds were discovered by Denny Bruce; and signed to his Takoma label in 1979. That year, *The Fabulous Thunderbirds a.k.a. Girls Go Wild* was issued and the band toured England with Dave Edmunds/NICK LOWE's Rockpile. Sharing an affinity, Lowe and Edmunds would remain involved with the T-Birds.

Jimmie and Kim moved the act to Chrysalis Records in 1980; Buck left, being replaced by ex-Roomful of Blues drummer Fran Christiana (b. Feb. 1, 1951, Westerly, RI). Before fame's knock, Ferguson left; replaced by bassist Preston Hubbard (b. Mar. 15, 1953, Providence, RI).

Three albums were issued for the label, with Lowe supplying tunes and Edmunds and Lowe alternating production work for the T-Birds. Sales were not sufficient said record company reps. From 1983 to 1986, they persisted, without benefit of a label. One of their tunes, however, was featured in the forgettable *Porky's II: The Next Night* (1983) and the group provided backup for Carlos Santana's *Havana Moon*.

The big break came in 1986, when Columbia Records signed the band. "Tuff Enuff" and its accompanying album were recorded in England; Edmunds produced.

Tuff Enough sold near a million copies. The T-Birds opened shows for Santana and the Rolling Stones. Their tune was featured in the flick *Gung Ho* (1986), and the group got to jam a song in the film *Light of Day* (1987).

"We do just whatever we like," said Wilson to *Creem*'s Iman Lababedi, "we're not going to bend over backwards for this bullshit Top 40. We want to swing everybody else onto our side, we want ours to be the most popular music . . . It's the only thing I know how to do; it's either this or being a trashman."

A take on Sam & Dave's "Wrap It Up," "Twist It Off," and others failed to repeat the fanfare. *Hot Number* sold well; *Powerful Stuff* proved the last T-Bird album to feature both Jimmie and Kim.

Jimmie left the band in 1990 to record with his brother Stevie Ray Vaughn. Buck went on to join Rounder Record act the Leroi Brothers; Ferguson formed the Tail Gators. Buck and Ferguson have been members of Big Guitar From Texas.

Kim Wilson with guitarists Doug "the Kid" Bangham and ex-Roomful of Blues founder Michael "Duke" Robillard carried the group name into the early 1990s. Kim has since ventured into a low-key solo career, recording albums and supplying session harp work for B. B. King, Pinetop Perkins, Bonnie Raitt, and Jimmy Rogers.

GRT
WHEN THE HEART RULES THE MIND
(Steve Hackett, Steve Howe)
Arista 9470
No. 14 *May 31, 1986*

Pundits proclaimed Hackett and Howe prime movers of pointless pomp. Before forming their GRT in 1985 Steve Hackett and Steve Howe had been to the pop cult pinnacle. Howe (b. Apr. 8, 1947, London) reeked of decades of success first with the psychedelic Tomorrow, lastly as co-founder of Asia, but primarily as the ax-lord who put the yazz in Yes; Hackett (b. Feb. 12, 1950, London), similarly, wheeled guitar for Genesis through its abundantly successful, spacey, progressive period.

By the mid-'80s—against a backdrop of rap, metal, and a growing alternative—such noodlin' seemed increasingly senseless. When the chance to be reborn as GRT arose, Hackett, who had been continuing his solo ventures—leaving Genesis in 1977—was weary; Howe, likewise, was world-worn. Said the guitar gurus, Howe, of his break from Asia: "Situations fall apart when people stop believing in each other . . . when you stop believing that it can get any better. All groups start out with good intentions."

With good intentions the two Steves joined forces, initially as a songwriting team. "That was the backbone of the project," said Howe to *Illinois Entertainer*'s Joan Tortorici Ruppert. "Then building a band around it seemed the most logical thing to do . . . Steve and I didn't want too many people from our past. This way we can maintain a sense of control and keep a newer sounding edge on the music." Added Phil Spaulding, GRT bassist, "The two guys [Hackett and Howe] could have got together and rung up their old mates, people who are sitting in castles or fields somewhere with a couple of million pounds." Instead the line-up was completed with Spaulding, Max Bacon (vocals), and ex-Marillion and lone American-born Jonathan Moore (drums).

A follow-up—"The Hunter" (#85, 1986)—and self-titled album, produced by former Yes man/one-time BUGGLES Geoff Downes were the group's last issuances. And what did GTR mean? Said Howe, "The name 'GTR' is even more obvious than it looks, if that's possible. Our name is nothing more than 'guitar' with the vowels taken out."

The "project" ended in 1987, with Howe returning to Yes conglomerated—billed Anderson, Bruford, Wakeman, Howe; still later, following legal actions, a reformed Yes.

Speaking of the fleeting GRT goal, when their single was on the charts, Howe has said, "Before Yes, I was in a band called Tomorrow, and even now I look back and marvel at what a great ego the band had . . . not a self-ego, but a terrific group ego about being good. I think that's what Yes had, and what Asia had . . . for a while. Maybe that's what GRT has going for it at the moment. If you can feel that, you can feel pretty good."

BLOW MONKEYS
DIGGIN' YOUR SCENE
(Robert Howard)
RCA 14325
No. 14 *June 14, 1986*

Bruce Robert Howard (b. May 2, 1961, Norfolk, England) is the core human in the seemingly odd-named group, the Blow Monkeys. "Dr. Robert," as Howard was fondly addressed by close ones, took the name for his group from the Australian slang for Aboriginal didgeridoo players, which was something he picked up on while a teenager living in Australia. Other circulating stories tell of a blow monkey being a jazz sax man with a mission. The Doctor bit of this bands' stick was pinned on to the Howard kid while he attending boarding school because he was noted as something of a ripe listener.

Completing the Blow Monkey line-up were saxman Neville Henry, bassist Mick Anter (b. July 2, 1957), and percussionist Tony Kiley (b. Feb. 16, 1962). In 1982, some rare experimental sides were recorded for Para-soul. Two years later, they had issued a number of nowhere going 45s for RCA with nifty titles: "Man From Russia," "Atomic Lullabye," "Forbidden Fruit." Their biggest United States charting happened in 1986 with "Digging Your Scene," apparently one of the earliest songs to deal with AIDS. The follow-up proved the band's biggest U.K. hit—the Top Five tune, "It Doesn't Have to Be That Way."

What followed largely was passed over by the American media. "(Celebrate) The Day After You," an anti-Thatcher complete with vocal input from soul legend Curtis Mayfield, was banned by the BBC. Their "You Don't Own Me" was utilized in the soundtrack to the hugely successful PATRICK SWAYZE flick *Dirty Dancing* (1987). After a few more minor European chartings, Dr. Roberts successfully remounted the British Top 10 with "Wait," a duet with Kym Mazelle. Months later, the Blow boys dueted with Sylvia Tella on "Slaves No More."

TIMEX SOCIAL CLUB
RUMORS
(Marcus Thompson, Michael Marshall, Alex Hill)
Jay 7001
No. 8 *July 12, 1986*

The lone moment was the creation of three buddies from Berkeley High in Sacramento, California—Michael Marshall, Alex Hill, and Marcus Thompson. Michael explained the song's birth to the authors of *The Billboard Book of Number One Rhythm & Blues Hits*: "You know how people talk too much and spread rumors. We used to hear them all the time and got inspired to write it. Most of the people in the song are from high school. I've always been a fan of Michael Jackson and, back then, there were always rumors about him. Then there were people at the school like Tina [the girl in the song]. It's a true, down to earth thing."

"Rumors" was first performed at a school function in the spring of 1984. The positive response was noted, and the tune was put to tape and given out to the local college station, KALX-FM in Berkeley.

Jay King, main man at tiny Jay/King Jay Records, based in Vallejo, California, home of the Con Fun Shun's Felton Pilate, caught a listen. "Everybody thought it sucked except me," said King. "I could hear what was happening, and I could hear it being a hit with some changes. We wanted to do it on Con Fun Shun, but Michael Cooper turned it down. So we called the guys who did the original and said they should record it."

"We made a lot of changes in the record." So Marcus, Michael, and Alex were concerned. "I told 'em, 'I'm spending the money, I'm the producer, I'm the record company. I'm not going to do anything to hurt your song; we're just trying to make it better. If it's a bomb, we'll take the blame; if it's a hit, we'll take the credit.'"

With no record companies interested, King issued the song on his Jay label. It clicked, and King did take too much of the credit—and too much of the money, some say. Before the chart ride was done, Timex Social Club was signed elsewhere to Danva Records. They experienced some R&B noise with their follow-up, "Thinkin' About You."

Tunes that King had planned for Timex Social Club to record were not wasted. King rounded up Thomas McElroy and Denzil Foster—the production team behind "Rumors"—plus sometime Timex madame Valerie Watson and lead singer Samuelle Prater and issued the stuff first as by Jet Set. Nothing charted, but nothing was lost. Noting King's skills, Warner Bros. set the man up with a national distribution affiliation.

King persisted, and within moments had hits galore. Jet Set was renamed Club Nouveau and became a chart-moving act, known nationally for "Jealousy," "Situation #9," and their revived dusting of Bill Withers's "Lean on Me." Prater, McElroy, and Foster left the group in 1988; the latter two found further action as Fmob and Foster/McElroy. As a production duo, they worked with Alexander O'Neal, Tony! Toni! Tone!; in 1990, they discovered and produced En Vogue.

REGINA
BABY LOVE
(Stephen Bray, Mary Kessler, Regina Richards)
Atlantic 89417
No. 10 *July 19, 1986*

"Queen for a Disk," said *Rolling Stone*, of Regina. "Madonna clone" said others. "When they find out what my history is," said Regina to *Rolling Stone*, "that will all change."

In the late '70s, with Madonna collaborator and sometime drummer Stephen Bray, Regina Richards (b. 1971, New York City) fronted for years a hot Big Apple club circuit band, Regina and the Red Hots. With a lot of musical mileage, the band was shelved in the early-to-mid '80s. Regina's attentions turned to songwriting. With numerous numbers to nail and mail, Doug Breibart, her manager, created West 78th Street Records in 1985 to issue "Baby Love" as her debut. Arrangements were made with George Hargraves with the U.K.-based Steiner label to put Regina's disk out first in England; making it available in the States as an import. For a fleeting moment in the mid-'80s, imported dance disks were given more immediate attention by the media than domestic releases. The ploy was to create the allusion of something exotic, foreign; it worked. "Baby Love," although soon released on Atlantic Records was viewed, at the start of its chart reign as an import. Regina had her debut disk become her first and only United States charting.

Why just be Regina, she was asked? Richards feels like a nice name. "That was against my will," she told *Rolling Stone*. "Regina means 'queen' in Latin. It was a gimmick used over in England, where the record was

released first. But next album, I'm gonna put my name back together. Just like John Cougar."

No further chartings happened; no other recordings are known to exist, by Regina, Regina Richards, even Regina and the Red Hots.

DOUBLE
THE CAPTAIN OF HER HEART
(Kurt Maloo, Felix Haugh)
A & M 2838
No. 16 *August 9, 1986*

Felix Haugh and Kurt Maloo made major moves to appear vague and mysterious. These efforts proved quite successful. Consequently, little is known about the Swiss duo.

As part of their on-going disguise, they appeared as a quartet on the cover of their debut album, *Blue*. Such behavior caused mass confusion when only two humans appeared for promotions and publicity stunts. Some say they were runaways from a jazz-pop entity called Ping Pong. Others claim that Felix had been a fleeting member of Yello with millionaire/pro-gambler/golf-pro Dieter Meier.

Guitar and vocalist Felix and percussion and keyboardist Kurt were signed to Germany's Metronome label in 1983; that much is certain. Kurt talked with *Billboard*'s Brian Chin on the creation of their lone moment: "We've known each other such a long time, we don't have to discuss ideas. Demo tapes were dispensed within the interest of spontaneity, and outside musicians were not involved until the final stages." "The Captain of Her Heart" was born of a one-take acoustic flourish by Felix. "We erase out-takes immediately. I was about to erase it when the engineer said to look at it again."

The duo believed in acting quickly. "We acted like children," said Felix. "The instruments were not mastered perfectly. But that gave us the chance to discover things."

Their massive—though mini-momentary—popularity was attributable, said their manager, Pete Zumsteg, "to a coordinated, consistent presentation." The group's name is pronounced doo-BLAY.

DON JOHNSON
HEARTBEAT
(Eric Kaz, Wendy Waldman)
Epic 06285
No. 5 *September 6, 1986*

Don Wayne Johnson was born in his grandma's house in the farming community of Galen, Missouri, on

December 15, 1950. His parents divorced when Don was 11. He blames the life-altering event as the cause of his hell-raising ways. "I realized then it was dog eat dog, every man for himself," Johnson told *Rolling Stone*'s Nancy Collins. "Most of the guys I hung out with are either dead or in jail."

Don spent time in juvenile detention for the theft of a car. At 16, he ran away from home, to Wichita, where he shared an apartment with a 26-year-old cocktail waitress, worked at a meat-packing plant, and attended high school. It was in his senior year that he signed up for a drama class. Said Don, "Acting struck something in me. . . . For the first time in my life, I felt that I belonged to something."

Johnson won a full drama scholarship to the University of Kansas. After two years, he moved to the American Conservatory Theatre in San Francisco. Two weeks later, Don had his professional debut in the company's production of *Your Own Thing*, a rock musical modeled after Shakespeare's *Twelfth Night*. His performance won him a part in Sal Mineo's staging of John Herbert's *Fortune and Men's Eyes*, a play about male homosexuality in prison. Months later MGM offered Don a contract and his first movie role in *The Magic Garden of Stanley Sweetheart* (1970), a period piece of turning on, tuning in, and dropping out.

The flick was panned, but further major roles in minor films followed—*Zachariah* (1971), *The Harrad Experiments* (1973), *Return to Macon County* (1975), *A Boy and His Dog* (1976). To fill time and the wallet, Don did guest spots on such TV dramas as "Police Story," "Young Doctor Kildare," "Kung Fu" and numerous made-for-TV flicks; notably "Elvis and The Beauty Queen" (1981), as the "King."

Five pilots were made for projected NBC series. All were turned down. "I would look around and see actors working who were no better than I was," he told Harry F. Waters, *Newsweek*. "I mean, I started when Jeff Bridges and Timothy Bottoms and all those guys started. But for some reason it didn't work out for me."

Johnson has admitted that he turned to years of abusing drugs and alcohol. "I think it was a reluctance to grow up, a fear of taking on responsibility of becoming successful," said Johnson to Collins." ". . . Stardom takes maturity, and I wasn't ready to deal with it. So drugs were a convenient way to . . . put that off."

By 1983, Don was recovering. What followed was Johnson's shot at stardom, and this time he was ready. "Miami Vice" debuted in September 1984, with Johnson starring as Detective James "Sonny" Crockett, an undercover cop. The series—featuring a chart-topping theme by JAN HAMMER—captured the moment, with guest spots for Leonard Cohen, Phil Collins, Miles Davis, TED NUGENT . . . and a cast position for Sheena Easton as rocker "Caitlin Davis."

By the time an offer as a sideline career as a rock singer was in place, co-star Phillip Michael Thomas had already tried and failed at making the transition. Don already had a $20 guitar, knew some chords, had hung out with Country Joe McDonald and Joe Walsh when filming *Zachariah*, and had even co-written a few tunes—"Blind Love" and "Can't Take It With You"—for the Allman Brothers with their guitarist Dickie Betts. Some session guys—JO JO GUNNE's Curley Smith and Son of Champlin's Bill Champlin—and a hoard of guesting notables—Willie Nelson, Bonnie Raitt, Stevie Ray Vaughn, Ron Wood, even Whoopi Goldberg—appeared and Don Johnson was a potential rock star.

"If it flies, great," said Don to *Rolling Stone*'s Kurt Loder. "If it doesn't, well I hope it sells enough so they'll let me make another one."

"Heartbeat" and a few other 45s charted; in particular a one-off duet with Barbra Streisand, "Till I Loved You" (#25, 1988).

Johnson's attention soon returned to movies and the small screen; most notably the mid-'90s TV series with Cheech Marin, "Nash Bridges." There was also *Hot Spot* (1990), *Dead Bang* (1989) and *Harley Davidson and the Motorcycle Man* (1991).

ORAN "JUICE" JONES
THE RAIN
(Vincent Bell)
Def Jam 06209
No. 9 *October 11, 1986*

Asked why he wanted to sing, Oran "Juice" Jones replied, "Money." The Houston-born, Harlem-raised "Juice" man explained to Adam White and Fred Bronson, authors of *The Billboard Book of Number One Rhythm & Blues Hits*, how he met Def Jam Records man Russell Simmons: "Hustling, man. We were selling jewelry and stuff, and Russell was putting together shows with Kurtis [Blow]. He had this group, Run-D.M.C., that he wanted to produce, and I was going to give him some money to produce them." The event didn't happen, though Russell asked the "Juice" if he would want to ply his vocal wares to a record. The response was "Oh, yeah," though the "Juice" man claims he never sang before; that is, outside of a public toilet.

Talking of his first encounter with a genuine recording studio, "Juice" said, "It was like "Star Trek." It was like we were on a spaceship . . . "The Rain" wasn't his initial vocal venture—"You Can't Hide From Love" (R&B: #75, 1986) charted; billing was simply "Juice." "The song didn't really hit me," White and Bronson were told. "I said, 'Man, there's something missing.' So,

I wrote this little monologue on the end of it—the talking part. I spent my money and booked the time and tagged that on the end of it." It's that monologue—based on true-to-life experiences, claims Jones, of guys whose "girlfriends were jerking them"—that "Juice" Jones feels sold the record.

"You can choose your own fate," he told Cynthia Horner, of *Right On!* "If you wake up in the morning and you don't have any money, and there's a gun nearby, you can go out there and rob, or you can choose not to. I pick up a pencil because I'd rather be remembered as a writer and a singer than as a stick-up kid."

Further R&B-only chartings fleshed out the '80s: "Curiosity" (#45, 1986), "Here I Go Again" (#45, 1987), "Cold Spendin' My $ Money" (#41, 1987), "Pipe Dreams" (#47, 1989). The latter was an extract from the "Juice's" third and much hoped for album, *To Be Immortal.*

Reflecting on his slot in the future, the "Juice" added: "Ten years from now, if somebody wanted to know what happened during the '80s, they could listen to a Juice album and know."

RIC OCASEK
EMOTION IN MOTION
(Ric Ocasek)
Geffen 28617
No. 15 *October 11, 1986*

"It may sound funny," said Ric Ocasek to Bill Flannagan, *Trouser Press*, "but I don't know what a hit is. I mean, I don't know exactly how to sit down and write them. Otherwise I could perpetuate my career forever. I stumble on them."

The Cars were a hit-making band; the first of the "new wave" bands to make it successful with the mainstream pop/rock audience. As their main wheel, Ocasek (b. Richard Otcasek, Mar. 23, 1949, Baltimore) drove four of the Cars' first five albums into the Top 10 of *Billboard's* top pop album charts; all eventually sold platinum. By the time the Cars were junked in 1988, 13 of their 45s had ranked well in the nation's Top 40.

"It's hard to be married to one person," explained Ocasek of the Car crash to *Musician's* Scott Isler. "It's harder to be married to five. Everybody eventually goes in different directions."

Ocasek took to music unknowingly and early. "When I was 14," he said to Holly Gleason, *Illinois Entertainer*," I bought a guitar, or I had someone buy me a guitar, I can't remember. But I played it for a whole year, and then I gave it up. Then when I was 18, I said to myself, 'I think I'd like to write songs.' It took me years to learn how and to develop a style, because I didn't want to be a cheap songwriter who'd throw together a few chords and some themes. I always cared . . ."

Ocasek added to Kelly Crowley, *Music Paper:* "It was Bob Dylan that gave me the fire. His words were amazing . . . When I started writing everything I did was an attempt to write as powerfully as Dylan."

Both Ric and fellow Car man BENJAMIN ORR (a.k.a. Benjamin Orzechowski) had gotten their start in an obscure band named Milkwood. A lone album—now highly collectible—was issued by Paramount in 1972. With the gathering of Elliot Easton (a.k.a. Elliott Shapiro), Greg Hawkes, and David Robinson—and a momentary moniker change to Cap'n Swing—the parts were in place for the musicians to be assembled as the Cars. Six albums were packaged and shipped before the act was scrapped for reasons of fatigue and perceived obsolescence.

Both Ocasek's debut album—*Beatitude* (1983)—and his hit-containing *This Side of Paradise* (1986)—produced by Tears for Fears producers Chris Hughes and Ross Cullium—were issued prior to the Cars shutdown; and proved hot sellers. Critics—while still interested— found both to be overly Car-like.

"I don't know why that surprises anyone," he told Crowley. "Who did all the writing for the Cars? I was being myself then, and I can't be anymore myself now. The only difference between The Cars and me is I am working with new musicians, except for Greg Hawkes."

Ocasek's post-Car collections, however, have been highly unsuccessful. Both 1991's *Fireball Zone*—a titled lifted from a Thomas Pynchon novel, *Gravity's Rainbow*—and its 1993 successor *Quick Change World* failed to even touch *Billboard's* Top 200 album listing.

Concurrent with his solo airing was Ric's fleshing out character roles in John Waters's flick *Hairspray* (1988) and *Made in Heaven* (1987) and his production work with Weezer, Alan Vega, Suicide, ROMEO VOID, Mercury Rev, Bad Brains, and IGGY POP.

"Independent records, like poetry and some other art forms, will never have a real widespread appeal," Ric told Crowley. "Bands and records with an independent twist will always have an audience looking for that little something different. It is a great feeling for me when I can help a band achieve the kind of sound they want to attract that type of crowd."

When asked in 1991 about the possibility of a Cars reunion, Ric responded, "I'm not sure what it would take . . . And I don't think I'd be interested 10 years from now [2001]."

In 1993, *Negative Theatre*, Ric's first book of poetry, was issued.

GREGORY ABBOTT
SHAKE YOU DOWN

(Gregory Abbott)
Columbia 06191
No. 1 *November 8, 1986*

Gregory Abbott was encouraged by his parents to acquire all of the education that he possibly could. After earning his B.A. in psychology from Boston University and a Master's in social psychology at California State University, Greg did graduate work in literature at Stanford and taught various classes at the University of California at Berkeley. When his huge international hit happened, Greg was at work attempting to complete his Ph.D. dissertation.

But what's a psychologist, a bookworm, an egghead got to do with making suggestive dance music? "I was raised in a household that put education first," Abbott explained to *Cashbox*'s Lee Jeske. "But in addition, my parents taught me that whatever you purse, you do it seriously. Even if it's a hobby. So I always took music and pursued it seriously; but more as an avocation.

"My mother sang, and she gave vocal training and piano training to me." When he was eight, he was a member of St. Patrick's Cathedral Choir, in New York City, singing for six years every Sunday mass and appearing on their annual television production and record album. Years later he got to meet Marvin Gaye, who showed Greg how to work the controls at his 24-track recording studio. Following a move to Los Angeles, Greg met, wooed, and wed soul singer Freda Payne. Surely, his life's path crossing with that of Marvin and Freda rekindled his hobby-like interests in making music. Payne went on to record some of his songs on her *Stares and Whispers* and *Supernatural High* albums.

Returning to Manhattan, Greg worked by day as a researcher for a Wall Street brokerage; by night he seriously tended to his hobby. When some investment bankers overheard some of Greg's demo materials, they financed a recording studio in his home as well as a record label, Gramercy Park Records. After recording a few aspiring acts for his label, Greg turned his attention to himself. "People would often ask who was singing on the demos I'd worked on," Abbott told David Nathan. "I figured it couldn't hurt to produce myself. After all, I know the artist in question pretty well—and I think he knows how to take direction."

Reportedly Greg spent three years writing songs for himself. Once 40 tunes were recorded, he selected the three best to submit to CBS Records. Label-heads were duly impressed and even allowed him to arrange, produce, and even play keyboards and drums on the debut, *Shake You Down*.

The title track was issued as Greg's first single and the response was instant and phenomenal. The album sold platinum; the single moved 2 million copies in no time. "'Shake You Down' "was an attempt to express how men feel when they see a woman they like," said Abbott to authors Adam White and Fred Bronson. The tune was not Abbott's favorite track.

Abbot only returned to *Billboard*'s Hot 100 with one more tune, "I Got the Feeling (It's Over)" (#56, 1987).

"The success of 'Shake You Down' certainly changed my life," said Abbott, to *Cashbox*. "It allowed me to participate on the highest level in the music business and make an impact all over the world. To go to a country where I've never been before and communicate through music to people who often don't speak English—that was an awesome feeling . . . the highlight of the 'Shake You Down' experience was the joy on the fans' faces when they saw me. Music makes me happy and when my music makes someone else happy, it's a total fulfillment."

TIMBUK 3
THE FUTURE'S SO BRIGHT,
I GOTTA WEAR SHADES

(Pat MacDonald)
I.R.S. 52940
No. 19 *November 22, 1986*

Misunderstood are Timbuk 3—Pat MacDonald, wife Barbara Kooyman MacDonald, and subset member "T3." "The U.S. Navy actually wanted to use that song ["The Future's So Bright, I'm Gonna Wear Shades"] for a recruitment commercial," said Pat to *Request*'s Michael Corcoran. "I guess I should take some of the blame, though, because I didn't set the record straight when people said it was cheerful. I hate explaining lyrics because they never sound as good. It's like having to repeat a punchline to a joke until people get it. By that time, it's not funny."

Pat (b. Aug. 6, 1952, Green Bay, WI, vocals, guitar, harmonica, bass) and Barb (b. Oct. 4, 1957, Wausau, WI, vocals, guitar, harmonica, violin, mandolin) met in Madison in 1978, both were students at the University of Wisconsin. Four years later they would marry, but prior to the occasion Pat worked the college clubs as a folkie, alone; then as front man with Texas guitarist Billy Logg in The Essentials—with Ken Heim (bass) and Michael Weiss (drums)—that got the chance in 1981 to record an album, *Lowdown*, for Mountain Railroad—a current collectible noted for such thinking-man tunes as "Einstein at the Pool Hall" and "Assholes on Parade."

"At one point, there was a vacancy in the band," said Pat to *Musician*'s Alan di Perna, "and Barbara [who had appeared with the group Cats Away] filled it. She was in it for two years. But by the time that it was over [around

1984], we knew we wanted to concentrate on our musical relationship without the constraints of having to deal with a band." A commemorative break-up EP was issued in 1983, *Essential Propaganda*.

They worked the streets of Manhattan, Pat, Barb, and a drum machine that came to be called "T3." Soon the duo and box moved to Austin, Texas, to perform at the Austin Outhouse and Hole in the Wall. As luck would have it, while gigging at the latter Timbuk 3 were to be "discovered" when MTV taped an episode of their series "The Cutting Edge" at the club. I.R.S. signed the act in 1986. In a few months, the single and debut album—*Greetings From Timbuk 3*—and the act known as Timbuk 3 were an international sensation.

As for their moniker, Pat told John Leland, of *Spin*, "The idea for it comes from this guy . . . Jim Spencer was his name. He was a real literate kind of guy and entertained himself with word plays. He had a whole religion called the Waslamic faith. The motto was, 'Waslam is as Islam was.' The spiritual mecca for the Waslamic faith was Timbuk 3."

Pat, Barb, and their noise box traveled the world— appeared on "Saturday Night Live," won a Grammy nomination—but all too soon realized they were being perceived by the masses as a novelty act. "No! We don't call the blaster, the 'jambox,' 'T3' anymore," said Pat to *Creem*'s Dave Kendall. "For awhile we had cute names for it, but it's so easy for articles about us to concentrate on the box as some kind of gimmick . . . We're trying to de-gimmickify it."

And then there's that song: "When I wrote it," explained Pat to Leland, "I never imagined there would be people who wouldn't see the irony in it, who would see it as a very optimistic anthem. . . . I'm just making fun not of naive optimism but blind ambition. That kind of thing is scary. I use nuclear science because of the idea of the future being bright, but possibly from an intense blast of radiation."

In 1988, *Eden Alley* was issued. Each of Timbuk 3's follow-up albums received still better reviews, but fewer sales. I.R.S. wanted hits. The pressure was on. "We'd turn in a record," said Pat to *Request*, "and they'd say, 'Where are the hits?' and then the album would become kind of invisible in their eyes. . . . The thing is, though, we weren't signed in the first place to have Top 40 success. That was kind of a fluke. We were supposed to make good albums, not hit singles."

No longer as one are Pat and Barb. Pat went on to co-write tunes with Aerosmith, Jill Sobule, Zucchero and to place tracks in such flicks as *Something Wild* (1986), *The Texas Chainsaw Massacre 2* (1986), *D.O.A.* (1988), and *Untamed Heart* (1993). In 1997, Pat had a first solo effort—*Pat MacDonald Sleeps With His Guitar*—issued by Ark 21.

GEORGIA SATELLITES
KEEP YOUR HANDS TO YOURSELF
(Dan Baird)
Elektra 69502
No. 2 *December 20, 1986*

They had lust and that silly grin and they played full-tilt bare-bones guitar rock'n'roll. As Keith and the Satellites they were formed in 1979; based in Atlanta. There was DAN BAIRD (vocals, guitar) and Rick Richards (guitar), then Mauro "Brains" Megellan (drums), and Rick Price (bass). Others passed through the line-up, including Keith Christopher—the Keith in the moniker. Four years they played the Atlanta bars and a steady gig called Hedgens Rock and Roll Tavern. They cut a six-song demo to no effect . . . and broke up. Don joined the Woodpeckers (later, simply the Woods); the rest went with the Hell Hounds.

The demo finally landed in England. Making Waves, a British independent label, gave a listen and financed a U.K. tour for the long-gone act; releasing the tentative tape as an EP, *Keeping the Faith*. Mauro and Price, also sometime members of the Mercury act Brains (known for "Money Changes Everything," popularized by Cyndi Lauper), rejoined for the projected tour that never happened. Meanwhile, the four Satellites are on course and settled in Nashville. Elektra "discovers" them and boom . . . the return of real rock'n'roll, "Keep Your Hands to Yourself."

"It's just a fun song I wrote years ago. People are going to roll their eyes and say, 'A fun song, what a horrible thing to have done,' explained Baird to *Creem*'s Michael Lipton on his "Hands to Yourself" song. "It's not like we were out there looking for some new thing. I tried that in my 20s. I figured it didn't have to have that bitter cynical quality that says, 'hey, hey, hey, I'm so smart.' Someone needed to write a song like that again—and I was just stupid enough to be smart."

They toured with Tom Petty, Bob Seger, Hank Williams, Jr. They trekked to Japan, Australia, Switzerland's Montreaux Pop Festival. Remakes of the Woods' "Battleship Chains" and THE SWINGING BLUE JEAN' "Hippy Hippy Shake" were sorely needed sounds for the growing numbers of cow-punks, retro-rockers, and country rock fans. They didn't chart, but they—a few other tracks and the *Open All Night* album—are deeply appreciated to this day to their cult followers.

In 1991, the Satellites splitted. Price played on Paul Westerberg's *14 Songs*; Don Baird recorded *Loves Songs for the Hearing Impaired*; becoming a One-Hit entry on his own with "I Love You Friend" (#26, 1992). Richards and Price reactivated the Georgia Satellites name in 1993.

BRUCE WILLIS
RESPECT YOURSELF
(Luther Ingram, Mack Rice)
Motown 1876
No. 5 *January 31, 1987*

"As a vocalist, the best that can be said of Willis is that he generally sings on key," reported *Rolling Stone*'s Kurt Loder on Bruce Willis's appearance at the Ritz, January 1987. "His voice lacks any sort of distinction, and as a live performer, he seems unacquainted with the concept of projection: beyond the first few rows it was hard to care what was happening onstage—which, at any given moment, wasn't much. This was a show with neither high points nor idiosyncratic lows. There was literally nothing to it."

Said Willis to the crowd at one point, "This beats the shit out of working on TV." "Unfortunately," wrote Loder, "this tiresome show was less interesting in every way than *watching* TV."

Bruce (b. Walter Willison, Mar. 19, 1955, Germany), the son of a welder, was raised among the chemical plants of Carney's Point, New Jersey. He was a student at Montclair State College, leaving to live in Hell's Kitchen in New York City to tend bar. Reportedly, Bruce was a real musician at some point: a sax player in a local thing called Loose Goose. If he's to be believed, this was his felt calling, but then an acting career started to take off, an acting career that greatly overshadowed any imprint he might marginally make on rock-'n'-roll music.

After minor roles in such flicks as *Ziegfield—The Man and His Woman* (1978), *The First Deadly Sin* (1980), *Prince of the City* (1981), and *The Verdict* (1985), Bruce hit the big time as the fast-talking, wisecracking "David Addison" opposite Cybill Shepherd on the witty ABC-TV classic "Moonlighting." The first in the highly successful *Die Hard* series of action films was issued in 1987, the same year Bruce married actress Demi Moore and returned to feel his rock'n'roll roots.

"Respect Yourself," a reworked take on the Staple Singers' classic, was the result of Bruce's TV special "The Return of Bruno." For the soundtrack, Willis rounded up many of the same Stax Record legends—Steve Crooper, Matt "Guitar" Murphy, Donald "Duck" Dunn—that a decade earlier had accompanied Dan Aykroyd and John Belushi in their Blues Brothers act.

Bruce's *The Return of Bruno* and remakes of the Coasters' "Youngblood" (#68, 1987) and the Drifters' "Under the Boardwalk" (#59, 1987) sold fairly well; the latter reportedly featured the assistance of the Temptations. Apparently having fulfilled his youthful dreams, Willis's attentions were turned elsewhere. There were blockbuster movies to be made: *Bonfires of the Vanities* (1990), *Hudson Hawke* (1991), *Pulp Fiction* (1994). . . .

"What's happened to me," said Willis to *Entertainment Weekly*, "is just an example of the American dream, of somebody busting their ass and working hard."

HIPSWAY
THE HONEYTHIEF
(John McElhone, Bill McLeod, Graham Skinner, Harry Travers)
Columbia 06579
No. 19 *March 14, 1987*

"People have terrible trouble describing us," said vocalist Grahame "Skin" Skinner to *Melody Maker*'s Teo Mico. "I suppose we're just not outrageous enough."

SPIN magazine's John Leland had no difficulty with his description: "Call it bubblegum or call it garbage, but this year's ranking One-Hit Wonder (after Robbie Nevil*) looks like an affably Scottish trio called Hipsway. The one hit, the three-minute alpha and omega of their cultural impact, a hit of proportions rivaling those of drummer Harry Travers's monstrous proboscis, is an infectious, lightly funky paean to hymen-snatching called 'The Honeythief.' Admit you like it and no one will ever think you cool again."

Hipsway was a Glasgow foursome comprised of "Skin" Skinner, Harry Travers, guitarist Pim Jones, and bassist John McElbone. "Skin" grew up listening to IGGY POP and ROXY MUSIC. Once he discovered the Glasgow R & B circuit, his views changed. Initially, there was the Jazzateers. "The idea was like a pastiche of Iggy, Bowie, and the New York Dolls," he told *Cashbox*. Next, "Skin" found Travers and the White Savages were formed.

By 1983, the two had found McElbone who had hooked up with Pim Jones. "We rehearsed and demoed some songs. Record companies came to Glasgow to see us rehearse . . . and we played terrible but the songs were good." Mercury/Phonogram signed the band now called Hipsway. It was the third 45, "Honeythief," the opening track on their self-titled debut album, that connected with Top 40 radio.

"'The Honeythief' is about the gaining of the cherry," explained Travers to *SPIN*. "It came to us in an art gallery in Glasgow where there's a painting called 'Cupid and the Honeythief.' I just thought it was an amazing concept . . . We took that and tied it together with the book *Lolita*. It's not fluffy. . . . You pop a cherry and it don't get any more real than that. That's gutsy stuff."

As a follow-up, "Ask the Lord" was reissued, then "Long White Car." Neither clicked and Hipsway fell by the media's wayside for three years. In Glasgow they were considered to be a manufactured band; not a hip thing to be in a community known for the Associates,

Simple Minds, and Orange Juice. "That's such a pile of crap!" responded "Skin" in *Melody Maker*. "If it was so easy to manufacture a band like us, why isn't everybody doing it? Just because we formed this band with the idea of getting a record deal and being successful and are on our way, other bands get really bitter."

In 1989, the band returned with "Young Love" and *Scratch the Surface*, their second and final album. Soon after Hipsway stopped; "Skin" Skinner and Jones went with Witness, McElbone joined Texas.

"I think that every band has one good song. The difference between Hipsway and the others is that Hipsway have loads of good songs," boasted "Skin." "It's hard to describe why we're going to be successful without sounding cliched and boring."

[*Leland, you may have hit the nail on its rhetorical helmet, but you're undebatably wrong about Robbie Nevil. With five Top 40 pop hits by mid-'96, Nevil is in no way to be considered a One-Hit Wonder.]

BREAKFAST CLUB
RIGHT ON TRACK
(Steve Bray, Steve Gilroy)
MCA 52954
No. 7 *April 11, 1987*

Madonna was introduced to Dan Gilroy in 1979. The introducer was a T-shirt designer named Norris Burroughs, a grown-weary paramour to Ciccone. Soon Madonna, Dan, brother Ed, and dancing friend of Madonna's Angie Smit were living together in the Gilroys' residence, an abandoned synagogue in Corona, Queens. The brothers had a stand-up comedy act they called "The Bil and Gil Show." With the dancers each attempting to learn an instrument—Angie, the bass, Madonna, drums—the Bil and Gil bit became the rock act Breakfast Club.

"It was Dan who was responsible for transforming Madonna from a dancer into a singer/musician," wrote

Mark Bego, author of *Madonna: Blond Ambition.* "Without him, the whole Madonna phenomenon might never have occurred."

Within months, Madonna was off to Paris for a year to be made a star by producers/financiers Jean Claude Pellerin and Jean Van Lieu, who were responsible for the success of German-born PATRICK HERNANDEZ.

On her return to the states, Madonna returned to the Gilroys'and the dream of fame. Madonna learned guitar, created songs, and practiced drums for hours per day. With Steve Bray and for a moment David Frank, later SYSTEM sideman, they as Breakfast Club appeared at rock clubs on the Lower East Side of Manhattan. Hidden behind the drums, Angie, not Madonna, got the stares. "Angie always dressed really sexy with see-through clothes, and she moved sensuously onstage," said Dan to Bego. Madonna noted all this. Asking to be let out from behind the drums to sing, the brothers agreed. Madonna wanted more attention. When the band vetoed her demand to be allowed to sing more, Bego reports, Madonna quit.

With Madonna's success and Breakfast Club's connections, their unveiling was orchestrated and duly noted by the music media. A promotional mailing of what *Billboard*'s Jim Bessman called an "unprecedented scope" was dispatched—a video of "Right on Track" was put in a "novel cereal box package," with the group's self-titled album, a bio, numerous photos, and a nightshirt complete with the band's logo in huge letters. Liz Heller, MCA's director of music videos, proudly revealed that six months of promotional planning preceded the act's debut. "We wanted to establish a look and an attitude for the band to go hand in hand with the record," said Heller to *Billboard*.

"I do hope that if we are successful we can get more black-white musical interaction," said Bray to *Billboard*'s Nelson George. "Sly & The Family Stone was a big influence on us, and on 'Right on Track' we and producer Jimmy Iovine wanted to echo Sly's music."

Only one follow-up single made the *Billboard* pop listings, "Kiss and Tell" (#48, 1987). Everyone except Bray returned to the void.

Steve Bray went on to score some of the soundtrack for the flicks *Beverly Hills Cop 2* (1987) and Madonna's *Who's That Girl* (1987).

SYSTEM
DON'T DISTURB THIS GROOVE
(David Frank, Mic Murphy)
Atlantic 89320
No. 4 *May 16, 1987*

David Frank's mother saw to it that he got piano lessons. By high school and the various R & B bands he

meandered through, Dave was classically trained. He attended the Berklee College of Music, took an interest in jazz, continued to write songs, made demos and diligently sent them off to record companies. For awhile nobody took much notice—outside of family and friends.

By the mid-'70s, Dave (b. Dayton, OH, synthesizer) moved to New York City and met what soon was to become the other half of the System, Mic Murphy (b. Raleigh, NC, vocals, guitar), a former roadie, soundman, and member of Mic & the Shakers. Discovering a mutual interest in the merging of soul and technology—what the pair would come to call "emotio electro" music—and late in '76 having some free studio time, the duo quickly assembled "I Only Want to Love You" (R&B: #88, 1977), released on the 20th Century Fox label as by Sass.

Writer/producers Patrick Adams and Greg Carmichael—noted for Disco-era studio acts Inner Life, Musique, Sine, and the Salsoul Orchestra—had luck in the spring of 1977 with a studio creation called "Dance and Shake Your Tambourine," issued as by the Universal Robot Band. The studio players noting the Robot Band's success and the camaraderie they shared decided to shake off Patrick and Greg and form their own unit—what would become the multi-hit-making Kleeer. It was as brief members of Kleeer—best remembered by dance fans for "Winners" (R&B: #23, 1980) and "Get Tough" (R&B: #15, 1981)—that Dave and Mic first considered creating the System.

"It's Passion," the pair's first System single was released in 1981, while still involved in the Kleeer klan. After a fleeting return to the Sass name—the following year for some noncharting sides for the 25 West label—Mic and Dave connected with R & B hitdom with "You Are in My System" (#68; R&B: #10, 1983). By years end, the intra-racial brothers had their performance of "Baptize the Beat" included in the Harry Belafonte produced *Street Beat* (1984).

To black radio, the act named for a line from some TV folder—"Honey, you just can't get him out of your system."—was anything but unknown. Both "The Pleasure Seekers (#21, 1985) and "This Is for You" (#8, 1985) had charted big time on *Billboard*'s R & B listings, prior to "Don't Disturb This Groove" (R&B: #1, 1987), their lone pop mega-moment.

"Our goal has always been the black chart. We reached our goal with 'Groove,' and now that it's done well on the pop chart, it's all just extra gravy," said Dave to *Billboard*'s Nelson George.

Neither Mic nor Dave had the notion during the creative act that "Groove" was to be the hit it became. "I worked on a musical track for two or three days, and I remember thinking, 'Why am I spending so much time on this? I don't know whether it's going to be good, it's a little bit too jazzy, and I'm probably making a mistake,'" said Dave to White and Bronson, authors of *The Billboard Book of Number One Rhythm & Blues*. "But I couldn't stop myself. I kept working on the track . . ."

The System's immediate follow-ups hit the R&B Top 10. "Nighttime Lover" (#7, 1987) and "Midnight Special" (#5, 1989). Their title tune to the Eddie Murphy flick *Coming to America* (1988) also made the R & B listings (R&B: #23).

As producer/writer, Mic and Dave went on to work with Howard Johnson, Chaka Khan, Evelyn "Champaign" King, Jeff Lorber, Nona Hendryx, GRAVIN CHRISTOPHER, and Angela Bofill. Dave, in the role of a multi-instrumentalist, did recording sessions for Phil Collins, Billy Idol, and Robert Palmer; the latter recharted the System's "You Are in My System" (#78, 1983).

PSEUDO ECHO
FUNKY TOWN
(Steven Greenberg)
RCA 5217
No. 6 *June 6, 1987*

They were a top Australian band in the early through mid-'80s; much like a down-under version of Duran Duran. Fronted by Bruce Canham, the Melbourne-based quartet's line-up changed often. Prior by only months to their isolated Stateside hit, Pseudo Echo made the United States listings with "Living in a Dream" (#57, 1987). "Funkytown," their big one, had been a chart-topping disco slice for LIPPS, INC. in the early months of 1980. Pseudo Echo's passed over follow-up, "Listening," was a track that had been successful for the act in its homeland in 1984.

Three albums were issued in the U.S. before the group's withdrawal from the game. Each presented the principle-free and overly malleable unit with a different collective persona—there was the lipstick, hair and synth-guitar stance, followed by a quickie as a dance-orientated pack of leather boys; and finally, they appeared all serious, long haired, and ready to riff.

Trouser Press founder Ira Robbins, in his *TP Record Guide* referred to them as "lame time-zone wrinkles," suggesting that given who they were they "consider going away."

Within months of their "Funky Town" flirt with fame, Pseudo Echo took the grand prize at the 18th World popular Song Festival held in Nippon Budokan Hall in Tokyo. The band won $10,000 for its performance of "Take on the World."

Nothing has been heard from Pseudo Echo since the changing of the decade.

T'PAU
HEART AND SOUL
(Carol Decker, Ronnie Rogers)
Virgin 99466
No. 4 *June 6, 1987*

"Our fans are a funny mix," said T'Pau front person Carol Deckers to *Q*'s Tom Hibbert, "because we do poppy, crappy throwaway songs, and we do songs that have a meaning in the lyrics, and we do love songs; and then there's banner wavers like 'China in Your Hand.' When we played Hammersmith recently, there was kids of 14 . . . children on their parents' shoulders, loving couples, and there were great big bikers. . . ."

T'Pau played "modern rock," they called it—raunchy guitars, heavy drums, layers of synthesizers. The five, largely nameless, guys behind screamin', screechin' Carol looked your average '80s rock star part. "Heart and Soul," their worldwide debut disk was initially passed over by all but American audiences who seemed taken in by Decker; who the media described as "a petite fireball," one feisty lady, ballsy.

T'Pau was formed in 1982 when Decker met and fell for guitarist Ronnie Rogers. Both had played in separate local bands to farmers in their home region of Wellington Shropshire, England. When Carol spotted Ron, he was playing licks in the Katz, a small-time comedic rock outfit. With the addition of Rogers, Deckers's Lazers became T'Pau—the name of a Vulcan princess and one-time associate of Mr. Spock's father on the TV series "Star Trek."

Five years of honing their craft in homeland dives—with frequent line-up changes—were to follow before T'Pau garnered the opening slot on a grueling tour of Canada and America with Brian Adams.

Once attention was won by the Stateside charting of "Heart and Soul," the single was dusted off and reissued in their homeland. Even "success" proved to be with price. "Most of the gigs we played in America were awful. Real toilets. We were there three months and even at the end, the biggest audience we were getting were less than a thousand," said Decker.

A half-dozen further chartings—including Top 10ers' "Valentine" and "China in Your Hand"—quickly following in Britain. Their debut album, *Bridge of Spies*, sold a million copies, but nothing further has charted in the United States.

Carol and Ronnie are still in love, still together, living in London's Kentish Town.

NYLONS
KISS HIM GOODBYE
(Gary DeCarlos, Dale Frashue, Paul Leka)
Open Air 0022
No. 12 *June 13, 1987*

Eking out a living in the theaters of Toronto were actors Paul Cooper, Marc Connors, and Claude Morrison. All shared a deep and secret passion that only surfaced publicly with the addition in March, 1981, of Arnold Robinson, a native of Wilmington, North Carolina, singer and one-time member of Sonny Turner's edition of the Platters/a.k.a. Sounds Unlimited. Soon it became common knowledge in Toronto that they loved to harmonize that good olde rock and pop, *a cappella*. Somehow via their talent and humor old was new and hip, again.

Before Arnold's arrival, the Nylons had a more liquid line-up that at times had included Dave Simpson and then Ralph Cole. Within months of their club circuit debut, Al Mair, president of Attic Records, began working with the boys to mix for vinyl their *a cappella* sounds with a percussion-only accompaniment. Their remake of the RAYS' "Silhouettes" and likewise the Tokens' "Lion Sleeps Tonight" almost clipped the *Billboard* charts. International attention was gathered for the Nylon men with the release of their fourth album, *Happy Together*. The first 45, "Kiss Him Goodbye," a revival of STEAM's "Na Na Hey Hey Kiss Him Goodbye," one critic referred to as "3 minutes and 23 seconds of possibly the most exciting power-packed harmony and percussion of any record of the '80s."

In 1986, they earned the "Best Singer Award" at the 15th Annual Tokyo Music Festival, for their take on the Supremes' "Up the Ladder to the Roof." They functioned as the opening act for the Pointer Sisters and Hall and Oates, and with the success of "Kiss Him Goodbye" toured the United States as a headliner.

While a large core fandom has remained stuck to the Nylons, follow-up 45s have yet to return the act to the charts.

Marc died March 25, 1991, of viral pneumonia. His replacement, Billy Newton-Davis, had recorded a few solo albums, winning three Juno Awards. Paul had left the group in 1990, to be replaced by Micah Barner. In 1992, a rejuvenated Nylons signed on with BMG Music.

SUZANNE VEGA
LUKA
(Suzanne Vega)
A & M 2937
No. 3 *July 4, 1987*

Widely considered one of the most brilliant songwriters of her generation. Jeremy Hellgar wrote in the *New York Review of Records*, "She's a contained maelstrom looking for a place to uncork. . . ."

Suzanne was born in Santa Monica, California, August 12, 1959, the eldest of four children and was raised in Spanish Harlem by her mother a musician and stepfather Fred Vega, a Puerto Rican teacher and writer of novels. Her stepdad encouraged her to write poetry, play the guitar, and to dance. At the High School of Performing Arts in Manhattan, she studied modern dance and composing. At 16, she began performing with guitar at folk festivals held at Columbia University and in Greenwich Village coffeehouses, notably Gerde's Folk City, where Dylan had made his debut decades before. "For the first time in my life," she told Anthony Scaduto, New York *Newsday*, "I found a scene I was happy in. I belonged there . . . I fit in."

A LOU REED concert she attended in 1979 proved a turning point. Said Vega, "His performance and his songs shocked me, disturbed me . . . I realized I too could write songs about things I experienced. The subways, the streets, lonely people, damaged people . . . I began to see that I could be a contemporary folksinger."

After graduating from Barnard College in 1982 with a degree in English, Suzanne worked as a receptionist for a lawyer, Ron Fierstein, and a producer, Steve Addabbo. The two formed a music promotion company and with their assistance Suzanne got a contract with A & M Records in 1984.

"What I'm aiming for is to be universal, but not in an obvious way where all the mystery is taken out of it," said Vega to Tina Clarke of *Music Express*.

". . . Put yourself in the position of the person speaking," said Suzanne Vega to *B-Side*'s Marcia B. Merson. "That's really what I'm asking the audience to do. I may be telling a truth in the song, I may not be. Usually, there's something not revealed. Some people seem to approach them as riddles—which is okay with me—that there is some kind of key information missing and that I'm asking the listener to provide."

In 1985, *Suzanne Vega*—produced by Lenny Kaye, critic and former PATTI SMITH GROUP guitarist—was issued to media acclaim. *Rolling Stone* included the Vega's debut in its "100 Best Albums of the 1980s."

A quarter million copies were sold in the United States; double that in England, where "Marlene on the Wall" became a hit single. Appearances at the prestigious Royal Albert Hall in London, Carnegie Hall, and Radio City Music Hall in New York City followed. Vega wrote the lyrics for two pieces in Phillip Glass's song cycle *Songs for Liquid Days*, and contributed "Left of Center" to the flick *Pretty in Pink* (1986). What followed would prove to be Vega's landmark; *Solitude Standing* was issued to even greater response—with sales reaching 3 million-plus and still selling. On the album is "Luka," Vega's only hit single—to date.

Suzanne Vega solitude standing

"Luka" was a tale of woe and of child abuse—from the child's view—set to a cheerful accompaniment. "I didn't want 'Luka' to be a self-pitying song about a boy sitting on a stoop feeling miserable," said Vega to Scaduto. "That kid had a dignity, as kids do, and that's what I wanted to come out . . . All I wanted to do was reveal his point of view . . . [The song is] unresolved, frustrating, like it is in real life."

"Luka" was nominated for a Grammy for "Record of the Year," "Song of the Year," and Vega, herself, for "Best Pop Female Vocalist."

Following this second album, Suzanne took a three-year hiatus. "I was very nervous at that point," said Vega to Don McLeese of the Chicago Tribune. "People were watching me in a certain way, giving me advice, giving me criticism and praise, alot of which I was very suspicious of. I was getting big audiences and people were very excited, but you don't know quite why. You're not sure whether they think you're something you're not, really."

Days of Open Road was warmly received in 1990. What followed in 1991, is any artist's dream: Vega had a hit record with a record that she had nothing to do with. Her a cappella reading of "Tom's Diner" from her Solitude Standing was, without her permission, given a hip-hop backing by D.N.A., a U.K. rap group. "If I thought it was bad," Vega told UPI, "I would have sued them." Elsewhere Vega said, "I was pleased that 'Tom's Diner' did what it did, because suddenly all these black kids in the neighborhood where I grew up in New York were listening to my songs."

A & M Records released Tom's Album, a compilation of a baker's dozen versions of "Tom's Diner" by such diversity as Michigan and Smiley and Bingo Hand Job.

Vega's 1992 release, 99.9 F, had varying musical contexts—industrial noise, girl group pop, and psychedelic. Critics approved, but sales have been diminishing.

LIVING IN A BOX
LIVING IN A BOX
(Marcus Vere, S. Piggot)
Chrysalis 43104
No. 17 *July 25, 1987*

"I know it's a strange story to listen to," Living in the Box keyboardist Marcus Vere said. "This is going to read like a best-selling novel: Young man goes from nothing to a Top Five hit . . . I've never been in any other group, never played in front of an audience, yet here I am."

It was in Manchester, England, in the summer of 1985 when Vere met drummer Anthony "Tich" Critchlow. "We met through friends," Vere told *Illinois Entertainer*'s Elianne Halbersberg, in 1987, "and figured that we should do something together." A month or two later, there was "the voice," Richard Darbyshire. "We found him via the advertising route. The two [tryouts] before him were completely and utterly hopeless!"

The three novices made a few demos and . . . "Two weeks later we were signed on the basis of our demos of 'Living in a Box.' Two further months were required to iron out the contractual small print supplied by Chrysalis Records, but by then Vere, Tich, and Darbyshire were due for stardom.

"We were born out of the studio," Vere explained. "Technology saved our skin. Eighty-five percent of the stuff we do is programmed. You can't tell it, or hear it. All that does is allow us to play something perfectly . . ."

During their moment of Top 40 peakdom, Vere met Elton John. "He was telling me how much he likes our record and he said, 'Savor your first success because you'll never feel that way again . . .'"

As for the future, Vere told Halbersberg: "Anything is possible. We're not going to write 10 more 'Living in a Boxes.'"

"So the Story Goes" (#81, 1987) was the group's last charting single.

GRATEFUL DEAD
TOUCH OF GREY
(Robert Hunter)
Arista 9606
No. 9 *August 15, 1987*

"We're overnight failures who have stuck with it," said Bob Weir to authors David Gans and Peter Simon. "We're the exception to just about every rule in the music business."

Said Jerry Garcia, the primal hippie and founding father of the greatest cult band the world has ever knwon, "The Grateful Dead just kind of grew out of the side of this social scene. There was no logic to it at all."

The Grateful Dead evolved out of Mother McRee's Uptown Jug Champions to become the Warlocks in 1965. The group's name, it is claimed, was randomly pulled from two dips into a copy of the *Oxford English Dictionary*. The Grateful Dead's original line-up included lead guitarist Garcia (b. Jerome John Garcia, Aug. 1, 1942, San Francisco), drummer Bill Kreutzmann (B. Apr. 7, 1946, Palo Alto, CA), bassist Phil Lesh (b. Phillip Chapman, Mar. 15, 1940, Berkeley, CA), keyboardist Ron "Pigpen" McKernan (b. Sept. 8, 1945, San Bruno, CA; d. Mar. 8, 1973), and rhythm guitarist Bob Weir (b. Robert Hall, Oct. 16, 1947, San Francisco).

From near its inception, the band was dead-set on playing long, meandering musical landscapes. "The challenging part," Garcia told David Gans and Peter Simon, the authors of *Playing in the Band*, "is coming up with structures that have the element of looseness to them, which means they can expand in any direction, go anywhere from anywhere—or come from anywhere—but also have enough form that we can lock into something."

"I just don't see why the bounds of popular music should be so constricted as to deny the possibility of, for instance, odd time signatures or harmonic modes," added Weir.

Although the band garnered a hardcore troop of farout fans from the get-go and their numerous albums sold fairly well, the Grateful dead never seemed to gather or much care about Top 40 radio and pop mainstream-ers as a lot took little notice of their seemingly endless trippy doings.

The band members' individual lives was the cosmic sounds they oozed; little else seemed to matter. "I can't do anything but lie," said Jerry Garcia, to authors Gans and Simon. "All talk is lying, and I'm lying now. And that's true, too. Go hear me play. That's me. That's the form my thoughts have taken. That's the Grateful Dead."

"To me," added Lesh, "the Grateful Dead is life, the life of the spirit and the mind, as opposed to standing in line and marking time in the twentieth century."

Garcia was found dead on the morning of August 9, 1995, in his room at Serenity Knolls, a treatment center in Forest Hills, California, where he had reportedly checked in to do battle with a heroin addiction.

LEVERT
CASANOVA
(Reggie Calloway)
Atlantic 89217
No. 5 *September 5, 1987*

Despite its lone pop hit status, LeVert remains one of the most consistently placing acts on the R & B charts. Between 1986 and 1993, Sean and Gerald LeVert and buddy Marc Gordon, as LeVert, secured 20 R & B chartings, a dozen of these placed in the Top 10; five of them, cherished chart-toppers—"(Pop, Pop, Pop, Pop) Goes My Mind," "Baby I'm Ready," "Just Cookin'," featuring Heavy D, "Addicted to Love," from the film *Coming to America* (1988), and their lone crossover hit, "Casanova." Another 11 singles placed as solo or duet efforts; notably, Gerald's number one R & B hits, "Private Life," and "Baby Hold on to Me"—the latter featuring the assistance of brother Sean.

Cleveland-born and based LeVert is Ohio Players' Eddie LeVert, Sr.'s sons Gerald (b. July 13, 1966, vocals) and Sean (b. Sept. 28, 1968, vocals), and neighborhood buddy Marc Gordon (b. Sept. 8, 1964, vocals, keyboards).

"We grew up fast," said Sean to John Swenson of UPI, "with my father being in the business. He would take us on the road in the summers when we were out of school. We learned a lot from that . . . My brother did sing with the O'Jays onstage, but I was always too scared."

In 1977, at a family gathering, the two brothers met Marc Gordon. "That happened through our mother," Sean told UPI. "She was real good friends with his mother, and she brought him over and he started playing the piano. We started writing songs then, and he became like our brother."

Sean said: "I was about 15 [about 1983] before I thought seriously about doing this. [By then,] we'd written a lot of songs together, so we sent some around and we got turned down a lot."

In late 1984, LeVert got the chance to record for the tiny Tempre label owned by the former Philadelphia International executive Harvy Coombs. *I Get Hot* was produced by soul vet Dexter Wansal. "I'm Still," their first single, charted (R & B: #70, 1985) and Atlantic Records took notice and signed the boys. *Bloodlines*, their debut album, yielded the R & B number one "(Pop, Pop, Pop, Pop) Goes My Mind."

The following year Reggie Calloway—then a member of MIDNIGHT STAR, later with brother Vincent, CALLOWAY—was brought in to produce LeVert's second LP, and to give the three some funk and some tunes. "Sometimes you write a song and you have no purpose for it," explained Reggie to authors Adam White and Fred Bronson on the creation of "Casanova." "It's just for your enjoyment. I came up with that song while on tour, riding down the highway on a tour bus. There are a lot of points where you don't see any houses. You don't see anything but road. I guess I have some country-western roots in me and 'Casanova' started out as one of my country-western songs."

Two other tracks from that album, *The Big Throwdown*, made the R & B Top 10 . . . and the chart action has yet to stop.

Said Marc to *Black Beat*, in 1987, in the first blush of success, "Our goal is to have our own production company, to be established across the country, and to be around for years like Gamble & Huff."

In 1988, Gerald and Marc formed Trevel Productions, a writing and producing team that worked with Anita Baker, Miki Howard, James Ingram, Men at Large, Stephanie Mills, Troop, and the O'Jays. Gerald, who has since forged a prominent solo career, found a new creative partner in Tony Nicholas. The pairing has found chart action for Gerald, with the DAVID FOSTER produced "I'd Give Anything" (R&B: #4, 1994)—reworked as "She'd Give Anything," a C & W Top 10 hit for Boy Howdy—and "Can't Help Myself" (R&B: #15, 1995) for the flick *Strapper* (1993), among others.

Speculating on LeVert's One-Hit status on the pop charts, Gerald told J. Wasser, *It's Hip*, their product may just be ". . . too black. It isn't just great music that sells records. You've got Frankie Beverley who doesn't sell more than 500,000, and Luther Vandross who doesn't have the major success that he should have . . . What you have is the whole music industry is . . . prejudice. Pop radio won't expose our music. It's frustrating."

ROGER
I WANT TO BE YOUR MAN
("Roger" Troutman, Larry Troutman)
Reprise 28229
No. 3 *February 13, 1988*

A lot of hard work went into creating, "I Want to Be Your Man," but upon its completion Roger Troutman knew one thing—he hated it. Roger recalls, "Lenny Waronker [Warner Bros. Records, President] called and said, 'This song is great . . . we want you to leave Warner Brothers Records and put it out on Reprise. Lenny and label chairman Mo Ostin wanted to reactivate Reprise and felt "I Want to Be" just might be strong enough to do the job." Roger reluctantly went along with their judgment.

"Guys have trouble committing, and women want us to commit," said Troutman of the theme behind the hit to authors Adam White and Fred Bronson. "Women want us to admit that we don't want to commit."

Roger's idea was converted into a song with the aid of brother Larry. Roger (b. Nov. 29, 1951, vocals, guitar) and brothers—Larry (congas), Lester (drums), and Terry "Zapp" (bass, keyboards)—grew up in a hardworking household in Hamilton, Ohio. With parental encouragement, he learned how to play the French horn, tuba, flute, harmonica, violin, keyboards, guitar, and pocket comb. By the late '70s, Roger found and overpopularized something called a vocoder, an electronic gadget that renders the human voice robotic.

A group he first formed in 1962 remained, though evolved through changes; in name they were the Veils, the Hungry People, the Human Body. Under the latter name, Roger and brothers put out an album—*Introducing Roger*—on their own Troutman Brothers label in 1975. Regionally, the disk was a success. Soon they were the opening act for their hero George Clinton and his Parliament/FUNKADELIC.

"It was about Bootsy, and it was about Sugarfoot and the Ohio Players, period," said Troutman to Rickey Vincent, author of *Funk*. "That was the origin of this sound. Point blank, that's it."

Through the group's connection with Clinton, the Human Body signed with Warner Brothers Records; though a name change was signaled. As Zapp—their new moniker, Terry's nickname—an album was issued to acclaim in 1980. Pulled from the package, "More Bounce to the Ounce" (#86, 1980) went to number two on *Billboard*'s R & B charts. Another extract, "Be Alright" (R&B: #26, 1980), as well as the album itself, *Zapp*, sold gold. Numerous R & B hits have continued through the '80s and up to the present; most notably, "Dance Floor (Pt. 1)" (R&B: #1, 1982), "Computer Love (Pt. 1)" (R&B: #8, 1986), "Slow and Easy" (R&B: #18, 1993).

Larry, Lester, and Terry left the Zapp fold in the late '80s to work with non-music-making brother Rufus, Jr., to run Troutman Enterprises, a mix of construction, real estate, and limousine services. Filling the void: Little Roger Jr. (guitar), Rufus III (keyboards, trumpet), and Funkadelic bass "Sting" Ray Davis.

Within a year of the initial Zapp album, Troutman had released his first in a series of Roger solo works. Sales have justified a continued stream of albums. More than a dozen Roger singles have made the R & B listings; including the Marvin Gaye remake "I Heard It on the Grapevine (Pt. 1)" (#1, 1981), "Do the Roger" (#24, 1981), "In the Mix" (#10, 1982), and a match-up with SCRITTI POLITTI, "Boom, There She Was" (#53; R&B: #19, 1988). Roger and Scritti Politti's David Gamson paired up again in 1993 for *Bridging the Gap*. His work as producer has included efforts made for Dayton, New Horizon, Sugarfoot, and sometime-Zapp singers Bobby Glover and Shirley Murdock.

"It's the black experience. It's the blues of the '80s," said Troutman to Vincent, of his personal style. "It has the same purpose with black people as blues had for black people when B. B. King started out, or Jimmy Reed."

M/A/R/R/S
PUMP UP THE VOLUME
(Steve Young, Andrew Briggs)
4th & Broadway 7452
No. 13 *February 20, 1988*

M/A/R/R/S was a U.K. electro-funk grouping that began as a friendly uniting of two sets of music-making brothers—Colourbox's Martyn and Steve Young and A. R. Kane's Alex and Rudi Kane. Both sibling sets were artists for England's independent 4AD Records.

The Young brothers, plus vocalist Lorita Grahame, recording briefly in the early '80s as Colourbox, worked their unique ways on reggae, industrial and '50s R & B, soul and whatever got in the way. When Colourbox is remembered in the United States, it is largely for their noxious experimental EP with the graphic depiction of horses mating on the cover and their screeching remake of the Supremes' "You Keep Me Holding On."

Alex and Rudi, recording as A. R. Kane, issued some late '80s Miles Davis-influenced albums, most notably *Sixty Nine*, described by *Trouser Press Record Guide* as containing "deep atmospherics and funk noise . . . with singing like some strange male siren calling from a cave." "Love From Outer Space" is a must to be treasured by all earthlings who have not experienced such festivities.

The intent of merging these two acts, in their entirety—minus Grahame—was not to be a one-off act, but to unleash some sounds unheard of prior. Said Martyn Young to *SPIN*'s David Toop: "We knew what we didn't want to end up with, but we didn't know what we would end up with. We didn't want it to end up sounding polished; we wanted it to sound . . . primitive."

By the time it became clear that the union was not working, "Pump Up the Volume" was nearly created. During the final moments, London DJ/journalist Dave Dorrel and scratch mixer Chris "C. J." Mackintosh were enlisted to provide scratching and cutting.

"Volume" became a sensation, but friction had arose during the recording and intensified once there was monies to divvy up. Matters were further complicated when All Boys Music Ltd. sued M/A/R/R/S and their record company claiming that "Volume" infringed on their copyright for a tune called "Roadblock."

Representatives for Alex and Rudi notified Martyn Young and Dave Dorrell—who insisted on reusing the M/A/R/R/S name with new product and no Kane brothers involvement—that they wanted 1 million pounds to be paid them for said purposes. "Basically, they can f**k off and die." was the response of Colourbox's manager, reported *Melody Maker*. "We're not gonna pay them.."

Trivia note: Before the group vanished, Martyn was asked by *SPIN* of the significance of their name. "We wanted to have a feeling of total anonymity," said Young. Most likely, the M stands for Martyn, S for Steve; with A and R for Alex and Rudi, respectively.

PATRICK SWAYZE, FEATURING WENDY FRASER
SHE'S LIKE THE WIND
(Patrick Swayze, Stacy Widelitz)
RCA 5563
No. 3 *February 27, 1988*

He was born in Houston, Texas, on August 18, 1954, to noted choreographer Patsy Swayze. He attended Harkness Ballet School, the Joffrey Ballet School, and San Jacinto College. Patrick got his start as a dancer in "Disney on Parade." After appearing in the Broadway production of *Grease*, he made his film debut in the little-noted *Skatetown U.S.A.* (1979). He starred in such screen successes as *Red Dawn* (1984), opposite Jennifer Grey as dance instructor "Johnny Castle" in *Dirty Dancing* (1987), and *Ghost* (1990). "She's Like the Wind," a duet with Wendy Frazer, represented Patrick's virgin voyage into rock/pop singing—a most successful debut. The soundtrack to *Dirty Dancing* went on to top the *Billboard* album charts for nine weeks, selling near 5 million copies; therein surpassing the chart achievements of such best-sellers as *Beverly Hill Cops*, *Flashdance*, and *Top Gun*.

No one could have figured that a '60s flashback flick, a coming-of-age drama set in the Catskills with greenery, dancing, and passion could possibly have been so well received. With their sounds present on the soundtrack, the CONTOURS and Bill Medley—the deep-voiced half of the Righteous Brothers—returned to the nation's Top 10 for the first time in three decades. Medley and dueting partner Jennifer Warnes topped the Top 40 with "(I've Had) The Time of My Life." Swayze told *Rolling Stone*'s Adam White: "If you'd have asked me about the movie before it was out, I'd have said, 'Who knows?' They certainly didn't reinvent the wheel."

Patrick has had his movie flops as well. *Road House* (1989), which featured some cameo footage of JEFF HEALEY, returned the now romantic lead to singing on screen. No further hits have resulted.

Trivia note: The flipside of Swayze's lone-moment was not another Swayze swinger, but a soundtrack cut—a reissue of MAURICE WILLIAMS & THE ZODIACS' 1960 chart-topper, "Stay."

SCARLETT & BLACK
YOU DON'T KNOW
(Robin Hild)
Virgin 99405
No. 20 *April 16, 1988*

Scarlett & Black were the British duo of Robin Hild and Sue West. Both songwriters and sometime session singers, they met in 1983 in the studio where psyche-delic, but pop-punchy Doctor & The Medics were recording their ARTHUR BROWN-stylized meanderings. Sue provided some of the act's back-up vocals; Robin, a keyboardist with his own mini-studio, had recorded some of the group's early demos. The Medics—fronted by a 6' 5" "real and live" physician named Clive Jackson—made strained and strange videos and a number one homeland charting with their remake of NORMAN GREENBAUM's "Spirit in the Sky."

"You Don't Know" was their first singles extraction from their debut and eponymously titled album for Virgin. The disk was produced by keyboardist/producer Paul Fox and featured the vocal assistance of ex-Go Go JANE WIEDLIN and on one cut, "Let Yourself Go," Yes' Chris Squire. Nothing further has placed on any of *Billboard*'s charts.

SUAVE
MY GIRL
(William Robinson, Ronald White)
Capitol 44124
No. 20 *May 14, 1988*

His dad was a member of GQ, a funky dance unit that had a major '70s hit with "Disco Nights (Rock-Freak)"; friends were members of the chart-swarming New Edition, but Suave (b. Waymond Anderson, Jr., Reno, NV, Feb. 22, 1966) had little interest in music and no musical training prior to his initial recording and lone pop hit, "My Girl."

"When [New Edition] moved out here to Los Angeles, we were reunited and started to play ball again together," Suave explained to *Cashbox*'s Bob Long and Brad Buchsbaum. "They began to talk about the music business, and I started to get more interested in it. I went home one day and told my father that I wanted to start singing and it was at the same time that New Edition was looking for a new member. I thought about joining a group situation, but I knew how my father's group broke up, and how many vocal groups get popular and then fall apart. I didn't want to get into a situation like that. So I chose to go the solo route."

Suave and cousin Dwayne Omarr began collaborating on a few songs that they then shopped around to the labels. "I started to put the demos together and the president of Capitol Records heard them. I wound up getting a 10 album deal, got my own production company, and my first number one record under my belt."

That "number one" disk (actually #3 on the R & B listings; #20 pop) was a remake of the Temptations' perennial "My Girl." Suave's reasons for reworking the dusty: "I dedicated 'My Girl' to my uncle. When I was little my father was always gone on the road, so my uncle raised me. He used to tell me stories about listening to 'My Girl' when he was in Vietnam, and he would play that song over and over again when I was growing up. When he passed away last year [1987] . . . the first thing I thought about was the song. They even played it at his funeral."

Despondent over the current music scene with its mechanical beats overlaid with thrown together words, Suave spoke of a mission. "My goal is to become the next TEDDY [PENDERGRASS] or Marvin [Gaye]. I admire people like that, and I try to rework those same ideas and feelings into my music."

"Shake Your Body," his immediate follow-up single, charted moderately well on the R & B listings (R&B #22, 1988). His debut album, *I'm Your Playmate*, gathered fans for soon to follow tours with ROGER (Troutman), GUY and Troop.

Suddenly, Suave's future plans were shaken to the core when in 1988, he was diagnosed with lung cancer. After two-plus years, *To the Maxx*, Suave's second album appeared. Involved were members of PORTRAIT, an act signed to Suave's company, First Productions. "It took the belief of everyone who was involved in making *To the Maxx*," said Suave in a bio handout from his label. "The whole concept of the title song is that I'm going to go all the way. I'm going to take my life to the maxx. I'm not going to give up."

The Gap Band's Charlie Wilson dueted with Suave on a core track, "Zero." Said Suave: "I was feeling down about myself, but Charlie put it to me straight when he said 'When you let your dreams die, you die.'"

Nothing further from Suave has yet to reach *Billboard*'s Hot 100.

DEELE
TWO OCCASIONS
(Darnell Bristol, Kenneth Edmonds)
Solar 70015
No. 10 *May 21, 1988*

They were from Cincinnati, met in high school, and quietly formed in 1981. Deele included Darnell "Dee" Bristol (vocals), Carlos "Satin" Greene (vocals), Kevin "Kayo" Roberson (bass), and Kenneth "Babyface" Edmonds (b. Apr. 10, 1959, vocals, guitar, keyboards),

SUAVE

formerly of Manchild; brother to After 7's Kevon and Melvin Edmonds, and Antonio "L.A." Marquis Reid (drums. percussion), the son of Herb Rooney and Brenda Reid of THE EXCITERS; cousin to After 7's Keith Mitchell and husband to Pebbles. Deele signed with Solar in 1983, recording *Street Beat*—produced by Reggie Calloway, of CALLOWAY, earlier MIDNIGHT STAR—as their debut. Two further LPs were released; most successfully the last, *Eyes of a Stranger*.

Before the act's break-up in the late '80s, Deele had eight R & B chartings; notably, "Body Talk" (#3, 1983), "Just My Luck" (#25, 1984), "Material Thangz" (#14, 1985), "Two Occasions" (#4, 1987) and "Shoot 'em Up Movies" (#10, 1988).

In 1988, the careers of Los Angeles and Babyface took off; the latter so nicknamed by FUNKADELIC wonder Bootsy Collins. The duo most successfully wrote and produced the Whispers' monster hit "Rock Steady," followed quickly by work on Bobby Brown's second album, *Don't Be Cruel*. Thereafter, the two were on constant call to produce/compose for the likes of Paula Abdul, the Boys, Boyz II Men, Tevin Campbell, Mariah Carey, Eric Clapton, Sheena Easton, Johnny Gill, Whitney Houston, the Jacksons, Midnight Star, TLC, Perri, Karyn White, and Los Angeles. Reid's spouse the multi-hit-maker Pebbles (a.k.a. Perri Aletta McKissack); known across the boards for "Girlfriend" . . . and even the "King of Pop," Michael Jackson.

Through all this, Babyface started an extremely successful solo career. By the mid-'90s, 20 disks had made their way onto and up the R & B listings; "It's No Crime" and "Tender Love," both checked in to the number one position. His voice has been heard on charting recordings by After 7, Toni Braxton, El DeBarge, Jon B., in duet with Lisa Stansfield, and on recordings included in Eddie Murphy's *Boomerang* (1992) and Macaulay Culkin's *The Pagemaster* (1994). Astonishing . . . it's a chick flick, but the bulk of the 16 songs present on the successful *Waiting to Exhale* soundtrack (1996) were written by none other than. . . Babyface; sales have passed 7 million copies.

In 1991, L.A. and Babyface started their own label, LaFace—affiliated with Arista—soon signed Jermaine Jackson and hit paydirt with Toni Braxton on her self-titled debut album in 1993.

Greg Knot of the *Chicago Tribune* claims that by January, 1997, Babyface had "written, produced, or performed on 111 Top 10 R & B hits, including 16 number one singles, and produced sales of 26 million singles and 72 million albums. . . ."

At press time, L.A. and Babyface continue to run the "Southern Motown," their LeFace label, but have shut down "one of the hippest and most successful production teams in the business."

MIDNIGHT OIL
BEDS ARE BURNING
(Midnight Oil)
Columbia 07433
No. 17 *July 2, 1988*

"We're the rogue dingo of Australian music," said Peter Garrett to *Music Express*. "We refuse to kow tow to peer pressure, fashion, and consensus. While knowing there is a built-in contradiction, we're still anti the commercialization of music. People can exploit that, and they will. Fine, that's the way we are."

It was no longer the "Summer of Love," but Midnight Oil persisted in behaving as a social force, a principled force—with songs that cried out against war, oppression, environment abuse and gave voice to the Koori (Australian aborigine) causes; with concerts for Greenpeace, the Tibet Council, Save the Whales, the anti-uranium mining movement . . .

They were formed originally as Farm, in Sydney, New South Wales, Australia, in 1975. From the onset, this was a band acting as if they had a mission. Said Rob Hirst (bass) to *Music Express*, "Jim [Moginie (guitar, keyboards)] and I and Andrew ["Bear"] Jones, who was our first bass player, organized tours on our holidays, while we were still in school. We played to surf audiences up and down the New South Wales coast; I used to book the venues myself and put the posters up. Eventually, I realized that I really didn't want to drum and sing so we advertised and Peter [Garrett, a bald-headed law graduate] joined. 'Round about that time [1977], Martin [Rotsey (lead guitar)] joined as well so the line-up's been the same since then except for the two changes on bass [added in 1980, Peter Gilfford; replaced 1990, Dwayne "Bones" Hillman]."

By 1977, they were Midnight Oil. Soon popular in concert, the band found itself in disfavor with local record companies. In 1978, they formed their own Powerworks label, issuing their debut self-titled album. With independent tours and political activities continuing, and a positive public response, their second album, *Head Injuries*, sold gold.

In 1981, they signed with Columbia Records. *10, 9, 8, 7, 6, 5, 4, 3, 2, 1*, their major label debut, made Midnight Oil homeland superstars; remaining on the Australian charts for a solid two years. The album featured songs about the environment and messages of anti-war, anti-nuclear, anti-establishment. They were becoming notorious for insisting on total control of their presentation, from record production to press releases, photos. Representing the Nuclear Disarmament Party, Garrett ran for a seat in the Australian Parliament in 1984; almost winning.

With the release of *Red Sails in the Sunset*, Midnight Oil toured Europe and the United States for the first time. *Rolling Stone* magazine anointed the album, "One of the best releases in 1985." *Diesel and Dust*, issued in 1987, and including "Beds Are Burning," became the act's highest charting disk in the United States.

The band was astonished. *SPIN*'s Toby Creswell asked Hirst why this response was so unexpected, "Because a song about an aboriginal land rights that features a tall, gangling bald bloke with a band that refuses to do X thousand TV shows and who have put everybody in the record company off side at some stage over the past tour or five years ended up with a hit single. I just didn't expect it."

Midnight Oil have continued into the '90s. *Blue Sky Mining*, followed its predecessor into the upper reaches of the *Billboard* album charts. Follow-up recordings have fared less well.

In 1990, the band-with-purpose staged a concert outside the Exxon Building in Manhattan to protest their anger at the Exxon *Valdez* oil spill in Alaska.

AL B. SURE!
NITE AND DAY
(Al B. Sure!, Kyle West)
Warner 28192
No. 7 *July 16, 1988*

"I think Al is what you call a born star," said DJ Eddie F., a childhood friend of Al B. Sure!, to authors Adam White and Fred Bronson. "He has that aura around him like he wants to be a celebrity or the center of attention. He has that charisma."

Born Al Brown, Jr., in Boston, sometime in 1971, Al B. Sure! cared little for music until just prior to his flash of pop fame—after all there was baseball, basketball, and football to occupy his time. "My whole family is into music," he told *Billboard*'s Bill Coleman. Everyone either plays piano or does something so I guess some of it rubbed off."

When 10 years old, Al lived in New Jersey and had a friend whose mother knew songwriting legend and half of the RAINDROPS, Ellie Greenwich. "Ellie heard us all singing one day and was in the middle of doing a soundtrack for the 'Sesame Street' parks," explained Al to White and Bronson, authors of *The Billboard Book of Number One Rhythm & Blues Hits*. "She had us sing on it and do the video, which I never got to see. I would love to see it."

While Al never forgot that moment in a real life recording studio, his interests were elsewhere. He became a star quarterback with his school, Mount Vernon High. By college, however, the turnabout happened and Al passed on a football scholarship to the University of Iowa to attend the Center for the Media Arts in New York City.

Prior to the career move, Al and cousin Kyle West found spare time to try and make music. "I would go over to his house after school, and we had my uncle Nick's organ in the basement and a little tape recorder," Al told White and Bronson. "We'd write and record our little songs. but it was just for fun."

Once in New York, Al met up with old buddy Eddie F., then a member of the rap act Heavy D and the Boys, who introduced him to their manager a former accountant at a gospel radio station, Andre Harrell. Heavy D. got signed to MCA. "I love popular music, but there's something I see that a lot of people are missing," Al told Coleman. "I can't name it but it's not there —and you can feel it in my music."

Said co-writer/producer Kyle West: "I'm still amazed at what he hears [with] a nontrained ear. He's able to produce things vocally that are amazing to me."

JANE WIEDLIN
RUSH HOUR
(Jane Wiedlin, Refelson)
EMI-Manhattan 50118
No. 9 *July 30, 1988*

"I didn't worry about the fact that we were girls and that we couldn't play," said Jane Wiedlin to author Irwin Stambler. "No one seemed very good either at the time. The important thing was just to get involved."

Jane Drano—as she initially billed herself—got her big break in an exceedingly inept novelty act that surprised all and tightened into the top all-girl rock band in the land. As rhythm guitarist with the California-based Go-Go's, Wiedlin (b. Oconomowoc, WI, May 20, 1958), Charlotte Cafferty, Belinda Carlisle, Kathy Valentine, and Gina Schock proved that fe-type-males could rock pop with the best. For three years (1982-1985), three albums (*Beauty and the Beast, Vacation, Talk Show*), three Top 15 singles ("We Got the Beat," "Vacation," "Head Over Heels"), Wiedlin and crew were at the center of rock music.

"I never thought about the future," said Jane to *Cashbox*'s Tom DeSabia. "Obviously I knew that there had to be life beyond the Go-Go's, but I didn't know what that life would be. I never, ever dreamed that I would be as happy as I am now. . . ."

Jane attended Taft High School in the San Fernando Valley community of Woodlawn Hills. After months with an unnamed punk band as Jane Drano, she enrolled in the Los Angeles Trade-Technical School, to study fashion.

"The ironic thing is that fashion got me back into music," she told the *Los Angeles Times*. "Through fashion magazines, I got interested in some of the punk things. I started going down to the Masque [an early

Hollywood punk palace] to check it out. Finally, some of us decided to start our own band"—the Go-Go's.

In 1983, two years before her departure from the Go-Go's, Wiedlin was featured as half of a one-off pairing with Sparks, a cult glam-rocker band with numerous British hits. "Cool Places" (#49, 1983), the Wiedlin-Sparks dueting almost relieved the latter of their no-hit status in the States. Jane is mum as to whether the sideline venture with Sparks was the cause, but early in 1985 Jane was the first of the Go-Go's to go. Months later, Carlisle departed and the Go-Go's became history.

I.R.S. Records issued Jane's self-titled solo debut album, late in 1985. Sales were disappointing, though the initial single—"Blue Tears" (#77, 1985)—did make the Hot 100. Jane now turned her attentions elsewhere.

"I've been a supporter of various animal rights groups for years," she told *Cashbox*. "After I left the Go-Go's, I decided to become more active and not just be a letter writer or a check writer—although that is important too—and I started going to demonstrations, and then I ended up getting arrested."

In 1987, Jane spent five days in jail for her participation in a demonstration. "Wearing fur coats is a matter of fashion, and I don't think anything deserves to die for fashion," she told the *Music Express*. "Humans don't have the right to exploit animals!"

"Rush Hour" (#9, 1988) and its immediate follow-up, "Inside a Dream" (#57, 1988), were extracts from her second album, *Fur*, a project for EMI-Manhattan that features Wiedlin and a baby bunny on the cover and a title take that deals with her continuing interests in animal rights.

Aside from the music and the rights movement, Jane has appeared in a number of flicks, including *Clue* (1985), starring Tim Curry and Christopher Lloyd; *Star Trek IV: The Voyage Home* (1986); and *Bill and Ted's Excellent Adventure (1989)*.

BOBBY MCFERRIN
DON'T WORRY BE HAPPY
(Bobby McFerrin)
EMI-Manhattan 50146
No. 1 *September 24, 1988*

"I consider myself a healer, using magic as a potent force to bring people joy," said Bobby to *People*'s Dianna Waggoner."

Bobby McFerrin (b. Mar. 11, 1950, New York City) was born to a musical family; both parents, Robert and Sara, were opera singers. His father sang leading roles with the New England Opera Company, the New York City Opera, the National Negro Opera Company, and in the mid-'50s became the first black man signed to a contract by the Metropolitan Opera. Robert was used

to dub Porky's singing voice for Sidney Poitier in the film version of George Gershwin's *Porky and Bess* (1959). Sara, a classically trained soprano, has been a voice teacher and chaired the vocal department of Fullerton Community College.

When six, Bobby began studying music theory at Julliard's preparatory division for the musically gifted. He formed the Bobby Mack Jazz Quintet in his senior year of high school. For a while, he was enrolled at the California State University as a music major; later Cerritos College, though he dropped out to play keyboards with various Top 40 bands and the Ice Follies.

Bobby married Debbie Lynn Green and moved to Salt Lake City, where for years he eked out a living playing piano bars. Then in 1977, Bobby had a life-altering moment, "I was feeling pretty burned out and wondering what my direction in life was going to be, when an inner voice told me I should sing," said McFerrin to *Rolling Stone*'s Francis Davis.

While touring with jazz legend, scat master Jon Hendricks, Bobby was spotted by BILL COSBY. Cosby recommended McFerrin for some nightclub gigs and a spot on the 1980 Playboy Jazz Festival; later asking him to sing the theme for "The Cosby Show." After a slot on the 1981 Kool Jazz concert tour, Bobby got to record his first album, a package that included only one unaccompanied tune, "Hallucinations."

Beginning in mid-'83, despite warnings that he might be seen as a novelty act, McFerrin started performing without accompaniment. Several clubs canceled Bobby's bookings when he went solo. One of McFerrin's West Germany shows was taped live in 1984 and released later that year as *The Voice*. "I knew that once I made a solo voice album, people would notice me," he said to Davis. *Downbeat* named him "Best Male Jazz Vocalist," an accolade that would be his for the next three years.

Spontaneous Invention was a collection of solo studies and improvised duets with Herbie Hancock, Wayne Shorter, and actor Robin Williams. McFerrin won his first two Grammy Awards, "Best Male Jazz Vocalist," and "Best Arranger," for his work on Manhattan Transfer's cut "Another Night in Tunisia."

"Because what I do is spontaneous," said McFerrin to *The New York Times*' Stephen Holden, "I've been called a jazz singer, but increasingly I've found the label restricting. I see myself as a performance artist. Although my work includes jazz and pop singing, it also involves mime, dance, storytelling, and creative work with the audience."

For mainstream pop and rock audiences, *Simple Pleasures* proved Bobby's break-through. The album featured his stylized renderings of the Beatles' "Drive My Car," Cream's "Sunshine of My Love" and his own "Don't Worry, Be Happy."

"It was just something that I started improvising on probably four or five years ago," said McFerrin to Dick Clark on "Countdown America," of his chart-happening. "And I didn't have any lyrics—I just had the phrase 'Don't Worry, Be Happy.' Occasionally I would sing it in clubs and make up a lyric as I went along."

Contributing to the number's stardom was its inclusion in the soundtrack of Tom Cruise's *Cocktail* (1988). Soon there were three more Grammys: "Best Male Pop Vocalist," "Best Song," "Record of the Year." To Bobby's dismay and without permission, the tune was used in George Bush's reelection committee.

"I think it was so popular because it went to the spirit," said Bobby at the 1989 Grammy Awards ceremony. "I think, given the mood at the time, it was such that people wanted something uplifting and jovial and funny." Soon after, Bobby McFerrin announced that he would not perform the song again.

Weary of touring, he took an indefinite leave. Bobby has returned to projects that he considers of merit. He has composed and performed selections from Rudyard Kipling's *Just So Serious*, for cable TV; created the score for the NBC-TV series "The Bronx Zoo," and appeared in commercials for Ocean Spray fruit juices and Levi's jeans.

"McFerrin's true art is his ability to make us all kids again," wrote *New York Newsday*'s Stephen Williams.

BOBBY MCFERRIN

GIANT STEP
ANOTHER LOVER
(Col Campsie, George McFarlane, Gardner Cole)
A & M 1226
No. 13 *November 12, 1988*

Col Campsie (vocals, guitar) and George McFarlane (guitar, bass, synthesizer) were masters of the name game. The U.K.-based studio duo got their start in the late '70s as members of Grand Hotel; a momentary act recorded by Columbia Records. By the early '80s, Col and George were Quick, club favorites with a few homeland chartings; most particularly, "Zulu" and "Rhythm of the Jungle." Two albums were issued—*Fascinating Rhythm* and *Wah Wah*. The latter contained the duo's last U.K. charting, "Down the Wire." Before shedding their persona to become Giant Step, Col and George wrote for Chaka Khan, and produced Blue Zoo, Haywoode, Second Image, and some tracks for George Michael bassist, DEON ESTUS.

In 1988, for reasons unknown, the U.K. twosome name changed to Giant Step. *The Book of Pride*, a debut album for A & M, contained their Stateside One-Hit as well as tracks produced by Bryan Loren (known for his work with Sting, Shanice Wilson) and Gardner Cole (Madonna, Brenda Russell). Their immediate follow-up, "Into You," charted (#58, 1989) and then Col and George were apparently off to seek further success under yet some other *nom de plum*.

WHEN IN ROME
THE PROMISE
(Clive Farrington, Michael Floreale, Andrew Mann)
Virgin 99323
No. 11 *December 10, 1988*

Initially, Clive Farrington (bass), Michael Floreale (keyboards), Andrew Mann (vocals), and sometime fashion designer Corinne Drewery (vocals) were the locally active Manchester, England-based Beau Leisure. Auxiliary members went and came and as all things are apt to do—Leisure turned to hard work; splintering in 1984, with Corinne joining Andrew Connell and Martin Jackson to become jazzy-pop Top 40 faves Swing Out Sister, known for "Breakout" and "Twilight World." Clive, Mick, and Andy clung together, renamed When in Rome.

Signed by Virgin U.K. subsidiary 10 Records, producers Ben Rogan (who had worked with Sade) and Richard Burgess (Five Star, LIVING IN A BOX) took special interest in the trio's "Promise," issued initially as a 12" dance disk. Because of immediate success topping *Billboard*'s "Dance Club Play" chart, Virgin ordered an album. "The Promise," remixed, was the initial single

from their debut and self-titled LP. Months later the trio touched *Billboard*'s pop chart's lower reaches for the last time with "Heaven Knows" (#95, 1990).

BOYS CLUB
I REMEMBER HOLDING YOU
(Joe Pasquale)
MCA 53430
No. 8 *January 14, 1989*

Joe Pasquale and Gene Hunt were buddies; Minneapolis raised. Their "pretty boy" pop act proved an ultra-brief affair. For mere months, teen mags ran their flashy photos with large-print, 100-word, no-depth interviews of the variety: Joe likes his dog Mike; Gene loves water-play and to watch girls. What's there to know? These boys were on a rocket to oblivion.

Gene apparently had a real history to tell. His real name is Eugene Wolfgramm. The name change to Gene Hunt came with the formation of Boys Club in 1988 seemingly as an effort—at least initially—to break from his popular past as a talented tyke. For at least a half decade, he had been a member of the Jets, a goody-goody family-only group, composed of Gene and 7 of his 14 siblings—Gene, Eddie, Elizabeth, Haini, Kathi, LeRoy, Monica, and Rudy—all multi-instrumentalists, ranging in age (in 1988) from 14 to 23. Together they rocked the charts with near-number one hits in the Ollie Brown (of OLLIE & JERRY notoriety) produced "Crush on You" (#3, 1986), "You Got It All" (#3, 1986), "Cross My Broken Heart" (#7, 1987), "Rocket 2 U" (#6, 1988), and "Make It Real" (#4, 1988).

The Wolfgramm family originated on the South Pacific island of Tonga. In the early '60s, they moved first to Salt Lake City, then Minneapolis. LeRoy, the oldest boy, took to music like a bee to honey, and joined his uncles in a club act when he was 11. In 1978, LeRoy and several sisters began performing in Polynesian nightspots as Quasar. Six years later the evolving act was spotted by Don Powell, once a manager for the Jackson Five. Noticing a similar marketable commodity, Powell signed the act up, eventually changing its name to the Jets and securing a contract with MCA.

Gene had left the Jets in 1988 just as the Jets' hit-streak was winding down to zip. "I Remember Holding You," their initial disk, supplied the doomed duo with a splash of fame. "The Same Love" (#87, 1989), their second and last hit, reached *Billboard*'s Hot 100 one year to the month after the Boys Club's only charting. The whereabouts of Gene Wolfgramm/Hunt and tunesmith Joe Pasquale are unknown.

SHERIFF
WHEN I'M WITH YOU
(Arnold Lanni)
Capitol 44302
No. 61 *May 14, 1983*
No. 1 *February 14, 1989*

Wolf Hassel (bass) and Arnold Lanni (guitar) were stranded in the Canadian Rockies by an avalanche . . . miles away Freddie Curci (lead singer) and Steve DeMarchi (guitar) delivered packages to make a living. Rob Elliot (drums) was cooling out, counting fingers, looking out the window, waiting on phone calls—and there it was. Their "When I'm With You" was number one on the *Billboard* pop charts.

How unlikely, how fictional—a number one record and the group, Sheriff, is a defunct band, with no record label, no management—and the disk is a dusty, forgotten seven-year-old tune.

The story goes . . . KZZP in Phoenix boisterously prided itself on reviving UB40's "Red Red Wine," rendering the one-time non-hit a current hit. Jay Taylor, the Music Director at KLUC in Las Vegas, KZZP's sister station, decided to see if he could spark some interest in what he considered a deserving oldie. "I always thought it should have been a big hit," Taylor told *Music Express*'s Keith Sharp. "When we put it back on the air the response was tremendous.

"Record companies love that when we do that. We really get them scrambling." And scramble Capitol did. It seemed the label had given up on Sheriff; dropping the group from the roster in 1985. Lanni and Hassel had formed another act, Frozen Ghost, a marginally happening act with Atlantic Records. Curci and DeMarchi were delivering and hoping to record their own album. Elliot was looking. . . .

The group's history began in the late '70s; with the line-up solidifying in 1979 with the addition of Lanni. By the early '80s, the band had met a Toronto couple, John and Helen Victor, who were starting up Reel Records. Their producer Stacey Heydon happened on to Sheriff. Capitol of Canada was sufficiently impressed with the resulting sides to issued a Sheriff LP and three singles; the last, "When I'm With You." The latter made mid-range on *Billboard*'s listing (#61) in May 1983 and then disappeared . . . as the group itself.

All had lost the faith. Musical differences . . . no money, no hits, their United States agent died of a heart attack . . . their manager left them, their record company dropped them.

Old wounds heal slowly. Curci, DeMarchi, and Elliot were eager to reform, tour, and carry on as Sheriff; not so with Hassel and Lanni who were working hard on getting their second Frozen Ghost record heard; their "Should I See" (#69) had charted moder-

ately in May '87. "It died in 1985," said Lanni. "Now all of a sudden, people want to exploit Sheriff. I could see us getting together for a one-off charity gig or something, but to me it's history, and I'd rather see it dead."

Curci, DeMarchi, and Elliot considered themselves 3/5 owners to the name and sought legal action, but to no avail. In 1990, Curci and DeMarchi along with three original members of Heart—Mike Derosier (drums), Roger Fisher (guitar), and Steve Fossen (bass)—signed with EMI as Alias. Both their "More Than I Can Say" and "Waiting for Love" have made *Billboard*'s Top 20.

EDIE BRICKELL & THE NEW BOHEMIANS
WHAT I AM
(Edie Brickell, Kenny Withrow)
Geffen 27696
No. 7 *March 4, 1989*

"She really runs away from the spotlight," said Tom Zutaut, Geffen Records A & R man, talking of Edie to Steve Pond, *Rolling Stone*. "She really wants to be part of the band, she doesn't want to be a star, and she makes her music because it's in her and it needs to come out . . . I don't think she could handle the attention by herself, without the band."

The tale is told that Edie (b. Mar. 10, 1966, Oak Cliff, TX)—whose mother is legally named Larry and whose father is a professional bowler—was "discovered" one night while working the redeye shift as a waitress. She was a college kid, attending Southern Methodist University, working to make ends meet when a shot of Jack Daniels kicked in and the chnace to jump up on the stage to ad-lib some lyrics with the New Bohemians happened. As legends have it, Brickell was immediately asked to join the band.

"There's really nothing to say about me, or the band, that's that interesting," said Edie to Pond. "We're just a bunch of normal kids who lucked into being a successful band . . . We shot rubber bands at the stars, and they hit."

"We were in the right place at the right time," explained Edie to Marie Woodhall of *Music Paper*. "This girl from MCA came into town. She just happened to come to this club that we were playing in. We hadn't sent out any tapes or anything. At that point, we were so inexperienced and disorganized; we hadn't done anything. She saw us play, and she wanted to sign us immediately, but MCA didn't like us. They thought we were unmarketable. Luckily, she knew people at Geffen. She told them about us, and they came to see us and they signed us."

Within months, Geffen Records had its folkie-jazzy-reggae product on the street. *Shoot Rubber Bands at the*

Moon and the extracted "What I Am" shocked all when they clicked.

"I didn't expect this success with this record," said Edie to Pond. "I thought we would be a band that would grow, like R.E.M. or Talking Heads. And that's what I really wanted, to be honest, because that's more real to me. Coming right out of the chute, bam, I feel like a joke or something."

"I don't want to get caught up in the whole music business," said Edie to *Creem*'s Bhargavi C. Mandava. "I just want to remain a songwriter. I realize where I've come from, and I don't want to be blinded by a lot of frosting: fame, good fortune, and that kind of stuff."

Geffen dropped the ball right from the start—figuring that Edie was the group; she penned the lyrics, co-wrote the tunes, and was the visual focal point. Geffen forced the New Bohemians—guitarist Wes Burt-Martin (b. May 28, 1964), drummer Matt Chamberlain (b. Apr. 17, 1967), bassist Brad Hauser (b. Sept. 7, 1960), and guitarist Kenny Withrow (b. Apr. 13, 1965)—to give Edie top billing, a maneuver that didn't sit well with any member, including Edie.

By the second album, the situation definitely was not right. *Ghost of a Dog* contained no hits and charted only moderately on *Billboard*'s Album listings.

"I'm wondering how many emotions there are in between all the extreme ones, and how we can get at them and express them," said Edie to Mark David Hendrickson of *Music Paper*. "That's what I'm interested in exploring in my songs."

In 1992, Edie married Paul Simon. In 1995, she released her solo effort, *Picture Perfect Morning*. Produced by her husband and Simon & Garfunkel producer Roy Halee, the acclaimed package featured support work from Dr. JOHN, the Dixie Cups, Art Neville, and Barry White.

KON KAN
BEG YOUR PARDON
(Barry Harris, Mark Goldenberg)
Atlantic 88969
No. 15 *March 11, 1989*

Kon Kan, it's surmised, is a derivative of the opposite of Can Con, short for Canadian Continent. As an act, Kon Kan was ultra-brief in its existence. It was a Canadian "project," born of a meeting in Toronto, in the mid-'80s of Barry Harris (piano, guitar) and Kevin Wayne (vocals). Little is known of the pairing or their individual pasts; even their former label officials claim ignorance.

A listen to "Beg Your Pardon," their historic trace, reveals the inclusion of several lines from LYNN ANDERSON's "Rose Garden." Nine months later, they returned to *Billboard*'s Hot 100 with "Puss N' Boots/These Boots

(Are Made for Walkin')" (#58, 1989), which made use of some clips from Led Zeppelin's "Immigrants Song" and Nancy Sinatra's "Boots" classic. What it all means is beyond research. Both men are musical absentees, no longer available for interrogation.

DEON ESTUS WITH GEORGE MICHAEL
HEAVEN HELP ME
(George Michael, Deon Estus)
Mika 871538
No. 5 *April 29, 1989*

For years before his moment in the floodlights, Deon was making uncredited hit records for others, as their behind-the-scenes bass man. Born and raised in Detroit, the musical kid dreamed daily of being a Motor City man. "Oh, to be able to touch the strings like James Jameson," the late Motown legendary bass great, he thought. Deon honed his skills and for a time was the bottom man for Brainstorm, known for the R & B hit "Lovin' Is Really My Game" (#14, 1977). After a late '70s tour with the outfit, opening for the Whispers and the Brothers Johnson, Deon became Marvin Gaye's bassist.

"I got this call from Marvin to go to Belgium," Deon told *Music Express*. "So I packed my bags and two hours later I was on a plane, and I've been gone for 10 years." When the tour ended, Estus moved to Dublin, eventually hooking up with U2 and Boomtown Rat Bob Geldof, organizer of Live Aid. Producer Steve Lillywhite connected him with Steve Brown, who had "this young guy George Michael, who's looking for a bass player and someone to write with. So I moved to London."

"Heaven Help Me"—an extract from *Spell*, his debut album, produced by Michael, David Z., and JELLYBEAN—featured pin-up pop idol George Michael on back-up vocals. Via his affiliation with Wham!, Deon had supplied the bass work for Michael's *Faith* package, the 1988 "Album of the Year" Grammy Award winner.

Evasive as to his future, Deon told *Music Express*: "I've always known the things I've wanted to do, and I've always done them. I've been fortunate that way."

SA-FIRE
THINKING OF YOU
(Wilma Cosme, DeSalvo, Steele)
Cutting 872502
No. 12 *May 5, 1989*

Born Wilma Cosme in Puerto Rico, Sa-Fire moved to East Harlem, New York, as a small child. She sang, danced, and entertained family and friends. In 1986, she successfully auditioned for Aldo Marin's Big Apple-based Cutting label. Her first single, "Don't Break My Heart," and its immediate follow-up, "Let Me Be the One," established her as a leading contender in the burgeoning "free-style movement."

She toured with Menudo and exposed her heart of gold via numerous benefit concerts for C.A.R.E., Muscular Dystrophy, and underprivileged children in Latin America; she received an award from the New York City Substance Abuse Anti-Drug Campaign, for her contributions. In 1988, Marin worked up a distribution arrangement with Mercury/PolyGram for Sa-Fire's self-titled debut album and subsequent singles. Success was hers with the first single, "Boy, I've Been Told" (#48, 1988), a solid club smash; followed by "Thinking of You," her lone pop Top 40 connection.

It was with "Thinking of You" that her career began to crumble. "Suddenly," she told *Cashbox*'s Larry Flick, "my eyes began to open. I woke up one day and felt like I was paralyzed, and at the mercy of these men who were out more for themselves than anyone else. I had to get out."

Without blatantly naming names to the press, the Latin diva engaged herself in a protracted legal wrangle with her former management and independent label, Cutting Records, and a bitter divorce from Albert Cabrera. "I made the mistake of not having a lawyer when I first signed with Cutting," she explained to *Rock* magazine. "Ignorance will really hurt you in this business. Don't let your dreams make you blind!"

Asserting her newfound will, she returned in the fall of 1989 as Sa-fire (with the hyphen removed to distinguish herself from what she now called the career's earlier phase) and signed directly to Mercury Records with a remaking of Gloria Gaynor's "I Will Survive" (#53, 1989)—utilized in the flick *She Devil* (1989).

Mercury quickly issued a new album, *I Wasn't Born Yesterday*, containing "I Will Survive" and what would become her final charting, "Make Up My Mind" (#82, 1991)—featuring the vocal support of GEORGE LAMOND and Cynthia (a.k.a. Cynthia Torres, known for her charting duet with Johnny "O," "Dream Boy-Dream Girl"). "I'm a much different person now than I was when my last album came out," Sa-fire said to *Cashbox*. "I feel like I've been to hell and back. I wanted this album to talk about that hell and how I survived." Sales were marginal.

BELLE STARS
IKO IKO
(Joe Jones, Marilyn Jones, Sharon Jones, Jessie Thomas)
No. 14 *May 13, 1989*

They were an all-female self-contained band, born of the new music scene in late '70s England. Initially called the Bodysnatchers, they played "ska" or "two-tone" music and were: Judy Parsons (drums), Miranda Joyce (saxophone), Sarah-Jane Owen (guitar), and "Stella" (b. Stella Barker, rhythm guitar). In 1980, they charted in their homeland on famed punk independent 2 Tone Records with "Lets Do Rock Steady" and "Easy Life."

In April 1981, the four women added three new members, known by first names only—Clare (b. Clare Hirst, saxophone), Jeannie (b. Jennie McKeown, vocals), Lesley (b. Lesley Shone, bass)—signed with Stiff Records and, for undisclosed reasons, renamed themselves the Belle Stars. Numerous Europe-only hits followed: "Sign of the Times," "Sweet Memory," "Indian Summer," "80's Romance," remakes of Shirley Ellis' "The Clapping Song," INEZ FOXX's "Mockingbird," and the Dixie Cups' "Iko Iko."

Between the homeland hits, the Belle Stars toured throughout Europe, often in support of the Beat, the Clash, Elvis Costello, the Police, and the Pretenders. After the dust seemed to have settled on their little-publicized career, a revised rendering of their first—a 1983—U.K. hit, "Iko Iko," was utilized in the Dustin Hoffman-Tom Cruise flick *Rain Man* (1988) and became a major stateside one-off hit. Unfortunately, by this point the Belle Stars were no more.

JIMMY HARNEN WITH SYNCH
WHERE ARE YOU NOW?
(Writer TK?)
TG 68625
No. 77 *March 1, 1986*
No. 10 *June 10, 1989*

It's said that beginning in the early '80s, Synch was a sextet from Wilkes-Barre, Pennsylvania, fronted and founded by lead vocalist Jimmy Harnen. Micki Records issued "Where Are You Now?" by the act—simply billed "Synch"—in the late months of 1984. Sales was such that months later Columbia Records became convinced of this tune's merit; issuing it by mid-'85. After three months on the charts, the highest position it had reached was number 77. Marginal success brought internal disintegration. No longer with a label and no longer together, Synch's dusty began getting airplay three years later. WTG Records reissued the exact recording, billing the act Jimmy Harnen With Synch. Before its demise "Where Are You Now?" remained on *Billboard*'s Hot 100 for six months, winning an accolade of sorts, "the slowest climb of any record into *Billboard*'s Top 10," 28 weeks.

With the belated success of the group's old records, Jimmy attempted to launch his singer career anew. To this day, pop historians are plagued by the questions "Who are Synch?" and "Where Are They Now?"

WATERFRONT
CRY
(Phil Cillia, Chris Duffy)
Polydor 871110
No. 10 *June 17, 1989*

Phil Cillia (guitar) and Chris Duffy (singer) were born and raised in Cardiff, Wales. They met at age 11, attended the same school, and began their friendship creating and selling a music magazine. As teenagers, they took to performing rock'n'roll at dances and holiday concerts as the Official Secrets. Phil and Chris moved to London, where they worked the nightclubs. A demo they created circulated for six months before finding a receptive earring (sic) at U.K. Polydor Records. Initially, Cillia and Duffy were signed as a songwriting duo; that soon changed. With the release of their eponymously titled and entirely self-composed debut album

—and renamed after the Marlon Brando flick, *On the Waterfront* (1954)—a first single was chosen, "Cry." The disk went Top 10 both in the States and abroad. "Nature of Love" (#70, 1989) sold modestly.

The Chris and Phil story, thus far, reads conflict-free. They did this, they did that, and up until their lone moment at the top of the heap all seemed—as presented here and there in the press—ever so effortless and idyllic. Nothing, however, has been heard of or from the British duo since.

JEFF HEALEY BAND
ANGEL EYES
(Jeff Healey)
Arista 9809
No. 5 *September 2, 1989*

"He's the undoubted wick of the guitar flame," wrote *Music Express*; the man to "revolutionize the way the guitar is played," said the late Stevie Ray Vaughn. The "white boy with fire in his fingers . . ." wrote Kerry Doole, *Music Express*. Jeff Healey, age 19, jammed with Albert Collins, then B. B. King; both praised him profusely—the former meeting Healey called "the most thrilling moment in my career." Ultra-impressed, George Harrison, Jeff Lynne, and Dire Straits' Mark Knopfler accompanied the blind guitarist on his second album—a package that much like his debut has sold more than 2 million copies.

"I have no use whatsoever for the job of 'guitar hero.'" said Healey to Jas Obrecht, *Guitar Player*. "That isn't why I play. I do it because I love good music. We're not in it to be stars; we don't crave the praise and fawning. Our aim is to be recognized as a band that can create good music. . . ."

Jeff (b. Mar. 25, 1966, Toronto, Canada) developed eye cancer and lost his sight when he was just a year old. His parents gave him his first instrument, a miniature Sears guitar, when he was three. By 11, he was quite accomplished and turned some of his attention to the trumpet, piano, and drums. At 15, he formed Blue Direction and played small-time gigs in the Toronto region.

"I was always listening to stuff. . . ." he told Doole. "My aunts and uncles grew up in the '30s and '40s, and I was fascinated by their records." Jeff is now a major record collector, with more than 10,000 vintage jazz and pop 78s.

Most notable about Healey is the manner in which he makes his music. He begins by placing his guitar across his lap, much like a lap steel guitar. The tuning is standard as is the use of his right hand which grips a pick. His left hand is the iconoclast; fretting from above, applying pressure to the strings much as a pianist would strike his keys. "I've never tried playing the guitar conventionally," he told *Musician*'s Ted Drozdowski. "I can play a few chords that way, but can't play lead to save my life."

Live Healey is a showman—tossing off speedball runs, plucking and pushing strings with his teeth, and dancing with abandonment.

Shortly after the meeting with Albert Collins, Jeff set about forming the Healey Band with Tom Stephen (b. Feb. 2, 1955, St. John, New Brunswick) and a session bassist, Joe Rockman (b. Jan. 1, 1957, Toronto). A few local singles were issued on their Forte label, before Arista Records signed the act in 1988. *See the Light*, containing "Angel Eyes," was put out the following year.

Before the album was even completed, the Healey band was asked to appear and perform in the PATRICK SWAYZE flick *Roadhouse* (1989).

Though Healey and band continued to record—and aside from album two, the harder-rockin' *Hell to Pay*—none has approached the popularity of their debut album and single.

GRAYSON HUGH
TALK IT OVER
(Grayson Hugh)
RCA 8802
No. 19 *September 9, 1989*

It has been said that the soul man has become a dinosaur. Al Green, Dennis Edwards, and James Brown have left the arena for the gospel, the grave, or jail and nostalgia. Dance and rap have largely rechanneled the raw youthful talent in other directions. . . . And then along came this white guy from Hartford, Connecticut.

When 31-year-old Grayson Hugh first appeared via a debut album—*Blind to Reason*— and "Talk It Over, a major mover in 1989, his label and the pop press presented the lad as the genre's savior. Grayson, shunning the label of "blue-eyed soul man number one," modestly referred to his offerings as "poetry with an attitude." That label I can live with, he told *Musician*'s Leonard Pitts, Jr.: "My music's loud, and it's a little audacious, and it's moody, and it's in the setting of a band playing live. It's not just a beat with empty words."

Where did this soul savior come from? Little was asked of him, and even less was learned. The gravel-voiced one admitted to savoring dusty disks by Sam Cooke, Soloman Burke, and the rest. He admitted to audaciously applying for a job—when in his early 20s—as pianist at a little black church. "Y'know, he said, "the first few times [I played] people were a little amazed to see me, being the only white and really young. But after two or three Sundays, I remember this woman, the mother of one of the singers, got up and just said, in the middle of the service, 'I know this boy is doing something a little different, but he sounds okay with me.'"

Nine months later, he was fired. "They really wanted an all-black church," said Grayson.

The immediate follow-up, "Bring It All Back (#89, 1989), charted fair. "How 'Bout Us" (#67, 1990), a duet with Betty Wright, did likewise; though it proved a moderate R & B hit (#30).

Hugh did something a bit different, but it sounded okay . . . for a moment.

JIVE BUNNY AND THE MIXMASTERS
SWING THE MOOD
(Garland, Razaf, Sigmond, Gray)
Music Factory 99140
No. 11 *November 25, 1989*

"Less a group than a marketing concept, Jive Bunny is a consortium of British DJs bent on turning cheap nostalgia into big bucks," wrote *Rolling Stone*'s music critic J. D. Considine. The magazine described "Swing the Mood" as "indescribably annoying."

Club DJ and ex-miner from Norway Les Hemstock and mixer and former electric store owner Johnny and son Andy Pickles, from Yorkshire, England, scored big with the concept, securing an unprecedented three number one U.K. hits on the BBC in less than five months. The idea behind "Swing the Mood," "That's What I Like," "Let's Party," and the rest: provide a disco drone filled with snippets of hit records from the '50s, '60s, and '70s. Stateside consumers went for the gimmick but once—"Swing the Mood," a electronically collaged mess of Glenn Miller's "In the Mood," Eddie Cochran's "C'mon Everybody," Chubby Checker's "Let's Twist Again," and some smidges of Bill Haley and Elvis nuggets.

Eight years prior Holland mastermind/producer and one-time Golden Earrings member Jaap Eggermont constructed Stars on 45. The idea was to assemble in a studio a cast of sound-alikes to impersonate noted rock'n'rollers on a medley of their hits. The concoction worked well worldwide; a trilogy of "Stars on 45" medleys went Top 10 in the U.K. Jive Bunny and his cohorts achieved the same effect, without even going through the hassle of hiring a bunch of wanna-bes (with the exception of Elvis, who proved to be a legitimate impostor).

Sales in the United States of the immediate follow-up, "That's What I Like," were only moderate (#69, 1990). Jive and his guys returned to the tried and true—Haley, Cochran, and even reused Chubby's "Let's Twist Again." A long-play package of the Mixmaster's dirty work, *The Album*, was reviewed by *Rolling Stone*. The verdict: "a world class pop excrescence . . . the best argument yet against sampling."

SYBIL
DON'T MAKE ME OVER
(Burt Bacharach, Hal David)
Next Plateau 325
No. 20 *December 2, 1989*

Sybil Lynch is from Paterson, New Jersey, where she lived, what she described to *Billboard*'s Larry Flick, as a "very traditional" lifestyle. With parental guidance, she sang in church and numerous school productions. "People were always coming up to me and saying, 'Sybil, you can sing. You have to do this professionally.' But it was more important for me to have something more stable. So when I went to college, I majored in speech and theater, with a minor in broadcasting. Eventually, I found myself working for a magazine."

On weekends, she sang with Kenny "Ce Ce" Rogers in something called Ce Ce & Company (no relation to the Detroit group, C. C. & Company, a.k.a. C. J. & Co.). While fronting that act, both were "discovered" and

hand-picked for solo careers. Rogers—nicknamed "Ce Ce" by "Soul Man No. 1," James Brown, for his dance steps that reminded the legend of a mini-Chubby Checker—was spotted by house musicmaker Marshall Jefferson and has had some U.K. successes. Sybil clicked immediately after signing with Next Plateau Records in 1986. The R & B chartings totaled a dozen-plus by the late 90s. Of particular note are the sparrow's duets with Salt-N-Pepper—"Crazy 4 U" (#19, 1990) and "Independent" (#85, 1991)—and her most successful renderings—"Don't Make Me Over" (R&B: #2, 1989) and "Walk on By" (R&B: #3, 1989), both remakes of Dionne Warwick's glories from the mid-'60s.

"Don't Make Me Over" had been recorded by Sybil two years prior to its charting for her debut album, *Let Yourself Go*. U.K. producer/remixer Tony King believed in the potential of the cut and restructured the instrumental base of the track for release as a single. "I've always loved that song," said Sybil. "The new mix is perfect. It's a lot grittier than most of my music."

On the possibility of being limited to mere moments of fickled fame, Sybil told *Billboard*: "I'm not afraid of the fact that I may someday be working at a magazine again someday. In fact, I might like that very much. But, for right now, I couldn't be happier."

KIX
DON'T CLOSE YOUR EYES
(Purnell, Halligan, Jr., Palumbo)
Atlantic 88902
No. 11 *December 16, 1989*

Asked how he wanted KIX to be remembered, lead screamer Steve Whiteman told *CAMM*'s Jeanena Spencer: "The band that hung around like a bad fart."

They were diehard hard-rockers from the get go, perversely out of step with the times. It was the late '70s—the era of punk noise and new wave minimalism—in Hagerstown, Maryland, when Whiteman, "Chocolate" Jimmy Chalfant (drums), Brian "Damage" Forsythe (guitar), Donnie "Nick Nack" Purnell (bass), and Ronnie "10/10" Younkins (guitar) formed a musical alliance. It would be more than a decade before the raucous band would acquire its only Top 40—with of all things a ballad.

They played arenas opening for Ratt and Whitesnake, but paid their dues slogging their way—nonstop touring through Baltimore, Philadelphia, Washington, DC, and the back street bars of Florida and North Carolina. "We've been arrested, we've had guns pulled on us by club owners, we've had vehicles stolen," said Whiteman. "It's been an endless loop of shit that happened to us!"

KIX

A live demo of naughty lyrics shouted over raw guitar squeals recorded off a nightclub soundboard got KIX signed to Atlantic Records. The group's 1981 self-titled debut album sold well, but only to the few who knew of them. *Cool Kids* (#177, 1983) leaned slightly in sound to new wave. "We were told we could have a hit album," Whiteman told Halbersberg, "and we fought like wild dogs, and lost." With *Midnight Dynamite* (1984): "We thought we had the one that could not miss . . . and it missed. Atlantic's format in breaking a band is basically to take the best chance for a radio song, push it, and if it goes, great. If it misses, 'Sorry—we tried and now you're on your own.'"

With no hits, the possibility of Atlantic Records cutting the boys free was at hand. To counteract—the band with the motto, "Never say die,"—stayed on the road playing the haunts that were receptive to the "KIX sound."

With the original line-up intact KIX broke into the big time with album number four, *Blow My Fuse*, and its "power ballad," "Don't Close Your Eyes."

But the road was taking its toll and thereafter KIX members tried to lighten their load. KIX never made the *Billboard* listings again.

"I don't think that we've changed our style that much over the last 10 years," said Whiteman to *Creem*'s Maxine Hillary J. "And when you look at bands like AC/DC and Aerosmith, they've stuck to their sound, too. We've never tried to write a hit song . . . if it happens, it happens. We just do what we do and hope people love it."

The 90s

BIZ MARKE
JUST A FRIEND
(Marcel Theo Hall)
Cold Chillin' 22784
No. 9 *March 17, 1990*

Marke has been called "the Inhuman Orchestra," for the use of his body as an instrument. Critics have called him "the weirdest of the hip-hop lot," but despite it all, Biz Marke has got his finger on some universal appeal.

"There are certain people Americans look at and don't see color—like BILL COSBY, Michael Jackson, Eddie Murphy—and Biz is another one who's going to appeal to everyone," said his manager to *Musician's* Celestine Ware.

Biz told *Cashbox*'s Joe Levy: "They call me the Eddie Murphy of rap. I'm like a comedian. I get on the mike and make everybody laugh . . . I'm like the class clown type."

He was born Marcell Hall, April 8, 1964, in Harlem and raised on Long Island. It was in the early '80s in downtown Manhattan that Biz got his start rappin' at the Roxie and Funhouse. In 1985, he met producer Marlon "Marley Marl" Williams—DJ for WBLS-FM/NYC rap radio show "Mr. Magic's Rap Attack," known for work with Big Daddy Kane, L. L. Cool J, Roxanne Shante—in the hallway of the Queensbridge Projects in Long Island City, Queens. The meeting got Biz the chance to make some demos; winning a slot on Shante's road crew, the Juice Crew All-Stars, which also featured Big Daddy Kane and M. C. Shan. The Marl connect soon got Biz a contract with Cold Chillin' Records. *Goin' Off*, his debut album, showcased his R & B charters, "Vapors" (R&B: #80, 1985) and "Make the Music With Your Mouth" (R&B: #84, 1985) and his honed abilities to gross out, "Picking Boogers."

The Biz Never Sleeps album included the big one, "Just a Friend," a rapped rendering of Freddie Scott's "(You've) Got What I Need." Disaster struck with album three, *Haircut*. "Alone Again" was included. The tune was built on an unauthorized sampling of the piano pattern underlining Gilbert O'Sullivan's chart-topping pop hit of 1972. O'Sullivan sued. And O'Sullivan won, in a landmark case the judge ruled against Biz and Warner Brothers, ordering the label to remove all copies of *Haircut* from circulation. Thereafter record companies would make greater efforts to gather permission before using any copyrighted materials.

Biz Marke charted moderately with "What Comes Around Goes Around" (R&B: #84, 1991) and in 1993 his first album since the legal wrangling, *All Samples Cleared!*

In 1993, Biz appeared in Robert Townsend's flick *The Meteor Man*. Two years later, Biz rapped on then 14-year-old Usher's "Think of You" (R&B: #8, 1995).

A Marke-conceived cartoon TV program, called "Mouth Man," was said to be in the works. "I want my own soft drink company, too," said Biz. "I not changing my music. I'll keep on rapping."

D-MOB, FEATURING CATHY DENNIS
C'MON AND GET MY LOVE
(Christina Ampnett, Thomas Kelly, William Steinberg)
FFRR 886798
No. 10 *March 17, 1990*

"We met all these radio programmers who said our records were 'radical'!" said Danny D to *Pulse*'s Perry Stern. "What's so radical about 'Come and Get My Love?' . . . "

Truth be known, D-Mob is the front, the moniker for "Dancin'" Danny D (b. Daniel Kojo Poku), who with much persistence made it big with his first love, funky sound production. Danny D notched a niche for himself, in the mid-'80s, DJing at London clubs. After some successful promotions for Full Force, Loose Ends, and Total Contrast, Danny D was offered an A & R position at Chrysalis Records. While there he remixed sides for Adeva, Eric B & Rakim, Kid N Play . . . Mild success met him from personal recordings as "the Tarus Boys."

In 1988, the first of his D-Mob disks—"We Call It Aceed"—went Top 10 in England; despite a BBC ban. The number, featuring vocals by Gary Haisman, was seen as an acid house tune that reeked of drug references. "It Is Time to Get Funky," featuring LRS and DC Sarome of the London Rhyme Syndicate, likewise charted Top 10 in the U.K. While both recordings moved freely in the United States dance charts—missing *Billboard*'s pop and R & B listings—record three, "Come and Get My Love, featuring the then-unknown Cathy Dennis, brought "Dancin'" Danny D's sounds into mainstream America.

"The great thing about me and Danny," said Dennis to Stern, "is that he gets a fantastic groove going, and I can come in and put something commercial—very commercial—on top."

The song "Come and Get My Love" received a tremendous shot in the arm when it was included in the soundtrack of the flick *She-Devil* (1989). Dennis remained the featured vocalist for one more D-Mob disk, "That's the Way of the World" (#59, 1990).

D-Mob has yet to return to the pop or R & B charts, but Danny D has gone on to fame-sustaining favor as a producer/remixer for Adeva, the Cookie Crew, Chaka Khan, MONIE LOVE, Juliet Roberts, Diana Ross, Jody Watley, Wee Papa Girls . . .

"What I do is find fun," said Danny D to *Melody Maker*. "It's enjoyment for me every time I go into the

studio—creating something new, feeling that this can happen . . ."

Dennis, meanwhile, has been on "The Oprah Winfrey Show," MTV, modeled for Vivienne Westwood, been photographed by David Bailey, and graced glossy mags as part of a Gap campaign—all while repeatedly returning to the United States pop charts: "Just Another Dream" (#9, 1990), "Touch Me (All Night Long)" (#2, 1991). "Too Many Walls" (#8, 1991) . . . In 1993, Dennis returned Danny D's favor—introduced her to stardom via "Come and Get My Love"—by recording again with his pseudo D-Mob. "Why" failed to chart.

"I don't take it all that seriously," said Danny D to *Billboard*'s Larry Flick, "because as quick as you can be a success, you can be a flop."

MICHAEL PENN
NO MYTH
(Michael Penn)
RCA 9111
No. 13 *March 24, 1990*

Michael Penn is surrounded by movie-making notoriety: his father is actor/director Leo Penn; his mother, actress Eileen Ryan; and his younger brothers are actors Christopher [*Footloose* (1984), *Reservoir Dogs* (1992)] and "Brat Pack" bad boy Sean Penn [*Bad Boys* (1983), *The Falcon & The Snowman* (1985), *Casualties of War* (1989); as director: *Carlo's Way* (1993)]. The only musicmaker in the family was momentary sister-in-law Madonna.

Penn was born in New York City's Greenwich Village and raised in Los Angeles. Mike's success was not an overnight occurrence. Back in junior high he discovered the guitar and was soon playing Bowie, Cream, and Stones cuts in a cover band. At Santa Monica High he sat near Terri Nunn, future lead singer of Berlin. With pen in hand, he created his first songs. "I leaned towards the gloomy and pretentious back then," he told *Rolling Stone*. Much of the '80s was spent in Doll Congress, a progressive band that included vocal stylist Gabriel Morgan and Patrick Warren. The outfit made an obscure EP, played the Los Angeles clubs—Madame Wong's West and Club Lingerie—and even opened for R.E.M. The act's money-making was minimal, and Penn earned extra as a service-relations representative for a photography company, and later as an extra on TV's "St. Elsewhere." By 1986, Penn and the Doll Congress had parted.

After a one-off appearance in 1987 as a member of a group billed the Pull on a "Saturday Night Live" episode hosted by brother Sean, Mike, and ex-Doll Congress keyboardist Patrick Warren got serious about creating some 4-track demos. Robbie Robertson's man-

ager, Nick Wechsler, brought the demos to the attention of Rick Dodd, RCA Record's General Manager and Senior VP for Promotions, and Penn was on his way to the charts with his first album, *March*, and single, "No Myth."

MTV accorded Penn the "Best New Artist Video Music Award." "This and That" (#53, 1990), a lesser charting followed, as did the album *Free for All*. The latter remained on the *Billboard*'s top pop album's chart for two weeks; peaking at number 160.

An obvious sore spot—the extant Michael's popularity is related to having Hollywood bad boy Sean Penn as brother. Mike told *Rolling Stone*'s David Wild: "I try not to go around sweeping my family underneath any carpet because of some great FRANK STALLONE fear. I love Sean, he's my brother, and I respect what he does. And the feeling is mutual. I'm trying to be polite and acknowledge it to a certain extent, but I just don't want it to become what it isn't—which is an issue."

"If his name were Michael Schwartz it would be just as good a record," explained RCA's Rick Dodds, to *It's Hip*, "and I think, frankly, just as many people would be playing it today."

Asked of Penn's potential future, Dodd said: "You never really know what people are going to like, and the biggest hits usually come from the left field. Artists who do something that's truly unique become the stars. When you go with artists that follow the trend, you're dead."

JANE CHILD
DON'T WANNA FALL IN LOVE
(Jane Child)
Warner 19933
No. 2 *April 14, 1990*

"I'm not suddenly famous," Child told *It's Hip*'s C. J. Hansen, "I've worked hard for this. I was classically trained on the piano at five, and I've been out on the road since I was 15. It's satisfying, I'm at peace now, ecstatic, happy. But there's a lot more to do."

She was noticeable right from the get go. Who could miss that spiked chain slung from her nose ring to her ear lobe, the corn-rowed "do," those piercing eyes? And as a classically trained kid, she eventually went on to arrange/produce and play almost every instrument on her debut, self-titled, hit-making album.

Child was born in the '60s to a musically sophisticated Toronto family. Daddy was a violinist and composer; Mommy, a vocalist and pianist. At 12, Child was singing in the Canadian Opera Company's children's chorus. Soon thereafter, she began her piano study via a scholarship at the Royal Conservatory of Music; studied harpsichord and composition with Samuel Dolin, the former Dean of the Canadian League of Composers. Rock music was a no-no in the Child household, though late at night in the privacy of her room, Jane picked up an R & B station beamed out of nearby Buffalo, New York.

"I was always going to be a concert pianist," she told Jeffery Ressner, *Rolling Stone.* "When I was 15, I needed a summer job and saw an ad in the paper for a keyboard player. I figured rock & roll couldn't be that difficult, and of course, I was wrong."

Two paths diverge . . . immediately, her life's course was irreparably altered. Jane Child was now a member of Summerhill, a locally known blues-rock unit. "It was great training," she told *Keyboard*'s Robert L. Doerschuk. "I played a lot of blues cliche piano and organ. It's a lot more fun to play the blues than to listen to it. It's a blast to play a I-IV-V. Really, it's just jerking off."

Through the years on the band circuit and later when she had returned to forge a solo career in Toronto, Jane regimented herself to write one song a day. In 1988, she completed a demo tape and caught the attention of Michael Ostin; soon her manager, later VP of A & R for Warner Bros. Records. The result: "Don't Wanna Fall in Love."

"I cried the first time I heard the song on the radio," Hansen was told. "There's just something about hearing it on the radio. When the single went to number one, that was a very satisfying moment, too."

"Welcome to the Real World" (#49, 1990) nearly nullified Child's status as a One-Hit artist. And though nothing further has approached the *Billboard* Hot 100, Child remains a singular musical being.

Doerschuk wrote of Child, "This is the key to Child: her balance of technique and spirit, glitz and substance. In an industry where image often carries more weight than talent, Child pays attention to both at the expense of neither."

SINEAD O'CONNOR
"NOTHING COMPARES 2 U"
(Prince)
Ensign 23488
No. 1 *April 21, 1990*

O'Connor, the baldheaded Irish vocalist, who is used to controversy, was born on December 12, 1966, in Glenageare, Eire. Before her debut album, *The Lion and the Cobra* (features guest appearance of ENYA), O'Connor sang with Ton Ton Macoute and did vocals for U2 guitarist The Edge's soundtrack for the flick *The Capture* (1986). The sales of her critically lauded albums have been marred by the artist's polarizing interviews and acts, such as ripping up a photo of the Pope on TV in 1992, and refusing to go on stage after "The Star Span-

SINEAD O'CONNOR

gled Banner" at Garden State Arts Center, New Jersey, in 1990. She has also appeared in the TV-film *Hush-a-Bye Baby* (1990). Her lone hit was written by Prince for his group Family.

A'ME LORAIN
WHOLE WIDE WORLD
(Elliot Wolff)
RCA 9098
No. 9 *April 28, 1990*

A'Me Lorain—a then 22 year old—from Simi Valley, California, was asked to record "Whole Wide World" for director Nancy Savoca's *True Love* (1989), about an atypical wedding day and the bride and groom's second thoughts. *True Love,* Savoca's first film, was created for a mere $750,000 and garnered the Grand Prize at the United States Film Festival. Despite it all though, the movie generated little interest and fears settled in that the tune would never see release on disk or cassette. More perceptive minds prevailed and RCA issued the cut. Though first shunned, "Whole Wide World"—co-written and produced by Elliott Wolff, known for his work with Paula Abdul—began gathering notice in the dance clubs in Boston and New York City, and later in San Francisco.

A'Me returned to *Billboard*'s Hot 100 months later with "Follow My Heartbeat" (#72, 1990). Director Savoca went on to further acclaim with her next films: *Dogfight* (1991) and *Household Saints* (1993).

CALLOWAY
I WANNA BE RICH
(Reginald Calloway, Vincent Calloway, Gentry, Lipscomb)
Solar 74005
No. 2 *May 5, 1990*

Vincent "Cino-vincent," Greg, and Reginald "Reggie" Calloway got their start beating on pots, pans, and garbage cans in Cincinnati, Ohio. "We were very imaginative kids," said Reggie to *It's Hip* magazine. "Grandmother had an old piano, which we'd play every now and then. Then in high school, we joined the choir . . ." The soon-to-be multi-instrumentalists played around separately in a succession of semi-pro bands. By the early '70s, the three bros were one act, Sunchild, a jazz-funk unit that often accompanied Sonny Stit.

In 1976, while attending Kentucky State University, Cino-vincent (trumpet, trombone, keyboards, flugelhorn) and Reggie (trumpet, flute, keyboards) formed MIDNIGHT STAR with fellow students. Before the brothers left the big-name R & B unit in 1988, numerous albums were successful and a dozen plus singles had charted on *Billboard*'s R & B listings: "Freak-a-Zoid" (#4, 1983), "Wet My Whistle" (#8, 1983), "Operator" (#1, 1984), "Headlines" (#3, 1986), "Midas Touch" (#7, 1986).

During their stay with the Midnight Star, together or apart, the Calloways produced/wrote for Natalie Cole ("Jump Start" . . .), DEELE, Klymaxx ("The Men All Pause". . .), Gladys Knight & The Pips, LEVERT ("Casanova". . .), TEDDY PENDERGRASS, The Whispers . . . "We've always seen ourselves as front men," said Cino-vincent. "But the production thing just blossomed, and we had to wait a little while. But, as you can probably tell, our hearts lie in [doing our own records]."

On the One-Hit pop success, said Cino-vincent: "The media so often focuses on the negatives in life. But with a song like 'I Wanna Be Rich,' for example, we got to speak for everyone who has a dream and is just going for it . . . Yeah, we wanna be rich, but more so successful at something that means so much to us."

"Our record is a mass appeal record," Reggie added. "That's why Calloway is doing so well."

"Sir Lancelot" (#19, 1990), "All the Way" (#33, 1990), and "Let's Get Smooth" (#39, 1992) charted fairly well on the R & B listings.

PARTNERS IN KRYME
TURTLE POWER!
(Peter Alpern, Richard Usher, Jr.)
SBK 07325
No. 13 *June 2, 1990*

A rap pack composed of DJ James Alpert and rapper Richard Usher. The NYC-based outfit met while attending Syracuse University. Both were communication majors. Less than little is known about how the duo got connected with the powers behind the flick *Teenage Mutant Ninja Turtles—The Movie* (1990), for which their "Turtle Power!" appeared in; still less is known about just who these two were and are. Follow-ups were apparently so underwhelming that they weren't noted by the reporting media.

It is known, trivia buffs, that Kryme, which was translated by the duo, meant: "Keep Rhythm Your Motivating Emotion."

PERFECT GENTLEMEN
OOH LA LA (I CAN'T GET OVER YOU)
(Larry Johnson)
Columbia 73379
No. 10 *June 2, 1990*

Maurice Starr is a songwriter and the founder/producer of a couple of highly successful Boston-based acts, New Edition and the New Kids on the Block. Seemingly in need of proving that he could deal with the gods and cause lightning to strike thrice, Starr assembled another trio, 11- to 13-year-olds, starting with son Maurice Starr, Jr. Much like Daddy Starr's previous acts, his intent was to assemble a catch of good-lookin' malleables. The goal was to mix mainstream pop with elements of rap and R & B to, hopefully, create a crossover success with the youthful pop and the R & B audience.

Completing the line-up were Starr Jr.'s neighbor Corey Blakely and Tyrone Stutton, a sometime member of other Boston groups. Daddy Starr arranged for a deal with Columbia Records and hooked the novice product up with the New Kids on the Block for a few months tour. Sandra Trim DaCosta, the label's director of marketing has said: "Maurice's got a winning formula, and he's capitalizing on it. He's creating music that works for all formulas."

The buzz around black radio was that these Starr protege's were the next New Kids, the African-American equivalent. Nothing further has charted on *Billboard*'s Hot 100. Before they vanished, "One More Chance" (#33, 1990) made a fair showing on the R & B listings.

GIANT
I'LL SEE YOU IN MY DREAMS
(Alan Pasqua)
A & M 1495
No. 20 *June 9, 1990*

Giant was a band of session vets, with an imposing list of jazz, rock, pop, and country credentials. Together, though more likely apart, they had recorded with Pat Benatar, Bob Dylan, John Fogerty, Sammy Hagar, Eddie Money, Santana, and Tony Williams's Lifetime.

The initial spark to get it all together came in 1985 when guitarist/lead singer Dann Huff met keyboardist Alan Pasqua at a Nashville recording session. Alan explained to *Keyboard*'s Alan di Perna: "We kept bumping into each other at sessions. One day, we got talking, and I said, 'Man, I don't want to be doing this. I want to get in a band.' Dann said, 'You're kidding! That's what I came out here to do!' We assembled a couple of different band situations before we got together with [bassist] Mike Brignardello and David Huff [Dann's brother and Giant's drummer]. The first time we played it really felt good. It had some of that 'I don't care' attitude . . . It wasn't about being schooled and polished, or playing each note perfectly. It was about emotions and digging in."

A & M Records gave them a chance. A self-titled debut album was released in mid-1988; "I'm a Believer," a reworked take on the Monkees' perennial was issued as the first 45. It peaked in the middle of *Billboard*'s Hot 100 and was followed six months later by what would be Giant's lone bell-ringer, "I'll See You in My Dreams."

Alan, who had studied classical piano, majored in music at Indiana University and the New England Conservatory of Music in Boston, was speaking for Giant members, when he told *Keyboard* their session days were a thing of the past. "The phone rings a lot, and it's a temptation. We've established comfortable session careers. But being a group is something we've wanted to do all our lives. It's what every kid dreams of, if he's into music."

LOUIE LOUIE
SITTIN' IN THE LAP OF LUXURY
(Louie Cordero)
WTG 73266
No. 19 *July 7, 1990*

He was born Louie Cordero, somewhere in southern California. His life—up until he met Madonna in 1984—is a blank. Once with the "Material Girl," Louie got the chance to show off his singing/dancing and songwriting abilities—principally as Madonna's boyfriend in the video for her "Borderline" hit. The

high visibility jolted, the now named Louie Louie, into a creative frenzy that culminated in a spray of co-written tunes, a demo tape, and back-up band to tour the L.A. club circuit. Martika, who had topped the pop charts in 1989 with "Toy Soldier," became an early admirer with clout. CBS Records listened when the former actress—known for her roles in the TV series "Kids Incorporated" and the flick *Annie* (1982)—fingered him as an up'n'comer.

Said Jerry Greenburg, senior VP at Louie Louie's label, WTG: "He's very unique—give 'em a boom box, put him on a corner, and he'll attract a crowd. Immediately, I signed him . . . I saw something different in him, something that came from the streets; the same reaction the first time I saw Chic in the early '70s."

"Sittin' in the Lap of Luxury"—the debut single from Louie Louie's funky-dance debut album, *The State I'm In*—featured trumpet blasts and some between take grumblings from legend Dizzy Gillespie. Louie's liner notes included thanks "to Jesus Christ for forgiving me." The 15-minute fame came quick and left silently, though just as quickly. Next up and out: "I Wanna Get Back With You," (#69, 1990) hung around the Hot 100's lower reaches for some weeks. Perhaps, Louie should have detoured with the ode to homelessness, a punchy LP cut, "Rodeo Clown," with lines: "I don't know if you can call it love/But she's campin' in my stable," complete with giddyaps and humorous horse sounds.

MELLOW MAN ACE
MENTIROSA
(Antonio Gonzalez, Sergio Reyes)
Capitol 44533
No. 14 *July 21, 1990*

Unlike a lot of rappers from Los Angeles, Mellow Man Ace—younger brother to Cypress Hill's Senen "Sen Dog" Reyes—is not mad as hell about living in the U.S.A. His prime motive has been to get down.

Ace also is one of but a handful of Latin rappers; laboring in anonymity had been pioneering Puerto Rican DJ Charlie Chase, Ruby D., Tito of the Fearless Four, and Prince Whipple Whip of the Fantastic Romantics MCs. For his forefront efforts and his across the board's success with "Mentirosa," Mellow Man has been labeled the "Ricky Ricardo of Rap," the "Babalu Bad Boy" . . . and he's proud.

"I realize controversy sells records, but most of the time I don't like to be controversial," Ace told Roy Trakin, *Music Express*. "I go outside and see enough harsh bullshit going on. I don't want to bring stuff like drive-by shootings into my music. Lotta times I just want to party."

Luck has been with Mellow Man—a black Hispanic rap-man, born Ulpiano Sergio Reyes in Cuba, April 12, 1967. When he was four, his family got to leave Havana on a "liberty flight," as a result of his birth date being picked in a random drawing run by the government to issue exit visas.

Ace never planned on being a musician; break dancing was his turn-on. When he no longer could keep pace with the steps being developed, he turned to rapping. It wasn't until 1985, when during some impromptu experiments at a Latin club that he rapped in Spanish. The audience response was instant. "People bugged out on it because it was so new and so different," he told *Request*'s Steve Appleford.

"When I put out 'Mentirosa,' I had no idea it would do what it did. You just put something out and hope it gets discovered by the widest possible audience." Ace acknowledged to Trakin that mass popularity can work against you. "Now people expect every song I do to sound like that, which is why I'm trying to break out . . . It's tough.

"I look at all this as a gift from God," said Mellow Man. "This land has given me the opportunity to be who I wanted to be, and to live freely and comfortably. To come from a country where you're held back by communism to one where if you strive for something and put in the time, it's bound to pay off . . . I thank God."

TYLER COLLINS
GIRLS NITE OUT
Tyler Collins
RCA 2630
No. 6 *August 4, 1990*

Big Apple-born and Motor City-raised Tyler Collins dreamt of stardom, more than a mite when just a wee size. She admired Dorothy Dandridge, Betty Boo, Aretha Franklin, and Chaka Khan. At age eight, she was dancing on stage; at 17, fronting a band called The Boys Next Door. Two years later, Tyler was off to fulfill that dream of solo stardom. By age 21, she was signed to one of the nation's six major recording complexes, RCA Records. Her debut album, *Girls Night Out*, contained a duet with Grady Harrell—then hot on the R & B listings with "Sticks and Stones" (#4)—and what would prove to be two Top 10 R & B tracks for Tyler— "Whatcha Gonna Do" (R&B: #8, 1989) and the title track, her lone pop Top 40 mark, "Girls Night Out" (R&B: #8, 1989).

"I stretch my resources from one extreme to the other," said Tyler to *Cashbox*'s Alex Henderson. "My natural voice is a big, straight-ahead stage voice. I had to learn to sing creatively, sometimes softly, and to work with technology."

Despite press praise from the R & B community, a promotion/publicity push from her label—that excitedly proclaimed her *the one* with "the beauty, the sound and all the right moves"—and three further mini-chartings—"Second Chance" (#53; R&B: #30, 1990), "Just Make Me the One" (R&B: #52, 1992), and "It Doesn't Matter" (#88; R&B: #93, 1992)—the titillatedly talented Tyler has yet to find that next major consumer-pleaser.

KYPER
TIC-TAC-TOE
Randall Kyper
Atlantic 87910
No. 14 *September 1, 1990*

Randall Kyper—it's a good guess—is now cracking books and performing drum riffs at sporting events. "Tic-Tac-Toe"—a pop-rap with a borrowed guitar line from Yes's "Owner of a Lonely Heart"—was a sizable pop hit, but didn't touch the R & B charts. And nothing has since shown up with his moniker on any chart.

Kyper was born in Baton Rouge, Louisiana, about 1961. Parents say he was a card even when quite young. He'd sing and hoof it for family and friends; he took up the drums in grammar school. In high school, Kyper played in the marching band and became something of a star attraction as a dancer during halftime shows. By his teen years, he was jotting down tunes and making tapes for any who would listen. His parents were educators and insisted that Kyper graduate from college and with good grades, too. Apparently someone with the power to make things happen, heard one of Kyper's demos. Atlantic Records offered to sign the lad up for a shot at stardom, and his parents gave their approval of his postponement of college.

As the sun sets in the west, it's imagined that Randall Kyper is as planned studiously studying for exams.

FAITH NO MORE
EPIC
(Faith No More)
Epic/Slash 19813
No. 9 *September 8, 1990*

Faith No More was formed in San Francisco in 1980. Each of the FNM men had seen service in the punk trenches of the late '70s. The initial line-up consisted of drummer Mike Bordin (b. Nov. 27, 1962, San Francisco), keyboardist Roddy Bottom (b. July 1, 1963, L.A.), bassist Bill Gould (b. Apr. 24, 1963, L.A.), guitarist James "Jim" Martin (b. Jul. 21, 1961, Oakland, CA), and vocalist Chuck Mosley (b. unknown). Bottom met

Gould while attending the same school. Bordin was discovered in a tribal rhythm class at Berkeley University. Gould had met Mosley in a club in L.A. Metallica's Clif Burton suggested that the group include Martin. Together they recorded a no-budget album for the tiny Mordam label. "We Care a Lot," the group's thrash-funk response to "We Are the World," received a great deal of college radio airplay. Soon after Slash, a Warner Brothers subsidiary, signed the band to cut its ground-breaking *Introduce Yourself.*

Internal squabbles caused Moseley to oust himself/be ousted from the whole affair. He went on for awhile with Bad Brains before forming his own Cement. His replacement was Mike Patton (b. Jan. 27, 1968, Eureka, CA), an even more flamboyant performer and former frontman for the bizarre Mr. Bungle, an act he would continue to work as a side activity. Rumors circulate that Courtney Love had auditioned with the group but was passed on. With Patton fronting Faith No More, *The Real Thing* was released to critical acclaim. Contained on it, the group's moment in the Top 40 sun, "Epic."

The band's style remained "different while commercial," or so say the scribes. Squabbles continued, however. For three years the band toured on with no further recordings, aside from a stop-gap live album, *Live at the Brixton Academy.* In 1991, patton recorded an album with Mr. Bungle. FNM contributed "The Perfect Crime" to the soundtrack of *Bill and Ted's Bogus Journey* (1991), with Martin fleshing out a walk-on role.

Martin left the fold in 1994 and was replaced by Dean Menta. Their *Songs to Make Love to* EP included takes on the Dead Kennedys' "Let's Lynch the Landlord and the Commodores' "Easy." The following year, *King for a Day, Fool for a Lifetime* was issued, but no singles chartings followed.

CANDYMAN
KNOCKIN' BOOTS
(Candyman, W. Clarke, A. Hamilton, T. Hamilton, Whitfield, R. Wiley, B. Wright)
Epic 73450
No. 9 *November 10, 1990*

"Contrary to what some people think, this is not my first record," said Candyman to *Billboard* magazine's Peter Wetherbee of "Knockin' Boots," his debut disk for Epic Records. "People think I went into the studio and got a hit, but I've made other records before on independents."

His birth name has been withheld. Info has been dispensed that he was born in Los Angeles on June 25, 1968, and his intention was to become the new "King of Rap." In 1983, fresh out of high school, Candy and part-

ner Johnny "J" got their start rappin' and writing songs; some included on *Ain't No Shame in My Game* (1990), Candyman's debut album. By 1986, Candy was recording his first demo's for Dr. Dre, who later experienced hip hop fame for his production work for Ice Cube, N.W.A., Michel'le, Snoop Doggy Dogg. Through Dre, Candyman got to record some tracks for Fila Al.

In 1987, Candyman hooked up with Tone Loc. Together they had a growing following in Los Angeles. When Tone Loc's "Wild Thing" scored big, Candyman was called upon to choreograph and help assemble his live show. The touring lasted into 1989.

At this point, Candyman got a chance by a major label to make it on his own. *Ain't No Shame in My Game* included "Knockin' Boots"—the allegory of just how you, me, he, and the rest got here . . . somebody knocked boots. For "Boots," Candyman, a professed "oldies" lover, utilized a remake of the chorus of Rose Royce's "Ooh Boy" and a sample of Betty Wright's "Tonight Is the Night." Months later, his "Melts in Your Mouth" (#69; R&B: #46, 1990) charted; followed by "Nightgown" (#91, 1991).

"Our sound is bringing back the old R & B and making it '90s rap," said Candyman to *Billboard.*

CONCRETE BLONDE
JOEY
(Johnette Napolitano)
I.R.S. 73014
No. 19 *November 10, 1990*

Johnette Napolitano (vocals, bass) was born in Hollywood. Her father cleaned the swimming pools for the stars. Bela Lugosi babysat for her. In Johnette's teen years, she learned how to play guitar from those *Play Guitar With the Ventures* album/books. "I had an aunt who used to be a dancer on "Shindig" and was engaged to Mickey Dolenz," said Johnette to *Creem* magazine's Amy Linden.

It's the late '70s, Los Angeles, and Jim Markley (guitar)—who with brother Earle was a founding member of Sparks—has joined Leon Russell as a bass player and engineer. Jim and Johnette met, there—she was acting as a self-described "office gopher, graphic artist, and general assistant." "It was just like one big family commune where he let everybody run free and explore their talents," she told Chris Helms, *Illinois Entertainer.* Leon moved to Nashville, but Jim and Johnette stayed in Los Angeles.

Together they worked the clubs and with auxiliary members going and coming, Jim and Johnette recorded an EP for a French label—Happy Hermit Records—as Dream 6. With the offer in 1985 from Miles Copeland at I.R.S. to record for his label and the addi-

tion of Harry Rushakoff, a Chicago drummer who had worked with the Nodes, Special Affect, the Dickies, Fear, A Drop in the Grey . . . Jim and Johnette were set to become, at R.E.M.'s Michael Stipe's suggestion, Concrete Blonde.

A critically acclaimed self-titled debut disk was issued in 1986, but plenty of problems ensued when legal wrangling between the group and label keep Concrete Blonde from recording again until 1989 and the release of *Free*. Added to the line-up was bassist Alan Bloch, freeing Johnette to giving full attention to her vocalizing and composing.

With *Bloodletting*, the album container for "Joey," Alan and Harry were gone; added is drummer Paul Thompson, formerly of ROXY MUSIC. Featured were guest appearances by R.E.M.'s Peter Buck, Dream Syndicates' Steve Wynn, and Wall of Voodoo's Andy Prieboy. While still in the charts, reflective Johnette told *It's Hip* the album was "a self-indulgent, miserable sort of record."

"I get weird on the road—I'm rude to people, and I get freaked out," said Johnette to Mary Dickie, *Music Express*. "I get isolated. I just don't want to be that way anymore. . . ." What followed was a hospital stay for

Napolitano. "For months afterward I was like a geriatric patient, . . . I couldn't get up and walk, do my dishes, take out my trash. . . ."

After a move to London, Jim and Johnette returned with *Walking in London* (1992), *Mexican Moon* (1993) . . . "At this point, I wouldn't mind making some money," said Johnette to Holly Gleason, *Illinois Entertainer*. "Look, we've done the rock thing, the band in the back of a van freezing cold. We want to keep it together. But we're not 15, and we don't like sleeping on people's floors."

DEEE-LITE
GROOVE IS IN THE HEART
(Dimitry Brill, Dong-Hwa Chung, Kamaal Fareed, Herbert Hancock, Kierin Kirby)
Elektra 64934
No. 4 *November 17, 1990*

From nowhere they came . . . "a delirious, appealing escapist fantasy," "a time-warped vacation," journalists have said. Their visual parade, a hodge-podge of '70s extremes—feather boas, hot pants, patterned stockings, platform shoes . . . ah, fabulashes . . . now they're gone.

Lady Miss Kier (b. Kier Kirby, Youngstown, OH) met Super DJ Dmitry (b. Dmitry Brill, Kirovograd, Ukraine) in New York City's Washington Square Park in 1982. Kier's mom had been an urban planner. Changes in residence were a constant. Settling in the city at age 18 to study textile design at the Fashion Institute of Technology, Kier soon found it necessary to work as a waitress and later as a ladies room attendant at the nightclub Area. Dmitry earned his keep DJing, running a restaurant, and working the coatcheck room at the Limelight nightclub.

Lady Miss Kier and Dmitry were working a club called Afro-chine when they happened on to Jungle DJ Towa Towa (b. Towa Tei, Tokyo)—a graphic design student, who sensed Dmitry's funky tastes and gave him a tape of his own compositions. Weeks would pass before either would give a listen, but once they did it was like "our destiny," said Kier.

The encounter shut down Dmitry's other sideline—Shazork, a psycho-Philly musical outfit composed of Dmitry and two drag queens, Lady Bunny and Sister Dimension, who would attempt to convince audiences that they were residents of the planet Shazork.

Their first gigs as Deee-lite—named after the Cole Porter perennial "It's De-lovely"—began in 1987 at the club Siberia. Wordsmiths labeled them nouveau-disco; Kier proclaimed their sound "holographic house groove." "The way Kier and Towa approach music has been an inspiration to me," said Dmitry, a classically trained pianist, to *Request*. "They don't approach it

from a musician's view. They take chances and break the rules. Their background in graphic art and fabric design has really helped the music 'visually' as well."

In 1990, Elektra Records signed the act. "Groove Is in the Heart" was the first single pulled from its debut album, *World Clique*. Before the recording session, Dmitry had written a letter—with tape—to Bootsy Collins. The parties had never met, but with a listen, Bootsy and JB legends Maceo Parker and Fred Wesley agreed to fly in and put some tasty sauce on the album.

"Power of Love" charted (#48, 1991), but two years passed before Deee-lite would return with album two, *Infinity Within*. Critics viewed the venture as "toned down," a let down with hippie polito-stuff about voting, the environment, and safe sex. Towa who left the unit in 1993 to pursue a career in computer graphics, was replaced on album three, 1994's *Dewdrops in the Garden*, by DJ Ani. Kier and Dmitry remain married and live in a small flat in New York City's Lower East Side.

SOHO
HIPPYCHICK
(Timothy Brunkhurst, Johnny Narr)
Savage/Atco 98908
No. 14 *November 24, 1990*

They were a British dance band composed of identical twin sisters Jacqueline, Jacquie Juanita Cuff, and Pauline, Pauline Osberga Cuff (b. Nov. 25, 1962, Wolverhampton, England), and guitarist Tim London (b. Timothy Brunkhurst, Nov. 20, 1960). For 10 years, the ladies helped others in a hospital setting. "We're trained nurses," said Jacqueline to *Creem*. "Our father died about a dozen years ago [1977, when we were 15], and our mother really couldn't afford to keep us at home. We were too young to train, so we were nurses' assistants until we were 18, and then we trained. We were psychiatric nurses until we got a record deal."

About the time they began nursing to others needs, the Cuff sisters met Tim London and formed a group called Groovalx; the band was soon retitled Tim London's Orgasm. For a moment, Bow Wow Wow's bass man was a member.

"We just liked going on stage and jumping about," Jacqueline told *Creem*. "Eventually we sort of learned to sing, because Tim got fed up. He told us we'd better start learning to sing and rehearse. We were really awful."

In 1988, as Soho, they were signed to Hedd, a Virgin subsidiary label, which rapidly issued "You Won't Hold Me Down," "Message From My Baby," and an album, *Noise*.

"We did the album; we knew it was crap," Jacqueline told *Vox*. Sales were poor and the three were dropped by the label.

The next year, they spent singing in Italian discos. Savage Tam Records gave them a try and with their second single, "Hippychick"—a house blast with a hypnotic beat that samples the Smiths' "How Soon Is Now"—sparks flew. "'Hippychick' is about a woman who's been on a demo, got it?" *Vox* was told. "And the policeman charging her turns out to be her ex-boyfriend, who tries to entice her into dropping charges. In the U.S. people are so dim they think it's about hippies."

Goddess, an album the sisters didn't dislike ("We did it with no money, and it's 100% us," they told *Vox.*), was issued, as were a few singles. Nothing charted and the group apparently parted. In 1993, Tim and Jacqueline had a daughter, Charlie. The following year, the couple, with sister Pauline returned to the studio as Dosh.

Soho never made the R & B listings. "A lot of the black media hated us from the start—they said that we were too white," said Pauline to *Vox*. "We were given a bubblegum, five minute pop group image, and we suffered for it."

2 IN A ROOM
WIGGLE IT
(George A. Morel, Rafael Vargas)
Cutting 98887
No. 15 *December 15, 1990*

Rafael "Dose" Vargas was a frustrated teen in need of some status. Born and raised in Washington Heights, New York, "Dose" had long been on the lookout for a claim to fame. "I needed something so I'd stand out on the street," he told *It's Hip*. To the dismay of his family, as a youth, he'd "drop beats," which is something you do when thumping and whacking on a kitchen table, or the like. When his brother acquired an electronic keyboard from Radio Shack, "Dose" settled into recording demos on an oversized boom box in the bathroom. The acoustics were a groove.

After a stay at an undisclosed Big Apple art school, "Dose" met Aldo Marin, the streetwise record man at Cutting Records. Marin heard untapped talent in the kid and connected him with Roger "Rog Nice" Paulette, a mixer with experience as a manager with Prime Cut Recording Studios. It's written that "Rog Nice" had worked on projects with Duran Duran, Debbie Gibson, Mantronix, and Echo & The Bunnymen.

"Wiggle It" was the duo's dance debut. "Booty Hump," "House Junkie" and the rest have yet to return "Dose" and "Rog Nice" to the listings. A press release in the early '90s indicated that the pair formed something called OSN Productions, to work with independent Cardiac Records.

CHRIS ISAAK
WICKED GAME
(Chris Isaak)
Reprise 19704
No. 6 *March 2, 1991*

With an Elvis look, melancholic lyrics, and a voice as lonely as a distant steam engine whistle on a foggy night, Chris Isaak has the market cornered on '50s cool. Despite his antiquated sounds, Isaak is media-defined as hip and current. Together his music and visual presentation are a '90s uniqueness.

Isaak was born on June 25, 1956, and raised in Stockton, California. As a child he listened to country and western and pop crooners, with a special interest in Louis Prima. At 20, Isaak took off for studies at the University of Tokyo, where he wound up on the boxing team. "It's a real tough racket," he told Kenny Doole at *Music Express*. "I'd spar with guys that were almost brain dead."

It was while in Japan that Isaak first heard and became obsessed with the Sun sides of Elvis Presley. On his return to San Francisco, he formed his group Silvertone and began making small club appearances. Erik Jacobson, known for his '60s work with NORMAN GREENBAUM, Tim Hardin, and The Lovin' Spoonful, helped arrange a recording deal with Warner Brothers. While the retro-rock of his first two LPs garnered critical acclaim, sales were slow in the United States. France picked up on "Blue Hotel," from Isaak's self-titled second album. European tours were met with success.

It wasn't until an Atlanta DJ caught the appearance of his "Wicked Game" in director David Lynch's *Wild at Heart* flick (1990), that United States. radio picked up on this haunting anachronistic style. The cut and *Heart Shaped World*, the album from which it was extracted, both charted Top 10. His follow-up album did not sell as well.

Reflecting on the real possibility of being relegated to cult status, Isaak said, "It's real easy—you're popular, and then you're not popular. And if you hang around long enough, you might come back again."

OLETA ADAMS
GET HERE
(Brenda Russell)
Fontana 878476
No. 5 *March 23, 1991*

"Miss O," a.k.a. Oleta Adams (b. Yakima, WA)—a vocalist/keyboardist with a unique slant on combining jazz, soul, and gospel into a sophisticated podge of contemporary pop—spent years honing her art. Since leaving high school, Oleta had been unceremoniously working the Midwest lounge circuit. One late night in 1985, at the bar in the Hyatt Regency Hotel in Kansas City, she was spotted by a twosome capable of providing career assistance. The Tears for Fears duo—Rolland Orzabal and Curt Smith, known universally for "Shout," "Everybody Wants to Rule the World, among others—were impressed. Both acts exchanged phone numbers and albums; Oleta had a tape issued locally. Two years later, Orzabal and Smith provided her with her first break recruiting her for touring purposes and back-up vocals on their LP, *The Seeds of Love*. In 1990, Orzabal produced her first international release, *Circle of One*. The disk included "The Rhythm of Life" and "Get Here." Oleta received two Grammy nominations—for the vocals on her lone hit, "Get Here" and her 1991 interpretation of Elton John and Bernie Taupin's "Don't Let the Sun Go Down."

Oleta has been called "a great pop singer with a vision" by *L.A. Times*' Robert Hilburn; "a jazz chanteuse and choir belter, an astute songwriter," by *People*; "a Whitney Houston with warmth, a Mariah Carey with charisma". . . , but has yet to return to the charts. *Los Angeles Times* critic Dennis Hunt described her as "one who walks the fine line between satisfying the pop fans while infusing enough tension and fire to woo the R & B crowd." Possibly her difficulty lies in meeting these diverse needs.

Adams lives quietly in Kansas City, with her husband, a drummer, John Cushon. *Moving On*, her third solo effort, was issued in 1996.

TONY TERRY
WITH YOU
(Robert Reeder, Jr.)
Epic 73713
No. 14 *April 27, 1991*

He was born to a religious family in Pinehurst, North Carolina, on March 12, 1964. By 1972, Tony Terry and family were living in the Washington, DC, area and were members of the Freedom Gospel Singers. "I grew up in the church, and listened to all the gospel greats," Terry explained to *Cashbox*'s Lee Jeske. "I'd close myself up in a room and listen to those guys for hours and hours, learning every riff from those records. And I just started incorporating the riffs—stealing them, basically—into my own thing."

By his mid-teens, Tony was singing secular music. "When I was 17, I did a musical in Washington called *Don't Bother Me I Can't Cope*, at the Ellington School of the Arts. I moved to New York after graduating from Ellington to do a gospel musical called *Black Nativity*. That led to a series of musicals at the Theatre of the Universal Image in Newark, New Jersey, and then I went on to *Mama, I Want to Sing*, an off-Broadway musical."

While hanging out at the Danceteria, Tony was spotted by producer Ted Currier (George Clinton, Sweet Sensation). Tony and Flame—Epic Recording artist, born Flame Braithwaite, daughter of jazz saxman George Braith—were exchanging vocalizations when Currier stopped them. "Currier was standing behind me, and asked me to sing it again. And I did, and he introduced himself and gave me his [business] card." Soon Currier was utilizing Tony for back-up work on sessions for Vanessa Bell Armstrong, the Boogie Boys, Sweet Sensation, and a charting dueted with Flame, "On the Strength" (R&B: #59, 1989).

By the mid-'90s, numerous Tony Terry disks had made the R & B listings; notably: "She's Fly" (#10, 1987), "Lovey Dovey" (#4, 1988), "Forever Yours" (#16, 1988), "Everlasting Love" (#6, 1991), and his lone major pop crossover, "With You" (R&B: #6, 1991).

"To tell you the truth," Tony told *Cashbox*, "I haven't really paid my dues. I've been blessed—I was put in the right situation at the right time with the right people."

KEEDY
SAVE SOME LOVE
(G. Gerard)
Arista 2153
No. 15 *May 11, 1991*

Kelly Keedy was born in Abilene, Texas, on July 26, 1965. Keedy's family moved to Milwaukee, Wisconsin, and enrolled her in numerous voice and dance lessons. In her teens, the mite-sized Keedy set out to become a opera singer. It's said in record company hand-outs that her cute but diminutive stature prevented her from pursuing an operatic career.

In the early '80s, she began fronting Gerard, a pop-oriented band with a huge area following. The act's moniker—Gerard—was taken from the founder/tunesmith Greg Gerard, who saw more than talent in his protege. Greg worked hard on perfecting Keedy's presentation. By the late '80s, the band was a Midwest favorite, performing more than 200 shows a year. A demo tape made its way to Mitchell Cohen, an A & R VP with Arista Records. After checking her out live, Mitchell signed not the band, but Keedy in 1990 to a recording contract.

"The first time I saw her," said Cohen to *Cashbox*'s Jim Richliano, "I could tell that she had her own style and personality—I wanted to capture her exuberance and energy, take a snapshot of it because it showed that there was a real artist persona behind her music."

Greg and Keedy are now husband and wife. He co-produced *Chase the Clouds*, her debut album, from which Keedy's lone hit moment was extracted.

DIVINYLS
I TOUCH MYSELF
(Christina Ampnett, Thomas Kelly,
Mark McEntee, William Steinberg)
Virgin 98873
No. 4 *May 18, 1991*

"Friends in Australia told us that this song would never be a hit in America—it's so risque," said guitar man Mark McEntree to *Music Connections'* Steven P. Wheeler. "But of course, the Americans just ate it up."

Jeremy Paul (bass) had been an original member of the Divinyls—as he had been with the band Air Supply; but when things started to come together, he took off to parts unknown leaving band members Mark McEntree (b. July 16, 1961, Perth, Australia/guitar), Christina Amphlett (b. Oct. 25, possibly 1960, Geelong, Victoria, Australia/vocals, covertly explicit postures), and the rest—Richard Harvey (drums) and Bjarne Ohlin (guitar, keyboards)—to work the sleazy bars of Sydney, Australia.

Raised in Perth, Christina had left school at 17 and traveled to Europe, where she was jailed in Barcelona, Spain, for street singing. Back in Sydney, she joined a church choir, to improve the upper reaches of her range, she has claimed. It was at this point that Christina met Mark and began a long but professed platonic relationship.

Within a year of their formation, film director Ken Cameron spotted Christina and the boys. Figuring that they had something he wanted to include in *Monkey Grip* (1982), Cameron approached them about creating a soundtrack for the film. "Boys in Town," was issued as their debut 45; followed by an EP, with four cuts from the flick. WEA took noticed, signed them, but dispensed with them when squabbles broke-out. With Rick Grossman replacing Paul and Chrysalis offering a multi-disk contract, *Desperate* was released in January, 1983.

About as close as the Divinyls got to a hit was the suggestive, S & M-laced ode, "Pleasure and Pain" (#76, 1986).

"I think I was a bit too much for everybody—wearing school uniforms with garters and sticking microphones up my dress," said Christina to *Details'* Lance Loud. "All hell broke loose when we came to America. It's taken a long time for people to accept that sort of outrageousness from girls."

After a disappointing run of three albums, not enough singles, and marginal sales, Chrysalis removed the band from its label.

The Divinyls, by this point, was reduced to Christina and Mark. Together they lived and wrote and reexamined their course to be taken. Demos of their new material was sent out. Virgin Records hearing something special in "I Touch Myself," responded.

"We were sitting, writing in a restaurant [Cat & Fiddle, on Sunset Blvd, in L.A.], and these two girls were listening, and I suppose we were just . . . being silly," said Christina to John Everson, *Illinois Entertainer,* explaining the song's creation. "No, wait, we weren't. But, it's just one of those songs that can be taken on different levels. And I think it's up to the listener's interpretation—if you're a nun, you're going to hear it one way, and if a stripper, another."

A self-title album was issued, graced with Christina in a fishnet dress. "Love School," the immediate follow-up, and others, flopped.

TRIPLETS
YOU DON'T HAVE TO GO HOME TONIGHT
(E. Lowen, D. Navarro, D. Villegas,
G. Villegas, V. Villegas)
Mercury 878864
No. 14 *May 18, 1991*

There's Diana, "the serious one," according to *Rolling Stone's* Michael Azerrad; Sylvia, "the rock and roll one"; and Vicky Villegas, "the bubbly one." They were born seven minutes apart, April 18, 1965, and raised in their father's native Mexico. Their mother American, a society figure from the North Shore of Chicago.

"We learned all the traditional music and the beauty of the Spanish language and culture," said Vicky to *Cashbox.* Their earliest memories were of traveling the backroads in the family Winnebago, singing bits of traditional tunes their dad taught them. By age 14, the three were as one vocally, singing on stage in small towns and at talent contests. "If they'd pay us, we'd sing," said Diana to *Music Connections'* Jonathan Widran.

In 1983, at age 17, they were drawn to New York City to seek fame and fortune. For awhile they played local nightspots. Word spread and they soon secured work as bilingual singers and writers for radio and TV commercials.

In 1986, the Triplets won MTV's "Basement Tapes Contest," a contest for the best self-financed/self-produced video. Jerry Love of Famous Music saw them sing original material at the Sanctuary, in Manhattan, in 1988. He signed them to a publishing deal and brought them to the attention of Wing/Mercury A & R director Tom Vickers. "You Don't Have to Go Home Tonight" was the first single pulled from their debut album, . . . *Thicker Than Water.*

"Our record is American pop music with the soul and the flavor of the Latin spirit," said Diana to Widran. Sylvia added: "Our two worlds, the Mexican and the American, do meet somewhere in our music." "There were a few people who said, 'You're not going to cross

over with Latin-influenced pop, it's not commercial,' Diana told *Billboard* magazine's Jim Richland. "But we knew with the success of Los Lobos and Linda Ronstadt that there is a large market out there for this type of music."

The foreshadowing of possible career problems was noted early, their label had even considered changing their name. Wrote Widran: "These three perky yet professional career girls are destined to receive their share of criticism, stemming from the public's perception of the three as just a gimmick capitalizing on their unique family ties . . . others will accuse them of trying to be the Wilson-Phillips of the year."

"Sure, the fact that we're real triplets is interesting, and it grabs people's attention, but eventually people will get past that, and the music will come to the forefront," said Diana in response to the question. "If anyone thinks there's anything wrong with families singing together, then I guess the Jacksons were also capitalizing on their harmonies."

QUEENSRŸCHE
SILENT LUCIDITY
(Christopher DeGarmo)
EMI 50345
No. 9 *June 1, 1991*

"If I had to play the same grunge music every day, it would drive me crazy," said guitarist Michael Wilton to *Guitar Player*'s Steve Peters. Queensrÿche—named for one of their early songs, "Queen of the Reich"—is a Seattle band, though it definitely is not perceived as such. "I've read tons of articles about this 'Seattle Sound,' and they mention Soundgarden, Alice in Chains, Mudhoney, Nirvana—every band from Seattle but Queensrÿche," said 'rÿche's vocalist Geoff Tate to Jeff Gilbert, *Request*. "I've learned to laugh at it, but it would be nice if people recognized our contributions . . ."

Wilton (b. Feb. 23, 1962, San Francisco/guitar), Tate (b. Jan. 14, 1959, Stuttgart, Germany/vocals), and the rest—Christopher DeGarmo (b. June 14, 1963,

Wenatchee, WA/guitar), Eddie Jackson (b. Jan. 29, 1961, Robstown, TX/bass), Scott Rockenfield (b. June 15, 1963, Seattle/drums)—have known each other since grade school days. Before they got it together, Tate—who had studied opera—sang with The Myth and most of the rest made rock sounds with The Mob.

In 1981 the operatic Tate and four others from the Seattle suburb of Bellevue recorded their a demo tape in Scott's parents basement. The four track found its way to Kim and Diana Harris, record shop owners, with an eye on managing the act. With the Harris' help, Queensrÿche formed 206 Records to issue an EP (*Queen of the Reich*) that eventually would secure a contract with EMI. The major label rereleased the band's EP as a self-titled package in 1983 and their first full album *The Warning* the following year. Critics took a pass on the latter, as well as its immediate successor, *Rage for Order* (1986). Despite opening for Kiss, Metallica, and Bon Jovi, fan appreciation was modest.

The George Orwell-inspired *Operation Mindcrime* (1988) and its follow-up—*Empire* with the hit, "Silent Lucidity"—launched the group into international stardom. With extensive MTV exposure for their hit, *Empire* sold double-platinum; *Billboard* named Grammy-nominated "Silent Lucidity" "the most popular rock song of 1991." No further recordings, however, have charted.

Becoming an album and cult fan band, Queensrÿche toured with the "Monsters of Rock Tour" in 1991, and released a critically approved *Operation Livecrime* album and a video recapping the in-concert *Mindcrime* song cycle. A four year layoff followed, before the release of *Promised Land*.

"It was just time for us to stop and think about, perhaps even remind ourselves of, why we are together," said DeGarmo in a publicity handout.

Queensrÿche came the closest to a hit single in 1993 with "Real Worth," a cut included in the Arnold Schwarzenegger flop *Last Action Hero* (1993).

"We can be a very dangerous band, a lot more dangerous that 2 Live Crew and their stupid use of foul language, because we have ideas," said Tate to *Request*. "We have philosophy. We know how to use propaganda and how to manipulate the media . . . But, we're from Seattle; we have a conscience."

RUDE BOYS
WRITTEN ALL OVER YOUR FACE
(Jacques Cameron)
Atlantic 87805
No. 16 *June 8, 1991*

The Rude Boys, a Cleveland vocal quartet, were named for a button Prince was once photographed flashing.

They were "discovered" singing in a local club by LEVERT members Marc Gordon and Gerald Levert, whose Trevel Productions produced the act's debut album, *Rude Awakening*.

Composed of brothers Edward Lee "Buddy" Banks and Joe'l Little III and Melvin Sephus and B. B. King cousin Larry Marcus, the Rude Boys were no novices. Buddy had recorded with local favorites the Latest, opening shows for the Average White Band, THE DAZZ BAND, and Kool & The Gang. B. B.'s cousin Larry received classical training on the guitar and had been a member of the Dazz Band. Melvin worked the cabaret shows at age six; later joining with Buddy and Joe'l in a church-hopping, talent contest-winning gospel group.

Initial confusion cost the act a pop hit with its debut single, "Come on Let's Do It." Joe'l believes consumers misconstrued the group's name to mean that they were a rap act. "Everything rude doesn't have to be bad," said Joe'l to *Cashbox*. After the fluke pop chart success with "Written All Over My Face," nothing further has made *Billboard*'s Hot 100, although R & B listeners have come to know and appreciate these smooth rude guys. "Heaven" (R&B: #15, 1991), "Are You Lonely for Me" (R&B: #1, 1991), and "My Kind of Girl" (R&B: #4, 1992) have all charted successfully with R & B listeners.

The act remained tight with their mentors Levert, often touring and opening for them. In 1994, Joe'l—now relabeled "J. Little"—left the Rude Boys for a solo career. An initial single, a rap, penned by Gerald Levert—"The Hump Is On" (#97, 1995)—made the lower *Billboard* R & B listings.

MARC COHN
WALKING IN MEMPHIS
(Marc Cohn)
Atlantic 87747
No. 13 *July 6, 1991*

The way Marc tells it, life's been rough. Others just listen to his voice and know . . . "Marc's got one of those voices," said John Leventhal, Cohen's guitarist, to Thom Duffy, *Musician*. "Marc could be singing the phone book and people would go, 'He's breaking my heart.'"

The success of "Walking in Memphis," Cohn's debut single, from a debut album, was phenomenal, earning him a Grammy as "Best New Artist, 1991."

Marc was born in Cleveland, July 5, 1959. His mother died when he was about two. "From age two I was completely obsessed with music," said Cohn to Elianne Halbersberg, the *Music Paper*. His father was a pharmacist who worked seven days a week. When he was 12, his dad remarried. Dad had a prized possession that seemed to drain him of money and emotions. Marc wrote about it and his clouded relationship with his father in "Silver Thunderbird" (#63, 1991), a follow-up attempt.

"I had a lot of personal things I needed to say," he told Fred L. Goodman, *Cashbox*. "But it doesn't matter if people know who the real characters are, or if they understand exactly what's behind the songs. If their emotions, as listeners, are anything like the feelings I have when I sing, then I think being a songwriter is a pretty noble profession."

Marc, a self-taught musician, began playing sets at Cleveland coffee bars when still a teen. He attended Oberlin College, graduated from UCLA, and began making demos for legends Jim Webb, Leiber & Stoller; providing session piano for Tracy Chapman's second album, *Crossroads*. After moving to New York City, Marc assembled a 14-piece horn band, the Supreme Court, and quickly gathered a following performing. Spotting them at the China Club, singer/songwriter Carly Simon recommended the outfit to Caroline Kennedy for her impending wedding. "There was a lot about the experience that I absolutely cherish," he told *Cashbox*. "Just being around the Kennedys is like being around mythology." From Jackie Onassis he received a handwritten letter: "You are the best singer I have ever heard."

After five performances total, Cohn quit the group and for the next 18 months committed himself to penning tunes and recording them as demos. "I picked the five or six I thought were the strongest and presented them to Atlantic [Records]," he told *Cashbox*. "It was the only company I gave the tape to initially."

It took two years, but late in 1990 the self-titled debut album and "Walking in Memphis" were issued.

"To me that song is about more than just Memphis as a place," he told Goodman. "It has something in it about a kind of spiritual awakening." Cohen told *Rolling Stone*'s David Wild: "The amazing thing is that since I wrote 'Memphis,' I haven't really come up with a lousy song. And this is after many years of nothing *but* lousy songs."

In 1993, *The Rainy Sea*, a second album, was put out, featuring guest appearances by David Crosby, GRA-HAM NASH, Bonnie Raitt, Heartbreaker Benmont Trench, and Los Lobos's David Hidalgo.

LISA FISCHER
HOW CAN I EASE THE PAIN
(Narada Michael Walden, Lisa Fischer)
Elektra 64897
No. 11 *July 6, 1991*

"I really wasn't looking for a record deal," said Lisa Fischer to *Billboard*'s Jim Richliano. "I was so comfortable being a featured singer in Luther Vandross's show; to me, that was the ultimate gig."

Lisa was born and raised in the Fort Greene section of Brooklyn, New York. She got her pop singing start as a "fill-in" for weather-worn members in such rock-'n'roll institutions as the Crystals and the Marvelettes; respectively of "He's a Rebel" and "Please, Mr. Post-man" fame. The acts recording days were done, but aging boomers still had that deep need to hear the classic hits in concert again and again. Her vocal talents were soon noticed by Billy Ocean and Melba Moore, who utilized her on their early '80s recordings. Ocean, himself a one-time session singer, was then in the midst of his major hits—"Caribbean Queen," "Loverboy," "Suddenly.". . . In 1984, Lisa was given the chance to audition for Luther, for a slot in his "Superstar Tour."

"He checked me out in New York, and after an hour of vocal workouts he said, 'If you can dance, you've got the job.' Lisa and Luther continued their professional relationship into the '90s, dating past her appearance on the Rolling Stones' 1990 "Steel Wheels" album and tour; the biggest grossing international tour of all time. She continued her studio work, providing vocal support for Chaka Khan, Dionne Warwick, and TEDDY PENDERGRASS; with the latter, she had her first chart experience, "Glad to Be Alive" (R&B: #31, 1990), a tune tapped for a slot in Andrew Dice Clay-Priscilla Presley flick *The Adventures of Ford Fairlane* (1990).

"How Can I Ease the Pain" was an extract from *So Intense*, her debut, album. Said Lisa: "'Pain' is an autobiographical account of a break-up—turned into a song worth celebrating."

Her immediate follow-ups—"Save Me" (R&B: #7, 1991) and "So Intense" (R&B: #15, 1991)—charted well with R&B listeners.

DAVID A. STEWART, INTRODUCING CANDY DULFER
LILY WAS HERE
(David A. Stewart)
Arista 2187
No. 11 *July 13, 1991*

"When we first recorded 'Lily,' I told Dave, 'I can't believe it. It has such a simple melody, too simple," explained Candy Dulfer to *Rolling Stone*'s Leslie Tucker. "And he said, 'No, you're wrong. It's going to be number one.' I was like 'Oh, sure, Dave.' Well, he's right. He's totally right about everything."

David A.Stewart (b. Sept. 9, 1952, Sunderland, Tyne & Wear, England/multi-instrumentalist) ran away from home at 15, when he stowed away in the back of the van for touring folkies, The Amazing Blondel. With Brian Harrison, he formed a duo and recorded an overlooked album. In 1973, he and his band Longdancer were signed to Elton John's Rocket label. Soon after he met

Annie Lennox, a student at the Royal Academy of Music in London. Together with Peter Coomes they toured as the Catch, later to evolve into the homeland successful Tourists. Before the breakup of both the band and David and Annie's romance in 1980, the Tourists charted in Britain with "So Good to Be Back Home Again" and a retake on Dusty Springfield's "I Only Want to Be With You."

As the Eurhythmics, David and Annie were one of the world's most successful rock acts of the '80s. Hits happened, albums sold in massive quantities, and Stewart went on to acclaim as a producer for Bob Dylan and Mick Jagger. In July, 1987, David and Siobhan Fahey of Bananarama, later of SHAKESPEAR'S SISTER, married.

"As much as I've enjoyed recording Eurythmics albums, I somehow felt disconnected," said Stewart to Keith Sharp, *Music Express*. "I guess there was the ego thing of being in the background. And also, I could only write 10 percent of the words, because Anne had to sing them. That obviously made it difficult for me to compose the right lyrics."

Dave had the confidence that he could write, but to sing his own words, well . . . "It's like the first time you hear your own voice on a tape recorder—you say, 'What the hell is that? It can't be me!' I thought my demos were awful. But friends like George [Harrison], Bob [Dylan], and Tom [Petty] heard them and encouraged me to give it a go. The [producer] Chris Thomas came over from Australia, and he agreed to produce the sessions."

With the Eurythmics shelved—possibly forever— David formed the anxious label, and the Spiritual Cowboys, and was soon involved in a side project, the soundtrack to a Dutch film *Lily Was Here* (1991), starring Marion van Thijn.

At this point Stewart discovered Candy Dulfer, a saxophonist from Amsterdam. The director Benford Long supplied Stewart with a copy of one of Dulfer's live performances, and Stewart was interested. A week later Dulfer was in the studio cutting the complete soundtrack with the Eurythmics. "It was really an extraordinary experience for me to improvise to the scenes in the film," said the Dutch born and bred Dulfer to Leslie Tucker, *Rolling Stone*. "Really great chemistry we had.

"Then the last five minutes before I had to leave, Dave came up with this song, 'Lily Was Here.' It's been Dave's idea and he's very—what I love about Dave— spontaneous. He likes to do things on the spot. That's exactly what 'Lily' is: a one-take recording."

Stewart and the Spiritual Cowboys—ex-Pretenders' Martin Chambers (drums), Chris James (bass), John Trubull (guitar)—experienced minor chart action in Britain with "Jack Talking." Bootsy Collins, Mick Jagger,

and David's wife guested on Stewart's 1994 issue, *Greetings from the Gutter*.

CORINA
TEMPTATION
(Aida Ayala, Carlos Berrios, Luis Duprey, Franc Reyes)
Cutting Records
No. 6 *August 10, 1991*

Record company handouts refer to Corina as a Manhattan-born, Bronx-raised beauty who went on to win second place in the 1983 Miss Puerto Rico pageant. Nothing is noted therein of her upbringing, or even her birth name. Despite her colossal crossover charting with "Temptation," her stardom was so brief that the print media seems to have completely missed her shooting star.

It is known that Corina met producer Carlos Berrios in 1987 and that her debut, "Out of Control," gathered a positive reaction from New York City dance clubs. Cutting Records' Aldo Marin spotted her at one of her local club appearances and signed her to the label, issuing "Give Me Back My Heart" and "Loving You Like Crazy"—all prior to "Temptation."

With "Temptation" a concerted effort was made to expand her attraction beyond the dance dens by supplying 12-inch promo copies to the nation's top 40 stations. Atco Records stepped in to provide distribution; a video for "Temptation" was completed, an album quickly packaged, and nothing has since been heard of the "Miss Puerto Rico" stand-by.

LENNY KRAVITZ
IT AIN'T OVER 'TIL IT'S OVER
(Lenny Kravitz)
Virgin 98795
No. 2 *August 24, 1991*

Lenny has been slammed for his apparent lifting of styles and stances from the psychedelic '60s and soulful '70s. "We should stop fooling ourselves," trumpeted Kravitz, in his defense, to Kim Neely, *Rolling Stone*. "The stuff was more happening then. People think, 'Oh, you have this romance with it, because you grew up with it; it's your background. Bullshit. I'm listening unprejudicedly to music. I don't care *when* it comes from—f**k that! I'm talking music, straight up."

Born Leonard Albert Kravitz in Brooklyn, New York, on May 26, 1964, to NBC-TV producer Sy Kravitz and actress Roxie Roker, who played "The Jeffersons" neighbor Helen on TV. Len claims that when he was small he sat on Duke Ellington's knee while the giant played the keyboards. Once Kravitz moved to Los

Angeles—for his mother to shoot the television series—he spent three years in the California Boys Chorale, where he participated in conductor Zubin Mehta's recording of Mahler's "Third Symphony." Len taught himself his way with the guitar, bass, keyboards, and drums, and attended Beverly Hills High School with Saul Hudson—that's "Slash," later of Guns n' Roses and Lone Justice's Maria McKee. For a brief time, from 1987 until what would prove to be a permanent separation in 1991, he was married to actress Lisa Bonet of "The Cosby Show."

Let Love Rule was issued in 1989 to much critical bickering. Spoilers said he sounded too much like the Beatles, Hendrix, Dylan, and Elvis Costello.

"Do I have to make up a new form of music? Is that my job? Everything's been done," Kravitz said. "The things that haven't been done, what is that? Playing furniture? Using your head as a drum? . . . I'm doing what God put in me. Besides, would you rather hear something innovative that sucked—or would you rather just hear a good old Motown song?"

Despite the rooster pecking, the album charted well (#67, 1989). The title track made the pop charts (#89, 1990) the following year, as did his produced and co-penned "Justify My Love," cut by Madonna. Prince's "discovery" Ingrid Chavez—costar with the "Artist Formerly Known As" in *Graffiti Bridge* (1990)—sued, claiming that she had co-written the tune with Kravitz. The situation was settled out of court, with Lenny admitting to her role in the creation.

In 1991, with the Persian Gulf War happening, Len recorded an all-star reworking of John Lennon's "Give Peace a Chance," as the Peace Choir, with support from Yoko and Sean Ono, L.L. Cool J, Peter Gabriel, Bonnie Raitt, Run-DMC, Slash, and the Red Hot Chili Peppers. Mick Jagger and Kravitz dueted on a revisit to Bill Withers's "Use Me" in 1993. Len also contributed a track to Aerosmith's *Get a Grip*.

Mama Said included what it hoped will not be Lenny's one hit, "It Ain't Over Till It's Over." The title track to his 1994 release, *Are You Gonna Go My Way*, was nominated for two Grammys.

Kravitz told Michael C. Davis at *Illinois Entertainer*: "I don't set out to do anything—I just do it. It's just a natural kind of thing. I don't say, 'Well, I have to go and do this, and touch this many people, make X amount of dollars.' I just do what I do. And I don't always know the outcome or even *why* I'm doing it. It all reveals itself in the end."

CHESNEY HAWKES
THE ONE AND ONLY
(Nik Kershaw)
Chrysalis 23730
No. 10 *November 2, 1991*

He was 19 and packaged as a pop pretty boy, a teen-idol in the making. Chesney Hawkes's father was revered beat group lead Len "Chip" Hawkes, whose group, the Tremeloes was responsible for such '60s staples as "Here Comes My Baby" (#13, 1967), "Silence Is Golden" (#11, 1967), and "Even the Bad Times Are Good" (#36, 1967).

Chesney first caught the bug to be a rock star at one of the Tremeloes' concerts. "That was a milestone for me. I knew I'd love it if somebody asked me for an autograph." He left school at age 16 to play in a band, Adrenalin. For awhile, he eked out a meager living playing piano in a wine bar. His parents weren't happy. To resolve family matters, Chesney was given two years to get a career going or he would return to the real world of school and a practical job.

Once it clicked, "One and Only" was hand-selected to be the title tune in Michael J. Fox's *Doc Hollywood* (1991). This was not Chesney's first brush with the movies. He was chosen to appear as ROGER DALTRY's son in the British-made flick *Buddy's Song* (1989), a tale of a vet rocker's infatuation with the legend of Buddy Holly. In support of Chesney's bubbling career the flick was reissued—packaged as primarily a Chesney Hawkes flick—and Roger trekked to the United States to help publicize the young wanna-be's career.

From the get-go, Chesney was perceived as a fluff artist, a pin-up with a so-so voice. "Obviously, if that's what it takes to start off in America, you can use that vehicle," he told *Cashbox*'s Thom Duffy. "The difference between me and a teen idol is that I can write my own stuff, and I hope to prove myself."

Asked what if the unspeakable happens and his career were to stop with this one-hit, Chesney said: "Then I'll try again. My philosophy is—and you might not believe me, a lot of people don't—nothing really matters. Whatever happens, if I'm still living and breathing, then I'm happy."

CURTIS STIGERS
I WONDER WHY
(Glen Ballard, Curtis Stigers)
Arista 12331
No. 9 *November 23, 1991*

For a moment, the media hype was that Curtis Stigers was to be the Next Big Thing, the next Michael Bolton.

"I have long hair, am a white guy, and am influenced vocally by some black artists," explained singer/songwriter Stigers to Q's Mat Snow.

Born in 1966 in Los Angeles, Stigers was raised in the modest surroundings of Boise, Idaho. "I started playing clarinet at grade school and drums with friends in rock bands, jamming badly. Then I settled on the saxophone," he said. After much effort his band, the High Tops, disbanded. "I got fed up with playing in smoky meat markets, and it got ugly with the other guys, who got preoccupied with family problems and drugs. Cocaine confused me because I tend to be hyper, and it just made me fall asleep. And I drank too much—the whole bar atmosphere got me down."

By 1987, Curtis had had enough. He moved to New York City to clean up and get his career goals in order. For awhile, he played the blues; then settled into alternating between light jazz and creating pop-soul; what he described as "singable songs, pop, rather than copying Muddy Waters."

It was a year's stay at Wilson's, a restaurant in Manhattan, as part of a jazz trio, that caught the ears of Fred Davis, an attorney with a vision. It was Davis who did the boy right—finding him a manager in Winston Simone, a publisher in Sony Tunes, and a label, Clive Davis' Arista. "Clive was transfixed by him," Arista A & R VP Michael Cohen told Billboard's Karen O'Connor."

Stigers's self-titled debut album for Arista contained his lone major moment. "You're All That Matters to Me" (#98, 1992) and "Sleeping With the Lights On" (#96, 1992) charted ever so slightly.

"I knew that I had the goods to be commercially viable as well as artistically impressive," said Stigers. "I know what a good song is."

*R*S*F (RIGHT SAID FRED)
I'M TOO SEXY
(Fred Fairbrass, Richard Fairbrass, Rob Manzoli)
Charisma 98671
No. 1 February 8, 1992

They got their unlikely moniker from an obscure British-only hit by Bernard Cribbins, a homeland TV personality—known there for "Hole in the Ground," "Gossip Calypso," and the 1962 Top 10 hit "Right Said Fred."

"I think we went for [the name] because we knew it was stupid," said Richard Fairbrass, 1/3 of the group *R*S*F, to author Fred Bronson, The Billboard Book of Number One Hits. "It had a good eccentric kind of English sound to it. . . ."

*R*S*F came together as a campy trio of music men in 1990. Composed of the brothers Richard (b. 1953, bass, vocals) and the much younger Fred (b. 1964, guitar), plus guitarist-of-sorts Rob Manzoli (b. 1955)—their goal was to make serious sounds, until Rich—at a rehearsal—came up with the basis of "I'm So Sexy." "We took a tea break and the computer was playing this loop round and round, and right out of the blue—I can't tell you where it came from—I started singing, 'I'm too sexy for my shirt,' and we all fell about laughing."

Later Rich was to realize that the theme for the tune probably came about due to the work he and his brother did as managers of the Dance Attic, in London. "If you work in a gymnasium or a health club or a dance studio, you see so much posing and so much attitude going on. We took the opportunity of using that as the raw material to work the song around. . . ."

A promo man named Guy Holmes heard their rough work-up on the tune and suggested that they alter it some and remix it. Help came when DJ/producer Tommy D. Holmes took the results around to the labels. "They said, 'This is rubbish, it's not a hit,' in the tradition of record company A & R men who cannot spot a hit if it disappears up their rear end." Charisma would later pick up the disk for distribution, but initially it was Holmes who believed in the number such that he formed Tug Records to issue it.

Overnight, *R*S*F were pop celebs in their homeland. Up was released to applauses; "Deeply Dippy" and "Don't Talk Just Kiss" continued their lascivious loopings. In 1993, Sex and Travel appeared; months later *R*S*F were involved in the Comic Relief fund-raiser "Stick It Out."

KATHY TROCCOLI
EVERYTHING CHANGES
(Diane Warren)
Reunion 19118
No. 14 April 25, 1992

"When I heard her voice, I got excited," said Diane Warren to Billboard's Glenn Darby. It was Warren—composer of such mega-hits as Milli Vanilli's chart-topper "Blame It on the Rain," Foreigner's "I Don't Want to Live Without Your Love," and Cher's "If I Could Turn Back Time"—who offered Kathy Troccoli her hit-to-be, "Everything Changes."

Troccoli began her career recording contemporary Christian albums in 1982. Four years later, following her third such release, Kathy moved from Nashville to New York City in an effort to expand her audience into the more mainstream, the more expansive pop field. While singing back-up vocals for Taylor Dayne's "Tell It to the Heart," Kathy met producer Ric Wake. Troccoli got the impression right off that Wake had a feel for what she was trying to accomplish. With the acceptance

JOE PUBLIC

of Dan Harrell and Mike Blanton, owners of Reunion
Records, a 10-year-old outfit constructed to issue non-
traditional Christian products, Troccoli and Wake set
about recording *Pure Attraction* and its accompanying
single "Everything Changes." Geffin Records distributed and promoted Kathy, much as Amy Grant, as a
potential crossover artist, as a secular-again artist. The
effort paid off, though Kathy Troccoli has yet to return
to the Top 40.

JOE PUBLIC
LIVE AND LEARN
(Joe Carter, Joseph Sayles, Nathan Sayles, Jr. Kevin Scott,
Dwight Wyatt)
Columbia 74012
No. 4 *May 23, 1992*

"F*#& 'em," wrote *SPIN*'s Bonz Malone of Joe Public's
debut and hit-containing self-titled album. "There'z no

flavor nor substance that spellz 'new.' The tracks are tired, even though the four guyz have a lot of energy. Who signed this group? Who gave them a record deal? What tha f#%* are they thinkin' up in thoze high rises? I don't believe theze guys deserve a second album after this schitt!"

Surely, this must be one of the most thumbs-down major-mag reviews a major-label hit-making act has yet received. Unkind, oh yes. Unfair, seemingly so . . . seeing that weeks later Joe Public made the nation's Top 20 with "Live and Learn."

Joe Public is a four-man funky/hip hop/R & B band from Brooklyn, New York. The group consists of Joe "JR" Carter (guitar, vocals), Joseph "Jake" Sayles (keyboards, vocals), Kevin "Kev" Scott (vocals, bass), and Dwight "Mr. Dew" Wyatt (drums).

"The feedback is very good," said Kev to *Billboard*'s Janine McAdams, more than likely unaware of the *SPIN* review. "Hopefully we'll inspire some of the younger kids to pick up instruments and get more interested in live instrumentation instead of sampling everything."

Joe Public began as two bands competing for the same limited nightspot slots in the Buffalo metro area. When JR's unit dismantled, Kev, Mr. Dew, and Jake invited him to join their variously named band. They honed their skills in parks and proms, even a boys' home. Finally, a steady name was needed to solidify their growing reputation. Since two guys were named Joe, they thought "Hey, why not be Joe Public?" "We looked up 'Public' in the dictionary just to be sure of the meaning," said Kev, "and one definition was: 'To serve the people.' So we were like hey!"

Lionel Job (producer: Third World, Keith Sweat, Sharon Bryant, Atlantic Starr) spotted the act at a "Battle of the Bands" show in Buffalo. "They just had something—a charisma magic going," said Job to *Billboard*, who immediately offered a management/production deal. "I pulled them away from gigging and said, 'I'll buy you the equipment, anything that you need, but you should go and work on your craft.' Job spent a year polishing up the act. "Without [Job's] help we probably won't even be here," said Mr. Dew.

Now all this—mind you—is the build up to that hit-containing debut album, of which the *SPIN* man wrote. Not every gem made it on to that album. Keith Sweat recorded one of Joe Public's tunes, "Keep It Comin.'" The band *SPIN* panned supplied the accompaniment and background vocals. The disk went Top 20, R & B. Two further Joe Public singles made *Billboard*'s Hot 100. In 1994, Joe Public returned to the R & B listings with "Easy Come, Easy Go" (#81), an extract from a similarly titled second album.

SIR MIX-A-LOT
BABY GOT BACK
(Anthony Ray)
Def Amer 18947
No. 1 *July 4, 1992*

If you chanced on the now-banned video, you know . . . "Baby Got Back" was "a public service announcement for the salacious wonder's of big butts and the African-American woman's physique," wrote *SPIN*'s Brian Keizer. It became MTV's most requested video. Charges of sexism and obscenity helped . . . sales mounted to 3 million; the number one pop position was granted and held for five weeks. The industry noted the excitement . . . and a Grammy was graciously given.

"I started rapping not because I liked it," said Sir Mix-A-Lot to *Request*'s Marty Hughley, "but because I thought a lot of the rappers weren't very good and I could do a better job."

Seattle's first rap star, Anthony Ray (b. August 12, 1963, Seattle, WA), got his moniker while DJing at an inner city club. Mix-A-Lot came to the attention of Ed Lock, head of Ed Lock Productions and future front for Nastymix Records, at a gig. His first single for Ed, "Square Dance Rap," grabbed a considerable response locally. "Iron Man," a rap version of Black Sabbath's metal staple, garnered more notice; "Posse on Broadway" clicked (R&B: #44, 1988). *Swass*, Mix-A-Lot's debut album, sold platinum; remaining on *Billboard*'s Black Music and Top Pop Albums for a year. Sir Mix toured with Public Enemy; did shows with N.W.A., and Ice-T. *Seminar*, went platinum, but Sir Mix in dispute with Lock over finances left Nastymix.

An arrangement was made with Def Jam co-founder/Def American founder Rick Rubins, and Mix-A-Lot was granted his own label, Rhyme Cartel. Next out, the platinum selling *Mack Daddy*, which contained Sir Mix's magic moment, "Baby Got Back." Despite the flak and controversy generated by the disk, Mix-A-Lot received a Grammy Award for "Best Rap Solo Performance" for the song.

"The song doesn't just say 'I like large butts,' you know? The song is talking about women who damn near kill themselves to try to look like these beanpole models that you see in *Vogue* magazine," said Sir Mix to Keizer. In 1993, Sir Mix was the executive producer of *Seattle: The Dark Side*, a packaged sampler of hometown rap acts. That same year, he and Seattle grunge rockers Mudhoney recorded "Freak Mama" for the Emilio Estevez-Cuba Gooding flick *Judgment Night* (1993). *Chief Boot Knocka*, yet another platinum generator, was issued in 1994.

For the dawning months of 1995, Mix-A-Lot hosted an unusual UPN-TV anthology series that was called "The Watcher."

Sir Mix doesn't see himself hanging out rapping for long. "Real estate, is my real dream," he said to Ernest Hardy, *Cashbox*.

BILLY RAY CYRUS
ACHY BREAKY HEART
(Donald L. Von Trees)
Mercury 866522
No. 4 *July 8, 1992*

"Some people look at me and say, 'Billy Ray Cyrus—overnight success,'" said Billy Ray to Kerry Doole, *Music Express*. "Man, I've been doing this as hard as I know for the last 12 years of my life. . . .

Some have called him "the new Elvis," others—in and outside the country establishment— have babbled that Billy boy ain't countrylike. Critics don't take to his hairdo, tanned bod, muscle ripples, gyrating hips, and all 'round dumb hunky looks. A One-Hit Wonder is what many have labeled him.

When asked for his thoughts on his lightning-fast success, Billy Ray told Doole, "I always learned from my Granpappy, 'as you sow, so shall ye reap,' It's what you sow in your life and in the mind and heart that are the things that will manifest in your life. And there's something that Thomas Edison said—'Failure is the most important ingredient for success.' He's thought of as one of the greatest successes in the world, but he said he'd failed more than any man he'd known. That same philosophy goes with me. I've certainly had many failures in this endeavor."

Billy Ray was born in Flatwoods, Kentucky, on August 25, 1961. One grandfather was a Pentecostal preacher; the other, a fiddle player. Billy Ray's father had a gospel quartet, and Billy Ray would often join in the singings. His parents divorced when he was six. Some say the boy dropped out of high school to head for California and fame as a movie star; others claim he won a scholarship to play baseball at Georgetown College. Either way, all reports agree that when Billy Ray was 20 he heard a "voice within" telling him to turn to music. Winning tickets to a Neil Diamond concert changed his life. So impressed was he that he bought a guitar and soon he and brother Kebo had a band named Sly Dog. The music stopped when a fire in 1984 took all of their equipment.

Billy Cyrus returned east and gigged five nights a week at the Ragtime Lounge, which is located in Huntington, West Virginia. Almost weekly, Billy Ray would drive to Nashville to knock on doors in search of country stardom. Forty-two treks, at his estimate, were made before Del Reeves—noted for "Girl on the Billboard"—introduced him to his former manager Jack McFadden; some say McFadden is a prime mover behind the successes had by MERLE HAGGARD and BUCK OWENS. Jack got the lad a spot opening for Reba McEntire. A rep from Mercury Records took notice . . . and the rest is history.

Within months "Achy Breaky Heart," which was both the Country Music Association's "Single of the Year" and the song responsible for the Line Dance craze, went platinum; *Some Gave All*, the debut album, was certified triple platinum. Sales of the album by 1995 were 9 million.

Billy Ray Cyrus isn't a one-hit wonder with country audiences. "Could Have Been Me," "She's Not Crying Anymore," "In the Heart of a Woman," "Somebody New". . . and others have won positions in *Billboard*'s C&W Top 10. Billy Ray's special "Dreams Come True" aired on ABC-TV in February, 1993. Months later, his second album, *It Won't Be the Last*, immediately sold certified platinum; "Live on Tour," his video, certified gold. In 1995, album number three, *Storm in the Heartland* was issued.

"Why am I the most disrespected entertainer since Elvis [more appropriately, Vanilla Ice]? Should I offer an apology," asked Cyrus of *New Country*'s John Swenson, "because my first album was the fastest-selling debut in history?"

TOM COCHRANE
LIFE IS A HIGHWAY
(Tom Cochrane)
Capitol 44815
No. 6 *August 22, 1992*

Tom Cochrane was born in the northern mining town of Lynn Lake, Manitoba, Canada, on May 13, 1953. As a youth, he was fascinated with the writings of Arthur Rimbaud and Pablo Neruda and dabbled in verse. Between eking out a living driving a cab and crewing on a ship in the Caribbean, Cochrane worked Toronto's Yorkville coffeehouses as a folkie. In 1973, at age 20, Tom had *Hang on to Your Resistance*, his first solo effort issued by Frank Davies on his Daffodil label. The following year Cochrane wrote and performed the soundtrack to Xaviera "The Happy Hooker" Hollander's autobiographical flick, *My Pleasure Is My Business* (1974).

Seeking fame and fortune, Tom Cochrane trekked to Los Angeles repeatedly. In 1977, back in Toronto, at the El Mocambo nightclub, Tom happened on to a struggling trio named Red Rider, an outfit that had opened for the Pure Prairie League and provided accompaniment for legend BO DIDDLEY. Rob Baker (drums), Peter Boynton (keyboards, vocals), and Ken Greer (guitar, vocals) asked Cochrane to join the group; soon musician Jeff Jones (bass) was added. Enter Vancouver-based management mogul Bruce Allen (Bryan Adams, Loverboy, PRISM) and Capitol Records.

Four albums were issued largely to homeland applause and big sales. Before 1990, the group would win a Juno Award as "Group of the Year" (1987), and Cochran would receive a Juno as "Composer of the Year" (1989). A half-dozen 45s went Top 10 in Canada; two singles—"White Hot" (#48, 1980) and "Young Thing, Wild Dreams (Rock Me)" (#71, 1984)—charted on *Billboard*'s Hot 100. All, however, was not well.

Red Rider was never able to duplicate the mass success of Allen's other acts—and Tom and crew felt the problem was largely due to Bruce Allen's divided attentions. With Tom Cochrane's name out in front of the group's name by 1986 three further albums were issued; the final effort being the *Symphony Sessions*, a collaboration with the Edmonton Symphony Orchestra.

By 1991, all Red Rider members were gone from Cochrane's life, and *Mad Mad World*—produced in Memphis's famed Ardent Studios by ex-Stax act Joe Hardy—was ready for release as his first solo release since 1973. "Life Is a Highway," a tune inspired by a fact-finding trip Cochrane made to Africa with the relief organization World Vision, was to be the first single and Cochrane's high point.

"It's easy for me to say I should have dumped those f**kers [Red Rider] long ago, but that wouldn't be fair," said Cochrane to *HMV*'s Keith Sharp within moments of his single breaking the Top 10. "I've grown a lot; I'm able to edit myself more. I've realized there's nothing wrong with writing songs for the masses instead of being self-indulgent. I want to reach a larger audience, and I'm not ashamed to admit it." "Washed Away," Tom's immediate follow-up charted briefly (#88, 1992). Red Rider's Ken Greer is involved in a solo career.

N2DEEP
BACK TO THE HOTEL
(Timothy Lyon, James Trujillo, John Zunino)
Profile 5367
No. 14 *August 22, 1992*

They were said to be a white rap act from Vallejo, California. It was at DJ/producer Johnny "Z" Zunino's instigation, when he found rappers "TL" Lyon and Jay "Tee" Trujillo that N2Deep was formed. Their lone moment in the limelight was the title track from off their debut album for Steve Plotnicki and Cory Robbins's Big Apple-based Profile Records. Their label, known for Rob Base, Dana Dana, Run-D.M.C., and Special Ed, passed on "Z," "Tee," and "TL"'s request to issue "What the F**k is Going On" as the initial or even subsequent release. "Toss Up" (R&B: #74, 1993), the eventual follow-up, did chart moderately on the R & B listings. Nothing further from the group has entered any of the *Billboard* listings.

SHAKESPEAR'S SISTER
STAY
(Mary Levy, David A. Stewart, Siobhan Stewart)
London 869730
No. 4 *September 19, 1992*

Siobhan Fahey told *Q*'s Adrian Deevoy of her performances with Shakespear's Sister: "I get totally out of it sometimes. I almost leave my body. I'm covered from head to toe in bruises. Every part of me. When I'm in the kind of state, I just smash into things and don't feel it at all. Until the next morning."

Fahey (b. Siobhan Marie Deidre Fahey-Stewart, Sept. 10, 1958, Dublin, Eire)—wife of former EURYTH-MIC DAVID A. STEWART—moved to Britain in the late '70s to work in the press office at Decca Records. For most of the '80s, Siobhan was a member of the highly successful Bananarama trio (a name—trivia fans—derived from a favorite kiddie show, "The Banana Splits," and the ROXY MUSIC tune "Pyjamarama"). The group had earthshakers in "Cruel Summer," "Venus," and "I Heard a Rumor."

"The reason I left that group," said Fahey to *Cashbox*'s Karen Woods, "was that I felt totally divorced from what I was doing musically. Because the group did change a lot. And what I became . . . I never wanted to be in that type of band. I wasn't inspired by it. I wasn't able to fulfill myself. They were really relieved, actually. I was a bit of a fly in the ointment for the last couple of years because I would argue about everything."

Besides Siobhan, Shakespear's Sister is composed of Marcella Detroit (b. Marcella Levy, June 21, 1959, Detroit), and some say songwriter Richard Feldman, an across-the-street neighbor of the Stewarts. Siobhan, fresh from a 1988 departure from Bananarama, sought out Feldman to make some demos and met Marcella.

Detroit gained first notice when 18 as a accompanist for Eric Clapton. In 1980, as Marcy Levy, she had an on-off duet charting with Bee Gee Robin Gibb, with "Help Me!' a tune taken from the Tim Curry flick *Times Square*. This was followed by studies and eventually—allegedly—the teaching of drama at the Lee Strasberg Institute in Los Angeles. During her teaching days, Detroit wrote songs for Chaka Khan and Al Jarreau; and during her nights with Clapton she co-wrote his Top 10 hit "Lay Down Sally."

On the writing of the rock staple, she told *Q*. ". . . and we were in the studio one day and he said, 'I want to write this song called "Lay Down Sally." So I went into the corner and came up with the melody. At first it had more of a Little Feat groove. But we worked at it all day and eventually Eric hit on the rhythm and I played keyboards, and we recorded the track. Then Eric said, 'Can you write some lyrics at home tonight?' So I did, and we recorded the vocals the next day. And a standard was born."

The group's intentionally misspelled moniker was taken from a Smiths' song, itself reportedly an extract from a Virginia Woolf essay bemoaning the lack of credit granted female artists. "Break My Heart (You Really)" charted, though the next song, "You're History" sold in quantities in Great Britain. *Sacred Heart* and *Hormonally Yours*—recorded while both official members were pregnant—won overseas accolades and big sales. "Stay" tiopped the listings in England, with follow-ups in "I Don't Care," "Goodbye Cruel World," "and Hello, Turn Your Radio On" registering good-sized hits there also.

In 1993, live on stage, without forewarning, Siobhan announced—to a surprised audience and an unaware Detroit —that she was disbanding Shakespear's Sister.

HOUSE OF PAIN
JUMP AROUND
(L. Maggenud, E. Schrody)
Tommy Boy 7526
No. 3 *October 10, 1992*

Irish-American rappers, that's the hype-handle on these House of Pain inducers. With a shamrock for a logo, abundant attitude, and a tad of a tale about drinking and scrapping, they appeared, for a minute.

"The Irish thing—I'm proud of it—but I don't want people to blow it out of proportion because we're not from Ireland," said House of Pain's Everlast to *SPIN*'s Jonathan Berstein.

Their origins have been traced to Taft High in Los Angeles, former home to Ice Cube and rap gurus Divine Styler. Members include lead rapper Everlast (b. Eric Schrody, Long Island, NY), his co-lyric man Danny Boy (b. Daniel O'Connor, Brooklyn, NY), and DJ Lethal (b. Leor DiMant, Latvia). Everlast's daddy was a construction worker; Danny Boy's was, per his report, "a drunk." "I'm not kidding," he said to *Melody Maker*, "he was a criminal, but I never really knew him." Both, with the lineage from the land of Guinness, and a residence in New York City prior, left school before it was time. Lethal is a Latvian, with Jewish ancestry. His family moved from Europe when he was small, and from New York City, when in fifth grade.

With high school behind them, they learned to rap. "It's just something you did when you grew up," said Everlast to *Melody Maker*. "You had to have a rap if you wanted to hang."

Everlast was formerly a member of Ice-T's rap stable Rhythm Syndicate and was accorded a solo album by Warner Brothers in 1990; with sales nil, the package went cut-out.

When House of Pain was called together, it was a punk unit and a name pulled from the movie The *Island of Dr. Moreau*. Guitars were put down when the gathering met Cypress Hill producer DJ Muggs. It was Muggs who gave the green-beer swilling pugs what probably will prove their biggest pop intrusion.

"Jump Around" was the act's first release, and its hit status surprised many, including Everlast. "When I was watching MTV and saw our video as one of the Top Five, then saw our single on the Top Five on the pop charts, I bugged," said Everlast to *Billboard*'s Gil Griffin. "The song wasn't even intended for pop radio. Our song is too hardcore with its sound and its language, that radio can't play our song to death. It's for the hip hop audience, not pop radio. . . ."

Soon House of Pain toured Europe, including a stopover in Dublin. "We played at a pub called the Irish Castle Inn," Everlast continued, "in front of 200 people. The whole front of the stage was a mosh pit. Kids came up to me and said, 'Welcome Home,' and brought me gifts. . . ."

On their return, House of Pain worked the Irish bit with tales of "Shamrocks and Shenanigans" and "Top O' the Morning to Ya."

"There's been a lot of people that have come up to us and said that we're the first white rap group they can really believe in," said Everlast to *Melody Maker*.

"This is it, you know," added Danny Boy to *Melody Maker*. "We are drunken Irish types. We're not gonna try and keep up with rappers on the righteous tip, like Public Enemy. How could we? Even the Beastie Boys, with their stupid little whiny voices, we couldn't beat them out of their thing. All rapping is talking shit. You may be saying things, but you're really just showing off. We're gonna keep doing what we do, which is jumpin', bitin' stuff."

Rumors of Everlast's death circulated before the release of *Same As It Ever Was*, in 1994. When spotted in 1995 by *Details* magazine, Everlast was under house arrest for reportedly** carrying a concealed weapon.

"Who knows? I might become some kind of Cat Stevens motherf***er," he told *Details*' R. J. Smith. "What he did was hardcore."

As for Danny Boy's future—"acting, yeah, acting, maybe," he said. It was Everlast, though, who appeared in flicks—*Who's the Man* (1993), opposite Public Enemy and Heavy D, and dumb devil-flick *Judgment Day* (1988).

K.W.S.
PLEASE DON'T GO
Harry Wayne Casey, Richard Finch
Next Plat. 339
No. 6 *October 17, 1992*

K.W.S. is Chris King, Winnie Williams, and "Mystic Meg" St. Joseph, a dance and vocal team from Nottingham, England. Chris, Winnie, and "Mystic Meg" were also B-Line, a yet-to-be successful act with Dave Barker and Neil Rushton's street-hip and sales-hot Birmingham-based Network Records.

For reasons now cloaked in mystery, when Neil noticed the club action that ZYX, a competing dance label was having with their version—an issuance by Double You?—of K.C. & The Sunshine Co.'s "Please Don't Go"—and Network was unsuccessful in acquiring the rights to releasing the disk on their label—B-Line was asked to quickly cover the tune, though incognito, as K.W.S., "Now there's a good name," was the thought. Winnie and the rest—lead vocals supplied by ex-T Cut F. Delroy Joseph—holed up in a bedroom until they had a complete release-ready rendition. The one-off bedroom session also produced what would prove—within the confines of Europe—to be a high charting reworking of the Sunshine Co.'s song "Rock Your Baby."

"Please Don't Go" topped the British charts for five straight weeks. The response from ZYX Records was nasty, a lawsuit, that as of this book's publication date has yet to be resolved. Network Records carried on, branching out with distribution deals with tiny independents and the creation or acquisition of various affiliated labels—as Serious Groove, Vinyl Addiction, Stafford South, Hidden Agenda—a partial buy-out from Sony and numerous street-smart success by the likes of Nexus 21/Altern 8, Bizarre Inc., MC Lethal, Sure Is Pure, Plant Four. B-Line, however, was not included among these power showings; likewise K.W.S. In 1994, the members of K.W.S. left Network to form X-Clusive.

HEIGHTS
HOW DO YOU TALK TO AN ANGEL
(Stephen Bilao, Barry Coffing, Stephanie Tyrell)
Capitol 44890
No. 1 *November 4, 1992*

Much as the syndicated "Catwalk" (1992) and CBS-TV's "Dreams" (1993), Heights was a Fox-Network series—unsuccessful, lasting only from August through November 1992—about the adventures of a fictional rock band. There was Alex Desert as "Stan Lee" (bass), Ken Ganto as "Dizzy" (drums), Cheryl Pollak as "Rita" (sax), Charlotte Ross as "Hope" (guitar), Shawn Thompson as "J. T. Banks" (lead vocals), and Zachary Throne as "Lenny" (keyboards). The series was a flop, but the Heights got a number one hit. Five weeks later, the series was canceled.

CHARLES & EDDIE
WOULD I LIE TO YOU?
(Michael Leeson, Peter Vale)
Capitol 44809
No. 13 *November 7, 1992*

It was a chance meeting. Philadelphia-born Charles Pettigrew met Oakland, California-native Eddie Chacon on a New York City subway, and both 28-year-old's lives were altered irreparably.

"Charles and I are both collectors of early '70s records," Eddie told *Music Express*' Jennie Punter. "He was on the subway with a copy of Marvin Gaye's *Trouble Man*, an original copy. And I just walked up and started rappin' with him, and realized we knew some of the same people, and we had done session work with the same people. We became best friends and started hanging out and then we started doing music. It was just a natural progression."

Both Charles and Eddie had separately drawn the attention of Capitol Records' A & R director Josh Deutsch. When the two became a duo, Josh signed them to the label. *Duophonic* was their debut album; "Would I Lie to You?" was the first single pulled from the package. Immediately, Capitol tagged their sound as "'90s Soul," "New Soul for the Modern Age."

"Revivalist, nostalgia, retro, call it what you want," said Charles, who had studied classical piano and jazz at Boston's Berklee College of Music, to Bessman. "We just want to make people appreciate music that means so much to us, by whatever path it takes."

Critics approved of the duo's embrace of the waning souls of Gaye, Al Green, and Sly Stone. The public, however, would have no further dealings with Charles & Eddie, no matter how soulful their sounds.

MAD COBRA
FLEX
(Ewart Brown, Clifton Dillon, Lowell Dunbar, Brian Thompson)
Columbia 74373
No. 13 *November 14, 1992*

"If you wanna make it [rappin'], learn and respect, keep the love going, and put God first in everything. And that's it," said Ewart Everton Brown, "Mad Cobra," to *Fresh!* magazine.

Cobra was born (Mar. 31, 1968) in Kingston, Jamaica. He was a studious teenager with a hobby for electronics. About 1987, the young man found himself with a dream developing, a dream of which his daddy disapproved. "I told him I'd like to be a DJ and he said 'Either go to school and choose some other trade or leave this house.'" Cobra stayed in school.

Shortly after, he attended his first live dancehall show. "Seeing it, I imagined myself onstage. I fell into a trance; I wished to be those artists. So, I left the dance, went straight home, and started writing lyrics. When I saw my friends the next day, I told them, 'I'm gonna be a DJ.' And they laughed."

Some years later, after completing high school, Cobra began DJing. A year later, he got to record "Respect Woman"—a homeland charter—and to sign to a major label and the shot at a album release. *Hard to Wet, Easy to Dry* sold better than any would have guessed. "Flex," a reggae rap record, won a slot in *Billboard*'s R & B Top 10. Follow-ups have yet to reconnect.

As for that Mad Cobra moniker, Ewart was a diehard fan of the G.I. Joe comics. "I use to love to draw that villain on the cover of my books," said Cobra. "When the teacher called on me, she didn't say my correct name, she said 'Cobra,' and everybody started calling me that."

If the hits don't start happening, Mad Cobra may return to heeding his father's hopes and study to be an architect.

PORTRAIT
HERE WE GO AGAIN!
(Susaye Greene, Phillip Johnson, Eric Kirkland, Michael Saulsberry, Stevie Wonder)
Capitol 44865
No. 11 *November 14, 1992*

"Our music is about portraying life as we see it, from different perspectives," wrote member Phillip Johnson (b. Aug. 26, Tulsa, OK/vocals), in a bio handout from their label, Capitol. "There's an East Coast flavor, a Midwest attitude, and West Coast style, all combined together. It's a mix, a fusion that comes from growing up in different places . . . and yet, there's a unity of spirit. We've lived together, argued, been hungry, laughed together; we've become best friends . . . and you can hear that bond in our music."

Portrait origins can be traced to a chance meeting in 1985 of Eric Kirkland (b. Feb. 6, L.A./vocals) and Michael Angelo Saulsberry (b. June 15, L.A./keyboards, drum programming). "[Soon], there was three of us: Michael was the musician, I was the singer," Eric explained in the handout, "and this other guy rapped." They saw themselves as funky-R & B hip hoppers and began getting it together with their own tunes by mid-'88. The "other guy" dropped out, being replaced by Irving Washington III (b. June 29, Providence, RI/vocals)—a vocalist on Suave's debut album—and soon Phillip Johnson. "I let Eric, Michael, and Irving hear my demo tape on the phone," explained Phillip. "They liked it. I came out to L.A. and auditioned, and by the fall of 1989 Portrait was in place."

Persistence and assertion paid off. "We came up to Capitol a few times and sang *a cappella* for different executives," wrote Irving. Adds Phillip: "We must have written about 100 songs up to that point. Then we got the green light to start the album in July '91. . . ." "Here We Go Again" was the first single to be pulled from the group's self-titled debut album.

Despite chemistry and a heavy initial response to follow-up "Honey Dip," a spring '93 release, Portrait have yet to work their self-described image of being "smooth, outgoing, positive and . . . full of humor" into further Hot 100 chartings.

TREY LORENZ
SOMEONE TO HOLD
(Mariah Carey, Trey Lorenz, Walter Afanasieff)
Epic 74482
No. 19 *November 21, 1992*

His big break came when he sang in an accompanist role to Mariah Carey on the Jackson Five chestnut "I'll Be There," for an MTV "Unplugged" segment. "Everybody kept asking, 'Who's the guy singing?'" said Carey, to *Billboard*'s Timothy White. "I really didn't want all the fun and interest behind him with the 'I'll Be There' record to go to waste, so we just went at it for about three months, worked at it real hard, and came up with this"—"Someone to Hold."

Trey first met Mariah in February 1990, when she was at work on her first and self-titled album; the particular track, "There's Got to Be a Way." One of her back-up singers was friends with Trey and had brought him down to the studio. "I heard someone singing all the high top notes with me," said Carey, "and I'm like, 'Who's is *that*?' I turn around, and it was Trey."

Trey remained in Carey's entourage recording back-up parts for her *Emotions* album, a tour through Europe, and the fated MTV "Unplugged" segment.

Mariah and Trey's dueting on the classic Jackson Five cut topped the *Billboard* pop charts for two weeks. Within six months, Lorenz would return to the Hot 100 for the first and last time as a solo artist, with the Mariah Carey co-produced "Someone to Hold."

Trey was born January 19, 1969, in Florence, South Carolina. Dad was the director of a local job-training program; Mom taught history at Wilson High. Both parents attended church on Sundays, as did Trey. By eighth grade, Trey was winning talent contests singing Eddie Rabbit and Crystal Gayle tunes. In high school, he was the vocalist/keyboardist with the Players, a local cover band. Just prior to his "discovery" by Carey, Trey was attending New Jersey's Fairleigh Dickinson University, majoring in advertising, and nightlighting in a band, Squeak & the Deep.

"Photograph of Mary" (R&B: #46, 1993) and "Just to Be Close to You" (R&B: #66, 1993)—both Mariah Carey productions—have since charted modestly on the R & B listings.

SAIGON KICK
LOVE IS ON THE WAY
(Jason Bieler)
Third Stone 98530
No. 12 *December 12, 1992*

Jason Bieler (guitar, vocals) and Matt Kramer (vocalist)—the core of what was to become Saigon Kick—met in a rock bar in Miami, Florida, in 1984. Jason had been picking a guitar for a long, long time.

Matt and Jason made rock sounds in various permutations for four years, until 1988, when bassist Tom DeFile and drummer Phil Varone completed what was to become the hit-making line-up. What was to follow was no picnic, as Miami was then no hardrock hotbed. Kramer told *CAMM* magazine, the band refused to play anything but their kind of music, their way. The price extolled: Saigon Kick got booted out of near every venue in town. Soon their integrity won them fans with FAITH NO MORE, the Godfathers, 24-7 Spyz.

By 1990, the tide had turned. Jason, Matt, and the rest were nominated for a number of honors at the First Annual South Florida Rock Awards. Via staff members for Skid Row, word reached Atlantic/Third Stone Records in New York City. A & R moguls David Feld and Jason Flom headed south to check out the act; soon after Dick Reynolds, president of Third Stone Records, and metal producer Michael Wagener (Extreme, Metallica, Motley Crue) followed. Four days later the band was walled up in a studio in Los Angeles; 11 days later its debut album was complete.

In rapid succession, the Saigon Kick played openers for bands as diverse as Ratt, the Ramones, Cheap Trick, King's X, plus a 25-date trek through Europe with Extreme, as well as two dates for OZZY OSBOURNE at Japan's Budokan. On their return, they dashed off *The Lizard* in 13 days, recorded in Stockholm.

The Lizard contained the group's pop peak, "Love Is on the Way." Matt was worried. The track was a ballad. "Releasing a ballad could throw us into a whole different ballpark," he told *CAMM's* D.J. Justice. "I hope it doesn't because we are a rock'n'roll band. . . ."

Saigon Kick never made the *Billboard* Hot 100 again. Within months of their success, Tom DeFile left the group. As for the group's name, Matt explained to *Rock's* Lee Sherman: "We were watching cable TV, and there were these previews for *Full Metal Jacket* and one of the guys in the room said 'Is Hollywood on some kind of Saigon Kick?'"

WRECKX-N-EFFECT
RUMP SHAKER
(Agil Davidson, Eldrap DeBarge, William DeBarge, Aton Hollins, Etterlene Jordan, David Porter, Demont Riley, Teddy Riley, David Wynn)
MCA 54388
No. 2 *December 26, 1992*

"We didn't think it was going to do this," said "Miggady-Mark" to *Fresh!* magazine, about the rapid rise of "Rump Shaker." "Not all butt songs do good. You've just got to do it the right way."

Hard times were no stranger to Wreckx-N-Effect (initially spelled Wrecks-N-Effect). The act was born in 1987 or so, in Harlem, in New York City's St. Nicholas Projects. There was vocalist Aquil "A Plus" Davidson (b. Aug. 2, 1972), vocalist Brandon Mitchell (d. 1990), lead MC and former member the Masterdon Committee, Keith KC (b. ca. 1967, and DJ Markell "Miggady-Mark" Riley (b. Dec. 5, 1970).

In the concrete jungle, just two floors above "A Plus" lived "Miggady-Mark," whose older brother proved to be producer/later GUY member, Teddy Riley. Teddy, who had done rap work with Doug E. Fresh, B-Fats, and Heavy D., got the foursome affiliated with Atlantic Records for a self-titled EP. The disk stiffed, as did a self-titled album for Motown. Tuff times got tuffer when legal battles with Motown ensued. Keith KC had left the group before the Motown move and Brandon was shot and killed in the spring of 1990, in a disagreement over a woman.

"New Jack City" (R&B: #14, 1989), a homage to Teddy Riley's rap/R & B/go-go musical merging, had charted well only on the R & B listings. The following year, Wrecks-N-Effect added some rap sounds to Troop's successful "That's My Attitude" (R&B: #14, 1990). Paired down to "A Plus" and Miggady-Mark," the act's luck changed in 1992 when Riley produced their *Hard or Smooth* album for his Future label. The video for "Rump Shaker," the album's initial single's extraction, featured such skimpy bikini-clad fanny dancers that MTV initially refused to air it, that is until the escapist excursion went Top 10 pop.

The album went platinum; "Rump Shaker" went multi-platinum. Despite only one further pop charting—"Knock-N-Boots" (#72, 1993)—Wreckx-N-Effect remain in the collective pop memory, though now largely for the fight the duo got into with Q-Tip, Ali, Jarobi, and Phife—A Tribe Called Quest, known to outsiders primarily for "I Left My Wallet in El Segundo"—at New York's Radio City Music Hall in April, 1993. The Nation of Islam negotiated a resolution between the two groups.

THE BOTTOM 20

JOHNNY ADAMS
RECONSIDER ME
No. 28 *June 28, 1969*

ADVENTURES OF STEVIE V
DIRTY CASH (MONEY TALKS)
No. 25 *July 21, 1990*

AFTERNOON DELIGHT
GENERAL HOSPI-TALE
No. 33 *October 3, 1981*

ARTHUR ALEXANDER
YOU BETTER MOVE ON
No. 24 *April 21, 1962*

DAVE ALLAN & THE ARROWS
BLUES THEME
No. 37 *September 23, 1967*

DEBORAH ALLEN
BABY I LIED
No. 26 *January 21, 1984*

DONNA ALLEN
SERIOUS
No. 21 *February 14, 1987*

STEVE ALLEN
AUTUMN LEAVES
No. 35 *December 10, 1955*

GENE ALLISON
YOU CAN MAKE IT IF YOU TRY
No. 36 *March 10, 1959*

AQUATONES
YOU
No. 21 *May 26, 1958*

RUSSELL ARMS
CINCO ROBLES (FIVE OAKS)
No. 22 *February 23, 1957*

ASTON, GARDNER & DYKE
RESURRECTION SHUFFLE
No. 40 *August 7, 1971*

AUTOGRAPH
TURN UP THE RADIO
No. 29 *December 22, 1984*

AVANT-GARDE
NATURALLY STONED
No. 40 *August 31, 1968*

JIM BACKUS & FRIEND
DELICIOUS
No. 40 *July 21, 1958*

DAN BAIRD
I LOVE YOU PERIOD
No. 26 *December 5, 1992*

BALANCE
BREAKING AWAY
No. 22 *September 26, 1981*

BALLOON FARM
A QUESTION OF TEMPERATURE
No. 37 *March 23, 1968*

DARRELL BANKS
OPEN THE DOOR TO YOUR HEART
No. 27 *October 1, 1966*

KEITH BARBOUR
ECHO PARK
No. 4 *November 1, 1969*

BARBUSTERS
LIGHT OF DAY
No. 33 *March 21, 1987*

BARDEUX
WHEN WE KISS
No. 36 *April 16, 1988*

H.B. BARNUM
LOST LOVE
No. 35 *February 6, 1961*

BARRY & THE TAMBERLANES
I WONDER WHAT SHE'S DOING
TONIGHT
No. 21 *December 7, 1963*

JOE BARRY
I'M A FOOL TO CARE
No. 24 *April 24, 1961*

CHRIS BARTLEY
THE SWEETEST THING THIS SIDE OF
HEAVEN
No. 32 *August 19, 1967*

BENNY BELL
SHAVING CREAM
No. 30 *April 26, 1975*

MADELINE BELL
I'M GONNA MAKE YOU LOVE ME
No. 26 *February 10, 1968*

TONY BELLUS
ROBBIN THE CRADLE
No. 25 *August 17, 1959*

VINCENT BELL
"AIRPORT" LOVE THEME
No. 31 *May 16, 1970*

JESSE BELVIN
GUESS WHO
No. 31 *March 30, 1959*

ELMER BERNSTEIN
MAIN THEME FROM "THE MAN
WITH THE GOLDEN ARM"
No. 32 *April 28, 1956*

BIG AUDIO DYNAMITE II
RUSH
No. 32 *September 21, 1991*

BINGOBOYS, FEATURING PRINCESSA
HOW TO DANCE
No. 25 *February 16, 1991*

CILLA BLACK
YOU'RE MY WORLD
No. 26 *July 7, 1964*

BLACK OAK ARKANSAS
JIM DANDY
No. 25 *December 15, 1973*

**JACK BLANCHARD
& MISTY MORGAN**
TENNESSEE BIRD WALK
No. 23 *April 25, 1970*

BLOODROCK
D.O.A.
No. 36 *March 6, 1971*

BLUE HAZE
SMOKE GETS IN YOUR EYES
No. 27 *January 13, 1973*

BLUE JAYS
LOVERS ISLAND
No. 31 *September 18, 1961*

JOHNNY BOND
HOT ROD LINCOLN
No. 26 *August 8, 1960*

BONEY M
RIVER OF BABYLON
No. 30 *August 26, 1978*

BRENT BOURGEOIS
DARE TO FALL IN LOVE
No. 32 *April 26, 1986*

BOURGEOIS TAGG
I DON'T MIND AT ALL
No. 38 *October 10, 1987*

BRAM TCHAIKOVSKY
GIRL OF MY DREAMS
No. 37 *September 1, 1979*

BRAT PACK
YOU'RE THE ONLY WOMAN
No. 36 *February 3, 1990*

BOB BRAUN
TILL DEATH DO US PART
No. 26 *September 1, 1962*

MARTIN BRILEY
THE SALT IN MY TEARS
No. 36 *July 30, 1983*

HERMAN BROOD
SATURDAY NIGHT
No. 35 *July 14, 1979*

BROTHER BEYOND
THE GIRL I USED TO KNOW
No. 27 *June 23, 1990*

AL BROWN'S TUNETOPPERS
THE MADISON
No. 23 *May 16, 1960*

BOOTS BROWN & HIS BLOCKBUSTERS
CERVEZA
No. 23 *September 29, 1958*

BUSTER BROWN
FANNIE MAE
No. 38 *May 2, 1960*

CHUCK BROWN & THE SOUL SEARCHERS
BUSTIN' LOOSE, PART 1
No. 34 *April 7, 1979*

NAPPY BROWN
DON'T BE ANGRY
No. 25 *May 7, 1955*

ROY BROWN
LET THE FOUR WINDS BLOW
No. 29 *July 1, 1957*

SHIRLEY BROWN
WOMAN TO WOMAN
No. 22 *December 7, 1974*

DAVE BRUBECK QUARTET
TAKE FIVE
No. 25 *October 9, 1961*

RAY BRYANT TRIO
THE MADISON TIME—PART 1
No. 30 *May 16, 1960*

SHARON BRYANT
LET GO
No. 34 *September 30, 1989*

BUCHANAN BROTHERS
MEDICINE MAN
No. 22 *July 5, 1969*

BUGGLES
VIDEO KILLED THE RADIO STAR
No. 40 *December 15, 1979*

BULL & THE MATADORS
THE FUNKY JUDGE
No. 39 *November 16, 1968*

BULLET
WHITE LIES, BLUE EYES
No. 28 *January 15, 1972*

DORSEY BURNETTE
(THERE WAS A) TALL OAK TREE
No. 23 *February 1, 1960*

LOU BUSCH
11TH HOUR MELODY
No. 35 *March 24, 1956*

KATE BUSH
RUNNING UP THE HILL
No. 30 *September 7, 1985*

BUSTERS
BUST OUT
No. 25 *September 7, 1965*

JONATHAN BUTLER
LICE
No. 27 *June 27, 1987*

TANE' CAIN
HOLDIN' ON
No. 37 *September 18, 1982*

J.J. CALE
CRAZY MAMA
No. 22 *January 29, 1972*

CANNIBAL & THE HEADHUNTERS
LAND OF A THOUSAND DANCES
No. 30 *April 17, 1965*

JIM CAPALDI
THAT'S LOVE
No. 28 *April 30, 1983*

CAREFREES
WE LOVE YOU BEATLES
No. 39 *April 11, 1964*

HENSON CARGILL
SKIP A ROPE
No. 25 *February 10, 1968*

ROSEANNE CASH
SEVEN YEAR ACHE
No. 22 *April 25, 1981*

CASHMAN & WEST
AMERICAN CITY SUITE
No. 27 *November 18, 1972*

BOOMER CASTLEMAN
JUDY MAE
No. 33 *June 14, 1975*

CATE BROS.
UNION MAN
No. 24 *May 22, 1975*

CAT MOTHER & THE ALL NIGHT NEWS BOYS
GOOD OLD ROCK AND ROLL
No. 21 *August 2, 1969*

CAUSE AND EFFECT
YOU THINK YOU KNOW HER
No. 38 *February 29, 1992*

C. COMPANY, FEATURING TERRY NELSON
BATTLE HYMN OF LT. CALLEY
No. 37 *May 1, 1971*

CELEBRATION, FEATURING MIKE LOVE
ALMOST SUMMER
No. 28 *April 29, 1978*

CERRONE
LOVE IN C MINOR - PART 1
No. 36 *April 9, 1977*

CHANGE
A LOVER'S HOLIDAY
No. 40 *July 19, 1980*

CHANSON
DON'T HOLD BACK
No. 21 *February 3, 1979*

SONNY CHARLES
PUT IT IN A MAGAZINE
No. 40 *January 22, 1983*

CHARLIE
IT'S INEVITABLE
No. 38 *August 13, 1983*

CHARTBUSTERS
SHE'S THE ONE
No. 33 *August 15, 1964*

CHASE
GET IT ON
No. 24 *July 31, 1971*

CHERRELLE WITH ALEXANDER O'NEAL
SATURDAY LOVE
No. 26 *June 5. 1982*

CHERI
MURPHY'S LAW
No. 39 *June 5, 1982*

CHICAGO LOOP
(WHEN SHE NEEDS GOOD LOVIN')
SHE COMES TO ME
No. 37 *December 3, 1966*

DESMOND CHILD
LOVE ON A ROOFTOP
No. 40 *June 22, 1991*

CHRIS CHRISTIAN
I WANT YOU, I NEED YOU
No. 37 *November 21, 1981*

CHRISTIE
YELLOW RIVER
No. 23 *November 28, 1970*

GAVIN CHRISTOPHER
ONE STEP CLOSER TO YOU
No. 22 *May 24, 1986*

CHURCH
UNDER THE MILKY WAY
No. 24 *April 9, 1988*

EUGENE CHURCH & THE FELLOWS
PRETTY GIRLS EVERYWHERE
No. 36 *March 2, 1985*

CITY BOY
5. 7. 0. 5.
No. 27 *October 14, 1979*

C.J. & CO.
DEVIL'S GUN
No. 36 *July 16, 1977*

TONY CLARKE
THE ENTERTAINER
No. 31 *May 8, 1965*

CLIMIE FISHER
LOVE CHANGES (EVERYTHING)
No. 23 *May 14, 1988*

CLIQUE
SUGAR ON SUNDAY
No. 22 *August 30, 1969*

BRUCE COCKBURN
WONDER WHERE THE LIONS ARE
No. 21 *June 7, 1980*

COCK ROBIN
WHEN YOUR HEART IS WEAK
No. 35 *June 15, 1985*

DAVE & ANSELL COLLINS
DOUBLE BARREL
No. 22 *August 7, 1971*

COMMUNDARDS
DON'T LEAVE ME THIS WAY
No. 40 *December 27, 1986*

COMPANY B
FASCINATED
No. 21 *May 9, 1987*

CHRIS CONNOR
I MISS YOU SO
No. 34 *March 16, 1957*

NORMAN CONNORS
YOU ARE MY STARSHIP
No. 27 *November 6, 1976*

LES COOPER & HIS SOUL ROCKERS
WIGGLE WOBBLE
No. 22 *January 12, 1963*

COVEN
ONE TIN SOLDIER
(THE LEGEND OF BILLY JACK)
No. 26 *November 27, 1971*
No. 79 *July 2, 1973*
No. 73 *December 29, 1973*

CRABBY APPLETON
GO BACK
No. 36 *July 18, 1970*

ROBERT CRAY BAND
SMOKING GUN
No. 22 *February 7, 1987*

MARSHALL CRENSHAW
SOMEDAY, SOMEWAY
No. 36 *August 28, 1982*

RODNEY CROWELL
ASHES BY NOW
No. 37 *May 10, 1980*

CRUSADERS
STREET LIFE
No. 36 *August 25, 1979*

MIKE CURB CONGREGATION
BURNING BRIDGES
No. 34 *February 27, 1971*

DADDY O'S
GOT A MATCH
No. 39 *July 7, 1958*

LIZ DAMON'S ORIENT EXPRESS
1900 YESTERDAY
No. 33 *February 13, 1971*

DANCER, PRANCER & NERVOUS
THE HAPPY REINDEER
No. 34 *December 28, 1959*

DANNY WILSON
MARY'S PRAYER
No. 23 *June 6, 1987*

DAS EFX
THEY WANT EFX
No. 25 *June 6, 1992*

DAVID & DAVID
WELCOME TO THE BOOMTOWN
No. 37 *October 4, 1986*

MORRIS DAY
FISHNET
No. 23 *February 20, 1988*

CHICO DEBARGE
TALK TO ME
No. 21 *November 8, 1986*

JOHNNY DEE
SITTIN' IN THE BALCONY
No. 38 *March 15, 1957*

DE LA SOUL
ME MYSELF AND I
No. 34 *June 3, 1989*

RICK DERRINGER
ROCK & ROLL, HOOTCHIE KOO
No. 23 *January 19, 1974*

DEVICE
HANGING ON A HEART ATTACK
No. 35 *June 14, 1986*

DEVOTIONS
RIP VAN WINKLE
No. 36 *April 4, 1964*

MANU DIBANGO
SOUL MAKOSSA
No. 35 *June 23, 1973*

DIESEL
SAUSALITO, SUMMERNIGHT
No. 25 *November 21, 1981*

KENNY DINO
YOUR MA SAID YOU CRIED
IN YOUR SLEEP LAST NIGHT
No. 24 *December 25, 1961*

PAUL DINO
GINNIE BELL
No. 38 *April 10, 1961*

**SENATOR EVERETT MCKINLEY
DIRKSEN**
GALLANT MEN
No. 29 *December 24, 1966*

**DR. BUZZARD'S ORIGINAL
"SAVANNAH"**
WHISPERING/CHERCHEZ
LA FEMME/SE SI BON
No. 27 *November 6, 1976*

DONNIE & THE DREAMERS
COUNT EVERY STAR
No. 35 *June 19, 1961*

HAROLD DORMAN
MOUNTAIN OF LOVE
No. 21 *May 23, 1960*

CHARLIE DRAKE
MY BOOMERANG WON'T COME BACK
No. 21 *March 17, 1962*

**PETE DRAKE & HIS
TALKING STEEL GUITAR**
FOREVER
No. 25 *April 25, 1964*

ROY DRUSKY
THREE HEARTS IN A TRIANGLE
No. 35 *June 26, 1961*

DUALS
STICK SHIFT
No. 25 *October 23, 1961*

DUBS
COULD THIS BE MAGIC
No. 23 *December 2, 1957*

DAVE DUDLEY
SIX DAYS ON THE ROAD
No. 32 *August 3, 1963*

EARL-JEAN
I'M INTO SOMETHING GOOD
No. 38 *August 8, 1964*

EARLS
REMEMBER WHEN
No. 24 *January 26, 1963*

EDSELS
RAMA LAMA DING DONG
No. 21 *June 19, 1961*

ELECTRONIC
GETTING AWAY WITH IT
No. 38 *March 31, 1990*

**LARRY ELGART & HIS MANHATTAN
SWING ORCHESTRA**
HOOKED ON SWING
No. 31 *July 24, 1982*

JIMMY ELLEDGE
FUNNY HOW TIME SLIPS AWAY
No. 22 *November 13, 1961*

EMERSON, LAKE & PALMER
FROM THE BEGINNING
No. 39 *August 26, 1972*

ENGLISH CONGREGATION
SOFTLY WHISPERING I LOVE YOU
No. 29 *March 4, 1972*

ENYA
ORINOCO FLOW (SAIL AWAY)
No. 24 *January 21, 1989*

EQUALS
BABY COME BACK
No. 32 *October 26, 1968*

E.U.
DA'BUTT
No. 35 *April 16, 1988*

EYE TO EYE
NICE GIRLS
No. 37 *July 24, 1982*

TOMMY FACENDA
HIGH SCHOOL U.S.A.
No. 28 *November 16, 1959*

FACE-TO-FACE
10-9-8
No. 38 *July 21, 1984*

FACTS OF LIFE
SOMETIMES
No. 31 *April 30, 1977*

DONALD FAGEN
I.G.Y. (WHAT A BEAUTIFUL WORLD)
No. 26 *October 9, 1982*

BARBARA FAIRCHILD
TEDDY BEAR SONG
No. 32 *June 2, 1973*

ADAM FAITH WITH THE ROULETTES
IT'S ALRIGHT
No. 31 *February 27, 1965*

BILLY FALCON
POWER WINDOWS
No. 35 *August 17, 1991*

AGNETHA FALTSKOG
CAN'T SHAKE LOOSE
No. 29 *November 5, 1983*

FASTER PUSSYCAT
HOUSE OF PAIN
No. 28 *February 24, 1990*

JOHNNY FERGUSON
ANGELA JONES
No. 27 *May 2, 1960*

MAYNARD FERGUSON
GONNA FLY NOW (THEME FROM
ROCKY)
No. 28 *April 23, 1977*

BRIAN FERRY
KISS AND TELL
No. 31 *February 27, 1988*

FIREFLIES
YOU WERE MINE
No. 21 *October 26, 1959*

ELISA FIORILLO
ON THE WAY UP
No. 27 *December 8, 1990*

FIRM
RADIOACTIVE
No. 28 *February 9, 1985*

FIRST CHOICE
ARMED AND EXTREMELY DANGEROUS
No. 28 *May 26, 1973*

FIVE BLOBS
THE BLOB
No. 33 *November 3, 1958*

FIVE FLIGHTS UP
DO WHAT YOU WANNA DO
No. 37 *October 17, 1970*

5000 VOLTS
I'M ON FIRE
No. 26 *December 13, 1975*

FLARES
FOOT STOMPIN'—PART 1
No. 25 *October 30, 1961*

FLASH
SMALL BEGINNINGS
No. 29 *August 26, 1972*

**FLASH CADILLAC & THE
CONTINENTAL KIDS**
DID YOU BOOGIE (WITH YOUR BABY)
No. 29 *October 23, 1976*

SHELBY FLINT
ANGEL ON MY SHOULDER
No. 22 *February 27, 1961*

FLIRTATIONS
NOTHIN' BUT A HEARTACHE
No. 34 *May 24, 1969*

DICK FLOOD
THE THREE BELLS
(THE JIMMY BROWN STORY)
No. 23 *September 14, 1959*

DEAN FRIEDMAN
ARIEL
No. 26 *June 25, 1977*

MAX FROST & THE TROOPERS
SHAPES OF THINGS TO COME
No. 22 *October 26, 1968*

FUNKADELIC
ONE NATION UNDER A GROOVE—
PART 1
No. 28 *September 16, 1978*

RICHIE FURAY
I STILL HAVE DREAMS
No. 39 *December 15, 1979*

FUZZ
I LOVE YOU FOR ALL SEASONS
No. 21 *May 22, 1971*

GADABOUTS
STRANDED IN THE JUNGLE
No. 39 *August 4, 1956*

FRANK GALLOP
THE BALLAD OF IRVING
No. 34 *May 28, 1966*

DAVE GARDNER
WHITE SILVER SANDS
No. 22 *July 29, 1957*

GET WET
JUST SO LONELY
No. 39 *May 30, 1981*

MICKEY GILLEY
STAND BY ME
No. 22 *May 17, 1980*

JAMES GILREATH
LITTLE BAND OF GOLD
No. 21 *May 11, 1963*

GLASS BOTTLE
I AIN'T GOT TIME ANYMORE
No. 36 *July 17, 1971*

GLENCOVES
HOOTENANNY
No. 38 *July 27, 1963*

GONE ALL STARS
7-11
No. 30 *March 3, 1958*

GONZALEZ
HAVEN'T STOPPED DANCING YET
No. 26 *March 10, 1979*

GRAHAM CENTRAL STATION
YOUR LOVE
No. 38 *September 20, 1975*

GERRY GRANAHAN
NO CHEMISE, PLEASE
No. 23 *June 9, 1959*

**ROCCO GRANATA & THE
INTERNATIONAL QUINTET**
MARINA
No. 31 *December 21, 1959*

JANIE GRANT
TRIANGLE
No. 29 *May 29, 1961*

CYNTHIA GRECO
MAKE OUR DREAMS COME TRUE
No. 25 *May 8, 1976*

BOBBY GREGG & HIS FRIENDS
THE JAM—PART 1
No. 29 *April 21, 1962*

VINCENT GUARALDI
CAST YOUR FATE TO THE WIND
No. 22 *February 23, 1963*

GUNHILL ROAD
BACK WHEN MY HAIR WAS SHORT
No. 40 *June 2, 1973*

JASMINE GUY
JUST WANT TO HOLD YOU
No. 34 *August 3, 1991*

MERLE HAGGARD
IF WE MAKE IT THOUGH DECEMBER
No. 28 *November 24, 1973*

HAIRCUT ONE HUNDRED
LOVE PLUS ONE
No. 37 *May 15, 1982*

JIMMY HALL
I'M HAPPY THAT LOVE
HAS FOUND YOU
No. 27 *November 22, 1980*

HALOS
NAG
No. 25 *September 18, 1961*

BOBBY HAMILTON
CRAZY EYES FOR YOU
No. 40 *August 4, 1958*

HARRIET
TEMPLE OF LOVE
No. 39 *February 16, 1991*

BETTY HARRIS
CRY TO ME
No. 25 *November 16, 1963*

EDDIE HARRIS
EXODUS
No. 36 *June 5, 1961*

EMMYLOU HARRIS
MISTER SANDMAN
No. 37 *February 28, 1981*

SAM HARRIS
SUGAR DON'T BITE
No. 36 *November 10, 1984*

RONNIE HAWKINS & THE HAWKS
MARY LOU
No. 26 *August 17, 1959*

DEANE HAWLEY
LOOK FOR A STAR
No. 29 *July 25, 1960*

JOEY HEATHERTON
GONE
No. 24 *August 12, 1972*

NEAL HEFTI
BATMAN THEME
No. 35 *March 12, 1966*

BOBBY HENDRICKS
ITCHY TWITCHY FEELING
No. 25 *October 6, 1958*

HEN HOUSE FIVE PLUS TWO
IN THE MOOD
No. 40 *February 5, 1977*

HESITATIONS
BORN FREE
No. 38 *February 17, 1968*

BUNKER HILL
HIDE & GO SEEK—PART 1
No. 33 *October 27, 1962*

JESSIE HILL
OOH POP PAH DOO—PART II
No. 28 *May 23, 1960*

SUSANNA HOFFS
MY SIDE OF THE BED
No. 30 *February 2, 1991*

AMY HOLLAND
HOW DO I SURVIVE
No. 22 *October 11, 1980*

EDDIE HOLLAND
JAMIE
No. 30 *March 24, 1962*

JENNIFER HOLLIDAY
AND I AM TELLING YOU I'M NOT
GOING
No. 22 *August 28, 1982*

HONEYMOON SUITE
FEEL IT AGAIN
No. 34 *March 8, 1986*

JIMMY BO HORNE
DANCIN' ACROSS THE FLOOR
No. 38 *June 24, 1978*

HOT LEGS
NEANDERTHAL MAN
No. 22 *September 26, 1970*

DAVID HOUSTON
ALMOST PERSAUDED
No. 24 *October 1, 1966*

FRED HUGHES
OO WEE BABY, I LOVE YOU
No. 23 *May 29, 1965*

HUGO & LUGI
JUST COME HOME
No. 35 *December 14, 1959*

**PAUL HUMPHREY &
THE COOL AID CHEMISTS**
COOL AID
No. 29 *March 13, 1971*

JOHN HUNTER
TRAGEDY
No. 39 *December 8, 1984*

ICICLE WORKS
WHISPER TO A SCREAM (BIRDS FLY)
No. 37 *June 9, 1984*

ILLUSION
DID YOU SEE HER EYES
No. 32 *July 5, 1969*

INDECENT OBSESSION
TELL ME SOMETHING
No. 31 *July 28, 1990*

INDEPENDENTS
LEAVING ME
No. 21 *June 2, 1973*

INNOCENCE
THERE'S GOT TO BE A WORD
No. 34 *January 14, 1967*

INTRIQUES
IN A MOMENT
No. 31 *October 11, 1969*

IRON BUTTERFLY
IN-DA-GADDA-DA-VIDA
No. 30 *August 24, 1968*

IRONHORSE
SWEET LUI-LOUISE
No. 36 *March 17, 1979*

BIG DEE IRWIN
SWINGIN' ON A STAR
No. 38 *July 13, 1963*

RUSS IRWIN
MY HEART BELONGS TO YOU
No. 28 *September 14, 1991*

J.J. JACKSON
BUT IT'S ALRIGHT
No. 22 *December 10, 1966*

REBBIE JACKSON
CENTIPEDE
No. 24 *October 6, 1984*

AMIES
SUMMERTIME, SUMMERTIME
No. 26 *September 22, 1958*
No. 38 *August 4, 1962*

JERRY JAYE
MY GIRL JOSEPHINE
No. 29 *May 27, 1967*

FRED WESLEY & THE J.B.'S
DOING IT TO DEATH
No. 22 *June 2, 1973*

JEFFERSON
BABY TAKE ME IN YOUR ARMS
No. 23 *February 14, 1970*

JIVE BOMBERS
BAD BOY
No. 36 *March 16, 1957*

J.J. FAD
SUPERSONIC
No. 30 *April 23, 1988*

JOBOXERS
JUST GOT LUCKY
No. 36 *November 19, 1983*

SAMI JO
TELL ME A LIE
No. 21 *April 20, 1974*

JOHN & ERNEST
SUPERFLY MEETS SHAFT
No. 31 *April 14, 1973*

TOM JOHNSON
SAVANNAH NIGHTS
No. 34 *November 11, 1979*

JO JO GUNNE
RUN RUN RUN
No. 27 *March 18, 1972*

JOMANDA
GOT A LOVE FOR YOU
No. 40 *July 6, 1991*

ETTA JONES
DON'T GO TO STRANGERS
No. 36 *December 12, 1960*

JONES GIRLS
YOU'RE GONNA MAKE ME LOVE
SOMEBODY ELSE
No. 38 *August 18, 1979*

LINDA JONES
HYPNOTIZED
No. 21 *August 26, 1967*

JUNIOR
MAMA USED TO SAY
No. 30 *April 24, 1982*

JUST US
I CAN'T GROW PEACHES
ON A CHERRY TREE
No. 34 *May 14, 1966*

KANE GANG
MOTORTOWN
No. 36 *October 17, 1987*

**KASENETZ-KATZ SINGING
ORCHESTRAL CIRCUS**
QUICK JOEY SMALL (RUN JOEY RUN)
No. 25 *October 5, 1968*

MONTY KELLY
SUMMER SET
No. 30 *February 29, 1960*

KERMIT
RAINBOW CONNECTION
No. 25 *November 24, 1979*

THEOLA KILGORE
THE LOVE OF A MAN
No. 21 *June 1, 1963*

ANDRIAN KIMBERLY
THE GRADUATION SONG...
POMP AND CIRCUMSTANCE
No. 34 *July 10, 1961*

FREDDY KING
HIDEAWAY
No. 29 *April 10, 1961*

PEGGY KING
MAKE YOURSELF COMFORTABLE
No. 30 *February 5, 1955*

KINGSMEN
WEEKEND
No. 35 *September 22, 1958*

KIRBY STONE FOUR
BAUBLES, BANGLES AND BEADS
No. 25 *July 28, 1958*

FREDERICK KNIGHT
I'VE BEEN LONELY FOR SO LONG
No. 27 *July 8, 1972*

MOE KOFFMAN QUARTETTE
THE SWINGIN' SHEPPARD BLUES
No. 23 *February 24, 1957*

KRAFTWERK
AUTOBAHN
No. 25 *March 15, 1975*

CHERYL LADD
THINK IT OVER
No. 34 *September 9, 1978*

LADY FLASH
STREET SINGIN'
No. 27 *September 18, 1976*

L.A. GUNS
THE BALLAD OF JAYNE
No. 33 *April 7, 1990*

LAID BACK
WHITE HORSE
No. 26 *May 12, 1984*

FRANCIS LAI
THEME FROM LOVE STORY
No. 31 *March 6, 1971*

GEORGE LAMOND
BAD OF THE HEART
No. 25 *May 12, 1990*

MICKEY LEE LANE
SHAGGY DOG
No. 38 *October 28, 1964*

K.D. LANG
CONSTANT CRAVING
No. 38 *August 1, 1992*

LARSEN-FEITEN BAND
WHO'LL BE THE FOOL TONIGHT
No. 29 *October 11, 1980*

DAVID LASLEY
IF I HAD MY WISH TONIGHT
No. 36 *March 13, 1982*

JAMES LAST
THE SEDUCTION (LOVE THEME)
No. 28 *May 24, 1980*

LATOUR
PEOPLE ARE STILL HAVING SEX
No. 35 *April 6, 1991*

ROD LAUREN
IF I HAD A GIRL
No. 31 *January 28, 1960*

LAURIE SISTERS
DIXIE DANNY
No. 30 *April 16, 1955*

EDDIE LAWRENCE
THE OLD PHILOSOPHER
No. 34 *September 1, 1956*

LEAVES
HEY JOE
No. 31 *July 9, 1966*

LAURA LEE
WOMAN'S LOVE RIGHTS
No. 36 *October 30, 1971*

A LIGHTER SHADE OF BROWN
ON A SUNDAY AFTERNOON
No. 39 *February 8, 1992*

LIGHTNING SEEDS
PURE
No. 31 *May 19, 1990*

LINDISFARNE
RUN FOR HOME
No. 33 *December 9, 1978*

LITTLE JOE & THE THRILLERS
PEANUTS
No. 22 *October 14, 1956*

LITTLE JOEY & THE FLIPS
BONGO STOMP
No. 33 *July 28, 1962*

LO-KEY?
I GOT A THANG 4 YOU
No. 27 *November 14, 1992*

DENISE LOPEZ
SAYIN' SORRY (DON'T MAKE IT RIGHT)
No. 31 *June 11, 1988*

**JEFF LORBER, FEATURING
KARYN WHITE**
FACTS OF LOVE
No. 27 *December 6, 1986*

LOST GENERATION
THE SLY,. THE SLICK, AND THE WICK
No. 30 *August 22, 1970*

JOHN D. LOUDERMILK
LANGUAGE OF LOVE
No. 32 *December 11, 1961*

LOVE
7 AND 7 IS
No. 33 *July 30, 1966*

LOVE & KISSES
THANK GOD IT'S FRIDAY
No. 22 *July 22, 1978*

MONIE LOVE
IT'S A SHAME (MY SISTER)
No. 26 *March 16, 1991*

GLORIA LYNNE
I WISH YOU LOVE
No. 28 *March 14, 1964*

MOMS MABLEY
ABRAHAM, MARTIN AND JOHN
No. 35 *July 19, 1969*

BETTY MADIGAN
DANCE EVERYONE DANCE
No. 31 *August 18, 1958*

MAGIC LATTERN
SHAME, SHAME
No. 29 *December 21, 1968*

GEORGE MAHARIS
TEACH ME TONIGHT
No. 25 *June 23, 1962*

MAJORS
A WONDERFUL DREAM
No. 22 *September 22, 1962*

BARBARA MANDRELL
(IF LOVING YOU IS WRONG)
I DON'T WANT TO BE RIGHT
No. 31 *March 17, 1979*

CARL MANN
MONA LISA
No. 25 *August 10, 1959*

BOBBY MARCHAN
THERE IS SOMETHING
ON YOUR MIND (PART 2)
No. 31 *June 13, 1960*

MARK IV
I GOT A WIFE
No. 24 *March 16, 1959*

**ZIGGY MARLEY & THE MELODY
MAKERS**
TOMORROW PEOPLE
No. 39 *May 14, 1988*

MARILYN MARTIN
NIGHT MOVES
No. 28 *January 18, 1986*

MOON MARTIN
ROLENE
No. 30 *October 13, 1979*

TRADE MARTIN
THAT STRANGER USE TO BE MY GIRL
No. 28 *November 17, 1962*

NANCY MARTINEZ
FOR TONIGHT
No. 32 *October 4, 1986*

MARVELOWS
I DO
No. 37 *July 3, 1965*

MASHMAKHAN
AS THE YEARS GO BY
No. 31 *November 21, 1970*

TOBIN MATHEWS & CO.
RUBY DUBY DOO
No. 30 *November 28, 1960*

MATTHEWS SOUTHERN COMFORT
WOODSTOCK
No. 23 *March 6, 1971*

**NATHANIEL MAYER & THE
FABULOUS TWILIGHTS**
VILLAGE OF LOVE
No. 22 *June 23, 1962*

MAC MCANALLY
IT'S A CRAZY WORLD
No. 37 *August 13, 1977*

M.C. BRAINS
OOCHIE COOCHIE
No. 21 *January 18, 1992*

ALTON MCCLAIN & DESTINY
IT MUST BE LOVE
No. 32 *June 9, 1979*

CHARLES MCDEVITT SKIFFLE GROUP
FREIGHT TRAIN
No. 40 *June 10, 1957*

BOB MCFADDEN & DOR
THE MUMMY
No. 39 *August 24, 1959*

MCGUINN, CLARK & HILLMAN
DON'T YOU WRITE HER OFF
No. 33 *May 12, 1979*

PHIL MCLEAN
SMALL SAD SAM
No. 21 *January 20, 1962*

LISETTE MELENDEZ
TOGETHER FOREVER
No. 35 *February 2, 1991*

MELLO-TONES
ROSIE LEE
No. 24 *May 13, 1957*

JOHN MILES
SLOW DOWN
No. 34 *June 11, 1977*

GARY MILLS
LOOK FOR A STAR
No. 26 *July 25, 1960*

MODELS
OUT OF MIND OUT OF SIGHT
No. 37 *April 26, 1986*

MOJO MEN
SIT DOWN, I THINK I LOVE YOU
No. 36 *March 18, 1967*

MELBA MONTGOMERY
NO CHARGE
No. 39 *April 13, 1974*

BOBBY MOORE & THE RHYTHM ACES
SEARCHING FOR A LOVE
No. 27 *August 13, 1966*

JACKIE MOORE
PRECIOUS, PRECIOUS
No. 30 *February 13, 1971*

GIORGIO MORODER
CHASE
No. 33 *March 31, 1979*

MOTT THE HOOPLE
ALL THE YOUNG DUDES
No. 37 *September 23, 1972*

MOUNTAIN
MISSISSIPPI QUEEN
No. 21 *April 4, 1970*

MOVING PICTURES
WHAT ABOUT ME
No. 29 *September 18, 1982*
No. 46 *August 12, 1989*

ALISON MOYET
INVISIBLE
No. 31 *May 4, 1985*

SHIRLEY MURDOCK
AS WE LAY
No. 23 *January 17, 1987*

MICKEY MOZART QUINTET
LITTLE DIPPER
No. 30 *July 6, 1959*

BILLY MYLES
THE JOKER (THAT'S WHAT
THEY CALL ME)
No. 25 *December 2, 1957*

GRAHAM NASH
CHICAGO
No. 35 *July 10, 1971*

NATURAL FOUR
CAN THIS BE REAL
No. 31 *February 16, 1974*

NEIGHBORHOOD
BIG YELLOW TAXI
No. 29 *August 22, 1970*

PETER NERO
THEME FROM 'SUMMER OF '42'
No. 21 *December 12, 1971*

**MICHAEL NESMITH & THE
FIRST NATIONAL BAND**
JOANNE
No. 21 *August 8, 1970*

IVAN NEVILLE
NOT JUST ANOTHER GIRL
No. 26 *October 8, 1988*

MICKEY NEWBURY
AN AMERICAN TRILOGY
No. 26 *January 1, 1972*

NEW ENGLAND
DON'T EVER WANNA LOSE YA
No. 40 *June 16, 1979*

JIMMY NEWMAN
A FALLEN STAR
No. 23 *June 10, 1957*

NIELSON/PEARSON
IF YOU SHOULD SAIL
No. 38 *November 22, 1980*

NIKKI
NOTICE ME
No. 21 *April 28, 1990*

NITEFLYTE
IF YOU WANT IT
No. 37 *December 1, 1979*

NITE-LITERS
K-JEE
No. 39 *September 11, 1971*

JACK NITZSCHE
THE LONELY SURFER
No. 39 *August 10, 1963*

**JACKY NOGUEZ & HIS MUSETTE
ORCHESTRA**
CIAO, CIAO BAMBINA
No. 24 *August 10, 1959*

FREDDIE NORTH
SHE'S ALL I GOT
No. 39 *November 27, 1971*

ALDO NOVA
FANTASY
No. 23 *May 29, 1982*

TED NUGENT
CAT SCRATCH FEVER
No. 30 *August 13, 1977*

NU-TORNADOS
PHILADELPHIA, U.S.A.
No. 26 *December 22, 1958*

JOHN O'BANION
LOVE YOU LIKE I NEVER LOVED BEFORE
No. 24 *May 16, 1981*

KENNY O'DELL
BEAUTIFUL PEOPLE
No. 38 *December 16, 1967*

ODYSSEY
NATIVE NEW YORKER
No. 21 *February 18, 1978*

SHAQUILLE O'NEAL
(I KNOW I GOT) SKILLZ
No. 35 *October 23, 1990*

ONE 2 MANY
DOWNTOWN
No. 37 *March 25, 1989*

ORIGINAL CAST
ONE TIN SOLDIER
No. 34 *February 14, 1970*

**ROBERT ELLIS ORRALL WITH
CARLENE CARTER**
I COULDN'T SAY NO
No. 32 *May 21, 1983*

BENJAMIN ORR
STAY THE NIGHT
No. 24 *November 8, 1986*

OZZY OSBOURNE
MAMA, I'M COMIN' HOME
No. 28 *February 15, 1992*

LITTLE JIMMY OSMOND
LONG HAIRED LOVER FROM LIVERPOOL
No. 38 *June 17, 1972*

OTHER ONES
HOLIDAY
No. 29 *August 1, 1987*

BUCK OWENS
I'VE GOT A TIGER BY THE TAIL
No. 25 *January 23, 1965*

DONNIE OWENS
NEED YOU
No. 25 *October 6, 1958*

OXO
WHIRLEY GIRL
No. 28 *April 23, 1983*

GRAHAM PARKER & THE SHOT
WAKE UP (NEXT TO YOU)
No. 39 *May 4, 1985*

PARTLAND BROTHERS
SOUL CITY
No. 27 *May 2, 1987*

PARTY
IN MY DREAMS
No. 34 *November 16, 1991*

PASTELS
BEEN SO LONG
No. 24 *March 10, 1958*

PASTEL SIX
CINNAMON CINDER
(IT'S A VERY NICE DANCE)
No. 25 *February 2, 1963*

ROBBIE PATTON
DON'T GIVE IT UP
No. 26 *August 22, 1981*

PATTY & THE EMBLEMS
MIXED-UP, SHOOK-UP GIRL
No. 37 *August 15, 1964*

RITA PAVONE
REMEMBER ME
No. 26 *July 11, 1964*

LESLIE PEARL
IF THE LOVE FITS WEAR IT
No. 28 *August 14, 1982*

ANN PEEBLES
I CAN'T STAND THE RAIN
No. 38 *December 22, 1973*

TEDDY PENDERGRASS
CLOSE THE DOOR
No. 25 *August 12, 1978*

PEPPERMINT RAINBOW
WILL YOU BE STAYING AFTER SUNDAY
No. 32 *May 3, 1969*

TONY PERKINS
MOONLIGHT SWIM
No. 24 *October 7, 1957*

BERNADETTE PETERS
GEE WHIZ
No. 32 *May 31, 1980*

PETS
CHA-HUA-HUA
No. 34 *June 9, 1958*

JOHN PHILLIPS
MISSISSIPPI
No. 32 *May 16, 1970*

RICK PINETTE & OAK
KING OF THE HILL
No. 36 *July 19, 1980*

PINK LADY
KISS IN THE DARK
No. 37 *August 4, 1979*

PIXIES THREE
BIRTHDAY PARTY
No. 40 *October 5, 1963*

POINT BLANK
NICOLE
No. 39 *September 9, 1981*

IGGY POP
CANDY
No. 28 *November 11, 1990*

PRELUDE
AFTER THE GOLDRUSH
No. 22 *October 5, 1974*

CHARLEY PRIDE
KISS AN ANGEL GOOD MORNING
No. 21 *February 5, 1972*

PRISM
DON'T LET HIM KNOW
No. 39 *March 13, 1982*

P.J. PROBY
NIKI HOEKY
No. 25 *January 28, 1967*

JEANNE PRUITT
SATIN SHEETS
No. 28 *July 14, 1973*

PSYCHEDELIC FURS
HEARTBREAK BEAT
No. 26 *March 14, 1987*

Q
DANCIN' MAN
No. 23 *May 4, 1977*

QUAKER CITY BOYS
TEASIN'
No. 39 *January 26, 1959*

RAINBOW
STONE COLD
No. 40 *April 24, 1982*

EDDIE RAMBEAU
CONCRETE AND CLAY
No. 35 *June 5, 1965*

RAMRODS
GHOST RIDERS IN THE SKY
No. 30 *February 20, 1961*

BOOTS RANDOLPH
YAKETY SAX
No. 35 *April 6, 1963*

DIANE RAY
PLEASE DON'T TALK TO THE
LIFEGUARD
No. 31 *September 21, 1963*

JAMES RAY
IF YOU GOT TO MAKE A
FOOL OF SOMEBODY
No. 22 *January 27, 1962*

GENE REDDING
THIS HEART
No. 24 *July 20, 1974*

REDEYE
GAMES
No. 27 *January 23, 1971*

DAN REED NETWORK
RITUAL
No. 38 *March 12, 1988*

RE-FLEX
THE POLITICS OF DANCING
No. 24 *March 17, 1984*

CLARENCE REID
NOBODY BUT YOU BABE
No. 40 *August 2, 1969*

REVELS
MIDNIGHT STROLL
No. 35 *November 30, 1959*

LAWRENCE REYNOLDS
JESUS IS A SOUL MAN
No. 28 *November 1, 1969*

RIFF
MY HEART IS FAILING ME
No. 25 *April 27, 1991*

CHERYL PEPSII RILEY
THANKS FOR MY CHILD
No. 32 *October 29, 1988*

RINKY DINKS
EARLY IN THE MORNING
No. 24 *August 11, 1958*

ROACHFORD
CUDDY TOY (FEEL FOR ME)
No. 25 *April 15, 1989*

ROAD APPLES
LET'S LIVE TOGETHER
No. 35 *January 10, 1976*

ROB BASE & D.J. E-Z ROCK
IT TAKES TWO
No. 36 *August 20, 1988*

ROBERT & JOHNNY
WE BELONG TOGETHER
No. 32 *March 3, 1958*

KANE ROBERTS
DOES ANYBODY REALLY FALL IN LOVE
ANYMORE?
No. 38 *April 27, 1991*

ROCHELL & THE CANDLES
ONCE UPON A TIME
No. 26 *April 10, 1961*

ROCKETS
OH WELL
No. 30 *September 1, 1979*

TIMMIE "OH YEAH" ROGERS
BACK TO SCHOOL AGAIN
No. 36 *November 18, 1958*

ROMEO VOID
A GIRL IN TROUBLE
(IS A TEMPORARY THING)
No. 35 *October 27, 1984*

ROXY MUSIC
LOVE IS A DRUG
No. 30 *December 27, 1975*

ROZALLA
EVERYBODY'S FREE (TO FEEL GOOD)
No. 37 *July 25, 1992*

RTZ
UNTIL YOUR LOVE COMES
BACK AROUND
No. 26 *January 18, 1992*

RUBETTES
SUGAR BABY LOVE DECEMBER 27, 1975
No. 37 *August 31, 1974*

RUBICON
I'M GONNA TAKE CARE OF
EVERYTHING
No. 28 *April 22, 1978*

RUGBYS
YOU, I
No. 24 *October 25, 1969*

PATRICE RUSHEN
FORGET ME NOT
No. 23 *July 3, 1982*

JENNIFER RUSH WITH ELTON JOHN
FLAMES OF PARADISE
No. 36 *May 15, 1987*

**CHARLIE RYAN & THE
TIMBERLANE RIDERS**
HOT ROD LINCOLN
No. 33 *September 5, 1960*

SAGA
ON THE LOOSE
No. 26 *February 26, 1983*

CAROL BAKER SAGER
STRONGER THAN BEFORE
No. 30 *July 11, 1981*

BUFFY SAINTE-MARIE
MISTER CAN'T YOU SEE
No. 38 *April 1, 1972*

SAMMY SALVO
OH JULIE
No. 23 *March 3, 1958*

SANDPEBBLES
LOVE POWER
No. 22 *January 27, 1968*

SAN REMO GOLDEN STRINGS
HUNGRY FOR LOVE
No. 27 *October 30, 1965*

LARRY SANTOS
WE CAN'T HIDE IT ANYMORE
No. 36 *April 10, 1976*

SAPPHIRES
WHO DO YOU LOVE
No. 25 *March 14, 1964*

TIMOTHY B. SCHMIT
BOYS NIGHT OUT
No. 25 *October 24, 1987*

EDDIE SCHWARTZ
ALL OUR TOMORROWS
No. 28 *December 12, 1981*

JOHNNY SEA
DAY OF DECISION
No. 35 *July 2, 1966*

SEEDS
PUSHING TOO HARD
No. 36 *December 24, 1966*

MARILYN SELLARS
ONE DAY AT A TIME
No. 37 *September 28, 1974*

PHIL SEYMOUR
PRECIOUS TO ME
No. 22 *March 28, 1981*

SHAMEN
MOVE ANY MOUNTAIN (PROGEN 91)
No. 38 *February 22, 1992*

SHANA
I WANT YOU
No. 40 *October 7, 1989*

TOMMY SHAW
GIRLS WITH GUNS
No. 33 *September 29, 1984*

SHELLS
BABY, OH BABY
No. 21 *January 16, 1961*

T. G. SHEPPARD
I LOVE 'EM EVERYONE
No. 37 *May 16, 1981*

SHERRYS
POP POP POP-PIE
No. 35 *November 11, 1962*

DON SHIRLEY
WATER BOY
No. 40 *October 9, 1961*

BUNNY SIGLER
LET THE GOOD TIMES ROLL & FEELS SO GOOD
No. 22 *August 9, 1967*

SILVER CONDOR
YOU COULD TAKE MY HEART AWAY
No. 32 *September 19, 1981*

SILVETTI
SPRING RAIN
No. 39 *January 22, 1977*

PATRICK SIMMONS
SO WRONG
No. 30 *March 18, 1983*

KYM SIMS
TOO BLIND TO SEE
No. 38 *November 16, 1991*

GORDON SINCLAIR
AMERICANS (A CANADIAN'S OPINION)
No. 24 *February 9, 1974*

SINGING DOGS
OH! SUSANNA
No. 22 *December 17, 1955*

SIOUXSIE & THE BANCHEES
KISS THEM FOR ME
No. 213 *August 17, 1991*

SIX TEENS
A CASUAL LOOK
No. 25 *September 1, 1956*

SKYY
CALL ME
No. 26 *March 6, 1982*

DAVID LASHLEY
IF I HAD MY WISH TONIGHT
No. 36 *May 1, 1982*

SLAVE
SLIDE
No. 32 *August 20, 1977*

FRANKIE SMITH
DOUBLE DUTCH BUS
No. 30 *August 15, 1981*

JIMMY SMITH
WALK ON THE WILD SIDE - PART 1
No. 21 *June 23, 1962*

RAY SMITH
ROCKIN' LITTLE ANGEL
No. 22 *February 22, 1960*

VERDELLE SMITH
TAR AND CEMENT
No. 38 *August 20, 1966*

SMOKIE
LIVING NEXT DOOR TO ALICE
No. 25 *February 26, 1977*

SNEAKER
MORE THAN JUST THE TWO OF US
No. 34 *January 23, 1982*

SOPWITH CAMEL
HELLO HELLO
No. 26 *February 11, 1967*

SOUL CHILDREN
I'LL BE THE OTHER WOMAN
No. 38 *February 16, 1974*

S.O.U.L. S.Y.S.T.E.M., INTRODUCING MICHELLE VISAGE
IT'S GONNA BE A LOVELY DAY
No. 34 *November 28, 1992*

SOUNDS OF SUNSHINE
LOVE MEANS (YOU NEVER HAVE TO SAY YOUR SORRY)
No. 39 *May 29, 1971*

SOUP DRAGONS
DIVING THING
No. 35 *September 19, 1992*

SOUTHER, HILLMAN, FURAY BAND
FALLING IN LOVE
No. 27 *October 5, 1974*

RED SOVINE
TEDDY BEAR
No. 40 *August 28, 1976*

JUDSON SPENCE
YEAH, YEAH, YEAH
No. 32 *November 26, 1988*

SPIDER
NEW ROMANCE (IT'S A MYSTERY)
No. 39 *June 7, 1980*

SPIRIT
I GOT A LINE ON YOU
No. 25 *January 18, 1969*

SPOKESMEN
THE DAWN OF CORRECTION
No. 36 *September 18, 1965*

SPYRO GYRA
MORNING DANCE
No. 24 *August 25, 1979*

STALLION
OLD FASHION BOY (YOU'RE THE ONE)
No. 37 *April 30, 1977*

JOE STAMPLEY
SOUL SONG
No. 37 *March 10, 1973*

BUDDY STARCHER
HISTORY REPEATS ITSELF
No. 39 *May 14, 1966*

STARGARD
THEME SONG FROM 'WHICH WAY IS UP'
No. 21 *April 1, 1978*

STARLETS
BETTER TELL HIM NO
No. 38 *June 19, 1961*

STARPOINT
OBJECT OF MY DESIRE
No. 25 *November 16, 1985*

RANDY STARR
AFTER SCHOOL
No. 32 *May 13, 1957*

STARZ
CHERRY BABY
No. 33 *May 7, 1977*

CANDI STATON
STAND BY YOUR MAN
No. 24 *August 29, 1970*

STEELHEART
I'LL NEVER LET YOU GO (ANGEL EYES)
No. 23 *March 16, 1991*

LOU STEIN
ALMOST PARADISE
No. 31 *April 6, 1957*

JIM STEINMAN
ROCK AND ROLL DREAMS
COME THROUGH
No. 32 *May 30, 1981*

VAN STEPENSON
MODERN DAY DELILAH
No. 22 *June 30, 1980*

STEREOS
I REALLY LOVE YOU
No. 29 *October 23, 1961*

GARY STITES
LONELY FOR YOU
No. 24 *June 1, 1959*

STONEBOLT
I WILL STILL LOVE YOU
No. 29 *October 28, 1978*

KIRBY STONE FOUR
BAUBLES, BANGLES AND BEADS
No. 25 *July 28, 1958*

PAUL STOOKEY
WEDDING SONG (THERE IS LOVE)
No. 24 *July 31, 1971*

STORM
I'VE GOT A LOT TO LEARN
ABOUT LOVE
No. 26 *October 26, 1991*

BILLY STORM
I'VE COME OF AGE
No. 28 *June 1, 1959*

STREET PEOPLE
JENNIFER TOMKINS
No. 36 *March 7, 1970*

BARRETT STRONG
MONEY
No. 23 *April 18, 1960*

STRYPER
HONESTY
No. 23 *December 26, 1987*

STYLE COUNCIL
MY EVER CHANGING MOOD
No. 29 *April 7, 1984*

SUGARHILL GANG
RAPPER'S DELIGHT
No. 36 *January 12, 1980*

SUNSHINE COMPANY
BACK ON THE STREET AGAIN
No. 36 *November 25, 1967*

SWEATHOG
HALLELUJAH
No. 33 *December 18. 1971*

SWINGIN' BLUE JEANS
HIPPY HIPPY SHAKE
No. 24 *April 4, 1964*

SWITCH
THERE'LL NEVER BE
No. 36 *December 9, 1978*

FOSTER SYLVERS
MISDEMEANORS
No. 22 *July 28, 1973*

TALK TALK
IT'S MY LIFE
No. 31 *May 19, 1984*

TA MARA & THE SEEN
EVERYBODY DANCE
No. 24 *October 12, 1985*

TAMI SHOW
THE TRUTH
No. 28 *August 3, 1991*

NORMA TANEGRA
WALKIN' MY CAT NAMED DOG
No. 22 *April 9. 1966*

ANDY TAYLOR
TAKE IT EASY
No. 24 *May 3, 1986*

BOBBY TAYLOR & THE VANCOUVERS
DOES YOUR MAMA KNOW ABOUT ME
No. 29 *April 20, 1968*

TECHNIQUES
HEY LITTLE GIRL
No. 29 *December 9, 1957*

TEEGARDEN & VAN WINKLE
GOD, LOVE & ROCK & ROLL
No. 22 *October 31, 1970*

TEMPOS
SEE YOU IN SEPTEMBER
No. 23 *September 7, 1959*

TEMPTATIONS
BARBARA
No. 29 *May 16, 1960*

TEN YEARS AFTER
I'D LOVE TO CHANGE THE WORLD
No. 40 *September 25, 1971*

ROBERT TEPPER
NO EASY WAY OUT
No. 22 *January 22, 1986*

THINK
ONCE YOU UNDERSTAND
No. 23 *May 15, 1971*
No. 53 *March 9, 1973*

3RD BASS
POP GOES THE WEASEL
No. 29 *August 19, 1991*

IAN THOMAS
PAINTED LADIES
No. 34 *January 12, 1974*

KAY THOMPSON
ELOISE
No. 39 *March 17, 1956*

THUNDERCLAP NEWMAN
SOMETHING IN THE AIR
No. 37 *November 1, 1969*
No. 120 *October 24, 1970*

TIMES TWO
STRANGE BUT TRUE
No. 21 *March 12, 1988*

NICK TODD
AT THE HOP
No. 21 *February 17, 1958*

TOM TOM CLUB
GENIUS OF LOVE
No. 31 *January 23, 1982*

OSCAR TONEY, JR.
FOR YOUR PRECIOUS LOVE
No. 23 *July 8, 1967*

TONY & JOE
THE FREEZE
No. 33 *August 4, 1958*

LIDELL TOWNSELL & M.T.F.
NU NU
No. 26 *February 29, 1992*

TRADE WINDS
NEW YORK IS A LONELY TOWN
No. 32 *March 6, 1964*

TURBANS
WHEN YOU DANCE
No. 33 *January 14, 1956*

TUXEDO JUNCTION
CHATTANOOGA CHOO CHOO
No. 32 *July 1, 1978*

TWISTED SISTER
WE'RE NOT GONNA TAKE IT
No. 21 *August 18, 1984*

TYCOON
SUCH A WOMAN
No. 26 *May 26, 1979*

THE BOTTOM 20

U-KREW
IF U WERE MINE
No. 24 *January 27, 1990*

UNDERGROUND SUNSHINE
BIRTHDAY
No. 26 *September 6, 1969*

UNIT 4 + 2
CONCRETE AND CLAY
No. 28 *June 12, 1965*

PHILIP UPCHURCH COMBO
YOU CAN'T SIT DOWN, PART 2
No. 29 *July 3, 1961*

URBAN DANCE SQUAD
DEEPER SHADE OF SOUL
No. 21 *December 15, 1990*

URIAH HEEP
EASY LIVIN'
No. 39 *July 29, 1972*

UTOPIA
SET ME FREE
No. 27 *February 23, 1980*

JOHN VALENTI
ANYTHING YOU WANT
No. 37 *November 6, 1976*

MARK VALENTINO
THE PUSH AND KICK
No. 27 *December 15, 1962*

VALJEAN
THEME FROM BEN CASEY
No. 28 *June 23, 1962*

VANDENBERG
BURNING HEART
No. 39 *March 12, 1983*

VAPORS
TURNING JAPANESE
No. 36 *November 29, 1980*

FRANKIE VAUGHN
JUDY
No. 22 *July 28, 1958*

VELVETS
TONIGHT (COULD BE THE NIGHT)
No. 26 *July 10, 1961*

VIK VENUS
MOONFLIGHT
No. 38 *August 9, 1969*

VISCOUNTS
HARLEM NOCTURNE
No. 39 *January 1, 1966*
No. 52 *February 1, 1960*

VOLUMES
I LOVE YOU
No. 22 *June 30, 1962*

ROGER VOUDOURIS
GET USE TO IT
No. 21 *June 16, 1979*

WAIKIKIS
HAWAII TATOO
No. 33 *December 5, 1964*

WAILERS
TALL COOL ONE
No. 36 *June 22, 1959*
No. 32 *May 30, 1964*

**JOHNNY WAKELIN &
THE KINSHASA BAND**
BLACK SUPERMAN—'MUHAMMAD ALI'
No. 21 *September 13, 1975*

CHRIS WALKER
TAKE TIME
No. 29 *April 18, 1992*

TRAVIS WAMMACK
(SHU-DOO-PA-POO-POOP)
LOVE BEING YOUR FOOL
No. 38 *August 16, 1975*

WALTER WANDERLEY
SUMMER SAMBA (SO NICE)
No. 26 *October 15, 1966*

DALE WARD
LETTER FROM SHERRY
No. 25 *December 28, 1963*

BABY WASHINGTON
THAT'S HOW HEARTACHES ARE MADE
No. 40 *March 23, 1963*

KEITH WASHINGTON
KISSING YOU
No. 40 *May 25, 1991*

WA WA NEE
SUGAR FREE
No. 35 *September 12, 1987*

WEDNESDAY
LAST KISS
No. 34 *March 2, 1974*

WHISTLE
ALWAYS AND FOREVER
No. 35 *April 7, 1990*

HARLOW WILCOX & THE OAKES
GROOVY GRUBWORM
No. 30 *December 13, 1969*

DON WILLIAMS
I BELIEVE IN YOU
No. 24 *December 20, 1980*

BRIAN WILSON
CAROLINE NO
No. 32 *March 26, 1966*

WILTON PLACE STREET BAND
DISCO LUCY (I LOVE LUCY THEME)
No. 24 *April 9, 1977*

JESSE WINCHESTER
SAY WHEN
No. 32 *June 13, 1981*

WIND
MAKE BELIEVE
No. 28 *October 25, 1969*

LAUREN WOOD
PLEASE DON'T LEAVE
No. 24 *November 24, 1979*

WORLD PARTY
SHIP OF FOOLS (SAVE ME FROM
TOMORROW)
No. 27 *February 14, 1987*

DALE WRIGHT WITH THE ROCK-ITS
SHE'S NEAT
No. 38 *February 24, 1958*

YELLOW BALLOON
YELLOW BALLOON
No. 25 *May 20, 1967*

YO YO
YOU CAN'T PLAY WITH MY YO YO
No. 36 *May 25, 1991*

PIA ZADORA
THE CLAPPING SONG
No. 36 *December 11, 1982*

MICHAEL ZAGER BAND
LET'S ALL CHANT
No. 36 *May 20, 1978*

RICKY ZAHND & THE BLUE JEANERS
(I'M GETTIN') NUTTIN' FOR CHRISTMAS
No. 21 *December 24, 1955*

FRANK ZAPPA
VALLEY GIRL
No. 32 *July 17, 1982*

WARREN ZEVON
WEREWOLVES OF LONDON
No. 21 *April 22, 1978*

ARTIST INDEX

SONG-TITLE INDEX

SONG-TITLE INDEX

34647875R00297

Made in the USA
Lexington, KY
13 August 2014